Publications of the

National Bureau of Economic Research, Inc.

Number 40

National Income and Its Composition, 1919–1938

Relation of the Directors
to the Work and Publications
of the National Bureau of Economic Research

1. The object of the National Bureau of Economic Research is to ascertain and to present to the public important economic facts and their interpretation in a scientific and impartial manner. The Board of Directors is charged with the responsibility of ensuring that the work of the National Bureau is carried on in strict conformity with this object.

2. To this end the Board of Directors shall appoint one or more Directors of Research.

3. The Director or Directors of Research shall submit to the members of the Board, or to its Executive Committee, for their formal adoption, all specific proposals concerning researches to be instituted.

4. No report shall be published until the Director or Directors of Research shall have submitted to the Board a summary drawing attention to the character of the data and their utilization in the report, the nature and treatment of the problems involved, the main conclusions and such other information as in their opinion would serve to determine the suitability of the report for publication in accordance with the principles of the National Bureau.

5. A copy of any manuscript proposed for publication shall also be submitted to each member of the Board. For each manuscript to be so submitted a special committee shall be appointed by the President, or at his designation by the Executive Director, consisting of three Directors selected as nearly as may be one from each general division of the Board. The names of the special manuscript committee shall be stated to each Director when the summary and report described in paragraph (4) are sent to him. It shall be the duty of each member of the committee to read the manuscript. If each member of the special committee signifies his approval within thirty days, the manuscript may be published. If each member of the special committee has not signified his approval within thirty days of the transmittal of the report and manuscript, the Director of Research shall then notify each member of the Board, requesting approval or disapproval of publication, and thirty additional days shall be granted for this purpose. The manuscript shall then not be published unless at least a majority of the entire Board and a two-thirds majority of those members of the Board who shall have voted on the proposal within the time fixed for the receipt of votes on the publication proposed shall have approved.

6. No manuscript may be published, though approved by each member of the special committee, until forty-five days have elapsed from the transmittal of the summary and report. The interval is allowed for the receipt of any memorandum of dissent or reservation, together with a brief statement of his reasons, that any member may wish to express; and such memorandum of dissent or reservation shall be published with the manuscript if he so desires. Publication does not, however, imply that each member of the Board has read the manuscript, or that either members of the Board in general, or of the special committee, have passed upon its validity in every detail.

7. A copy of this resolution shall, unless otherwise determined by the Board, be printed in each copy of every National Bureau book.

(Resolution adopted October 25, 1926 and revised February 6, 1933 and February 24, 1941)

National Income

and Its Composition, 1919-1938

by Simon Kuznets

assisted by Lillian Epstein

and Elizabeth Jenks

VOLUME I

National Bureau of Economic Research

NEW YORK · 1954

22749

Contents

PART TWO

Changes in National Income, 1919–1938

VOLUME II

PART THREE

Characteristics of the Estimates

PART FIVE

Supplementary Data
See list of tables, p. xxiii

INDEX

List of Tables

xiii

MANUFACTURING

CONSTRUCTION

Preface

IN RECENT years national income has been widely used to gauge the performance of the country's economic system. Statesmen and economists, politicians and journalists, reformers and cranks, defenders of group interests and advocates of special policies—in short, nearly everyone concerned with the workings of the economy—have at one time or another cited the billion dollar figures to proper or improper ends. They have been used to measure changes in the economy's total accomplishment in relation to factors observers select as strategic; to serve as a quantitative framework within which to judge policies proposed or opposed; to diagnose progress or retrogression; to claim credit or cast blame.

Such bandying about of national income estimates is to be expected in a society interested in the material results of man's activity. Nor is it surprising that national income figures have become more prominent in public discussion in recent years, if only because more trustworthy estimates have been prepared at more frequent intervals. Not the least of other reasons is the pronounced disturbance in the country's economic life caused by wars and the recent great depression and the consequent need for public action in the light of as much economic intelligence as can be mustered.

Their comprehensive character and quantitative definiteness make national income estimates useful as a standard by

which to judge economic processes or policies. Yet several
vital aspects of the estimates frequently tend to be overlooked
in popular discussion. The natural desire to have a single
measure and to read an unequivocal meaning into it often
leads to the treatment of national income as the uniquely objective measure of economic achievement rather than as an
appraisal based upon criteria that may differ from country
to country, group to group, and time to time. A national total
facilitates the ascription of independent significance to that
vague entity called the national economy and may induce
neglect of the patent fact that this entity comprises millions
of individuals and firms, and scores of industries, economic
groups, and regions whose efforts add up to the national income total. Interest in changes in national income during the
current short run pushes into the background the longer term
movements and cyclical fluctuations to which the economy has
been subject in the observable past, cognizance of which would
enable the observer to distinguish persistent from transient
changes. Finally, the quantitative definiteness of the estimates
makes it easy to forget their dependence upon imperfect data
and the consequently wide margins of possible error to which
both totals and components are liable.

The main objective of the investigation summarized in this
report was to arrive at annual estimates of national income
for this country since the 1914–18 war. It was carried out in
awareness of the matters just mentioned: that national income is an appraisal based upon criteria that help to differentiate economic and productive activities from others; that
segregation of significant components is essential; that analysis
of the longer term movements and cyclical fluctuations in national income and its components is desirable; and that
because the estimates depend upon necessarily incomplete
data a detailed description of sources and methods is indispensable.

The same considerations led us to do more in this report
than present estimates of totals or even of their numerous

components. In Chapter 1 we discuss at length the problems involved in defining national income; in Chapter 2, the difficulties inherent in the proper delimitation of significant components; and in Chapter 3 we sketch the bases of the estimates and of the limitations arising from lacunae in the data. Part Two analyzes both longer term changes and fluctuations during business cycles. Part Three explains the derivation of the estimates, their margins of error, and how and why they differ from other estimates. Part Four presents in detail the estimates by industries and types of income, describing the sources and methods used in deriving each total. Part Five assembles some supplementary data outside the scope of the basic totals and components, yet deemed of interest.

Naturally the detail with which these various phases of national income could be discussed and measured was predetermined by the data and the practical exigencies of completing a task with the resources at hand. Consideration of other definitions to which the choice of different criteria of national income gives rise could not be implemented with corresponding estimates. Distributions by significant components had to be restricted to those by industrial source, type of income, and such categories of final use as the capital formation study had established. Analysis of temporal changes in the totals and in their components was handicapped by their annual form and because there are estimates for only two decades (for some estimates, for three). The description of technical features, comparisons with other estimates, and the evaluation of the margins of error, while fairly detailed, are not complete. It would be almost impossible to examine all the feasible methods, push the comparisons to the point of accounting for all the differences, or refine the evaluation of the margins of error beyond the crude measures of informed opinion here ventured. Similarly, the tables and notes in Part Four and the supplementary data in Part Five are not exhaustive. But such limitations are unavoidable. Statistical measures and analysis are always conditioned by the stock of data and theoretical tools which, at any given time, falls short of an easily conceived perfectionist ideal.

A critical and patient reader will become aware of the defects in the estimates and in their analysis as he reads; the less critical and impatient will have to take the conclusions and this warning on faith. Both may wonder whether our treatment of one aspect of national income may not negate or render superfluous our analysis of other aspects. For example, in demonstrating that, in all cases including the present, national income is essentially an appraisal concept we concluded that it inevitably reflects the judgment of society at large as to what economic production is, a judgment that admits of several variants even for a given society at a given time. Why analyze temporal changes or worry about the quantitative accuracy of estimates so dependent upon debatable criteria of social judgment? Why, in view of the approximate character and the wide margin of error, go to the trouble of analyzing the estimates in terms of long time movements and cyclical fluctuations and treat them as if they were records of carefully organized and controlled observations?

Such doubts would be justified were the penumbra of conceptual and statistical vagueness not dispelled by delimiting the scope of the estimates and by taking into account the influence of possible errors. Once we have reviewed the various definitions of national income in the light of the criteria that underlie them and chosen one or a group of related criteria, there is no reason why we should not scrutinize and try to interpret the changes in the totals based on them. Obviously, one concept or group of concepts of national income is chosen because changes in the totals estimated on that basis facilitate understanding of economic reality; if the choice is valid, analysis of the results is called for. Likewise, even though our estimates cannot be precise, we should still try to analyze temporal changes. Only by so doing can we probe the limitations of the estimates and single out their substantive indications.

Our estimates, being for a definite period, may well require reinterpretation when the period is viewed as one panel of a much longer historical canvas. They are also bound to become obsolete as times and criteria of social valuation change, new components emerge, and experience and perspective widen. Indeed, the author cannot but hope that this study and whatever questions it raises may in themselves contribute to improvements in data and analysis that will render it obsolete.

An investigation such as this could not be carried out unless the author had the constant and expert help of people familiar with the sources and procedures. I have been fortunate in being assisted throughout the study by Lillian Epstein and Elizabeth Jenks who have shouldered the burden of assembling the data, making the computations, checking the results and their interpretation in the text, and putting the manuscript through its various versions. Miss Epstein is also responsible for the preparation of the detailed notes in Part Four, which required meticulous care.

The preliminary versions were read by the advisory committee of the National Bureau's research staff. I have especially profited from the comments by Milton Friedman, and received several useful suggestions from Solomon Fabricant. Wesley C. Mitchell contributed greatly to the improvement of Chapter 1 and upon his recommendation, a separate chapter dealing, among other topics, with business savings, was added. Of the Directors of the National Bureau I am indebted for valuable comments to George O. May, W. Leonard Crum, C. Reinold Noyes, and Harold M. Groves. Albert G. Hart of Iowa State College, Raymond Goldsmith of the Securities and Exchange Commission, and John L. Martin, formerly of the Department of Commerce, also made constructive criticisms.

In the preparation of the estimates the National Income

Unit of the United States Department of Commerce has been our generous ally. The discussions at the meetings of the Conference on Research in Income and Wealth served to clarify some of the theoretical issues and supplied some relevant statistical measures beyond the scope of our own investigations. The final manuscript has been patiently edited by Martha Anderson.

To all these individuals and organizations I am sincerely grateful.

Simon Kuznets

July 1, 1941

PART ONE

Concepts, Classifications, and Procedures

CHAPTER 1

Concept of National Income

1 National Income an Appraisal Notion

NATIONAL income may be defined as the net value of all economic goods produced by the nation. Each term in this definition—'net value', 'economic goods', 'produced', 'nation' —is circumscribed by a wide area of reference accepted by common agreement and a substantial periphery subject to controversy and treated differently from time to time, country to country, and investigator to investigator.

When any estimate is examined critically, it becomes evident that the maker, wittingly or unwittingly, has used one or more criteria of productivity. The statistician who supposes that he can make a purely objective estimate of national income, not influenced by preconceptions concerning the 'facts', is deluding himself; for whenever he includes one item or excludes another he is implicitly accepting some standard of judgment, his own or that of the compiler of his data. There is no escaping this subjective element in the work, or freeing the results from its effects. In consequence, all national income estimates are appraisals of the end products of the economic system rather than colorless statements of fact; and, like all appraisals, they are predetermined by criteria that are at worst a matter of chance, at best a matter of deliberate choice.

This thesis may be disputed. It may be contended that national income can be so measured as to be an objective record

3

of the net product of all activities that eventuate on the market, plus some of the non-market goods whose value is measurable: all inclusive, the estimate would involve no selection and, therefore, no criteria based upon some ethical notion of productivity.

But if no criteria of social productivity are used, national income becomes a mechanical total of all net receipts of individuals and business agencies, regardless for what activity or even whether there is any activity. It would include the compensation of robbers, murderers, drug peddlers, and smugglers, differential gains from the transfer of claims, and pure transfers such as gifts and contributions, which, in the absence of a productivity criterion, cannot be distinguished from payments for services. Such a judgmentless estimate would be of little use, since, to measure all market transactions, some gross rather than net total is requisite. It would measure neither the positive contribution of the country's economic system to the needs of its members for purposes of consumption or capital formation nor the sum total of what the inhabitants of the country *think* their income is. Any claim to significance such a total would have would lie in its presumptive usefulness as an appraisal of the contribution of economic activity to the welfare of the country's inhabitants, present and future. Consequently, to include such items as smuggling and robbery would have ethical implications-just as truly as trying to exclude everything except 'economic goods'—implications that exist whether the compiler recognizes them or not.

Whatever the criteria, they imply an underlying scheme of values or social philosophy. The part of wisdom is to make this scheme of values explicit and allow it to guide the procedure. An investigator can decide intelligently what items to include and how to treat each only by formulating criteria of productivity and the principles of valuation to be applied. To do without this preliminary and decide each issue as it arises in accordance with 'common sense' is to conceal from himself and others what rules he follows, and to run grave risks of vitiating his results by inconsistencies. The proper role of common sense is to aid in choosing the fundamental principles of selection and valuation and in deciding just how they can best be applied to imperfect or recalcitrant sections of the data.

For those not intimately acquainted with this type of work it is difficult to realize the degree to which estimates of national income have been and must be affected by implicit or explicit value judgments. The items about which estimators using different criteria reach conflicting conclusions may seem to be of little moment theoretically and to involve magnitudes picayune in comparison with those beyond controversy. But such an impression is misleading. Unless the cases that lie on the borderlines are considered, the very areas that are beyond dispute are obscure; and analysis of the borderline cases themselves usually shows that they are far reaching. Correspondingly, the magnitudes involved increase as the search for a substantive meaning of the estimates becomes more thoroughgoing. The apparent relative unanimity produced by empirical writings on national income is due largely to the estimators' unconscious acceptance of one social philosophy and their natural reluctance to face such fundamental issues as would reveal that estimates are conditioned by controversial criteria.

The demonstration of the conditional character of the national income concept and hence of national income estimates is neither thankless nor purely destructive. It is necessary for a proper interpretation of national income estimates because they are used extensively in controversial issues. It is also a stimulus toward their improvement in two respects, consistency and explicitness. First, all questions of scope must be decided consistently and can be only if the reasons for the decisions are clear. Second, national income estimates must be presented in explicit detail and in several variants. The purposes these variants may serve must be kept in mind when the criteria are set up.

2 *Economic Goods*

The chief characteristic of goods is that they are sources of satisfaction. Most of such sources are economic in that they are relatively scarce and at the disposal of the active unit (individual, enterprise, nation) in economic life. The goods may assume the tangible form of a commodity, appear in more elusive form as a service separable from its material source, or be perceived as a social or personal arrangement inseparable from the human beings that constitute society. Underlying the variety of their manifestations and the qualitative diversity of physical shape are the scarcity and disposability of these sources of satisfaction, characteristics without which they would not be involved in economic behavior or give rise to social relations that are the concern of economic study.

This description of economic goods indicates their broadest characteristics, but is too wide for a measurable concept of national income. First, it covers many services and arrangements and some commodities that result from the general functioning of individuals in aspects of everyday life not usually associated with economic activity and not considered germane to the understanding of economic reality. Second, it provides no basis for deciding how to treat a commodity, service, or arrangement that is a source of satisfaction to some people and of dissatisfaction to others. We discuss separately the two groups of items that consequently should be considered for exclusion, the first under the head of non-market goods, the second, of non-productive activities.

A NON-MARKET GOODS

An individual spends most of his time producing scarce and disposable sources of satisfaction. In accordance with the above definition, most acts that might be called 'personal', such as washing, shaving, and playing for amusement on the piano would be treated as economic activity and their results as economic goods, since, when judged by the attributes of satisfaction-yielding, scarcity, and disposability, they do not differ from the same activities carried on for money as services to other people (nursing, barbering, and giving concerts). Every canon of proper definition would be violated if we included almost all active life under economic activity and all its positive results under economic goods.

To draw a line between economic activity and economic goods on the one hand and active life in general and its stream of satisfactions on the other is the more difficult the greater the diversity of social experience for which the distinction is to be valid. It would not be easy to formulate a distinction that would be valid for both the primitive tribes in the wildernesses of Africa and South America and the nations of North America and Western Europe; or for the institutional settings of European society in both the tenth and the twentieth centuries. Fortunately, the practical purposes of our estimates, which are for recent years and a highly developed national economy, enable us to simplify the task by drawing the line between economic activity and active life in general in a way that will fit the experience of recent decades alone and be valid solely for mature economies.

For this range of experience the most distinctive attribute of economic activity, not considered heretofore, is its close connection with the market; and the most conspicuous characteristic of economic goods, not mentioned so far, is that they usually appear on the market. It is the market, with its vast mechanism for the disposition of diverse goods, that reveals the ties binding the separate units in the economic system and segregates economic goods from others. Therefore, we define economic goods as commodities, services, arrangements, etc. that are dealt in on the market; and since the attributes mentioned earlier are implicit in marketability we can dispense with them. Unless an object is a source of satisfaction, relatively scarce, and disposable, it is not bought or sold. Marketability implies these three attributes and adds an important fourth, viz., that the goods are involved in the complex of social relations that are of especial concern to economic study.

But if the market is considered as a complex of social relations of a certain type, and marketability as the characteristic of goods involved in them, it must be recognized that there are different kinds of market expressive of significantly different underlying social relations. In an attempt to assure meaning for the distinction, and essential homogeneity for the realm of economic life, the definition may be narrowed still further, restricting economic goods to those that appear on markets of one specific type. For example, some investigators confine the concept to results of private industry, excluding the activities of public agencies.

We are now in a position to see clearly the limits within which the national income investigator can choose his definition of economic goods. He can restrict the concept to goods dealt in on markets of the types that seem to him most expressive of the essential features of the economic system under study. For the modern economy these would presumably be the competitive markets of the private business system. Or he can accept the broadest definition and make economic activity almost co-extensive with active, satisfaction-producing life.

These two concepts are not the horns of an either/or dilemma, but rather the limits of a range within which significant stages can be distinguished. Obviously, differences in the scope of the concept of economic goods will produce corresponding differences in the scope of the national income estimate, and no one variant of national income along this range is best for all purposes. The stages in the full range of variants are described in the accompanying tabular arrangement which shows the groups of goods that are to be added progressively to the narrowest concept.

The investigator should recognize this variety of concepts and purposes and so arrange his data that variants of totals can be derived along the entire range from the narrowest to the broadest. But complete coverage of the possible variants is an

VARIANTS OF DEFINITION OF ECONOMIC GOODS	ADDITIONAL GROUPS OF GOODS
I (narrowest)—goods exchanged for money on private markets	1 goods sold by public agencies on markets characterized by compulsory powers of public authorities
II (I) + (1)—all goods exchanged for money on all markets of the country	2 goods entering barter exchange (payments in kind by enterprises to employees or other participants in their activity)
III (II) + (2)—all goods exchanged on all markets, whether for money or by barter	3 goods not appearing on markets a products retained by producers for their own consumption (especially important for farmers) b services and products of individuals outside the market system, flowing to other individuals (especially services of housewives and other members of households)
IV (III) + (3a) + (3daa) + (3e)—all products of the business and public economy but excluding most products of the family economy	c services of individuals outside the market system to themselves (largely personal self-service which accounts for a great deal of active life outside 'working' hours)
V (I) + (1 + 2 + 3)—all economic goods most broadly defined	d services of commodities owned and used by consumers aa residential real estate bb other consumers' durable commodities cc other consumers' goods e services of publicly owned commodities to ultimate consumers and business agencies, e.g., roads

ideal that cannot be attained, partly because data are lacking and partly because some groups of goods included in the broader variants are not measurable. As far as we could, we based our estimates on a definition corresponding to Variant IV, omitting item 3e. It includes all goods appearing on the markets of the country (subject to restrictions imposed by other issues), whether exchanged for money or for other goods, plus the retained products of activities most of which result in marketable goods, plus the imputed return from a type of consumer good whose services are in large degree separable from the commodity itself and are bought and sold on markets.

The other items under 3 cannot be estimated adequately on a continuous basis, although in Chapter 9 we indicate the approximate magnitudes of most items mentioned. On the other hand, we do attempt to break down the national income total so that each item added in passing from the narrowest concept to the broadest measured can be subtracted, thus making it possible to measure variants based on somewhat less inclusive definitions of economic goods.

The national total just described may seem at first to be an arbitrary stopping point between the two extremes. But it is more than that. It is essentially an appraisal of the final net product of the business and public economies of the country, two of the three important social institutions that contribute to the production of economic goods; and excludes completely the product of the third—the family. This sweeping statement is true with the relatively minor exceptions that some interpretations would classify the services of houses to owners who inhabit them as products of the family rather than the business economy; and that free services of publicly owned commodities to ultimate consumers are not included.

Exclusion of the products of the family economy, characteristic of virtually all national income estimates, seriously limits their validity as measures of all scarce and disposable goods produced by the nation. The line of division between the business and the family economy differs from country to country, and for the same country from time to time. The temporal differences are especially important for our estimates, since they occur not only over long periods but also, given violent cyclical fluctuations, over short. A severe depression with its attendant unemployment may force many individuals to return to household tasks that in prosperity are performed by hired labor or by manufacturing enterprises; and an opposite shift may take place during prosperity. Over longer periods distinct secular shifts occur in the relative contributions of the business and the family economy to the total of economic goods, most broadly defined. One must, therefore, guard against the common tendency to consider national income totals as all inclusive summaries of the scarce and disposable sources of satisfaction produced by the nation. Such summaries would become practicable only if the data improved substantially or if the family disappeared entirely as a producer of goods.

B NON-PRODUCTIVE ACTIVITIES

The assumption implicit in our discussion so far, that all money and barter transactions on markets involve goods and hence should be included in national income, is far from true. While all goods that pass through markets are economic, not all the *quid pro quos* changing hands on markets are necessarily goods; and not all money and barter transactions involve *quid pro quos*. The exclusion of these marketable non-goods and of transfers raises one of the most complex problems in defining national income.

Since we aim to ascertain, as accurately as we can, the contribution of economic activities to the consumption of the inhabitants of the country and to their stock of capital goods, our estimates must exclude results of market transactions that do not add to the flow of goods at their disposal. The application of this criterion of productivity leads to excluding from national income the results of transfer transactions when carried on for philanthropic (contributions, etc.), business (capital gains), or mixed motives (gambling, etc.); and the monetary equivalents of activities that may directly and explicitly be recognized as unproductive (theft, etc.).

No theoretical difficulties stand in the way of excluding from national income the results of such transactions as gifts, contributions, and relief payments. It is of their essence that no productive service is rendered by the recipient, even though he may so expend the proceeds of the gift, contribution, or relief payment as to induce the production of new goods. True, the donor may derive satisfaction from making the gift, contribution, etc., and the willingness of the recipient to accept the transfer may be viewed as a source of this new satisfaction. But our aim in measuring national income is not to gauge the flow of satisfactions from all sources, but rather to record the production of tangible and observable sources of satisfaction attained by the use of scarce and disposable resources—among which willingness to receive gifts is obviously not one. Contributions, gifts, and similar transfers should, therefore, be treated as a redistribution of goods produced currently or in the past, rather than as the production of new goods. Proceeds from gambling of various sorts, in which goods already produced are redistributed, the gains of some individuals being offset by the losses of others and the net gains not representing any services rendered by the gainers to the losers or to society at large, should be treated similarly.

Gains and losses on capital, i.e., on assets of various types, may be actually realized or merely imputed. At least realized gains and losses on sales of assets are often included in national income because individuals tend to think of national income as an exact analogue to their incomes; and both individuals and taxation laws in this country consider gains on sales of assets as *bona fide* income. Yet capital gains and losses are not increments to or drafts upon the heap of goods produced by the economic system for consumption or for stock destined for future use, and they should be excluded.

Most broadly conceived, capital gains and losses result from changes in the value of a given capital asset, whether or not due to its physical transformation. These changes may, in turn, reflect changes in the general price level, caused by changes in the supply of the monetary media and of all assets: or they may be specific to a given group of assets or even a single asset, caused by changes either in demand for the asset itself or in the number of effective units in it. Obviously, an increase or decrease in the price of a capital asset, caused by a general change in the price level arising from monetary inflation or deflation, is not evidence of any production or productive consumption of goods; therefore, the resulting gain or loss should not be included in national income. Nor is a change in the price of a given asset due to a shift in demand evidence of production or consumption although it may mean an accretion to or depletion of the country's stock of wealth. If for some reason consumers lose interest in maple furniture and acquire a passionate liking for mahogany, the consequent losses and gains in value do not in themselves represent any extraordinary consumption of maple furniture or new production of mahogany. In other words, autonomous changes in consumers' tastes, i.e., changes not brought about by the expenditures of enterprises, are not part of economic activity and should be excluded. Fully aware that we thereby exclude sources of changes in the value of wealth that lie beyond the production process proper, we decided to confine national income to the net product of economic activity of production processes broadly conceived.

Similar reasoning applies when the number of effective units in an asset changes either because of previous investment or disinvestment or because of discovery or other accidental causes outside the regular production process. The rise in the value of a farm due to the expenditure of preceding years' income to increase the herd and add machinery has already been included in national income for these years, and to include the capital gain once more when it is realized or recognized as accrued would be double counting. The rise in the value of a corporation due to the ploughing back of profits in preceding years has already been included in national income for these years and it would be duplication to include realized or unrealized capital gains by holders of this corporation's securities. Any real investment made in the course of a fortunate discovery that enhances the value of a given asset has already been recorded under preceding years' income; and so far as the appreciation in value actually exceeds this previous investment, it cannot be considered a part of continuous economic activity. It may best be treated as an accidental shift in technical conditions of production, similar to the autonomous shift in consumers' tastes. Likewise, capital losses due to regular and forecastable functions of productive operation that can be offset by depreciation, insurance premiums, etc. are taken account of in calculating the net income for each current year of operation. And any losses sustained above that amount because of floods, hurricanes, and other acts of God can best be treated as accidental shifts in conditions of production, outside economic activity proper. Here again, as in the case of autonomous changes in consumers' demand, we limit national income to results of productive activity broadly defined; and exclude exogenous, accidental changes on both the demand and supply sides, changes that nevertheless affect the value of wealth at the disposal of the inhabitants of the country.

There is general agreement, we believe, that gains and losses on capital assets arising from the previous disposition of income (i.e., previous investment and disinvestment) should not again be included in national income; also, that in measuring the real contents of national income, gains and losses on capital assets arising from general shifts in price levels should be excluded. The issue then reduces itself to the treatment of changes in the value of capital assets that arise from autonomous changes in consumers' tastes and in conditions of production, autonomous meaning in both cases outside the processes of economic production (extraction, fabrication, transportation, trade, direct services of various types). The concept of production could be extended to include changes in consumers' tastes and such extraordinary events as great discoveries, floods, and hurricanes. But we prefer to confine it to those numerous production processes in which there is some pattern of regularity and some effective control by individual producers and hence some economic rationality in their behavior. The narrower definition yields estimates that can more easily be interpreted in terms of a contribution by the economic system and removes possible fluctuations in national income estimates from year to year that would be introduced by external, ungovernable, disturbing factors.[1]

While gifts, contributions, and relief payments are not tokens of productive services rendered by their recipients, and appreciation and depreciation of assets likewise cannot be included under national income as we define it, the activities that facilitate the administration of relief or charity and the realization of gains and losses from sales of assets are productive, unless characterized otherwise on grounds different from the ones adduced. It may seem absurd to declare a given activity unproductive and an activity intended to facilitate it, productive. But this absurdity is merely apparent. If individuals derive satisfaction from gambling and from other methods of transferring money without a *quid pro quo* in terms of goods, these activities are unproductive in the sense that the monetary gains realized by the lucky members of the group do not measure any goods produced by them. But so far as gambling and similar pursuits are pleasurable, and the balance of satisfaction they render is positive, the provision of facilities for them must be considered productive and included under national income. Similar reasoning applies to the administration of charity or relief, as well as to any receipts representing gains by a broker on the sale of assets.

We pass now to the more difficult case of market transactions involving objects that are sources of satisfaction to some members of society but of dissatisfaction to others. Few goods, no matter how universally their usefulness is recognized, escape being sources of dissatisfaction to some members of society; and the issue, therefore, affects a major proportion of all objects that are exchanged on the market. We speak glibly of marketable commodities, services, etc. as positive magnitudes, partly because of a ready acceptance of willingness-to-pay as the ultimate test of what economic goods are, and of a

[1] Analysis at this point bears almost as much upon the meaning of 'produced' as of 'economic goods', but it is impossible to discuss productivity without at the same time elucidating production.

tendency to read rationality into the arrangements of a social order to which we are accustomed; partly because of the inter-changeability of marketable objects and the individualistic argument that no matter how useless or even harmful a specific object may seem to us, so long as it fetches a price it can be exchanged for a useful one. Neither view can be followed in arriving at a national income concept valid for the social system as a whole.

The problem might conceivably be treated in either of two ways. The first, theoretically more desirable but impossible in practice, would be to weigh for each object (commodity, service, arrangement, etc.) both the satisfactions and the dis-satisfactions it renders; and then include in national income only the net balance. Could this be done, some objects might appear in the final addition with a negative sign, thereby re-ducing the positive balances contributed by others. But neither social institutions nor scientific disciplines have as yet evolved a calculus by which the various products of economic activity can be measured as sources of satisfaction or dissatis-faction to all members of a society. The market mechanism does not provide such evaluation. The price an object fetches on the market is determined in general by costs on the supply side, and preferences, backed by means of purchase, on the demand side. The parties affected indirectly by the object do not usually participate in the transaction, and except when society intervenes legally, have no effect on it.

We must, therefore, adopt the second method, namely, con-sider whether, from the viewpoint of society at large, the net balance of satisfactions and dissatisfactions the object as an economic good gives is positive or negative or neutral. It is thus the sign, rather than both the sign and the size, of the net balance that is decisive. If the sign is positive, the object is declared to be an economic good and its full value included in national income; conversely, its value is excluded if the satisfactions yielded are more than outweighed by the dissatis-factions, or if no element of satisfaction is perceptible.

But how does one decide whether an object bought and sold on the market yields a positive balance of satisfaction? Upon what basis are some activities that fetch a price on the market and a fairly substantial price at that, considered unproductive by important groups in our society? Upon what basis do we often go even further and grade productive activities according to some more or less common scale of the satisfaction their products render?

The variety of answers to these questions is well evidenced by the diversity of ways in which productivity has been defined by economists since the days of the Classical School and by the substantial list of activities that have been classified as unproductive by national income investigators for various countries and at various times. Differences in viewpoint, determined largely by differences in social organization and by class or group interests, affect national income estimates markedly. Except for activities directly concerned with the production of the commodities that constitute necessities of life, all economic activities have probably at some time or other, by one investigator or another, been treated as unproductive.

Here again, as in the case of non-market goods, the national income investigator can lighten the burden of definition by so arranging his data that both productive and non-productive activities are measured. Users of the estimates can then derive various totals in accordance with their own notions of productivity. But this procedure does not obviate the necessity of clarifying notions of productivity, since they must serve as guides to classifying the components of the most inclusive national income total. Moreover, practical considerations force the investigator to adopt, consciously or unconsciously, some criterion of productivity to guide his efforts to measure the parts that are germane to national income as a concept of net product and keep him from wasting efforts on measuring activities whose productive character is doubtful.

In general, two types of decision concerning the criterion of productivity can be made. One is to accept the notions that have been expressed overtly by the body social in prohibiting some activities and encouraging others: illegal activities would be classified as unproductive; and any activities that are both legal and marketable would be classified as productive and their products included under national income. The other type of decision would entail the formulation of criteria of productivity with merely partial or no reference to the overt notions of society as expressed in its laws.

Either decision means approaches so complex that an investigator who conscientiously tried to carry out all their implications would never arrive at a national income estimate. The first, to take as the framework of one's concept the overt opinion of the body social as expressed in its legal statutes, seems to have the advantage of utilizing a recorded set of rules, especially definite with respect to items and activities that should be excluded as unproductive. But even brief and amateur consideration of the meaning of legality and illegality would immediately reveal a host of difficulties. Illegality ranges all the way from barring itinerant shoe shining or keeping a dog without a license to killing your neighbor. Quite frequently activities that seem equivalent in both substance and economic meaning are prohibited if performed in one way and permitted if performed in another. If the concept of illegality is to be taken literally, many economic activities accepted by the body social as productive would have to be declared unproductive. If, however, we try to distinguish among degrees of illegality by the severity of the penalty or some other feature, we become bewildered in a maze of equivocations and are likely to emerge with results that will be both arbitrary and subject to erratic changes from time to time or country to country.

The second decision, to set up substantive criteria of productivity with little or no reference to the consensus of the body social, is even more difficult. It may be easy to single out a few activities of so clearly an unproductive character that they would be classified as such by any set of criteria. But it is doubtful that objective standards of satisfaction can be worked out that would allow us to classify properly the thousand and one activities whose results appear on the market; and even were it possible, such standards might not be acceptable to society at large, nor might national income estimates built on them be acceptable appraisals of the past performance of the economic system or bases for more intelligent consideration of public policy.

The ideal solution would be to attempt both approaches: to study in detail how the legal system expresses the judgment of society concerning the productive character of activities; to explore the various bases of objective and widely acceptable substantive criteria of productivity; and to implement these analyses by statistical measures of productive and unproductive activities thus distinguished. But such a solution is far beyond the scope of our investigation. With the data and time we had, we thought it most practicable to follow the first type of decision, i.e., to base the criterion of productivity upon the judgment of the body social as expressed in laws. This application does not mean that we classified all illegal activities as unproductive. We rejected as unproductive only those few activities—theft, robbery, organized private murder, forbidden drug peddling, and the like—whose detrimental character is obvious enough to preclude any doubt that it was the basis for the legal prohibition. A rather broadly inclusive concept of national income results: it excludes few activities and includes many that may seem from any long range viewpoint of social utility to be not only non-productive but actually harmful.

This aspect of our decision must be clearly borne in mind. The criterion of productivity followed in our estimates, chosen in line with current social opinion, classifies as productive activities that, for a society organized differently from the United States in this century, might well be considered worthless and even harmful. It swells national income with items that represent what many citizens condemn as a misuse of energy and the inadequacies of the existing social structure. It includes dreadnoughts, bombing planes, poison gas, and patent medicines because they are rated economic goods in our country today. Obviously, national income estimates based upon formal criteria of productivity retain meaning only so long and so far as the legal structure of a society reflects fairly accurately the opinions of the body social and so long as these opinions correspond, however crudely, to standards of satisfaction that can be established objectively. They are the results of a compromise that any critic who has time and data can supplement or replace by criteria of productivity that go far beyond the notion represented by the attributes of marketability and legality. It may well be that social standards will be so modified as to reduce our present estimates to absurdity. If so, all we can claim is that they have historical validity.

To summarize: our estimates cover primarily the product of the business and public economies. Of the goods not appearing on the market they include only those retained by producers for their own consumption, payments in kind to employees, and imputed rent on owner-occupied houses. On the other hand, of the net money receipts by individuals from ordinary market transactions or other sources the following are excluded: (a) receipts from pure transfers, such as relief payments, contributions, gifts, and gambling debts; (b) gains or losses on already existing assets, whether actually realized on their sale or accrued because of changed valuation; (c) products of illegal activities, such as smuggling, racketeering, bootlegging, and drug peddling.

Only the *direct* value of these receipts is omitted: net monetary receipts from transfers or non-productive marketable activities and, in the case of non-market goods, imputed values. Even though racketeering is not productive, and the income originating in it is excluded, we cannot eliminate the indirect effects, e.g., racketeers' demand for steel. Likewise, gains from sales of assets, as well as the activity of the family economy outside the market, affect market activity, and hence the goods included in national income. Since the business, public, and family economies are closely interrelated with the various parts of the market mechanism, the indirect consequences of the excluded activities on activities whose products are properly included in national income are far.reaching and it would be exceedingly difficult to eliminate them. But elimination of the indirect effects of the excluded activities on the areas covered, though a challenging task, is not indispensable. For what we measure is the net product of the economic system, regardless of its causal factors. Important as estimates of capital gains and losses and products of illegal activities may be in explaining how the national income came to be what it is, an estimate that omits them is useful; and when explanation is attempted, such factors as are comprised under the family economy, transfers of claims, or illegal activities, will have to be considered together with many others not mentioned here.

3 Economic Value

In discussing the inclusion and exclusion of certain groups of items, we touched indirectly upon how the items included among economic goods and hence in national income are to be combined. The diversity of physical shapes economic goods display and of wants they serve compels us to express them in terms of a common unit that will reveal their economic significance and allow them to be added and subtracted in various combinations. This measurable aspect, common to all economic goods and revealing their economic significance, we designate 'economic value'.

The yardstick of economic value is fashioned on the market place. It is in markets that economic goods are brought together and their relative importance gauged for purposes of sale and purchase; that the members of the community vote, in terms of the common currency unit, upon the relative value to them of various commodities, services, and arrangements.

In fact, to identify economic value with market price is, at least as the first step, the one possible solution of the problem. Nevertheless, market prices are a somewhat defective yardstick. Though unable to remedy its defects, we discuss them here to give a better understanding of the totals and subtotals derived with its help.

A   GOODS NOT APPEARING ON THE MARKET

Strictly speaking, there are no prices for non-market goods. How then should the value of goods that do not appear on the market be measured? The usual answer is that almost all non-market goods have their counterparts on the market and that they should be assigned the prices their counterparts fetch. For example, the value of payments in kind to employees is to be measured at the market prices of the goods distributed; the value of housewives' services, at prices paid domestic servants.

Though the only practicable one, this solution overlooks an important element making for lack of comparability between non-market goods and seemingly identical market goods. The purchaser of the latter ordinarily has considerable freedom of choice and opportunity to change his mind; the recipient of the former usually does not. For example, a household can choose among many types of servant, hire on trial, and dismiss as often as it is so inclined; a gentleman would not treat his wife so summarily. An employee receiving payments in kind as part of his wages may put a low valuation upon them and might not purchase them if he had to buy them at their market price. Were he to receive cash instead, he might be willing to accept less than the equivalent of the market price. Thus by assigning the full price of their market counterparts to non-market goods we may overvalue them. A similar conclusion would apply to almost all other non-market goods whose counterparts appear on the free markets of the business economy. The only items to which it does not apply are products retained by producers for their own consumption.

Moreover, prices of market goods, whether or not counterparts of non-market goods, are affected by the fact that of a given volume of goods produced, all is not put on the market to compete with market products. We should perhaps evaluate both non-market goods and all others at prices we think they would fetch if all goods were offered for sale. The amount of money remaining the same, the addition to the goods on the supply side would lower the prices of all goods. But, other conditions being equal, the decline in market prices might be greater for those goods a large share of which do not ordinarily appear on the market. If this reasoning is valid, then the application of existing market prices to non-market goods overvalues them on two counts: first, because of the distinct probability that they are of lower quality than the market goods with which they are *at all* comparable; second, because withholding them from the market may have served to maintain the prices of their *exact* counterparts at a level, relative to the prices of all other goods, higher than it might otherwise have been.

In addition to goods withheld from the market, a considerable quantity is in production and does not appear on the market by the end of the period for which national income is estimated. Some may never appear on the market in the exact form in which they are completed by their producers (e.g., a machine built by an enterprise for its own use); others will appear shortly after their completion (e.g., goods in process). Such uncompleted production must, nevertheless, be recorded and evaluated. In the absence of current market prices for them, the only basis for measurement is outlays incurred, i.e., essentially past market prices of the components of these uncompleted products.

Evaluating uncompleted products at cost and completed products at current market prices introduces an element of incomparability. In general, costs are less sensitive to changing conditions than current market prices; and the price set upon uncompleted goods evaluated on a cost basis may be quite

different from the price actually realized when they are completed and sold. This element of incomparability is minor if
the value of uncompleted goods is small relative to that of completed and marketed goods. But the shorter the interval for
which national income is estimated, the greater the ratio of
uncompleted to completed goods tends to be; and the larger
the element of incomparability introduced by using the two
bases of evaluation.

B   PECULIARITIES OF THE MARKET MECHANISM
But how valid is market price as a measure of the value even
of marketed goods? Does the price a commodity or service
fetches reflect faithfully its importance relative to other commodities and services, when judged from the viewpoint of
society at large? Though markets are the sole mechanism by
which goods are compared for purposes of exchange, and hence
market prices are the sole directly available measure of the
relative economic importance of diverse goods, they may distort economic value judged by any substantive criterion.
Indeed, closer scrutiny of the market mechanism reveals
numerous peculiarities that indicate that market prices do not
accurately measure how well goods and services satisfy the
needs of the body social. We describe these peculiarities
briefly, primarily in order that the necessity of using market
prices to evaluate the components of national income may not
be misunderstood.

   1) It is axiomatic that economic goods derive their values
from the contributions they are deemed capable of making
directly or indirectly to the satisfaction of present or future
needs. Yet, because no practical calculus of satisfaction has
been devised, we cannot appraise 'the net value of all economic goods produced' in terms of this fundamental criterion;
instead we must use price as the criterion. We realize that we
thereby accept the institutionalized valuations of a society in
which market demand reflects human needs only so far as they
are backed by purchasing power. No one supposes that the

distribution of income parallels the distribution of wants or satisfactions. At one end of the scale are people whose incomes are insufficient to buy adequate food, clothing, and shelter; at the other end are people whose incomes suffice to satisfy not merely the imperious necessities of life, but also the innumerable less intense wants men conceive when they are well fed, well clothed, and well housed. Therefore we cannot claim that our estimates of national income, based as they must be upon market valuations, evaluate goods as means of satisfying directly or indirectly the present or future needs of the population.

Within the limits of their purchasing power consumers exercise their buying rights in accordance with their preferences and what they think their needs are. Just as one may be critical of the effects on market valuation of an uneven distribution of purchasing power, so one may doubt the wisdom of consumers in their choice of goods and services. From the standpoint of objectively established tests and criteria of what people should demand and how they should apportion their resources, the behavior of consumers may seem irrational.[2] It may be argued, therefore, that whatever the effect of consumers' purchases on market valuation, it does not lead to estimates that reveal accurately how well various goods satisfy social needs objectively and scientifically determined.

But if we accept society's classification of activities as productive and unproductive, we must accept the market mechanism as it functions: with the exercise of unevenly distributed purchasing power and of free if irrational choices (limited for only a very few commodities, such as poisonous drugs) by ultimate consumers. We make the statement here to emphasize

2 This statement, as well as some of the discussion in Section 2 B above, implies that objective standards of needs are possible. This possibility could scarcely be denied for some of the more elemental needs of sustaining and reproducing life, but, of course, is more remote for other needs and wants. The reference to such objective standards and tests should not be interpreted as an assertion that they exist now, that they can be so formulated as to be studied in detail, or that they should be imposed upon society.

how a viewpoint penetrates the entire network of definition and procedures; and again call attention to other viewpoints and the differences in quantitative results they are likely to cause.

2) Under conditions of effective competition, prices are set at the intersection of the supply curve with the demand curve; i.e., where the quantity of products turned out is as great as will be purchased by people wanting them and able to pay a price neither smaller nor greater than the marginal cost. With the development of significant departures from competitive conditions, there are corresponding changes in the mechanism of market prices. A distinctive feature of monopolistic conditions on the supply side is that an individual producer can alter prices for his product by putting a larger or smaller volume of goods on the market. More specifically and simply, he can restrict the total output of his product and charge a higher price per unit. If all other conditions remain the same, the monopolist's price is likely to be above marginal cost to him and also above marginal competitive cost.

There is another closely related feature of monopolistic behavior. Unlike a competitive producer, a monopolist can charge discriminatory prices, i.e., demand and obtain different prices for goods of one and the same kind from would-be purchasers of different classes. This substitution of several prices for the single price of a competitive market does not often invalidate the statement made above that, in general, monopolized goods are valued on the market at prices substantially higher than they would have fetched under competitive conditions;[3] but 'prices' must be a weighted average of all the monopolist's prices for the product, not any single price charged by him. In addition, the varying degree to which monopolists can charge different customers different rates becomes in itself a factor in setting the weighted prices of

[3] In some cases, however, it may reverse the result and lead to an average price lower than that charged for a competitive product.

monopolized products at certain levels above their competitive counterparts.

It may be argued that 'economic value' is measured properly only in competitive markets, for only here are real costs and returns (qualified by the distribution of purchasing power) allowed full play; that the existence of monopolies distorts price relationships and introduces an element of incomparability between goods sold on competitive and on monopolistic markets. And were one to meet the requirement of homogeneity of the competitive structure of markets, it would be exceedingly difficult to correct for this peculiarity of market prices, for competitive or monopolistic prices would have to be constructed in areas where they do not exist, causing a realignment throughout the price system.

The real question, however, is whether, recognizing this peculiarity of market prices as a limitation of the market mechanism when viewed as a way of determining values in some ideal system, we should not also admit it as part and parcel of a functioning society, which accepts it. Whether or not the investigator as an individual considers this aspect of the price structure beneficial, he must accept prices as they function, including their structural imperfections, if he bases his estimates upon the accepted notions of society. This is, perhaps, all the more true since monopolistic features have been directly attacked by society, which exercises whatever power it sees fit in governing price and other policies. In a sense, monopoly prices, although not determined by exactly the same processes as competitive prices and having a somewhat different meaning, do represent the valuation that society allows to be assigned a given category of goods or activities.

3) Almost all market transactions take place with the help of money, the exchange of one good for another being split into two separate acts of sale for and purchase with money. In comparisons at a given time, the possibility that money itself is an independent factor in determining market prices remains elusive: a universally accepted and all pervading

medium of exchange, money seems at any instant to be merely
the unit of accounting, a transparent veil through which the
relations among diverse goods can be seen but which in itself
has no effect on these relations. When changes over time are
considered, this impression proves erroneous. Market values,
all expressed in terms of money, can fluctuate because of fluctuations in monetary conditions, even if the supply of goods remains constant. And money, understood in the broad sense
as all means of payment in market transactions, is itself subject to several independent influences though they may on
second or third remove originate in the circulation of goods.

The most immediate effect of monetary fluctuations on
market prices is to make market value totals unreliable guides
to temporal changes in the quantity of goods on the market.
The instability of the unit by which market value is measured
at different times is an obvious defect of current prices, and
one for which statistical and economic analysis has most ardu-
ously attempted to adjust.

But there is another and much less obvious effect of fluctuations in money. The shift in the level of market prices they
cause does not affect the prices of various goods either simul-
taneously or equally. Since fluctuations in money, as well as
other disturbances, are not infrequent, relations between
market prices are continually being modified by differences in
the time and amplitude of the reaction. Consequently in
temporal comparisons price changes caused by fluctuations
in the value of money are not uniform among economic goods;
and any attempt to adjust for fluctuations in the value of
money is, therefore, much more difficult than if we could
assume a uniform rise or decline of all prices.

The devices used to evaluate the real contents of monetary
transactions vary in complexity and accuracy. The most common is to measure fluctuations in the value of money or in the
general price level. Prices at successive points of time are
recorded for one and the same group of economic goods.
An index constructed from the observable fluctuations in

them is assumed to measure fluctuations in the general price level or in the value of money. With its help, totals of market values in current prices are adjusted for fluctuations in prices.[4]

The numerous practical difficulties that arise in compiling price indexes need not be discussed here. We note merely that the all inclusive character of national income totals makes especially difficult the compilation of indexes that reflect changes in the prices of all goods entering them. Of more immediate interest is a difficulty central to the entire procedure: the conflict between the requirement that the index cover prices of the goods included in national income and the impossibility of meeting the requirement, owing to qualitative changes in the goods.

As noted above, the prices of diverse goods react with different intensity and timing to current or prospective changes in monetary conditions. If, therefore, the index is to measure fluctuations in prices common to all goods and hence ascribable to fluctuations in money, it cannot be computed for merely a part of the price universe. The assumption that prices of goods not included in the index move in the same direction and to the same extent as the prices included is dangerous. Such a selective coverage would be justified only if we could classify goods according to the responsiveness of their prices to fluctuations in money. The goods from each class included in the index could then be assigned a weight determined by the importance of the class as a whole. Since a reasonably complete classification of this type is not available, a price index cannot be satisfactory unless it has relatively complete coverage.

But prices can be compared at successive points of time only if goods of identical type appear on the market. Yet changes in technology and in the tastes of ultimate consumers spell qualitative changes over time. As some commodities (e.g., buggies, certain types of attire) disappear, new ones (auto-

[4] Another device is to construct indexes of output. The problems are analogous to those for indexes of the general price level.

mobiles, radios, etc.) appear; and some are so subject to qualitative changes that, while called by the same name, the unit of 1921 is hardly the same as that of 1941 (e.g., certain types of industrial machinery). Thus, even for commodities, prices comparable for a substantial period exist solely for goods that undergo merely minor qualitative changes and that are in active market circulation throughout the period. Among services it is still more difficult to establish qualitative homogeneity; qualitative changes are rather likely, and shifts into and out of markets frequent.

A further difficulty arises even for those goods for which comparable prices exist for a period. All are in active circulation during the period but the relative quantities in which they are produced and appear on the market, needed as weights in combining the prices into a general index, are not constant. Which set of quantities is to be used? If those of year 1 are used, then the measure of price changes assumes as basic the goods-basket in year 1; similarly for years 2, 3, etc. Since one and only one set of quantities can be used in an index, the measure of changes in the price level is always based upon some past, present, or intermediate basket of goods whose validity is confined to the point of time to which it refers.

In sum, even if all possible price data are at hand and no effort is spared, the measurement of temporal changes in prices and hence the possibility of establishing comparability in 'heterotemporal' comparisons is qualified by the limitation of prices to a body of goods appearing on the market throughout the period and by the necessity of choosing a single set of quantities as weights. The difficulty is practical: the choice is between presenting national income estimates solely in terms of current, fluctuating market prices, and attempting a necessarily imperfect correction for movements common to all prices and thus ascribable to fluctuations in the value of money. When changes in the general price level are appreciable, it is obviously better to make even an imperfect adjustment than to leave national income totals affected by fluctuations that express changes in neither the quantity of goods nor the substantively defined value per unit.

C VALUATION OF GOVERNMENTAL SERVICES

If governmental activities are treated as unproductive, as they have been by many national income investigators in the more distant past, no problem of valuation arises: by definition, the value of governmental services is zero. Such a treatment is manifestly invalid: governmental activities contribute too much to the satisfaction of needs and are too closely interwoven with the entire network of market relations for their role as economic and productive pursuits to be ignored.[5] But on what basis are they to be evaluated?

One basis, to treat value of governmental services as meas-

[5] It could hardly be denied that the services of the post office, judiciary, etc. represent productive activities and contribute to the satisfaction of the needs of society at large. Doubts, however, have often been expressed concerning the validity of including the services of police or armed forces in national income; and many estimators have explicitly excluded payments of interest on government debt created by wars, on the assumption that no productive services correspond to them and that they are, therefore, mere transfers.

One can easily see the reason for such treatment if an investigator adopts criteria of productivity in the light of which he can modify judgments expressed by an overt act of the body social. However, only the acceptance of criteria of productivity different from those applied by society at large would justify this treatment. Since the estimators or analysts who advocate it usually profess to accept the dictates of the market place, the exclusion of services of governmental agencies such as police or armed forces and of interest payments on government debt seems inconsistent. If the activities of the private police used by many large corporations are productive, why not those of municipal police? And if of domestic police, why not of international police, i.e., the armed forces of the nation? If capital invested in industrial plants is productive, why not capital sunk in the preservation of the country's economic system or in securing to it economic privileges that affect the welfare of all enterprises or inhabitants? The objection that private enterprises cease paying interest on capital when it ceases to be productive, that they retire the debt or cancel it through default is not valid; governmental agencies act in like manner, though with a greater lag. Indeed, there is considerable parallelism between governments and private corporations in their expenditures on policing, economic warfare, their financial structure, and their policies with respect to debt.

ured by payments to governments by enterprises and individuals, is similar to that applied to other goods entering national income. The implication is either that, as on the private markets of the economy, individuals and enterprises pay the amounts governmental services are specifically worth to each of them; or that while neither individuals nor enterprises determine singly and individually how much governmental services are worth to them, society at large, through its established agencies for the expression of public opinion, does determine the total value of governmental services and sets the payment for them accordingly.

This treatment is questionable. The market on which governments sell their services is, with a few important exceptions, one where the suppliers (i.e., governments) have the power to fix an obligatory payment (in the form of taxes, fees, assessments, etc.). On the markets where the prices of other goods are determined, on the contrary, the potential purchaser is free to buy or abstain from buying. Consequently, can the payments governments exact be regarded as prices measuring the economic value of their services to society at large? Are the prices comparable to prices set on private markets? The strongest doubt concerns the tax paid by a given individual or business firm. Does it measure accurately the value of the services rendered by government to this particular payer?

It has been suggested that instead of evaluating governmental services at payments made to governments it would be better to use the cost principle. The implication is that the conditions under which governments buy and use production factors such as labor and materials are more similar to those of private markets than those under which they sell services or determine the payment to be made.

The choice between the two principles is largely between two evils, for neither is adequate. Costs adjust themselves more slowly to changing economic conditions than payments; moreover, an enterprise may sustain a net gain or loss, either inadvertently or as a matter of policy. Both are disadvantages of the cost principle as applied to governmental activities; in addition, since all other goods are evaluated, as far as possible, at current market prices, the application of the cost principle to governmental services introduces an element of incomparability among the components of national income. On the other hand, the payment-price approach to governmental services is arbitrary because of the enforcement power of governmental agencies and because the relations between governments and citizens are hardly characterized by the same spirit of calculation and economic rationality that prevails in private markets.

Two considerations tip the balance in favor of the payment-price basis of evaluation. First, the difference between the results of the two bases would obviously be great chiefly for short periods, when governments may sustain large deficits or surpluses not offset by equivalent additions to or drafts upon tangible assets. But for short term changes the lag in costs and their insensitivity to changes in the market situation are especially conspicuous defects. Since the purpose of studying short term changes is to ascertain how the economic system responds to varying conditions, it seems preferable to use a valuation basis that is more sensitive to changing conditions.

Second, in estimating national income we need not be concerned whether a principle of valuation is efficient as applied to discrete units of goods and services passing through the market. We should judge its efficiency in measuring total national income and its significant components. For example, we should ask ourselves whether the payment-price is a valid basis when we consider the price paid by society at large for all governmental services,[6] not whether it is valid when applied to the prices (taxes) paid by Mr. Jones or Mr. Smith. When thus viewed in application to the whole complex of governmental services, the payment-price approach gives more reasonable results and has certain other advantages over the cost basis.

[6] Or more correctly, prices paid by ultimate consumers as a whole separately from those paid by all enterprises; see Section 4.

The piling up of deficits during depressions, which allows the market value of governmental services to fall below the cost value, is obviously in response to the changed market situation, and may be interpreted as reflecting a lower current valuation placed by society on governmental services. The case seems to be parallel to that of business corporations whose costs also tend to exceed returns during depressions, indicating that the valuation placed by society upon their products has declined compared with that implied in the past outlay. The difference is that whereas services of corporations are evaluated by the large body of consumers acting separately through private and free markets, the services of governments are evaluated by political agencies whose basic function is to express the consensus of opinion of the body social. But this difference does not seem to justify the adoption of the cost principle of valuation.

For these reasons, in our estimates governmental services are valued by the payment-price approach. But since the difference between the two approaches lies in an item estimated separately, viz., net savings of governmental agencies, anyone so inclined can substitute the cost approach.

4 Distinction between Net and Gross

We have defined national income as the *net* value of all goods produced by the nation during a given time unit. The emphasis on net and the need of distinguishing between gross and net values become clear from two observations. First, national income measures the results of economic activity cumulated over a finite period, rather than the state of the economic system at any one time. Second, the production of economic goods, both within separate enterprises and for the economic system as a whole, involves the use and consumption of already existing goods, products of time units preceding the one whose products are being measured or of this time unit itself. Since the full value of any good includes the value of other goods absorbed in its production, it would not do to count in national

income the full value of A as well as the value of B consumed
in the process of producing A.

The distinction between gross and net is clearest in the case
of a single enterprise. In performing its productive functions
during a given period, an enterprise almost inevitably consumes products of past periods and of other enterprises. Its
specific contribution to the value of goods made available during the current period for purposes of consumption and addition to stock is the value of its products *over and above* the
value of products of past periods and of other enterprises consumed in the production process. Thus the *net* value of the
enterprise's product is the full or *gross* value minus the value
consumed by it, i.e., the cost of commodities and of services of
other enterprises used up in the production process. The factors in a given enterprise that give rise to the excess of the gross
value of product over the value of products consumed can be
identified: they are labor, services of managerial and entrepreneurial personnel and of capital. The net value of product
is thus the value of production specifically attributable to
labor, capital, and entrepreneurial ability engaged in the
enterprise.

This description can be extended to the national economy
as a whole. The sum of the net values of products turned out
by the enterprises that comprise the economic system is the
net total that constitutes national income; and the sum of the
full values of products of the various enterprises yields a gross
national product total. The difference between national income and this gross national product is the value of products
of enterprises consumed in the productive activity of all enterprises that comprise the national economy. In other words, net
national product or national income is the value of product
specifically attributable to labor, capital, and entrepreneurial
ability.

Two types of difficulty arise in following this definition. The
first concerns the meaning and scope of 'enterprise' and 'consumption'. The relation of net to gross varies with the defini-

tion of these terms because of differences in items deducted from gross to obtain net. Again the problem is one of inclusion and exclusion, similar to that encountered in Section 2 in the discussion of the concept of economic goods, except that here inclusion and exclusion apply to deduction items and have an opposite effect on national income. The second difficulty arises when the items subject to deduction have already been defined: it is not always feasible to estimate their value in a way consonant with the evaluation of total product.

A INTERMEDIATE AND ULTIMATE CONSUMPTION

The meaning of the term enterprise is far from unique and specific. An economic enterprise in general, including such non-profit organizations as governmental agencies, may be described as a unit set up for production processes that result in economic goods. What then prevents us from classifying each wage earner as a separate economic enterprise whose primary purpose is to render labor services at the highest possible price? If this were done, the net value of products turned out by a factory would have to exclude wages paid to wage earners, since such payments would represent the value of consumed products of other enterprises. Instead we would have to add the net value of products of the various enterprises called wage earners. This net value would equal not the full amount of wages received (the *gross* value of the product of these wage-earning enterprises), but wages minus the cost of products wage-earning enterprises buy from other enterprises and consume in the process of producing labor power (food, clothing, and other means of maintenance and reproduction). Consequently, this extension of the concept of enterprise would materially reduce both the net value of goods produced by the economic system and national income.

Similar reasoning can be applied to other elements now commonly included in national income. Each salary earner, entrepreneur, holder of a managerial and executive position can be conceived of as an independent enterprise; the compensation for the products of each should be deducted from the gross value of products of the business or other unit in which each is employed, and from the total receipts of each should be subtracted the cost of maintaining and reproducing his capacity of rendering services of various types. Even for purely property income a case can be made for subtracting from total payments received the cost of maintaining a degree of abstinence and farsightedness indispensable for savings and investments. This extension of the concept of enterprise widens the scope of intermediate consumption, i.e., consumption of goods for the purpose of producing other goods, at the expense of ultimate consumption, i.e., consumption for carrying on life in its broadest aspects; and reduces the net national product or national income to that exceedingly minor magnitude that may be considered as *not* involved in the replacement of all goods, human capacity included, consumed in the process of economic production.

No purely analytical or empirical consideration can invalidate this extension of the concept of enterprise: it is largely a terminological question. But were this extension made and national income given the narrow scope and meaning, it would no longer reflect prevailing notions of the distinction between economic activity and life in general; and we should become more concerned with estimating the type of gross national product that corresponds to what we now call national income. Essentially we are interested in the type of national income we estimate because it corresponds broadly to current social philosophy, evolved from the basic assumptions of the modern social structure. We do not look upon human beings as enterprises, as units for the production of other goods; consequently, we do not view the raising and education of the younger generation or the sustenance of the working population as intermediate consumption destined to produce or sustain so many machines for performing labor, management, entrepreneurial, or capital-saving functions. It is this idea of economic goods existing for men, rather than men for economic goods, that gives point to the concept of ultimate consumption and special interest to national income as usually defined. In this definition intermediate consumption is confined to the consumption, in the production process carried on by business and public enterprises, as the term is usually understood, of commodities and of services of other enterprises.

It may be contended that the attribution of primacy to the ultimate consumer is an idealization and that the corresponding national income concept suffers from the incongruity of combining the *net* return from the use of capital with the total or *gross* return from the direct use of human services. We do not deny the incongruity; its corollary is that we estimate national income on the assumption that the capital of business and public enterprises is kept intact, but do not apply such a criterion to capital represented by human capacity. To repeat, the one justification for formulating the national income concept in this way is the general notion that it should measure the positive contribution of the economic system to the satisfaction of present and future needs of the nation as a body of ultimate consumers; and this notion of ultimate consumption is essentially derivable only from the view that goods exist for men, not men for goods. It is immaterial whether this view is realistic in the sense of being embodied in all the institutions of modern economic society; that it is not, many observers have declared. The point is that national income is an appraisal notion of this type and our task is to reveal its implications.

Other concepts of national income are of course not thereby barred; various types of gross and net national product may be as useful as 'national income' as we define it. It would be of great utility to measure the entire range of possible totals, beginning with the gross national product in which duplication is most extensive and ending with the narrowest net national product representing the broadest interpretation of the term 'enterprise'. If subtrahend and minuend are estimated separately, as they naturally would be in a whole series of totals ranging from the 'grossest' to the 'nettest', we would have a most illuminating picture of the working of the economic system. Among our estimates, for the parts of the economy for which data are available, are estimates of the gross value of product. And if in measuring net national product, we define intermediate consumption as the consumption by business and public enterprises, as the term is usually understood, of commodities and of services of other enterprises, it is because with the data and time at our disposal, we, in common with other investigators, consider this particular concept best suited to the basic criterion of appraisal, viz., provision of goods for the satisfaction of ultimate consumers of the present and future.

Application of these concepts of enterprise and intermediate consumption shows that some intermediate consumption by enterprises takes the form of consumption by individuals. But, when we try to differentiate between ultimate consumption as the basis of life in its broadest aspects and consumption forced upon individuals by the performance of specific productive functions, and hence eligible for classification as intermediate consumption, we are faced with analytical difficulties arising from the close interrelation in individuals' lives of occupation and other factors and from the impossibility of disentangling the purely economic elements in the organic pattern of life. Both tax laws and common sense treat the traveling expenses of salesmen as business expenses and intermediate consumption; but what about the expenses of commuting, which the tax laws do not recognize as deductible? Should the cost of work clothing or the differential cost of clothing demanded by occupational status be considered a 'business' expense and deducted in establishing the net national product? What of the expenses of special types of education? of special medical care needed to offset the incidence of specific occupations?

For lack of data (which is, in turn, due partly to the analytical difficulties just mentioned), we deduct practically no occupational expenses. Entrepreneurs constitute the sole important exception, but even for them only outlays reported under business expenses are deducted. Direct outlays on intermediate consumption, usually designated 'occupational expenses', are largest, both absolutely and relatively, for individuals engaged in rendering direct labor or other services; and are negligible for individuals in their capacity as savers and investors. Disregard of occupational expenses makes the service income items in national income 'gross' compared with the property income items in two respects: (1) the maintenance and reproduction of human capital is not allowed for; (2) even the outlays by service income earners incurred in specific connection with their productive functions are not deducted.

A much simpler problem of inclusion and exclusion hinges upon the meaning of 'consumption' when we speak of deducting intermediate consumption in deriving the net value product. By 'consumption' we typically mean a decline in the value of a good sustained in the process of utilization. This process of utilization associated with intermediate consumption is usually the process of production, of turning out the gross value product. But obviously, goods belonging to enterprises may lose value through events that cannot be interpreted as representing the process of production or of intermediate consumption: declines in value that may reflect sudden changes on the demand side or in the physical conditions of production, as well as changes in price levels, general or specific. Sudden shifts in consumers' tastes, fires, strikes, riots, wars, earthquakes and other acts of God may cause material declines in the value of goods ordinarily utilized by enterprises in the production process. Intermediate consumption includes only those declines that represent the ordinary and calculable hazards of active participation in the production process. Other changes, even though they have substantial effect on the economic welfare of individual enterprises are not part of the continuous and organized process of production. And just as we exclude from national income gains in capital value arising from such events, so we exclude from intermediate consumption any declines in value caused by them.

B ESTIMATING INTERMEDIATE CONSUMPTION

Once the distinction between intermediate and ultimate consumption and the meaning of the latter term have been established, national income can be computed by subtracting the magnitude representing intermediate consumption from the full or gross value of goods produced. This derivation of the *net* value of the national product by subtraction is not avoided even if the net values are given directly in the data, for in that case the subtraction has been done by the agencies providing the data, and we would still have to test the procedure by which intermediate consumption and the full value of products have been estimated by them. Of the specific questions that may arise in estimating the value of intermediate consumption we discuss two: (a) the consumption of durable products and of materials; (b) the measurement of those governmental services that represent intermediate consumption.

a) When the process of intermediate consumption involves the complete physical disappearance of the good, or, more accurately, such substantial transformation that we cease to recognize the good, its full value measures the magnitude of the consumption. But when the physical transformation in the process of utilization takes long, there is no quantitative evidence of consumption for relatively short intervals. All fixed, durable capital goods are in this category; and one of the first difficulties encountered in estimating national income for an interval as short as a year is to get annual values of the intermediate consumption of such goods.

What fraction of the durable capital good is consumed during the given period? The signs that would indicate that this or that fraction of a machine's total useful life or capacity has been absorbed are few. There are few reliable data even on total useful life and capacity.[7] Consequently, estimates by business enterprises of current consumption of durable capital are exceedingly crude, and many enterprises to which no immediate advantage would accrue from making them, do not. The investigator must accept these estimates, crude as they are, for he cannot hope to improve upon the practice of business units vitally concerned with a proper determination of the costs of their activity. But he must himself estimate durable capital consumption for the other parts of the business and public economy, even though entrepreneurs and public agencies themselves do not. To prevent distortion of the national income total and its distribution, estimates of intermediate consumption must be complete.

The fractions of durable capital goods consumed during a given period having been established and those for non-durable goods being known to equal 1, to what values should these fractions be applied in estimating intermediate consumption? Since it is to be deducted from the total value of products to yield the net, it should be as far as possible in terms of the yardstick used for the full value of completed products—the current market price, with whatever modifications needed to adjust for changes over time or to cover uncompleted production.

This conclusion is so obvious as to seem axiomatic. Yet it is not the practice followed by business enterprises and other producing agencies that estimate intermediate consumption. They usually calculate the consumption of durable capital as a fraction of the original cost of acquisition, except when it has been reappraised or revalued. Materials carried in inventories are usually charged at either original cost or market price, whichever is lower. For both groups of goods, substantial changes in price levels may bring about considerable disparities between the estimates of intermediate consumption ac-

---

[7] Indeed, it may be argued that any allowance of a fraction for a given year involves a forecast of the future, a forecast of the expected decline in capital value. Data for such forecasts are necessarily few.

tually made by business and other enterprises and the estimates that would be obtained by valuation based on current market prices. We attempt to adjust items in national income that reflect the prevalent practices of enterprises for the effect of departures from the principle of valuing all items at the prices they currently fetch on the market.

b) In estimating intermediate consumption it is assumed that outlays can be directly connected with the gross value of product originating, in that the former were incurred by the enterprise in order to obtain the latter. This assumption is manifestly valid for most outlays: a firm consumes durable capital equipment, raw materials, services of other enterprises, in order to produce gross and net income; and refrains from outlays that are not likely to increase gross, and consequently perhaps net, profit. But this is true solely of the intermediate consumption over which the enterprise has discretion, in the sense of opportunity to incur or refrain from the outlay.

Here, as in the valuation of governmental services, the exercise of governmental control over enterprises renders dubious assumptions readily accepted for private market activities. It may be argued that governments can and do levy taxes on enterprises greater than the value of their services to enterprises; and that consequently some income payments flow *via* governmental channels from enterprises to ultimate income recipients. If this is true, we cannot treat payments by enterprises to governments as a measure of intermediate consumption: they would be larger than intermediate consumption of governmental services and net national product would be undervalued if they were deducted. Obviously, the opposite may also be true: enterprises may pay governments less than the value of the services rendered them by governments; these payments may, therefore, understate the intermediate consumption of governmental services and net national product would be overvalued if they were deducted.

This argument implies that distinct groups of governmental services (e.g., those rendered enterprises as distinct from those rendered ultimate consumers) should be valued on a basis other than the payments made for them. Such valuation is not incompatible with valuing total governmental services on the basis of payments. It may be argued that society at large determines the *total* value of governmental services by determining how much will be paid for them, but that the apportionment of services and payments among specific groups of recipients and payers need not follow the principle of identity of value rendered and payment exacted. Both administrative and social policy considerations may require that enterprises be subject to greater or smaller assessments than they would be on the basis of services received, no matter how valued.

If governmental services to enterprises are separated from those to ultimate consumers, then, even if *total* governmental services are assumed equal to payments by enterprises and individuals, intermediate consumption might still be unequal to payments by enterprises. It might be claimed that the cost (or any other aspect called x) of various services indicates their relative value (implying that any difference between total cost (or x) and total payment value may be apportioned among various items in constant proportion to cost (or x) incurred); and that on this basis, payments by enterprises to governments contain a hidden transfer to ultimate consumers, or fail to reveal a hidden draft upon ultimate consumers by enterprises. In practice, this would mean the segregation of governmental services to enterprises from those to ultimate consumers; and the determination of the value of the two groups by apportioning total value (i.e., total payments) according to costs or any other basis. If intermediate consumption so determined is less than payments by enterprises, national income is increased; if it is greater, national income is reduced.

However, this treatment implies that we can separate governmental services to enterprises and to ultimate consumers. For some governmental activities such as information service to business concerns, on the one hand, and provision of public parks, on the other, we can, but for most essential governmental activities the line of demarcation between services to enterprises and to ultimate consumers is faint. For example, it would be exceedingly difficult to apportion between enterprises and individuals the services of the army and navy, the legislature, the public utility divisions of governments (streets, roads, etc.), activities designed to meet the needs of the community at large. And even many governmental services that seem at first to be directly of benefit to either enterprises or individuals cannot easily be classified under one or the other head. Relief payments are presumably services to individuals, but they also help to preserve the labor supply, a service to enterprises. Research into quality standards is presumably of direct utility to enterprises, but it also benefits ultimate consumers.

The difficulties of differentiating between services to individuals and to enterprises make any apportionment of governmental activities arbitrary. Any estimate of intermediate consumption of governmental services would in turn be arbitrary. Under the circumstances it seemed best to adopt the most easily obtainable: taxes and other payments by enterprises to governments. Manifestly a compromise, it may distort total national income and the proportion of industrial components. But it seemed the most expedient in view of the inadequacy of data on governmental outlays and the analytical difficulty of separating governmental services to enterprises and to individuals.[8]

8 Since the total value of all governmental services is measured by payments to governments by individuals and business enterprises, and since the value of governmental services to business enterprises is measured by payments of the latter to governments, the value of governmental services to individuals is measured by payments by individuals to governments. This equivalence is assumed for the broad groups *in toto;* not, of course, for payments by and services to any specific individual or business enterprise.

Thus our national income total includes all payments by enterprises to individuals. In estimating income flow to individuals, taxes paid by them, being payments for services rendered, are not subtracted any more than are payments for bread or medical services.

5   The Meaning of 'Produced'

The meaning of 'produced' and 'production' has been discussed at several points. We could not define the concepts of productivity and intermediate consumption properly without defining production. For example, we had to exclude changes in capital value whenever they seemed to be caused by factors outside the regular processes we associate with production—extracting, transforming, transporting, and distributing commodities and rendering services. But we have not yet discussed the validity of defining national income as the value of goods *produced,* rather than as the value of these goods at some stage in their circulation in the economic system. Nor have we established the time at which goods may be considered to be 'produced'.

A   'PRODUCED', 'PAID OUT', 'SPENT', 'CONSUMED'

Is it the value of goods *produced* that leads to the most valid appraisal of the positive contents of economic activity? Since the final aim is to satisfy the wants of ultimate consumers, we might perhaps more properly center attention on ultimate consumption. Instead of defining national income as the value of goods produced, we should perhaps define it as the value of goods consumed by ultimate consumers.

Between the completion of production and ultimate consumption two intervening stages can be distinguished. The first is that of disbursements by producing enterprises to ultimate consumers, largely in compensation for productive services rendered by them or their capital. Most of the total money value of goods produced during a year is distributed in payments to ultimate consumers, and these payments constitute the principal, although not the only, means of purchase at their disposal. The second stage is that at which ultimate consumers spend the money. For any given period the total of such expenditures on the purchase of finished goods is not necessarily equal to the payments received from the producing establishments or to the value of products actually consumed by ultimate consumers.[9]

We may describe national income as the net value of goods produced, or as total payments by producing enterprises to individuals largely in return for the productive services of the latter or of their property, or as total outlay by ultimate consumers on finished goods, or as the total value of goods consumed by the nation's ultimate consumers. For any reasonably short period, no two of the four totals will be the same; and between some pairs of totals the differences are substantial for any period. While the choice is largely terminological, the way in which national income is defined affects the total and its variability over time.

Several choices are possible. First, national income may be used as a generic term to designate all or any of the four totals, the totals being differentiated by a qualifying adjective. We may speak of 'national income produced', 'national income paid out', 'national income spent', and 'national income consumed'. While this usage has the advantage of stressing the essential multiplicity of possible totals corresponding to the variety of uses to which they may be put, it has obvious disadvantages. It tends to create confusion, for in seeking to appraise the results of economic activity there is a natural and justifiable tendency to look for a single total of general acceptability and validity. Moreover, it is awkward to speak of national income 'paid out' or 'spent': the term 'income' indicates an inflow; expenditures or payments, an outflow.

It is therefore preferable to confine 'national income' to one total, the net value of goods produced. The first and foremost reason is that it is a more comprehensive concept than any of the other three: what enterprises produce is the only source from which, in the long and often in the short run, ultimate consumers derive the means of payment they spend or save. In our economic system the net value of goods pro-

[9] These four stages are analytical, not chronological. At any given time goods are being produced, disbursements made, incomes spent, and goods consumed.

duced is usually, though not in every year, greater than payments to individuals; and still greater than consumers' outlay for goods or ultimate consumption. The practical advantage of designating the statistically larger total as national income is that it increases the probability that the other totals, which are components, will be estimated. In addition, it is the meaning of the term most consonant with usage in both economic literature and everyday discourse.

Nevertheless, the utility of the other totals and the advantage of estimating them are obvious. Aggregate payments to individuals, consumers' expenditures or outlay, and the total value of products actually consumed by individuals and households are all essential in interpreting national income as the measure of goods made available for ultimate consumption, present or future. As far as we can, we estimate not only the net value of goods produced but also aggregate payments to individuals and consumers' outlay; and only the absence of reliable continuous series prevents us from measuring the total value of goods consumed by individuals and households.

B THE TIMING OF PRODUCTION

For any period for which income is estimated, some production processes are incomplete and goods are maturing whose production was initiated during a preceding period. When may a good be considered to be 'produced'? In our decision, due weight must be given to the necessity of establishing net values primarily on the basis of current market prices.

One of two lines of treatment may be followed in dealing with uncompleted production or results of production processes initiated in preceding periods. The first is to consider a good as produced only when it actually appears on the market and there fetches the current price that reveals its economic value. All the prior processes of physical transformation are treated as preparatory to 'production', not as in themselves constituting production. National income would then exclude all uncompleted production, i.e., the output of commodities and services that had not yet reached the market.

This treatment has the advantage that the principle of valuation based on current market prices can be consistently applied, except to goods retained by producers for their own consumption. However, the disadvantages more than counterbalance this advantage. The production process, which for many goods takes place over a considerable period, is telescoped into a single point of time—when the goods appear on the market. The procedure neglects substantial additions to or drafts upon stock completed or in process during a given year as well as the large differences that may exist between the value of such uncompleted production or production for stock and the value of production brought over from preceding years. Finally, as long as we do not confine national income to consumers' outlay or ultimate consumption but include also investment and savings, it would obviously be highly inconsistent to use a narrow concept of production in which sale on the market is the distinctive mark of completion.

The other line of treatment has already been suggested: to admit the results of production processes before the products appear on the market; to measure uncompleted production on the best basis feasible, that of costs incurred; and to exclude from any given year's value production that was going on during a preceding year but was not yet completed, and was taken into account then. Although this treatment necessarily increases the area in which a principle other than current market price is applied, it seems better to record net production during a given interval, even though its parts are somewhat incommensurable, than to neglect a part of a given year's production and include parts of production of preceding years.

Whether this treatment can be applied in statistical practice depends largely on when producing enterprises themselves recognize that production is completed. If their accounts are kept on an accrual basis and record an increase in the value of stock as further work is done and costs are incurred on uncompleted production, we can include uncompleted production at cost. If the enterprises themselves do not acknowledge the existence of production until the good appears on the market, an estimate of all production, whether or not the good is on the market, is virtually impossible. The practices of business enterprises differ. The accrual basis is usual when the production process is relatively long and there is distinct physical evidence of transformation in the goods as a result of the production process (e.g., construction); the cash market basis, when the process is relatively short and there is little physical evidence of accrual of value (e.g., trade). National income estimates represent a mixture of the two treatments, a point to be kept in mind especially in interpreting estimates as indicators of short term changes in the value of the net product of economic activity.

The treatment adopted for timing the production of goods should be applied also to the timing of intermediate consumption in ascertaining the *net* values involved. Since goods that are completed within the year are evaluated at prices current when they appear on the market, their gross or full value should be reduced by intermediate consumption evaluated at the prices of goods consumed current at the time the final product appears on the market. And since uncompleted production is evaluated at cost, the associated intermediate consumption should also be evaluated at cost. The combination of the current market price and cost methods of valuation and the mixture of the two treatments in the timing of production should affect in equal degree the gross value of both goods produced and intermediate consumption sustained in producing them.

6 National Economy as Object of Measurement
The adjective 'national' used to characterize income estimates for various countries is not quite accurate. A nation may be defined as a group endowed with a common history, language, and cultural heritage, and a consciousness of kind, but not

necessarily possessed of a country with a sovereign government. All so-called national income estimates refer, however, not to the total income of national groups but to the total income of countries, each constituting a sovereign state. Some of these state units comprise more than one nation (e.g., pre-1918 Austria-Hungary); others represent only part of a national group (e.g., Great Britain). The corresponding estimates of income should perhaps rather be designated as 'statewide'. But the present terminology is too deeply intrenched to be susceptible to easy change.

The definition raises immediately the larger question of the utility and validity of striking off income totals for economic activities circumscribed by the boundaries of a sovereign state. Why choose state units at all? Since they do not always constitute self-contained economic systems, the unit chosen is not necessarily a natural one. i.e., one that would be defined by a student delimiting an economic region. A great deal of arbitrariness and historical accident, and a marked absence of historical continuity, may characterize the territorial composition of any given sovereign state. True, every sovereign state attempts to inculcate a feeling of unity and continuity in its citizens. But should economic science further such attempts by accepting these doctrines at their face value, couching all its discourse in terms of statewide economies, and making its basic estimates in terms of national totals, i.e., totals for the relatively artificial boundaries of states? Why should we segregate a particular group of individuals and enterprises, subsumed under the state, for the purpose of adding the net product of their activity and of their property; and especially why should we accept the judgments of this particular group of people concerning productivity and economic value?

It may well be contended that our *national* totals suffer from two limitations. First, they are artificial because they combine products and activities of groups that lack cohesion and homogeneity. One could argue that it might be more effective to study income totals by occupational-industrial groups, no matter in what country they reside. We would then be dealing with world farm income, world industry income, etc. Second, national totals include products that may be considered goods from the standpoint of each state unit separately but not from the standpoint of the world as a whole. It might be argued justifiably that such products as poison gas, tanks, and other armaments would be excluded from any estimates made from a viewpoint other than that of a single state unit.

While neither limitation can be denied, the effect of both can be overcome, at least partly. The effect of the first can be reduced by dividing the national totals into regional or other components and by supplementing totals for a given country with totals for other countries. The second can be partly overcome by segregating the net results of activities that, while appearing productive from the viewpoint of the given nation, are decidedly unproductive from the viewpoint of the world as a whole. Both these refinements and extensions of measurement are difficult, and we attempted neither. But the need for them should be recognized as the one way in which the undesirable limitations and implications of *national* income estimates can be removed.

On the other hand, it cannot be denied that state organization influences economic activity, canalizing it in certain directions; that the authority of the state often lends considerable independence and autonomy to the economic life within its borders; and that states impress upon their inhabitants a consciousness of kind that stimulates a desire to appraise the results of economic activity within their boundaries. It is of the essence of the state that it sets itself up as the sovereign authority, and hence the authority to guide and manage economic destinies; and since national income estimates, as well as other quantities in economic measurement, are indispensable guides to such policy, they should be for units corresponding to the areas within which state power can be exercised. Income totals are for national units because so much of our economic and social activity and of our thinking runs in these terms.

But granted that statewide estimates of income are of considerable utility, more specific questions arise in determining the precise scope of national income as the net product of a statewide economic system. The territorial principle of location of productive agencies or the political principle of state allegiance of individuals or institutions owning them may be applied. National income could be defined as the net value of products of productive agencies located within the territorial boundaries of a country, or as the net value of productive agencies owned by the citizens of that country, or in terms of some intermediate concept.

The variety of possible choices may be illustrated by the accompanying classification of productive agencies by their location, and the location and political allegiance of their owners. The strictly political definition would include I-1 and II-1, i.e., all agencies owned by the subjects of the given state. A somewhat more realistic but still political definition, determined by the possibility of reaching the income during any given year for purposes of taxation, would comprise (I-1) + (I-2) + (II-1a) + (II-2a); or the same total without I-2b. The strictly territorial concept would include all items under I, but none under II. Finally, if one conceives of the nation as a group of people residing within a given country, national income is (I-1a) + (I-2a) + (II-1a) + (II-2a).

I PRODUCTIVE AGENCIES LOCATED WITHIN THE BOUNDARIES OF A STATE	II PRODUCTIVE AGENCIES LOCATED OUTSIDE THE BOUNDARIES OF A STATE
1 Owned by subjects of given state residing a within b outside	1 Owned by subjects of given state residing a within b outside
2 Owned by aliens residing a within b outside	2 Owned by aliens residing a within b outside

The variety of choice is due largely to ambiguity concerning the limits of sovereign powers with respect to economic activity. Moreover, with the changing tenor of international relations and fluctuations in the level of international honesty and goodwill, these limits shift from time to time. For those decades in which international economic obligations were still respected by most nations, it was valid to exclude from the national income for a given country the yield of productive agencies located within its boundaries but owned by non-resident aliens; and to include the yield of productive agencies located outside the country but owned by its residents. In recent years, when many states bar almost completely any outward ˙flow of funds and make it impossible to maintain payments on international obligations, a definition based on a more strictly territorial principle is perhaps the only valid one.

Intended to reflect the kind of international relations that prevailed during most of the nineteenth and into the twentieth century, our estimates follow a combination of the territorial and political principles. They include the products of productive agencies located within the country and owned by its residents, (I-1a) + (I-2a); and those of productive agencies located outside the country but owned by its residents, (II-1a) + (II-2a). We define a nation as the group of individuals domiciled within the country's territorial boundaries, and estimate national income in terms of this group.

We cannot always estimate accurately the national income total suggested, since most data, especially in this country, are for productive agencies located within the country's boundaries but do not show ownership. Also, as already indicated, changes in the rules of international intercourse will invalidate within a short time any basis chosen for the determination of scope. Therefore, so far as possible, we present our estimates in such a way as to segregate those elements which account for the differences among some of the several variants of 'nation' and 'national' total.

7 Summary

In attempting to define national income as the net value of all goods produced by the nation, we had in turn to define 'economic goods', 'economic value', 'net' and 'gross' value, 'production', and 'nation'. We noted the criteria or assumptions that could be used to answer some of the fundamental questions raised by these terms and indicated how these answers lead to the inclusion or exclusion of certain items, to the selection of the basis of measurement, and to the drawing of temporal and spatial limits of the totals. Here we summarize first our conclusions, then give the broader assumptions and their implications.

Limiting national income to results of economic and productive pursuits forced us to exclude many satisfaction-yielding activities, primarily those conducted within the family, that may be considered part of life in general rather than economic activity proper. Included are results of pursuits whose products appear on markets. The only non-monetary items included are goods retained by producers for their own consumption, payments in kind by enterprises to ultimate consumers, and imputed income on owner-occupied houses. Results of some activities carried on for monetary returns are excluded as unproductive: gains in the value of assets not due to the production process; and receipts from gambling and pursuits definitely prohibited by society as harmful. Finally, pure transfers (contributions, relief payments, etc.) are excluded as duplications.

Goods that appear on the market are valued at market prices; goods that do not actually appear on the market (retained by producers for their own consumption, imputed rent, etc.) at the prices of their marketed counterparts; and governmental services at the total payments made for them by individuals and enterprises respectively. Uncompleted goods are valued at cost. Market prices are of course a far from perfect measure of how well goods satisfy society's needs. But they are the sole practicable basis if the estimator is to follow the consensus of social opinion. The one adjustment of market prices intended and made is for temporal changes in the general level of prices or in the value of the monetary unit.

In accordance with common usage, 'enterprise' was defined to comprise private and public producing units (including governments) and to exclude individuals, except in their capacity as entrepreneurs. Net value produced in a country was defined and measured as the difference between the full or gross value of all products and the value of commodities and of services of enterprises consumed in the production process (intermediate consumption). No occupational expenses of individuals could be deducted except the expenses entrepreneurs entered under their production costs. Intermediate consumption of governmental services is measured by payments to governments by business enterprises. All intermediate consumption is valued, as far as possible, on the basis of market prices current at the time the final product (from whose gross value intermediate consumption is deducted) is completed.

Production was confined to the regular processes of extraction, transformation, transportation, and distribution of commodities and rendering services. Mere changes in capital value due to changes in monetary conditions or to extraordinary events that cannot be anticipated or regarded as calculable hazards of productive activity were not considered part of production, and hence were not included under gross value or intermediate consumption. 'National income' was confined to the most comprehensive total, that of net value *produced,* and production was estimated, as far as possible, for all phases of the continuous flow from raw materials to finished products. Hence national income for any year includes goods not as yet on the market (uncompleted production, estimated at cost) as well as goods, parts of which were produced in the preceding period (value for current year to include only the production that took place during that year).

In setting spatial boundaries to national income, we included the income of residents of this country, from both their personal activity and their property, whether located here or abroad. Property income originating in enterprises located here but owned abroad is excluded.

Many of our decisions are not binding upon the user of our estimates, i.e., with the details presented he can derive estimates corresponding to somewhat different definitions. We give estimates of aggregate payments to individuals and of consumers' outlay as well as of national income. Governmental services can be evaluated on a cost or a payment-price basis. Income originating in enterprises located within the boundaries of this country, excluding income transfers abroad or receipts from abroad, can be estimated. But other controversial items are estimated on only one basis since any other would be impossible or too costly of time in the present state of data. We give no continuous estimates of excluded items (housewives' services, etc.) or alternative estimates of intermediate consumption, allowing for expenses of labor. No basis of valuation other than market prices is used.

While the procedures summarized above are due to a mixture of theoretical considerations and practical limitations, we stress the basic analytical assumptions that underlie them and the bearing of these assumptions upon the interpretation of our estimates. In defining national income the fundamental distinctions between: (a) economic and other activities, (b) productive and unproductive activities, and (c) regular processes of production and extraneous factors imply fundamental notions concerning the meaning of economic productivity— notions that represent a social philosophy. These notions may seem axiomatic, but they are essentially assumptions, not observations; and they are not in the nature of scientific statements subject to test.

In formulating these notions we attempted in general to hold consistently to two theses. The first is that needs of ultimate consumers provide the touchstone by which the results of economic activity are to be judged; that 'productive' designates the positive contents of economic activity viewed in terms of the satisfaction of recognized needs of ultimate consumers, present and future. Accordingly we assumed that goods are for men and that the members of the body social cannot be

treated as tools for the production of other goods; and consequently recognized wide areas in which ultimate consumption
occurs, in which activities that are not productive are compensated by monetary gains, and in which activities that are not
economic produce satisfaction.

The second thesis is that in judging relevance to needs, the
overt expression of social judgment, the standards followed by
society in its economic institutions are to be accepted as a guide.
For this reason we excluded only such activities as are considered harmful or not productive by society, and adopted the
market price basis of valuation. This decision does not mean
that we, as investigators, could find a clear-cut and detailed
consensus of opinion in the light of which specific questions
could be answered. It means merely that in the broad decisions
of inclusion, exclusion, and valuation, the generally accepted
notions of society as expressed in its social institutions were
followed.

Other positions could be taken with respect to both theses.
The definition of 'economic' and 'productive' could be broad-
ened to include all activities yielding satisfaction to any one
individual, or narrowed in accordance with some more restric-
tive criteria of productivity that prevailed among the early
economists of the Physiocratic and Classical Schools. It might
be possible, though difficult, to set up criteria of the needs of
society distinct from the criteria based on the market place, and
revalue all products of economic activity accordingly. Both
concept and estimates would differ substantially from ours.
Any validity that may be claimed for our concept and estimate
depends upon acceptance of the assumptions underlying the
definition. And as already admitted, such validity is only historical, in the sense that it attempts to reflect the prevailing
viewpoint on the contents of economic activity.

What is the utility of such national income estimates?
Grounded as they are upon arbitrary notions of productivity
and of the difference between economic and non-economic that

cannot be applied consistently, can they serve economic analysis? Are they suitable for any other purposes?

First, precisely because the estimates are based upon fundamental criteria that are widely accepted, they fulfill what we conceive as their basic purpose: to appraise the workings of the economic system. Much, if not most discussion, planning, and social strife are in the interest of making economic activity yield the largest positive contribution in terms of the criteria our national income concept uses, viz., to satisfy the needs of ultimate consumers at present and in the immediate future. The social utility of expressing quantitatively the current successes attained by these efforts is beyond question.

Second, if national income constitutes an appraisal of the results of economic activity, is it not useful in economic analysis? One basic aim of economics is to study the factors that make for changes in the net product of economic activity and analyze the ways in which it is distributed, consumed, and reproduced. An estimate of national income for a substantial period and based upon a consistent application of one and the same set of criteria can be of high utility.

Stated differently, the criteria on which a national income estimate as an appraisal notion is based are in fair consonance not only with the prevailing social attitude but also with the criteria that economics finds useful in the selective recording of the objects it studies. The estimates serve directly as guide posts in both scientific and everyday treatment of economic problems. And although we cannot always adhere strictly to our principles, approximations are better than no guides.

But for both scientific and lay analysis global estimates, single totals without subdivisions, are not sufficient, even if they cover substantial periods or several countries. As indicated repeatedly, the controversial issues of definition call for estimates in several variants corresponding to different solutions, variants that are components of the most comprehensive total. In addition, other subdivisions and classifications are needed to interpret changes in totals or differences among estimates

for different countries. We must know in what branches of the
productive system national income originates; how its monetary equivalents are distributed; and what the apportionment
is between savings and ultimate consumption of various types.
A national income total is like an amalgam of metals in unknown quantities that must be analyzed before meaningful
statements can be made concerning its composition or changes
in it.

Now that we have explored the outside boundaries of the
national income total in terms of the concept, we turn to its
internal composition.

CHAPTER 2

Distribution of National Income

A NATIONAL income total for a given country and period can be apportioned among smaller spatial units or shorter periods. For example, national income for the United States can be apportioned according to its origin in the various states or in still smaller territorial units. An annual total can be apportioned among quarters or months to give a more sensitive record of temporal changes. But we are not concerned with such distributions, largely because our estimates are for the country as a whole and annual. Our interest lies instead in distributions that reflect substantive rather than formal characteristics. To what uses is the monetary equivalent of national income put; by what industries is the net national product turned out; what are the attributes of the various factors in the production process and the qualities of goods comprising national income?

Three main types of distribution based on these characteristics are attempted in our estimates: (1) among withholdings, disbursements, and consumers' outlay; (2) by industrial origin; (3) by type of income or payment, representing compensation for various kinds of productive service. They are discussed here in order to clarify the meaning of the constituents of each classification; to indicate the difficulties encountered in defining these classifications precisely; and to explain how exigencies force us to depart at some points from the allocations that would best serve the purpose underlying the classification.

61

*1 Among Withholdings, Disbursements, and Consumers'
Outlay*

In the preceding chapter (Sec. 5 A) we mentioned that between
the completion of the production process, whose net yield
constitutes national income, and the end of the process of
ultimate consumption, there are two intermediate phases at
which we can measure aggregate payments to individuals and
consumers' outlay. Treating these two and ultimate consumption as parts of national income, we arrange in the accompanying tabulation the complementary categories which,
together with payments, outlay, or consumption, add up to
national income. The order on the left side is dichotomous
for each of the four larger magnitudes; on the right side it is
sequential, showing the number of categories (over two) into
which national income can be divided.

I National Income

1 Aggregate payments to individuals

2 Net savings of corporations and
governments

*II Aggregate Payments to Individuals
and Savings of Entrepreneurs*

1 Consumers' outlay

2 Net savings of individuals and entrepreneurs

*III Aggregate Payments to
Individuals*

1 Consumers' outlay

2 Net savings of individuals

IV Consumers' Outlay

1 Ultimate consumption

2 Net changes in consumers' inventories

National Income

1 Net savings of corporations and
governments

2 Net savings of individuals and entrepreneurs

3 Consumers' outlay

National Income

1 Net savings of all enterprises

2 Net savings of individuals

3 Consumers' outlay

National Income

1 Net savings of all enterprises

2 Net savings of individuals

3 Net changes in consumers' inventories

4 Ultimate consumption

A INCOME PAYMENTS AND SAVINGS OF ENTERPRISES

Enterprises do not necessarily disburse to individuals amounts equal to the net product originating during the year. A business corporation may not pay to individuals in wages, salaries, dividends, interest, etc. a sum exactly equal to the difference between the gross value of its product and the value of goods consumed in turning out this product. In prosperous years corporations often disburse less than this difference, retaining some positive net savings; in poor years they often disburse more, sustaining negative net savings. Any enterprise whose activity is included in national income may have different amounts of net income originating and total payments to individuals.

The distinction seems simple, but its application is not. How should we treat payments to individuals that cannot be interpreted as compensation for their services or the services of their property utilized in current production? Obviously, such payments may be of two types: (1) Enterprises may make payments which, while not in compensation for services to *current* production, may yet be in payment for *past* services (or sometimes even *future*). A clear case is that of pensions paid by business firms to their retired employees. (2) Enterprises may make payments whose connection with past, present, or future production is tenuous; e.g., contributions by business firms to community chests or other charities, or relief and public assistance payments by governments.

In either type we can include the disbursements under aggregate payments to individuals and estimate the net savings of the disbursing enterprises after the deduction of these disbursements; or exclude them from aggregate payments to individuals and estimate net savings prior to their deduction. Whichever we do, they are included or excluded under national income as they are or are not paid out of the current net value product.

Our practice has been to include such disbursements as pensions, contributions, and relief under aggregate payments to individuals and estimate net savings of enterprises after their deduction. For pensions and similar payments connected with past or future services, we can readily justify our practice. It is never too easy to say that any payment is necessarily in compensation for services in *current* production (consider dividends paid by a corporation in a year of greatly reduced activity, i.e., payment of a discretionary character for the use of a property that fails to earn a corresponding return); and it is more practicable to allow for discrepancies in timing between payments and current production. But an even better reason for including such disbursements under aggregate payments to individuals is that, unlike other net savings (which ordinarily assume the form of cash, inventory, equipment, or reduction in net indebtedness), they do flow to individuals and are not retained by enterprises; and that we are interested in all payments by enterprises to individuals, so long as the nexus between the two is one of some sharing by individuals in the production processes of the enterprises.

The case for the inclusion of contributions and relief and public assistance payments under aggregate payments to individuals is less clear, although even here some connection may be found with past or future services of individuals in the production process. Yet the alternative, i.e., to include them under net savings of enterprises, would yield more misleading results. Of course, these disbursements could be omitted from both payments to individuals and net savings of enterprises and treated as an inevitable cost of carrying on the production process. But this treatment would be even more misleading since it would understate national income and fail to measure properly disbursements by enterprises to individuals. For these reasons, we included relief and similar payments under aggregate payments to individuals and estimated net savings of enterprises after the corresponding deductions.

Our aggregate payments, consequently, include all disbursements by enterprises to individuals *qua* individuals, and since some represent compensation for current services and others have merely an indirect relation to them we must classify all in more detail (Sec. 3).

The distinction between income payments and net savings seems clear for business corporations, difficult as it may be to establish statistically. But for governmental agencies and unincorporated firms it is more complicated. The distinction between payments to individuals and net savings of enterprises implies that the gross value of product, minus the cost of goods consumed, can be compared with aggregate payments to individuals *qua* individuals. However, in the case of governmental agencies it may be argued that total receipts do not measure the gross value of product and that the latter should be measured by some other yardstick. If the cost of governmental activity is the yardstick, then net income originating and aggregate payments by governments to individuals must be equal.

In the preceding chapter (Sec. 3 C) we gave our reasons for using the payment-price basis for valuing governmental services. If this decision is accepted, the distinction between payments to individuals and net savings by governments parallels that for business enterprises. We mention it here in order to emphasize that the application of the dichotomy under discussion is dependent upon how governmental services are valued.

In an unincorporated firm the entrepreneur is both the recipient of disbursements from it and the man who decides how much of its net income should be withdrawn and how much should remain as its net savings. Can we differentiate between net income originating and income payments to the entrepreneur? It may be argued that the latter comprise the entire residue of net income originating, after payments to other productive factors have been made; that the entrepreneur whose firm has positive or negative savings is like any other ultimate recipient of income payments who may decide to reinvest part of his income in the enterprise that employs him or to withdraw part of his accumulated savings. If the argument is valid, there is still a significant difference between entrepreneurial withdrawals for consumption (or investment elsewhere) and the total net income accruing to the entrepreneur in his firm. But the difference is similar to that between total payments to ultimate recipients and consumers' outlay, and should not be treated as if it were similar to the difference between net savings of enterprises and payments to individuals.

Or, it may be argued that savings of unincorporated enterprises are different from savings of individuals as individuals. For the latter, saving is the result of decisions made with reference to a freely disposable income. An individual receives a salary, wage, dividend or withdraws a certain amount from his firm. The payments are usually in the form of freely disposable means; and although the income of every individual is subject to many unavoidable drafts, there is a freedom of disposition that is one of the consequences of a fully developed monetary system and a distinguishing feature of an actual payment received. On the other hand, considered as an addition to the individual entrepreneur's disposable income, the savings, whether positive or negative, of the firm itself are partly an accounting fiction. The savings that appear at the end of the year may be due to an improvement in accounts receivable or inventory position; and it would be difficult to claim that the entrepreneur, after calculating the net income that accrues to him during the year, decided to reinvest part of it in additional accounts receivable or inventories, a decision similar to one made by an individual investing freely disposable funds in stocks or bonds. Net savings of unincorporated firms can, therefore, be viewed as arising from the same mixture of discretion and helplessness as net savings in most business enterprises. Consequently, entrepreneurial net income should be differentiated from entrepreneurial withdrawals, and net savings of unincorporated firms included in net savings of enterprises and excluded from aggregate payments to individuals.

Since it seems to us that the balance of analytical considerations is in favor of treating net savings of unincorporated firms as savings of enterprises rather than of individuals, we have tried to separate entrepreneurial net savings from withdrawals; although in the present state of the data the measurement of the differences is exceedingly rough and tentative. We give estimates of savings of all enterprises and payments to individuals, excluding entrepreneurial net savings. But since the alternative viewpoint is tenable, we give also estimates corresponding to it and allow for it in the classification above. In this alternative treatment payments to individuals include net savings of unincorporated firms; net savings of enterprises exclude them; and income payments to entrepreneurs are considered to be equal to the total net income of entrepreneurs, including savings of their firms.

B CONSUMERS' OUTLAY AND INDIVIDUALS' NET SAVINGS

Aggregate payments to individuals represent the means of payment the economic system places at the disposal of ultimate consumers, constituting their main, but not sole, source of purchasing power: consumers may draw upon their accumulated assets or use credit to supplement their current income.

Consumers' outlay designates the sum spent by ultimate consumers during the year on finished commodities and services. It can be either smaller or larger than aggregate payments to individuals. Ultimate consumers, singly or *in toto,* can spend less than they receive from producing enterprises, realizing positive net savings and improving their net monetary or claims position; or they can spend more, sustaining negative savings and worsening their net monetary or claims position. Since consumers' outlay measures expenditures on finished consumer goods, and individuals' savings are the main source from which capital formation is financed, we divide aggregate payments to individuals into these two parts.

Two observations should be made about this dichotomy. First, the distinction between consumers' outlay and individuals' savings rests, in the final count, upon the definition of ultimate consumption and finished goods. If we consider education as ultimate consumption, then expenses for it become part of consumers' outlay. But if education is treated purely as preparation for economic activity and consequently a species of investment, expenses for it should properly be treated as part of individuals' net savings. The conclusion we reached in the preceding chapter (Sec. 4), that only such consumption is intermediate as represents utilization by business and public enterprises of commodities and of services of other enterprises, is relevant here. In accordance with it, consumers' outlay comprises all expenditures by individuals and households on products of enterprises except those incurred by the former as members of business and public enterprises; individuals' savings are, then, the difference between aggregate payments and consumers' outlay.[1]

The second observation relates to the measurement of both consumers' outlay and individuals' savings when the immediate payment does not cover the full price of the product. If a household buys an automobile or refrigerator on an installment basis, should consumers' outlay for the year include the full value of the purchase or only the amount actually paid during the year? How should purchases on which there was no payment at all during the year, but only a corresponding increase in consumers' debts, be treated?

The questions are similar to those discussed in establishing the timing of production (see Ch. 1, Sec. 5 B). But the argument that production is a continuous process and cannot be treated as occurring only at the instant the product appears on the market cannot be applied to purchasing. It would be unrealistic to assert that purchasing is a continuous process, and that a man who buys a car on an installment basis is engaged in continuous purchasing during the entire period he is making payments. Nor is it realistic to assert that a purchase or outlay takes place at the time the payment is made rather

1 Since we include net imputed rent from owner-occupied houses in national income, the owner-occupied unit is treated as an enterprise. Purchases of houses represent, therefore, use of savings, not consumers' outlay.

than at the time the good changes hands and the purchaser assumes the obligation to pay. The distinction between consumers' outlay and individuals' savings is consequently a more useful tool in economic analysis if the outlay includes the value of all goods that pass from the effective possession of enterprises to that of ultimate consumers, and if accordingly total individuals' savings are scaled down by the value of obligations that ultimate consumers may have assumed in purchasing goods on credit. This interpretation, modified by exigencies of data, is followed in deriving our estimates.[2]

c ULTIMATE CONSUMPTION AND CHANGES IN CONSUMERS' INVENTORIES

The services of finished goods purchased by ultimate consumers are not absorbed immediately, i.e., they are not immediately and exhaustively applied to the satisfaction of consumers' wants. The interval between the dates of purchase and of the exhaustion of services is relatively brief for perishable goods but substantial for others. If a smaller amount of goods is consumed during the year than is purchased, the stock held by ultimate consumers, viz., consumers' inventories, increases. Or, to the extent that consumers' inventories exist at the beginning of the year, ultimate consumption may exceed consumers' outlay, causing a decline in consumers' inventories.

Obviously, changes in consumers' inventories must be analyzed if the structure of ultimate demand and fluctuations in it are to be understood. Unfortunately, relevant data are few and not easy to obtain. Ultimate consumption and changes in consumers' inventories occur entirely within the household economy; economic study, on the contrary, tends to concentrate on processes observable in the market place.

In dividing consumers' outlay into ultimate consumption and changes in inventories, the major task, if we disregard the almost complete absence of relevant statistical data, is to esti-

2 Such treatment implies that a return to a business enterprise of goods bought by an ultimate consumer should enter consumers' outlay with a negative sign.

mate the current consumption of durable goods. As in the case of productive enterprises using durable capital equipment, it is difficult to estimate consumption for time units shorter than the entire life of the good. Moreover, ultimate consumers, unlike business enterprises, are not forced by necessities of accounting and taxation procedure to estimate such consumption; and the calculation of current depreciation and obsolescence is often neglected even for such goods as a house or a passenger car, let alone other finished goods that represent a smaller outlay.

Another factor that makes it difficult if not impossible to estimate the current consumption of consumers' durable goods is the luxury quality many of them have, in consequence of which their utilization has a strong flavor of ostentation. In times of stress an ultimate consumer may use his car or house much longer than otherwise and forego the kudos enjoyed by possession of a new one. Since durable equipment used by business enterprises seldom possesses such luxury elements, its consumption is more strictly controlled by the calculation of costs and returns and, as a result, is a more nearly determinable quantity than the consumption of consumers' durable goods.

Nevertheless, consumption and changes in consumers' inventories can now be measured for some commodities, and will become measurable for more as data accumulate. At present the data are too meager for us to estimate consumers' outlay other than as a whole. But there are strong indications that the increasing prominence of durable goods in the expenditure pattern of ultimate consumers will stimulate the measurement of changes in consumers' inventories.

2 By Industrial Origin

Industries differ in the raw materials utilized, production processes carried on, and products turned out. Raw materials differ in the degree to which their sources are concentrated territorially; in reproducibility and susceptibility to technical control; in exhaustibility and tendencies toward increasing costs or diminishing returns; in perishability, quality, and many other technological properties. Production processes differ in the size of the unit that can most advantageously be operated; in the ratio of direct labor and durable capital equipment to raw materials consumed; in the extent to which physical transformation of raw materials takes place; in the temporal continuity of operations; in the relation of vital phases of the process to skill, etc. Completed products of industries differ in their distance from the stage at which they are ready for ultimate consumption; in perishability over time and in durability in the process of use; in the primacy and urgency of the ultimate needs they satisfy; and so on through the various physical characteristics of products distinguishable according to their final use.

Superimposed upon these purely technological characteristics of materials, processes, and products are the peculiarities of social and economic organization, which also differ fundamentally from industry to industry. Some industries have mainly country sites; others are perforce concentrated in big cities. In some industries numerous small unincorporated enterprises predominate; in others, entrepreneurs do not exist and control is concentrated in huge semi-public or public corporations. In some industries competition among enterprises is fairly effective, in others there is no competition. In some industries overhead costs are minor compared with direct costs; in others, the opposite is true. Some industries cater to recipients of large incomes; others depend upon the mass demand of moderate and low income groups.

This combination of differences in technological characteristics and social and economic organization is an important datum in the understanding and measurement of economic phenomena. If measurement is to be helpful in revealing the factors that make for change and the way economic changes take place, study of how industries differ is indispensable: the technological characteristics of materials, processes, and products and the peculiarities of economic organization spell differences in response during both short and long periods. If an appraisal is involved, as in national income measurement, industrial differences must be kept in mind, for they reveal the areas in which the common yardstick used may have somewhat different meanings, and suggest the group composition of the body social for whose satisfaction national income is used.

A NATIONAL INCOME

The distribution of national income among industries is of the net value originating, not of the total value of an industry's product. For some purposes, such as estimating waste involved in an 'unproductive' industry, this is a disadvantage since we need the gross value. Net income originating in various industries may be interpreted as the contribution of each to the common pool of goods we call national income; or may be considered a measure of the cost to society of the activities carried on by each. Both interpretations are applicable to income originating in any single industry, and care must be taken not to switch, without good reason, from the one interpretation for one industry to the other for another industry.

Interest in ascertaining how much various industries contribute to a given national net product or how much they claim in compensation for their activity stems largely from the differences in their activities. An increase or decrease in national income arising from a corresponding change in the net value originating in agriculture is not open to the same interpretation as an equal change in national income attributable to an increase or decrease in the net value originating in finance.

If an industrial distribution is to provide bases for proper understanding, each category in it must be well defined. Similar productive activities should not be included under different industrial divisions; no divisions should include essentially different activities; the classification should be complete, i.e., not exclude activities of some importance in the economic system; and should contain no false categories that would give to purely transfer and auxiliary functions the semblance of a separate industry. To establish an industrial classification free from such defects is exceedingly difficult because (1) diverse productive activities are carried on in one operating or business unit; (2) productive activities and purely ownership functions are carried on in one business unit; (3) the productive activities carried on by operating and management units ostensibly belonging to one and the same industry change.

1) One operating unit often carries on diverse productive activities, e.g., both extractive and manufacturing activities or both manufacturing activities and trading functions; or combines the production of commodities, transportation, and power with construction. The activities are significantly disparate. Mining is different from manufacturing in that location and exhaustibility of natural resources are more vital to the former than to the latter. The functions performed by steam railroads and other public utility industries are continuous; construction is seasonal. Manufacturing is concerned with changing the form of commodities; merchandising, with their distribution. Yet within operating units, i.e., within the establishments directly engaged in production, a mixture of these productive activities is common. To allocate the net income originating in the enterprise among the different productive functions is a task obviously beyond the powers of a national income investigator, since it would require exceedingly detailed cost accounting and some arbitrary allocation of joint costs.

Business or management units carry on diverse productive functions even more commonly than operating units. An enterprise, whether incorporated or unincorporated, may comprise several plants, offices, agencies, which are often engaged in production of different types, though usually complementary to one another. Certain components of net income originating in the enterprise—property income, overhead salaries and, of course, net savings—are ordinarily not allocated to the various operating units, but are given for the enterprise as a whole. Consequently, in distributing them, and hence national income, by industries, we encounter a mixture of productive functions within larger business units even more frequently than within operating units.

2) Enterprises can act not only as producing entities but also as ownership units. A corporation may receive dividends and interest from other business enterprises, and in turn pay dividends and interest to them. Do the payments received represent compensation for goods produced by it or payments to it as an investor, i.e., as a possessor of property and funds it does not itself utilize? If the payment is to the enterprise as a *producer*, the net income to which it gives rise may be considered to originate in the receiving enterprise. But if the payment is to the enterprise purely as an *owner*, the net income to which it gives rise obviously originates in the paying enterprise.

This distinction demands that we answer two questions when we attempt an industrial distribution of a national income total. First, how shall we treat enterprises obviously engaged in productive activity but still deriving part of their gross revenue from ownership, i.e., receiving income on investments? In this case income in the form of dividends and interest originates in the paying enterprise, not in the receiving. Accordingly, in establishing net income originating in a given economic unit we must subtract from its gross receipts not only the cost of goods consumed but also the part of the gross receipts that represents compensation for pure ownership. So far as data are available on inter-enterprise receipts of dividends and interest, we can and do follow this procedure.

Second, how shall we treat enterprises that are largely ownership units and in which the share of productive activity in total income may be relatively small? Savings banks and insurance companies, which are engaged primarily in placing the accumulated savings of individuals at the disposal of industry, are good illustrations. In the process of mobilizing individuals' savings and selecting the place for investment, they produce net income, i.e., the net value of the services of individuals and capital engaged in them. In addition, they earn net income, part of which may be retained temporarily but the bulk of which goes to policyholders and depositors. Can interest paid to depositors by savings banks and the net savings of the latter be considered as arising in the banking industry? Or the payments to policyholders by insurance companies and the net savings of the latter as arising in the insurance industry? A similar question can be raised about payments to investors by all institutions engaged in placing idle balances at the disposal of productive enterprises.

Unless the industrial distribution of national income is to lose most of its meaning, it cannot be so applied as to attribute net savings and payments to depositors by banks, insurance companies, etc. to the banking and insurance industries. If this is done, what is to bar an interpretation of investment as an industry, and of dividends and interest received by wealthy families (who may have formed a personal corporation) as income originating in the 'investment' industry? We must recognize the possibility that payments may be transferred from one group of enterprises to another, and that a given group of enterprises may be, with respect to some of the income streams passing through them, not much more than an association of individuals in their capacity as investors and ultimate income recipients.

Hence, income originating in such industries as savings banks and insurance is confined to the net value of the services of individuals engaged in them, and excludes payments to depositors and policyholders as well as the net savings of the enterprises. These payments and savings are treated as originating in the industries from whose stocks and bonds the enterprises receive their revenue.[3]

3) The effect of carrying on diverse productive functions

---

[3] This does not dispose of some technical difficulties introduced by the absence of relevant data or of questions arising in connection with the treatment of rent. The latter are discussed in Section 3 A; the former, in Part Four.

within operating or business units and of combining productive activities with purely ownership functions within one
enterprise would be reduced appreciably if they always remained the same. But they are susceptible to change. Changes
in technology make for shifts in the relative importance of
various types of productive function within one operating
unit. Shorter term cyclical fluctuations lead to fluctuations in
the distribution of the working personnel and of the active
time a single plant devotes to turning out the finished product
and auxiliary operations such as repairs and construction; or
to production and merchandising. The housing of several operating units within one enterprise is the result and the essence
of the process of industrial integration that developed rapidly
during the last decades of the nineteenth century and is still
proceeding at a fast pace. Inter-enterprise payments of dividends and interest arising from interlocking ownership are
another facet of the same process. And the extent to which
individuals place their savings with insurance companies, savings banks, and similar institutions is also changing. Since
complete adjustment is impossible, the industrial distribution
is not precise and the blurred area changes from one period
to another.

Moreover, comparisons over time must also take account of
the changes that may have occurred in the productive activities
classified as belonging to one and the same industry. The
functions of retail trade, professional service, government, and
many other branches of the productive system are quite different today from what they were fifty years ago. The name
remains the same, but activities subsumed under it change,
without necessarily reducing or increasing the mixture of types
of productive activity.

Any distribution of national income by industrial origin
is thus subject to serious qualifications. In the nature of the
case, it cannot be accurate for clearly demarcated functional
types of productive activity. At best it is a distribution among
the institutional categories designated as industries, and its

interpretation must be qualified accordingly. For example, if the estimates show that manufacturing accounts for x and trade for y per cent of national income, this does not mean that x measures accurately the share of activity concerned with transforming commodities, or y the share concerned with the exchange and distribution of commodities among enterprises and between enterprises and households. Some trading functions may be performed by 'manufacturing' and some manufacturing activity by 'trade'. Similarly, an increase in the share of trade and a decrease in the share of manufacturing does not necessarily mean that distributive activity contributes or claims an increasing share of the national product, and manufacturing activity a declining share. It may well be that certain distributive functions formerly carried on by manufacturing enterprises and included under manufacturing have been shifted to wholesalers and retailers, thereby swelling net income originating in trade. Similarly, an increase in the share of income originating in governmental activity does not necessarily mean that either the price or quantity of governmental services proper has increased relatively to the price or quantity of goods provided by the private business system. It may mean merely that governmental agencies have taken over some activities formerly pursued by private business, or have been forced into new activities.

Since the shifts and overlapping are minor in comparison with the persistent and significant differences among categories, these limitations do not render an industrial distribution of national income worthless. The institutions called agriculture, mining, manufacturing, steam railroading, etc., while containing enterprises that combine productive activities of diverse types, are largely dominated by distinctive productive functions. The element of pure trading is minor in manufacturing, as is the element of pure manufacturing in trade. When really significant changes do occur, the institutional categories also shift, i.e., new industries are recognized and old industries dropped. The lack of strict correspondence between the institutional categories and the strictly functional segregation of types of productive activity is important merely as a qualification that should prevent erroneous interpretations of differences or changes in the estimates.

B SAVINGS OF ENTERPRISES AND AGGREGATE PAYMENTS TO IN-
    DIVIDUALS

Net savings of enterprises suggest the amount of funds made available for investment without recourse to banks and the outside money market, or the amount of disinvestment sustained. The amounts have a high prognostic value, since usually enterprises that enjoy large positive net savings demonstrate thereby their favorable market position and are likely to expand their activities in the future; while enterprises sustaining large negative savings will naturally be forced to curtail their activities. What is true of enterprises is, somewhat less directly, true of industries. Therefore, the industrial distribution of net savings of enterprises reveals one of the prime factors making for changes in the relative importance of various industries in the country's total. It is subject to the same qualifications as a distribution of national income by industrial origin.

Somewhat similar reasoning can be applied to suggest why we allocate aggregate payments to individuals by industries. So far as changes in total payments differ from industry to industry, the analysis of aggregate payments must rest upon its distribution among industrial branches. The use of an industrial distribution of aggregate payments is thus coordinate with that of national income, and is also subject to all the limitations discussed above.

A distribution of aggregate payments to individuals by industrial origin may serve also to demarcate groups in the body social. Most of the people who derive their income from agriculture reside in the country and pursue a mode of life quite different from that followed by people attached to other industries and dependent upon income payments originating in them. Similarly, miners, employees of manufacturing enterprises, people engaged in trade or in professional pursuits, etc. form fairly distinct social groups. Since the pattern of expenditures and savings may well differ for each group, an industrial distribution of payments would assist not only in understanding the background of conflict and cooperation within at least one set of social groups but also in analyzing changes and differences in the division of payments between consumers' outlay and net savings and the apportionment of consumers' outlay among finished goods of various types.

A distribution of income payments by industrial *origin* is, however, merely a rough approximation to what is wanted and fails to conform to two essential conditions. If our interest lies in the income of various social groups differentiated largely by their industrial attachment, we should estimate *total* income payments received by each, and exclude income payments that cannot be interpreted as receipts by members of a group with a given industrial attachment. For example, by estimating income payments originating in agriculture we account for the major part of farmers' current income and segregate the part of aggregate income payments that is received primarily by a social group called farmers. But total income payments originating in agriculture are both too small and too large for our purpose: too small because they cover only payments farmers receive from agriculture and exclude payments farmers receive as compensation either for direct services to other industries or for property invested otherwise than in agriculture; too large because they include payments not only to farmers but also to individuals who have little connection with agriculture and do not depend upon it for their income, e.g., holders of farm mortgages. For any industry the amount of payments originating tends to differ in these two respects from the total income of the group attached to it.

The industrial allocation of property income, dividends, interest, and to some extent rent is especially difficult to interpret in terms of social groups, for the recipients do not actively participate in the industries that are the sources of this income. When merely a minor portion of the income of individuals or households is derived from property, where it originated does not help in classifying recipients by social groups. When property is the major source, receipts are likely to come from diverse industrial sources, and dependence upon a single industry is probably uncommon.

The industrial distribution of aggregate payments to individuals is more significant when applied solely to payments that represent compensation for direct services. The industrial distributions of wages, salaries, and entrepreneurial income reflect the apportionment of the proceeds of industry to groups differentiated by their industrial attachment. But even this narrowing of the scope of payments to be allocated still leaves the distribution merely an approximation. It is not unusual for an individual to derive income from more than one industry (either from seasonal or part-time jobs or from divers industrial attachments, common among the professions). Such inter-industry combinations are even more common within households or economic families, in which one income earner may be engaged in one industry and another in a different one. And the household as consumer rather than the individual as producer is the unit by which income receipts of social groups are classified.

Despite these limitations, the second meaning of the industrial distribution of aggregate payments to individuals is significant. Payments originating in an industry are a tolerable approximation to the total receipts of people attached to it; and can be derived in large part from the body of data upon which the industrial distribution of national income rests.

3 Of Income Payments by Type

The classification of income payments by type is based largely upon differences in the functions performed by the recipients. Differentiation among these functions is based in turn upon whether the recipient himself engages in the production process or participates solely through his property; upon the directness of his participation, if active; upon the extent to which he shares in the management and disposition of the enterprise's activities; upon the character of his property claims. Applying these criteria yields the usual classification of income payments by type—wages, salaries, other income of employees, entrepreneurial withdrawals or net income, dividends, interest, rent, royalties, etc.

A   PAYMENTS FOR SERVICES OF INDIVIDUALS AND OF PROPERTY
The most fundamental distinction is perhaps between payments for the services of individuals and of property. The former are based on direct participation in the production process—the commonest form of economic activity, absorbing the major part of active economic agents' attention, imposing a pattern on the life they and their families lead, and demanding at times considerable sacrifice. Participation through investment, the source of property income receipts, does not require similar activity on the part of individuals and is compatible with extensive participation in other activities. To be sure, property investment is sometimes embodied in the individual's training and skill, and the return for the services of individuals contains a substantial element of return for the services of property. Yet the difference between income payments in compensation for direct activity by individuals and for the services of their property holds for a wide range of comparisons.

One type of compensation for individuals' services may be designated labor income; another, entrepreneurial income. The former represents compensation for services rendered by individuals who have little voice in the decisions an enterprise makes and can easily be separated from it. The latter includes compensation for the making of all the responsible decisions in the management of the enterprise.

This tripartite division into labor, entrepreneurial, and property income payments seems at first well represented by institutional categories of income streams to individuals, i.e., by wages and salaries, entrepreneurial net income or withdrawals, and dividends, interest, and rents and royalties. But further consideration reveals a lack of correspondence.

Entrepreneurial net income, as measured, is what accrues to entrepreneurs after the payment of all production costs. Entrepreneurial withdrawals are the amounts retained by entrepreneurs for their own consumption and for investment outside their firms. These income payments or withdrawals, as they accrue to or are made by groups of entrepreneurs (farmers, miners, retail traders, small construction contractors, etc.) are, from the viewpoint of the functions they represent, a hybrid of all three types. A majority of entrepreneurs perform actual, physical productive functions that, under a different form of business organization, are performed by wage earners or salaried employees. All entrepreneurs exercise managerial discretion and make the decisions vital to the enterprise both internally and in its relations with other enterprises. An overwhelming proportion of entrepreneurs have a net property investment in their enterprise. The relative importance of these three forms of entrepreneurs' participation varies from industry to industry; but dividing entrepreneurial income or withdrawals into labor, entrepreneurial, and property income would be so arbitrary as to serve no useful purpose. What the preponderant element in it is for the country as a whole is hard to say; but since in the group receiving entrepreneurial income farmers, retail merchants, small construction contractors, and professional people predominate, the category is by and large that of service rather than of property income; and perhaps preponderantly that of labor income rather than of entrepreneurial income.

Rent raises a somewhat different question. Net rent paid to individuals is largely for urban real estate, that flowing from farm property and other extractive sources being relatively minor. Recipients of rent typically take a more active part in managing their property than holders of stocks or bonds, who merely draw dividends or interest. Hence the category is a combination of property and entrepreneurial income. If the element of entrepreneurial activity were substantial enough, a recipient of rent could be classified as an entrepreneur in real estate rather than as an individual recipient of property income originating in whatever industry pays the rent. If this were done, rent would not be classified as a separate type of payment but would become an income stream from one industrial branch in our classification. Alternatively, rent could be treated as purely property income and its origin traced to various industries, among which residential real estate is one. There may also be intermediate treatments. For example, rent from agriculture can be considered property income originating in agriculture, and all other rent, entrepreneurial income from real estate; or all rent can be classified as property income but assigned to real estate.

There is no decisive reason for our choice of the last-mentioned method. Had we the proper data, we could perhaps segregate the net rent that represents purely property income from that which is compensation largely for entrepreneurial activity. Since such data are lacking, it seemed best to treat rent as property income, comparable with dividends and interest. As property income, rent should have been apportioned among the industries in which it originated (similarly to dividends and interest); but for lack of continuous data on rent originating in the various industries (except in agriculture and one or two other branches) all rent had to be assigned to real estate.

There is little information on royalties with which we could segregate, estimate, or classify them definitely as property or entrepreneurial income. They are probably almost entirely a return on property, acquired either through direct monetary outlay or an outlay of labor, although some royalties imply more entrepreneurial activity than is manifested by recipients of dividends and interest. The item is so small that it can be disregarded and since it cannot be estimated separately on a continuous annual basis, we omit it.

In the total income of employees, how should we treat 'other income' and to what extent are elements of entrepreneurial and property income contained in wages and salaries, particularly the latter? 'Other income' is a miscellaneous category made up of pensions, compensation for injury,[4] and relief payments. The second alone has a close connection with *current* services rendered in the production process. But all three are based upon a substantial connection with active participation in the production process in the past. If we disregard timing, it is reasonable to describe all three as payments to individuals for their services rather than for the services of their property. In this respect they are similar to wages and salaries. Consequently we designate them as 'other income of *employees*' and include them in our estimates under the more comprehensive total, employee compensation.

There is one substantial element of property income in both wages and salaries, and at least two minor ones in salaries. The important factors in higher rates of compensation to some wage earners and salaried employees are their education and training and the scarcity of the natural capacities needed for the service they render relative to demand. The part of wages and salaries derived from higher rates of compensation due to these factors may be considered property income payments, i.e., returns on the investment made in the past in education and training or on the value of a natural resource monopolized by its possessor. The share of wages, and more especially, of salaries, that could be interpreted as property income is often substantial, e.g., among professional employees.

Of the other elements of property income in salaries the first and more obvious is contained in the compensation paid

4 The one industry for which we show this item is steam railroads, Pullman, and express. Compensation paid to persons other than employees is included, since it could not be segregated. The amount in question is probably relatively small.

for a sinecure obtained by a property investment, rather than for any productive activity or only in minor degree for services rendered. A job is awarded to someone who has made or is making a property investment to the benefit of the groups in control of the appointment. Theoretically, such payments are on a par with charity contributions by enterprises on the one hand, with dividends and interest on the other. Data do not admit of their segregation, but their total is probably not large.

The second additional element of property income in salaries is in the compensation of corporation executives. When the owners of a corporation are also officials, their salaries are identical with entrepreneurial withdrawals; and to the extent that entrepreneurial withdrawals include an element of property income, so do salary payments to the owners of these pseudo-corporate units. This item also cannot be segregated but is probably relatively minor. It is absolutely much larger in big corporations: the executive personnel, though theoretically subordinate to the stockholders, are actually very influential in making decisions and are, to all intents and purposes, the entrepreneurs. The main distinction lies not in their presumed subordination to the controlling bodies, but in the size of the enterprise. Any enterprise that has attained a certain size must rely for its entrepreneurial functions not on an individual and mortal owner, but on a more powerful and self-perpetuating group of executives.

In large enterprises the necessity of apportioning entrepreneurial functions among many people makes for gradations of power among employees, and the point at which a given employee ceases to be an entrepreneur and becomes a subordinate is often not apparent. The part of salaries that represents compensation for entrepreneurial activity, therefore, cannot be calculated precisely, but it can be approximated and we must not forget that salaries, which are often treated as representing labor income, include substantial elements of entrepreneurial income.

Thus the distinction between payments for services and for property cannot be clearly drawn on the basis of the institutionally prevalent types of payment. There are elements of property income in salaries and in entrepreneurial net income or withdrawals; and an element of service income in rent. Yet by and large, wages, all except executive salaries, and most entrepreneurial net income or withdrawals, are preponderantly service income; dividends, interest, and rent are even more preponderantly property income. If compensation for purely entrepreneurial functions is to be distinguished from other service income, elements of it will be found in salaries, rent, and, to a minor extent, even in dividends; but there is no single, institutionally recognized type of payment in which it is quantitatively predominant.

B WAGES AND SALARIES

As already mentioned, salaries include a more substantial element of property and entrepreneurial income than wages. But this difference is too elusive and variable to serve as the basis for the segregation by enterprises of these two types of payment. The salary of a filing clerk or of a typist includes perhaps a smaller element of property and entrepreneurial income than the wages of many a skilled worker.

Of the various bases on which the two might be distinguished—proximity to and directness of participation in the production process; manual and non-manual character of the services rendered; training and education required; method of payment (piece or time); periodicity of payment (hour, day, week, month, year, etc.); size of compensation—none seems adequate by itself. Some employees participating in the auxiliary functions of the enterprise are classified as wage earners (e.g., construction workers in a factory, repair men, watchmen). Some salaried employees seem to perform primarily manual functions (e.g., multigraph machine operators, draftsmen). The education and training required of many skilled wage earners is not substantially less, and is sometimes more, than that required of recipients of salaries. Many wage earners are paid on a time basis; many salaried employees are virtually on a day and hour payment basis; others (e.g., salesmen) may be on a commission basis.

The answer seems to lie in a combination of these criteria, of which proximity to and directness of participation in the production process and the manual character of operations seem to have most weight. These two factors constitute the basis for other differences between wages and salaries. The manual character of operations explains the fewer prerequisites of education and training that differentiate most wage-earning jobs from most salaried occupations. Directness of participation in the production process explains a piece rate basis of wages in many industries and the payment of wages for time units much shorter than those used for salaries in most industries. Finally, direct manual participation in the production process usually means that wage earners do not engage in administrative and entrepreneurial functions, renders wages largely prime rather than overhead costs, and, demanding as it does few prerequisites of education and training, is a factor making for the lower levels of most wages as compared with salaries.

The distinction between wages and salaries is not worth making in all industries. There is little meaning in it when the production process does not involve much manual labor. For example, banks, insurance companies, educational institutions, professional enterprises, governmental agencies, and even trade, draw no clear-cut line between wages and salaries. The term 'wages' in such industries is confined to the compensation of the few employees who perform manual labor (construction and repair men, charwomen, etc.), and applies to so small a part of total payments to employees that the distinction is not important. Even industries that employ a large amount of manual labor in extracting, transforming, and transporting commodities make the distinction only if, in addition to employees engaged directly in these processes, there is a substantial group performing administrative, research, supervisory, or entrepreneurial functions. Where, as in agriculture, such a group is absent or exceedingly small because the size of the entrepreneurial unit reduces such functions to a minimum and leads to their performance by the entrepreneurs themselves, the distinction between wages and salaries again is not worth while. For this reason, our estimates segregate wages from salaries for only such industries as mining, manufacturing, construction, and steam railroads.

The distinction between wages and salaries in some industries forces us to segregate these industries, one by one. In others the characteristics of the functions compensated by the combined wage and salary or salary payments vary considerably. The very factors that force the separation of wages and salaries in industries like mining and manufacturing make desirable an industrial allocation of total employee compensation among trade, personal service, government, etc.

It would be illuminating also to have wages classified on the basis of skill and training, occupation in primary or auxiliary functions, method of payment (piece or time), and amount of compensation. Similarly, it would be useful to have salaries divided into their property and entrepreneurial elements; among various types of administrative, supervisory, etc. activities; by basis and level of compensation; and by the degree to which they represent prime or overhead costs. Such classifications, with the possible exception of the segregation of compensation of corporation officers from other salaries, are barred by lack of data. This lack of data is not accidental: the allocations suggested demand a close analysis of employee compensation within each enterprise. Only when the need for such an analysis is forced upon an enterprise by its own development or by the concern of public agencies for the stability of employee compensation (as under social security legislation) are some of the allocations suggested made.

C DIVIDENDS AND INTEREST

The distinction between interest and dividends reflects the character of the obligations assumed by the paying enterprise. The obligations giving rise to interest are rigidly fixed with reference to the repayment of principal (as in savings banks), or to the continuous payment of interest (as in non-redeemable bonds), or to both (as in practically all bonds issued by business enterprises). The payment of dividends reflects no such obligations. Though many business units pursue a policy of maintaining stable dividends in order to remove speculative elements from the purchase or holding of their stocks, they are in a position to vary disbursements when conditions are markedly above or below ordinary levels, and usually do so. By contrast, even when there is no definite obligation to pay interest the existence of an obligation to repay the principal is conducive to a conservative investment policy and to a temporal stability of interest payments. Since dividends fluctuate and interest is relatively stable we separate these two types of property income.

With this basic difference between interest and dividends two others are associated. The first is the presence in dividends, but not in interest, of an appreciable element of entrepreneurial income. Short term changes in dividends distributed by enterprises reflect the skill with which they have met changing economic conditions and fluctuations in the markets. And if under entrepreneurial income we include, among other elements, compensation for their success or failure, dividends obviously contain a substantial share of entrepreneurial income. On the other hand, interest on bonds, which carry legal obligations, can reflect business conditions only when default occurs, a concomitant of that extreme failure of entrepreneurial activity that occurs chiefly during depressions.

A corollary aspect of the difference between interest and dividends is that they go largely to people in substantially different income groups. Dividends represent a return on the more speculative investment, requiring a discernment and knowledge of opportunities that possessors of small savings usually do not have, and bestowing a right to participate in the affairs of the enterprises not desired by a small investor or accessible to one who holds only a few shares of stock. For these reasons the great bulk of stocks are held by large investors; and at least in this country, by far the major portion of all dividends disbursed to individuals is received by people enjoying incomes well above the average. Interest paying investments, on the other hand, appeal to small investors; and a large share of interest paid to individuals is received by people with moderate incomes.

While this generalization is on the whole true, two qualifications must be kept in mind. The first and more important is that the groups of people receiving interest and those receiving dividends overlap considerably, not only because the same individual may receive both, but also because some individuals with low incomes receive dividends and some with high incomes receive interest. The second is that interest and, to a much smaller extent, dividends, frequently flow from enterprises to individuals *via* some agency such as a savings bank or insurance company rather than directly. When such agencies intervene and we cannot separate the interest flow to them from their payments to individuals, interest does not necessarily measure current interest receipts by individuals, and cannot be compared with dividends. The intervening agencies may retain a part of the payments originating in the industries proper, or add to them from accumulated reserves; and there may be some disparities between actual receipts by individuals and the estimated net interest originating in the economic system.

D   DISTRIBUTION OF PAYMENTS BY SIZE

The usefulness of the distribution of family income receipts by size classes cannot be realized fully unless it is supplemented by a distribution of the size and other characteristics of the family, of other economic resources at the disposal of families, and of the sacrifices incurred in obtaining income.

Yet its value in the treatment of various problems ot economic analysis and in the interpretation of changes and differences in national income totals is great, even when it alone is available. Its contribution to any interpretation of the welfare equivalents of the income flowing to individuals from economic enterprises is patent. Its importance in the social conflict economic activity engenders between the 'haves' and 'have-nots' is equally clear.

To construct this distribution we need to know how much income each family received. It is not sufficient to know the distribution by size of each type of payment separately, since many individuals and families receive more than one type. The ideal, of course, would be to have the distribution by size combined with that by type, cross-classified by industrial origin. Such a combination of characteristics—size, type, and industrial origin —would shed light not only on differentiae with respect to current income receipts but, by segregating property income, would suggest the existence or absence of additional resources, and would also indicate differences,in the standard of living of recipients and the sacrifices implied in the process of earning. However, the unit in this distribution would still be the family, not the industry or enterprise in which payments originate.

It is this circumstance that makes the construction of a distribution of payments by size so difficult. As indicated in the next chapter, most of the continuous, comprehensive data for this country are for activities of enterprises and industries; and records of income receipts of individuals or families have, until very recent years, been confined to the small group that file income tax returns. Direct and comprehensive information on the distribution of income receipts by size is not available even for a single year, let alone continuously. We must therefore consider substitutes and approximations.

The first and most obvious substitute is the distribution by type of payment. As noted, one criterion of distinction between wages and salaries is the size of average payment; and one difference between dividends and interest is that a preponderant part of the former is received by people with incomes much larger than those of people who draw the preponderant part of the latter. Entrepreneurial income or withdrawals also are the source of low average incomes, being in the main receipts of small proprietors. Indeed, a great deal of the public interest in the distribution of payments by type lies in its identification with a distribution by size and among social groups. Shifts in the share of wages are interpreted as changes in the shares of the low income groups; and similar interpretations are applied to changes in the distribution between service and property income, or between entrepreneurial withdrawals and property income.

We have already indicated how crudely an allocation by type approximates a distribution by size. We point out here merely. that departures from a true distribution by size are greater when it is among family units than when it is among individuals. Among the former there is more opportunity for income from several sources and greater possibility that substantial incomes from a combination of wages and/or salaries will raise a family to a higher income category than it would be in if classified by any one source. Moreover, although incomes from wages and salaries, or interest and dividends, or labor and property differ greatly, the hybrid category of entrepreneurial income or withdrawals is not so clearly separable from the others with respect to the income size class to which it gives rise. In some industries entrepreneurial income payments or withdrawals are akin to wages; in others, to salaries; in still others they tend to yield high bracket incomes.

This suggests one more reason for cross-classifying types of payment by industrial origin. Differences in average levels of wages and salaries prevail from industry to industry; and the like, as just indicated, is still more true of entrepreneurial income or withdrawals. Even dividends and interest may differ in this respect among industries, because of differences in the speculative character of the industries and in the net property return they yield. Thus the multiplication of cells serves to suggest more accurately differences in size categories within total income payments to individuals and families. True, an increase in subdivisions increases the probability that one individual or family will draw income from more than one cell. But the possibly increased overlapping is surely more than off-set by the greater precision with which differences among payments by size classes would be revealed.

4 Summary

Four types of classification may be used in studying the composition of the national income total: analytical, evaluative, empirical, and institutional. Analytical classifications are based upon the analysis of economic reality provided by economic theory and its various applications, analysis that attempts to establish the various factors making for stability and change and the interrelations among them in determining economic phenomena. Distributions like that among labor, entrepreneurial, and property income types, or between monopolistic and competitive industries are good examples.

The evaluative type distinguishes categories within which, for substantial or imaginary reasons, the contents of national income are to be evaluated differently. Extreme examples arise from violent prejudices or partisanship. If one happens to believe that blondes form a distinct and exalted group, then income payments should be apportioned between fair-haired and other recipients. But usually the grounds of distinction are somewhat more cogent, resting upon a recognition that types of activity or groups of individuals should be segregated for substantial reasons of similarities and differences in pattern of life and consciousness of kind. A good illustration is the distribution of income payments among social groups (farmers, urban manual workers, white collar employees, small business men, etc.).

The empirical type of classification is based upon categories that have behaved in significantly different ways in the past and hence should be segregated for the present and future as

a help in diagnosing changes in the national total. It is difficult
to find an illustration of a purely empirical classification, but it
could be exemplified by the hypothetical case of an investigator
who classifies data on net values originating in each enterprise
of the country into groups exclusively by the way they changed
in the past.

The institutional classifications are based upon the categories
in which the statistical data come. They follow the divisions
determined by the institutional framework of economic
activity as reflected in current statistics, which, while often suf-
fering from sins of omission, rarely err by departing from institutional categories. Any book on national income affords
numerous illustrations of such institutional classifications.

While these four types of allocation differ sufficiently to warrant their separation, they have a great deal in common. Economic analysis is not an exercise of the imagination detached
from reality, but must consider the institutional framework of
economic activity and deal with the institutions that are reflected in the statistical data. Nor are the factors analyzed without influence upon the groups or types singled out in evaluative classifications: they are at least one among several sets of
factors that differentiate one social group or one type of activity
from another. Whatever other factors are involved in such
evaluative classifications, a goodly proportion must be reflected
in the data and hence in the institutional classifications. The
purely empirical allocations also have considerable kinship
with the analytical and institutional: they are usually based
upon institutional categories characteristic of the statistical
data in the past, and if consistently observed, give clues to combinations of factors susceptible to economic analysis.

The investigator must perforce adhere to institutional
classifications. Purely empirical allocations are few and unreliable, since adequately accurate estimates of national income do
not cover a period or a number of countries sufficient to yield
empirically established distinctions. And in order to assign
quantitative counterparts to analytical or evaluative categories,

he should either be able to go behind the published summary statistics and reclassify the original returns from enterprises or individuals, or be in a position, by expenditure of time and ingenuity, so to readjust the institutional divisions in the published data as to get good approximations to analytical and evaluative categories. The former opportunity is usually lacking and the latter severely limited.

For this reason our estimates present chiefly the institutional classifications of industrial origin and type of payment, with a single and broad analytical allocation among withholdings, disbursements, and consumers' outlay. For the same reason we discuss in this chapter primarily these three classifications. The classification among withholdings, disbursements, and outlay, being largely analytical and having been made by means of extensive readjustments and recalculations, is discussed in order to show clearly the lines drawn between the various categories and the allocation of doubtful items. In the classifications by industrial origin and by type of payment there was no need to clarify the distinctions made familiar by everyday discourse. The main purpose was to indicate the extent to which these institutional classifications conform to or differ from the analytical and evaluative ones they approximate but with which they are often treated as identical. Thus, a distribution among industries is not synonymous with that among types of productive activity or among social groups characterized by their industrial attachment. Similarly, the distribution among wages and salaries, entrepreneurial net income or withdrawals, and dividends plus interest and rent is not identical with the analytical distinction between labor, entrepreneurial, and property incomes. Even though, without actually carrying through the analytical and evaluative classifications, we cannot indicate how far the institutional classifications depart from them, we must not forget that they do. Finally, we suggested the possible combinations of classifications and indicated their use in translating the institutional allocations into the analytical and evaluative categories they approximate.

CHAPTER 3

Methods of Measurement

ALTHOUGH repeatedly deploring the limitations imposed by lack of data, we have not explained how the stock of data affects our estimates. It is decisive, since a national income investigator must rely on adequate and fairly accurate information in assigning magnitudes to the categories he sets up; and such information is a matter of laborious accumulation by many agencies rather than the work of an individual.

The general characteristics of continuous data serve to determine the approach. But even after the approach has been chosen in conformity with the data that are most plentiful and continuous, approximations must be made when data are lacking. In attempting to bridge gaps, in estimating one cell after another, the investigator must have at hand some controlling figures to test whether he has attained the countrywide total or whether parts are missing. In trying to make continuous annual estimates he finds that some parts of the total are recorded for some years and not for others.

We therefore discuss briefly the approach, the approximation of parts, the controlling totals, and the preparation of continuous annual estimates. In a sense this chapter is a summary of the description of sources and procedures given in detail in Volume II, emphasizing only the salient points at which the stock of data conditioned our estimates.

1 The Approach

The primary data needed to measure national income may be reported by enterprises or by individuals and families. Information from enterprises may be submitted by producing or proprietorship units, with effects on the distribution by industrial origin already discussed. If it is in terms of the gross value of products without classification of products by type, and of the cost of goods consumed in the production process, net value originating in an industrial division can be estimated by subtracting the cost of goods consumed from the gross value of products; national income is then the sum of these net values. If such net values are reported directly by type of payment and the net savings that comprise them, national income can be distributed not only by industrial origin but also between withholdings and disbursements and by type of payment. If the flow of commodities and services is reported in considerable detail, national income can be divided between consumers' outlay and net capital formation and both can be distributed by type of commodity and service. Indeed, of the classifications discussed in the preceding chapter, the only one that cannot readily be derived from reports by enterprises is that of payments by size among individuals or families.

A distribution of payments by size could be most easily derived from an estimate of national income based on reports by individuals or families, for the first item of information requested would be total payments received by each. If, in addition, the industrial characteristics of the paying enterprises, the type of payment, the division of receipts between expenditures and savings, and the apportionment of expenditures among commodities and services of diverse types were covered, most of the breakdowns mentioned in the preceding chapter could be carried through. But two important items would be missing. First, net savings of enterprises could not be estimated, since they are revealed solely by the accounting of enterprises themselves. Second, the commodity and service counterparts of individuals' net savings, the larger portion of which is expended by enterprises rather than by individuals, could not be ascertained.

In this country, as in many others, primary data sufficiently comprehensive to estimate national income are reported by enterprises. The censuses of agriculture, mining, manufacturing, electrical and communication industries, and for recent years, of construction, trade, and service cover at not too infrequent intervals the major part of the country's productive system. In addition, the Interstate Commerce Commission publishes continuous and complete reports on steam railroads and most other public utilities; the federal income tax authorities publish summaries of the annual reports of business corporations; and there is continuous information on various activities of government and many semi-public agencies. Continuous information reported by individuals or families, in contrast, has been exceedingly meager and incomplete, at least until very recent years.

Continuous and complete primary data solely from enterprises do not in themselves determine how to estimate national income and to classify its components. As already indicated, they may give us any one approach or all three: (1) the gross-net product, (2) the industrial payments, (3) the finished products. By means of the first, from the value of the gross product of enterprises in various industries and of the materials and products consumed by them in the production process we can estimate national income and gross product totals distributed by industrial source; by means of the second, from income payments and net savings originating in various industries, we can estimate national income (but not necessarily a gross product total) distributed by both industrial source and type of income; by means of the third, from detailed data on the products of enterprises, we can estimate national income, divided into consumers' outlay and capital formation, with these two broad components further subdivided by various categories of goods.

Could we use all three approaches we could check the accuracy of our estimates of national income as well as make distributions that would be complementary and constitute a useful blueprint of the workings of the national economy. However, the second approach alone is feasible for the period under study. Information on gross product, especially on products consumed in the production process, is still lacking for most industries. Data on the finished products of various industries have become relatively abundant since 1929, and it would be feasible to approximate national income for recent years by the finished products method. Even so, the margin of error would be greater than in estimates derived by the industry payments approach; and the relatively better supply of data for the latter approach becomes more decisive for the years before 1929.

Therefore, we used the industry payments approach. We began with agriculture and attempted to estimate wages, salaries, other compensation of employees, dividends, interest, entrepreneurial withdrawals or income, and net savings of enterprises. The combined total of these items is net income originating in agriculture. Then we proceeded similarly for mining, manufacturing, construction, and all other industries that can be singled out, until the contents of the country's economic system had been covered. National income is the sum of all the parts, adjusted for the flow of property income payments into and out of the country.

Abundant as the data are for this method, formidable difficulties must be overcome before we arrive at complete and continuous annual estimates of national income distributed by industrial origin and type of income.

2   The Approximation of Parts

A   DIFFICULTIES OF MEASUREMENT ENCOUNTERED IN MOST INDUSTRIES

Data are most abundant for industrial divisions concerned with the extraction, fabrication, and transportation of commodities

or the provision of publicly regulated services, and characterized by the corporate form of organization—mining, manufacturing, steam railroads, electrical industries (electric light and
power, electric railroads), and communication (telephone and
telegraph). With occasional lapses (such as the omission of
petroleum mining by the *Census of Mines* in 1929), the industrial censuses and Interstate Commerce Commission reports
cover these divisions fairly adequately, showing the number
and compensation of employees and the proportion of incorporated and unincorporated enterprises. Since the corporation
predominates in these industries, their property income and
net savings are reported rather fully on federal corporate income tax returns. In addition, special governmental agencies
(such as the Bureau of Mines and the Interstate Commerce
Commission) report supplementary information that can be
used in deriving estimates of gross income or of net income for
some industry type of income cells.

But difficulties arise even in these industrial divisions. First,
there are few data on receipts by employees of incomes other
than monetary wages and salaries: perquisites and other payments in kind, gratuities, compensation for injury, pensions.
For some industries, such as steam railroads, the items are reported; for others it is almost impossible to obtain them. Whenever feasible, these payments were estimated. Since they are
small, discretion seemed the better part of statistical valor for
industries for which great effort would have to be expended to
achieve even rough approximations. For these industries 'other'
payments to employees were omitted; and to that extent employee compensation is incompletely estimated.

Second, while in all industries discussed here corporations
predominate, some activity in mining and manufacturing is
still carried on by unincorporated establishments. The industrial censuses report the wages and salaries paid by such establishments but not the incomes of the proprietors. Nor are they
given adequately in *Statistics of Income,* the annual statistical
compendium of information reported on federal income tax

returns by individuals and corporations. The various means devised to estimate the total net income of these entrepreneurs and to divide it between entrepreneurial withdrawals and net savings, based largely upon some use of corporate data, are described in the notes to the tables in Part Four. The resulting estimates are crude, but the totals for these unincorporated firms are very small compared with the totals for the corporate, and any error in the former is not likely to affect the total for each industry greatly.

Third, *Statistics of Income* reports for the various industrial divisions total annual dividends and interest paid, but the payments are to other enterprises as well as to individuals. These inter-enterprise payments must be excluded if duplication is to be avoided. For dividends the adjustment can readily be made because *Statistics of Income* reports also dividends received by corporations. The difference between dividend receipts and payments is the net amount contributed by each industrial division to total dividends received by individuals, but it is the amount of net dividends *originating* rather than the amount actually *paid* by the industry *directly to individuals*.

The adjustment of interest is harder because the only long term interest receipts reported separately by corporations to the federal income tax authorities and published by the latter are those on government bonds; and total interest paid as reported in *Statistics of Income* is not divided between interest on short and long term debt. Our solution is based upon rather heroic assumptions; namely, that all interest on short term debt by corporations other than those representing aggregations of individuals (savings banks, insurance companies, etc.) is paid to enterprises, and that interest on long term debt is paid to individuals; and that, therefore, total interest paid on bonds minus interest received on government bonds is a good approximation to net interest originating and paid to individuals. Accordingly, we estimated interest on long term debt by applying an average rate of return derived from an extensive corporate sample to the total corporate long term debt outstanding shown by *Statistics of Income,* revised for a minor shortage in coverage. From these payments we subtracted receipts on government bonds held by corporations. Our estimate of interest payments to individuals is undoubtedly an approximation much cruder than our estimate of net dividend disbursements.

Fourth, the reported industrial classifications of employee income (and the less important entrepreneurial income) are not comparable with those of property income and corporate net savings. The former are from industrial censuses, the latter from *Statistics of Income,* and the two are not identical. This difficulty is, however, minor, especially when we discuss the broad industrial divisions. More important is the fact that payments to employees are based on primary information classified by producing establishments, i.e., plants at specified locations, while property income and corporate net savings are reported by corporations which, until 1934, were permitted by federal tax authorities to file consolidated statements for the parent corporation and its affiliates. Even single corporations having no affiliates frequently control several producing establishments engaged in diverse productive activities and classified in the industrial censuses in more than one industrial division. Among consolidated corporations this is the rule rather than the exception. Federal tax authorities classify each reporting unit in the industrial division from which it derived the major part of its income. This means that a corporation devoting a considerable part of its resources to oil mining or distribution in one year may be classified under chemical manufactures; in another year, with a slight increase in the relative importance of its mining or distributive operations, it may be classified under mining or trade.

A national income investigator cannot unscramble this mixture. It is an onerous task even for the management of an enterprise to determine accurately what part of its net revenue can be attributed to the various activities pursued or the different products turned out. Such a calculation is impossible from totals by industrial divisions in which reports of individual corporations are consolidated and from primary data for each corporation already combined for the various industrial activities represented. All we can do is to admit that property income and net savings of enterprises cannot be distributed by industrial divisions with the same thoroughness as payments to employees; and that consequently too much reliance cannot be placed on small differences among industrial divisions in the relative shares of property and service incomes or in the apportionment between aggregate payments to individuals and net savings of enterprises.[1]

The four types of difficulty in estimating income originating in mining, manufacturing, electrical industries and communication, and steam railroads (including Pullman and express), all industrial divisions for which data are relatively complete, are met also in most other industrial branches. The first, that relating to 'other' income of employees, is solved in these other industries along the lines already indicated: whenever possible we attempted to include these items, but we could not always attain complete coverage. However, when the payments are really substantial (e.g., relief disbursements, or subsistence for army and navy employees) the information is usually available

[1] The effect of the consolidation of reports on the industrial classification is revealed by a comparison made possible for 1934 by a change in the law restricting the right to file consolidated returns for income tax purposes (see *Statistics of Income* for 1934, Part 2, Tables 2, 10, and 13). The 1934 information is given for corporations classified by industrial divisions based on consolidated returns in 1933 and by industrial divisions based on separate returns in 1934. For net dividends originating (i.e., dividends paid minus dividends received) by major industrial groups, agriculture, manufacturing, and construction show minor changes from one classification to the other. But in dividends originating in mining, transportation and public utilities, and trade there is a significant decline (over 20 per cent) from the consolidated classification to the non-consolidated; and there is a striking increase in net dividends originating in finance. The apparent reason is that holding companies, formerly classified in the industrial division of their affiliates, are now segregated in finance and their dividend disbursements swell the item for that group. Of course, there may have been other substantial shifts not revealed in a classification by broad industrial groups.

and the items can be estimated. The omissions are therefore relatively minor. The third, estimating net interest payments to individuals, is also encountered in all other industries except government and those that represent transitional stages in the flow of property income to ultimate recipients, and is treated similarly. The last difficulty, fitting property income and net savings of enterprises into the moulds of the industrial classification in the same way as service income, is also present in the other industries; and there also little can be done beyond admitting it as a qualification of our estimates. The second difficulty, estimating entrepreneurial net income and its breakdown, assumes much greater proportions in most of the other industries than in those discussed and is aggravated by new problems.

B ADDITIONAL PROBLEMS IN AGRICULTURE, CONSTRUCTION, AND
   TRADE

The substantial part of activity in agriculture, construction, and trade carried on by unincorporated firms makes it especially necessary to estimate entrepreneurial net income more precisely than for industries in which unincorporated firms are relatively few; but for these three industries, to attain comprehensive coverage of any aspect of activity and of any type of income is far from easy.

This question of comprehensiveness might have been raised about the industrial divisions discussed first. Can it be assumed that the industrial censuses cover exhaustively the industries they purport to describe? Or that all active business corporations report to the federal income tax authorities as they are required to by law? Obviously some shortage in coverage may be expected, greater in some industries than in others. For example, while the reporting for steam railroads, electrical, and communication industries may be assumed to be complete, not all manufacturing and mining enterprises are covered; the censuses themselves expressly exempt establishments with a gross value of product under a low minimum. Also, there may be some evasion in reporting by corporations. But the magnitudes involved probably have so slight an effect on the estimates of income originating that it did not seem worth while to strive for more complete coverage.

The situation is quite different in agriculture, construction, and trade. Even when census surveys have been made we cannot be sure that the coverage is reasonably complete or consistent. In agriculture, for which a census has been taken at regular intervals for several decades, grounds for suspicion lie first in the difficulty of distinguishing between a *bona fide* farm, i.e., a productive unit devoted exclusively or preponderantly to agricultural activity, and a farm that is the country residence of people whose major activity is elsewhere or a place of refuge from urban centers during depressions. Furthermore, coverage may vary from one census year to the next because of differences in the time it is taken, the money spent, and the enumerator's method. Finally, there is the ever present difference between information reported to enumerators by farmers and that submitted to authorities by business corporations. The former is in large degree a matter of rough calculations on the part of the farmer; and sometimes, as in the case of a new tenant reporting on activity for the preceding year, i.e., before he took over the given farm, hearsay evidence.[2] Fortunately, the Department of Agriculture, especially the Bureau of Agricultural Economics, supplements the censuses by special studies and attempts to provide continuous series of comparable scope. It is this Bureau's estimates of income originating in agriculture that, with slight changes, we present here.

The deficiencies of coverage in construction and trade are much more serious. Unlike farms, many firms in contract construction and not a few in trade have no clearly recognizable,

[2] For the difficulties of defining a farm unit see J. D. Black and R. H. Allen, 'The Counting of Farms in the United States', *Journal of the American Statistical Association*, Sept. 1937; and Karl Brandt, 'Fallacious Census Terminology and its Consequences in Agriculture', *Social Research*, Feb. 1938. On the whole subject of estimating income from agriculture see the Social Science Research Council monograph, *Research in Agricultural Income* (June 1933).

identifiable location, and can easily be overlooked in any countrywide survey. A contractor or a broker who has his office 'in his hat', or a tradesman who has a stand in the lobby of an apartment hotel, is operating a genuine business that is perhaps his sole source of income as well as that of one or two employees. But the Census Bureau or any other agency can scarcely be expected to comb these fields so finely as to turn up all these elusive units. Complete coverage would be especially improbable in a first census, without the benefit of experience, or in a survey that had no legal power to compel the giving of information—characteristics of the more recent censuses of construction and trade. Furthermore, high mortality, both secular and seasonal, is common among construction and trade units. Consequently, a census for a given year would necessarily miss the activity of the units that were seasonally idle when it was taken or no longer in existence. Finally, in view of the primitive methods of accounting prevailing among small tradesmen and construction contractors, the trustworthiness of the information collected is subject to considerable doubt.

Although the business units omitted are small, their number may be large, and the consequent deficiency in the coverage of income and expense items rather substantial. Since the censuses collect the basic information on employee income, as well as on the gross volume of activity (used subsequently to estimate entrepreneurial incomes), we attempted to adjust for the shortage in coverage in contract construction and retail trade. In construction it was substantial and we raised the wage, salary, and other items reported in the Census for 1929, the basic figures in our estimates. The shortage for retail trade was much smaller, and because the approximation was rough, we decided to adhere to the Census totals of the number and compensation of employees. Whatever shortage there may be in our estimates for trade proper is, at least in some degree, caught in 'miscellaneous industries', the division in which we attempt to make up for the shortcomings of our approximations by parts and which is thus a patent measure of our failure to carry out the classification adopted.

Entrepreneurial income, the major type in agriculture and the preponderant one in construction and trade, is not reported in any industrial census and must be approximated. We have already suggested that the approximation based on corporate data—the means we used to estimate this item in mining and manufacturing—is too crude for industries in which unincorporated firms predominate. For instance, it would be nonsensical to try to approximate incomes of individual farmers from data for agricultural corporations. But can other information be found for estimating entrepreneurial income and its division between withdrawals and net savings?

The answer varies from industry to industry. The Census reports salaries paid to proprietors in many large construction firms. The salaries of executive officers may be used to approximate entrepreneurial withdrawals in wholesale trade. Besides, in 1929 corporate activity accounted for about 50 per cent of construction and of retail trade; 80 per cent of wholesale trade. We used corporate data to approximate total entrepreneurial net income in these three branches; and the reported salaries, salaries of corporation executives, or average salaries and wages, to approximate entrepreneurial withdrawals.

The expenses incurred by farmers in the conduct of their business are usually collected on a voluntary basis, and reported in terms of percentages of gross receipts. These reports are based on a sample of units that have fairly good accounting methods; such units are likely to be among the more successful and the larger units in the industry. The samples thus tend to exaggerate incomes and minimize losses; and their application to the countrywide totals leads to an exaggerated estimate of entrepreneurial net income. Nevertheless since with them a better approximation to the total net income of entrepreneurs in agriculture can be made than with the corporate reports in *Statistics of Income*, they were used by the Department of Agriculture, whose estimates we adopted. Entrepreneurial income totals have been further divided into withdrawals and net savings by estimating the former on the basis of farm workers' wages raised to represent the higher standard of living of independent farmers.

C SPECIAL PROBLEMS OF THE SERVICE INDUSTRIES

The industrial divisions discussed under Sections A and B comprise almost all the commodity producing, transporting, and distributing industries. The other industries in the country's productive system, except a few branches of transportation (pipe lines, water transportation, motor trucking, local cartage), are concerned with the provision of services: government, finance (banking, insurance, real estate), and service industries proper (professional, amusement, personal, domestic, business, etc.). Finally there is always the miscellaneous group which supplements the parts approximated specifically.

These diverse industries can be divided roughly into two large groups: those in which corporations or some other non-personal form of organization are common—water transportation, motor trucking, cartage, aviation, pipe lines, banking, insurance, government, educational service, and some parts of real estate, personal, amusement, and other service; and those characterized by the prevalence of individually owned enterprises—some small subdivisions under banking (private investment banks, brokerage houses, etc.), the part of real estate represented by net rent received by individuals, professional, domestic, and parts of personal, amusement, and other service industries.

For practically all industries in both groups a comprehensive and reliable estimate of net income originating is difficult. Educational institutions alone have been covered by a census at fairly regular intervals; and even its information on employee compensation is incomplete. Census surveys for other industries have either not been made or were made too early (e.g., for water transportation in 1916) or too late (for several service industries in 1935), contain insufficient information, and are inadequate in coverage. The 1935 *Census of Business* is especially deficient for those branches in which there are a multitude of small business units even more elusive than in contract construction and retail trade.

Thus for both groups, considerable difficulty is encountered in estimating employee, entrepreneurial, and property incomes. In the first group, that in which corporations and nonpersonal organizations predominate, little trouble is encountered in estimating property income originating: it is reported in *Statistics of Income* or elsewhere (as in the case of government debt and interest), or need not be considered at all since property income payments are interpreted as transfers of payments originating elsewhere in the productive system (e.g., in savings banks and life insurance companies). And since there are practically no unincorporated establishments, the main task is to estimate employee compensation. In the industries of the second group the main task is to estimate entrepreneurial net income. Employee income is a smaller though still considerable magnitude, and segregable property income is usually negligible.

We cannot describe adequately here the means by which we bridged gaps in information. Varying greatly according to the data used and in complexity, they yield final approximations of diverse reliability. But some general indications that suggest the main characteristics of the estimates can be given.

The estimates of payments to employees in the first group of industries utilize all or some of the following data: questionnaires sent to enterprises on the number and compensation of employees, the resulting sample raised to cover the total for the country; actual count of employees in a sample of enterprises, often reported in directories and manuals, raised to cover the entire industry, and multiplied by a sample average compensation; sample studies showing income paid to employees as a percentage of all operating expenses or all gross revenue; number of employees attached to the industry (according to the *Census of Population*), reduced by estimated unemployment, and multiplied by average compensation derived on the basis of samples or assumed to be equal to average compensation in a related industrial branch; estimates of the capital equipment of the industry, multiplied by the complement or crew of employees needed to man the equipment and their compensation. In general we estimated income originating for divisions as narrow as possible. Wide as the margin of error may be within them, to estimate for narrow divisions is the one way to arrive at a more reliable estimate for larger divisions, the one approach that assures estimates whose validity can be appraised by a critical student.

For the second group of industries measurement is more complicated and the estimates even cruder. Not only employee compensation but also the more important item, entrepreneurial net income, must be estimated. And adequate samples cannot be taken of the numerous small, unincorporated enterprises. Questionnaires become expensive if a large sample is attempted and yield treacherous results if a small sample is used. The absence of big, non-personal organizations means the absence of information that such organizations usually collect and publish incident to the discharge of public obligations; and that, while not relating directly to income, does afford some basis for approximating its size. Finally, the great differences in net income known to exist among entrepreneurs in the industries in this group, or among enterprises in this and other groups, bar an acceptance of averages for the industries covered by available data as valid for industries for which no direct information exists.

Consequently, only crude approximations could be made for industries in the second group. Estimates of total entrepreneurial income were usually computed by multiplying the number of entrepreneurs, obtained either from the *Census of Population* or from directories, by average net income, derived from sample studies of widely diverse coverage. The procedure followed for net rent receipts by individuals was to estimate as comprehensively as we could total gross rent payments, subtract gross rent received by corporations, and reduce gross rent received by individuals to net rent on the basis of sample studies. Finally, employee compensation was determined partly on the basis of census information, partly on the basis of sample returns from individual employers, partly on the crude basis of estimating the number attached (from the *Census of Population*), reducing it to the number employed, and multiplying the latter by an average compensation derived either from a sample for the specific industry or from information for related or similar industrial branches.

This description conveys an inadequate notion of the devices used to compensate for the paucity of data. The main point is that ingenuity cannot fully or effectively compensate for lack of basic information. Most of the estimates for this group of industries are susceptible to a wide margin of error. And for many industrial branches in it a specific estimate had to be given up as hopeless. These were thrown into the miscellaneous group. Because the industries that had to be treated in this manner were large and because we had controlling totals for most of the service industries proper, a division of 'miscellaneous service' was established for all service industries for which we could not make separate estimates.

The 'miscellaneous service' as well as the general 'miscellaneous' division could more properly be designated 'all other service' and 'all other industries'. They comprise the segments of national income obtained by subtracting net income originating in the industrial branches for which specific estimates proved feasible from the totals that constitute the most comprehensive estimate of income in the field of service or of the total national product. The characteristics of these controlling totals and their effect on the scope of national income estimates are now considered.

3 The Controlling Totals

A THE NATURE OF THE TOTALS

The device of controlling totals is used commonly to approximate totals for industry type of income cells. Whenever detailed and complete information can be had for only a portion of the area under study, it is usual to find some other attribute by which the area of partial coverage can be compared with the entire area. The total of this attribute for the entire area becomes the controlling magnitude; and all totals derived from data covering a portion of the area are adjusted to correspond with it.

However, we are concerned here with countrywide controlling totals, not with those for any specific industrial division or industry type of income cell. Since the approximation by parts proceeds from one industrial division to the next, i.e., each category of payments and net savings of enterprises is estimated first in one industry, then in another, the countrywide controlling totals must, if possible, be given separately for each type of payment and for the net savings of enterprises. From a controlling total for employee income for the country as a whole and the payments accounted for in each industry we derived the payments to employees in the miscellaneous industrial group; and proceeded likewise for the other types of income.[3]

The controlling total for payments to employees was the number of gainfully occupied persons, exclusive of individual proprietors, reported in the *Census of Population*. A gainfully occupied person is one who, though he may not be employed or otherwise engaged in a gainful pursuit at the time the Census is taken, is ordinarily so engaged. The number of gainfully occupied employees reported by the Census, if the Census is at all

[3] The discussion that follows relates to the countrywide controlling totals used to derive the estimates for the miscellaneous industries group. The controlling totals for the service industry, used to derive 'miscellaneous service' and thus complete the estimate for the service group, are similar and need not be discussed here. They are described in detail in Part Four, in the notes appended to the tables that give estimates for miscellaneous service.

complete, thus represents the maximum number likely to receive wages and salaries; maximum since it includes persons ordinarily employed but who may have been inactive, either voluntarily or involuntarily, at the time the Census was taken.[4]

Consequently, the total must be adjusted for unemployment, even before it can be used to control the *number* receiving employee compensation. We attempted this adjustment as follows. For each industry covered in the approximation by parts, we estimated the number employed. The sum of these totals was subtracted from total gainfully occupied employees reduced by the number fully unemployed: the remainder is the number employed in the miscellaneous group. Since it still included some partly unemployed, it was reduced to equivalent full-time employment on the basis of ratios for other industries.

Total entrepreneurs were also estimated from the *Census of Population* but somewhat differently from employees. It was not feasible to compare the overall total of proprietors reported in the Census with the number accounted for in the industrial branches for which specific estimates had been made, because for some branches the estimates of entrepreneurs were the crudest of approximations. But since the latest *Census of Population* reports occupations by industries, we could obtain the number of proprietors in the industrial divisions for which no specific estimates of entrepreneurial income had been made. This number, unadjusted, is given as the number of entrepreneurs in the miscellaneous group. Total unemployment is infrequent among entrepreneurs so long as they remain entrepreneurs; and partial unemployment has little meaning in this type of gainful pursuit.

The number of equivalent full-time employees and of entrepreneurs in the miscellaneous group determined, the estimates

4 Actually the Census is not complete in that it omits at least recipients of casual and part-time incomes, who would not classify themselves as gainfully occupied. For a brief discussion of this and other omissions see Section 3 C below and Chapter 9.

of employee compensation and entrepreneurial income originating in this residual group were dependent upon an average compensation per employee and an average net income per entrepreneur. Direct data from which such averages could be computed are not available; if they were, there would be no need for a miscellaneous division. Any averages that could be used would necessarily be arbitrary. Such arbitrariness was lessened by examining the nature of the industries included in this miscellaneous group, by finding similarities between them and other industries for which fairly acceptable estimates of service income had been made, and by using for some industries scattered data for 1929 and later years. Separate averages were applied to the number of employees and of entrepreneurs. Since those averages were at best merely reasonable guesses, we pressed the approximation by parts as far as we could, thereby reducing to a minimum the area covered by the residual miscellaneous industrial division.

The controlling total for net rent received by individuals was derived chiefly from (a) rent paid by corporations (*Statistics of Income* for recent years), raised whenever possible to cover unincorporated establishments; (b) rent paid by all enterprises in trade (*Census of Distribution*); (c) total residential rent (derived from the *Census of Population*, 1929); (d) rent originating in agriculture and paid to non-farmers as estimated by the Bureau of Agricultural Economics. From this total of gross rent (excluding rent from agriculture) we subtracted rent received by corporations (*Statistics of Income*); and to the residual gross rent received by or imputed to individuals we applied a ratio of net to gross rent, derived from samples of operating and maintenance expenditures for real estate, to obtain net non-farm rent. To the latter we added net farm rent.

Comprehensive totals of dividends and corporate net savings are given in *Statistics of Income* but we preferred to use for public utilities information reported by the Bureau of the Census and the Interstate Commerce Commission; consequently, the derivation of dividends and net savings in the residual miscellaneous division by subtraction yields in several years patently absurd results. We therefore estimated dividends and net savings for this miscellaneous division directly, by using data from *Statistics of Income* on the industries specifically included. In that sense there is no single controlling total for either dividends or corporate savings. For both, the countrywide totals consist of *Statistics of Income* totals for all except the public utilities covered by the Bureau of the Census and the Interstate Commerce Commission, and the latter totals for them. In addition, net savings are estimated for unincorporated firms, for which the controlling total is essentially the number of entrepreneurs; and for governments, for which the controlling totals are, on the one hand, net public construction and, on the other, the net public debt of all governments.

The countrywide total of interest includes: (1) interest on long term debt for all corporations except public utilities, reported in *Statistics of Income* and raised to allow for a slight shortage in coverage, multiplied by a rate of interest derived from an extensive corporate sample, minus interest received by corporations on government bonds; (2) long term interest paid by public utilities, as reported by the Interstate Commerce Commission and the *Census of Electrical Industries*, minus all long term interest received; (3) interest payments originating in agriculture and real estate; (4) interest payments by governmental agencies. Interest payments in miscellaneous industries are estimated from *Statistics of Income* data for industries specifically covered, not by subtraction from a single controlling total.

The totals of interest and of net savings are, perhaps, the least comprehensive. The former explicitly omits interest paid by unincorporated firms to individuals—a presumably small item that cannot be gauged with the existing data. Estimates of net savings of enterprises are probably deficient for unincorporated firms.

B EFFECT ON TERRITORIAL COVERAGE

The controlling totals determine the territorial coverage of national income estimates. While the industrial and other censuses record some service income that may flow to people residing outside this country, the controlling total for this type of payment is the number of persons gainfully occupied reported in the *Census of Population*. Since this Census, as well as all the industrial censuses, cover only people residing in the continental United States (i.e., the forty-eight states and the District of Columbia), and exclude such outlying territorial possessions as Alaska, Hawaii, the Virgin Islands, and Puerto Rico, the service income total is for this territorial area. If the service income in the various industrial branches except miscellaneous does cover some people residing outside the continental United States, there will be an offsetting reduction in the service income originating in the residual, the miscellaneous division. Full coverage of the number of employees drawing wages and salaries, the number of entrepreneurs, and the activity of unincorporated enterprises, is also for the continental United States.

At first sight, net rent received by individuals seems to have the same coverage, since the global totals are derived largely from the *Census of Population* and the industrial censuses. But it must be remembered that rent, though *paid* by individuals and business organizations domiciled in the continental United States, may flow to people residing abroad; conversely, residents of this country may receive rent from abroad. This is possible so far as we conceive of net rent as purely property income, not calling for participation by the recipient in activity within the country. Since the flow of net rent across international boundaries is relatively minor and can be neglected, we accept the total originating in the continental United States as identical with the total received by its residents, although this treatment results in greater error than a similar procedure for employee compensation or entrepreneurial income.

The basic totals for dividends, interest, and corporate net

savings are from *Statistics of Income,* which covers Alaska and
Hawaii in addition to the continental United States. The cor-
·porations are classified by the states and territories in which the
principal place of business or principal office or agency is located. Adjustment for the inclusion of Alaska and Hawaii to
assure strict identity of territorial coverage with that of service
income is both difficult and relatively unimportant. In the
case of dividends and interest we wish to know how much
individuals residing in the United States receive; and the fact
that the principal agency, office, or place of business of a corporation is in Alaska or Hawaii is no assurance that its dividends and interest are received largely by individuals residing
outside the continental United States. A better case can be
made for the exclusion of the net savings of corporations in
Alaska and Hawaii. But the corporations classified under these
two territories are such a small fraction of the total (for 1936
their net income and net deficit combined accounted for less
than one-half of one per cent of a similar total for the continental United States), and their exclusion would entail so
many minor and arbitrary reductions in the industrial divisions that it did not seem worth while. Consequently, the totals
of corporate net savings include corporations domiciled in the
continental United States, Alaska, and Hawaii.

The totals of dividends and interest received by individuals
discussed so far *originate* in enterprises domiciled in the continental United States, Hawaii, and Alaska. But some of these
payments are received by residents of foreign countries; conversely, residents of this country receive some interest and
dividends from abroad. Our definition of national income demands an estimate of dividends and interest received by the
residents of this country, preferably residents of the continental
United States. Figures for the adjustment, that for the flow of
property income into and out of the country, are from the
study of the balance of international payments, in the course
of which the Department of Commerce estimates the returns
on investments in this country by foreigners and by Americans

abroad. These investments are largely in securities; and while direct investments (in such properties as real estate) are also estimated by the Department of Commerce, they are small and the estimates do not cover the entire period. The final adjustment was to subtract from total dividends and interest originating the payments flowing to foreigners and to add the payments received from abroad by residents of this country.

However, the territorial area, for purposes of this adjustment, is even wider than that covered in *Statistics of Income*. "In addition to continental United States, our balance-of-payments area includes Alaska, Hawaii, Puerto Rico and the Virgin Islands. The Philippine Islands and the Panama Canal Zone fall outside this area and are therefore considered foreign countries" (*Foreign Investment in the United States,* prepared under the direction of A. E. Taylor, Department of Commerce, Washington, 1937, p. 3, note 1). It would be difficult to modify this adjustment to reduce the area it covers, and the change would be too slight to affect the totals significantly.

To sum up: In view of the dominance of employee compensation and entrepreneurial income, total national income is almost exclusively for the continental United States. Dividends, interest, and corporate net savings cover a somewhat larger area; but the additional coverage probably amounts to less than one-half of one per cent of the respective type of income totals.

C RESULTING EXCESSES AND OMISSIONS

The national income estimates, as described in the approximation by parts and delimited by the controlling totals, include some items that should be omitted and omit others that should be included. Their excesses and omissions are not to be confused with under- or overvaluations in the estimates themselves. We do not deal here with such questions as whether wages and salaries for various industrial divisions are larger or smaller than they should be. We are concerned with the possible omission of some group of employees, a certain type of income, some industry; or the inclusion of items that definitely do not belong in national income.

Activities whose compensation should be omitted are likely to be included because people engaged in pursuits upon which society frowns cannot be expected to report them under their real name. Peddlers of pernicious and prohibited drugs, panders, professional assassins are loathe to admit their true occupations to Census enumerators; and if recorded, they will appear under some occupation that meets with social approval or tolerance. Similarly, many people, corporations, or individual firms engaged in occupations that are innocuous, or at least not prohibited, but are recognized by society at large as not contributing to the positive contents of national income, may try, sometimes in vain, to evade Census surveys as they do the vigilance of authorities. Hence, the controlling totals undoubtedly include some activities whose compensation should be excluded from national income. This over-inclusion cannot be even roughly approximated, but it can be assumed to be minor relative to the total.

The omissions due to lack of data are more numerous and the items are larger. Reasonably complete coverage of goods that do not appear on the market is attained only for products retained by farmers for their own consumption and the services of houses inhabited by their owners. Payments in kind to employees are covered for only a few industries, and have to be omitted for most. None of the other activities whose products do not appear on the market (listed in Ch. 1) is included in national income. The size of these omissions depends mainly upon which of these non-market goods one thinks belong in national income. If a most inclusive viewpoint is adopted, the shortage in our total is relatively large.[5]

Some significant groups of monetary income payments are omitted. We have already noted that 'other' income of employees cannot be fully estimated except for a few industries.

[5] For a suggestion of the magnitudes involved see Chapter 9.

A much larger omission is income from casual or secondary occupations, either combined with a full-time pursuit or engaged in by persons not usually gainfully occupied and of a type not sufficiently important to place their performers in the category of gainfully occupied. For example, a full-time worker in a factory may earn some occasional income by doing repair work for a householder. The net value of his activity is recorded in our estimates in connection with his full-time job. But his additional earnings, derived from occasional repair jobs, stand little chance of being recorded anywhere. They cannot be retrieved through comparison of the number gainfully occupied and employed: the household does not report its expenditure on this job, and the worker is unlikely to be subject to an income tax or to report his earnings. Other not uncommon instances are those of professional salaried people deriving fees from lecturing, writing, and other free lance jobs; proceeds from the sale of products by people to whom gardening, flower raising, or owning a milch cow is a secondary pursuit, etc.

Illustrations of incomes earned by people not classified as gainfully occupied are also plentiful. Many minors in urban communities deriving small incomes from occasional jobs (bootblacking, newspaper selling, fruit gathering, etc.) also stand little chance of being recorded among the gainfully occupied in the *Census of Population.* Many a housewife, especially among the lower income families, takes in a boarder or two without thereby converting the household into a professional boarding house and considering herself, or being considered by statistical authorities, as gainfully occupied; the same is true of occasional charring, laundry work, and similar domestic jobs. Finally, a gainfully occupied person, entirely or partly unemployed, may find an occasional job that yields a small income. He does not thereby fall out of the unemployed classification, and his income is not recorded anywhere. Each of these omissions, which are partly employee compensation and partly entrepreneurial income, is fairly small, but they are numerous and may well add up to a substantial sum. Uncertain as the amount is, it is probably not large relative to total recorded payments to employees and entrepreneurial income.

Some items are omitted from property income. As indicated in Chapter 2 (Sec. 3 A), royalties cannot be estimated. The item is reported by individuals who file federal income tax returns, but the authorities combine it with net rent receipts in their publications. We noted also that interest paid to individuals by unincorporated firms cannot be estimated. But it is not a large amount, relatively. The chief shortcoming of our estimates of property income arises because we cannot trace its flow through institutions such as banks and insurance companies. In it we include all dividends and long term interest received by these institutions and interpret their receipt as an accrual to the account of the ultimate recipient. However, we cannot ascertain whether the actual net disbursement to the ultimate recipients by these institutions is larger or smaller than the flow of dividends and long term interest to them.

Finally, all our estimates may have a shortage over and above that due to the items we are aware we omit, for the controlling totals, no matter how comprehensive, may fail to cover some parts of the country's economic activity. Some residents and gainfully occupied persons may elude the Census enumerator; some corporations may not be recorded in *Statistics of Income*. The bias is toward omission rather than over-inclusion, for the obvious reason that it is easier for a census, as for any statistical survey, to miss units than to count those that do not exist.

Most of the omissions are vague or unknown quantities, and one cannot do more than conjecture what they amount to. They are noted here primarily to indicate the scope of our national income total, and to emphasize that we can estimate recordable, 'professional' economic activities alone. Products of activities so far removed from the market as to have an uncertain market value, products of casual and secondary pursuits, and the margin of unknown that always remains, even after assiduous effort at completeness, are perforce excluded.

4 Continuous Annual Estimates

A THE NEED

Estimating national income for a single hypothetical year, assumed to be most advantageous from the viewpoint of the supply of basic data, is easy compared with preparing reliable totals covering each year in a period. Do we really need continuous annual estimates? Since they are necessarily approximate and only rough guides in a study of short term changes in the economic scene, would it not be sufficient to estimate national income for single years at substantial intervals, preferably those for which censuses are taken—1909, 1919, 1929?

Several reasons may be suggested for declaring such an intermittent series unsatisfactory and for estimating national income continuously on an annual and perhaps even shorter time unit basis. First and foremost is that estimates for any single year are inevitably affected by the economic conditions peculiar to it: the phase of the business cycle through which the country was passing and the conjuncture of events. For example, from estimates for 1919 and 1929, the character of the changes during the decade could scarcely be inferred; and from estimates for a single year, it would be impossible to infer which magnitudes and relations are persistent and which contingent upon conditions peculiar to it. To differentiate between transient and persistent elements we must have estimates for several time units.

Consequently, whether one is content with annual estimates at decennial, quinquennial, or biennial intervals or strives for a continuous annual series depends primarily upon the period for which one wishes to establish significant changes or differences in national income and its components. From decennial estimates we can establish tendencies free from cyclical and casual disturbances only for sixty years or more, and must treat the entire period as a unit, since we cannot isolate the secular changes peculiar to any part. With quinquennial estimates we can study the non-cyclical, persistent movements during a shorter period, say thirty to forty years; from annual estimates we can approximate secular movements for still shorter periods. In other words, cyclical and other transient changes can be the better distinguished and the persistent movements for shorter periods studied with greater accuracy the shorter (up to a certain limit) the intervals separating the estimates. The same holds *pari passu* for comparisons among countries or regions, since the impact of cyclical and other transient disturbances varies with the area. Here again a series composed of estimates for not too infrequent time units is needed in order to separate the persistent from the transient differences and study the former closely during relatively brief intervals.

Second, we may be interested in these transient changes or differences themselves. If so, we may consider national income estimates as attempts to synthesize diverse movements occurring at any given time in the various parts of the economic system. While approximate and too broad for a proper measurement of cyclical and other short term changes in economic conditions, still, in the absence of more comprehensive estimates for briefer time units, annual estimates are of some use for the study of short term changes or differences. For such purposes continuous estimates are indispensable.

This aspect of national income estimates accounts for the powerful incentive to bridge long intervals in any series. When a series contains an estimate for a year close to the present, the incentive is dormant. But if the estimate is for some year in the past, we are impelled to bring it up to date, to ascertain what happened in the years immediately preceding and what is happening at present. For example, were we to estimate national income for 1940, by 1942 or 1943 we would want to know what had happened meanwhile. This desire will be the stronger the more accurately the estimates reflect the conditions during the one year they cover and the greater the apparent changes since. Both factors, the accuracy of the estimates and the sensitivity of the economic system to short term disturbances, have during recent years made more desirable national income estimates at close intervals.

Finally, there is the purely practical consideration that any interval longer than a year, combined with any choice of dates, would not be the best for all parts of the economic system. For example, if decennial intervals and the years 1909, 1919, 1929 were chosen, it would be unfortunate for estimates of electrical industries and communication, the censuses of which are for 1917, 1922, 1927, 1932, etc.; of water transportation, the census of which, when taken, covers the sixth year of the decade; and for any information on wealth, the census of which (*Wealth, Debt, and Taxation*) is taken decennially in the second year of the decade. Continuous annual estimates free us from the quandary of what intervals and dates to select.

B THE PREPARATION

The difficulties arising in the preparation of continuous series for this country apply exclusively to employee compensation, entrepreneurial income, and rent. Dividends, interest, and corporate net savings can be derived, for almost the entire period covered by us, from *Statistics of Income* and other reports published annually; and their measurement on a continuous annual basis involves few additional difficulties. The only point to be noted is that while our estimates are for calendar years, some corporations report for fiscal years. However, the proportion is small (for 1933 about 10 per cent of all corporations, accounting for about 12 per cent of combined net income and net deficit). The consequent blurring of the temporal limits of the year is not material.

To prepare continuous annual estimates of other income types is not simple, because censuses are taken at decennial, quinquennial, or biennial intervals. We must either bridge the temporal gaps between the census years, when several fall within the period, or extrapolate a census figure for a single year backward and/or forward until the entire period is covered. Either choice reduces itself to the acceptance of the census figure, adjusted or unadjusted, as the basic quantity; finding a related series, usually of much narrower coverage but continuous, and using it as an index of changes which, when applied to the census figures for one year or several, yields the continuous annual estimate of that particular group of income payments.

Our first task is to choose a continuous series which, when converted to an index, can be taken to represent annual changes in the total. The choice is seldom among several continuous series for the same group of wages, salaries, or entrepreneurial income. It is more often a matter of deciding what, in the absence of continuous series relating directly to the industry in question, we should choose to construct the interpolating or extrapolating index. In this choice we resorted to various expedients. If continuous direct series were reported for wages but not for salaries in a given industry, we used a ratio of salaries to wages in a related industry. If there were no indexes for total payments to employees but we could estimate annual gross sales in a given industry, as well as in a related one for which employee compensation could be estimated annually, we based the interpolation index on the ratio of employee compensation to gross sales. When continuous series were reported for the number employed but not for their compensation, we estimated the change in the per capita figure on the basis of a sample narrower in coverage than that for the number employed or of changes in the per capita figure for a related industry. For entrepreneurial income there were also either sample series relating directly to the industry concerned or estimates of the number based on the number of unincorporated firms, the latter interpolated between Census dates by an index based on the number of failures; and estimates of withdrawals per entrepreneur based largely on the movement of per capita salaries. In general we used all sample data that applied specifically to the industrial division or type of payment to be estimated, and only in their absence, sample information for related industries, converting it to some ratio basis before using it as an index.

The supply of such continuous series is governed by the factors that determine the availability of basic information. Primarily for enterprises rather than for individuals and households, they are most plentiful for the industrial divisions for which the basic information is best, i.e., mining, manufacturing, and public utilities, and for the same reasons. The factors limiting the supply of comprehensive, basic data in such industries as contract construction and trade also affect the supply of continuous annual series and are aggravated by the lack of a census for these two industries before 1929. Again the absence of data is most acute in the service industries, in which unincorporated enterprises predominate. This similarity of the stocks of continuous sample series to that of intermittent Census data is to be expected not only because the same factors are operative, but also because regular censuses in themselves constitute an incentive to collect sample data. In industries for which censuses are not taken, or are recent, there is little incentive to collect continuous samples, since there are no basic totals in conjunction with which sample data could be used or by which they could be tested and improved.

Our second task was to decide how to treat industry type of income cells for which a crude but tolerable approximation could be made for a single year but for which data were insufficient for acceptable annual series. Such cells or branches were usually transferred to 'miscellaneous', a fate that befell fisheries, motor transportation, and aviation. The alternative, to make estimates for the more recent years for which they are feasible and change the industrial classifications for the various parts of the period under study, would increase the cumbersomeness of the classification and the difficulties of temporal comparison. It would be worth while only if the period covered by the specific estimates were substantial and the estimates themselves fully trustworthy.

This consideration indicates one reason why our estimates

begin in 1919. The decennial census is for 1919, which is also
the year when new continuous sample data on employment
began to be collected on a large scale. *Statistics of Income*
tabulations start in 1916. If one were to go beyond 1919, especially to the somewhat abnormal war years, numerous series
would cease to be available and the breakdown of national
income could not be as detailed. On the other hand, there
would be small gain in the amount of data continuously available had we begun after 1919, unless we had shifted all the
way to 1929, another year that serves as the initial date for an
appreciable amount of additional information.

Once we had chosen the continuous series to be used in extending the basic magnitudes over time, we had to decide upon
the method of interpolation and extrapolation. The theoretically possible variety of methods is wide. In extrapolating, one
can make various assumptions concerning the way in which
changes in the area to be estimated are reflected in the sample
series used as an index. We might assume that the sample is
strictly proportional, the simplest possible hypothesis; or that
it is too sensitive or not sufficiently sensitive to short term oscillations, so that its oscillations would be damped or intensified
when we transfer them to the estimated area; or that it has an
upward or downward bias as compared with the basic area
studied, and allow for it in using the sample as an index. Similar assumptions may be made to modify the application of the
continuous sample in interpolation, i.e., estimating the totals
between two given magnitudes; and various interpolation
formulae, expressive of different assumptions concerning the
underlying line of movement and the relation between the
sample series and the successive basic magnitudes, may be used.

But the choice presupposes more exact knowledge of the
relation between the sample and the total area to be estimated
than is possessed by the national income investigator. Even
when the continuous series are based on data relating directly
to the industry or type of income to be estimated, it is difficult
to know precisely in what way the sample may not record the

relative changes in the magnitudes to be extrapolated or interpolated. When the index is based on data from other industries or types of income, no precise judgment is possible. For
these reasons the simplest methods of extrapolation and interpolation were followed: for the former we assumed that the
relative changes in the sample series describe exactly the relative changes in the basic figure; for the latter, that the average
relative error of the index, as compared with the two basic
totals, is distributed equally over the intervening years. Only
in the interpolation between biennial Census totals was another method of interpolation sometimes used.

5 Concluding Comments

For an adequate account of how the supply of data conditioned
our estimates of national income and of its components, a
critical reader should consult the comments on the characteristics of the industrial and type of income classifications followed
(Ch. 8), review the tentative magnitudes suggested for the various items omitted (Ch. 9), compare our estimates with those
published by the National Bureau in the past and by the Department of Commerce at present (Ch. 10), inspect critically
our classification of underlying data and the analysis of the interpolation and extrapolation procedures (Ch. 11), observe the
relative margins of error we set for the various industry type
of income cells that comprise national income in each year
(Ch. 12), refer to the tables and notes in Part Four, and finally
glance at the supplementary materials in Part Five.

Obviously, not much would be gained by trying to summarize this chapter, already a summary of Part Four. Instead,
we speculate briefly upon the factors that determine the supply
of income data in this country. The decisions it imposes have
been stressed. Statistical information for so comprehensive a
total cannot be collected by one investigator or research agency,
but is the cumulative product of continuous and extensive
collection largely by governmental agencies, which have the
power to demand information and are impelled to do so by

considerations of public policy and administrative needs. Why are income data in this country so much more plentiful from enterprises than from individuals and households? Why are those from enterprises primarily suitable for the industry payments approach rather than for the gross-net product or finished product approaches?

In answer to the first question, several, necessarily tentative, suggestions can be advanced. First, there is the greater ease with which reports can be obtained from enterprises than from individuals or families, partly a matter of sheer numbers, partly of how well informed the reporter is. In recent years about 450,000 corporations reported to the federal income tax authorities. The families whose livelihoods were derived from these corporations must have numbered over fifteen million. In 1929 the *Census of Manufactures* reported about 211,000 manufacturing establishments. In April 1930 the *Census of Population* reported over eleven million persons usually engaged in manufacturing. Moreover, enterprises are in direct contact with production processes, sales, and payments, and have systems of accounting and control that place them in a much better position to provide accurate information than are individuals as ultimate consumers and members of households.

Second, much of governmental regulation is aimed directly at enterprises, rather than at individuals or families; and a large part of our statistical information on economic matters is a byproduct of such administrative efforts. This is especially true for public utilities, foreign trade, and business corporations subject to taxation. On the other hand, not until recent years have governments even tried to collect information on the incomes of individuals and households or the ways in which they disposed of payments received from enterprises, except when the incomes were above the taxable minimum. As they became more concerned with the temporal stability and the sufficiency of individuals' incomes, they began, through their social security administration, to collect comprehensive information on incomes. Even now, for technical reasons, they prefer to obtain it from enterprises.

Finally, both the public at large and students of economic problems have tended, and perhaps still tend, to emphasize production, neglecting distribution and consumption. With the rapid extensive and intensive progress that characterized this country through most of its history, the existence of frontiers to be conquered and the need to raise the industrial arts to the level of the more advanced countries, the pressing problems seemed to be in production; and the problems created by the distribution of national income and its utilization by ultimate consumers seemed relatively minor and soluble in the upward rush of industrial production. This viewpoint put a premium on information on productive activity, on the achievements of the industrial system in terms of goods produced, men employed, values added, etc., rather than on goods consumed or the shares of inhabitants in the national total. Obviously, information on productive activity can be supplied only by the enterprises that organize and control it. The recent shift in viewpoint, toward greater concern over the distribution of national income among ultimate consumers and between consumption and savings, presages a change in the emphasis on what questions should be asked and an increase, already apparent, in information reported in terms of individuals and household units.

These suggestions serve to explain also why we know so much more about some industries than about others. Information is richest for industries in which corporations, especially of the type that are subject to more rigid control by public authority (public utilities), are most common; and poorest for industries in which the predominant unit is the unincorporated firm. Here again the difference is due to the smaller number of corporations, their better accounting systems, their more rigid control by governmental and administrative agencies. Information is more plentiful for enterprises that deal with commodities, especially extraction, fabrication, and transportation (agriculture, mining, manufacturing, construction, steam railroads), than for enterprises engaged in the provision of services that have no material embodiment (trade, direct service, finance, government, etc.). Here again emphasis on the productive accomplishments of the economic system in a society which, at least in the past, tended to identify them with increase in material wealth, led to a greater interest in commodity production than in services.

These comments suggest the answer to the second question: why data on income type are more abundant than on the value of products consumed or on finished products. Public interest, whether social or administrative, naturally lies chiefly in the productive system as a source either of employment and occupational possibilities, thereby establishing a link between population as a productive factor and total output, or of taxable income. The industrial censuses record employment and employee compensation, and the population censuses, occupations; *Statistics of Income* and similar byproducts of administrative agencies record dividends, interest, and corporate savings. To require reports on gross product, especially on the full value of products of other enterprises consumed, would mean demanding more from economic units than many could easily give and would serve no clear social or administrative purpose. Similarly, detailed reports on finished products would require a more comprehensive coverage of interrelations among enterprises and of purely service activities than seems warranted in a society whose industrial production is growing rapidly and the welfare of whose inhabitants is apparently increasing. Only concern over the adequacy of ultimate consumption, greater attention to service activities closer to the passage of goods into households, greater concern over the adequacy of capital formation, and emphasis on the *utilization* rather than on the *production* of income render detailed reports on finished products of sufficient importance for public agencies to attempt to procure them and for enterprises and society at large to recognize that their value justifies the effort.

Our discussion of the factors that determine the stock of income data in this country, sketchy and speculative though it is, perhaps attempts to explain too much. But the main conclusion seems valid: the stock, which can be accumulated only at appreciable cost to society, is far from being due to chance. It is rather due to factors deeply seated in social organization and the outlook of society at large. Some determine the extent to which the final units in social life—ultimate consumers, business enterprises, public organizations—record in their operations and define in their everyday discourse the figures from which estimates can be made. Others determine the extent to which these final units, which are at the same time units of reporting and observation, recognize that the information desired is indispensable from the viewpoint of the body social, whether for purposes of administration, legislation, or any other form of action by society at large, and hence are willing to provide it. Finally, more specific factors come into play in actuating governmental agencies, the only ones that can gather the continuous and comprehensive information requisite to estimate national income.

Again we stress the dependence of the supply of economic data in general, and income data in particular, upon the organization of the units of observation; upon the viewpoint entertained by society at large as to the relative urgency of various economic problems and hence as to the need for various types of data; upon the responsiveness of governmental agencies to the demands of public administration and social policy. Just as in defining his concepts and classifications, the investigator operates within a frame of reference determined by the viewpoint of the society whose economic activities he measures, so his actual statistical work is conditioned by the social organization and viewpoint that are reflected in the statistics for the period with which he is concerned. There is an obvious interplay among the factors that determine both the conceptual framework and the statistical bricks of the national income estimates.

Changes in National Income, 1919–1938

National Income, Aggregate Payments, and Consumers' Outlay

1 The Totals in Current Prices

As WE define it, national income (Table 1, col. 1) is the net value of the services individuals and their property contribute to the production of economic goods; or the value of commodities and services produced by the country's economic system minus the costs of the commodities (raw materials and capital equipment) and of services of enterprises consumed in the production process.

National income does not measure the *gross* value of all industrial and financial transactions. A given commodity or service, or its components, may be bought and sold several times during the year, entering repeatedly into total transactions. But the only part that enters national income is the net value of the services of labor, capital, and enterprise embodied in the given commodity or service in its flow to ultimate consumers or in its entrance into the inventory holdings of enterprises or in the balance of international payments. Compared with the value of transactions or of gross product, which may differ with the amount of duplication involved, national income or net product is a much smaller and a single value total.

Furthermore, national income does not include the net value of *all* commodities and services produced in the country during the year. A considerable group of services and some commodities, e.g., housewives' services and hobby products, are excluded because their production is outside the field of economic activity proper. Some minor activities on the borderline between economic and non-economic, e.g., urban gardening or cow keeping, and many occasional and incidental earnings are omitted for lack of data (see Ch. 9). Still other activities, which yield income to some individuals, are excluded because they do not contribute to the country's output of economic goods.

National income may also be described as the sum of all payments by enterprises to individuals as individuals (not as entrepreneurs) and of the savings of enterprises after all costs and disbursements sustained in the production process have been deducted. Payments to individuals are predominantly in compensation for services rendered either by the individuals themselves or by their property—wages, salaries, entrepreneurial withdrawals, interest, dividends, rent. They include, however, some few payments that are not in compensation for any activity of either individuals or their property, but that must be taken into account as part of the net value product of enterprises (pensions, compensation for injury, direct relief payments, etc.). Whether net savings of entrepreneurs should be included under disposable payments to individuals or be treated, similarly to the savings of corporations, as undistributed income, is another matter. The broader aggregate of payments to individuals, including entrepreneurial savings, is shown in Table 1, column 2; that excluding entrepreneurial savings, in column 3.

The commodities and services that comprise the net product of the nation's economic activity during the year may pass to ultimate consumers to satisfy their wants, be added to the stocks of goods held by enterprises within the country, or flow abroad, adding to the claims against foreign countries. The last two uses represent additions to the country's capital goods, a process the quantitative aspects of which are discussed in *Commodity Flow and Capital Formation*, Volume One. The totals of net capital formation given there can be subtracted from the national income totals to yield the value of goods and

services flowing to ultimate consumers—consumers' outlay
(Table 1, col. 4).[1]

We present aggregate payments and consumers' outlay as
components of the more comprehensive total, national income.
Yet they may be regarded as in some respects better indicators

TABLE 1

National Income, Aggregate Payments to Individuals,
and Consumers' Outlay, Current Prices, 1919–1938

	BILLIONS OF DOLLARS				INDEXES (1919–38 = 100)			
		Agg. pay. to individuals				Agg. pay. to individuals		
	National income	incl. entrep. savings	excl. entrep. savings	Con- sumers' outlay	National income	incl. entrep. savings	excl. entrep. savings	Con- sumers' outlay
	(1)	(2)	(3)	(4)	(5)	(6)	(7)	(8)
1919	64.2	64.5	59.0	53.9	96.2	97.0	89.4	87.2
1920	74.2	70.1	68.5	62.9	111.3	105.4	103.8	101.7
1921	59.4	57.7	57.1	56.1	89.1	86.8	86.5	90.7
1922	60.7	59.6	59.7	56.2	91.0	89.7	90.4	90.9
1923	71.6	69.0	67.9	63.0	107.4	103.8	102.8	101.9
1924	72.1	70.0	69.1	66.2	108.1	105.2	104.6	107.1
1925	76.0	73.6	72.0	66.8	114.0	110.7	109.0	107.9
1926	81.6	77.1	75.0	72.3	122.2	115.9	113.6	116.9
1927	80.1	77.2	76.1	71.9	120.0	116.1	115.3	116.2
1928	81.7	78.9	77.9	74.3	122.4	118.6	118.1	120.1
1929	87.2	83.5	82.4	77.2	130.8	125.5	124.8	124.8
1930	77.3	75.9	76.5	73.1	115.9	114.1	115.9	118.2
1931	60.3	63.0	65.1	60.2	90.4	94.7	98.5	97.3
1932	42.9	48.6	52.1	47.1	64.3	73.1	78.9	76.1
1933	42.2	46.3	48.7	45.8	63.2	69.6	73.7	74.1
1934	49.5	53.4	53.8	52.1	74.3	80.3	81.4	84.3
1935	54.4	58.2	58.0	53.7	81.5	87.6	87.9	86.8
1936	62.9	65.8	64.5	57.5	94.2	98.9	97.7	93.0
1937	70.5	71.4	71.0	64.1	105.7	107.4	107.5	103.7
1938	65.5	66.3	66.1	62.6	98.1	99.7	100.1	101.2
Average								
1919–28	72.2	69.8	68.2	64.4	108.2	104.9	103.4	104.1
1929–38	61.3	63.2	63.8	59.3	91.8	95.1	96.6	95.9
1919–38	66.7	66.5	66.0	61.9	100.0	100.0	100.0	100.0
Percentage change 1919–28 to								
1919–38	−15.1	−9.4	−6.5	−7.8				

In the estimates of national income and of aggregate payments to individuals
including entrepreneurial savings, shown here and in subsequent tables of
Chapter 4, savings of enterprises are adjusted for (a) effects of changes in inventory valuation, (b) disparity between depreciation charges on cost and on
reproduction bases, (c) gains and losses on sales of capital assets. All four totals
include Social Security contributions of employers. They differ from totals used
in Chapters 5 and 6, in which, except when noted, net savings are unadjusted
and Social Security contributions are omitted.

1 See also *Bulletin 74*, Commodity Flow and Capital Formation in the Recent
Recovery and Decline, 1932–1938. Revised estimates of capital formation have
been used to pass from national income to consumers' outlay.

of the net contribution of the economic system. If our interest is primarily in the current contribution of the nation's economy to the purchasing power of its inhabitants, aggregate payments to individuals are a somewhat better gauge than national income, since net savings of enterprises, or at least of corporations, are not means of payment flowing to ultimate consumers and cannot immediately and directly affect their share in the nation's product. It may be argued that the amounts received by individuals but not spent on consumption goods do not represent a current contribution to individuals' welfare; and that consumers' outlay is a better measure of what the economic system yields currently to individuals.[2]

The annual average of national income, 1919–38, was $66.7 billion; of aggregate payments to individuals including entrepreneurial savings, $66.5 billion; of aggregate payments excluding entrepreneurial savings, $66.0 billion; and of consumers' outlay, $61.9 billion. These averages conceal marked fluctuations. The broad movement over the period is clearly downward in all four, the decline from the first decade to the second amounting to 15 per cent of national income, 9 per cent of aggregate payments including entrepreneurial savings, and to a somewhat smaller percentage of the other two totals. But this movement is obviously dominated by the severe contraction that developed after 1929. The greater severity of this contraction in national income explains why the decline for the period as a whole is more pronounced in it than in the other three totals.

That this decline can hardly be considered an approximation to the secular trend is seen when we go further back. With the help of W. I. King's estimates [3] we constructed a roughly continuous series for one of the income totals, aggre-

2 Estimates of consumers' outlay are subject to a wider relative margin of error than estimates of national income or of aggregate payments, especially in year to year fluctuations.
3 *The National Income and Its Purchasing Power* (National Bureau of Economic Research, 1930).

gate payments to individuals excluding entrepreneurial savings, since 1909 (Table 2). The broad sweep over the thirty years is upward, and the long term significance of the decline from the second to the third decade is extremely uncertain. Of course, it is possible that the downward movement of the more recent years will continue. But it seems more plausible to view it as the downward phase of a prolonged swing which may soon be succeeded by a resumption of the long term rise.

The totals in current prices reflect fluctuations during busi-

TABLE 2

Aggregate Payments to Individuals excluding Entrepreneurial Savings, King's and Present NBER Estimates
Current Prices, Selected Periods, 1909–1938

	AVERAGE VALUE PER YEAR (billions of dollars)		INDEXES (1919–23 = 100)	
	Based on King (1)	Present NBER estimates (2)	Based on King (3)	Present NBER estimates (4)
1909–13	30.7		47.7	
1911–15	33.0		51.3	
1914–18	41.7		64.7	
1916–20	53.3		82.7	
1919–23	64.5	62.5	100.0	100.0
1921–25	69.3	65.2	107.4	104.3
1924–28		74.0		118.6
1926–30		77.6		124.3
1929–33		64.9		104.0
1931–35		55.5		88.9
1934–38		62.7		100.3
1909–18				56.2
1919–28				109.3
1929–38				102.2

Entries in col. 1 are based upon King's estimates adjusted to assure greater conformity in scope with our estimates (see Ch. 10, Sec. 3, and its Appendix). The indexes in col. 3 are based upon the assumption that the relative discrepancy between King's and our estimates for 1919–23 would also characterize his estimates for the years before 1919. It might have been more reasonable to ascribe such validity to the discrepancy between King's and our estimates for 1919–20 alone. On this assumption, the entry in col. 1 for 1919–23 would be $62 billion and the indexes for earlier years in col. 3 would be raised accordingly. But this small change would not affect the broad picture revealed by Table 2.

ness cycles. Some, such as the decline from 1920 to 1921, the
sustained rise from 1921 to 1929, and the drastic contraction
from 1929 to 1932, are obvious. Others can be established only
upon further analysis. A simple measure of the fluctuations
during business cycles is given in Table 3.[4]

TABLE 3

National Income, Aggregate Payments to Individuals, and
Consumers' Outlay, Changes during Business Cycles
Current Prices, 1919–1938

All measures of change are on a per year basis and are in percentages of the
average value of the series for each full reference cycle. The dates used are
those established by Wesley C. Mitchell and Arthur F. Burns in the National
Bureau's study of business cycles.

| | NATIONAL INCOME (1) | AGGREGATE PAYMENTS TO INDIVIDUALS | | CONSUMERS' OUTLAY (4) |
		Incl. entrep. savings (2)	Excl. entrep. savings (3)	
Cycle 1919–21				
Change, 1919–20	+14.7	+8.5	+15.1	+15.2
Change, 1920–21	−21.8	−18.8	−18.1	−11.5
Difference	−36.5	−27.3	−33.2	−26.7
Cycle 1921–24				
Change, 1921–23	+9.2	+8.8	+8.5	+5.8
Change, 1923–24	+0.7	+1.4	+1.9	+5.3
Difference	−8.5	−7.4	−6.6	−0.5
Cycle 1924–27				
Change, 1924–26	+6.0	+4.8	+4.0	+4.4
Change, 1926–27	−1.9	+0.1	+1.5	−0.6
Difference	−7.9	−4.7	−2.5	−5.0
Cycle 1927–32				
Change, 1927–29	+4.8	+4.3	+4.3	+3.8
Change, 1929–32	−20.1	−16.0	−13.8	−14.6
Difference	−24.9	−20.3	−18.1	−18.4
Cycle 1932–38				
Change, 1932–37	+9.9	+7.8	+6.4	+6.2
Change, 1937–38	−9.1	−8.6	−8.2	−2.9
Difference	−19.0	−16.4	−14.6	−9.1
Average for 5 business cycles				
Change during expansion	+8.9	+6.8	+7.7	+7.1
Change during contraction	−10.4	−8.4	−7.3	−4.9
Difference	−19.4	−15.2	−15.0	−11.9

[4] See *Bulletin 57*, The National Bureau's Measures of Cyclical Behavior.

Every reference cycle established for the American economy since 1919 is reflected in our four totals. All rise during each expansion and decline during contractions except the mild recession from 1926 to 1927 and, more surprisingly, the contraction from 1923 to 1924. Uniformly, the fluctuations in national income are greater than in aggregate payments or in consumers' outlay. There is less difference in this respect between the two totals of aggregate payments; but, by and large, the total including entrepreneurial savings seems to fluctuate more during business cycles than the total excluding them. Both fluctuate more than does consumers' outlay, except during the 1924–27 cycle. These differences, as well as the consistency with which the various income totals reflect business cycles, conform to expectations based upon other knowledge concerning the cyclical behavior of net business savings, income payments, and consumers' outlay.

2 Adjustment for Price Changes

The estimates discussed above are in current prices, measuring the net value of product at the changing price levels that prevailed on the market during each year; totaling payments to individuals without allowance for changes in their purchasing power; gauging the value of consumers' outlay at prices varying from year to year. Obviously, any change in these totals cannot be interpreted as a change in the basket of commodities and services unless some allowance is made for the effect of fluctuations in prices on the purchasing power of money.

Adjustment for price changes may, however, be made for various purposes, which will, or should, find expression in different procedures. And while the choice is severely limited by the available data, we venture a few comments on the possibilities.

Whether we are concerned with the effects of changes in prices of groups of goods or in the more nebulous general price level, no adjustment can be expected to correct for the fundamental effects of price fluctuations on output and economic activity at large. One can merely conjecture what national income, aggregate payments, or consumers' outlay would have been had no commodity or service changed in price. The output of goods would have been vastly different, but from the output of the economy as it actually operated under conditions of fluctuating price levels there is no way of inferring its quantity, in tolerably precise terms. Even were it possible, there is independent utility in the kind of correction for price changes that we make.

Granted that changes in the amount of commodities and services comprised in the income totals have been·determined in the past by fluctuating price levels (among other factors), how can we measure changes in the real contents of these current value totals separately from the changes in prices at which the commodities and services are weighted? The answer depends largely upon the choice of the basket of goods to be taken into account in measuring price changes and adjusting the totals expressed in dollars of current purchasing power. An investigator can attempt to take into account commodities and services in the varieties and quantities that actually characterized the economy in the years under study or he can attempt to adjust for the fluctuating prices of some hypothetical basket of goods, whether definitely specified or only vaguely implied. To adjust consumers' outlay (for illustrative purposes, the most simple total) by the first method would demand (1) a breakdown of total consumers' outlay in current prices into as many groups of commodities and services as can be distinguished, based on data that reflect changes throughout the period; (2) indexes of prices of each category of commodities and services. Adjustment would be carried through for each category, and the adjusted total of consumers' outlay obtained by addition. The second type of adjustment would begin by assuming a hypothetical basket of goods, let us say that comprised in a standard subsistence budget for a family of five of a specified age and sex composition. The cost of goods bought on this budget would then be evaluated at current prices for each year in the period, and a price index derived; its application to total consumers' outlay in current prices would yield outlay in dollars of constant purchasing power.

Since we wish to measure the actual course of the economy, taking into account the full variety of the changes, the adjustment we attempt is of the first type. If we could, we would distinguish all the various groups of commodities and services that enter consumers' outlay, are bought with the aggregate receipts by individuals from enterprises (including investment goods), or are comprised in national income. But limitations of data necessitate a compromise. We are forced to use approximate price indexes for large groups of goods in which the prices of various goods are given weights not necessarily conforming to the quantities currently appearing in the income totals and which, therefore, may give an 'economic' bias [5] to the price indexes. However, as will be seen below, the price measures used have implicit weights, most of which are quantities of goods relating to the period covered by the income estimates, or to a period close to it; and the brevity of the period covered by our estimates lessens the danger of substantial bias arising from improper weighting.

We began with the adjustment of consumers' outlay for price changes, carrying through two variants. For the first (Table 4, col. 1), expenditures on passenger cars were corrected for price changes on the basis of the Bureau of Labor Statistics index. For the rest of consumers' outlay an index was derived by weighting, by non-farm population, the BLS cost of living index, and, by farm population, the Bureau of Agricultural Economics index of prices paid by farmers for subsistence

[5] Because relative changes in prices cause changes in quantities demanded and produced. Treating quantities as constant may underweight the importance of goods whose price (relative to the prices of other goods) has declined and the demand for which has in consequence increased. On the other hand, prices may decline when demand slackens. If so, a lowering of the price relative to the prices of other goods may be correlated with a diminution rather than an increase in the quantity produced.

goods. The second variant (col. 2) was based largely upon the price adjustment work in the capital formation study. The flow to consumers of perishable, semidurable, and durable commodities was estimated in 1929 prices. The only part of consumers' outlay that still had to be adjusted for price changes was the outlay on services not embodied in new commodities. For this purpose we utilized the various group indexes in the BLS cost of living index, choosing those that represented preponderantly direct services.[6] The differences between the indexes in the two variants are minor. We used both to reduce consumers' outlay in current prices to 1929 prices,[7] and averaged the two sets of results (Table 5, col. 4; the corresponding price index appears in Table 4, col. 3).

From consumers' outlay in 1929 prices we derived national income in 1929 prices by adding net capital formation in 1929 prices to it. The implicit price index is given in Table 4, column 6.

The differences between national income and both totals of aggregate payments, as well as between the latter and consumers' outlay, represent shares in net capital formation. These shares, in current prices, can be derived (from the estimates in Table 1) by simple subtraction. To obtain the two totals of aggregate payments in 1929 prices we assumed that the shares of entrepreneurial savings and of individuals' savings (i.e., the difference between the two totals of aggregate payments and that between aggregate payments, excluding entrepreneurial savings, and consumers' outlay) in total net capital formation were, for each year in the period, the same for values in both current and 1929 prices. While this assumption may be erroneous in that savings of individuals, of entrepreneurs, and of corporations may be embodied in types of

---

[6] With weights as provided in BLS bulletins. The groups chosen were rent, fuel and light, and miscellaneous (made up chiefly of services).

[7] We chose 1929 as the base year because it was the basic year in the capital formation study from which most of the price adjustments were derived. But the price level for that single year is only slightly different from the average for 1924–26, and even for 1919–28.

TABLE 4

Comprehensive Price Indexes Compared (1929 = 100)

INDEXES IMPLICIT IN THE ADJUSTMENT OF INCOME
TOTALS FOR PRICE CHANGES

| | CONSUMERS' OUTLAY | | | Agg. pay. to individuals incl. entrep. savings | excl. entrep. savings | National income | BLS INDEXES | |
| | Var. I | Var. II | Avg. | | | | Cost of living | Wholesale price |
	(1)	(2)	(3)	(4)	(5)	(6)	(7)	(8)
1919	111.4	109.2	110.3	112.8	111.6	112.7	101.6	145.4
1920	124.5	122.7	123.6	125.9	125 5	127.1	116.9	162.0
1921	104.0	105.4	104.7	104.9	104.8	105.2	104.2	102.4
1922	98.2	99.9	99.0	99.6	99.7	99.8	97.7	101.5
1923	99.9	101.7	100.8	101.2	101.1	101.3	99.5	105.6
1924	99.9	100.3	100.1	100.4	100.4	100.6	99.8	102.9
1925	102.4	102.9	102.6	102.8	102.8	102.8	102.4	108.6
1926	102.3	103.3	102.8	103.0	102.9	103.2	103.2	104.9
1927	100.7	100.2	100.4	100.5	100.5	100.5	101.2	100.1
1928	100.2	101.1	100.6	100.7	100.7	100.7	100.1	101.5
1929	100.0	100.4	100.2	100.2	100.2	100.2	100.0	100.0
1930	96.5	97.0	96.8	96.7	96.7	96.7	97.5	90.7
1931	86.6	87.6	87.1	86.7	86.4	87.1	88.7	76.6
1932	77.1	77.0	77.1	77.0	76.9	77.2	79.7	68.0
1933	74.0	74.6	74.3	74.3	74.2	74.4	75.4	69.2
1934	78.3	80.4	79.3	79.1	79.1	79.8	78.1	78.6
1935	80.2	84.6	82.3	86.0	85.8	82.9	80.1	83.9
1936	80.4	85.3	82.8	84.3	84.1	83.8	80.9	84.8
1937	83.5	89.1	86.2	87.4	87.3	87.3	83.8	90.6
1938	81.5	83.7	82.6	82.9	82.9	82.8	82.3	82.5
Average								
1919–28	104.4	104.7	104.5	105.2	105.0	105.4	102.7	113.5
1929–38	83.8	86.0	84.9	85.5	85.4	85.2	84.6	82.5
1919–38	94.1	95.3	94.7	95.3	95.2	95.3	93.7	98.0
Percentage change 1919–28 to								
1929–38	−19.7	−17.9	−18.8	−18.7	−18.7	−19.1	−17.6	−27.3

capital formation characterized by diverse price movements,
absence of information led us to accept it as a plausible basis
for the most consistent procedure. Accordingly, we applied to
net capital formation in 1929 prices the percentages of net
capital formation in current prices that could be attributed in
each year to entrepreneurial and individuals' savings. This
gave us the amounts of these two types of savings embodied in
net capital formation in 1929 prices; adding the second to
consumers' outlay in 1929 prices yielded aggregate payments
excluding entrepreneurial savings; adding the first to this total
yielded aggregate payments including entrepreneurial savings,
both in 1929 prices. The implicit price indexes are given in
Table 4, columns 4 and 5.

All indexes in Table 4 show a declining trend over the period as a whole and fairly similar patterns of shorter term movements: a decline from a peak in 1920 to a trough in 1922; a relatively moderate rise to a peak in 1925–26; a drastic fall to a trough in 1932 or 1933; a recovery to a peak in 1937; and a decline from 1937 to 1938.

The indexes implicit in the four income totals (cols. 1–6) move in close conformity to business cycles. That implicit in national income declines somewhat more from 1920 to 1922 than the other three; and that implicit in consumers' outlay rises somewhat more from 1922 to 1926. But the differences are minor for the simple reason that consumers' outlay and aggregate payments alike constitute such a large percentage of national income. More significant differences appear between the indexes implicit in the income totals and those representing wholesale commodity prices and wage earners' cost of living. In general, the income price indexes show movements over the period or cyclical variations intermediate in amplitude between those in wholesale commodity prices and the cost of living. The decline from the first to the second decade in the income price indexes is not as great as in wholesale commodity prices but greater than in the cost of living. The cyclical rises and declines in the income price indexes are uniformly less than in wholesale commodity prices, but greater than in the cost of living (except the rise from 1919 to 1920 and from 1922 to 1926). These differences are to be expected since the income totals include both consumers' outlay, made at retail prices represented in the cost of living index, and capital formation, investment outlays made at wholesale prices represented in the wholesale commodity price index.

3 The Totals in 1929 Prices

Adjustment for price changes has several effects (Table 5). It alters materially the general trend, canceling the decline apparent in the four totals in Table 1. Tables 1, 4, and 5 indicate clearly that the downward movement of the totals in current prices was due to a decline in the price level, not in real product.

TABLE 5

National Income, Aggregate Payments to Individuals, and Consumers' Outlay, 1929 Prices, 1919–1938

| | BILLIONS OF DOLLARS | | | | INDEXES (1919–38 = 100) | | | |
| | | Agg. pay. to individuals | | | | | Agg. pay. to individuals | | |
	National income (1)	incl. entrep. savings (2)	excl. entrep. savings (3)	Con-sumers' outlay (4)	National income (5)	incl. entrep. savings (6)	excl. entrep. savings (7)	Con-sumers' outlay (8)
1919	57.0	57.2	52.9	48.9	81.4	81.6	75.7	74.4
1920	58.4	55.7	54.6	50.9	83.5	79.4	78.2	77.4
1921	56.5	55.0	54.5	53.6	80.7	78.5	78.0	81.5
1922	60.8	59.8	59.9	56.8	86.9	85.4	85.8	86.4
1923	70.7	68.2	67.1	62.5	101.0	97.3	96.1	95.1
1924	71.7	69.7	68.8	66.2	102.4	99.4	98.5	100.6
1925	73.9	71.6	70.1	65.1	105.6	102.1	100.3	99.0
1926	79.0	74.9	72.9	70.3	112.9	106.8	104.4	107.0
1927	79.6	76.8	75.8	71.6	113.8	109.6	108.4	108.9
1928	81.1	78.3	77.4	73.8	115.8	111.7	110.8	112.3
1929	87.1	83.3	82.2	77.0	124.4	118.8	117.7	117.2
1930	79.9	78.4	79.1	75.5	114.2	111.9	113.2	114.9
1931	69.3	72.7	75.3	69.1	99.0	103.7	107.8	105.1
1932	55.6	63.1	67.7	61.1	79.5	90.0	96.9	93.0
1933	56.7	62.3	65.6	61.6	81.0	88.9	93.8	93.8
1934	62.1	67.5	68.0	65.7	88.8	96.3	97.3	100.0
1935	65.6	67.7	67.6	65.2	93.7	96.6	96.7	99.2
1936	75.0	78.1	76.8	69.5	107.2	111.3	109.9	105.7
1937	80.8	81.7	81.3	74.4	115.4	116.5	116.3	113.1
1938	79.0	80.0	79.7	75.8	112.9	114.1	114.1	115.3
Average								
1919–28	68.9	66.7	65.4	62.0	98.4	95.2	93.6	94.3
1929–38	71.1	73.5	74.3	69.5	101.6	104.8	106.4	105.7
1919–38	70.0	70.1	69.9	65.7	100.0	100.0	100.0	100.0
Percentage change 1919–28 to 1929–38	+3.3	+10.1	+13.6	+12.2				

The upward trend in the totals in 1929 prices is least pronounced in national income and most pronounced in aggregate payments excluding entrepreneurial savings. The rise in consumers' outlay is somewhat smaller than in the latter.

Here again we take advantage of King's estimates for years prior to 1919 to paint a broader picture of the movement of an income total adjusted for changes in the price level (Table 6). First, while the rise in aggregate payments excluding entrepreneurial savings for the period is not as marked as in the

totals in current prices (see Table 2), it is still substantial even
after adjustment for the effects of a rising price level—more
than 50 per cent over 25 years (from 1909–13 to 1934–38), or
on the basis of decennial averages, more than 40 per cent over
20 years (from 1909–18 to 1929–38). Second, while the percentage rise from the second to the third decade is smaller than
from the first to the second, the quinquennial averages suggest
that this retardation is due exclusively to the pronounced depression of 1929–32. Thus the rise from 1909–13 to 1919–23
is relatively less than that from 1919–23 to 1929–33, even
though the latter quinquennium is already affected by the
great contraction that followed 1929; and the decline from
1926–30 to 1931–35 may be regarded as offsetting the rapid
rates of growth from 1919–23 to 1926–30. Third, against the
background of the rise over the longer period, the decline
during the recent quinquennia takes on the appearance of
a small break. These three conclusions would probably hold
for consumers' outlay also; but would have to be modified
somewhat for national income, in view of its more drastic decline after 1929.

Adjustment for price changes affects also the consistency and
intensity with which the income totals fluctuate during business cycles (Table 7). In 1929 prices national income still reflects each of the five business cycles, but each of the other three
totals fails to respond in one: aggregate payments including
entrepreneurial savings in 1919–21, aggregate payments excluding entrepreneurial savings in 1924–27, and consumers'
outlay in 1919–21. The amplitudes of fluctuations are
greatly reduced by the adjustment for price changes: in 1929
prices the averages are from less than one-half to less
than one-fourth of those in current prices. The relative decrease in amplitude due to the adjustment for price changes,
greatest for consumers' outlay and smallest for national income, is inversely correlated with the amplitude and conformity
of fluctuations during business cycles. The greater the
conformity and the amplitude of fluctuation in values in cur-

TABLE 6

Aggregate Payments to Individuals excluding Entrepreneurial
Savings, King's and Present NBER Estimates
1929 Prices, Selected Periods, 1909–1938

	AVERAGE VALUE PER YEAR (billions of dollars)		INDEXES (1919–23 = 100)	
	Based on King (1)	Present NBER estimates (2)	Based on King (3)	Present NBER estimates (4)
1909–13	52.2		84.8	
1911–15	54.9		89.3	
1914–18	58.3		94.8	
1916–20	58.5		95.1	
1919–23	61.5	57.8	100.0	100.0
1921–25	68.8	64.1	111.7	110.9
1924–28		73.0		126.3
1926–30		77.5		134.0
1929–33		74.0		128.0
1931–35		68.8		119.1
1934–38		74.7		129.1
1909–18				89.8
1919–28				113.1
1929–38				128.6

Entries in col. 1 are based upon King's adjusted estimates. The correction for
price changes was carried through with the help of King's index of prices of
consumers' goods, the index transferred from the 1913 to the 1929 base on
the assumption that no change took place between 1928 (last year for which
it is given) and 1929. For further explanations see the note to Table 2.

rent prices, the less the relative decrease introduced by price
changes.

As a result, adjustment for price changes accentuates the
differences in fluctuation during business cycles among the
various income totals. During the five business cycles national
income in 1929 prices varies more, on the average and for each
cycle, than any of the other three income totals. On the basis
of averages but not necessarily for each cycle, this is true of
aggregate payments including entrepreneurial savings compared with aggregate payments excluding them; and of the
latter compared with consumers' outlay. The increase in these
differences caused by the adjustment for price changes is clear
when we compare the average cyclical swings in current and

TABLE 7

National Income, Aggregate Payments to Individuals, and
Consumers' Outlay, Changes during Business Cycles
1929 Prices, 1919–1938

	NATIONAL INCOME (1)	AGGREGATE PAYMENTS TO INDIVIDUALS		CONSUMERS' OUTLAY (4)
		Incl. entrep. savings (2)	Excl. entrep. savings (3)	
Cycle 1919–21				
Change, 1919–20	+2.5	−2.7	+3.2	+3.8
Change, 1920–21	−3.4	−1.1	−0.3	+5.4
Difference	−5.9	+1.6	−3.5	+1.6
Cycle 1921–24				
Change, 1921–23	+10.8	+10.4	+10.0	+7.5
Change, 1923–24	+1.5	+2.3	+2.7	+6.1
Difference	−9.3	−8.1	−7.3	−1.4
Cycle 1924–27				
Change, 1924–26	+4.8	+3.6	+2.8	+3.0
Change, 1926–27	+0.8	+2.7	+4.0	+1.8
Difference	−4.0	−0.9	+1.2	−1.2
Cycle 1927–32				
Change, 1927–29	+4.8	+4.2	+4.2	+3.8
Change, 1929–32	−13.6	−8.8	−6.3	−7.3
Difference	−18.4	−13.0	−10.5	−11.1
Cycle 1932–38				
Change, 1932–37	+7.4	+5.2	+3.8	+3.9
Change, 1937–38	−2.6	−2.4	−2.1	+2.1
Difference	−10.0	−7.6	−5.9	−1.8
Average for 5 business cycles				
Change during expansion	+6.1	+4.1	+4.8	+4.4
Change during contraction	−3.5	−1.5	−0.4	+1.6
Difference	−9.5	−5.6	−5.2	−2.8

Based on entries in Table 5; see the notes to Table 3.

in 1929 prices: in current prices, that in national income is less
than twice that in consumers' outlay; in 1929 prices the ratio
is almost 4 to 1.

4 Income per Population Unit

It is the country's population that helps to produce national
income, receives payments from enterprises, and consumes the
major part of the resulting product. A broad picture of changes

in national income, aggregate payments, and consumers' outlay is not complete until these changes are compared with those in the population as a body of producers and consumers.

Table 8 presents measures of population in terms of units

TABLE 8

Population in Units relevant to the Production
and Consumption of Income, 1919–1938

| | TOTALS IN MILLIONS | | | | RATIO OF: | | |
	Population [1] (1)	Gainfully occupied [2] (2)	Engaged [3] (3)	Consuming units [4] (4)	Col. 2 to col. 1 (5)	Col. 3 to col. 1 (6)	Col. 4 to col. 1 (7)
1919	105.0	41.3	39.8	74.8	39.3	37.9	71.3
1920	106.5	42.3	40.2	75.9	39.7	37.7	71.2
1921	108.2	43.2	36.5	77.2	39.9	33.7	71.4
1922	109.9	43.8	38.0	78.5	39.9	34.6	71.5
1923	111.5	44.7	40.8	80.0	40.1	36.6	71.7
1924	113.2	45.7	40.6	81.4	40.4	35.9	72.0
1925	114.9	46.4	41.3	82.7	40.4	36.0	72.0
1926	116.5	47.2	42.8	84.0	40.5	36.7	72.1
1927	118.2	47.9	42.9	85.2	40.5	36.3	72.1
1928	119.9	48.7	43.2	86.4	40.6	36.0	72.1
1929	121.5	49.4	44.9	87.6	40.7	37.0	72.0
1930	123.1	50.2	42.8	88.7	40.8	34.8	72.0
1931	124.1	50.8	39.4	89.6	41.0	31.7	72.2
1932	125.0	51.4	36.0	90.6	41.1	28.8	72.5
1933	125.8	52.0	36.0	91.5	41.3	28.7	72.7
1934	126.6	52.6	38.5	92.3	41.5	30.4	72.9
1935	127.5	53.2	39.8	93.1	41.7	31.2	73.0
1936	128.4	53.8	41.8	94.0	41.9	32.6	73.2
1937	129.3	54.5	43.8	94.9	42.1	33.9	73.4
1938	130.2	55.1	41.4	95.8	42.4	31.8	73.6
Average							
1919–28	112.4	45.1	40.6	80.6	40.1	36.1	71.7
1929–38	126.2	52.3	40.5	91.8	41.4	32.1	72.8
1919–38	119.3	48.7	40.5	86.2	40.8	34.1	72.2
Percentage change							
1919–28 to							
1929–38	+12.3	+15.9	−0.4	+13.9	+3.2	−11.1	+1.5

[1] Annual midyear estimates prepared by the Bureau of the Census and published in the *Statistical Abstract*.
[2] Estimates by Daniel Carson of the National Research Project in *Labor Supply and Employment, Preliminary Statement of Estimates Prepared and Methods Used* (WPA, mimeo., Nov. 1939).
[3] See Tables 51 and 53.
[4] The age and sex distributions of the population are those of W. S. Thompson and P. K. Whelpton of the Scripps Foundation, Miami, Ohio. The consuming equivalents are from their monograph, *Population Trends in the United States* (McGraw-Hill, 1933), p. 169. The data in this column are not strictly comparable with those in column 1 because the basic total population figures are slightly different.

relevant to the production and consumption of income. Total population (col. 1) is the crudest gauge for the purpose at hand: while it is a count of the individual members of the nation, it includes as equivalent units men and women, in both productive and unproductive years and at ages of both high and low consumption needs. A somewhat better approximation to population as a body of producers is the number gainfully occupied (col. 2), adults who ordinarily engage in economic pursuits, whether or not they happen to be employed when a census is taken. This measure of the available productive population should not be confused with another—the number actually employed, in the case of employees, and engaged, in the case of entrepreneurs (col. 3). Employees are in terms of equivalent full-time units, i.e., after an approximate reduction of the partly employed to the number estimated on the assumption of full employment. But partial unemployment is allowed for only so far as it is reflected in the data. Changes in the working time of a fully employed person, such as the secular decline in the length of the working day or reductions during a severe depression that may result from attempts to 'spread' work, are not allowed for. Consequently the number engaged or employed is not an accurate measure of man-hours of productive effort, although it is better than the number gainfully occupied. A fourth way to express population is in terms of equivalent consuming units, i.e., by allowing for differences among various age and sex groups in subsistence needs (col. 4).

It will be seen at a glance that total population, persons gainfully occupied, and the number of consuming units are characterized primarily by sustained long term movements and do not reflect shorter term cyclical fluctuations. All three totals rose steadily, but at a slower pace during the second half of the period. The rate of increase was fairly rapid, the rise from the first to the second decade exceeding 10 per cent. It was significantly higher in both gainfully occupied and the number of consuming units than in total population, reflecting a shift in the age distribution in favor of the adult producing and heavily consuming ages.

The total engaged is the only measure in Table 8 that reflects cyclical changes, declining from 1920 to 1921, 1923 to 1924, 1937 to 1938, and especially severely from 1929 to 1932.

This susceptibility to cyclical fluctuations accounts for its slight downward movement over the period.

For comparison with changes in population, income estimates in 1929 prices alone are relevant, since our purpose is to ascertain changes in productivity per employed or available unit of the human factor or in the supply of goods per consuming unit; i.e., in terms of commodities and services, not in monetary units of fluctuating purchasing power.

National income in 1929 prices can be compared with all four population measures (Table 9): since it is a comprehen-

TABLE 9

National Income per Population Unit, 1929 Prices, 1919–1938

	Capita	INCOME IN DOLLARS PER Gainfully occupied	Engaged	Consuming unit
	(1)	(2)	(3)	(4)
1919	543	1,380	1,431	761
1920	548	1,380	1,453	770
1921	522	1,308	1,547	732
1922	553	1,388	1,599	774
1923	634	1,582	1,732	884
1924	633	1,569	1,764	880
1925	644	1,592	1,789	894
1926	678	1,675	1,847	941
1927	674	1,661	1,856	934
1928	676	1,665	1,879	938
1929	716	1,761	1,938	994
1930	649	1,591	1,869	901
1931	558	1,362	1,758	773
1932	445	1,082	1,545	614
1933	451	1,091	1,573	620
1934	491	1,181	1,612	673
1935	515	1,233	1,648	705
1936	584	1,394	1,793	798
1937	625	1,483	1,844	852
1938	607	1,433	1,909	825
Average				
1919–28	610	1,520	1,690	851
1929–38	564	1,361	1,749	776
1919–38	587	1,441	1,719	813
Percentage change				
1919–28 to				
1929–38	—7.6	—10.5	+3.5	—8.9

sive gauge of net value product it can be compared not only
with the number actually participating in the production process but also with the potential number; and since it may be
treated also as a type of maximum fund for current consumption it can be compared with consuming units.

National income per capita, per person gainfully occupied,
and per consuming unit decline from the first to the second
decade about one-tenth or somewhat less, because the increase
in population—total, gainfully occupied, or converted to consuming units—was, over the period, appreciably greater than
in total national income in 1929 prices. While this decline
from the first to the second decade in the per unit figures was
due to the severe depression of 1929–32, it is noteworthy that
in 1937, the latest peak year, national income per capita was
still about 13 per cent below that in the preceding peak year
(1929); that national income per person gainfully occupied in
1937 was still 16 per cent below that in 1929; and that national
income per consuming unit in 1937 was still 14 per cent below
that of 1929. If we compare these figures with the secular rise
that would ordinarily be expected in the real national product
per population unit, we see the substantial degree to which by
1937 the recovery from the 1929–32 depression was still incomplete.

The pattern traced by national income per equivalent full-
time unit engaged was significantly different. It rose 3.5 per
cent from the first to the second decade. While this rise was in
contrast to the substantial decline over the period in national
income per capita, per person gainfully occupied, and per
consuming unit, the annual figures in column 3 show that even
on a per person engaged basis the entry for the recent highest
year, 1938, was about 1.5 per cent below that for 1929. The
increase in the decennial averages is thus due exclusively to
the rise from the first to the second half of the 1920's.

The cyclical behavior of national income per person engaged deserves attention. Income per capita, per person gainfully occupied, and per consuming unit fluctuated in close

conformity with business cycles: per capita income declined significantly from 1920 to 1921, 1929 to 1932, and 1937 to 1938, and very slightly from 1923 to 1924 and 1926 to 1927; and rose during each reference expansion. Income per person gainfully occupied and per consuming unit display equally marked conformity to business cycles. But income per person engaged declined only from 1929 to 1932; and rose substantially in other contractions, in some at a rate greater than the annual rise in the preceding expansion. These movements are plausible. During contractions the labor force is reduced by the elimination of the less efficient, and capital per worker employed is increased, causing a rise in the net product (in constant prices) per unit of work. While, as already indicated, our figures on equivalent full-time units engaged do not reflect faithfully variations in the units of work (such as man-hours), their failure to take cognizance of changes in the number of hours in a full-time month and of some types of partial unemployment is not, during brief contractions, sufficiently great to offset the rise in the product per unit of work; hence the rise in column 3 during the brief contractions of 1920–21, 1923–24, 1926–27, and 1937–38. But during the severe and prolonged depression of 1929–32 the reduction in the hours of full-time workers and increase in partial unemployment not reflected in our figures more than offset the increase that may have occurred in real product per unit of work, causing national income per person engaged to decline.[8]

It did not seem necessary to show annual figures on per unit aggregate payments or consumers' outlay: these can easily be derived from Tables 5 and 8, and they tend to duplicate the evidence of Table 9, differing from national income in pattern, as already noted in the discussion of Table 5. We therefore

---

[8] It is also possible that in a severe contraction real product per work unit declines. This may occur if business enterprises keep employees on largely in order to maintain a skeleton force, the hours of work being partly devoted to tasks whose current net value (disregarding price changes) is appreciably lower than that of tasks to which the hours would have been devoted under conditions of fuller employment.

confined Table 10 to summary measures of changes in per unit aggregate payments and consumers' outlay: consumers' outlay is compared solely with total population and consuming units, since little meaning is to be attached to consumers' outlay per person gainfully occupied or engaged.

TABLE 10

Aggregate Payments and Consumers' Outlay per Population Unit
1929 Prices, Selected Periods, 1919–1938

	AVERAGES (DOLLARS)			% CHANGE 1919–28 to 1929–38	VALUES (DOLLARS) AT RECENT PEAKS		% CHANGE COL. 6 TO COL. 5
	1919–38 (1)	1919–28 (2)	1929–38 (3)	1929–38 (4)	Latest (5)	1929 (6)	(7)
Aggregate payments incl. entrepreneurial savings per							
Capita	587	592	583	−1.5	632 (1937)	685	−7.7
Gainfully occupied	1,440	1,473	1,406	−4.6	1,500 (1937)	1,685	−11.0
Engaged	1,725	1,637	1,813	+10.7	1,932 (1938)	1,855	+4.2
Consuming unit	813	824	801	−2.9	861 (1937)	951	−9.5
Aggregate payments excl. entrepreneurial savings per							
Capita	585	580	590	+1.7	629 (1937)	677	−7.1
Gainfully occupied	1,433	1,444	1,423	−1.5	1,492 (1937)	1,664	−10.3
Engaged	1,721	1,605	1,837	+14.4	1,925 (1938)	1,831	+5.1
Consuming unit	809	808	810	+0.3	857 (1937)	939	−8.7
Consumers' outlay per							
Capita	550	549	551	+0.3	582 (1938)	634	−8.2
Consuming unit	762	765	758	−1.0	791 (1938)	880	−10.1

In the changes from the first to the second decade the differences among the various per unit figures are similar to those in national income. Aggregate payments including entrepreneurial savings per capita, per person gainfully occupied, and per consuming unit decline, on the whole, slightly; aggregate payments excluding entrepreneurial savings per capita rise a little and per person engaged, substantially. All these measures of rise and decline over the period are algebraically larger than the corresponding measures for national income, reflecting, of course, the greater rise in each total over the period than in national income. Comparison for the reference peak years shows that during the last decade the decline per capita, per person gainfully occupied, and per consuming unit was much greater and the rise per person engaged much less than from the first to the second decade (col. 5–7). Aggregate payments and consumers' outlay per capita in 1937 or 1938 were from 7 to 8 per cent lower than in 1929; aggregate payments per person gainfully occupied in 1937, from 10 to 11 per cent lower; and aggregate payments and consumers' outlay per consuming unit in 1937 or 1938, from 9 to 10 per cent lower. Aggregate payments per person engaged were from 4 to 5 per cent higher in 1938 (the latest peak year) than in 1929. The failure of the other three totals to regain the per unit levels reached during 1929 confirms the evidence of national income that by 1937–38 the recovery from the 1929–32 depression was far from complete.

In conclusion, with the aid of Dr. King's estimates we trace the movement of aggregate payments excluding entrepreneurial savings per capita and per person gainfully occupied since 1909 (Table 11). While there is a secular rise, it is quite moderate. In the comparison by decades the rise in aggregate payments per capita during twenty years is about 11 per cent, and per person gainfully occupied only about 7 per cent. One would be inclined to infer that for national income the per capita and per person gainfully occupied averages would not rise significantly over the period as a whole, if at all. Much as this result may be affected by the severity of the recent depression, it does suggest that any secular rise in the real net product per capita or per person gainfully occupied could not have been appreciable during the period under review.

Moreover, the rise in the per unit figures is concentrated between 1919–23 and 1924–28, more specifically between 1921 and 1929. Before 1921 there was little significant rise in the real value of aggregate payments per capita and per person gainfully occupied, and one is inclined to infer that the same must have been true of national income and of consumers' outlay. Because the rise occurs only during the 1920's one is all the more justified in discounting the effect of the recent severe depression on the trends over the period as a whole. In other words, there is more reason to attribute some secular significance to the small rise in the per unit figures of aggregate payments and to the inferentially probable stability of national income per capita or per person gainfully occupied.

TABLE 11

Aggregate Payments to Individuals excluding Entrepreneurial
Savings, per Capita and per Gainfully Occupied
King's and Present NBER Estimates
1929 Prices, Selected Periods, 1909–1938

	PER CAPITA		PER GAINFULLY OCCUPIED	
	Based on King (1)	Present NBER estimates (2)	Based on King (3)	Present NBER estimates (4)
	DOLLARS			
1909–13	556		1,463	
1911–15	566		1,487	
1914–18	573		1,503	
1916–20	562		1,474	
1919–23	568	533	1,502	1,341
1921–25	615	574	1,625	1,430
1924–28		626		1,547
1926–30		647		1,591
1929–33		598		1,460
1931–35		547		1,325
1934–38		581		1,385
	INDEXES (1919–23 = 100)			
1909–13	97.9		97.4	
1911–15	99.6		99.0	
1914–18	100.9		100.1	
1916–20	98.9		98.1	
1919–23	100.0	100.0	100.0	100.0
1921–25	108.3	107.7	108.2	106.6
1924–28		117.4		115.4
1926–30		121.4		118.6
1929–33		112.2		108.9
1931–35		102.6		98.8
1934–38		109.0		103.3
1909–18		99.3		98.7
1919–28		108.8		107.7
1929–38		110.6		106.1

The estimates of population and of persons gainfully occupied used to derive the per unit figures based on King's data are those prepared by Dr. King and published in his *National Income and Its Purchasing Power* (Table I, p. 47). For derivation of the income totals based on King's data, see the notes to Tables 2 and 6.

5 *Summary*

a) Over the twenty years 1919–38 national income in current prices averaged $66.7 billion per year; both totals of aggregate payments to individuals only slightly less; and consumers' outlay, $61.9 billion. In 1929 prices the annual averages of national income and of aggregate payments were roughly $70 billion, and of consumers' outlay, $65.7 billion.

b) All income totals in current prices declined over the two decades. But study of one total since 1909 suggests a substantial rise over the thirty years in all the totals, even when expressed in current prices.

c) The decline from 1919–29 to 1929–38 in the totals in current prices is due exclusively to the downward tilt of the price levels. When adjusted for price changes, the income totals rise from the first to the second decade. The rise in national income is moderate (3 per cent); that in aggregate payments and consumers' outlay, substantial (over 10 per cent). But for all totals the rise is concentrated in the decade of the 1920's; and in the most recent peak year, 1937 (1938, for consumers' outlay), no total had regained the 1929 level, even though adjustment is made for the decline in prices since 1929.

d) Population, the number of persons gainfully occupied and of consuming units grew from the first to the second decade at a rate appreciably greater than national income (in 1929 prices); the number of equivalent full-time units employed declined slightly. As a result, national income per capita, per person gainfully occupied, and per consuming unit declined over the period; national income per unit employed rose. The other totals per unit (in 1929 prices) described similar patterns, except that the declines were less appreciable and the rises more pronounced than in national income per unit.

e) Over the thirty years 1909–38 aggregate payments excluding entrepreneurial savings in 1929 prices rose substantially. But since population and the number of gainfully occupied also grew rapidly, aggregate payments per capita and per person gainfully occupied rose only moderately (about 11 and 7 per cent respectively). National income per capita or per person gainfully occupied must have risen even less, if at all.

f) All totals in current prices fluctuate in close conformity with business cycles. The amplitude of conforming movements is greatest in national income; greater in aggregate payments including entrepreneurial savings than in aggregate payments excluding them; and greater in either total of aggregate payments than in consumers' outlay.

g) Adjustment for price changes sharply reduces amplitudes. But in 1929 prices all totals still reflect business cycles, and the difference between national income and the other three totals in amplitude of conforming movements is even greater for the totals in 1929 than in current prices.

h) Since population, the number of gainfully occupied and of consuming units are not greatly affected by business cycles, movements in the income totals divided by these units and in the undivided totals are quite similar during business cycles. But the number of equivalent full-time engaged rises during expansions and declines during contractions. National income and aggregate payments in 1929 prices, when calculated on a per person engaged basis, rise during four contractions and decline only from 1929 to 1932 (aggregate payments excluding entrepreneurial savings, from 1931 to 1935). These movements during contractions suggest rises in real product per worker due to greater efficiency and an increase in capital per worker. That such a rise did not occur from 1929 to 1932 may be due partly to the failure of the number engaged to reflect fully reduction in hours and certain forms of partial unemployment and partly to a genuine decline in real product per man-hour employed that may result from attempts to maintain a minimum labor force in the face of a drastic curtailment of output.

CHAPTER 5

Distribution by Industrial Source

1 Annual Distribution of National Income

How THE stock of data conditioned our industrial classification is recounted at length in Chapter 8. Here we may say in general that it is not feasible to distribute national income or its components precisely among the productive functions that form the basis of our industrial classification; that, for savings of enterprises and property income payments particularly, the shares attributed to a given industry may contain substantial amounts of income from productive factors engaged in other industries; and that even compensation of employees and entrepreneurs can be attributed precisely to only a few industrial divisions.

These qualifications lessen but do not destroy the essential usefulness of the distribution by industrial source. The resulting divisions of the national product reflect differences in the economic conditions of the people who derive most of their livelihood from them; represent segments susceptible in varying degree to the benefits of economic progress and to the disturbing effects of business cycles; and in divers ways reveal the capacity of the nation to sustain itself and its role in the concert of nations.

As has been indicated, net income originating may be interpreted as a measure of a given industry's contribution to or draft upon the total net product of the nation. We might consider income from agriculture and the percentage it constitutes of national income as measuring the amount and share that productive factors—labor, capital, and enterprise engaged in agriculture—contributed to the total value of that hypothetical heap of goods we call national income; or as measuring how much they succeeded in wresting from the common pot in return for their services, i.e., the total price they forced society to pay. The two interpretations are equally cogent if we define the value of any good, of any positive economic contribution, as the price it fetches on the market.

Under either interpretation income originating in the several industries measures results of interdependent processes; and this interdependence implies the contingency of one value upon others. During a given phase of economic and social development, a phase that may last several decades, some relations among activities representing various industrial functions tend to persist; for example, between functions of government and those of the private economic system or between amounts spent upon construction and capital formation and upon immediate consumption. Consequently, the percentage distribution of national income by industrial source tends to vary within narrow limits, especially when it is of averages for broad industrial groups for a long period.[1] If a large or small amount of income originates in an industry, a correspondingly large or small amount originates in other industries. In this sense a given industry that contributes to or draws from national income a certain net value product does so only because and so long as the other industries contribute or draw corresponding net value products.

For this reason the easiest and most promising way to analyze the distribution by industrial source is to emphasize that in percentage terms. Fluctuations in the totals have already been considered in Chapter 4. Here we try to answer two questions: What was the industrial composition of national income and of various types of income during the period as a whole? What

[1] This is especially true for a large and relatively self-contained national economy, like that of the United States.

TABLE 12

National Income * and its Percentage Distribution by Major Industrial Divisions, 1919–1938

	AGR. (1)	MINING (2)	MFG. (3)	CONSTR. (4)	TRANSP. AND OTHER PUB. UTIL. (5)	TRADE (6)	FINANCE (7)	SERVICE (8)	GOV. (9)	MISC. (10)	TOTAL (11)
					TOTALS (billions of dollars)						
1919	10.9	1.8	16.2	2.0	6.0	10.2	6.8	6.1	3.8	2.2	65.9
1920	9.1	2.3	19.8	2.6	7.4	11.5	7.4	6.8	7.0	2.4	76.4
1921	5.5	1.7	12.6	2.0	6.3	9.5	7.8	6.7	6.2	2.0	60.3
1922	5.9	1.3	13.1	2.3	6.2	8.6	8.3	7.4	6.1	2.3	61.5
1923	6.7	2.0	16.8	3.3	7.1	10.1	8.8	8.3	7.0	2.7	72.9
1924	7.1	1.7	15.5	3.7	7.1	9.8	9.6	8.6	7.3	2.8	73.4
1925	7.9	1.8	16.8	4.0	7.6	10.2	9.8	9.3	7.4	3.1	77.8
1926	7.5	2.2	18.1	4.3	7.9	11.5	9.8	10.1	8.1	3.2	82.8
1927	7.5	1.9	17.2	4.1	7.8	10.6	10.3	10.3	8.5	3.3	81.4
1928	7.3	1.6	17.9	4.0	8.0	11.0	10.9	10.7	8.3	3.7	83.4
1929	7.7	1.8	19.8	4.1	8.5	11.4	10.9	11.3	8.9	3.5	87.8
1930	5.8	1.4	16.3	3.5	7.7	11.0	9.7	10.4	8.9	2.9	77.6
1931	4.0	0.83	11.0	2.2	6.5	9.0	7.9	8.8	7.4	2.6	60.3
1932	2.8	0.48	6.3	1.1	4.9	6.3	5.9	6.5	6.2	2.1	42.6
1933	3.6	0.48	6.6	0.71	4.7	5.2	5.2	5.8	7.5	2.0	41.8
1934	4.7	0.83	9.0	0.83	4.8	7.0	5.1	6.8	8.2	2.3	49.5
1935	5.4	0.92	11.4	1.0	5.2	7.4	5.7	7.4	7.5	2.6	54.4
1936	6.1	1.2	14.2	1.6	5.8	8.5	6.0	8.3	8.2	2.9	62.7
1937	6.3	1.4	15.9	1.8	6.1	9.0	6.6	9.1	10.7	3.2	70.1
1938	5.5	1.1	12.6	1.7	5.5	9.3	6.5	8.9	10.8	3.0	64.9

TABLE 12 (concl.)

	AGR. (1)	MINING (2)	MFG. (3)	CONSTR. (4)	TRANSP. AND OTHER PUB. UTIL. (5)	TRADE (6)	FINANCE (7)	SERVICE (8)	GOV. (9)	MISC. (10)	TOTAL (11)
					PERCENTAGE DISTRIBUTION						
1919	16.5	2.7	24.6	3.0	9.0	15.5	10.3	9.3	5.7	3.4	100.0
1920	11.9	3.0	25.9	3.5	9.7	15.0	9.7	9.0	9.2	3.1	100.0
1921	9.2	2.8	20.9	3.3	10.5	15.8	12.9	11.1	10.3	3.3	100.0
1922	9.5	2.2	21.3	3.8	10.1	14.0	13.4	12.0	10.0	3.7	100.0
1923	9.2	2.8	23.0	4.6	9.7	13.9	12.1	11.3	9.7	3.7	100.0
1924	9.7	2.3	21.3	5.1	9.7	13.4	13.1	11.8	9.9	3.8	100.0
1925	10.2	2.4	21.6	5.1	9.8	13.1	12.5	12.0	9.5	3.9	100.0
1926	9.1	2.6	21.9	5.2	9.5	13.9	11.9	12.2	9.8	3.9	100.0
1927	9.2	2.3	21.1	5.1	9.6	13.0	12.7	12.7	10.4	4.0	100.0
1928	8.8	2.0	21.5	4.8	9.6	13.2	13.0	12.8	9.9	4.4	100.0
1929	8.8	2.1	22.5	4.6	9.7	13.0	12.4	12.8	10.1	4.0	100.0
1930	7.5	1.8	20.9	4.5	10.0	14.1	12.6	13.4	11.5	3.7	100.0
1931	6.7	1.4	18.3	3.7	10.7	15.0	13.1	14.6	12.3	4.3	100.0
1932	6.6	1.1	14.7	2.6	11.5	14.8	13.9	15.3	14.5	5.0	100.0
1933	8.5	1.1	15.8	1.7	11.3	12.5	12.4	13.9	17.9	4.8	100.0
1934	9.6	1.7	18.2	1.7	9.7	14.2	10.2	13.6	16.5	4.6	100.0
1935	9.9	1.7	20.9	1.9	9.5	13.6	10.4	13.5	13.8	4.7	100.0
1936	9.7	1.9	22.6	2.5	9.3	13.5	9.5	13.2	13.1	4.7	100.0
1937	8.9	2.0	22.7	2.6	8.8	12.8	9.5	13.0	15.3	4.5	100.0
1938	8.4	1.7	19.4	2.6	8.5	14.3	10.1	13.7	16.7	4.6	100.0

* Unadjusted for the disparity between depreciation and depletion charges at cost and reproduction prices, and gains and losses from sales of capital assets before 1929. Social Security contributions of employers are omitted.

changes occurred in the relative weight of the different industries in national income and in the countrywide totals of
various types of income?

Table 12 answers both questions in a preliminary fashion.
But for close analysis the distribution shown is unsatisfactory
in several respects. First, only national income is apportioned;
changes in it cannot be clearly understood until they are seen
as changes in the industrial apportionment of the constituent
types. Second, the industrial classification omits the minor
industrial divisions. Third, and most important, it follows institutional lines which, while interesting in themselves, should
perhaps be recast in order to satisfy more directly analytical
purposes. Such recasting can, of course, be done only by combining the minor industrial divisions into broader analytical
categories, since it is impossible to subdivide them further.

2 Average for the Period

Table 13 presents percentage distributions of national income
and of its components by major and minor industrial divisions,
based on arithmetic means of the totals for the two decades,
1919–38. Serving to introduce the countrywide totals of national income and the components whose industrial distribution can be studied, it reveals the composition of some of the
major industrial groups; although omitting several industry
type of income cells, it suggests the multitude of separate elements of which national income and other countrywide income totals are composed. Chiefly for reference, enabling the
reader to gauge the relative importance of the various cells in
the industrial type of income structure, it calls for no extended
comment.

We should note, however, the striking differences in the
shares of one and the same industry in the countrywide totals
of various types of income; for example, while agriculture accounts for about 10 per cent of national income, it accounts
for less than 3 per cent of wages and salaries, over 40 per cent
of entrepreneurial income, and for slightly over 3 per cent of

TABLE 13

National Income and its Components, Percentage Distribution by Industrial Source, Based on Average Values for 1919–1938

	NATIONAL INCOME	AGGREGATE PAYMENTS Incl. entrep. savings	AGGREGATE PAYMENTS Excl. entrep. savings	WAGES AND SALARIES	ENTREPRENEURIAL Withdr.	ENTREPRENEURIAL Net income	SERVICE INCOME Incl. entrep. savings	SERVICE INCOME Excl. entrep. savings	DIVIDENDS	INTEREST	PROPERTY INCOME INCL. RENT
	(1)	(2)	(3)	(4)	(5)	(6)	(7)	(8)	(9)	(10)	(11)
I Agriculture	9.6	9.6	10.0	2.6	45.2	41.9	11.1	11.6	0.43	8.6	3.3
II Mining	2.2	2.5	2.5	3.3	0.20	0.19	2.6	2.6	5.2	0.84	2.0
1 Anthracite coal	0.33	0.35	0.36	0.54	...[1]	...[1]	0.40	0.41	0.17	0.21	0.14
2 Bituminous coal	0.96	1.0	1.0	1.6	0.04	0.04	1.2	1.2	0.49	0.23	0.24
3 Metal	0.30	0.36	0.36	0.39	0.01	0.01	0.30	0.30	1.9	0.11	0.65
4 Oil & gas	0.35	0.45	0.46	0.52	0.14	0.13	0.42	0.43	1.6	0.17	0.58
5 Other	0.21	0.26	0.26	0.30	0.02	0.02	0.23	0.23	1.1	0.12	0.39
III Manufacturing[2]	21.0	21.0	21.1	28.6	2.9	3.2	22.3	22.4	44.0	3.4	15.5
1 Food & tobacco[2]	2.6	2.5	2.6	3.1	0.98	0.96	2.5	2.5	7.3	0.74	2.7
2 Textile & leather[2]	3.9	3.9	3.9	5.7	0.76	0.84	4.5	4.5	4.4	0.12	1.5
3 Constr. mat. & furn.[2]	2.4	2.5	2.5	3.6	0.33	0.38	2.8	2.8	3.5	0.28	1.2
4 Paper[2]	0.61	0.60	0.60	0.82	0.03	0.04	0.63	0.63	1.2	0.24	0.47
5 Printing[2]	1.6	1.6	1.6	2.3	0.34	0.40	1.8	1.8	1.9	0.17	0.69
6 Metal[2]	7.2	7.1	7.1	9.8	0.22	0.30	7.5	7.5	15.2	0.97	5.3
7 Chemical[2]	1.5	1.6	1.6	1.7	0.12	0.13	1.3	1.3	8.2	0.55	2.9
8 Misc. & rubber[2]	1.2	1.2	1.2	1.7	0.12	0.13	1.3	1.3	2.3	0.30	0.87
IV Construction	3.8	3.8	3.8	5.3	2.9	3.0	4.7	4.6	0.90	0.16	0.35

V Transp. & other pub. util.	9.8	9.6	9.6	11.1	0.05	0.05	8.6	8.6	21.1	8.6	19.2	14.0
1 Elec. light & power	1.4	1.3	1.3	0.82	0.02	0.01	0.62	0.63	7.2	0.62	5.0	4.2
2 Mfd. gas	0.25	0.27	0.27	0.22			0.17	0.17	1.3	0.17	0.75	0.69
3 Steam rr., Pull., & exp.	5.4	5.3	5.3	6.7			5.2	5.2	5.9	5.2	10.2	5.7
4 Street rwy.	0.74	0.75	0.75	0.88	0.03	0.04	0.66	0.67	0.88	0.66	2.2	1.1
5 Water transp.	0.73	0.75	0.75	1.1			0.86	0.86	0.62	0.86	0.22	0.28
6 Pipe lines	0.20	0.19	0.19	0.10			0.07	0.07	2.0	0.07	0.03	0.68
7 Telephone	0.94	0.92	0.92	1.1			0.83	0.84	3.0	0.84	0.78	1.3
8 Telegraph	0.16	0.16	0.16	0.22			0.17	0.17	0.21	0.17	0.05	0.08
VI Trade	13.5	13.6	13.4	15.5	18.4	19.4	16.0	15.7	10.3	15.7	0.86	3.7
VII Finance	11.9	12.2	12.3	5.1	1.8	1.7	4.2	4.3	10.9	4.3	32.4	46.0
1 Banking	1.4	1.3	1.3	1.4			1.1	1.1	7.4	1.1		2.4
2 Insurance	1.6	1.7	1.7	2.2			2.0	2.0	0.93	2.0	−0.49	0.12
3 Real estate	8.9	9.2	9.3	1.5	1.8	1.7	1.1	1.2	2.5	1.2	32.9	43.5
VIII Service	12.6	12.8	12.4	12.8	25.0	26.8	15.5	15.1	1.9	15.1	1.4	1.1
1 Professional				2.5		17.2	5.7					
2 Personal				3.7		6.6	4.3					
3 Domestic				3.8			2.8					
4 Misc.				2.8		3.0	2.7					
IX Government	11.6	10.6	10.7	10.9			10.6	10.7			29.0	10.8
1 Federal		5.2	5.2	3.6			4.9	4.9			17.6	6.5
2 State		0.55	0.56	0.73			0.64	0.64			0.55	0.20
3 County		0.58	0.58	0.72			0.55	0.55			1.9	0.70
4 City incl. pub. educ.		4.3	4.3	5.8			4.5	4.6			8.9	3.3
X Miscellaneous	4.0	4.3	4.2	4.8	3.7	3.8	4.5	4.5	5.2	4.5	4.1	3.2
Total	100.0	100.0	100.0	100.0	100.0	100.0	100.0	100.0	100.0	100.0	100.0	100.0

TABLE 13 (concl.)

	NATIONAL INCOME (1)	AGGREGATE PAYMENTS Incl. entrep. savings (2)	Excl. entrep. savings (3)	WAGES AND SALARIES (4)	ENTREPRENEURIAL Withdr. (5)	Net income (6)	SERVICE INCOME Incl. entrep. savings (7)	Excl. entrep. savings (8)	DIVI-DENDS (9)	INTEREST (10)	PROPERTY INCOME INCL. RENT (11)
CLASSIFICATION A BY CHARACTER OF PRODUCTIVE FUNCTION											
1 Commodity producing	38.2	38.5	39.0	40.8	51.1	48.2	41.4	42.0	59.0	18.7	26.1
2 Commodity transp. & distr.	19.8	19.8	19.6	23.4	18.4	19.5	22.1	21.9	18.9	11.3	10.3
3 Services	41.9	41.7	41.4	35.8	30.5	32.3	36.5	36.1	22.1	70.0	63.6
CLASSIFICATION B BY DURABILITY OF PRODUCT											
1 Non-durable	43.2	43.9	44.0	32.6	72.6	71.2	40.2	40.3	33.9	48.2	59.3
2 Durable	13.9	14.0	14.0	19.3	3.4	3.7	15.4	15.5	22.5	1.6	7.9
3 Mixed	42.9	42.1	42.0	48.0	24.0	25.1	44.3	44.2	43.6	50.2	32.8
4 Non-durable as % of durable & non-durable	75.7	75.8	75.9	62.8	95.5	95.1	72.3	72.2	60.1	96.8	88.2
CLASSIFICATION C BY TYPE OF BUSINESS ORGANIZATION											
1 With large proportion of individual firms	52.4	53.3	53.1	42.5	95.1	94.9	52.9	52.6	21.3	48.1	55.2
2 Private corp.	23.2	23.5	23.6	31.9	3.1	3.4	24.9	25.0	49.2	4.2	17.5
3 Semi-public corp.	12.8	12.6	12.6	14.7	1.8	1.8	11.6	11.7	29.5	18.7	16.5
4 Public	11.6	10.6	10.7	10.9			10.6	10.7		29.0	10.8

1 Less than 0.005 per cent.

2 Including salaries of employees at central administrative offices.

property income. The share of the electric light and power industry in property income is about seven times its share in service income. Indeed the net income of few industries has a composition similar to that of national income. This diversity betokens the great diversity among industries in the character of their business organization, which determines the relative importance of entrepreneurial income; in the ratio of direct labor to capital, which largely determines the importance of wages and salaries compared to property income; in the relative availability of various types of long term credit, which determines the relative importance of interest and dividends, etc. These differences in the composition of income by type among industries are measured directly and treated in more detail in Chapter 6, but they necessarily appear here in the distribution of national income components by industrial source.

The three new classifications into which we combined the major and minor industrial divisions, based on significant characteristics, are useful in economic analysis; their composition is revealed in the accompanying tabular exhibit.

Classification A is based on the nature of the productive function, not the physical characteristics of the industry's product. A portion of governmental and banking services is embodied in the commodity whose production governmental administration or the credit activity of banks has helped promote; and the value of the commodity certainly embodies the cost of governmental or banking activities. But the productive function of government or banks is not part of the physical process of extraction or fabrication, and it is the substantive nature of the production process that is the basis of the distinction.

Viewed in this light, the classification is obviously rough. Agricultural and manufacturing enterprises, and the corresponding industries as a whole, engage in transportation, distribution, and services that are only indirectly related to the physical process of production, as well as in the extraction and

Composition of Groups in the Industrial Classifications by Character of Productive Function, Durability of Product, and Type of Business Organization

A   BY CHARACTER OF PRODUCTIVE FUNCTION

Commodity Producing	*Commodity Transport- ing and Distributing*	*Services*
Agriculture (I)	Steam rr., Pullman, &	Street rwy. (V-4)
Mining (II)	express (V-3)	Telephone (V-7)
Manufacturing (III)	Water transp. (V-5)	Telegraph (V-8)
Construction (IV)	Pipe lines (V-6)	Finance (VII)
Elec. lt. & power (V-1)	Trade (VI)	Service (VIII)
Mfd. gas (V-2)		Government (IX)
		Misc. (X)

B   BY DURABILITY OF PRODUCT

Non-durable	*Durable*	*Mixed*
Agriculture (I)	Metal mining (II-3)	Bituminous coal (II-2)
Anthracite coal (II-1)	Other mining (II-5)	Misc. & rubber mfg.
Oil & gas (II-4)	Construction materials	(III-8)
Food & tobacco (III-1)	& furniture (III-3)	Elec. lt. & power (V-1)
Textile & leather	Metal mfg. (III-6)	Steam rr., Pullman, &
(III-2)	Construction (IV)	express (V-3)
Paper (III-4)		Water transp. (V-5)
Printing (III-5)		Telephone (V-7)
Chemical (III-7)		Telegraph (V-8)
Mfd. gas (V-2)		Trade (VI)
Street rwy. (V-4)		Banking (VII-1)
Pipe lines (V-6)		Insurance (VII-2)
Real estate (VII-3)		Government (IX)
Service (VIII)		Misc. (X)

C   BY TYPE OF BUSINESS ORGANIZATION

With Large Proportion of Individual Firms	*Private Corporations*	*Semi-public Corporations*	*Public*
Agriculture (I)	Mining (II)	Transp. & other pub.	Government (IX)
Construction (IV)	Mfg. (III)	util. (V)	
Trade (VI)		Banking (VII-1)	
Real estate (VII-3)		Insurance (VII-2)	
Service (VIII)			
Misc. (X)			

The roman and arabic numerals in parentheses designate the line number of the industrial division in Table 13.

fabrication of commodities. On the other hand, governmental agencies and some public utilities carry on some commodity production, e.g., by engaging in construction on force account. Yet the distinction is real in that in agriculture and manufacturing, transportation, distribution, and service are subsidiary to extraction and fabrication; likewise, in telephone companies and governmental agencies commodity production is secondary and auxiliary.[2]

It is the physical characteristics of the final product, including both the finished product and the materials that eventually enter it, that underlie Classification B. The criterion of durability is whether the product, in its utilization by the ultimate user, ordinarily lasts longer than three years; and by ultimate use we mean not only consumption by ultimate consumers but also the utilization by enterprises of such durable capital as buildings and machinery.[3]

Unfortunately, the industrial division followed in our estimates is not fine enough for a clear-cut classification by durability; indeed, no purely *industrial* (rather than *product*) classification could be. We could not separate perishable product from semidurable product industries; and more important, we had to classify industries by the characteristics of the preponderant part of their product, without further division of the latter. Even on this crude basis, we could classify only a majority of industries. A substantial number in which the proportion of durable or of non-durable products was too large to be ignored had to be placed in a mixed category.

Classification C, by type of prevailing organizational unit, distinguishes industries in which a substantial proportion of

[2] The inclusion of electric light and power and manufactured gas under commodity production may be questioned. Yet it is perhaps more questionable to include them under services. They are admittedly borderline industries. The Pullman Company should properly be excluded from commodity production and distribution and put under services. But the items involved are so minor that it was not considered worth while to make the necessary calculations.
[3] For a more detailed discussion of this classification see *National Income and Capital Formation, 1919–1935*, pp. 35–7.

the field is still in the hands of entrepreneurs from others in which large private corporations, corporations of more public character and hence subject to governmental regulation, and governmental agencies predominate to the virtual exclusion of individual proprietorship. This also is a rough classification. We disregarded the formally corporate character of numerous one-man corporations in such fields as trade, construction, or service, and we may have put too much weight on the fact that in such fields as steam railroading or banking, corporations are subject to more public control than in mining or manufacturing; yet these two groups differ significantly in flexibility and freedom in price, production, and cost policies.

Commodity producing industries account for about two-fifths of national income, aggregate payments to individuals, and wages and salaries, a somewhat larger share of entrepreneurial withdrawals, and a smaller share of property income. Commodity transporting and distributing industries account for roughly one-fifth of national income and aggregate payments, a larger share of wages and salaries, a smaller share of entrepreneurial withdrawals, and half as large a share of property income. Service industries account for the remaining two-fifths of national income and aggregate payments, a larger share of property income, and smaller shares of entrepreneurial withdrawals and wages and salaries.

The significant aspect of Classification A is the substantial proportion of total net product accounted for by activities that are not production, transportation, or distribution of commodities. It is perhaps exaggerated in Table 13, since commodity producing activities in the service industries may be greater than purely service activities in the other industries. Yet the exaggeration cannot be so large as to invalidate the inference that at least one-third of the net national product is accounted for by services that do not contribute directly to the increase in commodity stocks or to their availability to ultimate users. Such a high proportion is undoubtedly possible only in communities of advanced economic development, since low productivity would compel greater concentration on the production and distribution of objects of prime necessity, the preponderant part of which is in the form of commodities.

In Classification B the share of industries that produce durable commodities mainly is small, amounting to 14 per cent of national income and of aggregate payments, a somewhat larger percentage of wages and salaries, and a somewhat smaller percentage of property income. The smallness of the share that, by the nature of the goods included, is a source of additions to the stock at the disposal of consumers and producers is partly determined by the definition: we assume that tangible goods alone can be durable, and classify as non-durable or mixed some products of service industries for which a claim of longevity may be made (e.g., education). And, of course, there may be a substantial share of durable products in the mixed category. Yet the proportion of durable goods, whether consumer or producer, in national income probably does not exceed one-fifth; the great majority of goods currently produced are obviously for fairly immediate consumption.[4]

The distribution in Classification C may seem at first to contradict the generally prevalent notion of the predominance of the corporate and non-personal form of organization in our economy: the share of industries in which entrepreneurs are numerous is slightly over one-half of national income, of aggregate payments, and of property income (including rent). But the contradiction is only apparent. Predominance need not be judged by the apportionment of the *net* product of the economy. Of gross volume of activity the share of industries in which corporations and non-personal forms of organization predominate is possibly larger than in Table 13; and the same is likely to be true of the share of material capital. Moreover,

[4] For reasons already indicated, no really satisfactory classification by durability can be derived by using the industry as the unit. Classification B is, therefore, omitted in the analysis of changes in the industrial composition over the period. We return to it in Chapter 7, where we analyze the distribution of national income by type of final product.

corporations and other non-personal organizations may exercise an effect on the course of economic affairs quite out of proportion to their share in net or gross income, or in the total of all physical resources. Nevertheless, for the understanding of changes in the national product it is worth noting that industries with large groups of entrepreneurs still play an important role. Also, a substantial share of the ultimate product is contributed by industries that are either completely public or under social control sufficient to affect greatly the freedom with which they can adapt their activity to market demand, and thus to the changing needs or wishes of ultimate users. The combined share of these two groups (public and semi-public corporations) average about one-fourth of national income.

Other classifications could probably be devised, despite the difficulty of fitting the unwieldy units of our industrial divisions into them neatly.[5] Broader groups could be based on differences in the spatial mobility of the product; on variations in the extent to which industries depend upon foreign countries, either as markets or as sources of supplies; on differences in the cost structure of industries, i.e., the ratio of capital to direct labor, etc.; or on differences in the pattern of secular or cyclical fluctuations. But some of these groupings are not relevant, in that they would not reveal any significant tendencies in the industrial distribution of the national product; while others will emerge in the analysis of temporal changes below. Classifications A, B, and C promise to add to the conclusions concerning the distribution of national income and of its components by industrial source. Even of these three, that by durability has to be abandoned in some of the analysis in this chapter; and the crudities in the other two make it necessary often to go behind the broad categories in order to check the conclusions suggested in terms of the minor and major industrial divisions of which they are composed.

[5] One that unfortunately could not be carried through satisfactorily is that between consumer and producer goods industries.

3 Changes over the Period

The percentage distribution of national income tends to reflect the structure of the nation's productive system and is not likely to show the pronounced and violent fluctuations that often characterize the totals. Yet even during a period as short as that since the first World War, the distribution by industrial source may have changed radically, especially as notable structural shifts took place, reflecting the post-War readjustment and new developments that led to the severe depression of 1929–32 and its aftermath. We therefore consider changes in the industrial distribution of income, first during the period as a whole, as possible indicators of secular movements in the industrial structure of the economy, then the shorter term cyclical fluctuations. To some degree we can make up for the shortness of the period by utilizing King's estimates back to 1909.

The basic series for establishing changes over the period in the distribution by industrial source are the annual percentage shares of major and minor industrial divisions in the country-wide totals, shown fully in the Statistical Appendix to Part Two. From these annual percentages we derive averages for longer periods in which the transient effects of business cycles are moderated and that should, therefore, reveal the longer term movements in the percentage distribution. After experimenting with various periods, we chose the decades 1919–28 and 1929–38, and, as a check on the decade measures for possible effects of the severe contraction of 1929–32, the quinquennia 1919–23 and 1934–38. By computing the arithmetic means [6]

[6] It would have been more proper to take geometric means. But the percentages do not show extreme variations and the minor improvement that would be effected by taking geometric means did not warrant the additional labor.

It would also have been possible to follow the procedure adopted in Table 13 and compute percentages based on arithmetic means of absolute values for decades or quinquennia. This is tantamount to computing arithmetic means of percentages, each percentage weighted by the base to which it is computed. But there did not seem to be sufficient reason why, in establishing average percentage shares for the study of changes in percentage distributions over the period, a percentage should be given greater weight because the absolute total from which it is derived is larger. Accordingly, in all subsequent calculations of percentages for them we obtained two measures of change in each percentage distribution—one, the difference between the arithmetic means for the two decades, the other, the difference between the arithmetic means for the two quinquennia.

These changes in average shares from the first decade to the second and from the first quinquennium to the last are usually in the same direction for one industry in one income total; but they vary in magnitude and direction among industries within the various totals.

To summarize the evidence most effectively and bring out clearly the most telling conclusions, we established the following broad categories of change: (a) a minor rise or decline over the period—both measures rise or decline, but neither more than one-tenth of the average share for 1919–38 (as given in Table 13); (b) a significant rise or decline—both measures rise or decline, one or both more than one-tenth of the average percentage for the entire period, but not more than four-tenths; (c) a large rise or decline—same as (b), but the rise or decline exceeds four-tenths of the average percentage for the period; (d) no definite movement—the two measures of change have opposite signs. In Tables 14, 15, and 16 changes of type (a) are designated by o with a sign attached to differentiate a minor rise from a minor decline; (b) is denoted by + if a rise and by — if a decline; (c) by + * if a rise and by — * if a decline; and (d) by an unadorned o.

Columns 1–4 of Table 14 illustrate the classification of direction and magnitude of change. The first column gives the percentage for the entire period accounted for by various industries in national income (from Table 13); the second column, the change from the arithmetic mean of percentages for 1919–28 to that for 1929–38; and the third, the change from

relating to changes in percentage distributions over the period we used arithmetic means of percentages rather than percentages of arithmetic means of absolute values. However, because changes in both percentages and/or their bases were fairly moderate within quinquennia or decades, the alternative procedure would reveal shifts in distribution similar to those shown by our present procedure.

the arithmetic mean of percentages for 1919–23 to that for 1934–38. The symbols in column 4 are derived by applying to columns 1–3 the rules formulated in the preceding paragraph; e.g., the entry for agriculture is — because the measures of change in columns 2 and 3 are both negative and one or both exceed one-tenth, but not four-tenths, of the percentage in column 1. The other entries in column 4 are similarly derived from columns 1, 2, and 3. Columns 5 and 6 contain the final entries—changes in the industrial distribution of the two totals of aggregate payments—derived by a procedure strictly analogous to that followed for the distribution of national income.

Three considerations must be borne in mind in interpreting the conclusions suggested by this and the following tables. First, since we are dealing with percentages, not with totals, an increase in the share of an industry does not necessarily mean an increase in the income originating in it. Second, the percentages are interdependent in that if the share of one industry rises during a period, the share of another *must* decline; i.e., the share of an industry depends upon the composition of the countrywide total and if percentages are based upon a total made up of different components, a different movement results. For example, the percentage that trade constitutes of national income declines from 14.1 for 1919–23 to 13.8 for 1934–38 because service and government are included. If for some reason they were excluded, it would be 17.6 and 19.2 respectively, thus increasing instead of decreasing. Third, and perhaps most important, the distributions in Table 14 and subsequent tables are of totals in current prices. Consequently we must not infer from a decrease or increase in the share of an industry that its share in the *goods* volume of the national product, i.e., in constant prices, changed similarly. Were it possible to adjust the incomes originating in the various industries for fluctuations in the specific price levels involved, the shifts in the distribution might differ from those in Table 14.

The industrial distributions of national income and of aggregate payments in current prices changed considerably

(Table 14). The shares of most commodity producing industries declined, some strikingly—not only those of the four major
divisions—agriculture, mining, manufacturing, and construction—but also those of most minor divisions under mining and
manufacturing. Under mining, the share of oil and gas alone
failed to decline over the period; under manufacturing, food
and tobacco, paper, printing, and chemicals are the sole increasing shares.

Although it is primarily the commodity producing industries whose shares decline, the shares of two other groups also
decline: the public utility—steam railroads, street railways, and
water transportation, forms of transportation whose development was distinctly retarded by new competitors; and the
finance—real estate and banking; on these two latter industries
the effect of the downward sweep of the cycle after 1928 may
perhaps have been greater and more prolonged than on others.

Other knowledge concerning the dark spots in the nation's
economic picture from 1919 to 1938 is corroborated by the
severe declines in the shares of anthracite coal, bituminous
coal, construction materials and furniture, construction, steam
railroads, street railways—the laggards in the productive
system.

The list of industries whose shares in national income and
aggregate payments increase is also familiar. In addition to food
and tobacco, paper, printing, and chemicals, it comprises electric light and power (large increase), manufactured gas, pipe
lines (large increase), telephones (large increase), insurance,
the service industries, total government and all its branches
(large increase), and miscellaneous. It thus includes the more
rapidly growing manufactures; the utilities that are not affected by new technical competitors but profit from technological progress and increasing urbanization; services (professional,
personal, etc.) the demand for which increases with an improvement in the standard of living; and government, whose
more vigorous participation in the economic life of the nation
is reflected in its increasing share in national income. The in-

TABLE 14

National Income and Aggregate Payments to Individuals Change over the Period in the Percentage Distribution by Industrial Source, 1919–1938

	NATIONAL INCOME			DIRECTION AND MAGNITUDE OF CHANGE	AGGREGATE PAYMENTS	
	AVG. % 1919-38	CHANGE FROM 1919-28 to 1929-38	1919-23 to 1934-38	NATIONAL INCOME	Incl. entrep. savings	Excl. entrep. savings
	(1)	(2)	(3)	(4)	(5)	(6)
Agriculture	9.6	−1.9	−2.3	−	−	—*
Mining	2.2	−0.83	−0.87	−	—*	—*
Anth. coal	0.33	−0.12	−0.19	—*	—*	—*
Bit. coal	0.96	−0.47	−0.61	—*	—*	—*
Metal	0.30	−0.13	−0.08	—*	—	—
Oil & gas	0.35	−0.04	+0.04	o	o	o
Other	0.21	−0.07	−0.04	−	−	−
Manufacturing	21.0	−2.4	−1.4	−	o −	o −
Food & tobacco	2.6	+0.42	+0.47	+	+	o +
Text. & leather	3.9	−0.72	−1.0	−	−	−
Constr. mat. & furn.	2.4	−1.2	−1.0	—*	−	—*
Paper	0.61	+0.05	+0.10	+	+	+
Printing	1.6	+0.32	+0.30	+	+	+
Metal	7.2	−1.1	−0.26	−	−	−
Chemical	1.5	+0.07	+0.24	+	+	+
Misc. & rubber	1.2	−0.28	−0.27	−	−	−
Construction	3.8	−1.5	−1.4	−	—*	−
Transp. & other pub. util.	9.8	+0.22	−0.88	o	−	−
Elec. light & power	1.4	+1.1	+1.1	+*	+*	+*
Mfd. gas	0.25	+0.07	+0.09	+	+*	+
Steam rr., Pull., & exp.	5.4	−1.3	−2.1	−	—*	—*
Street rwy.	0.74	−0.20	−0.38	—*	—*	—*
Water transp.	0.73	−0.05	−0.12	−	−	−
Pipe lines	0.20	+0.11	+0.10	+*	+*	+*
Telephone	0.94	+0.46	+0.46	+*	+*	+*
Telegraph	0.16	0.0	−0.01	o −	+	o +
Trade	13.5	−0.08	−0.31	o −	o −	o +
Finance	11.9	−0.90	−2.1	−	−	−
Banking	1.4	−0.24	−0.19	−	o	o
Insurance	1.6	+0.67	+0.78	+*	+	+
Real estate	8.9	−1.3	−2.7	−	−	−
Service	12.6	+2.3	+2.5	+	+	+
Government	11.6	+4.8	+5.7	+*	+*	+*
Federal					+*	+*
State					+*	+*
County					+*	+*
City incl. pub. educ.					+*	+*
Miscellaneous	4.0	+0.35	+1.1	+	+	+

TABLE 14 (concl.)

	NATIONAL INCOME			DIRECTION AND MAGNITUDE OF CHANGE AGGREGATE PAYMENTS		
		CHANGE FROM			Incl.	Excl.
	AVG. % 1919–38	*1919–28* *to* *1929–38*	*1919–23* *to* *1934–38*	NATIONAL INCOME	entrep. savings	entrep. savings
	(1)	(2)	(3)	(4)	(5)	(6)

CLASSIFICATION A   BY CHARACTER OF PRODUCTIVE FUNCTION

Commodity prod.	38.2	—5.5	—4.8	—	—	—
Commodity transp. & distr.	19.8	—1.3	—2.5	—	—	—
Services	41.9	+6.8	+7.3	+	+	+

CLASSIFICATION C   BY TYPE OF BUSINESS ORGANIZATION

With large proportion of individual firms	52.4	—2.1	—3.1	0 —	0 —	0 —
Private corp.	23.2	—3.3	—2.3	—	—	—
Semi-public corp.	12.8	+0.65	—0.29	0	0	0
Public	11.6	+4.8	+5.7	+*	+*	+*

The symbols are based upon the direction and magnitude of change in the average percentages from 1919–28 to 1929–38 and from 1919–23 to 1934–38: o means that the signs of change in the two comparisons are different; o + or o —, that the change, in the same direction for both comparisons, is in both less than 10 per cent of the average percentage for 1919–38; + or — , that the change in one or both comparisons is more than 10 per cent but less than 40 per cent of the average percentage for the period; +* or —*, that the change in one or both comparisons is more than 40 per cent of the average percentage for the period.

crease in the share of the miscellaneous division seems to be due largely to the inclusion of some industries for which, because of their very rapid growth, continuous estimates for the period could not be made: motor transportation, aviation, and brokerage.

These movements in the shares of specific industries cause changes in the relative distribution among categories of Classifications A and C. In Classification A the share of commodity producing industries declines, of course; that of commodity transporting and distributing industries also declines since its two chief components, steam railroads and trade, decline markedly and slightly, respectively. The share of service industries rises significantly.

In Classification C the share of industries in which private corporations predominate (i.e., mining and manufacturing) declines significantly. That of industries with a large proportion of individual firms also declines, but slightly; the marked decline in the shares of agriculture and construction and the slight decline in that of trade tend to be offset by the rise in the share of professional, personal, and other service industries in which individual firms are numerous. The share of semi-public corporations shows no definite movement, increases in the shares of some public utilities and divisions of finance offset-

TABLE 15

Aggregate Payments to Individuals excluding Entrepreneurial Savings, Change over the Period in the Percentage Distribution by Industrial Source, King's and Present NBER Estimates, 1909–1938

	PERCENTAGE SHARES 1919-23		INDEXES (1919-23 = 100)			DIRECTION AND MAGNITUDE OF CHANGE [1]		
						1909-18 to 1919-28	*1919-28 to 1929-38*	*1909-18 to 1929-38*
	King (1)	Present NBER (2)	*1909-18* (3)	*1919-28* (4)	*1929-38* (5)	(6)	(7)	(8)
1 Agriculture	12.2	12.7	101.9	90.2	67.2	—	—	—
2 Mining	2.8	3.1	105.7	93.5	63.6	—	—	—•
3 Manufacturing	21.8	22.5	93.0	97.7	88.6	o +	o —	o —
4 Construction	3.1	3.8	140.6	117.8	77.5	—	—	—•
5 Steam rr.	6.3	6.5	101.0	93.0	68.3	o —	—	—
6 Street rwy.	0.98	0.94	111.2	92.5	67.6	—	—	—•
7 Water transp.	1.1	0.91	72.7	88.2	76.8	+	—	o +
8 Communication	0.84	0.80	76.2	110.3	160.0	+	+•	+•
9 Elec. light & power	0.60	0.63	66.7	138.3	279.8	+•	+•	+•
10 Trade	13.0	13.4	93.8	99.2	101.4	o +	o +	o +
11 Banking	1.3	1.3	95.4	103.5	104.1	o +	o +	o +
12 Rent	9.9	8.9	114.0	102.1	80.7	—	—	—
13 Government	9.0	8.4	72.6	97.9	162.8	+·	+•	+•
14 All other	17.2	16.1	112.8	110.3	136.4	o —	+	+

CLASSIFICATION A [2] BY CHARACTER OF PRODUCTIVE FUNCTION

	King (1)	Present NBER (2)	(3)	(4)	(5)	(6)	(7)	(8)
15 Commodity prod. (1 + 2 + 3 + 4 + 9)	40.5	42.7	99.8	97.5	82.2	o —	—	—
16 Commodity transp. & distr. (5 + 7 + 10)	20.3	20.8	95.4	96.8	89.9	o +	o —	o —
17 Services (6 + 8 + 11 + 12 + 13 + 14)	39.2	·36.4	102.5	104.7	126.6	o +	+	+

CLASSIFICATION C [2] BY TYPE OF BUSINESS ORGANIZATION

	King (1)	Present NBER (2)	(3)	(4)	(5)	(6)	(7)	(8)
18 With large proportion of individual firms (1+4+10+12+14)	55.4	54.9	107.7	102.1	98.8	o —	o —	o —
19 Private corp. (2 + 3)	24.6	25.6	94.4	97.2	85.5	o +	—	o —
20 Semi-public corp. (5+6+7+8+9+11)	11.1	11.1	94.9	97.6	91.8	o +	o —	o —
21 Public (13)	9.0	8.4	72.6	97.9	162.8	+	+•	+•

[1] See note to Table 14.
[2] Classifications A and C are not strictly comparable with those in other tables. Manufactured gas is excluded from line 15, pipe lines from line 16, and both are included in line 17. Manufactured gas, pipe lines, and insurance are excluded from line 20 and included in line 18. Rent, here, is the sum of rent received by individuals, imputed rent, and real estate interest.

ting declines in the shares of others. The public sector, i.e.,
government, rises markedly.

For the distribution of aggregate payments excluding entrepreneurial savings we extend the analysis to 1909 by using
King's estimates (Table 15). The first two columns show the
differences in the industrial distributions, which are roughly
continuous for the three decades, during the quinquennium
for which the two series of estimates can be compared. The
symbols in columns 6–8 are determined by a procedure analogous to that used in Table 14, except that the distinctions
between slight, significant, and large changes are based upon
a comparison of the change with the average percentage share
in the middle decade, 1919–28.

The movements in the shares of several industries during
the last two decades characterized also the longer span of three
decades: the shares of agriculture, mining, construction, steam
railroads, street railways, and rent (roughly comparable to real
estate in the other tables) declined not only from 1919–28 to
1929–38 but also from 1909–18 to 1919–28; the shares of electric light and power, communication (largely telephone),
trade, banking, and government increased not only from
1919–28 to 1929–38 but also from 1909–18 to 1919–28. In other
industries the change from the first to the second decade was
in the opposite direction from that from the second to the
third: the shares of manufacturing and water transportation
rose from 1909–18 to 1919–28 but declined from 1919–28 to
1929–38; that of the 'all other' division declined from 1909–18
to 1919–28 and rose from 1919–28 to 1929–38. Comparison of
column 8 in Table 15, recording the movement from the first
to the third decade, with column 6 in Table 14, showing
changes in the industrial distribution of the same total during
two decades, indicates similarity for comparable industrial
branches. The only difference is that the share of water transportation rises slightly in Table 15, i.e., over the three decades,
and declines in Table 14; and that the share of banking rises
slightly in Table 15 but not at all in Table 14.

The decline in the share of commodity producing industries (Classification A) was persistent, although less from the first to the second decade than from the second to the third; the share of commodity transporting and distributing industries increased slightly between 1909–18 and 1919–28, the decline developing only after the first World War; and the share of service industries rose persistently, although more markedly during the third than during the earlier decades. In Classification C the share of industries in which individual firms predominate declined slightly but consistently; and the share of government rose throughout but especially during the recent decades. The shares of industries in which private corporations predominate and of semi-public industries rose from 1909–18 to 1919–28 and declined from 1919–28 to 1929–38.

Having established that the shares of commodity producing industries, of the older public utilities, and of real estate declined in national income and aggregate payments, while the shares of some public utilities, direct service industries, and government rose, we now inquire whether similar declines and rises characterized their shares in the countrywide totals of wages and salaries, entrepreneurial income, dividends, interest, etc. (Table 16). The symbols that indicate slight, significant, and large rises; slight, significant, and large declines; and no movement, are determined by a procedure analogous to that used in Table 14. The one minor modification was to disregard shares that, for the period as a whole, averaged less than one-tenth of one per cent of the countrywide total. Changes in such minute shares are likely to be extremely erratic; they are designated 'a', which means that for the given industry the type of income or payment does not exist, is not estimated, or changes in its share are not classified.

a) The first impression conveyed by Table 16 is that in few industries do their shares in various types of income move similarly. If we assume as the criterion of consistency the same sign in all the columns (excluding those marked a), whether it follows o (designating a slight change), stands by itself (desig-

TABLE 16: Direction and Magnitude of Change * over the Period in the Percentage Distribution by Industrial Source of Types of Income, 1919–1938

	WAGES & SALARIES (1)	ENTREPRENEURIAL Withdr. (2)	ENTREPRENEURIAL Net income (3)	SERVICE INCOME Incl. entrep. savings (4)	SERVICE INCOME Excl. entrep. savings (5)	DIVIDENDS (6)	INTEREST (7)	DIVIDENDS & INTEREST (8)	PROPERTY INCOME INCL. RENT (9)	NATIONAL INCOME (10)
Agriculture	−*	−*	o	−*	−*	o	−*	−*	−*	−*
Mining										
Anthracite coal	−*	a	a	−*	−*	−*	−*	−*	−*	−*
Bituminous coal	−*	a	a	−*	−*	−*	−*	−*	−*	−*
Metal	−*	a	a	−*	−*	−*	o	−*	−*	−*
Oil & gas	o	−*	−*	o	o	o	o	o	o*	o
Other	−*	a	a	−*	−*	o	+	−*	+	−*
Manufacturing										
Food & tobacco	o	−*	o	o	o	o*	+	+	+	+
Textile & leather	o	−*	+	−*	−*	+	+	−*	+	−*
Constr. mat. & furn.	−*	−*	−*	−*	−*	−*	+	−*	+	−*
Paper	o	a	a	+	+	+	+	+	+	+
Printing	+	−*	−*	+	+	+	+	o	+	+
Metal	o	−*	−*	o*	o	o	+	+	+	−*
Chemical	+	−*	o	+	+	+	o	o	o	+
Misc. & rubber	o	−*	−*	−*	−*	−*	+	+	+	−*
Construction	−*	o	o	−*	−*	−*	−*	−*	−*	−*
Transp. & other pub. util.	+*	a	a	−*	−*	+	o*	+	o	o*
Elec. light & power	−*	a	a	+	+*	+	+	+	+	+*
Mfd. gas	o+	a	a	o*	o*	+	+	+	+	+
Steam rr., Pull., & exp.	−*	a	a	−*	−*	−*	−*	+	−*	+
Street rwy.	−*	a	a	−*	−*	−*	−*	−*	−*	−*
Water transportation	−*	a	a	a	a	a	a	−*	−*	−*
Pipe lines	−*	a	a	+	+	+	o	+	+	+*
Telephone	++	a	a	+	o*	+	o*	+	+	+*
Telegraph	o+	a	a	+	+	o	a	−*	a	o*

Trade	o	+	o	o	o	o	o	o	o	o +
Finance										
Banking	+	*	*	*	*	•	•	•	•	+ + +
Insurance	-	+	+	+	+	+	+	+	+	o +
Real estate	+	a	*	a	+	o	+	+	+	+
Service										
Professional	-	a	+	+	+	+	+	+	+	* + + -
Personal	+	a	a	a	a	a	a	a	a	*
Domestic	a	a	a	a	a	a	a	a	a	+
Misc.	-	a	a	a	a	a	a	a	a	* + + +
Government										
Federal	+	a	+	+	*	a	*	+	+	* + + + + +
State	a	a	a	a	*	a	*	+	o	-
County	+	a	a	a	*	a	+	+	o	+
City incl. pub. education	+	a	a	a	*	a	+	+	+	+
Miscellaneous	+	+	*	+	+	+	+	-	o	+

CLASSIFICATION A   BY CHARACTER OF PRODUCTIVE FUNCTION

Commodity producing	-	-	o	-	-	-	o	o	o
Commodity transp. & distr.	+	*	*	+	+	+	+	+	+
Services	+	+	+	+	+	+	+	o	+

CLASSIFICATION C   BY TYPE OF BUSINESS ORGANIZATION

With large proportion of individual firms	o	o	o	o	o	o	o	o	o
Private corp.	-	*	-	-	-	-	-	o	-
Semi-public corp.	*	a	*	+	a	a	a	a	a
Public	+	a	+	+	+	•	o	o	+

* See note to Table 14. An entry of 'a' signifies that the corresponding type of income is either absent, has not been estimated, or is less than 0.1 per cent of the countrywide total.

nating a significant change), or has an asterisk (designating a
large change), we find that the shares of anthracite coal, bituminous coal, textiles and leather, miscellaneous and rubber
manufacturing, steam railroads, Pullman, and express, and
street railways declined consistently. The shares of electric
light and power, pipe lines, and state, county, and city subdivisions of government rose. Thus of 42 major and minor industrial divisions and 7 categories in Classifications A and C, the
shares of only 11 in national income and all its components
rose or declined consistently. Naturally enough, these 11 are
the industries whose shares in national income rose or declined
most over the period.

b) In some industries an increase or lack of change in their
shares in wages and salaries is accompanied by a decrease in
their shares in either entrepreneurial withdrawals or net income or both: oil and gas, food and tobacco, printing, chemicals, and trade (col. 1, 2, and 3). In other industries the movements are in the same direction, but the change over the period
in their shares in entrepreneurial withdrawals and net income
is algebraically smaller than in wages and salaries: total manufacturing, textile and leather, construction materials and furniture, metal, miscellaneous and rubber manufacturing, professional, personal, and miscellaneous service. The major
factor in these differences is the declining relative importance
of unincorporated firms. The greater decrease in the share of
entrepreneurial withdrawals in oil and gas, various branches
of manufacturing, trade, and some divisions of direct service
industries than in other industries in which unincorporated
firms predominate is due to the more rapidly diminishing scope
of the noncorporate form of organization in these fields. On
the other hand, for agriculture, the one industry in which unincorporated firms predominate and in whose relative importance no notable reduction occurred, the change in its share in
entrepreneurial withdrawals or net income is algebraically
greater than in wages and salaries.

c) Because in most industries wages and salaries (including

or excluding other compensation of employees) are so much greater than either entrepreneurial withdrawals or net income, the industrial distributions of total service income and of wages and salaries are similar; consequently, changes over the period in them are also similar. When we compare columns 4 and 5 with column 1 we find divergence in sign for merely a few industries: oil and gas, food and tobacco, paper, trade, and, naturally enough, the category of industries in Classification C in which unincorporated firms predominate.

d) Changes in the industrial distributions of dividends and interest are divergent (col. 6 and 7). In oil and gas, total manufacturing, construction materials and furniture, paper, metal manufacturing, total finance, real estate, and direct service industries a decline or no movement in their shares in dividends is accompanied by a rise in their shares in interest. In anthracite coal, metal mining, and steam railroads a decline in their shares in dividends is accompanied by a less notable decline (or absence of decline) in their shares in interest. In printing and chemicals a rise in their shares in dividends is accompanied by a much more pronounced rise in their shares in interest. On the other hand, in a few but important industries the change in their shares in dividends is algebraically greater than in their shares in interest: agriculture, food and tobacco, construction, total transportation and public utilities, telephone, and miscellaneous.

These divergent changes over the period in the industrial distributions of dividends and interest arise from several factors. In many industries one or both of these income types are so small that changes in the industry shares in the country-wide totals are likely to be erratic: e.g., the share of agriculture in dividends and of service industries in both. In industries in which dividends were much more severely affected by the depression of the 1930's, even changes over the period would reveal the greater decline (or smaller rise) in their shares in dividends compared with their shares in interest. In other industries fixed interest indebtedness may have been reduced and replaced by dividend paying stocks.

e) Because of the divergence in changes in the industrial distributions of these two types of property income, and the shift in their relative weight, changes in the industrial distribution of dividends and interest combined are unlike those in either. The inclusion under property income of rent and its assignment to real estate cause another big difference. Since rent declined much more than interest and dividends the algebraic value of the change in all industries except real estate is raised, i.e., any decline in their shares in total property income is reduced and any increase, augmented (col. 8 and 9).

f) Perhaps the most interesting comparison is between changes in the industrial distributions of service income (col. 4 and 5) and property income (col. 8 and 9). In oil and gas, other mining (non-metal mines and quarries), total manufacturing, food and tobacco, metal manufacturing, transportation and other public utilities, and water transportation a decline in their shares in service income is accompanied by a rise or absence of decline in their shares in interest and dividends combined. In chemicals, manufactured gas, telephone, and service an absence of decline or a rise in their shares in service income is accompanied by a distinct or greater rise in their shares in dividends and interest combined. Industries in which changes in their shares in service income exceed algebraically the changes in their shares in dividends and interest combined are chiefly in the finance and government groups.

Since for most industries the change in their shares in property income including rent is algebraically greater than in their shares in property income made up of dividends and interest alone, the conclusions drawn from comparing columns 4 and 5 with column 8 are strengthened in the comparison with column 9. In the preponderant majority of cases the decrease in the share of an industry in total service income is accompanied by a smaller decrease (or no decrease, or an increase) in its share in total property income; and an increase in its share in total service income is often accompanied by a larger increase in its share in total property income. The notable exceptions are textiles and leather, miscellaneous and rubber manufacturing, total finance and its subgroups, and total and federal government.

g) In Classification A the shares of commodity producing industries in wages and salaries combined, entrepreneurial withdrawals and net income, and in both totals of service income decline. Their shares in dividends and in property income including rent rise, but their share in interest declines slightly. The shares of commodity transporting and distributing industries in all totals except entrepreneurial withdrawals and property income including rent decrease; those of service industries in all except dividends and property income including rent increase.

h) In Classification C the shares in the various totals of industries in which unincorporated firms predominate change only slightly. The one significant decrease is in their share in property income including rent. The industries in which private corporations predominate account for decreasing shares in service income and its components, and for a relatively unchanging share in property income (but an increasing share in property income including rent). The semi-public industries account for a decreasing share in wages and salaries, and surprisingly enough, for an increasing share in entrepreneuriaı net income; but their share in the latter countrywide total is so slight that the increase is of no moment. The shares of gov ernment behave most consistently, increasing over the period in the various type of income totals (except interest) to which government contributes.

Table 16 shows clearly that a decline or rise in the share of an industry in national income or aggregate payments does not necessarily mean a similar change in the relative importance of that industry as a source of wages and salaries, of entrepreneurial income, or of property income. This conclusion is not unexpected. That an industry whose share in national income decreases may yet have an increasing share in total wages and salaries or dividends is not a matter for surprise. For even if the composition of national income by type were to remain constant, i.e., even if the percentage share in national income of wages and salaries, entrepreneurial income, dividends, etc., were to remain exactly the same over the period, the direction and magnitude of industry shares might still diverge because of changes in the relative importance of various types of income within each industry. For example, if the share of wages and salaries in national income were to remain constant, a decrease in its share and an increase in the share of dividends in net income originating in manufacturing could cause a decrease in the share of manufacturing in total wages and salaries, an increase in its share in total dividends, and either movement in its share in national income. Such shifts within industries are common because of changes in the organization of an industry, in the composition of its productive resources (between direct labor and capital), and in its disbursement policy with respect to types of income. If, in addition to these shifts within industries, we consider that the relative distribution of national income by type of income or payment also changed, the reasons for divergence in the movement of the shares of one and the same industry in various countrywide type of income totals become abundant.

If we were to treat the type of income composition of national income as constant, changes in the industrial distribution of national income (or of aggregate payments) would be different from those in Table 14. If the industrial composition of the various countrywide type of income totals changed similarly, changes in the type of income composition of national income could not affect changes in its industrial composition; i.e., shifts in the type of income composition would mean changing weights, all applied to one and the same series of figures measuring changes in the industrial composition of the various type of income totals. But the differences among columns in Table 16 mean that, if the distribution of national income or aggregate payments by type of income or payment changed, their industrial composition would also be affected. For example, since the share of manufacturing in wages and salaries declined, and that in interest rose, a shift in the composition of national income in favor of interest, reducing the share of wages and salaries, would raise algebraically the change in the share of manufacturing in national income.

If we assumed that the percentage distribution of national income by type of income remains constant, we could calculate changes in its industrial distribution, allowing the industrial distribution of each type of income total to vary from year to year. But this assumption is unrealistic: there is no discernible mechanism in society that either consciously or unconsciously operates to hold the distribution of national income by type constant.[7] Nor is the industrial distribution of an income type a sufficiently realistic concept to be worth pushing far: all people receiving entrepreneurial income from various industries hardly constitute a homogeneous group. We therefore considered it unnecessary to carry out laborious calculations in order to derive an industrial distribution of national income or of aggregate payments, on the assumption of constancy over the period in their relative distributions by type.

4 Changes during Business Cycles

The brevity of the period covered, the time unit used, the crude and approximate character of the estimates for some of the industry type of income cells—all bar detailed analysis of cyclical fluctuations in the income flows. Yet we can perhaps answer a few questions concerning their cyclical behavior, and

[7] Some mechanisms of this type may be evolving. The attempt of governments to maintain the purchasing power of the farming population relative to that of urban may be interpreted as an effort to hold the ratio of entrepreneurial income in farming constant relative to all other components of national income. The relief policy of the government is essentially an attempt to maintain the relative share of wages. But these attempts are for much narrower groups than those in our type of income or payment classification. With the detailed estimates in Volume II any student willing to formulate the assumptions and undertake the labor involved, can make the necessary calculations.

take advantage of the comprehensiveness of the estimates to study areas for which more adequate data are not yet available.

How do the income totals of various types that originate in the various industries of the nation change during business cycles? Do they rise during expansions, decline during contractions, and do their rates of movement decline from expansion to contraction? If they rise and decline in fair conformity with expansions and contractions in the nation's economy at large, do some rise or decline more than others?

With the help of reference cycle dates established in the National Bureau's study of business cycles, we determined the direction of change in the income totals during each expansion and contraction, and the sign of the differential movement, i.e., the difference in the rate of change *per year* between each expansion and the following contraction. An increase was credited with + 1; a decline, with — 1; no movement, with 0. Then the scores were added algebraically for the five expansions, the five contractions, and the five differential movements, i.e., the five differences in the annual rate of movement between an expansion and the following contraction. Thus, if an income total originating in a given industry rose during each expansion, its score is + 5; if it rose in four and declined in one, its score is + 3; if it rose in three, declined in one, and failed to change in one, its score is + 2; if it rose in three and declined in two, its score is + 1; and similarly for the behavior during the five contractions and cycles. A plus or minus sign indicates the direction of the preponderant number of changes in a given income during the reference periods.

The scores can, of course, range from — 5 to + 5, with every intervening integer and 0. However, for net income originating in each industry, 5 and 3 predominate, and 1 and 0 are rare, the values and signs indicating that net income originating in each industry tends to increase during expansions, decrease during contractions, and that its differential movement is negative (Table 17, col. 1, 3, and 5). Such scores suggest consistent positive conformity to business cycles.

TABLE 17

Direction of Movement during Business Cycles in Totals and
Percentage Shares of Net Income Originating in
Industrial Divisions, 1919–1938

	EXPANSION		CONTRACTION		DIFFERENTIAL	
	Total value	Percent-age share	Total value	Percent-age share	Total value	Percent-age share
	(1)	(2)	(3)	(4)	(5)	(6)
Agriculture	+3	−3	−3	−3	−5	+1
Mining	+5	+3	−5	−5	−5	−5
Anth. coal	+1	−3	−3	+1	−3	+3
Bit. coal	+3	+3	−5	−5	−5	−3
Metal	+5	+5	−5	−5	−5	−5
Oil & gas	+5	+5	−5	−3	−5	−5
Other	+3	+3	−3	−3	−5	−5
Manufacturing	+5	+3	−5	−5	−5	−5
Food & tobacco	+3	−1	−1	+3	−3	+3
Text. & leather	+1	−1	−3	−1	−3	+1
Constr. mat. & furn.	+5	+1	−5	−5	−5	−5
Paper	+5	+3	−3	−3	−5	−5
Printing	+5	+1	−1	+5	−5	+5
Metal	+5	+5	−5	−5	−5	−5
Chemical	+5	+3	−1	−3	−5	−5
Misc. & rubber	+5	+1	−3	−3	−5	−3
Construction	+5	+1	−3	−1	−5	−3
Transp. & other pub. util.	+5	+1	−5	−1	−5	+1
Elec. light & power	+5	+3	+1	+5	−5	+5
Mfd. gas	+3	−1	+1	+5	−3	+3
Steam rr., Pull., & exp.	+5	−3	−5	−3	−5	−1
Street rwy.	+1	−3	−5	+1	−5	+5
Water transp.	+3	−1	−3	−1	−3	−1
Pipe lines	+5	+3	−1	+3	−3	+1
Telephone	+5	+1	+1	+5	−5	+5
Telegraph	+5	−1	−3	+1	−5	+2
Trade	+3	−3	−5	−1	−5	+1
Finance	+5	−3	+1	+5	−1	+5
Banking	+5	+1	−1	+3	−1	+3
Insurance	+5	−1	+3	+5	−1	+5
Real estate	+3	−3	+1	+5	−1	+5
Service	+5	+1	−1	+5	−5	+3
Government	+5	−1	+1	+5	−5	+3
Miscellaneous	+5	+3	−1	+3	−5	+1
Total	+5		−3		−5	

Lack of such conformity to expansions or contractions is associated in part with pronounced long term rises or declines in the totals. We noted in the preceding section that the shares in national income of anthracite coal, textiles and leather, and street railways declined markedly over the period. Since national income in current prices also declined, the drop in these shares must have meant an even more marked decline in the totals in current prices. But it is these three industries that have the lowest score for rises during expansions (col. 1). Similarly, among the industries whose scores for contractions are algebraically greater than — 5 or — 3 there are many whose shares in national income, as shown in the preceding section, rose markedly over the period: food and tobacco, printing, chemicals, electric light and power, manufactured gas, pipe lines, telephones, total finance, banking, real estate, the direct service industries, government. Because of this effect of longer term movements on conformity to either expansions or contractions, the 'purest' indicator of behavior during business cycles is the score for the direction of the differential movement: a long term movement would affect approximately equally changes during an expansion and the following contraction, and should, therefore, have little effect on the difference.

When the effects of long term changes during expansions and contractions are reduced the income totals conform better (col. 5). Of the 35 entries in columns 1, 3, and 5 respectively, there are 24 maximum entries in column 1, only 11 in column 3, and 25 in column 5. Of the ten industries whose score in column 5 is algebraically greater than — 5, four are finance and its three subdivisions, industries that are either not too responsive to business cycles (such as insurance) or are susceptible to cycles different in timing from those characterizing general business conditions (real estate). Of the other six exceptions, four are purely consumer goods industries: anthracite coal, food and tobacco, textiles and leather, manufactured gas. On the other hand, industries that conform most consistently during expansion, contraction, and the full cycle (i.e., + 5 in

col. 1, — 5 in col. 3, and — 5 in col. 5) are chiefly those concerned with the production or transportation of industrial raw
materials or durable goods—total mining, metal mining, oil
and gas, total manufacturing, construction materials and furniture, metal manufacturing, and steam railroads.

While the entries in columns 1, 3, and 5 reveal the movement
of the totals, they do not indicate whether some industries rise
more or less than others during expansions; whether they decline more or less than others during contractions; or whether
their differential movements are greater than those of others.
Such differences in amplitude of conforming fluctuations could
be ascertained by directly computing for each income series its
changes in terms of the average value for the reference cycle:
the change from trough to peak dates, from peak to trough
dates, and the change in the rate of movement from expansion
to contraction. However, since we already had percentage distributions of the countrywide totals by industrial branches, we
approximated the differential amplitude of conforming fluctuations without going through the laborious direct computations.

Given a percentage distribution of an income total by industrial source, we can study the movements of the *percentages*
during expansions, contractions, and full cycles. If the *percentage* share of an industry in national income increases
during an expansion, the relative increase in net income originating in it is greater than the relative increase in national income (or decline in the former less than the decline in the latter). If the *percentage* share decreases, the underlying total
increases less or decreases more, relatively, than the countrywide total to which the percentage is related. Knowing from
columns 1, 3, and 5 in Table 17 that national income increases
during each expansion, decreases during four of the five contractions, and that its differential movement is negative in each
cycle, we also know how to interpret the movements in the percentage shares in this total. But whatever the movement of the
countrywide total to which the percentage shares are related,

an *increase* in the percentage share of an industry during expansions means that the total originating in it is more responsive to cyclical expansions than the countrywide total of all industries and we describe it below as a conforming movement or fluctuation of wider amplitude than in the countrywide total; that a *decrease* in the percentage share of an industry during contractions means greater responsiveness to cyclical contractions, i.e., a conforming movement of wider amplitude than in the countrywide total; and that a negative differential movement (as compared with the countrywide total) means greater responsiveness of the percentage share of a given industry to the change in the rate of activity that is associated with a complete business cycle.[8]

We therefore scored the movements of the percentage shares of various industries during expansions, contractions, and full cycles in a fashion exactly analogous to that used to record the movements of the totals (Table 17, col. 2, 4, and 6).

The entries in columns 2 and 4, for expansions and contractions, are affected by longer term changes, in this case in the percentage shares rather than in the totals themselves. When such changes are pronounced, it is the differential movement that reveals most clearly behavior during business cycles (col. 6). The industries in whose net incomes conforming fluctua-

[8] It must be emphasized that changes in percentage shares are used here to study only greater or less responsiveness to business cycles. A statement that an income flow X exhibits conforming movements of a wider amplitude than income flow Y does not mean, therefore, that the cyclical fluctuations characterizing X are of wider amplitude than those in Y. It means only that during reference cycle phases for which a rise in the rate of economic activity is assumed, the change in X is algebraically greater than in Y (although this change itself may be either a rise or decline); and that during reference cycle phases or swings for which a decline in the rate of economic activity is assumed, the change in X is algebraically smaller than in Y. This meaning of the expression 'conforming movements' or 'fluctuations' and of their amplitude must be kept in mind in the discussion here and in Chapter 6.

However, since most income totals show fairly high positive conformity to business cycles, a conforming movement during reference expansions does denote a rise in most cases; and during contractions or in the differential movement over the whole cycle, it frequently does denote a decline.

tions are consistently of wider amplitude than in national income are total mining, metal mining, oil and gas, 'other' mining, total manufacturing, construction materials and furniture, paper, metal manufacturing, and chemicals—a list that includes most of the industries known to reflect business cycles most sensitively because of their concern with industrial materials and durable products. The industries in whose net incomes conforming fluctuations are consistently of narrower amplitude than in national income are anthracite coal, food and tobacco, textiles and leather, printing, total transportation and public utilities, electric light and power, manufactured gas, street railways, pipe lines, telephones, telegraph, trade, finance and its various subdivisions, direct service industries, and government. The list includes consumer goods industries and industries the character of whose very organization makes their incomes less sensitive to business cycles.

Table 17 presents the full set of measures for the industrial components and percentage shares of national income only. We now consider changes during business cycles in the industrial components and percentage shares of other countrywide income totals, such as aggregate payments, wages and salaries, and entrepreneurial net income, emphasizing the behavior of income totals in their origin in the various industries, and deferring analysis of the cyclical behavior of various types of income to Chapter 6.

A IN INCOME TOTALS

Totals of income originating in the various industries (Table 17, col. 1, 3, and 5) moved in consistent conformity with business cycles: a preponderant number of entries were + 3 or + 5 for expansion, — 3 or — 5 for the differential movement. The same conformity is largely true of business savings, payments to individuals, wages and salaries, and other income types.

Since we cannot attribute much significance to the difference between + 5 and + 3 or — 5 and — 3, we classified the two positive entries as expressing conformity of movement during

TABLE 18

Industrial Divisions and Types of Income whose Totals Fail to Conform to Business Cycles, 1919–1938

FAIL TO RISE DURING EXPANSIONS

NET INCOME (1)	CORP. & GOV. SAVINGS (2)	TOTAL PAY. TO INDIVIDUALS EXCL. ENTREP. SAVINGS (3)	WAGES & SALARIES (4)	ENTREPRENEURIAL NET INCOME (5)	DIVIDENDS (6)	INTEREST (7)	PROPERTY INCOME INCL. RENT (8)
Anth. coal	Text. & leather	Anth. coal	Anth. coal	Manufacturing	Agriculture	Agriculture	Agriculture
Text. & leather	Misc. & rubber	Street rwy.	Street rwy.	Food & tobacco	Anth. coal	Mining	Anth. coal
Street rwy.	Construction	Fed. gov.	Fed. gov.	Text. & leather	Transp. & other pub. util.	Anth. coal	Transp. & other pub. util.
	Street rwy.			Misc. & rubber	Mfd. gas	Bit. coal	Mfd. gas
	Trade			Construction	Pipe lines	Metal	Steam rr.
	Finance			Elec. lt. & power	Telephone	Manufacturing	Street rwy.
	Banking			Trade	Telegraph	Food & tob.	Pipe lines
	Insurance					Text. & leather	Telegraph
	Real estate					Paper	Finance
	Service					Printing	Insurance
						Chemical	Real estate
						Misc. & rubber	Fed. gov.
						Construction	
						Mfd. gas	
						Steam rr.	
						Street rwy.	
						Water transp.	
						Pipe lines	
						Telephone	
						Trade	
						Insurance	
						Service	
						Fed. gov.	

FAIL TO DECLINE DURING CONTRACTIONS

Food & tobacco	Bit. coal	Anth. coal	Anth. coal	Oil & gas	Agriculture	Mining	Agriculture
Printing	Food & tobacco	Printing	Printing	Construction	Anth. coal	Anth. coal	Anth. coal
Chemical	Construction	Transp. & other	Elec. lt. & power	Finance	Other mining	Bit. coal	Other mining
Elec. lt. & power	Mfd. gas	pub. util.	Mfd. gas	Insurance	Food & tob.	Metal	Food & tobacco
Mfd. gas	Street rwy.	Elec. lt. & power	Telephone	Service	Printing	Oil & gas	Printing
Pipe lines	Finance	Mfd. gas	Finance	Professional	Metal mfg.	Other	Metal mfg.
Telephone	Banking	Pipe lines	Banking	Miscellaneous	Construction	Manufacturing	Construction
Finance	Real estate	Telephone	Insurance		Transp. & other	Food & tob.	Transp. & other
Banking	Service	Finance	Real estate		pub. util.	Text. & leather	pub. util.
Insurance	Government	Real estate	Service		Elec. lt. & power	Constr. mat. &	Elec. lt. & power
Real estate		Service	Professional		Mfd. gas	furn.	Mfd. gas
Service		Government	Personal		Steam rr.	Paper	Steam rr.
Government		Federal	Domestic		Pipe lines	Printing	Pipe lines
Miscellaneous		State	Misc.		Telephone	Metal	Telephone
		County	Government		Telegraph	Chemical	Telegraph
		City	Federal		Trade	Misc. & rubber	Trade
		Miscellaneous	State		Finance	Construction	Finance
			County		Banking	Transp. & other	Banking
			City		Insurance	pub. util.	Insurance
			Miscellaneous		Service	Elec. lt. & power	Real estate
					Miscellaneous	Mfd. gas	Service
						Steam rr.	Government
						Water transp.	State
						Pipe lines	County
						Telephone	City
						Telegraph	Miscellaneous
						Trade	
						Finance	
						Real estate	
						Service	
						Government	
						State	
						County	
						City	
						Miscellaneous	

TABLE 18 (concl.)

NET INCOME (1)	CORP. & GOV. SAVINGS (2)	TOTAL PAY. TO INDIVIDUALS EXCL. ENTREP. SAVINGS (3)	WAGES & SALARIES (4)	ENTREPRENEURIAL NET INCOME (5)	DIVIDENDS (6)	INTEREST (7)	PROPERTY INCOME INCL. RENT (8)
				RATE OF MOVEMENT FAILS TO DECLINE FROM EXPANSION TO CONTRACTION			
Finance	Text. & leather	Anth. coal	Anth. coal	Text. & leather	Agriculture	Agriculture	Anth. coal
Banking	Mfd. gas	Mfd. gas	Telephone		Anth. coal	Mining	Food & tobacco
Insurance	Telegraph	Pipe lines	Finance		Construction	Anth. coal	Construction
Real estate	Finance	Telephone	Banking		Transp. & other pub. util.	Bit. coal	Transp. & other pub. util.
	Banking	Finance	Real estate		Elec. lt. & power	Metal	Elec. lt. & power
	Insurance	Banking	Prof. service		Mfd. gas	Manufacturing	Mfd. gas
	Real estate	Real estate	Misc. service		Steam rr.	Food & tob.	Steam rr.
		Government	Government		Pipe lines	Text. & leather	Street rwy.
		Federal	Federal		Telephone	Constr. mat., & furn.	Pipe lines
		State	State		Banking	Printing	Telephone
		County	County		Insurance	Metal	Telegraph
		City	City		Miscellaneous	Chemical	Finance
						Misc. & rubber	Banking
						Construction	Insurance
						Transp. & other pub. util.	Real estate
						Elec. lt. & power	Fed. gov.
						Mfd. gas	State
						Steam rr.	County
						Street rwy.	City
						Water transp.	Miscellaneous
						Pipe lines	
						Telephone	
						Telegraph	

INTEREST (concl.) (7)

Trade
Finance
Insurance
Real estate
Service
Fed. gov.
State
County
City
Miscellaneous

expansions, the two negative entries as expressing conformity during contractions and conformity to the expected change in the differential movement. Applying this criterion to the scores established for various type of income totals originating in the different industries, we find that in the overwhelming majority they conform. We therefore present in Table 18 the industries in which they do not conform. A score of less than + 3 for expansion, or algebraically greater than — 3 for contraction and for the differential movement indicates lack of conformity.

Anthracite coal, textiles and leather, and street railways are conspicuous in that several of the type of income totals originating in them fail to conform during expansions. For other industries in the table, only one or two income types are listed, but even these industries, such as the federal government, agriculture, and finance, belong to the group that does not reflect sensitively fluctuations in general business activity.

The type of income totals of more industries fail to conform consistently to contractions, partly because of their upward trend in several industries, partly because of the relative brevity of most expansions during the period (of the five expansions, four last just one year when dated on an annual basis). But the list is again dominated by consumer goods industries, such public utilities as are insensitive to transient changes in business conditions, and government.

Among the industries whose type of income totals fail to conform in differential movement most consistently are anthracite coal, manufactured gas, telephones, construction, finance and its three subdivisions, and government.

Table 18 is by major and minor industrial divisions, not by the categories of Classifications A and C. Even so, it includes relatively few industries. Indeed, the more important evidence it provides is not the specific industries whose type of income totals fail to conform to business cycles, but rather the brevity of the list. For comprehensive totals such as net income, total payments, wages and salaries, entrepreneurial net income, and some of the narrower but sensitive income types such as corporate savings and dividends, the industries failing to follow consistently cyclical swings in general business activity are few. For interest alone, a type relatively insensitive to business cycles, is the list of industries failing to conform long.

For the categories of the broader industrial classifications it is practicable to go further and present the actual measures of the direction of movement of the income totals during expansions, contractions, and full cycles (Table 19). We include Classification B, since the apportionment of the mixed group would not greatly affect the short term cyclical changes in the totals for the non-durable and durable groups whereas differences in the cyclical behavior of these two groups are prominent.

There is a general tendency toward high conformity, the entries for expansions being preponderantly either + 5 or + 3; for contractions, either — 5 or — 3; and for the differential movement, either — 5 or — 3. The differences in the scores among the various groups also are as we would expect, especially if we take into account the long term changes that characterize the income totals in the various industrial categories. Thus the score for the commodity producing group during expansions is in general higher than those for the commodity transporting and distributing group and for the service industries. Since this is true under conditions of smaller increase or greater decline over the period in the income totals originating in the commodity producing industries their closer conformity during expansions is all the more significant. Similarly, during contractions commodity producing industries have a more consistently negative score, which may partly be due to the lower rate of their movement over the period. In the most telling comparison, that for the differential movement, commodity producing industries have the highest conformity in accordance with expectations based on general knowledge.

In Classification B durable product industries conform better than non-durable industries during contractions and dur-

TABLE 19

Direction of Movement during Business Cycles in Income Totals Originating in Broad Industrial Divisions, 1919–1938

	NET INCOME (1)	CORP. & GOV. SAVINGS (2)	TOTAL PAY. TO INDIVIDUALS EXCL. ENTREP. SAVINGS (3)	WAGES & SALARIES (4)	ENTREP. NET INCOME (5)	DIVIDENDS (6)	INTEREST (7)	PROP. INCOME INCL. RENT (8)
EXPANSION								
Classification A By Character of Productive Function								
Commodity producing	+5	+3	+5	+5	+3	+5	+3	+5
Commodity transp. & distr.	+3	+3	+5	+5	+1	+3	+1	+3
Services	+5	+3	+5	+5	+3	+3	+3	+3
Classification B By Durability of Product								
Non-durable	+3	+3	+5	+5	+3	+5	+3	+5
Durable	+5	+3	+5	+5	+1	+5	+1	+5
Classification C By Type of Business Organization								
With large proportion of individual firms	+3	−1	+5	+5	+3	+5	+3	+3
Private corp.	+5	+3	+5	+5	+3	+5	−1	+5
Semi-public corp.	+5	+3	+5	+5	+5	+1	+1	+3
Public	+5	+3	+5	+3			+5	+5
Total	+5	+5	+5	+5	+3	+5	+3	+5
CONTRACTION								
Classification A By Character of Productive Function								
Commodity producing	−5	−5	−5	−5	−3	−3	+3	−3
Commodity transp. & distr.	−5	−5	−3	−5	−3	−1	+3	−1
Services	−1	−1	+3	+1	−1	+1	+1	+1
Classification B By Durability of Product								
Non-durable	−1	−5	−1	−1	−3	−3	+1	+1
Durable	−5	−5	−5	−5	−3	−1	−1	−1
Classification C By Type of Business Organization								
With large proportion of individual firms	−3	−3	−1	−1	−3	−1	+1	+1
Private corp.	−5	−5	−5	−5	−5	−3	+1	−3
Semi-public corp.	−1	−5	−1	−1	−1	−1	+3	+1
Public	+1	−1	+5	+5			+1	+1
Total	−3	−5	−1	−3	−3	−3	+1	+1
DIFFERENTIAL MOVEMENT								
Classification A By Character of Productive Function								
Commodity producing	−5	−5	−5	−5	−5	−5	+3	−5
Commodity transp. & distr.	−5	−3	−5	−5	−3	−3	+1	−1
Services	−5	−5	−3	−1	−5	−3	−1	−3
Classification B By Durability of Product								
Non-durable	−5	−3	−3	−3	−5	−5	+1	−3
Durable	−5	−5	−5	−5	−5	−5	−1	−5
Classification C By Type of Business Organization								
With large proportion of individual firms	−5	−3	−5	−5	−5	−5	+1	−1
Private corp.	−5	−5	−5	−5	−5	−5	+3	−5
Semi-public corp.	−5	−3	−5	−5	−3	−1	+3	−1
Public	−5	−5	+3	+3			−3	−3
Total	−5	−5	−5	−5	−5	−5	+1	−3

ing the complete cycle; but there is no evidence of their more consistent conformity during expansions.

In Classification C government naturally conforms least consistently to cyclical changes. Of the other three groups, industries in which private corporations predominate (mining and manufacturing) conform most consistently; there seem to be no significant differences in conformity between industries in which unincorporated firms are still numerous and those in which semi-public corporations predominate.

Because of the generally high conformity of the totals and the crudity of the measures, merely the most striking instances of failure to rise and decline in unison with the rate of general economic activity are revealed by the consistency with which the *totals* conform. To detect the industries whose incomes rise or decline in conformity with business cycles at a more or less rapid rate than the countrywide income totals we must study the percentage shares.

B   IN PERCENTAGE SHARES OF VARIOUS INDUSTRIES

How shares of various industries in national income change during business cycles has already been discussed in connection with Table 17. We now consider their shares in other countrywide income totals (Table 20). For the sake of brevity, Table 20 is confined to measuring the consistency of the differential movement in the shares of industries in such countrywide totals as themselves conform adequately to business cycles during the entire period. It was observed in Table 19 that national income, aggregate payments, wages and salaries, entrepreneurial net income, and dividends all conform perfectly in their differential movements, whereas property income including rent has a score of — 3. Hence any departure from conformity in all except the last column of Table 20, i.e., any score that is algebraically greater than — 5, indicates that the component in question failed in at least one business cycle to decline from expansion to contraction as much as the total for all industries in the country. Similarly, an entry algebraically

TABLE 2 0

Direction of Differential Movement during Business Cycles in Percentage Shares of Industrial Divisions in Countrywide Income Totals, 1919–1938

	NATIONAL INCOME	AGG. PAY. TO INDI- VIDUALS	WAGES & SAL- ARIES	ENTREP. NET INCOME	DIVI- DENDS	PROP. INCOME INCL. RENT
	(1)	(2)	(3)	(4)	(5)	(6)
Agriculture	+1	+3	−1	−1	+3	+3
Mining	−5	−5	−5	−5	−1	−5
Anthracite coal	+3	+3	+3	−4	+1	+3
Bituminous coal	−3	−3	−3	−5	+1	−5
Metal	−5	−5	−5	−3	−1	−3
Oil & gas	−5	−5	−3	−5	+1	−3
Other	−5	−5	−3	−5	+3	−5
Manufacturing	−5	−5	−3	−3	−5	−5
Food & tobacco	+3	+5	+5	−1	+3	+1
Text. & leather	+1	−3	−1	−1	−1	−3
Constr. mat. & furn.	−5	−5	−5	−5	−5	−5
Paper	−5	−5	−3	−5	−1	−3
Printing	+5	+1	+5	−1	−1	−3
Metal	−5	−5	−5	−5	−3	−3
Chemical	−5	−5	−5	−5	+1	−5
Misc. & rubber	−3	−5	−3	−3	−3	−5
Construction	−3	−5	−5	−1	−1	−3
Transp. & other pub. util.	+1	+3	+3	−5	+5	+5
Elec. light & power	+5	+5	+3	+5	+3	+1
Mfd. gas	+3	+5	+5		+5	+3
Steam rr.	−1	−1	−1		+1	+3
Street rwy.	+5	+5	+5		+3	+3
Water transp.	−1	−1	+1	−5	−3	−3
Pipe lines	+1	+3	+3		+3	+3
Telephone	+5	+5	+5		+5	+3
Telegraph	+2	−3	+1		+1	+1
Trade	+1	+3	+3	+3	+1	−3
Finance	+5	+3	+5	+5	−1	+3
Banking	+3	+5	+5		+5	+3
Insurance	+5	+5	+5	+5	+1	+1
Real estate	+5	+3	+3		−3	+3
Service	+3	+5	+5	+3	−1	−1
Professional			+5	+1		
Personal			+5	+3		
Domestic			+1			
Misc.			+1	+3		
Government	+3	+5	+5			−1
Federal		+5	+5			−1
State		+5	+5			+1
County		+5	+5			+3
City		+5	+5			+3
Miscellaneous	+1	+5	+3	+3	+3	+3

greater than — 5 in the last column means that the income total in question failed in at least one business cycle to decline as much as (or rose more than) total property income. Relative intensity of change during business cycles is thus gauged in Table 20 by the negative score: the smaller the score (algebraically) the wider the amplitude of conforming fluctuations recorded for income flows in a given industry during business cycles, *wider in comparison with other industry entries in the same column.*

Keeping in mind that comparisons of scores among industries should be within rather than among columns, i.e., vertically among the rows, we group the industries according to the amplitude of their conforming fluctuations during business cycles: wide (score — 5 or — 3), narrow (score + 5 or +3), or an amplitude not significantly different from those for the respective countrywide income totals (scores from — 2 to + 2). We first use as a basis of classification the entries for national income and aggregate payments (excluding all savings of enterprises); then the two large components of national income: wages and salaries and property income. In the first classification we place an industry among those showing wide amplitude if the score for its share in national income or aggregate payments does not rise above — 3 (algebraically); in the second classification, if the score for its share in wages and salaries or property income is either — 5 or — 3; and likewise for the placing of industries in the narrow amplitude or intermediate groups.

The two groupings are similar. In general, industries whose incomes display conforming fluctuations of widest amplitude during business cycles are extractive, manufacturing, or construction, industries concerned with the production of industrial raw materials and durable commodities. Among the industries whose incomes fluctuate more than the countrywide totals, there is not one from other than the commodity producing category. On the other hand, industries whose incomes are distinctly less variable in conformity with business cycles

DISTRIBUTION BY INDUSTRIAL SOURCE 207

Classification of Industries by the Movement of Their Shares in Countrywide Income Totals

AMPLITUDE OF CONFORMING FLUCTUATIONS
DURING BUSINESS CYCLES

WIDER THAN FOR THE COUNTRYWIDE TOTAL	NARROWER THAN FOR THE COUNTRYWIDE TOTAL	INTERMEDIATE

IN NATIONAL INCOME AND/OR AGGREGATE PAYMENTS
(EXCLUDING SUBDIVISIONS OF GOVERNMENT)

Mining	Anthracite coal	Agriculture
Bituminous coal		
Metal	Food & tobacco	Text. & leather
Oil & gas		Printing
Other	Elec. light & power	
	Mfd. gas	Transp. & other pub. util.
Manufacturing	Street rwy.	Steam rr.
Constr. mat. & furn.	Telephone	Water transp.
Paper		Pipe lines
Metal	Finance	Telegraph
Chemical	Banking	
Misc. & rubber	Insurance	Trade
	Real estate	
Construction		Miscellaneous
	Service	
	Government	

IN WAGES AND SALARIES AND PROPERTY INCOME INCLUDING RENT
(INCLUDING SUBDIVISIONS OF GOVERNMENT)

Mining	Anthracite coal	Agriculture
Bituminous coal		
Metal	Transp. & other pub. util.	Food & tobacco
Oil & gas	Mfd. gas	Text. & leather
Other	Street rwy.	Printing
	Pipe lines	
Manufacturing	Telephone	Elec. light & power
Constr. mat. & furn.		Steam rr.
Paper	Finance	Water transp.
Metal	Banking	Telegraph
Chemical	Real estate	
Misc. & rubber		Trade
	County gov.	
Construction	City incl. pub. educ.	Insurance
	Misc.	Service
		Government
		Federal
		State

than the countrywide totals are largely consumer goods industries producing non-durable goods; or private or public service
industries. The group with intermediate amplitude of conforming fluctuations comprises industries concerned with both
producer and consumer goods, such as printing, trade, steam
railroads, and water transportation; and industries whose incomes while having cycles of their own, do not fluctuate in
close conformity to cycles in general business conditions (agriculture).

The differential movements established for the major and
minor industrial divisions in Table 20 determine the differences in variability among the categories of Classifications A,
B, and C. In Table 21 these differences are measured directly,
as are also the movements during expansions and contractions.
The greater variability in conformity with business cycles of
income flows from commodity producing industries stands out
clearly. They rise more than those from other industries during
expansions; decline more than those from other industries
during contractions; and of course their differential movement
is greater. The only exception is their share in entrepreneurial
net income during expansions, possibly because of the non-
conforming movement in farmers' net income. The shares of
the commodity transporting and distributing industries in the
various income types vary more in conformity with business
cycles than do those of the service industries.

An even greater contrast in amplitude of conforming movement during business cycles is presented by the non-durable
and durable goods industries. The latter uniformly rise more
than the countrywide totals during expansions, uniformly
decline more during contractions, and their differential movement is greater. The non-durable goods industries rise less
during expansions than the countrywide totals, decline less during contractions, and their differential movement is smaller.
But this narrower amplitude of fluctuation in income flows
from non-durable goods industries is not so consistent as the
wider amplitude of conforming fluctuations in the durable.

TABLE 21

Direction of Movement during Business Cycles in Percentage Shares of Broad Industrial Divisions in Countrywide Income Totals, 1919–1938

	NATIONAL INCOME (1)	AGG. PAY. TO INDIVIDUALS (2)	WAGES & SALARIES (3)	ENTREP. NET INCOME (4)	DIVIDENDS (5)	PROP. INCOME INCL. RENT (6)
EXPANSION						
Classification A By Character of Productive Function						
Commodity producing	+3	+3	+1	−3	+5	+5
Commodity transp. & distr.	−3	−1	−3	−3	−3	−1
Services	−3	−3	−1	+1	+1	−3
Classification B By Durability of Product						
Non-durable	−5	−5	−3	+1	+1	−3
Durable	+5	+5	+5	+1	+5	+5
Classification C By Type of Business Organization						
With large proportion of individual firms	−5	−3	+3	0	+3	−5
Private corp.	+5	+5	+3	−1	+3	+5
Semi-public corp.	+1	−1	−3	+1	−5	+1
Public	−1	−3	−1			−1
CONTRACTION						
Classification A By Character of Productive Function						
Commodity producing	−5	−5	−5	−1	−5	−3
Commodity transp. & distr.	−1	−1	+1	−1	+1	−1
Services	+5	+5	+5	+3	+3	+3
Classification B By Durability of Product						
Non-durable	+5	+3	+5	+1	−1	+1
Durable	−5	−5	−5	−1	−1	−3
Classification C By Type of Business Organization						
With large proportion of individual firms	+5	+3	+3	+5	−1	+1
Private corp.	−5	−5	−5	−5	−5	−5
Semi-public corp.	+5	+5	+3	+5	+5	+5
Public	+5	+5	+5			+1
DIFFERENTIAL MOVEMENT						
Classification A By Character of Productive Function						
Commodity producing	−5	−5	−5	−1	−5	−5
Commodity transp. & distr.	+1	+1	+1	+3	+5	+3
Services	+5	+5	+5	+3	+3	+5
Classification B By Durability of Product						
Non-durable	+5	+5	+5	−3	−1	+5
Durable	−5	−5	−5	−3	−3	−5
Classification C By Type of Business Organization						
With large proportion of individual firms	+5	+5	+1	+5	+1	+3
Private corp.	−5	−5	−5	−5	−5	−5
Semi-public corp.	+5	+3	+3	+5	+5	+5
Public	+3	+5	+5			−1

The public category is distinguished by the failure of its income flow to respond to business cycles with as wide an amplitude as the countrywide totals. Industries in which private corporations predominate are at the other extreme: the income flows from them fluctuate in conformity with business cycles much more than the countrywide totals. Income flows from the other two groups in Classification C, industries in which unincorporated firms are still numerous and semi-public industries, tend to increase less than the countrywide totals during expansions, decrease less during contractions, and have a smaller differential movement. No significant differences in the amplitude of conforming movements during business cycles between the two groups can be observed on the basis of Table 21.

5 Summary

All statements below concerning the industrial distribution of income are for totals in current prices.

a) From 1919 to 1938 commodity producing industries accounted on the average for two-fifths of national income, aggregate payments, and wages and salaries, a somewhat larger share of entrepreneurial income, and a smaller share of property income. Industries concerned with commodity transporting and distributing accounted for one-fifth of national income and aggregate payments, a somewhat larger share of wages and salaries, and a smaller share of entrepreneurial and property income. The service industries accounted for the remaining two-fifths of national income and aggregate payments, a somewhat larger share of property income, and smaller shares of wages and salaries and of entrepreneurial income.

b) Industries that could be directly classified as producing preponderantly durable goods accounted on the average for 14 per cent of national income and of aggregate payments, a larger share of wages and salaries, for only 3 to 4 per cent of entrepreneurial income, and for 8 per cent of property income (including rent). Industries that could be directly classified as producing non-durable goods accounted for 43 to 44 per cent of national income and of aggregate payments, a somewhat smaller share of wages and salaries, a much larger share of entrepreneurial income, and a somewhat larger share of property income. With the addition of durable products from the mixed group, industries producing durable goods would perhaps account for not much more than one-fifth of national income or aggregate payments.

c) Industries in which unincorporated firms are still numerous accounted on the average for over half of national income and aggregate payments; those in which private corporations predominate, for 23 per cent, those in which semi-public corporations predominate, for 13 per cent, and government, for 11 to 12 per cent. The shares of these broad groups in the component income totals vary somewhat, but the distributions of wages and salaries and of property income tend to be roughly similar to those of national income and aggregate payments.

d) The industries whose shares in national income, aggregate payments, and *all* the component income totals declined over the period are anthracite coal, bituminous coal, textiles and leather, miscellaneous and rubber manufacturing, steam railroads, Pullman, and express, and street railways. The industries whose shares in *all* the comprehensive and component income totals rose are electric light and power, pipe lines, state, county, and city divisions of the government. In all other industries a rise or decline of shares in some countrywide income totals was accompanied by a decline or rise of shares in other totals. But if only national income and aggregate payments are considered, a significant decline occurred in the shares of the following industries (in addition to those listed above): agriculture, total mining, metal mining, 'other' mining, total manufacturing, construction materials and furniture, metal manufacturing, contract construction, water transportation, total finance, and real estate. The industries (in addition to those listed above) whose shares in national income and aggregate payments rose significantly are manufactured gas, telephones, insurance, total service, total government (and all its subdivisions), and miscellaneous.

e) The shares of commodity producing industries in national income, aggregate payments, and some important component income totals decreased over the period, 1919–1938, as did those of commodity transporting and distributing industries, although not so much. The shares of service industries increased. The share of commodity producing industries in aggregate payments excluding entrepreneurial savings decreased also from 1909–18 to 1919–28, although not so markedly as from 1919–28 to 1929–38; that of commodity transporting and distributing industries increased from the first to the second decade, and decreased only from the second to the third; and that of service industries increased from 1909–18 to 1919–28, although not so markedly as from 1919–28 to 1929–38.

f) In national income, aggregate payments, and some component totals the shares of the two groups in Classification C in which unincorporated firms or private corporations predominate declined during the two recent decades; those of semi-public industries did not change significantly; and those of public industries rose markedly. In aggregate payments excluding entrepreneurial savings the decline in the share of industries with many unincorporated firms and the rise in the share of public industries characterized also the change from 1909–18 to 1919–28; but the shares of the other two groups (private and semi-public corporations) did not move consistently.

g) The divergence in movement among shares of one industry in countrywide income type totals arises from changes in the relative importance of the income types within industries and of total net income originating in the different industries. For most industries or industrial groups a decrease or increase in their shares in national income or in aggregate payments cannot be interpreted as a decrease or increase in their shares in each component—wages and salaries, entrepreneurial income, dividends, and interest.

h) Total net income and the income type totals originating

in the different industries fluctuate, on the whole, in close conformity with business cycles. The industries whose income type totals fail significantly to conform are anthracite coal, manufactured gas, telephones, contract construction, total finance and its subdivisions, and government. These are industries producing consumer goods, or so organized as to be unresponsive to transient changes in economic conditions, or having cycles of their own. The list of industries failing significantly to conform is longest for the industrial distribution of interest, a countrywide total itself insensitive to business cycles.

i) Income totals of various types originating in the broader industrial groups conform well to business cycles, showing the expected differences in degree. Incomes originating in the commodity producing group fluctuate in greater conformity than those originating in either the commodity transporting and distributing or service group; incomes originating in durable goods industries, than those originating in non-durable; incomes originating in industries in which private corporations predominate, than those originating in the other industry groups in Classification C.

j) Incomes originating in various industries differ greatly in the amplitude of their conforming fluctuations during business cycles. Wide amplitudes of conforming fluctuations characterize such commodity producing industries as are concerned with industrial raw materials and durable products (total mining, bituminous coal, metal mining, oil and gas, 'other' mining, total manufacturing, construction materials and furniture, metal manufacturing, chemicals, miscellaneous and rubber manufacturing, contract construction). Narrow amplitudes characterize industries concerned exclusively with consumer goods of the non-durable type or the more rigidly organized industries unresponsive to business cycles (anthracite coal, food and tobacco, electric light and power, manufactured gas, total finance and its subdivisions, government and some of its subdivisions). In the group with intermediate amplitudes of conforming fluctuations are agriculture, steam railroads, trade, and telegraph, industries concerned with both consumer and producer goods or having cycles of their own.

k) Differences in amplitude of conforming fluctuations during business cycles appear again among incomes originating in the broad industrial groups. Incomes originating in commodity producing industries have much wider amplitudes than those originating in either the commodity transporting and distributing or service group. Incomes originating in durable goods industries have an even greater excess of amplitude over those originating in non-durable. Finally, incomes originating in industries in which private corporations predominate fluctuate in conformity with business cycles with a wider amplitude than incomes originating in any other group in Classification C.

CHAPTER 6

Distribution by Type of Income

1 Annual Distribution of National Income
OUR CLASSIFICATION of income by type (Table 22) reflects several principles or bases of distinction. First, there is the separation of income flows that are actual payments to ultimate income recipients from items that are accruals, i.e., of income payments from savings of enterprises. There is the further differentiation among the factors of production whose compensation the various types of income represent—labor, capital, and enterprise. Employee compensation may thus be taken to represent compensation of labor; dividends and interest, of capital; net savings, of enterprise; and entrepreneurial withdrawals or income, of all three, with labor preponderant. Finally, there is a third aspect of the classification relevant to income payments alone: its significance in differentiating among groups of income recipients at different average income levels. Wages are, by and large, the major source of income to the lowest income groups, while salaries are the major return to groups with distinctly higher average incomes. Dividends and interest, especially the former, are a major source of income to the high income groups. Entrepreneurial withdrawals are between the extremes represented by wages and dividends. In some industries entrepreneurial income constitutes the major return to groups whose average income is not much higher than that of wage earners; in others, it is high enough to raise the per capita income of entrepreneurs well above the average for the salaried group.

TABLE 22

National Income[1] and its Percentage Distribution by Type of Income, 1919–1938

A TOTALS (billions of dollars)

	WAGES & SALARIES (1)	OTHER PAY. TO EMPL. (2)	ENTREPRENEURIAL Withdr. (3)	ENTREPRENEURIAL Savings (4)	RENT (5)	DIVIDENDS[2] (6)	INTEREST (7)	CORP. NET SAVINGS (8)	GOV. NET SAVINGS (9)	NATIONAL INCOME (10)
1919	36.7	0.43	11.8	5.5	4.0	2.9	3.2	1.0	—1.3	64.2
1920	43.3	0.57	13.5	1.6	4.3	3.2	3.7	2.2	1.9	74.2
1921	34.9	0.60	10.3	0.63	4.5	3.0	3.9	0.71	0.96	59.4
1922	36.4	0.60	10.8	—0.09	4.9	3.0	4.0	0.23	0.85	60.7
1923	42.7	0.62	11.3	1.2	5.2	3.8	4.2	0.97	1.6	71.6
1924	42.7	0.62	11.9	0.87	5.6	3.8	4.4	0.42	1.7	72.1
1925	44.4	0.61	12.5	1.6	5.5	4.4	4.6	0.83	1.6	76.0
1926	47.4	0.62	12.5	2.1	5.1	4.7	4.7	2.3	2.2	81.6
1927	47.8	0.65	12.6	1.1	5.1	5.1	4.9	0.56	2.3	80.1
1928	48.7	0.66	12.9	0.91	4.9	5.5	5.3	0.92	1.9	81.7
1929	51.5	0.69	13.4	1.1	4.9	6.3	5.6	1.5	2.2	87.2
1930	47.0	0.73	12.8	—0.64	4.3	6.0	5.7	—0.67	2.1	77.3
1931	39.6	0.88	11.2	—2.0	3.0	4.6	5.7	—3.1	0.34	60.3
1932	30.7	0.98	9.7	—3.5	2.1	3.0	5.5	—4.8	—0.91	42.9
1933	28.2	1.9	9.0	—2.4	2.1	2.5	5.0	—4.0	—0.11	42.2
1934	32.1	2.8	9.1	—0.35	1.9	3.0	4.8	—3.3	—0.58	49.5
1935	35.0	2.9	9.5	0.23	2.1	3.8	4.6	—2.1	—1.7	54.4
1936	38.9	3.9	10.1	1.2	2.2	4.8	4.6	—0.71	—2.2	62.9
1937	43.5	4.0	11.2	0.44	2.6	4.9	4.7	—1.4	0.50	70.5
1938	39.7	4.7	11.1	0.27	2.6	3.5	4.6	—0.70	—0.18	65.5

B PERCENTAGE SHARES OF COMPONENTS

1919	57.2	0.68	18.4	8.5	6.2	4.5	5.0	1.6	—2.0	100.0
1920	58.4	0.77	18.2	2.1	5.8	4.3	4.9	3.0	2.6	100.0
1921	58.8	1.0	17.3	1.1	7.5	5.0	6.5	1.2	1.6	100.0
1922	60.0	0.99	17.8	—0.15	8.1	5.0	6.6	0.38	1.4	100.0
1923	59.6	0.86	15.8	1.6	7.2	5.4	5.9	1.4	2.2	100.0
1924	59.2	0.86	16.6	1.2	7.8	5.3	6.1	0.58	2.4	100.0
1925	58.4	0.80	16.4	2.1	7.2	5.8	6.0	1.1	2.1	100.0
1926	58.1	0.76	15.3	2.5	6.3	5.8	5.8	2.8	2.6	100.0
1927	59.7	0.81	15.8	1.3	6.3	6.3	6.2	0.70	2.9	100.0
1928	59.6	0.81	15.8	1.1	6.0	6.7	6.5	1.1	2.3	100.0
1929	59.1	0.79	15.3	1.2	5.6	7.2	6.4	1.8	2.6	100.0
1930	60.8	0.94	16.5	—0.83	5.5	7.8	7.4	—0.86	2.7	100.0
1931	65.6	1.5	18.6	—3.4	5.0	7.7	9.5	—5.1	0.57	100.0
1932	71.6	2.3	22.7	—8.1	4.9	7.0	12.8	—11.1	—2.1	100.0
1933	66.8	4.4	21.4	—5.6	5.0	5.9	11.9	—9.5	—0.27	100.0
1934	64.8	5.6	18.4	—0.71	3.8	6.1	9.8	—6.6	—1.2	100.0
1935	64.3	5.4	17.5	0.43	3.9	6.9	8.5	—3.9	—3.2	100.0
1936	61.8	6.2	16.1	2.0	3.5	7.7	7.3	—1.1	—3.5	100.0
1937	61.7	5.7	15.9	0.62	3.7	7.0	6.7	—2.0	0.70	100.0
1938	60.6	7.1	16.9	0.41	3.9	5.3	7.0	—1.1	—0.27	100.0

¹ Includes Social Security contributions of employers and is adjusted for the effects on net savings of corporations and other business firms of gains and losses from sales of capital assets; of inventory revaluations; and of the use of cost rather than reproduction basis for depreciation charges. In all other tables in this chapter the unadjusted series excluding Social Security contributions of employers is used.
² Includes balance of international payments.

T A B L E 22 (concl.)

C PERCENTAGE SHARES OF SUBTOTALS OF COMPONENTS

	EMPL. COMP.	ENTREP. INCOME	SERVICE INCOME		PROP. INCOME		AGGREGATE PAYMENTS	
			Excl. entrep. savings	Incl. entrep. savings	Incl. rent	Excl. rent	Excl. entrep. savings	Incl. entrep. savings
	(1)	(2)	(3)	(4)	(5)	(6)	(7)	(8)
1919	57.8	26.9	76.2	84.7	15.7	9.5	91.9	100.4
1920	59.1	20.3	77.3	79.4	15.0	9.3	92.3	94.4
1921	59.8	18.4	77.1	78.2	19.0	11.5	96.1	97.2
1922	61.0	17.6	78.7	78.6	19.6	11.6	98.4	98.2
1923	60.5	17.4	76.3	78.0	18.4	11.2	94.8	96.4
1924	60.1	17.8	76.7	77.9	19.2	11.4	95.8	97.0
1925	59.2	18.6	75.6	77.8	19.0	11.8	94.7	96.8
1926	58.9	17.8	74.2	76.7	17.9	11.6	92.0	94.6
1927	60.5	17.1	76.3	77.6	18.8	12.5	95.1	96.4
1928	60.4	16.9	76.2	77.3	19.2	13.2	95.4	96.5
1929	59.9	16.6	75.2	76.4	19.3	13.6	94.5	95.7
1930	61.8	15.7	78.3	77.5	20.7	15.1	99.0	98.1
1931	67.1	15.2	85.7	82.3	22.2	17.2	107.9	104.5
1932	73.8	14.6	96.5	88.4	24.7	19.9	121.3	113.2
1933	71.2	15.8	92.6	87.1	22.7	17.7	115.4	109.8
1934	70.4	17.7	88.8	88.1	19.7	15.9	108.5	107.8
1935	69.7	17.9	87.2	87.6	19.4	15.5	106.6	107.1
1936	68.1	18.1	84.2	86.1	18.5	15.0	102.7	104.6
1937	67.4	16.5	83.3	84.0	17.3	13.7	100.7	101.3
1938	67.8	17.3	84.6	85.1	16.3	12.3	100.9	101.3

As explained in Chapter 2 (Sec. 3), our classification does not follow faithfully any of the principles mentioned. Even in separating actual payments from an accrual item such as net savings, there is considerable blurring, not only because it is difficult to separate entrepreneurial withdrawals from net savings, but also because the estimates of dividends and interest include portions that do not reach the ultimate income recipients directly but are credited to their accounts in insurance companies, savings banks, and similar 'associations of individuals'. In differentiating among payments to various production factors the classification also leaves much to be desired, if only because it includes entrepreneurial income, which necessarily includes compensation of more than one production factor, as a single category. Moreover, employee compensation includes some items, such as payments to principal corporation executives, that can hardly be considered reward for labor alone; and dividends are presumably a mixture of a 'pure' return on capital with some return to enterprise. Finally, the classification by type is obviously defective as a grouping of returns to recipients at significantly different average income levels. Employee compensation is paid to some people with high incomes; a substantial portion of interest goes to low income groups; while entrepreneurial incomes are scattered among people in income groups at diverse levels.

These defects can be partly overcome by a cross-classification of income types with the several industrial divisions, and by a segregation, whenever data are available, of principal corporation officers' salaries. Even with these refinements, the distribution by type still retains some weaknesses, stemming from the institutional lines our estimates perforce follow. Nevertheless, it does reflect, if sometimes obscurely, various bases: temporal differences in levels in the distribution within industries roughly approximate differences between payments and net savings, among compensation of various production factors, and among payments to groups of recipients at significantly different average income levels.

As in the distribution by industrial source, we discuss the distribution by type of income largely in percentage terms. Conversion to percentages eliminates the changes in the totals treated in Chapter 4, and reveals more clearly the relative importance of various production factors and of payments to groups receiving incomes of varying size and description. In Table 22 B and C the percentages are of national income alone, and are adequate for a preliminary study of the distribution by type. But subsequently we discuss the distribution of aggregate payments by type as well. The chief reason for basing a percentage distribution on aggregate payments is that in measuring the relative importance of payments to various groups it is the distribution of aggregate payments, not of national income, that is desired. Net savings of enterprises, especially of corporations and of other non-personal organizations, cannot be assigned to any one group of income recipients; and if they are considered, as perhaps they should be, of equal relative importance to the fortunes of all income recipients attached to an industry, their percentage distribution becomes identical with that of aggregate payments. Since we have two variants of aggregate payments, one including and the other excluding entrepreneurial savings, we have two variants of the percentage distribution. In both, net savings are taken into account and, like all types of payments, expressed as percentages of aggregate payments.

The distribution in Table 22 B reveals obvious shifts in the percentage shares in national income. The share of wages and salaries rises; that of other employee compensation rises even more, reflecting the marked increase in work and other relief payments in the 1930's and the inclusion of Social Security contributions of employers. The share of entrepreneurial withdrawals declines, as do the shares of entrepreneurial net savings and rent. The share of dividends rises, and that of interest, even more. The shares of corporate and government net savings decline.

These categories, the most detailed in the distribution of

national income by type, are combined into broader divisions in Table 22 C. The share of total employee compensation, a sum of wages, salaries, and other compensation, rises markedly. The share of entrepreneurial income, a sum of withdrawals and savings, declines markedly. Total service income, a sum of compensation of employees and of entrepreneurs, seems to rise in relative importance, although not markedly when entrepreneurial savings are included. The share of property income excluding rent rises markedly; but when rent is included, the rise becomes negligible. Aggregate payments, whether including or excluding entrepreneurial savings, are smaller than national income during the first decade and larger during the second—a direct reflection of the fact that net savings of enterprises were positive during the 1920's and negative during the 1930's.

The shares of these various components in aggregate payments may behave quite differently from their shares in national income. Furthermore, analysis of the percentage distribution of any income flow cannot be confined to the comprehensive totals. We now consider the distribution within each division of the nation's productive system and attempt to survey its aspects in a manner similar to that followed in the analysis by industrial source. First, the average distribution for the entire period is examined; next, changes over the period; finally, changes during business cycles.

2 Average for the Period

Table 23 presents distributions of net income originating for the country as a whole and for individual industries, based upon the arithmetic means of the totals for 1919–38. Similar distributions could be presented for total payments including or excluding entrepreneurial savings, but since for the period as a whole they would differ little from the distributions of net income, we omit them.

In Table 23 rent is included in property income under real estate largely because it cannot be allocated by industrial divi-

TABLE 23

Net Income Originating in Industrial Divisions, Percentage Distribution by Type, Based on Average Values for 1919–1938

	EMPL. COMP.	ENTREPRENEURIAL Withdr.	ENTREPRENEURIAL Net income	DIVIDENDS	INTEREST	PROP. INCOME INCL. RENT	AGG. PAY. TO INDIV. EXCL. ENTREP. NET SAVINGS	NET SAVINGS OF Corp. & gov.	NET SAVINGS OF All enterprises
	(1)	(2)	(3)	(4)	(5)	(6)	(7)	(8)	(9)
Agriculture	16.4	80.6	76.9	0.27	6.4	6.6	103.7		−3.7
Mining	94.4	1.6	1.6	14.9	2.7	17.6	113.6	−13.6	−13.6
Manufacturing	83.0	2.4	2.7	12.9	1.1	14.0	99.4	0.24	0.56
Food & tobacco	72.3	6.5	6.6	17.5	2.0	19.6	98.4	1.5	1.6
Text. & leather	90.7	3.4	3.9	7.0	0.22	7.2	101.3	−1.8	−1.3
Constr. mat. & furn.	89.4	2.3	2.8	8.9	0.81	9.7	101.4	−1.9	−1.4
Paper	82.1	0.88	1.2	11.8	2.8	14.5	97.5	2.1	2.5
Printing	85.7	3.6	4.4	7.4	0.74	8.2	97.4	1.8	2.6
Metal	83.5	0.52	0.74	13.1	0.95	14.0	98.0	1.8	2.0
Chemical	66.2	1.3	1.5	33.1	2.5	35.7	103.2	−3.4	−3.2
Misc. & rubber	84.4	1.6	1.8	11.5	1.7	13.2	99.1	0.64	0.86
Construction	84.7	12.9	13.8	1.4	0.30	1.7	99.4	−0.24	0.65
Transp. & other pub. util.	70.1	0.08	0.10	13.3	13.8	27.0	97.2	2.8	2.8
Elec. light & power	35.2	0.18	0.18	31.4	24.6	56.0	91.4	8.6	8.6
Mfd. gas	55.3			32.0	21.5	53.5	108.8	−8.8	−8.8
Steam rr., Pull., & exp.	77.3			6.7	13.3	20.0	97.3	2.7	2.7
Street rwy.	71.8			7.3	21.3	28.6	100.4	−0.44	−0.44
Water transp.	94.0	0.74	0.96	5.3	2.2	7.4	102.2	−2.4	−2.2
Pipe lines	29.2			63.0	1.0	64.0	93.2	6.8	6.8
Telephone	71.4			19.7	5.8	25.5	97.0	3.0	3.0
Telegraph	85 1			7.8	2.0	9.8	94.8	5.2	5.2

	1	2	3	4	5	6	7	8	9
Trade	70.0	23.2	25.3	4.7	0.45	5.1	98.3	−0.42	1.7
Finance	26.1	2.5	2.5	5.7	19.2	73.4	102.0	−2.0	−2.0
Banking	61.6		18.9	33.2		33.2	94.8	5.2	5.2
Insurance	84.0			3.6	−2.2	1.4	104.4	−4.4	−4.4
Real estate	10.3			1.8	25.9	92.4	102.7	−2.7	−2.7
Service	61.9	34.0	37.5	0.93	0.79	1.7	97.6	−1.1	2.4
Government	73.8				17.6	17.6	91.5	8.5	8.5
Miscellaneous	74.6	15.8	16.8	8.1*	7.4	15.4	105.8	−6.8	−5.8
Total	63.1	17.1	17.6	6.2*	7.1	19.0	99.2	0.31	0.82

CLASSIFICATION A BY CHARACTER OF PRODUCTIVE FUNCTION

	1	2	3	4	5	6	7	8	9
Commodity prod.	65.2	22.9	22.2	9.5	3.5	13.0	101.1	−0.40	−1.1
Commodity transp. & distr.	72.4	15.8	17.3	5.9	4.0	9.9	98.1	0.42	1.9
Services	56.7	12.4	13.6	3.3	11.8	28.8	98.0	0.90	2.0

CLASSIFICATION C BY TYPE OF BUSINESS ORGANIZATION

	1	2	3	4	5	6	7	8	9
With large proportion of individual firms	49.5	31.0	31.9	2.5	6.5	20.0	100.5	−1.4	−0.52
Private corp.	84.1	2.3	2.6	13.1	1.3	14.4	100.8	−1.0	−0.76
Semi-public corp.	70.9	2.4	2.4	14.2	10.3	24.5	97.8	2.2	2.2
Public	73.8				17.6	17.6	91.5	8.5	8.5

In those instances in which employee compensation includes 'other' payments to employees, the percentage of wages and salaries is:

Transp. and other pub. util.	68.9
Steam rr., Pull., & exp.	75.4
Telephone	70.2
Telegraph	82.6
Government	57.3
Total	61.0

CLASSIFICATION A BY CHARACTER OF PRODUCTIVE FUNCTION

Commodity transp. & distr.	71.9
Services	52.1

CLASSIFICATION C' BY TYPE OF BUSINESS ORGANIZATION

Semi-public corp.	70.0
Public	57.3

* Includes balance of international payments.

sions. Also, the subdivisions of mining were not retained: for
these five subdivisions the estimates of income other than wages
and salaries for the years before 1929 were derived by distributing the totals for the mining group in proportion to wages and
salaries. Since the percentage distribution among types of income within each subdivision of mining is not significant for
the early years in the period, Classification B, which is subject
to the difficulties mentioned in Chapter 5, is also omitted.

Employee compensation accounts, on the average, for
slightly less than two-thirds of national income. But in agriculture, electric light and power, manufactured gas, pipe lines,
and real estate its share is well below this average. These industries obviously belong to two distinct categories. In the first,
represented by agriculture and real estate, the prevailing type
of business organization is the unincorporated enterprise of
small average size or the individual property holder. Hence
entrepreneurial income or rent bulks so large in net income
originating that employee compensation must necessarily be
a relatively limited fraction. In the second, to which electric
light and power, manufactured gas, and pipe lines belong, the
dominant form of organization is corporate, and capital used in
production is so large relative to direct labor that a major portion of net income is a return on the capital invested and only a
small portion is compensation for the direct services of employees. On the other hand, in mining, textiles and leather,
construction materials and furniture, printing, water transportation, and telegraph the share of employee compensation
exceeds 85 per cent. In these industries the entrepreneur either
does not appear or plays a minor role; and the use of capital is
small relative to that of direct labor.

In agriculture, service, and trade the proportion of entrepreneurial withdrawals is above the average for the country,
17.1 per cent; in government, the public utilities, finance,
manufacturing, mining, and construction, below. We have already mentioned the industries with a large proportion of
property income. In general, industries in which entrepre-

neurs predominate, or in which the capital investment is small relative to direct labor, or in which entrepreneurs do not have to pay returns on past investment, or in which by definition there cannot be large property returns (such as insurance) have low ratios of property income to net income originating (agriculture, construction, trade, insurance, and service).

The average shares of dividends and of interest in national income are about the same, but within industries they differ markedly. In some industries, such as government and agriculture, dividends are absent or negligible, either because there are no private enterprises or because small private enterprises, for which credit without security and fixed interest obligation is impracticable, predominate. As industries approach either extreme—absence of a variable entrepreneurial revenue because of a controlled market or preponderance of small units —interest tends to constitute a relatively greater share than dividends. Public utilities, such as steam railroads, represent the first extreme; real estate, the second. On the other hand, in industries in which the private business enterprise is large and continuously active in a competitive market, the share of dividends tends to be relatively greater (mining, manufacturing).

The share of savings of enterprises for the country as a whole is, on the average, small, amounting to somewhat less than 1 per cent of national income. But the percentages vary strikingly among industries. In general, the industries that, as shown by our analysis in Chapter 5, rose in relative importance in the income structure, were the ones for which the ratio of net savings to net income was well above the average: food and tobacco, paper, printing, electric light and power, pipe lines, telephone, telegraph, service, and government. Most of the industries whose relative shares in the countrywide income totals declined were characterized by a lower than average ratio of net savings to net income originating: agriculture, mining, total manufacturing, and construction. Although not perfect, the correlation is nevertheless sufficient to suggest that the relative magnitude of net savings of enterprise is a fair index of the shift in an industry's share in national income and aggregate payments.

In Classification A the highest percentage of property income and the lowest percentage of employee compensation and entrepreneurial withdrawals are within the service industries; the commodity transporting and distributing industries are at the other extreme in these respects, except for entrepreneurial withdrawals; while the commodity producing group occupies an intermediate position. The share of dividends is highest in commodity producing industries and the share of interest lowest—the opposite being true of the service industries.

The greatest differences in the distribution by type are in Classification C. Industries in which entrepreneurs are still numerous are characterized by the largest share of entrepreneurial withdrawals, the smallest of employee compensation, and a share of property income close to that for the country as a whole. The largest share of employee compensation and the greatest dominance of dividends over interest are in industries in which private corporations predominate. In industries with a semi-public status, property income accounts for a larger proportion of income originating than elsewhere. The public category naturally does not have any entrepreneurial income or dividends.

3 Changes over the Period

A IN COMPREHENSIVE TOTALS

In studying changes in the distribution by type over the period we use averages of percentage shares free from the effects of the more transient cyclical fluctuations. As in the distribution by industrial source, we computed two sets of averages: one for the two decades, 1919–28 and 1929–38, the other for the terminal quinquennia, 1919–23 and 1934–38.

Again, as in the distribution by industrial source, our conclusions are summarized by differentiating broad classes by the sign and magnitude of the changes in the averages. A plus or minus sign indicates that the share increases or decreases and that the change is in the same direction in both the decennial and quinquennial averages; if the two sets of averages disagree in this respect, no definite direction is assigned the movement over the period and the entry is o. Changes are classified as minor if the estimates for both the decennial and the quinquennial averages rise or decline less than one-tenth of the average share for 1919–38 (denoted by o + or o —); as significant if either estimate changes more than one-tenth of the average share for the period but not more than two-fifths (denoted by + or —); and as large if either estimate changes more than two-fifths of the average share for the period (denoted by + * or — *). Table 24 demonstrates the procedure and reveals several significant shifts in the shares of various income types in each of the three comprehensive income totals.

Wages and salaries increase significantly as a share in national income, but not in aggregate payments including entrepreneurial savings, i.e., when net savings of corporations and government are omitted from the comprehensive total. When we exclude from the latter entrepreneurial savings also, the share of wages and salaries declines slightly but unmistakably. The increase in this share in any of the three comprehensive income totals is thus due largely to the increase in wages and salaries relative to that in net savings of business enterprises and government.

The share of other compensation of employees in all three comprehensive income totals, however, increases owing primarily to the introduction of relief payments and Social Security contributions in the latter part of the second decade and to the maintenance, if not increase, of other types of compensation (pensions and compensation for injury). The share of total compensation, the sum of wages and salaries and other compensation, increases as a percentage of all three comprehensive totals; but the increase from the first to the second decade in its share in aggregate payments excluding entrepreneurial savings is so small as to be insignificant.

TABLE 24 : National Income and Aggregate Payments to Individuals
Change over the Period in the Percentage Distribution by Type, 1919–1938

	PERCENTAGE OF NATIONAL INCOME			PERCENTAGE OF AGGREGATE PAYMENTS TO INDIVIDUALS					
	CHANGE FROM		DIRECTION & MAGNITUDE OF CHANGE	INCL. ENTREP. SAVINGS			EXCL. ENTREP. SAVINGS		
				CHANGE FROM		DIRECTION & MAGNITUDE OF CHANGE	CHANGE FROM		DIRECTION & MAGNITUDE OF CHANGE
	1919–28 to 1929–38	1919–23 to 1934–38		1919–28 to 1929–38	1919–23 to 1934–38		1919–28 to 1929–38	1919–23 to 1934–38	
	(1)	(2)	(3)	(4)	(5)	(6)	(7)	(8)	(9)
Wages & salaries	+6.3	+3.2	+	+0.46	−0.38	0	−1.7	−1.3	0
Other comp. of empl.	+2.8	+4.4	+*	+2.6	+4.2	+*	+2.6	+4.2	+*
Empl. comp.	+9.1	+7.6	+	+3.1	+3.8	0 +	+0.89	+2.9	0 +
Entrep. withdr.	+1.6	−0.71	0	−0.07	−1.7	0 −	−0.72	−2.0	0 −
Entrep. savings	−3.7	−1.4	−*	−3.5	−1.5	−*	−3.5	−1.7	−*
Entrep. net income	−2.0	−2.1	−	−3.6	−3.2	−	−4.2	−3.8	−
Service inc. excl. entrep. savings	+10.7	+6.9	+	+3.0	+2.1	0 +	+0.17	+0.85	0 +
Service inc. incl. entrep. savings	+7.0	+5.5	0 +	−0.51	+0.60	0	−3.3	−0.87	0 −
Dividends	+1.6	+1.7	+	+1.0	+1.4	+	+0.84	+1.3	+
Interest	+3.0	+2.0	++	+2.2	+1.6	++	+1.9	+1.5	++
Dividends & interest	+4.6	+3.7	+*	+3.2	+2.9	++	+2.8	+2.8	++
Rent	−2.2	−3.2	−*	−2.7	−3.5	−*	−2.9	−3.7	−*
Prop. income incl. rent	+2.4	+0.44	+	+0.51	−0.60	0	−0.17	−0.85	0
Corp. net savings	−7.2	−3.3	−*	−6.7	−3.4	−*	−6.6	−3.5	−*
Gov. net savings	−2.2	−2.7	−*	−2.2	−2.6	−*	−2.2	−2.6	−*
Net savings of all enterprises	−13.1	−7.3	−	−12.4	−7.5	−	−12.4	−7.9	−
Agg. pay. excl. entrep. savings	+13.1	+7.3	+	+3.5	+1.5	0 +	−3.5	−1.7	0 −
Agg. pay. incl. entrep. savings	+9.4	+6.0	0 +						
National income				−8.9	−6.0	0 −	−12.4	−7.9	−

The symbols are based upon the direction and magnitude of change in the average percentages from 1919–28 to 1929–38 and from 1919–23 to 1934–38: o means that the signs of change in the two comparisons are different; o + or o −, that the change, in the same direction for both comparisons, is in both less than 10 per cent of the average percentage for 1919–38; + or − , that the change in one or both comparisons is more than 10 per cent but less than 40 per cent of the average percentage for the period; + * or − *, that the change in one or both comparisons is more than 40 per cent of the average percentage for the period.

The share of entrepreneurial withdrawals in national income shows no definite movement but in both aggregate payments totals it decreases. Entrepreneurial savings, however, decrease drastically and constitute a decreasing share of all three comprehensive income totals. Hence, total entrepreneurial income, the sum of entrepreneurial withdrawals and savings, also accounts for a decreasing share of each.

Since employee compensation is far bigger than either entrepreneurial withdrawals or income it largely determines total service income. The share of the latter, excluding entrepreneurial savings, in all three comprehensive income totals increases, significantly as a share in national income and much less so as a share in aggregate payments. When entrepreneurial savings are included in service income, its share in national income still increases; its share in aggregate payments including entrepreneurial savings shows no definite change; and its share in aggregate payments excluding entrepreneurial savings actually decreases.

Of the three types of property income, the share of interest increases most and consistently in all three comprehensive income totals; that of dividends, somewhat less; that of rent decreases markedly. Hence total property income including rent, while accounting for an increasing share in national income, constitutes a decreasing share in aggregate payments excluding entrepreneurial savings. However, the decrease is small and is perhaps no more worth noting than the increase in the share of employee compensation from 1919–28 to 1929–38.

Since the shares of corporate, government, and entrepreneurial net savings in all three comprehensive income totals decrease markedly, the share of the combined total of net savings of all enterprises decreases markedly; and since these items of savings constitute the differences among the three comprehensive income totals, the movements of the latter are determined by these declines. The total that excludes all or any of these savings items increases relatively to the total that includes them.

For the distribution of aggregate payments excluding entrepreneurial savings we extend the analysis to 1909 by using
King's estimates (Table 25). The shares of employee compensation and of interest increase not only from 1919–28 to
1929–38 but also from 1909–18 to 1919–28, the former much
more from the first to the second decade than from the second
to the third. Likewise, the shares of entrepreneurial withdrawals and rent decline from the first to the second decade, as
they do from the second to the third, indeed much more. The
only type of payment for which such consistency of movement
is not true is dividends (and, consequently, dividends and interest): its share declines from 1909–18 to 1919–28, probably
owing to the unusually high levels it attained during the war
years 1914–18.

In Table 25 there is some suggestion of secular tendencies in
the shares of employee compensation, entrepreneurial withdrawals, interest, and rent. The rise in the share of employee
compensation and the decline in that of entrepreneurial withdrawals could be expected over long periods in view of the decrease in unincorporated firms and the corresponding increase
in corporate and other forms of organization that pay wages,
salaries, etc. The rise in the share of interest may well be associated partly with the waxing importance of industries (government, public utilities) in which this type of property income predominates; partly, for this specific historical period,
with a declining price level and the naturally greater resistance
of interest to reduction. The reason for the decline in the share
of rent is not so clear, unless it is because the main source, residential housing, is not among the rapidly developing industries.

B   IN TYPE OF INCOME TOTALS WITHIN INDUSTRIES

To determine shifts in the distribution by type within the
industrial divisions we measure shares of various components
in both net income originating and total payments. When used
as a base for this relative distribution the latter ordinarily ex-

TABLE 25

Aggregate Payments to Individuals excluding Entrepreneurial Savings

Change over the Period in the Percentage Distribution by Type

King's and Present NBER Estimates, 1909–1938

	PERCENTAGE DISTRIBUTION 1919–23		CHANGES IN PERCENTAGES				DIRECTION AND MAGNITUDE OF CHANGE [1]			
	King (1)	Present NBER (2)	1909–18 to 1919–28 (3)	1919–28 to 1929–38 (4)	1909–18 to 1929–38 (5)	1909–13 to 1934–38 (6)	1909–18 to 1919–28 (7)	1919–28 to 1929–38 (8)	1909–18 to 1929–38 (9)	1909–13 to 1934–38 (10)
Employee compensation	59.0	63.0	+8.4	+0.89	+9.3	+11.9	+	0+	+	+
Entrep. withdrawals	21.8	18.5	−5.8	−0.72	−6.5	−7.7	−	0−	−	−
Service income	80.9	81.5	+2.7	+0.17	+2.8	+4.2	0+	0+	0+	0
Dividends	4.9	5.1	−0.66	+0.84	+0.17	+0.54	−	+	0+	+
Interest	4.3	4.5	+0.23	+0.89	+1.1	+0.85	0+	+	0	+
Dividends & interest	9.2	9.6	−0.44	+1.8	+1.4	+1.4	0−	+	+	+
Rent [2]	9.9	8.9	−2.2	−1.9	−4.1	−5.6	−	−	*−	*−
Property income incl. rent	19.1	18.5	−2.7	−0.17	−2.8	−4.2	−	0−	−	−

[1] See note to Table 24.
[2] Sum of rent received by individuals, imputed rent, and interest in the real estate industry.

clude entrepreneurial savings, but for the few industries in
which unincorporated firms are numerous and the inclusion of
entrepreneurial savings might affect the distribution, additional entries, with total payments including entrepreneurial
savings as base, are given. The conclusions are summarized in
Tables 26–29 by the symbols signifying positive and negative,
and minor, significant, and large changes.

In mining, various subdivisions of manufacturing, construction, and steam railroads we can separate wages from salaries
(Table 26). In other industries the combined total alone can
be studied. In the former there are significant differences in
the movement of the shares of wages and salaries in both net
income originating and total payments. As shares in net income originating, wages rise in textiles and leather, construction materials and furniture, paper, and miscellaneous and
rubber manufacturing; but as shares in total payments, they
decline except in textile and leather manufacturing, in which
they rise slightly. The share of salaries in both net income
originating and total payments rises in most industries: in net
income originating it declines in food and tobacco alone; and
in total payments it declines only in food and tobacco and
chemical manufacturing. Comparison of wages and salaries industry by industry indicates that the share of salaries in both
net income originating and total payments either increases
more or declines less in all industries except food and tobacco.

We can now test the showing of Table 24—that the share of
wages and salaries in national income increased, whereas in
aggregate payments excluding entrepreneurial savings it declined; and that the share of employee compensation in both
totals rose—by observing whether similar movements occurred
in each industry in Table 26.

The shares of wages and salaries and of employee compensation in net income originating do increase in total manufacturing, some of its subdivisions (textile and leather, construction
materials and furniture, paper, printing, and miscellaneous
and rubber), and in street railways, water transportation,

TABLE 26

Employee Compensation, Direction and Magnitude of Change * over the Period in its Share in Net Income and Total Payments, by Industrial Divisions, 1919–1938

| | SHARE IN NET INCOME | | | | SHARE IN TOTAL PAYMENTS EXCL. ENTREPRENEURIAL SAVINGS | | | |
| | Wages | Salaries | Wages & salaries | Empl. comp. | Wages | Salaries | Wages & salaries | Empl. comp. |
	(1)	(2)	(3)	(4)	(5)	(6)	(7)	(8)
Agriculture	a	a	—	—	a	a	—	—
Mining	o	+*	o	o	—	+	o—	o—
Manufacturing	o	+	+	+	o—	+	o—	o—
Food & tobacco	o—	—	—	—	o—	—	o—	o—
Text. & leather	+	+	+	+	o+	o+	o+	o+
Constr. mat. & furn.	+	+*	+	+	o—	+	o—	o—
Paper	o+	+	+	+	o—	+	o+	o+
Printing	o	+	o+	o+	—	+	o	o
Metal	o	+*	o	o	o—	+	o—	o—
Chemical	o	o	o	o	—	—	—	—
Misc. & rubber	+	+	+	+	o	+	o+	o+
Construction	o	+	o	o	—	+	—	—
Transp. & other pub. util.	a	a	—	—	a	a	—	—
Electric light & power	a	a	—	—	a	a	—	—
Mfd. gas	a	a	—	—	a	a	—	—
Steam rr., Pull., & exp.	—	+	o	o	—	+	o—	o—
Street rwy.	a	a	o+	o+	a	a	o—	o—
Water transp.	a	a	o+	o+	a	a	o—	o—
Pipe lines	a	a	—	—	a	a	—*	—*
Telephone	a	a	o—	o—	a	a	—	—
Telegraph	a	a	+	+	a	a	o+	o+
Trade	a	a	+	+	a	a	o	o
Finance	a	a	+*	+*	a	a	+*	+*
Banking	a	a	+*	+*	a	a	+	+
Insurance	a	a	o	o	a	a	o+	o+
Real estate	a	a	+*	+*	a	a	+	+
Service	a	a	o+	o+	a	a	o—	o—
Government	a	a	o	+	a	a	—	o+
Federal	a	a	a	a	a	a	—*	+
State	a	a	a	a	a	a	o+	—
County	a	a	a	a	a	a	o—	o—
City	a	a	a	a	a	a	o—	o—
Miscellaneous	a	a	+	+	a	a	o+	o+
Total	a	a	+	+	a	a	o—	o+

CLASSIFICATION A	BY CHARACTER OF PRODUCTIVE FUNCTION							
Commodity producing	a	a	o	o	a	a	o—	o—
Commodity transp. & distr.	a	a	o+	o+	a	a	o—	o—
Services	a	a	+	+	a	a	o+	+

TABLE 26 (concl.)

	SHARE IN NET INCOME				SHARE IN TOTAL PAYMENTS EXCL. ENTREPRENEURIAL SAVINGS			
	Wages	Salaries	Wages & salaries	Empl. comp.	Wages	Salaries	Wages & salaries	Empl. comp.
	(1)	(2)	(3)	(4)	(5)	(6)	(7)	(8)
CLASSIFICATION C BY TYPE OF BUSINESS ORGANIZATION								
With large proportion of individual firms	a	a	+	+	a	a	o+	o+
Private corp.	a	a	+	+	a	a	o—	o—
Semi-public corp.	a	a	o—	o—	a	a	—	o—
Public	a	a	o	+	a	a	—·	o+

Supplementary data for industries in which individual firms predominate:

	SHARE IN TOTAL PAYMENTS INCL. ENTREP. SAVINGS Employee Compensation		SHARE IN TOTAL PAYMENTS INCL. ENTREP. SAVINGS Employee Compensation
Agriculture	—	Real estate	+
Construction	o	Service	o+
Trade	o+	Miscellaneous	+

* See note to Table 24. An entry of 'a' means that the corresponding type of income is either absent, has not been estimated, or is less than 0.1 per cent of net income or total payments.

telegraph, trade, finance, service, and miscellaneous; but in several important industries (agriculture, food and tobacco, the transportation and public utility total, electric light and power, manufactured gas, telephones, and pipe lines) they decline. As shares in total payments, wages and salaries and employee compensation decline in many more industrial divisions (mining, total manufacturing and several of its subdivisions, construction, almost all the public utility subdivisions, and service). The rise in the shares of wages and salaries and of employee compensation in national income is thus not uniformly true of the distribution of net income originating for all industries; nor is the increase in the share of employee compensation in aggregate payments true of the share in total payments in most industries; and the mild decline in the share of wages and salaries in aggregate payments becomes marked in the share in total payments in several industries.

In general the shares of both wages and salaries and employee compensation tend to increase less or decline more in the commodity producing industries and the public utilities than in the comprehensive totals; and in the service industries they increase more or decline less than in the comprehensive totals. Thus in Classification A the shares in both net income originating and total payments for the service group rise more than the shares for the commodity producing and transporting and distributing groups (if the latter rise at all). In Classification C it is the semi-public group, primarily public utilities, that is characterized by declining shares of wages and salaries and of employee compensation. For the other groups in Classification C the changes in the shares in net income and total payments differ, and in the public industry group the change in the shares of wages and salaries in net income and total payments differs from that in the shares of employee compensation. The reasons for these divergences are obvious. The effect of negative business savings in the 1930's on the distribution of net income originating in the group in which private corporations predominate (i.e., mining and manufacturing) causes the share of employee compensation to rise; when we omit net savings the share in total payments declines. In the public category it is the addition of relief and other compensation that causes the share of total employee compensation to rise; the share of wages and salaries alone does not rise. Finally, if we omit net savings from income originating in the group in which unincorporated firms are still numerous, the rise in the share of employee compensation becomes smaller.

The shares of entrepreneurial withdrawals and net income in the comprehensive income totals decline; and when we examine their shares in net income originating and total payments industry by industry we find that the decline is fairly widespread (Table 27). Only in agriculture and finance do the shares of entrepreneurial income in net income originating and of withdrawals in total payments rise, and for agriculture even these rises are mild. In construction and service the share of withdrawals in total payments rises also, that in construction markedly. In all other industries in which entrepreneurial income and withdrawals exist, the component constitutes a declining share in net income originating and in total

TABLE 27

Entrepreneurial and Service Incomes, Direction and Magnitude of Change * over the Period in their Shares in Net Income and Total Payments, by Industrial Divisions, 1919–1938

	SHARE IN NET INCOME			SHARE IN TOTAL PAYMENTS EXCL. ENTREP. SAVINGS	
		SERVICE INCOME			Service income
	Entrep. income	Incl. savings	Excl. savings	Entrep. withdr.	excl. savings
	(1)	(2)	(3)	(4)	(5)
Agriculture	o +	o	o	o +	o —
Mining	— *	o	o	—	o —
Manufacturing	— *	+	+	— *	o —
Food & tobacco	—	—	—	— *	—
Textile & leather	— *	+	+	— *	o +
Constr. mat. & furn.	— *	+	+	— *	o —
Paper	— *	+	+	— *	o +
Printing	— *	o +	o +	— *	o —
Metal	— *	o	o	— *	o —
Chemical	—	o	o	— *	—
Misc. & rubber	— *	+	+	—	o +
Construction	o	o +	+	+ *	o —
Transp. & other pub. util.	a	—	—	a	—
Elec. light & power	— *	—	—	— *	—
Manufactured gas	a	—	—	a	—
Steam rr., Pull., & exp.	a	o	o	a	o —
Street rwy.	a	o +	o +	a	o —
Water transp.	—	o	o	— *	o —
Pipe lines	a	—	—	a	— *
Telephone	a	o —	o —	a	—
Telegraph	a	+	+	a	o +
Trade	—	o	+	—	o —
Finance	+ *	+ *	+ *	+ *	+ *
Banking	a	+ *	+ *	a	+
Insurance	o —	o	o	o —	o +
Real estate	a	+ *	+ *	a	+
Service	o —	o +	+	+	o —
Government	a	+	+	a	o +
Federal	a	a	a	a	+
State	a	a	a	a	—
County	a	a	a	a	o —
City incl. pub. educ.	a	a	a	a	o —
Miscellaneous	o	+	+	+	o +
Total	—	o +	+	—	o +

	SHARE IN NET INCOME			SHARE IN TOTAL PAYMENTS EXCL. ENTREP. SAVINGS	
		SERVICE INCOME			Service income
	Entrep. income	Incl. savings	Excl. savings	Entrep. withdr.	excl. savings
	(1)	(2)	(3)	(4)	(5)
CLASSIFICATION A BY CHARACTER OF PRODUCTIVE FUNCTION					
Commodity producing	o —	o	o	—	o —
Commodity transp. & distr.	—	o +	+	o	o —
Services	o —	+	+	+	+
CLASSIFICATION C BY TYPE OF BUSINESS ORGANIZATION					
With large proportion of individual firms	o —	o +	+	o	o +
Private corp.	—*	o	o	—*	o —
Semi-public corp.	+	o	o	+	o —
Public	a	+	+	a	o +

Supplementary data for industries in which individual firms predominate:

	SHARE IN TOTAL PAYMENTS INCL. ENTREPRENEURIAL SAVINGS	
	Entrepreneurial net income	Service income incl. savings
Agriculture	o +	o
Construction	o	o —
Trade	—	o —
Real estate	a	+
Service	—	o —
Miscellaneous	—	o +

* See notes to Tables 24 and 26.

payments. This is reflected in Classifications A and C where the only increase is in entrepreneurial withdrawals as a share in total payments in the service industries and as a share in both income totals in the semi-public industries (entrepreneurs in the latter are so few that the entries for this group can be discounted).

The share of service income, including or excluding entrepreneurial savings, in net income originating rises in most industries but declines in food and tobacco and several public utilities. Its share in aggregate payments rises slightly, and in total payments, declines in the majority of industries. Indeed, the increase in its share in the comprehensive total is due largely to the increase in its share in the service category; in the commodity producing and transporting and distributing categories its share declines. Thus the share of service income, like that of employee compensation and unlike that of entrepreneurial income or withdrawals, shows considerable diversity of movement, with a preponderance of declines in the several industries as a share in total payments, in contrast to its mild rise as a share in the comprehensive total.

The share of dividends in net income originating increases in most industries as well as for the country as a whole (Table 28). The few industries in which it does not—textiles and leather, paper, miscellaneous and rubber manufacturing, steam railroads, telegraph, finance and its subgroups—are, for the most part, industries that are losing weight in the industrial structure (see Ch. 5). As a share in total payments, dividends do not rise so consistently from industry to industry but the exceptions are not many more than for the share in net income originating. In all groups of Classifications A and C, except service (in which dividends are small) and public industries (in which they do not exist), the share of dividends in both net income originating and total payments rises.

The increase in the share of interest is as widespread among industries as that in the share of dividends. In the share in net income originating it does not occur in only nine industries: agriculture, food and tobacco, textiles and leather, miscellaneous and rubber manufacturing, construction, telephone, insurance, government, and miscellaneous; and in at least two, interest is a rather important item. In total payments the share of interest fails to rise in one or two more industries. But Table 28 conveys the definite impression that the pronounced rise in the share of interest in all three comprehensive totals is characteristic of most industries. In Classification C this increase in the share of interest in net income originating is absent in the public industries alone; and in its share in total payments, only in the commodity transporting and distributing group of Classification A and the public industry group of Classification C.

Since the shares of both dividends and interest in net income

TABLE 28

Property Income, Direction and Magnitude of Change * over the
Period in its Share in Net Income and Total Payments, by
Industrial Divisions, 1919–1938

	SHARE IN NET INCOME			SHARE IN TOTAL PAYMENTS EXCL. ENTREP. SAVINGS		
	Dividends (1)	Interest (2)	Dividends & interest (3)	Dividends (4)	Interest (5)	Dividends & interest (6)
Agriculture	+*	o	o	+*	o	+
Mining	+*	+*	+*	+*	+*	+*
Manufacturing	+	+*	+	+	+*	+
Food & tobacco	+*	o	+*	+*	—	+*
Text. & leather	—	—*	—	—	—*	—
Constr. mat. & furn.	+*	+*	+*	+	+*	+
Paper	o —	+*	+	—	+*	o —
Printing	+	+*	+	+	+*	+
Metal	+*	+*	+*	+	+*	+
Chemical	+*	+*	+*	+	+*	+
Misc. & rubber	o	o	o	—	o	—
Construction	+*	o .	+*	+*	o	+*
Transp. & other pub. util.	+*	+	+*	+*	+	+*
Elec. light & power	+	+	+	+	o+	+
Mfd. gas	+*	+*	+*	+	+*	+
Steam rr., Pull., & exp.	o —	+*	+	—	+	+
Street rwy.	+	+	+	+	+	+
Water transp.	+*	+*	+*	+*	+*	+*
Pipe lines	+*	+*	+*	+	+*	+
Telephone	+*	—	+*	+*	—	+*
Telegraph	—*	+*	o	—*	+*	—
Trade	+*	+*	+*	+	o	+
Finance	o	+*	+*	—	+*	+*
Banking	o	a	o	—	a	—
Insurance	—	o —	—*	—	—	—*
Real estate	o —	+*	+*	—	+*	+*
Service	+	+*	+*	o	+*	+*
Government	a	—	—	a	—	—
Federal	a	a	a	a	—*	—*
State	a	a	a	a	+*	+*
County	a	a	a	a	o+	o+
City incl. pub. educ.	a	a	a	a	+	+
Miscellaneous	+	o	o	—	—*	—
Total	+	+*	+	+	+	+

TABLE 28 (concl.)

	SHARE IN NET INCOME			SHARE IN TOTAL PAYMENTS EXCL. ENTREP. SAVINGS		
	Dividends (1)	Interest (2)	Dividends & interest (3)	Dividends (4)	Interest (5)	Dividends & interest (6)
CLASSIFICATION A BY CHARACTER OF PRODUCTIVE FUNCTION						
Commodity producing	+*	+*	+*	+*	+*	+*
Commodity transp. & distr.	+	+	+	+	o	+
Services	o	+	+	−	+	o +
CLASSIFICATION C BY TYPE OF BUSINESS ORGANIZATION						
With large proportion of individual firms	+	+*	+*	+	+	+
Private corp.	+	+*	+	+	+*	+
Semi-public corp.	+	+	+	+	+	+
Public	a	−	−	a	−	−

* See notes to Tables 24 and 26.

originating and total payments rise in most industries, the share of their combined total also rises in most industries. As all rent is assigned to real estate this sum of dividends and interest is the one total of property income that can be studied for the several industries. Thus the inclusion of rent under property income affects the distribution by type only for real estate and for groups of industries including it. The effect is of course great: whereas in real estate the share of interest and dividends together in net income originating and total payments rises markedly, total property income including rent rises slightly as a share in net income originating and declines slightly as a share in total payments.

Thus, while the share of property income including rent in aggregate payments tends to decline over the period, its share in national income and for most industries in both net income originating and total payments rises. This difference may be partly due to our inability to apportion rent among the various industries in which it may originate. Yet, compared with interest and dividends combined, rent is probably a small item in many industries, for most rent originates in connection with residential housing. It is therefore reasonable to assume that even if we could distribute rent among the industries in which it originates the share of property income in total payments in most industries would still rise, while in aggregate payments it declines—obviously because the declining property income component (rent) is concentrated in one or two industries and the rising property income components (dividends and interest) are distributed widely among industries.

We conclude the survey of changes over the period in the distribution by type within industries by observing the share of net savings in net income originating and total payments (Table 29). To complement net savings we record the share of total payments (exclusive of all net savings) in net income originating.

As a share in net income originating and total payments net savings of corporations and government decline significantly in practically all industries, industrial divisions, and Classifications A and C. The two exceptions are food and tobacco and insurance, both growing industries not too sensitive to cyclical disturbances. This widespread decline is characteristic also of net savings of all enterprises (including entrepreneurial savings).

Since the share of net savings of all enterprises in net income originating declines in practically all industries and industrial groups, the share of total payments must rise.

C EFFECTS OF INTRA- AND INTER-INDUSTRY SHIFTS

The share of any component, such as wages and salaries or entrepreneurial income, in a comprehensive income total is the product of two factors: (1) the share of the component in net income or total payments originating in each industry; (2) the share of net income or total payments originating in each industry in national income or aggregate payments. Changes in the distribution of comprehensive totals by type may, therefore, be due to changes in the distribution by type of net income or total payments originating in each industry; or, with a constant distribution by type within each industry but dif-

TABLE 29

Savings and Total Payments, Direction and Magnitude of Change [1]
over the Period in their Shares in Net Income and of Savings in
Total Payments, by Industrial Divisions, 1919–1938

	SHARE IN NET INCOME			SHARE IN TOTAL PAYMENTS EXCL. ENTREP. SAVINGS NET SAVINGS	
	NET SAVINGS		Total payments excl. entrep. savings		
	Corp. & gov.	All enterprises		Corp. & gov.	All enterprises
	(1)	(2)	(3)	(4)	(5)
Agriculture	a	o	o	a	o
Mining	—*	—*	+	—*	—*
Manufacturing	—*	—*	+	—*	—*
Food & tobacco	o	o	o	—*	o
Textile & leather	—*	—*	+	—*	—*
Constr. mat. & furn.	—*	—*	+	—*	—*
Paper	—*	—*	+	—*	—*
Printing	—*	—*	+	—*	—*
Metal	—*	—*	+	—*	—*
Chemical	—*	—*	+	—*	—*
Misc. & rubber	—*	—*	+	—*	—+*
Construction	—*	—*	+	—*	—*
Transp. & other pub. util.	—*	—*	o+	—*	—*
Electric light & power	—*	—*	o+	—*	—*
Mfd. gas	—*	—*	+	—*	—*
Steam rr., Pull., & exp.	—*	—*	o+	—*	—*
Street rwy.	—*	—*	+	—*	—*
Water transp.	—*	—*	o+	—*	—*
Pipe lines	—*	—*	+	—*	—*
Telephone	—*	—*	o+	—*	—*
Telegraph	—*	—*	+	—*	—*
Trade	—*	—*	+	—*	—*
Finance	—*	—*	o+	—*	—*
Banking	—*	—*	+*	—*	—*
Insurance	o	o	o	o	o
Real estate	—*	—*	o+	—*	—*
Service	—*	—*	+	—*	—*
Government	—*	—*	+	—*	—*
Miscellaneous	—*	—*	+	—*	—*
Total	—*	—*	+	—*	—*
CLASSIFICATION A BY CHARACTER OF PRODUCTIVE FUNCTION					
Commodity producing	—*	o	o	—*	—*
Commodity transp. & distr.	—*	—*	+	—*	—*
Services	—*	—*	+	—*	—*
CLASSIFICATION C BY TYPE OF BUSINESS ORGANIZATION					
With large proportion of individual firms	—*	—*	+	—*	—*
Private corp.	—*	—*	+	—*	—*
Semi-public corp.	—*	—*	o+	—*	—*
Public	—*	—*	+	—*	—*

Supplementary data for industries in which individual firms predominate:

	SHARE IN NET INCOME Total payments incl. entrep. savings
Agriculture	.. [2]
Construction	o +
Trade	o +
Real estate	o +
Service	o +
Miscellaneous	+

[1] See notes to Tables 24 and 26.
[2] Net income and total payments including entrepreneurial savings are identical.

ferent distributions from industry to industry, to changes in the relative importance of industries as measured by their shares in national income or aggregate payments; or to both.

As we have seen, changes in the distribution of income by type occurred over the period not only in national income and aggregate payments but also in net income and total payments originating in each industry. Yet it is not clear whether the intra-industry shifts account fully for the changes in the distribution by type of national income and aggregate payments or whether shifts in the relative importance of industries also contribute. This question is analogous to that raised in Chapter 5 (Sec. 3) where we indicate that changes in the industrial distribution could be due to changes in the industrial distribution of each component or to shifts in the relative importance of income types, or to both. We did not implement these alternatives by analysis, since it did not seem to us that the relation could be conceived as extending from the distribution of the comprehensive income total by type as a cause to the industrial distribution as an effect; nor that there were mechanisms by which efforts would be made to maintain or alter the relative distribution among income types with consequences to the distribution by industrial source. But the question concerning the effects of inter- and intra-industry shifts upon the distribution of comprehensive income totals by type does seem realistic enough to warrant further investigation.

The active units in economic life are attached to and operate within the framework of individual industries; there is inter-industry competition, i.e., conscious or unconscious attempts on the part of one industry to gain at the expense of other industries; industries differ markedly in their responses to economic conditions; given inter-industry shifts as cause, changes in the distribution by type of comprehensive income totals may well be treated as effects. Moreover, attachment to industries does give rise to significant differences among groups of income recipients, and the distribution by type within individual industries is of considerable interest.

On the basis of the analysis already carried through in the preceding sections of this chapter and Chapter 5 the simplest way to explore more directly the effects of intra- and inter-industry shifts on changes over the period in the distribution of comprehensive income totals by type is the following. We measure the change from 1919–28 to 1929–38 in the average share in national income (or aggregate payments) of the various income components. This change can be viewed as the product of the changes in the shares of each within the several industries and the changes in the shares of the respective industries in national income (or aggregate payments). But instead of weighting the change in the share of a given income type in each industry by *changes* in the shares of the respective industries in national income (or aggregate payments), we can weight them by the *average share* for 1919–38 of the respective industries, and divide the sum of the products by 100, i.e., the sum total of the weights. By this method we approximate the change from 1919–28 to 1929–38 in the share of the given income type in national income (or aggregate payments), on the assumption that the relative importance of industries remained constant over the period, i.e., that there were no shifts in the industrial distribution. If this result is subtracted from the change in the share of this income type shown in Table 24, the residual approximates the change in the share of the given income type in national income (or aggregate payments) that is due exclusively to shifts in the relative importance of various industries.

TABLE 30

Effects of Inter- and Intra-Industry Shifts upon the Change
over the Period in the Distribution of National Income
by Type, 1919–1938

	CHANGE FROM 1919–28 TO 1929–38			CHANGE FROM 1919–23 TO 1934–38		
		CHANGE DUE TO			CHANGE DUE TO	
	TOTAL CHANGE	Intra-industry shifts	Inter-industry shifts (1 — 2)	TOTAL CHANGE	Intra-industry shifts	Inter-industry shifts (4 — 5)
	(1)	(2)	(3)	(4)	(5)	(6)
Wages & salaries	+6.3	+7.7	−1.4	+3.2	+1.8	+1.4
Employee compensation	+9.1	+9.6	−0.5	+7.6	+5.0	+2.6
Entrep. withdrawals	+1.6	+2.6	−1.0	−0.71	+0.20	−0.91
Entrep. net income	−2.0	−1.4	−0.6	−2.1	−1.1	−1.0
Service income excl. entrep. savings	+10.7	+12.2	−1.5	+6.9	+5.2	+1.7
Service income incl. entrep. savings	+7.0	+8.2	−1.2	+5.5	+3.9	+1.6
Dividends	+1.6	+1.8	−0.2	+1.7	+1.5	+0.2
Interest	+3.0	+2.6	+0.4	+2.0	+1.8	+0.2
Prop. income incl. rent	+2.4	+2.9	−0.5	+0.44	+1.7	−1.3
Agg. pay. excl. entrep. savings	+13.1	+15.2	−2.1	+7.3	+6.9	+0.4
Total net savings	−13.1	−15.2	+2.1	−7.3	−6.9	−0.4
Corp. & gov. net savings	−9.4	−11.1	+1.7	−6.0	−5.5	−0.5

Columns 1 and 4 of Table 30 measure changes in shares
shown by the direct distribution of national income and are
identical with the entries in Table 24. Columns 2 and 5 were
obtained by weighting the changes for each industry (using the
most detailed industrial classification) by the average share
of the industries in national income (from Table 13) and
dividing the sum of the products by 100. The entries show
what would have been the changes in the shares of wages and
salaries, employee compensation, etc. in national income if its
industrial distribution were held constant year in, year out at
the 1919–38 average level, and if, therefore, changes in the
shares of income types in it were caused by changes in the distribution of net income by type within each industry alone.
Columns 2 and 5 thus measure the effects of *intra-industry*
shifts on changes in the distribution of national income by
type. Columns 3 and 6, obtained by subtracting columns 2 and
5 from 1 and 4, measure the effects of shifts in the industrial
composition of national income, i.e., of *inter-industry* shifts.

For the income components and their subtotals in Table 30 the conclusions concerning changes from 1919–28 to 1929–38 are clear. For all types of income, except interest and the two net savings items, the total change is algebraically smaller than the change ascribable to intra-industry shifts. This means that the shifts in relative importance among industries caused the shares in national income of all income types, except interest and net savings, to decline. In other words, industries in which the average shares of such components as wages and salaries, employee compensation, entrepreneurial withdrawals or net income, and dividends were above the countrywide average shares lost relatively to industries in which they were below. But for interest and net savings, the reverse occurred: industries in which the average shares of these two components were above the countrywide average shares gained relatively to industries in which they were below.

This conclusion can be checked by comparing the industries in Tables 23 and 14. However, correlating industries by two of their characteristics: (1) the excess or shortage of the average share of an income type in the net income originating in the various industries compared with its average share in national income; (2) the sign and magnitude of the change in the share of the industry in national income from 1919–28 to 1929–38, would mean a needless multiplication of detail and would merely demonstrate what must arithmetically follow from the differences between columns 1 and 2, Table 30. Even without such a demonstration the reason for the relations between columns 1, 2, and 3 of Table 30 is obvious. For example, a relative decline in net savings from the first to the second decade in any industry in excess of the decline for the country would reduce the weight of that industry in national income. It would tend also to give that industry a small average share of net savings in net income originating. Hence there would be positive correlation between a small share of net savings in an industry and the decline in the weight of that industry in national income; or between a large share of net savings in an industry and the increase in the weight of that industry in national income. Similarly, the industries in which the share of interest in national income is relatively large have increased in weight: government, electric light and power, manufactured gas. Obviously this increase was insufficiently offset by a decline in the shares in national income of other industries with relatively large shares of interest (steam railroads, street railways, real estate) and was reenforced by the decline in the shares of industries in which interest is negligible (manufacturing, mining, and construction).

Changes from the first to the last quinquennium differ. Here again the effect of inter-industry shifts was to increase the share of interest in national income and to reduce the shares of entrepreneurial withdrawals and of net income. But these effects of shifts in the industrial composition of national income upon changes in its distribution by type were more moderate between 1919–23 and 1934–38 than between 1919–28 and 1929–38. Furthermore, the shift in the industrial composition tended to *reduce* the share of net savings and to *increase* the shares of wages and salaries and of dividends from the first to the last quinquennium, whereas it tended to increase the share of net savings and to reduce those of wages and salaries and of dividends from the first to the second decade. The increase in the share of wages and salaries from the first to the last quinquennium is due largely to the remarkable recovery in the last quinquennium of commodity producing industries with their large shares of wages and salaries and of employee compensation (mining, manufacturing, and construction); the loss in their share in national income was therefore much less when measured from 1919–23 to 1934–38 than from 1919–28 to 1929–38. As some industries with high ratios of wages and salaries and employee compensation declined less in relative importance and other industries with high ratios (government, trade, telephone) increased, inter-industry shifts between 1919–23 and 1934–38 raised the shares of wages and salaries and of employee compensation in national income.

In one respect the analysis of changes between the two decades and the two quinquennia in Table 30 yields similar results: the removal of the effects of inter-industry shifts and the confining of changes in the shares of income types to those caused by intra-industry shifts does not materially influence the changes in the distribution of national income by type. When we compare columns 1 and 2 for the changes from 1919– 28 to 1929–38, not one income component or subtotal alters its sign. Thus were we to consider only intra-industry shifts in shares of income types, disregarding the effects of inter-industry shifts, the shares in national income of wages and salaries, employee compensation, entrepreneurial withdrawals, both totals of service income, dividends, interest, property income including rent, and aggregate payments excluding entrepreneurial savings would still rise significantly; and those of entrepreneurial net income and the various savings totals would still decline significantly. In the comparison for 1919–23 and 1934–38 the sign is reversed in the share of entrepreneurial withdrawals alone; but the change in its share in national income is minor anyway, whether inter- and intra-industry shifts are combined or the effects of intra-industry shifts alone are considered. In short, while shifts in the industrial composition of national income had some effect on changes in the distribution by type, it was moderate.

When changes over the period in the distribution by type of aggregate payments excluding entrepreneurial savings are similarly analyzed, the results are significantly different (Table 31). The entries in Table 31 were derived by a procedure analogous to that used in Table 30, except that changes within each industry were measured for shares in total payments and the weights used were the average share for 1919–38 of each industry in aggregate payments.

Changes in the industrial composition of aggregate payments, both from 1919–28 to 1929–38 and from 1919–23 to 1934–38, were such as to raise the shares of wages and salaries, employee compensation, total service income excluding entre-

TABLE 31

Effects of Inter- and Intra-Industry Shifts upon the Change over the Period in the Distribution of Aggregate Payments, excluding Entrepreneurial Savings, by Type, 1919–1938

	CHANGE FROM 1919–28 TO 1929–38			CHANGE FROM 1919–23 TO 1934–38		
		CHANGE DUE TO			CHANGE DUE TO	
	TOTAL CHANGE	Intra-industry shifts	Inter-industry shifts (1 − 2)	TOTAL CHANGE	Intra-industry shifts	Inter-industry shifts (4 − 5)
	(1)	(2)	(3)	(4)	(5)	(6)
Wages & salaries	−1.7	−2.4	+0.7	−1.3	−3.0	+1.7
Employee compensation	+0.89	−1.1	+2.0	+2.9	−0.87	+3.8
Entrep. withdrawals	−0.72	+0.69	−1.4	−2.0	+0.43	−2.4
Service income excl. entrep. savings	+0.17	−0.43	+0.60	+0.85	−0.44	+1.3
Dividends	+0.84	+0.65	+0.19	+1.3	+1.2	+0.1
Interest	+1.9	+0.17	+1.7	+1.5	+1.3	+0.2
Prop. income incl. rent	−0.17	+0.43	−0.60	−0.85	+0.44	−1.3
Total net savings	−12.4	−13.3	+0.9	−7.9	−8.2	+0.3
Corp. & gov. net savings	−8.8	−9.5	+0.7	−6.2	−6.2	0.0

preneurial savings, dividends, and interest. In other words, industries characterized by larger than average shares of these income components gained compared with industries characterized by smaller than average shares. Shifts in the industrial composition tended to depress the shares of entrepreneurial withdrawals and of property income including rent. By and large, the effects of inter-industry shifts upon changes in the distribution of aggregate payments by type are greater than the effects of shifts within industries; and also than the total change in the distribution of aggregate payments by type.

Consequently, for several income type components in Table 31 the total change in the share in aggregate payments is in the opposite direction to that caused by the change in the distribution by type within industries (col. 1, 2, 4, and 5). Thus in the comparisons for both decades and quinquennia the total change in the share of employee compensation in aggregate payments is upward, while in the distribution by type within industries the share of employee compensation declines; and only shifts in industrial composition raise it in the comprehensive total. Likewise, the decline in the share of entrepre-

neurial withdrawals in aggregate payments is due exclusively
to shifts in industrial composition in favor of industries characterized by small shares; intra-industry shifts alone would
cause a small rise. There are similar reversals in the sign of the
change characterizing the share of total service income excluding entrepreneurial savings. Finally, the total change in the
share of property income including rent is negative, but only
because of shifts in the industrial composition of aggregate
payments. Within industries changes in the distribution by
type cause a small rise in the share of property income including rent.

In the light of Table 31 the conclusions concerning shifts in
the distribution of aggregate payments by type may be restated.
In the countrywide distribution the rise in the shares of employee compensation and of service income excluding entrepreneurial savings and the decline in the shares of entrepreneurial withdrawals and of property income including rent
are due exclusively to shifts in the industrial composition of
aggregate payments. If these shifts were removed and only the
change within industries taken into account, the shares of
wages and salaries, employee compensation, and total service
income would decline; and the shares of entrepreneurial withdrawals, dividends, interest, and total property income including rent, would rise.

4 Changes during Business Cycles

A IN COUNTRYWIDE TOTALS

As in the analysis of changes in national income and in its industrial distribution during business cycles we are concerned
here with answering two questions. First, how do the various
income type components, either in the country at large or
within industries, change during expansions and contractions
in the country's economic activity? Second, are there any significant differences among the components, either country-

wide or within industries, in the intensity with which they respond to changes associated with business cycles?

The cyclical behavior of income type components is analyzed by a procedure strictly analogous to that used in Chapters 4 and 5: the chronology of reference periods is the same, as is the method of scoring. We therefore introduce Table 32 without further explanation.

The totals were studied in Chapter 5 and require no comment. We merely note that by and large the countrywide type of income totals rise fairly consistently during expansions; decline somewhat less consistently during contractions; and that in most, the differential movement is consistently negative. Nevertheless, significant differences appear in the behavior of the totals themselves. For example, wages conform to business cycles more consistently than salaries; employee compensation, than entrepreneurial withdrawals. The most conspicuous lack

TABLE 32

Direction of Movement during Business Cycles in Types of Income and in their Percentage Shares of National Income and Aggregate Payments, 1919–1938

	TOTAL			% OF NATIONAL INCOME			% OF AGG. PAY. EXCL. ENTREP. SAVINGS		
	Expansion (1)	Contraction (2)	Differential (3)	Expansion (4)	Contraction (5)	Differential (6)	Expansion (7)	Contraction (8)	Differential (9)
Wages & salaries	+5	−3	−5	−1	+3	+3	+3	−5	−5
Wages *	+5	−5	−5	−3	+3	+3	+1	−5	−5
Salaries *	+5	−1	−3	−1	+5	+5	−3	+5	+5
Employee compensation	+5	−3	−5	−1	+3	+3	+3	−3	−5
Entrep. withdrawals	+5	−1	−3	−3	+5	+3	−5	+1	+3
Entrep. net income	+3	−3	−5	−1	−1	−1	+1	−1	−3
Service income excl. entrep. savings	+5	−1	−5	−3	+5	+3	+3	−1	−1
Service income incl. entrep. savings	+5	−3	−5	−5	+5	+5	+1	−3	−3
Dividends	+5	−3	−5	+1	+1	+1	+3	−1	−3
Interest	+3	+1	+1	−1	+5	+5	−3	+5	+5
Dividends & interest	+5	−1	−5	+1	+3	+5	−1	+3	+1
Rent	+1	−1	−1	−3	+1	+5	−5	+1	+3
Property income incl. rent	+5	+1	−3	−1	+3	+5	−3	+1	+1
Net savings	+3	−5	−5	+3	−5	−5	+3	−5	−5

* Based on data for mining, manufacturing, construction, and steam railroads, Pullman, and express, the only industries for which this breakdown is possible.

of conformity is in interest, an income type whose character and industrial source (government, agriculture, and real estate are the important sources) make it less responsive to short term fluctuations in economic conditions.

The movements of the shares in national income indicate which income type components respond to business cycles with a wider amplitude and which with a narrower. For reasons repeatedly indicated, the differential movement is the measure of behavior during business cycles least affected by longer term changes. Net savings, which fluctuate violently, so dominate the movements of the other components of national income that most have narrower amplitudes than national income (col. 6). In other words, net savings affect conforming fluctuations in national income during business cycles so much that, by comparison, conforming fluctuations of the other income components seem to have narrower amplitudes. The only exception is entrepreneurial net income, a component itself affected by entrepreneurial savings.

Only by excluding net savings and studying the movements in the percentage distribution of aggregate payments can we discover which type of payment components are most responsive to business cycles (col. 9). Wages and salaries, employee compensation, wages (but not salaries), and dividends have conforming fluctuations of wider amplitudes than aggregate payments. Salaries, entrepreneurial withdrawals, interest, and rent have consistently narrower amplitudes. The insignificant scores for the more inclusive totals, such as service income or property income including rent, indicate such inconsistency in the movement of their percentage shares that it is difficult to say whether on the whole their conforming fluctuations have wider or narrower amplitudes than aggregate payments. This is, of course, because the subtotals include components that behave in different ways during business cycles: service income includes the responsive and sensitive wages and the less responsive salaries and entrepreneurial withdrawals;

property income includes the responsive and sensitive dividends and the less responsive interest and rent.

The differences in amplitude of conforming fluctuations among the income type components are not unexpected. But we must test them by studying the behavior of income type components within industries as well. We consider first the totals, then the percentage distribution by type of net income originating in each industry, and finally the percentage distribution of total payments by type within industries.

B IN TYPE OF INCOME TOTALS WITHIN INDUSTRIES

The consistency of movement during business cycles of income type totals by industries and major industrial groups is analyzed in Chapter 5.[1] Tables 18 and 19 can be used here to establish the movements of the totals within industries.

Table 19 shows that, on the whole, similarities and differences observed for countrywide income type totals (in Table 32) persist within the groups of Classifications A and C. The differential movement indicates that net savings conform most consistently to business cycles; interest, least consistently; indeed, in most industrial groups the latter rises from expansion to contraction. Dividends, wages and salaries, and entrepreneurial withdrawals move in conformity with business cycles, but not as consistently as net savings.

The differences among the groups reflect essential differences in sensitivity to business cycles among industrial groups (e.g., commodity producing on the one hand and service industries on the other; private corporations and public industries, etc.) superimposed upon essential differences in such sensitivity among income type components. Measured again, by the differential movement, wages and salaries reflect business cycles quite consistently in the commodity producing and com-

[1] Entrepreneurial net income and corporate and government savings, rather than entrepreneurial withdrawals and net savings of enterprises, are given in Tables 18 and 19, but the movements are similar. Presentation of similar tables here, which would duplicate much of the material, was considered superfluous.

modity transporting and distributing groups, but much less
consistently in the service industries. Also, wages and salaries
have scores of high positive conformity in the first three groups
of Classification C but not in the group of public industries (for
which the entry + 3 for the differential movement indicates
inverse conformity). Entrepreneurial income conforms well in
all the groups in which it exists, except the commodity transporting and distributing group in Classification A. Dividends
also conform fairly consistently in all groups except the semi-
public in Classification C. Interest, which conforms poorly or
inversely in most groups, conforms fairly well and positively in
the public industries group of Classification C. Finally, net savings conform closely in all groups.

The components of our more detailed industrial classification move on the whole in consistent conformity with business cycles. Table 18 lists the industries and components that
do not show significant conformity to business cycles (i.e., are
measured by differential scores other than — 5 or — 3). All
components, with the sole exception of interest, in most industries conform significantly to business cycles. But interest in
many does not: in agriculture, mining, manufacturing and
most of its subdivisions, transportation and public utilities and
most of its subdivisions, construction, trade, finance, service,
and government. The widespread conformity of wages and
salaries, entrepreneurial withdrawals, dividends, and net savings is thus confirmed, as well as the lack of definite conformity
of interest in almost all industries.

C IN PERCENTAGE SHARES OF NET INCOME ORIGINATING
For most groups in Classifications A and C the shares of the
various income types as percentages of net income originating
decline during expansions, rise during contractions, and their
differential movements are positive (Table 33). The outstanding exception is net savings of enterprises, whose share moves
in consistent positive conformity to business cycles. Obviously
the amplitude of their conforming fluctuations so influences

TABLE 33

Direction of Movement during Business Cycles in Percentage
Shares of Types of Income in Net Income Originating
Broad Industrial Divisions, 1919–1938

| | CLASSIFICATION A | | | CLASSIFICATION C | | | |
	Commodity producing (1)	Commodity transp. & distr. (2)	Services (3)	With large proportion of indiv. firms (4)	Private corp. (5)	Semi-public corp. (6)	Public (7)
EXPANSION							
Wages & salaries	−3	0	−1	+1	−3	−3	−3
Entrep. withdrawals	−3	−3	+1	−3	−5	+1	
Dividends	+1	+1	+3	+3	+1	+1	
Interest	−3	−3	−3	+1	−1	−5	−5
Net savings	+3	+1	+3	+1	+3	+3	+3
CONTRACTION							
Wages & salaries	+3	+5	+5	+3	+5	−1	+5
Entrep. withdrawals	+5	+5	+1	+3	+5	+5	
Dividends	+1	+1	−1	−1	+3	+5	
Interest	+5	+3	+3	+5	+5	+5	−1
Net savings	−5	−5	−5	−5	−5	−5	−1
DIFFERENTIAL MOVEMENT							
Wages & salaries	+5	+1	+5	+1	+5	+3	+5
Entrep. withdrawals	+5	+3	+3	+3	+5	+3	
Dividends	+3	+1	+1	−1	+3	+3	
Interest	+5	+5	+5	+5	+5	+5	+1
Net savings	−5	−3	−5	−3	−5	−3	−5

net income originating that the amplitudes of conforming
movements in all other income components must be narrower.
In this respect Table 33 corroborates Table 32.

But the responses of the various income type components
within the industrial groups differ. Wages and salaries in the
commodity transporting and distributing group of Classification A and in the first group of Classification C do not show
consistently narrower conforming amplitudes than net income
originating. The same is true of dividends in all except the
commodity producing group of Classification A. Apparently
therefore, at least in some groups, wages and salaries and dividends fluctuate in conformity with business cycles with sufficient amplitude even in comparison with net savings to cause,
in at least some cycles, their percentage shares to show positive
conformity.

Not many shares of income type components in net income originating in the individual industries conform consistently, positively or negatively (i.e., with a score of either + 5 or + 3 or — 5 or — 3). We therefore list in Table 34 the industries and components for which adequate positive or negative conformity in the differential movement is recorded. As might have been expected, all components except net savings have largely entries with positive scores, indicating that the amplitudes of their conforming movement during business cycles are narrower than in net income originating in the industry and still narrower than in net savings. The negative entries under net savings indicate that consistent positive conformity is established only because this component fluctuates in conformity with business cycles uniformly more violently than net income originating.

In almost every industry interest, if it responds to business cycles, has an amplitude narrower than net income originating; net savings just as consistently respond with wider amplitude than net income originating. For wages and salaries, entrepreneurial withdrawals, and dividends, industries with consistent scores are fewer, and the last-mentioned component in several industries responds to business cycles with wider amplitude than net income originating. Most of the industries with consistently negative scores are of the type that do not respond sensitively to business cycles (insurance, finance, textiles and leather, printing, water transportation, real estate, service). It is tempting to infer that among the industries with positive scores under wages and salaries, entrepreneurial withdrawals, and dividends, the preponderant majority would be of the type that is sensitive to business cycles: mining; manufacturing and such of its divisions as metals, chemicals, miscellaneous and rubber; steam railroads, etc. A positive score would indicate that conforming fluctuations in the three income type components are of narrower amplitude than in net income originating and it might well be expected that conforming fluctuations in wages and salaries, entrepreneurial withdrawals, and

TABLE 34

Industrial Divisions whose Shares of Types of Income in Net Income Originating Conform Adequately to Business Cycles (Based on the Differential Movement), 1919–1938

WAGES & SALARIES (1)	ENTREP. WITHDRAWALS (2)	DIVIDENDS (3)	INTEREST (4)	NET SAVINGS (5)
Mining (+)	Finance (−)	Text. & leather (−)	Agriculture (+)	Agriculture (−)
Mfg. (+)	Insurance (−)	Printing (−)	Mining (+)	Mining (−)
Food & tobacco (+)	Agr. (+)	Water transp. (−)	Mfg. (+)	Mfg. (−)
Constr. mat. & furn. (+)	Mining (+)	Finance (−)	Food & tobacco (+)	Food & tobacco (−)
Paper (+)	Mfg. (+)	Real estate (−)	Constr. mat. & furn. (+)	Constr. mat. & furn. (−)
Printing (+)	Food & tobacco (+)	Service (−)	Paper (+)	Paper (−)
Metal (+)	Constr. mat. & furn. (+)	Mfg. (+)	Printing (+)	Printing (−)
Chemical (+)	Paper (+)	Metal (+)	Metal (+)	Metal (−)
Misc. & rubber (+)	Printing (+)	Chemical (+)	Chemical (+)	Chemical (−)
Transp. & other pub. util. (+)	Metal (+)	Transp. & other pub. util. (+)	Misc. & rubber (+)	Misc. & rubber (−)
Steam rr., Pull., & exp. (+)	Chemical (+)	Pipe lines (+)	Construction (+)	Transp. & other pub. util. (−)
Water transp. (+)	Misc. & rubber (+)	Telephone (+)	Transp. & other pub. util. (+)	Elec. light & power (−)
Gov. (+)	Construction (+)	Banking (+)	Elec. light & power (+)	Mfd. gas (−)
Misc. (+)	Elec. light & power (+)	Misc. (+)	Mfd. gas (+)	Steam rr., Pull., & exp. (−)
	Trade (+)		Steam rr., Pull., & exp. (+)	Street rwy. (−)
	Service (+)		Street rwy. (+)	Water transp. (−)
	Misc. (+)		Water transp. (+)	Pipe lines (−)
			Telephone (+)	Telephone (−)
			Telegraph (+)	Telegraph (−)
			Trade (+)	Trade (−)
			Insurance (+)	Service (−)
			Service (+)	Gov. (−)
			Misc. (+)	Misc. (−)

(+) means that the amplitude of conforming fluctuations is narrower than in net income originating.

(−) means that the amplitude of conforming fluctuations is wider than in net income originating.

dividends would have narrower amplitudes than in net income originating chiefly in industries in which net income originating is itself highly sensitive to business cycles. But such a conclusion is barred since among the industries with components that have narrower amplitudes than net income originating not a few are none too sensitive (agriculture, service, etc.). Apparently, therefore, the responsiveness of income type totals cannot be interpreted solely in terms of differences among industries in sensitivity to business cycles.

D IN PERCENTAGE SHARES OF TOTAL PAYMENTS

Changes in the percentage distribution of total payments (excluding entrepreneurial savings) by type within broad industrial groups indicate that wages and salaries, dividends, and of course net savings have conforming fluctuations of wider amplitudes than total payments; entrepreneurial withdrawals and interest, on the contrary, have conforming fluctuations of narrower amplitudes (Table 35).

However, the amplitudes of conforming fluctuations in various income type components are different in different groups. For example, wages and salaries have wider amplitudes than total payments in the commodity producing and commodity transporting and distributing groups in Classification A; in the group of service industries the indication of wider amplitude is not significant. In the group with a large proportion of unincorporated firms and in the semi-public group, but not in the public industry group or in that in which private corporations predominate, in Classification C, wages and salaries have a wider amplitude than total payments. Entrepreneurial withdrawals usually have a narrower amplitude than total payments; but in the service industries group in Classification A, in which entrepreneurial withdrawals are substantial, their amplitude is wider. The amplitude of conforming fluctuations in the share of dividends is narrower than in total payments in the commodity transporting and distributing group in Classification A, the first group in Classification C

TABLE 35

Direction of Movement during Business Cycles in Percentage
Shares of Types of Income in Total Payments
Broad Industrial Divisions, 1919–1938

	CLASSIFICATION A				CLASSIFICATION C		
	Com-modity producing	Com-modity transp. & distr.	Services	With large proportion of indiv. firms	Private corp.	Semi-public corp.	Public
	(1)	(2)	(3)	(4)	(5)	(6)	(7)
EXPANSION							
Wages & salaries	+3	+5	+1	+5	—1	—1	—1
Entrep. withdrawals	—5	—3	+1	—5	—5	+3	
Dividends	+3	+5	+3	+5	+3	+1	
Interest	—1	—5	+1	—1	—1	—3	—1
Net savings	+3	+1	+3	+1	+3	+3	+3
CONTRACTION							
Wages & salaries	—5	—3	—1	—3	—1	—3	—1
Entrep. withdrawals	+3	+3	+1	+1	+3	+5	
Dividends	—1	+1	—1	—1	—1	+3	
Interest	+5	+3	+1	+5	+5	+3	—3
Net savings	—5	—5	—5	—5	—5	—5	—1
DIFFERENTIAL MOVEMENT							
Wages & salaries	—5	—5	—1	—5	+1	—5	+1
Entrep. withdrawals	+5	+5	—3	+3	+5	+1	
Dividends	—3	+1	—5	—1	—3	+1	
Interest	+5	+5	+1	+5	+5	+5	—3
Net savings	—3	—3	—5	—3	—5	—3	—5

(in which, however, such payments are negligible), and the
semi-public group.

These differences can perhaps be explained in terms of the
differing sensitivity of industrial groups and of their income
type components to business cycles. In the commodity transporting and distributing group public utilities are important,
and for various reasons their dividend disbursement policy is
none too sensitive to shorter business cycles; hence the positive
scores for differential movements in dividends in both the second group in Classification A and the semi-public group in
Classification C. The third group in Classification A comprises
governments and some public utilities that are not too sensitive to business cycles, as well as private service industries
with many entrepreneurs whose incomes are more sensitive.
As a result, wages and salaries in this group are not too respon-

sive, since they originate to a large extent in governments and
the cyclically insensitive public utilities; and the scores are
low for the differential movements of wages and salaries in
both this and the public industries groups. Entrepreneurial
withdrawals in the service group, coming from its private industry sector, are more sensitive than total payments. Finally,
the peculiarly low score for wages and salaries in the second
group in Classification C (mining and manufacturing) may be
due to the extreme sensitivity of dividends originating in these
two industries; but this explanation may be inadequate.

In observing the shares of income type components in total
payments industry by industry we again list only industries
for which the behavior of the given share is fairly consistently
in one direction (Table 36). Table 36 confirms the indication
of Table 34: in almost all industries conforming movements of
interest are of an amplitude narrower than in total payments;
those in net savings are just as consistently of a wider amplitude. But there is one negative entry under interest: in government, significantly enough, the conforming fluctuations in
interest are of wider amplitude than in total payments.

Again as we might have expected, most of the entries under
wages and salaries and dividends are negative, and those under entrepreneurial withdrawals, positive. However, in some
industries wages and salaries and dividends conform with narrower amplitudes than total payments; and entrepreneurial
withdrawals, with a wider amplitude. Most of the industries
in which wages and salaries and dividends respond with narrower amplitudes and entrepreneurial withdrawals with wider
are rather insensitive to business cycles (finance, insurance,
water transportation, pipe lines). On the other hand, we cannot say with assurance that industries in which wages and
salaries and dividends had conforming fluctuations with consistently wider amplitudes than total payments and in which
the conforming fluctuations in entrepreneurial withdrawals
were of narrower amplitudes than in total payments are necessarily characterized by sensitivity to business cycles; for agricul-

TABLE 36

Industrial Divisions whose Shares of Types of Income in Total Payments Conform Adequately to Business Cycles (Based on the Differential Movement), 1919–1938

WAGES & SALARIES (1)	ENTREP. WITHDRAWALS (2)	DIVIDENDS (3)	INTEREST (4)	NET SAVINGS (5)
Agriculture (−)	Transp. & other pub. util. (−)	Mfg. (−)	Government (−)	Agriculture (−)
Construction (−)	Finance (−)	Text. & leather (−)	Agriculture (+)	Mining (−)
Transp. & other pub. util. (−)	Insurance (−)	Constr. mat. & furn. (−)	Mining (+)	Mfg. (−)
Elec. light & power (−)	Agriculture (+)	Printing (−)	Mfg. (+)	Food & tobacco (−)
Steam rr., Pull., & exp. (−)	Mining (+)	Water transp. (−)	Food & tobacco (+)	Constr. mat. & furn. (−)
Pipe lines (−)	Mfg. (+)	Finance (−)	Constr. mat. & furn. (+)	Paper (−)
Telephone (−)	Food & tobacco (+)	Real estate (−)	Printing (+)	Printing (−)
State gov. (−)	Text. & leather (+)	Service (−)	Metal (+)	Metal (−)
Misc. (−)	Printing (+)	Pipe lines (+)	Chemical (+)	Chemical (−)
Constr. mat. & furn. (+)	Metal (+)	Telephone (+)	Misc. & rubber (+)	Misc. & rubber (−)
Water transp. (+)	Chemical (+)		Construction (+)	Transp. & other pub. util. (≤)
Insurance (+)	Misc. & rubber (+)		Transp. & other pub. util. (+)	Elec. light & power (−)
	Construction (+)		Elec. light & power (+)	Steam rr., Pull., & exp. (−)
	Trade (+)		Mfd. gas (+)	Street rwy. (−)
	Misc. (+)		Steam rr., Pull., & exp. (+)	Water transp. (−)
			Street rwy. (+)	Pipe lines (−)
			Water transp. (+)	Telephone (−)
			Telephone (+)	Service (−)
			Telegraph (+)	Gov. (−)
			Trade (+)	Misc. (−)
			Finance (+)	
			Service (+)	
			Misc. (+)	

(+) means that the amplitude of conforming fluctuations is narrower than in total payments.

(−) means that the amplitude of conforming fluctuations is wider than in total payments.

ture, construction, and real estate are included as well as manufacturing and some of its sensitive subdivisions. Apparently then, there are differences in the responsiveness of wages and salaries and dividends on the one hand and of entrepreneurial withdrawals on the other, apart from the differences in the cyclical responsiveness of industries in which these types of payment are prominent.

5 *Summary*

a) During 1919–38 wages and salaries accounted on the average for 61 per cent of national income; employee compensation, for 63 per cent; entrepreneurial withdrawals, for 17 per cent; and entrepreneurial net income including savings, for 17.6 per cent. Thus total service income constituted on the average about 81 per cent of national income. Total property income including rent was slightly less than one-fifth of national income. Of the three types, dividends averaged 6 per cent of national income, interest, 7, and rent, 6. Net savings of corporations and government averaged (algebraically) less than one-half of one per cent of national income, and net savings of all enterprises, less than one per cent.

The average percentage distribution by type of aggregate payments, including or excluding entrepreneurial savings, was similar to the distribution of national income.

b) The average distribution of both net income originating and total payments by type varied among industries. Organizational characteristics affect the share of entrepreneurial income or of interest compared with dividends; technological characteristics of the production processes affect the share of compensation for direct labor (wages, salaries, etc.) compared with payments for capital (interest, dividends, rent); various other characteristics (accessibility to sources of capital supply, relative importance of different types of labor or capital, etc.) determine the relative importance of different types of income. Because of such differences in the type of income structure among industries, shifts in the industrial composition of the countrywide income totals are bound to influence greatly changes in their distribution by type.

c) The shares of both wages and salaries and employee compensation in national income increased significantly over the period. In most industries, a similar increase occurred in their shares in net income originating although in several the shares declined. The effects of shifts in industrial composition upon changes in these shares were minor: wages and salaries and employee compensation would have increased relatively to national income even had there been no shifts in its industrial composition.

d) The share of employee compensation in aggregate payments, including or excluding entrepreneurial net savings, increased; but the share of wages and salaries decreased slightly. In the majority of industries the shares of both wages and salaries and employee compensation in total payments including or excluding entrepreneurial savings decreased. Shifts in the industrial composition of aggregate payments excluding entrepreneurial savings tended to raise the shares of wages and salaries and of employee compensation in aggregate payments; were the effects of these inter-industry shifts removed, the shares of both would decrease.

e) For the few industries for which wages and salaries could be separated the share of salaries in both net income originating and total payments increased significantly more or declined significantly less than the share of wages. Hence, in these industries, with the single exception of food and tobacco manufacturing, the distribution changed markedly in favor of salaries.

f) The share of entrepreneurial withdrawals in national income showed no definite movement over the period; its share in both totals of aggregate payments declined. The share of entrepreneurial income (i.e., withdrawals plus savings) in both national income and aggregate payments declined. Were the effects of inter-industry shifts removed, the conclusions concerning movements in the shares of both entrepreneurial withdrawals and income in national income would remain the same. But were the shifts in the industrial distribution of aggregate payments excluding entrepreneurial savings removed, the share of entrepreneurial withdrawals in aggregate payments would rise instead of decline.

g) The share of interest and dividends in national income and both aggregate payments totals increased significantly over the period in the preponderant majority of industries. Even were we to correct for the effect of changes in industrial composition, the rise would still remain significant.

h) The share of rent in national income and both aggregate payments totals declined. When this component is added to interest and dividends to form total property income, the share of the latter in national income still increases; but in aggregate payments excluding entrepreneurial savings it decreases.

Since all rent is assigned to one industry, real estate, the share of total property income in both net income originating and total payments increased in the preponderant majority of industries. Were the effects of shifts in industrial composition removed, its share in both national income and aggregate payments would still rise.

i) Net savings constitute a strikingly declining share of national income and of both aggregate payments totals. It would not be much affected by allowance for the effects of shifts in industrial composition. In most industries a similar decline occurred in the share of net savings in both net income originating and total payments.

j) The countrywide totals of wages and salaries, entrepreneurial withdrawals, etc. show fairly consistent conformity to business cycles; i.e., they rise during expansions, decline during contractions, and their differential movement is negative. The one conspicuous exception is interest.

This generally conforming behavior of all income types except interest is true also of the components within industries. However, in some industries usually unresponsive to business cycles (e.g., government) even income types that ordinarily conform may not conform consistently.

k) The conforming fluctuations of net savings of enterprises are of especially wide amplitude. This type of income contributes so much to the variability during business cycles of net income originating that the amplitudes of conforming fluctuations in any and all other types are, for the country as a whole and in most industries, narrower than in net income originating.

l) When net savings are omitted and we compare the amplitudes of conforming fluctuations in the various types of payment, we find that wages and salaries and dividends display conforming movements of wider amplitude than total payments both for the country as a whole and in most industries; and that entrepreneurial withdrawals and interest have narrower amplitudes than aggregate payments.

m) Since there is naturally some tendency for these differences in the amplitude of conforming changes of income types to be merged with the differences in the amplitude of conforming changes of various industries, we cannot say that one income type will always show conforming changes of wider amplitude than another. But in industries usually sensitive to business cycles the various types of income differ markedly and on the whole persistently in their responsiveness: net savings are especially sensitive, and interest, insensitive; wages and salaries and dividends are more sensitive than entrepreneurial withdrawals.

CHAPTER 7

Distribution by Type of Final Product

CHAPTERS 5 and 6 deal with the origin of national income in the country's industrial system and the distribution of the monetary counterpart among types of income and payment. We now consider the various categories of final goods turned out and ascertain how national income, originating in various industries and distributed in various types of payment or accruals, is utilized.

By final goods we mean commodities and services in the form in which, without further modification or movement, they are used by ultimate consumers in households or by consumers of durable equipment in business and other economic enterprises. They include fully finished consumer goods reaching ultimate consumers, fully finished construction of all types, and durable capital equipment reaching the economic enterprises that use it in the production process. The gross value of fully finished consumer goods reaching households during the year is consumers' outlay, an item already measured and discussed in Chapter 4. The values of construction and durable equipment are net, i.e., the remainder left after an allowance has been made for the construction and equipment consumed during the year, and constitute the major part of net capital formation. But the gross value of finished consumer goods reaching ultimate consumers and the net value of construction and durable equipment reaching the economic enterprises that use them do not exhaust the full contents of national income. Unfinished commodities may be produced in excess of their consumption, making net additions to inventories in the hands of economic enterprises. And more goods may be transferred from domestic consumers to foreign countries than are received by domestic consumers from foreign countries, making net additions to claims against foreign countries. Hence, net capital formation includes net changes in inventories of all economic enterprises (but not of households) and net changes in claims against foreign countries as well as the net value of construction and producers' durable equipment. National income is by definition equal to the sum of consumers' outlay and net capital formation.

It is theoretically possible to subdivide both consumers' outlay and net capital formation into various categories. In consumers' outlay commodities could be separated from services; various groups of either according to their place in consumers' scales of wants, the characteristics of demand for them, the distinctive features of the goods themselves such as durability, divisibility into small units, and mobility. For net capital formation under each of the four categories—construction, durable equipment, inventories, and claims against foreign countries—numerous subdivisions could be introduced separating more specific commodity groups, the various industries or countries to whose stock of goods capital formation adds, and the like. But such detailed analysis is barred by limitations of data, and the few divisions by type of final product in this chapter are the only ones possible with the combination of data and analysis utilized in the National Bureau's studies of national income and capital formation.

Unlike the distributions by industrial origin and type of income, the distribution by type of final product must use the results of both studies. Since the errors of estimate in the two studies are not likely to be in the same direction and, more important, cannot be appraised as accurately as errors attaching to estimates all made within the framework of one study, this chapter is subject to more severe qualification than the preceding. Yet within these limitations, from the combined results of the two studies we can observe what shares net capital formation and its various components constitute of national income and how these shares change over time; how net capital formation is apportioned to various accounts; how consumers' outlay is distributed among various groups of goods; and finally, how national income itself is apportioned among various types of final product.

1 Capital Formation by Type of Product
Net capital formation as part of national income is discussed implicitly in Chapter 4, in the comparison of national income and consumers' outlay. In Table 37 we make a direct comparison, which reveals the level of net capital formation and its temporal fluctuations. The first impression conveyed by Table 37 is the smallness of the share of net capital formation in national income: in current and 1929 prices it accounts on the average for approximately 6 per cent. Thus for the period as a whole, real savings, i.e., savings that found embodiment in additions to the stock of equipment and commodities or to claims against foreign countries, amounted to appreciably less than one-tenth of national income. The year by year comparison of totals adjusted for price changes and thus relatively free from the distorting effects of fluctuating price levels indicates that net capital formation has not exceeded 15 per cent of national income.

1 Capital formation is measured here on a *net* basis, after an allowance for depreciation, depletion, and regularly accountable obsolescence of capital equipment and construction. So far as new capital goods, whose value is offset by deductions for current consumption, may represent additions to productive power greater than the losses such deductions measure, even complete absence of net capital formation may mean a greater rather than constant productive power of durable capital. If it does, addition to the productive power of capital goods may be composed of two parts: (a) excess efficiency of new capital goods whose value is offset by the allowance for depreciation, etc.; (b) total efficiency of new capital goods, whose value constitutes net capital formation as here measured. It is exceedingly difficult to approximate the relative magnitudes of items (a) and (b), but it is likely that our estimates of net capital formation

TABLE 37

National Income and Capital Formation
Current and 1929 Prices, 1919–1938

	CURRENT PRICES			1929 PRICES		
	National income [1] (billions of dollars)	Capital formation	Capital formation as % of national income	National income [1] (billions of dollars)	Capital formation	Capital formation as % of national income
	(1)	(2)	(3)	(4)	(5)	(6)
1919	64.2	10.3	16.0	57.0	8.1	14.1
1920	74.2	11.4	15.3	58.4	7.5	12.9
1921	59.4	3.3	5.5	56.5	2.9	5.1
1922	60.7	4.5	7.4	60.8	4.0	6.6
1923	71.6	8.6	12.0	70.7	8.2	11.5
1924	72.1	5.9	8.1	71.7	5.5	7.7
1925	76.0	9.3	12.2	73.9	8.9	12.0
1926	81.6	9.2	11.3	79.0	8.7	11.0
1927	80.1	8.2	10.2	79.6	8.0	10.1
1928	81.7	7.4	9.0	81.1	7.3	8.9
1929	87.2	10.0	11.5	87.1	10.0	11.5
1930	77.3	4.2	5.4	79.9	4.4	5.5
1931	60.3	0.1	0.2	69.3	0.2	0.2
1932	42.9	—4.2	—9.7	55.6	—5.5	—9.9
1933	42.2	—3.6	—8.6	56.7	—5.0	—8.8
1934	49.5	—2.6	—5.2	62.1	—3.6	—5.8
1935	54.4	0.7	1.3	65.6	0.4	0.6
1936	62.9	5.4	8.5	75.0	5.6	7.4
1937	70.5	6.4	9.0	80.8	6.4	7.9
1938	65.5	2.9	4.4	79.0	3.2	4.1
Average [2]						
1919–23	66.0	7.6	11.2	60.7	6.1	10.0
1924–28	78.3	8.0	10.2	77.1	7.7	9.9
1929–33	62.0	1.3	—0.2	69.7	0.8	—0.3
1934–38	60.6	2.5	3.6	72.5	2.4	2.8
1919–28	72.2	7.8	10.7	68.9	6.9	10.0
1929–38	61.3	1.9	1.7	71.1	1.6	1.3

[1] As in Chapter 4, but not as in Chapters 5 and 6, national income in this and other tables includes the Social Security contributions of employers and is adjusted for the effects on net savings of corporations and other business firms of gains and losses on sales of capital assets, of inventory revaluations, and of the use of a cost rather than a reproduction basis for depreciation charges. These adjustments are indispensable in establishing the comparability of national income and capital formation totals.

[2] As in all measures of change in percentage shares, we use here arithmetic means of percentages rather than percentages based on arithmetic means of totals. The alternative set of percentages (which can easily be computed from entries in col. 1 and 2, 4 and 5), would show movements in the same direction but more moderate from period to period.

Over the period as a whole the share of net capital formation in national income declines significantly. The decline, to be sure, is caused largely by the severe contraction of 1929–32, but even in the latest peak year, 1937, the share is smaller than in the 1920's. Subsequent analysis reveals the importance of construction, which is susceptible to pronounced cycles well over ten years in duration, in net capital formation. For these reasons, one cannot attribute much secular significance to estimated changes in the share of net capital formation in national income for a period as short as two decades.

Both national income and net capital formation conform closely to business cycles, but the fluctuations in capital formation are greater than in national income. In each of the five business cycles the share of net capital formation in national income falls markedly during contractions, and the amplitude of the swing is wide indeed. The timing of the cyclical fluctuations in net capital formation diverges once or twice from the chronology of cycles in general business conditions: for example, net capital formation (in 1929 prices) fails to rise from 1919 to 1920, reaches a peak in 1925 and a trough in 1928 rather than in 1926 and 1927 respectively. But these departures from reference cycle chronology, due primarily to the influence of construction which is subject to cycles of its own, are minor, and the violent fluctuations in net capital formation and in its share in national income increase the sensitivity of national income to cyclical swings.

There is a highly variable relation between changes in net capital formation and in national income. Indeed, in several years an increase in net capital formation is accompanied by a decrease in national income, or vice versa (1924, 1926, 1928, 1933, and others). While some of these divergences may be

---

undervalue relative additions to the productive power of the country's stock of capital. However, there is no reason to assume that the changes over time in items (a) and (b) are inversely related. If they are not, then rises and declines in new capital formation, as here estimated in 1929 prices, would indicate rises and declines in the rate of addition to the productive power of the stock of capital goods in the country.

due to crudities of the estimates, they are indicative of the looseness of correlation between changes in capital formation and in national income. The impression is the same when we compare only upward changes; for example, from 1921 to 1922 capital formation in current prices increased $1.2 billion, national income, $1.3 billion; from 1922 to 1923 the former increased $4.1 billion, the latter, $10.9 billion. Thus the ratio of the increase in national income to the increase in net capital formation was only 1.1 in 1921–22, and 2.7 in 1922–23. There are similar variations in the ratio in other years, which remain even if we compare changes in gross capital formation with changes in gross national income, i.e., include in both the allowance for consumption of capital goods, or if we omit certain items, such as changes in claims against foreign countries, from both capital formation and national income. The estimates in Table 37 fail to support an assumption of constancy in the ratio of *changes* in capital formation to *changes* in national income (or of capital formation to national income), in either the rising or declining phases of business cycles, a constancy that seems to be implicit in most discussions of 'the multiplier'.

Estimates of net capital formation enable us to separate: (a) net value of producers' durable equipment combined with the net value of business construction; (b) net value of residential construction; (c) net value of public construction, i.e., all construction done by and for the account of governmental agencies; (d) net changes in business inventories (excluding inventories of households and, for lack of data, inventories in the hands of non-business economic enterprises); (e) changes in claims against foreign countries. In Table 38 we can observe the shares formed by these various components of net capital formation in national income. The comparison is confined to estimates in 1929 prices, in order to reveal the movement of shares in real product; but if the estimates were computed in current prices the results would be roughly similar.

The most striking feature for the period as a whole is the large share of public construction and the small share of residential construction. Ranked in order of relative importance of the average share for the period are public construction, producers' durable goods and business construction, net flow to inventories, changes in claims against foreign countries, and residential construction. The ranking would be entirely

TABLE 38

Percentage Shares of Type of Product Components
of Capital Formation in National Income
1929 Prices, 1919–1938

	PRODUCERS' DURABLE INCL. BUSINESS CONSTRUCTION	CONSTRUCTION Residential	Public	CHANGE IN BUSINESS INVENTORIES	CHANGE IN CLAIMS AGAINST FOREIGN COUNTRIES
	(1)	(2)	(3)	(4)	(5)
1919	3.0	—0.4	2.8	4.9	3.7
1920	3.2	—1.1	1.0	7.2	2.5
1921	0.7	0.04	2.1	—0.1	2.3
1922	1.3	2.1	2.0	0.5	0.7
1923	3.3	2.5	1.4	4.0	0.3
1924	3.2	3.2	1.7	—1.3	0.9
1925	3.9	3.6	2.0	2.2	0.4
1926	4.3	3.2	1.8	1.5	0.1
1927	4.2	2.7	2.1	0.5	0.6
1928	4.2	2.2	2.2	—0.5	0.8
1929	4.9	1.3	2.1	2.8	0.5
1930	3.3	—0.1	2.8	—1.3	0.9
1931	—0.3	—1.0	3.2	—1.9	0.4
1932	—4.3	—2.8	2.8	—5.7	0.1
1933	—4.4	—3.1	1.5	—3.0	0.3
1934	—2.1	—3.2	2.3	—3.6	0.7
1935	—0.6	—2.4	1.9	2.0	—0.3
1936	1.9	—1.2	3.3	3.8	—0.5
1937	3.2	—0.7	2.4	3.2	—0.1
1938	0.7	—0.8	3.3	—0.4	1.3
Average					
1919–23	2.3	0.6	1.9	3.3	1.9
1924–28	4.0	3.0	2.0	0.5	0.6
1929–33	—0.2	—1.1	2.5	—1.8	0.4
1934–38	0.6	—1.7	2.6	1.0	0.2
1919–28	3.1	1.8	1.9	1.9	1.2
1929–38	0.2	—1.4	2.6	—0.4	0.3

See notes to Table 37.

different were components of gross capital formation compared, and it would be more trustworthy than that based upon Table 38, since the estimates of net values of residential and public construction are subject to especially wide errors because of conceptual and statistical difficulties in establishing the annual consumption of already existing construction. Also, the higher average share of *net* public construction is accounted for largely by its rise during the depressed decade of the 1930's. Nevertheless, the conclusion contains an undeniable kernel of significance: public construction had considerable weight in net capital formation during the last two decades while net residential construction was of relatively small weight.

The share of each component, except public construction, declined significantly from the first to the second decade. The quinquennial averages, and especially the annual figures (with due allowance for cyclical fluctuations), indicate that the movement of the shares of at least three components over the period is sufficiently consistent to claim secular significance. The rise in the share of public construction in both national income and capital formation is consistently suggested by the quinquennial averages, and there are many indications that, like the rise in the share of government in national income, it is in the nature of a secular tendency. Similarly, the share in national income of net flow to inventories declined fairly consistently, while the share of changes in claims against foreign countries did not regain the levels of 1919–20. In the shares of both inventories and claims against foreign countries the downward tilt is accentuated by the high levels attained immediately after the first World War. It is possible that this downward movement is a declining phase of a long cycle in inventory holdings (associated with a downward sweep of the price level) and in foreign trade (associated with a passing of the exceptional position of the United States in 1919–21 as the only large exporter in a weary and exhausted world).

The components of capital formation differ significantly in the degree to which their shares in national income reflect cyclical fluctuations. The component whose share conforms perfectly to business cycles and whose amplitudes are widest is the net flow to business inventories. Its share rises during every expansion and declines during every contraction, the differential movement ranging well above 5 per cent of national income. Another component whose share moves in perfect conformity to business cycles is producers' durable goods plus business construction; and its fluctuations would be greater could we confine it to producers' durable equipment excluding business construction. For various reasons, the shares of the other three components conform much less closely and have narrower amplitudes; residential construction because of a pronounced cycle of its own, with a trough in 1920, a peak in 1925, and the next trough in 1934; public construction because of its lack of susceptibility to transient changes in general business conditions, not to mention its use as a counterbalance to severe depressions; and changes in claims against foreign countries because of their dependence upon business conditions, not only in the United States but also in other countries whose business cycles do not necessarily coincide with American.

In the light of Table 38 some of the conclusions derived from Table 37 concerning the behavior of the share of net capital formation in national income may be reinterpreted. The decline over the period is due solely to the decline in the shares of capital formation of private types, notably residential construction, net flow to inventories, and producers' durable equipment including business construction. The marked conformity of fluctuations in the share of capital formation to business cycles and their wide amplitude are due largely to two components: net flow to inventories and the net flow of producers' durable equipment plus business construction.

2 *Capital Formation by Various Savings Accounts*
So far we have compared capital formation with national income as congeries of final products or forms of the disposition

of real product. We now attempt to study capital formation as the investment of a share of the monetary equivalent of national income, i.e., part of the total flow of various types of payment and income distinguished in Chapter 6. Viewed in this way net capital formation and its share in national income remain, of course, as they appeared in Table 37, but the divisions of net capital formation are different from those in Table 38. Instead of forming *material* or *channel of utilization* categories, we now set up divisions according to the type of income that became embodied in capital formation, i.e., according to the groups to whose savings we should attribute various parts of capital formation—corporations, governments, and unincorporated business firms.

Since savings of enterprises were so estimated as to exclude items that do not represent a flow to or from the stock of capital goods as estimated in capital formation (i.e., gains and losses from sales of capital assets, book gains and losses due to revaluation of inventories, gains and losses due to the difference between cost and reproduction bases of depreciation charges), we can interpret them as parts of the current national product that became embodied in current capital formation. If corporate savings are positive, as they were in 1919 to the extent of $1.0 billion, we may say that of the national product, $1.0 billion of current corporate net income became embodied in net capital formation; and that the rest of net capital formation represents net savings of governments, of unincorporated firms, or of individuals. Negative corporate savings may likewise be interpreted as indicating that not only did current income contribute nothing to net capital formation but actually that a net draft was made upon the existing stock of durable goods.

By using our estimates of net savings and of net capital formation we can apportion net capital formation among various accounts, i.e., among the groups whose savings became embodied in additions to the stock of capital goods in the country or to claims against foreign countries (Table 39). By

TABLE 39

Capital Formation by Type of Savings, Current Prices
1919–1938 (billions of dollars)

	CAPITAL FORMATION	Corp.	Gov.	SAVINGS OF Corp. & gov. (2 + 3)	Indiv. & entrep. (6 + 7)	Entre- preneurs	Individ- uals
	(1)	(2)	(3)	(4)	(5)	(6)	(7)
1919	10.3	1.0	—1.3	—0.3	10.6	5.5	5.1
1920	11.4	2.2	1.9	4.1	7.2	1.6	5.6
1921	3.3	0.7	1.0	1.7	1.6	0.6	1.0
1922	4.5	0.2	0.9	1.1	3.4	—0.1	3.5
1923	8.6	1.0	1.6	2.6	6.0	1.2	4.9
1924	5.9	0.4	1.7	2.1	3.7	0.9	2.9
1925	9.3	0.8	1.6	2.4	6.8	1.6	5.2
1926	9.2	2.3	2.2	4.4	4.8	2.1	2.7
1927	8.2	0.6	2.3	2.9	5.3	1.1	4.2
1928	7.4	0.9	1.9	2.8	4.6	0.9	3.6
1929	10.0	1.5	2.2	3.8	6.3	1.1	5.2
1930	4.2	—0.7	2.1	1.4	2.8	—0.6	3.4
1931	0.1	—3.1	0.3	—2.7	2.8	—2.0	4.9
1932	—4.2	—4.8	—0.9	—5.7	1.5	—3.5	5.0
1933	—3.6	—4.0	—0.1	—4.1	0.5	—2.4	2.9
1934	—2.6	—3.3	—0.6	—3.9	—1.3	—0.4	1.6
1935	0.7	—2.1	—1.7	—3.8	4.6	0.2	4.3
1936	5.4	—0.7	—2.2	—2.9	8.3	1.2	7.0
1937	6.4	—1.4	0.5	—0.9	7.3	0.4	6.8
1938	2.9	—0.7	—0.2	—0.9	3.7	0.3	3.5
Average							
1919–23	7.6	1.0	0.8	1.8	5.8	1.7	4.0
1924–28	8.0	1.0	1.9	2.9	5.0	1.3	3.7
1929–33	1.3	—2.2	0.7	—1.5	2.8	—1.5	4.3
1934–38	2.5	—1.6	—0.8	—2.5	5.0	0.4	4.7
1919–28	7.8	1.0	1.4	2.4	5.4	1.5	3.9
1929–38	1.9	—1.9	—0.05	—2.0	3.9	—0.6	4.5

subtracting corporate savings from net capital formation we obtain the savings by governments, entrepreneurs, and individuals that became embodied in capital formation. By subtracting savings of governments and entrepreneurs from the remainder we obtain the savings of individuals entering net capital formation.

Several qualifications must be stressed in order to avoid misinterpretation of the distributions in Tables 39 and 40. The first and most obvious is that the estimates are subject to fairly wide margins of error. The second is that corporate, government, entrepreneurial, and individuals' savings that became embodied in capital formation should not be confused with the amounts that accrued to the stock of capital goods at the disposal of these various groups. A corporation may have sustained negative savings but the stock of real capital goods at its disposal may have increased by purchases with borrowed funds; and the same is true of governments, unincorporated firms, and individuals. On the other hand, a corporation may have enjoyed positive net savings without itself using the surplus to finance additions to its capital goods. Such savings may have been used by other enterprises to finance capital investment through direct or indirect loans or investments made by the saver corporation. Third, net savings of economic enterprises (corporate and unincorporated firms, governments) are defined here to exclude several items usually included under such savings, and to that extent differ from what the enterprises themselves consider their net savings to be. Finally, and most important, individuals' savings embodied in net capital formation are significantly different from what individuals conceive their savings to be and from savings as usually measured in estimates under that label. The estimates in Table 39 exclude all capital gains and losses, i.e., gains and losses on sales of capital assets. They are the remainder after the amounts allocated as depreciation charges (over and above regular maintenance charges) against residential and other property owned by individuals have been subtracted, an adjustment not usually made in estimates of individuals' savings. They include amounts accruing to individuals as depositors in savings banks and other savings institutions and as holders of policies in life insurance companies, whether or not these amounts have been distributed to the depositors or policyholders; but exclude insurance benefit payments. They exclude amounts individuals may consider savings but that have failed to find expression in capital formation, either because they were appropriated by the transmitting agencies or because some delay may have occurred in their being used to finance additions to the stock of capital goods or to claims against foreign countries.

But while the estimates in Table 39 differ significantly from what enterprises and individuals conceive their savings to be; while they cannot be used to gauge the propensity of enterprises and individuals to save, they do reflect approximately the shares of net capital formation, i.e., of real investment financed from the current income of different groups of enterprises and individuals. In that sense they measure the contribution of various types of savings from current income to additions to the stock of the nation's capital goods.

Because net capital formation totals themselves, and still more frequently some of the components in Table 39, are often negative, we cannot establish annual percentage distributions of capital formation among components financed by savings of various types. But from the decennial averages we can gain some idea of the relative importance of various categories. In the decade 1919–28, when capital formation was at a relatively high level, corporate net savings accounted for only one-eighth of it; and if savings of unincorporated firms were added, the share of all business savings would rise to somewhat less than one-third of the total. Net savings of governments accounted for somewhat over one-sixth; while the share of individuals' savings was the largest, amounting to one-half of net capital formation. In the next decade, when savings of enterprises were negative and average net capital formation was positive, individuals' savings were the sole source of financing capital formation.[2]

The same decennial averages, supplemented by quinquennial averages, reveal the marked contrast in movement over

2 Although our estimates of savings of unincorporated firms are subject to a wide margin of error (see Ch. 12), we use them to separate this type of savings from individuals' savings embodied in capital formation. The total of savings of individuals and unincorporated firms combined (Table 39, col. 5), derived by subtracting from total net capital formation the savings of corporations and governments, is more reliable than that of either component.

the period between the shares of net capital formation attributable to individuals' savings and to savings of enterprises. Savings of corporate and unincorporated firms, and even of governments, decline markedly from the first to the second decade; and the average for the last quinquennium, 1934–38, is decidedly lower in all three series than for the first or second. No such decline occurs in capital formation attributable to individuals' savings, the average for 1929–38 being slightly higher than that for 1919–28, and the average for the last quinquennium, highest. The decline in net savings of enterprises needs no detailed comment. We note merely that with respect to them government has no advantage over private enterprise: changes in business conditions that affect private incorporated and unincorporated firms also affect tax and other revenue receipts of governments and hence their net savings. The absence of decline in individuals' savings embodied in capital formation is unexpected, but we postpone its discussion for a moment.

It is not surprising that savings of incorporated and of unincorporated firms fluctuate in close conformity to business cycles: they reflect clearly cyclical expansions (except that from 1919 to 1920 in entrepreneurial savings) and contractions (except that from 1937 to 1938 in corporate savings). And since government savings depend upon receipts that are largely determined by business conditions, we would expect them to reflect at least the more pronounced business cycles. Despite the wide margin of error and regardless of the movement in individuals' savings shown by the more customary indexes, individuals' savings embodied in capital formation also conform closely to fluctuations in general business conditions: the entries in column 7 reflect clearly the expansions of 1919–20, 1921–23, 1924–26, 1927–29, and 1932–37, although in the third and last the timing is somewhat different. Every contraction stands out.

We now turn to the intriguing question raised by the movement of the share of capital formation attributable to individu-

als' savings. As said, this share did not decline over the period
and was highest in the last quinquennium, 1934–38. When
we compare individuals' savings embodied in net capital
formation with aggregate payments to individuals (Table 40,
col. 1–4), both including savings of unincorporated firms, the
results are not unlike those of the business savings series in
Table 39: total savings and their share in aggregate payments
decline over the period, and the average for the last quinquennium is lower than that for 1919–23. The percentage
shares in columns 2 and 4 have a slightly higher average level
than the percentages of net capital formation in national income in Table 37, ranging about 6.5 per cent. Even in this
comparison the ratio of savings to aggregate payments in 1936
and 1937 was close to the peak (1919) and higher than during
the 1920's.

The second comparison in Table 40 (col. 5–8), of savings of
individuals, but not of unincorporated firms, embodied in net
capital formation, with aggregate payments to individuals excluding entrepreneurial savings is more striking. As already
indicated in Table 39, such savings in current prices rise
slightly from the first to the second decade. As a percentage
of aggregate payments, their share increases from the first to
the second decade and is highest in the last quinquennium.
When adjusted for price changes, they are considerably larger
in the second than in the first decade, and their share in aggregate payments increases markedly.

The conclusion that they were larger during the depressed
1930's than during the prosperous 1920's, and that as a share
in aggregate payments to individuals they were at least about
the same during the last decade of depression and recovery
as during the first decade of prosperity, is confirmed by a comparison of the recent years of cyclical expansion, 1936 and
1937, with the years of cyclical peaks in the 1920's. In 1929
prices individuals' savings embodied in capital formation were
highest in 1936 and 1937; for their percentage shares in aggregate payments also, these were among the highest years.

TABLE 40

Individuals' and Entrepreneurial Savings Embodied in
Capital Formation and their Percentage Share of
Aggregate Payments to Individuals, 1919–1938
Current and 1929 Prices (absolute figures in billions of dollars)

	PAYMENTS AND SAVINGS INCL. ENTREPRENEURIAL SAVINGS				PAYMENTS AND SAVINGS EXCL. ENTREPRENEURIAL SAVINGS			
	CURRENT PRICES		1929 PRICES		CURRENT PRICES		1929 PRICES	
	Savings	Savings as % of agg. pay.	Savings	Savings as % of agg. pay.	Savings	Savings as % of agg. pay.	Savings	Savings as % of agg. pay.
	(1)	(2)	(3)	(4)	(5)	(6)	(7)	(8)
1919	10.6	16.4	8.3	14.5	5.1	8.6	4.0	7.5
1920	7.2	10.3	4.8	8.6	5.6	8.2	3.7	6.9
1921	1.6	2.8	1.4	2.6	1.0	1.7	0.9	1.6
1922	3.4	5.7	3.1	5.1	3.5	5.8	3.1	5.3
1923	6.0	8.7	5.7	8.4	4.9	7.2	4.6	6.9
1924	3.7	5.3	3.5	5.0	2.9	4.1	2.7	3.9
1925	6.8	9.3	6.6	9.2	5.2	7.3	5.0	7.1
1926	4.8	6.2	4.5	6.0	2.7	3.6	2.6	3.5
1927	5.3	6.9	5.2	6.8	4.2	5.6	4.2	5.5
1928	4.6	5.8	4.5	5.7	3.6	4.7	3.6	4.6
1929	6.3	7.5	6.3	7.5	5.2	6.3	5.2	6.3
1930	2.8	3.6	2.9	3.7	3.4	4.4	3.6	4.5
1931	2.8	4.5	3.6	5.0	4.9	7.5	6.2	8.3
1932	1.5	3.1	2.0	3.1	5.0	9.6	6.6	9.7
1933	0.5	1.1	0.7	1.1	2.9	5.9	3.9	6.0
1934	1.3	2.4	1.7	2.6	1.6	3.0	2.2	3.3
1935	4.6	7.8	2.5	3.7	4.3	7.5	2.4	3.5
1936	8.3	12.6	8.6	11.0	7.0	10.9	7.3	9.5
1937	7.3	10.2	7.3	9.0	6.8	9.6	6.9	8.5
1938	3.7	5.6	4.2	5.3	3.5	5.3	3.9	4.9
Average								
1919–23	5.8	8.8	4.7	7.8	4.0	6.3	3.3	5.6
1924–28	5.0	6.7	4.9	6.5	3.7	5.1	3.6	4.9
1929–33	2.8	4.0	3.1	4.1	4.3	6.7	5.1	7.0
1934–38	5.0	7.7	4.9	6.3	4.7	7.3	4.5	5.9
1919–28	5.4	7.7	4.8	7.2	3.9	5.7	3.4	5.3
1929–38	3.9	5.8	4.0	5.2	4.5	7.0	4.8	6.4

Furthermore, even in the depressed years 1931–33 the share
of individuals' savings in aggregate payments was as high as
during the prosperous 1920's. As reiterated again and again,
estimates of individuals' savings embodied in capital formation are subject to serious qualifications. But distortions caused
by errors in estimates are not sufficiently great to invalidate
the general import of the conclusion.

Even the statement that individuals' savings embodied in

capital formation, both absolutely and as percentages of aggregate payments were, in 1929 prices, at least about the same during the 1930's as during the more prosperous 1920's may seem inexplicable; yet such behavior might well have been expected. The assumption of large savings by individuals in prosperous times is contingent upon the inclusion of capital gains of various types and a disregard of the extent to which an increase in individuals' indebtedness (a common occurrence during recent expansions) means an increase in consumption that leaves small margin for savings. It is not unlikely that during the 1920's, especially in the later years of the decade, when speculative gains were enormous and people spent as if good times would continue indefinitely, 'real' savings, i.e., savings available for capital formation, were much smaller absolutely and relatively than they seemed. It is beyond doubt that a large portion of what individuals themselves considered savings were illusory capital gains, investments of the type that could never constitute real additions to capital goods; and that 'real' savings by consumers as a whole were materially offset by an increase in consumers' and individuals' indebtedness.

In the 1930's the situation was different. The pressure for liquidation of individuals' indebtedness must surely have been a powerful incentive to curtail consumption and save more, even on smaller incomes. The absence of speculative gains and a dull stock market were not conducive to spending at the expense of saving and greatly lessened the chance that individuals' monetary savings would be dissipated in stock market losses. With the passing of the banking crisis in 1933 the tendency to save must have been strengthened considerably by the experience of the depression and by a desire to attain greater security against future calamities. Thrift, together with fewer opportunities to pursue capital gains or speculate, might well explain why savings embodied in capital formation were not lower in the 1930's than in the 1920's, and were higher in the peak years 1936 and 1937, and why they constituted a larger proportion of aggregate payments to individuals. Above all, it must not be overlooked that aggregate payments per capita in the second decade (in 1929 prices) were slightly higher, not lower, than in the first; and that under such conditions, the change in the factors affecting the flow of individuals' savings into capital formation might easily have given rise to the movements shown in Table 40. At any rate, the evidence must be accepted at least tentatively and as at least warranting a hypothesis that the relative level of individuals' 'real' savings was not lower and perhaps was slightly higher during the 1930's than during the 1920's.

3 Consumers' Outlay by Type of Product

The capital formation study yields estimates of consumers' outlay on perishable commodities, defined as lasting usually less than six months (food products, fuel, drugs, and the like); on semidurable, lasting between six months and three years (chiefly clothing, shoes, and some light household articles); and on durable, lasting more than three years (passenger cars, heavy household equipment such as washing machines, stoves, refrigerators, and furniture). The estimates are approximate in that no allowance is made for minor fractions of consumer goods sold to units other than ultimate consumers. But they do gauge roughly what consumers spend on these various categories of commodities; and by subtracting these amounts from total consumers' outlay we get a rough estimate of consumers' expenditures on services not embodied in new commodities (payments for rent, for professional and personal services, to governments, etc.).

In the annual apportionment of consumers' outlay among the four categories errors are substantial enough to cause year to year changes in the outlay on services that are not corroborated by other knowledge. For example, the estimated outlay on services not embodied in new commodities increases during all contractions except the very severe one from 1929 to 1932; probably because estimates of consumers' outlay on commodities exaggerate their levels during expansions and underestimate them during contractions, since the shares of these commodities sold to enterprises (for which no allowance is made) are likely to be higher in prosperity than in depression. While these errors are minor compared with amounts spent on finished commodities or with total consumers' outlay, they loom large in the estimate of outlay on services, computed as the difference between consumers' outlay and the outlay on all commodities. For this reason we thought it best to confine the study of the apportionment of consumers' outlay to periods in which the effects of movements during cyclical swings could be averaged out—the five reference cycle periods, the four quinquennia, and the two decades (Table 41).

Expenditure on commodities accounts, on the whole, for about two-thirds of consumers' outlay, expenditure on services not embodied in new commodities, for one-third. This apportionment is not unlike that of national income between commodity producing and commodity transporting and distributing industries on the one hand (60 per cent) and the service industries on the other (40 per cent) (Ch. 5). However, the distribution of national income by type of productive operation need not resemble that of consumers' outlay by type of product: service industries may contribute to the value of commodities so far as services become embodied in new commodities, thereby raising the cost of the latter to ultimate consumers.

By far the largest part of consumers' outlay is on perishable commodities—about 40 per cent of total outlay. Somewhat more goes for semidurable than for consumers' durable, the former accounting for over 15 per cent of total outlay, the latter for slightly over 10 per cent.

In current prices the share of semidurable commodities decreases over the period; the share of services not embodied in new commodities increases. The share of perishable commodities shows no definite movement, although the averages for the first four reference cycles decline continuously. How-

TABLE 41

Consumers' Outlay and its Percentage Distribution by Type of Product

Current and 1929 Prices, Selected Periods, 1919–1938

	CURRENT PRICES					1929 PRICES				
	CONSUMERS' OUTLAY (billions of dollars)	PERCENTAGE SHARE				CONSUMERS' OUTLAY (billions of dollars)	PERCENTAGE SHARE			
		Perishable	Semi-durable	Consumers' durable	Services		Perishable	Semi-durable	Consumers' durable	Services
	(1)	(2)	(3)	(4)	(5)	(6)	(7)	(8)	(9)	(10)
Average										
1919–21	57.6	42.8	18.7	10.7	27.8	51.3	41.1	14.4	10.0	34.6
1921–24	60.4	37.4	17.3	11.4	33.9	59.4	39.8	15.1	10.6	34.5
1924–27	69.3	37.1	16.6	12.8	33.6	68.2	38.4	15.0	13.2	33.4
1927–32	67.3	36.9	15.5	10.9	36.7	71.2	38.5	15.6	11.0	35.0
1932–38	54.7	41.0	14.8	10.0	34.1	66.4	42.2	15.4	9.4	32.9
1919–23	58.4	40.6	18.4	11.1	29.9	54.4	40.4	15.0	10.5	34.1
1924–28	70.3	37.1	16.6	12.7	33.7	69.2	38.1	15.2	13.1	33.6
1929–33	60.7	37.4	14.8	9.9	37.9	68.7	40.1	15.2	9.6	35.1
1934–38	58.0	41.8	15.0	10.7	32.4	68.5	41.6	15.5	10.1	32.8
1919–28	64.4	38.8	17.5	11.9	31.8	61.8	39.3	15.1	11.8	33.9
1929–38	59.3	39.6	14.9	10.3	35.2	68.6	40.8	15.4	9.8	33.9

ever, in the last cycle the share is not significantly lower than
at the beginning of the period. The share of consumers'
durable commodities likewise shows no significant trend, the
averages for the successive cycles first rising, then declining.

Adjustment for fluctuations in prices suggests that a substantial part of the change over the period in the apportionment of consumers' outlay in current prices is due to differences in price movements among the various commodity and
service groups. In the apportionment in 1929 prices the share
of perishable commodities again fails to reveal a trend, but
even the changes in the cyclical and quinquennial averages are
smaller than in the percentage distribution of totals in current
prices. The share of semidurable commodities in 1929 prices
does not decline, the averages for reference cycles and quinquennia suggesting, if anything, a slight rise. Consequently
the decline in the share of semidurable commodities in current prices seems to be due to the greater decline in the prices
of this group than in those of other commodity and service
groups. The share of consumers' durable commodities in 1929
prices shows the same rise and decline as in current prices,
and while the average for the second decade is lower than for
the first, the decline over the period is not sufficiently consistent
to be attributed much secular significance. Finally, the averages for both reference cycles and quinquennia of the share
of services not embodied in new commodities in 1929 prices
show no distinct movement over the period and there is no
change from the first to the second decade.

Thus, when the differential movements in the price levels of
various commodity and service groups are allowed for, there
seem to be no significant shifts in the apportionment of consumers' outlay. Although our estimates are crude, the conclusion
seems reasonable in the light of what little we know about the
stability of the composition of consumers' budgets in terms of
large categories of commodities and services. Greater use of durable commodities tends to be accompanied by larger outlay on
such non-durable goods as are involved in their utilization; for

example, greater use of passenger cars means larger consumption of gasoline and oil, more demand for services not embodied in new commodities (repair services, etc.) and even for semidurable goods (such as tires and tubes). On the other hand, any increase in the relative importance of non-durable goods is limited in that a rising standard of living is ordinarily accompanied by an increase in the demand for durable goods. Indeed, consumers' demand for goods of varying durability is perhaps governed by the rather fixed patterns of life in general, patterns determined by persistent rhythms of daily, seasonal, and secular wants that do not allow for substantial shifts in relative weight among goods that must be consumed within periods of significantly varying length.

4 National Income by Type of Product

By combining the subdivisions under net capital formation and under consumers' outlay we get a twofold apportionment of national income (Table 42): one separating all non-durable types of final products, whether commodities or services, from durable; the other separating all commodities from services not embodied in new commodities. In the first, non-durable types comprise perishable and semidurable commodities and services not embodied in new commodities; and durable comprise construction, consumers' and producers' durable. This still leaves a minor portion of national income not allocated by durability, viz., net flow to inventories and changes in claims against foreign countries. In the second classification the commodities group comprises not only all categories of commodities and construction but also net flow to inventories; the group of services is naturally confined to services not embodied in new commodities; and the unallocable portion is represented by changes in claims against foreign countries, a mixture of commodity and service transactions. In Table 42 the percentages are shown for periods for which most of the cyclical swing is averaged out, since the crudeness of the estimate of services precludes valid annual comparisons.

TABLE 42

National Income, Percentage Distribution by Type of Product
Current and 1929 Prices, Selected Periods, 1919–1938

| | BY DURABILITY | | | BETWEEN COMMODITIES AND SERVICES | | |
| | Non-durable | Durable | Unal-locable | Com-modities | Services | Unal-locable |
	(1)	(2)	(3)	(4)	(5)	(6)
		CURRENT	PRICES			
Average						
1919–21	78.4	12.8	8.8	72.0	24.6	3.4
1921–24	81.3	16.6	2.1	67.9	31.1	1.0
1924–27	78.2	20.5	1.4	69.4	30.0	0.5
1927–32	85.2	15.3	—0.5	64.3	35.2	0.5
1932–38	90.1	10.0	—0.1	65.4	34.4	0.2
1919–23	78.9	14.5	6.6	71.0	26.7	2.2
1924–28	78.5	20.3	1.2	69.1	30.3	0.6
1929–33	90.5	11.0	—1.4	61.5	38.1	0.4
1934–38	86.2	12.4	1.4	68.4	31.4	0.2
1919–28	78.7	17.4	3.9	70.1	28.5	1.4
1929–38	88.3	11.7	0.0	65.0	34.8	0.3
		1929	PRICES			
1919–21	80.5	12.7	6.8	66.2	30.9	2.8
1921–24	82.4	15.7	1.8	67.2	31.8	1.0
1924–27	78.0	20.8	1.2	69.5	30.0	0.5
1927–32	85.2	15.2	—0.5	66.0	33.4	0.6
1932–38	91.2	9.1	—0.3	66.6	33.2	0.2
1919–23	80.5	14.2	5.2	67.4	30.7	1.9
1924–28	78.3	20.7	1.1	69.2	30.3	0.6
1929–33	90.9	10.5	—1.4	64.5	35.1	0.4
1934–38	87.3	11.5	1.2	67.9	31.9	0.2
1919–28	79.4	17.4	3.1	68.3	30.5	1.2
1929–38	89.1	11.0	—0.1	66.2	33.5	0.3

The relative importance of non-durable types is quite high,
averaging about 85 per cent of national income for the period.
Thus the preponderant part of the economy's current product
is consumed within a short time, an indication of the extent
to which maintenance of current consumption depends upon
maintenance of national income. The share of non-durable
products increased over the period. Although the rise did not
begin until the 1930's, still since the averages for the last reference cycle and quinquennium are higher than for the first,

and similar movements appear in the percentage shares even after adjustment for price changes, it attains some significance. It might be offset substantially by an allowance for the portion of non-durable products in the unallocable item, flow to inventories, and changes in claims against foreign countries. And, correspondingly, the share of durable commodities does not decline as much as the share of non-durable rises. The movement of the former, with the long cycle it seems to describe, suggests the influence of construction. Yet the five cyclical averages do indicate a rather significant drop in the share of durable commodities in national income. Whether this is transient, due to a lag in the recovery of the construction cycle and in general recovery from the 1929–32 contraction, or whether it is indicative of a more persistent trend toward an increasing share of non-durable products (especially services not embodied in new commodities) only the future can tell.

Roughly two-thirds of our current product assumes the form of commodities. In current prices the share declines markedly over the period, and the share of services not embodied in new commodities rises. Since the unallocated remainder is small, the relative loss in the share of commodities and the relative gain in the share of services would not be affected much, even if it were added fully to one or the other. The change in the apportionment in current prices is thus similar to that observed in Chapter 5 for the distribution of national income among industries classified by type of productive operation— a decline in the share of commodity producing industries and a rise in the share of service industries.

After adjustment for price changes, the decline in the share of commodities and the rise in the share of services become much less marked. Indeed, the averages for both business cycles and quinquennia indicate such a small decline in the share of commodities that it may be treated as insignificant. The share of services not embodied in new commodities still rises, but much less than the share in current prices. It would seem, therefore, that a major part of the shift in the shares of com-

modities and of services in national income in current prices
is due to the differences in movement between prices of commodities and of services; and that after adjustment for price
changes, the decline in the share of commodities and the rise
in the share of services are so small as to be of doubtful significance.

5 *Summary*

a) Net capital formation averaged over the period about 6
per cent of national income; and it is this low fraction that
measures the share of the economy's net current product that
was added to the stock of capital goods in the country or to
claims against foreign countries.

b) The share of net capital formation in national income
declined over the period by reason of the extremely severe
contraction in 1929–32 and the failure of capital formation to
recover sufficiently to offset fully the effects of that contraction.

c) Net capital formation fluctuates more violently than national income during business cycles, causing its share in
national income to fluctuate in close conformity to them.

d) The decline over the period in the share of capital formation in national income is accounted for by the decline in the
share of private capital formation. The share of public construction, the only non-private component of capital formation
that can be segregated, does not decline.

e) The great sensitivity of capital formation to business
cycles is due largely to the close conformity of two of its chief
components, net flow to inventories and net value of producers' durable goods, to business cycles. Of the other components, public construction and changes in claims against
foreign countries are least responsive.

f) When net capital formation is apportioned among savings of various types, the share attributable even during 1919–
28 to corporate savings amounts to less than 15 per cent; to
savings of unincorporated firms, to about 20 per cent; to savings of governments, to more than 15 per cent; and to indi-

viduals' savings, to 50 per cent. This dominance of the share attributable to individuals' savings was even more marked in the second decade, when savings of enterprises became negative.

g) The decline from the first to the second decade in the shares of net capital formation attributable to savings of enterprises (private and public) is quite marked. There is a correspondingly sharp increase in the share attributable to individuals' savings.

h) The crude estimates of individuals' savings embodied in net capital formation suggest that, in 1929 prices, they were, on the average, not lower in the 1930's than in the 1920's; and their share in aggregate payments to individuals was at least about the same during the second as during the first decade. We did not attempt to estimate the amounts individuals think they saved, or individuals' savings as reflected by records of financial institutions, records that usually disregard several positive and negative components of savings in their bearing upon capital formation.

i) In the apportionment of consumers' outlay by type of product the share of perishable commodities averages over 40 per cent; of semidurable commodities, somewhat over 15 per cent; of durable commodities, about 11 per cent; and of services not embodied in new commodities, about 33 per cent.

j) In current prices the share of semidurable commodities in consumers' outlay declines over the period; that of services not embodied in new commodities, rises; that of perishable commodities shows no definite movement; and that of durable commodities declines, although far from consistently. Adjustment for price changes reduces these shifts appreciably and suggests that, since the first World War, there have been no significant long term changes in the apportionment of consumers' outlay in 1929 prices among the four categories of goods classified by durability.

k) Non-durable goods constitute the overwhelming proportion of national income, averaging about 85 per cent. In both

current and 1929 prices the share of non-durable goods seems
to increase over the period; that of durable to decline.

l) Commodities seem to account on the average for two-
thirds of national income; in current prices their share declines appreciably over the period; that of services not embodied in new commodities rises. With the adjustment for
price changes the loss in the share of commodities and the
gain in that of services are materially reduced, although there
are still traces of a decline in the share of commodities and a
somewhat more obvious indication of a rise in the share of
services. However, the shifts are so minor that they cannot be
attributed much significance.

*Appendix to Chapter 7: Comparison with Published Estimates
of Individuals' Savings*
The crudeness of our estimates of individuals' savings embodied in capital formation, the importance of the subject, and
the interest that attaches to any evidence that bears upon it
led us to compare our estimates with others. Because of differences in concept and scarcity of reliable data, such comparisons cannot serve as valid checks upon the accuracy of any
one set of estimates. But they should reveal the substantial
differences, suggest reasons for them, and be conducive to more
intelligent interpretation and use.

1 Consumer Expenditures Study Estimate for 1935–36
The most recent and perhaps most thorough estimate of individuals' savings in this country is for a year extending
roughly from the middle of 1935 to the middle of 1936 by
the National Resources Committee (*Consumer Expenditures
in the United States;* Washington, 1939). Based largely upon

1 I am indebted to A. G. Hart of Iowa State College, and Raymond Goldsmith
and Irwin Friend of the Securities and Exchange Commission, for valuable
suggestions in connection with parts of this Appendix.

a sample study of how families and individuals, including also entrepreneurs, spend their income, they are, except for items noted below, roughly comparable to our estimate of individu-als' and entrepreneurs' savings embodied in capital formation.

Savings are defined in the report (p. 22) as "net change in assets and liabilities of the family (or single individual) during the year, exclusive of gains and losses from revaluation of assets". Appreciation and depreciation of assets, whether real-ized or not, are not allowed for in either income or savings; and it is stated that the definition of savings "conforms to the accepted rule that savings equals income less expenditures for current consumption and for gifts and personal taxes" (p. 22). However, profits and losses on assets bought and sold within the year are included in income and hence in savings.

After examining the questionnaire on changes in assets and liabilities and the description of various concepts involved in determining savings we concluded that savings as estimated by the National Resources Committee differ from our individ-uals' (including entrepreneurs') savings embodied in capital formation in the following important respects:

a) The N.R.C. estimate does not allow for the depreciation of residential real estate owned by individuals and inhabited by its owners. The imputed rental value was added to income and included again under expenditures. There seems to be no provision in the balance sheet of assets and liabilities for depreciation on real estate. To the extent that it is not allowed for, the N.R.C. total savings is larger than our savings em-bodied in net capital formation.

b) It is not clear whether in the N.R.C. estimate expendi-tures incurred in investment (brokerage fees, interest on loans made to carry securities) are allowed for and whether purchases of various types of assets on the positive side of the balance sheet include charges in addition to the net value of the asset. Consequently the N.R.C. estimate of savings may be inflated by using the cost of assets purchased instead of the net market value of assets

c) If savings, expenditures, and family income were reconciled, and gains and losses from sales of assets were included in income, they must have been included also under savings (and no figures are given to indicate gains and losses or whether they were positive or negative).

d) Both family income and savings, in the case of entrepreneurs, include net profit or loss from business; and net profit and loss reported on the schedules presumably reflect customary practices of business accounting. Therefore, in contrast to our estimate of savings embodied in net capital formation, the N.R.C. estimate of individuals' savings is affected by gains and losses on sales of capital assets, revaluation of inventories, and the use of the cost basis in estimating depreciation. However, the N.R.C. report states explicitly that only quantity changes in farmers' inventories are taken into account (p. 22, footnote 27).

e) The treatment of savings in connection with life insurance, building and loan associations, and similar savings institutions suggests that the N.R.C. estimates omit an item included in ours—the accrual to individuals' savings derived from the excess of receipts, by life insurance companies and other associations, over and above current costs of operation. In the N.R.C. estimates, payments of premiums or new payments to associations are alone considered evidence of savings. While annuities and benefits are included in income, the balance sheets would not reveal payments of annuities or of benefits as a source of savings since there would be a corresponding reduction in assets outstanding. In our estimate such net receipts are included under individuals' savings, just as much as their actual in-payments (both, of course, so far as they are embodied in net capital formation).

When we try to express these differences in scope quantitatively, we find that there is no way, with the present data, of approximating costs of investment or savings and losses from purchases and sales of assets for 1935–36 (items b and c). But it may reasonably be assumed that both amounts and their sum are small compared to total individuals' savings.

The other items may be roughly approximated: (a) Depreciation on owner-occupied residential real estate in 1935–36 is approximately $800 million (derived from an estimate of depreciation on all residential property, minus an allowance for residential property owned by corporations, the remainder apportioned on the basis of ratios of imputed to money rent received by individuals). (d) Estimated from the national income study to be about $120 million, the excess of the accounting measure of entrepreneurial net savings over adjusted net savings (average of items for 1935 and 1936). (e) Estimated to be roughly $1,000 million, the excess of receipts, by life insurance companies and other associations of individuals, of dividends, interest, rent, and all forms of property income over current costs of operation (wages, salaries, materials, and dividends to stockholders, but, of course, excluding payments of annuities and benefits).[2] The adjusted estimate of savings on the basis of the N.R.C. study for 1935–36 would then be, in millions of dollars:

Present N.R.C. estimate	5,978
Minus depreciation	800
Minus adjustment of entrepreneurial savings	120
Plus accruals of life insurance companies and similar institutions	1,000
Net total	6,058

Our estimates of individuals' savings embodied in capital formation are $4.6 billion for 1935 and $8.3 billion for 1936. If we average these totals in accordance with the distribution of monthly income payments, as shown for these two years in Department of Commerce reports, we obtain the following: ratio of the last six months in 1935 to the annual total, 0.518; ratio of the first six months in 1936 to the annual total, 0.473; total for 1935–36, $6.31 billion.

2 This is the estimate made in the N.R.C. report, in the reconciliation with the Department of Commerce national income total (see *Consumer Incomes in the United States*, p. 35, footnote 5.)

According to these calculations, our estimate exceeds that of the N.R.C. by at least $0.25 billion. The errors accounting for the difference may be in both sets of estimates. The N.R.C. estimates of income (and hence of savings) are some 3 per cent less than the comparable Department of Commerce estimates, excluding the shortage due to the failure to take into account accruals by insurance companies and similar institutions (see *Consumer Incomes in the United States,* p. 35); and this alone would lead us to raise the N.R.C. estimate of savings by another $200 million, thereby canceling the difference. It is also possible that savings embodied in net capital formation were much more heavily concentrated in the second half of 1936 than were monthly income payments, which would reduce our estimate of savings for 1935–36 to less than $6.31 billion.

It can therefore be said that comparison with the N.R.C. estimate does not reveal any significant evidence that our estimate of individuals' savings embodied in capital formation for 1935–36 is either too high or too low.

2 The Brookings Estimate for 1929

In *America's Capacity to Consume,* Maurice Leven estimates individuals' savings (including entrepreneurial) to be $17.8 billion for both families and unattached individuals in 1929 (see Tables 5, 6, 9, pp. 260, 261, 265). Our estimate of savings embodied in net capital formation (individuals' plus entrepreneurs') in 1929 is only $6.3 billion. A large proportion of this striking difference is easily accounted for. The Brookings estimate includes in individuals' income gains on sales of assets to the tune of $6.2 billion in 1929 (see Table 13, p. 163). Since such gains, even though affecting consumers' expenditures, cannot be included in the latter total, their appearance under income in the Brookings study means that they were included in the savings of families and individuals that had them (mostly in the higher income brackets). Accordingly, we subtract the capital gains from both income and savings, which reduces distributed income to $86.8 billion and savings to $11.6 billion (for the former figure see Table 39, p. 229).

But even after this adjustment, the Brookings estimate of income is larger than our aggregate payments including entrepreneurial savings ($83.3 billion), owing chiefly to the inclusion of income from odd jobs, gardens, etc. (see Table 13, p. 163). If we assume that the proportion of this additional income saved is the same as of savings to total income after the exclusion of capital gains, the excess in savings is about 4 per cent, or $0.4 billion, reducing the Brookings estimate to $11.2 billion.

This residual Brookings estimate exceeds our estimate of individuals' savings embodied in capital formation for the following reasons: (a) So far as it is based upon consumer budget samples, it does not allow fully for depreciation on owner-occupied residential property, or even for depreciation on all residential property owned by individuals. Savings items reported in budget studies are ordinarily derived from financial data relating to the family without a careful calculation of costs or reconciliation of income and expenditures. (b) It does not allow for commissions on purchases of assets and losses on fraudulent securities. (c) It takes into account entrepreneurial net savings before the adjustments involved in making them comparable with net capital formation.

Item (a), for *all* residential property owned by individuals, may be estimated for 1929 as between $1.8 and $2.5 billion, with $2 billion as a roughly acceptable figure. Item (b) is estimated by Clark Warburton to be $2 billion (see *Studies in Income and Wealth*, Vol. One, p. 109). Item (c), however, is negative for 1929, about — $0.1 billion. The total adjustment for these three items in the Brookings figures is $3.9 billion; and the estimate is accordingly reduced to $7.3 billion.

Thus, after such adjustments as we can make, the Brookings estimate of savings for 1929 still exceeds our estimate of savings embodied in net capital formation by about $1 billion. Whether this excess is due to the assumption of too high a savings ratio in the Brookings estimate (especially for the upper income groups, for which data were perforce scanty) or to deficiencies in our estimate, cannot be ascertained with the present data. The significant conclusion, however, is that the huge difference is to be ascribed largely to significant differences in scope; and that after adjustment the residual discrepancy is not more than 16 per cent of our total, a relatively small difference in view of the essential differences in the materials upon which the two estimates are based.

3 Lough's Estimates for 1919–31

In preparing his estimates of consumption and individuals' savings (*High Level Consumption,* McGraw-Hill, 1935) William H. Lough made some attempt to segregate the latter from those of business and government. But it is not clear to what extent savings of unincorporated firms were excluded from his estimates of savings proper. His estimates are based upon a study of movements in bank deposits, outstanding currency, issuance of securities, acquisitions, etc. Inspection of the procedures (see especially Table 33, pp. 284–5, which describes in detail the derivation of the savings estimate for 1929) suggests that, on the whole, savings of unincorporated firms must have been included with individuals' savings. However, it is likely that several forms of savings by firms (additions to inventories, reductions of debt, and the like) were not covered; other forms, such as acquisition of securities or additions to bank deposits and purchase of farms, on the other hand, probably were.

It seems reasonable to treat Lough's estimates as most nearly comparable with our estimates of individuals' savings, including those of unincorporated firms. The divergences in scope are as follows: (a) Lough's estimates, based upon records of financial institutions and study of the acquisition of assets, omit an adjustment for depreciation chargeable to all residential and other property held by individuals. (b) In estimating payments by individuals for securities, Lough uses the *Commercial and Financial Chronicle* series on non-refunding issues, whereas, according to more recent studies, a considerable proportion of even these non-refunding issues does not represent flow into real investment and capital formation.[3] (c) Lough allows for changes in individuals' debts only in connection with real estate and in estimating security takings, and it is not clear that this allowance covers changes in consumer debt not connected with the purchase or holding of real estate securities. (d) Lough's estimates do not include savings of unincorporated firms in the form of additions to their stocks of goods (inventories or equipment) or changes in their debt. (e) Lough does not allow for accruals to individuals *via* life insurance companies, although he has taken such changes in building and loan associations and other savings organizations into account. In contrast to other estimates, Lough's seem to exclude from savings costs of investment transactions (since the net market value of securities and other assets purchased is used and divided between individuals and enterprises).

It is possible to adjust roughly for item (a) on the basis of depreciation attributable to residential real estate (and residential alone); for (b), since 1921, on the basis of the ratio of Moody's productive issues to the *Chronicle* total of non-refunding issues;[4] for (c), since 1924, by allowing for changes in consumers' debt. No allowance is possible for (d), for, while we have estimates of entrepreneurial net savings, we cannot divide them into the various forms in which they were embodied. Item (e) can be estimated roughly, but not as an annual series.

Lough's estimates, the various adjustments to them, and a comparison with our estimates of individuals' net savings embodied in net capital formation are shown in the accompanying table. The comparison, after all the adjustments, is still between estimates of which one (Lough's) excludes at least a substantial part of net savings of unincorporated firms and

---

[3] See 'Security Issues and Real Investment in 1929', by George A. Eddy, *Review of Economic Statistics*, May 1937.

[4] *Ibid.*, p. 91.

	LOUGH'S ESTIMATES[1] (1)	DEPRECIATION (2)	ALLOWANCE FOR NON-PRODUCTIVE ISSUES[2] (3)	CONSUMER CREDIT[3] (4)	TOTAL ADJUSTMENT (2 + 3 − 4) (5)	LOUGH'S ESTIMATES, ADJ. (1 − 5) (6)	NBER ESTIMATES (7)	DIFFERENCE (6 − 7) (8)
			(billions of dollars)					
1919	9.4	1.8					10.6	
1920	10.1	2.4					7.2	
1921	6.5	1.7	0.7		2.4	4.1	1.6	+2.5
1922	5.4	1.6	0.5		2.1	3.3	3.4	−0.1
1923	7.8	1.9	0.7		2.6	5.2	6.0	−0.8
1924	8.7	1.9	0.7	−0.3	2.9	5.8	3.7	+2.1
1925	10.6	1.9	1.9	−0.8	4.6	6.0	6.8	−0.8
1926	10.6	2.0	2.1	−0.6	4.7	5.9	4.8	+1.1
1927	10.4	2.1	2.3	−0.2	4.6	5.8	5.3	+0.5
1928	8.5	2.1	3.3	−0.8	6.2	2.3	4.6	−2.3
1929	9.3	2.2	4.7[4]	−1.0	7.9[4]	1.4[4]	6.3	−4.9
1930	8.5	2.1	1.8	+0.6	3.3	5.2	2.8	+2.4
1931	4.1	1.8	0.5	+1.1	1.2	2.9	2.8	+0.1

[1] *High Level Consumption*, Table 41, p. 306.
[2] Obtained by correcting Table 38 of *High Level Consumption*. The ratio of productive issues to total non-refunding issues (*Review of Economic Statistics*, May 1937, p. 91) was applied to lines 1, 4, and 11 and the new totals derived as outlined by Lough. The entries in col. 3 are the difference between Lough's original estimates of payments by individuals for securities and our new estimates of these values, derived, as just stated, by a further allowance for non-productive, non-refunding issues.
[3] Rolf Nugent, *Consumer Credit and Economic Stability* (Russell Sage Foundation, 1940), Table 10, p. 116.
[4] The Eddy figure for the *Chronicle* total issues less refunding series is $9.2 billion; the Lough, $7.8. In all other years the difference is slight. The use of the Eddy figure for 1929 would reduce the allowance for non-productive issues to $4.3 billion, making the total adjustment $7.5 billion, Lough's adjusted estimates $1.8 billion, and the difference (col. 8), −$4.5 billion.

accruals to the benefit of individuals on the books of life insurance companies.

In view of the crudeness of the adjustments and the consequently erratic annual movement of Lough's adjusted estimates, we may properly compare only the average level of the two series. For 1921–31 our estimates are only $0.2 billion larger than Lough's adjusted (col. 6), a truly insignificant difference. Correction for the accrual to individuals of assets on books of life insurance companies would make Lough's estimates about $0.4 billion *per year* more than ours; allowance for part of net savings of unincorporated firms might add to the average excess of Lough's estimates over ours. One may contend also that at least part of the change in consumers' credit (col. 4) has already been taken into account in Lough's estimates, and that the corresponding downward adjustment of Lough's estimates has, therefore, been too large. But it is doubtful that the inclusion of these elements would make Lough's estimates more than $0.5 billion per year greater than ours. On the other hand, the adjustment for depreciation chargeable to real estate held by individuals is probably too small, since it excludes non-residential real estate owned by individuals; there is no allowance for an increase in individuals' indebtedness before 1924; and the adjustments are so crude that we should not ascribe any significance to an average difference of some $0.5 billion per year, which amounts to no more than about 10 per cent of the average value of either total.

The comparison therefore does not cast serious doubt upon the correctness of the average level or the general movement of our estimates. Nor does the movement of the differences between the two series suggest that our estimates are too low for the 1920's and too high for the 1930's.

4 Goldsmith's Estimates for 1933–37

In a report to the Conference on Research in Income and Wealth, Raymond Goldsmith presented in detail his **estimates** of savings for 1933–37 (see *Studies in Income and Wealth*, Vol. Three, pp. 217–315). Based upon an attempt to take into account movements in individuals' balances in banks, building and loan associations, insurance and pension reserves, absorption of securities and various forms of consumer goods, they measure also business savings of agriculture, but not of unincorporated enterprises in other industries.

Goldsmith's estimates of individuals' savings (excluding their savings invested in automobiles and other consumer durable goods, but including their savings invested in dwellings) plus savings in agriculture are strikingly lower than our estimates of individuals' savings (including entrepreneurial savings) embodied in capital formation. The difference may be due partly to a difference in scope: our estimates attempt to cover fully entrepreneurial net savings (crude and approximate as the estimates necessarily are), whereas Goldsmith's

	1933	*1934*	*1935*	*1936*	*1937*	*Total*
			(billions of dollars)			
Goldsmith (see p. 237)	—1.3	+0.5	+0.9	+6.7	+3.9	+10.7
Present NBER	+0.5	+1.3	+4.6	+8.3	+7.3	+22.0
Difference	—1.8	—0.8	—3.7	—1.6	—3.4	—11.3

Dr. Goldsmith has informed me that his estimates are being revised. The revised figures, however, were not available when this chapter went to press.

estimates of individuals' savings include some forms of entre-preneurial savings (cash, securities, etc.) and exclude others (inventories, debt, construction, fixtures, etc. for non-farmers). It is quite possible that during 1935, 1936, and 1937 there were substantial additions to the inventories and equipment of entrepreneurs that were not offset by increases in debt; and that for the period as a whole (1933–37) this item, omitted in Goldsmith's estimates, amounted to some two or three billion dollars. If this is true, adjustment for the difference in scope would reduce the difference in the years in which it is espe-cially marked—1935, 1936, and 1937.

But even after this adjustment, a substantial difference would still remain between the two series. It may be due to an excess in our estimates, a shortage in the Goldsmith estimates, or to both. The excess in our series of individuals' savings embodied in capital formation may be due largely to an under-estimate of corporate savings, arising from (a) the tendency of corporations to understate their net income to taxing authori-ties and to include under current maintenance the cost of cer-tain capital goods which we include in gross capital formation; and (b) our failure to adjust corporate net savings properly for such items as gains and losses from sales of capital assets, effects of inventory revaluation, and the disparity between deprecia-tion charges on cost and reproduction bases. Sources of under-estimates of corporate savings (a) would not affect our esti-mates of capital formation; which means that individuals' savings embodied in capital formation (the difference between net capital formation and corporate and government savings) would be overestimated.

This possibility of an exaggeration of the average level of our estimates of individuals' savings embodied in capital formation would go far to explain the continuous excess of our estimates over Goldsmith's. Yet in the present state of our knowledge, such a possibility can only be conjectured; it can neither be demonstrated nor adjusted for. What is more to the point, this bias toward exaggerating individuals' savings embodied in capital formation would be most pronounced during periods of prosperity, when corporate net profits are high. Hence, the overestimate of individuals' savings, if there is one, should be greater in the 1920's than in the 1930's, and correction would only strengthen our conclusion that individuals' savings did not decline during the depressed 1930's.

On the other hand, as Dr. Goldsmith himself recognizes (see pp. 234–6), there are possible shortages in his estimates. Perhaps the most important source is that he does not take into account reductions in individuals' debts, except for the debt connected with passenger cars (directly) and real estate (see comments by A. G. Hart, *Studies in Income and Wealth*, Vol. Three, pp. 303–4). Hart mentions a decline of $6.2 billion (an admittedly crude guess) in individuals' short term debts during 1933–35; Goldsmith shows a few million dollars of increase in individuals' debt from changes in installment debt (for consumers' durable goods) and shrinkage in security loans. This enormous difference would account in large part for the difference between Goldsmith's and our estimates, although it probably would not affect years after 1935, in which the differences are substantial.

Why should estimates derived by a careful scrutiny of financial accounts run lower than those obtained by subtracting from net capital formation the net savings of corporations and governments? More data and study are obviously needed to effect a reconciliation, but even if there is some excess in our estimates of individuals' savings embodied in capital formation, the trend in this bias is only likely to confirm our tentative conclusion concerning the relative levels of these savings in the 1920's and the 1930's.

5 Other Estimates

We mention three other estimates, although no comparison with our estimates is possible or needed. The first is that of Mordecai Ezekiel, made largely by the application of the savings-income ratio in the Brookings study to the distribution of income in the upper brackets as shown by federal income tax returns (see 'An Annual Estimate of Saving by Individuals', *Review of Economic Statistics*, Nov. 1937). Since the estimates include capital gains, are subject to all the deficiencies of the income concept as defined in tax returns, and apply solely to savings of individuals who file income tax returns, they cannot be compared with any estimate of individuals' savings embodied in capital formation.

The second estimate is that recently published by Gainsbrugh and Osborne of the National Industrial Conference Board staff (see The Conference Board *Economic Record*, March 22, 1940 and April 22, 1940). Savings are shown separately for unincorporated enterprises and for individuals; for the latter the estimates are derived by methods essentially similar to those used by Goldsmith. But whereas individuals' savings are defined as "the difference between consumption expenditures of individuals and earned income received by individuals in that year" (see April 22 issue, p. 180), comparison of income received by individuals (Table 1, p. 181) with consumption expenditures (Conference Board *Economic Bulletin*, Aug. 24, 1939) indicates a total of individuals' savings significantly and inexplicably different from the total given directly and based upon financial and other records. The difference remains whether we consider individuals' savings alone or include also savings of unincorporated enterprises. Since it is not explained, we do not attempt a comparison of the estimates with ours.

Gordon S. Fulcher's method (*Review of Economic Statistics,* Feb. 1941) is essentially similar to ours, since he derives estimates of individuals' savings by subtracting corporate and government savings from capital formation. But by using estimates of gross capital formation and corporate and government gross savings he derives gross savings of individuals, somewhat modified (in comparison with our estimates) by a partial inclusion of capital gains. The general result of Fulcher's analysis is, however, quite similar to ours in indicating a level of individuals' savings in the 1930's not much lower than in the 1920's and a ratio of individuals' savings to total income in 1934–37 about the same as in 1926–29 (Fulcher's estimates cover only the years since 1926).

6 Concluding Comments

a) Only our estimates of individuals' savings, including savings of entrepreneurs, can be tested by comparison with other published estimates of individuals' savings. The reasons that make it difficult to estimate savings of unincorporated enterprises make it almost impossible to segregate entrepreneurial savings from other savings in any study based upon records of banking and savings institutions, absorption of securities, etc.

b) The closest comparison that can be made is between our estimates and those based upon a study of how income was spent or saved, provided, of course, that the income concepts are similar. Comparisons with estimates of savings based upon records of financial and other institutions are, however, unsatisfactory, because such records are not explicit concerning elements that may represent depreciation and other reserves rather than savings, and are necessarily incomplete in their coverage of unincorporated firms and of the individuals' complete network of claims and obligations.

c) As far as valid comparisons can be made, the difference between our estimates of individuals' savings embodied in capital formation and other estimates of individuals' savings is fairly small, after adjustments for differences in scope. There is no significant evidence that the average level shown by our estimates is either too high or too low.

d) It is possible that our estimates of savings embodied in capital formation are somewhat too low in the second half of the 1920's and somewhat too high in the second half of the 1930's. But no evidence substantial enough to affect the broad conclusions in the text concerning the movement of individuals' savings (including entrepreneurial savings) embodied in capital formation has been uncovered.

Statistical Appendix to Part Two

National Income and its Components
by Major Industrial Divisions, 1919–1938

TABLES 43–56

Whenever two entries are made for 1934 the first is comparable with those for preceding years in that the *Statistics of Income* data used are based on the old industrial classification; the second is comparable with those for succeeding years in that the *Statistics of Income* data used are based on the new industrial classification.

Net savings and net income, adjusted, exclude gains and losses from sales of capital assets, 1929–38, and from changes in inventory valuation, 1919–38. Net savings and net income without any specific designation are unadjusted, i.e., include these two types of gain and loss.

TABLE 43

Net Income Originating, Adjusted (millions of dollars)

	1919	1920	1921	1922	1923	1924	1925	1926	1927
Agr.	10,862	9,077	5,538	5,861	6,729	7,114	7,946	7,534	7,458
Mining	1,752	2,323	1,666	1,332	2,026	1,706	1,838	2,157	1,855
Mfg.	16,180	19,802	12,627	13,083	16,785	15,603	16,829	18,105	17,200
Constr.	2,002	2,642	1,984	2,327	3,337	3,732	3,957	4,264	4,111
Transp. & other pub. util.	5,958	7,418	6,337	6,209	7,057	7,094	7,600	7,905	7,829
Trade	10,205	11,472	9,527	8,630	10,143	9,813	10,166	11,516	10,568
Finance	6,819	7,418	7,770	8,255	8,809	9,608	9,762	9,837	10,312
Service	6,115	6,847	6,673	7,381	8,258	8,647	9,311	10,120	10,320
Gov.	3,768	7,017	6,205	6,136	7,042	7,277	7,365	8,113	8,483
Misc.	2,241	2,365	1,974	2,297	2,723	2,782	3,068	3,248	3,258
Total *	65,904	76,385	60,304	61,513	72,912	73,380	77,845	82,802	81,397

* Excluding Social Security contributions of employers.

TABLE 44

Net Income Originating (millions of dollars)

	1919	1920	1921	1922	1923	1924	1925	1926	1927
Agr.	10,862	9,077	5,538	5,861	6,729	7,114	7,946	7,534	7,458
Mining	1,723	2,488	1,352	1,456	1,975	1,697	1,886	2,172	1,749
Mfg.	17,082	17,702	9,814	13,455	16,914	15,427	16,880	17,323	16,817
Constr.	2,070	2,610	1,859	2,358	3,382	3,712	3,952	4,240	4,036
Transp. & other pub. util.	5,963	7,348	6,087	6,215	7,094	7,080	7,564	7,888	7,790
Trade	11,111	9,498	6,788	8,964	10,154	9,886	10,481	10,658	10,390
Finance	6,899	7,471	7,682	8,258	8,793	9,600	9,740	9,815	10,311
Service	6,129	6,852	6,652	7,382	8,260	8,644	9,306	10,114	10,318
Gov.	3,768	7,017	6,205	6,136	7,042	7,277	7,365	8,113	8,483
Misc.	2,245	2,341	1,954	2,303	2,722	2,782	3,072	3,247	3,258
Total *	67,854	72,408	53,934	62,390	73,068	73,223	78,195	81,107	80,613

* Excluding Social Security contributions of employers.

TABLE 45

Corporate and Government Net Savings,* Adjusted (millions of dollars)

	1919	1920	1921	1922	1923	1924	1925	1926	1927	1928
Mining	14.1	−6.5	−155	−269	−243	−287	−114	−111	−174	−175
Mfg.	1,521	2,765	710	686	1,295	920	1,286	1,799	788	918
Constr.	−6.3	26.7	17.5	−1.2	9.7	54.8	43.3	61.7	76.3	28.4
Transp. & other pub. util.	121	175	317	221	410	386	680	704	481	684
Trade	314	910	622	174	456	275	253	646	261	348
Finance	201	43.1	80.4	22.6	1.6	83.5	104	161	307	408
Service	35.1	0.6	−4.0	24.9	40.9	47.2	60.5	29.1	−4.4	13.0
Gov.	−1,303	1,894	958	854	1,611	1,717	1,614	2,151	2,293	1,897
Misc.	182	94.7	−126	73.8	114	72.0	131	117	49.0	276
Total *	1,079	5,904	2,421	1,787	3,697	3,269	4,060	5,560	4,079	4,398

* Excluding net savings of agricultural corporations which are included with entrepreneurial net savings.

TABLE 43

Net Income Originating, Adjusted (millions of dollars)

1928	1929	1930	1931	1932	1933	1934		1935	1936	1937	1938
7,330	7,708	5,814	4,041	2,821	3,554	4,749	4,749	5,380	6,089	6,274	5,457
1,638	1,805	1,381	825	480	479	831	819	922	1,173	1,399	1,096
17,924	19,794	16,257	11,047	6,253	6,625	9,046	8,935	11,377	14,198	15,910	12,574
3,990	4,071	3,486	2,228	1,102	711	844	808	1,048	1,557	1,792	1,703
8,030	8,505	7,744	6,452	4,911	4,709	4,802	4,764	5,165	5,834	6,141	5,529
10,977	11,374	10,978	9,031	6,298	5,224	7,036	7,058	7,399	8,498	8,961	9,277
10,874	10,910	9,740	7,894	5,905	5,191	5,071	5,071	5,680	5,976	6,636	6,538
10,686	11,266	10,424	8,798	6,502	5,811	6,746	6,759	7,369	8,284	9,105	8,869
8,289	8,873	8,920	7,410	6,175	7,503	8,188	8,188	7,504	8,216	10,724	10,815
3,653	3,476	2,856	2,579	2,127	2,008	2,138	2,393	2,567	2,921	3,171	3,005
83,396	87,787	77,604	60,309	42,579	41,819	49,454	49,546	54,413	62,749	70,116	64,866

TABLE 44

Net Income Originating (millions of dollars)

1928	1929	1930	1931	1932	1933	1934		1935	1936	1937	1938
7,330	7,708	5,814	4,041	2,821	3,554	4,749	4,749	5,380	6,089	6,274	5,457
1,661	1,821	1,319	738	463	513	910	898	950	1,210	1,440	1,099
17,949	19,504	14,094	9,307	5,380	7,480	10,039	9,928	11,816	14,322	16,237	11,959
4,014	4,085	3,377	2,124	1,042	727	894	856	1,062	1,584	1,842	1,691
8,045	8,511	7,625	6,366	4,867	4,720	4,876	4,833	5,149	5,843	6,212	5,513
10,840	11,105	9,225	7,410	5,453	6,128	7,339	7,368	7,721	8,563	9,156	8,863
10,870	11,134	9,761	7,591	5,493	4,833	5,035	5,035	5,731	6,112	6,651	6,551
10,680	11,289	10,411	8,727	6,398	5,771	6,746	6,758	7,363	8,298	9,130	8,872
8,289	8,873	8,920	7,410	6,175	7,503	8,188	8,188	7,504	8,216	10,724	10,815
3,653	3,866	2,595	1,855	1,453	1,435	1,862	2,367	2,629	3,012	3,178	3,013
83,336	87,901	73,144	55,572	39,548	42,669	50,639	50,982	55,308	63,253	70,847	63,836

TABLE 45

Corporate and Government Net Savings,* Adjusted (millions of dollars)

1929	1930	1931	1932	1933	1934		1935	1936	1937	1938
−178	−245	−311	−290	−286	−190	−286	−236	−176	−177	−156
1,472	250	−1,206	−2,145	−1,722	−1,358	−1,363	−480	62.6	−171	219
31.6	19.5	−25.6	−105	−89.1	−55.9	−62.1	−34.7	−29.6	−32.5	1.6
751	250	−118	−431	−203	−291	−285	−203	203	50.6	−72.8
200	261	−207	−621	−778	−260	−294	−274	−32.0	−165	237
−153	−409	−639	−747	−600	−621	−621	−386	−176	−39.1	−121
−7.9	−67.2	−135	−372	−317	−239	−238	−206	−213	−194	−172
2,225	2,104	344	−906	−113	−575	−575	−1,736	−2,196	497	−175
−106	−478	−407	−345	−326	−251	−218	−269	−193	−177	−178
4,233	1,685	−2,708	−5,965	−4,436	−3,844	−3,945	−3,828	−2,750	−410	−417

TABLE 46

Entrepreneurial Net Savings,* Adjusted (millions of dollars)

	1919	*1920*	*1921*	*1922*	*1923*	*1924*	*1925*	*1926*	*1927*	*1928*
Agr.*	2,275	—898	—1,443	—907	—645	—357	420	—115	—124	—237
Mining	10.7	14.1	0.8	—8.3	—3.4	—3.0	15.6	23.7	14.2	13.9
Mfg.	319	297	157	112	200	104	146	161	114	71.4
Constr.	141	94.0	52.2	22.4	47.7	209	208	175	159	82.1
Transp. & other pub. util.	8.2	5.4	—1.6	—0.5	0.1	0.6	1.1	1.3	0.2	1.2
Trade	1,830	1,491	1,195	381	833	449	364	815	380	437
Service	1,079	826	708	383	798	566	584	1,031	604	637
Misc.	157	127	101	25.1	88.3	53.7	52.3	111	50.6	45.9
Total *	5,820	1,958	770	8.0	1,319	1,023	1,792	2,206	1,199	1,052

* Including net savings of agricultural corporations.

TABLE 47

Corporate and Government Net Savings * (millions of dollars)

	1919	*1920*	*1921*	*1922*	*1923*	*1924*	*1925*	*1926*	*1927*	*1928*
Mining	—12.9	147	—449	—153	—291	—295	—69.4	—97.9	—273	—154
Mfg.	2,305	914	—1,760	1,014	1,410	762	1,332	1,090	441	941
Constr.	21.7	11.7	—28.5	7.8	22.7	49.8	42.3	54.7	51.3	36.4
Transp. & other pub. util.	126	105	67.6	227	447	372	644	687	442	699
Trade	624	8.5	—462	306	460	305	393	235	173	278
Finance	281	96.1	—7.6	25.6	—14.4	75.5	82.3	139	306	404
Service	49.1	5.6	—25.0	25.9	42.9	44.2	55.5	23.1	—6.4	7.0
Gov.	—1,303	1,894	958	854	1,611	1,717	1,614	2,151	2,293	1,897
Misc.	186	70.7	—146	79.8	113	72.0	135	116	49.0	276
Total *	2,277	3,254	—1,853	2,388	3,803	3,103	4,231	4,401	3,478	4,385

* Excluding net savings of agricultural corporations which are included with entrepreneurial savings.

TABLE 48

Entrepreneurial Net Savings * (millions of dollars)

	1919	*1920*	*1921*	*1922*	*1923*	*1924*	*1925*	*1926*	*1927*	*1928*
Agr.*	2,275	—898	—1,443	—907	—645	—357	420	—115	—124	—237
Mining	8.1	25.1	—19.2	—0.3	—6.4	—4.0	18.6	24.7	7.2	15.9
Mfg.	437	48.8	—184	156	214	86.6	151	88.8	78.7	73.4
Constr.	181	77.0	—26.8	44.4	79.7	194	204	158	109	98.1
Transp. & other pub. util.	8.2	5.4	—1.6	—0.5	0.1	0.6	1.1	1.3	0.2	1.2
Trade	2,426	419	—458	583	840	492	539	368	290	370
Service	1,079	826	708	383	798	566	584	1,031	604	637
Misc.	157	127	101	25.1	88.3	53.7	52.3	111	50.6	45.9
Total *	6,572	631	—1,324	284	1,369	1,032	1,971	1 670	1,016	1,005

* Including net savings of agricultural corporations.

TABLE 46

Entrepreneurial Net Savings,* Adjusted (millions of dollars)

1929	1930	1931	1932	1933	1934		1935	1936	1937	1938
77.0	−1,335	−1,780	−1,671	−491	340	340	639	1,045	624	−83.0
21.8	−12.4	−24.1	−29.5	−25.2	−13.4	−14.2	−11.7	−2.9	3.5	5.4
85.5	34.6	−60.3	−150	−81.1	−48.7	−52.1	27.5	120	34.3	15.9*
89.2	24.2	−42.0	−195	−167	−127	−146	−80.3	−60.5	−59.3	8.4
1.9	−1.6	−1.8	−2.1	0.4	0.3	1.5	2.7	3.6	4.3	0.4
308	297	−2.0	−438	−554	−136	−132	−121	60.2	−28.0	182
518	383	−103	−935	−1,013	−318	−337	−195	105	−49.4	217
29.5	7.9	−31.0	−101	−91.5	−35.7	−37.3	−26.5	−9.0	−19.4	−5.7
1,132	−601	−2,044	−3,525	−2,403	−340	−378	234	1,261	510	340

TABLE 47

Corporate and Government Net Savings * (millions of dollars)

1929	1930	1931	1932	1933	1934		1935	1936	1937	1938
−166	−304	−392	−306	−253	−119	−213	−210	−142	−138	−153
1,209	−1,738	−2,812	−2,948	−935	−438	−447	−75.8	177	129	−346
36.5	−28.9	−70.6	−126	−84.1	−43.5	−49.2	−30.8	−21.8	−18.8	−0.7
756	131	−203	−475	−190	−217	−215	−218	211	120	−89.1
68.8	−640	−985	−1,037	−266	−65.8	−100	−71.2	11.7	−42.5	−29.0
70.4	−388	−943	−1,158	−957	−658	−658	−336	−39.6	−24.0	−108
15.1	−79.7	−206	−476	−357	−240	−239	−211	−199	−169	−169
2,225	2,104	344	−906	−113	−575	−575	−1,736	−2,196	497	−175
283	−739	−1,131	−1,018	−900	−527	−244	−207	−102	−169	−169
4,499	−1,684	−6,400	−8,453	−4,059	−2,886	−2,743	−3,097	−2,300	183	−1,241

TABLE 48

Entrepreneurial Net Savings * (millions of dollars)

1929	1930	1931	1932	1933	1934		1935	1936	1937	1938
77.0	−1,335	−1,780	−1,671	−491	340	340	639	1,045	624	−83.0
24.9	−15.7	−29.9	−31.5	−23.5	−6.4	−9.0	−9.5	−0.4	6.2	6.1
58.8	−139	−194	−221	−12.3	24.3	25.3	61.8	130	60.1	−33.0
98.6	−36.9	−101	−234	−155	−91.0	−110	−70.2	−41.7	−23.0	−1.3
2.0	−1.8	−2.6	−2.3	−0.4	0.4	1.5	0.8	3.8	4.5	0.4
171	−553	−846	−868	−141	−27.8	−17.9	−2.3	82.4	43.9	34.9
518	383	−103	−935	−1,013	−318	−337	−195	105	−49.4	217
29.5	7.9	−31.0	−101	−91.5	−35.7	−37.3	−26.5	−9.0	−19.4	−5.7
981	−1,691	−3,088	−4,067	−1,929	−114	−145	398	1,315	646	135

TABLE 49

Total Payments to Individuals (millions of dollars)

	1919	1920	1921	1922	1923	1924	1925	1926	1927
Agr.	8,587	9,975	6,981	6,768	7,374	7,471	7,526	7,649	7,582
Mining	1,727	2,315	1,820	1,609	2,273	1,997	1,937	2,245	2,015
Mfg.	14,339	16,739	11,760	12,284	15,289	14,578	15,396	16,143	16,296
Constr.	1,868	2,522	1,915	2,306	3,279	3,468	3,706	4,027	3,875
Transp. & other pub. util.	5,828	7,237	6,021	5,988	6,647	6,707	6,919	7,199	7,347
Trade	8,061	9,070	7,708	8,074	8,853	9,089	9,548	10,053	9,926
Finance	6,618	7,375	7,689	8,233	8,808	9,525	9,657	9,675	10,005
Service	5,000	6,020	5,968	6,973	7,419	8,033	8,666	9,059	9,720
Gov.	5,071	5,123	5,247	5,282	5,431	5,560	5,751	5,962	6,190
Misc.	1,901	2,143	1,999	2,198	2,520	2,656	2,884	3,019	3,158
Total *	59,004	68,523	57,111	59,718	67,895	69,088	71,992	75,035	76,119

* Excluding Social Security contributions of employers.

TABLE 50

Employee Compensation (millions of dollars)

	1919	1920	1921	1922	1923	1924	1925	1926	1927
Agr.	1,515	1,780	1,159	1,122	1,219	1,224	1,243	1,326	1,280
Mining	1,479	2,035	1,557	1,407	1,980	1,705	1,588	1,846	1,669
Mfg.	12,468	14,609	9,891	10,480	13,021	12,396	12,960	13,504	13,539
Constr.	1,608	2,253	1,651	1,963	2,929	3,030	3,070	3,556	3,398
Transp. & other pub. util.	4,607	6,026	4,807	4,630	5,166	5,100	5,170	5,382	5,339
Trade	5,430	6,052	5,171	5,682	6,389	6,531	6,986	7,423	7,200
Finance	1,379	1,651	1,729	1,745	1,816	1,973	2,028	2,241	2,434
Service	3,256	4,072	4,203	4,498	4,925	5,238	5,520	5,905	6,351
Gov.	4,026	3,877	3,982	3,956	4,099	4,281	4,467	4,680	4,936
Misc.	1,369	1,531	1,384	1,517	1,791	1,842	1,984	2,150	2,194
Total *	37,139	43,890	35,536	37,003	43,339	43,323	45,019	48,017	48,433

* Excluding Social Security contributions of employers.

TABLE 51

Employees * (thousands)

	1919	1920	1921	1922	1923	1924	1925	1926	1927
Agr.	2,091	2,144	2,045	2,036	1,985	1,945	1,935	2,036	1,975
Mining	1,078	1,197	889	879	1,116	1,014	1,016	1,155	1,061
Mfg.	9,866	9,756	7,574	8,351	9,492	8,890	9,144	9,364	9,228
Constr.	1,031	1,171	1,064	1,345	1,614	1,663	1,649	1,900	1,769
Transp. & other pub. util.	3,262	3,502	3,006	3,024	3,341	3,245	3,241	3,325	3,278
Trade	3,882	4,269	3,819	4,029	4,370	4,514	4,589	4,729	4,878
Finance	940	1,017	1,007	979	1,037	1,099	1,100	1,209	1,306
Service *	3,629	3,767	3,810	4,055	4,351	4,513	4,692	4,956	5,147
Gov.	3,497	2,820	2,787	2,685	2,715	2,826	2,891	2,937	3,007
Misc.	1,163	1,164	1,109	1,198	1,325	1,355	1,419	1,506	1,549
Total *	30,443	30,811	27,114	28,585	31,351	31,068	31,680	33,121	33,201

* Equivalent full-time units. Excluding salaried engineers and employees in hand trades and including entrepreneurs in automobile repair shops and garages.

TABLE 49

Total Payments to Individuals (millions of dollars)

1928	1929	1930	1931	1932	1933	1934		1935	1936	1937	1938
7,567	7,631	7,149	5,821	4,492	4,045	4,409	4,409	4,741	5,044	5,650	5,540
1,800	1,962	1,639	1,160	800	790	1,035	1,120	1,170	1,352	1,573	1,247
16,934	18,236	15,972	12,314	8,550	8,428	10,453	10,350	11,831	14,015	16,047	12,339
3,880	3,950	3,443	2,296	1,403	967	1,028	1,016	1,163	1,647	1,883	1,693
7,344	7,752	7,495	6,572	5,345	4,912	5,093	5,048	5,366	5,627	6,087	5,601
10,191	10,865	10,419	9,241	7,359	6,537	7,433	7,486	7,795	8,469	9,155	8,857
10,466	11,064	10,149	8,534	6,652	5,791	5,693	5,693	6,067	6,152	6,675	6,659
10,036	10,755	10,108	9,036	7,810	7,142	7,304	7,334	7,770	8,392	9,348	8,824
6,392	6,648	6,816	7,066	7,081	7,616	8,763	8,763	9,240	10,412	10,227	10,990
3,331	3,553	3,327	3,017	2,574	2,427	2,425	2,648	2,863	3,124	3,367	3,189
77,944	82,421	76,520	65,061	52,069	48,658	53,639	53,870	58,008	64,238	70,016	64,942

TABLE 50

Employee Compensation (millions of dollars)

1928	1929	1930	1931	1932	1933	1934	1935	1936	1937	1938
1,268	1,284	1,134	847	584	517	558	639	690	794	758
1,481	1,530	1,325	962	664	666	875	932	1,080	1,223	992
13,863	14,911	12,795	9,918	7,024	7,049	8,800	9,897	11,217	13,205	10,521
3,438	3,441	2,945	1,976	1,157	764	801	897	1,261	1,487	1,290
5,308	5,489	5,073	4,310	3,302	3,040	3,272	3,508	3,877	4,280	3,937
7,521	8,012	7,644	6,644	5,136	4,513	5,293	5,502	5,848	6,450	6,258
2,637	2,856	2,650	2,385	1,967	1,743	1,858	1,952	2,017	2,120	2,149
6,433	6,893	6,390	5,574	4,415	3,919	4,395	4,792	5,304	5,914	5,610
5,152	5,385	5,549	5,788	5,716	6,154	7,194	7,751	8,874	8,546	9,301
2,256	2,409	2,259	2,061	1,731	1,684	1,837	2,057	2,311	2,550	2,413
49,361	52,214	47,767	40,468	31,699	30,054	34,888	37,929	42,484	46,574	43,231

TABLE 51

Employees * (thousands)

1928	1929	1930	1931	1932	1933	1934	1935	1936	1937	1938
1,963	1,971	1,863	1,759	1,616	1,590	1,537	1,618	1,637	1,680	1,675
978	1,033	963	829	690	706	830	848	897	942	818
9,245	9,890	8,799	7,452	6,331	6,791	7,890	8,390	9,063	9,917	8,332
1,778	1,827	1,610	1,179	784	656	723	780	985	1,047	941
3,206	3,269	3,043	2,626	2,228	2,126	2,192	2,183	2,303	2,415	2,158
4,929	5,184	4,980	4,433	3,833	3,794	4,207	4,224	4,383	4,611	4,403
1,398	1,500	1,453	1,346	1,234	1,178	1,222	1,240	1,272	1,319	1,307
5,234	5,536	5,338	4,979	4,479	4,279	4,783	5,094	5,447	5,724	5,538
3,080	3,162	3,213	3,254	3,251	3,199	3,296	3,457	3,675	3,801	3,860
1,580	1,684	1,617	1,566	1,491	1,519	1,571	1,644	1,734	1,813	1,767
33,394	35,059	32,882	29,426	25,940	25,841	28,254	29,482	31,400	33,272	30,802

TABLE 52

Entrepreneurial Withdrawals (millions of dollars)

	1919	1920	1921	1922	1923	1924	1925	1926	1927
Agr.	6,699	7,749	5,316	5,120	5,630	5,745	5,806	5,859	5,828
Mining	30.9	39.7	32.1	29.5	31.7	28.0	26.3	25.6	24.4
Mfg.	523	534	404	388	385	374	371	369	365
Constr.	240	242	223	307	306	397	567	418	419
Transp. & other pub. util.	10.8	8.9	7.2	7.7	7.3	5.8	5.9	5.7	5.1
Trade	2,197	2,594	2,176	2,050	2,072	2,137	2,091	2,133	2,109
Finance	121	147	144	148	172	189	211	226	234
Service	1,699	1,853	1,681	2,404	2,397	2,691	3,012	3,000	3,199
Misc.	259	307	282	333	340	375	410	413	435
Total	11,781	13,477	10,269	10,788	11,345	11,945	12,503	12,452	12,621

TABLE 53

Entrepreneurs * (thousands)

	1919	1920	1921	1922	1923	1924	1925	1926	1927
Agr.	6,393	6,406	6,443	6,400	6,328	6,319	6,313	6,252	6,216
Mining	22.3	21.6	20.4	20.1	19.7	18.2	17.2	16.6	15.8
Mfg.	250	221	172	160	148	140	133	133	132
Constr.	96.7	90.3	74.4	108	126	159	193	174	166
Transp. & other pub. util.	2.5	2.4	2.3	2.2	2.0	1.7	1.5	1.3	1.0
Trade	1,149	1,179	1,210	1,240	1,270	1,300	1,330	1,361	1,391
Service *	1,222	1,229	1,220	1,250	1,284	1,324	1,361	1,396	1,433
Misc.	236	249	262	275	288	301	313	326	339
Total *	9,374	9,400	9,405	9,457	9,467	9,565	9,664	9,661	9,696

* Excluding entrepreneurs in insurance, estimates for which are not available, and entrepreneurs in automobile repair shops and garages; and including salaried engineers and employees in hand trades.

TABLE 54

Dividends (millions of dollars)

	1919	1920	1921	1922	1923	1924	1925	1926	1927
Agr.	16.0	16.0	16.0	16.0	16.0	15.0	18.0	16.0	29.0
Mining	194	209	193	139	223	212	269	326	278
Mfg.	1,261	1,488	1,325	1,310	1,763	1,652	1,910	2,118	2,227
Constr.	15.3	20.9	32.4	30.3	37.5	32.4	58.4	41.3	47.4
Transp. & other pub. util.	530	486	455	566	637	707	816	866	1,038
Trade	400	382	320	302	369	389	440	471	495
Finance	335	405	410	472	531	506	554	549	545
Service	29.0	80.4	65.7	48.8	68.0	71.2	92.1	105	106
Misc.	74.5	82.8	75.5	77.2	97.7	96.1	111	120	150
Total	2,857	3,172	2,894	2,962	3,745	3,683	4,270	4,615	4,918

TABLE 52

Entrepreneurial Withdrawals (millions of dollars)

1928	1929	1930	1931	1932	1933	1934		1935	1936	1937	1938
5,832	5,899	5,579	4,541	3,502	3,166	3,500	3,500	3,775	4,028	4,546	4,492
22.9	21.4	20.8	18.6	15.1	14.3	14.9	14.9	15.5	16.5	18.2	18.3
368	372	326	268	206	183	176	181	197	241	266	264
380	436	397	266	216	175	205	197	244	347	352	371
5.2	5.7	5.7	4.2	3.0	2.5	2.6	2.6	2.9	3.0	3.2	2.9
2,127	2,231	2,209	2,144	1,948	1,796	1,816	1,816	1,822	1,921	2,048	2,085
245	260	252	229	195	176	191	191	201	201	225	217
3,430	3,658	3,505	3,295	3,230	3,093	2,780	2,799	2,818	2,872	3,218	3,052
463	499	476	440	429	411	402	404	438	488	550	552
12,876	13,384	12,773	11,207	9,747	9,019	9,090	9,108	9,516	10,119	11,227	11,056

TABLE 53

Entrepreneurs * (thousands)

1928	1929	1930	1931	1932	1933	1934	1935	1936	1937	1938
6,229	6,234	6,286	6,406	6,569	6,691	6,741	6,771	6,776	6,778	6,836
15.0	14.1	14.0	14.1	13.6	13.4	13.2	12.8	12.8	12.8	12.8
133	133	118	103	84.2	72.3	76.5	81.5	90.6	99.3	99.3
163	167	167	149	121	108	120	134	151	151	151
1.0	0.9	0.8	0.8	0.7	0.6	0.7	0.6	0.6	0.6	0.6
1,421	1,452	1,448	1,444	1,440	1,436	1,394	1,351	1,389	1,410	1,416
1,441	1,486	1,499	1,509	1,509	1,557	1,594	1,623	1,646	1,664	1,672
352	365	357	343	322	319	339	358	378	397	412
9,756	9,854	9,892	9,971	10,062	10,199	10,280	10,332	10,445	10,525	10,601

TABLE 54

Dividends (millions of dollars)

1928	1929	1930	1931	1932	1933	1934		1935	1936	1937	1938
25.0	12.0	7.0	14.0	6.0	0.02	17.0	17.0	19.0	37.0	32.0	22.0
253	365	249	138	81.6	75.3	114	190	185	215	295	204
2,518	2,743	2,616	1,895	1,119	1,010	1,297	1,224	1,583	2,411	2,434	1,413
51.4	60.0	85.0	40.1	19.2	18.7	13.0	15.2	20.7	36.6	42.1	29.4
1,047	1,287	1,426	1,254	974	830	833	818	932	865	948	849
499	565	496	386	214	178	275	339	438	669	624	482
660	764	664	593	370	204	260	260	277	270	285	291
99.1	116	112	73.7	54.5	33.9	41.8	50.6	54.3	113	120	69.0
189	202	110	−30.7	−87.0	−100	−121	164	218	242	240	168
5,344	6,117	5,768	4,345	2,752	2,251	2,731	3,079	3,729	4,861	5,022	3,530

TABLE 55

Interest (millions of dollars)

	1919	1920	1921	1922	1923	1924	1925	1926	1927
Agr.	357	430	490	510	509	487	459	448	445
Mining	23.3	30.4	38.3	33.2	37.3	51.3	53.9	46.5	43.7
Mfg.	86.7	107	138	105	117	154	153	151	163
Constr.	4.0	4.9	7.8	4.4	6.0	7.8	10.4	11.0	11.3
Transp. & other pub. util.	679	714	751	784	835	893	926	945	965
Trade	33.1	41.7	40.0	39.2	22.0	30.7	30.7	24.6	30.8
Finance	815	882	935	970	1,121	1,223	1,396	1,516	1,712
Service	15.9	14.9	18.1	22.8	28.0	33.2	41.0	47.7	62.7
Gov.	1,044	1,246	1,264	1,326	1,331	1,279	1,284	1,281	1,254
Misc.	169	178	188	183	197	213	223	225	245
Total	3,228	3,652	3,872	3,979	4,206	4,374	4,579	4,698	4,935

TABLE 56

Property Income * (millions of dollars)

	1919	1920	1921	1922	1923	1924	1925	1926	1927
Agr.	373	446	506	526	525	502	477	464	474
Mining	217	240	231	172	260	263	323	373	321
Mfg.	1,348	1,595	1,463	1,416	1,881	1,806	2,064	2,270	2,391
Constr.	19.3	25.8	40.2	34.8	43.4	40.2	68.7	52.4	58.7
Transp. & other pub. util.	1,210	1,201	1,207	1,350	1,473	1,601	1,742	1,811	2,003
Trade	433	423	360	341	391	420	470	495	526
Finance *	5,117	5,576	5,816	6,339	6,818	7,361	7,417	7,208	7,336
Service	44.9	95.2	83.8	71.6	96.0	104	133	153	169
Gov.	1,044	1,246	1,264	1,326	1,331	1,279	1,284	1,281	1,254
Misc.*	273	304	332	347	388	438	488	455	528
Total *	10,082	11,155	11,306	11,925	13,211	13,818	14,469	14,565	15,065

* Including, under miscellaneous, international dividend and interest payments, and, under finance, rent received by individuals (cash and imputed)

TABLE 55

Interest (millions of dollars)

1928	1929	1930	1931	1932	1933	1934		1935	1936	1937	1938
442	436	429	419	400	362	334	334	308	289	278	268
42.0	44.7	44.5	41.7	39.5	34.1	30.0	39.2	37.0	40.6	35.8	31.4
184	209	233	231	200	185	179	144	152	145	141	140
10.0	13.2	15.3	13.5	10.3	8.6	8.2	1.7	1.2	1.9	2.0	2.0
983	970	990	1,023	1,065	1,038	984	954	923	882	854	812
43.0	55.6	68.7	66.1	60.5	49.1	47.0	36.3	32.1	30.1	31.5	31.3
1,981	2,266	2,316	2,298	2,028	1,552	1,478	1,478	1,493	1,475	1,465	1,426
73.0	87.0	99.0	93.7	110	95.3	86.9	88.7	104	101	95.6	92.9
1,240	1,263	1,266	1,278	1,364	1,461	1,568	1,568	1,489	1,537	1,681	1,689
272	258	256	246	236	211	199	135	107	104	102	99.0
5,272	5,604	5,720	5,712	5,515	4,999	4,915	4,780	4,648	4,608	4,688	4,593

TABLE 56

Property Income * (millions of dollars)

1928	1929	1930	1931	1932	1933	1934		1935	1936	1937	1938
467	448	436	433	406	362	351	351	327	326	310	290
295	410	293	180	121	109	144	229	222	255	331	236
2,703	2,952	2,849	2,127	1,319	1,196	1,476	1,368	1,736	2,556	2,576	1,553
61.4	73.2	100	53.6	29.5	27.3	21.2	16.9	22.0	38.4	44.1	31.4
2,031	2,257	2,416	2,257	2,039	1,869	1,818	1,773	1,855	1,747	1,803	1,661
542	621	565	452	274	227	322	375	470	699	656	513
7,583	7,947	7,246	5,918	4,489	3,870	3,644	3,644	3,913	3,933	4,329	4,293
172	203	211	167	164	129	128	139	159	215	215	161
1,240	1,263	1,266	1,278	1,364	1,461	1,568	1,568	1,489	1,537	1,681	1,689
611	643	591	516	413	331	185	407	367	324	267	223
15,707	16,822	15,978	13,384	10,622	9,585	9,661	9,873	10,562	11,633	12,214	10,654

National Income and Aggregate Payments by Type, 1919–1938

Whenever two entries are made for 1934 the first is comparable with those for preceding years in that the *Statistics of Income* data used are based on the old industrial classification; the second is comparable with those for succeeding years in that the *Statistics of Income* data used are based on the new industrial classification.

TABLE 57

Aggregate Payments [3] by Type of Payment (millions of dollars)

	1919	1920	1921	1922	1923	1924	1925	1926	1927
Empl. comp.[1], [3]	37,139	43,890	35,536	37,003	43,339	43,323	45,019	48,017	48,433
Entrep. withdr.[2]	11,781	13,477	10,269	10,788	11,345	11,945	12,503	12,452	12,621
Dividends	2,857	3,172	2,894	2,962	3,745	3,683	4,270	4,615	4,918
Interest	3,228	3,652	3,872	3,979	4,206	4,374	4,579	4,698	4,935
Div. and int., internat.	29.0	43.0	69.0	86.0	94.0	129	154	110	132
Net rent recd. by indiv.	3,966	4,287	4,470	4,896	5,165	5,631	5,465	5,141	5,078
Prop. income	10,082	11,155	11,306	11,925	13,211	13,818	14,469	14,565	15,065
Agg. pay. to indiv.	59,004	68,523	57,111	59,718	67,895	69,088	71,992	75,035	76,119

[1] Including entrepreneurial withdrawals in automobile garages and repair shops.
[2] Including compensation of salaried engineers and of employees in hand trades.
[3] Including Social Security contributions of employers.

TABLE 58

National Income,[4] Aggregate Payments, and Savings of Enterprises (millions of dollars)

	1919	1920	1921	1922	1923	1924	1925	1926	1927
Agg. pay. to indiv.	59,004	68,523	57,111	59,718	67,895	69,088	71,992	75,035	76,119
Net savings of enterprises [1]	8,850	3,885	—3,177	2,672	5,173	4,135	6,202	6,071	4,494
Nat. income [1]	67,854	72,408	53,934	62,390	73,068	73,223	78,195	81,107	80,613
Net savings of enterprises [2]	6,900	7,862	3,192	1,795	5,017	4,292	5,852	7,766	5,278
Nat. income [2]	65,904	76,385	60,304	61,513	72,912	73,380	77,845	82,802	81,397
Net savings of enterprises [3]	5,199	5,709	2,301	989	3,730	3,007	4,055	6,515	3,932
Nat. income [3]	64,203	74,232	59,412	60,707	71,626	72,095	76,047	81,551	80,051

[1] Unadjusted.
[2] Adjusted for gains and losses from sales of capital assets, 1929–38, and from inventory holdings, 1919–38.
[3] Including the adjustment for the difference between depreciation and depletion at cost and at current reproduction prices, and for gains and losses from sales of capital assets, 1919–28, in addition to the adjustments mentioned in footnote 2.
[4] Including Social Security contributions of employers.

TABLE 57

Aggregate Payments [3] by Type of Payment (millions of dollars)

1928	1929	1930	1931	1932	1933	1934	1934	1935	1936	1937	1938
49,361	52,214	47,767	40,468	31,699	30,054	34,891	34,891	37,937	42,783	47,524	44,351
12,876	13,384	12,773	11,207	9,747	9,019	9,090	9,108	9,516	10,119	11,227	11,056
5,344	6,117	5,768	4,345	2,752	2,251	2,731	3,079	3,729	4,861	5,022	3,530
5,272	5,604	5,720	5,712	5,515	4,999	4,915	4,780	4,648	4,608	4,688	4,593
149	183	224	301	264	220	108	108	41.0	—23.0	—76.0	—44.0
4,941	4,917	4,265	3,026	2,090	2,114	1,905	1,905	2,143	2,186	2,579	2,575
15,707	16,822	15,978	13,384	10,622	9,585	9,661	9,873	10,562	11,633	12,214	10,654
77,944	82,421	76,520	65,061	52,069	48,658	53,643	53,874	58,015	64,537	70,966	66,061

TABLE 58

National Income, [4] Aggregate Payments, and Savings of Enterprises (millions of dollars)

1928	1929	1930	1931	1932	1933	1934	1934	1935	1936	1937	1938
77,944	82,421	76,520	65,061	52,069	48,658	53,643	53,874	58,015	64,537	70,966	66,061
5,391	5,480	—3,375	—9,489	—12,520	—5,989	—3,000	—2,888	—2,699	—985	830	—1,105
83,336	87,901	73,144	55,572	39,548	42,669	50,642	50,985	55,316	63,552	71,797	64,955
5,451	5,365	1,084	—4,752	—9,490	—6,839	—4,184	—4,324	—3,594	—1,488	100	—76.3
83,396	87,787	77,604	60,309	42,579	41,819	49,458	49,550	54,421	63,049	71,066	65,985
3,733	4,813	799	—4,761	—9,137	—6,476	—4,141	—4,280	—3,610	—1,673	—472	—600
81,678	87,234	77,319	60,300	42,932	42,183	49,502	49,594	54,406	62,864	70,494	65,461

National Income and its Components
Percentage Distribution by Major and
Minor Industrial Divisions, 1919–1938

TABLE 59

National Income *

	1919	1920	1921	1922	1923	1924	1925	1926	1927
Total ($000,000)	67,855	72,409	53,934	62,390	73,069	73,224	78,195	81,108	80,614
Agriculture	16.0	12.5	10.3	9.4	9.2	9.7	10.2	9.3	9.3
Mining	2.5	3.4	2.5	2.3	2.7	2.3	2.4	2.7	2.2
Anth. coal	0.35	0.38	0.51	0.30	0.41	0.46	0.31	0.44	0.37
Bit. coal	1.2	1.7	1.4	1.2	1.5	1.1	1.0	1.1	0.92
Metal	0.50	0.53	0.23	0.26	0.31	0.30	0.39	0.33	0.29
Oil & gas	0.35	0.59	0.22	0.34	0.30	0.27	0.41	0.54	0.32
Other	0.19	0.29	0.14	0.20	0.23	0.23	0.29	0.29	0.26
Manufacturing	25.2	24.4	18.2	21.6	23.1	21.1	21.6	21.4	20.9
Food & tobacco	2.8	2.4	2.3	2.6	2.4	2.4	2.3	2.3	2.3
Textile & leather	5.4	4.2	4.4	4.8	4.6	3.7	3.9	3.5	4.0
Constr. mat. & furn.	2.8	3.2	2.4	2.9	3.3	3.0	3.0	3.0	2.7
Paper	0.57	0.76	0.48	0.55	0.59	0.56	0.56	0.60	0.60
Printing	1.1	1.3	1.6	1.5	1.4	1.5	1.5	1.6	1.6
Metal	9.2	9.3	5.1	6.2	7.9	7.3	7.6	7.6	7.0
Chemical	1.5	1.5	1.1	1.5	1.4	1.4	1.5	1.7	1.4
Misc. & rubber	1.7	1.7	0.92	1.5	1.6	1.3	1.3	1.2	1.2
Construction	3.1	3.6	3.4	3.8	4.6	5.1	5.1	5.2	5.0
Transp. & other pub. util.	8.8	10.1	11.3	10.0	9.7	9.7	9.7	9.7	9.7
Electric light & power	0.48	0.53	0.76	0.80	0.87	1.0	1.0	1.2	1.3
Mfd. gas	0.15	0.16	0.21	0.19	0.20	0.20	0.32	0.26	0.28
Steam rr., Pull., & exp.	5.8	6.7	7.1	6.1	6.1	5.8	5.7	5.8	5.5
Street rwy.	0.78	0.87	1.1	1.0	0.89	0.86	0.79	0.74	0.73
Water transp.	0.87	1.1	0.99	0.75	0.66	0.70	0.65	0.66	0.61
Pipe lines	0.10	0.13	0.13	0.16	0.14	0.15	0.17	0.16	0.19
Telephone	0.48	0.55	0.80	0.76	0.72	0.77	0.80	0.82	0.87
Telegraph	0.14	0.16	0.18	0.17	0.16	0.15	0.16	0.17	0.18
Trade	16.4	13.1	12.6	14.4	13.9	13.5	13.4	13.1	12.9
Finance	10.2	10.3	14.2	13.2	12.0	13.1	12.5	12.1	12.8
Banking	1.3	1.3	1.7	1.5	1.3	1.4	1.4	1.5	1.6
Insurance	1.0	1.0	1.4	1.3	1.1	1.2	1.3	1.4	1.6
Real estate	7.8	8.0	11.2	10.5	9.6	10.5	9.7	9.3	9.6
Service	9.0	9.5	12.3	11.8	11.3	11.8	11.9	12.5	12.8
Government	5.6	9.7	11.5	9.8	9.6	9.9	9.4	10.0	10.5
Miscellaneous	3.3	3.2	3.6	3.7	3.7	3.8	3.9	4.0	4.0

* Excluding Social Security contributions of employers.

TABLE 59

National Income *

1928	1929	1930	1931	1932	1933	1934	1935	1936	1937	1938
83,336	87,902	73,145	55,572	39,549	42,670	50,811	55,309	63,253	70,847	63,836
8.8	8.8	7.9	7.3	7.1	8.3	9.3	9.7	9.6	8.9	8.5
2.0	2.1	1.8	1.3	1.2	1.2	1.8	1.7	1.9	2.0	1.7
0.36	0.30	0.36	0.37	0.35	0.29	0.30	0.23	0.20	0.15	0.12
0.76	0.73	0.68	0.65	0.58	0.59	0.79	0.78	0.81	0.78	0.67
0.33	0.41	0.21	0.07	—0.04	0.05	0.17	0.22	0.31	0.45	0.30
0.30	0.40	0.33	0.07	0.20	0.22	0.38	0.34	0.40	0.44	0.44
0.25	0.23	0.22	0.17	0.09	0.05	0.14	0.14	0.20	0.21	0.18
21.5	22.2	19.3	16.7	13.6	17.5	19.6	21.4	22.6	22.9	18.7
2.4	2.4	2.6	2.7	2.8	3.0	3.2	3.1	3.0	2.6	2.8
3.6	3.5	2.8	3.1	2.8	4.2	3.9	4.1	3.9	3.5	3.1
2.6	2.5	2.1	1.4	0.61	1.2	1.5	1.8	2.1	2.2	1.9
0.59	0.59	0.59	0.57	0.49	0.66	0.72	0.70	0.70	0.72	0.59
1.7	1.7	1.9	2.0	2.1	1.8	1.7	1.7	1.7	1.6	1.7
7.7	8.4	6.8	4.8	2.7	4.2	5.9	7.1	8.1	9.2	6.1
1.8	1.9	1.6	1.1	1.2	1.4	1.5	1.6	1.7	1.8	1.5
1.2	1.1	0.93	0.96	0.77	1.0	1.1	1.3	1.3	1.3	1.1
4.8	4.6	4.6	3.8	2.6	1.7	1.7	1.9	2.5	2.6	2.6
9.7	9.7	10.4	11.5	12.3	11.1	9.6	9.3	9.2	8.8	8.6
1.4	1.6	2.0	2.5	2.9	2.4	2.0	1.9	1.8	1.7	1.8
0.23	0.21	0.26	0.28	0.40	0.37	0.30	0.26	0.25	0.26	0.27
5.4	5.3	5.3	5.4	5.3	5.0	4.4	4.4	4.4	4.1	3.8
0.68	0.64	0.72	0.80	0.86	0.71	0.63	0.59	0.54	0.49	0.53
0.62	0.61	0.64	0.68	0.71	0.72	0.67	0.72	0.77	0.80	0.76
0.21	0.23	0.24	0.31	0.34	0.35	0.25	0.23	0.23	0.23	0.21
0.91	0.96	1.1	1.4	1.6	1.4	1.2	1.1	1.1	1.1	1.2
0.17	0.17	0.17	0.20	0.19	0.18	0.16	0.16	0.15	0.14	0.13
13.0	12.6	12.6	13.3	13.8	14.4	14.5	14.0	13.5	12.9	13.9
13.0	12.7	13.3	13.7	13.9	11.3	9.9	10.4	9.7	9.4	10.3
1.7	1.6	1.6	1.3	1.0	0.68	0.96	1.3	1.4	1.2	1.3
1.7	1.7	1.8	2.1	2.4	2.0	2.0	2.0	1.8	1.8	2.0
9.6	9.4	10.0	10.2	10.5	8.6	6.9	7.1	6.5	6.4	7.0
12.8	12.8	14.2	15.7	16.2	13.5	13.3	13.3	13.1	12.9	13.9
9.9	10.1	12.2	13.3	15.6	17.6	16.1	13.6	13.0	15.1	16.9
4.4	4.4	3.5	3.3	3.7	3.4	4.2	4.8	4.8	4.5	4.7

TABLE 60

Aggregate Payments including Entrepreneurial Savings *

	1919	1920	1921	1922	1923	1924	1925	1926	1927
Total ($000,000)	65,577	69,154	55,788	60,002	69,266	70,121	73,964	76,706	77,136
Agriculture	16.6	13.1	9.9	9.8	9.7	10.1	10.7	9.8	9.7
Mining	2.6	3.4	3.2	2.7	3.3	2.8	2.6	3.0	2.6
Anth. coal	0.36	0.38	0.56	0.32	0.47	0.52	0.34	0.47	0.42
Bit. coal	1.2	1.7	1.6	1.4	1.6	1.2	1.1	1.2	1.0
Metal	0.52	0.50	0.38	0.32	0.42	0.41	0.43	0.39	0.36
Oil & gas	0.37	0.56	0.40	0.43	0.42	0.38	0.46	0.61	0.51
Other	0.20	0.27	0.26	0.25	0.32	0.32	0.33	0.31	0.30
Manufacturing	22.5	24.3	20.7	20.7	22.4	20.9	21.0	21.2	21.2
Food & tobacco	2.6	2.6	2.6	2.5	2.4	2.4	2.2	2.2	2.3
Textile & leather	4.7	4.6	4.6	4.6	4.6	3.9	4.0	3.8	4.0
Constr. mat. & furn.	2.6	3.1	2.5	2.8	3.1	3.0	3.0	3.1	2.9
Paper	0.51	0.64	0.58	0.54	0.58	0.54	0.58	0.57	0.58
Printing	1.1	1.3	1.5	1.5	1.4	1.5	1.5	1.6	1.6
Metal	8.2	8.9	6.2	6.1	7.5	7.1	7.1	7.3	7.1
Chemical	1.4	1.6	1.5	1.4	1.4	1.3	1.4	1.4	1.4
Misc. & rubber	1.4	1.6	1.3	1.4	1.4	1.2	1.2	1.2	1.3
Construction	3.1	3.8	3.4	3.9	4.8	5.2	5.3	5.5	5.2
Transp. & other pub. util.	8.9	10.5	10.8	10.0	9.6	9.6	9.4	9.4	9.5
Electric light & power	0.44	0.49	0.66	0.72	0.81	0.95	1.0	1.1	1.2
Mfd. gas	0.20	0.20	0.22	0.20	0.20	0.24	0.24	0.24	0.24
Steam rr., Pull., & exp.	5.9	7.0	6.8	6.2	6.0	5.7	5.6	5.5	5.6
Street rwy.	0.79	0.88	1.0	1.0	0.90	0.88	0.82	0.78	0.75
Water transp.	0.86	1.1	1.0	0.81	0.72	0.74	0.68	0.69	0.65
Pipe lines	0.09	0.09	0.12	0.16	0.12	0.11	0.15	0.13	0.17
Telephone	0.47	0.56	0.74	0.74	0.71	0.77	0.78	0.79	0.83
Telegraph	0.12	0.15	0.16	0.15	0.14	0.14	0.14	0.16	0.16
Trade	16.0	13.7	13.0	14.4	14.0	13.7	13.6	13.6	13.2
Finance	10.1	10.7	13.8	13.7	12.7	13.6	13.1	12.6	13.0
Banking	1.0	1.1	1.5	1.4	1.3	1.3	1.3	1.3	1.4
Insurance	1.0	1.1	1.5	1.5	1.3	1.4	1.5	1.5	1.6
Real estate	8.1	8.4	10.8	10.9	10.2	10.9	10.3	9.8	10.0
Service	9.3	9.9	12.0	12.3	11.9	12.3	12.5	13.2	13.4
Government	7.7	7.4	9.4	8.8	7.8	7.9	7.8	7.8	8.0
Federal	4.9	4.3	4.9	4.3	3.7	3.6	3.4	3.3	3.3
State	0.28	0.32	0.47	0.44	0.42	0.47	0.43	0.37	0.40
County	0.29	0.32	0.47	0.47	0.44	0.47	0.47	0.48	0.49
City incl. pub. educ.	2.3	2.5	3.5	3.6	3.3	3.4	3.5	3.6	3.8
Miscellaneous	3.1	3.3	3.8	3.7	3.8	3.9	4.0	4.1	4.2

* Excluding Social Security contributions of employers

TABLE 60

Aggregate Payments including Entrepreneurial Savings *

1928	1929	1930	1931	1932	1933	1934	1935	1936	1937	1938
78,950	83,402	74,829	61,972	48,002	46,729	53,625	58,407	65,554	70,663	65,078
9.3	9.2	7.8	6.5	5.9	7.6	8.9	9.2	9.3	8.9	8.4
2.3	2.4	2.2	1.8	1.6	1.6	2.0	2.0	2.1	2.2	1.9
0.39	0.33	0.35	0.35	0.33	0.29	0.30	0.25	0.21	0.18	0.17
0.85	0.82	0.76	0.68	0.60	0.65	0.81	0.79	0.83	0.82	0.69
0.37	0.48	0.36	0.24	0.15	0.15	0.18	0.23	0.33	0.46	0.33
0.41	0.48	0.45	0.32	0.34	0.38	0.51	0.47	0.46	0.51	0.51
0.28	0.27	0.25	0.24	0.19	0.17	0.19	0.25	0.24	0.26	0.23
21.5	21.9	21.2	19.6	17.4	18.0	19.4	20.4	21.6	22.8	18.9
2.4	2.4	2.6	2.6	2.7	2.8	3.0	2.8	2.8	2.7	2.8
3.9	3.8	3.4	3.5	3.2	3.8	3.8	3.9	3.7	3.6	3.2
2.8	2.7	2.4	1.9	1.4	1.4	1.6	1.8	2.0	2.2	1.8
0.59	0.58	0.60	0.60	0.58	0.64	0.67	0.66	0.66	0.70	0.62
1.6	1.7	1.9	1.9	1.9	1.7	1.7	1.6	1.6	1.6	1.6
7.5	8.0	7.2	5.9	4.8	4.7	5.9	6.7	7.6	8.8	6.1
1.6	1.6	1.9	1.9	1.7	1.8	1.6	1.7	1.8	1.8	1.6
1.2	1.2	1.2	1.2	1.0	1.1	1.1	1.2	1.2	1.3	1.1
5.0	4.9	4.6	3.5	2.4	1.7	1.7	1.9	2.4	2.6	2.6
9.3	9.3	10.0	10.6	11.1	10.5	9.5	9.2	8.6	8.6	8.6
1.3	1.4	1.7	2.1	2.3	2.2	1.8	1.7	1.6	1.6	1.7
0.23	0.24	0.28	0.34	0.46	0.43	0.35	0.33	0.29	0.28	0.30
5.2	5.1	5.2	5.1	4.9	4.6	4.3	4.2	4.1	4.1	3.8
0.71	0.68	0.69	0.74	0.79	0.71	0.65	0.60	0.56	0.52	0.56
0.65	0.62	0.66	0.66	0.66	0.69	0.67	0.78	0.77	0.81	0.78
0.17	0.20	0.25	0.28	0.40	0.31	0.24	0.32	0.19	0.19	0.21
0.86	0.90	1.0	1.2	1.4	1.4	1.2	1.1	1.0	1.0	1.2
0.16	0.17	0.20	0.20	0.18	0.16	0.16	0.15	0.14	0.14	0.14
13.4	13.2	13.2	13.5	13.5	13.7	13.9	13.3	13.0	13.0	13.7
13.3	13.3	13.6	13.8	13.9	12.4	10.6	10.4	9.4	9.4	10.2
1.4	1.4	1.6	1.7	1.7	1.4	1.3	1.2	1.1	1.0	1.1
1.7	1.7	1.9	2.1	2.3	2.2	2.0	1.9	1.7	1.7	1.9
10.1	10.1	10.1	9.9	9.8	8.9	7.4	7.3	6.6	6.7	7.2
13.5	13.5	14.0	14.4	14.3	13.1	13.0	13.0	13.0	13.2	13.9
8.1	8.0	9.1	11.4	14.8	16.3	16.3	15.8	15.9	14.5	16.9
3.2	3.1	3.5	4.4	5.8	7.7	8.9	8.8	9.3	7.9	9.4
0.42	0.41	0.50	0.65	0.87	0.89	0.82	0.82	0.78	0.80	0.92
0.52	0.55	0.62	0.76	0.97	0.93	0.81	0.76	0.70	0.67	0.75
4.0	3.9	4.5	5.6	7.1	6.8	5.8	5.4	5.1	5.1	5.8
4.3	4.3	4.5	4.8	5.2	5.0	4.7	4.9	4.8	4.7	4.9

TABLE 61

Aggregate Payments excluding Entrepreneurial Savings *

	1919	1920	1921	1922	1923	1924	1925	1926	1927
Total ($000,000)	59,004	68,523	57,112	59,718	67,896	69,088	71,993	75,036	76,119
Agriculture	14.6	14.6	12.2	11.3	10.9	10.8	10.5	10.2	10.0
Mining	2.9	3.4	3.2	2.7	3.3	2.9	2.7	3.0	2.6
Anth. coal	0.40	0.39	0.57	0.32	0.48	0.53	0.34	0.48	0.42
Bit. coal	1.3	1.7	1.6	1.4	1.7	1.2	1.1	1.2	1.0
Metal	0.58	0.50	0.37	0.33	0.42	0.42	0.44	0.40	0.37
Oil & gas	0.40	0.54	0.42	0.44	0.43	0.39	0.46	0.60	0.51
Other	0.22	0.27	0.26	0.25	0.32	0.33	0.33	0.32	0.30
Manufacturing	24.3	24.4	20.6	20.6	22.5	21.1	21.4	21.5	21.4
Food & tobacco	2.9	2.7	2.7	2.5	2.4	2.4	2.3	2.2	2.3
Textile & leather	4.8	4.7	4.5	4.5	4.5	4.0	4.0	3.9	4.0
Constr. mat. & furn.	2.9	3.1	2.5	2.8	3.1	3.1	3.1	3.1	2.9
Paper	0.56	0.63	0.57	0.54	0.59	0.55	0.59	0.58	0.59
Printing	1.1	1.3	1.4	1.5	1.4	1.5	1.5	1.6	1.6
Metal	9.0	8.9	6.1	6.1	7.6	7.2	7.2	7.4	7.2
Chemical	1.6	1.6	1.5	1.4	1.4	1.3	1.4	1.5	1.4
Misc. & rubber	1.5	1.6	1.3	1.4	1.4	1.2	1.2	1.3	1.3
Construction	3.2	3.7	3.4	3.9	4.8	5.0	5.1	5.4	5.1
Transp. & other pub. util.	9.9	10.6	10.5	10.0	9.8	9.7	9.6	9.6	9.7
Electric light & power	0.49	0.49	0.64	0.73	0.82	0.96	1.0	1.1	1.2
Mfd. gas	0.23	0.20	0.21	0.20	0.21	0.24	0.25	0.24	0.25
Steam rr., Pull., & exp.	6.6	7.1	6.7	6.2	6.1	5.8	5.7	5.6	5.6
Street rwy.	0.87	0.89	1.0	1.0	0.92	0.90	0.84	0.79	0.76
Water transp.	0.95	1.1	0.98	0.81	0.73	0.75	0.70	0.70	0.66
Pipe lines	0.10	0.09	0.12	0.16	0.12	0.11	0.15	0.13	0.17
Telephone	0.53	0.57	0.72	0.74	0.73	0.78	0.80	0.81	0.84
Telegraph	0.14	0.15	0.16	0.15	0.14	0.14	0.15	0.16	0.16
Trade	13.7	13.2	13.5	13.5	13.0	13.2	13.3	13.4	13.0
Finance	11.3	10.8	13.5	13.8	13.0	13.8	13.4	12.9	13.1
Banking	1.1	1.1	1.4	1.4	1.3	1.3	1.3	1.3	1.4
Insurance	1.1	1.2	1.5	1.5	1.3	1.4	1.5	1.6	1.7
Real estate	9.0	8.5	10.6	10.9	10.4	11.1	10.6	10.0	10.1
Service	8.5	8.8	10.5	11.7	10.9	11.6	12.0	12.1	12.8
Government	8.6	7.5	9.2	8.8	8.0	8.0	8.0	7.9	8.1
Federal	5.4	4.3	4.8	4.4	3.8	3.6	3.5	3.4	3.3
State	0.31	0.33	0.46	0.44	0.43	0.47	0.44	0.38	0.40
County	0.32	0.32	0.46	0.47	0.44	0.48	0.48	0.49	0.50
City incl. pub. educ.	2.5	2.5	3.4	3.6	3.3	3.5	3.6	3.7	3.9
Miscellaneous	3.2	3.1	3.5	3.7	3.7	3.8	4.0	4.0	4.1

* Excluding Social Security contributions of employers.

TABLE 61

Aggregate Payments excluding Entrepreneurial Savings *

1928	1929	1930	1931	1932	1933	1934	1935	1936	1937	1938
77,945	82,421	76,520	65,061	52,070	48,659	53,755	58,009	64,238	70,016	64,942
9.7	9.3	9.3	8.9	8.6	8.3	8.2	8.2	7.9	8.1	8.5
2.3	2.4	2.1	1.8	1.5	1.6	2.0	2.0	2.1	2.2	1.9
0.39	0.34	0.35	0.33	0.31	0.28	0.30	0.25	0.22	0.18	0.17
0.86	0.83	0.74	0.66	0.56	0.63	0.81	0.80	0.85	0.82	0.69
0.38	0.49	0.35	0.23	0.14	0.15	0.18	0.24	0.33	0.46	0.33
0.40	0.46	0.46	0.34	0.36	0.40	0.52	0.48	0.47	0.51	0.50
0.28	0.27	0.25	0.24	0.18	0.17	0.19	0.25	0.24	0.27	0.23
21.7	22.1	20.9	18.9	16.4	17.3	19.4	20.4	21.8	22.9	19.0
2.4	2.4	2.5	2.6	2.6	2.7	2.9	2.8	2.8	2.7	2.8
3.9	3.8	3.4	3.5	3.1	3.6	3.8	3.9	3.8	3.7	3.2
2.8	2.7	2.4	1.9	1.4	1.4	1.6	1.8	2.1	2.2	1.8
0.59	0.58	0.59	0.58	0.54	0.61	0.67	0.66	0.67	0.70	0.63
1.6	1.7	1.8	1.8	1.8	1.6	1.7	1.6	1.6	1.6	1.7
7.5	8.1	7.1	5.7	4.4	4.6	5.9	6.7	7.7	8.9	6.1
1.6	1.6	1.9	1.8	1.6	1.8	1.6	1.7	1.8	1.8	1.6
1.2	1.2	1.2	1.1	0.99	1.0	1.1	1.2	1.3	1.3	1.1
5.0	4.8	4.5	3.5	2.7	2.0	1.9	2.0	2.6	2.7	2.6
9.4	9.4	9.8	10.1	10.3	10.1	9.4	9.3	8.8	8.7	8.6
1.3	1.4	1.7	2.0	2.2	2.1	1.8	1.7	1.6	1.6	1.7
0.23	0.25	0.28	0.32	0.43	0.41	0.35	0.34	0.29	0.28	0.30
5.3	5.2	5.1	4.9	4.5	4.5	4.3	4.2	4.2	4.1	3.8
0.72	0.68	0.68	0.70	0.73	0.68	0.64	0.60	0.57	0.53	0.56
0.66	0.63	0.64	0.63	0.61	0.67	0.67	0.79	0.78	0.81	0.78
0.18	0.20	0.24	0.27	0.36	0.30	0.24	0.32	0.19	0.19	0.21
0.87	0.91	1.0	1.1	1.3	1.3	1.2	1.1	1.0	1.0	1.2
0.16	0.17	0.19	0.18	0.16	0.15	0.16	0.15	0.14	0.14	0.14
13.1	13.2	13.6	14.2	14.1	13.4	13.9	13.4	13.2	13.1	13.6
13.4	13.4	13.3	13.1	12.8	11.9	10.6	10.5	9.6	9.5	10.3
1.5	1.4	1.5	1.6	1.6	1.3	1.3	1.2	1.1	1.1	1.2
1.7	1.7	1.9	2.0	2.2	2.1	2.0	1.9	1.8	1.8	1.9
10.2	10.3	9.9	9.5	9.0	8.5	7.3	7.3	6.7	6.7	7.2
12.9	13.0	13.2	13.9	15.0	14.7	13.6	13.4	13.1	13.4	13.6
8.2	8.1	8.9	10.9	13.6	15.7	16.3	15.9	16.2	14.6	16.9
3.3	3.1	3.4	4.2	5.3	7.4	8.9	8.9	9.5	8.0	9.4
0.42	0.42	0.48	0.62	0.80	0.86	0.82	0.82	0.80	0.81	0.93
0.52	0.55	0.61	0.72	0.89	0.89	0.81	0.77	0.71	0.68	0.76
4.0	4.0	4.4	5.4	6.6	6.5	5.8	5.5	5.2	5.1	5.9
4.3	4.3	4.3	4.6	4.9	5.0	4.7	4.9	4.9	4.8	4.9

TABLE 62

Wages and Salaries

	1919	1920	1921	1922	1923	1924	1925	1926	1927
Total ($000,000)	36,706	43,319	34,932	36,403	42,724	42,708	44,413	47,399	47,787
Agriculture	4.1	4.1	3.3	3.1	2.9	2.9	2.8	2.8	2.7
Mining	4.0	4.7	4.5	3.9	4.6	4.0	3.6	3.9	3.5
Anth. coal	0.61	0.58	0.86	0.50	0.72	0.80	0.51	0.71	0.62
Bit. coal	2.1	2.6	2.4	2.1	2.6	1.9	1.7	1.8	1.6
Metal	0.64	0.57	0.39	0.38	0.46	0.46	0.46	0.44	0.41
Oil & gas	0.46	0.64	0.47	0.54	0.51	0.46	0.52	0.62	0.55
Other	0.27	0.33	0.30	0.32	0.38	0.39	0.38	0.37	0.35
Manufacturing	34.0	33.7	28.3	28.8	30.5	29.0	29.2	28.5	28.3
Food & tobacco	3.6	3.3	3.4	3.2	2.9	2.9	2.7	2.6	2.7
Textile & leather	6.6	6.4	6.5	6.5	6.4	5.7	5.8	5.5	5.8
Constr. mat. & furn.	4.2	4.4	3.7	4.1	4.4	4.4	4.4	4.3	4.1
Paper	0.76	0.83	0.76	0.76	0.78	0.77	0.79	0.79	0.78
Printing	1.6	1.8	2.0	2.1	1.9	2.1	2.1	2.2	2.2
Metal	13.2	13.0	8.7	8.9	10.7	10.0	10.0	9.9	9.5
Chemical	1.9	1.9	1.6	1.6	1.6	1.5	1.5	1.5	1.5
Misc. & rubber	2.1	2.1	1.7	1.8	1.8	1.7	1.7	1.7	1.7
Construction	4.4	5.2	4.7	5.4	6.9	7.1	6.9	7.5	7.1
Transp. & other pub. util.	12.4	13.7	13.6	12.6	11.9	11.8	11.5	11.2	11.0
Electric light & power	0.38	0.41	0.53	0.53	0.59	0.70	0.70	0.75	0.77
Mfd. gas	0.21	0.19	0.22	0.22	0.22	0.24	0.24	0.23	0.24
Steam rr., Pull., & exp.	8.6	9.4	8.8	8.1	7.8	7.4	7.2	7.0	6.8
Street rwy.	1.0	1.1	1.3	1.2	1.0	1.0	0.98	0.91	0.88
Water transp.	1.4	1.6	1.5	1.2	1.1	1.2	1.1	1.0	0.99
Pipe lines	0.07	0.08	0.09	0.09	0.09	0.08	0.08	0.09	0.10
Telephone	0.64	0.71	0.92	0.96	0.90	0.98	0.98	0.97	1.0
Telegraph	0.19	0.22	0.23	0.22	0.20	0.20	0.21	0.22	0.21
Trade	14.8	14.0	14.8	15.6	15.0	15.3	15.7	15.7	15.3
Finance	3.8	3.8	5.0	4.8	4.3	4.6	4.6	4.7	5.1
Banking	1.0	1.1	1.5	1.4	1.3	1.4	1.4	1.4	1.4
Insurance	1.5	1.5	2.0	1.9	1.6	1.8	1.9	2.0	2.1
Real estate	1.3	1.2	1.5	1.4	1.4	1.5	1.3	1.4	1.6
Service	8.9	9.4	12.0	12.4	11.5	12.3	12.4	12.5	13.3
Professional	1.5	1.4	2.0	2.1	1.9	2.1	2.1	2.1	2.2
Personal	2.8	3.1	3.6	3.8	3.3	3.5	3.5	3.5	3.8
Domestic	3.1	3.0	4.1	4.3	4.0	4.2	4.3	4.2	4.3
Miscellaneous	1.4	1.9	2.4	2.2	2.3	2.5	2.6	2.7	3.0
Government	9.9	7.8	9.8	9.4	8.3	8.7	8.9	8.8	9.2
Federal	5.6	3.5	3.8	3.1	2.7	2.8	2.8	2.7	2.7
State	0.42	0.42	0.55	0.54	0.48	0.52	0.56	0.50	0.55
County	0.41	0.41	0.60	0.61	0.54	0.58	0.56	0.55	0.59
City incl. pub. educ.	3.5	3.5	4.9	5.1	4.6	4.9	5.0	5.0	5.3
Miscellaneous	3.7	3.5	4.0	4.2	4.2	4.3	4.5	4.5	4.6

TABLE 62

Wages and Salaries

1928	1929	1930	1931	1932	1933	1934	1935	1936	1937	1938
48,703	51,521	47,040	39,587	30,721	28,194	32,124	34,998	38,863	43,503	39,693
2.6	2.5	2.4	2.1	1.9	1.8	1.7	1.8	1.8	1.8	1.9
3.0	3.0	2.8	2.4	2.2	2.4	2.7	2.7	2.8	2.8	2.5
0.58	0.49	0.52	0.50	0.47	0.44	0.47	0.38	0.32	0.28	0.25
1.3	1.2	1.1	1.0	0.88	1.0	1.3	1.3	1.3	1.3	1.1
0.39	0.40	0.36	0.26	0.18	0.19	0.22	0.26	0.32	0.43	0.33
0.44	0.55	0.52	0.40	0.42	0.49	0.55	0.53	0.54	0.56	0.59
0.33	0.29	0.30	0.27	0.22	0.22	0.23	0.24	0.26	0.27	0.24
28.5	28.9	27.2	25.1	22.9	25.0	27.4	28.3	28.9	30.4	26.5
2.8	2.7	2.8	2.9	3.0	3.4	3.5	3.4	3.2	3.2	3.4
5.5	5.5	5.0	5.2	4.9	5.8	5.9	6.0	5.6	5.3	4.9
3.9	3.8	3.3	2.7	2.0	2.2	2.4	2.6	2.9	3.1	2.7
0.78	0.78	0.80	0.80	0.79	0.90	0.95	0.93	0.92	0.92	0.92
2.3	2.4	2.6	2.7	2.7	2.5	2.5	2.4	2.3	2.3	2.4
10.0	10.6	9.3	7.6	6.3	6.9	8.5	9.4	10.3	11.9	8.8
1.5	1.6	1.7	1.6	1.6	1.8	1.9	1.8	1.8	1.8	1.8
1.7	1.7	1.6	1.6	1.5	1.6	1.7	1.7	1.7	1.8	1.5
7.1	6.7	6.3	5.0	3.8	2.7	2.5	2.6	3.2	3.4	3.2
10.7	10.5	10.6	10.7	10.5	10.5	10.0	9.8	9.8	9.6	9.7
0.82	0.84	0.96	1.1	1.1	1.1	1.1	1.0	1.0	1.0	1.1
0.22	0.20	0.21	0.21	0.24	0.27	0.25	0.23	0.22	0.21	0.23
6.5	6.3	6.1	5.9	5.5	5.5	5.3	5.2	5.3	5.1	4.9
0.84	0.80	0.81	0.85	0.88	0.81	0.74	0.68	0.62	0.56	0.60
0.99	0.93	0.96	0.96	0.95	1.1	1.0	1.1	1.1	1.2	1.1
0.10	0.10	0.09	0.10	0.10	0.11	0.11	0.11	0.11	0.11	0.12
1.1	1.1	1.3	1.3	1.5	1.4	1.3	1.2	1.2	1.2	1.3
0.22	0.23	0.25	0.26	0.25	0.24	0.24	0.22	0.21	0.21	0.21
15.4	15.6	16.3	16.8	16.7	16.0	16.5	15.7	15.0	14.8	15.8
5.4	5.5	5.6	6.0	6.4	6.2	5.8	5.6	5.2	4.9	5.4
1.4	1.4	1.5	1.6	1.8	1.7	1.5	1.4	1.3	1.2	1.4
2.2	2.2	2.4	2.7	3.0	3.0	2.7	2.6	2.4	2.3	2.6
1.8	1.9	1.7	1.7	1.6	1.5	1.5	1.5	1.4	1.3	1.4
13.2	13.4	13.6	14.1	14.4	13.9	13.7	13.7	13.6	13.6	14.1
2.4	2.4	2.6	3.1	3.7	3.8	3.3	3.2	3.1	2.9	3.3
3.6	3.8	4.0	4.1	4.2	3.9	4.1	4.1	4.1	3.9	4.2
4.2	4.2	3.9	3.6	3.4	3.3	3.3	3.2	3.2	3.4	3.3
3.1	3.1	3.1	3.2	3.0	3.0	3.0	3.1	3.3	3.3	3.3
9.4	9.3	10.4	12.6	15.7	15.5	14.0	14.0	13.7	12.9	14.8
2.8	2.7	3.0	3.6	4.4	4.3	4.4	4.8	4.9	4.4	4.9
0.58	0.58	0.67	0.85	1.1	1.2	1.1	1.1	1.1	1.1	1.3
0.62	0.63	0.72	0.91	1.1	1.1	1.0	0.96	0.92	0.88	1.0
5.4	5.4	6.0	7.2	9.0	8.9	7.5	7.2	6.9	6.5	7.6
4.6	4.7	4.8	5.2	5.6	6.0	5.7	5.9	5.9	5.9	6.1

TABLE 63

Employees (full-time equivalents)

	1919	1920	1921	1922	1923	1924	1925	1926	1927
Total (000)	30,444	30,811	27,114	28,586	31,351	31,068	31,680	33,121	33,202
Agriculture	6.9	7.0	7.5	7.1	6.3	6.3	6.1	6.1	5.9
Mining	3.5	3.9	3.3	3.1	3.6	3.3	3.2	3.5	3.2
Anth. coal	0.51	0.48	0.62	0.36	0.51	0.54	0.35	0.49	0.50
Bit. coal	1.9	2.2	1.7	1.6	1.9	1.6	1.6	1.7	1.5
Metal	0.48	0.47	0.29	0.36	0.42	0.42	0.42	0.40	0.37
Oil & gas	0.37	0.44	0.36	0.43	0.42	0.39	0.43	0.52	0.46
Other	0.28	0.33	0.30	0.32	0.36	0.36	0.36	0.34	0.34
Manufacturing	32.4	31.7	27.9	29.2	30.3	28.6	28.9	28.3	27.8
Food & tobacco	3.7	3.5	3.4	3.4	3.1	3.0	3.0	2.8	2.9
Textile & leather	7.3	7.1	7.4	7.5	7.5	6.8	6.9	6.7	6.8
Constr. mat. & furn.	4.3	4.2	3.9	4.6	4.6	4.6	4.6	4.5	4.2
Paper	0.77	0.83	0.77	0.77	0.79	0.78	0.80	0.79	0.77
Printing	1.4	1.5	1.5	1.6	1.5	1.6	1.6	1.5	1.6
Metal	10.9	10.7	7.5	8.0	9.2	8.5	8.6	8.5	8.1
Chemical	1.7	1.5	1.4	1.4	1.5	1.4	1.4	1.4	1.4
Misc. & rubber	2.1	2.0	1.7	1.8	1.8	1.7	1.7	1.7	1.7
Construction	3.4	3.8	3.9	4.7	5.1	5.4	5.2	5.7	5.3
Transp. & other pub. util.	10.7	11.4	11.1	10.6	10.7	10.4	10.2	10.0	9.9
Electric light & power	0.36	0.39	0.46	0.48	0.57	0.62	0.63	0.68	0.71
Mfd. gas	0.21	0.18	0.20	0.20	0.21	0.22	0.22	0.22	0.22
Steam rr., Pull., & exp.	7.0	7.3	6.9	6.3	6.6	6.3	6.1	6.0	5.8
Street rwy.	0.97	0.98	1.0	1.0	0.93	0.90	0.85	0.80	0.77
Water transp.	0.96	1.2	1.1	1.1	1.0	1.0	0.94	0.93	0.90
Pipe lines	0.06	0.06	0.07	0.08	0.08	0.07	0.08	0.08	0.09
Telephone	0.92	0.99	1.1	1.1	1.1	1.1	1.1	1.1	1.1
Telegraph	0.25	0.25	0.27	0.24	0.24	0.25	0.26	0.26	0.25
Trade	12.8	13.9	14.1	14.1	13.9	14.5	14.5	14.3	14.7
Finance	3.1	3.3	3.7	3.4	3.3	3.5	3.5	3.6	3.9
Banking	1.0	1.1	1.3	1.2	1.1	1.2	1.2	1.2	1.2
Insurance	0.99	1.0	1.3	1.2	1.1	1.2	1.3	1.3	1.4
Real estate	1.1	1.1	1.2	1.1	1.1	1.2	1.0	1.2	1.3
Service	11.9	12.2	14.1	14.2	13.9	14.5	14.8	15.0	15.5
Professional	2.0	1.9	2.2	2.3	2.3	2.5	2.5	2.5	2.6
Personal	3.0	3.1	3.4	3.6	3.4	3.5	3.7	3.7	3.8
Domestic	5.6	5.5	6.4	6.4	6.3	6.5	6.6	6.5	6.7
Miscellaneous	1.4	1.7	2.0	1.8	1.9	2.1	2.1	2.2	2.4
Government	11.5	9.2	10.3	9.4	8.7	9.1	9.1	8.9	9.1
Federal	5.9	3.4	3.7	3.0	2.6	2.7	2.6	2.5	2.5
State	0.53	0.55	0.61	0.58	0.53	0.58	0.62	0.56	0.61
County	0.49	0.51	0.61	0.61	0.57	0.61	0.58	0.57	0.59
City incl. pub. educ.	4.6	4.7	5.4	5.2	5.0	5.2	5.3	5.2	5.4
Miscellaneous	3.8	3.8	4.1	4.2	4.2	4.4	4.5	4.5	4.7

TABLE 63

Employees (full-time equivalents)

1928	1929	1930	1931	1932	1933	1934	1935	1936	1937	1938
33,394	35,059	32,882	29,426	25,941	25,842	28,254	29,483	31,400	33,272	30,802
5.9	5.6	5.7	6.0	6.2	6.2	5.4	5.5	5.2	5.0	5.4
2.9	2.9	2.9	2.8	2.7	2.7	2.9	2.9	2.9	2.8	2.7
0.48	0.44	0.44	0.44	0.40	0.35	0.37	0.33	0.30	0.28	0.26
1.4	1.4	1.4	1.5	1.4	1.5	1.6	1.5	1.5	1.4	1.4
0.35	0.36	0.34	0.28	0.21	0.21	0.24	0.27	0.32	0.39	0.32
0.37	0.47	0.42	0.33	0.35	0.40	0.46	0.44	0.45	0.45	0.46
0.33	0.31	0.31	0.31	0.28	0.28	0.30	0.29	0.29	0.28	0.26
27.7	28.2	26.8	25.3	24.4	26.3	27.9	28.5	28.9	29.8	27.1
2.9	2.9	3.0	3.0	3.1	3.4	3.6	3.5	3.4	3.4	3.5
6.6	6.5	6.2	6.5	6.6	7.5	7.4	7.5	7.3	7.1	6.7
4.0	3.9	3.4	2.9	2.4	2.6	2.8	3.0	3.2	3.4	3.1
0.76	0.76	0.78	0.77	0.79	0.87	0.92	0.90	0.88	0.89	0.89
1.6	1.6	1.7	1.7	1.7	1.6	1.6	1.6	1.6	1.7	1.7
8.3	8.8	8.0	6.9	6.3	6.6	7.7	8.2	8.7	9.6	7.7
1.4	1.5	1.5	1.4	1.4	1.6	1.7	1.6	1.6	1.5	1.5
1.7	1.6	1.6	1.6	1.5	1.7	1.7	1.8	1.7	1.8	1.6
5.3	5.2	4.9	4.0	3.0	2.5	2.6	2.6	3.1	3.1	3.1
9.6	9.3	9.3	8.9	8.6	8.2	7.8	7.4	7.3	7.3	7.0
0.75	0.78	0.85	0.88	0.87	0.83	0.80	0.78	0.78	0.77	0.80
0.21	0.18	0.19	0.18	0.18	0.19	0.18	0.17	0.17	0.16	0.16
5.5	5.2	5.0	4.8	4.4	4.2	4.0	3.8	3.8	3.8	3.4
0.73	0.69	0.68	0.68	0.67	0.61	0.56	0.52	0.48	0.44	0.44
0.89	0.83	0.84	0.81	0.80	0.88	0.84	0.84	0.84	0.86	0.83
0.09	0.08	0.08	0.08	0.07	0.08	0.08	0.08	0.08	0.08	0.08
1.2	1.2	1.3	1.2	1.3	1.2	1.1	1.0	0.97	0.98	1.0
0.26	0.27	0.28	0.28	0.26	0.25	0.25	0.23	0.23	0.23	0.22
14.8	14.8	15.1	15.1	14.8	14.7	14.9	14.3	14.0	13.9	14.3
4.2	4.3	4.4	4.6	4.8	4.6	4.3	4.2	4.1	4.0	4.2
1.2	1.2	1.2	1.2	1.2	1.0	1.0	0.92	0.86	0.84	0.91
1.4	1.4	1.5	1.7	1.9	1.8	1.7	1.7	1.6	1.5	1.7
1.5	1.6	1.6	1.7	1.7	1.7	1.6	1.6	1.6	1.6	1.6
15.7	15.8	16.2	16.9	17.3	16.6	16.9	17.3	17.3	17.2	18.0
2.8	2.8	3.0	3.4	3.8	3.8	3.5	3.5	3.5	3.4	3.8
3.8	4.0	4.2	4.4	4.7	4.3	4.7	4.8	4.7	4.7	4.9
6.7	6.6	6.5	6.5	6.4	6.1	6.3	6.3	6.4	6.4	6.3
2.5	2.5	2.4	2.6	2.5	2.4	2.4	2.6	2.8	2.8	3.0
9.2	9.0	9.8	11.1	12.5	12.4	11.7	11.7	11.7	11.4	12.5
2.5	2.5	2.7	3.0	3.3	3.3	3.3	3.6	3.7	3.6	3.9
0.62	0.61	0.68	0.81	0.94	0.94	0.92	0.96	0.96	0.98	1.1
0.62	0.62	0.68	0.79	0.92	0.90	0.84	0.83	0.82	0.81	0.91
5.5	5.3	5.8	6.5	7.4	7.2	6.6	6.4	6.2	6.1	6.7
4.7	4.8	4.9	5.3	5.8	5.9	5.6	5.6	5.5	5.5	5.7

TABLE 64

Entrepreneurial Net Income

	1919	1920	1921	1922	1923	1924	1925	1926
Total ($000,000)	18,355	14,108	8,945	11,073	12,715	12,978	14,475	14,123
Agriculture	48.9	48.6	43.3	38.0	39.2	41.5	43.0	40.7
Mining	0.21	0.46	0.14	0.26	0.20	0.18	0.31	0.36
Anth. coal	...*	...*	...*	...*	...*	...*	...*	...*
Bit. coal	0.04	0.08	0.03	0.07	0.05	0.04	0.06	0.07
Metal	0.02	0.03	0.01	0.01	0.01	0.01	0.01	0.01
Oil & gas	0.14	0.32	0.09	0.17	0.12	0.12	0.21	0.24
Other	0.02	0.03	0.01	0.02	0.02	0.02	0.03	0.03
Manufacturing	5.2	4.1	2.5	4.9	4.7	3.6	3.6	3.2
Food & tobacco	1.1	0.79	0.55	1.2	1.1	1.1	0.85	0.91
Textile & leather	2.3	0.98	0.93	1.7	1.4	0.73	1.0	0.67
Constr. mat. & furn.	0.57	0.87	0.23	0.70	0.86	0.58	0.57	0.51
Paper	0.06	0.12	0.02	0.05	0.05	0.04	0.04	0.05
Printing	0.34	0.52	0.58	0.61	0.48	0.47	0.43	0.42
Metal	0.56	0.51	0.08	0.30	0.44	0.37	0.40	0.38
Chemical	0.17	0.11	0.05	0.15	0.14	0.13	0.13	0.15
Misc. & rubber	0.21	0.22	0.02	0.20	0.20	0.17	0.18	0.15
Construction	2.3	2.3	2.2	3.2	3.0	4.6	5.3	4.1
Transp. & other pub. util.	0.10	0.10	0.06	0.06	0.06	0.05	0.05	0.05
Electric light & power	0.02	0.02	0.04	0.03	0.02	0.02	0.02	0.01
Water transp.	0.09	0.08	0.02	0.04	0.04	0.03	0.03	0.04
Trade	25.2	21.4	19.2	23.8	22.9	20.3	18.2	17.7
Finance	0.66	1.0	1.6	1.3	1.4	1.5	1.5	1.6
Insurance	0.66	1.0	1.6	1.3	1.4	1.5	1.5	1.6
Service	15.1	19.0	26.7	25.2	25.1	25.1	24.8	28.6
Professional	8.5	9.5	13.0	15.7	15.2	15.8	16.5	18.5
Personal	4.6	6.3	9.3	6.1	6.7	6.2	5.6	7.1
Miscellaneous	2.0	3.2	4.4	3.3	3.3	3.1	2.8	3.0
Miscellaneous	2.3	3.1	4.3	3.2	3.4	3.3	3.2	3.7

* Less than 0.005 per cent.

TABLE 64

Entrepreneurial Net Income

1927	1928	1929	1930	1931	1932	1933	1934	1935	1936	1937	1938
13,637	13,881	14,366	11,083	8,119	5,680	7,090	8,970	9,914	11,435	11,875	11,192
41.8	40.3	41.6	38.3	34.0	32.2	37.7	42.8	44.5	44.4	43.5	39.4
0.23	0.28	0.32	0.04	—0.14	—0.29	—0.13	0.08	0.06	0.14	0.21	0.22
...*	...*	...*	...*	...*	...*	...*	...*	...*	...*	...*	...*
0.05	0.05	0.06	0.01	—0.02	—0.03	—0.01	0.01	0.01	0.01	0.02	0.02
0.01	0.01	0.01	...*	...*	—0.01	...*	...*	...*	...*	0.01	0.01
0.16	0.20	0.23	0.03	—0.10	—0.23	—0.10	0.06	0.05	0.11	0.16	0.17
0.02	0.02	0.03	...*	—0.01	—0.02	—0.01	0.01	0.01	0.01	0.02	0.02
3.3	3.2	3.0	1.7	0.91	—0.28	2.4	2.3	2.6	3.3	2.7	2.1
0.90	0.96	0.93	1.0	0.94	0.84	1.0	1.2	1.1	1.2	0.88	0.83
1.0	0.76	0.65	—0.11	—0.24	—0.61	0.80	0.41	0.55	0.76	0.52	0.53
0.35	0.39	0.35	0.08	—0.18	—0.49	—0.03	0.08	0.16	0.32	0.33	0.15
0.05	0.04	0.04	0.03	0.01	—0.01	0.03	0.03	0.03	0.04	0.04	...*
0.40	0.42	0.40	0.37	0.31	0.29	0.40	0.30	0.31	0.34	0.31	0.24
0.29	0.34	0.38	0.19	—0.02	—0.26	0.01	0.08	0.22	0.34	0.39	0.12
0.12	0.14	0.14	0.12	0.10	0.08	0.12	0.12	0.13	0.15	0.14	0.09
0.14	0.13	0.11	0.02	—0.02	—0.11	0.04	0.07	0.14	0.16	0.14	0.12
3.9	3.4	3.7	3.3	2.0	—0.32	0.28	1.1	1.8	2.7	2.8	3.3
0.04	0.05	0.05	0.04	0.02	0.01	0.03	0.04	0.04	0.06	0.06	0.03
0.01	0.01	0.01	0.01	0.01	0.01	0.01	0.01	0.01	0.01	0.01	0.01
0.03	0.04	0.05	0.03	0.01	...*	0.02	0.03	0.03	0.05	0.06	0.02
17.6	18.0	16.7	14.9	16.0	19.0	23.3	20.0	18.4	17.5	17.6	18.9
1.7	1.8	1.8	2.3	2.8	3.4	2.5	2.1	2.0	1.8	1.9	1.9
1.7	1.8	1.8	2.3	2.8	3.4	2.5	2.1	2.0	1.8	1.9	1.9
27.9	29.3	29.1	35.1	39.3	40.4	29.3	27.5	26.5	26.0	26.7	29.2
18.0	19.7	19.8	23.7	26.4	27.7	20.3	18.1	17.6	17.3	18.1	19.6
7.0	6.7	6.5	8.0	8.9	8.6	6.0	6.6	6.3	6.3	6.0	7.0
2.9	2.9	2.7	3.4	4.0	4.2	3.0	2.8	2.6	2.5	2.6	2.6
3.6	3.7	3.7	4.4	5.0	5.8	4.5	4.1	4.2	4.2	4.5	4.9

TABLE 65

Entrepreneurial Withdrawals

	1919	1920	1921	1922	1923	1924	1925	1926
Total ($000,000)	11,782	13,477	10,269	10,789	11,345	11,946	12,503	12,452
Agriculture	56.9	57.5	51.8	47.5	49.6	48.1	46.4	47.1
Mining	0.26	0.30	0.31	0.27	0.28	0.24	0.21	0.20
Anth. coal	...*	...*	...*	...*	...*	...*	...*	...*
Bit. coal	0.04	0.05	0.07	0.07	0.07	0.05	0.04	0.04
Metal	0.02	0.02	0.02	0.01	0.01	0.01	0.01	0.01
Oil & gas	0.18	0.20	0.20	0.17	0.17	0.15	0.14	0.14
Other	0.02	0.02	0.02	0.02	0.02	0.02	0.02	0.02
Manufacturing	4.4	4.0	3.9	3.6	3.4	3.1	3.0	3.0
Food & tobacco	1.6	1.3	1.3	1.2	1.1	0.98	0.88	0.90
Textile & leather	1.2	1.0	1.1	1.0	0.92	0.84	0.85	0.84
Constr. mat. & furn.	0.48	0.52	0.45	0.45	0.42	0.40	0.40	0.39
Paper	0.04	0.05	0.05	0.04	0.04	0.03	0.03	0.03
Printing	0.34	0.40	0.45	0.42	0.38	0.37	0.35	0.34
Metal	0.38	0.34	0.28	0.25	0.26	0.25	0.23	0.22
Chemical	0.19	0.17	0.16	0.15	0.14	0.12	0.12	0.11
Misc. & rubber	0.16	0.16	0.15	0.14	0.13	0.13	0.12	0.12
Construction	2.0	1.8	2.2	2.9	2.7	3.3	4.5	3.4
Transp. & other pub. util.	0.09	0.07	0.07	0.07	0.06	0.05	0.05	0.04
Electric light & power	0.03	0.03	0.03	0.03	0.02	0.02	0.02	0.02
Water transp.	0.06	0.04	0.04	0.04	0.04	0.03	0.03	0.03
Trade	18.6	19.3	21.2	19.0	18.3	17.9	16.7	17.1
Finance	1.0	1.1	1.4	1.4	1.5	1.6	1.7	1.8
Insurance	1.0	1.1	1.4	1.4	1.5	1.6	1.7	1.8
Service	14.4	13.7	16.4	22.3	21.1	22.5	24.1	24.1
Miscellaneous	2.2	2.3	2.7	3.1	3.0	3.1	3.3	3.3

* Less than 0.005 per cent.

TABLE 65

Entrepreneurial Withdrawals

1927	1928	1929	1930	1931	1932	1933	1934	1935	1936	1937	1938
12,621	12,876	13,385	12,774	11,208	9,747	9,019	9,099	9,516	10,120	11,228	11,056
46.2	45.3	44.1	43.7	40.5	35.9	35.1	38.5	39.7	39.8	40.5	40.6
0.19	0.18	0.16	0.16	0.17	0.16	0.16	0.16	0.16	0.16	0.16	0.17
...*	...*	...*	...*	...*	...*	...*	...*	...*	...*	...*	...*
0.04	0.03	0.03	0.02	0.02	0.02	0.02	0.02	0.02	0.02	0.02	0.01
0.01	0.01	...*	...*	...*	...*	...*	...*	...*	0.01	0.01	0.01
0.13	0.12	0.11	0.12	0.13	0.12	0.12	0.13	0.13	0.13	0.13	0.13
0.02	0.02	0.01	0.01	0.02	0.01	0.01	0.01	0.01	0.02	0.02	0.02
2.9	2.9	2.8	2.6	2.4	2.1	2.0	2.0	2.1	2.4	2.4	2.4
0.95	0.99	0.98	0.92	0.90	0.82	0.73	0.72	0.67	0.78	0.83	0.86
0.81	0.75	0.72	0.64	0.61	0.48	0.52	0.50	0.54	0.61	0.55	0.54
0.34	0.34	0.33	0.28	0.23	0.17	0.15	0.17	0.19	0.24	0.25	0.24
0.03	0.03	0.02	0.02	0.02	0.02	0.02	0.02	0.03	0.03	0.03	0.03
0.34	0.32	0.30	0.30	0.29	0.34	0.34	0.26	0.29	0.31	0.30	0.31
0.21	0.20	0.21	0.18	0.15	0.11	0.11	0.13	0.16	0.20	0.21	0.20
0.11	0.10	0.11	0.10	0.10	0.08	0.08	0.08	0.10	0.11	0.10	0.11
0.11	0.12	0.11	0.11	0.10	0.08	0.08	0.08	0.10	0.11	0.11	0.11
3.3	3.0	3.3	3.1	2.4	2.2	1.9	2.2	2.6	3.4	3.1	3.4
0.04	0.04	0.04	0.04	0.04	0.03	0.03	0.03	0.03	0.03	0.03	0.03
0.01	0.01	0.01	0.01	0.01	0.01	0.01	0.01	0.01	0.01	0.01	0.01
0.03	0.03	0.03	0.04	0.03	0.02	0.02	0.02	0.02	0.02	0.02	0.02
16.7	16.5	16.7	17.3	19.1	20.0	19.9	20.0	19.1	19.0	18.2	18.9
1.9	1.9	1.9	2.0	2.0	2.0	2.0	2.1	2.1	2.0	2.0	2.0
1.9	1.9	1.9	2.0	2.0	2.0	2.0	2.1	2.1	2.0	2.0	2.0
25.4	26.6	27.3	27.4	29.4	33.1	34.3	30.7	29.6	28.4	28.7	27.6
3.5	3.6	3.7	3.7	3.9	4.4	4.6	4.4	4.6	4.8	4.9	5.0

TABLE 66

Entrepreneurs

	1919	1920	1921	1922	1923	1924	1925	1926
Total (000)	9,374	9,401	9,405	9,457	9,468	9,566	9,664	9,662
Agriculture	68.2	68.1	68.5	67.7	66.8	66.1	65.3	64.7
Mining	0.24	0.23	0.22	0.21	0.21	0.19	0.18	0.17
Anth. coal	...*	...*	...*	...*	...*	...*	...*	...*
Bit. coal	0.04	0.04	0.04	0.05	0.05	0.04	0.04	0.04
Metal	0.02	0.02	0.01	0.01	0.01	0.01	0.01	0.01
Oil & gas	0.15	0.15	0.14	0.14	0.13	0.12	0.12	0.11
Other	0.02	0.02	0.02	0.02	0.02	0.02	0.02	0.02
Manufacturing	2.7	2.4	1.8	1.7	1.6	1.5	1.4	1.4
Food & tobacco	0.85	0.73	0.57	0.53	0.50	0.46	0.42	0.43
Textile & leather	0.43	0.41	0.38	0.36	0.34	0.32	0.29	0.30
Constr. mat. & furn.	0.55	0.45	0.27	0.25	0.22	0.22	0.22	0.20
Paper	0.01	0.01	0.01	0.01	0.01	0.01	0.01	0.01
Printing	0.32	0.29	0.23	0.21	0.19	0.19	0.19	0.19
Metal	0.30	0.28	0.22	0.20	0.17	0.16	0.14	0.14
Chemical	0.07	0.06	0.05	0.05	0.04	0.04	0.04	0.04
Misc. & rubber	0.14	0.12	0.09	0.09	0.08	0.08	0.08	0.07
Construction	1.0	0.96	0.79	1.2	1.3	1.7	2.0	1.8
Transp. & other pub. util.	0.03	0.03	0.03	0.02	0.02	0.02	0.02	0.01
Electric light & power	0.02	0.02	0.02	0.01	0.01	0.01	0.01	0.01
Water transp.	0.01	0.01	0.01	0.01	0.01	0.01	0.01	0.01
Trade	12.3	12.5	12.9	13.1	13.4	13.6	13.8	14.1
Service	13.0	13.1	13.0	13.2	13.6	13.8	14.1	14.5
Professional	4.8	4.8	4.9	5.0	5.2	5.3	5.4	5.6
Personal	4.3	4.3	4.2	4.5	4.8	5.0	5.3	5.5
Miscellaneous	4.0	3.9	3.8	3.7	3.6	3.5	3.4	3.3
Miscellaneous	2.5	2.7	2.8	2.9	3.0	3.1	3.2	3.4

* Less than 0.005 per cent.

TABLE 66

Entrepreneurs

1927	1928	1929	1930	1931	1932	1933	1934	1935	1936	1937	1938
9,696	9,757	9,854	9,893	9,971	10,062	10,199	10,280	10,333	10,445	10,525	10,601
64.1	63.8	63.3	63.5	64.2	65.3	65.6	65.6	65.5	64.9	64.5	64.5
0.16	0.15	0.14	0.14	0.14	0.14	0.13	0.13	0.12	0.12	0.12	0.12
...*	...*	...*	...*	...*	...*	...*	...*	...*	...*	...*	...*
0.04	0.03	0.03	0.03	0.03	0.02	0.02	0.02	0.02	0.02	0.02	0.01
0.01	...*	...*	...*	...*	...*	...*	...*	...*	...*	...*	...*
0.11	0.10	0.09	0.09	0.09	0.09	0.09	0.09	0.09	0.09	0.09	0.09
0.02	0.02	0.02	0.02	0.02	0.02	0.02	0.02	0.02	0.02	0.02	0.02
1.4	1.4	1.4	1.2	1.0	0.84	0.71	0.74	0.79	0.87	0.94	0.94
0.44	0.44	0.45	0.41	0.35	0.30	0.25	0.24	0.24	0.29	0.34	0.33
0.31	0.29	0.27	0.24	0.20	0.16	0.14	0.14	0.14	0.15	0.15	0.15
0.18	0.21	0.24	0.19	0.15	0.10	0.07	0.09	0.11	0.12	0.13	0.13
0.01	0.01	0.01	0.01	0.01	0.01	...*	0.01	0.01	0.01	0.01	0.01
0.19	0.17	0.15	0.14	0.13	0.12	0.11	0.12	0.13	0.14	0.14	0.14
0.14	0.13	0.12	0.12	0.10	0.09	0.08	0.08	0.09	0.09	0.09	0.09
0.03	0.04	0.04	0.03	0.03	0.03	0.02	0.02	0.03	0.03	0.03	0.03
0.07	0.07	0.07	0.06	0.05	0.04	0.04	0.04	0.05	0.05	0.05	0.05
1.7	1.7	1.7	1.7	1.5	1.2	1.1	1.2	1.3	1.4	1.4	1.4
0.01	0.01	0.01	0.01	0.01	0.01	0.01	0.01	0.01	0.01	0.01	0.01
...*	...*	...*	...*	...*	...*	...*	...*	...*	...*	...*	...*
0.01	0.01	0.01	0.01	0.01	...*	...*	...*	...*	...*	...*	...*
14.3	14.6	14.7	14.6	14.5	14.3	14.1	13.6	13.1	13.3	13.4	13.4
14.8	14.8	15.1	15.2	15.1	15.0	15.3	15.5	15.7	15.8	15.8	15.8
5.8	6.0	6.1	6.3	6.4	6.5	6.5	6.6	6.7	6.8	6.9	7.0
5.8	5.7	6.0	5.9	5.8	5.8	6.0	6.2	6.3	6.3	6.2	6.2
3.2	3.1	3.0	2.9	2.9	2.8	2.7	2.7	2.7	2.7	2.7	2.6
3.5	3.6	3.7	3.6	3.4	3.2	3.1	3.3	3.5	3.6	3.8	3.9

TABLE 67

Service Income including Entrepreneurial Savings *

	1919	1920	1921	1922	1923	1924	1925	1926
Total ($000,000)	55,495	57,998	44,482	48,077	56,055	56,302	59,494	62,140
Agriculture	18.9	14.9	11.3	11.1	11.1	11.7	12.6	11.4
Mining	2.7	3.6	3.5	3.0	3.6	3.1	2.7	3.1
Anth. coal	0.40	0.44	0.68	0.38	0.55	0.61	0.38	0.54
Bit. coal	1.4	1.9	1.9	1.6	2.0	1.4	1.3	1.4
Metal	0.43	0.44	0.31	0.29	0.36	0.35	0.35	0.34
Oil & gas	0.35	0.56	0.39	0.44	0.41	0.38	0.44	0.52
Other	0.18	0.26	0.24	0.24	0.30	0.30	0.29	0.29
Manufacturing	24.2	26.2	22.7	22.9	24.3	22.8	22.7	22.5
Food & tobacco	2.7	2.6	2.8	2.7	2.5	2.4	2.3	2.2
Textile & leather	5.1	5.0	5.3	5.3	5.2	4.5	4.6	4.3
Constr. mat. & furn.	2.9	3.5	2.9	3.2	3.5	3.5	3.4	3.4
Paper	0.52	0.65	0.60	0.59	0.60	0.60	0.60	0.61
Printing	1.2	1.5	1.7	1.7	1.6	1.7	1.7	1.8
Metal	8.9	9.8	6.8	6.8	8.3	7.6	7.6	7.6
Chemical	1.3	1.4	1.2	1.2	1.2	1.1	1.1	1.2
Misc. & rubber	1.5	1.6	1.4	1.4	1.4	1.3	1.3	1.3
Construction	3.7	4.4	4.2	4.8	5.9	6.4	6.5	6.7
Transp. & other pub. util.	8.3	10.4	10.8	9.6	9.2	9.1	8.7	8.7
Electric light & power	0.26	0.31	0.42	0.41	0.46	0.53	0.52	0.58
Mfd. gas	0.14	0.14	0.18	0.17	0.17	0.18	0.18	0.18
Steam rr., Pull., & exp.	5.7	7.2	7.0	6.2	6.1	5.7	5.5	5.4
Street rwy.	0.66	0.80	0.99	0.90	0.78	0.78	0.73	0.70
Water transp.	0.92	1.2	1.2	0.95	0.83	0.88	0.81	0.80
Pipe lines	0.05	0.06	0.07	0.07	0.07	0.06	0.06	0.07
Telephone	0.43	0.54	0.73	0.73	0.70	0.75	0.74	0.75
Telegraph	0.13	0.17	0.18	0.17	0.16	0.16	0.16	0.18
Trade	18.1	15.6	15.5	17.3	16.6	16.3	16.2	16.0
Finance	2.7	3.1	4.2	3.9	3.5	3.8	3.8	4.0
Banking	0.69	0.82	1.1	1.1	0.97	1.0	1.0	1.0
Insurance	1.2	1.4	1.9	1.8	1.5	1.7	1.8	1.9
Real estate	0.83	0.93	1.2	1.1	1.0	1.1	0.96	1.1
Service	10.9	11.6	14.8	15.2	14.5	15.1	15.3	16.0
Government	7.3	6.7	9.0	8.2	7.3	7.6	7.5	7.5
Federal	4.3	3.3	4.0	3.3	2.8	2.8	2.8	2.8
State	0.34	0.40	0.61	0.55	0.51	0.57	0.51	0.43
County	0.27	0.31	0.48	0.47	0.42	0.45	0.42	0.42
City incl. pub. educ.	2.3	2.6	3.9	3.9	3.6	3.8	3.8	3.9
Miscellaneous	3.2	3.4	4.0	3.9	4.0	4.0	4.1	4.3

* Excluding Social Security contributions of employers.

TABLE 67

Service Income including Entrepreneurial Savings *

1927	1928	1929	1930	1931	1932	1933	1934	1935	1936	1937	1938
62,070	63,243	66,580	58,851	48,588	37,379	37,144	43,858	47,844	53,920	58,449	54,424
11.3	10.9	10.9	9.1	7.4	6.5	8.6	10.0	10.6	10.7	10.2	9.5
2.7	2.4	2.4	2.3	2.0	1.7	1.8	2.0	2.0	2.0	2.1	1.9
0.48	0.44	0.38	0.41	0.40	0.38	0.34	0.34	0.28	0.23	0.20	0.18
1.2	1.0	0.96	0.90	0.81	0.72	0.78	0.92	0.93	0.96	0.96	0.80
0.32	0.30	0.31	0.29	0.22	0.14	0.14	0.16	0.19	0.23	0.32	0.24
0.46	0.38	0.48	0.42	0.31	0.31	0.35	0.42	0.40	0.41	0.45	0.47
0.28	0.26	0.23	0.24	0.22	0.18	0.16	0.17	0.17	0.19	0.20	0.18
22.5	22.6	23.0	22.1	20.6	18.8	19.4	20.5	21.2	21.5	23.2	19.8
2.3	2.3	2.3	2.5	2.5	2.6	2.7	2.8	2.7	2.6	2.6	2.7
4.7	4.4	4.4	4.0	4.2	3.9	4.5	4.4	4.5	4.2	4.1	3.7
3.2	3.1	3.0	2.7	2.1	1.6	1.6	1.8	1.9	2.1	2.4	2.0
0.61	0.61	0.61	0.65	0.66	0.65	0.69	0.70	0.69	0.67	0.70	0.67
1.8	1.9	1.9	2.2	2.2	2.3	2.0	1.9	1.8	1.7	1.8	1.8
7.4	7.7	8.3	7.5	6.2	5.2	5.2	6.3	6.9	7.5	8.9	6.4
1.2	1.2	1.3	1.3	1.3	1.4	1.4	1.4	1.4	1.3	1.4	1.4
1.4	1.4	1.3	1.3	1.3	1.2	1.2	1.2	1.3	1.3	1.3	1.1
6.3	6.2	6.0	5.6	4.4	3.0	2.1	2.1	2.2	2.9	3.1	3.1
8.6	8.4	8.3	8.6	8.9	8.8	8.2	7.5	7.3	7.2	7.3	7.2
0.60	0.64	0.65	0.77	0.87	0.94	0.86	0.79	0.76	0.74	0.76	0.81
0.18	0.17	0.15	0.17	0.17	0.20	0.20	0.18	0.17	0.16	0.16	0.17
5.4	5.1	5.0	5.0	4.9	4.7	4.4	4.0	4.0	3.9	4.0	3.8
0.68	0.64	0.62	0.65	0.69	0.72	0.61	0.54	0.49	0.45	0.42	0.43
0.77	0.77	0.73	0.77	0.78	0.78	0.82	0.75	0.81	0.83	0.88	0.84
0.08	0.08	0.08	0.08	0.08	0.08	0.08	0.08	0.08	0.08	0.08	0.08
0.79	0.83	0.89	1.0	1.1	1.2	1.1	0.95	0.90	0.86	0.90	0.99
0.17	0.17	0.18	0.21	0.22	0.21	0.19	0.18	0.17	0.16	0.16	0.16
15.6	15.8	15.6	15.8	16.3	16.6	16.6	16.2	15.3	14.6	14.6	15.4
4.3	4.6	4.7	4.9	5.4	5.8	5.2	4.7	4.5	4.1	4.0	4.3
1.1	1.1	1.1	1.2	1.3	1.5	1.3	1.1	1.0	0.96	0.92	1.0
2.0	2.1	2.1	2.4	2.7	3.0	2.7	2.4	2.3	2.1	2.1	2.3
1.2	1.4	1.5	1.4	1.4	1.3	1.2	1.1	1.1	1.0	0.96	1.0
16.4	16.6	16.6	17.5	18.0	18.0	16.2	15.6	15.5	15.4	15.5	16.3
8.0	8.1	8.1	9.4	11.9	15.3	16.6	16.4	16.2	16.5	14.6	17.1
2.9	2.9	2.9	3.3	4.4	5.7	7.7	9.0	9.1	9.8	8.0	9.5
0.47	0.49	0.49	0.59	0.75	0.99	0.97	0.86	0.88	0.85	0.88	1.0
0.46	0.48	0.50	0.59	0.75	0.95	0.87	0.74	0.71	0.67	0.66	0.75
4.2	4.3	4.2	4.9	6.0	7.6	7.0	5.8	5.5	5.2	5.1	5.9
4.3	4.4	4.4	4.7	5.1	5.5	5.4	5.0	5.2	5.2	5.3	5.4

TABLE 68

Service Income excluding Entrepreneurial Savings *

	1919	1920	1921	1922	1923	1924	1925	1926
Total ($000,000)	48,922	57,367	45,806	47,793	54,685	55,269	57,523	60,470
Agriculture	16.8	16.6	14.1	13.1	12.5	12.6	12.3	11.9
Mining	3.1	3.6	3.5	3.0	3.7	3.1	2.8	3.1
Anth. coal	0.46	0.44	0.66	0.38	0.57	0.62	0.40	0.55
Bit. coal	1.6	1.9	1.9	1.6	2.0	1.5	1.3	1.4
Metal	0.48	0.44	0.30	0.30	0.36	0.36	0.36	0.35
Oil & gas	0.39	0.53	0.40	0.45	0.43	0.39	0.43	0.51
Other	0.20	0.26	0.23	0.24	0.30	0.31	0.30	0.29
Manufacturing	26.6	26.4	22.5	22.7	24.5	23.1	23.2	22.9
Food & tobacco	3.1	2.8	2.9	2.7	2.5	2.4	2.3	2.2
Textile & leather	5.3	5.1	5.2	5.1	5.2	4.6	4.7	4.5
Constr. mat. & furn.	3.2	3.4	2.9	3.2	3.5	3.5	3.5	3.5
Paper	0.58	0.64	0.59	0.59	0.61	0.60	0.61	0.62
Printing	1.3	1.4	1.7	1.7	1.6	1.7	1.7	1.8
Metal	10.0	9.9	6.7	6.8	8.4	7.7	7.8	7.8
Chemical	1.5	1.5	1.2	1.2	1.3	1.2	1.2	1.2
Misc. & rubber	1.6	1.6	1.4	1.4	1.4	1.3	1.4	1.4
Construction	3.8	4.4	4.1	4.8	5.9	6.2	6.3	6.6
Transp. & other pub. util.	9.4	10.5	10.5	9.7	9.5	9.2	9.0	8.9
Electric light & power	0.29	0.31	0.41	0.41	0.47	0.54	0.54	0.59
Mfd. gas	0.16	0.15	0.17	0.17	0.17	0.18	0.18	0.18
Steam rr., Pull., & exp.	6.5	7.2	6.8	6.3	6.2	5.8	5.7	5.6
Street rwy.	0.75	0.81	0.96	0.91	0.80	0.80	0.75	0.72
Water transp.	1.0	1.2	1.2	0.96	0.85	0.90	0.83	0.82
Pipe lines	0.06	0.06	0.07	0.07	0.07	0.06	0.06	0.07
Telephone	0.49	0.55	0.71	0.74	0.71	0.76	0.76	0.77
Telegraph	0.15	0.17	0.18	0.17	0.16	0.16	0.16	0.18
Trade	15.6	15.1	16.0	16.2	15.5	15.7	15.8	15.8
Finance	3.1	3.1	4.1	4.0	3.6	3.9	3.9	4.1
Banking	0.78	0.82	1.1	1.1	1.0	1.0	1.1	1.1
Insurance	1.3	1.4	1.8	1.8	1.6	1.7	1.9	1.9
Real estate	0.94	0.94	1.2	1.1	1.1	1.1	0.99	1.1
Service	10.1	10.3	12.8	14.4	13.4	14.3	14.8	14.7
Government	8.2	6.8	8.7	8.3	7.5	7.7	7.8	7.7
Federal	4.9	3.4	3.8	3.3	2.9	2.9	2.9	2.9
State	0.38	0.41	0.59	0.55	0.52	0.58	0.52	0.44
County	0.31	0.31	0.47	0.47	0.43	0.46	0.44	0.43
City incl. pub. educ.	2.7	2.7	3.8	3.9	3.7	3.9	3.9	4.0
Miscellaneous	3.3	3.2	3.6	3.9	3.9	4.0	4.2	4.2

* Excluding Social Security contributions of employers.

TABLE 68

Service Income excluding Entrepreneurial Savings *

1927	1928	1929	1930	1931	1932	1933	1934	1935	1936	1937	1938
61,054	62,238	65,599	60,542	51,676	41,447	39,073	43,988	47,446	52,604	57,802	54,288
11.6	11.4	11.0	11.1	10.4	9.9	9.4	9.2	9.3	9.0	9.2	9.7
2.8	2.4	2.4	2.2	1.9	1.6	1.7	2.0	2.0	2.1	2.1	1.9
0.49	0.45	0.39	0.40	0.38	0.35	0.32	0.34	0.28	0.24	0.21	0.18
1.2	1.0	0.97	0.88	0.77	0.66	0.75	0.92	0.94	0.99	0.96	0.80
0.32	0.30	0.31	0.28	0.20	0.13	0.14	0.16	0.19	0.24	0.33	0.24
0.46	0.37	0.46	0.43	0.33	0.34	0.38	0.43	0.42	0.42	0.44	0.46
0.28	0.26	0.23	0.23	0.21	0.17	0.16	0.17	0.18	0.20	0.21	0.18
22.8	22.9	23.3	21.7	19.7	17.4	18.5	20.4	21.3	21.8	23.3	19.9
2.3	2.4	2.3	2.4	2.4	2.5	2.6	2.7	2.6	2.5	2.6	2.7
4.7	4.5	4.4	4.0	4.1	3.7	4.3	4.4	4.5	4.3	4.1	3.7
3.3	3.1	3.0	2.7	2.1	1.5	1.6	1.8	1.9	2.2	2.4	2.0
0.62	0.62	0.62	0.63	0.62	0.59	0.65	0.70	0.69	0.68	0.70	0.68
1.8	1.9	1.9	2.1	2.1	2.1	1.9	1.9	1.8	1.8	1.8	1.8
7.5	7.8	8.3	7.3	5.8	4.7	5.0	6.2	7.0	7.7	9.0	6.5
1.2	1.2	1.3	1.3	1.3	1.2	1.3	1.4	1.4	1.3	1.4	1.4
1.4	1.4	1.3	1.3	1.2	1.1	1.2	1.2	1.3	1.3	1.4	1.1
6.3	6.1	5.9	5.5	4.3	3.3	2.4	2.3	2.4	3.1	3.2	3.1
8.8	8.5	8.4	8.4	8.3	8.0	7.8	7.4	7.4	7.4	7.4	7.3
0.60	0.65	0.66	0.75	0.82	0.85	0.81	0.78	0.76	0.75	0.77	0.82
0.18	0.17	0.15	0.16	0.16	0.18	0.19	0.18	0.17	0.16	0.16	0.17
5.4	5.2	5.0	4.8	4.6	4.2	4.1	4.0	4.0	4.0	4.0	3.8
0.69	0.65	0.63	0.63	0.65	0.65	0.58	0.54	0.50	0.46	0.42	0.44
0.78	0.78	0.74	0.75	0.74	0.71	0.78	0.75	0.81	0.84	0.89	0.84
0.08	0.08	0.08	0.07	0.08	0.07	0.08	0.08	0.08	0.08	0.08	0.08
0.80	0.85	0.90	0.99	1.0	1.1	1.0	0.95	0.90	0.88	0.91	0.99
0.17	0.17	0.18	0.20	0.21	0.19	0.18	0.18	0.17	0.16	0.16	0.16
15.4	15.5	15.6	16.3	17.0	17.1	16.1	16.2	15.4	14.8	14.7	15.4
4.4	4.6	4.8	4.8	5.1	5.2	4.9	4.7	4.5	4.2	4.1	4.4
1.1	1.1	1.1	1.2	1.2	1.3	1.2	1.1	1.1	0.98	0.94	1.0
2.0	2.1	2.1	2.3	2.5	2.7	2.6	2.4	2.4	2.2	2.2	2.3
1.3	1.4	1.5	1.3	1.3	1.2	1.1	1.1	1.1	1.0	0.97	1.1
15.6	15.8	16.1	16.3	17.2	18.4	17.9	16.3	16.0	15.5	15.8	16.0
8.1	8.3	8.2	9.2	11.2	13.8	15.8	16.4	16.3	16.9	14.8	17.1
2.9	2.9	2.9	3.2	4.1	5.2	7.3	9.0	9.2	10.0	8.1	9.5
0.48	0.50	0.50	0.57	0.71	0.89	0.92	0.86	0.88	0.87	0.89	1.0
0.46	0.49	0.50	0.57	0.70	0.86	0.82	0.74	0.72	0.68	0.67	0.75
4.2	4.4	4.3	4.8	5.7	6.9	6.7	5.8	5.5	5.3	5.1	5.9
4.3	4.4	4.4	4.5	4.8	5.2	5.4	5.1	5.3	5.3	5.4	5.5

TABLE 69

Number Engaged (employees on full-time equivalent basis)

	1919	1920	1921	1922	1923	1924	1925	1926
Total (000)	39,818	40,212	36,519	38,043	40,819	40,634	41,344	42,783
Agriculture	21.3	21.3	23.2	22.2	20.4	20.3	19.9	19.4
Mining	2.8	3.0	2.5	2.4	2.8	2.5	2.5	2.7
Anth. coal	0.39	0.37	0.46	0.27	0.39	0.41	0.27	0.38
Bit. coal	1.5	1.7	1.3	1.2	1.4	1.2	1.3	1.4
Metal	0.37	0.36	0.22	0.27	0.32	0.32	0.32	0.31
Oil & gas	0.32	0.37	0.30	0.36	0.35	0.32	0.36	0.43
Other	0.22	0.26	0.23	0.25	0.28	0.28	0.28	0.27
Manufacturing	25.4	24.8	21.2	22.4	23.6	22.2	22.4	22.2
Food & tobacco	3.0	2.8	2.7	2.7	2.5	2.4	2.4	2.3
Textile & leather	5.7	5.5	5.6	5.7	5.8	5.3	5.4	5.2
Constr. mat. & furn.	3.4	3.3	3.0	3.5	3.6	3.5	3.6	3.5
Paper	0.59	0.64	0.57	0.58	0.61	0.60	0.61	0.62
Printing	1.2	1.2	1.2	1.2	1.2	1.2	1.2	1.2
Metal	8.4	8.3	5.6	6.0	7.1	6.6	6.6	6.6
Chemical	1.3	1.2	1.1	1.1	1.1	1.1	1.1	1.1
Misc. & rubber	1.6	1.6	1.3	1.4	1.4	1.3	1.4	1.3
Construction	2.8	3.1	3.1	3.8	4.3	4.5	4.5	4.8
Transp. & other pub. util.	8.2	8.7	8.2	8.0	8.2	8.0	7.8	7.8
Electric light & power	0.28	0.30	0.34	0.36	0.44	0.48	0.48	0.53
Mfd. gas	0.16	0.14	0.14	0.15	0.16	0.17	0.17	0.17
Steam rr., Pull., & exp.	5.3	5.6	5.1	4.8	5.0	4.8	4.7	4.6
Street rwy.	0.74	0.75	0.77	0.77	0.71	0.69	0.66	0.62
Water transp.	0.74	0.90	0.84	0.84	0.78	0.77	0.72	0.72
Pipe lines	0.05	0.04	0.06	0.06	0.06	0.05	0.06	0.06
Telephone	0.70	0.76	0.80	0.82	0.83	0.85	0.87	0.86
Telegraph	0.19	0.19	0.20	0.18	0.18	0.19	0.20	0.20
Trade	12.6	13.6	13.8	13.9	13.8	14.3	14.3	14.2
Finance	2.4	2.5	2.8	2.6	2.5	2.7	2.7	2.8
Banking	0.78	0.86	0.93	0.87	0.85	0.88	0.89	0.91
Insurance	0.76	0.80	0.94	0.90	0.86	0.93	0.97	1.0
Real estate	0.83	0.86	0.89	0.81	0.84	0.89	0.80	0.92
Service.	12.2	12.4	13.8	13.9	13.8	14.4	14.6	14.8
Professional	2.6	2.6	2.9	3.0	3.0	3.1	3.2	3.2
Personal	3.3	3.4	3.6	3.8	3.7	3.8	4.0	4.1
Domestic	4.3	4.2	4.7	4.8	4.8	5.0	5.0	5.1
Miscellaneous	2.0	2.2	2.5	2.3	2.3	2.4	2.4	2.5
Government	8.8	7.0	7.6	7.1	6.7	7.0	7.0	6.9
Federal	4.5	2.6	2.7	2.2	2.0	2.0	2.0	1.9
State	0.40	0.42	0.46	0.43	0.41	0.44	0.48	0.43
County	0.38	0.39	0.46	0.46	0.44	0.47	0.45	0.44
City incl. pub. educ.	3.5	3.6	4.0	3.9	3.8	4.0	4.0	4.1
Miscellaneous	3.5	3.5	3.8	3.9	4.0	4.1	4.2	4.3

TABLE 69

Number Engaged (employees on full-time equivalent basis)

1927	1928	1929	1930	1931	1932	1933	1934	1935	1936	1937	1938
42,898	43,151	44,913	42,775	39,398	36,003	36,041	38,534	39,815	41,846	43,797	41,403
19.1	19.0	18.3	19.1	20.7	22.7	23.0	21.5	21.1	20.1	19.3	20.6
2.5	2.3	2.3	2.3	2.1	2.0	2.0	2.2	2.2	2.2	2.2	2.0
0.39	0.37	0.34	0.34	0.33	0.29	0.25	0.27	0.25	0.23	0.21	0.19
1.2	1.1	1.1	1.1	1.1	1.0	1.1	1.2	1.1	1.1	1.1	1.0
0.29	0.27	0.28	0.26	0.21	0.15	0.15	0.18	0.20	0.24	0.30	0.24
0.38	0.31	0.38	0.35	0.27	0.28	0.31	0.36	0.35	0.36	0.36	0.36
0.27	0.26	0.24	0.24	0.24	0.21	0.21	0.22	0.22	0.22	0.22	0.20
21.8	21.7	22.3	20.8	19.2	17.8	19.0	20.7	21.3	21.9	22.9	20.4
2.3	2.4	2.4	2.4	2.3	2.3	2.5	2.7	2.6	2.6	2.7	2.7
5.4	5.2	5.1	4.8	4.9	4.8	5.4	5.5	5.6	5.5	5.4	5.0
3.3	3.1	3.1	2.7	2.2	1.8	1.9	2.1	2.2	2.5	2.6	2.3
0.60	0.59	0.59	0.60	0.58	0.57	0.62	0.68	0.67	0.66	0.68	0.66
1.2	1.3	1.3	1.4	1.3	1.3	1.2	1.2	1.2	1.2	1.3	1.3
6.3	6.4	6.9	6.2	5.2	4.6	4.7	5.7	6.1	6.5	7.3	5.8
1.1	1.1	1.2	1.2	1.1	1.0	1.2	1.2	1.2	1.2	1.2	1.1
1.3	1.3	1.3	1.2	1.2	1.1	1.2	1.3	1.3	1.3	1.4	1.2
4.5	4.5	4.4	4.2	3.4	2.5	2.1	2.2	2.3	2.7	2.7	2.6
7.6	7.4	7.3	7.1	6.7	6.2	5.9	5.7	5.5	5.5	5.5	5.2
0.55	0.58	0.61	0.66	0.66	0.63	0.59	0.59	0.58	0.59	0.59	0.60
0.17	0.16	0.14	0.15	0.14	0.13	0.14	0.13	0.13	0.12	0.12	0.12
4.5	4.3	4.1	3.9	3.6	3.2	3.0	2.9	2.8	2.8	2.9	2.6
0.59	0.57	0.54	0.52	0.51	0.48	0.44	0.41	0.38	0.36	0.33	0.33
0.70	0.69	0.65	0.65	0.61	0.58	0.63	0.62	0.62	0.63	0.66	0.62
0.07	0.07	0.06	0.06	0.06	0.05	0.06	0.06	0.06	0.06	0.06	0.06
0.88	0.91	0.97	1.0	0.93	0.93	0.86	0.79	0.75	0.73	0.74	0.77
0.20	0.20	0.21	0.22	0.21	0.19	0.18	0.18	0.17	0.17	0.17	0.16
14.6	14.7	14.8	15.0	14.9	14.7	14.5	14.5	14.0	13.8	13.7	14.1
3.0	3.2	3.3	3.4	3.4	3.4	3.3	3.2	3.1	3.0	3.0	3.2
0.94	0.96	0.94	0.94	0.89	0.85	0.75	0.73	0.68	0.65	0.64	0.68
1.1	1.1	1.1	1.2	1.3	1.4	1.3	1.3	1.2	1.2	1.2	1.3
1.0	1.2	1.3	1.3	1.3	1.2	1.2	1.2	1.2	1.2	1.2	1.2
15.3	15.5	15.6	16.0	16.5	16.6	16.2	16.6	16.9	17.0	16.9	17.4
3.3	3.5	3.5	3.8	4.2	4.5	4.5	4.3	4.3	4.3	4.2	4.6
4.3	4.2	4.4	4.6	4.8	5.0	4.8	5.1	5.2	5.1	5.0	5.2
5.2	5.1	5.1	5.0	4.9	4.6	4.4	4.6	4.7	4.8	4.8	4.7
2.6	2.6	2.6	2.6	2.6	2.5	2.5	2.5	2.6	2.8	2.7	2.9
7.0	7.1	7.0	7.5	8.3	9.0	8.9	8.6	8.7	8.8	8.7	9.3
1.9	1.9	1.9	2.0	2.2	2.4	2.4	2.4	2.6	2.8	2.7	2.9
0.47	0.48	0.47	0.52	0.60	0.68	0.68	0.67	0.71	0.72	0.74	0.81
0.46	0.48	0.48	0.52	0.59	0.66	0.65	0.62	0.62	0.61	0.62	0.68
4.2	4.2	4.2	4.4	4.8	5.3	5.2	4.8	4.7	4.7	4.6	5.0
4.4	4.5	4.6	4.6	4.8	5.0	5.1	5.0	5.0	5.0	5.0	5.3

TABLE 70

Dividends

	1919	1920	1921	1922	1923	1924	1925	1926
Total ($000,000)	2,887	3,216	2,963	3,049	3,839	3,813	4,425	4,725
Agriculture	0.55	0.50	0.54	0.52	0.42	0.39	0.41	0.34
Mining	6.7	6.5	6.5	4.6	5.8	5.6	6.1	6.9
Anth. coal	0.18	0.16	0.30	0.12	0.19	0.22	0.15	0.30
Bit. coal	0.68	0.75	0.91	0.55	0.75	0.55	0.54	0.82
Metal	3.4	2.7	2.4	1.6	2.2	2.2	2.4	1.8
Oil & gas	1.4	1.8	1.6	1.3	1.4	1.3	1.6	2.9
Other	1.0	1.1	1.3	0.96	1.3	1.3	1.4	1.1
Manufacturing	43.7	46.3	44.7	43.0	45.9	43.3	43.2	44.8
Food & tobacco	5.3	6.1	5.4	5.0	5.8	6.5	6.3	5.8
Textile & leather	8.7	8.6	6.8	6.9	6.4	5.3	4.9	4.4
Constr. mat. & furn.	3.2	3.9	3.7	4.0	4.6	4.2	4.2	5.2
Paper	1.6	1.9	1.7	1.1	1.5	0.97	1.4	1.0
Printing	1.2	1.3	1.9	2.2	1.8	1.7	2.0	2.0
Metal	13.2	13.2	13.3	12.1	14.2	16.4	15.1	16.9
Chemical	6.9	7.8	8.7	7.0	7.0	6.4	7.2	7.3
Misc. & rubber	3.6	3.5	3.4	4.5	4.7	1.9	2.1	2.2
Construction	0.53	0.65	1.1	0.99	0.98	0.85	1.3	0.88
Transp. & other pub. util.	18.4	15.1	15.4	18.6	16.6	18.6	18.5	18.3
Electric light & power	2.4	2.2	2.8	4.0	4.2	4.9	5.2	5.2
Mfd. gas	1.5	1.1	0.86	0.73	0.87	1.3	1.1	1.0
Steam rr., Pull., & exp.	8.9	7.3	7.0	7.4	6.6	7.3	6.7	7.1
Street rwy.	1.2	1.0	0.91	1.5	1.2	1.2	1.1	0.99
Water transp.	1.6	0.88	0.61	0.60	0.49	0.35	0.41	0.43
Pipe lines	1.1	0.96	1.2	2.0	1.1	1.2	1.6	1.2
Telephone	1.4	1.3	1.6	2.0	1.9	2.2	2.1	2.1
Telegraph	0.35	0.31	0.33	0.32	0.24	0.25	0.21	0.25
Trade	13.9	11.9	10.8	9.9	9.6	10.2	9.9	10.0
Finance	11.6	12.6	13.8	15.5	13.9	13.3	12.5	11.6
Banking	9.6	9.3	10.5	10.8	8.5	8.6	7.7	7.5
Insurance	0.64	0.60	0.78	1.5	1.0	0.88	0.87	0.91
Real estate	1.4	2.8	2.5	3.3	4.4	3.8	3.9	3.2
Service	1.0	2.5	2.2	1.6	1.8	1.9	2.1	2.2
Miscellaneous	3.6	3.9	4.9	5.4	5.0	5.9	6.0	4.9

TABLE 70

Dividends

1927	1928	1929	1930	1931	1932	1933	1934	1935	1936	1937	1938
5,051	5,493	6,300	5,993	4,646	3,016	2,472	3,014	3,770	4,838	4,947	3,486
0.57	0.46	0.19	0.12	0.30	0.20	0.00	0.57	0.50	0.76	0.65	0.63
5.5	4.6	5.8	4.2	3.0	2.7	3.0	5.0	4.9	4.4	6.0	5.9
0.25	0.25	0.25	0.22	0.20	0.20	0.03	0.07	0.07	0.06	0.02	0.02
0.68	0.36	0.43	0.40	0.34	0.22	0.17	0.77	0.29	0.34	0.24	0.25
1.5	1.8	3.1	1.5	0.81	0.37	0.54	0.79	1.1	1.6	2.6	2.2
2.0	1.3	1.1	1.3	0.80	1.2	1.5	2.6	1.9	1.4	1.9	2.0
0.99	0.94	0.93	0.67	0.83	0.70	0.76	0.79	1.5	0.96	1.3	1.4
44.1	45.8	43.5	43.7	40.8	37.1	40.9	42.0	42.0	49.8	49.2	40.5
6.5	6.4	6.4	7.2	7.9	9.7	11.3	10.5	8.9	9.2	8.3	9.9
4.2	4.2	3.4	2.8	2.7	2.5	3.1	3.8	3.0	3.6	3.4	2.4
4.3	4.0	3.5	3.0	2.3	1.6	1.7	2.6	2.5	3.5	3.7	2.3
1.1	1.2	0.91	0.86	0.79	0.68	1.1	1.3	1.2	1.3	1.5	0.76
2.2	1.8	2.1	2.1	2.0	2.0	1.4	2.1	1.9	2.2	1.9	2.1
17.1	17.4	17.7	15.9	13.5	10.0	9.0	12.7	14.1	18.3	19.8	12.1
6.6	9.0	7.7	10.0	9.9	9.3	12.0	7.7	8.3	9.4	8.4	8.3
2.1	1.8	1.9	1.7	1.6	1.4	1.4	1.3	2.0	2.3	2.1	2.6
0.94	0.94	0.95	1.4	0.86	0.64	0.76	0.47	0.55	0.76	0.85	0.84
20.6	19.1	20.4	23.8	26.6	32.3	33.6	27.5	24.7	17.9	19.2	24.4
5.6	6.5	7.1	9.0	11.5	14.3	15.1	10.9	8.8	7.1	8.0	10.8
0.92	0.70	1.1	1.1	1.7	2.9	2.5	1.9	1.7	1.2	1.2	1.7
8.6	6.7	7.0	7.4	5.5	2.5	3.1	4.2	3.4	3.0	3.3	2.4
0.93	0.84	0.77	0.65	0.61	0.59	0.62	0.64	0.57	0.65	0.77	1.0
0.38	0.40	0.45	0.50	0.42	0.41	0.32	0.58	1.5	0.83	0.83	0.87
1.6	1.6	1.8	2.4	2.9	5.2	4.4	3.0	3.8	1.6	1.7	2.5
2.2	2.1	2.0	2.5	3.8	6.2	7.6	6.3	4.8	3.5	3.3	5.1
0.25	0.24	0.33	0.37	0.22	0.10	0.01	0.02	0.12	0.01	0.04	−0.02
9.8	9.1	9.0	8.3	8.3	7.1	7.2	10.2	11.6	13.8	12.6	13.8
10.8	12.0	12.1	11.1	12.8	12.3	8.3	8.7	7.4	5.6	5.8	8.4
7.6	8.0	7.2	7.5	8.8	9.3	6.4	6.2	5.0	4.0	4.1	5.6
1.1	1.2	1.1	1.0	1.3	1.0	0.66	0.75	1.0	0.45	0.43	1.1
2.2	2.8	3.8	2.6	2.6	2.0	1.2	1.7	1.4	1.1	1.3	1.6
2.1	1.8	1.9	1.9	1.6	1.8	1.4	1.5	1.4	2.3	2.4	2.0
5.6	6.2	6.1	5.6	5.8	5.9	4.8	4.0	6.9	4.5	3.3	3.6

TABLE 71

Interest

	1919	1920	1921	1922	1923	1924	1925	1926
Total ($000,000)	3,229	3,653	3,872	3,980	4,206	4,374	4,579	4,699
Agriculture	11.1	11.8	12.7	12.8	12.1	11.1	10.0	9.5
Mining	0.72	0.83	0.99	0.84	0.89	1.2	1.2	0.99
Anth. coal	0.18	0.18	0.33	0.19	0.24	0.38	0.28	0.24
Bit. coal	0.22	0.29	0.33	0.29	0.31	0.32	0.33	0.22
Metal	0.14	0.13	0.10	0.10	0.11	0.16	0.18	0.11
Oil & gas	0.11	0.15	0.14	0.15	0.13	0.17	0.22	0.21
Other	0.07	0.08	0.09	0.10	0.10	0.15	0.17	0.21
Manufacturing	2.7	2.9	3.6	2.7	2.8	3.5	3.4	3.2
Food & tobacco	0.78	0.97	0.93	0.77	0.75	0.92	0.95	0.78
Textile & leather	0.40	0.31	0.36	0.30	0.09	0.07	0.10	0.05
Constr. mat. & furn.	0.18	0.18	0.19	0.22	0.22	0.26	0.24	0.25
Paper	0.12	0.10	0.11	0.16	0.19	0.19	0.21	0.26
Printing	0.08	0.05	0.09	0.04	0.03	0.04	0.09	0.11
Metal	0.81	0.77	0.86	0.47	0.92	1.2	1.1	0.97
Chemical	0.01	0.08	0.53	0.31	0.32	0.47	0.46	0.46
Misc. & rubber	0.30	0.47	0.49	0.40	0.27	0.32	0.24	0.35
Construction	0.12	0.14	0.20	0.11	0.14	0.18	0.23	0.24
Transp. & other pub. util.	21.0	19.6	19.4	19.7	19.9	20.4	20.2	20.1
Electric light & power	2.4	2.3	2.4	2.9	3.4	4.1	4.3	4.8
Mfd. gas	0.45	0.43	0.48	0.38	0.36	0.38	0.47	0.56
Steam rr., Pull., & exp.	13.5	12.6	12.3	12.3	11.9	12.0	11.7	11.2
Street rwy.	3.5	3.0	3.0	3.2	3.2	3.0	2.7	2.4
Water transp.	0.30	0.26	0.26	0.25	0.24	0.21	0.17	0.17
Pipe lines	...*	...*	...*	0.01	0.01	0.01	0.01	0.01
Telephone	0.94	0.92	0.92	0.73	0.75	0.75	0.88	0.86
Telegraph	−0.05	−0.04	...*	...*	...*	0.01	0.01	0.02
Trade	1.0	1.1	1.0	0.99	0.52	0.70	0.67	0.52
Finance	25.3	24.2	24.2	24.4	26.7	28.0	30.5	32.3
Insurance	−0.42	−0.46	−0.48	−0.49	−0.47	−0.50	−0.49	−0.48
Real estate	25.7	24.6	24.6	24.9	27.1	28.5	31.0	32.8
Service	0.49	0.41	0.47	0.57	0.66	0.76	0.90	1.0
Government	32.3	34.1	32.7	33.3	31.7	29.3	28.0	27.3
Federal	25.5	27.7	25.7	25.7	23.8	20.9	18.8	17.3
State	−0.18	−0.23	−0.18	−0.01	0.10	0.19	0.31	0.33
County	1.2	1.1	1.2	1.3	1.6	1.8	2.1	2.2
City incl. pub. educ.	5.9	5.5	5.9	6.2	6.3	6.4	6.8	7.4
Miscellaneous	5.3	4.9	4.9	4.6	4.7	4.9	4.9	4.8

* Less than 0.005 per cent.

TABLE 71

Interest

1927	1928	1929	1930	1931	1932	1933	1934	1935	1936	1937	1938
4,936	5,273	5,605	5,720	5,712	5,516	4,999	4,848	4,649	4,609	4,689	4,593
9.0	8.4	7.8	7.5	7.3	7.3	7.2	6.9	6.6	6.3	5.9	5.8
0.89	0.80	0.80	0.78	0.73	0.72	0.68	0.72	0.80	0.88	0.76	0.68
0.22	0.21	0.14	0.14	0.16	0.18	0.20	0.21	0.23	0.23	0.19	0.19
0.20	0.17	0.27	0.26	0.22	0.20	0.18	0.16	0.16	0.16	0.14	0.12
0.09	0.07	0.04	0.06	0.08	0.10	0.11	0.09	0.10	0.17	0.14	0.12
0.18	0.18	0.17	0.16	0.17	0.17	0.16	0.20	0.22	0.22	0.19	0.14
0.18	0.17	0.17	0.16	0.10	0.06	0.04	0.05	0.09	0.11	0.10	0.10
3.3	3.5	3.7	4.1	4.1	3.6	3.7	3.3	3.3	3.2	3.0	3.1
0.79	0.80	0.77	0.84	0.79	0.66	0.64	0.59	0.59	0.53	0.56	0.57
0.10	0.14	0.19	0.16	0.13	0.01	—0.02	—0.01	0.04	0.06	0.08	0.07
0.28	0.33	0.40	0.45	0.46	0.33	0.32	0.27	0.24	0.24	0.16	0.15
0.27	0.25	0.27	0.32	0.30	0.30	0.33	0.28	0.24	0.24	0.27	0.23
0.18	0.21	0.23	0.26	0.27	0.26	0.27	0.22	0.18	0.19	0.19	0.21
0.74	0.91	1.1	0.98	0.92	0.90	1.0	1.0	1.1	1.1	1.1	1.1
0.59	0.52	0.46	0.72	0.85	0.91	0.89	0.69	0.66	0.56	0.50	0.56
0.37	0.36	0.32	0.34	0.34	0.26	0.28	0.28	0.23	0.19	0.14	0.14
0.23	0.19	0.24	0.27	0.24	0.19	0.17	0.10	0.03	0.04	0.04	0.04
19.6	18.7	17.3	17.3	17.9	19.3	20.8	20.0	19.9	19.1	18.2	17.7
5.1	5.1	5.0	5.1	5.6	6.2	6.9	6.4	6.4	6.2	5.7	5.8
0.57	0.68	0.67	0.81	0.86	1.1	1.3	1.1	1.0	1.0	0.95	0.95
10.7	10.0	9.1	9.1	9.1	9.2	9.5	9.2	9.0	8.6	8.4	7.6
2.2	2.0	1.8	1.7	1.6	1.7	1.8	1.8	2.0	2.0	1.9	1.9
0.16	0.13	0.11	0.11	0.15	0.20	0.25	0.27	0.33	0.33	0.32	0.35
0.01	0.01	0.01	0.01	0.04	0.05	0.08	0.06	0.08	0.07	0.06	0.04
0.81	0.66	0.56	0.46	0.51	0.77	0.93	0.96	0.92	0.81	0.81	0.84
0.03	0.04	0.04	0.06	0.06	0.07	0.08	0.09	0.11	0.11	0.10	0.10
0.62	0.82	0.99	1.2	1.2	1.1	0.98	0.86	0.69	0.65	0.67	0.68
34.7	37.6	40.4	40.5	40.2	36.8	31.0	30.5	32.1	32.0	31.3	31.1
—0.48	—0.45	—0.57	—0.42	—0.38	—0.38	—0.42	—0.52	—0.57	—0.60	—0.66	—0.67
35.2	38.0	41.0	40.9	40.6	37.2	31.5	31.0	32.7	32.6	31.9	31.7
1.3	1.4	1.6	1.7	1.6	2.0	1.9	1.8	2.3	2.2	2.0	2.0
25.4	23.5	22.6	22.1	22.4	24.7	29.2	32.4	32.0	33.4	35.9	36.8
15.4	13.4	12.0	10.9	10.8	11.7	14.5	17.2	16.9	17.7	19.6	20.5
0.32	0.36	0.37	0.46	0.64	0.85	1.1	1.3	1.3	1.2	1.1	1.0
1.9	1.9	2.2	2.1	1.8	2.0	2.2	2.2	2.2	2.1	1.9	1.8
7.7	7.8	8.0	8.7	9.1	10.2	11.3	11.6	11.7	12.4	13.3	13.5
5.0	5.2	4.6	4.5	4.3	4.3	4.2	3.4	2.3	2.3	2.2	2.2

TABLE 72

Dividends and Interest

	1919	1920	1921	1922	1923	1924	1925	1926
Total ($000,000)	6,116	6,868	6,836	7,029	8,046	8,187	9,004	9,424
Agriculture	6.1	6.5	7.4	7.5	6.5	6.1	5.3	4.9
Mining	3.6	3.5	3.4	2.5	3.2	3.2	3.6	4.0
Anth. coal	0.18	0.17	0.31	0.16	0.22	0.30	0.22	0.27
Bit. coal	0.44	0.50	0.58	0.40	0.52	0.43	0.44	0.52
Metal	1.7	1.3	1.1	0.76	1.1	1.1	1.3	0.97
Oil & gas	0.73	0.91	0.79	0.66	0.73	0.68	0.88	1.5
Other	0.52	0.58	0.61	0.47	0.67	0.70	0.78	0.65
Manufacturing	22.0	23.2	21.4	20.1	23.4	22.1	22.9	24.1
Food & tobacco	2.9	3.4	2.9	2.6	3.2	3.5	3.6	3.3
Textile & leather	4.3	4.2	3.1	3.2	3.1	2.5	2.4	2.2
Constr. mat. & furn.	1.6	1.9	1.7	1.9	2.3	2.1	2.2	2.7
Paper	0.80	0.92	0.78	0.59	0.81	0.55	0.78	0.64
Printing	0.62	0.64	0.89	0.97	0.86	0.80	1.0	1.1
Metal	6.6	6.6	6.2	5.5	7.3	8.3	8.0	8.9
Chemical	3.2	3.7	4.1	3.2	3.5	3.2	3.8	3.9
Misc. & rubber	1.8	1.9	1.8	2.2	2.4	1.1	1.1	1.3
Construction	0.32	0.38	0.59	0.50	0.54	0.49	0.76	0.56
Transp. & other pub. util.	19.8	17.5	17.7	19.2	18.3	19.6	19.4	19.2
Electric light & power	2.4	2.3	2.6	3.4	3.8	4.4	4.7	5.0
Mfd. gas	0.92	0.76	0.65	0.53	0.60	0.79	0.80	0.79
Steam rr., Pull., & exp.	11.3	10.2	10.0	10.2	9.4	9.8	9.2	9.2
Street rwy.	2.4	2.1	2.1	2.5	2.3	2.2	1.9	1.7
Water transp.	0.91	0.55	0.41	0.40	0.36	0.28	0.29	0.30
Pipe lines	0.52	0.45	0.51	0.86	0.55	0.55	0.81	0.59
Telephone	1.2	1.1	1.2	1.3	1.3	1.4	1.5	1.5
Telegraph	0.14	0.12	0.15	0.14	0.12	0.12	0.11	0.14
Trade	7.1	6.2	5.3	4.9	4.9	5.1	5.2	5.3
Finance	18.8	18.8	19.7	20.5	20.6	21.1	21.7	21.9
Banking	4.5	4.3	4.6	4.7	4.0	4.0	3.8	3.8
Insurance	0.08	0.04	0.06	0.36	0.24	0.14	0.18	0.22
Real estate	14.2	14.4	15.1	15.5	16.3	17.0	17.7	17.9
Service	0.73	1.4	1.2	1.0	1.2	1.3	1.5	1.6
Government	17.1	18.2	18.5	18.9	16.6	15.6	14.3	13.6
Federal	13.4	14.7	14.6	14.6	12.4	11.1	9.5	8.6
State	−0.10	−0.12	−0.10	−0.01	0.05	0.10	0.16	0.16
County	0.62	0.59	0.70	0.76	0.81	0.95	1.1	1.1
City incl. pub. educ.	3.1	2.9	3.3	3.5	3.3	3.4	3.5	3.7
Miscellaneous	4.5	4.4	4.9	4.9	4.8	5.4	5.4	4.8

TABLE 72

Dividends and Interest

1927	1928	1929	1930	1931	1932	1933	1934	1935	1936	1937	1938
9,987	10,766	11,905	11,713	10,358	8,532	7,471	7,862	8,419	9,447	9,636	8,079
4.7	4.3	3.8	3.7	4.2	4.8	4.8	4.5	3.9	3.5	3.2	3.6
3.2	2.7	3.4	2.5	1.7	1.4	1.5	2.4	2.6	2.7	3.4	2.9
0.24	0.23	0.20	0.18	0.18	0.19	0.14	0.16	0.16	0.14	0.11	0.12
0.44	0.27	0.36	0.33	0.27	0.21	0.18	0.39	0.22	0.25	0.19	0.18
0.83	0.95	1.7	0.82	0.41	0.20	0.25	0.36	0.56	0.92	1.4	1.0
1.1	0.74	0.66	0.75	0.45	0.54	0.62	1.1	0.98	0.84	1.0	0.96
0.59	0.56	0.57	0.42	0.43	0.29	0.28	0.33	0.72	0.54	0.70	0.67
23.9	25.1	24.8	24.3	20.5	15.5	16.0	18.1	20.6	27.1	26.7	19.2
3.7	3.7	3.7	4.1	4.0	3.8	4.2	4.4	4.3	5.0	4.5	4.6
2.2	2.2	1.9	1.5	1.3	0.88	1.0	1.4	1.4	1.9	1.8	1.1
2.3	2.2	2.0	1.7	1.3	0.78	0.76	1.2	1.3	1.9	2.0	1.1
0.70	0.72	0.61	0.60	0.52	0.44	0.59	0.67	0.69	0.77	0.91	0.46
1.2	1.0	1.2	1.2	1.1	0.86	0.66	0.95	0.96	1.2	1.1	1.0
9.0	9.3	9.9	8.6	6.6	4.1	3.6	5.5	6.9	10.0	10.7	5.8
3.6	4.9	4.3	5.5	4.9	3.9	4.6	3.3	4.1	5.1	4.6	3.9
1.3	1.1	1.1	1.1	0.91	0.68	0.64	0.67	1.0	1.3	1.2	1.2
0.59	0.57	0.62	0.86	0.52	0.35	0.37	0.24	0.26	0.41	0.46	0.39
20.1	18.9	19.0	20.6	21.8	23.9	25.0	22.9	22.0	18.5	18.7	20.6
5.3	5.8	6.1	7.1	8.2	9.1	9.6	8.1	7.5	6.7	6.9	8.0
0.75	0.69	0.87	0.98	1.2	1.7	1.7	1.4	1.3	1.1	1.1	1.3
9.7	8.3	8.0	8.2	7.5	6.9	7.4	7.3	6.5	5.8	5.8	5.4
1.6	1.4	1.3	1.2	1.2	1.3	1.4	1.4	1.4	1.3	1.3	1.5
0.27	0.27	0.29	0.31	0.27	0.28	0.27	0.39	0.85	0.58	0.58	0.57
0.81	0.82	0.95	1.2	1.3	1.9	1.5	1.2	1.8	0.87	0.88	1.1
1.5	1.4	1.3	1.5	2.0	2.7	3.1	3.0	2.7	2.2	2.1	2.7
0.14	0.14	0.19	0.22	0.13	0.08	0.06	0.06	0.11	0.06	0.07	0.04
5.3	5.0	5.2	4.8	4.4	3.2	3.0	4.4	5.6	7.4	6.8	6.4
22.6	24.5	25.5	25.4	27.9	28.1	23.5	22.1	21.0	18.5	18.2	21.3
3.8	4.1	3.8	3.8	4.0	3.3	2.1	2.4	2.2	2.1	2.1	2.4
0.31	0.39	0.32	0.32	0.38	0.12	−0.06	−0.03	0.13	−0.06	−0.10	0.10
18.5	20.1	21.3	21.3	23.6	24.7	21.5	19.8	18.7	16.5	16.2	18.7
1.7	1.6	1.7	1.8	1.6	1.9	1.7	1.7	1.9	2.3	2.2	2.0
12.6	11.5	10.6	10.8	12.3	16.0	19.6	20.0	17.7	16.3	17.4	20.9
7.6	6.6	5.6	5.3	6.0	7.6	9.7	10.6	9.3	8.6	9.5	11.6
0.16	0.17	0.17	0.23	0.35	0.55	0.76	0.78	0.70	0.58	0.54	0.60
0.95	0.94	1.1	1.0	1.0	1.3	1.5	1.4	1.2	1.0	0.92	1.0
3.8	3.8	3.7	4.2	5.0	6.6	7.6	7.2	6.5	6.1	6.5	7.7
5.3	5.7	5.4	5.0	5.0	4.8	4.4	3.7	4.4	3.4	2.8	2.8

TABLE 73

Property Income including Rent

	1919	1920	1921	1922	1923	1924	1925	1926
Total ($000,000)	10,082	11,156	11,306	11,925	13,211	13,819	14,470	14,566
Agriculture	3.7	4.0	4.5	4.4	4.0	3.6	3.3	3.2
Mining	2.2	2.2	2.0	1.4	2.0	1.9	2.2	2.6
Anth. coal	0.11	0.10	0.19	0.09	0.13	0.18	0.14	0.18
Bit. coal	0.27	0.31	0.35	0.24	0.31	0.25	0.27	0.34
Metal	1.0	0.82	0.66	0.45	0.67	0.66	0.79	0.63
Oil & gas	0.44	0.56	0.48	0.39	0.44	0.40	0.55	1.0
Other	0.32	0.35	0.37	0.28	0.41	0.42	0.48	0.42
Manufacturing	13.4	14.3	12.9	11.9	14.2	13.1	14.3	15.6
Food & tobacco	1.8	2.1	1.7	1.5	1.9	2.1	2.2	2.1
Textile & leather	2.6	2.6	1.9	1.9	1.9	1.5	1.5	1.4
Constr. mat. & furn.	0.98	1.2	1.0	1.1	1.4	1.2	1.4	1.8
Paper	0.48	0.57	0.47	0.35	0.49	0.33	0.49	0.41
Printing	0.37	0.40	0.54	0.57	0.52	0.47	0.64	0.70
Metal	4.0	4.1	3.8	3.2	4.4	4.9	5.0	5.8
Chemical	2.0	2.3	2.5	1.9	2.1	1.9	2.4	2.5
Misc. & rubber	1.1	1.2	1.1	1.3	1.5	0.63	0.70	0.82
Construction	0.19	0.23	0.36	0.29	0.33	0.29	0.48	0.36
Transp. & other pub. util.	12.0	10.8	10.7	11.3	11.2	11.6	12.0	12.4
Electric light & power	1.5	1.4	1.6	2.0	2.3	2.6	2.9	3.3
Mfd. gas	0.56	0.47	0.39	0.31	0.37	0.47	0.50	0.51
Steam rr., Pull., & exp.	6.9	6.3	6.1	6.0	5.7	5.8	5.7	5.9
Street rwy.	1.5	1.3	1.3	1.5	1.4	1.3	1.2	1.1
Water transp.	0.55	0.34	0.25	0.23	0.22	0.16	0.18	0.19
Pipe lines	0.31	0.28	0.31	0.51	0.33	0.32	0.50	0.38
Telephone	0.71	0.67	0.74	0.75	0.78	0.83	0.92	0.96
Telegraph	0.08	0.08	0.09	0.08	0.07	0.07	0.07	0.09
Trade	4.3	3.8	3.2	2.9	3.0	3.0	3.3	3.4
Finance	50.8	50.0	51.4	53.2	51.6	53.3	51.3	49.5
Banking	2.7	2.7	2.8	2.8	2.5	2.4	2.4	2.4
Insurance	0.05	0.02	0.04	0.21	0.15	0.08	0.11	0.14
Real estate	48.0	47.3	48.6	50.2	49.0	50.8	48.8	46.9
Service	0.44	0.85	0.74	0.60	0.73	0.76	0.92	1.1
Government	10.4	11.2	11.2	11.1	10.1	9.3	8.9	8.8
Federal	8.2	9.1	8.8	8.6	7.6	6.6	5.9	5.6
State	—0.06	—0.08	—0.06	...*	0.03	0.06	0.10	0.11
County	0.38	0.36	0.42	0.45	0.49	0.56	0.67	0.72
City incl. pub. educ.	1.9	1.8	2.0	2.1	2.0	2.0	2.2	2.4
Miscellaneous	2.7	2.7	2.9	2.9	2.9	3.2	3.4	3.1

* Less than 0.005 per cent.

Property Income including Rent

1927	1928	1929	1930	1931	1932	1933	1934	1935	1936	1937	1938
15,065	15,707	16,822	15,978	13,385	10,623	9,585	9,767	10,563	11,634	12,215	10,655
3.1	3.0	2.7	2.7	3.2	3.8	3.8	3.6	3.1	2.8	2.5	2.7
2.1	1.9	2.4	1.8	1.3	1.1	1.1	1.9	2.1	2.2	2.7	2.2
0.16	0.16	0.14	0.13	0.14	0.15	0.11	0.13	0.13	0.12	0.08	0.09
0.29	0.18	0.25	0.24	0.21	0.17	0.14	0.32	0.18	0.20	0.15	0.14
0.55	0.65	1.2	0.60	0.32	0.16	0.20	0.29	0.44	0.75	1.1	0.76
0.74	0.50	0.47	0.55	0.35	0.43	0.48	0.91	0.78	0.68	0.82	0.73
0.39	0.38	0.40	0.31	0.33	0.23	0.22	0.27	0.58	0.44	0.55	0.51
15.9	17.2	17.6	17.8	15.9	12.4	12.5	14.6	16.4	22.0	21.1	14.6
2.4	2.5	2.6	3.0	3.1	3.1	3.2	3.5	3.4	4.1	3.6	3.5
1.4	1.5	1.4	1.1	0.99	0.71	0.79	1.2	1.1	1.5	1.4	0.82
1.5	1.5	1.4	1.3	1.0	0.63	0.59	0.94	1.0	1.6	1.6	0.83
0.46	0.50	0.43	0.44	0.40	0.35	0.46	0.54	0.55	0.62	0.72	0.35
0.79	0.70	0.87	0.90	0.83	0.69	0.51	0.77	0.76	0.98	0.84	0.78
6.0	6.4	7.0	6.3	5.1	3.3	2.8	4.4	5.5	8.1	8.5	4.4
2.4	3.3	3.0	4.0	3.8	3.1	3.6	2.7	3.3	4.1	3.6	3.0
0.83	0.75	0.81	0.78	0.70	0.55	0.50	0.54	0.81	1.0	0.92	0.91
0.39	0.39	0.44	0.63	0.40	0.28	0.28	0.20	0.21	0.33	0.36	0.29
13.3	12.9	13.4	15.1	16.9	19.2	19.5	18.4	17.6	15.0	14.8	15.6
3.5	4.0	4.3	5.2	6.4	7.3	7.5	6.6	6.0	5.4	5.4	6.1
0.50	0.47	0.62	0.72	0.94	1.4	1.3	1.1	1.1	0.88	0.85	0.96
6.4	5.7	5.6	6.0	5.8	5.5	5.8	5.9	5.2	4.7	4.6	4.1
1.0	0.96	0.90	0.84	0.90	1.0	1.1	1.1	1.1	1.1	1.0	1.2
0.18	0.18	0.21	0.23	0.21	0.22	0.21	0.32	0.68	0.48	0.46	0.43
0.54	0.56	0.67	0.89	1.0	1.5	1.2	0.96	1.4	0.70	0.69	0.82
1.0	0.96	0.92	1.1	1.5	2.2	2.4	2.4	2.1	1.8	1.7	2.0
0.10	0.10	0.14	0.16	0.10	0.07	0.05	0.05	0.09	0.04	0.06	0.03
3.5	3.5	3.7	3.5	3.4	2.6	2.4	3.6	4.5	6.0	5.4	4.8
48.7	48.3	47.2	45.3	44.2	42.3	40.4	37.3	37.1	33.8	35.4	40.3
2.5	2.8	2.7	2.8	3.1	2.6	1.6	1.9	1.8	1.7	1.6	1.8
0.20	0.26	0.22	0.23	0.29	0.09	−0.05	−0.02	0.11	−0.05	−0.08	0.07
46.0	45.2	44.3	42.3	40.9	39.5	38.8	35.4	35.2	32.2	33.9	38.4
1.1	1.1	1.2	1.3	1.3	1.6	1.3	1.4	1.5	1.8	1.8	1.5
8.3	7.9	7.5	7.9	9.5	12.8	15.3	16.1	14.1	13.2	13.8	15.9
5.1	4.5	4.0	3.9	4.6	6.1	7.6	8.5	7.4	7.0	7.5	8.8
0.10	0.12	0.12	0.17	0.27	0.44	0.60	0.63	0.56	0.47	0.42	0.45
0.63	0.64	0.75	0.76	0.79	1.0	1.2	1.1	0.98	0.83	0.72	0.77
2.5	2.6	2.6	3.1	3.9	5.3	5.9	5.8	5.1	4.9	5.1	5.8
3.5	3.9	3.8	3.7	3.9	3.9	3.5	3.0	3.5	2.8	2.2	2.1

Net Income and Total Payments Originating within Industrial Divisions

Percentage Distribution by Type, 1919–1938

TABLES 74–76

The estimates for total manufacturing include and those for manufacturing subdivisions exclude salaries of employees at central administrative offices.

TABLE 74

Net Income Originating, Percentage Distribution by Type

	1919	1920	1921	1922	1923	1924	1925	1926	1927
1 Agriculture									
Total ($000,000)	10,862	9,077	5,538	5,861	6,729	7,114	7,946	7,534	7,458
Total net savings	20.9	−9.9	−26.1	−15.5	−9.6	−5.0	5.3	−1.5	−1.7
Total payments	79.1	109.9	126.1	115.5	109.6	105.0	94.7	101.5	101.7
Empl. comp.	13.9	19.6	20.9	19.1	18.1	17.2	15.6	17.6	17.2
Entrep. withdr.	61.7	85.4	96.0	87.4	83.7	80.8	73.1	77.8	78.1
Dividends	0.15	0.18	0.29	0.27	0.23	0.21	0.23	0.21	0.39
Interest	3.3	4.7	8.8	8.7	7.6	6.8	5.8	5.9	6.0
2 Mining									
Total ($000,000)	1,723	2,488	1,352	1,456	1,976	1,697	1,887	2,172	1,749
Entrep. net savings	0.47	1.0	−1.4	−0.02	−0.32	−0.24	0.99	1.1	0.41
Corp. net savings	−0.75	5.9	−33.2	−10.5	−14.7	−17.4	−3.7	−4.5	−15.6
Total payments	100.3	93.1	134.6	110.5	115.1	117.7	102.7	103.4	115.2
Wages	76.8	73.0	104.4	86.3	90.7	90.1	74.6	75.8	84.4
Salaries	9.1	8.8	10.7	10.4	9.5	10.4	9.5	9.2	11.0
Entrep. withdr.	1.8	1.6	2.4	2.0	1.6	1.7	1.4	1.2	1.4
Dividends	11.3	8.4	14.3	9.6	11.3	12.5	14.3	15.0	15.9
Interest	1.4	1.2	2.8	2.3	1.9	3.0	2.9	2.1	2.5
3 Manufacturing									
Total ($000,000)	17,083	17,703	9,815	13,455	16,914	15,427	16,880	17,323	16,817
Entrep. net savings	2.6	0.28	−1.9	1.2	1.3	0.56	0.90	0.51	0.47
Corp. net savings	13.5	5.2	−17.9	7.5	8.3	4.9	7.9	6.3	2.6
Total payments	83.9	94.6	119.8	91.3	90.4	94.5	91.2	93.2	96.9
Wages	56.7	65.4	76.0	59.4	60.1	61.5	59.1	59.6	60.1
Salaries	16.3	17.1	24.8	18.5	16.9	18.8	17.6	18.4	20.4
Entrep. withdr.	3.1	3.0	4.1	2.9	2.3	2.4	2.2	2.1	2.2
Dividends	7.4	8.4	13.5	9.7	10.4	10.7	11.3	12.2	13.2
Interest	0.51	0.61	1.4	0.79	0.70	1.0	0.91	0.88	0.98
3a Food and tobacco									
Total ($000,000)	1,896	1,675	1,196	1,570	1,744	1,762	1,744	1,801	1,827
Entrep. net savings	0.24	−3.9	−7.2	0.30	1.0	1.2	0.80	0.90	0.13
Corp. net savings	12.0	−3.7	−17.7	6.4	6.4	7.7	5.9	8.6	4.4
Total payments	87.8	107.6	124.9	93.3	92.6	91.1	93.3	90.5	95.5
Wages	50.1	62.4	72.9	54.5	52.9	51.5	52.1	50.9	51.1
Salaries	18.1	20.8	24.3	19.1	17.9	16.5	16.3	16.1	17.7
Entrep. withdr.	10.1.	10.6	11.3	8.0	7.2	6.7	6.3	6.2	6.6
Dividends	8.1	11.7	13.4	9.8	12.8	14.1	16.0	15.2	18.0
Interest	1.3	2.1	3.0	1.9	1.8	2.3	2.5	2.0	2.1

Net Income Originating, Percentage Distribution by Type

1928	1929	1930	1931	1932	1933	1934	1935	1936	1937	1938
7,330	7,708	5,814	4,041	2,821	3,554	4,749	5,380	6,089	6,274	5,457
—3.2	1.0	—23.0	—44.0	—59.2	—13.8	7.2	11.9	17.2	9.9	—1.5
103.2	99.0	123.0	144.0	159.2	113.8	92.8	88.1	82.8	90.1	101.5
17.3	16.7	19.5	21.0	20.7	14.5	11.8	11.9	11.3	12.7	13.9
79.6	76.5	96.0	112.4	124.1	89.1	73.7	70.2	66.2	72.5	82.3
0.34	0.16	0.12	0.35	0.21	0.00	0.36	0.35	0.61	0.51	0.40
6.0	5.7	7.4	10.4	14.2	10.2	7.0	5.7	4.7	4.4	4.9
1,662	1,821	1,319	738	463	513	904	950	1,210	1,440	1,100
0.96	1.4	—1.2	—4.1	—6.8	—4.6	—0.85	—1.0	—0.04	0.43	0.55
—9.3	—9.1	—23.1	—53.2	—66.1	—49.5	—18.4	—22.2	—11.7	—9.6	—14.0
108.3	107.8	124.3	157.2	172.8	154.0	119.3	123.2	111.8	109.2	113.4
78.4	73.4	87.1	111.0	120.0	111.1	84.2	84.7	77.7	74.1	77.3
10.7	10.6	13.4	19.2	23.4	18.8	12.7	13.5	11.6	10.9	12.9
1.4	1.2	1.6	2.5	3.3	2.8	1.6	1.6	1.4	1.3	1.7
15.2	20.1	18.9	18.8	17.6	14.7	16.9	19.5	17.8	20.5	18.6
2.5	2.5	3.4	5.6	8.5	6.7	3.8	3.9	3.4	2.5	2.9
17,949	19,505	14,094	9,307	5,380	7,480	9,984	11,817	14,323	16,237	11,960
0.41	0.30	—0.99	—2.1	—4.1	—0.16	0.25	0.52	0.91	0.37	—0.28
5.2	6.2	—12.3	—30.2	—54.8	—12.5	—4.4	—0.64	1.2	0.80	—2.9
94.3	93.5	113.3	132.3	158.9	112.7	104.2	100.1	97.9	98.8	103.2
56.8	55.9	62.9	72.0	85.8	66.0	63.7	61.9	59.1	62.3	64.5
20.4	20.6	27.9	34.6	44.8	28.2	24.4	21.9	19.3	19.0	23.4
2.0	1.9	2.3	2.9	3.8	2.4	1.8	1.7	1.7	1.6	2.2
14.0	14.1	18.6	20.4	20.8	13.5	12.6	13.4	16.8	15.0	11.8
1.0	1.1	1.7	2.5	3.7	2.5	1.6	1.3	1.0	0.87	1.2
1,966	2,038	1,827	1,439	1,074	1,259	1,611	1,656	1,871	1,826	1,743
0.28	0.12	—0.40	—1.7	—3.0	0.65	2.5	2.5	2.9	0.62	—0.13
7.2	5.7	—2.7	—10.7	—18.6	—2.8	3.8	2.9	2.5	—3.3	—1.9
92.6	94.2	103.1	112.4	121.6	102.1	93.7	94.6	94.6	102.7	102.1
48.7	49.2	52.1	56.4	61.0	53.6	51.9	52.2	49.6	57.6	58.5
17.3	16.8	18.2	20.4	22.6	18.7	16.3	16.6	15.6	16.2	16.8
6.5	6.4	6.5	7.0	7.5	5.2	4.0	3.9	4.2	5.1	5.4
18.0	19.7	23.8	25.5	27.2	22.1	19.7	20.3	23.9	22.4	19.8
2.1	2.1	2.6	3.1	3.4	2.5	1.8	1.7	1.3	1.4	1.5

TABLE 74 (cont.)

Net Income Originating, Percentage Distribution by Type

	1919	1920	1921	1922	1923	1924	1925	1926	1927
3b Textile and leather									
Total ($000,000)	3,622	3,022	2,339	2,982	3,344	2,642	2,997	2,781	3,164
Entrep. net savings	7.6	0.04	—1.2	2.8	2.3	—0.23	1.2	—0.32	1.1
Corp. net savings	15.2	—5.2	—7.9	8.3	6.7	—2.6	2.8	—2.9	3.5
Total payments	77.3	105.2	109.1	88.8	91.0	102.8	96.0	103.2	95.4
Wages	53.4	76.0	79.8	64.6	66.9	75.2	70.4	76.2	70.5
Salaries	12.6	15.1	15.4	13.1	13.5	16.0	14.6	15.7	14.8
Entrep. withdr.	4.0	4.5	4.8	3.6	3.1	3.8	3.6	3.7	3.2
Dividends	7.0	9.2	8.6	7.1	7.4	7.7	7.2	7.5	6.7
Interest	0.35	0.38	0.60	0.40	0.12	0.12	0.15	0.08	0.16
3c Construction materials and furniture									
Total ($000,000)	1,894	2,332	1,264	1,780	2,352	2,181	2,303	2,382	2,139
Entrep. net savings	2.5	2.3	—2.0	1.6	2.6	1.2	1.4	0.98	0.23
Corp. net savings	9.4	8.5	—10.7	6.4	9.1	3.3	3.6	2.2	—2.2
Total payments	88.1	89.3	112.7	92.0	88.3	95.5	95.0	96.8	101.9
Wages	66.6	68.6	80.9	66.6	65.7	70.6	69.2	68.6	72.2
Salaries	13.3	12.0	19.0	15.2	12.7	14.9	15.1	15.3	16.9
Entrep. withdr.	3.0	3.0	3.6	2.7	2.0	2.2	2.2	2.1	2.0
Dividends	4.9	5.4	8.6	6.9	7.5	7.3	8.1	10.3	10.2
Interest	0.32	0.29	0.58	0.50	0.40	0.52	0.47	0.50	0.65
3d Paper									
Total ($000,000)	383	544	256	339	425	403	446	475	477
Entrep. net savings	1.4	2.0	—1.2	0.39	0.62	0.39	0.55	0.54	0.57
Corp. net savings	13.2	19.6	—23.4	5.7	6.5	7.1	5.8	9.3	8.3
Total payments	85.4	78.4	124.5	94.0	92.9	92.5	93.7	90.1	91.2
Wages	55.9	54.6	79.7	62.1	59.4	62.4	59.8	59.2	57.6
Salaries	15.4	10.9	22.2	18.5	17.2	18.0	17.2	17.5	18.1
Entrep. withdr.	1.3	1.2	1.8	1.2	0.98	0.98	0.90	0.86	0.78
Dividends	11.7	11.0	19.1	10.3	13.4	9.1	13.7	10.0	11.9
Interest	1.0	0.69	1.7	1.9	1.9	2.0	2.2	2.6	2.8
3e Printing and publishing									
Total ($000,000)	729	938	821	944	995	1,071	1,126	1,214	1,225
Entrep. net savings	2.9	2.0	0.64	2.4	1.8	1.6	1.7	1.4	0.96
Corp. net savings	7.5	7.1	1.8	8.1	5.9	6.2	4.8	4.5	2.6
Total payments	89.6	90.9	97.6	89.5	92.4	92.2	93.6	94.1	96.4
Wages	48.2	53.2	52.8	47.5	49.4	48.4	48.0	47.6	47.7
Salaries	30.6	27.2	31.7	30.0	31.7	33.6	33.5	34.5	35.5
Entrep. withdr.	5.6	5.8	5.7	4.7	4.4	4.1	3.8	3.5	3.5
Dividends	4.8	4.5	7.0	7.1	6.8	5.9	7.8	8.0	9.0
Interest	0.35	0.21	0.43	0.15	0.12	0.18	0.35	0.43	0.72

TABLE 74 (cont.)

Net Income Originating, Percentage Distribution by Type

1928	1929	1930	1931	1932	1933	1934	1935	1936	1937	1938
2,947	2,992	1,971	1,668	1,076	1,750	1,913	2,193	2,424	2,426	1,938
0.31	−0.09	−4.8	−5.3	−7.6	0.56	−0.45	0.14	1.0	−0.01	−0.01
−0.84	−1.6	−23.7	−25.8	−37.9	1.8	−5.1	−1.4	0.70	−3.7	−5.0
100.5	101.7	128.5	131.0	145.5	97.6	105.6	101.3	98.3	103.7	105.0
72.2	73.3	90.9	93.9	105.5	73.5	80.2	78.2	73.7	79.8	82.2
17.0	17.6	24.4	25.0	28.6	17.1	17.1	15.4	14.6	14.2	15.3
3.3	3.2	4.2	4.1	4.4	2.7	2.4	2.3	2.5	2.5	3.1
7.8	7.2	8.6	7.5	6.9	4.4	6.0	5.2	7.3	7.0	4.3
0.25	0.36	0.47	0.44	0.06	−0.05	−0.04	0.09	0.11	0.16	0.17
2,141	2,172	1,452	757	211	481	730	951	1,322	1,557	1,154
0.48	0.25	−1.9	−5.3	−21.1	−3.2	−1.2	−0.23	0.85	0.77	−0.84
0.71	0.50	−18.5	−49.3	−200.0	−33.7	−15.8	−5.1	0.91	1.1	−0.39
98.8	99.2	120.4	154.6	321.1	136.9	117.0	105.3	98.2	98.1	101.2
68.8	68.5	78.7	97.1	194.9	91.3	78.1	72.9	67.5	69.1	72.4
17.1	17.6	25.2	36.4	86.6	31.0	24.2	19.4	15.2	15.0	18.9
2.0	2.1	2.5	3.4	7.8	2.7	2.2	1.9	1.9	1.8	2.3
10.2	10.0	12.3	14.3	23.2	8.5	10.7	9.9	12.8	11.7	7.1
0.80	1.0	1.8	3.5	8.5	3.3	1.8	1.2	0.82	0.49	0.61
476	498	414	303	183	271	352	377	434	498	367
0.43	0.35	−0.02	−0.51	−1.4	−0.01	0.23	0.20	0.35	0.40	−0.81
5.6	7.2	−5.1	−18.3	−46.6	−6.0	1.2	0.49	2.9	2.7	−6.9
94.0	92.4	105.1	118.8	148.0	106.0	98.6	99.3	96.7	96.9	107.7
57.5	58.0	64.5	70.7	88.8	63.7	60.2	62.6	60.0	61.7	74.4
19.4	19.2	23.1	29.5	37.8	25.5	22.9	20.6	19.4	16.8	22.2
0.74	0.68	0.76	0.89	1.2	0.72	0.61	0.66	0.69	0.67	0.91
13.6	11.5	12.5	12.1	11.3	10.0	11.0	12.5	14.1	15.1	7.2
2.8	3.1	4.4	5.6	9.1	6.1	3.8	3.0	2.6	2.5	2.9
1,308	1,408	1,304	1,052	765	711	828	912	1,007	1,091	1,004
1.3	1.2	0.21	−0.68	−2.2	−0.38	0.43	0.37	0.70	0.29	−0.77
6.6	4.7	−1.7	−6.3	−13.2	−4.0	−3.1	0.61	0.29	−0.34	−1.1
92.1	94.1	101.5	107.0	115.4	104.4	102.6	99.0	99.0	100.0	101.9
45.2	45.2	47.6	51.2	54.1	50.0	49.7	48.9	48.2	48.8	50.7
35.2	35.6	40.0	42.2	47.2	43.1	41.0	38.2	36.3	38.7	39.5
3.2	2.9	2.9	3.1	4.4	4.4	2.9	3.0	3.1	3.1	3.4
7.6	9.4	9.8	9.0	7.8	5.0	7.7	7.9	10.4	8.6	7.4
0.86	0.93	1.2	1.5	1.8	1.9	1.3	0.90	0.86	0.83	0.96

TABLE 74 (cont.)

Net Income Originating, Percentage Distribution by Type

	1919	1920	1921	1922	1923	1924	1925	1926	1927
3f Metal									
Total ($000,000)	6,175	6,665	2,717	3,793	5,726	5,250	5,862	6,038	5,559
Entrep. net savings	0.93	0.40	—0.79	0.16	0.46	0.35	0.50	0.43	0.25
Corp. net savings	14.3	8.9	—25.7	5.1	10.1	6.5	12.0	9.1	3.6
Total payments	84.8	90.7	126.5	94.8	89.5	93.1	87.5	90.4	96.1
Wages	63.9	68.5	83.2	66.2	64.1	63.1	60.1	61.2	62.3
Salaries	13.6	14.7	26.6	17.7	14.6	16.6	14.7	14.8	17.2
Entrep. withdr.	0.73	0.68	1.0	0.70	0.52	0.57	0.49	0.46	0.47
Dividends	6.2	6.4	14.5	9.7	9.5	11.9	11.4	13.2	15.5
Interest	0.42	0.42	1.2	0.49	0.68	1.0	0.84	0.75	0.65
3g Chemical									
Total ($000,000)	1,030	1,073	559	934	975	999	1,162	1,364	1,073
Entrep. net savings	0.87	—0.66	—2.2	0.10	0.20	0.23	0.41	0.51	0.23
Corp. net savings	11.7	0.34	—45.7	14.8	2.3	10.2	13.4	20.5	0.20
Total payments	87.5	100.3	147.9	85.1	97.5	89.6	86.2	79.0	99.6
Wages	45.0	53.1	63.4	39.9	46.2	42.5	38.8	35.4	44.6
Salaries	21.0	21.5	31.9	19.3	20.9	19.1	16.9	15.6	20.1
Entrep. withdr.	2.2	2.1	3.0	1.7	1.6	1.4	1.3	1.0	1.3
Dividends	19.2	23.3	45.9	23.0	27.4	24.5	27.5	25.3	30.9
Interest	0.04	0.28	3.7	1.3	1.4	2.0	1.8	1.6	2.7
3h Miscellaneous and rubber									
Total ($000,000)	1,154	1,234	487	935	1,145	906	1,015	967	967
Entrep. net savings	1.6	0.86	—2.9	0.74	0.88	0.72	1.1	0.58	0.55
Corp. net savings	21.1	13.5	—47.1	13.7	15.6	9.3	12.5	3.5	2.4
Total payments	77.3	85.7	150.0	85.6	83.5	90.0	86.4	95.9	97.0
Wages	48.6	57.0	91.6	52.1	51.3	60.9	57.8	62.9	62.7
Salaries	17.2	16.5	30.5	15.5	14.2	17.7	17.1	19.1	19.9
Entrep. withdr.	1.6	1.7	3.3	1.6	1.3	1.7	1.5	1.6	1.5
Dividends	9.0	9.1	20.7	14.7	15.8	8.1	9.0	10.7	11.0
Interest	0.83	1.4	3.9	1.7	0.99	1.5	1.1	1.7	1.9
4 Construction									
Total ($000,000)	2,071	2,611	1,860	2,358	3,382	3,713	3,952	4,240	4,036
Entrep. net savings	8.7	2.9	—1.4	1.9	2.4	5.2	5.2	3.7	2.7
Corp. net savings	—1.0	0.45	—1.5	0.33	0.67	1.3	1.1	1.3	1.3
Total payments	90.2	96.6	103.0	97.8	97.0	93.4	93.8	95.0	96.0
Wages	65.9	74.9	73.0	69.8	75.7	70.0	67.1	71.7	71.9
Salaries	11.8	11.5	15.8	13.5	10.9	11.6	10.5	12.1	12.3
Entrep. withdr.	11.6	9.3	12.0	13.1	9.1	10.7	14.3	9.9	10.4
Dividends	0.74	0.80	1.7	1.3	1.1	0.87	1.5	0.98	1.2
Interest	0.19	0.19	0.42	0.19	0.18	0.21	0.26	0.26	0.28

TABLE 74 (cont.)

Net Income Originating, Percentage Distribution by Type

1928	1929	1930	1931	1932	1933	1934	1935	1936	1937	1938
6,224	7,225	4,797	2,544	987	1,718	2,912	3,837	5,045	6,365	3,775
0.34	0.38	−0.04	−0.71	−2.6	−0.54	−0.15	0.19	0.37	0.36	−0.24
7.6	10.4	−8.9	−39.3	−121.0	−24.3	−5.7	1.2	3.1	3.9	−2.5
92.1	89.3	109.0	140.1	223.7	124.8	105.9	98.6	96.5	95.7	102.7
59.2	57.2	64.2	79.3	125.5	79.9	69.2	65.2	62.5	64.1	67.8
16.4	15.4	23.3	33.3	61.6	28.6	21.4	17.9	15.0	15.0	21.8
0.42	0.38	0.48	0.65	1.1	0.58	0.40	0.38	0.39	0.36	0.59
15.4	15.4	19.8	24.7	30.4	12.9	13.1	13.8	17.6	15.4	11.2
0.77	0.85	1.2	2.1	5.1	2.9	1.7	1.3	1.0	0.83	1.3
1,451	1,610	1,108	582	467	595	754	866	1,065	1,224	952
0.41	0.37	0.06	−0.44	−0.71	0.22	0.45	0.46	0.58	0.42	−0.22
14.5	18.6	−25.8	−93.0	−73.4	−40.2	−11.7	−12.2	−8.3	−0.01	−7.9
85.1	81.0	125.8	193.4	174.2	139.9	111.3	111.8	107.7	99.6	108.1
32.9	33.1	44.6	68.7	67.0	55.7	52.4	48.7	42.9	45.3	52.6
15.3	15.3	22.1	35.5	34.9	25.7	23.7	22.3	18.8	17.4	21.1
0.93	0.88	1.1	1.9	1.6	1.2	1.0	1.0	1.0	0.96	1.2
34.1	30.2	54.2	79.0	59.8	49.9	29.8	36.2	42.6	34.0	30.5
1.9	1.6	3.7	8.4	10.8	7.4	4.4	3.6	2.4	1.9	2.7
961	961	646	504	282	411	562	694	810	874	686
0.29	0.11	−1.8	−2.5	−5.0	−1.1	−0.25	0.51	0.84	0.46	0.16
1.5	−1.9	−30.3	−38.0	−69.4	−16.9	−2.3	1.2	2.1	0.12	−0.85
98.2	101.8	132.2	140.6	174.4	118.0	102.6	98.3	97.1	99.4	100.7
64.3	64.8	79.8	83.0	102.0	75.4	69.4	62.9	61.5	65.3	62.4
20.0	21.2	31.1	36.6	49.0	29.2	22.5	21.7	19.4	19.8	22.4
1.6	1.6	2.1	2.2	2.8	1.7	1.4	1.4	1.4	1.4	1.7
10.4	12.4	16.2	14.9	15.5	8.2	6.9	10.8	13.7	12.2	13.1
1.9	1.9	3.0	3.8	5.1	3.5	2.4	1.6	1.1	0.73	0.96
4,015	4,086	3,377	2,124	1,042	728	875	1,062	1,584	1,842	1,691
2.4	2.4	−1.1	−4.8	−22.5	−21.4	−11.6	−6.6	−2.6	−1.2	−0.08
0.91	0.89	−0.86	−3.3	−12.1	−11.6	−5.3	−2.9	−1.4	−1.0	−0.04
96.6	96.7	101.9	108.1	134.6	133.0	116.9	109.5	104.0	102.3	100.1
72.2	71.6	71.2	74.2	84.2	77.6	73.5	68.2	65.4	67.2	62.6
13.5	12.7	16.0	18.8	26.8	27.5	18.2	16.2	14.3	13.6	13.7
9.5	10.7	11.8	12.6	20.8	24.1	23.0	23.0	21.9	19.1	22.0
1.3	1.5	2.5	1.9	1.8	2.6	1.6	2.0	2.3	2.3	1.7
0.25	0.32	0.45	0.64	0.99	1.2	0.56	0.12	0.12	0.11	0.12

TABLE 74 (cont.)

Net Income Originating, Percentage Distribution by Type

	1919	1920	1921	1922	1923	1924	1925	1926	1927
5 Transportation and other public utilities									
Total ($000,000)	5,963	7,348	6,087	6,215	7,094	7,080	7,564	7,888	7,791
Entrep. net savings	0.14	0.07	—0.03	—0.01	...*	0.01	0.01	0.02	...*
Corp. net savings	2.1	1.4	1.1	3.7	6.3	5.3	8.5	8.7	5.7
Total payments	97.7	98.5	98.9	96.4	93.7	94.7	91.5	91.3	94.3
Wages & salaries	76.4	80.9	78.1	73.6	71.9	71.1	67.3	67.2	67.4
Empl. comp.	77.3	82.0	79.0	74.5	72.8	72.0	68.4	68.2	68.5
Entrep. withdr.	0.18	0.12	0.12	0.12	0.10	0.08	0.08	0.07	0.06
Dividends	8.9	6.6	7.5	9.1	9.0	10.0	10.8	11.0	13.3
Interest	11.4	9.7	12.3	12.6	11.8	12.6	12.2	12.0	12.4
5a Electric light and power									
Total ($000,000)	325	382	410	503	635	730	818	944	1,032
Corp. net savings	11.0	11.8	11.0	13.6	12.1	9.2	9.8	12.0	12.5
Total payments	89.0	88.2	89.0	86.4	87.9	90.8	90.2	88.0	87.5
Wages & salaries	43.0	46.3	45.1	38.6	39.7	40.8	37.9	37.7	35.6
Entrep. withdr.	0.99	0.90	0.83	0.64	0.45	0.36	0.28	0.20	0.15
Dividends	20.9	18.7	20.4	24.5	25.4	25.4	28.1	26.1	27.5
Interest	24.1	22.3	22.7	22.7	22.4	24.3	23.9	24.0	24.2
5b Manufactured gas									
Total ($000,000)	99	114	114	118	143	150	252	210	222
Corp. net savings	—34.7	—20.4	—7.5	0.33	0.95	—11.3	29.7	12.7	15.6
Total payments	134.7	120.4	107.5	99.7	99.1	111.3	70.3	87.3	84.4
Wages & salaries	77.8	74.1	68.7	67.9	65.3	68.0	41.7	51.9	50.6
Dividends	42.3	32.5	22.5	18.9	23.3	32.2	20.0	22.9	21.0
Interest	14.6	13.8	16.3	12.8	10.5	11.1	8.6	12.5	12.7
5c Steam railroads, Pullman, and express									
Total ($000,000)	3,938	4,845	3,815	3,824	4,439	4,266	4,487	4,668	4,465
Corp. net savings	1.5	—0.13	—0.14	2.8	6.4	5.7	8.5	9.2	3.9
Total payments	98.5	100.1	100.1	97.2	93.6	94.3	91.5	90.8	96.1
Wages	62.5	66.4	59.5	55.4	55.7	53.7	51.8	51.5	52.5
Salaries	17.1	17.8	21.5	21.9	19.6	20.4	19.5	19.1	20.1
Empl. comp.	80.9	85.7	82.2	78.5	76.7	75.5	73.0	72.3	74.4
Dividends	6.5	4.9	5.5	5.9	5.7	6.5	6.6	7.2	9.8
Interest	11.1	9.5	12.5	12.8	11.3	12.3	12.0	11.3	11.8
5d Street railways									
Total ($000,000)	528	629	611	625	649	627	619	602	585
Corp. net savings	2.2	3.5	4.6	2.7	4.1	1.3	2.2	1.2	1.6
Total payments	97.8	96.5	95.4	97.3	95.9	98.7	97.8	98.8	98.4
Wages & salaries	69.9	73.8	71.8	69.4	67.7	70.3	70.1	71.9	71.8
Dividends	6.7	5.1	4.4	7.5	7.3	7.5	7.7	7.8	8.0
Interest	21.2	17.6	19.2	20.4	20.9	21.0	20.0	19.1	18.7

* Less than 0.005 per cent.

TABLE 74 (cont.)

Net Income Originating, Percentage Distribution by Type

1928	1929	1930	1931	1932	1933	1934	1935	1936	1937	1938
8,046	8,511	7,625	6,366	4,867	4,721	4,855	5,149	5,843	6,212	5,513
0.02	0.02	—0.02	—0.04	—0.05	—0.01	0.02	0.02	0.06	0.07	0.01
8.7	8.9	1.7	—3.2	—9.8	—4.0	—4.5	—4.2	3.6	1.9	—1.6
91.3	91.1	98.3	103.2	109.8	104.0	104.4	104.2	96.3	98.0	101.6
65.0	63.5	65.4	66.4	66.4	62.9	65.9	66.5	65.0	66.9	69.6
66.0	64.5	66.5	67.7	67.8	64.4	67.4	68.1	66.4	68.9	71.4
0.06	0.07	0.08	0.06	0.06	0.05	0.05	0.06	0.05	0.05	0.05
13.0	15.1	18.7	19.4	20.0	17.6	17.0	18.1	14.8	15.3	15.4
12.2	11.4	13.0	16.1	21.9	22.0	20.0	17.9	15.1	13.8	14.7
1,205	1,380	1,452	1,379	1,145	1,029	996	1,042	1,112	1,189	1,143
14.5	15.7	11.6	7.4	1.6	—0.40	1.1	4.7	7.7	6.7	4.8
85.5	84.3	88.4	92.6	98.4	100.4	98.9	95.3	92.3	93.3	95.2
33.3	31.3	31.2	30.6	30.6	30.8	34.6	34.7	35.6	37.5	38.6
0.11	0.09	0.07	0.06	0.06	0.06	0.06	0.06	0.06	0.07	0.07
29.6	32.5	37.0	38.6	37.8	36.2	33.0	31.8	31.0	33.2	33.1
22.5	20.3	20.2	23.3	30.0	33.4	31.3	28.7	25.7	22.4	23.5
194	184	186	155	159	159	152	143	160	182	174
6.5	—11.0	—14.6	—35.7	—39.5	—26.5	—24.8	—35.5	—17.7	—6.8	—11.0
93.5	111.0	114.6	135.7	139.5	126.5	124.8	135.5	117.7	106.8	111.0
55.2	54.7	53.1	54.2	46.5	47.6	53.1	56.7	53.4	49.7	51.9
19.9	36.0	36.5	49.8	54.9	38.2	36.0	44.7	35.2	32.7	34.0
18.4	20.4	25.0	31.7	38.1	40.7	35.7	34.0	29.1	24.4	25.1
4,483	4,653	3,871	2,974	2,090	2,121	2,231	2,410	2,811	2,928	2,416
8.0	8.7	—0.30	—6.8	—11.6	—2.3	—4.2	—1.4	5.1	1.5	—2.6
92.0	91.3	100.3	106.8	111.6	102.3	104.2	101.4	94.9	98.5	102.6
50.5	50.1	51.6	53.2	53.7	50.0	52.2	52.6	52.3	54.3	56.0
19.9	19.2	22.0	25.2	27.0	23.6	23.5	23.3	20.9	21.5	25.1
72.0	70.9	75.5	80.7	83.5	76.3	78.5	78.8	75.6	79.4	84.6
8.2	9.4	11.4	8.6	3.7	3.6	5.6	5.3	5.2	5.7	3.5
11.8	11.0	13.4	17.4	24.4	22.5	20.0	17.3	14.1	13.4	14.5
567	566	523	442	339	302	320	324	345	345	338
1.6	0.51	1.0	—3.3	—12.0	9.4	—8.3	—8.0	—5.8	—7.3	—6.8
98.4	99.5	99.0	103.3	112.0	109.4	108.3	108.0	105.8	107.3	106.8
71.7	72.7	73.2	76.0	79.8	75.3	74.4	72.9	69.9	70.4	69.9
8.2	8.6	7.5	6.5	5.3	5.0	6.0	6.7	9.1	11.0	10.7
18.5	18.2	18.3	20.9	26.9	29.0	27.9	28.5	26.8	25.9	26.3

TABLE 74 (cont.)

Net Income Originating, Percentage Distribution by Type

	1919	1920	1921	1922	1923	1924	1925	1926	1927
5e Water transportation									
Total ($000,000)	589	771	535	470	485	516	507	531	494
Entrep. net savings	1.4	0.71	−0.29	−0.11	0.01	0.12	0.21	0.25	0.03
Corp. net savings	3.7	2.5	−4.6	−3.0	−2.2	−0.94	0.12	0.68	−1.7
Total payments	94.9	96.8	104.9	103.1	102.1	100.8	99.7	99.1	101.7
Wages & salaries	84.2	91.2	98.9	96.2	95.3	95.8	93.8	93.0	95.4
Entrep. withdr.	1.3	0.71	0.71	0.95	0.93	0.61	0.71	0.71	0.72
Dividends	7.8	3.7	3.4	3.9	3.9	2.6	3.6	3.8	3.9
Interest	1.7	1.2	1.9	2.1	2.1	1.8	1.5	1.5	1.6
5f Pipe lines									
Total ($000,000)	66	92	69	97	106	112	134	129	150
Corp. net savings	11.4	29.9	3.6	3.3	22.7	30.0	17.3	24.8	13.8
Total payments	88.6	70.1	96.4	96.7	77.3	70.0	82.7	75.2	86.2
Wages & salaries	40.8	36.6	45.9	34.7	35.7	30.0	28.1	32.1	32.6
Dividends	47.6	33.4	50.3	61.8	41.3	39.7	54.4	42.8	53.4
Interest	0.18	0.12	0.18	0.26	0.38	0.35	0.29	0.25	0.25
5g Telephone									
Total ($000,000)	325	397	433	473	524	566	622	668	701
Corp. net savings	4.4	2.2	5.2	6.5	6.0	5.1	7.9	9.1	8.5
Total payments	95.6	97.8	94.8	93.5	94.0	94.9	92.1	90.9	91.5
Wages & salaries	72.7	77.9	74.4	73.6	73.4	73.8	69.9	69.1	69.0
Empl. comp.	73.6	78.9	75.4	74.6	74.3	74.6	70.7	69.9	69.9
Dividends	12.6	10.3	11.2	12.7	13.6	14.5	15.0	15.0	15.9
Interest	9.4	8.5	8.2	6.1	6.0	5.8	6.5	6.0	5.7
5h Telegraph									
Total ($000,000)	92	118	100	106	113	113	125	136	141
Corp. net savings	12.3	10.6	7.8	15.2	13.4	12.5	15.9	11.0	15.3
Total payments	87.7	89.4	92.2	84.8	86.6	87.5	84.1	89.0	84.7
Wages & salaries	76.7	80.4	80.2	73.6	76.1	76.6	73.9	77.7	72.5
Empl. comp.	78.4	82.1	82.3	75.6	78.3	78.8	76.0	79.7	74.4
Dividends	11.0	8.6	9.9	9.2	8.2	8.3	7.6	8.7	9.1
Interest	−1.7	−1.3	0.09	−0.04	0.16	0.37	0.52	0.63	1.1
6 Trade									
Total ($000,000)	11,111	9,498	6,788	8,964	10,155	9,887	10,482	10,658	10,390
Entrep. net savings	21.8	4.4	−6.7	6.5	8.3	5.0	5.2	3.5	2.8
Corp. net savings	5.6	0.09	−6.8	3.4	4.5	3.1	3.8	2.2	1.7
Total payments	72.5	95.5	113.6	90.1	87.2	91.9	91.1	94.3	95.5
Wages & salaries	48.9	63.7	76.2	63.4	62.9	66.1	66.6	69.7	70.2
Entrep. withdr.	19.8	27.3	32.1	22.9	20.4	21.6	20.0	20.0	20.3
Dividends	3.6	4.0	4.7	3.4	3.6	3.9	4.2	4.4	4.8
Interest	0.30	0.44	0.59	0.44	0.22	0.31	0.29	0.23	0.30

TABLE 74 (cont.)

Net Income Originating, Percentage Distribution by Type

1928	1929	1930	1931	1932	1933	1934	1935	1936	1937	1938
519	535	468	376	280	306	341	398	489	564	484
0.23	0.38	−0.38	−0.68	−0.83	−0.13	0.26	0.20	0.77	0.80	0.09
0.72	2.5	−4.8	−8.9	−12.2	−5.7	−5.7	−14.8	−2.9	−1.7	−4.2
99.1	97.2	105.2	109.6	113.0	105.8	105.4	114.6	102.1	100.9	104.1
92.8	89.8	96.4	101.3	103.8	98.6	95.8	96.0	90.4	90.5	94.1
0.74	0.85	0.99	0.88	0.82	0.60	0.58	0.56	0.47	0.44	0.44
4.3	5.3	6.5	5.2	4.4	2.6	5.2	14.2	8.2	7.3	6.2
1.3	1.1	1.4	2.2	3.9	4.0	3.9	3.8	3.1	2.7	3.3
176	205	176	170	134	149	129	126	144	163	135
22.4	20.2	−5.6	−2.9	−41.6	3.2	0.16	−47.6	14.3	17.9	0.77
77.6	79.8	105.6	102.9	141.6	96.8	99.8	147.6	85.7	82.1	99.2
27.5	24.5	24.9	23.3	22.8	20.3	27.2	29.8	28.8	30.0	34.2
49.8	55.0	80.5	78.4	116.7	73.9	70.4	114.9	54.6	50.4	63.6
0.29	0.24	0.20	1.2	2.1	2.6	2.2	3.0	2.3	1.7	1.4
757	840	823	762	646	578	602	619	688	744	739
10.4	11.1	6.1	2.0	−7.2	−9.7	−8.4	−5.6	3.0	2.2	−2.0
89.6	88.9	93.9	98.0	107.2	109.7	108.4	105.6	97.0	97.8	102.0
68.7	69.7	71.9	69.8	70.2	67.6	67.8	67.6	65.6	68.7	71.0
69.6	70.6	72.8	71.0	71.6	69.1	69.4	69.3	67.3	70.4	72.8
15.4	14.7	17.9	23.1	29.1	32.6	31.2	29.4	24.3	22.2	24.0
4.6	3.7	3.2	3.8	6.6	8.1	7.8	6.9	5.4	5.1	5.2
144	149	126	109	74	76	84	86	96	98	84
15.0	4.0	−16.4	−10.1	−16.2	2.5	−1.4	−3.1	4.7	−2.3	−6.8
85.0	96.0	116.4	110.1	116.2	97.5	101.4	103.1	95.3	102.3	106.8
72.6	78.5	93.8	94.5	102.5	87.9	92.0	88.9	86.6	92.0	98.7
74.5	80.6	96.4	97.7	106.7	91.5	95.4	92.2	89.9	95.3	102.6
9.2	14.0	17.5	9.2	4.2	0.43	0.63	5.0	0.27	2.2	−1.0
1.3	1.4	2.5	3.3	5.3	5.5	5.4	5.8	5.2	4.8	5.3
10,840	11,106	9,225	7,410	5,453	6,129	7,354	7,722	8,564	9,157	8,863
3.4	1.5	−6.0	−11.4	−15.9	−2.3	−0.31	−0.03	0.96	0.48	0.39
2.6	0.62	−6.9	−13.3	−19.0	−4.4	−1.1	−0.92	0.14	−0.46	−0.33
94.0	97.8	112.9	124.7	135.0	106.7	101.4	101.0	98.9	100.0	99.9
69.4	72.1	82.9	89.7	94.2	73.6	72.0	71.3	68.3	70.4	70.6
19.6	20.1	23.9	28.9	35.7	29.3	24.7	23.6	22.4	22.4	23.5
4.6	5.1	5.4	5.2	3.9	2.9	4.2	5.7	7.8	6.8	5.4
0.40	0.50	0.74	0.89	1.1	0.80	0.57	0.42	0.35	0.34	0.35

TABLE 74 (cont.)

Net Income Originating, Percentage Distribution by Type

	1919	1920	1921	1922	1923	1924	1925	1926	1927
7 Finance									
Total ($000,000)	6,899	7,472	7,682	8,259	8,794	9,601	9,740	9,816	10,312
Corp. net savings	4.1	1.3	—0.10	0.31	—0.16	0.79	0.84	1.4	3.0
Total payments	95.9	98.7	100.1	99.7	100.2	99.2	99.2	98.6	97.0
Wages & salaries	20.0	22.1	22.5	21.1	20.7	20.6	20.8	22.8	23.6
Entrep. withdr.	1.8	2.0	1.9	1.8	2.0	2.0	2.2	2.3	2.3
Dividends	4.9	5.4	5.3	5.7	6.0	5.3	5.7	5.6	5.3
Interest	11.8	11.8	12.2	11.7	12.8	12.7	14.3	15.5	16.6
Rent	57.5	57.4	58.2	59.3	58.7	58.7	56.1	52.4	49.3
7a Banking									
Total ($000,000)	868	958	921	924	971	1,035	1,132	1,181	1,282
Corp. net savings	24.2	19.6	10.9	8.7	10.2	12.5	16.3	15.6	17.6
Total payments	75.8	80.4	89.1	91.3	89.8	87.5	83.7	84.4	82.4
Wages & salaries	44.0	49.3	55.2	55.8	56.3	56.0	53.4	54.3	52.6
Dividends	31.8	31.1	33.9	35.5	33.5	31.5	30.3	30.1	29.8
7b Insurance									
Total ($000,000)	706	727	742	784	777	866	1,032	1,127	1,288
Corp. net savings	6.3	—8.9	—11.8	—12.0	—13.5	—12.5	—4.9	—4.1	2.3
Total payments	93.7	108.9	111.8	112.0	113.5	112.5	104.9	104.1	97.7
Wages & salaries	75.8	88.3	91.8	89.9	88.7	89.3	82.8	82.2	77.1
Entrep. withdr.	17.2	20.3	19.5	18.9	22.3	21.9	20.5	20.1	18.2
Dividends	2.6	2.7	3.1	5.7	5.1	3.9	3.7	3.8	4.2
Interest	—1.9	—2.3	—2.5	—2.5	—2.6	—2.5	—2.2	—2.0	—1.8
7c Real estate									
Total ($000,000)	5,325	5,787	6,019	6,552	7,046	7,699	7,577	7,508	7,742
Corp. net savings	0.50	—0.46	—0.34	0.61	—0.12	0.70	—0.68	0.02	0.66
Total payments	99.5	100.5	100.3	99.4	100.1	99.3	100.7	100.0	99.3
Wages & salaries	8.7	9.3	9.0	8.0	8.2	8.1	7.5	9.0	9.9
Dividends	0.76	1.5	1.2	1.5	2.4	1.9	2.3	2.0	1.4
Interest	15.6	15.5	15.9	15.1	16.2	16.2	18.7	20.5	22.4
Rent	74.5	74.1	74.3	74.7	73.3	73.1	72.1	68.5	65.6
8 Service									
Total ($000,000)	6,129	6,853	6,652	7,383	8,260	8,644	9,306	10,114	10,318
Entrep. net savings	17.6	12.1	10.6	5.2	9.7	6.6	6.3	10.2	5.9
Corp. net savings	0.80	0.08	—0.38	0.35	0.52	0.51	0.60	0.23	—0.06
Total payments	81.6	87.9	89.7	94.5	89.8	92.9	93.1	89.6	94.2
Wages & salaries	53.1	59.4	63.2	60.9	59.6	60.6	59.3	58.4	61.6
Entrep. withdr.	27.7	27.0	25.3	32.6	29.0	31.1	32.4	29.7	31.0
Dividends	0.47	1.2	0.99	0.66	0.82	0.82	0.99	1.0	1.0
Interest	0.26	0.22	0.27	0.31	0.34	0.38	0.44	0.47	0.61

TABLE 74 (cont.)

Net Income Originating, Percentage Distribution by Type

1928	1929	1930	1931	1932	1933	1934	1935	1936	1937	1938
10,871	11,135	9,762	7,591	5,494	4,834	5,035	5,731	6,113	6,651	6,551
3.7	0.63	—4.0	—12.4	—21.1	—19.8	—13.1	—5.9	—0.65	—0.36	—1.7
96.3	99.4	104.0	112.4	121.1	119.8	113.1	105.9	100.6	100.4	101.7
24.3	25.7	27.2	31.4	35.8	36.1	36.9	34.1	33.0	31.9	32.8
2.3	2.3	2.6	3.0	3.6	3.7	3.8	3.5	3.3	3.4	3.3
6.1	6.9	6.8	7.8	6.7	4.2	5.2	4.8	4.4	4.3	4.4
18.2	20.4	23.7	30.3	36.9	32.1	29.4	26.1	24.1	22.0	21.8
45.5	44.2	43.7	39.9	38.1	43.7	37.9	37.4	35.8	38.8	39.3
1,401	1,390	1,139	735	415	290	490	709	882	875	814
18.5	14.6	—2.0	—43.1	101.3	—119.2	—39.2	2.9	19.3	15.4	8.2
81.5	85.4	102.0	143.1	201.3	219.2	139.2	97.1	80.7	84.6	91.8
50.2	52.6	62.6	87.2	133.8	164.8	101.0	70.5	58.7	61.7	67.7
31.3	32.8	39.4	55.9	67.5	54.4	38.2	26.5	22.0	22.9	24.1
1,436	1,484	1,327	1,161	937	865	1,041	1,105	1,145	1,273	1,275
6.1	3.7	—7.4	—14.7	—19.7	—16.6	—2.3	—2.2	0.03	3.1	1.8
93.9	96.3	107.4	114.7	119.7	116.6	102.3	102.2	100.0	96.9	98.2
73.9	76.2	85.6	91.5	97.7	96.7	84.2	83.0	82.9	80.0	80.5
17.1	17.5	19.1	19.8	20.9	20.4	18.4	18.2	17.6	17.7	17.0
4.6	4.7	4.6	5.2	3.3	1.9	2.2	3.4	1.9	1.7	3.0
—1.7	—2.2	—1.8	—1.9	—2.2	—2.5	—2.4	—2.4	—2.4	—2.4	—2.4
8,034	8,261	7,296	5,696	4,141	3,678	3,503	3,917	4,086	4,503	4,463
0.71	—2.3	—3.7	—8.0	—13.4	—12.7	—12.6	—8.5	—5.1	—4.4	—4.4
99.3	102.3	103.7	108.0	113.4	112.7	112.6	108.5	105.1	104.4	104.4
10.9	12.0	11.0	12.0	12.0	11.7	13.9	13.7	13.5	12.5	12.8
1.9	2.9	2.1	2.1	1.4	0.82	1.4	1.3	1.3	1.4	1.3
25.0	27.8	32.1	40.7	49.5	42.8	42.9	38.8	36.8	33.2	32.7
61.5	59.5	58.5	53.1	50.5	57.5	54.4	54.7	53.5	57.3	57.7
10,680	11,290	10,412	8,727	6,398	5,772	6,752	7,364	8,298	9,130	8,872
6.0	4.6	3.7	—1.2	—14.6	—17.6	—4.9	—2.6	1.3	—0.54	2.5
0.06	0.13	—0.77	—2.4	—7.4	—6.2	—3.5	—2.9	—2.4	—1.9	—1.9
94.0	95.3	97.1	103.5	122.1	123.7	108.4	105.5	101.1	102.4	99.5
60.2	61.1	61.4	63.9	69.0	67.9	65.1	65.1	63.9	64.8	63.2
32.1	32.4	33.7	37.8	50.5	53.6	41.3	38.3	34.6	35.2	34.4
0.93	1.0	1.1	0.84	0.85	0.59	0.68	0.74	1.4	1.3	0.78
0.68	0.77	0.95	1.1	1.7	1.7	1.3	1.4	1.2	1.0	1.0

TABLE 74 (concl.)

Net Income Originating, Percentage Distribution by Type

	1919	1920	1921	1922	1923	1924	1925	1926	1927
9 Government									
Total ($000,000)	3,768	7,018	6,206	6,136	7,042	7,278	7,365	8,114	8,484
Net savings	−34.6	27.0	15.4	13.9	22.9	23.6	21.9	26.5	27.0
Total payments	134.6	73.0	84.6	86.1	77.1	76.4	78.1	73.5	73.0
Wages & salaries	96.8	48.2	55.3	55.6	50.4	51.3	53.5	51.1	51.6
Empl. comp.	106.9	55.2	64.2	64.5	58.2	58.8	60.7	57.7	58.2
Interest	27.7	17.8	20.4	21.6	18.9	17.6	17.4	15.8	14.8
10 Miscellaneous									
Total ($000,000)	2,245	2,341	1,954	2,303	2,723	2,782	3,072	3,248	3,258
Entrep. net savings	7.0	5.4	5.2	1.1	3.2	1.9	1.7	3.4	1.6
Corp. net savings	8.3	3.0	−7.5	3.5	4.2	2.6	4.4	3.6	1.5
Total payments	84.7	91.5	102.3	95.4	92.6	95.5	93.9	93.0	96.9
Wages & salaries	61.0	65.4	70.8	65.9	65.8	66.2	64.6	66.2	67.3
Entrep. withdr.	11.6	13.1	14.4	14.5	12.5	13.5	13.4	12.7	13.4
Dividends	4.6	5.4	7.4	7.1	7.0	8.1	8.6	7.1	8.7
Interest	7.6	7.6	9.6	8.0	7.2	7.7	7.3	6.9	7.5

TABLE 74 (concl.)

Net Income Originating, Percentage Distribution by Type

1928	1929	1930	1931	1932	1933	1934	1935	1936	1937	1938
8,290	8,874	8,920	7,410	6,175	7,504	8,188	7,504	8,216	10,724	10,816
22.9	25.1	23.6	4.6	−14.7	−1.5	−7.0	−23.1	−26.7	4.6	−1.6
77.1	74.9	76.4	95.4	114.7	101.5	107.0	123.1	126.7	95.4	101.6
55.2	53.8	55.0	67.3	77.9	58.2	55.0	65.3	64.9	52.2	54.2
62.2	60.7	62.2	78.1	92.6	82.0	87.9	103.3	108.0	79.7	86.0
15.0	14.2	14.2	17.2	22.1	19.5	19.2	19.8	18.7	15.7	15.6
3,654	3,867	2,596	1,855	1,454	1,435	2,115	2,629	3,012	3,179	3,013
1.3	0.76	0.31	−1.7	−7.0	−6.4	−1.7	−1.0	−0.30	−0.61	−0.19
7.6	7.3	−28.5	−61.0	−70.1	−62.7	−19.3	−7.9	−3.4	−5.3	−5.6
91.2	91.9	128.2	162.6	177.0	169.1	121.1	108.9	103.7	106.0	105.8
61.7	62.3	87.0	111.1	119.1	117.4	88.2	78.2	76.7	80.2	80.1
12.7	12.9	18.4	23.7	29.5	28.6	19.3	16.7	16.2	17.3	18.3
9.3	10.0	12.9	14.6	12.2	8.3	5.4	9.9	7.3	5.2	4.1
7.5	6.7	9.9	13.3	16.3	14.8	8.2	4.1	3.5	3.2	3.3

TABLE 75

Total Payments including Entrepreneurial Savings
Percentage Distribution by Type

	1919	1920	1921	1922	1923	1924	1925	1926	1927
1 Construction									
Total ($000,000)	2,049	2,599	1,888	2,350	3,359	3,663	3,910	4,185	3,985
Wages & salaries	78.5	86.7	87.4	83.5	87.2	82.7	78.5	85.0	85.3
Entrep. net income	20.6	12.3	10.4	15.0	11.5	16.2	19.7	13.8	13.3
Property income	0.94	0.99	2.1	1.5	1.3	1.1	1.8	1.3	1.5
2 Trade									
Total ($000,000)	10,487	9,490	7,250	8,657	9,695	9,581	10,088	10,422	10,217
Wages & salaries	51.8	63.8	71.3	65.6	65.9	68.2	69.3	71.2	71.4
Entrep. net income	44.1	31.8	23.7	30.4	30.1	27.4	26.1	24.0	23.5
Property income	4.1	4.5	5.0	3.9	4.0	4.4	4.7	4.8	5.1
3 Service									
Total ($000,000)	6,080	6,847	6,677	7,357	8,217	8,600	9,251	10,091	10,325
Wages & salaries	53.6	59.4	63.0	61.1	59.9	60.9	59.7	58.5	61.5
Entrep. net income	45.7	39.1	35.8	37.9	38.9	37.9	38.9	40.0	36.8
Property income	0.74	1.4	1.3	0.97	1.2	1.2	1.4	1.5	1.6
4 Miscellaneous									
Total ($000,000)	2,059	2,271	2,101	2,223	2,609	2,710	2,936	3,131	3,209
Wages & salaries	66.5	67.4	65.9	68.3	68.7	68.0	67.6	68.7	68.4
Entrep. net income	20.2	19.2	18.2	16.1	16.4	15.8	15.8	16.8	15.1
Property income	13.3	13.4	15.8	15.6	14.9	16.2	16.6	14.6	16.5

For agriculture, the percentage distribution is identical with that of net income originating since savings are all considered entrepreneurial; for real estate, it is identical with that for total payments excluding entrepreneurial savings since the latter were not estimated.

TABLE 75

Total Payments including Entrepreneurial Savings
Percentage Distribution by Type

1928	1929	1930	1931	1932	1933	1934	1935	1936	1937	1938
3,978	4,049	3,406	2,195	1,169	812	922	1,093	1,606	1,861	1,692
86.4	85.0	86.5	90.0	99.0	94.2	87.0	82.1	78.6	80.0	76.3
12.0	13.2	10.6	7.5	—1.5	2.4	10.9	15.9	19.0	17.7	21.9
1.5	1.8	2.9	2.4	2.5	3.4	2.1	2.0	2.4	2.4	1.9
10,562	11,037	9,866	8,395	6,491	6,395	7,437	7,793	8,552	9,199	8,892
71.2	72.6	77.5	79.2	79.1	70.6	71.2	70.6	68.4	70.1	70.4
23.7	21.8	16.8	15.5	16.6	25.9	24.1	23.4	23.4	22.7	23.8
5.1	5.6	5.7	5.4	4 2	3.6	4.7	6.0	8.2	7.1	5.8
10,673	11,275	10,492	8,934	6,875	6,129	6,992	7,576	8,497	9,299	9,042
60.3	61.1	60.9	62.4	64.2	63.9	62.9	63.3	62.4	63.6	62.0
38.1	37.0	37.1	35.7	33.4	33.9	35.2	34.6	35.0	34.1	36.2
1.6	1.8	2.0	1.9	2.4	2.1	1.9	2.1	2.5	2.3	1.8
3,378	3,583	3,335	2,986	2,472	2,336	2,501	2,836	3,115	3,348	3,183
66.8	67.3	67.7	69.0	70.0	72.1	73.6	72.5	74.2	76.2	75.8
15.1	14.8	14.5	13.7	13.2	13.7	14.7	14.5	15.4	15.9	17.2
18.1	18.0	17.7	17.3	16.7	14.2	11.7	12.9	10.4	8.0	7.0

TABLE 76

Total Payments excluding Entrepreneurial Savings
Percentage Distribution by Type

	1919	1920	1921	1922	1923	1924	1925	1926	1927
1 Agriculture									
Total ($000,000)	8,587	9,975	6,981	6,768	7,374	7,471	7,526	7,649	7,582
Empl. comp.	17.6	17.8	16.6	16.6	16.5	16.4	16.5	17.3	16.9
Entrep. withdr.	78.0	77.7	76.2	75.6	76.3	76.9	77.1	76.6	76.9
Dividends	0.19	0.16	0.23	0.24	0.22	0.20	0.24	0.21	0.38
Interest	4.2	4.3	7.0	7.5	6.9	6.5	6.1	5.9	5.9
Net savings	26.5	—9.0	—20.7	—13.4	—8.7	—4.8	5.6	—1.5	—1.6
2 Mining									
Total ($000,000)	1,728	2,315	1,821	1,610	2,273	1,997	1,937	2,246	2,016
Wages	76.6	78.5	77.6	78.0	78.8	76.6	72.7	73.4	73.2
Salaries	9.0	9.4	8.0	9.4	8.3	8.8	9.3	8.9	9.6
Entrep. withdr.	1.8	1.7	1.8	1.8	1.4	1.4	1.4	1.1	1.2
Dividends	11.3	9.1	10.6	8.6	9.8	10.6	13.9	14.5	13.8
Interest	1.3	1.3	2.1	2.1	1.6	2.6	2.8	2.1	2.2
Entrep. net savings	0.47	1.1	—1.1	—0.02	—0.28	—0.20	0.96	1.1	0.36
Corp. net savings	—0.75	6.4	—24.7	—9.5	—12.8	—14.8	—3.6	—4.4	—13.6
3 Manufacturing									
Total ($000,000)	14,340	16,740	11,760	12,285	15,289	14,578	15,396	16,143	16,296
Wages	67.5	69.2	63.4	65.1	66.5	65.1	64.8	63.9	62.1
Salaries	19.4	18.1	20.7	20.2	18.7	19.9	19.3	19.7	21.0
Entrep. withdr.	3.6	3.2	3.4	3.2	2.5	2.6	2.4	2.3	2.2
Dividends	8.8	8.9	11.3	10.7	11.5	11.3	12.4	13.1	13.7
Interest	0.60	0.64	1.2	0.86	0.77	1.1	1.0	0.94	1.0
Entrep. net savings	3.1	0.29	—1.6	1.3	1.4	0.59	0.98	0.55	0.48
Corp. net savings	16.1	5.5	—15.0	8.3	9.2	5.2	8.7	6.8	2.7
3a Food and tobacco									
Total ($000,000)	1,664	1,802	1,494	1,465	1,615	1,605	1,627	1,630	1,744
Wages	57.1	58.0	58.4	58.4	57.1	56.6	55.9	56.3	53.5
Salaries	20.6	19.3	19.4	20.4	19.3	18.1	17.5	17.8	18.5
Entrep. withdr.	11.5	9.8	9.1	8.5	7.7	7.3	6.7	6.9	6.9
Dividends	9.3	10.9	10.7	10.5	13.8	15.5	17.2	16.8	18.8
Interest	1.5	2.0	2.4	2.1	2.0	2.5	2.7	2.2	2.2
Entrep. net savings	0.28	—3.6	—5.8	0.32	1.1	1.3	0.86	1.0	0.13
Corp. net savings	13.6	—3.4	—14.2	6.8	6.9	8.5	6.4	9.5	4.6

TABLE 76

Total Payments excluding Entrepreneurial Savings
Percentage Distribution by Type

1928	1929	1930	1931	1932	1933	1934	1935	1936	1937	1938
7,567	7,631	7,149	5,821	4,492	4,045	4,409	4,741	5,044	5,650	5,540
16.8	16.8	15.9	14.6	13.0	12.8	12.7	13.5	13.7	14.1	13.7
77.1	77.3	78.0	78.0	78.0	78.3	79.4	79.6	79.9	80.5	81.1
0.33	0.16	0.10	0.24	0.13	0.0	0.39	0.40	0.73	0.57	0.40
5.8	5.7	6.0	7.2	8.9	8.9	7.6	6.5	5.7	4.9	4.8
—3.1	1.0	—18.7	—30.6	—37.2	—12.1	7.7	13.5	20.7	11.0	—1.5
1,800	1,962	1,640	1,161	801	791	1,078	1,171	1,352	1,573	1,247
72.4	68.1	70.1	70.6	69.4	72.1	70.7	68.8	69.5	67.8	68.2
9.9	9.9	10.8	12.2	13.6	12.2	10.7	10.9	10.4	9.9	11.4
1.3	1.1	1.3	1.6	1.9	1.8	1.4	1.3	1.2	1.2	1.5
14.1	18.6	15.2	11.9	10.2	9.5	14.0	15.8	15.9	18.8	16.4
2.3	2.3	2.7	3.6	4.9	4.3	3.2	3.2	3.0	2.3	2.5
0.88	1.3	—0.96	—2.6	—3.9	—3.0	—0.71	—0.81	—0.03	0.39	0.49
—8.6	—8.5	—18.6	—33.8	—38.2	—32.1	—15.3	—18.0	—10.5	—8.8	—12.3
16,935	18,237	15,972	12,315	8,550	8,429	10,402	11,831	14,015	16,048	12,339
60.2	59.8	55.5	54.4	54.0	58.6	61.2	61.8	60.4	63.0	62.6
21.6	22.0	24.6	26.1	28.2	25.0	23.4	21.9	19.7	19.3	22.7
2.2	2.0	2.0	2.2	2.4	2.2	1.7	1.7	1.7	1.7	2.1
14.9	15.0	16.4	15.4	13.1	12.0	12.1	13.4	17.2	15.2	11.5
1.1	1.1	1.5	1.9	2.3	2.2	1.6	1.3	1.0	0.88	1.1
0.43	0.32	—0.87	—1.6	—2.6	—0.15	0.24	0.52	0.93	0.37	—0.27
5.6	6.6	—10.9	—22.8	—34.5	—11.1	—4.3	—0.64	1.3	0.81	—2.8
1,819	1,919	1,884	1,617	1,306	1,286	1,510	1,566	1,770	1,876	1,779
52.6	52.2	50.5	50.2	50.2	52.4	55.4	55.2	52.4	56.1	57.3
18.6	17.8	17.6	18.1	18.6	18.3	17.4	17.6	16.5	15.8	16.5
7.0	6.8	6.3	6.2	6.1	5.1	4.3	4.1	4.5	5.0	5.3
19.4	20.9	23.1	22.7	22.4	21.7	21.0	21.4	25.2	21.8	19.4
2.3	2.2	2.6	2.8	2.8	2.5	1.9	1.7	1.4	1.4	1.5
0.30	0.13	—0.38	—1.5	—2.5	0.64	2.7	2.7	3.0	0.60	—0.12
7.7	6.1	—2.6	—9.5	—15.3	—2.7	4.1	3.1	2.6	—3.3	—1.9

TABLE 76 (cont.)

Total Payments excluding Entrepreneurial Savings
Percentage Distribution by Type

3b Textile and leather	1919	1920	1921	1922	1923	1924	1925	1926	1927
Total ($000,000)	2,800	3,178	2,552	2,649	3,045	2,717	2,875	2,870	3,019
Wages	69.1	72.3	73.2	72.7	73.5	73.1	73.4	73.9	73.9
Salaries	16.3	14.4	14.1	14.8	14.9	15.6	15.3	15.2	15.5
Entrep. withdr.	5.1	4.3	4.4	4.1	3.4	3.7	3.7	3.6	3.4
Dividends	9.0	8.7	7.9	8.0	8.1	7.5	7.5	7.3	7.0
Interest	0.46	0.36	0.55	0.45	0.13	0.12	0.16	0.08	0.16
Entrep. net savings	9.8	0.04	—1.1	3.2	2.5	—0.22	1.3	—0.31	1.2
Corp. net savings	19.6	—5.0	—7.2	9.4	7.3	—2.5	2.9	—2.8	3.6

3c Construction materials and furniture

	1919	1920	1921	1922	1923	1924	1925	1926	1927
Total ($000,000)	1,668	2,081	1,425	1,638	2,078	2,083	2,187	2,306	2,180
Wages	75.6	76.8	71.8	72.4	74.4	73.9	72.8	70.9	70.8
Salaries	15.1	13.4	16.9	16.5	14.4	15.6	15.9	15.8	16.6
Entrep. withdr.	3.4	3.4	3.2	3.0	2.3	2.3	2.3	2.1	1.9
Dividends	5.6	6.0	7.6	7.5	8.5	7.6	8.5	10.6	10.0
Interest	0.36	0.32	0.51	0.55	0.45	0.54	0.50	0.52	0.63
Entrep. net savings	2.9	2.5	—1.8	1.8	2.9	1.3	1.5	1.0	0.23
Corp. net savings	10.7	9.5	—9.5	6.9	10.3	3.5	3.8	2.3	—2.1

3d Paper

	1919	1920	1921	1922	1923	1924	1925	1926	1927
Total ($000,000)	327	427	319	318	395	373	418	428	435
Wages	65.5	69.7	64.0	66.1	64.0	67.4	63.8	65.7	63.2
Salaries	18.1	13.9	17.8	19.7	18.5	19.4	18.3	19.4	19.9
Entrep. withdr.	1.5	1.5	1.5	1.3	1.1	1.1	0.97	0.95	0.85
Dividends	13.7	14.0	15.3	11.0	14.4	9.9	14.6	11.1	13.0
Interest	1.2	0.88	1.3	2.0	2.1	2.2	2.3	2.8	3.1
Entrep. net savings	1.7	2.6	—0.93	0.41	0.67	0.42	0.59	0.60	0.63
Corp. net savings	15.5	25.0	—18.8	6.0	7.0	7.6	6.2	10.4	9.1

3e Printing

	1919	1920	1921	1922	1923	1924	1925	1926	1927
Total ($000,000)	653	853	802	845	920	988	1,054	1,142	1,181
Wages	53.9	58.5	54.1	53.1	53.5	52.5	51.3	50.6	49.5
Salaries	34.2	29.9	32.5	33.6	34.3	36.4	35.8	36.7	36.8
Entrep. withdr.	6.2	6.4	5.8	5.3	4.7	4.5	4.1	3.8	3.6
Dividends	5.4	4.9	7.1	7.9	7.4	6.4	8.4	8.5	9.3
Interest	0.39	0.23	0.44	0.16	0.13	0.20	0.37	0.46	0.75
Entrep. net savings	3.3	2.2	0.65	2.7	1.9	1.7	1.8	1.5	1.0
Corp. net savings	8.4	7.8	1.8	9.0	6.3	6.7	5.1	4.8	2.7

TABLE 76 (cont.)

Total Payments excluding Entrepreneurial Savings
Percentage Distribution by Type

1928	1929	1930	1931	1932	1933	1934	1935	1936	1937	1938
2,963	3,044	2,532	2,185	1,565	1,708	2,020	2,221	2,382	2,515	2,035
71.8	72.1	70.7	71.7	72.5	75.3	75.9	77.2	75.0	77.0	78.2
16.9	17.3	19.0	19.1	19.7	17.5	16.2	15.3	14.9	13.7	14.5
3.3	3.2	3.2	3.1	3.0	2.8	2.2	2.3	2.6	2.4	2.9
7.8	7.1	6.7	5.7	4.8	4.5	5.7	5.2	7.4	6.8	4.1
0.25	0.35	0.37	0.33	0.04	−0.05	−0.03	0.09	0.12	0.15	0.16
0.31	−0.09	−3.7	−4.0	−5.2	0.58	−0.42	0.14	1.1	−0.01	−0.01
−0.83	−1.6	−18.4	−19.7	−26.0	1.8	−4.9	−1.4	0.71	−3.5	−4.8
2,116	2,156	1,748	1,171	676	658	854	1,001	1,299	1,527	1,168
69.6	69.1	65.4	62.8	60.7	66.7	66.7	69.2	68.7	70.5	71.5
17.3	17.7	20.9	23.5	27.0	22.7	20.7	18.5	15.5	15.3	18.7
2.1	2.1	2.1	2.2	2.4	2.0	1.8	1.8	1.9	1.8	2.3
10.3	10.1	10.2	9.2	7.2	6.2	9.2	9.4	13.1	11.9	7.0
0.81	1.0	1.5	2.2	2.7	2.4	1.5	1.1	0.84	0.50	0.60
0.48	0.25	−1.6	−3.4	−6.6	−2.3	−1.0	−0.22	0.87	0.78	−0.83
0.72	0.51	−15.3	−31.9	−62.3	−24.6	−13.5	−4.8	0.93	1.1	−0.38
448	461	435	360	272	288	347	374	420	482	395
61.2	62.7	61.3	59.5	60.0	60.0	61.1	63.0	62.0	63.7	69.1
20.6	20.8	21.9	24.9	25.5	24.0	23.2	20.7	20.1	17.4	20.6
0.79	0.73	0.72	0.75	0.78	0.68	0.62	0.66	0.71	0.70	0.84
14.5	12.4	11.9	10.2	7.6	9.5	11.2	12.6	14.6	15.6	6.7
2.9	3.3	4.2	4.7	6.1	5.8	3.9	3.0	2.6	2.6	2.7
0.46	0.38	−0.02	−0.43	−0.97	−0.01	0.24	0.20	0.36	0.42	−0.76
5.9	7.8	−4.8	−15.4	−31.5	−5.7	1.2	0.50	3.0	2.8	−6.4
1,205	1,324	1,323	1,125	883	742	850	903	997	1,092	1,023
49.1	48.1	46.9	47.8	46.9	47.9	48.4	49.4	48.7	48.8	49.7
38.3	37.9	39.4	39.4	40.9	41.3	39.9	38.6	36.7	38.7	38.8
3.5	3.0	2.9	2.9	3.8	4.2	2.8	3.1	3.2	3.1	3.3
8.2	10.0	9.7	8.5	6.7	4.8	7.5	8.0	10.5	8.6	7.2
0.94	0.99	1.1	1.4	1.6	1.8	1.3	0.91	0.87	0.83	0.94
1.4	1.3	0.21	−0.63	−1.9	−0.37	0.42	0.37	0.71	0.29	−0.76
7.2	5.0	−1.7	−5.9	−11.4	−3.8	−3.0	0.62	0.29	−0.34	−1.1

TABLE 76 (cont.)

Total Payments excluding Entrepreneurial Savings
Percentage Distribution by Type

	1919	1920	1921	1922	1923	1924	1925	1926	1927
3f Metal									
Total ($000,000)	5,235	6,046	3,437	3,595	5,124	4,890	5,131	5,461	5,344
Wages	75.4	75.5	65.8	69.8	71.7	67.7	68.7	67.6	64.8
Salaries	16.0	16.2	21.0	18.7	16.3	17.8	16.7	16.4	17.9
Entrep. withdr.	0.86	0.75	0.83	0.74	0.58	0.61	0.56	0.51	0.49
Dividends	7.3	7.0	11.4	10.2	10.6	12.8	13.1	14.6	16.2
Interest	0.50	0.47	0.98	0.52	0.76	1.1	0.96	0.83	0.68
Entrep. net savings	1.1	0.44	—0.62	0.17	0.51	0.37	0.58	0.48	0.26
Corp. net savings	16.9	9.8	—20.3	5.3	11.2	7.0	13.7	10.1	3.8
3g Chemical									
Total ($000,000)	901	1,076	827	795	951	894	1,001	1,077	1,069
Wages	51.4	52.9	42.9	46.9	47.4	47.5	45.0	44.9	44.8
Salaries	24.1	21.5	21.6	22.6	21.5	21.3	19.6	19.8	20.2
Entrep. withdr.	2.5	2.1	2.0	2.0	1.6	1.6	1.5	1.3	1.3
Dividends	22.0	23.2	31.0	27.0	28.1	27.3	31.9	32.1	31.0
Interest	0.04	0.27	2.5	1.5	1.4	2.3	2.1	2.0	2.7
Entrep. net savings	0.99	—0.66	—1.5	0.11	0.20	0.26	0.48	0.64	0.23
Corp. net savings	13.3	0.34	—30.9	17.3	2.3	11.4	15.5	26.0	0.20
3h Miscellaneous and rubber									
Total ($000,000)	891	1,057	730	800	956	815	877	927	938
Wages	63.0	66.5	61.1	60.9	61.4	67.7	66.9	65.6	64.6
Salaries	22.2	19.2	20.3	18.1	17.0	19.7	19.8	19.9	20.5
Entrep. withdr.	2.1	2.0	2.2	1.9	1.6	1.9	1.7	1.6	1.5
Dividends	11.6	10.6	13.8	17.2	18.9	9.0	10.4	11.1	11.4
Interest	1.1	1.6	2.6	2.0	1.2	1.7	1.2	1.8	2.0
Entrep. net savings	2.1	1.0	—1.9	0.86	1.0	0.80	1.3	0.61	0.57
Corp. net savings	27.3	15.7	—31.4	16.0	18.7	10.3	14.4	3.7	2.5
4 Construction									
Total ($000,000)	1,868	2,522	1,915	2,306	3,280	3,469	3,706	4,027	3,876
Wages	73.0	77.5	70.9	71.4	78.1	74.9	71.6	75.5	74.9
Salaries	13.1	11.9	15.3	13.8	11.2	12.4	11.2	12.8	12.8
Entrep. withdr.	12.9	9.6	11.7	13.3	9.4	11.5	15.3	10.4	10.8
Dividends	0.82	0.83	1.7	1.3	1.1	0.93	1.6	1.0	1.2
Interest	0.21	0.20	0.41	0.19	0.18	0.23	0.28	0.27	0.29
Entrep. net savings	9.7	3.1	—1.4	1.9	2.4	5.6	5.5	3.9	2.8
Corp. net savings	1.2	0.46	—1.5	0.34	0.69	1.4	1.1	1.4	1.3

TABLE 76 (cont.)

Total Payments excluding Entrepreneurial Savings
Percentage Distribution by Type

1928	1929	1930	1931	1932	1933	1934	1935	1936	1937	1938
5,732	6,449	5,228	3,563	2,208	2,144	3,083	3,783	4,870	6,092	3,878
64.2	64.1	58.9	56.6	56.1	64.0	65.4	66.1	64.7	67.0	66.0
17.8	17.3	21.4	23.8	27.5	22.9	20.2	18.1	15.6	15.6	21.2
0.46	0.43	0.44	0.46	0.50	0.47	0.38	0.39	0.40	0.38	0.57
16.7	17.3	18.2	17.7	13.6	10.4	12.4	14.0	18.2	16.1	10.9
0.83	0.95	1.1	1.5	2.3	2.3	1.6	1.4	1.1	0.87	1.3
0.36	0.42	—0.04	—0.51	—1.2	—0.43	—0.14	0.20	0.38	0.37	—0.24
8.2	11.6	—8.2	—28.1	—54.1	—19.4	—5.4	1.2	3.2	4.1	—2.4
1,234	1,305	1,393	1,126	814	832	840	968	1,147	1,219	1,030
38.7	40.9	35.5	35.5	38.5	39.8	47.2	43.6	39.8	45.5	48.7
17.9	18.9	17.6	18.4	20.0	18.4	21.3	19.9	17.4	17.5	19.5
1.1	1.1	0.90	0.98	0.94	0.87	0.91	0.94	0.95	0.97	1.1
40.1	37.2	43.1	40.8	34.4	35.6	26.6	32.4	39.6	34.2	28.2
2.2	2.0	3.0	4.3	6.2	5.3	3.9	3.2	2.3	1.9	2.5
0.48	0.46	0.05	—0.23	—0.41	0.16	0.40	0.41	0.54	0.42	—0.20
17.1	22.9	—20.5	—48.1	—42.2	—28.7	—10.4	—11.0	—7.7	—0.01	—7.3
944	978	854	708	491	484	576	682	787	869	690
65.5	63.7	60.4	59.0	58.5	63.9	67.6	64.0	63.4	65.7	62.0
20.3	20.8	23.5	26.0	28.1	24.8	22.0	22.0	20.0	19.9	22.3
1.6	1.5	1.6	1.6	1.6	1.5	1.3	1.4	1.4	1.4	1.7
10.5	12.1	12.2	10.6	8.9	6.9	6.7	11.0	14.1	12.2	13.0
2.0	1.8	2.3	2.7	2.9	2.9	2.4	1.6	1.1	0.73	0.96
0.30	0.11	—1.4	—1.8	—2.8	—0.93	—0.24	0.52	0.86	0.47	0.16
1.6	—1.8	—22.9	—27.1	—39.8	—14.3	—2.3	1.2	2.1	0.12	—0.84
3,880	3,951	3,443	2,297	1,404	968	1,022	1,163	1,648	1,884	1,693
74.7	74.0	69.8	68.7	62.5	58.3	62.9	62.3	62.9	65.7	62.5
14.0	13.1	15.7	17.4	19.9	20.7	15.6	14.8	13.7	13.3	13.7
9.8	11.0	11.5	11.6	15.4	18.1	19.7	21.0	21.1	18.7	22.0
1.3	1.5	2.5	1.7	1.4	1.9	1.4	1.8	2.2	2.2	1.7
0.26	0.33	0.44	0.59	0.74	0.89	0.48	0.11	0.12	0.11	0.12
2.5	2.5	—1.1	—4.4	—16.7	—16.1	—9.9	—6.0	—2.5	—1.2	—0.08
0.94	0.92	—0.84	—3.1	—9.0	—8.7	—4.5	—2.6	—1.3	—1.0	—0.04

TABLE 76 (cont.)

Total Payments excluding Entrepreneurial Savings
Percentage Distribution by Type

	1919	1920	1921	1922	1923	1924	1925	1926	1927
5 Transportation and other public utilities									
Total ($000,000)	5,829	7,237	6,021	5,988	6,647	6,707	6,919	7,200	7,348
Wages & salaries	78.1	82.2	79.0	76.4	76.7	75.0	73.6	73.6	71.5
Empl. comp.	79.1	83.3	79.8	77.3	77.7	76.0	74.7	74.8	72.7
Entrep. withdr.	0.19	0.12	0.12	0.13	0.11	0.09	0.08	0.08	0.07
Dividends	9.1	6.7	7.6	9.5	9.6	10.6	11.8	12.0	14.1
Interest	11.7	9.9	12.5	13.1	12.6	13.3	13.4	13.1	13.1
Entrep. net savings	0.14	0.08	—0.03	—0.01	...*	0.01	0.02	0.02	...*
Corp. net savings	2.2	1.5	1.1	3.8	6.7	5.6	9.3	9.5	6.0
5a Electric light and power									
Total ($000,000)	290	337	365	434	558	663	737	831	903
Wages & salaries	48.3	52.5	50.7	44.7	45.1	44.9	42.0	42.8	40.7
Entrep. withdr.	1.1	1.0	0.93	0.74	0.51	0.40	0.31	0.23	0.17
Dividends	23.5	21.2	22.9	28.3	28.9	28.0	31.2	29.7	31.5
Interest	27.0	25.3	25.5	26.3	25.5	26.7	26.5	27.3	27.6
Corp. net savings	12.3	13.4	12.3	15.7	13.7	10.1	10.9	13.6	14.3
5b Manufactured gas									
Total ($000,000)	134	137	122	117	142	167	177	183	187
Wages & salaries	57.7	61.6	63.9	68.2	65.9	61.1	59.4	59.5	60.0
Dividends	31.4	27.0	21.0	19.0	23.5	28.9	28.4	26.2	24.9
Interest	10.9	11.5	15.2	12.9	10.6	9.9	12.2	14.3	15.1
Corp. net savings	—25.8	—16.9	—7.0	0.33	0.96	—10.2	42.3	14.6	18.5
5c Steam railroads, Pullman, and express									
Total ($000,000)	3,880	4,852	3,821	3,718	4,156	4,024	4,105	4,239	4,289
Wages	63.5	66.3	59.4	57.0	59.5	56.9	56.6	56.7	54.7
Salaries	17.4	17.8	21.4	22.5	20.9	21.6	21.4	21.1	21.0
Empl. comp.	82.1	85.6	82.1	80.8	81.9	80.1	79.7	79.6	77.5
Dividends	6.6	4.9	5.5	6.1	6.1	6.9	7.2	8.0	10.2
Interest	11.2	9.5	12.5	13.1	12.0	13.1	13.1	12.4	12.3
Corp. net savings	1.5	—0.13	—0.14	2.9	6.8	6.0	9.3	10.1	4.1
5d Street railways									
Total ($000,000)	516	607	583	608	622	620	605	595	576
Wages & salaries	71.4	76.4	75.3	71.3	70.6	71.2	71.7	72.8	72.9
Dividends	6.9	5.3	4.6	7.7	7.6	7.6	7.9	7.9	8.1
Interest	21.7	18.2	20.1	20.9	21.8	21.3	20.4	19.3	19.0
Corp. net savings	2.3	3.6	4.9	2.8	4.3	1.3	2.3	1.2	1.6

* Less than 0.005 per cent.

TABLE 76 (cont.)

Total Payments excluding Entrepreneurial Savings
Percentage Distribution by Type

1928	1929	1930	1931	1932	1933	1934	1935	1936	1937	1938
7,345	7,752	7,496	6,572	5,345	4,912	5,071	5,367	5,628	6,087	5,602
71.2	69.7	66.6	64.4	60.5	60.5	63.1	63.8	67.5	68.3	68.5
72.3	70.8	67.7	65.6	61.8	61.9	64.5	65.4	68.9	70.3	70.3
0.07	0.07	0.08	0.06	0.06	0.05	0.05	0.05	0.05	0.05	0.05
14.3	16.6	19.0	18.8	18.2	16.9	16.3	17.4	15.4	15.6	15.2
13.4	12.5	13.2	15.6	19.9	21.1	19.1	17.2	15.7	14.0	14.5
0.02	0.03	−0.02	−0.04	−0.04	−0.01	0.02	0.02	0.07	0.07	0.01
9.5	9.8	1.8	−3.1	−8.9	−3.9	−4.3	−4.1	3.8	2.0	−1.6
1,030	1,162	1,284	1,277	1,127	1,033	985	993	1,026	1,109	1,088
38.9	37.2	35.3	33.1	31.1	30.7	35.0	36.4	38.5	40.3	40.6
0.13	0.10	0.08	0.07	0.06	0.06	0.06	0.07	0.07	0.07	0.07
34.6	38.6	41.8	41.7	38.4	36.0	33.3	33.4	33.6	35.6	34.7
26.4	24.1	22.8	25.2	30.5	33.2	31.6	30.1	27.8	24.0	24.7
17.0	18.7	13.1	8.0	1.6	−0.40	1.1	4.9	8.3	7.2	5.0
182	205	213	210	222	201	189	194	188	194	193
59.1	49.2	46.3	40.0	33.3	37.6	42.4	41.9	45.3	46.5	46.7
21.3	32.4	31.8	36.7	39.4	30.2	29.0	33.0	29.9	30.6	30.6
19.7	18.3	21.8	23.4	27.3	32.2	28.6	25.1	24.7	22.9	22.7
6.9	−9.9	−12.7	−26.3	−28.3	−20.9	−19.8	−26.2	−15.1	−6.4	−9.9
4,123	4,250	3,883	3,175	2,332	2,171	2,324	2,445	2,667	2,883	2,477
54.9	54.9	51.4	49.9	48.1	48.8	50.1	51.9	55.1	55.1	54.6
21.6	21.1	22.0	23.6	24.2	23.1	22.6	23.0	22.0	21.8	24.5
78.3	77.7	75.3	75.6	74.8	74.6	75.3	77.7	79.6	80.6	82.5
8.9	10.3	11.4	8.1	3.3	3.5	5.4	5.2	5.5	5.7	3.4
12.8	12.0	13.4	16.3	21.9	21.9	19.2	17.0	14.9	13.7	14.2
8.7	9.5	−0.30	−6.3	−10.4	−2.3	−4.0	−1.4	5.4	1.5	−2.5
558	563	518	457	379	331	347	350	365	370	361
72.9	73.1	74.0	73.5	71.3	68.9	68.7	67.5	66.1	65.6	65.4
8.3	8.6	7.6	6.2	4.7	4.6	5.5	6.2	8.6	10.3	10.0
18.8	18.3	18.5	20.2	24.0	26.5	25.8	26.4	25.3	24.1	24.6
1.6	0.51	1.0	−3.2	−10.7	−8.6	−7.7	−7.4	−5.5	−6.8	−6.4

TABLE 76 (cont.)

Total Payments excluding Entrepreneurial Savings
Percentage Distribution by Type

	1919	1920	1921	1922	1923	1924	1925	1926	1927
5e Water transportation									
Total ($000,000)	559	747	562	484	495	520	505	526	503
Wages & salaries	88.7	94.2	94.3	93.3	93.3	95.0	94.2	93.9	93.9
Entrep. withdr.	1.4	0.73	0.68	0.92	0.91	0.61	0.72	0.72	0.71
Dividends	8.2	3.8	3.2	3.7	3.8	2.6	3.6	3.9	3.9
Interest	1.7	1.3	1.8	2.0	2.0	1.8	1.5	1.5	1.6
Entrep. net savings	1.5	0.73	—0.28	—0.10	0.01	0.12	0.21	0.25	0.03
Corp. net savings	3.9	2.5	—4.4	—2.9	—2.1	—0.94	0.12	0.68	—1.7
5f Pipe lines									
Total ($000,000)	58	65	67	94	82	79	111	97	130
Wages & salaries	46.0	52.2	47.7	35.9	46.1	42.8	33.9	42.7	37.8
Dividends	53.8	47.6	52.2	63.9	53.4	56.7	65.7	57.0	61.9
Interest	0.20	0.18	0.19	0.27	0.49	0.51	0.35	0.34	0.29
Corp. net savings	12.8	42.7	3.8	3.4	29.3	42.9	20.9	33.0	16.0
5g Telephone									
Total ($000,000)	311	388	410	442	493	537	573	607	641
Wages & salaries	76.0	79.7	78.5	78.7	78.1	77.7	75.8	76.0	75.4
Empl. comp.	77.0	80.8	79.5	79.8	79.1	78.6	76.7	76.9	76.4
Dividends	13.2	10.5	11.8	13.6	14.5	15.3	16.3	16.5	17.4
Interest	9.8	8.7	8.7	6.6	6.4	6.1	7.0	6.7	6.2
Corp. net savings	4.6	2.3	5.5	6.9	6.4	5.3	8.5	10.0	9.3
5h Telegraph									
Total ($000,000)	81	105	92	90	98	99	105	121	119
Wages & salaries	87.5	89.9	86.9	86.7	87.9	87.5	87.8	87.3	85.6
Empl. comp.	89.5	91.8	89.2	89.2	90.3	90.1	90.4	89.5	87.9
Dividends	12.5	9.6	10.7	10.9	9.5	9.5	9.0	9.7	10.7
Interest	—2.0	—1.5	0.10	—0.05	0.18	0.42	0.62	0.71	1.3
Corp. net savings	14.0	11.9	8.4	17.9	15.4	14.3	18.9	12.4	18.1
6 Trade									
Total ($000,000)	8,061	9,071	7,708	8,074	8,854	9,089	9,548	10,053	9,926
Wages & salaries	67.4	66.7	67.1	70.4	72.2	71.9	73.2	73.8	73.5
Entrep. withdr.	27.3	28.6	28.2	25.4	23.4	23.5	21.9	21.2	21.2
Dividends	5.0	4.2	4.2	3.7	4.2	4.3	4.6	4.7	5.0
Interest	0.41	0.46	0.52	0.49	0.25	0.34	0.32	0.24	0.31
Entrep. net savings	30.1	4.6	—5.9	7.2	9.5	5.4	5.7	3.7	2.9
Corp. net savings	7.7	0.09	—6.0	3.8	5.2	3.4	4.1	2.3	1.8

TABLE 76 (cont.)

Total Payments excluding Entrepreneurial Savings
Percentage Distribution by Type

1928	1929	1930	1931	1932	1933	1934	1935	1936	1937	1938
514	520	492	412	317	324	360	456	499	569	504
93.6	92.4	91.6	92.4	91.9	93.1	90.8	83.8	88.5	89.7	90.4
0.74	0.88	0.94	0.80	0.73	0.57	0.55	0.49	0.46	0.43	0.43
4.3	5.5	6.1	4.8	3.9	2.5	4.9	12.4	8.0	7.2	6.0
1.3	1.2	1.3	2.0	3.5	3.8	3.7	3.3	3.0	2.7	3.2
0.24	0.39	−0.36	−0.62	−0.74	−0.12	0.25	0.17	0.75	0.79	0.09
0.72	2.5	−4.6	−8.14	−10.8	−5.4	−5.4	−12.9	−2.8	−1.7	−4.0
136	163	186	175	190	144	129	186	123	133	134
35.4	30.7	23.5	22.6	16.1	21.0	27.3	20.2	33.6	36.6	34.4
64.2	69.0	76.3	76.2	82.4	76.4	70.5	77.8	63.7	61.4	64.1
0.38	0.30	0.19	1.2	1.5	2.6	2.2	2.0	2.7	2.0	1.4
28.9	25.3	−5.3	−2.8	−29.4	3.3	0.16	−32.3	16.7	21.8	0.78
678	747	773	746	692	634	652	654	668	728	754
76.7	78.3	76.6	71.2	65.5	61.6	62.5	64.0	67.7	70.3	69.6
77.8	79.4	77.6	72.5	66.7	63.0	64.0	65.7	69.4	72.1	71.4
17.2	16.5	19.0	23.6	27.1	29.7	28.8	27.8	25.1	22.7	23.5
5.1	4.2	3.4	3.9	6.1	7.3	7.2	6.5	5.6	5.2	5.1
11.6	12.4	6.5	2.1	−6.7	−8.8	−7.7	−5.3	3.1	2.3	−1.9
123	143	147	121	86	74	85	89	91	101	90
85.5	81.8	80.6	85.8	88.2	90.1	90.7	86.2	90.9	89.9	92.4
87.7	83.9	82.8	88.7	91.8	93.9	94.0	89.5	94.3	93.1	96.0
10.8	14.6	15.0	8.3	3.6	0.44	0.62	4.9	0.29	2.2	−0.94
1.5	1.5	2.2	3.0	4.5	5.7	5.4	5.6	5.4	4.7	4.9
17.7	4.2	−14.1	−9.2	−13.9	2.6	−1.4	−3.0	4.9	−2.2	−6.4
10,191	10,865	10,419	9,241	7,359	6,537	7,460	7,795	8,470	9,155	8,857
73.8	73.7	73.4	71.9	69.8	69.0	71.0	70.6	69.1	70.5	70.7
20.9	20.5	21.2	23.2	26.5	27.5	24.4	23.4	22.7	22.4	23.5
4.9	5.2	4.8	4.2	2.9	2.7	4.1	5.6	7.9	6.8	5.4
0.42	0.51	0.66	0.72	0.82	0.75	0.56	0.41	0.36	0.34	0.35
3.6	1.6	−5.3	−9.2	−11.8	−2.2	−0.31	−0.03	0.97	0.48	0.39
2.7	0.63	−6.1	−10.7	−14.1	−4.1	−1.1	−0.91	0.14	−0.46	−0.33

TABLE 76 (cont.)

Total Payments excluding Entrepreneurial Savings
Percentage Distribution by Type

	1919	1920	1921	1922	1923	1924	1925	1926	1927
7 Finance									
Total ($000,000)	6,618	7,376	7,690	8,233	8,808	9,525	9,658	9,676	10,005
Wages & salaries	20.8	22.4	22.5	21.2	20.6	20.7	21.0	23.2	24.3
Entrep. withdr.	1.8	2.0	1.9	1.8	2.0	2.0	2.2	2.3	2.3
Dividends	5.1	5.5	5.3	5.7	6.0	5.3	5.7	5.7	5.4
Interest	12.3	12.0	12.2	11.8	12.7	12.8	14.5	15.7	17.1
Rent	59.9	58.1	58.1	59.5	58.6	59.1	56.6	53.1	50.8
Corp. net savings	4.3	1.3	—0.10	0.31	—0.16	0.79	0.85	1.4	3.1
7a Banking									
Total ($000,000)	658	770	821	843	871	906	947	996	1,056
Wages & salaries	58.1	61.3	62.0	61.1	62.7	64.0	63.8	64.3	63.8
Dividends	41.9	38.7	38.0	38.9	37.3	36.0	36.2	35.7	36.2
Corp. net savings	31.9	24.4	12.3	9.5	11.4	14.3	19.5	18.5	21.4
7b Insurance									
Total ($000,000)	662	792	830	878	882	974	1,082	1,174	1,258
Wages & salaries	80.9	81.0	82.1	80.3	78.2	79.3	79.0	79.0	78.9
Entrep. withdr.	18.4	18.6	17.4	16.9	19.6	19.5	19.6	19.3	18.6
Dividends	2.8	2.4	2.8	5.1	4.5	3.4	3.6	3.7	4.3
Interest	—2.0	—2.1	—2.3	—2.2	—2.2	—2.2	—2.1	—1.9	—1.9
Corp. net savings	6.7	—8.2	—10.6	—10.7	—11.9	—11.2	—4.7	—3.9	2.3
7c Real estate									
Total ($000,000)	5,298	5,814	6,039	6,512	7,055	7,645	7,628	7,506	7,691
Wages & salaries	8.7	9.2	8.9	8.1	8.2	8.1	7.5	9.0	10.0
Dividends	0.76	1.5	1.2	1.5	2.4	1.9	2.3	2.0	1.4
Interest	15.6	15.5	15.8	15.2	16.2	16.3	18.6	20.5	22.6
Rent	74.9	73.7	74.0	75.2	73.2	73.7	71.7	68.5	66.0
Corp. net savings	0.51	—0.46	—0.34	0.61	—0.12	0.71	—0.68	0.02	0.66
8 Service									
Total ($000,000)	5,001	6,021	5,969	6,974	7,419	8,034	8,667	9,059	9,721
Wages & salaries	65.1	67.6	70.4	64.5	66.4	65.2	63.7	65.2	65.3
Entrep. withdr.	34.0	30.8	28.2	34.5	32.3	33.5	34.8	33.1	32.9
Dividends	0.58	1.3	1.1	0.70	0.92	0.89	1.1	1.2	1.1
Interest	0.32	0.25	0.30	0.33	0.38	0.41	0.47	0.53	0.64
Entrep. net savings	21.6	13.7	11.9	5.5	10.8	7.1	6.7	11.4	6.2
Corp. net savings	0.98	0.09	—0.42	0.37	0.58	0.55	0.64	0.26	—0.07

TABLE 76 (cont.)

Total Payments excluding Entrepreneurial Savings
Percentage Distribution by Type

1928	1929	1930	1931	1932	1933	1934	1935	1936	1937	1938
10,466	11,064	10,150	8,534	6,653	5,791	5,694	6,067	6,152	6,675	6,660
25.2	25.8	26.1	28.0	29.6	30.1	32.6	32.2	32.8	31.8	32.3
2.3	2.4	2.5	2.7	2.9	3.1	3.4	3.3	3.3	3.4	3.3
6.3	6.9	6.5	7.0	5.6	3.5	4.6	4.6	4.4	4.3	4.4
18.9	20.5	22.8	26.9	30.5	26.8	26.0	24.6	24.0	22.0	21.4
47.2	44.4	42.0	35.5	31.4	36.5	33.5	35.3	35.5	38.6	38.7
3.9	0.64	−3.8	−11.1	−17.4	−16.5	−11.6	−5.5	−0.64	−0.36	−1.6
1,142	1,188	1,162	1,051	836	636	683	688	712	741	748
61.6	61.6	61.3	60.9	66.5	75.2	72.5	72.7	72.8	72.9	73.8
38.4	38.4	38.7	39.1	33.5	24.8	27.5	27.3	27.2	27.1	26.2
22.7	17.0	−2.0	−30.1	−50.3	−54.4	−28.2	3.0	23.9	18.1	8.9
1,348	1,428	1,425	1,331	1,121	1,008	1,065	1,129	1,145	1,233	1,251
78.7	79.2	79.7	79.8	81.6	82.9	82.3	81.2	82.9	82.5	82.0
18.2	18.2	17.7	17.2	17.5	17.5	17.9	17.8	17.6	18.3	17.3
4.9	4.9	4.3	4.6	2.8	1.6	2.1	4.4	1.9	1.7	3.1
−1.8	−2.2	−1.7	−1.6	−1.9	−2.1	−2.3	−3.4	−2.4	−2.5	−2.5
6.5	3.9	−6.9	−12.8	−16.4	−14.2	−2.2	−2.1	0.03	3.2	1.9
7,976	8,449	7,563	6,152	4,696	4,147	3,946	4,250	4,296	4,701	4,661
11.0	11.8	10.6	11.1	10.6	10.3	12.3	12.6	12.8	12.0	12.3
2.0	2.8	2.0	2.0	1.3	0.72	1.3	1.2	1.3	1.4	1.2
25.1	27.2	31.0	37.7	43.6	37.9	38.1	35.8	35.0	31.8	31.3
62.0	58.2	56.4	49.2	44.5	51.0	48.3	50.4	50.9	54.9	55.3
0.72	−2.2	−3.5	−7.4	−11.8	−11.3	−11.2	−7.8	−4.9	−4.2	−4.2
10,036	10,756	10,108	9,037	7,811	7,142	7,319	7,771	8,392	9,349	8,824
64.1	64.1	63.2	61.7	56.5	54.9	60.1	61.7	63.2	63.3	63.6
34.2	34.0	34.7	36.5	41.4	43.3	38.1	36.3	34.2	34.4	34.6
0.99	1.1	1.1	0.82	0.70	0.48	0.63	0.70	1.3	1.3	0.78
0.73	0.81	0.98	1.0	1.4	1.3	1.2	1.3	1.2	1.0	1.1
6.4	4.8	3.8	−1.1	−12.0	−14.2	−4.5	−2.5	1.3	−0.53	2.5
0.07	0.14	−0.79	−2.3	−6.1	−5.0	−3.3	−2.7	−2.4	−1.8	−1.9

TABLE 76 (concl.)

Total Payments excluding Entrepreneurial Savings
Percentage Distribution by Type

	1919	1920	1921	1922	1923	1924	1925	1926	1927
9 Government									
Total ($000,000)	5,071	5,124	5,248	5,282	5,431	5,561	5,751	5,963	6,191
Wages & salaries	71.9	66.1	65.4	64.6	65.4	67.1	68.5	69.6	70.7
Empl. comp.	79.4	75.7	75.9	74.9	75.5	77.0	77.7	78.5	79.7
Interest	20.6	24.3	24.1	25.1	24.5	23.0	22.3	21.5	20.3
Net savings	—25.7	37.0	18.3	16.2	29.7	30.9	28.1	36.1	37.0
9a Federal government									
Total ($000,000)	3,210	2,948	2,755	2,608	2,571	2,491	2,515	2,548	2,540
Wages & salaries	64.4	51.9	47.9	43.6	44.5	47.2	49.2	50.4	51.3
Empl. comp.	74.4	65.7	63.9	60.7	61.1	63.4	65.8	68.1	70.0
Interest	25.6	34.3	36.1	39.3	38.9	36.6	34.2	31.9	30.0
9b State government									
Total ($000,000)	182	225	263	264	289	328	315	281	306
Wages & salaries	85.4	79.8	73.5	74.1	71.1	68.2	78.3	84.5	86.0
Empl. comp.	103.2	103.7	102.6	100.1	98.6	97.4	95.5	94.5	94.9
Interest	—3.2	—3.7	—2.6	—0.12	1.4	2.6	4.5	5.5	5.1
9c County government									
Total ($000,000)	189	220	261	280	301	330	349	366	378
Wages & salaries	79.0	80.2	80.2	79.6	76.9	74.9	71.0	70.7	74.3
Empl. comp.	80.0	81.5	81.8	80.9	78.3	76.4	72.1	71.4	75.0
Interest	20.0	18.5	18.2	19.1	21.7	23.6	27.9	28.6	25.0
9d City government including public education									
Total ($000,000)	1,490	1,730	1,969	2,130	2,270	2,412	2,573	2,767	2,967
Wages & salaries	85.6	86.7	86.8	87.1	86.7	86.5	85.9	85.5	85.3
Empl. comp.	87.2	88.3	88.4	88.3	88.4	88.4	87.8	87.4	87.1
Interest	12.8	11.7	11.6	11.7	11.6	11.6	12.2	12.6	12.9
10 Miscellaneous									
Total ($000,000)	1,901	2,143	1,999	2,198	2,520	2,657	2,884	3,019	3,158
Wages & salaries	72.0	71.4	69.3	69.0	71.1	69.3	68.8	71.2	69.5
Entrep. withdr.	13.6	14.4	14.1	15.2	13.5	14.1	14.2	13.7	13.8
Dividends	5.4	5.9	7.2	7.4	7.6	8.5	9.2	7.6	9.0
Interest	8.9	8.3	9.4	8.4	7.8	8.0	7.7	7.5	7.8
Entrep. net savings	8.3	5.9	5.1	1.1	3.5	2.0	1.8	3.7	1.6
Corp. net savings	9.8	3.3	—7.3	3.6	4.5	2.7	4.7	3.9	1.6

TABLE 76 (concl.)

Total Payments excluding Entrepreneurial Savings
Percentage Distribution by Type

1928	1929	1930	1931	1932	1933	1934	1935	1936	1937	1938
6,393	6,649	6,816	7,066	7,081	7,617	8,763	9,240	10,412	10,227	10,991
71.6	71.8	72.0	70.6	67.9	57.3	51.4	53.0	51.2	54.7	53.3
80.6	81.0	81.4	81.9	80.7	80.8	82.1	83.9	85.2	83.6	84.6
19.4	19.0	18.6	18.1	19.3	19.2	17.9	16.1	14.8	16.4	15.4
29.7	33.5	30.9	4.9	−12.8	−1.5	−6.6	−18.8	−21.1	4.9	−1.6
2,535	2,580	2,586	2,741	2,780	3,597	4,788	5,152	6,079	5,588	6,096
53.0	54.1	55.1	52.6	48.8	33.9	29.6	32.6	31.1	34.1	31.7
72.1	74.0	75.9	77.5	76.8	79.8	82.6	84.8	86.6	83.6	84.6
27.9	26.0	24.1	22.5	23.2	20.2	17.4	15.2	13.4	16.4	15.4
329	345	371	403	417	418	441	478	514	568	601
85.8	85.9	85.0	83.6	81.4	79.0	78.5	79.8	81.3	82.8	83.6
94.3	94.0	92.9	90.9	88.7	86.3	86.0	87.8	89.3	90.9	92.0
5.7	6.0	7.1	9.1	11.3	13.7	14.0	12.2	10.7	9.1	8.0
408	455	466	468	465	433	434	444	457	475	491
74.5	71.6	73.2	76.6	75.3	73.4	74.1	75.8	78.0	80.3	82.2
75.2	72.3	74.0	77.5	76.3	74.2	75.0	76.7	78.9	81.3	83.3
24.8	27.7	26.0	22.5	23.7	25.8	25.0	23.3	21.1	18.7	16.7
3,122	3,269	3,393	3,454	3,419	3,169	3,100	3,166	3,362	3,596	3,803
84.8	84.4	83.2	82.5	80.8	78.8	78.1	79.1	79.3	78.9	79.5
86.8	86.4	85.4	85.0	83.6	82.1	81.8	82.8	83.0	82.7	83.7
13.2	13.6	14.6	15.0	16.4	17.9	18.2	17.2	17.0	17.3	16.3
3,332	3,553	3,327	3,017	2,574	2,427	2,537	2,863	3,124	3,368	3,189
67.7	67.8	67.9	68.3	67.3	69.4	72.6	71.8	74.0	75.7	75.7
13.9	14.1	14.3	14.6	16.7	16.9	15.9	15.3	15.6	16.3	17.3
10.2	10.8	10.1	9.0	6.9	4.9	4.8	9.1	7.0	4.9	3.9
8.2	7.3	7.7	8.2	9.2	8.7	6.7	3.7	3.3	3.1	3.1
1.4	0.83	0.24	−1.0	−4.0	−3.8	−1.4	−0.93	−0.29	−0.58	−0.18
8.3	8.0	−22.2	−37.5	−39.6	−37.1	−15.5	−7.2	−3.3	−5.0	−5.3

PART THREE

Characteristics of the Estimates

CHAPTER 8

Classification by Industrial Source and Type of Income

1 Industrial

A GENERAL CHARACTERISTICS

THE general characteristics of the industrial classification followed in our estimates may be presented conveniently in tabular form. For most of the period covered, 1919–38, we allocated the several types of income from most industrial groups to the major divisions listed in the second column of the summary. A few income types we allocated to more detailed industrial divisions, which are also summarized.

The classification reflects the compromise we had to make between what would be desirable for analytical purposes and what was possible with the data at our disposal. On the one hand, some industrial groups we now treat as units —agriculture, construction, wholesale trade, retail trade— should but cannot be further subdivided, owing to absence of data for a sufficiently long period and often even for a single year. On the other hand, we refrained from presenting all the detail available for some industries; for example, we estimate but do not present separately income originating in the Pullman Company and railway express. Both are closely related to steam railroads and income from them is small compared with that from some broader categories that could not be subdivided.

The miscellaneous group is vastly different from the others

in that it is a hodge-podge of industries as diverse as taxicabs and brokerage, aviation and fisheries, autobus transportation and finance companies. The one feature characterizing all is the impossibility, because of lack of data, of making tolerably good estimates of income originating in each, either separately or as part of the wider industrial group to which it properly belongs. Consequently in contrast to the other groups and divisions, which have a positive meaning in the classification, the miscellaneous group has a negative meaning: it is the part of national income that cannot be properly allocated by industrial source.

INDUSTRIAL GROUP	MAJOR DIVISION	NOTES ON COVERAGE
Agriculture	None	Excl. agriculture not on farms. The Census defines a farm as any tract of land of 3 or more acres; & incl. under 'farms' those with less acreage if agricultural products in the year covered were valued at $250 or more (1925, 1930, 1935); or if the continuous service of at least one person was required for agricultural operations.
Mining	Anthracite coal Bituminous coal Oil & gas Metal Other minerals	Incl. sand & stone, oil & gas throughout. The Census excl. bituminous coal mines with an output of less than 1,000 tons; production of sand & gravel by enterprises whose output was less than 25,000 tons; production of other mining & quarrying enterprises whose output was valued at less than $500 (1919) & $2,500 (1929), or, if not producing, whose development work cost less than $5,000 (1919) & $2,500 (1929); mining of placer gold & hunting for precious stones by itinerant individuals & miners employing no help; production of stone, sand, & gravel by rr. & public utility plants for their own consumption; production by governmental enterprises of all minerals except coal.
Manufacturing	Food & tobacco Textile & leather Construction materials & furniture Paper Printing Metal & metal products Chemical Misc. & rubber	Excl. automobile repairing (1919), mfd. gas, motion picture production, rr. repair shops; incl. ship building. With a few exceptions the Census incl. establishments reporting products valued at $5,000 or more. In the 1919 Census, however, data were obtained from all establishments reporting products valued at $500 or more.
Construction	None	Contract construction alone. Excl. construction on force account. The Census has no size limitations but is admittedly incomplete.

INDUSTRIAL GROUP	MAJOR DIVISION	NOTES ON COVERAGE
Transportation & other public utilities	Electric light & power & mfd. gas Steam rr., Pullman, & rwy. express Other transp. (water transp., street rwy., pipe lines) Communication (telephone, telegraph)	Excl. minor public utilities, such as air transportation, autobus lines, taxicabs, cartage & storage, radio broadcasting, water companies. There are no coverage limitations except for water transportation, from which the Census excl. all vessels & craft of less than 5 tons net register; yachts of 15 gross tons and under; stationary wharf boats, scows, or craft used for storage purposes; house boats, without propelling machinery; craft operating exclusively in the waters of the Philippine Islands, or between those islands and foreign ports; non-commercial vessels owned by the federal government; American owned vessels under foreign registry.
Trade	Wholesale Retail	Excl. itinerant hucksters & peddlers; stands in hotels; restaurants. The Census has no coverage limitations but is admittedly incomplete, specifically for milk dealers & other dispersed transient & minor retail units.
Finance	Banking Insurance Real estate	Excl. stock & bond brokers; loan & finance companies; investment banks & trusts, etc. Incl., under real estate, rents received by individuals from all real property owned by them as well as imputed rent on owner-occupied houses.
Service	Professional Personal Domestic Misc.	Incl. restaurants & motion picture production. Excl. all service pursuits attached to other industries. The Census has no coverage limitations but is admittedly incomplete.
Government	Federal State County City Public education	
Misc.	None	Incl. the various industries indicated specifically above as omitted and not incl. elsewhere; the fractions of industries measured separately but not incl. because of coverage limitations; in short, the residue that cannot be allocated by industrial source.

The classification is applicable in varying detail to the different types of income. Only for estimates of employee compensation can we give several minor and some major industrial divisions. In the groups in which wages can be measured separately from salaries, e.g., manufacturing, it is the former that can be divided into the minor categories; salaries must be combined into broader groups. In some groups, such as government, finance, service, and trade throughout the period, and mining during the later part of the period, wages and salaries combined are given by minor industrial divisions. On the other hand, for entrepreneurial income and especially for property income and business net savings the allocation by industrial source cannot be as detailed.

INDUSTRIAL GROUP & MAJOR DIVISION	MINOR INDUSTRIAL DIVISION						
	(1)	(2)	(3)	(4)	(5)	(6)	(7)
Manufacturing							
Food & tobacco	Food	Tobacco					
Textile & leather	Wearing apparel	Textile fabrics	Other leather goods				
Wearing apparel	Boots & shoes, other than rubber	Boots & shoes, rubber	Hosiery & knit goods	Men's clothing	Women's clothing	Millinery	Other wearing apparel
Textile fabrics	Woolen goods	Cotton goods	Silk & rayon	Dyeing & finishing	Other textile fabrics		
Construction materials & furniture	Lumber	Stone, clay, glass	Heating apparatus	Other construction materials	Furniture		
Metal	Iron & steel	Non-ferrous metals	Motor vehicles	Machinery			
Machinery	Machinery proper	Ship building	Other transp. equipment, excl. motor vehicles	Hardware			
Chemical	Petroleum refining	Other chemicals					
Misc. & rubber	Rubber, excl. boots & shoes	Misc.					

INDUSTRIAL GROUP & MAJOR DIVISION	MINOR INDUSTRIAL DIVISION						
	(1)	(2)	(3)	(4)	(5)	(6)	(7)
Transportation & other public utilities							
Elec. light & power, & mfd. gas	Elec. light & power	Mfd. gas					
Other transp.	Street rwy.	Water transp.	Pipe lines				
Communication	Telephone	Telegraph					
Finance							
Banking	Commercial, incl. stock savings	Mutual savings	Federal Reserve	Insolvent			
Insurance	Life	Other than life	Agencies				
Service							
Professional	Private education	Religious	Curative	Other			
Personal	Hotels	Restaurants	Power laundries, & clean. & dye.	Other			
Government							
Federal	Legislative	Judicial	Executive	Military			

B PROPERTY INCOME AND BUSINESS SAVINGS

Since industries are differentiated chiefly by the characteristics of the transforming operations that constitute their productive function and of goods in which these operations result, it is natural to assume that income originating in a given industry represents the value (at market prices) of the services of labor, capital, and enterprise devoted to a specific series of operations performed on a given, well defined category of goods. Thus, it is assumed that income originating in

manufacturing represents the net market value of the services
of the various production factors consumed in transforming
raw materials into movable fabricated commodities.

This interpretation is largely correct but is subject to some
qualifications. Even of total wages, some fraction represents
payment for participation in auxiliary rather than primary
functions of the industry; e.g., all commodity producing industries and public utilities engage in construction activity
with their own forces, some on a considerable scale. In many
industries the maintenance of plants and buildings often de-
velops into substantial real estate management. In some ostensibly purely service branches, such as trade, auxiliary manufacturing operations are carried on. Consequently, wages
paid out in any single branch, as well as salaries, wages and
salaries combined, and entrepreneurial withdrawals even to
a greater extent than wages, represent payments for a mixture
of operations, of which only the preponderant part is peculiar
to the given branch.

A second and much more important source of 'impurity'
affects the classification of dividends, interest, corporate net
savings and, in less degree, net income of unincorporated
firms. A single corporation (and, to a less extent, an unincorporated firm) may comprise under one proprietorship and
management unit establishments that engage in different production operations and belong to different industrial divisions. In such cases property income and net savings originating in a given corporation (or unincorporated firm) include
payments for services of production factors engaged in several industrial divisions and cannot be allocated.

This difficulty was discussed in Chapter 3, Section 2 A and
is recalled here only to indicate its effect upon our estimates.
For all except three industrial groups—agriculture, transportation and other public utilities, and government—our
data on dividends, interest, and corporate savings (and, indirectly, savings of unincorporated firms) come from *Statistics
of Income*, i.e., from returns filed by corporations for income

tax purposes. During 1919–33, the greater part of the period under consideration, the income tax law permitted consolidated returns, i.e., a single return for a corporation and the various subsidiaries which, while separate legal entities, were under its financial control. The Bureau of Internal Revenue entered each return under the industrial division from which the major part of the gross and net income of the consolidated group of corporations was derived during the given year.

Consequently during most of the period covered by our estimates the industrial classification of property income and business net savings is subject to two qualifications. First, the practice of filing consolidated returns increased considerably the mixture of industrial affiliations occasioned by the fact that even a single corporation can comprise producing establishments belonging to more than one industrial division. Some corporations availed themselves of the privilege of filing consolidated returns: there were 6,462 such returns in 1933 and 418,602 non-consolidated returns. But the former naturally accounted for a greater proportion of gross income than of the number of returns: $24.5 billion, out of a total gross income of all corporations of $73.6 billion.[1] Second, the degree and character of the mixture of industrial affiliation in the data on property income and business net savings must have changed from year to year, partly because of the practice of classifying each return by the industrial source of the major share of income *during any given year,* partly because of changing extent and direction of consolidation within single corporate units, and partly because of changing extent and direction of consolidation represented by consolidated returns.

Since 1934 the law has required a separate return for each corporation and expressly forbade the filing of consolidated returns (except by railroads). This eliminated only one source of the mixture of industrial affiliations in the reporting of property income and business savings. The other source, the

[1] The number and amounts are for all corporations excluding public utilities.

combination of establishments pursuing different industrial activities under the aégis of a single corporation,
still remains, and has perhaps been intensified by the change
in the law, since the advantages, for purposes of taxation, of
filing a single return may have forced into a single corporation several that were formerly legally independent.

The 'unconsolidation' of consolidated returns increased the
reported value of certain income items, such as gross dividend
and interest payments; as well as the reported value of certain offsetting items, such as dividends received. Were the
Bureau of Internal Revenue the sole source of our data on
corporate incomes and income payments, the grand totals for
1934 on consolidated and non-consolidated bases would be
identical, so far as they refer to *net* income originating or to
net business savings. But since the data for transportation and
other public utilities are based on Interstate Commerce Commission records, which are more satisfactory, even the grand
totals for 1934 on the two bases differ somewhat. On a non-
consolidated basis, they are somewhat larger for dividends and
corporate net savings and somewhat smaller for interest.

In the industrial classification of these totals a more important difficulty inheres. The Bureau of Internal Revenue classified the returns for 1934 of corporations that filed consolidated returns in 1933 according to business: (a) reported on
a non-consolidated basis in 1934, the basis that prevails for
years since 1934; (b) reported on a consolidated basis in 1933.
Shifting from a consolidated to a non-consolidated basis increased substantially amounts under construction, trade, service, and finance, and reduced amounts under mining, manufacturing, and transportation and other public utilities. On the
basis of the two classifications we prepared two sets of estimates
of dividends, interest, corporate net savings, and entrepreneurial net income and savings: one, using classification (a)
above, the non-consolidated classification of 1934 comparable
with the estimates for the years since 1934; the other, using

classification (b) above, of 1934 returns on the 1933 basis comparable with the estimates for the years prior to 1934.

This double set of estimates for 1934, which appears in our tables for dividends, interest, net savings, and all the totals that include these items for all industrial divisions except agriculture, public utilities reporting to the Interstate Commerce Commission, finance, and government, provides the sole connecting link between two somewhat different industrial allocations of national income: one for the years before 1934, the other for the years after 1934. No other way of obviating the difficulties raised by the non-comparability of the industrial allocation seems possible with the available data. It is impracticable to assume that the absolute and relative discrepancies between the 1934 estimates for the industrial divisions with the same name would be characteristic of other years, and accordingly extrapolate either discrepancy to the years prior or subsequent to 1934. On the contrary, it is much more likely that the difference caused by the shift from a consolidated to a non-consolidated basis would vary from year to year with the state of business conditions and the progress of the consolidation movement. These differences could be ascertained only by an intensive study of Bureau of Internal Revenue files for years other than 1934. However, the differences for 1934 are not strikingly large, and in most industrial divisions are minor.[2] The notable exceptions are in the miscellaneous division, which is of little importance in the industrial classification.

C NUMBER EMPLOYED AND ENGAGED

The allocation of the number employed and engaged naturally reflects the peculiarities of the allocation of wages and salaries and of entrepreneurial income, since the same industrial divisions are used. But in addition, our estimates of the number employed and engaged have peculiarities of their own. First and foremost, they are in terms of theoretical units,

[2] *Statistics of Income* for 1934, Part 2, pp. 19-29.

not *persons*. The number employed in a given industry is not the number of individuals who, during the year, received wages and salaries from enterprises belonging to it. The figures represent theoretical, fully employed units, i.e., the number of persons that would have been employed if each employee worked full-time during the year, no more and no less; if there were no changes in personnel; and if each employee held only one job. The number of entrepreneurs in our estimate is a somewhat closer approximation to the actual number of persons involved, but even here a person included in a given industry may possibly be partly covered as a fraction of a full-time employed unit in another industry. A rigorous classification of persons among the industries in which they are engaged would encounter the difficulties of how to treat those who held jobs in more than one industry and how to combine those engaged on a full-time basis with those engaged only part-time. Our apportionment avoids these difficulties by using equivalent full-time units, a concept that is a direct derivative of and corollary to that of the income flow.

Second, we present no estimates of the number of persons receiving property income corresponding to the flow of property income. It is impossible to estimate the number of persons who depend entirely upon receipts of property income or the total number of property income recipients. Either total would be of doubtful value compared with that of the number of theoretical full-time units in receipt of service income.

D GENERAL QUALIFICATIONS

Before concluding the discussion of the industrial classification, we may summarize, at the risk of tiresome repetition, some of the major qualifications upon the significance of our allocation by industrial source.

i) Strictly, income originating is allocated neither among distinct types of productive function nor among activities concerned with distinct types of economic goods. Any single income flow represents compensation for activities of which that peculiar to the industrial division to which it is traced back is only the preponderant part, not the whole. Thus not all wages paid in manufacturing are for purely *manufacturing* functions; nor is all property income originating in manufacturing the compensation of capital employed only in manufacturing uses.

ii) This mixture of industrial activities and affiliations is most heterogeneous for property income and net savings of both incorporated and unincorporated firms. For these income types the institutional categories of the classification do not coincide with the analytical categories by type of productive function; also, incomes are reported for establishments that may belong to several, institutionally different, industrial divisions.

iii) Income payments originating in an industry should not be identified with the amounts actually disbursed by the enterprises classified under it. For wages and salaries the differences (e.g., gratuities, deductions for social security) are not likely to be large. For dividends and interest the estimates are of net amounts originating, not totals disbursed directly to individuals.[3]

iv) Income payments should not be confused with the total income receipts of people attached to a given industry, not only for the reasons indicated under (iii) but also because people attached to any given industry may derive income from other sources. For example, income originating in agriculture is not the sole income of farmers, nor do farmers receive the entire amount; and wages paid in mining may not be the sole income of mine workers.

v) The number employed or engaged, estimated for a given industrial division, should not be identified with the number of *persons* who drew wages, salaries, or entrepreneurial income from it. The figures represent theoretical units of fully

[3] For further discussion of this point, see Sec. 2 C.

employed or engaged, and are bound to be smaller than the number of persons.

vi) The varying adequacy of data affects the trustworthiness of the industrial classification in numerous respects. In some cases estimates of changes over time have to be based on data not for the industry in question but for other industries. Relative changes in the totals for divisions for which specific data are lacking (e.g., some divisions under service, and practically all miscellaneous) are therefore subject to wide margins of error, which, of course, affect the percentage allocation of national income among the industrial branches as well.

2 *By Type of Income*

A GENERAL CHARACTERISTICS

The types of income differentiated in our estimates for most industries are outlined herewith. Their characteristics, as reflected in our estimates, are commented on in detail below. A few general observations are made here.

I *Income Payments*

  A *Service Income*
    1 Wages, including: (a) gratuities, (b) compensation in kind
    2 Salaries, including: (a) compensation in kind, (b) commissions
    3 Other compensation of employees, including: (a) pensions, (b) compensation for injury, (c) relief
    4 Entrepreneurial withdrawals

  B *Property Income*
    1 Dividends
    2 Interest
    3 Rent

II *Undistributed Income*
    1 Net savings of corporations and of government
    2 Net savings of entrepreneurs (this item combined with A-4 yields net income of entrepreneurs)

Like the allocation by industrial source, that by type of income represents merely what is practicable with the present data, not all that is desirable from the viewpoint of analysis and evaluation. It would have been desirable to estimate separately wages of skilled and unskilled workers; and the compensation of those salaried employees who, owing to their position in the corporation, are virtually independent entrepreneurs separately from the compensation of purely subordinate salaried employees. It would have been of interest to segregate withdrawals by and the net income of entrepreneurs into parts that correspond to compensation for their services and to returns on their property investment. There might have been some value in separating dividends on preferred and common stock, especially when voting privileges are attached to the latter alone; or various categories of interest according to the character of the underlying debt. But with the available data such distinctions cannot be made for enough industries or years to warrant allowance for them in the general classification by type of income.[4]

Especially to be noted is the treatment of rents and royalties. Royalties are an exceedingly minor item and cannot be estimated by years.[5] But net rents over the period were about as large as dividends and slightly less than interest. Unfortunately it is not possible to estimate net rent originating in each industrial branch. We might treat rent as a return for entrepreneurial activity in the real estate industry or as property income arising in the several industrial divisions. Because of lack of data, however, we are forced to assign all rent, even as property income, to the real estate industry. Were it possible to apportion rent by industrial source, national income would be somewhat differently allocated by industries than it is in the tables in Part Four. The share of the real estate industry

[4] Data on the compensation of corporation officers and on salaries of executive employees in selected industries make possible some breakdown of total salaries (or of salaries and wages combined). The series are presented in Part Five, Table I.
[5] See their tentative evaluation in Ch. 9.

would naturally be smaller, since it would be confined to residential properties; and the relative shares of industries in which the practice of renting is extensive, such as agriculture, would be larger.

Finally, as already indicated, the classification by type of income is applicable in varying detail to the different industries. In general, more data are available for the commodity producing industries and the established public utilities. For the former, separation of wages from salaries is practicable because of the clear distinction between the actual production process and the auxiliary and managerial functions; and the basic data make it possible also to segregate unincorporated firms. From the relatively plentiful data for the long established public utilities the various types of income can be estimated separately. In other industries the difficulties of differentiating among types of income and the relative scarcity of relevant data forced us to combine related types and use fewer categories.

B SERVICE INCOME

The industrial classification can be carried through with most detail for wages and salaries since data are relatively plentiful, especially when the two types of payment are combined. But our estimates even of wages and salaries are incomplete. They should include not only regular wages and salaries but also bonuses, commissions, compensation in kind, expense accounts, gratuities, discounts of various types, etc. Bonuses and commissions are included, so far as they are reported in basic sources; gratuities are estimated whenever they seem to be an important source of income; compensation in kind for industries in which it is common (agriculture, water transportation, restaurants, hotels, domestic service, military service, etc.) is also measured, although as in the case of gratuities, the estimates are necessarily rough. It may be assumed that the items omitted would add up to a sum small in comparison with the large total of wages and salaries recorded in our estimates, although it is improbable that the available data cover exhaustively the numerous forms in which compensation flows from enterprises to employees.

Our estimates of other compensation of employees probably omit a large proportion of the amounts disbursed in this form. However, since the items are small and any estimates that could be computed for them would necessarily be crude, we considered it inadvisable to go beyond the few industries for which the essential data were readily available. Our estimates therefore cover pensions and compensation for injury paid out in merely a few industries, but the omitted totals are insignificant compared with *total* employee compensation recorded.

The estimates of entrepreneurial withdrawals are subject to an entirely different and a much more serious qualification. What we want to ascertain are the amounts individual entrepreneurs withdraw, in the form of either money or goods, to be used for living expenses or any other purpose that cannot be interpreted as an expense of carrying on the business. But such withdrawals are not reported on any scale, comprehensive or narrow; their exact size is known to merely a small fraction of the entrepreneurs themselves; and their measurement would, in a large majority of firms, require considerable intensive analysis In this quandary, our sole recourse is to bold assumptions; and the results are exceedingly crude. The assumptions are described in detail in the comments on sources and methods in Part Four. Here we need merely state that the estimates are subject to a larger relative error than any other group in the total, except possibly net savings of enterprises.

Finally, no sharp line should be drawn between employee compensation and entrepreneurial withdrawals, because frequently one who may appear to be an entrepreneur is really an employee. The most conspicuous case is in agriculture. The Census of Agriculture treats as independent farm operators both farmers who own their land and renters and share-croppers. But sharecroppers, whose farming activity is under the direction of farm proprietors and who contribute little, if anything, beyond labor, are virtually employees whose compensation takes the form of a share in the crop. Similarly, a considerable proportion of renters who are not sharecroppers and who contribute neither capital nor entrepreneurial direction to the conduct of their agricultural activity must be in much the same category.[6]

Similar overlapping may be encountered in mining, retail trade, and some service and miscellaneous industries, where also entrepreneurial withdrawals include a part that should properly be considered employee compensation. On the other hand, salaries may and do include items that represent entrepreneurial withdrawals; for example, compensation of executive officers in large corporations and payments to officers in one-man corporate units. It is doubtful that whatever overlapping there is would affect materially the larger category, wages and salaries, except possibly in agriculture. But it may constitute a substantial fraction of the smaller total, entrepreneurial withdrawals, in many industries.

[6] According to the 1930 *Census of Agriculture* there were about 776,000 share-croppers and 1,399,000 "all other tenants, including those giving a share of the products for the use of the land or a share for part and cash for part" (IV, 145). It is impossible to say how many of these 'other' tenants are, like sharecroppers, really employees working under direction and with the capital of the land-owner. But even if we classify only sharecroppers as employees, somewhat less than 40 per cent is added to the two million estimated full-time equivalents of farm wage earning labor; and on the assumption of a per capita income of sharecroppers equal to that of farm workers, about $0.5 billion would be added to employee compensation in 1929, with a corresponding deduction from entrepreneurial withdrawals and a significant increase in the per capita income of independent farm operators.

According to the recent report by the National Resources Committee, *Consumer Incomes in the United States* (Washington, 1938), of 6,167,000 farm families living in rural areas in 1935–36, 732,000 were sharecropper. The median income per sharecropper family in the South, the only region in which share-cropper income was segregated, was $530; independent farm operators in the South earned $902; all farm families in the country, $965 (see Tables 9, 10B, 18B, and 28B).

Finally, there is lack of comparability between the number of employed wage and salary earners and of entrepreneurs. Our estimates of the former are in terms of fully employed units, an attempt being made to adjust for partial employment; and the coverage of the number of employees is as complete as that of the flow of income to them. In the case of entrepreneurs we assumed, in the absence of other information, that all reported as entrepreneurs are fully employed. When, in addition, the impossibility of estimating properly the number corresponding to the flow of property income is considered, it becomes obvious that the apportionment in our estimates of the number by categories of employment or work status is too crude to merit analysis.

C PROPERTY INCOME

In estimating income payments we attempt to gauge the amount paid by enterprises to individuals in compensation for services rendered either by the individuals themselves or by their property. Accordingly, in estimating dividends and interest by industrial divisions we attempt to gauge the amount paid to individuals as individuals (not as entrepreneurs) by enterprises classified under each industrial division. The data needed for this purpose are, therefore, not total dividends and interest, but the amounts paid to and received by individuals.

With the single exception of interest on government debt, for which we have data on total payments and on receipts by corporations (so that by subtraction, we can obtain receipts by individuals, including entrepreneurs), no such data are available. Individuals' federal income tax returns cover a large proportion of dividends and interest received by all income recipients in this country; but the fraction covered varies and its magnitude cannot be determined unless the countrywide total can somehow be estimated. Besides, the data do not admit of a breakdown by industrial source. The annual comprehensive tabulations for corporations in *Statistics of Income* show total dividends paid and received and total interest paid, but do not separate payments to individuals from payments to enterprises.

For dividends the difficulty is solved by subtracting dividends received from dividends paid by enterprises in each industrial division. The remainder is not the amount paid to individuals by the enterprises in the division, but the amount contributed by the latter to the countrywide pool of dividend payments to individuals.[7] Dividends are derived in this manner for all industrial divisions except two: life insurance companies and banks. For these it is impossible to ascertain net income payments to individual policyholders or depositors; it is therefore impossible to estimate what part of the dividends received from other enterprises is passed on to the ultimate consumers who eventually benefit from them. Under these circumstances, dividends received by banks and life insurance companies cannot be subtracted, and they are thus automatically included in total net dividend payments to individuals. Hence, the estimated total of dividends may differ from the amount actually received by individuals.

For interest payments further difficulties arise because while *Statistics of Income* reports total interest paid by corporations, the only long term interest receipts recorded are those on tax-exempt government securities. Since a substantial fraction of total interest payments must be short term interest paid to banks and other enterprises, it is impossible to assume that the total paid out closely approximates the total received by individuals. It is also impossible to adopt the procedure used in estimating net dividend payments.

The procedure actually followed assumes that short term interest is usually paid by corporations to other economic enterprises, but that long term interest is paid either directly to individuals or to enterprises that can be treated as associations of individuals, such as life insurance companies, savings

7 Gross dividends paid and dividends received are given in Part Five, Table III.

banks, and philanthropic institutions. In other words, inter-corporate (exclusive of the institutions just mentioned) hold-ings of long term debt are assumed to be negligible; and short term interest payments are assumed to flow to enterprises which disburse them in the form of other income payments or accumulate them as savings. Hence we estimate the outstand-ing long term debt of all corporations (excluding associations of individuals); multiply it by an interest rate paid by a sam-ple of corporations; from the product, gross interest payments, we subtract interest received on government securities. For public utilities alone do we have data with which we can ad-just for receipts of interest on all long term obligations held. For agriculture, in which corporations and corporate debt are negligible, the method of estimating interest payments is somewhat different.[8]

These assumptions undoubtedly do some violence to the actualities, and our estimates of net interest paid to individ-uals may deviate from the true totals. They may be under-estimates so far as they omit: (i) possible payments of interest by unincorporated firms directly to individuals; (ii) payments by other enterprises to individuals in the form of short term interest. On the other hand, they are overestimates so far as intercorporate holdings of long term debt (excluding public utilities and associations of individuals) are not considered and payments on them are assumed to enter the total paid to indi-viduals. The item (i) omitted is likely to be rather small; and *total* short term interest paid by corporations in mining, man-ufacturing, construction, trade, service, and transportation and other public utilities seems to have ranged from $950 million in 1929 to $520 million in 1934. The net shortage in our estimates, if there is a shortage, is probably not great.

As noted, rent is treated as property income in the real estate industry. It includes both money rent received by indi-

8 Series on gross long term interest paid and on interest received by corpora-tions are given in Part Five, Table III.

viduals and imputed rent of individuals residing in their own houses. The estimates are based upon gross rent and expenses chargeable as proper deductions from the latter. The difficulties involved in measuring properly both the minuend and the subtrahend further qualify the estimates of net rent.

D NET SAVINGS

Income payments by any given group of enterprises do not necessarily add up to the net value of product originating, i.e., the gross value of product minus the cost of raw materials, equipment, and services of other enterprises consumed in the production process. The difference between income payments and net value product constitutes the last category in our classification by type of income, net savings. Our information on this item, except for agriculture, government, and some public utilities, comes from corporation reports for income tax purposes, summarized annually in *Statistics of Income*. If the accounting practices of corporations conformed in all respects to the economist's definition of net value product, no difficulty would arise in estimating corporate net savings. They would be accurately represented by the reported net profit or loss, after payment of dividends. But since the prevailing accounting practices depart in several respects, especially for certain cost items, from those conforming to the concepts appropriate for purposes of economic analysis, we made several adjustments in the reported amounts of net profit or loss after payment of dividends.

i) The reported amounts include gains and losses on sales of capital assets. For reasons presented in Chapter 1, Section 2 B, such gains and losses are not considered part of national income. They should, therefore, be eliminated from total profit and loss reported by corporations. But since data for making this adjustment by industrial divisions are available only since 1929, our estimates for the earlier years for the separate industries had to be left unadjusted in this particular respect.[9] The items in question are not large (see Part Five, Table IV), but fluctuate cyclically. Failure to exclude them for years before 1929 probably exaggerates the cyclical fluctuations in our estimates of net savings by industries.

ii) Business enterprises commonly compute the cost of materials consumed by adding to the value of inventory at the beginning of the year (at beginning of year valuation) the value of materials purchased during the year (at cost of purchase), and then subtracting the value of the inventory at the end of the year (at end of year valuation). Since, by definition, the cost of any material consumed should be taken at its market value at the time the production of the good into which it enters is completed, this accounting method of computing costs of materials consumed would yield a correct estimate only on the improbable assumption that prices are constant through the year (or of some equally improbable combination of price rise and decline within the year). Actually, during periods of rising prices this method underestimates costs of materials consumed and correspondingly overestimates net income and net savings; and during periods of declining prices it overestimates costs of materials consumed and underestimates net income and net savings. By converting inventories at the beginning and end of the year to the same valuation level and converting the difference between them to price levels prevailing during the year, we obtain a correct estimate of the value of the part of inventory that was consumed during the year in the production process (or purchased and added to inventory). Subtracting it from the difference between inventories at the beginning and end of the year, taken at their current and hence different valuations (as they are in the accounting procedure described above), yields the approximate gain or loss on inventory holdings included in the reported net income of enterprises. By using the National Bureau's study of commodity flow and capital formation, we carried

---

[9] For the earlier years we did make a rough approximation of gains and losses on sales of capital assets for all industries combined.

through this adjustment for most industrial divisions for the entire period covered by our estimates.[10]

iii) In calculating the cost of durable capital equipment consumed during the year, the accounting practice of corporations is to apply some apportionment rate (based on estimated life and an apportionment formula) to the value of durable equipment based on original cost of acquisition. But on the principle that costs should be taken at the current market value of materials consumed, the proper estimate is the product of the rate and the value of durable equipment based on its market or reproduction price. And while for this item the disparity between the accounting and the economic measures is not as great or as variable as that between the two measures of inventories, it is sufficient to call for adjustment.

Given the current value of durable capital equipment, as well as an index of value based on original cost, total depreciation and depletion charges based on current valuation can be computed. The difference between the latter and total depreciation and depletion charges actually reported in the various accounts based on original cost (the annual rates being the same in the calculation of the two totals) can be used as an adjustment factor to be applied to net income as reported by enterprises. These various calculations have been carried out by Dr. Fabricant, and their results used to adjust our estimates.[11] However, unlike the adjustments listed under (i) and (ii), which were made for the several industrial divisions, the correction for the disparity in depreciation charges between cost and reproduction bases can be carried through only for the private business system as a whole.

The three adjustments described above are the only ones applied to reported net income, after payment of dividends, to derive an approximation of corporate net savings. No ad-

[10] The data underlying this adjustment are presented in Part Five, Table VII. The problem is discussed in detail in *Studies in Income and Wealth* (National Bureau of Economic Research, 1937), Vol. One, Part Four.

[11] See *Capital Consumption and Adjustment* (National Bureau of Economic Research, 1938), especially Tables 29 and 31.

justment of reported net income is made for the bad debts, taxes, and philanthropic contributions that have already been deducted. These items are proper deductions in estimating net savings, but as explained in Chapter 9, their positive counterparts are not fully recorded as additions to income elsewhere in our estimates. A more serious qualification of corporate net savings is that they may be subject to a downward bias especially in years of prosperity. Reporting for income tax purposes tends to minimize gains; and it is not safe to assume that the vigilance of income tax authorities and the dictates of conscience fully offset the effects of a desire to save on tax payments.[12] At any rate, comparisons of reports to the Bureau of Internal Revenue and reports published by the same corporations suggest that net income reported to the former is smaller.[13] While this is no positive proof of a downward bias in the basic data in *Statistics of Income*, the possibility should be considered in interpreting our estimates, although little can be done in the way of testing or adjusting them.

So far our discussion has been largely in terms of net income reported by corporations, and of the adjustments needed to arrive at a proper estimate of corporate net savings. To obtain

[12] The tabulations in *Statistics of Income* are from unaudited returns, and any upward revisions of net income figures that may result from auditing are not available to allow revision of the estimates. The amount of depreciation alone that was disallowed in each fiscal year ending June 30, 1934–38 was approximately $250 million. Correspondingly, there was a revision upward of about the same amount in taxable net income. It is probable, though no definite evidence is available, that such disallowances were considerably smaller before 1934. There is no information concerning other expense items that may have been lowered by audits or income items that may have been raised. Cursory examination of published corporate reports, including those to the Securities and Exchange Commission, in which statements are made concerning additional income taxes assessed upon audit of tax returns, suggests that for years prior to 1934 no serious revisions would be made even were audited figures available.
[13] See 'Income Forecasting by the Use of Statistics of Income Data' by J. F. Ebersole, S. S. Burr, and G. M. Peterson, *Review of Economic Statistics*, Nov. 1929.

net savings of unincorporated firms we subtract entrepreneurial withdrawals from the total net income of entrepreneurs. But the latter is measured, in most industries, on the basis of certain items in corporation accounts, including net profit and loss. Hence whatever adjustments are applied to the net income reported by corporations are, in most industries, applied also to net income and net savings of unincorporated firms. In agriculture alone is the net income of entrepreneurs obtained directly by subtracting current expenses from current gross income.

The item 'net savings by governments' is called for by our decision to evaluate governmental services on the basis used in evaluating the services of production factors in all other branches of the economic system, viz., market value. This market value of governmental services is gauged by current payments by the community—taxes, fees, etc. But like all other economic agencies, governments can expend on the production factors used in turning out the current product an amount larger or smaller than they take in, thus realizing a net saving or sustaining a net dissaving. And like other economic agencies, they can borrow money, either to cover their net dissaving or to invest in additions to their assets.

Since it is difficult to estimate net governmental savings directly, we adopted a somewhat circuitous procedure. We estimated net additions to governmental assets and to governmental debts. We then derived positive net savings as the excess of the former over the latter, negative net savings as the excess of the latter over the former.[14] These estimates are crude, owing to the sparsity of relevant data; and numerous questions arise about the items that may properly be treated as governmental assets or liabilities (consider debts owed by foreign governments). Yet it seemed to us that allowing for these net savings yielded a total of net income from govern-

14 Net savings in other industries could be estimated similarly, were it possible to calculate net additions to assets exclusive of changes in the reported figures caused by changing valuation.

mental activity more nearly comparable with net income for other branches of the economic system than a total excluding this net savings item would have been.

In Part Four we give fully both the unadjusted and the adjusted estimates of net savings and in Part Five the basis of the adjustments in detail, whenever they are not already available elsewhere. The definition and proper method of estimating net savings (including the adjustments made to reported net income after payment of dividends) is perhaps the most controversial issue in the whole field of national income and the estimates naturally reflect all the difficulties and controversial points in the definition of net value product. Of course our estimates reflect also our judgments concerning these moot points and it seemed advisable to provide the detail that would make possible the estimation of net savings and net income according to other concepts. Furthermore, the computations of net profit or loss reported in accordance with accounting practice, diverging as they do from business net savings as defined here, are of interest and value in their own right: they show what the business community conceives net profit or loss to be and the estimates it uses in arriving at decisions concerning the present and future.

3 Territorial Coverage and Year

A THE AREA

As indicated in Chapter 3, Section 3 B, the area to which our estimates of national income apply is largely the continental United States; total service income is made up of payments to residents of that area alone; property income covers payments to residents of the same area and also to residents of some territorial possessions; corporate net savings are for corporations located within the continental United States and Alaska, Hawaii, and Puerto Rico.

The classifications by industrial source and by type of income, as described above, appear to be all inclusive, in the sense that all industrial divisions combined and all types of income combined account for total national income. But this inclusiveness is real only for the classification by type of income, and even there only for the broader categories; for the simple reason that the controlling totals are available for these broad type of income categories alone. Therefore, the apportionment of the national total among these larger groups (service income, comprising employee compensation and entrepreneurial withdrawals, property income, and net savings of enterprises) is for the continental United States, in that each category actually covers this area or some close approximation to it.

As said above, the miscellaneous division has no positive meaning; it represents merely the part of the national income total that cannot be properly allocated by industrial source. But it contains the adjustments yielding the desired territorial coverage of total national income. Wages and salaries, entrepreneurial withdrawals, dividends, and interest, as they are estimated for all the industrial divisions except the miscellaneous, represent payments by enterprises domiciled in the United States to any and all individual recipients, whether they are residents of the United States or of another country. In the miscellaneous division alone, by estimating the service income of the gainfully occupied and employed residing within the continental United States and not accounted for in the other industrial divisions, do we make the proper adjustment; the resulting total of service income covers residents of the continental United States alone. Similarly, it is in the miscellaneous division that we take account of the net balance of the international flow of property income payments during the year; by adding it to dividends and interest paid by domestic corporations in all industrial divisions (including domestic enterprises comprised under miscellaneous), we obtain total property income paid to the residents of the balance-of-payments area (a total close to that for residents of the continental United States).

It must therefore be remembered in interpreting our estimates that the allocation by industrial source applies not to total income paid to residents of the United States but to all income payments originating in enterprises located in the United States. And since this is true of the industrial allocation, it is true also of the industrial type of income cells. Thus wages and salaries originating in manufacturing, water transportation, or government may include payments to individuals residing outside the United States. And, on the other hand, earnings of residents in the United States employed by manufacturing, water transportation, or governmental enterprises of foreign countries may be included in the wage and salary totals in the miscellaneous industrial division.

B THE YEAR

We attempted throughout to adhere to the calendar year basis. But in many cases crude adjustments had to be made to attain that end; and in some no adjustment could be made, so that minor departures from the calendar year basis remain in our estimates.

For employee compensation the calendar year basis of reporting prevails for most industries. There are, however, notable exceptions. For governments, which report on a fiscal year basis, the calendar year figures we show are averages of fiscal years. A similarly crude procedure had to be followed for estimates for education, since the basic data are reported for school years. But since in both government and education year to year changes are either minor or regular, our procedures do not damp pronounced cyclical fluctuations, as they might in some other industries.

Most of the basic information on dividends, interest, and business savings, derived from corporate data primarily, is for calendar years. However, a fraction of corporations do report for fiscal years; e.g., for 1929, about 11 per cent of all corporations did so, accounting for 10.4 per cent of the net income of all corporations reporting net income and 14.4 per cent of the net deficit of all corporations reporting no net income. To the extent suggested by these figures, our estimates of property income and corporate savings depart from the calendar year basis for all industries for which we utilize *Statistics of Income* data (i.e., all except agriculture, transportation and other public utilities, and government).

To the extent that entrepreneurial withdrawals are based upon wage and salary data, the estimates tend to follow the calendar year basis; and to the extent that estimates of net income and business savings of unincorporated firms are based on corporate data, they reflect the departure from the calendar year basis indicated above.

The departures from the calendar year basis that characterize the underlying data and survive in our estimates are small, and certainly minor compared with the other limitations that result from lack of specific data for some industrial divisions or types of income.

CHAPTER 9

Items Omitted from the Estimates

1 General Characteristics

THE preceding chapter discussed the contents of our estimates, noting only incidentally the items omitted. The limitations of our estimates cannot be made clear without an explicit statement concerning the items that had to be omitted but that might or should have been included if national income is conceived broadly along the lines discussed in Chapter 1. These omissions can be conveniently summarized as:

A Flow from Enterprises

I Service Income

1 Employees' pensions, compensation for injury, compensation in kind, expense accounts, discounts, etc.
2 Entrepreneurial income from
  a Roomers and boarders
  b Gardens and poultry and cows
3 Casual service income of
  a Gainfully occupied and employed
  b Gainfully occupied unemployed and of non-gainfully occupied

II Property Income

1 Royalties

III Other Income (Hidden Payments)

1 Bad debts
2 Taxes paid by business enterprises
3 Contributions by business enterprises

B Incomes within the Family Economy

1 Imputed income from services of
  a Housewives
  b Other members of family
2 Imputed income from durable commodities other than houses

These items are not all that might be considered from one viewpoint or another parts of national income, or all that have actually been included by other estimators; for example, some estimates have included gains and losses on capital assets, whether realized or not. Claims have been made that income from certain illegal activities, such as bootlegging during Prohibition, should be included. We confine discussion to the items that should be included if the criterion of productivity is interpreted broadly rather than abandoned, for once it is abandoned, the list of possible omissions becomes impracticably long.

The nature of the items omitted is described, their probable size indicated, and the probable temporal changes in them compared with temporal changes in the totals covered in our estimates. But the very fact that the items were omitted largely because available data made satisfactory estimates impossible means that the figures cited are much more uncertain than most of our estimates; and the statements concerning changes in their size are perforce exceedingly tentative.

2 Service Income (A-I)

In the first category under this heading, A-I-1, are the shortages in our estimates of employee compensation, already indicated in Chapter 8, Section 2 B. Pensions, compensation for injuries, and direct compensation in kind are covered for only a few industries. Other forms of compensation received by employees from enterprises are not covered at all: expense accounts, stipends for additional training, lower prices on the products of the employing or related enterprises, and other benefits derived from employers. In a sense, some of these income flows to employees are counterparts, within the business system, of benefits derived from domestic activities, and, like them, tend to elude reporting and measurement.

It is difficult even to guess the size of the items in this category. For only two, pensions and compensation for injury, can we indicate the shortage in our estimates. For 1929 the Department of Commerce estimates 'other labor income' for industrial divisions not covered by us at $217 million.[1] But this figure does not show the full shortage in our estimate for this category alone, for even the Department of Commerce estimate is incomplete. The shortage for other compensation of employees may amount, in a year like 1929, to a billion dollars, and may be much larger.

For entrepreneurial incomes, A-I-2, our information is somewhat more adequate. Income from roomers and boarders is omitted from our estimates primarily because it is a return on an activity that is rather casual and unorganized, is not reported in any industrial census, and is received by people who are not likely to be classified in the *Census of Population* as gainfully employed. Hence there are no basic data for a continuous estimate that could be included in our national income total. But since lower income families frequently take roomers and boarders, income from this source has been segregated in studies of consumer expenditures and costs of living. An estimate based upon recent data on consumer expenditures evaluates net income from boarders and lodgers at $300 million in 1935–36.[2] That based upon sample data for earlier years and applied to 1929 evaluated *gross* rent paid by lodgers at $1,086 million. Net income from lodgers alone (excluding net income from boarders) was estimated at $746 million ($85 per room for 4 million rooms was deducted to cover the pro-

1 From unpublished data underlying 'National Income at Nearly 70 Billion Dollars in 1939', *Survey of Current Business*, June 1940.
2 National Resources Committee, *Consumer Incomes in the United States* (Washington, 1938), p. 35, note 4.

portion of house rent and other costs of residential maintenance for lodgers in private rooms).[3]

Of the other forms of income from entrepreneurial activity
that is carried on largely within the family economy but possibly has regular connections with the outside market we have
estimates for urban poultry and gardens and for cow keeping.
W. I. King's preliminary estimates for 1927 are for the former
item, $136 million, and for the latter, $109 million.[4] If these
estimates can be accepted, the corresponding figure for the
two items for 1929 would be about $250 million, since it is
probable that no major changes occurred between 1927 and
1929.

The basic reason for not covering casual service income
(A-I-3), i.e., all receipts from odd jobs or activities whether
performed in the capacity of employee or entrepreneur, is, of
course, lack of information. This arises from two sources.
First, casual and odd jobs may be performed by people who
are already gainfully occupied and fully employed, and whose
main income is thus presumably included in our estimates.
Information concerning this kind of casual income is scarce
because enterprises that pay it (whether or not incorporated)
may not report it. Second, casual and odd jobs may be per-

[3] *Studies in Income and Wealth,* Vol. Three, 'Three Estimates of the Nation's
Output of Commodities and Services—a Comparison', by Clark Warburton;
Table 11.
[4] *National Income and Its Purchasing Power* (National Bureau of Economic
Research, 1930), Table CXXXIII, p. 379. The estimate of profit from urban
cow keeping is based on the number of cows not on farms (reported in the 1920
Census of Agriculture) and the profit per cow (changes in the latter estimated
on the basis of changes in the prices of dairy products); see *Income in the
Various States* (National Bureau of Economic Research, 1925), p. 245. The basic
figure on profit per cow is for 1917, from a study of South Carolina mill villages
by the U. S. Public Health Service. Dr. King's estimate of profit from urban
poultry and gardens was based on the assumption that one-half of the families
in towns of 10,000 and under, one-third in towns of 10,000–50,000, one-fourth in
towns of 50,000–100,000, one-eighth in towns of 100,000–250,000, and one-
sixteenth in larger cities produced enough poultry and garden crops to give an
average net gain of $25 per family in 1909. This estimate was extrapolated by
changes in total city and village population and in wholesale prices.

formed by a gainfully occupied person who reports himself as unemployed or by a person who is not classified in the *Census of Population* as gainfully occupied. In the second case the income is not covered in our estimates largely because the person slips out of our controlling totals of gainfully occupied. But even in this case, the income would be included were it reported by the enterprise that paid it.

The variety of these odd jobs and income producing activities is enormous, ranging from newspaper vending and bootblacking by urchins to occasional paid lectures by professors or statesmen; from selling apples and ice cream on street corners during the depression to attending board of directors meetings (paid for by fees). To measure the income involved is all the more difficult because our aim is not the total of all secondary, auxiliary, and casual incomes but only the part that is not covered by the basic data and hence is omitted from our estimates. The only relevant estimate is that in *America's Capacity to Consume* which sets earnings from odd jobs of otherwise employed persons in 1929 at $700 million.[5] The National Resources Committee publication, already referred to, accepted this estimate, and suggested a corresponding figure of $500 million for 1935–36 (p. 35, note 4).

To sum up: total income from the items omitted under service income from enterprises, partly domestic, may, in a year like 1929, have amounted to not much less than $3 billion, and perhaps appreciably more. The exceedingly uncertain nature of the estimates underlying this figure cannot be overemphasized. Nor can a definite statement be made concerning temporal changes in them, as compared with the changes in the service incomes included in our estimates. But two tentative suggestions can be advanced.

First, it is doubtful that the rate of long time rise in most of the omitted service incomes is as great as may be assumed to exist in those reported. The upward trend in the national

5 Brookings Institution, 1934, p. 163. No explanation of how the item was derived is given.

product was accompanied by a rise in income per family and decreasing need for minor and auxiliary jobs. Moreover, all income payments, service incomes among them, are more completely reported than formerly. And the vestiges of agricultural activities in non-farm localities have become fewer.[6] These trends apply to items I-3, I-2-b, and in some degree even to I-2-a. Of item I-1 alone it is impossible to suggest even tentatively the relative long time movement.

Second, the omitted items probably reflect cyclical fluctuations less sensitively than total recorded service incomes. Some could be assumed to move against the cycle in general business conditions, since the need for casual and supplementary activities increases when main income sources contract. Others, such as pensions and compensation for injury, would tend to resist short term fluctuations in business conditions more than wages and salaries.[7]

3 Property Income (A-II)

Royalties and net rents are combined in the tabulation of federal income tax returns by individuals. Because of the incomplete coverage of these returns, other sources of information must be used. Additional data are available for net rents, although even on these a great deal of labor and statistical ingenuity must be spent in order to arrive at approximations. But these approximations could be used in conjunction with income tax data to calculate royalties only if we knew the percentage of total net rents that is reported on tax returns.

Some assistance can be found in tax data for states whose income tax laws have a wider relative coverage than the federal; for example, in Wisconsin, in recent years, royalties have been tabulated separately.

---

[6] This consideration may have little bearing upon recent decades during which there was no appreciable rise in real income per capita.

[7] Of course, a great deal depends upon the relative importance of the omitted items in the total for A-I. One source of the difficulty in arriving at conclusions concerning changes from one period to another arises from the lack of weights, which could be provided only by a greater knowledge of the size of the items.

Of a total income of $809,246,000 in 1936, $911,000 were reported in royalties—a ratio of only 0.11 per cent.[8] Royalties are relatively better covered than total income since most royalties are presumably received in the higher income brackets. But even if we apply this exaggerated percentage to total national income in 1929 estimated royalties would approximate only $100 million. Another estimate, made by deriving the Wisconsin ratio of royalties to the combined total of royalties and rents reported on all Wisconsin returns with incomes of $5,000 and over and applying it to break down the combined total reported on all federal income tax returns, gives royalties of $282 million in 1929. Still another estimate gives $175 million. It is derived by first approximating the amount of royalties reported on federal returns with net incomes of $5,000 and over (by applying to the combined total of rents and royalties the breakdown ratio derived for Wisconsin returns with net incomes of $5,000 and over); and then raising this amount by the ratio of royalties reported on all Wisconsin returns to the amount reported on Wisconsin returns with net incomes of $5,000 and over. Finally, from Delaware state income tax data for 1936, which report rents and royalties combined but for a coverage that extends to an overwhelming majority of income recipients and a high percentage of total income received in the state, we obtain an estimate for 1929 of combined rents and royalties of some $1,996 million and of royalties alone of some $100 million. The latter is derived by applying to the 1936 ratio of the Delaware state total to the Delaware total reported on federal income tax returns the Wisconsin breakdown ratio, according to which in 1936 royalties constituted 5 per cent of the combined total.

Thus, the various scanty data available suggest that total royalties in a year like 1929 would range from $100 to $300 million. In other years they would vary with changes in business conditions, reflecting particularly the economic fortunes

8 *Wisconsin Individual Income Tax Statistics,* Vol. I, Table 2.

of the mining industries from which a large part of the countrywide total is probably derived.

4 Hidden Payments (A-III)

Most of the costs sustained by enterprises in the conduct of their business represent outflows in the form either of income payments to individuals, accounted for in our estimates, or of payments for products of other enterprises, which in turn make income payments to individuals (or other enterprises). But some costs represent transfers that may be received by individuals in a form not discussed in Chapter 8 and that may be omitted from our estimates: deductions in the income accounts of enterprises for (a) bad debts; (b) taxes; (c) contributions. Such circuitous flows from enterprises to individuals must be considered, even though they cannot be segregated and measured accurately.

At first sight they seem to be legitimate costs of carrying on business and properly deducted in the computation of the net income and savings of enterprises. Losses from bad debts are expected in the ordinary course of business and are usually provided for in the calculation of costs, prices, and plans for the future. Taxes are payments to governmental agencies for their services; and when they are notably higher than the cost of specific governmental services given in return, enterprises that produce goods like tobacco, liquor, and gasoline include them in the price of the goods, and their net income is usually not affected. Contributions to philanthropic institutions may seem to be a more discretionary type of expenditure than bad debts or taxes, as are advertising and many other undoubtedly proper expenses incurred in the conduct of business. Such contributions may be interpreted by enterprises as investment in goodwill.

Nevertheless, it can be argued that these three types of expenditure do not represent, at least to the full amount reported, materials consumed in the production process. Unlike payments for materials that are destroyed in the production process, they are not fully offset by services rendered to an enterprise and consumed by it in turning out its product. To that extent they should be included under net income originating in the industrial branch to which the enterprise belongs. While they cannot be reincluded in net savings, since they are not amounts retained by the enterprise that makes the deduction, they should be added to other income disbursements, perhaps forming a category of their own. And yet, as will be seen, our estimates omit them. The reasons for this omission vary from one type of deduction to the next and can best be discussed separately.

A BAD DEBTS

The debtors whose bad debts are written off by the creditor enterprises may be either business enterprises or ultimate consumers. If a deduction for a bad debt has as a concomitant the final cancellation of the liability of the debtor to an equal amount, then obviously the latter derives an increase in his net worth not unlike that resulting from receipt of income. And yet our estimates do not record this flow, for estimates of income payments nowhere include the benefits derived by individual debtors (i.e., ultimate consumers) from the cancellation of their debts. And net savings of enterprises, the difference between gross receipts and costs, would hardly reflect any reduction in liability resulting from cancellation of their debts by creditors.

There are, however, grounds for denying that cancellation of a liability is a type of income and should be included in national income totals. First, it is doubtful that the amount written off as bad debts represents the amount of liability that is completely cancelled: a substantial part of it may hang over for years as a potential liability of a debtor against whom a judgment is taken out.[9] Second, the benefit to the debtor even in case of complete cancellation can hardly be compared to a receipt of income or an increase in net savings out of

[9] This is true, largely, for individual debtors.

current activity; for much as losses on bad debts may be
treated, within limits, as ordinary business expenses, gains
from the cancellation of debts are irregular and unexpected,
more comparable to changes in the valuation of assets and
liabilities due to striking and unforeseen changes in circumstances, i.e., a change in the balance position not resulting
from the disposition of income. Consequently, we consider
deductions for bad debts as *post facto* revaluations of the price
at which the goods were sold, i.e., *post facto* reductions in the
net income of the creditor enterprise.

For these reasons, even though *Statistics of Income* reports
deductions by corporations for bad debts (by industrial divisions since 1927), we thought it best to exclude the item from
our estimates.[10] The corporate totals ranged from about $800
million in 1927 and 1928 to $1.3 billion in 1932. Since they
tend to decline during prosperity and rise during depression,
their inclusion would reduce somewhat the cyclical variability
of our national income estimates.

B TAXES

The problem with respect to taxes paid by enterprises is somewhat different. The transfer that may take place arises because
enterprises may pay to federal, state, and local governments
an amount greater than the cost and value of governmental
services to them, and because part of these taxes is spent by
the governments for the benefit of ultimate consumers. It may
then be claimed that so far as proceeds from taxes paid by all
business enterprises are spent by governmental agencies for
the benefit of ultimate consumers, without a corresponding
amount of the proceeds from taxes paid by ultimate consumers being spent by governmental agencies for the benefit of
business enterprises, a transfer of income produced to ulti-

[10] For those students who think otherwise, the amounts in question (for corporations only) are presented in Part Five, Table V. It would be difficult to
cover losses on bad debts by unincorporated firms, unless it were assumed that
the ratio of losses on bad debts to gross sales is the same for unincorporated as
for incorporated enterprises.

mate consumers really occurs; and such income received by the latter should be included in national income.

The exact nature of the item presumably omitted from our estimates can now be seen. In measuring net income of enterprises we deduct all taxes paid by them.[11] Part of these taxes may go to finance governmental services to ultimate consumers. This part then represents a flow from enterprises, *via* government, to ultimate consumers, a flow not recorded by us anywhere. On this interpretation, it should be added to both aggregate income flows to individuals and to total national income. The amounts are fairly substantial; for example, Gerhard Colm concludes that national income produced in 1932 is really about $5 billion larger than in our calculation. Clark Warburton calculates that in 1929 the cost of governmental services to consumers exceeded their tax payments by some $3 billion.[12] Since there were positive governmental savings in 1929 this flow of $3 billion to consumers may be assumed to have come from taxes paid by enterprises.[13]

The general assumption of this argument is that it is possible to distinguish between governmental services to enterprises and to ultimate consumers; but one of the most distinctive characteristics of governmental activity is that it is designed to serve society at large, not specific groups. It is true that in extreme cases, such as relief on the one hand and information service on business matters on the other, there does

[11] So far as data make it possible, tax payments by individual entrepreneurs considered as business enterprises (e.g., farmers) are treated similarly. Tax payments by individuals are not deducted from their incomes; they are treated either as payments for services rendered by government or as transfers to other individuals not recorded elsewhere. Series on taxes paid by agriculture and by non-agricultural corporations are given in Part Five, Table VI.

[12] *Studies in Income and Wealth,* Vol. One, Part Five, p. 213; Vol. Three, Part Five, p. 360.

[13] See the discussion of Colm's paper, *ibid.,* Vol. One, pp. 233-6. This question of the possibility of distinguishing in governmental activities between services to consumers and to enterprises should not be confused with the question whether the value of governmental services should be evaluated on a cost or market price basis.

seem to be a distinct difference in that the former benefits directly and primarily ultimate consumers, and the latter, enterprises. But in most essential governmental functions—legislation, administration, justice, police, post office, public education, military affairs—the benefits to ultimate consumers and to business enterprises are inextricably intertwined.

The position taken here is perhaps biased by a realization of the enormous statistical difficulties of classifying governmental expenditures, in their present composition and with the present data, as services to individuals or to enterprises. But if further development of governmental activity results in an increased relative importance of expenditures that can clearly be put in one category or the other and if information on government expenditures improves in quality and quantity, it may become feasible to attempt the allocation.[14]

G CONTRIBUTIONS

Contributions by enterprises either directly to individuals or to non-profit institutions, which in turn distribute them to ultimate consumers, represent a flow of funds from the business system to individuals. Our estimates do not cover this flow, for while they do include the incomes paid by non-profit institutions to their employees, these payments represent compensation for services rendered by the latter *in addition to* those net values which the contributing enterprises produced but passed on in the form of contributions. Hence, net income originating in the contributing enterprises is undervalued to the extent that contributions by them do not represent services consumed in the production process. A correct treatment would demand the inclusion of contributions as part of net income, but not of net savings, originating in

[14] Many of the difficulties that would be encountered and the necessarily arbitrary character of their solution are revealed in 'Allocation of Benefits from Government Expenditures', by R. W. Nelson and Donald Jackson, *ibid.*, Vol. Two, Part Six.

the industrial branches to which the contributing enterprises belong.[15]

Prior to 1936 the income tax law permitted deduction of contributions only if they were either for the direct benefit of employees and their dependents or were made with a reasonable expectation of commensurate financial returns to the enterprise.[16] Hence, all other donations were included under corporate net income and our estimates cover them. The only difficulty is that these amounts should have been classified under payments either to individuals or other organizations, and so far as such organizations may have been recorded by us elsewhere as income sources, some duplication in the estimates has taken place. However, the amounts involved are small both relatively and absolutely.[17]

5 Imputed Income from Services

It may be doubted that the productive activities of housewives and other members of the family, rendered within the family circle, can be characterized as economic processes whose net product should be evaluated and included in national income. The conditions under which they are carried on and the factors that affect the amount of income from them are so vastly different from those that bear upon activities whose products usually appear on the market place that it seems best to exclude them.[18] But it cannot be denied that they are an important complement to the market-eventuat-

---

[15] The same argument would apply to the part of taxes that does not represent payment for governmental services consumed by enterprises in the production process, could it be segregated. For reasons submitted above, the argument does not apply to deductions for bad debts.

[16] See Article 23 (O)-2, *Regulations 86*, Revenue Act of 1934.

[17] In both 1936 and 1937 those 'pure' deductions allowed by the new law were reported as about $30 million. We reincluded these amounts in net income, to retain comparability over the period.

[18] This refers to activities constituting part of family life, not to participation by family members in a family enterprise. The latter (such as labor by members of the farmer's family on the farm) is included under net income originating in such family enterprises.

ing processes in supplying goods to ultimate consumers, and should be considered in any attempt to evaluate the net product of the social system in terms of satisfying wants with scarce means. Moreover, there seem to be distinct and significant shifts over time in the relative importance of activities within the domestic circle as compared with the activities that eventuate in marketable products and are included under national income. The tendency is for the business system to take over many activities formerly carried on within the domestic circle and considered part of everyday family life (e.g., canning, baking, laundering, dressmaking) rather than of a family business enterprise. As a result, the importance of domestic activities relative to those that are part of the business system declines in the long run. In the shorter term cyclical fluctuations, expansion and contraction in general business activity mean expansion and contraction in the importance of activities eventuating in a marketable product relative to those within the family. It is especially noted that during severe depressions a drastic contraction in employment and incomes is accompanied by a significant expansion of activities within the household. Therefore, we approximated the order of magnitude of these activities within the domestic circle and compared them with the activities whose end products are covered in our estimates.

This approximation had to be based on market values, and there are no market values for activities that are the exact counterpart of the productive functions of family members within the household. For non-farm housewives there may be some ground for taking the average compensation for domestic service, and for the housewife in a farm family, of farm workers. Both procedures do violence to many of the social and emotional factors involved, but they seem to be the only way of even approximating the order of magnitude involved. The average compensation in 1929 for domestic service was roughly $900 and of farm workers, roughly $600. According to the *Census of Population*, Vol. II, there were on

April 1, 1930, 27,547,000 families of two members or more, of which 6,261,000 were farm and 21,286,000 non-farm. If we assume that the figures for 1929 are roughly 6 and 21 million respectively, the rough dollar equivalent of house-wives' services amounted to some $23 billion, or somewhat more than one-fourth of total national income in 1929.[19]

For the imputed income of other members of the family from domestic activities even such an approximate figure cannot be suggested. The *Census of Population* reports for April 1930 76.2 million people between the ages of 15 and 60, of whom 44.2 million were classified as gainfully occupied. From the residual 32 million we should subtract about 27 million housewives whose domestic activities have presumably already been taken into account. This leaves about 5 million adults not reported as gainfully occupied who, in addition to housewives, may have performed services within the domestic circle. Moreover, gainfully occupied persons, even if employed and especially when unemployed (of whom there may have been another 2 million in 1929), are also in a position to contribute services in the course of family life. But it is impossible even to approximate the amount of income involved.

6 Imputed Income from Property
One's own property, used within the household for living, may be a source of net income, just as much as is the property of a business enterprise used for a similar purpose. Net income derived by an owner from occupying his own house

19 An earlier estimate sets the conjectural total value of housewives' services in 1919 at $18.45 billion (*Income in the United States;* National Bureau of Economic Research, 1921, I, 59). This would constitute somewhat less than one-third of the measurable total for that year. This higher relative estimate seems to be the result of using a per housewife compensation larger than that for domestic service or of farm workers. Some allowance should be made also for households where all domestic labor is performed by hired help. The proportion of such households to the total must, however, be low; and in a crude estimate of the type submitted an adjustment does not seem advisable.

is not essentially different from that of an owner who rents his house to a tenant. Net income derived from the possession and use of a passenger car is not much different from that of taxicab companies or companies that rent out automobiles. Most property used within the household is not, however, employed in an activity that enters directly into market transactions; and performance of activities in the household for which there is some counterpart in the market is no evidence of income production. With the exception of net income from owner-occupied houses, which is included in our estimates, imputed income from goods used by the family may properly be excluded from national income.

For the omitted item, income from durable goods, other than houses, used by the family, estimates were given by W. I. King in *National Income and Its Purchasing Power*. The preliminary figures for 1926 and 1927 were each slightly over $3 billion.[20] If these estimates can be accepted, the approximate total for a year like 1929 would be well over $3 billion. And it may be surmised that the item, whatever its long term movement as compared to that of total national income, would be less responsive to short term fluctuations in economic conditions than are the current income payments or the net savings of enterprises.

7 Summary

a) The total of the omitted items for a year like 1929 may be assumed to amount to more than $33 billion, or about 40 per cent of the national income actually recorded in our estimates. Of this tentative total of omitted items, by far the largest is that for housewives' services, $23 billion. Omitted

[20] P. 379. The estimates are based upon the application of an interest rate to an estimated value of all durable goods held by ultimate consumers. The basic figure for the latter value was taken from the *Census of Wealth, Public Debt, and Taxation* for 1922. It was extrapolated to other years by an index obtained by multiplying estimated population by the price indexes of furniture, clothing, and automobiles. A constant interest rate of 6 per cent was assumed.

service incomes and imputed income from durable goods other than houses are each somewhat more than $3 billion; bad debts and hidden payments *via* taxes paid, about $4 billion. An estimate of the net value of services of family members other than housewives is not attempted. The margin of error in the total of omitted items (again excepting services of other family members) is such that the true total may well be $15 billion above or below the figure cited. And, of course, the total would vary with inclusion and exclusion of items.

b) It is reasonable to assume that the ratio of this total of omitted items to national income would have a declining secular trend because functions formerly performed in the home tend to be taken over by commercial enterprises; minor entrepreneurial activities have less importance than formerly; and coverage of the data is gradually improving.

c) It is probable that in short term cyclical fluctuations, the omitted total fluctuates less with changes in business conditions than national income, partly because of a complementary relation between the omitted items and those included in national income, which tends to force the former to expand when the latter contract and vice versa; partly because the omitted items are less responsive to business cycles, owing to the relatively minor role the profit motive and business calculation play in determining their course.

CHAPTER 10

Comparisons with Other Estimates

WERE there no controversial questions concerning the scope of national income and its components, and were the data for the various parts of the countrywide totals complete and accurate, estimates, even when prepared by different investigators, would necessarily be identical. An investigator would not need to compare his estimates with those of others or to juxtapose the results of his most recent and previous efforts. But since national income investigators still disagree on many issues of inclusion and evaluation, and since data are still inadequate, varying in this respect from year to year, it is incumbent upon a student of national income who presents a new set of estimates to compare them with such others as merit scrutiny and can be analyzed.

In this chapter we compare our most recent estimates, designated as 'present NBER' or 'our', with three other sets: (1) the preliminary estimates published in *National Income and Capital Formation, 1919–1935* (National Bureau of Economic Research, 1937) (designated as 'preliminary NBER'); (2) the estimates currently published by the Department of Commerce (designated as 'D of C'); (3) the estimates published in *National Income and Its Purchasing Power,* by W. I. King (designated as 'King'). The purpose of the first comparison is to indicate briefly the chief changes in scope and basis of estimation made since our preliminary estimates were completed four years ago. In a sense, it is the least important of the three comparisons, since the present estimates replace those published in *National Income and Capital Formation* and render them obsolete. But it is useful in revealing the extent of revisions that accretion of data and experience can cause, and suggesting the extent of revisions to which the present estimates may be subject in the future. The second comparison shows the major respects in which the present NBER estimates differ from the most widely used current estimates and suggests the magnitudes of the discrepancies to be taken into account in splicing them to ours back to 1919. The third comparison indicates similarly the major differences in scope and basis of King's and the present NBER sets, and should be helpful in any attempt to use the two as one continuous series back to 1909.

The comparisons are not exhaustive in the sense that the difference in every cell is accounted for to the last million dollars. To do so would involve us in details of differences, changes, and revisions that result from minor and gradual accretion of data. The attempt here is to indicate and to account for only the salient points of difference.

1 Preliminary Estimates in National Income and Capital Formation, 1919–1935

National income and aggregate payments to individuals, as published in preliminary form in *National Income and Capital Formation,* and as they appear in this report, are compared in Table 77. The preliminary estimates of national income are smaller in every year. While the relative discrepancy is not large, amounting at its greatest to less than 8 per cent of the present estimate and averaging about 3 per cent, the shortage is sufficient to call for analysis.

Aggregate payments to individuals differ less, and the last column of Table 77 indicates clearly that changes in net savings made by recent revisions are much greater relative to the total than those in aggregate payments. Accumulation of data and development in the theoretical treatment of national in-

come thus affect much more conspicuously the controversial
and obscure area of savings of enterprises than income payments, the concept of which is more definite and the data for
which are less open to improvement.

TABLE 77

National Income and Aggregate Payments to Individuals
Preliminary and Present NBER Estimates Compared
1919–1935 (millions of dollars)

	NATIONAL INCOME			AGG. PAY. EXCL. ENTREP. SAVINGS			DIF. IN NET SAVINGS
	Prelim. NBER	Present NBER	(1 − 2)	Prelim. NBER	Present NBER	(4 − 5)	(3 − 6)
	(1)	(2)	(3)	(4)	(5)	(6)	(7)
1919	59,926	64,203	−4,277	57,499	59,004	−1,505	−2,772
1920	72,386	74,232	−1,846	67,056	68,523	−1,467	−379
1921	58,343	59,412	−1,069	55,177	57,112	−1,935	+866
1922	59,706	60,707	−1,001	58,041	59,718	−1,677	+676
1923	69,706	71,626	−1,920	65,854	67,896	−2,042	+122
1924	70,369	72,095	−1,726	66,763	69,088	−2,325	+599
1925	74,846	76,047	−1,201	69,921	71,993	−2,072	+871
1926	79,477	81,551	−2,074	72,823	75,036	−2,213	+139
1927	77,429	80,051	−2,622	73,381	76,119	−2,738	+116
1928	80,397	81,678	−1,281	75,823	77,945	−2,122	+841
1929	83,424	87,234	−3,810	79,808	82,421	−2,613	−1,197
1930	72,940	77,319	−4,379	73,620	76,520	−2,900	−1,479
1931	56,010	60,300	−4,290	62,565	65,061	−2,496	−1,794
1932	39,628	42,932	−3,304	49,785	52,070	−2,285	−1,019
1933	39,283	42,183	−2,900	47,880	48,659	−779	−2,121
1934 *	47,849	49,548	−1,699	52,385	53,758	−1,373	−326
1935	53,035	54,406	−1,371	56,287	58,016	−1,729	+358
Average 1919–35	64,397	66,796	−2,398	63,804	65,820	−2,016	−382
Avg. disregarding signs			2,398			2,016	922

* Present estimates for 1934 in this and subsequent tables are arithmetic means of the two
estimates for that year appearing in the tables in the Statistical Appendix to Part Two and
in Part Four.

Since the greater relative revision was in total net savings
we analyze the main sources of the change in this item first
(Table 78). The greatest difference in it is in net savings of
governmental agencies. Our preliminary estimates of net governmental savings are the difference between changes in
governmental debt and in tangible assets; in the present estimates account is also taken of changes in the security assets

held by governmental agencies. In the early years of the period these changes in security assets, whose accretion is primarily to the credit of the federal government, were largely increases in claims against foreign governments; and in the later part of the period, i.e., since 1931, increases in claims against public corporations financed and supported by the federal government. We did not originally take these intangible assets into account because we doubted their real worth, a doubt that can still be entertained with reference to claims against foreign governments. Since omission of changes in these assets caused erratic fluctuations in the total net value of governmental services, we finally decided to include them, just as we include in business net savings changes in claims by business establishments. If such claims are not eventually substantiated, the fact will be reflected in revaluations of assets; and such revaluations, like other changes in assets that do not arise from current productive operations, cannot properly be included in current net income. A further revision was introduced by the substitution of new estimates of public construction for those previously available, in preparing the figures on tangible assets. The basic data now used are from Lowell J. Chawner's *Construction Activity in the United States, 1915–37* (Washington, 1938). These modifications in treatment raised savings of government and of enterprises in most years of the period; and this rise accounts for most of the shortage in the preliminary estimates of net savings.

The other revisions in the estimates of net savings were smaller. That in agriculture ranks second and is the result of replacing the preliminary estimates of gross income and expenses by the estimates prepared by the Bureau of Agricultural Economics in connection with the study of Income Parity for Agriculture. The changes in the gross income figures were relatively small but bore heavily upon the residual item, net savings, since the subtrahend (current expenses and income payments) was revised only slightly.

Modifications of the preliminary estimates of savings in con-

TABLE 78

Main Differences in Components of Net Savings
Preliminary and Present NBER Estimates Compared,
1919–1934 (millions of dollars)

	DIFFERENCE IN UNADJUSTED SAVINGS BY INDUSTRIAL DIVISIONS						DIF. IN UNADJ. SAVINGS FOR ALL INDUSTRIAL DIVISIONS	DIF. DUE TO CHANGES IN ADJ.
	Agr.	Constr.	Serv.	Gov.	Misc.	Total		
	(1)	(2)	(3)	(4)	(5)	(6)	(7)	(8)
1919	+481	−87	+97	−2,976	+31	−2,454	−2,410	−362
1920	+127	−55	−107	−287	+65	−237	−173	−206
1921	+1,077	+15	−546	−298	+172	+618	+640	+226
1922	+385	−16	+54	+148	−45	+508	+512	+164
1923	+313	−35	−51	−186	−39	+2	−9	+131
1924	+588	−104	−7	−252	−27	+198	+184	+415
1925	+152	−116	+15	−43	−82	−76	−108	+979
1926	+58	−98	−107	−274	−22	−443	−490	+629
1927	−10	−65	−80	−276	−14	−443	−593	+709
1928	+191	−51	−53	−153	−238	−284	−292	+1,133
1929	−200	−58	−88	−718	−232	−1,246	−1,074	−123
1930	+228	+89	−155	−1,129	−644	−1,671	−1,615	+136
1931	+10	+73	−251	−1,044	−704	−1,916	−1,894	+100
1932	−188	+157	−122	−500	−605	−1,258	−1,221	+202
1933	−242	+68	−675	−705	−499	−2,053	−2,126	+5
1934	−216	+103	−317	−606	+206	−850	+149	−475
Average 1919–34	+172	−14	−155	−580	−167	−724	−658	+229
Avg. disregarding signs	279	69	155	598	226	890	843	375

As in Tables 77 and 79, from the preliminary estimates the present estimates are subtracted. Col. 8: difference between col. 7 of Table 77 and col. 7 of Table 78.

struction were due largely to the revision of the estimate for total construction that utilized the recent estimates of Mr. Chawner. The value of construction was raised in most years, and since net savings in this industry are derived as a ratio to total value, they also were raised.

Preliminary estimates of net savings for the service division were revised partly because of a revision in the average net income of several professional groups. This revision was, in turn, due partly to the accretion of sample data collected by the Department of Commerce and other agencies, and to the recalculation by Milton Friedman of the averages with more careful consideration of the biases of the samples, partly to the revision of the extrapolating series for 1919–28, and partly to the change in the ratio of savings to net income for the combined total of mining, manufacturing, construction, and trade—a ratio that is one of the bases for estimating net savings in the service industries.

Net savings in the miscellaneous industrial division were substantially revised for the years since 1929, owing chiefly to a change in method. In the preliminary estimates we attempted, for the years since 1929, to make corporate net savings check with that in *Statistics of Income*. Accordingly, corporate net savings for miscellaneous industries were estimated as the difference between total net savings accounted for in the specific industries (except agriculture and life insurance) and the overall total in *Statistics of Income*. In the present estimates we abandoned this attempt, concluding that since our estimates of net savings in public utilities are derived from the *Census of Electrical Industries,* sample corporate data, and Interstate Commerce Commission reports, to use the *Statistics of Income* total as a controlling one was undesirable. Hence for the years since 1926 net savings for the miscellaneous industries were estimated on the basis of the item for the specific industries reported in *Statistics of Income* and included by us under the miscellaneous division; and for the earlier years were extrapolated on the basis of the movement of the item in all other industrial divisions.[1]

Finally, changes were made in the adjustment of net savings for profit and loss from sales of capital assets, the effects of revaluation of inventories, and the difference between depreciation charges at original and reproduction costs. The series on profit and loss from sales of capital assets was extended to cover the entire period. In our preliminary estimates the adjustment was made for 1929 and later years only. The revision of the inventory adjustment was due largely to a change in the coverage of trade and construction. When the estimates of activity in these two industries published in *Commodity Flow and Capital Formation* (National Bureau of Economic Research, 1938), Vol. One, were used (in a somewhat revised form), estimates of total inventories and hence of the effects of changing inventory valuations on net savings had to be revised. The changes in the depreciation adjustment were due in part to slight revisions in Dr. Fabricant's estimates of depreciation charges; his final estimates were published in *Capital Consumption and Adjustment*. Other changes were due to our exclusion of the estimated depreciation adjustment on farmers' property, since our agricultural savings are derived after deducting depreciation charges on a current price basis.

The total difference in unadjusted savings for the five industrial divisions given in Table 78 (col. 6) accounts for an overwhelming proportion of the difference between the present and preliminary estimates of the countrywide total of unadjusted net savings (col. 7). The only part of the difference not accounted for, in 1934, arises from the use, in the latter, of sample corporate data and, in the former, of *Statistics of Income* data.

We now turn to an analysis of the sources of the difference between the preliminary and present estimates of aggregate payments to individuals excluding entrepreneurial savings (Table 79). Most of the revisions are due to the appearance

[1] See Part Four, notes to Table Ms 1.

TABLE 79

Main Differences in Components of Aggregate Payments to Individuals
Preliminary and Present NBER Estimates Compared, 1919–1934 (millions of dollars)

	AGR. (1)	MINING (2)	CONSTR. (3)	TRADE (4)	INS. (5)	REAL ESTATE (6)	SERV. (7)	GOV. (8)	MISC. (9)	TOTAL (10)	TOTAL UNACCOUNTED FOR (11)
1919	−107	+68	−327	−27	−152	−1,243	+201	+131	−8	−1,464	−41
1920	−218	+179	−429	−32	−177	−1,292	+281	+175	−13	−1,526	+59
1921	−389	+40	−292	−32	−195	−1,245	+81	+244	−131	−1,919	−16
1922	−418	+93	−531	−42	−204	−1,188	+276	+271	−95	−1,638	−39
1923	−352	+155	−623	−52	−111	−1,269	+83	+297	−145	−2,017	−25
1924	−377	+102	−767	−60	−120	−1,422	+157	+335	−149	−2,301	−24
1925	−329	+117	−854	−70	−127	−1,254	+286	+307	−125	−2,049	−23
1926	−298	+136	−1,076	−83	−129	−1,124	+182	+304	−145	−2,233	+20
1927	−249	+95	−967	−119	−144	−1,191	−226	+323	−210	−2,688	−50
1928	−239	+86	−817	−161	−166	−1,003	+61	+348	−159	−2,050	−72
1929	−277	+97	−920	−215	−155	−1,189	−5	+379	−128	−2,413	−200
1930	−532	+72	−925	−241	−162	−1,240	−133	+593	+7	−2,761	−139
1931	−563	+25	−658	−515	−164	−1,055	+55	+275	−21	−2,416	−80
1932	−451	−2	−571	−343	−158	−802	−5	+184	−75	−2,223	−62
1933	−232	−1	−174	−298	−149	−846	+973	+281	−227	−733	−46
1934	−257	+33	−84	−711	−154	−961	+811	+211	−207	−1,319	−51
Average 1919–34	−330	+81	−613	−175	−154	−1,145	+192	+275	−114	−1,984	−49
Avg. disregarding signs	330	81	613	175	154	1,145	238	275	115	1,984	59

Col. 11: difference between col. 6 of Table 77 and col. 10 of Table 79.

of new and more comprehensive data. The Department of Agriculture's estimates of gross income and expenses in agriculture have replaced the data formerly used in the agricultural estimates. The 1935 *Census of Business* segregated for the first time wages paid by mining contractors (for anthracite coal), thereby making it possible to revise the earlier estimate, which was based on statements from Bureau of Mines authorities. Also, contract work in oil and gas wells, which is apparently primarily construction and drilling of wells rather than production of oil and gas, was transferred to construction. For construction the more comprehensive estimates of Mr. Chawner were used. The estimates for trade were raised to include employee compensation at central administrative offices of retailers. There also were revisions in the 1930's owing to new Census data. The 1935 Census collected new data on payrolls in insurance agencies. For real estate the revision was extensive. D. L. Wickens' data on the ratio of average to median rents (from a special tabulation of Census data) and on rent-value ratios for specific Real Property Inventory cities led to an upward revision in most years. The use of the Department of Commerce study of individuals' long term debt raised the estimates of interest. The ratio of net to gross rent, applied to imputed rent, was raised, resulting in increased estimates of imputed rent in all years. For service, new sample data and Mr. Friedman's recomputation of the averages led to a downward revision of the preliminary estimates. In estimating net government interest we deducted receipts of interest by state and local governments. A second revision in government was the elimination, from pensions, of contributions by employees to pension funds. Finally, in the miscellaneous division, the new treatment of dividends and interest (see comments above on net savings) and a more careful estimate for such industries as could be segregated resulted in larger totals in most years.

The differences in Table 79 and the comments just made account for all except a minor part of the total differences be-

tween our preliminary and present estimates. For 1929 and
1930 a substantial discrepancy between the two sets is still un-
accounted for (see col. 11). This discrepancy, almost entirely
in the estimates for manufacturing, is due in part to a correction in *Statistics of Income* for 1929 and in part to estimating
by detailed parts rather than as a whole.

2 *Department of Commerce Estimates*

The present estimates cannot be expected to agree as closely
with those of the Department of Commerce. Estimates by different investigators usually reflect differences in the treatment
of controversial questions and in the extent to which they
venture to stretch inadequate data in order to attain comprehensive scope. Also, since the Department of Commerce estimates cover only the years since 1929, whereas we attempt a
continuous coverage back to 1919, differences in details of
classification and in some specific aspects of methods are inevitable. Discrepancies between the two sets, due to a cumu-
lation of minor differences in methods and data, are therefore inevitably larger than between our own two sets, and
our accounting for them cannot be as fine.

The differences between the Department of Commerce and
our estimates of national income are much more substantial
than between the two estimates of payments to individuals
(Table 80), indicating clearly that there is a major discrepancy in the estimates of net savings of enterprises. By and
large, the Department of Commerce totals for both national
income and payments to individuals are smaller than ours.
The differences average about 3 per cent of either total of
national income and of aggregate payments to individuals.

Our estimates include three items omitted by the Department of Commerce: imputed rent on owner-occupied houses,
direct relief payments, and net savings of governmental
agencies. Furthermore, the Department of Commerce ad-
justs business savings for gains and losses on sales of capital
assets, but not for gains and losses on inventory holdings or

TABLE 80

National Income and Aggregate Payments to Individuals

Department of Commerce and Present NBER Estimates Compared, 1929–1938 (millions of dollars)

	1929	1930	1931	1932	1933	1934	1935	1936	1937	1938	AVG. 1929–38	AVG. DISREGARDING SIGNS
National income												
1 D of C	82,885	68,901	54,310	40,074	42,430	50,347	55,860	64,936	71,028	63,547	59,432	
2 Present	87,234	77,319	60,300	42,932	42,183	49,548	54,406	62,864	70,494	65,461	61,274	
3 (1 − 2)	−4,349	−8,418	−5,990	−2,858	+247	+799	+1,454	+2,072	+534	−1,914	−1,842	2,864
Aggregate payments excl. entrepreneurial savings												
4 D of C	80,611	74,211	62,816	49,289	45,515	51,788	55,886	63,922	70,118	64,944	61,910	
5 Present	82,421	76,520	65,061	52,070	48,659	53,758	58,016	64,537	70,966	66,061	63,807	
6 (4 − 5)	−1,810	−2,309	−2,245	−2,781	−3,144	−1,970	−2,130	−615	−848	−1,117	−1,897	1,897
Net savings												
7 Difference (3 − 6)	−2,539	−6,109	−3,745	−77	+3,391	+2,769	+3,584	+2,687	+1,382	−797	+55	2,708

All Department of Commerce estimates in this and subsequent tables are based upon unpublished data underlying 'National Income at Nearly 70 Billion Dollars in 1939', *Survey of Current Business*, June 1940.

for the difference between depreciation charges at original and reproduction costs. Although the Department of Commerce estimates of pensions and similar other income of employees are of distinctly broader industrial coverage than ours we include the military and naval compensation and pensions reported by the Veterans' Administration and consequently our estimates of 'other labor income' are larger than those of the Department of Commerce.

When these differences in definitions and coverage are taken into account (Table 81), the discrepancy between the two sets, so much larger in Table 80, shrinks to moderate proportions. The residual difference between the two national income totals ranges from $76 million to $2.0 billion, and at its largest is less than 3 per cent of either. The residual difference between the two totals of payments to individuals is still smaller, ranging from $17 million to $1.4 billion, and at its largest is only slightly over 2 per cent of either. The residual discrepancy in the two estimates of net savings is sizable, although far smaller than that in Table 80.

But since small overall differences may conceal large differences for industrial divisions, we compare the two sets of estimates in greater detail. Agriculture, transportation and other public utilities, service, and miscellaneous are the divisions for which the two sets of estimates of net savings differ markedly (Table 82), for various reasons. For agriculture the difference is in entrepreneurial withdrawals. Our estimates assume that withdrawals per farmer equal full-time compensation per farm worker plus some allowances for (a) family labor and (b) the difference between average consumption expenditures of farm operators and farm workers. The Department of Commerce estimates do not provide for the second allowance (b). Consequently our estimate of farmers' withdrawals is distinctly larger, and since net income originating is approximately the same in the two sets, the Department of Commerce estimate of net savings is much larger.

The comparison for transportation and other public utili-

TABLE 81

Differences due to Differences in Definitions and Coverage
Department of Commerce and Present NBER Estimates Compared, 1929–1938 (millions of dollars)

	1929	1930	1931	1932	1933	1934	1935	1936	1937	1938	AVG. 1929–38	AVG. DISREGARDING SIGNS
1 Imputed rent	−2,337	−2,283	−1,789	−1,284	−1,216	−1,048	−1,107	−1,115	−1,315	−1,421	−1,486	1,486
2 Relief payments					−482	−657	−834	−439	−407	−476	−330	330
3 Dif. in coverage of other empl. comp.	−261	−278	−377	−416	−317	−248	−273	−506	−425	−347	−345	345
4 Gov. savings	−2,225	−2,104	−344	+906	+113	+575	+1,736	+2,196	−497	+175	+53	1,087
5 Adj. for gains on inventory holdings	−702	−4,115	−3,290	−1,471	+2,273	+1,487	+724	+164	+635	−1,104	−534	1,590
6 Adj. of depreciation item	+553	+286	+9	−353	−364	−44	+15	+185	+572	+524	+138	290
7 Total dif. (1 — 6)	−4,972	−8,494	−5,681	−2,618	+7	+65	+261	+485	−1,487	−2,649	−2,503	2,667
8 Residual dif. in nat. income: (3) of Table 80 minus (7)	+623	+76	−309	−240	+240	+734	+1,193	+1,587	+1,971	+735	+661	771
9 Dif. affecting agg. pay. (1 — 3)	−2,598	−2,561	−2,116	−1,700	−2,015	−1,953	−2,214	−2,060	−2,147	−2,244	−2,161	2,377
10 Residual dif. in agg. pay: (6) of Table 80 minus (9)	+788	+252	−129	−1,081	−1,129	−17	+84	+1,445	+1,299	+1,127	+264	735
11 Residual dif. in net savings (8 minus 10)	−165	−176	−180	+841	+1,369	+751	+1,109	+142	+672	−392	+397	580

ties is not quite exact, because the Department of Commerce coverage is somewhat broader: it includes and we exclude motor transportation, public warehousing, and air transportation. But according to unpublished Department of Commerce detail, net savings in motor and air transportation were consistently negative from 1929 to 1938, ranging from — $8 million in 1929 to — $82 million in 1932. Hence the difference between the two estimates would, for a comparable area, be about the same as that indicated in Table 82. The reason for this difference is that our estimates of net savings in transportation and other public utilities are based largely upon Interstate Commerce Commission reports and the *Census of Electrical Industries* while the Department of Commerce estimates are based largely on *Statistics of Income*. The former, obtained from standardized accounting forms and not subject to the bias from which all reporting for income tax purposes is likely to suffer, seemed preferable to *Statistics of Income,* although their use does disturb somewhat the comparability of the resulting estimates with those for the industrial divisions for which *Statistics of Income* is used.

The Department of Commerce coverage of the service group is also different from ours, including accounting, chambers of commerce, trade associations, other miscellaneous business service, and various repair services. Another source of difference is that we include all professional service industries, while the Department of Commerce includes only religious, curative, legal, and engineering service, and private education. A third source is the Department of Commerce assumption that the total net income of professional entrepreneurs is withdrawn by them. We estimated the savings of professional entrepreneurs on the basis of the ratio of savings to net income for manufacturing, mining, construction, and trade.

The discrepancy between the two estimates of net savings in the miscellaneous division is more apparent than real. If we added to the Department of Commerce totals the net savings arising in motor and air transportation (which we in-

TABLE 82

Main Differences in Components of Net Savings due to Differences in Methods of Estimation
Department of Commerce and Present NBER Estimates Compared, 1929–1938 (millions of dollars)

	1929	1930	1931	1932	1933	1934	1935	1936	1937	1938	AVG. 1929–38	AVG. DISREGARDING SIGNS
Agriculture												
1 D of C	935	−277	−1,016	−1,058	161	966	1,364	1,805	1,713	887	548	
2 Present	77	−1,335	−1,780	−1,671	−491	340	639	1,045	624	−83	−264	
3 (1 − 2)	+858	+1,058	+764	+613	+652	+626	+725	+760	+1,689	+970	+812	812
Transportation and other public utilities												
4 D of C	460	−368	−636	−848	−436	−475	−481	−123	−183	−416	−351	
5 Present	757	131	−194	−474	−176	−221	−197	213	122	−90	−13	
6 (4 − 5)	−297	−499	−442	−374	−260	−254	−284	−336	−305	−326	−338	338
Service												
7 D of C	−18	−388	−594	−787	−410	−268	−232	−220	−196	−226	−334	
8 Present	511	301	−268	−1,321	−1,314	−556	−403	−107	−228	39	−335	
9 (7 − 8)	−529	−689	−326	+534	+904	+288	+171	−113	+32	−265	+1	385
Miscellaneous												
10 D of C	−89	−432	−391	−290	−286	−126	260	−352	−290	−339	−234	
11 Present	−77	−473	−440	−448	−416	−270	−296	−202	−198	−184	−300	
12 (10 — 11)	−12	+41	+49	+158	+130	+144	+556	−150	−92	−155	+67	149
13 Total dif. (3 + 6 + 9 + 12)	+20	−89	+45	+931	+1,426	+804	+1,168	+161	+724	+224	+541	559
14 Residual dif. in net savings: (11) of Table 81 minus (13)	−185	−87	−225	−90	−57	−53	−59	−19	−52	−616	−144	144

All estimates of savings presented above are adjusted only for gains and losses on sales of capital assets. Line 4 includes savings of motor transportation, public warehousing, and air transportation, which are excluded from line 5. These industries are included in line 11 but not in line 10.

clude under the miscellaneous division), the discrepancy would become insignificant.

Between the two sets of estimates of payments to individuals the main differences are in entrepreneurial withdrawals in agriculture, rent paid to individuals, total manufacturing, total construction, total service, and total miscellaneous (Table 83). In the other divisions the differences are minor; and their total combined discrepancy ranges from $3 million to $307 million, an exceedingly small part of aggregate payments to individuals or of the total payments originating in these industries. The reason for the large excess in our estimate of withdrawals by farmers has already been indicated. The difference in net rent (paid, not imputed) received by individuals arises from a difference in the estimated ratio of net to gross rent. The ratio underlying the Department of Commerce estimate is 50 per cent, derived from a "consensus of authorities". In our estimates the ratio is based upon samples of operating expenses for apartment and office buildings which suggest an appreciably lower ratio. The difference in the manufacturing estimates is due to the inclusion by the Department of Commerce of payments to employees in distributing offices, canvassed for the first time in the *Census of Business,* 1935. These employees are covered by us in the miscellaneous division. The reason for the excess in our estimates for construction is that our basic figures on the value of construction include contracts for private maintenance construction whereas the Department of Commerce figures cover new private construction only. Since employee compensation is derived by applying to the value of construction the ratio of wages and salaries to value, total payments reflect the difference in the value estimates. Our inclusion of miscellaneous professional services (mentioned above in connection with the coverage of service) accounts in large part for our higher total service (line 15).

The higher Department of Commerce estimate for the miscellaneous division (including motor transportation, pub-

TABLE 83

Main Differences in Components of Aggregate Payments to Individuals due to Differences in Methods of Estimation Department of Commerce and Present NBER Estimates Compared, 1929–1938 (millions of dollars)

	1929	1930	1931	1932	1933	1934	1935	1936	1937	1938	AVG. 1929–38	AVG. DISREGARDING SIGNS
Entrepreneurial withdrawals, agriculture												
1 D of C	4,693	4,429	3,565	2,719	2,464	2,760	3,016	3,219	3,622	3,553	3,404	
2 Present	5,899	5,579	4,541	3,502	3,166	3,500	3,775	4,028	4,546	4,492	4,303	
3 (1 − 2)	−1,206	−1,150	−976	−783	−702	−740	−759	−809	−924	−939	−899	899
Rent paid to individuals												
4 D of C	3,364	2,674	2,036	1,224	1,208	1,455	1,691	1,909	2,113	1,975	1,965	
5 Present	2,581	1,982	1,288	807	898	857	1,036	1,071	1,264	1,154	1,294	
6 (4 − 5)	+783	+692	+748	+417	+310	+598	+655	+838	+849	+821	+671	671
Total payments, manufacturing												
7 D of C	19,097	16,763	12,926	8,872	8,817	10,917	12,424	14,672	16,770	13,068	13,433	
8 Present	18,237	15,972	12,315	8,550	8,429	10,402	11,831	14,015	16,048	12,339	12,814	
9 (7 − 8)	+860	+791	+611	+322	+388	+515	+593	+657	+722	+729	+619	619
Total payments, construction												
10 D of C	3,591	2,739	1,938	1,147	707	843	1,017	1,621	1,935	1,769	1,731	
11 Present	3,951	3,443	2,297	1,404	968	1,022	1,163	1,648	1,884	1,693	1,947	
12 (10 − 11)	−360	−704	−359	−257	−261	−179	−146	−27	+51	+76	−217	242
Total payments, service												
13 D of C	9,606	9,084	7,908	6,388	5,705	6,421	7,031	7,833	8,644	8,261	7,683	
14 Present	10,756	10,108	9,037	7,811	7,142	7,319	7,771	8,392	9,349	8,824	8,651	
15 (13 − 14)	−1,150	−1,024	−1,129	−1,473	−1,437	−898	−740	−559	−705	−563	−968	968
Total payments, miscellaneous												
16 D of C	5,173	4,971	4,300	3,445	3,145	3,410	3,293	4,239	4,548	4,436	4,096	
17 Present	3,553	3,327	3,017	2,574	2,427	2,537	2,863	3,124	3,368	3,189	2,998	
18 (16 − 17)	+1,620	+1,644	+1,283	+871	+718	+873	+430	+1,115	+1,180	+1,247	+1,098	1,098
19 Total dif. (3 + 6 + 9 + 12 + 15 + 18)	+547	+249	+178	−903	−984	+169	+33	+1,215	+1,173	+1,371	+305	682
20 Residual dif. in agg. pay: (10) of Table 81 minus (19)	+241	+3	−307	−178	−145	−186	+51	+230	+126	−244	−41	171

Line 16 is the sum of total payments in miscellaneous industries, motor transportation and public warehousing, and air trans portation. Lines 7, 10, 13, and 16 exclude 'other labor income', differences in this item having already been considered.

lic warehousing, and air transportation) is due to a larger estimated number of employees and entrepreneurs attached to it. The difference is due partly to the inclusion, under the Department of Commerce miscellaneous division, of a few professional service industries and partly to our method of computing the number attached to the miscellaneous division. By subtracting from an overall measure of gainfully occupied those attached to the specific industries whose income activities have already been accounted for we estimate the number of persons engaged in the miscellaneous industries in 1929 as 2.0 million. The corresponding Department of Commerce estimate, based on data for the miscellaneous division, is 2.2 million.

3 King's Estimates

Since the estimates prepared under the direction of W. I. King and published in *National Income and Its Purchasing Power* were completed more than a decade ago many new data, of both comprehensive Census and sample coverage, have become available. While most are for recent years, making possible estimates for industrial divisions that could not be measured separately before, they provide basing points, with the help of which better estimates can be derived for the earlier years covered by King.

We therefore found, as we expected, that King's estimates differ much more from ours than do those of the Department of Commerce. But large as the differences are, a major proportion of the industrial divisions covered by King is truly comparable with ours both as to scope and the character of the underlying data; and for these divisions the differences, while still large, do not bar using one set of estimates as a continuation of the other.

The totals of national income, aggregate payments to individuals, and net savings are compared in Table 84. The differences between the two estimates of national income, if we accept in both instances the most comprehensive concept,

TABLE 84

National Income, Aggregate Payments to Individuals, and Net Savings

King's and Present NBER Estimates Compared, 1919–1925 (millions of dollars)

	1919	1920	1921	1922	1923	1924	1925	AVG. 1919–25	AVG. DISREGARDING SIGNS
National income									
1 King [1]	54,058	72,659	88,254	75,416	72,819	90,191	85,369	76,967	
2 Present	64,203	74,232	59,412	60,707	71,626	72,095	76,047	68,332	
3 (1 — 2)	−10,145	−1,573	+28,842	+14,709	+1,193	+18,096	+9,322	+8,635	11,983
Aggregate payments excl. entrepreneurial savings									
4 King [2]	65,949	73,999	63,371	65,925	74,337	77,135	81,931	71,807	
5 Present	59,004	68,523	57,112	59,718	67,896	69,088	71,993	64,762	
6 (4 — 5)	+6,945	+5,476	+6,259	+6,207	+6,441	+8,047	+9,938	+7,045	7,045
Difference due to net savings									
7 (3 — 6)	−17,090	−7,049	+22,583	+8,502	−5,248	+10,049	−616	+1,590	10,162
Net savings and gains in property values									
8 King [3]	−11,891	−1,340	+24,884	+9,490	−1,518	+13,056	+3,438	+5,160	10,162
9 Present net savings, adj.	+5,199	+5,709	+2,301	+989	+3,730	+3,007	+4,055	+3,570	
10 (8 — 9)	−17,090	−7,049	+22,583	+8,501	−5,248	+10,049	−617	+1,590	10,162
11 Present net savings, unadj.	+8,851	+3,886	−3,177	+2,672	+5,173	+4,136	+6,203	+3,963	
12 (8 — 11)	−20,742	−5,226	+28,061	+6,818	−6,691	+8,920	−2,765	+1,197	11,318

Lines 1, 4, and 8 are from W. I. King, *National Income and Its Purchasing Power*, Table LII. All subsequent citations of King's estimates (tables numbered with Roman numerals) are from the same source.

1 Income of all people.
2 Entire realized income.
3 Gains in purchasing power of property values.

are striking indeed. At their largest, in 1921, they amount to almost one-half of our estimate; and they average, signs disregarded, about 17 per cent of the average of our estimates of national income. But an important source of the difference lies in the estimates of net savings, since they are based upon different concepts. King's concept of savings as an item complementary to payments to individuals led him to interpret them as gains in purchasing power of property values held by individuals. We, on the other hand, treat them as part of current net value product retained by enterprises. It is this difference in concept that causes the huge discrepancies in lines 10 and 12 of Table 84, since changes in property values are bound to fluctuate much more violently than net savings of enterprises, tracing a different pattern.[2]

While the difference in the savings item accounts for a substantial part of the difference between the two estimates of national income, King's 'entire realized income' is consistently larger than our 'aggregate payments to individuals', comparable concepts. The excess ranges between $5.5 and $7 billion from 1919 through 1923, and increases markedly in 1924 and 1925. We trace its sources and show its effect on the relative apportionment of the two totals by industrial source and type of payment, treating first the differences that arise from differences in coverage (Table 85).

King's 'entire realized income' includes three items omitted from our 'aggregate payments to individuals': (a) net income from urban poultry and gardens; (b) net income from urban cow keeping; (c) interest on durable goods accruing to owner-users. The totals under these heads, as estimated by King, amount to about $3 billion annually (except in 1920 when

2 Our concept of net savings of enterprises (unadjusted) is identical with that used in the first income study of the National Bureau of Economic Research, *Income in the United States*, 1909–1919. The algebraic sum of changes in property values from 1919 to 1925 differs from that of unadjusted savings of enterprises by an annual average of only $1 billion. This small difference may be accidental, although there are reasons to assume that over a long period the average value of the two items should be fairly close.

TABLE 85

Differences in Aggregate Payments to Individuals due largely to Differences in Coverage King's and Present NBER Estimates Compared, 1919-1925 (millions of dollars)

	1919	1920	1921	1922	1923	1924	1925	AVG. 1919–25	AVG. DISREGARDING SIGNS
Items incl. by King and omitted by us									
1 Urban poultry & gardens	197	187	117	120	128	132	147	147	
2 Urban cow keeping	126	135	100	85	97	95	96	105	
3 Int. on durable goods	2,740	3,717	3,015	2,596	2,834	2,923	3,000	2,975	
4 Total	3,063	4,039	3,232	2,801	3,059	3,150	3,243	3,227	3,227
Total payments, agriculture									
5 King	11,009	9,864	5,831	6,284	7,017	7,276	8,016	7,900	
6 Present	8,587	9,975	6,981	6,768	7,374	7,471	7,526	7,812	
7 (5 − 6)	+2,422	−111	−1,150	−484	−357	−195	+490	+88	
8 Est. net savings in agr. (King)	3,151	898	−1,870	−848	−358	−250	461	169	744
Total payments, manufacturing									
9 King	15,941	19,356	13,080	13,757	16,631	16,071	16,661	15,928	
10 Present	14,340	16,740	11,760	12,285	15,289	14,578	15,396	14,341	
11 (9 − 10)	+1,601	+2,616	+1,320	+1,472	+1,342	+1,493	+1,265	+1,587	
12 Est. duplication in King	797	+1,041	+755	+677	+868	+762	+762	+809	809
13 Residual excess in King [transferred to 'all other', Table 87, (2)]	+804	+1,575	+565	+795	+474	+731	+503	+778	
14 Excess accounted for (4 + 7 + 12)	+6,282	+4,969	+2,837	+2,994	+3,570	+3,717	+4,495	+4,123	4,123
15 Residual excess: (6) of Table 84 minus (14)	+663	+507	+3,422	+3,213	+2,871	+4,330	+5,443	+2,921	2,921

Lines 1–3: Table CXXXIII.

Line 5: King's estimate of realized income (Table XIV), excluding rent paid to non-farmers (Table XCVIII).

Line 9: King's estimate of realized income (Table XIV), excluding rent paid (from original source books).

Line 12: wages and salaries in steam and electric railroad repair shops, reported for 1919, 1921, 1923, and 1925 in the *Census of Manufactures* and interpolated between 1919 and 1923 by the Federal Reserve Board payrolls index for car building and repairing and between 1923 and 1925 by the Bureau of Labor Statistics payrolls index for railroad repair shops.

they were over $4 billion) and account for almost one-half of the difference between the two estimates of payments to individuals.

Furthermore, King includes under income realized from agriculture rent paid to non-farmers and net savings of farm operators. Since we include the former item under real estate, we transferred King's estimate of it to this division in Tables 86-90. And since we exclude completely farmers' net savings from the narrower total of payments to individuals we computed them by estimating farmers' withdrawals on the basis of King's figures on the number of farmers and average compensation of farm workers; and subtracting these withdrawals from King's total net income of farm operators. The results (Table 85, line 8) indicate that the major part of the difference in the two estimates for agriculture for 1919, 1921, 1923, 1924, and 1925 is due to the inclusion, in King's total, of net savings. The residual difference under agriculture, averaging about $81 million, is a relatively small part of the total and is due largely to our use of more recent and more comprehensive data on gross income and expenses.

King's estimates for manufacturing had to be adjusted in two respects to be comparable with ours. First, they include wages and salaries in repair shops of steam and electric railroads, apparently duplicating this item under transportation and public utilities. The correction is entered in line 12 of Table 85. Second, King includes under manufacturing custom grist and saw mills, manufactured gas, power laundries, and motion pictures—industries included by us under other divisions. Since other incomes in King's estimate for manufacturing agree fairly closely with ours, we thought it best to ascribe the entire excess in his estimates (remaining after the correction for duplication) (line 13) to wages and salaries, and transfer it to the 'all other' division in Table 87 (line 2).

With these differences in coverage and classification (as well as the basis of the estimate in agriculture) accounted for, the excess of King's 'entire realized income' over our 'aggregate

TABLE 86

Income Payments Originating in Directly Comparable Industrial Divisions

King's and Present NBER Estimates Compared, 1919–1925 (millions of dollars)

	1919	1920	1921	1922	1923	1924	1925	AVG. 1919–25	AVG. DISREGARDING SIGNS
Mining									
1 King	1,675	2,050	1,660	1,518	2,128	1,800	1,914	1,821	
2 Present	1,728	2,315	1,821	1,610	2,273	1,997	1,937	1,954	
3 (1—2)	—53	—265	—161	—92	—145	—197	—23	—134	134
Construction									
4 King	1,846	1,895	1,740	2,198	2,465	2,974	3,458	2,368	
5 Present	1,868	2,522	1,915	2,306	3,280	3,469	3,706	2,724	
6 (4—5)	—22	—627	—175	—108	—815	—495	—248	—356	356
Steam railroad, Pullman, & express									
7 King	3,856	4,818	3,801	3,689	4,128	3,999	4,073	4,052	
8 Present	3,880	4,852	3,881	3,718	4,156	4,024	4,105	4,079	
9 (7—8)	—24	—34	—20	—29	—28	—25	—32	—27	27
Street railways									
10 King	552	652	646	627	671	671	668	641	
11 Present	516	607	583	608	622	620	605	594	
12 (10—11)	+36	+45	+63	+19	+49	+51	+63	+47	47
Water transportation									
13 King	710	896	741	555	563	602	587	665	
14 Present	559	747	562	484	495	520	505	553	
15 (13—14)	+151	+149	+179	+71	+68	+82	+82	+112	112
Communication									
16 King	406	518	528	568	626	679	719	578	
17 Present	392	493	502	532	591	636	679	546	
18 (16—17)	+14	+25	+26	+36	+35	+43	+40	+31	31

Electric light and power

19 King	267	323	365	413	505	571	679	446	
20 Present	290	337	365	434	558	663	737	483	
21 (19 — 20)	—23	—14	0	—21	—53	—92	—58	—37	37
Trade									
22 King	7,517	8,192	7,872	8,077	10,130	10,362	11,261	9,059	
23 Present	8,061	9,071	7,708	8,074	8,854	9,089	9,548	8,629	
24 (22 — 23)	—544	—879	+164	+3	+1,276	+1,273	+1,713	+429	836
Banking									
25 King	646	775	848	930	997	1,029	1,094	903	
26 Present	658	770	821	843	871	906	947	831	
27 (25 — 26)	—12	+5	+27	+87	+126	+123	+147	+72	75
Rent									
28 King	5,368	6,200	6,620	6,781	6,842	7,117	7,322	6,607	
29 Present rent	3,967	4,288	4,470	4,897	5,165	5,632	5,466	4,841	
30 Present interest, real estate	829	900	954	990	1,141	1,245	1,419	1,068	
31 Present total (29 + 30)	4,796	5,188	5,424	5,887	6,306	6,877	6,885	5,909	
32 (28 — 31)	+572	+1,012	+1,196	+894	+536	+240	+437	+698	698
Government									
33 King	6,136	5,311	5,629	5,792	5,783	5,896	6,130	5,811	
34 Present	5,071	5,124	5,248	5,282	5,431	5,561	5,751	5,353	
35 (33 — 34)	+1,065	+187	+381	+510	+352	+335	+379	+458	458
36 Total difference (3 + 6 + 9 + 12 + 15 + 18 + 21 + 24 + 27 + 32 + 35)	+1,160	—396	+1,680	+1,370	+1,401	+1,338	+2,500	+1,293	1,406
37 Dif: Table 85, (15)	+663	+507	+3,422	+3,213	+2,871	+4,330	+5,443	+2,921	2,921
38 Residual dif. (37 — 36)	—497	+903	+1,742	+1,843	+1,470	+2,992	+2,943	+1,628	1,770

Lines 1, 4, 7, 10, 13, 16, 19, 22, 25, 33: Table XIV, excluding estimates of rent originating (from original source books).
Line 28: sum of estimates of rent for agriculture, mining, manufacturing, express, electric railways, telegraphs, mercantile, unclassified, leased houses not on farms, and imputed rent on owner-occupied urban houses. Of these only the first and the last two are given in King's published report (see Tables XCVIII and CXXXIII).

payments to individuals' is cut in half. The residual difference
(line 15) is about $500 million in 1919 and 1920, about $3
billion in 1921 through 1923, and about $5 billion in 1924
and 1925.

The industrial divisions for which the two sets of estimates
can be compared directly, without any adjustment for coverage, are listed in Table 86. Our attempt to correct for interest
receipts on government securities and pension contributions
by employees lessens slightly the comparability of King's and
our estimates by industrial divisions. Nevertheless in the industrial divisions for which few new data have accumulated
since King completed his report—mining, the combined
groups of transportation and communication (exclusive of
pipe lines and manufactured gas), banking, and government
(except for 1919)—the differences are moderate.

In construction, trade, and rent the differences are consistently substantial. The difference in construction seems to
be due primarily to the difference in the value of construction. Our estimates are based on data collected recently. That
in trade seems to be due largely to a difference in the trend of
sales. King's total sales rise much more steeply from 1919 to
1925 than ours, which are from the commodity flow and capital formation study. As a result, his income payments rise
much more rapidly. Our smaller totals for rent seem to be
due largely to the much lower ratio of net to gross rent in
our calculations. In many components of the rent total (estimated by King for each industrial division in which it is assumed to originate), the figure for gross rent is used for net.
In other components of the rent total, the ratio of net to gross
is less than 100 per cent, but is still appreciably higher than
that derived from operating expense samples which we used.[3]

The discrepancies in directly comparable industrial divi-

[3] In order to assure comparability with King's estimate, we include not only
net rent received by individuals and imputed rent but also interest originating.
King seems not to have differentiated between these two types of income
derived by individuals from real estate.

sions account for a substantial part of the total excess of King's estimate of income payments over ours. But even when added to those previously accounted for in Table 85, they do not account fully for the difference between the two totals of payments to individuals. The residual difference (Table 86, line 38) is substantial, and still rises rapidly from the earlier to the later years of the period covered by the comparison. Its source, of course, is largely in the difference between King's 'all other' and our estimates for industrial divisions (including our 'miscellaneous') for which there is no comparable, segregable division in King's total (Table 87).

TABLE 87

Income Payments Originating in the 'All Other' Comparable Industries, King's and Present NBER Estimates Compared 1919–1925 (millions of dollars)

	1919	1920	1921	1922	1923	1924	1925	AVG. 1919–25
King 'All other'								
1 Unclassified	6,977	9,120	10,785	11,579	12,424	14,552	15,685	11,589
2 Residual from mfg.	804	1,575	565	795	474	731	503	778
3 Net income from foreign investments	−17	−8	−7	354	369	390	419	214
4 Total	7,764	10,687	11,343	12,728	13,267	15,673	16,607	12,581
Present 'All other'								
5 Mfd. gas	134	137	122	117	142	167	177	142
6 Pipe lines	58	65	67	94	82	79	111	79
7 Insurance	662	792	830	878	882	974	1,082	871
8 Real estate other than covered	502	626	615	625	749	768	743	661
9 Service	5,001	6,021	5,969	6,974	7,419	8,034	8,667	6,869
10 Misc.	1,901	2,143	1,999	2,198	2,520	2,657	2,884	2,329
11 Total	8,258	9,784	9,602	10,886	11,794	12,679	13,664	10,952
12 Difference * (4 − 11)	−494	+903	+1,741	+1,842	+1,473	+2,994	+2,943	+1,629

Line 1: Table XIV, excluding rent originating (from original source books).
Line 2: Table 85, (13).
Line 3: Table CXXXIII.
Line 8: sum of our estimates of employee compensation and dividends in real estate.
* Average for 1919–25, disregarding signs, is $1,770 million.

By far the largest component in King's 'all other' is total payments originating in the unclassified division. Estimated as a unit, it is largely the product of a single average compensation figure and the number of employees and entrepreneurs

estimated as attached to and employed in this carry-all residual industrial division. But our corresponding 'all other',
the miscellaneous division, estimated similarly, accounts on
the average for about one-fifth of the total for the group. The
rest is estimated by parts, i.e., on the basis of specific data for
each part. It is this difference in the method of estimation and
the character of the underlying data that accounts for the
substantial and varying difference between the two estimates.
A large part of the *increase* over the period in the excess of
King's total payments to individuals over our estimates is due
to this discrepancy of the totals for the 'all other' or miscellaneous divisions.[4]

We now compare the percentage distributions of the two
totals by industrial divisions (Table 88). In deriving the percentage distribution of King's total, the following adjustments, already explained, were made: (a) from his 'entire
realized income' we subtracted the items we excluded—income
from urban poultry, gardens, and cows, interest on durable
goods utilized by their owners, net savings in agriculture, and
the duplication of railroad repair shops; (b) for his manufacturing total we substituted our total and transferred the difference (remaining after the adjustment for duplication) to
his 'all other' division; (c) we excluded from the total for all
industrial divisions the item 'rent originating', and transferred the amounts to a separate rent category. The only adjustment we made in our own estimates was to include under
rent not only rent received by individuals and imputed rent
but also interest originating in real estate.

After these minor adjustments, the percentage distributions
of the two totals by industrial source show small differences,
especially in the averages for the period as a whole. The share
of the commodity producing industries—agriculture, mining,
manufacturing, construction—is consistently smaller in King's
estimates. But the difference is moderate, averaging about
6 per cent of the total share. Similarly, the share of the com-

4 The other factor is the divergency in trend of the two totals for trade.

TABLE 88: Payments to Individuals

Percentage Distribution by Industrial Divisions

King's and Present NBER Estimates Compared, 1919–1925

	1919	1920	1921	1922	1923	1924	1925	AVG. 1919–25	AVG. DISRE- GARDING SIGNS
Agriculture									
1 King	13.3	13.2	12.6	11.3	10.4	10.2	9.8	11.5	
2 Present	14.6	14.6	12.2	11.3	10.9	10.8	10.5	12.1	
3 (1 — 2)	—1.3	—1.4	+0.4	0.0	—0.5	—0.6	—0.7	—0.6	0.7
Mining									
4 King	2.8	3.0	2.7	2.4	3.0	2.4	2.5	2.7	
5 Present	2.9	3.4	3.2	2.7	3.3	2.9	2.7	3.0	
6 (4 — 5)	—0.1	—0.4	—0.5	—0.3	—0.3	—0.5	—0.2	—0.3	0.3
Manufacturing									
7 King	24.3	24.6	19.2	19.4	21.6	19.8	19.9	21.3	
8 Present	24.3	24.4	20.6	20.6	22.5	21.1	21.4	22.1	
9 (7 — 8)	0.0	+0.2	—1.4	—1.2	—0.9	—1.3	—1.5	—0.9	0.9
Construction									
10 King	3.1	2.8	2.8	3.5	3.5	4.0	4.5	3.5	
11 Present	3.2	3.7	3.4	3.9	4.8	5.0	5.1	4.2	
12 (10 — 11)	—0.1	—0.9	—0.6	—0.4	—1.3	—1.0	—0.6	—0.7	0.7
Steam railroad, Pullman, & express									
13 King	6.5	7.1	6.2	5.8	5.8	5.4	5.3	6.0	
14 Present	6.6	7.1	6.7	6.2	6.1	5.8	5.7	6.3	
15 (13 — 14)	—0.1	0.0	—0.5	—0.4	—0.3	—0.4	—0.4	—0.3	0.3
Street railways									
16 King	0.9	1.0	1.1	1.0	0.9	0.9	0.9	1.0	
17 Present	0.9	0.9	1.0	1.0	0.9	0.9	0.8	0.9	
18 (16 — 17)	0.0	+0.1	+0.1	0.0	0.0	0.0	+0.1	+0.1	0.1
Water transportation									
19 King	1.2	1.3	1.2	0.9	0.8	0.8	0.8	1.0	
20 Present	0.9	1.1	1.0	0.8	0.7	0.8	0.7	0.9	
21 (19 — 20)	+0.3	+0.2	+0.2	+0.1	+0.1	0.0	+0.1	+0.1	0.1
Communication									
22 King	0.7	0.8	0.9	0.9	0.9	0.9	0.9	0.9	
23 Present	0.7	0.7	0.9	0.9	0.9	0.9	0.9	0.8	
24 (22 — 23)	0.0	+0.1	0.0	0.0	0.0	0.0	0.0	0.0	0.0
Electric light and power									
25 King	0.5	0.5	0.6	0.7	0.7	0.8	0.9	0.7	
26 Present	0.5	0.5	0.6	0.7	0.8	1.0	1.0	0.7	
27 (25 — 26)	0.0	0.0	0.0	0.0	—0.1	—0.2	—0.1	—0.1	0.1
Trade									
28 King	12.8	12.0	12.9	12.8	14.3	14.1	14.5	13.3	
29 Present	13.7	13.2	13.5	13.5	13.0	13.2	13.3	13.3	
30 (28 — 29)	—0.9	—1.2	—0.6	—0.7	+1.3	+0.9	+1.2	0.0	1.0

TABLE 88 (concl.)

		1919	1920	1921	1922	1923	1924	1925	AVG. 1919–25	AVG. DISRE- GARDING SIGNS
	Banking									
31	King	1.1	1.1	1.4	1.5	1.4	1.4	1.4	1.3	
32	Present	1.1	1.1	1.4	1.4	1.3	1.3	1.3	1.3	
33	(31 — 32)	0.0	0.0	0.0	+0.1	+0.1	+0.1	+0.1	+0.1	0.1
	Rent									
34	King	9.1	9.1	10.8	10.7	9.7	9.7	9.5	9.8	
35	Present	8.1	7.6	9.5	9.9	9.3	10.0	9.6	9.1	
36	(34 — 35)	+1.0	+1.5	+1.3	+0.8	+0.4	—0.3	—0.1	+0.7	0.8
	Government									
37	King	10.4	7.8	9.2	9.2	8.2	8.0	7.9	8.7	
38	Present	8.6	7.5	9.2	8.8	8.0	8.0	8.0	8.3	
39	(37 — 38)	+1.8	+0.3	0.0	+0.4	+0.2	0.0	—0.1	+0.4	0.4
	'All other'									
40	King	13.2	15.7	18.5	20.1	18.7	21.3	21.4	18.4	
41	Present	14.0	14.3	16.8	18.2	17.4	18.4	19.0	16.9	
42	(40 — 41)	—0.8	+1.4	+1.7	+1.9	+1.3	+2.9	+2.4	+1.5	1.8

CLASSIFICATION A   BY CHARACTER OF PRODUCTIVE FUNCTION

		1919	1920	1921	1922	1923	1924	1925	AVG. 1919–25	AVG. DISRE- GARDING SIGNS
	Commodity producing									
43	King	44.0	44.1	37.9	37.3	39.2	37.2	37.6	39.6	
44	Present	45.5	46.6	40.0	39.2	42.3	40.8	40.7	42.2	
45	(43 — 44)	—1.5	—2.5	—2.1	—1.9	—3.1	—3.6	—3.1	—2.5	2.5
	Commodity transporting and distributing									
46	King	20.5	20.4	20.3	19.5	20.9	20.3	20.6	20.4	
47	Present	21.2	21.4	21.2	20.5	19.8	19.8	19.7	20.5	
48	(46 — 47)	—0.7	—1.0	—0.9	—1.0	+1.1	+0.5	+0.9	—0.2	0.9
	Services									
49	King	35.4	35.5	41.9	43.4	39.8	42.2	42.0	40.0	
50	Present	33.4	32.1	38.8	40.2	37.8	39.5	39.6	37.3	
51	(49 — 50)	+2.0	+3.4	+3.1	+3.2	+2.0	+2.7	+2.4	+2.7	2.7

CLASSIFICATION C   BY TYPE OF BUSINESS ORGANIZATION

		1919	1920	1921	1922	1923	1924	1925	AVG. 1919–25	AVG. DISRE- GARDING SIGNS
	With large proportion of individual firms									
52	King	51.5	52.8	57.6	58.4	56.6	59.3	59.7	56.6	
53	Present	53.6	53.4	55.4	56.8	55.4	57.4	57.5	55.6	
54	(52 — 53)	—2.1	—0.6	+2.2	+1.6	+1.2	+1.9	+2.2	+0.9	1.7
	Private corporations									
55	King	27.1	27.6	21.9	21.8	24.6	22.2	22.4	23.9	
56	Present	27.2	27.8	23.8	23.3	25.8	24.0	24.1	25.1	
57	(55 — 56)	—0.1	—0.2	—1.9	—1.5	—1.2	—1.8	—1.7	—1.2	1.2
	Semi-public corporations									
58	King	10.9	11.8	11.4	10.8	10.5	10.2	10.2	10.8	
59	Present	10.7	11.4	11.6	11.0	10.7	10.7	10.4	10.9	
60	(58 — 59)	+0.2	+0.4	—0.2	—0.2	—0.2	—0.5	—0.2	—0.1	0.3
	Public									
61	King	10.4	7.8	9.2	9.2	8.2	8.0	7.9	8.7	
62	Present	8.6	7.5	9.2	8.8	8.0	8.0	8.0	8.3	
63	(61 — 62)	+1.8	+0.3	0.0	+0.4	+0.2	0.0	—0.1	+0.4	0.4

modity handling industries—transportation, communication, and trade—is somewhat smaller in King's estimates, but the difference is much less than for the commodity producing industries. The share of the service industries in King's total is larger than in ours. Similar minor differences are true of the apportionments among the broader groups by character of organization. The two totals are sufficiently similar in industrial composition for the industrial allocation to be treated as continuous in rough comparison.

While the industrial categories are more numerous and hence can be compared in more detail, we compare the two sets of estimates by type of payment also (Table 89).[5] After the necessary adjustments, all of which have been indicated, moderate differences appear between the two sets of estimates of dividends and interest. There are sizable differences between the two totals of employee compensation, although the algebraic mean difference for the period is small compared with the totals. But King's rent is about 12 per cent and his entrepreneurial withdrawals are from 10 to 35 per cent larger than ours, obviously because trade, real estate, and the 'all other' industrial divisions, for which the bases of his estimates differ so significantly from ours, dominate these categories.

The differences in the totals of payments to individuals (Table 89) are naturally reflected in the differences in the percentage distributions by type of payment (Table 90). The share of employee compensation is lower in King's total; the share of entrepreneurial withdrawals higher. The shares of the combined total of service income are fairly close in the two sets; and so are, naturally, the shares of property income. But the persistence of the difference between the apportionments of the two totals during the years covered by both makes it feasible to use King's figures for rough comparisons, even without adjustments for the trade, rent, and unclassified items.

[5] Comparisons by type of payment were omitted from the preceding sections of this chapter because the differences would have been minor or were already indicated in the industry by industry comparisons.

TABLE 89

Payments to Individuals by Type of Payment King's and Present NBER Estimates Compared 1919–1925 (millions of dollars)

	1919	1920	1921	1922	1923	1924	1925	AVG. 1919–25	AVG. DIS-REGARDING SIGNS
Employee compensation									
1 King	35,399	42,283	36,213	37,700	42,893	44,493	46,855	40,834	
2 King, adj. for duplication	34,602	41,242	35,458	37,023	42,025	43,731	46,093	40,025	
3 Present	37,140	43,890	35,537	37,004	43,340	43,324	45,019	40,751	
4 (2 − 3)	−2,538	−2,648	−79	+19	−1,315	+407	+1,074	−726	1,154
Dividends incl. international payments									
5 King	3,209	3,103	2,951	3,003	3,715	3,899	4,577	3,494	
6 Present	2,887	3,216	2,963	3,049	3,839	3,813	4,425	3,456	
7 (5 − 6)	+322	−113	−12	−46	−124	+86	+152	+38	122
Interest									
8 King	2,585	2,706	2,773	2,872	2,889	2,846	2,892	2,795	
9 Present	3,229	3,653	3,872	3,980	4,206	4,374	4,579	3,985	
10 Present excl. real estate int.	2,400	2,753	2,918	2,990	3,065	3,129	3,160	2,916	
11 (8 − 10)	+185	−47	−145	−118	−176	−283	−268	−122	175
Rent									
12 King	5,368	6,200	6,620	6,781	6,842	7,117	7,322	6,607	
13 Present	4,796	5,188	5,424	5,887	6,306	6,877	6,885	5,909	
14 (12 − 13)	+572	+1,012	+1,196	+894	+536	+240	+437	+698	698

Entrepreneurial withdrawals

15 Comp. of entrep. & property owners (King)	30,550	31,716	27,157	28,225	31,444	32,642	35,076	30,973	
16 Items omitted by us & net savings in agr.	6,214	4,937	1,362	1,953	2,701	2,900	3,704	3,396	
17 Div., int., & rent	11,162	12,009	12,344	12,656	13,446	13,862	14,791	12,896	
18 Withdrawals (King) (15 — 16 — 17)	13,174	14,770	13,451	13,616	15,297	15,880	16,581	14,681	
19 Present	11,782	13,477	10,269	10,789	11,345	11,946	12,503	11,730	
20 (18 — 19)	+1,392	+1,293	+3,182	+2,827	+3,952	+3,934	+4,078	+2,951	2,951
21 Total dif. (4 + 7 + 11 + 14 + 20)	−67	−503	+4,142	+3,576	+2,873	+4,384	+5,473	+2,840	3,003
Totals paid out									
22 Realized income (King)	65,949	73,999	63,371	65,925	74,337	77,135	81,931	71,807	
23 Items omitted by us & net savings in agr.	6,214	4,937	1,362	1,953	2,701	2,900	3,704	3,396	
24 Duplication in mfg.	797	1,041	755	677	868	762	762	809	
25 King's total comparable with ours (22 — 23 — 24)	58,938	68,021	61,254	63,295	70,768	73,473	77,465	67,602	
26 Present	59,004	68,523	57,112	59,718	67,896	69,088	71,993	64,762	
27 (25 — 26)	−66	−502	+4,142	+3,577	+2,872	+4,385	+5,472	+2,840	3,002

Line 1: Table XIX.
Line 2: difference between (1) and Table 85, (12).
Line 5: Tables XXXVII, XXXVIII, CXXXIII.
Line 8: Tables XXXVI, CXXXVII, XCVIII.

Line 12: Table 86, (28).
Line 15: Table XVII.
Line 16: Table 85, (4 + 8).
Line 24: Table 85, (12).

TABLE 90

Payments to Individuals

Percentage Distribution by Type of Payment

King's and Present NBER Estimates Compared, 1919–1925

		1919	1920	1921	1922	1923	1924	1925	AVG. 1919–25	AVG. DISREGARDING SIGNS
	Employee compensation									
1	King	58.7	60.6	57.9	58.5	59.4	59.5	59.5	59.2	
2	Present	62.9	64.1	62.2	62.0	63.8	62.7	62.5	62.9	
3	(1 − 2)	−4.2	−3.5	−4.3	−3.5	−4.4	−3.2	−3.0	−3.7	3.7
	Entrepreneurial withdrawals									
4	King	22.4	21.7	22.0	21.5	21.6	21.6	21.4	21.7	
5	Present	20.0	19.7	18.0	18.1	16.7	17.3	17.4	18.2	
6	(4 − 5)	+2.4	+2.0	+4.0	+3.4	+4.9	+4.3	+4.0	+3.6	3.6
	Service income									
7	King	81.1	82.3	79.8	80.0	81.0	81.1	80.9	80.9	
8	Present	82.9	83.7	80.2	80.0	80.5	80.0	79.9	81.0	
9	(7 − 8)	−1.8	−1.4	−0.4	0.0	+0.5	+1.1	+1.0	−0.1	0.9
	Dividends incl. international payments									
10	King	5.4	4.6	4.8	4.7	5.2	5.3	5.9	5.1	
11	Present	4.9	4.7	5.2	5.1	5.7	5.5	6.1	5.3	
12	(10 − 11)	+0.5	−0.1	−0.4	−0.4	−0.5	−0.2	−0.2	−0.2	0.3
	Interest									
13	King	4.4	4.0	4.5	4.5	4.1	3.9	3.7	4.2	
14	Present	4.1	4.0	5.1	5.0	4.5	4.5	4.4	4.5	
15	(13 − 14)	+0.3	0.0	−0.6	−0.5	−0.4	−0.6	−0.7	−0.4	0.4
	Dividends and interest									
16	King	9.8	8.6	9.3	9.2	9.3	9.2	9.6	9.3	
17	Present	9.0	8.7	10.3	10.1	10.2	10.0	10.5	9.8	
18	(16 − 17)	+0.8	−0.1	−1.0	−0.9	−0.9	−0.8	−0.9	−0.5	0.8
	Rent									
19	King	9.1	9.1	10.8	10.7	9.7	9.7	9.5	9.8	
20	Present	8.1	7.6	9.5	9.9	9.3	10.0	9.6	9.1	
21	(19 − 20)	+1.0	+1.5	+1.3	+0.8	+0.4	−0.3	−0.1	+0.7	0.8
	Property income									
22	King	18.9	17.7	20.2	20.0	19.0	18.9	19.1	19.1	
23	Present	17.1	16.3	19.8	20.0	19.5	20.0	20.1	19.0	
24	(22 − 23)	+1.8	+1.4	+0.4	0.0	−0.5	−1.1	−1.0	+0.1	0.9

4 Summary Note

It is not possible, or intended here, to summarize the several comparisons just made in detail. But it seems pertinent to point out that they show that our estimates differ from each of the three others in much the same items. Thus, of the various types of income, the greatest relative discrepancies occur in all three comparisons for the controversial area of net savings; and of the various types of payment, the greatest discrepancy is in entrepreneurial withdrawals. Of the estimates for the various industries, those for branches covered by well established censuses, such as mining and manufacturing, agree best; greater discrepancies exist among the service industries, real estate, and the miscellaneous divisions, areas in which the paucity of data leaves wide room for differences in methods.

Appendix to Chapter 10: King's Estimates, 1909–1919

Comparison of King's and our estimates for the few years covered by both indicates substantial disparities. But a large part is due to differences in coverage that can be eliminated; and after adjustment the comparable totals of payments to individuals are fairly close. More important, the distributions of the two totals by industrial source and type of payment are sufficiently similar to allow using both sets in exploring changes in the distribution over periods extending beyond that covered by each separately.

Tables 84–90 compare only the years since 1919 for which both sets are available. But for analysis of temporal changes it would obviously be useful to have King's estimates for earlier years, modified by adjustments similar to those followed above to make them as comparable with our estimates as possible without cardinal revision. We therefore give King's estimates of payments to individuals for 1909–19, modified by the three revisions noted: (a) omission of the items we ex-

TABLE 91

King's Estimates of Income Payments by Industrial Divisions, Adjusted to Conform in Coverage with Present NBER Estimates, 1909–1919 (millions of dollars)

	1909	1910	1911	1912	1913	1914	1915	1916	1917	1918	1919
Items to be omitted from King											
1 Urban poultry and gardens	70	75	72	80	78	82	85	100	211	281	197
2 Urban cow keeping	52	56	54	59	61	61	62	66	86	109	126
3 Int. on durable goods	850	932	966	1,018	1,070	1,116	1,187	1,334	1,625	2,302	2,740
4 Total	972	1,063	1,092	1,157	1,209	1,259	1,334	1,500	1,922	2,692	3,063
Agriculture											
5 Income pay. incl. savings	4,360	4,547	4,095	4,594	4,412	4,547	4,737	5,819	8,272	10,182	11,009
6 Est. net savings	510	770	138	553	243	257	567	1,275	2,679	3,658	3,151
7 Adj. income pay. (5 − 6)	3,850	3,777	3,957	4,061	4,169	4,110	4,170	4,544	5,593	6,524	7,858
Manufacturing											
8 Income pay.	5,405	6,123	6,167	6,749	7,238	6,816	7,261	10,145	12,355	14,661	15,941
9 Est. duplication	214	244	245	273	295	279	308	425	543	697	797
10 Residual excess (transferred to line 24)	276	512	514	344	369	347	369	516	627	741	804
11 Adj. income pay. (8 − 9 − 10)	4,915	5,567	5,608	6,132	6,574	6,190	6,584	9,204	11,185	13,223	14,340
Income payments											
12 Mining	760	839	834	916	1,054	884	883	1,309	1,597	1,795	1,675
13 Construction	1,692	1,580	1,607	1,742	1,527	1,412	1,394	1,516	1,206	1,207	1,846
14 Steam rr., Pullman, & express	1,800	1,961	2,017	2,110	2,211	2,142	2,165	2,345	2,668	3,584	3,856
15 Street rwy.	306	330	348	366	388	410	414	438	454	488	552
16 Water transp.	211	232	289	241	250	252	276	339	436	504	710
17 Communication	154	169	187	205	221	226	226	265	301	342	406
18 Elec. light & power	93	99	117	126	139	152	166	182	204	232	267
19 Trade	3,377	3,417	3,704	3,695	4,126	4,373	4,437	4,899	5,896	6,358	7,517
20 Banking	337	389	409	429	455	454	463	480	509	572	646
21 Rent	3,292	3,483	3,592	3,716	3,903	4,027	4,164	4,412	4,691	4,960	5,368
22 Government	1,554	1,678	1,767	1,862	1,981	2,095	2,192	2,397	3,044	6,278	6,136

All other

23 Unclassified	5,364	5,596	5,775	6,156	6,702	6,886	7,161	7,388	7,829	6,579	6,977
24 Residual from mfg.	276	312	314	344	369	347	369	516	627	741	804
25 Net income from foreign investments	−74	−78	−82	−86	−90	−85	−68	−46	−51	−26	−17
26 Income pay. (23 + 24 + 25)	5,566	5,830	6,007	6,414	6,981	7,148	7,462	7,858	8,405	7,294	7,764
27 Total income pay. (7 + 11 + 12 + 13 + 14 + 15 + 16 + 17 + 18 + 19 + 20 + 21 + 22 + 26)	27,907	29,351	30,383	32,013	33,977	33,873	34,996	40,088	46,187	53,361	58,941
28 Total realized income	29,605	31,430	31,858	33,977	35,723	35,647	37,205	43,288	51,331	60,408	65,949
29 Total income pay. (28 − 4 − 6 − 9)	27,909	29,355	30,383	32,014	33,976	33,872	34,996	40,088	46,187	53,361	58,938

Lines 1–3: Table CXXXIII.

Line 5: difference between realized income from Table XIV and rent paid.

Line 6: difference between entrepreneurial net income (realized income, Table XCVIII, col. C. Table XVII, less interest and rent payments to non-farmers, Table XCVIII) and withdrawals as estimated by us (see notes to Vol. II, Part Four, Table A 2).

Lines 8, 12, 14, 15, 17, 19, 23: realized income from Table XIV less rent paid (original source books).

Line 9: wages and salaries in railroad repair shops, reported for 1909, 1914, and 1919 in the *Census of Manufactures* and interpolated by King's estimates of manufacturing employee compensation.

Line 10: difference in 1919 between the present estimate and (8 − 9) extrapolated by (8 − 9) for the earlier years.

Lines 13, 16, 18, 20, 22, 28: Table XIV.

Line 21: sum of estimates of rent in agriculture, mining, manufacturing, express, street railways, telegraphs, mercantile, unclassified, leased houses, and imputed rent on owner-occupied houses. Only the first and the last two are given in King's published report (Tables XCVIII and CXXXIII).

Line 25: Table CXXXIII.

TABLE 92

King's Estimates of Income Payments, Adjusted to Conform in Coverage with Present NBER Estimates
Percentage Distribution by Industrial Divisions, 1909–1919

	1909	1910	1911	1912	1913	1914	1915	1916	1917	1918	1919
1 Agriculture	13.8	12.9	13.0	12.7	12.3	12.1	11.9	11.3	12.1	12.2	13.3
2 Mining	2.7	2.9	2.7	2.9	3.1	2.6	2.5	3.3	3.5	3.4	2.8
3 Manufacturing	17.6	19.0	18.5	19.2	19.3	18.3	18.8	23.0	24.2	24.8	24.3
4 Construction	6.1	5.4	5.3	5.4	4.5	4.2	4.0	3.8	2.6	2.3	3.1
5 Steam rr., Pullman, & express	6.4	6.7	6.6	6.6	6.5	6.3	6.2	5.8	5.8	6.7	6.5
6 Street rwy.	1.1	1.1	1.1	1.1	1.1	1.2	1.2	1.1	1.0	0.9	0.9
7 Water transp.	0.8	0.8	0.8	0.8	0.7	0.7	0.8	0.8	0.9	0.9	1.2
8 Communication	0.6	0.6	0.6	0.6	0.7	0.7	0.6	0.7	0.7	0.6	0.7
9 Electric light & power	0.3	0.3	0.4	0.4	0.4	0.4	0.5	0.5	0.4	0.4	0.5
10 Trade	12.1	11.6	12.2	11.5	12.1	12.9	12.7	12.2	12.8	11.9	12.8
11 Banking	1.2	1.3	1.3	1.3	1.3	1.3	1.3	1.2	1.1	1.1	1.1
12 Rent	11.8	11.9	11.8	11.6	11.5	11.9	11.9	11.0	10.2	9.3	9.1
13 Government	5.6	5.7	5.8	5.8	5.8	6.2	6.3	5.7	6.6	11.8	10.4
14 All other	19.9	19.9	19.8	20.0	20.5	21.1	21.3	19.6	18.2	13.7	13.2
15 Total	100.0	100.0	100.0	100.0	100.0	100.0	100.0	100.0	100.0	100.0	100.0
CLASSIFICATION A BY CHARACTER OF PRODUCTIVE FUNCTION											
16 Commodity prod.	40.5	40.5	39.9	40.6	39.6	37.6	37.7	41.9	42.8	43.1	44.0
17 Commodity transp. & distri.	19.3	19.1	19.6	18.9	19.3	19.9	19.7	18.8	19.5	19.5	20.5
18 Services	40.2	40.5	40.4	40.4	40.9	42.4	42.6	39.3	37.8	37.4	35.4
CLASSIFICATION C BY TYPE OF BUSINESS ORGANIZATION											
19 With large proportion of individual firms	63.7	61.7	62.1	61.2	60.9	62.2	61.8	57.9	55.9	49.4	51.5
20 Private corp.	20.3	21.9	21.2	22.1	22.4	20.9	21.3	26.3	27.7	28.2	27.1
21 Semi-public corp.	10.4	10.8	10.8	10.8	10.7	10.6	10.6	10.1	9.9	10.6	10.9
22 Public	5.6	5.7	5.8	5.8	5.8	6.2	6.3	5.7	6.6	11.8	10.4

TABLE 93

King's Estimates of Income Payments by Type of Payment,
Adjusted to Conform in Coverage with Present NBER Estimates, 1909–1919 (millions of dollars)

	1909	1910	1911	1912	1913	1914	1915	1916	1917	1918	1919
1 Empl. comp.	15,090	16,266	16,498	17,587	18,822	18,516	19,561	22,470	25,802	32,324	35,399
2 Duplication	214	244	245	273	295	279	308	425	543	697	797
3 Empl. comp. adj. for duplication (1 − 2)	14,876	16,022	16,253	17,314	18,527	18,237	19,053	22,045	25,259	31,627	34,602
4 Div. incl. international pay.	1,496	1,761	1,799	1,885	2,097	1,970	2,006	3,290	3,723	3,518	3,209
5 Interest	1,211	1,269	1,388	1,374	1,436	1,464	1,575	1,631	1,760	1,967	2,585
6 Rent	3,292	3,485	3,592	3,716	3,903	4,027	4,164	4,412	4,691	4,960	5,368
7 Realized income of entrep. & property owners	14,515	15,163	15,360	16,390	16,901	17,131	17,845	20,817	25,529	28,084	30,550
8 Items omitted by us & net savings in agr.	1,482	1,833	1,230	1,690	1,452	1,496	1,901	2,775	4,601	6,550	6,214
9 Entrep. withdr. (7 − 4 − 5 − 6 − 8)	7,034	6,817	7,411	7,725	8,013	8,174	8,199	8,709	10,754	11,289	13,174
10 Total (3 + 4 + 5 + 6 + 9)	27,909	29,352	30,383	32,014	33,976	33,872	34,997	40,087	46,167	53,561	58,938

Line 1: Table XIX.
Line 2: see Table 91, (9).
Line 4: Tables XXXVII, XXXVIII, CXXXIII.
Line 5: Tables XXXVI, CXXVII, XCVIII.
Line 6: see Table 91, (21).
Line 7: Table XVII.
Line 8: see Table 91, (4) and (6).

TABLE 94

King's Estimates of Income Payments, Adjusted to Conform in Coverage with Present NBER Estimates
Percentage Distribution by Type of Payment, 1909–1919

	1909	1910	1911	1912	1913	1914	1915	1916	1917	1918	1919
1 Empl. comp.	53.2	54.5	53.5	54.1	54.5	53.8	54.4	55.0	54.7	59.3	58.7
2 Entrep. withdr.	25.2	23.2	24.4	24.1	23.6	24.1	23.4	21.7	23.3	21.2	22.4
3 Service income (1 + 2)	78.5	77.8	77.9	78.2	78.1	78.0	77.9	76.7	78.0	80.4	81.1
4 Dividends	5.4	6.0	5.9	5.9	6.2	5.8	5.7	8.2	8.1	6.6	5.4
5 Interest	4.3	4.3	4.4	4.3	4.2	4.3	4.5	4.1	3.8	3.7	4.4
6 Rent	11.8	11.9	11.8	11.6	11.5	11.9	11.9	11.0	10.2	9.3	9.1
7 Prop. income (4 + 5 + 6)	21.5	22.2	22.1	21.8	21.9	22.0	22.1	23.3	22.0	19.6	18.9
8 Total	100.0	100.0	100.0	100.0	100.0	100.0	100.0	100.0	100.0	100.0	100.0

clude; (b) exclusion of entrepreneurial savings in agriculture; (c) adjustment for duplication and wider coverage in King's estimates for manufacturing. Table 91, which lists the items excluded and gives payments by industrial source, thus parallels and supplements Tables 85, 86, and 87. Table 92, which gives the percentage distribution of the revised total among payments originating in the several industries, supplements Table 88. Table 93 gives payments by type of income; and Table 94 the corresponding percentage distribution of aggregate payments to individuals. Tables 93 and 94 supplement Tables 89 and 90.

The estimates in Tables 91–94, together with those in Tables 85–90, provide the basis for some of the analysis of changes in the income totals and in their distribution developed in Chapters 4–6.

CHAPTER 11

Characteristics of the Data and Procedures

1 The Underlying Data

ON THE simplest possible basis the information that underlies our estimates may be classified into three broad groups: (a) Data that result from an attempt by the collecting agency to cover exhaustively the area to which our estimates refer; e.g., Interstate Commerce Commission data on income originating in the steam railroad industry; Census reports on wages and salaries of employees in manufacturing, mining, and trade; Bureau of Internal Revenue data on corporate incomes. (b) Data that explicitly cover only a part of the area measured in the given industry type of income cell; and since this partial coverage is intentional and is recognized by the collecting agency, it is usually well defined. To this category belong statistics for several states on payrolls in various industries; information gathered from sample collections of corporate reports; results of questionnaire surveys necessarily partial in coverage. (c) Data that do not relate directly to the industry type of income cell for which the estimate is being made, but whose magnitude or changes are assumed to be similar to the magnitude or changes that are to be estimated.

Within each category of underlying data some are more complete and reliable than others. The collecting agencies are not always successful in attaining complete coverage and accurate reports. The degree of success depends upon the number and size of reporting units in the field, the power of

475

regulation and control exercised by the collecting agency, and the intensity of the factors that make for bias in reporting. Within the first broad category some data are complete and reliable, e.g., employee compensation reported by steam railroads to the Interstate Commerce Commission. Some are incomplete in certain minor respects, because it was not deemed advisable to spend the labor and time necessary to obtain exhaustive coverage; e.g., the *Census of Mines and Quarries* does not segregate the labor cost included in contract work or cover individual placer miners. Some Census reports were intended to be complete but, because of the large number of small units in the field and lack of authority to enforce reporting, they are manifestly incomplete, e.g., the *Census of Business* for 1935. Finally, some data are complete in terms of the number of reporting units, but may suffer from a bias, varying in direction or magnitude from year to year and difficult to measure; e.g., reports on income submitted by corporations to tax authorities.

In the second category, the degree of admittedly partial coverage varies. A given sample may be based on reports for a few states, on information from the larger economic units that publish their income accounts and balance sheets, or on a questionnaire study conducted under specific conditions of sampling, editing of returns, etc. The magnitude and direction of the probable bias and the basis of the adjustment by which complete coverage can be attained differ from one group of data to another.

Even in the third category, information *not* relating to the particular area to be measured, data may vary in pertinence. If for two related industries we have estimates that are similar in magnitude or in fluctuations for some years, we base estimates for the missing years for the one industry upon those for the other. If we lack such a quantitative foundation we may base an estimate upon qualitative knowledge of kinship between the cell to be measured and the cells for which we have estimates. This qualitative knowledge of kinship, especially with reference to industrial divisions, may be specific, relating estimates for one industry to those for another, or general, relating estimates for one industry or homogeneous combination of industries to those for a fairly heterogeneous combination of industries.

Most estimates are based upon data that belong to several of these three broad categories and the groups within them. Estimates of manufacturing wages for intercensal years are based upon Census reports (first category) and sample data on payrolls (second category). Entrepreneurial withdrawals in some industries for some years are estimated from (a) complete data on number in one year; (b) sample data on changes in number; (c) average withdrawals based upon average salaries, thus combining data belonging to all three broad categories. For only a few cells, notably employee compensation in manufacturing for Census years, dividends for most industries in recent years, and income originating in some public utilities, are our estimates based entirely upon data belonging to the first broad category.

The reason is obvious. No final estimates can rest upon data belonging exclusively either to the second or third category: by definition, they are either incomplete or do not relate directly to the area under measurement. And from the first category only data that are complete in coverage and unbiased can be used directly for our final estimates. Such data are to be had for most cells for only a few years, and often not at all. So far as they can be obtained for at least one year, the incomplete and biased information for other years must be adjusted to the complete data in order to derive the final estimate. In other words, the partial data in the second category, the indirectly related data in the third, and data in the first category that have gaps or biases cannot be used by themselves. They are either adjusted to compensate for their bias or incompleteness or used as indicators of fluctuations but not of magnitude, i.e., as indexes for interpolating and extrapolating beyond the years for which complete data are to be had.

2 *Adjustment, Interpolation, Extrapolation*

A ADJUSTMENT

By adjustment we mean that a given total or ratio, reported in
the data and considered either incomplete or excessive, is revised in an attempt to approximate the true figure. It is not
intricate and presents no technical difficulties if the shortage
or excess is known; otherwise, it is almost impossible. The
overall controlling totals, effective as they are in adjusting the
combined coverage of the specific cells to a national income
total, are of no use in adjusting estimates within industrial
divisions and type of income categories.

Most of the adjustments we made were upward, since the
common defect of reported data is a shortage in coverage. We
made no qualitative adjustments; i.e., we made adjustments
solely for areas for which a definite quantitative basis could be
found. This means that in several industrial divisions the
data as reported in the basic source were used unchanged, even
though there were grounds for suspecting incompleteness of
coverage. But since in almost all cases a quantitative basis for
adjustment was available for only a few years or a single year
in the period, and in several cases only for an industry as a
whole, not for the various types of income originating in it,
we had to apply the same relative adjustment to all years in
the period or to all types of income in the industry. We did
this, however, only when the adjustments were relatively
minor, and when there was no evidence that they would differ
from year to year or be substantially different within the industry for different types of income.

Adjustments are illustrated in the procedures by which,
from Census totals of contract construction, we derived a more
comprehensive total for the construction industry; by which
the reported balance sheet totals of long term interest-bearing
securities of corporations in *Statistics of Income* were raised to
the more complete coverage of the income accounts; or by
which the totals for interstate pipe lines reporting to the In-

terstate Commerce Commission were raised to include all pipe lines in the country.

B   INTERPOLATION

Interpolation is used when final and complete estimates for a given cell are available for more than one year in a period, but not for successive years. By it partial but directly related data, indirectly related data, or other information are used to derive estimates for the intervening years.

Interpolation may be based upon specific data, whether directly or indirectly related to the area estimated, or upon general assumptions concerning the character of changes during the intervening years. Since we deal with irregularly changing quantities, rather than with paths of mathematical functions, we avoided interpolation based upon general assumptions concerning the character of changes between the two terminal years. When neither direct nor indirect data were available, straight line interpolation was used, usually to derive not the final magnitudes themselves but subsidiary ratios or numbers. We used the straight line procedure because in the absence of specific information concerning the character of changes during the intervening years, it was most convenient to assume the simplest type of movement.

When specific data were available, interpolation was most frequently by the simple ratio procedure:

Let A and E be the complete totals available, and B, C, and D the estimated totals for the intervening years; let a, b, c, d, and e be the partial direct, or indirect, data available for all years. Then

$$A = a \ \frac{A}{a} = A$$

$$B = b \left(\frac{A}{a} + \frac{\frac{E}{e} - \frac{A}{a}}{4} \right) = b \left(\frac{3A}{4a} + \frac{E}{4e} \right)$$

$$C = c \left(\frac{A}{2a} + \frac{E}{2e} \right)$$

$$D = d \left(\frac{A}{4a} + \frac{3E}{4e} \right)$$

$$E = e \, \frac{E}{e} = E$$

This method apportions any change in the relative disparity between the partial or indirect data and the complete direct data in the two terminal years along an arithmetic straight line. It might be more consistent with the relative character of the disparity to apportion any change along a logarithmic straight line. Then

$$B = b \, \frac{A}{a} \sqrt[4]{\frac{E}{e} \div \frac{A}{a}} = b \, \sqrt[4]{\frac{E}{e} \times \left(\frac{A}{a} \right)^3}$$

$$C = c \, \sqrt[4]{\left(\frac{E}{e} \right)^2 \times \left(\frac{A}{a} \right)^2}$$

$$D = d \, \sqrt[4]{\left(\frac{E}{e} \right)^3 \times \left(\frac{A}{a} \right)}$$

$$E = e \, \sqrt[4]{\left(\frac{E}{e} \right)^4} = E$$

But the logarithmic straight line would have entailed more laborious calculations, and since the assumption as to the way any change in the relative disparity at the two terminal years should be apportioned among the intervening years is necessarily arbitrary, it was considered justifiable to choose the procedure that required fewer calculations.

In a few instances an interpolation that may be designated proportional was used.

$$B = A + \left[(E-A) \times \frac{(b-a)}{(e-a)} \right] = E - \left[(E-A) \times \frac{(e-b)}{(e-a)} \right]$$

$$C = A + \left[(E-A) \times \frac{(c-a)}{(e-a)} \right] = E - \left[(E-A) \times \frac{(e-c)}{(e-a)} \right]$$

$$D = A + \left[(E-A) \times \frac{(d-a)}{(e-a)} \right] = E - \left[(E-A) \times \frac{(e-d)}{(e-a)} \right]$$

$$E = A + \left[(E-A) \times \frac{(e-a)}{(e-a)} \right] = E - \left['(E-A) \times \frac{(e-e)}{(e-a)} \right] = E$$

The advantage of proportional interpolation is that it does *not* assume, as does the simple ratio method, a progressive movement over the intervening years of the change from one terminal year to the other in the relative discrepancy between the basic and the partial (or indirect) data. It assumes that the proportional distribution among the intervening years of the total change from one terminal year to the other is portrayed accurately by the partial or indirect data upon which the interpolation is based. Such an assumption is preferable for short periods marked by a sustained cyclical rise or decline. Over such periods the total rise or decline in the sample data may be smaller or larger than in the universe, but the change in the disparity from one terminal year to the other need not be at the same rate per intervening year. It is assumed that the annual pattern of the cyclical expansion or contraction, as far as its proportional distribution among the intervening years is concerned, is faithfully revealed by the sample data.[1]

[1] The difference between the ratio and the proportional methods may be illustrated by the following simple example. Let us assume the values for the universe at two terminal years to be 100 and 200. The values for the sample for the same years are 50 and 90. The value for the intervening year in the sample is 70. Then, the value for the intervening year in the universe will be interpolated as follows:

By the ratio method:

$$70 \left[\left(\frac{1}{2} \times \frac{100}{50} \right) + \left(\frac{1}{2} \times \frac{200}{90} \right) \right] = 70 \times 2.1111 = 147.7777$$

But the proportional is to be preferred to the ratio method solely under three conditions. The first, already mentioned, is that the period of interpolation is brief; for when it is long,

By the proportional method:

$$100 + \left[(200 - 100) \times \frac{70 - 50}{90 - 50} \right] = 150$$

Of course, if there is no change in the relative disparity between the sample and the universe from one terminal year to the other, the ratio and the proportional methods are bound to yield the same results, as can be demonstrated:

Assume that $\dfrac{A}{a} = \dfrac{E}{e}$

Then $\dfrac{a}{A} = \dfrac{e}{E}$ $\qquad\qquad e = \dfrac{Ea}{A}$ $\qquad\qquad a = \dfrac{Ae}{E}$

By the ratio method: $B = b\left(\dfrac{3A}{4a} + \dfrac{E}{4e} \right) = b\dfrac{A}{a}$

By the proportional method: $B = A + \left[(E-A) \times \dfrac{b-a}{e-a} \right]$

$$= A + \left[(E-A) \times \frac{b - A\dfrac{e}{E}}{E\dfrac{a}{A} - A\dfrac{e}{E}} \right]$$

$$= A + \left[(E-A) \times \frac{b - A\dfrac{a}{A}}{(E-A)\dfrac{a}{A}} \right]$$

$$= A + \frac{b - A\dfrac{a}{A}}{\dfrac{a}{A}} = \frac{A\dfrac{a}{A} + b - A\dfrac{a}{A}}{\dfrac{a}{A}}$$

$$= \frac{b}{\dfrac{a}{A}} = b\dfrac{A}{a}$$

one should assume some progressive change in the relative disparity between the sample and the universe from one terminal year to the other. Second, the total change in the sample and in the universe must be substantial and in the same direction. For unless it is substantial, the percentage distribution in the proportional method is likely to be erratic; and unless the change in the sample and the universe are in the same direction, there is no basis for assuming similarity in the percentage distribution of the change. Finally, the changes in the sample during the intervening years should all be in the same direction, i.e., either positive or negative, since the percentage distributions of totals whose components are different in sign are likely to be erratic.

These three conditions limited severely the use of the proportional method. As a result, it was applied in our estimates largely to interpolate manufacturing wages and salaries for intercensal years; and even then only for those items in which the changes conformed to the conditions just described. For all other interpolations the ratio method was used.

C EXTRAPOLATION

Extrapolation is used when the period for which the estimates are to be derived on the basis of partial or indirect data or assumptions concerning the character of change has an open end. The need for this device arises when the basic and complete figures cover only part of the period and *all* preceding or *all* succeeding years must be derived with the help of samples or on some other basis.

Like interpolation, from which it differs solely by the absence of a second basic terminal value, extrapolation can be carried through by assuming a general pattern of change over the missing years. This assumption can be based on the behavior of the complete figures available for part of the period; e.g., one may assume that the relative change from year x to year x + 1 is the same as that from x − 1 to x. Or a mathematical formula can be fitted to the period covered by the

complete figures and values for earlier or later years extrapolated. But for obvious reasons such assumptions were
avoided and an effort was made to find specific data, either
partial or indirectly related, upon which extrapolation could
be based. In only a very few instances, and for relatively minor
quantities, was extrapolation based on the assumption that
values for a missing (usually earlier) year were equal to the
figures available for the nearest year.

When direct data were used, extrapolation was based upon
the assumption that the relative change in them from the
terminal year to the years to be estimated accurately portrayed
the relative change in the values to be estimated. This was,
of course, one of many assumptions that might have been
made. But lacking information that would lead to a choice of
any other procedure, we used the simplest. Its implication is
that the relative disparity in the terminal year between the
complete figure and the partial or indirect data remained constant over the years for which values were extrapolated. Since
such an assumption is valid for only a short period, we tried to
confine such extrapolation to periods not exceeding two years.
Most uses of extrapolation in our estimates are, as a matter of
fact, for only the most recent year or two.

3 Data, Procedures, and Margins of Error
Originally we intended to classify the estimates for the various
industry type of income cells according to the character of the
underlying data and the procedure used. Such a classification
might have spared us the delicate task of assigning specific
values to the error margins of the various estimates. An estimate based on complete Census totals is subject to a narrower
relative error than one based on incomplete data or data not
directly related to the given industry type of income cell.
Similarly, the very reason for adjustment, interpolation, or
extrapolation—lack of complete and directly related data—
means that the estimate is subject to a wider margin of error
than an estimate obtained by direct use of comprehensive

figures. Furthermore, differences in the reliability of the groups within the three broad categories of underlying data may spell differences in the reliability of estimates derived from them. Similarly, all other conditions being equal, an interpolation is likely to yield more reliable estimates than an extrapolation; an interpolation based upon a directly related and large sample will yield more reliable estimates than a straight line interpolation; and so on.

Had our experiment proved successful we might have presented the classification as an adequate indication of the accuracy of the estimates. It would have served as an effective summary of our detailed notes in Part Four. But we could not classify the estimates according to the reliability of the data and procedures, for two reasons. First, the number of classes that could and had to be made was unmanageably large. As already indicated, for few cells are the estimates based directly and exclusively upon comprehensive data: for most, data from more than one category are used, and the combinations vary considerably. In some cases a single adjustment or extrapolation of basic Census totals is used; in others, dollar values are derived through estimates of the number of persons engaged and of per capita averages, each of these in turn based upon complex combinations of data in various categories. The attempt to classify the interpolation and extrapolation procedures, whenever these were used, was no more successful, since they may be applied to derive the final estimate directly or to obtain one or several subsidiary quantities from which in turn the final estimate is derived. A complete description of this variety of combinations of data and procedures yields a complex classification having slight advantage over the detailed notes to the basic tables in Part Four.

The second and even more important difficulty was that the tentative classification by character of data and procedures did not represent definite classes of error margins. Even relatively complete data differ in the relative undercoverage or bias to which they are subject; the coverage of partly complete data may range all the way from 1 to 99 per cent; and there is no inherently uniform relation between the coverage of a sample and the reliability of estimates based upon it. Straight line interpolation may mean one range of error when applied directly to obtain the estimate itself, and another when used to derive a subsidiary quantity from which the estimate is made; and similar variations in the margin of error may accompany differences in the duration and character of the period covered. As a consequence, a classification based on characteristics of data and procedures would have to have subdivisions for the differences in reliability, among and within its groups. In other words, it proved difficult to evaluate margins of error on the basis of classes of underlying data and procedures, since *within* each class the various estimates still differed in reliability, and *among* some there were no apparent differences in reliability. Therefore, we had to evaluate the margins of error *directly*, fully aware that they represent at best merely an informed opinion. Sample classifications, one for all 1929 estimates and the other for estimates based on interpolation and extrapolation only, for several industries for all years, demonstrated clearly the difficulties discussed above and proved of small use (compared to the detailed description of procedures in Part Four) in judging the margins of error in the final estimates. The procedure we finally adopted and the results are described in detail in Chapter 12. But first we give briefly the results of a preliminary test that was applied to some of the interpolations and extrapolations, a test which, like the comparisons in Chapter 10, suggests the margins of error to which our estimates are subject.

4 Test of Selected Interpolations and Extrapolations
For several industries we have for the period studied at least three Census values, as well as directly related samples upon which we base interpolation for non-Census years. It is then possible to test our estimates by comparing, with the Census figure for the intermediate year, an estimate that is derived for

the intermediate Census year by interpolation. To illustrate: the *Biennial Census of Manufactures* reports salaries in 1919, 1921, and 1923. We use sample data to interpolate salaries for the intercensal years 1920 and 1922. The same sample data can be used to estimate salaries for 1921 by interpolating between the Census values for 1919 and 1923; and this interpolated value for 1921 can then be compared with the Census figure for 1921.

A somewhat similar procedure can be used when only two Census values are reported, but then the reliability of an extrapolation alone can be tested. To illustrate: if Census values are reported for 1929 and 1935, and we have interpolated the intervening years on the basis of sample data, we can test the goodness of this sample by extrapolating, from the 1929 Census value, a 1935 estimate for comparison with the 1935 Census value (or by extrapolating the 1935 Census value back to 1929 for comparison with the 1929 Census value). This procedure tests the sample data as a basis for an extrapolation, not an interpolation, index.

Neither procedure is an infallible test. Both necessarily exaggerate the errors in our estimates, since the first assumes a gap in the data wider than that actually filled; and the second tests a sample as a basis for an extrapolation index whereas it is actually used for an interpolation. Yet, when such tests can be applied to only one rather than several time units, they may yield accidentally a favorable showing that is not necessarily valid for other years in which the sample has been applied to derive estimates. Finally, the test can be applied to merely a few extrapolations and interpolations, since for many others *no* basic comprehensive data are reported for more than one time unit. The results of these tests are presented to indicate those cells for which interpolation rests upon several comprehensive totals; and to suggest the margin of error that may arise from the use of sample data in estimating values for non-Census years.

Table 95 presents tests of interpolation when at least three

Tests of Selected Indexes used for Interpolation during Periods containing at least Three Census Values

INDUSTRY AND TYPE OF INCOME OR PERSONS ENGAGED (1)	YEAR FOR WHICH TEST IS MADE (2)	BASIC DATA (3)	ESTIMATED DATA (4)	% DIF. (5)	TERMINAL YEARS (6)		INDEX TESTED (7)	INDEX DESCRIBED IN NOTES TO Table	Col.
Anthracite coal									
Wage earners	1929	144,761	144,585	−0.12	1919	1935	Wage earners, sample, 1919–29; BLS, employment, 1929–35	Q 9	1
Salaried workers	1929	8,495	8,277	−2.84	1919	1935	Salaried workers, sample	Q 9	7
Wages ($000)	1929	233,123	235,670	+1.09	1919	1935	Wages, sample, 1919–21; FRB, wages, 1921–29; BLS, wages, 1929–35	Q 4	1
Salaries ($000)	1929	21,626	20,556	−4.95	1919	1935	Salaries, sample	Q 4	7
Bituminous coal									
Wage earners	1929	459,552	473,520	+3.04	1919	1935	Our employment index, 1919–29; BLS, employment, 1929–35	Q 9	2
Salaried workers	1929	23,724	21,690	−8.57	1919	1935	Ratio *	Q 9	8
Salaries ($000)	1929	58,751	57,388	−2.32	1919	1935	Avg. salary, sample	Q 4	8
Men's clothing mfg.									
Wage earners	1921	245,661	244,774	−0.36	1919	1923	BLS, men's clothing combined with shirts & collars	M 23	6
Wages ($000)	1921	265,732	261,857	−0.72	1919	1923	}	M 6	6
Other wearing apparel mfg.									
Wage earners	1921	48,988	59,777	+22.02	1919	1923	BLS, wearing apparel	M 23	9
Wages ($000)	1921	49,570	62,074	+25.22	1919	1923	BLS, wearing apparel	M 6	9
Woolen goods mfg.									
Wage earners	1921	194,500	196,245	+1.00	1919	1923	BLS, woolen & worsted goods combined with carpets & rugs	M 23	11
Wages ($000)	1921	213,682	214,996	+0.61	1919	1923	}	M 6	11
Other textile fabrics mfg.									
Wage earners	1921	77,576	82,506	+6.37	1919	1923	BLS, textile fabrics	M 23	15
Wages ($000)	1921	75,406	77,757	+3.09	1919	1923	BLS, textile fabrics	M 6	15

Lumber mfg.								
Wage earners	1925	585,827	577,836	−1.28	1923 1927	BLS, sawmills, combined with millwork	M 23	18
Wages ($000)	1925	603,308	602,495	−0.13	1923 1927	BLS, sawmills, combined with millwork	M 6	18
Stone, clay, & glass mfg.								
Wage earners	1925	386,232	338,050	+0.54	1923 1927	BLS, brick, tile, & terra cotta, combined with glass & cement	M 23	19
Wages ($000)	1925	444,079	448,206	+0.93	1923 1927		M 6	19
Heating apparatus mfg.								
Wage earners	1925	95,860	95,151	−0.74	1923 1927	BLS, steam & hot water apparatus & steam fittings, combined with stoves	M 23	20
Wages ($000)	1925	138,350	137,450	−0.65	1923 1927		M 6	20
Other construction materials mfg.								
Wage earners	1925	115,248	106,989	−7.17	1923 1927	BLS, structural & ornamental metalwork, combined with cast iron pipe	M 23	21
Wages ($000)	1925	169,389	156,208	−7.78	1923 1927		M 6	21
Printing								
Wage earners	1925	314,021	314,001	−0.01	1923 1927	BLS, book & job printing, combined with newspaper & periodical printing	M 22	5
Wages ($000)	1925	540,826	542,078	+0.23	1923 1927		M 5	5
Iron & steel mfg.								
Wage earners	1925	538,021	542,300	+0.80	1923 1927	BLS, blast furnaces, steel mills, & rolling mills	M 23	24
Wages ($000)	1925	846,256	849,227	+0.35	1923 1927	BLS, blast furnaces, steel mills, & rolling mills	M 6	24
Other transp. equipment mfg.								
Wage earners	1925	83,244	81,862	−1.66	1923 1927	BLS, cars, combined with locomotives	M 23	27
Wages ($000)	1925	120,281	116,898	−2.81	1923 1927	BLS, cars, combined with locomotives	M 6	27
Non-ferrous metal mfg.								
Wage earners	1927	272,667	267,696	−1.83	1925 1929	BLS, brass, bronze, & copper products, combined with stamped & enamelled ware	M 23	31
Wages ($000)	1927	383,185	371,519	−3.04	1925 1929		M 6	31

Table 95 (cont.)

INDUSTRY AND TYPE OF INCOME OR PERSONS ENGAGED (1)	YEAR FOR WHICH TEST IS MADE (2)	BASIC DATA (3)	ESTIMATED DATA (4)	% DIF. (5)	TERMINAL YEARS (6)		INDEX TESTED (7)	INDEX DESCRIBED IN NOTES TO Table	Col.
Misc. excl. rubber mfg.									
Wage earners	1921	341,108	335,595	−1.62	1919	1923	BLS, all mfg.	M 23	35
Wages ($000)	1921	371,115	345,619	−6.87	1919	1923	BLS, all mfg.	M 6	35
Food & tobacco mfg.									
Salaried workers	1921	149,400	154,780	+3.60	1919	1923	Ratio *	M 24	1
Salaries ($000)	1921	290,528	291,479	+0.3?	1919	1923	Avg. salary, sample	M 7	1
Wearing apparel mfg.									
Salaried workers	1921	101,878	121,174	+18.94	1919	1923	Ratio *	M 25	3
Salaries ($000)	1921	209,640	225,558	+7.59	1919	1923	Avg. salary, sample	M 8	3
Textile fabrics mfg.									
Salaried workers	1921	50,441	51,218	+1.54	1919	1923	Ratio *	M 25	4
Salaries ($000)	1921	129,491	132,811	+1.03	1919	1923	Avg. salary, sample	M 8	4
Leather mfg.									
Salaried workers	1921	8,058	9,657	+19.84	1919	1923	Ratio *	M 25	5
Salaries ($000)	1921	19,927	19,855	−0.36	1919	1923	Avg. salary, sample	M 8	5
Lumber & furniture mfg.									
Salaried workers	1921	51,309	54,309	+5.85	1919	1923	Ratio *	M 25	6, 11
Salaries ($000)	1921	114,058	114,673	+0.54	1919	1923	Avg. salary, sample	M 8	6, 11
Stone, clay, & glass mfg.									
Salaried workers	1921	28,919	32,859	+13.62	1919	1923	Ratio *	M 25	7
Salaries ($000)	1921	65,258	63,680	−2.42	1919	1923	Avg. salary, sample	M 8	7
Heating apparatus mfg.									
Salaried workers	1921	12,923	14,445	+11.78	1919	1923	Ratio *	M 25	8
Salaries ($000)	1921	30,797	25,600	−16.88	1919	1923	Avg. salary, sample	M 8	8

Other construction materials mfg.									
Salaried workers	1921	12,888	13,310	+3.27	1919	1923	Ratio *	M 25	9
Salaries ($000)	1921	30,404	31,073	+2.20	1919	1923	Avg. salary, sample	M 8	9
Paper & printing									
Salaried workers	1921	156,500	162,374	+3.75	1919	1923	Ratio *	M 24	4, 5
Salaries ($000)	1921	317,375	321,138	+1.19	1919	1923	Avg. salary, sample	M 7	4, 5
Metal mfg.									
Salaried workers	1921	300,727	338,174	+12.45	1919	1923	Ratio *	M 24	6
Salaries ($000)	1921	721,796	659,494	−8.63	1919	1923	Avg. salary, sample	M 7	6
Chemical mfg., excl. petroleum ref.									
Salaried workers	1921	64,422	67,015	+4.03	1919	1923	Ratio *	M 25	16
Salaries ($000)	1921	143,975	140,053	−2.72	1919	1923	Avg. salary, sample	M 8	16
Petroleum refining									
Salaried workers	1921	13,705	22,494	+64.13	1919	1923	Ratio *	M 25	17
Salaries ($000)	1921	34,633	28,109	−18.84	1919	1923	Avg. salary, sample	M 8	17
Rubber tire mfg.									
Salaried workers	1921	12,526	18,924	+51.08	1919	1923	**Ratio ***	M 25	18
Misc. mfg., excl. rubber									
Salaried workers	1921	55,311	58,329	+5.46	1919	1923	Ratio *	M 25	19
Salaries ($000)	1921	118,719	121,408	+2.27	1919	1923	Avg. salary, sample	M 8	19
Food & tobacco mfg.									
Entrepreneurs	1921	53,406	69,279	+29.72	1919	1923	Failures, milling, bakers, liquors, & tobacco	M 28	1
Textile & leather mfg.									
Entrepreneurs	1921	35,538	38,344	+7.90	1919	1923	Failures, woolens, woolen goods, cotton, etc.	M 28	2

Table 95 (concl.)

INDUSTRY AND TYPE OF INCOME OR PERSONS ENGAGED (1)	YEAR FOR WHICH TEST IS MADE (2)	BASIC DATA (3)	ESTIMATED DATA (4)	% DIF. (5)	TERMINAL YEARS (6)		INDEX TESTED (7)	INDEX DESCRIBED IN NOTES TO Table	Col.
Construction materials & furniture mfg.									
Entrepreneurs	1921	25,795	40,273	+56.13	1919	1923	Failures, lumber & lumber products, etc.	M 28	3
Printing									
Entrepreneurs	1921	22,024	26,514	+20.39	1919	1923	Failures, printing & engraving	M 28	5
Metal mfg.									
Entrepreneurs	1921	20,868	24,986	+19.73	1919	1923	Failures, iron & steel, machinery & tools	M 28	6
Chemical mfg.									
Entrepreneurs	1921	5,020	5,822	+15.98	1919	1923	Failures, chemicals, drugs, paints & oils	M 28	7
Misc. & rubber mfg.									
Entrepreneurs	1921	8,841	11,166	+26.30	1919	1923	Failures, all other mfg.	M 28	8
Elec. light & power									
Employees	1927	234,747	230,049	−2.00	1922	1932	Employment index, sample states, 1922–29; BLS, elec. light & power & gas, 1929–32	P 20	1
Wages & salaries ($000)	1927	367,652	372,074	+1.21	1922	1932	Avg. pay index, sample states, 1922–29; BLS, payrolls for elec. light & power & gas, 1929–32	P 7	1
Dividends paid ($000)	1927	338,239	338,163	−0.02	1922	1932	Dividend pay., sample	P 10	1
Mfd. gas									
Employees	1927	74,155	69,469	−6.32	1925	1929	Am. Gas Asso. employment estimates	P 20	2
Wages & salaries ($000)	1927	113,255	116,349	+3.65	1925	1929	Payrolls index, elec. light & power & gas, sample	P 7	2
Street rwy.									
Employees	1927	254,364	254,786	+0.17	1922	1932	Am. Transit Asso. employment estimates	P 20	4
Wages & salaries ($000)	1927	419,990	423,227	+0.77	1922	1932	Am. Transit Asso. payroll estimates	P 7	4

Telephone										
Employees	1927	375,272	381,280	+1.87	1922	1932	Employees, sample, 1922–27; employees reported to ICC, 1927–32	P	20	6
Wages & salaries ($000)	1927	483,524	488,434	+1.02	1922	1932	Wages & salaries, sample	P	7	6
Telegraph										
Employees	1927	83,483	82,988	−0.59	1922	1932	Employees, sample, 1922–27; employees reported to ICC, 1927–32	P	20	7
Wages & salaries ($000)	1927	102,078	105,416	+3.27	1922	1932	Wages & salaries, sample	P	7	7
Dividends paid ($000)	1927	14,199	13,071	−7.94	1922	1937	Div. reported to ICC, 1922–27; div. reported to ICC, plus Com'l Cable Co. div., 1927–37	P	10	7
Wholesale trade										
Employees	1933	1,136,679	1,168,554	+2.80	1929	1935	BLS, employment	T	5	1
Wages & salaries ($000)	1933	1,714,109	1,807,010	+5.42	1929	1935	BLS, payrolls	T	4	1
Retail trade										
Employees	1933	2,563,989	2,666,164	+3.99	1929	1935	BLS, employment	T	5	2
Wages & salaries ($000)	1933	2,648,704	2,783,989	+5.11	1929	1935	BLS, payrolls	T	4	2
Restaurants										
Employees	1933	388,769	470,280	+20.97	1929	1935	BLS, employment, retail trade	S	9	6

* Salaried workers to wage earners, sample.

TABLE 96

Tests of Selected Indexes used for Interpolation during Periods containing Two Census Values

INDUSTRY AND TYPE OF INCOME OR PERSONS ENGAGED (1)	YEAR FOR WHICH TEST IS MADE (2)	BASIC DATA (3)	ESTIMATED DATA (4)	% DIF. (5)	TERMINAL YEARS (6)		INDEX TESTED (7)	INDEX DESCRIBED IN NOTES TO Table	Col.
A									
Telephone									
Interest ($000)	1937	42,806	44,190	+4.45	1922	1937	Int. paid, sample	P	12 6
'Other' mining									
Wage earners	1929	96,478	163,061	+69.01	1929	1935	BLS, employment	Q	9 4
Salaried workers	1929	11,679	11,095	−5.00	1929	1935	Ratio,* sample	Q	9 11
Oil & gas mining									
Salaried workers	1935	20,315	17,506	−13.83	1919	1935	Ratio,* selected industry	Q	9 10
Salaries ($000)	1935	41,113	46,034	+11.97	1919	1935	Avg. salary, selected industry	Q	4 10
'Other' personal service									
Employees	1935	261,011	250,274	−4.11	1933	1935	Employees, selected industry	S	9 8
Advertising									
Wages & salaries ($000)	1935	140,423	112,683	−19.75	1933	1935	Avg. salary, selected industries	S	5 6
B									
Bituminous coal mining									
Wages ($000)	1929	575,792	617,717	+7.28	1919	1929	Ratio, wages to value of product, sample	Q	4 2
Wages ($000)	1929	575,792	575,409	−0.07	1929	1935	BLS, payrolls	Q	4 2

							Q
Metal mining							
Wage earners	1929	1929	116,484	114,937	−1.33	300-day workers	Q 9 3
Wage earners	1929	1935	115,486	155,053	+34.26	BLS, employment	Q 9 3
Salaried workers	1929	1919	9,864	7,874	−20.17	Ratio,* selected industry	Q 9 9
Salaried workers	1929	1935	9,732	9,008	−7.44	Ratio,* selected industry	Q 9 9
Wages ($000)	1929	1919	179,498	167,761	−6.54	Wage per day, sample	Q 4 3
Wages ($000)	1929	1929	178,110	222,083	+24.69	BLS, payrolls	Q 4 3
Salaries ($000)	1929	1919	27,680	28,576	+3.24	Avg. salary, selected industries	Q 4 9
Salaries ($000)	1929	1935	27,210	26,617	−2.18	Avg. salary, selected industries	Q 4 9
'Other' mining							
Wages ($000)	1929	1919	117,534	128,351	+9.20	Ratio, wages to value of product, sample	Q 4 5
Wages ($000)	1929	1929	118,922	200,456	+68.56	BLS, payrolls	Q 4 5
Salaries ($000)	1929	1919	31,832	33,131	+4.08	Avg. salary, sample	Q 4 11
Salaries ($000)	1929	1929	32,300	33,016	+2.22	Avg. salary, sample	Q 4 11

* Salaried workers to wage earners.

Census values are connected by one type of sample data. But
the table is not complete. First, when the indexes used for interpolation had already been adjusted by the compiling authorities to conform to Census data (e.g., the Bureau of Labor
Statistics indexes of employment and payrolls of wage earners
and the Bureau of Agricultural Economics indexes of farm
income), it seemed unnecessary to test them by the procedure
suggested. Exceptions were made, however, whenever these
indexes were combined for purposes of interpolation in such
a way that their scope did not exactly fit the industrial group
whose number or value we had to estimate. Since this occurred
in several of our manufacturing groups, there are tests in
Table 95 of BLS indexes of wage earners' employment and
payrolls. Second, for manufacturing industries the frequency
of Census values meant that the testing procedure could be
applied to more than one time unit. But it seemed unnecessary to test more than one year; and we selected 1921 because
it is in a period for which sample data are weakest, the gyra-
tions of the basic data greatest, and hence the possible error
in the interpolation highest. Third, for some series three
Census values were reported, but the interpolating samples
used between each pair of Census values were different. Since
such conditions were more comparable to the existence of two
sets of two Census values each, they are given in Table 96.
Finally, we have omitted from Table 95 interpolations whose
results appear in the final estimates in combination with results of other procedures that cannot be similarly tested. For
example, it is possible to test estimates of the number of entrepreneurs for some divisions of mining. But since we combine
these in a final total for all mining with estimates for other
subdivisions for which no Census values are reported, the final
total belongs to the category that could not be tested because
only one Census value is reported. Table 96 presents tests
when only two Census values are reported (Section A), or
when three Census values are treated as two pairs of values,
each pair being connected by a different interpolation index

(Section B). It excludes interpolations whose results do not enter directly into our estimates.

Thus the interpolation procedures can be tested for only a few industries and types of income or employment. In general, mining, manufacturing, and the public utilities are well represented, with some sprinkling of trade and service. Government, finance, construction, and the miscellaneous division are completely absent. Estimates for agriculture had already been adjusted to the Census data by the compiling authority. For the commodity producing and public utility industries alone are censuses taken in two, three, or more years during the period covered. For such important divisions as government, finance, and most of service there is either none or only one Census value during the twenty years covered by our estimates. Consequently, a large proportion of the estimates for these industrial divisions, being based on extrapolation by sample data throughout, rest upon a much less secure foundation than most of the estimates tested in Tables 95 and 96.

Tests are more numerous for estimates of the number of employees and of employee compensation than of entrepreneurs and other types of income flow because the industrial censuses, which provide the controlling figures, rarely present information on dividends or interest and practically never on net income. This does not necessarily mean that the estimates of dividends, interest, and net income are less reliable than those of employment and payrolls. For years for which *Statistics of Income* provides data on dividends or for the public utility industries covered by the Interstate Commerce Commission, annual estimates are easily derived and are of a fair degree of accuracy. But it does mean that in other cases whenever interpolation and extrapolation are based on sample data they cannot be tested by the procedures used in preparing Tables 95 and 96; and it is likely that the resulting estimates are not as reliable as those derived by the interpolation and extrapolation procedures tested in these two tables.

To ascertain the margins of errors revealed by the tests a frequency distribution of entries by classes of size of error was constructed (Table 97). All entries were included, even though there is some duplication within Table 96, and the cells to which the entries refer differ considerably in relative size.

TABLE 97

Distribution of Entries in Tables 95 and 96 by Size of Error

GROUPS OF ENTRIES	CLASSES OF SIZE OF ERROR					
	0 to 5	5 to 10	10 to 20	20 to 40	40 to 80	Total
Table 95						
Wage earners	12	2		1		15
Salaried workers	6	3	5		2	16
Employees	6	1		1		8
Entrepreneurs		1	2	3	1	7
Wages	11	2		1		14
Salaries	11	2	2			15
Empl. compensation	5	2				7
Dividends	1	1				2
Total	52	14	9	6	3	84
Table 96						
Wage earners	1			1	1	3
Salaried workers	1	1	1	1		4
Employees	1					1
Wages	1	3		1	1	6
Salaries	4		1			5
Empl. compensation			1			1
Interest	1					1
Total	9	4	3	3	2	21

By and large the preponderant number of tests suggest relatively moderate errors. Of the entries in Table 95 about two-thirds show errors of 5 per cent or less, and only slightly over one-tenth, errors in excess of 20 per cent. Even in Table 96 over 40 per cent of the entries show errors of 5 per cent or less. Table 95 has many more small errors than Table 96, and would have, even were we to omit from it tests of the number of wage earners and of wages in manufacturing (based on adjusted BLS indexes). It is obvious that the error in an interpolation between two Census values is likely to be much less than in an extrapolation from one Census value.

Of the seven entries for number of entrepreneurs four show errors in excess of 20 per cent. Although tests in Table 95 for number of entrepreneurs are relatively few, yet the greater error shown indicates that the estimates are less reliable than other estimates tested.

Our interpolation of the number of salaried employees is subject to a greater error than our interpolation of per capita salary. Of all entries in Tables 95 and 96 for the number of salaried employees (20), less than four-tenths show errors of 5 per cent or less; of all entries for salaries (20), over seven-tenths show errors of 5 per cent or less. The test for number is of the indexes of number of salaried employees; for salaries, of indexes of compensation per employee, the number given in the Census year being accepted as reported. Hence the test is of the reliability of the estimates of number and of per capita salary, not of our final estimates of total salaries.[2]

The evidence presented above could be expanded by including other years to which the procedure can be applied (e.g., for number of salaried employees and salaries in manufacturing); or, by studying the changes that had to be introduced into the BLS indexes of employment and payrolls for the purpose of establishing conformity to new Census figures whenever these appeared. But the results of tests of this kind, like those in the tables, would be merely illustrative and suggestive: they could not demonstrate with any precision the margins of error in the final estimates.

Two important qualifications must be noted, particularly with reference to the small error the tests reveal. First, so far

[2] The errors that would be shown by a test of estimates of salaries, regardless of number, as given in the Census are suggested by combining the errors in Tables 95 and 96 shown separately for the number of salaried employees and for salaries. These combined errors, which bear more directly upon the reliability of our final estimates of total salaries than the present entries, indicate that in most cases the error in the estimates of total salaries is greater than that in the estimates of the number of salaried employees.

as the tests are interpreted in their bearing upon the estimates derived with the help of the interpolations tested, the entries in Tables 95 and 96 are likely to be overestimates. The tests necessarily disregard the fact that the interpolations actually made are for shorter periods than is assumed in Table 95; and that they are interpolations rather than extrapolations, as is assumed in Table 96. This qualification also means that the differences in the magnitude of error shown between entries in Tables 95 and 96 are suggestive of differences between interpolations and extrapolations, but not between interpolations applying to periods of different duration. Second, the errors revealed by the tests apply only to interpolations based upon two Census values or to extrapolations based upon one Census value. They do not reveal the errors that may characterize estimates based on other than Census data; or, of course, those in which availability of direct and comprehensive data makes it possible for us to dispense with the use of samples.

CHAPTER 12

Reliability of the Estimates

FOR reasons indicated in Chapter 11, the reliability of the estimates for the numerous cells that make up the income total year by year cannot be revealed clearly in a classification based on the character of the underlying data and procedures. To get a quantitative measure the margins of error must be evaluated by those who, being familiar with the estimates, dare to surmise how far wrong they may be. In the first two sections of this chapter we describe in detail the procedure by which the investigators who participated actively in the preparation of the estimates and hence know them best evaluated their margins of error. The evaluation concerns the margin of error that could be assigned to each total for the various cells making up national income in each year and cannot be applied *directly* to the changes from year to year or to differences among estimates for various cells. We discuss in the third section the margins of error that could be assigned to the estimated *changes* from year to year, or to *differences* among totals for the various important industrial divisions or types of income within national income.

1 Reliability of the Totals—The Procedure

In general, the procedure consists in classifying, by the size of the error margins, the estimates within cells formed by the combination of the allocation by industrial source with the classification by type of income. The industrial divisions were:

1 Agriculture	21 Street railways
2 Mining, total	22 Water transportation
3 Anthracite coal	23 Pipe lines
4 Bituminous coal	24 Telephone
5 Metal mining	25 Telegraph
6 Oil and gas	26 Trade
7 Other mining	27 Banking
8 Manufacturing, total	28 Insurance
9 Food & tobacco	29 Real estate
10 Textile & leather	30 Service, total
11 Construction materials & furniture	31 Professional
12 Paper	32 Personal
13 Printing	33 Domestic
14 Metal mfg.	34 Miscellaneous service
15 Chemical	35 Government, total
16 Miscellaneous & rubber	36 Federal
17 Construction	37 State
18 Electric light & power	38 County
19 Manufactured gas	39 City incl. public education
20 Steam railroads, Pullman, & express	40 Miscellaneous

The type of income and employment categories were:

a Wages	h Net savings, entrepreneurial
b Salaries	i Net income originating
c Employee compensation	j Wage earners
d Entrepreneurial withdrawals	k Salaried employees
e Dividends	l Total employees
f Interest	m Entrepreneurs
g Net savings, corporate & government	

The 40 industry and 13 type of income or employment categories make up a total of 520 cells for each year. Of course, for no year in the period were estimates available for all 520 cells; and some cells are interdependent in the sense that the estimate for one is a sum of estimates for several others. But all the available estimates, both components and totals, were classified, since the margin of error for the total is not necessarily the sum of the margins of error for the components.

The various estimates in these industry type of income or employment cells were then classified under one of four categories by the size of the probable maximum error: [1]

[1] The margin classes used originally in these classifications were from 3 to 7, 8 to 12, 13 to 27, and 28 to 52 (with central values of 5, 10, 20, and 40). A subse-

I An error of 5 to 10 per cent, with 7.5 as the average. If the margin appeared to be less than 5 per cent, the estimate was put in this category.

II An error of 11 to 20 per cent, with 15 as the average.

III An error of 21 to 40 per cent, with 30 as the average.

IV An error of 41 to 80 per cent, with 60 as the average. If the margin appeared to be greater than 80 per cent, the estimate was put in this category.

The margin of error was judged on the basis of what the estimate was, rather than what it should have been conceptually. For example, our estimate of net dividends originating in each industrial division was classified by its maximum error as a measure of net dividends, not of dividends paid directly to individuals by enterprises in the industrial division. But we did assign a larger margin of error to estimates of dividends, interest, and business savings originating in the various industrial divisions because of the distortion in the industrial allocation caused by consolidated returns.

Our classification was based upon maximum errors, not minimum or average errors; i.e., we were concerned with how large the error could be. An error of 5 per cent meant that this was the maximum error to which the estimate was likely to be subject. The minimum error for each estimate is zero and the average error too indefinite to estimate.

The setting up of error classes, with fairly wide class limits, might be interpreted in two ways: it may be thought: (1) that we know precisely what the probable maximum error for each estimate is but, for the sake of economy in presentation, forbear to give the exact figures, grouping them into four classes; or (2) that we do *not* know precisely what the probable maximum error is, but can approximate it within certain limits. If we put an estimate in Class I, we mean that its probable maximum error is between 1 and 10 per cent.

Of these two interpretations of our procedure the second

---

quent upward revaluation of error margins resulted in the classes above; see below.

is valid. We do *not* know the precise percentage at which to set
the probable maximum error for each estimate; and we established error classes in order to allow a range for the maximum
error. In subsequent calculations, it is true, we assume a single
central value for each class; but this is a simplification, needed
to arrive at compact results. It does not mean that for every
estimate in Class I the most probable value of the maximum
error is 7.5 per cent. On the contrary, there are appreciable
differences in the relative accuracy of estimates in Class I (from
a maximum error of 1 or 2 to 10 per cent), and especially in
the upper error classes with their wide range between class
limits. But for purposes of calculation a single central value is
assigned to each class, and the probable maximum error of
the combined estimates in the class is assumed to be this central value.

Since the ranges indicated above represent both positive
and negative errors, estimates included in Class I, for example, may be from 1 to 10 per cent greater or less than the true
value. This would seem to indicate that the maximum
range of Class I is from — 10 to + 10. As a matter of fact the
maximum errors are in one direction for a majority of the
estimates. Thus the error in our estimate of employee compensation for manufacturing, in Census years, is likely to be
negative, i.e., our estimate is probably always somewhat less
than the true one. But it would bring us upon too uncertain
ground were we to distinguish positive and negative errors,
and try to set up classes accordingly.

The estimates were classified by the four error classes inde-
pendently by each of the three investigators who participated
most directly in the study and were most familiar with sources
and methods.[2] It was thought that a combination of independent classifications would reduce any bias that might result from pessimism or optimism of the individual investigator. The three evaluations of estimates by classes of probable

[2] Lillian Epstein, Elizabeth Jenks, and the author.

maximum errors—all for identical estimates in identical industry type of income or employment cells—were used in all further calculations of error margins. No attempt was made to reconcile them or change them in any way: it was thought best to use them in the form that corresponds most closely to their real meaning—appraisals by individual investigators familiar with the estimates.

The procedure was followed with one significant exception: we raised all margins of error by one-half [3] because we found that all three investigators tended to underestimate the errors attaching to the results of their labors. The original sets of evaluations were based on the working tables used in preparing the estimates and the detailed description of methods and data in Part Four, but without consulting the comparisons in Chapter 10 or using the tests of interpolation and extrapolation procedures discussed in Chapter 11. Reference to these materials indicated that the margins of error, as originally calculated, were, on the whole, too low, but the relative differences were not affected by the additional information in Chapters 10 and 11.

The estimates were classified by each investigator for every year in the period and, for purposes of analysis, averages, unweighted geometric means of the central values of error classes, were computed for 1919–28, 1929–35, and 1919–35.[4] These average margins [5] for net income originating, for

[3] This uniform adjustment may have resulted in an overestimate of the margins of error for some cells. It is likely that the margins as now presented, even for some of the more comprehensive totals, are somewhat too high, since the estimates placed in Class I may have a mean margin of error somewhat lower than the mid-value used in further computations (i.e., 7.5) and the resulting exaggeration of the margin of error may not be offset by an excess over 60 per cent of the average margin of error of estimates in Class IV.

[4] The computation was made before the estimates for 1936-38 were completed. It was felt that the additional labor necessitated by the inclusion of data for these recent years was not warranted since the margins of error would be affected only slightly.

[5] In subsequent discussion the central values of error classes and the averages derived from them are referred to as margins of error.

number engaged by industrial divisions, and for the countrywide totals of the various types of income and employment are shown in Tables 98–100.

Margins of error were calculated not only for the estimates within each industry type of income cell, but also for certain composite totals; e.g., for wages and salaries in total manufacturing as well as for those in its subdivisions. As mentioned above, most of the composite totals were classified by error classes directly, and are assigned a margin of error that is not derived from the errors of their components. But this procedure was subject to significant exceptions. First, the maximum error of total net income originating in each industrial branch was evaluated both directly and by weighting error margins assigned to the various type of income components. Second, a weighted margin of error of the countrywide totals of each type of income and each category of number engaged was derived from the error margins for the several industrial components, in two variants, one using the ten major industrial divisions, the other, the minor industrial divisions.

The calculation of these weighted entries followed a few standard rules. First, the weights throughout were the average absolute values of the estimates whose margins of error were compounded into averages. When these absolute values were either positive or negative, as in the case of savings of enterprises, the average value was computed with signs disregarded. Second, the weighted mean margins of error were computed from the means for the periods, not from entries for each year; e.g., the weighted mean for the countrywide total for 1919–28 was derived from the error margins computed for 1919–28 for wages and salaries in each industrial division, the absolute average value for each wage and salary industry cell for the decade being used as weights. Third, the margins of error thus weighted were averaged by taking an arithmetic mean. The arithmetic mean was used because a geometric mean would underestimate the total absolute and relative margin of error.[6] Fourth, in obtaining weighted margins of error for the estimates of net income originating in each industry, the most detailed list of components was used, i.e., wages, salaries, entrepreneurial withdrawals, dividends, interest, net savings of corporations and government, and net savings of entrepreneurs. Similar rules were followed in deriving weighted margins of error for the estimates of the number engaged or employed.

Since the evaluations are essentially opinions, they are presented separately in Tables 98–100 to reveal the full extent of agreement or disagreement. But it was thought that some consensus of opinion would be helpful. For this purpose we summarized the evaluations by the three investigators by taking a geometric mean of the margins of error they assigned to the various components and totals over the long periods covered. For each cell we averaged the three error margins; and these geometric means are presented in the tables.

Equal weight was assigned to the three evaluations of error margins. While it cannot be assumed that the three investigators were equally familiar with the estimates of each and every component of national income and of the total employed and engaged, the differences were so vague that it was impossible to assign any weight to them. In addition, each investigator had at hand not only the general rules of classification set forth above, but also the detailed description of sources and methods in Part Four. This description was con-

---

[6] This can be shown by the following illustration:

Cell	True Value	Estimated Maximum Error	Maximum Possible Value	Minimum Possible Value
a	1,000	15%	1,150	850
b	2,000	30%	2,600	1,400
Total	3,000		3,750	2,250

The maximum possible error is 750/3,000 or 25 per cent. This result would be obtained by weighting 15 per cent by 1 and 30 per cent by 2, and taking the arithmetic mean (dividing by 3). But the geometric mean would be 23.8 per cent, i.e., too low.

tinually referred to as a basis for classification. A greater degree of agreement would have been possible by elucidation of the reasons that led to the differences. But in such a discussion unaccountable personal influences and factors are likely to play a part; and it was thought preferable to avoid the introduction of such elements. The present evaluations have, we believe, a more objective meaning than would evaluations modified after conference.

Finally, we summarized not only the margins of error assigned to each estimate by the three investigators, but also the extent of agreement or divergence. For this purpose, the computation of the geometric means of the error margins was accompanied by a computation of the logarithmic average deviations. The antilogs of these average deviations represent the geometric mean *relative* deviations of the three error margins for each cell from the geometric mean margins of error. These geometric mean relative deviations, expressed as percentages, also appear in the tables. The deviations for the weighted entries were computed directly from the weighted geometric means already established by each investigator.

2 Reliability of the Totals—The Results

In interpreting the results of our attempt to evaluate the margins of error, it is imperative to remember that these evaluations are nothing more than informed opinions, since no exact criteria or specific empirical evidence were at hand by which to measure the errors precisely. Consequently, the values in the tables are themselves subject to a considerable margin of error. It is perhaps narrower for the combined judgment of the three investigators than for each separately, but is probably substantial even for the former.

Although the absolute error margins are surrounded by a large zone of doubt and uncertainty, the differences among them are significant. If, for example, the average margin of error for an estimate is 7.5 per cent, the mid-point of Class I, the true error may well be somewhat smaller or larger. But substantial differences in error margins are significant indicators of substantial differences in the reliability of estimates.

Furthermore, we must warn the reader not to apply margins of error to aspects of the estimates to which they do not refer directly. For example, the weighted average margins are averages of error margins for the components, and since the error margins for the components may partly cancel one another, the weighted average margins may exaggerate the error for the composite total. For this reason a weighted error should often be scaled down, if it is to be interpreted as a margin of error for the composite total; and for such composite totals a directly evaluated margin of error that is appreciably smaller than the weighted mean of the components is the more significant measure of the two.

A   INDUSTRIAL DIVISIONS

The margins of error in estimates for various industrial divisions are shown for the income totals in Table 98 and for the number employed or engaged in Table 99. Brief inspection of Table 98 reveals three distinct groupings of industries. In the first, with a margin of error well below 15 per cent, are the basic branches of manufacturing and several public utilities (electric light and power, steam railroads, street railways, telephone, telegraph), industries for which the high reliability of the estimates is largely explained by the frequency of the industrial censuses and availability of comprehensive data from the Interstate Commerce Commission. In the second group, with margins of error of about 15 per cent but well below 30, are agriculture, mining, manufactured gas, pipe lines, trade, banking, insurance, and government—industries for which information is extensive but not complete. In the third group, with margins of error of about 30 per cent and higher, are the dark spots in the statistical picture of the income of the nation—construction.

TABLE 98

Net Income Originating, Margins of Error by Industrial Divisions, 1919–1935

	DIRECTLY ESTIMATED					ESTIMATED BY PARTS				
	INVESTIGATOR					INVESTIGATOR				
	A	B	C	Mean	Relative deviation	A	B	C	Mean	Relative deviation
	(1)	(2)	(3)	(4)	(5)	(6)	(7)	(8)	(9)	(10)
					I 1919–1928					
Agriculture	15.00	15.00	7.50	11.91	36	31.51	51.38	8.43	23.90	100
Mining, total	14.00	27.99	7.50	14.32	56	23.99	28.07	12.65	20.42	38
Mfg., total	7.50	15.00	7.50	9.45	36	11.45	10.44	7.76	9.75	17
Food & tobacco	7.50	15.00	7.50	9.45	36	18.61	11.97	19.98	16.45	24
Textile & leather	7.50	15.00	7.50	9.45	36	13.34	10.63	7.90	10.39	20
Construction materials & furniture	7.50	15.00	7.50	9.45	36	12.69	10.20	7.79	10.03	18
Paper	7.50	15.00	7.50	9.45	36	15.16	17.93	7.64	10.65	27
Printing	7.50	15.00	7.50	9.45	36	14.68	11.24	7.94	10.94	24
Metal	7.50	15.00	7.50	9.45	36	13.69	9.88	7.58	10.08	23
Chemical	15.00	15.00	15.00	15.00	0	29.36	11.06	28.21	20.92	53
Misc. & rubber	7.50	15.00	7.50	9.45	36	17.30	10.77	9.50	12.10	27
Construction	30.00	30.00	30.00	30.00	0	31.66	30.90	29.62	30.70	2
Electric light & power	13.06	15.00	7.50	11.37	32	13.24	18.10	7.53	12.17	38
Mfd. gas	15.00	15.00	30.00	18.90	36	30.21	16.04	18.02	20.59	29
Steam rr., Pullman, & express	7.50	7.50	7.50	7.50	0	7.50	7.50	7.50	7.50	0
Street railways	13.06	13.06	7.50	10.86	28	13.06	13.12	7.50	10.88	28
Water transportation	30.00	30.00	30.00	30.00	0	32.64	30.34	30.00	30.98	4
Pipe lines	22.74	21.21	11.37	17.64	34	18.08	18.29	8.80	14.27	38
Telephone	7.50	7.50	7.50	7.50	0	7.50	7.50	7.50	7.50	0
Telegraph	7.50	7.50	7.50	7.50	0	7.50	8.77	7.50	7.90	7

Trade	30.00	30.00	12.18	22.22	49	33.64	37.79	20.66	29.72	27
Banking	15.00	15.00	24.38	17.64	24	17.36	14.09	21.47	17.38	15
Insurance	15.00	15.00	15.00	15.00	0	18.76	17.79	17.23	17.92	3
Real estate	30.00	30.00	60.00	37.80	36	29.69	34.42	56.90	38.74	29
Service, total	30.00	30.00	30.00	30.00	0	41.54	41.42	59.25	46.71	17
Government, total	16.08	16.08	30.00	19.80	32	26.17	24.90	24.26	25.10	3
Miscellaneous	60.00	60.00	60.00	60.00	0	60.46	57.22	57.52	58.39	2
Total, based on major divisions	20.44	20.48	20.83	20.59	1	26.36	29.02	24.50	26.56	6
Total, based on minor divisions	20.60	20.64	20.98	20.74	1	27.26	29.08	25.16	27.12	5

II 1929–1935

Agriculture	20.19	15.00	7.50	13.14	45	33.47	52.57	9.05	25.16	98
Mining, total	13.59	15.00	7.50	11.52	33	25.49	14.73	11.67	16.36	34
Mfg., total	7.50	15.00	7.50	9.45	36	11.43	10.22	7.69	9.65	16
Food & tobacco	7.50	15.00	7.50	9.45	36	16.23	10.75	15.20	13.84	18
Textile & leather	7.50	15.00	7.50	9.45	36	14.36	10.40	7.82	10.53	23
Construction materials & furniture	7.50	15.00	7.50	9.45	36	17.23	10.67	7.74	11.25	33
Paper	7.50	15.00	7.50	9.45	36	13.88	9.69	7.57	10.06	24
Printing	7.50	15.00	7.50	9.45	36	12.80	10.76	7.78	10.23	20
Metal	7.50	15.00	7.50	9.45	36	15.33	9.68	7.55	10.39	30
Chemical	12.30	15.00	12.30	14.64	9	27.56	10.36	21.04	18.18	46
Misc. & rubber	7.50	15.00	7.50	9.45	36	16.59	10.34	8.79	11.47	28
Construction	30.00	15.00	27.16	23.04	33	31.70	20.14	26.54	25.68	18

Table 98 (concl.)

	DIRECTLY ESTIMATED					ESTIMATED BY PARTS				
	INVESTIGATOR			Mean	Relative deviation	INVESTIGATOR			Mean	Relative deviation
	A	B	C		1929–1935	A	B	C		
	(1)	(2)	(3)	(4)	(5)	(6)	(7)	(8)	(9)	(10)
				II		(concl.)				
Electric light & power	13.59	15.00	7.50	11.52	33	18.03	14.61	8.80	13.24	31
Mfd. gas	15.00	15.00	20.19	16.56	14	29.50	14.45	15.82	18.89	35
Steam rr, Pullman, & express	7.50	7.50	7.50	7.50	0	7.50	7.50	7.50	7.50	0
Street railways	13.59	13.59	7.50	11.14	30	13.88	13.94	7.50	11.32	32
Water transportation	30.00	30.00	15.00	23.80	36	34.64	17.63	15.90	21.34	38
Pipe lines	15.00	15.00	7.50	11.91	36	15.00	15.00	7.50	11.90	36
Telephone	7.50	7.50	7.50	7.50	0	7.50	7.50	7.50	7.50	0
Telegraph	7.50	7.50	7.50	7.50	0	7.50	7.96	7.50	7.65	3
Trade	30.00	27.16	7.50	18.28	81	26.32	22.52	11.52	18.98	39
Banking	15.00	12.30	12.30	13.14	9	17.97	11.50	10.02	12.75	26
Insurance	15.00	15.00	13.59	14.52	4	18.74	17.63	15.12	17.09	9
Real estate	30.00	27.16	54.34	35.38	33	29.70	36.92	48.97	37.72	19
Service, total	30.00	30.00	15.00	23.80	36	31.42	31.03	29.30	30.57	3
Government, total	15.00	15.00	15.00	15.00	0	20.21	19.02	13.58	17.35	18
Miscellaneous	60.00	60.00	30.00	47.62	36	58.46	36.50	29.43	39.74	29
Total, based on major divisions	21.22	20.21	14.97	18.58	16	24.27	23.45	17.05	21.33	16
Total, based on minor divisions	21.40	20.25	15.10	18.70	15	25.24	23.52	17.56	21.85	16
III 1919–1935										
Agriculture	16.95	15.00	7.50	12.40	40	32.14	51.78	8.65	24.32	99
Mining, total	13.83	21.64	7.50	13.10	45	24.04	19.79	12.20	17.97	29

Mfg., total	7.50	15.00	7.50	9.45	36	11.62	10.34	7.73	9.76	17
Food & tobacco	7.50	15.00	7.50	9.45	36	17.72	11.48	17.86	15.38	21
Textile & leather	7.50	15.00	7.50	9.45	36	13.66	10.51	7.88	10.42	20
Construction materials & furniture	7.50	15.00	7.50	9.45	36	14.12	10.36	7.77	10.43	22
Paper	7.50	15.00	7.50	9.45	36	14.71	10.06	7.61	10.41	26
Printing	7.50	15.00	7.50	9.45	36	13.93	11.00	7.88	10.64	22
Metal	7.50	15.00	7.50	9.45	36	14.26	9.79	7.57	10.18	25
Chemical	13.83	15.00	13.83	14.20	4	28.56	10.87	25.47	19.92	50
Misc. & rubber	7.50	15.00	7.50	9.45	36	16.94	10.52	10.54	12.34	24
Construction	30.00	22.54	28.80	26.91	12	31.64	25.42	28.35	28.36	8
Electric light & power	13.28	15.00	7.50	11.43	32	14.66	16.22	7.94	12.36	34
Mfd. gas	15.00	15.00	25.48	17.90	27	30.29	15.78	17.57	20.32	30
Steam rr., Pullman, & express	7.50	7.50	7.50	7.50	0	7.50	7.50	7.50	7.50	0
Street railways	13.28	13.28	7.50	10.98	29	13.39	13.45	7.50	11.06	30
Water transportation	30.00	30.00	22.54	27.27	14	33.34	23.71	22.92	26.26	17
Pipe lines	19.16	18.39	9.58	15.00	35	16.43	16.54	8.07	12.99	37
Telephone	7.50	7.50	7.50	7.50	0	7.50	7.50	7.50	7.50	0
Telegraph	7.50	7.50	7.50	7.50	0	7.50	8.38	7.50	7.78	5
Trade	30.00	28.80	9.98	20.50	62	30.55	30.22	16.58	24.82	31
Banking	15.00	13.83	18.39	15.63	11	17.62	12.87	15.63	15.25	12
Insurance	15.00	15.00	14.40	14.80	2	18.75	17.72	16.90	17.56	5
Real estate	30.00	28.80	57.60	36.78	35	29.69	35.48	53.47	38.33	25
Service, total	30.00	30.00	22.54	27.27	14	36.86	36.65	44.27	39.10	9
Government, total	15.63	15.63	22.54	17.66	18	23.54	22.31	47.94	29.31	39
Miscellaneous	60.00	60.00	45.10	54.56	14	58.73	47.14	43.44	49.36	12
Total, based on major divisions	20.88	21.83	18.16	20.23	7	25.40	26.36	21.12	24.18	9
Total, based on minor divisions	21.04	21.87	18.31	20.35	7	26.34	26.43	22.13	24.88	8

TABLE 99

Number Employed, Margins of Error by Industrial Divisions, 1919–1935

	EMPLOYEES					ENTREPRENEURS				
	INVESTIGATOR			Mean	Relative deviation	INVESTIGATOR			Mean	Relative deviation
	A	B	C			A	B	C		
	(1)	(2)	(3)	(4)	(5)	(6)	(7)	(8)	(9)	(10)
					I 1919–1928					
Agriculture	26.12	15.00	7.50	14.32	54	7.50	13.06	7.50	9.03	28
Mining, total	14.00	14.00	7.50	11.37	32	52.23	14.00	7.50	17.64	106
Anthracite coal	7.50	7.50	7.50	7.50	0					
Bituminous coal	14.00	14.00	7.50	11.37	32					
Metal	14.00	14.00	7.50	11.37	32					
Oil & gas	26.12	26.12	14.00	21.21	32					
Other	14.00	15.00	7.50	11.64	34					
Mfg, total	7.50	7.50	7.50	7.50	0	10.60	10.60	7.50	9.45	17
Food & tobacco	7.50	7.50	7.50	7.50	0	10.60	10.60	7.50	9.45	17
Textile & leather	7.50	7.50	7.50	7.50	0	10.60	10.60	7.50	9.45	17
Construction materials & furniture	7.50	7.50	7.50	7.50	0	10.60	10.60	7.50	9.45	17
Paper	7.50	7.50	7.50	7.50	0	10.60	10.60	7.50	9.45	17
Printing	7.50	7.50	7.50	7.50	0	10.60	10.60	7.50	9.45	17
Metal	7.50	7.50	7.50	7.50	0	10.60	10.60	7.50	9.45	17
Chemical	7.50	7.50	7.50	7.50	0	10.60	10.60	7.50	9.45	17
Misc. & rubber	7.50	7.50	7.50	7.50	0	10.60	10.60	7.50	9.45	17
Construction	30.00	30.00	30.00	30.00	0	30.00	27.99	26.12	27.99	5

Electric light & power	13.06	22.74	7.50	13.06	45	52.23	26.12	15.00	27.34	54
Mfd. gas	10.60	10.60	7.50	9.45	17					
Steam rr., Pullman, & express	7.50	7.50	7.50	7.50	0					
Street railways	13.06	13.06	7.50	10.86	28					
Water transportation	30.00	30.00	30.00	30.00	0	60.00	60.00	15.00	37.80	85
Pipe lines	15.00	22.74	11.37	15.70	28					
Telephone	7.50	7.50	7.50	7.50	0					
Telegraph	7.50	7.50	7.50	7.50	0					
Trade	27.99	30.00	12.18	21.70	47	27.99	30.00	15.00	23.26	34
Banking	15.00	30.00	30.00	23.80	36					
Insurance	15.00	30.00	30.00	23.80	36					
Real estate	30.00	30.00	26.12	28.65	6					
Service, total	30.00	30.00	30.00	30.00	0	30.00	30.00	30.00	30.00	0
Professional	30.00	30.00	60.00	37.80	36	30.00	30.00	60.00	37.80	36
Personal	30.00	30.00	15.00	23.80	36	30.00	30.00	15.00	23.80	36
Domestic	30.00	30.00	30.00	30.00	0					
Misc.	60.00	30.00	30.00	37.80	36	60.00	60.00	30.00	47.62	36
Government, total	15.00	16.08	15.00	15.34	3					
Federal	16.08	16.08	15.00	15.70	3					
State	15.00	14.00	39.58	20.25	56					
County	30.00	26.12	39.58	31.42	17					
City, incl. public education	15.00	14.00	24.38	17.24	26					
Miscellaneous	60.00	60.00	60.00	60.00	0	60.00	60.00	60.00	60.00	0
Total, based on major divisions	19.78	19.85	16.31	18.58	9	15.50	19.34	13.52	15.94	14
Total, based on minor divisions	20.58	19.84	17.34	19.21	7	16.58	20.41	14.42	16.96	13

Table 99 (cont.)

	EMPLOYEES					ENTREPRENEURS				
	INVESTIGATOR					INVESTIGATOR				
	A	B	C	Mean	Relative deviation	A	B	C	Mean	Relative deviation
	(1)	(2)	(3)	(4)	(5)	(6)	(7)	(8)	(9)	(10)
					II 1929–1935					
Agriculture	24.62	15.00	7.50	14.04	52	12.30	12.30	7.50	10.44	25
Mining, total	13.59	12.30	7.50	10.78	27					
Anthracite coal	7.50	7.50	7.50	7.50	0					
Bituminous coal	13.59	12.30	7.50	10.78	27					
Metal	13.59	12.30	7.50	10.78	27					
Oil & gas	27.16	13.59	7.50	14.04	55					
Other	13.59	12.30	7.50	10.78	27					
Mfg., total	7.50	7.50	7.50	7.50	0	10.10	12.30	7.50	9.76	19
Food & tobacco	7.50	7.50	7.50	7.50	0	10.10	12.30	7.50	9.76	19
Textile & leather	7.50	7.50	7.50	7.50	0	10.10	12.30	7.50	9.76	19
Construction materials & furniture	7.50	7.50	7.50	7.50	0	10.10	12.30	7.50	9.76	19
Paper	7.50	7.50	7.50	7.50	0	10.10	12.30	7.50	9.76	19
Printing	7.50	7.50	7.50	7.50	0	10.10	12.30	7.50	9.76	19
Metal	7.50	7.50	7.50	7.50	0	10.10	12.30	7.50	9.76	19
Chemical	7.50	7.50	7.50	7.50	0	10.10	12.30	7.50	9.76	19
Misc. & rubber	7.50	7.50	7.50	7.50	0	10.10	12.30	7.50	9.76	19
Construction	30.00	15.00	15.00	18.90	96	30.00	27.16	13.59	22.29	39

Electric light & power	13.59	13.59	7.50	11.14	30	54.34	27.16	15.00	28.08	55
Mfd. gas	10.10	13.59	7.50	10.10	22					
Steam rr., Pullman, & express	7.50	7.50	7.50	7.50	0					
Street railways	13.59	13.59	7.50	11.14	30					
Water transportation	30.00	15.00	15.00	18.90	36	60.00	49.22	15.00	35.38	77
Pipe lines	15.00	15.00	7.50	11.91	36					
Telephone	7.50	7.50	7.50	7.50	0					
Telegraph	7.50	7.50	7.50	7.50	0					
Trade	22.29	11.14	7.50	12.30	49	22.29	22.29	7.50	15.51	62
Banking	15.00	20.19	12.30	15.51	19					
Insurance	15.00	27.16	13.59	17.68	33					
Real estate	30.00	30.00	15.00	23.80	36					
Service, total	30.00	30.00	15.00	23.80	36	30.00	30.00	15.00	23.80	36
Professional	30.00	30.00	30.00	30.00	0	30.00	30.00	30.00	30.00	0
Personal	22.29	22.29	7.50	15.51	62	30.00	30.00	7.50	18.90	85
Domestic	30.00	30.00	27.16	29.02	4					
Misc.	30.00	30.00	15.00	23.80	36	60.00	60.00	15.00	37.80	85
Government, total	15.00	15.00	7.50	11.91	36					
Federal	15.00	15.00	7.50	11.91	36					
State	15.00	15.00	30.00	18.90	36					
County	30.00	30.00	60.00	37.80	36					
City, incl. public education	15.00	15.00	15.00	15.00	0					
Miscellaneous	60.00	33.12	30.00	39.06	33	33.12	33.12	30.00	32.04	4
Total, based on major divisions	19.83	15.81	10.54	14.90	26	17.48	17.46	9.54	14.28	31
Total, based on minor divisions	19.72	15.62	12.59	15.71	16	18.35	18.33	10.08	15.02	30

Table 99 (concl.)

III 1919–1935

	EMPLOYEES					ENTREPRENEURS				
	INVESTIGATOR			Mean	Relative deviation	INVESTIGATOR			Mean	Relative deviation
	A	B	C			A	B	C		
	(1)	(2)	(3)	(4)	(5)	(6)	(7)	(8)	(9)	(10)
Agriculture	25.48	15.00	7.50	14.20	53	9.20	12.75	7.50	9.58	21
Mining, total	13.83	13.28	7.50	11.13	30					
Anthracite coal	7.50	7.50	7.50	7.50	0					
Bituminous coal	13.83	13.28	7.50	11.13	30					
Metal	13.83	13.28	7.50	11.13	30					
Oil & gas	26.55	19.95	10.83	17.90	40					
Other	13.83	13.83	7.50	11.28	31					
Mfg., total	7.50	7.50	7.50	7.50	0	10.40	11.28	7.50	9.58	18
Food & tobacco	7.50	7.50	7.50	7.50	0	10.40	11.28	7.50	9.58	18
Textile & leather	7.50	7.50	7.50	7.50	0	10.40	11.28	7.50	9.58	18
Construction materials & furniture	7.50	7.50	7.50	7.50	0	10.40	11.28	7.50	9.58	18
Paper	7.50	7.50	7.50	7.50	0	10.40	11.28	7.50	9.58	18
Printing	7.50	7.50	7.50	7.50	0	10.40	11.28	7.50	9.58	18
Metal	7.50	7.50	7.50	7.50	0	10.40	11.28	7.50	9.58	18
Chemical	7.50	7.50	7.50	7.50	0	10.40	11.28	7.50	9.58	18
Misc. & rubber	7.50	7.50	7.50	7.50	0	10.40	11.28	7.50	9.58	18
Construction	30.00	22.54	22.54	24.80	14	30.00	27.64	19.95	25.48	18

Electric light & power	13.28	18.39	7.50	12.24	39	53.08	26.55	15.00	27.64	54
Mfd. gas	10.40	11.74	7.50	9.70	19					
Steam rr., Pullman, & express	7.50	7.50	7.50	7.50	0					
Street railways	13.28	13.28	7.50	10.98	29					
Water transportation	30.00	22.54	22.54	24.80	14	60.00	55.30	15.00	36.78	82
Pipe lines	15.00	19.16	9.58	14.01	29					
Telephone	7.50	7.50	7.50	7.50	0					
Telegraph	7.50	7.50	7.50	7.50	0					
Trade	25.48	19.95	9.98	17.19	44	25.48	26.62	11.28	19.68	45
Banking	15.00	25.48	20.79	19.95	21					
Insurance	15.00	28.80	21.64	21.08	25					
Real estate	30.00	30.00	20.79	26.55	18					
Service, total	30.00	30.00	22.54	27.27	14	30.00	30.00	22.54	27.27	14
Professional	30.00	30.00	45.10	34.36	20	30.00	30.00	45.10	34.36	20
Personal	26.55	26.55	11.28	19.95	46	30.00	30.00	11.28	21.64	54
Domestic	30.00	30.00	28.80	29.60	2					
Misc.	45.10	30.00	22.54	31.24	28	60.00	60.00	22.54	43.30	54
Government, total	15.00	15.63	11.28	13.83	15					
Federal	15.63	15.63	11.28	14.01	16					
State	15.00	14.40	35.31	19.68	48					
County	30.00	27.64	46.98	33.90	24					
City, incl. public education	15.00	14.40	19.95	16.28	15					
Miscellaneous	60.00	46.98	45.10	50.28	13	46.98	46.98	45.10	46.35	2
Total, based on major divisions	19.77	17.73	13.57	16.82	15	16.07	18.52	11.62	15.13	19
Total, based on minor divisions	20.18	17.65	15.10	17.52	10	17.06	19.51	12.36	16.02	19

water transportation, real estate, direct service industries, and, of course, the miscellaneous division.

The margins of error in the estimates of the number employed or engaged (Table 99) naturally reveal the same grouping of industries. The basic data for service income, the preponderant part of total income originating in each industry, are also a source of information on the number employed and engaged. In fact, information on number is in some instances somewhat more complete than on income flows, e.g., the number of entrepreneurs as compared with their total income in manufacturing. For this reason, some of the income estimates are derived by applying to the number of entrepreneurs (or employees) a per capita income figure. It is, therefore, not surprising that the margins of error in the estimates of the number employed or engaged are often lower than those in the estimates of the corresponding income flows. This is especially true of the number of entrepreneurs as compared with their income, but can be observed also for some of the estimates of the number and income of employees (mining, construction, real estate, service). On the other hand, for some industries information on income flows is more complete than on number, with consequent effects on the respective margins of error (banking, insurance).

Comparison of the directly evaluated average margins of error for estimates of net income by industrial divisions with those obtained by weighting the errors of the components shows that in several industries (agriculture, mining, trade, service, government) the former are significantly lower. This difference arises largely because in the direct evaluation the separate errors attaching to the estimates of entrepreneurial withdrawals and of entrepreneurial net savings partly cancel one another, whereas they are added without any cancellation in the weighted mean of the errors in the components. On the other hand, in pipe lines and miscellaneous industries the directly evaluated margins of error are somewhat greater than those obtained by weighting parts, even when averaged for the error margins calculated by the three investigators. But these differences are of doubtful significance, as are also the exceedingly minor differences between the two sets of error margins observed for other industries not mentioned. The weighted margins of error for national income, whether on the basis of the ten major industrial divisions or of the more numerous minor divisions, are distinctly smaller when derived from the margins for each industrial division evaluated directly than when derived from the margins for each industrial division obtained by weighting the errors attached to the estimates of the components.

To show changes in the margins of error from the first part of the period to the second (Tables 98 and 99, Sec. I and II) we compare the weighted error margins for net income originating in each industry, because these are more sensitive than those based on direct evaluation. In mining, construction, water transportation, pipe lines, trade, various branches of finance, total service, government, and miscellaneous, the margin of error declined markedly from the average for 1919–28 to that for 1929–35, partly because of the extension of Census coverage in these industries since 1929, partly because of the greater detail in the presentation of data in *Statistics of Income* and employment and payroll samples of the Bureau of Labor Statistics, partly because of special studies, conducted primarily by the Department of Commerce in connection with its estimates of national income. For similar reasons, the margins of error for the number employed in the various industries declined.

Agreement among the three investigators in their evaluation of the margins of error was high for some estimates and low for others. The relative deviation from the geometric mean margin of error in net income ranges from zero for the steam railroad and telephone industries to 99 per cent for agriculture. These variations in the degree of agreement reveal several general features. First, there seems to be a posi-

tive association between the geometric mean margin of error
and the size of the *relative* deviation which measures the extent of divergence in the evaluations of the three investigators. This association is suggested by the coefficient of rank
correlation computed for the weighted margins of error for
the net income totals and for the margins of error directly
evaluated for the number of employees. When the underly-

**Coefficient of Rank Correlation between Geometric Mean
Margins of Error and Mean Relative Deviations**

	NO. OF PAIRS OF ITEMS	*1919– 1935*	*1919– 1928*	*1929– 1935*
1 Net income estimates, by industrial division, weighted by parts *	27	+0.28	+0.13	+0.40
2 Estimates of number of employees, by industrial division *	27	+0.22	+0.16	+0.43

* The subdivisions of mining and manufacturing were excluded from line 2 to
reduce the number of entries of identical magnitude. The two countrywide
totals were excluded from both lines to prevent duplication.

ing data are not sufficiently comprehensive and exact to yield
an estimate with a narrow margin of error, there is apparently a greater possibility of disagreement among the investigators as to what margin of error to assign. This does not
mean that for weak estimates there cannot be perfect agreement on margins of error. But the estimates whose weakness
is so apparent as to compel all three investigators to assign
uniformly large margins of error are few. And when unre-
liability is not obvious, significant disagreement in the evaluation of error arises more easily.

A corollary result is revealed when the relative deviations
about the geometric mean error are compared for the two
parts of the period. The divergence in the three evaluations
is larger for 1929–35 than for 1919–28, and this increase in
the relative deviations is concentrated in a few industrial divisions: construction, water transportation, and the miscellaneous (for both net income and number employed), trade (for

net income), real estate and service (for number employed). The margin of error for these industries declined markedly from 1919–28 to 1929–35. What obviously happened is that, with the accretion of new data, the estimates passed out of the definitely weak category to a somewhat superior standing with respect to reliability; and concurrently with this change appeared a greater opportunity for divergence in the evaluation of the error margins.[7]

B TYPES OF INCOME AND EMPLOYMENT

For the countrywide totals of income by type and of the number employed and engaged it was not feasible to evaluate the margins of error directly. Hence, the evaluations of these estimates in Table 100 are all weighted means of error margins assigned to income or number for the various industrial divisions. Since it is likely that errors in the estimates for a given type of income or of employment in the various industries may partly cancel one another, the margins of error in Table 100 exaggerate the errors for the countrywide totals.[8] This is especially likely to be true for property income, for which differentiation among various industries is more difficult than for service income. It is quite possible that the margins of error in the estimates of dividends and interest are appreciably below 15 to 18 per cent for the former and 25 per cent for the latter.

This qualification may be sufficiently great to affect the difference in the margins of error between the estimates of employee compensation on the one hand and of dividends and interest on the other. As the weighted means stand, the margins of error for the estimates of employee compensation, 1919–35, are slightly wider than those for dividends and signifi-

[7] It is obviously this factor, i.e., the unanimity of opinion for especially weak estimates that lowers the association established just above between margins of error and mean relative deviations.

[8] This inference is supported by the fact that the weighted means based on ten major industrial divisions are, by and large, smaller than those derived from the more numerous minor divisions.

TABLE 100

Income Types and Categories of Employment, Margins of Error, 1919–1935

DERIVED FROM ESTIMATES FOR

	MAJOR INDUSTRIAL DIVISIONS					MINOR INDUSTRIAL DIVISIONS				
	INVESTIGATOR			Relative		INVESTIGATOR				Relative
	A	B	C	Mean deviation	deviation	A	B	C	Mean	deviation
	(1)	(2)	(3)	(4)	(5)	(6)	(7)	(8)	(9)	(10)
					I 1919–1928					
Wages	12.20	12.41	10.20	11.56	9	12.22	12.15	10.27	11.51	8
Salaries	11.68	12.18	9.56	11.08	10	11.92	12.20	9.66	11.20	10
Employee compensation	19.66	19.85	20.13	19.88	1	20.52	19.77	20.06	20.12	1
Entrepreneurial withdrawals	35.90	50.80	31.93	38.76	20	35.90	50.80	31.93	38.76	20
Dividends	18.56	14.79	16.90	16.68	8	24.02	14.79	24.20	20.48	19
Interest	23.90	26.12	24.02	24.66	4	22.99	27.10	25.43	25.12	6
Net savings, corporate & government	45.42	36.32	36.02	39.02	11	53.74	35.96	38.72	42.14	18
Net savings, entrepreneurial	60.00	60.00	44.54	54.33	14	60.00	60.00	44.32	54.24	14
National income estimated directly	20.44	20.48	20.83	20.59	1	20.60	20.64	20.98	20.74	1
National income estimated by parts	26.36	29.02	24.50	26.56	6	27.26	29.08	25.16	27.12	5
Wage earners	12.70	11.07	9.50	11.01	10	12.74	11.11	9.56	11.06	10
Salaried employees	13.11	12.17	9.16	11.36	15	13.32	12.18	9.22	11.44	15
Total employees	19.78	19.85	16.31	18.58	9	20.58	19.84	17.34	19.21	7
Entrepreneurs	15.50	19.34	13.52	15.94	14	16.58	20.41	14.42	16.96	13

Wages	11.40	9.13	9.52	9.97	11.50	9.08	9.52	9.71	10
Salaries	11.23	12.68	8.92	10.83	11.53	12.74	9.16	11.04	13
Employee compensation	18.97	14.94	13.59	15.68	19.00	14.88	14.40	15.97	12
Entrepreneurial withdrawals	31.34	44.65	22.76	31.70	31.34	44.65	22.76	31.70	26
Dividends	14.72	11.21	11.60	12.41	18.27	11.21	16.60	15.04	22
Interest	23.82	27.51	24.43	25.20	23.46	29.45	25.70	26.09	8
Net savings, corporate & government	41.68	25.18	23.30	29.02	49.99	25.02	25.59	31.75	35
Net savings, entrepreneurial	60.00	60.00	26.55	45.72	60.00	60.00	26.45	45.67	44
National income estimated directly	21.22	20.21	14.97	18.58	21.40	20.25	15.10	18.70	15
National income estimated by parts	24.27	23.45	17.05	21.33	25.24	23.52	17.56	21.85	16
Wage earners	12.25	9.55	8.08	9.82	12.32	9.51	8.08	9.82	16
Salaried employees	12.97	12.88	8.02	11.02	13.39	12.96	8.14	11.22	16
Total employees	19.83	15.81	10.54	14.90	19.72	15.62	12.59	15.71	24
Entrepreneurs	17.48	17.46	9.54	14.28	18.35	18.33	10.08	15.02	30

Wages	11.92	10.75	9.94	10.84	11.98	10.59	9.98	10.82	7
Salaries	11.50	12.31	9.26	10.94	11.76	12.36	9.43	11.11	12
Employee compensation	19.34	17.23	17.09	17.86	19.82	17.14	17.40	18.08	6
Entrepreneurial withdrawals	34.10	48.40	28.16	35.96	34.10	48.40	28.16	35.96	22
Dividends	16.64	13.01	14.24	14.56	21.27	13.01	20.67	17.89	24
Interest	23.09	26.75	24.01	24.57	22.46	28.11	25.36	25.21	8
Net savings, corporate & government	43.72	31.10	30.66	34.67	52.09	30.83	32.98	37.56	24
Net savings, entrepreneurial	60.00	60.00	36.69	50.92	60.00	60.00	36.52	50.85	25
National income estimated directly	20.88	21.83	18.16	20.23	21.04	21.87	18.31	20.35	7
National income estimated by parts	25.40	26.36	21.12	24.18	26.34	26.43	22.13	24.88	8
Wage earners	12.52	10.30	8.78	10.42	12.56	10.30	8.80	10.45	13
Salaried employees	13.05	12.41	8.61	11.18	13.34	12.46	8.71	11.31	19
Total employees	19.77	17.73	13.57	16.82	20.18	17.65	15.10	17.52	19
Entrepreneurs	16.07	18.52	11.62	15.13	17.06	19.51	12.36	16.02	19

cantly narrower than those for interest. Since the difficulty of proper industrial apportionment is greater for property income than for employee compensation, it is quite possible that a correct direct evaluation of the countrywide totals would yield significantly lower margins of error for the estimates of dividends and of interest. But there is little doubt that the margins of error in the estimates of entrepreneurial withdrawals and net savings of enterprises are significantly greater than in those of payments to employees and property income; and that for industries in which wages and salaries can be estimated separately, the latter are subject to wider margins of error than the former.

For the countrywide total of employees the weighted margin of error is about 17 per cent, surprisingly greater than for the countrywide total of entrepreneurs. But this may be due to the large weight in total entrepreneurs of the agricultural group, for which adequate data are available throughout the period.

Changes in the error margins over time for the various type of income and employment groups were similar to those for net income originating in the several industrial divisions. In most groups the margins of error declined from 1919–28 to 1929–35, the decline being especially great in estimates of entrepreneurial withdrawals, dividends, and net savings of enterprises. In the estimate of total interest the margin of error increased from the first part of the period to the second, but in most branches it declined. The rise in the weighted mean for the country is obviously due to a shift in the distribution of interest toward industries for which the margin of error is greater than the average for the country.

In the association between the error margins and the extent of divergence in the evaluations by the three investigators, the results for various types of income and categories of employment also confirm those for the industrial divisions. The greatest divergence is in the income totals the components of which are subject to the widest margins of error: entrepreneurial withdrawals, net savings of corporations and government and of unincorporated enterprises. But the association is far from perfect, since the divergence is less for the wider margin of error in the estimate of interest than for the narrower margin of error in the estimate of salaries, and is least for the relatively wide margin of error in the estimate of employee compensation. The geometric mean relative deviation is greater for the narrower error margin in the estimate of entrepreneurs than for the wider error margin for the number of employees.

Finally, as already observed for the industrial divisions, the mean relative deviations increase from the first part of the period to the second. The increase in extent of disagreement is greatest in the relative deviations for entrepreneurial withdrawals, dividends, interest, and savings of enterprises—all categories of estimates whose margin of error declined significantly from 1919–28 to 1929–35. In this respect also, the results for types of income confirm the conclusions drawn for the movement of evaluations of income estimates by industrial divisions.

C NATIONAL INCOME AND NUMBER ENGAGED

The weighted margin of error for the estimate of national income (Table 100, Sec. III) is about 20 per cent (10 major divisions estimated directly). A similar margin for the number employed and engaged, if computed, would approximate 16 per cent. But it is obvious from the preceding discussion that both figures exaggerate the margins of error that would be assigned by the investigators directly to the two comprehensive totals. The merging of the estimates of dividends and of interest each into a countrywide total would appreciably reduce the margins of error assigned to the estimates by industrial divisions, with the result that the error margins for these two countrywide totals would be much lower than the percentages now appearing in Table 100, Section III. Similarly, the merging of entrepreneurial withdrawals with entrepreneurial net savings would cancel a substantial part of the error margins assigned to these two totals taken separately. Even for employee compensation, the weighted mean of errors attached to the estimates by industrial divisions exaggerates the margin of error that would be applied directly to the countrywide total. Similar considerations bear upon the margins of error in the countrywide total of number employed and engaged. It is reasonable to infer that for the estimates of national income and number employed and engaged the average margin of error is not much above 10 per cent, and perhaps somewhat less.

For both totals the weighted margin of error declines from 1919–28 to 1929–35. The decline has been reduced by the shift in the industrial composition of national income and of the number employed and engaged in favor of industries the data for which are least comprehensive and the estimates for which are therefore assigned rather wide margins of error. As noted in Chapter 5, the relative share of commodity producing industries in national income declined from 1919–28 to 1929–38, and that of industries engaged in service activities increased; and the movements would be even more pronounced in a comparison of 1919–28 with 1929–35. This shift meant a decline in the importance of industries for which estimates were fairly exact and reliable (mining and manufacturing) and a rise in the importance of industries for which information was less adequate and error margins wider (service and government). The decline from 1919–28 to 1929–35 in the weighted error margins for national income and number employed and engaged is all the more significant in that it occurred in the face of this adverse shift in the industrial composition of the two totals.

The mean relative deviations of the weighted error margins in the estimates of national income are moderate; but, as already suggested, they increase from 1919–28 to 1929–35. However, here again the weighted measures exaggerate considerably the true magnitudes that would result from direct evaluation. They reflect the average divergence in the evaluation of error margins in the estimates for the many components, and, of course, for each component the range and grounds for disagreement are more extensive than in a direct evaluation of comprehensive totals. It is reasonable to assume that direct evaluations of the error margins in the estimates of national income and the number employed and engaged would disagree even less than the weighted means in Table 100, Section III. The increase in disagreement from 1919–28 to 1929–35 now shown for the weighted means in Sections I and II might not occur with direct evaluation.

3 Reliability of Changes and Differences Revealed by the Estimates

The margins of error apply to the totals for the various cells. In evaluating these margins the investigators asked what maximum percentage error could be assumed for each amount of income or employment in a given year in a given industry. But for many uses to which these estimates are put totals may be less important than *differences* among them for industries or types of income, or *changes over time*. The relation of the error margins established for the totals to the error margins of differences among them or of the changes in them over time can best be elucidated by a symbolic exposition.

Let x_1 and x_2 be the totals and e_1 and e_2 the relative error margins. We can then calculate the *relative* error in the relative difference between the two totals as follows:

1) Observed relative difference (i.e., including error) will be:

$$\frac{x_2 + e_2 x_2}{x_1 + e_1 x_1} - 1$$

2) True relative difference:

$$\frac{x_2}{x_1} - 1$$

3) *Absolute* error in the relative difference:

$$\left(\frac{x_2 + e_2 x_2}{x_1 + e_1 x_1} - 1\right) - \left(\frac{x_2}{x_1} - 1\right) = \frac{x_2\,(e_2 - e_1)}{x_1\,(1 + e_1)}$$

4) *Relative* error in the relative difference:

$$\left(\frac{x_2\,(e_2 - e_1)}{x_1\,(1 + e_1)}\right) : \left(\frac{x_2}{x_1} - 1\right) = \frac{x_2\,(e_2 - e_1)}{(x_2 - x_1)\,(1 + e_1)}$$

Expression (4) defines the relative error in which we are interested, viz., the relative error of a percentage difference between two totals whose relative errors are known and given. From expression (4) it may be seen that this relative error of a percentage difference depends upon four factors:

a) First and foremost is the correlation in sign between the errors in the totals compared. If the given error of one is negative and that of the other positive, then the numerator of the equation is a sum rather than a difference.

b) If the correlation in sign between e_1 and e_2 is positive, the relative size of the errors is also important. If the two errors are close in size, then obviously the difference between them will be small. If e_1 and e_2 are equal, the numerator becomes zero and there is no relative error in the percentage difference between the two totals compared.

c) The larger the ratio of x_2 to $(x_2 - x_1)$ the larger the relative error of the relative difference; in other words, the smaller the relative difference revealed by the two totals the larger the relative error in the observed difference (other conditions being equal).

d) All other conditions being equal, the relative error will be smaller if e_1 is positive (i.e., if the absolute value in the base year is exaggerated) and larger if e_1 is negative (i.e., if the absolute value in the base year is underestimated).

One could easily set up cases in which the derived relative error of the difference is small when the relative errors in two totals themselves are substantial; as well as cases in which the errors of the difference would be many times as large as the relative errors in two totals.[9]

We now consider the characteristics of our estimates with respect to the factors that determine how one can pass from the relative errors in the totals to the relative errors of relative differences. Since base years may be reversed without impairing the value of the comparison, the sign of the error in the base year magnitude is of little interest. We must, therefore, consider only (1) the correlation of the signs of the relative errors of totals compared, (2) the size of the relative errors, and (3) the size of the relative difference itself.

1) In dealing with changes from one year to the next, it can be assumed that the errors in totals tend to be of the same sign. If the data lead to an over- or underestimate in a given year and if the error assigned is substantial, it is unlikely that any new error, resulting from the use of an extrapolation or interpolation index, will produce in the next year's estimate an error with the opposite sign. Since most estimates are derived by applying interpolation and extrapolation indexes to some basic, comprehensive value, there is a natural tendency for the error implicit in the basic quantities to persist through the period covered. This makes for a positive correlation of the signs of errors for adjacent time units when the error margins in the totals are at all substantial.

For differences between two totals for the same year the case for the correlation of signs of errors is not quite so clear. When totals of employee compensation, entrepreneurial withdrawals, and number employed or engaged are compared

[9] E.g., if we assume that both e_1 and e_2 are 0.2, x_1 is 10, and x_2 is 5, and that the correlation in sign between the e's is positive, the relative error of the relative difference would be zero. If under the same conditions, e_1 is 0.1 and e_2 is 0.2, the relative error of the relative difference would become 0.09. If we assume that both e_1 and e_2 are 0.2 and the correlation in sign is negative, the relative error would become (with e_1 negative) 0.5. Finally, if we assume e_1 is $-$ 0.2, e_2 is $+$ 0.2, and the corresponding x's are 10 and 9 respectively, the relative error of the relative difference becomes 4.5, or 22.5 times as great as the relative error in either of the two totals.

by industrial divisions, we may expect identity in the signs of the errors, since there is a general tendency toward an underestimate arising from the bias of Census data toward undercoverage. Similarly, there is a bias in some of the property income estimates toward negative errors, since their common source is income tax returns, in which there is a tendency to minimize taxable items. But these tendencies toward identity in the signs of errors assigned to various totals for a given year are subject to numerous exceptions. It is not at all unlikely that in many industries entrepreneurial withdrawals or income are overestimated whereas employee compensation is underestimated; or that in some years income originating in the service industries is overestimated whereas income originating in real estate may be underestimated. At any rate, the likelihood of opposite signs of error seems to be greater in comparisons of totals for the various cells for a given year than in comparisons of totals for one and the same cell for successive years.

2) There is a similar contrast between changes over time and differences among cells in the relative error margins assigned to the two totals compared. In comparisons over time, the error margins change relatively little. Of course, our use of mid-values of wide error classes in deriving Tables 98–100 conceals the changes that may occur in the margin of error in an estimate from one year to the next, changes that we cannot gauge with any degree of accuracy. But it is reasonable to assume that these changes in error margins over time are relatively small, and our tests of interpolations and extrapolations in Chapter 11 tend to support this assumption.

Differences in the relative error in the totals for various cells in the same year are quite substantial (see Tables 98–100). This means that even when the correlation in the *sign* of the relative errors in two totals is positive, the difference in size may yield a substantial numerator in equation (4) above, and a large relative error in the relative difference between the two totals.

3) This undesirable result in comparisons of totals for various cells at a given point of time is offset somewhat by the correlation between differences in the size of relative errors and differences in the size of the totals themselves. The size of the total is one of several factors that guide an estimator in his evaluation of a relative error: the smaller the total the more likely a large percentage error. As a result, large items of $(e_2 - e_1)$ are correlated with fairly high ratios of $(x_2 - x_1)$ to x_2. But in comparisons at a given point of time *small* relative differences may be subject to relative errors much greater than those attached to the totals compared.

The size of the relative difference may seem to be of no importance in considering relative errors in percentage changes over time. This would be true if the hypothesis suggested above, viz., that in such comparisons relative errors are correlated in sign and tend to be approximately equal in size, were always valid. If we could say that in these changes the relative errors in the totals compared are invariably correlated in sign (positively) and are invariable in size, then the size of the difference observed would be of no importance —for the simple reason that under these conditions the relative error of the relative difference would always be zero.

But we cannot assume that the relative error in the totals remains constant from year to year; and the size of the relative change is, therefore, an important factor in the relative error that can be assigned to it. If the error in the total changes even slightly from one year to the next, the estimate of the change may contain a much larger relative error, provided the change itself is merely a small fraction of the total: e.g., if e_1 is 0.20, e_2 is 0.18, and x_1 is 100, then the relative error of the change from x_1 to x_2 will vary much as the change itself varies. Thus if we have a decline to 95, the relative error of that decline of 5 points will be 0.32 (or 32 per cent). But if we have a decline to 50, the relative error of that decline of 50 points will be only 0.02 (or 2 per cent).

Consequently, even for changes over time, it may be said that in general small changes are greatly affected by slight shifts in the error to be attached to the totals compared. In other words, the relative errors in the totals can be applied to changes over time only when the latter constitute substantial proportions of the former. When they are relatively small, their relative errors may be much greater than those in the totals from which they are derived.

The statements above are advanced as tentative conjectures that can serve as a basis for passing from the error margins in totals to errors in changes in or differences among totals.

With respect to changes over time, the following conclusion is suggested. In view of the tendency toward positive correlation in the signs of errors of successive quantities and the minor character of changes that may be assumed to occur in the size of the error in successive years, the error in the totals can be treated, at least provisionally, as a maximum of the relative errors in the changes over time in successive pairs of these totals. When the changes are substantial fractions of the totals themselves there is considerable likelihood that the relative error in the percentage change will be smaller than the relative errors in the totals themselves. But it would be dangerous to assume that a decline or rise of 2 or 3 per cent, or even of 5 per cent, is subject to the same relative error as the totals from which it was derived, or to a smaller relative error.

For differences between totals for a given unit of time there is some basis for a conclusion similar to that made for changes over time, but there is greater likelihood that the errors in the two totals compared may not be the same in sign.

A similar analysis could be carried forward for more complicated comparisons, e.g., for changes over time not between successive time units but between averages for periods separated by a substantial interval; or for changes over time shown by differences, absolute or relative, between two totals. But the general principles are clear enough. Changes between averages, provided the error margins of the averages are known, will have to be deduced from assumptions concerning the correlation of errors in sign, the relative size of errors, and the relative size of the difference or change. Changes over time in percentages will also have to be tested in the light of the same three considerations. The logic involved is clear enough for any student to follow; and our specific knowledge concerning the applicability of the necessary assumptions is not any greater than that an intelligent reader could himself acquire from perusal of the tables and notes in Parts Four and Five

4 Concluding Comments

To analyze the reliability of data and procedures used to derive national income totals and their components is essentially an insoluble task. Were we able to ascertain the sign and size of error for any given estimate, we could, of course, correct for this error and there would be no need to retain it. Were our procedures or data of such a controlled character that we could make specific assumptions concerning the distribution of errors, if not concerning each single error, it would be possible to apply to our task the full armory of weapons of statistical analysis of sampling errors and limits of inference. But dealing as we do with data that are partly a byproduct of administrative activity, partly a result of direct observation of complex phenomena without controls designed to reduce the variations observed, the best that we can do is to express an opinion in quantitative form.

This we did by setting margins of maximum relative errors for the various cells in the nationwide totals. Even in so doing we have perhaps overstepped the limits to which one should go in assigning a quantitative expression to what are essentially personal judgments, based to a large extent on intuition and guess (although the judgment of more than one investigator and some knowledge of the extent to which estimates of various cells have been revised in the past have possibly produced evaluations that are a bit more than arbitrary opinions). But we did not evaluate margins of errors in differences, percentage shares, changes over time, changes in percentages, etc., partly because of the greater variability of errors attaching to these aspects of measurement and partly because the 'remove' of these aspects from the single absolute amount, which is the first result of our estimating, made evaluation of error difficult. We describe, therefore, in general the theoretical relation between relative errors in totals and relative errors in differences, changes, etc.; and offer a few tentative suggestions as to the character of the factors that govern this relation (correlation in sign among successive errors, similarity in size, etc.) for the estimates that comprise our nationwide totals.

This, perforce inadequate, analysis of the reliability of our estimates has, however, a fairly solid core: the general order of differences in degree of reliability of the various parts of our estimated totals is reasonably reliable. The comparison of various published estimates in Chapter 10; the results of the tests of interpolations and extrapolations in Chapter 11; and the similarity of judgments of the individual investigators in Tables 98–100 support the established differences in reliability among estimates in various industry or type of income or employment categories. While some of this supporting evidence is duplicated, it points to conclusions concerning differences in the reliability of estimates that seem to be significant, much more significant than the results relating to the absolute levels of error margins.

The size of the error margins may raise questions in the minds of students concerning the utility of the estimates and the progress that can be made toward more reliable estimates. As to the possibility that the usefulness of the estimates is fatally impaired by the wide margins of error attributable to them, the only relevant comment is that we believe our estimates to be as good as can be made from available data. Of course, any individual investigator or group of investigators can commit indiscretions of judgment, overlook possible sources of information, or neglect potentialities of fruitful procedures. But such sins of omission and commission have, we hope, been kept within reasonable bounds; and by far the major source of possible error in our estimates is the inadequacies of existing data. The choice is, therefore, not between present estimates and better estimates: it is largely between present estimates, inadequate as they are, worse estimates, or no estimates at all. For many purposes for which national income estimates are used this set is a significant advance over everyday knowledge which people tend to acquire and use without careful reference to basic data and without any attempt to piece together and collate the evidence.

An extensive and intensive utilization of the data, together with a critical evaluation of their inadequacies, is a step in their better utilization and in furthering the collection of more adequate data. Even more effective than a recital of inadequacies of existing information is an attempt to use it and the resulting tentative revelation of some important finding: this provides an effective stimulus to a quest for further data and for an improvement of procedures. It is thus important to use the data already available, with complete recognition of their faults but without giving way to perfectionist despair. Many of our estimates will prove inadequate in the light of fuller information in the future. But this means only that the present, like all, national income estimates reflect current knowledge, just as they are based upon the current social standards that determine which of the numerous activities in the nation are economic, productive, and hence a source of national income.

Basic Data, Sources, and Methods

PART FOUR presents, in sections devoted to major industrial groups, our estimates in detail. Notes to the tables give the sources and the methods by which the data were combined or adjusted to obtain the estimates. In both tables and notes the order is more or less the same for all major industrial divisions. First are estimates of gross income, but only when data are easily accessible. No effort has been made to derive a comprehensive estimate of gross income comparable to that of net income originating. For most major groups the table on gross income is followed by a table giving estimates of total payments originating in the broad industrial group as a whole. Next two sets of estimates of net savings of corporations and of entrepreneurs are given: one unadjusted, the other adjusted for gains and losses from sales of capital assets and for the effects of changing valuation of inventories. The sum of these savings and total payments to individuals is net income originating in the broad industrial group as a whole.

Whenever a broad industrial group can be subdivided, types of income for which more detailed estimates are possible are presented by minor industrial divisions. The order for each minor industrial group is net income originating, wages, salaries, employee compensation, entrepreneurial withdrawals, dividends, interest, property income, corporate net savings, and entrepreneurial net savings. In the last tables are estimates of the number of employees, converted to equivalents of full-time employment, and of the number of entrepreneurs, for both the broad industrial group as a whole and those subdivisions that can be measured separately.

The tables present the components of total national income

539

and two closely related items—gross income and number of persons engaged. Other subsidiary data and some detailed estimates for a few industries or years are presented in Part Five which, in a sense, is an appendix to Part Four.

The discussion in the notes to the numbered columns of each table varies in detail with the variety of our sources, the complexity of the method, and the extent to which a procedure has already been used and described elsewhere. For one industrial group, agriculture, our notes are especially brief, because we have taken over for most years the estimates prepared by the Department of Agriculture, Bureau of Agricultural Economics, and to describe at length its methods and original data seemed unnecessary. Several procedures used fairly uniformly for the various industrial groups were discussed in Part Three and are not referred to in Part Four: (1) the adjustment of business savings for gains and losses from sales of capital assets, effects of changing valuation of inventories, and the disparity between depreciation charges on cost and reproduction bases (discussed in Ch. 3, Sec. 2 D; subsidiary data presented in Part Five, Tables IV, VII, and VIII); (2) the preparation of two sets of estimates of dividends, interest, and net savings for 1934 (discussed in Ch. 8, Sec. 1 B); (3) the methods of interpolation and extrapolation (discussed in Ch. 11, Sec. 2).

A clear understanding of the methods and characteristics of the estimates can be gained only by reading the notes in Part Four in conjunction with the discussion in Part Three and the subsidiary data in Part Five. Even these do not always give a reader a complete description of how some estimates were derived. Practical considerations forbade this elaboration which would have entailed a description not only of the actual procedures but also of alternatives that were tried and discarded, as well as the presentation in much greater detail of the various subsidiary data and devices used. Instead we confine ourselves to a statement of our essential procedures and of our basic sources.

Agriculture

TABLES A1 – A3

A 1 Gross Income and Payments to Other Industries (millions of dollars)

	GROSS INCOME [3] (1)	CURRENT EXPEND. [2,4] (2)	DECREASE IN VALUE OF LIVESTOCK (3)	NET RENT TO NON-FARMERS (4)	TAXES [4] (5)	SHORT TERM INT. [4] (6)	PAY. TO OTHER INDUSTRIES (7)	NET INCOME (8)
1919	17,472	4,176	596	1,113	352	373	6,610	10,862
1920	15,805	4,552	474	801	438	463	6,728	9,077
1921	10,606	3,313	347	578	496	334	5,068	5,538
1922	10,902	3,197	299	632	509	404	5,041	5,861
1923	11,907	3,280	301	688	513	396	5,178	6,729
1924	12,532	3,528	284	729	514	363	5,418	7,114
1925	13,421	3,653	302	654	514	352	5,475	7,946
1926	13,076	3,742	342	594	521	343	5,542	7,534
1927	13,114	3,723	384	687	535	327	5,656	7,458
1928	13,402	4,089	442	655	550	336	6,072	7,330
1929	13,646	3,944	435	648	562	349	5,938	7,708
1930	11,153	3,626	352	476	567	318	5,339	5,814
1931	8,264	2,865	243	286	546	283	4,223	4,041
1932	6,286	2,352	182	190	493	248	3,465	2,821
1933	6,905 [1]	2,285	144	273	429	220	3,351	3,554
1934	8,350 [1]	2,430	203	382	392	194	3,601	4,749
1935	9,443 [1]	2,690	299	500	389	185	4,063	5,380
1936	10,457 [1]	2,930	345	525	396	172	4,368	6,089
1937	11,118 [1]	3,312	366	593	403	170	4,844	6,274
1938	10,016 [1]	3,056	336	562	415	190	4,559	5,457

[1] Including rental and benefit payments amounting to $131 million in 1933, $447 million in 1934, $573 million in 1935, $287 million in 1936, $367 million in 1937, and $482 million in 1938.

[2] Including depreciation on buildings and machinery.

[3] Including rental value of operators' homes.

[4] Including expenses of non-farmer landlords.

A 2   Net Income Originating by Type (millions of dollars)

	WAGES (1)	ENTREP. WITHDR. (2)	DIVIDENDS (3)	INT. ON MTGE. (4)	PAY. TO INDI- VIDUALS (5)	NET SAVINGS (6)	ENTREP. NET INCOME (7)	NET INCOME (8)
1919	1,515	6,699	16	357	8,587	2,275	8,974	10,862
1920	1,780	7,749	16	43c	9,975	—898	6,851	9,077
1921	1,159	5,316	16	490	6,981	—1,443	3,873	5,538
1922	1,122	5,120	16	510	6,768	—907	4,213	5,861
1923	1,219	5,630	6	509	7,374	—645	4,985	6,729
1924	1,224	5,745	15	487	7,471	—357	5,388	7,114
1925	1,243	5,806	18	459	7,526	420	6,226	7,946
1926	1,326	5,859	16	448	7,649	—115	5,744	7,534
1927	1,280	5,828	29	445	7,582	—124	5,704	7,458
1928	1,268	5,832	25	442	7,567	—237	5,595	7,330
1929	1,284	5,899	12	436	7,631	77	5,976	7,708
1930	1,134	5,579	7	429	7,149	—1,335	4,244	5,814
1931	847	4,541	14	419	5,821	—1,780	2,761	4,041
1932	584	3,502	6	400	4,492	—1,671	1,831	2,821
1933	517	3,166	0.02	362	4,045	—491	2,675	3,554
1934	558	3,500	17	334	4,409	340	3,840	4,749
1935	639	3,775	19	308	4,741	639	4,414	5,380
1936	690	4,028	37	289	5,044	1,045	5,073	6,089
1937	794	4,546	32	278	5,650	624	5,170	6,274
1938	758	4,492	22	268	5,540	—83	4,409	5,457

A 3 Persons Engaged (thousands)

| | EMPLOYEES | | | |
| | Wage earners | Salaried | Total | ENTREPRENEURS |
	(1)	(2)	(3)	(4)
1919	1,996	95	2,091	6,393
1920	2,048	96	2,144	6,406
1921	1,957	88	2,045	6,443
1922	1,958	78	2,036	6,400
1923	1,914	71	1,985	6,328
1924	1,883	62	1,945	6,319
1925	1,876	59	1,935	6,313
1926	1,974	62	2,036	6,252
1927	1,910	65	1,975	6,216
1928	1,895	68	1,963	6,229
1929	1,899	72	1,971	6,234
1930	1,789	74	1,863	6,286
1931	1,688	71	1,759	6,406
1932	1,550	66	1,616	6,569
1933	1,526	64	1,590	6,691
1934	1,476	61	1,537	6,741
1935	1,559	59	1,618	6,771
1936	1,581	56	1,637	6,776
1937	1,624	56	1,680	6,788
1938	1,619	56	1,675	6,836

The preponderant part of the basic materials used in preparing
the estimates of net income originating in agriculture is taken from
Income Parity for Agriculture, a study by the Department of Agriculture, Bureau of Agricultural Economics. Its estimates are *tentative* and subject to revision. In the specific notes below, BAE data
are so specified and the description of their derivation can be
obtained from the Bureau of Agricultural Economics. All *other*
estimates are described fully.

TABLE A 1

Gross Income and Payments to Other Industries

Col. 1 Gross income: (BAE) sum of cash income, farm value of products consumed, government benefit payments, and rental value of operators' homes.

Col. 2 Current expenditures: (BAE) cost of feed, seed, and fertilizer; livestock purchases; operation of automobiles, trucks and tractors; cotton ginning, binder twine, containers, insecticides; veterinary service and medicine, horseshoeing, electricity, insurance, irrigation and drainage, grazing, and toll for sugar crops, and also the estimated depreciation on buildings and machinery.

Col. 3 Decrease in value of livestock on farms: the figures for 1919–34 are published in *Capital Consumption and Adjustment*, by Solomon Fabricant (National Bureau of Economic Research, 1938). Estimates for later years were made by methods similar to those outlined there.

Col. 4 Net rent paid to non-farmer landlords: (BAE) a net figure after expenses have been deducted. Since expenses paid by non-farmer landlords are included in the totals for the various expense items (col. 2, 5, and 6), only net rent is shown as an additional expense of farmers.

Col. 5 Taxes: (BAE)

Col. 6 Short term interest: (BAE) mortgage interest paid by non-farmer landlords included as well as short term interest paid by farmers. The BAE in its current work does not separate mortgage interest into that paid by farmers and by non-farmers. We have assumed that one-fourth is paid by non-farmers (see *Crops and Markets*, Sept. 1936).

Col. 7 Total payments to other industries: sum of col. 2–6.

Col. 8 Net income originating: difference between col. 1 and 7.

TABLE A 2

Net Income Originating by Type

Col. 1 Wages: (BAE data published in *Income Parity for Agriculture*, Part II, Sec. 1) allowance for board and other perquisites included.

Col. 2 Entrepreneurial withdrawals: a preliminary figure is derived by multiplying the number of farmers including salaried employees (see the notes to Table A 3) by the average annual wage without board; the product is raised by 22 per cent to allow for unpaid family labor. The resulting estimate in turn is raised by 25 per cent to allow for the difference in expenditure levels between farm operators and hired men. The second adjustment factor is derived from data in Department of Agriculture Bulletin 1466, *The Farmer's Standard of Living,* and in Iowa Agricultural Experiment Station Bulletin 237, *Cost of Living on Iowa Farms,* both of which give expenditure figures for farm operators and for farm hired men. The final estimates of per capita withdrawals are, on the whole, confirmed by the *Study of Consumer Purchases* (WPA), which collected data on farmers' incomes and expenditures.

Col. 3 Dividends: difference between total dividends paid and dividends received. Both are reported for 1926–37 in the special tabulation by minor industrial divisions of *Statistics of Income* data. The 1938 estimate is extrapolated from 1937 by a corporate sample for the industry. The 1926 figures are extrapolated to 1922 by total dividends paid and dividends received by agriculture and related industries, as recorded in *Statistics of Income.* Net dividends in 1919, 1920, and 1921 are assumed to be the same as in 1922.

Col. 4 Interest: (BAE) see the notes to Table A 1, col. 6.

Col. 5 Total payments: sum of col. 1–4.

Col. 6 Net savings: difference between net income originating (Table A 1, col. 8) and total payments (col. 5, above).

Col. 7 Entrepreneurial net income: sum of col. 2 and 6.

Col. 8 Net income originating: sum of col. 5 and 6.

TABLE A 3

Persons Engaged

Col. 1 Wage earners: number obtained by dividing the total cash wage bill plus allowance for board by the average annual wage without board. Annual wage rates are from *Agricultural Statistics, 1939.*

Col. 2 Salaried employees: number for 1930 is from the 1930 *Census of Population,* Vol. V, Ch. 7. It is extrapolated for all other years by the number of managers and foremen. Basic data for the number of managers and foremen are reported for 1910, 1920, and 1930 in the occupation statistics of the *Census of Population*. Interpolation between these years and extrapolation of the 1930 figures are by the number of managed farms. The number of managed farms in 1910, 1920, 1925, 1930, and 1935 is reported in the *Census of Agriculture*. Interpolation is along a straight line and it is assumed that the average annual decline from 1935 to 1936 is the same as from 1930 to 1935. The 1937 and 1938 figures are assumed to be the same as the 1936.

Col. 3 Employees: sum of col. 1 and 2.

Col. 4 Entrepreneurs: the number of all farms, January 1, is published by the BAE in *Income Parity for Agriculture,* Part V, Sec. 1. By subtracting our estimates of the number of managed farms (see the notes to col. 2) we obtain the number of owners and tenants. Annual figures are averages of year-end figures.

Mining

TABLES Q1–Q9

Whenever two entries are made for 1934 the first is comparable with those for preceding years in that the *Statistics of Income* data used are based on the old industrial classification; the second is comparable with those for succeeding years in that the *Statistics of Income* data used are based on the new industrial classification.

Net savings and net income, adjusted, exclude gains and losses from sales of capital assets, 1929–38, and from changes in inventory valuation, 1919–38. Net savings and net income without any specific designation are unadjusted, i.e., include these two types of gain and loss.

Q 1   Gross Income (millions of dollars)

	C O A L Anth. (1)	Bit. (2)	METAL (3)	OIL & GAS (4)	OTHER (5)	TOTAL (6)
1919	364	1,146	549	890	206	3,155
1920	433	2,110	716	1,513	295	5,068
1921	451	1,192	267	938	230	3,079
1922	273	1,269	406	1,052	273	3,275
1923	505	1,512	625	1,156	351	4,152
1924	476	1,064	513	1,210	362	3,626
1925	327	1,064	578	1,517	387	3,875
1926	473	1,191	591	1,708	400	4,365
1927	420	1,039	516	1,419	401	3,796
1928	392	945	547	1,333	396	3,615
1929	384	966	628 *	1,596	413 *	3,989
1930	354	805	413	1,345	360	3,278
1931	296	595	235	731	261	2,119
1932	222	409	116	828	166	1,744
1933	206	448	166	759	182	1,763
1934	244	630	215	1,071	226	2,389
1935	210	658	285	1,142	254	2,551
1936	227	771	426	1,403	313	3,142
1937	197	864	578	1,733	326	3,701
1938	180	655	351	1,579	288	3,054

* Comparable with the figures for 1930–38. Since several of the minor metals were classified with non-metals in the 1935 Census the 1929 figures also were reclassified. The 1929 figures comparable with those for 1919–28 are Metal, 633; 'Other' mining, 407.

Q 2   Total Payments by Type (millions of dollars)

	WAGES (1)	SALARIES (2)	EMPL. COMP. (3)	ENTREP. WITHDR. (4)	DIVI- DENDS (5)	INTER- EST (6)	PROP. INCOME (7)	PAY. TO INDI- VIDUALS (8)
1919	1,322	156	1,479	30.9	194	23.3	217	1,727
1920	1,817	218	2,035	39.7	209	30.4	240	2,315
1921	1,412	145	1,557	32.1	193	38.3	231	1,820
1922	1,256	151	1,407	29.5	139	33.2	172	1,609
1923	1,792	188	1,980	31.7	223	37.3	260	2,273
1924	1,529	175	1,705	28.0	212	51.3	263	1,997
1925	1,407	180	1,588	26.3	269	53.9	323	1,937
1926	1,647	199	1,846	25.6	326	46.5	373	2,245
1927	1,476	193	1,669	24.4	278	43.7	321	2,015
1928	1,303	178	1,481	22.9	253	42.0	295	1,800
1929	1,336	193	1,530	21.4	365	44.7	410	1,962
1930	1,148	176	1,325	20.8	249	44.5	293	1,639
1931	820	142	962	18.6	138	41.7	180	1,160
1932	555	108	664	15.1	81.6	39.5	121	800
1933	570	96.7	666	14.3	75.3	34.1	109	790
1934	761	114	875	14.9	114	30.0	144	1,035
1934	761	114	875	14.9	190	39.2	229	1,120
1935	804	127	932	15.5	185	37.0	222	1,170
1936	940	140	1,080	16.5	215	40.6	255	1,352
1937	1,067	156	1,223	18.2	295	35.8	331	1,573
1938	850	142	992	18.3	204	31.4	236	1,247

Q 3 Net Income Originating (millions of dollars)

	PAY. TO INDI- VIDUALS	NET SAVINGS			NET INCOME	NET SAVINGS, ADJUSTED			NET INCOME, ADJ.
		Entrep.	Corp.	Total		Entrep.	Corp.	Total	
	(1)	(2)	(3)	(4)	(5)	(6)	(7)	(8)	(9)
1919	1,727	8.1	—12.9	—4.8	1,723	10.1	14.1	24.2	1,752
1920	2,315	25.1	147	172	2,488	14.1	—6.5	7.7	2,323
1921	1,820	—19.2	—449	—468	1,352	0.8	—155	—154	1,666
1922	1,609	—0.3	—153	—153	1,456	—8.3	—269	—277	1,332
1923	2,273	—6.4	—291	—297	1,975	—3.4	—243	—246	2,026
1924	1,997	—4.0	—295	—299	1,697	—3.0	—287	—290	1,706
1925	1,937	18.6	—69.4	—50.7	1,886	15.6	—114	—98.7	1,838
1926	2,245	24.7	—97.9	—73.2	2,172	23.7	—111	—88.2	2,157
1927	2,015	7.2	—273	—266	1,749	14.2	—174	—160	1,855
1928	1,800	15.9	—154	—138	1,661	13.9	—175	—161	1,638
1929	1,962	24.9	—166	—141	1,821	21.8	—178	—156	1,805
1930	1,639	—15.7	—304	—320	1,319	—12.4	—245	—258	1,381
1931	1,160	—29.9	—392	—422	738	—24.1	—311	—335	825
1932	800	—31.5	—306	—337	463	—29.5	—290	—319	480
1933	790	—23.5	—253	—277	513	—25.2	—286	—311	479
1934	1,035	—6.4	—119	—125	910	—13.4	—190	—203	831
1934	1,120	—9.0	—213	—222	898	—14.2	—286	—300	819
1935	1,170	—9.5	—210	—220	950	—11.7	—236	—248	922
1936	1,352	—0.4	—142	—142	1,210	—2.9	—176	—179	1,173
1937	1,573	6.2	—138	—132	1,440	3.5	—177	—173	1,399
1938	1,247	6.1	—153	—147	1,099	5.4	—156	—150	1,096

MINING

Q 4 Wages and Salaries (millions of dollars)

	WAGES						SALARIES					
	COAL		Metal	Oil & gas	Other	Total	COAL		Metal	Oil & gas	Other	Total
	Anth. (1)	Bit. (2)	(3)	(4)	(5)	(6)	Anth. (7)	Bit. (8)	(9)	(10)	(11)	(12)
1919	211	684	209	135	82.5	1,322	13.0	68.9	24.4	33.9	15.9	156
1920	237	1,008	220	229	122	1,817	15.0	103	28.3	49.5	22.0	218
1921	283	791	119	131	85.6	1,412	18.4	60.8	16.1	31.7	17.8	145
1922	165	717	121	155	96.2	1,256	17.3	57.5	18.2	39.8	18.9	151
1923	289	1,016	172	174	139	1,792	20.3	77.7	25.6	41.1	23.8	188
1924	319	737	172	159	141	1,529	21.8	63.0	25.7	39.2	26.0	175
1925	206	691	178	189	142	1,407	21.7	64.4	26.4	42.0	25.5	180
1926	311	765	184	238	147	1,647	22.8	71.7	24.6	53.9	26.1	199
1927	274	682	170	212	135	1,476	23.7	61.3	26.3	49.7	32.0	193
1928	258	581	163	172	127	1,303	22.3	56.7	25.8	42.0	31.5	178
1929	233	575	178 *	231	118 *	1,336	21.6	58.8	27.2 *	54.0	32.3 *	193
1930	223	477	144	198	105	1,148	20.1	49.7	25.7	47.0	34.0	176
1931	178	352	86.4	124	78.0	820	18.5	43.1	18.7	33.1	28.7	142
1932	129	287	43.2	98.8	46.5	555	14.3	32.0	11.3	29.9	21.0	108
1933	113	261	42.7	110	42.8	570	12.2	29.0	10.1	27.0	18.3	96.7
1934	138	368	57.3	142	55.3	761	12.5	35.8	11.7	34.9	19.8	114
1935	120	403	75.3	144	61.5	804	12.2	39.1	14.5	41.1	20.9	127
1936	114	475	107	164	78.0	940	12.1	42.7	18.2	43.1	24.0	140
1937	107	509	164	194	91.0	1,067	11.6	47.0	23.7	47.8	26.2	156
1938	87.9	390	112	189	70.4	850	10.7	42.7	19.8	46.1	22.8	142

* Comparable with the figures for 1930–38. Since several of the minor metals were classified with non-metals in the 1935 Census the 1929 figures also were reclassified. The 1929 figures comparable with those for 1919–28 are: Wages: metal, 179; 'other' mining, 117; Salaries: metal, 27.7; 'other' mining, 31.8.

MINING

Q 5 Dividends and Interest (millions of dollars)

| | DIVIDENDS | | | | | | INTEREST | | | | | |
| | COAL | | | | | | COAL | | | | | |
	Anth. (1)	Bit. (2)	Metal (3)	Oil & gas (4)	Other (5)	Total (6)	Anth. (7)	Bit. (8)	Metal (9)	Oil & gas (10)	Other (11)	Total (12)
1919						194						23.3
1920						209						30.4
1921						193						38.3
1922						139						33.2
1923						223						37.3
1924						212						51.3
1925						269						53.9
1926	53.2[1]	....[2]	86.3	135	51.8	326	21.8[1]	....[2]	5.2	9.7	9.9	46.5
1927	47.0[1]	....[2]	78.2	103	49.8	278	21.1[1]	....[2]	4.6	9.0	9.1	43.7
1928	13.7	20.0	98.5	69.8	51.4	253	20.1[1]	....[2]	3.7	9.4	8.8	42.0
1929	15.6	26.8	195	69.4	58.4	265	8.0	15.4	2.2	9.4	9.7	44.7
1930	13.2	24.0	92.6	79.0	40.2	249	8.2	15.0	3.2	8.9	9.2	44.5
1931	9.4	15.6	37.8	37.2	38.5	138	9.3	12.8	4.5	9.5	5.7	41.7
1932	6.1	6.7	11.1	36.4	21.2	81.6	10.1	11.1	5.5	9.6	3.2	39.5
1933	0.8	4.2	13.3	38.1	18.9	75.3	9.9	9.0	5.5	7.9	1.9	34.1
1934	1.4	18.6	16.7	60.6	17.4	114	9.6	6.8	4.8	7.2	1.6	30.0
1935	2.7	28.1	31.6	97.3	30.7	190	11.1	8.7	4.1	12.2	3.0	39.2
1935	2.7	11.0	42.3	72.8	56.6	185	10.6	7.7	4.5	10.1	4.2	37.0
1936	3.1	16.4	79.5	69.6	46.5	215	10.4	7.4	7.8	9.9	5.0	40.6
1937	1.1	11.7	128	91.6	62.4	295	9.1	6.5	6.6	8.8	4.8	35.8
1938	0.5	8.8	75.3	70.8	49.4	204	8.8	5.7	5.5	6.6	4.7	31.4

1 Including figures for bituminous.

2 Included with figures for anthracite.

MINING

Q 6 Employee Compensation and Property Income (millions of dollars)

| | EMPLOYEE COMPENSATION | | | | | | PROPERTY INCOME | | | | | |
| | COAL | | | | | | COAL | | | | | |
	Anth. (1)	Bit. (2)	Metal (3)	Oil & gas (4)	Other (5)	Total (6)	Anth. (7)	Bit. (8)	Metal (9)	Oil & gas (10)	Other (11)	Total (12)
1919	224	753	233	169	98.4	1,479						217
1920	252	1,111	248	278	144	2,035						240
1921	301	852	136	163	103	1,557						231
1922	182	774	139	195	115	1,407						231
1923	309	1,093	198	216	163	1,980						172 260
1924	341	800	198	198	167	1,705						263
1925	228	755	204	231	168	1,588						323
1926	334	837	209	291	173	1,846	75.0 [2]	.... [3]	91.5	145	61.6	373
1927	298	744	196	262	167	1,669	68.1 [2]	.... [3]	82.8	112	58.9	321
1928	280	638	189	214	159	1,481	53.9 [2]	.... [3]	102	79.2	60.1	295
1929	254	634	205 [1]	284	151 [1]	1,530	23.6	42.2	197	78.8	68.1	410
1930	243	527	170	245	139	1,325	21.4	39.0	95.7	88.0	49.5	293
1931	197	395	105	157	106	962	18.7	28.4	42.2	46.7	44.1	180
1932	144	269	54.5	128	67.4	664	16.2	17.9	16.6	46.0	24.4	121
1933	125	290	52.9	137	61.1	666	10.7	13.2	18.8	46.0	20.8	109
1934	150	404	69.1	177	75.1	875	11.0	25.4	21.6	67.8	18.9	144
1934							13.8	36.8	35.7	109	33.7	229
1935	132	442	89.8	185	82.4	932	13.3	18.7	46.7	82.9	60.7	222
1936	126	518	125	207	102	1,080	13.6	23.8	87.3	79.5	51.4	255
1937	119	556	188	242	117	1,223	10.2	18.3	135	100	67.2	331
1938	98.6	433	132	235	93.2	992	9.3	14.5	80.8	77.4	54.0	296

1 Comparable with the figures for 1930–38. Since several of the minor metals were classified with non-metals in the 1935 Census the 1929 figures also were reclassified. The 1929 figures comparable with those for 1919–28 are Metal, 207; 'Other' mining, 149.

2 Including figures for bituminous.

3 Included with figures for anthracite.

Q 7 Total payments to Individuals (millions of dollars)

	COAL Anth. (1)	Bit. (2)	METAL (3)	OIL & GAS (4)	OTHER (5)	TOTAL (6)
1919						1,727
1920						2,315
1921						1,820
1922						1,609
1923						2,273
1924						1,997
1925						1,937
1926	1,251 [1]	... [2]	301	454	238	2,245
1927	1,115 [1]	... [2]	280	390	228	2,015
1928	977 [1]	... [2]	291	309	221	1,800
1929	278	680	403	379	221	1,962
1930	264	569	266	348	190	1,639
1931	215	426	147	218	152	1,160
1932	160	289	71.5	186	93.0	800
1933	136	305	71.9	194	83.0	790
1934	161	431	91.0	256	95.3	1,035
1934	164	442	105	298	110	1,120
1935	145	462	136	280	144	1,170
1936	139	544	213	300	155	1,352
1937	129	576	323	357	186	1,573
1938	108	449	213	327	148	1,247

Q 8 Total Net Savings (millions of dollars)

	CORPORATE COAL Anth. (1)	Bit. (2)	Metal (3)	Oil & gas (4)	Other (5)	Total (6)	ENTREP. (7)	TOTAL (8)
1919						—12.9	8.1	—4.8
1920						147	25.1	172
1921						—449	—19.2	—468
1922						—153	—0.3	—153
1923						—291	—6.4	—297
1924						—295	—4.0	—299
1925						—69.4	18.6	—50.7
1926	—20.3 [1]	... [2]	—37.8	—36.9	—3.0	—97.9	24.7	—73.2
1927	—70.8 [1]	... [2]	—45.0	—140	—16.7	—273	7.2	—266
1928	—8.9	—44.3	—14.9	—74.7	—11.5	—154	15.9	—138
1929	—13.3	—39.4	—45.8	—48.6	—19.1	—166	24.9	—141
1930	—5.5	—66.0	—113	—94.5	—25.2	—304	—15.7	—320
1931	—11.2	—62.2	—107	—157	—54.0	—392	—29.9	—422
1932	—22.6	—56.8	—88.7	—83.8	—54.0	—306	—31.5	—337
1933	—11.8	—51.0	—49.9	—82.1	—59.0	—253	—23.5	—277
1934	—11.8	—28.6	—1.6	—56.1	—20.9	—119	—6.4	—125
1934	—10.9	—37.1	—25.7	—102	—37.3	—213	—9.0	—222
1935	—18.6	—27.8	—15.8	—83.8	—64.5	—210	—9.5	—220
1936	—14.4	—30.8	—18.0	—48.6	—30.2	—142	—0.4	—142
1937	—20.7	—21.6	—6.7	—53.2	—36.5	—138	6.2	—132
1938	—28.2	—21.6	—18.5	—51.5	—33.9	—153	6.1	—147

[1] Including figures for bituminous.   [2] Included with figures for anthracite.

MINING

Q 9 Persons Engaged (thousands)

	WAGE EARNERS						SALARIED EMPLOYEES						ENTRE-PRENEURS
	COAL		Metal	Oil & gas	Other	Total	COAL		Metal	Oil & gas	Other	Total	Total
	Anth.	Bit.					Anth.	Bit.					
	(1)	(2)	(3)	(4)	(5)	(6)	(7)	(8)	(9)	(10)	(11)	(12)	(13)
1919	147	547	135	93.7	76.3	1,001	7.4	33.7	10.8	18.0	7.9	77.7	22.3
1920	139	630	133	114	92.4	1,109	7.5	40.3	10.3	19.8	9.6	87.5	21.6
1921	159	439	71.9	84.9	73.1	829	8.3	25.4	6.1	12.9	7.8	60.5	20.4
1922	96.2	430	95.8	106	84.1	813	7.7	25.3	7.2	17.5	8.3	66.1	20.1
1923	150	552	121	111	102	1,037	8.8	31.4	9.4	19.6	9.8	79.0	19.7
1924	158	460	119	102	101	942	9.1	26.0	9.4	17.7	10.2	72.4	18.2
1925	102	494	123	118	102	941	9.0	27.3	9.9	18.1	10.1	74.3	17.2
1926	153	545	123	149	102	1,073	9.5	30.3	9.2	22.8	10.2	82.0	16.6
1927	157	481	112	131	101	984	9.7	25.4	9.6	20.6	11.7	77.1	15.8
1928	150	445	108	104	98.9	908	8.7	23.0	9.2	17.5	11.5	70.0	15.0
1929	144	459	115*	139	96.5*	956	8.5	23.7	9.7*	23.6	11.7*	77.3	14.1
1930	137	441	101	118	90.7	890	8.4	21.7	9.8	20.8	12.7	73.3	14.0
1931	121	408	76.0	81.6	80.0	767	7.7	19.7	7.5	14.9	11.5	61.3	14.1
1932	98.1	350	49.4	76.3	63.6	638	6.2	16.8	5.1	14.2	9.9	52.2	13.6
1933	85.4	367	49.1	90.3	63.2	655	6.0	16.4	5.2	13.2	10.1	50.8	13.4
1934	99.4	424	61.8	112	74.3	772	5.9	18.9	5.7	17.1	10.5	58.1	13.2
1935	92.4	436	73.3	108	75.0	785	5.8	19.3	6.7	20.3	10.5	62.6	12.8
1936	89.3	448	93.5	119	80.7	830	5.8	20.7	8.0	21.1	10.8	66.4	12.8
1937	86.0	456	119	126	83.8	872	5.7	21.5	10.0	22.5	10.9	70.6	12.8
1938	74.7	398	91.5	119	69.0	753	5.2	20.0	8.6	21.2	10.1	65.1	12.8

* Comparable with the figures for 1930–38. Since several of the minor metals were classified with non-metals in the 1935 Census the 1929 figures also were reclassified. The 1929 figures comparable with those for 1919–28 are: Wage earners: metal, 116; 'other' mining, 95.5; Salaried employees: metal, 9.9; 'other' mining, 11.5.

TABLE Q 1

Gross Income

Col. 1 and 2 Coal: data for 1919 and 1929 are from the *Census of Mines and Quarries* and for 1935 from mimeographed reports of the *Census of Business.* Interpolation between Census years is by Bureau of Mines value of production figures (*Mineral Resources* and the *Minerals Yearbook*). This series is used also for the 1936–38 estimates.

Col. 3 Metal: for 1919–29 the metals covered are those classified as such in the *Census of Mines and Quarries* for 1919 and 1929. Interpolation between Census years is by Bureau of Mines value of metal production figures.

For 1930–38 five minor metals are included with non-metals: manganese, molybdenum, titanium, tungsten, and vanadium. The 1929 figure is adjusted (see the notes to col. 5) to exclude these five metals. Interpolation between the adjusted and the 1935 figure (reported in the *Census of Business*) and the extrapolation for 1936–38 are by Bureau of Mines value of production figures.

Col. 4 Oil and gas: Bureau of Mines figures on the value of petroleum, natural gas, and natural gasoline. The values are those at the wells and differ in this respect from those in the summary table in the *Minerals Yearbook.*

Col. 5 Other mining: for 1919–29 'other' mining covers the mining of non-metals classified as such in the 1929 *Census of Mines and Quarries.* For 1929 and later years 'other' mining includes, in addition to the non-metal total reported in the 1929 Census, manganese, molybdenum, titanium, tungsten, and vanadium. The 1935 *Census of Business* covers in its non-metal section all the items included in 1929 except titanium, vanadium, tungsten, sulphur and pyrites which we estimate for 1935 as follows:

a) *Titanium and vanadium:* from the 1929 *Census of Mines and Quarries* combined total for molybdenum, titanium, and vanadium we subtract the value of molybdenum (*Mineral Resources*) to obtain the value of titanium and vanadium in 1929. Their value in 1935 is estimated by multiplying tonnage produced by the price per ton. Tonnage production of vanadium and titanium in 1929 and 1935 is derived on the basis of data for other years and of text discussion on activity in this field in the *Minerals Yearbook.* It is used to extrapolate the 1929 Census quantity figure (after subtracting molybdenum as reported by the Bureau of Mines). The price per ton in 1929 is derived from the Census; for 1935 it is estimated on the basis of the change from 1929 to 1935 in the price per ton of tungsten.

b) *Tungsten:* the value of tungsten produced in 1929 is reported in the *Census of Mines and Quarries;* for 1935 it is estimated on the basis of the change from 1929 to 1935 in the value of concentrated tungsten ores produced, as reported by the Bureau of Mines.

c) *Sulphur and pyrites:* the value and quantity of sulphur and pyrites produced in 1929 are reported in the *Census of Mines and Quarries.* The quantity figure is estimated for 1935 on the basis of the change from 1929 to 1935 in production as reported by the Bureau of Mines; and to it is applied the price per ton as derived from the 1929 data to obtain value in 1935. According to the Bureau of Mines, the price of crude sulphur f.o.b. mines remained constant over the period; and although the price of pyrites declined slightly from 1929 to 1935, this change in price is disregarded since the value of pyrites is less than 2 per cent of the total value of sulphur and pyrites in 1929.

Interpolation for all other mining for 1920–28 and 1930–34 and extrapolation for 1936–38 are by Bureau of Mines figures on the value of non-metallic production other than coal, petroleum, natural gas, and natural gasoline (*Mineral Resources* and the *Minerals Yearbook*).

Col. 6 Total mining: sum of col. 1–5.

TABLE Q 2

Total Payments by Type

Col. 1 and 2 Wages and salaries: see the notes to Table Q 4.

Col. 3 Employee compensation: sum of col. 1 and 2.

Col. 4 Entrepreneurial withdrawals: sum of entrepreneurial withdrawals for each industrial subgroup, obtained by multiplying the average wage in the field by the estimated number of entrepreneurs (see the notes to Tables Q 4 and Q 9).

Col. 5 and 6 Dividends and interest: see the notes to Table Q 5.

Col. 7 Property income: sum of col. 5 and 6.

Col. 8 Total payments: sum of col. 3, 4, and 7.

TABLE Q 3

Net Income Originating

Col. 1 Total payments: see the notes to Table Q 2, col. 8.
Col. 2 Entrepreneurial net savings: see the notes to Table Q 8, col. 7.
Col. 3 Corporate net savings: see the notes to Table Q 8.
Col. 4 Total net savings: sum of col. 2 and 3.
Col. 5 Net income originating: sum of col. 1 and 4.

TABLE Q 4

Wages and Salaries

WAGES

Col. 1 Anthracite: payments to contract and to non-contract workers. Wages to non-contract workers in 1919 and 1929 are from the *Census of Mines and Quarries,* and in 1935, from the *Census of Business.* The latter reports also wages paid under contract work in 1935. The sum of the various costs under contract work as reported in the *Census of Business* is raised to the total value of contract work in 1935 by the ratio of the cost of goods sold to total sales of anthracite corporations filing income tax returns. The ratio of contract wages to value of contract work is derived for 1935, extrapolated for 1919 and 1929 by the corresponding ratio for non-contract work, and applied to the value of contract work, as reported in the *Census of Mines and Quarries,* for those years to obtain wages paid under contract work. Interpolation of total wages between 1919 and 1929 is by total wages, recorded annually in the Pennsylvania *Report on Productive Industries, Public Utilities and Miscellaneous Statistics.* Interpolation between 1929 and 1935 and extrapolation for 1936–38 are by the BLS payrolls index.

Col. 2 Bituminous: wages in producing and in non-producing mines, basic data for which are reported in the *Census of Mines and Quarries* for 1919 and 1929 and in the *Census of Business* for 1935, and estimated wages paid under contract work. For 1919 and 1929 the latter are obtained by applying to the value of contract work, as reported in the Census, the ratio of contract wages to the value of contract work. This ratio is estimated on the assumption that its relation to the similar ratio for non-contract work is the same as for anthracite coal. The 1935 Census covers producing mines alone. Estimates of wages paid in non-producing mines and under contract work are based on their ratios to the 1929 producing mines figures.

Estimates for 1920–28 are based on the ratio of wages to value of product, derived for Census years and interpolated by the average ratio for Ohio, Pennsylvania, Tennessee, and Indiana. For all four states the value of product is from *Mineral Resources*. The Pennsylvania wage data are from the Pennsylvania *Report on Productive Industries,* the Ohio data from *Statistics of Ohio Coal Mines and Quarries,* the Tennessee data from the *Annual Report of the Mineral Resources of Tennessee* and the *Annual Report of the Department of Labor* of that state, and the Indiana data from the Indiana *Year Book.* Interpolation between 1929 and 1935 and extrapolation for 1936–38 are by the BLS payrolls index.

Col. 3 Metal: wages in producing and in non-producing mines, reported in the 1919 and 1929 *Census of Mines and Quarries* and in the 1935 *Census of Business,* and wages paid under contract work. The 1929 figure comparable with that for 1919 covers all the metals classified as such in the 1929 Census. The 1929 figure comparable with that for 1935 excludes manganese, molybdenum, tungsten, titanium, and vanadium.

Wages paid under contract work in 1935 are covered in total wages reported, as are wages in non-producing mines. For 1919 and 1929 wages paid under contract work are obtained by applying to the value of contract work, as reported in the Census, the ratio of contract wages to the value of contract work. This ratio is estimated on the assumption that its relation to the similar ratio for non-contract work is the same as for anthracite coal.

Total wages, 1920–28, are the product of the number of man-shifts and the average wage per man-shift. The number of man-shifts in metal mines is reported annually by the Bureau of Mines in *Metal-Mine Accidents.* The average wage per man-shift in Census years, obtained by dividing the total wage bill by the number of man-shifts, is interpolated by the average daily wage in iron mines in Itasca County, Minnesota (*Biennial Report of the Department of Labor and Industry* of Minnesota). Interpolation of total wages between 1929 and 1935 and extrapolation for 1936–38 are by the BLS payrolls index.

Col. 4 Oil and gas: basic data, covering petroleum, natural gas, and natural gasoline producing and non-producing wells, for 1919 are from the *Census of Mines and Quarries,* and for 1935 from the *Census of Business.* The 1935 wage figure is extrapolated to 1933 by the BLS payrolls index. From 1933 to 1929 the estimate is extrapolated by wages paid by sample companies reporting to the Bureau of Foreign and Domestic Commerce, National Income Division, raised by the ratio of the total value of product to the value of product for the sample companies.

Interpolation between the 1919 and the estimated 1929 figures is by applying, to the total value of product, the ratio of wages to value of product. The ratio of wages to value of product is derived from Census data for 1919 and 1929 and interpolated by the similar ratio for petroleum refining. The 1936–38 estimates are the product of the number of wage earners (see the notes to Table Q 9) and the average wage. The average wage in 1935, derived from the Census, is extrapolated by the ratio of the BLS payrolls index to its employment index.

Col. 5 Other mining: wages in producing and in non-producing mines, reported in the 1919 and 1929 *Census of Mines and Quarries,* and in the 1935 *Census of Business,* and wages paid under contract work. The 1929 figure comparable with that for 1919 covers the non-metals listed as such in the 1929 Census. The 1929 figure comparable with that for 1935 includes the five metals that were not segregable in 1935: manganese, molybdenum, tungsten, titanium, and vanadium. The 1919 figure includes an estimate for wages in the sand and gravel, glass and molding sand industries which were canvassed in 1929 but not in 1919. This estimate is obtained by applying, to the value of product reported in the 1929 Census and extrapolated by the Bureau of Mines value of production figure, the ratio of wages to value of product derived from the 1929 Census and extrapolated by the ratio for Pennsylvania; the latter ratio was computed from data recorded in the Pennsylvania *Report on Productive Industries, Public Utilities and Miscellaneous Statistics.* Wages paid under contract work are included in the 1935 Census wage figure and are estimated for 1919 and 1929 by the procedure described for col. 3.

Wages for the total 'other' mining group, 1920–28, are obtained by multiplying the value of product by the ratio of wages to it. The ratio of wages to value of product is derived from Census data for 1919 and 1929 and interpolated by the corresponding ratio for Pennsylvania and Tennessee for 1919–29; for 1921–29 Wisconsin is added: for 1924–29 Ohio is added. The Pennsylvania, Tennessee and Ohio data are from the sources cited in the notes to col. 2. The Wisconsin wage figure is the 1929 Census figure extrapolated by an index derived from month to month percentage changes for stone crushing and quarrying (*Wisconsin Labor Market*).

The 1935 figure as reported in the *Census of Business* does not include sulphur and pyrites, tungsten, titanium, and vanadium. Estimates for these items are based on their ratio of wages to value of product in 1929, adjusted by the percentage change in the ratio for non-metals covered in both 1929 and 1935. Interpolation between 1929 and 1935 and extrapolation for 1936–38 are by the BLS payrolls index.

Col. 6 Total mining: sum of col. 1–5.

SALARIES

Col. 7 Anthracite: basic data for 1919 and 1929 are from the *Census of Mines and Quarries,* for 1935 from the *Census of Business,* and cover salaries paid in producing mines, central administrative offices, and under contract work. Salaries paid under contract work are reported for 1935 in the Census and estimated for 1919 and 1929 by applying to the estimated wages paid under contract work the ratio of salaries to wages paid under contract work in 1935, extrapolated by the ratio of salaries to wages for non-contract work. Interpolation for 1920–28 and 1930–34 and extrapolation for 1936–38 are by salaries recorded in the Pennsylvania *Report on Productive Industries, Public Utilities and Miscellaneous Statistics.*

Col. 8 Bituminous: basic data are from the sources cited for col. 2 and cover salaries paid in producing and in non-producing mines, central administrative offices, and under contract work. Salaries paid under contract work in 1919, 1929, and 1935 are estimated by applying, to estimated contract wages, the ratio of contract salaries to contract wages. This ratio is derived on the assumption that its relation to the similar ratio for non-contract work is the same as for anthracite coal.

Total salaries in intercensal years and 1936–38 are obtained by multiplying the average salary by the estimated number of salaried employees (see the notes to Table Q 9). The average salary is derived for Census years and interpolated by the average salary computed from data in the Pennsylvania *Report on Productive Industries, Public Utilities and Miscellaneous Statistics.*

Col. 9 Metal: basic data are from the sources cited for col. 3 and cover salaries paid in producing and in non-producing mines, central administrative offices, and under contract work. For the adjustment of the 1929 figure for comparability with the 1935 see the notes to col. 3. The 1935 figure, as reported, covers all the above items except salaries at central administrative offices. The latter are estimated by applying to other salaries their 1929 ratio to other salaries. Salaries paid under contract work in 1919 and 1929 are derived by the method described for bituminous coal.

Total salaries in intercensal years and 1936–38 are obtained by multiplying the average salary by the number of salaried employees (see the notes to Table Q 9). The average salary is derived for Census years and interpolated by the weighted average salary for anthracite, bituminous, and 'other' mining.

Col. 10 Oil and gas: basic data for 1919 are from the *Census of Mines and Quarries,* for 1935 from the *Census of Business,* and cover salaries at producing wells and central administrative offices. For 1935 the salaries paid at central administrative offices are given for only some natural gasoline plants. The ratio of the average salary at the central administrative offices to the average salary at the wells for these plants is applied to the average salary excluding central administrative offices for the entire oil and gas field. The product of the resulting average and the estimated number of salaried employees in central administrative offices (see the notes to Table Q 9) is the estimated salary bill for these offices.

Total salaries, 1920–34 and 1936–38, are obtained by multiplying the average salary by the estimated number of salaried workers (see the notes to Table Q 9). The average salary is derived for 1919 and 1935 and interpolated and extrapolated by the average salary paid in petroleum refining.

Col. 11 Other mining: basic data are from the sources cited for col. 5 and cover salaries paid in producing and in non-producing mines, central administrative offices, and under contract work. The 1919 figure is raised to include salaries in the sand and gravel, glass and molding sand industries, which are the product of the estimated number of salaried employees and the average salary. The latter is computed for 1929 and estimated for 1919 on the basis of the percentage change from 1919 to 1929 in the average salary paid in these industries in Pennsylvania. The 1935 figure, as reported, covers all the above items except salaries at central administrative offices, which are estimated by the procedure outlined for col. 9. The 1935 figure is raised further to include an estimate of salaries for sulphur and pyrites, titanium, tungsten, and vanadium (not covered by the Census in that year). This adjustment is made by applying to the estimated wages for these items in 1935 their 1929 ratio of salaries to wages, modified by the percentage change in the ratio of salaries to wages of the other non-metals from 1929 to 1935. Salaries paid under contract work in 1919 and 1929 are estimated by the method described for col. 8.

Total salaries in intercensal years and 1936–38 are obtained by multiplying the average salary by the number of salaried employees (see the notes to Table Q 9). The average salary is derived for Census years and interpolated by the average salary in Pennsylvania mines other than coal, as estimated from data in the Pennsylvania *Report on Productive Industries, Public Utilities and Miscellaneous Statistics*. Extrapolation of the average salary for 1936–38 is by the Pennsylvania data and, in addition, Ohio data, published annually in *Statistics of Ohio Coal Mines and Quarries*.

Col. 12 Total mining: sum of col. 7–11.

TABLE Q 5

Dividends and Interest

Col. 1–6 Dividends: net originating in the industry, the difference between total dividends paid and dividends received. The division of the total into five subgroups for 1928–37 and into four for 1926 and 1927 is from the special tabulation of *Statistics of Income* data. The 1926–33 and 1934 (new classification) –37 figures are taken directly from these tabulation sheets. The 1938 estimates are extrapolated from 1937 by the corporate samples for the five subgroups.

For 1922–25 both dividends paid and received are reported for the entire mining industry in *Statistics of Income*. Dividends paid, 1919–21, are extrapolated from 1922 by dividend payments of a corporate sample for the industry. Dividends received, 1919–21, are extrapolated from 1922 by dividend receipts of all corporations as reported in *Statistics of Income*.

Col. 7–12 Interest: net originating in the industry, the difference between estimated interest paid on long term debt and interest received on holdings of government obligations.

For 1919–28 interest is estimated for the mining industry as a whole. From the capital stock tax returns published in *Statistics of Income* long term debt is obtained for December 31, 1921, 1923, and 1924. The 1921 figures are assumed to be complete. The figures for 1923 and 1924 are raised by the ratio of the fair value of total stock to the fair value of the stock of corporations submitting statements of assets and liabilities, to yield total long term debt. Long term debt outstanding at the end of each year, 1926–28, reported in *Statistics of Income*, is raised by the 1931 ratio of total compiled receipts to compiled receipts of corporations reporting balance sheet items. Interpolation for the December 31, 1922 and 1925 figures is by the long term debt of a corporate sample for the industry. To the average of the final December 31 figures are applied the interest rates derived from sample corporations. The 1922 interest figure is extrapolated to 1919 by the long term interest payments of the corporate sample for the industry.

The division for 1926–28 of total interest paid by mining into the industrial subgroups is derived from the percentage distributions of preliminary estimates. The latter are based on the par value of long term debt outstanding, available by subgroups for 1924 from capital stock tax returns, and for 1929 as described below. Long term debt for the subgroups, 1926–28, is obtained by multiplying total long term debt for mining by the ratios of the subgroups to it. The ratios, calculated for 1924 and 1929, are interpolated along a straight line for the intervening years. The interest rates applied to these estimates of long term debt are those for the industrial subgroups in 1929 extrapolated by the change in the rate for all mining. The percentage distributions of these estimates for 1926, 1927, and 1928 are applied to the estimated total for all mining to yield total interest paid by the subgroups.

Interest received on tax-exempt obligations is reported for total mining for 1922–25 in *Statistics of Income* and for 1926–28 in the special tabulation of *Statistics of Income* data. For 1919–21 it is extrapolated from 1922 by total tax-exempt interest received by all corporations as reported in *Statistics of Income.*

For 1929–36 the procedure is similar to that for the earlier period for total mining, except that the estimates are made for the minor industrial divisions directly. The 1929 value of long term debt outstanding for each subgroup is assumed to be the same percentage of the total for all mining as in 1930. The 1930–33 and 1934 (new classification)–36 data are taken from the special tabulation of *Statistics of Income* data, which gives total long term debt on December 31 of each year for the companies that report assets and liabilities. These are raised by the ratio, for the entire mining group, of compiled receipts of all companies to compiled receipts of companies reporting assets and liabilities, to yield total long term debt. The December 31, 1934 figures comparable with the reported 1933 figures and the December 31, 1933 figures comparable with the reported 1934 figures are based on the percentage change in corporate sample data for the industry. The December 31 figures are averaged to yield the average outstanding during the year, to which the average interest rate of the corporate sample for the industry is applied to obtain total long term interest paid.

Interest received on tax-exempt obligations by minor industrial divisions also is reported for 1929–33 and 1934 (new classification)–37 in the special tabulation of *Statistics of Income* data.

The estimates of interest paid, 1937 and 1938, and of interest received, 1938, are extrapolated from 1936 and 1937 by the corporate samples for the five subdivisions.

TABLE Q 6
Employee Compensation and Property Income

Col. 1–6 Employee compensation: see the notes to Table Q 4.
Col. 7–12 Property income: see the notes to Table Q 5.

TABLE Q 7
Total Payments to Individuals

Sum of employee compensation (Table Q 4), property income (Table Q 5), and entrepreneurial withdrawals (Table Q 2, col. 4).

TABLE Q 8

Total Net Savings

Col. 1–6 Corporate net savings: for 1919–25, estimated for mining as a whole; for 1926–38, for the minor industrial divisions.

Corporate net savings are the difference between net profits after taxes and total dividends paid. For the derivation of dividends paid, see the notes to Table Q 5. Net profits after taxes are reported for 1922–37 in *Statistics of Income* and in the special tabulation of *Statistics of Income* data. For 1919–21 they are the sum of statutory net income after taxes (*Statistics of Income*) and interest and dividends received (see the notes to Table Q 5). For 1938, except in the case of bituminous coal, they are extrapolated from 1937 by the corporate sample for the industries. Corporate net savings for bituminous coal in 1938 are assumed to be the same as in 1937.

Col. 7 Entrepreneurial net savings: difference between entrepreneurial net income and withdrawals (see the notes to Table Q 2, col. 4). Net income is derived by applying an estimated net income ratio to the non-corporate value of product.

a) Non-corporate value of product: the 1919 and 1929 figures are derived from data on the character of ownership in the *Census of Mines and Quarries*. The ratio of non-corporate to total value of product in the oil and gas field, from the Census for 1919, is extrapolated to 1929 by the percentage change in the ratio for the other mining divisions. The ratio for sand and gravel, from the Census for 1929, is estimated for 1919 by the same procedure. The resulting ratio for mining as a whole is interpolated along a straight line between 1919 and 1929, then kept constant. Non-corporate value of product is estimated by applying to the total value of product the ratio so derived.

b) Net income ratio: on the basis of corporate data a preliminary net income ratio is estimated as the ratio of statutory net income before taxes (from *Statistics of Income*) plus officers' compensation (from *Statistics of Income*) plus total long term interest (see the notes to Table Q 5) to gross sales (from *Statistics of Income*). Officers' compensation, not reported for 1925–27, is estimated by the ratio to gross sales in 1924 and 1928, interpolated along a straight line. Gross sales, not reported for 1919–21, are extrapolated from

1922 by corporate gross income for the industry (from *Statistics of Income*). The net income ratio so derived is applied to the non-corporate value of product to yield entrepreneurial net income. This method is used for 1919–37, except that to derive a figure for 1934 comparable with that for 1933 the 1933 ratio is extrapolated. by the percentage change in the similar ratio for corporations filing unconsolidated returns in 1933 and 1934.

Since, for 1919–29, the results obtained by the method outlined above seemed unreasonably low, they were raised in each year by the average of the difference for the 11 years between this estimate and a second, based on net income from the mining business reported on individual income tax returns in *Statistics of Income*, which for 1919–25 cover all returns, and for later years cover only those with net incomes of $5,000 and over. For 1925 and 1928 both the total and those with incomes of $5,000 and over are reported. The 1926, 1927, and 1929 figures as reported are raised to the totals on the basis of the 1925 and 1928 ratios. To the resulting net income figure we apply a raising ratio—the ratio of the final estimate for entrepreneurial net income in printing for 1919–29 (see the notes to Table M 18) to the entrepreneurial net income in printing estimated from individual income tax returns, for the same period. The printing industry is selected because average value of production per entrepreneur is approximately the same as in mining.

Entrepreneurial net income in 1938 is assumed to be the same as in 1937.

Col. 8 Total net savings: sum of col. 6 and 7.

TABLE Q 9
Persons Engaged

Sources for the basic data for employees are the same as those cited in the notes to Table Q 4 and cover the same items. For all industrial divisions for the three Census years, except anthracite coal in 1935, the number of wage earners and salaried employees under contract work is obtained by dividing total contract pay by the average pay of those working directly for the mine, on the assumption that the average compensation of contract and non-contract workers is the same. For anthracite coal in 1935 the number of employees under contract work is reported in the Census.

WAGE EARNERS

Col. 1 Anthracite: interpolation for 1920–28 is by the number of wage earners recorded in the Pennsylvania *Report on Productive Industries, Public Utilities and Miscellaneous Statistics.* That for 1929–35 and extrapolation for 1936–38 are by the BLS employment index.

Col. 2 Bituminous: interpolation for 1920–28 is by the product of the number of underground and surface employees and of days the mine operates. Both series are from *Mineral Resources.* Interpolation between 1929 and 1935 and extrapolation for 1936–38 are by the BLS employment index.

Col. 3 Metal: interpolation for 1920–28 is by Bureau of Mines figures for 300-day workers in metal mines (*Metal-Mine Accidents*). Interpolation between 1929 and 1935 and extrapolation for 1936–38 are by the BLS employment index.

Col. 4 Oil and gas: the 1935 figure is extrapolated to 1933 and 1934 by the BLS employment index. The 1933 figure is extrapolated to 1929 by a preliminary estimate, based on the data for the sample companies reporting to the Bureau of Foreign and Domestic Commerce, National Income Division, raised by the ratio of total value of product to the value of product of reporting companies. Estimates for 1920–28 are obtained by dividing the total wage bill (see the notes to Table Q 4) by the estimated average wage. The average wage is derived from Census data for 1919 and 1929 and interpolated by the average wage paid in petroleum refining.

The estimates for 1936 and 1937 are based on the number of workers in the field, reported in *Recent Trends in Employment and Productivity in the Oil and Gas Fields* (Bureau of Mines, Mineral Market Report 728) and adjusted to exclude salaried employees. The 1938 figure is extrapolated from 1937 by the BLS employment index.

Col. 5 Other mining: for 1919–29 estimates are made separately for non-metals other than sand and gravel and for sand and gravel. Interpolation for non-metals other than sand and gravel is by Bureau of Mines figures on 300-day workers in non-metal mines and in quarries (*Metal-Mine Accidents* and *Quarry Accidents*). The number of wage earners in sand and gravel is reported for 1929 and is estimated for the earlier years on the basis of output and the ratio of the number of wage earners to it. The 1929 ratio is extrapolated by the ratio for Pennsylvania and Ohio. Pennsylvania wage earners in glass sand and sand and gravel are from the Pennsylvania *Report on Productive Industries, Public Utilities and Miscellaneous Statistics;* Ohio wage earners in sand and gravel excavation are from BLS Bulletin 553. Output for Pennsylvania and Ohio as well as for the United States is from *Mineral Resources.*

The 1935 figure as reported in the Census is adjusted to include wage earners producing the minerals not covered, by applying the ratio of wage earners to output, as reported in the 1929 Census, to output as estimated from Bureau of Mines data for the specific minerals. Interpolation between 1929 and 1935 and extrapolation for 1936–38 are by the BLS employment index.

Col. 6 Total: sum of col. 1–5.

Col. 7 Anthracite: interpolation between 1919 and 1929, 1929 and 1935, and extrapolation for 1936–38 are by the number of salaried employees as recorded in the Pennsylvania *Report on Productive Industries, Public Utilities and Miscellaneous Statistics.*

Col. 8 Bituminous: estimates for intercensal years are the product of the number of wage earners and the ratio of salaried employees to wage earners. This ratio is derived from Census data and interpolated by the similar ratio for Pennsylvania, West Virginia, and Illinois. The Pennsylvania data appear in the Pennsylvania *Report on Productive Industries, Public Utilities and Miscellaneous Statistics;* the West Virginia data in the *Annual Report of the Department of Mines* of that state; and the Illinois data in the *Coal Report of Illinois.* For 1923 and 1924 Illinois data are not available. For 1936–38 the basic data include figures for Ohio reported in the *Statistics of Ohio Coal Mines and Quarries.*

Col. 9 Metal: estimates for intercensal years are the product of the number of wage earners and the ratio of salaried employees to wage earners. For 1920–28 this ratio is interpolated by the ratio for iron and steel manufacturing. It is interpolated for 1930–34 and extrapolated for 1936–38 by the ratio for 'other' mining.

Col. 10 Oil and gas: the number of salaried employees in the 1935 Census is adjusted to include central administrative employees by applying to total salaried employees, excluding those at central administrative offices, reported for petroleum, natural gas, and natural gasoline the ratio, for natural gasoline plants reporting, of salaried employees at central administrative offices to other salaried employees. Estimates for 1920–34 are the product of the number of wage earners and the ratio of salaried employees to wage earners. The ratio is interpolated by the ratio of salaried employees to wage earners in petroleum refining.

The 1936 and 1937 estimates are extrapolated from 1935 by the number of salaried employees in the field, obtained by subtracting the number of wage earners from the total in the Bureau of Mines report cited in the notes to col. 4. The 1938 figure is extrapolated from 1937 by the BLS employment index.

Col. 11 Other mining: estimates for intercensal years are the product of the number of wage earners and the ratio of salaried employees to wage earners. The ratio is interpolated by the ratio derived from data in the Pennsylvania *Report on Productive Industries, Public Utilities and Miscellaneous Statistics* and extrapolated for 1936–38 by the ratio for Pennsylvania and Ohio. The Ohio data are reported in *Statistics of Ohio Coal Mines and Quarries.*

Col. 12 Total: sum of col. 7–11.

Col. 13 Entrepreneurs, total: sum of the estimates for the minor divisions.

a) Anthracite: data for 1919 and 1929 are from the *Census of Mines and Quarries,* and for 1935 from the NRP report, *Employment and Related Statistics of Mines and Quarries, 1935: Coal.* Interpolation is by the number of establishments in Pennsylvania (*Report on Productive Industries, Public Utilities and Miscellaneous Statistics*). Since 1935 the number of entrepreneurs has been kept constant.

b) Bituminous: the sources of the basic data are the same as for (a). Interpolation for 1920–28 is by the number of commercial mines in operation, and for 1930–34 by the number of Class 5 mines. The number of mines is recorded in *Mineral Resources* and the *Minerals Yearbook.* Since 1935 the number of entrepreneurs has been kept constant.

c) Metal: data for 1919 and 1929 are from the *Census of Mines and Quarries.* Interpolation between 1919 and 1929 and extrapolation through 1934 are by the number of active operators of metal mines as reported in *Metal-Mine Accidents*. Since 1934 the number of entrepreneurs has been kept constant.

d) Oil and gas: the figure for 1919 is from the *Census of Mines and Quarries,* that for 1929, from the 1930 *Census of Population,* Vol. V. Interpolation between 1919 and 1929 is along a straight line. Since 1929 the number of entrepreneurs has been kept constant.

e) Other mining: data for 1919 and 1929 are from the *Census of Mines and Quarries.* Interpolation between 1919 and 1929 and extrapolation through 1934 are by the sum of non-metal mine operators (*Metal-Mine Accidents*), and of quarry operators (*Quarry Accidents*). Since 1934 the number of entrepreneurs has been kept constant.

Manufacturing

TABLES M1–M28

Whenever two entries are made for 1934 the first is comparable with those for preceding years in that the *Statistics of Income* data used are based on the old industrial classification; the second is comparable with those for succeeding years in that the *Statistics of Income* data used are based on the new industrial classification.

Net savings and net income, adjusted, exclude gains and losses from sales of capital assets, 1929–38, and from changes in inventory valuation, 1919–38. Net savings and net income without any specific designation are unadjusted, i.e., include these two types of gain and loss.

M 1 Gross Income by Major Industrial Divisions
(millions of dollars)

	(1)	(2)	(3)	(4)	(5)	(6)	(7)	(8)	(9)
1919	14,239	12,271	4,487	1,261	1,762	18,290	5,341	2,856	60,509
1920	12,768	12,959	6,191	1,928	2,268	18,328	6,219	2,995	63,659
1921	9,402	8,891	3,696	1,088	2,068	10,526	4,123	2,099	41,897
1922	9,810	9,858	4,723	1,230	2,225	10,717	4,995	2,483	46,045
1923	10,658	10,881	5,753	1,480	2,306	18,472	5,207	2,739	57,499
1924	11,118	10,409	5,689	1,421	2,488	17,072	4,983	3,001	56,184
1925	11,587	11,442	6,056	1,576	2,583	18,634	5,952	2,998	60,831
1926	11,674	11,537	6,306	1,785	2,762	18,257	6,071	3,343	61,739
1927	12,267	11,409	5,723	1,812	2,846	17,798	5,847	3,078	60,783
1928	12,688	11,426	5,796	1,863	3,049	19,620	6,345	3,099	63,889
1929	13,324	11,709	5,704	1,909	3,170	22,669	6,876	3,104	68,468
1930	11,876	9,085	4,241	1,674	2,990	15,834	6,129	2,568	54,399
1931	9,451	7,386	2,807	1,357	2,497	10,173	4,438	2,029	40,141
1932	7,221	5,223	1,678	1,031	1,802	5,574	3,714	1,389	27,635
1933	7,519	6,025	1,800	1,172	1,733	7,161	3,703	1,440	30,557
1934	10,220	6,076	2,375	1,333	2,011	9,911	4,285	1,699	37,913
1935	10,636	7,600	2,792	1,523	2,165	13,273	4,942	2,061	44,993
1936	11,944	8,876	3,819	1,836	2,378	17,834	5,887	2,403	54,981
1937	12,568	8,926	4,266	2,060	2,585	20,939	6,674	2,690	60,712

Column
1 Food and tobacco
2 Textile and leather
3 Construction materials and furniture
4 Paper
5 Printing

Column
6 Metal
7 Chemical
8 Miscellaneous and rubber
9 Total

MANUFACTURING

M 2 Net Income Originating by Major Industrial Divisions (millions of dollars)

	(1)	(2)	(3)	(4)	(5)	(6)	(7)	(8)	(9)	(10)
1919	1,895	3,622	1,893	382	728	6,175	1,030	1,153	16,882	16,180
1920	1,674	3,022	2,331	544	938	6,665	1,072	1,234	17,483	19,802
1921	1,195	2,339	1,263	256	821	2,717	559	486	9,039	12,627
1922	1,569	2,982	1,779	338	943	3,793	933	934	13,275	13,083
1923	1,744	3,343	2,352	425	995	5,726	975	1,145	16,708	16,785
1924	1,762	2,641	2,181	403	1,071	5,250	998	906	15,214	15,603
1925	1,744	2,996	2,302	445	1,126	5,862	1,161	1,014	16,654	16,829
1926	1,801	2,781	2,382¹	475	1,213	6,037²	1,364	966	17,022	18,105
1927	1,826	3,164	2,139	476	1,224	5,558	1,073	966	16,430	17,200
1928	1,965	2,947	2,141	476	1,308	6,224	1,450	961	17,474	17,924
1929	2,038	2,992	2,172	498	1,407	7,224	1,609	960	18,904	19,794
1930	1,827	1,970	1,451	413	1,303	4,797	1,107	645	13,518	16,257
1931	1,438	1,667	757	303	1,051	2,544	582	503	8,848	11,047
1932	1,074	1,075	210	183	765	987	467	281	5,044	6,253
1933	1,258	1,749	480	271	711	1,717	594	410	7,194	6,625
1934	1,619	1,913	732	353	831	2,915	788	563	9,717	9,046
1934	1,602	1,912	727	351	824	2,909	718	559	9,606	8,935
1935	1,655	2,192	950	376	912	3,836	866	693	11,484	11,377
1936	1,870	2,423	1,322	434	1,007	5,045	1,064	810	13,978	14,198
1937	1,825	2,426	1,556	498	1,091	6,365	1,223	874	15,861	15,910
1938	1,742	1,938	1,154	367	1,004	3,775	952	685	11,619	12,574

Column
1 Food and tobacco
2 Textile and leather
3 Construction materials and furniture
4 Paper
5 Printing

Column
6 Metal
7 Chemical
8 Miscellaneous and rubber
9 Total excl. central administrative offices
10 Total, adj., incl. central administrative offices

¹ Comparable with the figures for 1927–38. Includes dividends, interest, and savings of metal building materials corporations which are excluded in the earlier years. The 1926 figure comparable with those for 1919–25 is $2,317 million.

² Comparable with the figures for 1927–38. Excludes dividends, interest, and savings of metal building materials corporations which are included in the earlier years. The 1926 figure comparable with those for 1919–25 is $6,102 million.

M 3　Total Payments by Type (millions of dollars)

	WAGES	SALARIES	WAGES & SALARIES	ENTREP. WITHDR.	DIVIDENDS	INTEREST	PROP. INCOME	PAY. TO INDIVIDUALS
	(1)	(2)	(3)	(4)	(5)	(6)	(7)	(8)
1919	9,682	2,785	12,468	523	1,261	86.7	1,348	14,339
1920	11,577	3,032	14,609	534	1,488	107	1,595	16,739
1921	7,460	2,431	9,891	404	1,325	138	1,463	11,760
1922	7,997	2,483	10,480	388	1,310	105	1,416	12,284
1923	10,160	2,861	13,021	385	1,763	117	1,881	15,289
1924	9,493	2,903	12,396	374	1,652	154	1,806	14,578
1925	9,981	2,978	12,960	371	1,910	153	2,064	15,396
1926	10,316	3,187	13,504	369	2,118	151	2,270	16,143
1927	10,115	3,424	13,539	365	2,227	163	2,391	16,296
1928	10,198	3,665	13,863	368	2,518	184	2,703	16,934
1929	10,898	4,013	14,911	372	2,743	209	2,952	18,236
1930	8,861	3,934	12,795	326	2,616	233	2,849	15,972
1931	6,701	3,217	9,918	268	1,895	231	2,127	12,314
1932	4,616	2,408	7,024	206	1,119	200	1,319	8,550
1933	4,940	2,109	7,049	183	1,010	185	1,196	8,428
1934	6,363	2,437	8,800	176	1,297	179	1,476	10,453
1934	6,363	2,437	8,800	181	1,224	144	1,368	10,350
1935	7,311	2,585	9,897	197	1,585	152	1,736	11,831
1936	8,460	2,757	11,217	241	2,411	145	2,556	14,015
1937	10,112	3,093	13,205	266	2,434	141	2,576	16,047
1938	7,719	2,801	10,521	264	1,413	140	1,553	12,339

M 4　Net Income Originating (millions of dollars)

	PAY. TO INDIVID- UALS	NET SAVINGS Entrep.	Corp.	Total	NET INCOME	NET SAVINGS, ADJUSTED Entrep.	Corp.	Total	NET INCOME, ADJ.
	(1)	(2)	(3)	(4)	(5)	(6)	(7)	(8)	(9)
1919	14,339	437	2,305	2,743	17,082	319	1,521	1,841	16,180
1920	16,739	48.8	914	963	17,702	297	2,765	3,063	19,802
1921	11,760	−184	−1,760	−1,945	9,814	157	710	867	12,627
1922	12,284	156	1,014	1,170	13,455	112	686	798	13,083
1923	15,289	214	1,410	1,625	16,914	200	1,295	1,496	16,785
1924	14,578	86.6	762	849	15,427	104	920	1,025	15,603
1925	15,396	151	1,332	1,484	16,880	146	1,286	1,433	16,829
1926	16,143	88.8	1,090	1,179	17,323	161	1,799	1,961	18,105
1927	16,296	78.7	441	520	16,817	114	788	903	17,200
1928	16,934	73.4	941	1,014	17,949	71.4	918	989	17,924
1929	18,236	58.8	1,209	1,268	19,504	85.5	1,472	1,557	19,794
1930	15,972	−139	−1,738	−1,878	14,094	34.6	250	285	16,257
1931	12,314	−194	−2,812	−3,007	9,307	−60.3	−1,206	−1,267	11,047
1932	8,550	−221	−2,948	−3,170	5,380	−150	−2,145	−2,296	6,253
1933	8,428	−12.3	−935	−948	7,480	−81.1	−1,722	−1,803	6,625
1934	10,453	24.3	−438	−414	10,039	−48.7	−1,358	−1,407	9,046
1934	10,350	25.3	−447	−422	9,928	−52.1	−1,363	−1,415	8,935
1935	11,831	61.8	−75.8	−14.0	11,816	27.5	−480	−453	11,377
1936	14,015	130	177	307	14,322	120	62.6	183	14,198
1937	16,047	60.1	129	189	16,237	34.3	−171	−137	15,910
1938	12,339	−33.0	−346	−379	11,959	15.9	219	235	12,574

M 5   Wages by Major Industrial Divisions (millions of dollars)

	(1)	(2)	(3)	(4)	(5)	(6)	(7)	(8)	(9)
1919	950	1,934	1,260	214	351	3,946	463	561	9,682
1920	1,045	2,297	1,599	297	498	4,566	569	703	11,577
1921	871	1,866	1,022	204	433	2,260	354	446	7,460
1922	855	1,926	1,185	210	448	2,510	372	487	7,997
1923	923	2,237	1,545	252	491	3,672	450	587	10,160
1924	908	1,986	1,539	251	518	3,312	424	552	9,493
1925	909	2,110	1,593	266	540	3,523	450	586	9,981
1926	917	2,119	1,635	281	578	3,693	483	607	10,316
1927	933	2,231	1,543	274	584	3,461	479	606	10,115
1928	956	2,126	1,472	273	591	3,681	476	618	10,198
1929	1,001	2,193	1,488	289	636	4,133	533	622	10,898
1930	951	1,790	1,142	266	620	3,080	494	515	8,861
1931	811	1,566	735	214	538	2,017	400	418	6,701
1932	655	1,134	410	162	414	1,238	313	287	4,616
1933	674	1,286	439	172	355	1,371	331	309	4,940
1934	836	1,533	570	212	411	2,016	393	389	6,363
1935	863	1,713	692	235	446	2,501	422	436	7,311
1936	927	1,786	892	260	486	3,152	456	498	8,460
1937	1,051	1,935	1,076	307	533	4,082	554	571	10,112
1938	1,019	1,592	835	273	508	2,561	501	428	7,719

Column

1 Food and tobacco
2 Textile and leather
3 Construction materials and furniture
4 Paper
5 Printing

Column

6 Metal
7 Chemical
8 Miscellaneous and rubber
9 Total

M 6   Wages by Minor Industrial Divisions (millions of dollars)

	(1)	(2)	(3)	(4)	(5)	(6)	(7)	(8)	(9)	(10)	(11)	(12)	(13)	(14)	(15)	(16)	(17)
1919	826	124	228	30.9	125	254	243	49.8	59.4	990	205	370	108	58.8	79.9	822	121
1920	901	144	247	29.9	160	328	263	59.8	64.9	1,154	253	472	126	69.0	93.9	1,015	127
1921	750	120	219	23.4	132	263	229	60.4	49.6	978	213	342	113	59.9	75.4	805	83.6
1922	741	114	241	28.3	152	278	223	60.1	53.4	1,037	221	333	103	60.0	77.8	796	92.7
1923	802	120	265	33.7	168	299	228	64.0	67.9	1,127	285	423	126	74.7	96.2	1,006	103
1924	793	115	237	23.3	149	266	210	60.1	61.7	1,009	254	353	121	71.8	85.2	885	91.9
1925	798	111	243	28.1	168	265	231	66.6	65.3	1,069	248	379	142	85.9	92.2	948	92.5
1926	810	106	242	28.8	177	268	236	65.8	65.4	1,084	226	380	140	88.0	106	940	94.9
1927	828	105	245	32.1	188	286	272	46.8	78.5	1,149	228	398	140	93.2	126	987	94.0
1928	857	99.6	252	30.4	187	276	284	46.1	76.4	1,133	213	334	139	93.4	121	902	90.3
1929	907	94.6	243	29.9	210	279	298	42.7	76.8	1,181	218	341	137	95.7	130	923	87.7
1930	867	84.0	200	21.9	176	221	269	36.4	62.6	987	161	264	113	83.4	104	727	75.8
1931	741	69.4	179	15.8	149	190	234	32.6	51.9	851	151	252	97.4	77.7	92.5	652	63.1
1932	599	55.7	149	12.0	122	154	159	25.0	37.3	639	100	167	63.0	56.7	61.9	449	46.0
1933	623	50.9	156	14.4	132	156	154	20.3	39.6	673	128	227	74.1	59.6	69.9	560	52.4
1934	777	58.4	186	16.5	162	196	212	23.2	48.2	844	129	257	90.5	66.1	83.2	626	62.5
1935	804	59.4	189	16.1	184	234	247	24.0	54.9	950	182	248	95.5	69.6	96.0	692	70.4
1936	864	63.3	188	18.5	194	243	261	23.5	60.5	989	180	278	86.3	73.8	104	723	74.0
1937	981	70.3	209	20.4	205	255	262	22.9	62.7	1,058	197	325	92.4	78.5	124	818	78.8
1938	951	67.9	185	13.7	182	203	237	21.9	53.6	897	144	250	67.5	69.4	99.0	630	64.2

Column
1 Food
2 Tobacco
3 Boots and shoes, other than rubber
4 Boots and shoes, rubber
5 Hosiery and knit goods
6 Men's clothing
7 Women's clothing
8 Millinery
9 Other wearing apparel

Column
10 Total wearing apparel (col. 3–9)
11 Woolen goods
12 Cotton goods
13 Silk and rayon goods
14 Dyeing and finishing
15 Other textile fabrics
16 Total textile fabrics (col. 11–15)
17 Other leather

M 6 Wages by Minor Industrial Divisions (millions of dollars)

(19)	(20)	(21)	(22)	(23)	(24)	(25)	(26)	(27)	(28)	(29)	(30)	(31)	(32)	(33)	(34)	(35)	
325	106	95.8	1,109	151	916	1,253	597	170	158	2,179	491	359	307	156	121	440	1919
413	151	155	1,400	198	1,101	1,638	372	214	161	2,386	592	486	367	202	152	550	1920
291	84.2	86.9	872	150	476	844	155	116	91.7	1,208	318	256	227	127	75.1	371	1921
317	88.0	106	1,004	182	599	872	81.3	103	109	1,167	430	312	241	130	93.8	393	1922
427	139	152	1,328	216	896	1,271	90.7	212	145	1,720	659	395	297	153	108	478	1923
436	132	155	1,323	215	826	1,171	76.4	142	136	1,526	594	365	288	136	107	444	1924
444	138	169	1,355	238	846	1,243	74.3	120	142	1,581	713	382	307	142	120	466	1925
460	145	181	1,380	254	881	1,372	81.2	125	150	1,729	687	394	330	153	120	487	1926
443	137	171	1,291	252	829	1,306	87.1	103	139	1,636	613	383	329	149	120	486	1927
405	130	168	1,229	242	867	1,372	68.4	84.8	130	1,655	748	410	334	143	131	487	1928
390	133	169	1,231	257	956	1,654	88.3	121	135	2,000	733	443	364	168	127	495	1929
314	100	142	957	185	767	1,247	91.5	106	102	1,548	431	332	327	167	89.0	426	1930
217	70.0	94.7	596	138	475	760	62.0	56.1	73.4	951	350	240	267	132	63.1	355	1931
125	42.5	46.7	329	81.0	257	438	43.6	41.2	49.4	572	255	153	205	108	46.2	241	1932
123	50.5	41.7	355	84.0	360	472	33.9	33.3	52.5	591	252	166	223	107	54.7	254	1933
169	64.4	54.2	470	99.3	489	703	47.4	54.8	70.0	876	423	227	268	125	73.0	316	1934
195	77.8	66.8	565	127	606	872	55.4	55.5	82.3	1,065	545	283	288	133	78.3	358	1935
248	101	92.4	732	159	830	1,097	78.1	80.8	100	1,357	626	338	312	144	92.5	406	1936
306	118	117	885	190	1,104	1,456	93.7	122	126	1,799	756	422	378	176	96.7	474	1937
238	82.3	87.6	690	145	639	949	83.4	75.9	85.2	1,194	421	305	326	174	67.2	360	1938

Column
18 Lumber
19 Stone, clay, and glass
20 Heating apparatus
21 Other construction materials
22 Total construction materials (col. 18–21)
23 Furniture
24 Iron and steel
25 Machinery proper
26 Shipbuilding
27 Other transportation equipment excl. motor
   vehicles

Column
28 Hardware
29 Total machinery (col. 25–28)
30 Motor vehicles
31 Non-ferrous metal
32 Chemical excl. petroleum refining
33 Petroleum refining
34 Rubber tires
35 Miscellaneous

MANUFACTURING

M 7 Salaries by Major Industrial Divisions (millions of dollars)

	(1)	(2)	(3)	(4)	(5)	(6)	(7)	(8)	(9)	(10)	(11)
1919	343	456	251	59.0	223	836	216	198	2,585	200	2,785
1920	348	456	279	59.5	255	979	231	203	2,812	219	3,032
1921	290	359	240	56.9	260	721	178	148	2,256	175	2,431
1922	299	391	270	62.6	283	670	180	144	2,303	179	2,483
1923	312	452	298	73.1	315	837	204	162	2,655	206	2,861
1924	290	423	324	72.5	359	869	190	160	2,690	213	2,903
1925	285	438	346	76.5	377	859	196	173	2,753	225	2,978
1926	290	435	364	83.0	418	896	213	184	2,886	301	3,187
1927	322	468	361	86.3	434	956	215	192	3,037	387	3,424
1928	339	500	365	92.2	461	1,019	221	191	3,190	474	3,665
1929	341	527	382	95.9	501	1,114	246	203	3,412	600	4,013
1930	331	481	365	95.4	521	1,117	244	200	3,359	575	3,934
1931	293	417	275	89.5	443	847	206	184	2,758	459	3,217
1932	242	308	182	69.3	361	608	163	198	2,072	335	2,408
1933	235	299	149	69.2	306	490	152	120	1,822	286	2,109
1934	262	327	177	80.6	339	624	178	126	2,115	322	2,437
1935	275	338	184	77.6	348	685	193	150	2,253	332	2,585
1936	292	354	201	84.3	366	757	200	157	2,412	344	2,757
1937	295	343	233	83.7	422	952	212	173	2,716	376	3,093
1938	292	295	218	81.6	396	822	200	153	2,462	339	2,801

Column
1 Food and tobacco
2 Textile and leather
3 Construction materials and furniture
4 Paper
5 Printing
6 Metal

Column
7 Chemical
8 Miscellaneous and rubber
9 Total excl. central administrative offices
10 Central administrative offices
11 Total incl. central administrative offices

MANUFACTURING

M 8 Salaries by Minor Industrial Divisions (millions of dollars)

	(1)	(2)	(3)	(4)	(5)	(6)	(7)	(8)	(9)	(10)	(11)	(12)	(13)	(14)	(15)	(16)	(17)	(18)	(19)
1919	316	27.2	278	145	31.8	78.4	68.4	30.9	30.1	207	43.5	153	493	94.8	94.4	172	43.9	54.9	143
1920	321	26.3	282	145	29.0	84.6	72.9	43.9	35.3	236	43.1	188	568	136	86.6	182	49.0	49.1	154
1921	265	24.7	209	129	19.9	74.3	65.3	30.8	30.4	200	39.8	130	431	81.4	77.8	144	34.6	29.8	118
1922	269	30.4	233	135	22.5	92.0	72.4	35.4	32.2	230	41.0	122	386	79.6	82.3	142	37.8	29.0	115
1923	283	28.5	268	160	23.4	91.1	82.4	54.7	40.2	248	50.0	150	485	101	99.4	163	40.8	28.8	133
1924	267	22.6	253	149	20.9	95.5	89.7	36.5	49.5	271	53.5	142	484	125	116	152	38.1	27.6	133
1925	262	22.4	255	160	22.3	100	95.3	40.6	48.8	285	61.3	144	491	119	103	160	36.1	32.4	141
1926	266	23.9	257	155	22.3	104	99.1	43.2	58.9	300	63.9	136	523	129	106	173	39.6	37.7	146
1927	299	23.3	270	174	23.0	94.4	102	42.4	56.5	295	65.6	154	564	120	117	175	39.7	40.4	151
1928	316	23.0	293	182	24.5	94.0	102	40.7	59.6	296	68.6	160	604	126	128	181	39.9	37.1	154
1929	318	23.0	309	192	24.6	102	99.2	42.6	61.7	306	76.0	170	662	137	143	200	45.5	31.1	172
1930	309	21.9	292	167	21.9	87.4	95.9	45.5	69.5	298	67.3	180	661	138	137	199	45.8	27.5	173
1931	276	16.4	241	158	18.0	59.7	73.4	42.9	49.6	225	50.1	132	483	115	116	167	39.1	21.0	163
1932	230	12.6	182	111	13.7	41.2	48.3	26.9	40.9	146	35.5	92.9	358	71.9	84.5	128	34.7	18.2	119
1933	223	11.6	174	110	14.5	33.4	42.8	22.1	20.2	118	30.7	84.5	281	57.5	67.2	124	28.3	17.2	102
1934	249	12.9	186	125	15.6	38.6	52.3	27.4	23.3	141	35.1	101	357	76.9	88.7	144	33.2	18.3	108
1935	263	11.9	196	126	15.9	42.3	56.8	24.8	25.9	149	35.1	122	394	76.1	92.3	152	40.8	18.8	131
1936	279	12.6	202	134	17.0	47.2	58.0	28.2	28.5	161	39.2	149	421	90.9	95.4	158	42.0	22.1	135
1937	285	12.1	194	134	15.7	54.4	64.9	32.9	34.7	187	39.6	194	528	115	95.4	168	44.7	25.3	147
1938	281	11.4	169	114	12.3	51.9	61.1	28.8	36.0	177	40.3	164	444	102	110	150	50.6	20.6	133

Column

1 Food
2 Tobacco
3 Wearing apparel
4 Textile fabrics
5 Other leather
6 Lumber
7 Stone, clay, and glass
8 Heating apparatus
9 Other construction materials
10 Total construction materials (col. 6–9)

Column

11 Furniture
12 Iron and steel
13 Machinery
14 Motor vehicles
15 Non-ferrous metal
16 Chemical excl. petroleum refining
17 Petroleum refining
18 Rubber tires
19 Miscellaneous

MANUFACTURING

M 9 Wages and Salaries by Major Industrial Divisions (millions of dollars)

	(1)	(2)	(3)	(4)	(5)	(6)	(7)	(8)	(9)	(10)
1919	1,293	2,391	1,512	273	574	4,783	680	759	12,267	12,468
1920	1,393	2,753	1,878	356	754	5,546	800	907	14,390	14,609
1921	1,162	2,225	1,263	261	694	2,981	533	594	9,716	9,891
1922	1,155	2,818	1,456	273	731	3,181	552	631	10,300	10,480
1923	1,235	2,690	1,843	325	807	4,509	654	749	12,815	13,021
1924	1,198	2,409	1,864	324	878	4,181	615	712	12,183	12,396
1925	1,194	2,549	1,940	343	918	4,382	646	760	12,734	12,900
1926	1,207	2,555	2,000	364	997	4,590	696	792	13,202	13,504
1927	1,256	2,699	1,904	361	1,019	4,418	694	798	13,152	13,539
1928	1,295	2,627	1,837	365	1,052	4,701	698	810	13,388	13,863
1929	1,343	2,720	1,870	385	1,138	5,247	779	826	14,311	14,911
1930	1,283	2,271	1,508	362	1,141	4,197	739	716	12,220	12,795
1931	1,104	1,984	1,011	303	981	2,865	606	602	9,459	9,918
1932	897	1,442	593	232	775	1,846	476	425	6,689	7,024
1933	909	1,585	588	242	662	1,861	484	429	6,763	7,049
1934	1,098	1,860	747	292	750	2,640	571	516	8,478	8,800
1935	1,138	2,052	877	313	795	3,186	615	586	9,564	9,897
1936	1,220	2,141	1,093	344	852	3,909	656	655	10,872	11,217
1937	1,347	2,279	1,309	391	955	5,035	767	744	12,829	13,205
1938	1,312	1,888	1,053	354	905	3,383	701	581	10,181	10,521

Column
1 Food and tobacco
2 Textile and leather
3 Construction materials and furniture
4 Paper
5 Printing

Column
6 Metal
7 Chemical
8 Miscellaneous and rubber
9 Total excl. central administrative offices (col. 1–8)
10 Total incl. central administrative offices

MANUFACTURING

M 10 Wages and Salaries by Minor Industrial Divisions (millions of dollars)

	(1)	(2)	(3)	(4)	(5)	(6)	(7)	(8)	(9)	(10)	(11)	(12)	(13)	(14)	(15)	(16)	(17)	(18)	(19)
1919	1,142	151	1,269	968	153	659	394	137	125	1,317	194	1,070	2,673	585	453	479	200	176	583
1920	1,222	170	1,436	1,160	156	765	486	195	190	1,657	241	1,290	2,954	728	573	549	251	201	705
1921	1,016	145	1,187	934	103	483	357	115	117	1,073	190	606	1,640	400	334	371	161	104	489
1922	1,010	145	1,271	931	115	583	390	121	138	1,234	222	722	1,553	510	395	384	168	122	508
1923	1,086	149	1,396	1,167	126	700	509	174	193	1,577	266	1,047	2,206	761	494	460	194	137	612
1924	1,060	137	1,262	1,035	112	694	525	169	205	1,595	268	969	2,011	719	481	440	174	135	577
1925	1,060	133	1,325	1,109	114	704	539	178	218	1,640	299	990	2,072	833	486	467	178	153	607
1926	1,077	130	1,341	1,096	117	697	559	188	235	1,681	318	1,017	2,253	817	501	503	192	158	654
1927	1,127	128	1,420	1,162	117	633	546	179	227	1,587	317	983	2,200	733	500	505	188	160	638
1928	1,173	122	1,426	1,085	114	619	508	171	227	1,526	311	1,028	2,260	874	538	515	182	168	642
1929	1,226	117	1,491	1,116	112	640	489	176	231	1,537	333	1,126	2,662	870	587	564	214	158	668
1930	1,177	105	1,279	894	97.8	486	410	145	212	1,255	252	948	2,309	569	469	526	215	116	599
1931	1,018	85.8	1,093	810	81.2	274	290	112	144	822	188	607	1,435	466	356	434	172	84.1	518
1932	829	68.3	821	561	59.7	156	173	69.4	77.2	476	116	350	931	327	237	333	143	64.4	360
1933	847	62.5	848	670	66.9	172	166	72.6	61.9	473	114	445	873	309	233	348	135	72.0	357
1934	1,027	71.3	1,030	751	78.1	221	221	91.8	77.5	612	134	591	1,233	500	516	413	158	91.5	424
1935	1,067	71.3	1,146	819	86.3	267	252	102	92.6	714	162	728	1,459	621	376	440	174	97.1	489
1936	1,144	75.9	1,191	858	91.0	337	306	129	120	894	198	980	1,778	717	433	470	186	114	541
1937	1,264	82.4	1,232	952	94.5	397	371	151	152	1,072	237	1,298	2,327	870	587	546	221	122	622
1938	1,233	79.3	1,066	745	76.5	335	299	111	125	867	185	804	1,638	524	416	477	224	87.8	494

Column

1 Food
2 Tobacco
3 Wearing apparel
4 Textile fabrics
5 Other leather
6 Lumber
7 Stone, clay, and glass
8 Heating apparatus
9 Other construction materials
10 Total construction materials (col. 6–9)

Column

11 Furniture
12 Iron and steel
13 Machinery
14 Motor vehicles
15 Non-ferrous metal
16 Chemical excl. petroleum refining
17 Petroleum refining
18 Rubber tires
19 Miscellaneous

M 11 Dividends by Major Industrial Divisions
(millions of dollars)

	(1)	(2)	(3)	(4)	(5)	(6)	(7)	(8)	(9)
1919	154	252	93.3	44.8	35.0	380	198	103	1,261
1920	196	276	125	59.7	42.1	425	249	112	1,488
1921	160	200	108	48.9	57.2	392	256	100	1,325
1922	154	211	122	34.9	66.7	368	214	137	1,310
1923	223	246	176	57.0	67.8	545	267	180	1,763
1924	248	202	159	36.9	63.5	624	244	73.4	1,652
1925	279	215	186	60.9	88.3	670	319	91.1	1,910
1926	274	208	245[1]	47.7	96.8	797[2]	345	103	2,118
1927	328	211	219	56.6	109	863	331	106	2,227
1928	353	231	217	65.0	99.2	957	495	99.5	2,518
1929	401	216	218	57.1	132	1,113	485	118	2,743
1930	434	168	178	51.6	127	951	600	104	2,616
1931	367	125	108	36.6	95.1	628	459	75.1	1,895
1932	292	74.3	48.9	20.7	59.6	300	279	43.7	1,119
1933	278	76.5	40.9	27.2	35.6	222	296	33.6	1,010
1934	296	115	79.2	38.2	61.6	379	286	40.8	1,297
1934	337	114	77.6	39.6	66.6	384	167	36.3	1,224
1935	335	114	94.2	47.0	72.4	530	313	75.0	1,583
1936	446	176	169	61.3	105	887	453	110	2,411
1937	408	170	182	75.4	93.9	980	416	106	2,434
1938	345	83.8	81.4	26.6	74.0	421	290	90.0	1,413

Column

1 Food and tobacco
2 Textile and leather
3 Construction materials and furniture
4 Paper
5 Printing

Column

6 Metal
7 Chemical
8 Miscellaneous and rubber
9 Total

[1] Comparable with the figures for 1927–38. Includes dividends of metal building materials corporations which are excluded in the earlier years. The 1926 figure comparable with those for 1919–25 is $210 million.

[2] Comparable with the figures for 1927–38. Excludes dividends of metal building materials corporations which are included in the earlier years. The 1926 figure comparable with those for 1919–25 is $832 million.

MANUFACTURING

M 12 Dividends by Minor Industrial Divisions (millions of dollars)

	(1)	(2)	(3)	(4)	(5)	(6)	(7)	(8)	(9)	(10)	(11)	(12)	(13)	(14)
1926	68.2	129	10.7	114	96.4	34.5	165	337	228	65.8	165	180	−4.0	107
1927	69.1	132	9.9	98.8	81.8	38.5	170	380	230	82.1	186	144	39.9	66.9
1928	81.0	138	12.0	103	79.5	34.2	185	395	279	96.2	232	262	8.0	91.6
1929	85.9	121	8.8	94.4	86.8	36.9	238	483	281	110	228	257	25.4	93.3
1930	72.2	89.0	7.4	63.6	75.7	38.8	217	417	234	82.1	278	322	24.6	79.8
1931	50.5	70.7	4.0	30.2	54.2	23.8	125	262	182	59.0	199	259	16.2	58.9
1932	31.1	40.6	2.6	14.3	27.9	6.7	55.3	125	76.6	43.4	170	109	11.0	32.8
1933	29.4	44.4	2.7	12.9	22.7	5.3	15.3	92.9	73.6	40.2	175	121	5.6	27.9

Column

1 Wearing apparel
2 Textile fabrics
3 Other leather
4 Lumber
5 Stone, clay, and glass
6 Metal building materials
7 Iron and steel

Column

8 Machinery
9 Motor vehicles
10 Non-ferrous metal
11 Chemical excl. petroleum refining
12 Petroleum refining
13 Rubber tires
14 Miscellaneous

M 13   Interest by Major Industrial Divisions
(millions of dollars)

	(1)	(2)	(3)	(4)	(5)	(6)	(7)	(8)	(9)
1919	25.3	12.8	6.0	4.0	2.6	26.1	0.4	9.6	86.7
1920	35.6	11.4	6.7	3.8	2.0	28.2	3.0	17.2	107
1921	36.0	14.0	7.3	4.3	3.5	33.5	20.5	19.1	138
1922	30.6	11.9	8.9	6.3	1.4	18.7	12.2	15.8	105
1923	31.5	3.8	9.4	8.1	1.2	38.8	13.6	11.3	117
1924	40.4	3.2	11.3	8.2	1.9	54.7	20.4	13.8	154
1925	43.6	4.5	10.9	9.7	3.9	49.4	21.1	10.8	153
1926	36.4	2.3	11.9[1]	12.2	5.2	45.5[2]	21.4	16.6	151
1927	39.1	5.0	13.8	13.3	8.9	36.4	29.2	18.3	163
1928	42.1	7.4	17.2	13.1	11.3	47.8	27.3	18.7	184
1929	43.0	10.6	22.4	15.3	13.1	61.3	25.6	17.8	209
1930	48.3	9.3	25.7	18.1	15.1	56.3	41.1	19.6	233
1931	44.9	7.3	26.2	17.0	15.5	52.6	48.6	19.2	231
1932	36.3	0.6	18.0	16.6	14.1	49.9	50.4	14.3	200
1933	31.9	—0.8	15.9	16.7	13.4	49.9	44.3	14.3	185
1934	31.2	—0.6	13.9	14.7	13.3	51.6	39.9	15.3	179
1934	26.5	—0.8	12.5	12.2	8.6	46.1	26.8	12.3	144
1935	27.4	2.0	11.2	11.4	8.2	51.1	30.8	10.8	152
1936	24.5	2.8	10.9	11.1	8.7	52.9	25.8	8.8	145
1937	26.4	3.8	7.6	12.5	9.0	52.9	23.2	6.4	141
1938	26.1	3.2	7.1	10.7	9.6	50.9	25.9	6.6	140

Column

1   Food and tobacco
2   Textile and leather
3   Construction materials and furniture
4   Paper
5   Printing

Column

6   Metal
7   Chemical
8   Miscellaneous and rubber
9   Total

[1] Comparable with the figures for 1927–38. Includes interest of metal building materials corporations which are excluded in the earlier years. The 1926 figure comparable with those for 1919–25 is $9.1 million.

[2] Comparable with the figures for 1927–38. Excludes interest of metal building materials corporations which are included in the earlier years. The 1926 figure comparable with those for 1919–25 is $48.4 million.

M 14 Property Income by Major Industrial Divisions
(millions of dollars)

	(1)	(2)	(3)	(4)	(5)	(6)	(7)	(8)	(9)
1919	179	265	99.3	48.8	37.6	406	198	112	1,348
1920	232	288	132	63.5	44.1	454	252	129	1,595
1921	196	214	115	53.2	60.7	426	277	119	1,463
1922	184	223	131	41.2	68.1	387	226	153	1,416
1923	255	249	185	65.2	69.0	584	280	191	1,881
1924	289	206	170	45.1	65.5	678	264	87.2	1,806
1925	322	219	197	70.6	92.3	719	340	101	2,064
1926	310	210	257[1]	59.9	102	843[2]	367	119	2,270
1927	367	216	232	69.9	118	899	360	125	2,391
1928	395	238	234	78.1	110	1,004	522	118	2,703
1929	444	227	240	72.4	146	1,174	511	136	2,952
1930	482	177	203	69.7	143	1,007	641	124	2,849
1931	412	132	134	53.6	110	681	508	94.3	2,127
1932	328	75.0	66.9	37.3	73.7	350	330	58.0	1,319
1933	310	75.6	56.9	43.9	49.0	271	340	47.8	1,196
1934	328	114	93.2	52.9	74.9	430	326	56.1	1,476
1934	364	113	90.1	51.8	75.2	430	194	48.5	1,368
1935	362	116	105	58.4	80.6	581	344	85.8	1,736
1936	471	179	180	72.4	113	940	479	119	2,556
1937	435	174	189	87.9	102	1,033	439	112	2,576
1938	371	87.0	88.5	37.3	83.7	472	316	96.6	1,553

Column		Column	
1	Food and tobacco	6	Metal
2	Textile and leather	7	Chemical
3	Construction materials and furniture	8	Miscellaneous and rubber
4	Paper	9	Total
5	Printing		

[1] Comparable with the figures for 1927–38. Includes dividends and interest payments of metal building materials corporations which are excluded in the earlier years. The 1926 figure comparable with those for 1919–25 is $219 million.

[2] Comparable with the figures for 1927–38. Excludes dividends and interest payments of metal building materials corporations which are included in the earlier years. The 1926 figure comparable with those for 1919–25 is $880 million.

M 15 Entrepreneurial Withdrawals
by Major Industrial Divisions (millions of dollars)

	(1)	(2)	(3)	(4)	(5)	(6)	(7)	(8)	(9)
1919	191	143	56.5	4.8	40.5	45.0	22.7	18.9	523
1920	176	137	70.1	6.4	54.4	45.4	23.0	20.9	534
1921	135	111	45.8	4.7	46.5	28.5	16.7	15.8	404
1922	125	107	48.8	4.0	44.8	26.7	15.8	15.0	388
1923	124	104	48.0	4.2	43.5	29.8	15.6	14.9	385
1924	117	100	48.3	4.0	44.1	30.0	14.4	15.5	374
1925	109	106	49.7	4.0	43.4	28.6	14.5	15.1	371
1926	112	104	49.1	4.1	42.9	27.8	13.9	15.1	369
1927	119	102	42.4	3.7	42.8	26.2	13.6	14.4	365
1928	127	96.6	43.4	3.5	41.6	26.3	13.4	15.1	368
1929	130	96.4	44.7	3.4	40.2	27.6	14.1	15.1	372
1930	117	82.1	35.9	3.1	38.4	23.0	12.5	13.6	326
1931	100	68.3	25.7	2.7	32.5	16.5	11.0	11.3	268
1932	80.1	47.3	16.5	2.1	33.6	11.0	7.7	7.9	206
1933	65.5	47.0	13.2	2.0	31.0	10.0	7.2	7.1	183
1934	65.2	45.0	15.3	2.1	22.8	11.4	7.4	7.3	176
1934	65.2	45.6	16.1	2.2	24.7	12.0	7.7	8.2	181
1935	64.0	51.5	18.4	2.5	27.6	14.7	9.1	9.9	197
1936	79.0	61.5	24.7	3.0	31.6	19.7	10.9	11.1	241
1937	92.9	61.4	27.6	3.4	33.5	23.3	11.8	12.2	266
1938	94.9	59.9	26.5	3.3	34.2	22.1	11.8	11.9	264

Column
1 Food and tobacco
2 Textile and leather
3 Construction materials and furniture
4 Paper
5 Printing

Column
6 Metal
7 Chemical
8 Miscellaneous and rubber
9 Total

M 16   Total Payments to Individuals
by Major Industrial Divisions (millions of dollars)

	(1)	(2)	(3)	(4)	(5)	(6)	(7)	(8)	(9)	(10)
1919	1,664	2,799	1,667	326	652	5,235	901	891	14,138	14,339
1920	1,802	3,178	2,081	426	852	6,045	1,076	1,057	16,520	16,739
1921	1,493	2,552	1,424	319	801	3,436	827	730	11,585	11,760
1922	1,464	2,649	1,637	318	844	3,594	795	800	12,104	12,284
1923	1,615	3,044	2,077	395	919	5,123	951	956	15,083	15,289
1924	1,604	2,716	2,082	373	987	4,890	894	815	14,365	14,578
1925	1,627	2,875	2,187	417	1,053	5,131	1,001	877	15,170	15,396
1926	1,630	2,869	2,306[1]	428	1,141	5,461[2]	1,077	927	15,842	16,143
1927	1,743	3,019	2,180	434	1,180	5,344	1,068	938	15,909	16,296
1928	1,819	2,962	2,115	447	1,204	5,732	1,233	943	16,459	16,934
1929	1,919	3,044	2,156	460	1,324	6,449	1,304	977	17,636	18,236
1930	1,884	2,531	1,747	435	1,323	5,228	1,393	853	15,397	15,972
1931	1,616	2,185	1,171	360	1,125	3,563	1,125	708	11,855	12,314
1932	1,306	1,565	676	271	882	2,207	814	491	8,214	8,550
1933	1,285	1,708	658	287	742	2,143	832	484	8,142	8,428
1934	1,491	2,020	855	347	848	3,083	905	579	10,131	10,453
1934	1,527	2,019	853	346	850	3,083	774	572	10,028	10,350
1935	1,565	2,220	1,001	374	903	3,782	968	682	11,498	11,831
1936	1,770	2,381	1,298	420	997	4,869	1,146	786	13,671	14,015
1937	1,875	2,515	1,527	482	1,091	6,091	1,218	869	15,671	16,047
1938	1,779	2,035	1,168	395	1,023	3,878	1,029	690	11,999	12,339

Column

1 Food and tobacco
2 Textile and leather
3 Construction materials and furniture
4 Paper
5 Printing
6 Metal

Column

7 Chemical
8 Miscellaneous and rubber
9 Total excl. central administrative
  offices (col. 1–8)
10 Total incl. central administrative
  offices

[1] Comparable with the figures for 1927–38. Includes dividends and interest of metal building materials corporations which are excluded in the earlier years. The 1926 figure comparable with those for 1919–25 is $2,268 million.

[2] Comparable with the figures for 1927–38. Excludes dividends and interest of metal building materials corporations which are included in the earlier years. The 1926 figure comparable with those for 1919–25 is $5,498 million.

M 17   Entrepreneurial Net Savings by Major Industrial Divisions (millions of dollars)

	(1)	(2)	(3)	(4)	(5)	(6)	(7)	(8)	(9)
1919	4.6	273	47.7	5.4	21.3	57.3	8.9	18.8	437
1920	—65.6	1.4	52.7	11.1	18.9	26.7	—7.1	10.6	48.8
1921	—86.0	—27.8	—25.5	—3.0	5.2	—21.4	—12.3	—14.0	—184
1922	4.7	84.5	28.9	1.3	22.8	6.3	0.9	6.9	156
1923	17.9	76.7	61.3	2.7	17.5	26.1	1.9	10.0	214
1924	20.9	—6.1	26.7	1.6	16.6	18.2	2.3	6.5	86.6
1925	14.0	37.4	33.0	2.5	18.9	29.6	4.8	11.1	151
1926	16.2	—8.8	23.5	2.6	16.6	26.2	6.9	5.6	88.8
1927	2.5	35.2	5.0	2.7	11.8	13.9	2.4	5.3	78.7
1928	5.4	9.1	10.2	2.0	16.9	20.9	6.0	2.8	73.4
1929	2.5	—2.6	5.4	1.8	17.3	27.4	6.0	1.1	58.8
1930	—7.2	—94.2	—27.6	—0.1	2.7	—1.9	0.7	—11.9	—139
1931	—24.5	—87.9	—40.1	—1.5	—7.1	—18.2	—2.6	—12.8	—194
1932	—32.4	—82.1	—44.4	—2.6	—17.1	—26.1	—3.3	—14.0	—221
1933	8.2	9.9	—15.2	...*	—2.7	—9.3	1.3	—4.5	—12.3
1934	36.8	—6.9	—8.7	0.9	8.0	—7.7	3.8	—1.9	24.3
1934	43.8	—10.3	—9.3	0.8	—0.8	—1.0	3.0	—0.9	25.3
1935	41.9	3.1	—2.2	0.8	3.4	7.4	4.0	3.5	61.8
1936	53.5	25.1	11.3	1.5	7.1	18.7	6.2	6.8	130
1937	11.4	—0.2	12.0	2.0	3.2	22.6	5.1	4.1	60.1
1938	—2.2	—0.2	—9.7	—3.0	—7.7	—9.1	—2.1	1.1	—33.0

* Loss of less than $50,000.

Column		Column	
1	Food and tobacco	6	Metal
2	Textile and leather	7	Chemical
3	Construction materials and furniture	8	Miscellaneous and rubber
4	Paper	9	Total
5	Printing		

M 18 Entrepreneurial Net Income by Major Industrial Divisions (millions of dollars)

	(1)	(2)	(3)	(4)	(5)	(6)	(7)	(8)	(9)
1919	195	417	104	10.2	61.8	102	31.6	37.7	960
1920	111	138	122	17.5	73.4	72.1	15.9	31.6	582
1921	49.4	83.4	20.3	1.8	51.8	7.1	4.4	1.8	220
1922	129	192	77.7	5.4	67.6	32.9	16.7	21.9	544
1923	142	181	109	6.8	61.1	55.9	17.5	25.0	599
1924	138	94.6	75.0	5.5	60.7	48.1	16.7	22.0	461
1925	123	144	82.6	6.5	62.3	58.2	19.3	26.2	522
1926	128	95.2	72.5	6.7	59.6	54.0	20.8	20.7	457
1927	122	137	47.4	6.4	54.5	40.0	16.0	19.7	444
1928	133	105	53.6	5.6	58.6	47.2	19.4	17.9	441
1929	133	93.8	50.1	5.1	57.5	55.0	20.1	16.2	431
1930	110	—12.1	8.4	3.0	41.1	21.1	13.2	1.7	187
1931	75.9	—19.6	—14.4	1.2	25.4	—1.6	8.4	—1.5	73.9
1932	47.7	—34.8	—27.9	—0.5	16.6	—15.1	4.4	—6.1	—15.7
1933	73.7	56.9	—2.0	1.9	28.3	0.7	8.5	2.7	170
1934	102	38.2	6.6	3.0	30.8	3.7	11.2	5.3	200
1934	108	35.3	6.9	3.0	23.9	11.0	10.7	7.3	207
1935	105	54.6	16.2	3.2	31.0	22.2	13.1	13.4	259
1936	132	86.6	36.0	4.5	38.6	38.4	17.1	17.9	371
1937	104	61.2	39.6	5.4	36.7	45.9	16.9	16.3	326
1938	92.7	59.7	16.8	0.4	26.5	13.0	9.8	13.0	231

Column		Column	
1	Food and tobacco	6	Metal
2	Textile and leather	7	Chemical
3	Construction materials and furniture	8	Miscellaneous and rubber
4	Paper	9	Total
5	Printing		

M 19 Corporate Net Savings by Major Industrial Divisions (millions of dollars)

	(1)	(2)	(3)	(4)	(5)	(6)	(7)	(8)	(9)
1919	226	548	178	50.6	54.6	882	120	243	2,305
1920	−62.2	−157	197	106	66.7	592	3.6	166	914
1921	−212	−185	−135	−59.9	14.5	−697	−255	−229	−1,760
1922	100	248	113	19.2	76.2	191	137	127	1,014
1923	111	222	213	27.5	58.3	576	22.1	179	1,410
1924	136	−68.8	71.9	28.6	66.5	341	101	84.2	762
1925	103	83.9	82.5	25.7	53.7	701	155	126	1,332
1926	154	−79.8	52.6[1]	44.4	55.0	550[2]	279	34.0	1,090
1927	80.5	110	−46.1	39.4	32.0	200	2.2	23.3	441
1928	140	−24.7	15.2	26.5	86.8	471	210	14.8	941
1929	116	−49.3	11.0	35.9	66.0	747	299	−18.1	1,209
1930	−49.5	−467	−268	−21.1	−22.1	−428	−286	−195	−1,738
1931	−153	−429	−373	−55.5	−66.4	−1,000	−541	−191	−2,812
1932	−199	−407	−421	−85.4	−100	−1,194	−343	−195	−2,948
1933	−35.2	31.5	−162	−16.4	−28.5	−416	−258	−69.4	−955
1934	90.6	−100	−114	4.9	−25.1	−160	−120	−13.7	−438
1934	31.1	−96.4	−116	3.6	−25.4	−173	−58.7	−12.6	−447
1935	48.1	−31.2	−48.4	1.9	5.6	46.3	−106	8.1	−75.8
1936	46.9	17.0	12.1	12.6	2.9	156	−88.1	16.9	177
1937	−61.1	−88.7	17.5	13.6	−3.7	250	−0.1	1.0	129
1938	−33.9	−96.9	−4.5	−25.4	−11.2	−93.6	−75.3	−5.8	−346

Column

1 Food and tobacco
2 Textile and leather
3 Construction materials and furniture
4 Paper
5 Printing

Column

6 Metal
7 Chemical
8 Miscellaneous and rubber
9 Total

[1] Comparable with the figures for 1927–38. Includes the savings of metal building materials corporations which are excluded in the earlier years. The 1926 figure comparable with those for 1919–25 is $25.3 million.

[2] Comparable with the figures for 1927–38. Excludes the savings of metal building materials corporations which are included in the earlier years. The 1926 figure comparable with those for 1919–25 is $577 million.

M 20 Corporate Net Savings by Minor Industrial Divisions (millions of dollars)

	(1)	(2)	(3)	(4)	(5)	(6)	(7)	(8)	(9)	(10)	(11)	(12)	(13)	(14)
1926	16.3	−95.3	−0.8	−29.4	54.7	27.2	140	220	154	35.4	108	171	2.3	31.7
1927	48.8	50.5	10.7	−80.8	29.8	5.0	19.9	113	40.3	27.0	70.2	−68.0	−10.1	33.4
1928	11.8	−33.0	−3.5	−45.8	43.6	17.4	126	238	29.2	77.5	96.5	114	−27.8	42.6
1929	7.9	−43.1	−14.0	−38.4	29.5	19.8	204	321	151	71.2	128	170	−26.4	8.3
1930	−121	−301	−13.3	−182	−44.6	−41.6	−98.5	−176	−96.3	−57.4	−59.9	−226	−77.3	−118
1931	−142	−246	−40.9	−214	−94.2	−64.9	−244	−497	−166	−92.2	−76.1	−465	−34.1	−157
1932	−152	−220	−34.2	−220	−124	−76.8	−320	−487	−270	−116	−126	−216	−38.7	−156
1933	−9.3	34.8	5.9	86.8	−45.9	−29.5	−119	−232	−49.6	−15.1	−44.6	−194	−6.1	−63.3

Column

1 Wearing apparel
2 Textile fabrics
3 Other leather
4 Lumber
5 Stone, clay, and glass
6 Metal building materials
7 Iron and steel

Column

8 Machinery
9 Motor vehicles
10 Non-ferrous metal
11 Chemical excl. petroleum refining
12 Petroleum refining
13 Rubber tires
14 Miscellaneous

M 21   Total Net Savings by Major Industrial Divisions
(millions of dollars)

	(1)	(2)	(3)	(4)	(5)	(6)	(7)	(8)	(9)
1919	231	822	225	56.0	75.9	940	129	262	2,743
1920	—127	—156	250	117	85.7	619	—3.4	176	963
1921	—298	—212	—160	—62.8	19.8	—719	—267	—243	—1,945
1922	104	332	142	20.5	99.0	198	138	134	1,170
1923	129	299	274	30.2	75.8	602	24.0	189	1,625
1924	157	—74.9	98.6	30.1	83.1	360	104	90.8	849
1925	117	121	115	28.2	72.6	731	160	137	1,484
1926	170	—88.6	76.0 [1]	46.9	71.6	576 [2]	286	39.7	1,179
1927	82.9	145	—41.1	42.2	43.8	214	4.6	28.6	520
1928	146	—15.6	25.4	28.6	103	492	216	17.6	1,014
1929	119	—51.9	16.3	37.7	83.4	775	305	—17.0	1,268
1930	—56.7	—561	—295	—21.2	—19.4	—430	—285	—207	—1,878
1931	—178	—517	—413	—57.1	—73.6	—1,018	—543	—204	—3,007
1932	—231	—489	—465	—88.1	—117	—1,220	—346	—209	—3,170
1933	—27.0	41.4	—177	—16.4	—31.2	—426	—237	—73.8	—948
1934	127	—107	—123	5.8	—17.1	—168	—116	—15.6	—414
1934	74.9	—106	—125	4.4	—26.3	—174	—55.8	—13.4	—422
1935	89.9	—28.1	—50.6	2.6	8.9	53.7	—102	11.6	—14.0
1936	100	42.2	23.4	14.2	10.0	175	—81.9	23.7	307
1937	—49.8	—88.9	29.5	15.7	—0.5	273	5.0	5.1	189
1938	—36.1	—97.2	—14.2	—28.4	—18.9	—102	—77.4	—4.7	—379

Column		Column	
1	Food and tobacco	6	Metal
2	Textile and leather	7	Chemical
3	Construction materials and furniture	8	Miscellaneous and rubber
4	Paper	9	Total
5	Printing		

[1] Comparable with the figures for 1927–38. Includes net savings of metal building materials corporations which are excluded in the earlier years. The 1926 figure comparable with those for 1919–25 is $48..8 million.

[2] Comparable with the figures for 1927–38. Excludes net savings of metal building materials corporations which are included in the earlier years. The 1926 figure comparable with those for 1919–25 is $603 million.

M 22   Wage Earners by Major Industrial Divisions (thousands)

	(1)	(2)	(3)	(4)	(5)	(6)	(7)	(8)	(9)
1919	930	2,041	1,172	209	301	2,895	406	526	8,482
1920	900	2,005	1,172	235	314	2,884	375	525	8,413
1921	781	1,856	948	186	281	1,734	302	396	6,487
1922	803	1,971	1,190	196	293	1,972	328	443	7,198
1923	833	2,141	1,313	221	307	2,520	371	496	8,206
1924	798	1,925	1,284	215	314	2,272	348	459	7,618
1925	800	2,015	1,323	224	314	2,358	360	477	7,873
1926	793	2,024	1,342	232	323	2,458	387	487	8,048
1927	812	2,082	1,252	226	327	2,303	381	481	7,866
1928	835	2,031	1,198	223	332	2,379	375	486	7,863
1929	872	2,097	1,217	234	358	2,687	422	498	8,386
1930	842	1,866	987	223	351	2,218	398	443	7,330
1931	753	1,746	730	194	316	1,696	342	398	6,179
1932	688	1,574	541	178	275	1,345	305	336	5,246
1933	755	1,807	596	196	264	1,452	346	369	5,787
1934	888	1,937	706	228	290	1,882	391	426	6,751
1935	890	2,054	790	235	304	2,085	397	444	7,203
1936	932	2,142	921	242	328	2,378	403	474	7,822
1937	982	2,210	1,028	264	353	2,796	420	513	8,569
1938	935	1,919	845	241	339	2,010	375	419	7,086

Column
1 Food and tobacco
2 Textile and leather.
3 Construction materials and furniture
4 Paper
5 Printing

Column
6 Metal
7 Chemical
8 Miscellaneous and rubber
9 Total

M 23 Wage Earners by Minor Industrial Divisions (thousands)

	(1)	(2)	(3)	(4)	(5)	(6)	(7)	(8)	(9)	(10)	(11)	(12)	(13)	(14)	(15)	(16)	(17)
1919	773	157	229	32.9	172	256	206	50.8	63.8	1,012	202	448	126	57.2	89.6	924	104
1920	746	154	212	28.1	179	274	195	52.5	59.5	1,002	188	449	129	54.3	88.2	910	92.8
1921	631	150	196	23.9	161	245	180	53.7	49.0	911	194	428	121	52.6	77.4	874	71.0
1922	656	146	216	26.5	193	268	168	53.4	55.9	982	214	431	118	56.1	83.2	904	83.8
1923	687	146	240	29.4	194	279	170	54.2	63.3	1,031	241	498	125	64.6	93.8	1,023	85.8
1924	661	136	220	21.0	175	253	158	49.8	57.3	936	218	432	119	62.1	83.7	915	74.9
1925	668	132	222	23.0	186	256	163	53.6	58.3	966	210	471	132	71.7	89.1	974	74.7
1926	668	125	221	23.9	187	262	169	51.5	60.1	979	193	474	129	73.0	100	969	75.2
1927	682	129	221	26.8	190	276	190	53.3	68.4	1,008	197	485	127	74.6	114	999	74.6
1928	709	125	215	26.4	190	275	206	53.6	67.6	1,015	189	438	127	75.5	111	943	73.0
1929	756	116	225	23.7	208	282	222	32.2	68.1	1,064	190	442	130	80.2	118	962	70.7
1930	733	108	210	20.6	190	254	215	29.0	59.6	980	153	372	119	73.8	103	822	63.7
1931	653	99.8	199	15.9	178	242	205	26.6	54.2	922	151	344	109	68.2	96.3	769	55.4
1932	598	90.8	196	15.0	174	221	176	23.5	49.3	855	124	309	93.0	61.2	81.4	670	48.8
1933	668	87.3	207	18.1	189	249	187	22.6	54.9	929	157	394	110	67.0	91.9	821	56.4
1934	794	94.3	220	19.5	204	269	223	23.2	58.8	1,019	151	410	119	72.6	99.7	853	64.1
1935	800	90.5	220	17.2	219	298	255	22.8	63.2	1,097	196	384	125	74.7	108	890	66.8
1936	840	91.4	223	18.7	234	314	277	22.2	73.8	1,163	193	407	114	75.7	117	909	69.2
1937	890	92.2	234	18.4	241	320	268	21.6	75.0	1,179	195	436	116	77.5	134	961	69.5
1938	845	90.2	221	13.7	215	277	242	21.1	66.5	1,057	154	373	90.2	71.2	114	803	58.7

Column

1 Food
2 Tobacco
3 Boots and shoes, other than rubber
4 Boots and shoes, rubber
5 Hosiery and knit goods
6 Men's clothing
7 Women's clothing
8 Millinery
9 Other wearing apparel

Column

10 Total wearing apparel (col. 3–9)
11 Woolen goods
12 Cotton goods
13 Silk and rayon goods
14 Dyeing and finishing
15 Other textile fabrics
16 Total textile fabrics (col. 11–15)
17 Other leather

M 23   Wage Earners by Minor Industrial Divisions (thousands)

(18)	(19)	(20)	(21)	(22)	(23)	(24)	(25)	(26)	(27)	(28)	(29)	(30)	(31)	(32)	(33)	(34)	(35)	
7	295	86.3	74.8	1,024	147	582	1,010	387	127	139	1,665	343	304	301	104	87.1	439	1919
6	304	96.2	94.0	1,011	161	605	1,116	207	129	137	1,590	354	334	277	98.1	81.9	443	1920
2	242	68.1	66.2	819	129	359	671	106	86.3	84.9	949	212	212	221	80.0	55.5	341	1921
8	284	87.3	85.3	1,035	155	461	708	60.2	93.8	105	967	289	253	240	87.8	69.7	373	1922
8	332	99.0	106	1,137	176	577	922	62.3	138	117	1,241	404	297	275	96.0	74.0	422	1923
5	324	92.1	109	1,111	173	533	833	50.7	95.7	109	1,088	376	273	261	87.4	71.6	387	1924
5	336	95.9	115	1,132	190	538	873	50.2	83.2	111	1,118	426	276	271	89.4	81.6	396	1925
1	348	99.6	123	1,142	199	553	949	52.9	87.5	111	1,201	422	281	291	96.0	79.8	407	1926
0	333	94.0	116	1,053	198	526	901	55.0	70.5	108	1,134	369	272	288	93.2	78.3	403	1927
5	304	90.4	113	1,004	194	529	925	43.2	58.5	101	1,128	434	286	287	88.2	83.2	403	1928
9	294	93.5	116	1,013	204	577	1,106	55.1	80.8	104	1,347	447	314	317	104	83.3	415	1929
1	248	78.7	103	822	164	505	905	58.4	72.1	90.9	1,127	322	262	295	102	59.8	383	1930
1	192	66.3	82.6	592	138	384	657	45.3	43.0	71.8	817	285	208	256	85.6	49.2	349	1931
9	139	50.1	55.1	433	108	324	476	36.3	34.5	60.0	607	243	170	226	78.8	45.3	291	1932
4	147	57.1	51.9	481	114	388	505	30.9	32.9	62.4	631	243	188	261	84.2	53.0	316	1933
9	188	67.0	59.4	584	122	476	665	40.6	50.3	75.7	831	341	232	295	95.7	60.8	365	1934
3	201	73.6	67.3	645	144	511	748	44.8	48.3	79.8	920	387	265	301	96.4	57.1	387	1935
3	233	86.2	82.6	755	165	611	855	57.4	66.0	88.0	1,066	405	294	304	99.1	59.3	415	1936
0	262	95.2	92.9	841	186	721	1,011	62.3	87.4	103	1,264	479	331	313	106	63.3	450	1937
0	215	72.3	76.6	694	150	532	741	54.4	57.3	77.9	931	283	263	274	101	47.4	371	1938

Column

18 Lumber
19 Stone, clay, and glass
20 Heating apparatus
21 Other construction materials
22 Total construction materials (col. 18–21)
23 Furniture
24 Iron and steel
25 Machinery proper
26 Shipbuilding
27 Other transportation equipment excl. motor vehicles

Column

28 Hardware
29 Total machinery (col. 25–28)
30 Motor vehicles
31 Non-ferrous metal
32 Chemical excl. petroleum refining
33 Petroleum refining
34 Rubber tires
35 Miscellaneous

MANUFACTURING

M 24 Salaried Employees by Major Industrial Divisions (thousands)

	(1)	(2)	(3)	(4)	(5)	(6)	(7)	(8)	(9)	(10)	(11)
1919	191	191	124	24.3	134	417	110	103	1,296	87.2	1,384
1920	176	181	124	20.6	138	421	99.4	96.4	1,258	84.3	1,343
1921	149	160	106	22.0	134	300	78.1	67.8	1,019	68.5	1,087
1922	158	177	120	23.4	150	303	79.5	66.8	1,080	72.4	1,152
1923	153	197	130	27.4	157	375	90.9	72.5	1,205	81.1	1,286
1924	140	184	135	27.2	170	379	82.8	68.6	1,188	84.3	1,272
1925	135	184	141	28.8	177	361	81.6	74.7	1,186	84.6	1,270
1926	137	179	145	30.6	184	363	87.3	78.7	1,207	108	1,316
1927	143	184	139	30.7	190	374	86.2	79.5	1,229	133	1,362
1928	143	184	135	31.6	191	387	84.8	78.1	1,238	143	1,381
1929	145	184	139	31.6	207	414	93.7	77.8	1,294	208	1,503
1930	141	172	133	31.7	212	410	93.0	77.1	1,271	196	1,468
1931	129	157	108	31.7	188	342	79.7	72.0	1,109	164	1,273
1932	115	134	85.3	27.5	170	285	69.2	64.3	951	134	1,085
1933	120	134	77.4	27.8	154	243	67.5	59.6	884	119	1,003
1934	131	148	88.7	31.0	170	299	77.4	61.8	1,009	129	1,138
1935	137	152	93.4	31.2	170	319	83.7	71.0	1,058	128	1,187
1936	143	154	99.3	32.3	180	344	86.2	72.9	1,113	127	1,241
1937	144	152	107	32.8	204	407	90.3	77.3	1,217	130	1,348
1938	139	134	105	32.2	188	369	85.1	70.5	1,124	121	1,246

Column
1 Food and tobacco
2 Textile and leather
3 Construction materials and furniture
4 Paper
5 Printing
6 Metal
7 Chemical
8 Miscellaneous and rubber
9 Total excl. central administrative offices
10 Central administrative offices
11 Total incl. central administrative offices

MANUFACTURING

M 25 Salaried Employees by Minor Industrial Divisions (thousands)

	(1)	(2)	(3)	(4)	(5)	(6)	(7)	(8)	(9)	(10)	(11)	(12)	(13)	(14)	(15)	(16)	(17)	(18)	(19)
1919	176	14.7	124	54.0	12.1	39.0	34.8	15.8	15.2	104	19.8	70.4	254	47.6	44.9	87.2	23.0	29.8	73.8
1920	162	14.3	117	52.8	10.7	39.7	32.4	18.8	15.2	106	18.6	69.5	257	54.2	39.8	80.3	19.2	23.3	73.1
1921	135	13.8	101	50.4	8.1	35.0	28.9	12.9	12.9	89.8	16.3	44.4	188	33.0	35.1	64.4	13.7	12.5	55.5
1922	141	16.6	116	52.5	9.3	41.4	32.2	14.7	14.2	102	18.0	49.1	186	32.9	34.8	65.4	16.1	12.3	54.5
1923	138	14.7	127	60.7	9.5	41.3	36.8	16.0	16.5	110	20.4	61.5	226	43.8	42.8	72.2	18.7	12.3	60.3
1924	127	13.2	119	55.8	8.5	42.3	37.4	15.4	18.6	113	21.4	57.1	227	50.3	44.3	66.4	16.3	12.0	56.6
1925	125	10.5	116	59.6	8.7	43.0	39.2	16.2	19.1	117	24.2	56.9	213	48.3	43.0	66.9	14.7	14.4	60.3
1926	124	13.1	114	57.2	8.4	43.1	40.6	16.8	21.0	121	24.0	53.7	228	45.0	36.7	71.6	15.7	16.7	62.0
1927	132	11.6	114	61.8	8.3	38.1	40.3	16.3	20.6	115	24.2	56.9	227	44.9	45.5	70.9	15.3	17.2	62.3
1928	133	10.1	115	62.2	8.2	36.9	38.2	15.0	20.6	110	25.2	55.7	239	44.9	47.6	69.4	15.4	15.6	62.5
1929	135	10.2	111	65.5	7.6	38.7	36.9	15.7	21.5	112	26.3	59.6	256	47.0	51.6	75.4	18.3	13.0	64.8
1930	133	8.1	107	57.5	6.8	33.5	35.8	16.0	24.6	109	23.8	63.5	247	47.4	51.6	74.5	18.5	11.5	65.5
1931	124	5.3	95.0	56.1	5.9	25.2	29.4	15.1	19.8	89.6	18.4	51.3	208	38.7	44.5	63.7	16.0	9.1	62.9
1932	110	4.4	82.2	46.9	5.2	20.9	21.7	11.6	15.4	69.7	15.6	43.9	172	30.4	38.4	54.4	14.8	8.3	55.9
1933	116	3.8	81.0	47.4	5.9	18.8	20.5	10.7	10.9	61.0	16.4	39.9	140	29.6	32.8	55.2	12.5	8.4	51.2
1934	126	4.9	87.7	54.6	6.5	20.7	24.9	12.5	12.1	70.2	18.4	44.5	175	39.1	40.3	63.0	14.5	8.5	55.3
1935	132	5.0	90.8	55.3	6.5	22.7	26.5	12.3	13.4	74.9	18.5	50.5	188	37.2	43.1	66.0	17.8	8.6	62.4
1936	137	5.7	91.9	55.7	6.5	24.5	26.8	13.4	14.4	79.2	20.1	62.5	195	43.9	42.8	68.1	18.1	9.8	63.2
1937	138	5.7	89.9	56.2	6.2	25.9	29.8	15.4	15.2	86.3	21.6	74.6	232	50.8	49.7	71.8	18.5	11.0	66.4
1938	134	5.4	80.4	49.0	4.9	24.5	29.5	14.5	16.4	84.6	20.4	66.1	205	48.0	50.2	64.7	20.5	9.5	61.0

Column

1 Food
2 Tobacco
3 Wearing apparel
4 Textile fabrics
5 Other leather
6 Lumber
7 Stone, clay, and glass
8 Heating apparatus
9 Other construction materials
10 Total construction materials (col. 6–9)

Column

11 Furniture
12 Iron and steel
13 Machinery
14 Motor vehicles
15 Non-ferrous metal
16 Chemical excl. petroleum refining
17 Petroleum refining
18 Rubber tires
19 Miscellaneous

MANUFACTURING

M 26 Employees by Major Industrial Divisions (thousands)

	(1)	(2)	(3)	(4)	(5)	(6)	(7)	(8)	(9)	(10)	(11)
1919	1,121	2,232	1,296	233	436	3,313	516	629	9,779	87.2	9,866
1920	1,077	2,186	1,297	255	453	3,305	475	621	9,672	84.3	9,756
1921	931	2,016	1,054	208	416	2,035	380	464	7,506	68.5	7,574
1922	961	2,149	1,311	219	444	2,275	407	510	8,278	72.4	8,351
1923	987	2,338	1,444	248	464	2,895	462	569	9,411	81.1	9,492
1924	938	2,110	1,419	242	484	2,651	431	527	8,806	84.3	8,890
1925	935	2,200	1,464	252	491	2,720	442	552	9,060	84.6	9,144
1926	931	2,203	1,487	262	507	2,822	474	566	9,256	108	9,364
1927	955	2,266	1,391	257	517	2,677	467	560	9,095	133	9,228
1928	979	2,215	1,334	255	524	2,767	460	564	9,101	143	9,245
1929	1,018	2,281	1,356	266	565	3,102	515	576	9,681	208	9,890
1930	983	2,038	1,121	255	563	2,628	491	520	8,602	196	8,799
1931	882	1,903	838	226	505	2,038	422	470	7,288	164	7,452
1932	803	1,709	626	205	445	1,630	374	400	6,197	134	6,331
1933	875	1,941	673	224	418	1,695	413	428	6,672	119	6,791
1934	1,019	2,086	795	259	461	2,181	468	488	7,760	129	7,890
1935	1,028	2,207	883	266	475	2,404	481	515	8,262	128	8,390
1936	1,075	2,296	1,020	274	508	2,723	489	547	8,935	127	9,063
1937	1,127	2,362	1,136	297	557	3,204	510	590	9,786	130	9,917
1938	1,075	2,054	950	273	527	2,380	460	489	8,211	121	8,332

Column
1 Food and tobacco
2 Textile and leather
3 Construction materials and furniture
4 Paper
5 Printing
6 Metal

Column
7 Chemical
8 Miscellaneous and rubber
9 Total excl. central administrative offices
10 Central administrative offices
11 Total incl. central administrative offices

M 27 Employees by Minor Industrial Divisions (thousands)

	(1)	(2)	(3)	(4)	(5)	(6)	(7)	(8)	(9)	(10)	(11)	(12)	(13)	(14)	(15)	(16)	(17)	(18)	(19)
1919	950	171	1,157	978	116	666	330	102	90.0	1,129	167	653	1,919	390	349	388	127	116	512
1920	908	168	1,119	963	103	556	336	115	109	1,117	180	674	1,848	409	374	357	117	105	516
1921	767	163	1,013	924	79.1	477	271	81.1	79.1	908	145	403	1,137	245	247	286	93.8	68.0	396
1922	798	163	1,098	957	93.1	619	317	102	99.4	1,138	173	510	1,154	322	288	303	103	82.0	428
1923	826	161	1,159	1,084	95.3	640	369	115	123	1,247	197	638	1,467	448	340	348	114	86.2	482
1924	788	149	1,055	970	83.4	627	361	107	127	1,224	194	590	1,816	427	317	327	103	83.6	444
1925	793	142	1,082	1,034	83.5	628	375	112	134	1,250	214	595	1,831	474	319	338	104	96.1	456
1926	792	138	1,093	1,026	83.6	614	389	116	144	1,264	223	607	1,429	467	318	362	111	96.5	469
1927	814	140	1,122	1,061	82.8	548	373	110	156	1,169	222	583	1,362	414	318	359	108	95.4	465
1928	843	135	1,129	1,005	81.1	552	342	105	154	1,114	219	585	1,368	479	334	356	103	98.8	465
1929	891	126	1,175	1,027	78.3	547	331	109	157	1,126	230	637	1,603	494	366	393	122	96.2	479
1930	867	116	1,088	879	70.5	425	284	94.7	128	932	188	569	1,375	370	313	370	121	71.4	448
1931	777	105	1,017	825	61.4	276	221	81.4	102	682	156	435	1,025	324	253	320	101	58.3	412
1932	708	95.2	938	717	54.1	210	161	61.8	70.4	503	123	368	779	273	208	281	93.6	53.6	347
1933	784	91.2	1,010	868	62.3	245	168	67.8	62.8	542	131	428	772	273	221	317	96.5	61.3	367
1934	920	99.2	1,107	907	70.7	290	213	79.5	71.5	655	140	520	1,007	380	272	358	110	69.3	418
1935	931	95.6	1,188	945	73.3	336	227	85.9	80.7	720	163	562	1,109	425	308	367	114	65.7	450
1936	978	97.1	1,255	964	75.7	378	260	99.6	97.0	834	185	674	1,262	449	337	372	117	69.1	478
1937	1,029	97.9	1,269	1,017	75.7	416	292	110	108	927	208	795	1,497	530	381	385	125	74.3	516
1938	979	95.6	1,138	852	63.6	354	245	86.6	93.0	779	171	598	1,136	331	314	338	121	56.9	432

Column

1 Food
2 Tobacco
3 Wearing apparel
4 Textile fabrics
5 Other leather
6 Lumber
7 Stone, clay, and glass
8 Heating apparatus
9 Other construction materials
10 Total construction materials (col. 6–9)

Column

11 Furniture
12 Iron and steel
13 Machinery
14 Motor vehicles
15 Non-ferrous metal
16 Chemical excl. petroleum refining
17 Petroleum refining
18 Rubber tires
19 Miscellaneous

M 28 Entrepreneurs by Major Industrial Divisions (thousands)

	(1)	(2)	(3)	(4)	(5)	(6)	(7)	(8)	(9)
1919	80.0	40.2	51.6	1.3	29.5	28.5	6.6	12.9	250
1920	69.0	38.6	42.1	1.3	27.6	25.9	6.1	11.2	221
1921	53.4	35.5	25.8	1.3	22.0	20.9	5.0	8.8	172
1922	50.3	33.9	23.4	1.2	19.9	18.6	4.5	8.3	160
1923	47.6	32.7	20.8	1.0	17.9	16.5	4.1	7.8	148
1924	44.3	30.1	20.8	1.0	18.1	15.0	3.8	7.6	140
1925	40.8	27.8	20.8	1.0	18.2	13.7	3.4	7.3	133
1926	41.5	29.0	19.2	0.9	18.3	13.6	3.4	7.2	133
1927	42.2	30.3	17.1	0.8	18.4	13.5	3.3	7.0	132
1928	43.3	28.4	20.7	0.8	16.6	12.9	3.5	6.9	133
1929	44.5	26.6	23.8	0.7	14.8	12.2	3.6	6.8	133
1930	40.1	23.7	18.9	0.7	14.1	11.4	3.4	6.0	118
1931	35.2	20.2	15.3	0.6	13.2	10.3	3.1	5.2	103
1932	29.6	15.9	10.4	0.5	11.9	8.8	2.6	4.4	84.2
1933	25.7	14.1	7.4	0.4	10.8	7.7	2.3	3.9	72.3
1934	25.2	14.3	9.3	0.5	11.8	8.2	2.6	4.6	76.5
1935	24.7	14.5	11.5	0.6	13.1	8.9	2.8	5.5	81.5
1936	30.1	15.4	12.6	0.6	14.2	9.3	2.9	5.5	90.6
1937	35.2	16.1	13.7	0.7	15.2	9.7	3.0	5.6	99.3
1938	35.2	16.1	13.7	0.7	15.2	9.7	3.0	5.6	99.3

Column
1 Food and tobacco
2 Textile and leather
3 Construction materials and furniture
4 Paper
5 Printing

Column
6 Metal
7 Chemical
8 Miscellaneous and rubber
9 Total

Classification of *Biennial Census of Manufactures* Industries by Industrial Divisions

The basic data for estimates of wages and salaries originating in manufacturing for both major and minor industrial divisions are reported for several hundred industries in the *Biennial Census of Manufactures*. The industrial divisions in our estimates have been formed by grouping numerous Census industries. Since the number of industries in the *Biennial Census of Manufactures* varies somewhat from year to year, the exact grouping into our industrial divisions also is subject to change from one Census year to the next. But as these changes are minor, it was deemed sufficient to give in detail the contents of our industrial divisions, in terms of Census industries, for one Census year alone. The classification below is for 1929, the year in which the Census was especially detailed.

Grouping of *Biennial Census of Manufactures* Industries for 1929 into Our Major and Minor Industrial Divisions

FOOD AND TOBACCO

FOOD
Baking powders, yeast & other leavening compounds
Beverages
Bread & other bakery products
Butter
Canning & preserving: fish, crabs, shrimps, oysters, & clams
Canning & preserving: fruits & vegetables; pickles, jellies, preserves, & sauces
Cereal preparations
Cheese
Chewing gum
Chocolate & cocoa products, excl. confectionery
Coffee & spice, roasting & grinding
Condensed & evaporated milk
Confectionery
Corn sirup, corn sugar, corn oil & starch
Feeds, prepared, for animals & fowls
Flavoring extracts & flavoring sirups
Flour & other grain mill products
Food preparations, n.e.c.
Ice cream

Ice, mfd.
Liquors, vinous
Macaroni, spaghetti, vermicelli, & noodles
Malt
Meat packing, wholesale
Oleomargarine, not made in meat packing establishments
Peanuts, walnuts, & other nuts, processed or shelled
Poultry killing, dressing, & packing, wholesale
Rice cleaning & polishing
Sausage, meat puddings, headcheese, etc., & sausage casings, not made in meat packing establishments
Shortenings (excl. lard) & vegetable cooking oils
Sugar, beet
Sugar, cane, excl. products of refineries
Sugar refining, cane
Vinegar & cider

TOBACCO
Cigars & cigarettes
Tobacco: chewing & smoking, & snuff

TEXTILE AND LEATHER

WEARING APPAREL
Boots and Shoes, other than Rubber
Boot & shoe cut stock, not made in
  boot & shoe factories
Boot & shoe findings. not made in boot
  & shoe factories
Boots & shoes, other than rubber

Boots and Shoes, Rubber
Boots & shoes, rubber

Hosiery and Knit Goods
Knit goods

Men's Clothing
Clothing (except work clothing),
  men's, youths', & boys', n.e.c.
Clothing, men's, buttonholes
Clothing, work (incl. sheep lined and
  blanket lined work coats but excl.
  shirts), men's
Collars, men's
Furnishing goods, men's, n.e.c.
Shirts
Suspenders, garters, & other elastic
  woven goods, made from purchased
  webbing

Women's Clothing
Clothing, women's, n.e.c.
Corsets & allied garments
Feathers, plumes & mfs. thereof
Fur goods
Furs, dressed

Millinery
Millinery

Other Wearing Apparel
Gloves & mittens, cloth or cloth &
  leather combined, made from pur-
  chased fabrics
Gloves & mittens, leather
Handkerchiefs
Hat & cap materials, men's
Hats & caps, except felt & straw, men's
Hats, fur felt
Hats, straw, men's
Hats, wool felt
Pocketbooks, purses, & cardcases
Umbrellas, parasols, & canes

TEXTILE FABRICS
Woolen Goods
Carpets & rugs, rag
Carpets & rugs. wool, other than rag

Felt goods, wool, hair, or jute
Woolen goods
Wool pulling
Wool scouring
Wool shoddy
Worsted goods

Cotton Goods
Cotton goods
Cotton small wares
Linen goods

Silk and Rayon Goods
Silk & rayon mfs.

Dyeing and Finishing
Cloth sponging & refinishing
Dyeing & finishing textiles

Other Textile Fabrics
Artificial & preserved flowers & plants
Artificial leather
Asphalted felt base floor covering
Awnings, tents, sails, & canvas covers
Bags, other than paper, not made in
  textile mills
Belting, other than leather & rubber.
  not made in textile mills
Cordage & twine
Embroideries
Flags & banners
Flax & hemp, dressed
Haircloth
Horse blankets, fly nets, & related
  products
House furnishing goods, n.e.c.
Jute goods
Lace goods
Linoleum
Mats & matting, grass & coir
Mattresses & bed springs, n.e.c.
Nets & seines
Oilcloth
Regalia, badges, & emblems
Trimmings (not made in textile mills)
  & stamped art goods for embroidering
Upholstering materials, n.e.c.
Waste

Other Leather Goods
Leather goods, n.e.c.
Leather: tanned, curried, & finished
Saddlery & harness
Trunks, suitcases, & bags
Whips

CONSTRUCTION MATERIALS AND FURNITURE

CONSTRUCTION MATERIALS
Lumber
Lumber & timber products, n.e.c.
Planing mill products (incl. general
mill work) not made in planing mills
connected with sawmills

Stone, Clay, and Glass
Asbestos products, other than steam
packing & pipe boiler covering
Cement
Clay products (other than pottery) &
non-clay refractories
Concrete products
Crucibles
Emery wheels & other abrasive &
polishing appliances
Glass
Glass products (except mirrors) made
from purchased glass
Graphite, ground & refined
Hones, whetstones, & similar products
Lime
Marble, granite, slate, & other stone
products
Minerals & earths, ground or other-
wise treated
Paving materials: asphalt, tar, crushed
slag, & mixtures
Roofing, built-up & roll; asphalt
shingles; roof coatings, other than
paint

Sand-lime brick
Wall plaster, wall board, insulating
board, & floor composition

Heating Apparatus
Steam & other packing, pipe & boiler
covering, & gaskets, n.e.c.
Steam fittings & steam & hot water
heating apparatus
Stoves and ranges (other than electric)
& warm-air furnaces

Other Construction Materials
Cast-iron pipe
Doors, shutters, & window sash &
frames, metal
Plumbers' supplies, excl. pipe or
vitreous-china sanitary ware
Structural & ornamental iron & steel
work, not made in plants operated in
connection with rolling mills
Window & door screens & weather strip

FURNITURE
Billiard & pool tables, bowling alleys,
& accessories
Furniture, incl. store & office fixtures
Mirror & picture frames
Mirrors, framed & unframed

PAPER

Bags, paper, excl. those made in paper
mills
Boxes, paper, n.e.c.
Cardboard, not made in paper mills
Card cutting & designing
Envelopes
Labels & tags

Paper
Pulp (wood & other fiber)
Paper goods, n.e.c.
Sandpaper, emery paper, & other
abrasive paper & cloth
Wall paper

PRINTING AND PUBLISHING

Bookbinding & blank-book making
Engravers' materials
Engraving (other than steel, copper-
plate, or wood), chasing, etching, &
diesinking
Engraving, steel & copperplate, & plate
printing
Engraving, wood
Lithographing
Photo-engraving, not done in printing
establishments

Printing & publishing, book & job
Printing & publishing, music
Printing & publishing, newspaper &
periodical
Printing materials, excl. type or ink
Stereotyping & electrotyping, not done
in printing establishments
Type-founding

METAL

IRON AND STEEL
Bolts, nuts, washers, & rivets, not made
    in plants operated in connection
    with rolling mills
Forgings, iron & steel, not made in
    plants operated in connection with
    rolling mills
Galvanizing & other coating, not done
    in plants operated in connection
    with rolling mills
Iron & steel: blast furnaces
Iron & steel: steel works & rolling mills
Iron & steel, processed
Nails, spikes, etc., not made in wire
    mills or in plants operated in con-
    nection with rolling mills
Screw-machine products & wood screws
Springs, steel, except wire, not made
    in plants operated in connection with
    rolling mills
Steel barrels, kegs & drums
Tin cans & other tin ware, n.e.c.
Wire, drawn from purchased bars or
    rods
Wirework, n.e.c.
Wrought pipe, welded & heavy riveted,
    not made in plants operated in con-
    nection with rolling mills

MACHINERY
Machinery, Proper
Agricultural implements
Cash registers & adding, calculating, &
    card-tabulating machines
Dairymen's supplies; creamery, cheese-
    factory, & butter factory equipment;
    poultrymen's & apiarists' supplies
Electrical machinery, apparatus, &
    supplies
Engines, turbines, tractors, & water
    wheels
Foundry & machine-shop products,
    n.e.c.
Gas machines, gas meters, & water &
    other liquid meters
Machine-tool accessories & small
    metal-working tools, n.e.c.
Machine tools
Pumps (hand & power) & pumping
    equipment
Refrigerators & refrigerator cabinets,
    exclusive of mechanical refrigerating
    equipment
Refrigerators, mechanical

Scales & balances
Sewing machines & attachments
Textile machinery & parts
Typewriters & parts
Washing machines, wringers, driers, &
    ironing machines, for household use
Windmills & windmill towers

Shipbuilding
Ship & boat building, steel & wooden,
    incl. repair work

*Other Transportation Equipment,
    excl. Motor Vehicles*
Aircraft & parts
Carriage, wagon, sleighs, & sled
    materials
Carriages & sleds, children's
Carriage, wagon, sleigh, & sled
Cars, electric & steam railroad, not
    built in railroad repair shops
Locomotives, not made in railroad
    repair shops
Motorcycles, bicycles, & parts

Hardware
Cutlery (excl. silver & plated cutlery)
    & edge tools
Files
Firearms
Hardware, n.e.c.
Safes & vaults
Saws
Tools, excl. edge tools, machine tools,
    files, or saws

Motor Vehicles
Motor-vehicle bodies & motor-vehicle
    parts
Motor vehicles, excl. motorcycles

Non-Ferrous Metal
Aluminum mfs.
Clocks, clock movements, time-record-
    ing devices, & time stamps
Collapsible tubes
Copper, tin, & sheet-iron work, incl.
    galvanized iron-work, n.e.c.
Electroplating
Fire extinguishers, chemical
Gas & electric fixtures; lamps, lanterns
    & reflectors
Gold leaf & foil

METAL *(concl.)*

Non-Ferrous Metal (concl.)
Gold, silver, & platinum, reducing &
  refining, not from the ore
Jewelry
Needles, pins, hooks & eyes, & snap
  fasteners
Non-ferrous-metal alloys & products,
  excl. aluminum products
Plated ware
Silversmithing & silverware
Smelting & refining, copper
Smelting & refining, lead

Smelting & refining, metals other than
  gold, silver, or platinum, not from
  the ore
Smelting & refining, zinc
Stamped ware, enameled ware, &
  metal stamping, enameling, japan-
  ning, & lacquering
Tin & other foils, excl. gold foil
Watch & clock materials & parts,
  except watch cases
Watch cases
Watches & watch movements

CHEMICAL, INCLUDING PETROLEUM REFINING

CHEMICAL, PROPER
Alcohol, ethyl, & distilled liquors
Ammunition & related products
Blacking, stains, & dressings
Bluing
Bone black, carbon black, & lamp
  black
Candles
Chemicals, n.e.c.
Cleaning & polishing preparations
Compressed & liquefied gases
Druggists' preparations
Drug grinding
Explosives
Fertilizers
Fireworks
Glue & gelatin
Grease & tallow, excl. lubricating
  grease
Ink, printing
Ink, writing
Mucilage, paste, & other adhesives,
  except glue & rubber cement
Oil, cake, & meal, cottonseed

Oil, cake, & meal, linseed
Oils, essential
Oils, n.e.c.
Paints & varnishes
Patent or proprietary medicines &
  compounds
Perfumes, cosmetics, & other toilet
  preparations
Rayon & allied products
Salt
Soap
Tanning materials, natural dyestuffs,
  mordants & assistants, & sizes
Turpentine & rosin
Wood distillation & charcoal manu-
  facture

PETROLEUM REFINING
Coke, excl. gas-house coke
Fuel: briquettes and boulets
Lubricating oils and greases, not made
  in petroleum refineries
Petroleum refining

MISCELLANEOUS AND RUBBER

RUBBER
Rubber tires & inner tubes

MISCELLANEOUS, PROPER
Artists' materials
Baskets & rattan & willow ware, excl.
  furniture
Belting, leather
Boxes, cigar, wooden
Boxes, wooden, except cigar boxes
Brooms
Brushes, other than rubber

Buttons
Carbon paper & inked ribbons
Caskets, coffins, burial cases, & other
  morticians' goods
China firing & decorating, not done in
  potteries
Combs & hairpins, not made from
  metal or rubber
Cooperage
Cork products
Dental goods & equipment
Excelsior

MISCELLANEOUS AND RUBBER (*concl.*)

MISCELLANEOUS, PROPER (*concl.*)
Fancy & miscellaneous articles, n.e.c.
Foundry supplies
Hair work
Hand stamps & stencils & brands
Instruments, professional & scientific
Ivory, shell, & bone work, excl.
  buttons, combs, or hairpins
Jewelry & instrument cases
Lapidary work
Lasts & related products
Matches
Models & patterns, excl. paper
  patterns
Musical instrument parts & materials:
  piano & organ
Musical instruments & parts &
  materials, n.e.c.
Musical instruments: organs
Musical instruments: pianos
Optical goods
Pencils, lead (incl. mechanical)
Pens, fountain & stylographic; pen
  points, gold, steel, & brass

Phonographs
Photographic apparatus & materials
Pipes (tobacco)
Pottery, incl. porcelain ware
Pulp goods
Rubber goods, other than tires, inner
  tubes, & boots & shoes
Signs & advertising novelties
Soda water apparatus
Sporting & athletic goods, excl. fire-
  arms or ammunition
Stationery goods, n.e.c.
Statuary & art goods, factory product
Surgical & orthopedic appliances, incl.
  artificial limbs
Theatrical scenery & stage equipment
Toys (excl. children's wheel goods or
  sleds), games, & playground equip-
  ment
Window shades & fixtures
Wood preserving
Wood turned & shaped & other
  wooden goods, n.e.c.

TABLE M 1

Gross Income by Major Industrial Divisions

The entries for odd years are the sums of value of product figures from the *Biennial Census of Manufactures* and grouped according to our classification. The intercensal year estimates, except that in col. 8 for 1924, are interpolated by corporate data on gross income for 1919–22 and on gross sales for 1922–33 and 1935–37 (*Statistics of Income*). Beginning with 1928 the estimates for the chemical group are the sum of the interpolated figures for petroleum refining and other chemicals. The estimates for 1934 are based on indexes derived by multiplying production indexes (the NBER series are those prepared by F. C. Mills) by wholesale price indexes, weighting in each case by the average of the 1933 and 1935 value of product figures for the specific Census group. The basic series are given in the accompanying table.

Production and Price Indexes Used in Estimating
Value of Product in *1934*

INDUSTRIAL DIVISION	PRODUCTION INDEX	WHOLESALE PRICE INDEX
1 Food & tobacco	FRB food	BLS food
	FRB tobacco	BLS tobacco
2 Textile & leather	FRB textiles	BLS textiles
	FRB leather	BLS leather
3 Construction materials & furniture	(sum of a and b)	
a Lumber	NBER lumber	BLS lumber
b Other construction materials	FRB cement	BLS cement
	FRB glass	BLS glass
4 Paper	NBER paper	BLS paper
5 Printing	*Publishers' Weekly* no. of editions printed	BLS book paper
	FRB newsprint consumption	BLS newsprint paper
6 Metal	NBER steel works & rolling mills	
	NBER blast furnaces	
	NBER cast iron pipe	
	NBER motor vehicles & bodies & parts	BLS metals
	NBER smelting & refining	
	NBER non-ferrous metals & alloys	
7 Chemical	(weighted avg. of a, b, and c)	
a Chemical	[weighted avg. of (1), (2), and (3)]	
1) Fertilizers	NBER fertilizers	
	NBER explosives	
	NBER cottonseed oil and cake	BLS chemicals, drugs, and fertilizers
	NBER wood distillation	
2) Paints & varnishes	NBER paints & varnishes	BLS paints and varnishes
	NBER turpentine & rosin	
3) Rayon	NBER rayon	BLS rayon
b Petroleum	FRB petroleum	BLS petroleum
c Coke	FRB coke	BLS coke
8 Misc. & rubber	FRB rubber tires & tubes	BLS rubber
	FRB total mfg.	BLS all commodities other than farm products

TABLE M 2

Net Income Originating by Major Industrial Divisions

Sum of payments to individuals (Table M 16) and net savings
(Table M 21).

TABLE M 3

Total Payments by Type

Col. 1 Wages: see Table M 5.
Col. 2 Salaries: see Table M 7.
Col. 3 Wages and salaries: sum of col. 1 and 2.
Col. 4 Entrepreneurial withdrawals: see Table M 15.
Col. 5 Dividends: see Table M 11.
Col. 6 Interest: see Table M 13.
Col. 7 Property income: sum of col. 5 and 6.
Col. 8 Total payments: sum of col. 3, 4, and 7.

TABLE M 4

Net Income Originating

Col. 1 Total payments: see Table M 3, col. 8.
Col. 2 Entrepreneurial net savings: see Table M 17.
Col. 3 Corporate net savings: see Table M 19.
Col. 4 Total net savings: sum of col. 2 and 3.
Col. 5 Net income originating: sum of col. 1 and 4.

TABLE M 5

Wages by Major Industrial Divisions

Col. 1 Food and tobacco: see Table M 6, col. 1 and 2.
Col. 2 Textile and leather: see Table M 6, col. 10, 16, and 17.
Col. 3 Construction materials and furniture: see Table M 6, col.
22 and 23.
Col. 4 Paper: the entries for odd years are the sums of wage figures
from the *Biennial Census of Manufactures* and grouped according

to our classification. Interpolation for intercensal years and extrapolation for 1938 are made separately for paper boxes and for other paper and are by BLS payrolls indexes for the specific groups.

Col. 5 Printing: see the notes to col. 4. For 1919–23 interpolation is by the BLS payrolls index for paper and printing; for 1924 and later years, by the weighted average of the BLS payrolls indexes for book and job printing and for newspaper and periodical printing. The weights for 1923–29 are the 1923 Census figures and for 1929 and later years, those given in BLS Bulletin 610.

Col. 6 Metal: see Table M 6, col. 24, 29, 30, and 31.

Col. 7 Chemical: see Table M 6, col. 32 and 33.

Col. 8 Misc. and rubber: see Table M 6, col. 34 and 35.

Col. 9 Total: sum of col. 1–8.

TABLE M 6

Wages by Minor Industrial Divisions

The entries for odd years are the sums of wage figures from the *Biennial Census of Manufactures* and grouped according to our classification. Except when indicated, interpolation for intercensal years and extrapolation for 1938 are by BLS payrolls indexes for the specific groups. When the interpolating series is a weighted average of two or more indexes, the weights used for 1923–29 are those in the *Federal Reserve Bulletin*, November 1929, and for 1929 and later years those in BLS Bulletin 610. The notes below refer only to exceptions to the general procedure just described.

Col. 4 Boots and shoes, rubber: for 1919–23 interpolation is by the BLS rubber boots and shoes index, available since 1923, extrapolated by the index for boots and shoes other than rubber.

Col. 6 Men's clothing: for 1919–31 interpolation is by the weighted average of the BLS indexes for men's clothing and for shirts and collars; for 1931 and later years, by the weighted average of the indexes for men's clothing, shirts and collars, and for men's furnishings.

Col. 8 Millinery: for 1919–26 lace goods and trimmings are included. The estimate for 1926 is extrapolated from 1925 by the same index.

Col. 9 Other wearing apparel: interpolation is by the BLS index for wearing apparel.

Col. 10 Total wearing apparel: sum of col. 3–9.

Col. 11 Woolen goods: for 1919–23 interpolation is by the BLS textile fabrics index; for 1923 and later years, by the weighted average of the BLS indexes for woolen and worsted goods and for carpets and rugs. The 1923 Census figures are used as weights for 1923–29.

Col. 12 Cotton goods: for 1919–31 interpolation is by the BLS index for cotton goods; for 1931 and later years, by the weighted average of the indexes for cotton goods and for cotton smallwares.

Col. 15 Other textile fabrics: interpolation is by the BLS index for textile fabrics.

Col. 16 Total textile fabrics: sum of col. 11–15.

Col. 18 Lumber: for 1919–23 interpolation is by the BLS index for lumber and allied products; for 1923 and later years, by the weighted average of the BLS indexes for sawmills and for millwork.

Col. 19 Stone, clay, and glass: for 1919–23 interpolation is by the BLS index for all stone, clay, and glass products; for 1923–31 by the weighted average of the BLS indexes for brick, tile and terra cotta, cement, and glass. The index for marble, granite, etc., was added for 1931 and later years.

Col. 20 Heating apparatus: for 1919–23 interpolation is by the BLS index for machinery excluding transportation equipment; for 1923 and later years, by the weighted average of the BLS indexes for steam and hot water heating apparatus and steam fittings, and for stoves.

Col. 21 Other construction materials: for 1919–23 interpolation is by the BLS index for iron and steel excluding machinery; for 1923–31 by the weighted average of the BLS indexes for structural and ornamental metal work and for cast iron pipe. The index for plumbers' supplies was added for 1931 and later years.

Col. 22 Total construction materials: sum of col. 18–21.

Col. 24 Iron and steel: for 1919–23 interpolation is by the BLS index for blast furnaces and products excluding machinery; for 1923–31, by the BLS index for blast furnaces, steel works, and rolling mills. For 1931 and later years the latter index is combined with those for bolts, nuts, etc., forgings, tin cans and other tinware, and wirework.

Col. 26 Shipbuilding: total wages in 1920 and 1922 are the product of the estimated number of wage earners (see the notes to Table M 23) and the estimated average wage. The average wage is interpolated between Census years by the weighted average of data for Massachusetts, New York, and Pennsylvania. For the sources of the state data and the weights used in combining them see the notes to Table M 23.

Col. 27 Other transportation equipment excluding motor vehicles: total wages in 1920 and 1922 are the product of the estimated number of wage earners (see the notes to Table M 23) and the estimated average wage. The average wage is interpolated between Census years by the weighted average of data for Pennsylvania transportation equipment, excluding shipbuilding and automobiles (*Report on Productive Industries, Public Utilities and Miscellaneous Statistics*), and New York railroad equipment and car repair shops (*Labor Market Bulletin,* Jan. 1919–Dec. 1920, and the N. Y. Department of Labor Special Bulletin 171). The weights are the employment figures reported in the 1923 *Biennial Census of Manufactures.*

For 1923–31 interpolation is by the weighted average of the BLS indexes for cars and for locomotives; for the years since 1931 the index for aircraft is added. The weights for 1923–29 are the 1923 Census figures.

Col. 28 Hardware: for 1919–31 interpolation is by the BLS index for hardware; for 1931 and later years, by the weighted average of the indexes for hardware, cutlery, and tools.

Col. 29 Total machinery: sum of col. 25–28.

Col. 31 Non-ferrous metal: for 1919–23 interpolation is by the FRB payrolls index for non-ferrous metals as given in the *Federal Reserve Bulletin,* November 1929; for 1923 and later years, by the BLS index for non-ferrous metals estimated for 1926, 1928, and 1930 on the basis of the weighted average of the indexes for brass, bronze, and copper products, and for stamped and enamelled ware.

Col. 32 Chemical excluding petroleum refining: for 1919–23 interpolation is by the FRB payrolls index for chemicals excluding petroleum refining as given in the *Federal Reserve Bulletin,* November 1929; for 1923 and later years, by the BLS index.

Col. 33 Petroleum refining: wages in 1920 and 1922 are interpolated by the sum of wages paid in Pennsylvania (*Report on Productive Industries, Public Utilities and Miscellaneous Statistics*) and Ohio petroleum refining. The Ohio data for 1919, 1920, 1921, and 1923 are from *Industrial and Commercial Ohio,* Vol. II, which reports wages also for all chemicals and allied products for 1921–23. Thẹ 1922 figure for Ohio petroleum refining is obtained by applying to the 1922 wages for all chemicals the average of the 1921 and 1923 ratios of petroleum refining wages to total chemical wages.

Col. 34 Rubber tires: total wages in 1920 and 1922 are interpolated by total wages paid in Ohio, Pennsylvania, and Massachusetts. Sources for Pennsylvania and Massachusetts data are those cited in the notes to Table M 23. Ohio data are reported in *Industrial and Commercial Ohio,* Vol. II, the 1922 figure being estimated on the basis of the average of the 1921 and 1923 ratios of wages for tires and tubes to wages for all rubber goods.

Col. 35 Miscellaneous: interpolation is by the BLS index for all manufacturing.

TABLE M 7

Salaries by Major Industrial Divisions

The entries for odd years, except 1931, are the sums of the salary figures from the *Biennial Census of Manufactures* and grouped according to our classification. The 1919, 1921, and 1923 figures reported are adjusted to exclude salaries paid at central administrative offices. The basis for this adjustment is the ratio, for all manufacturing, of the total excluding central administrative offices to the total including central administrative offices as reported for 1925 in the *Biennial Census of Manufactures.* Salaries, as reported for 1933 in the *Biennial Census of Manufactures,* exclude salaries of principal officers. These we estimate on the basis of the ratio of salaries of principal officers to other salaries as reported in the 1935 *Biennial Census of Manufactures.*

The method of estimating salaries for intercensal years is the same, in general, for all industrial divisions: multiplying the number of salaried workers (see the notes to Table M 24) by the average salary. The average salary is computed for Census years and interpolated for intercensal years by average salary data for Pennsylvania, Ohio, and New York. The Pennsylvania figures are from the Pennsylvania *Report on Productive Industries, Public Utilities and Miscellaneous Statistics* and advance tables for recent years from the Department of Internal Affairs; those for Ohio, from the Department of Industrial Relations. The New York figures are obtained by multiplying by 52 the weekly earnings of office workers as reported in the *Industrial Bulletin*. The specific data used for each industrial branch are indicated below.

Col. 1 Food and tobacco: interpolation of the average salary for food and tobacco combined, 1919–29, is by the average salary for food and tobacco in Pennsylvania and New York. For 1929–38 data for the Ohio food and tobacco groups are added.

Col. 2 Textile and leather: see Table M 8, col. 3–5.

Col. 3 Construction materials and furniture: see Table M 8, col. 10 and 11.

Col. 4 and 5 Paper and printing: salaries for intercensal years are estimated for paper and printing combined. The industrial distribution of the total is based on the ratio of salaries in each industry to total salaries. This ratio, derived for Census years, is interpolated for other years by state data.

Interpolation of the average salary for paper and printing combined, 1919–29, is by the average salary in New York pulp and paper, and printing and paper goods, and Pennsylvania paper boxes, paper bags, cutting and designing, labels and tags, paper (building, printing, stationery, toilet, tissue, wrapping, miscellaneous), pulp goods, sand and emery paper, wall and roofing paper, electroplating, photo-engraving, printing and publishing, stereotyping, and for 1921 and later years, bookbinding. For 1929 and later years Pennsylvania sand and emery paper and electroplating are excluded and typefounding is included; fibreboard and fibre containers are added in 1933. In addition, for 1929–37, Ohio data for paper boxes, paper bags, envelopes, paper, photo-engraving, printing and publishing, stereotyping and electrotyping are included; labels and tags were added in 1933 and later years.

In estimating salaries for each branch of paper and printing Pennsylvania data are used for 1919–29 and 1938, and Pennsylvania and Ohio data for 1929–37; the products are those covered in the average salary series.

Col. 6 Metal: interpolation of the average salary, 1919–29, is by the average salary in the New York metals and machinery group and in the following industries in Pennsylvania classified by the groups used to subdivide total salaries:

Iron and steel: bars, billets, ferro-alloys, ingots, pig iron, plates, sheets, tinplate, wire rods, bolts, nuts, castings, forgings, nails and spikes, springs and wire products

Machinery: refrigerators, washing machines, agricultural implements, elevators, engines, machinery, machine tools, meters, motors, pumps, scales, typewriters, carriages, sleds, bicycles (through 1923 only), cars, railroad engines, and shipbuilding, axes and edge tools, cutlery, files, firearms (through 1921 only), hardware, horseshoes, safes, saws and shovels

Motor vehicles: automobiles, automobile bodies, automobile parts

Non-ferrous: aluminum, babbitt metal, brass and bronze products, cornices, fixtures, needles, silverware, smelting and refining, tinware, enamelware, watches, jewelry and gold and silver leaf and foil, and from 1921 on, copper, zinc, gold, etc.

For 1929 and later years the Pennsylvania iron and steel group has, in addition, rails, axles, chains, frogs and switches, hoops, bands and cotton ties, shafting and shapes, but excludes iron rods. The machinery group, for 1929 and later years, excludes horseshoes, and includes pulleys, apiarists', dairymen's, and poultrymen's supplies, railroad supplies, aircraft and parts, and, since 1933, includes electric refrigerators. Additions to the non-ferrous group, for 1929 and later years, are sheet metal products, n.e.c., welding and brazing, manganese-ferro, magnesia products, lamps, chimneys and reflectors, and electroplating. Data for the following Ohio industries are also included for 1929–37:

Iron and steel: blast furnace products, bolts and nuts, forgings, springs, steel works and rolling mills, tinplate and terneplate, wire, wirework

Machinery: calculating machines, foundry and machine shop products, gas engines and tractors, pumps, agricultural implements, batteries, electric machines, washing machines, clothes wringers, scales and balances, dairymen's supplies, the vehicle group excluding automobiles, cutlery and tools, safes and vaults

Motor vehicles: automobiles and parts

Non-ferrous: total non-ferrous group excluding metal caskets and furniture

Col. 7 Chemical: see Table M 8, col. 16 and 17.

Col. 8 Misc. and rubber: see Table M 8, col. 18 and 19.

Col. 9 Total: sum of col. 1–8.

Col. 10 Central administrative offices: salaries for 1919, 1921, 1923 are estimated on the basis of the 1925 ratio to total salaries, including those at central administrative offices; for 1925, 1929, and 1937 they are reported in the *Biennial Census of Manufactures.* For all other years they are interpolated and extrapolated by total salaries excluding those at central administrative offices.

Col. 11 Total: sum of col. 9 and 10.

TABLE M 8

Salaries by Minor Industrial Divisions

The procedure followed in estimating salaries paid by minor industrial divisions is that described for Table M 7. The specific data used for each minor industrial division are indicated below.

Col. 1 and 2 Food and tobacco: total salaries for food and tobacco (see Table M 7) are distributed on the basis of the ratio of salaries in each industry to total salaries. This ratio, derived for Census years, is interpolated for intervening years by Pennsylvania data for 1919–29 and 1938, and Pennsylvania and Ohio data for 1929–37; the products are those covered in the average salary series.

Col. 3 Wearing apparel: interpolation of the average salary, 1919–29, is by the average salary in Pennsylvania men's clothing, women's clothing, corsets, gloves other than leather, hats and caps, hosiery and knit goods, millinery, neckwear, overalls, shirts, shirtwaists, underwear, leather boots and shoes, sole leather, handkerchiefs, umbrellas and parasols; and in New York furs, leather and rubber, and clothing and millinery. For 1929 and later years data for the following Pennsylvania industries are also included: leather gloves, fur goods, men's furnishing goods, n.e.c., and suspenders. For 1929–37 data for the following Ohio industries are included: men's and women's clothing, hosiery and knit goods, and boots and shoes.

Col. 4 Textile fabrics: interpolation of the average salary, 1919–29, is by the average salary in Pennsylvania awnings, bags, blankets, braids, carpets, cordage and twine, cotton goods and yarn, curtains, dyeing and finishing textiles, flags, haircloth, lace goods, shoddy and waste, silk goods and yarns, woolen yarns, woolen goods, wool pulling, artificial flowers, house furnishings, n.e.c., mattresses and oilcloth, and in New York textiles. For 1929 and later years the Pennsylvania data for plush and velvet are also included, and for 1933 and later years, jute and burlap. Included also for 1929–37 are Ohio data for awnings, flags, banners and regalia, mattresses and pillows, oilcloth and linoleum (through 1933 only), silk and silk goods, woolens and worsteds, and house furnishing goods (through 1933 only).

Col. 5 Other leather: interpolation of the average salary, 1919–29, is by the average salary in Pennsylvania tanned leather, trunks, miscellaneous or unclassified leather goods. For 1929 and later years Pennsylvania data for hides and skins are also included, and for 1929–37 Ohio data for the leather and leather products group, excluding boots and shoes.

Col. 6 Lumber: salaries for intercensal years are estimated for lumber and furniture combined. The industrial distribution of the total is made by the method described in the notes to col. 1 and 2.

Interpolation of the average salary for lumber and furniture combined, 1919–21, is by the average salary in Pennsylvania lumber and timber products, planing mill products, mirrors, billiard tables, frames and furniture, and in New York wood manufactures. In 1921–29 Pennsylvania data on billiard tables and frames are dropped. In 1929 and later years beds and bed springs are included; in 1933 and later years metal furniture; and in 1929–37 Ohio sawmill and planing mill products and furniture, wooden and metal.

Col. 7 Stone, clay, and glass: interpolation of the average salary, 1919–29, is by the average salary in New York stone, clay, and glass products; and in Pennsylvania artificial stone, building brick, cement, crucibles, emery wheels, plate glass, window glass, lime, paving brick, other paving materials, and asbestos products; in 1921 ganister brick is added; in 1927 artificial stone is dropped and concrete added. In 1929 and later years Pennsylvania terra cotta, etc., and wallplaster are included also, and for 1929–37 Ohio roofing materials and the stone, clay, and glass group, excluding pottery.

Col. 8 Heating apparatus: interpolation of the average salary for the entire period is by the average salary for Pennsylvania radiators, stoves, etc. and steam packing; in 1929–37 Ohio stoves and furnaces are included.

Col. 9 Other construction materials: interpolation of the average salary, 1919–29, is by the average salary in Pennsylvania fire escapes, plumbers' supplies, boilers, tanks, etc., cornices, ornamental iron and steel; in 1921 structural iron and steel is added. In 1929 and later years Pennsylvania pipes and tubing, and tinners' and roofers' supplies are included also; and in 1929–37, Ohio steel works and rolling mills, doors and shutters, and boilers and tanks.

Col. 10 Total construction materials: sum of col. 6–9.

Col. 11 Furniture: see the notes to col. 6.

Col. 12, 13, 14, and 15 Iron and steel, machinery, motor vehicles, and non-ferrous metal: see the notes to col. 1 and 2 for the procedure by which total metal salaries (see Table M 7, col. 6) are distributed among the minor industrial divisions.

Col. 16 Chemical excluding petroleum refining: interpolation of the average salary, 1919–29, is by the average salary in the Pennsylvania chemical group, excluding gasoline and lubricating oil, and in the New York chemical group. In 1929–37 the Ohio chemical group, excluding petroleum refining, is added. From the Pennsylvania sample for 1929 and later years data for fuel oil are excluded; and after 1933 kerosene oil also.

Col. 17 Petroleum refining: interpolation of the average salary, 1919–29, is by the average salary in Pennsylvania gasoline, lubricating oil, coke, and manufactured fuel; in 1929–37 the average salary in Ohio petroleum refining is included; and in 1933 and later years, Pennsylvania kerosene oil.

Col. 18 Rubber tires: interpolation of the average salary for 1926 and for 1938 is by the average salary in Pennsylvania rubber tires and tubes. In 1929–37 Ohio rubber tires and tubes are included. The estimates for 1920, 1922, 1924, and 1928 are interpolated along a straight line.

Col. 19 Miscellaneous: interpolation of the average salary, 1919–29, is by the average salary in Pennsylvania glass bottles, cut glass, decorative glass, table glass, leather belting, rubber goods excluding tires and tubes, hose, barrels, bobbins, cigar boxes, packing boxes, pulp goods, models (not paper), wood (turned), professional and scientific instruments, pens, and the miscellaneous group excluding apiarists' supplies, artificial flowers, awnings, asbestos products, coke, flags (when given), manufactured fuel, gold and silver leaf (when given), house furnishings, mattresses, oilcloth, steam packing, shipbuilding, and laundry work (when given). In 1929 and later years the Pennsylvania industries for which the average salary is used are glass bottles and jars, cut glass, decorative glass, glass tableware, miscellaneous glass, leather belting, unclassified rubber, rubber hose, barrels, bobbins, cigar boxes, packing boxes, models and patterns, wood turned and carved, instruments, pens, advertising novelties, artificial limbs, baskets, brooms, brushes, buttons, caskets, cork, curled hair, dental supplies, fancy articles, hair work, hand stamps, musical instruments, optical goods, lead pencils, phonographs, photographic apparatus, pianos, signs, soda water apparatus, sporting and athletic goods, statuary and art goods, surgical appliances, teeth, toys and games, window shades, pottery, stationery goods, n.e.c., and radios. In 1929–37 the Ohio lumber group excluding furniture and sawmill products, metal caskets, the rubber group excluding tires and tubes, pottery, the miscellaneous group excluding agricultural implements, dairymen's supplies, electrical machines, ice, roofing materials, batteries, and washing machines are included.

TABLE M 9

Wages and Salaries by Major Industrial Divisions

Sum for each industrial division of wages (Table M 5) and salaries (Table M 7).

TABLE M 10

Wages and Salaries by Minor Industrial Divisions

Sum for each industrial division of wages (Table M 6) and salaries (Table M 8).

TABLE M 11

Dividends by Major Industrial Divisions

Net dividends are the difference between total dividends paid and dividends received by corporations. Dividends paid, 1922–37, are from *Statistics of Income*. The estimates of dividends paid,

1919–21, are obtained by extrapolating the 1922 figures, and for 1938 by extrapolating the 1937 figures by the dividend payments of a corporate sample for the industry.

Dividends received, 1922–37, are also from *Statistics of Income*. The 1919–21 estimates are made on the assumption that the industrial distribution of dividends received by all corporations, as reported in *Statistics of Income*, is the same as in 1922. The 1938 estimates are assumed to have the same relation to dividends paid as in 1937.

Col. 3 Construction materials and furniture: includes net dividends paid by metal building materials corporations in 1926 and later years. They are covered by *Statistics of Income* in the metals group but are reported separately for 1926–34 in the special tabulation of *Statistics of Income* data. The 1934 estimate, by the classification by business reported for 1933, is obtained by applying to the total for the metals group, by the same classification, the ratio of the metal building materials group to the total for the metals group by the classification by business reported for 1934. The same method is used in estimating later years.

Col. 6 Metal: excluded, in 1926 and later years, are net dividends paid by metal building materials corporations (see the notes to col. 3). Included are net dividends paid by shipbuilding corporations, covered in *Statistics of Income* under construction. The figures are reported for 1926–37 in the special tabulation of *Statistics of Income* data (except for 1934 classified by business reported in 1933, in which case the method outlined in col. 3 for metal building materials corporations is applied). For the years before 1926 the estimates are extrapolated by preliminary estimates obtained by applying, to total dividends paid and received by all construction corporations, the ratio of shipbuilding gross income to total construction gross income. The data are reported in *Statistics of Income*.

Col. 9 Total: sum of col. 1–8.

TABLE M 12

Dividends by Minor Industrial Divisions

The method is outlined in the notes to Table M 11; the source is the special tabulation of *Statistics of Income* data.

TABLE M 13

Interest by Major Industrial Divisions

Net long term interest is the difference between total interest paid on long term debt and interest received on tax-exempt obligations. Total interest, 1922–35, is estimated by applying to the par value of long term debt the average interest rate of the corporate sample for the industry. Long term debt outstanding on December 31, 1921, 1923, 1924, 1926–35 is reported in *Statistics of Income*. The 1921 figures as reported in capital stock tax returns are assumed to be complete; the 1923 and 1924 figures are raised by the ratio of the fair value of the stock of all corporations to the fair value of the stock of corporations reporting assets and liabilities. For 1926–31 the reported figures on par value of long term debt are raised by the 1931 ratio of compiled receipts of all corporations to compiled receipts of corporations reporting assets and liabilities. The compiled receipts ratios for 1932–35 are used to raise the reported figures for the respective years.

Long term debt outstanding on December 31, 1922 and 1925 is interpolated by the corporate sample for the industry, when available, and along a straight line, in other cases. The year-end figures are averaged to give average long term debt outstanding during the year; multiplying these averages by the estimated interest rates yields total long term interest, 1922–35. The estimates of total long term interest, 1919–21 and 1936–38, are extrapolated from 1922 and 1935 respectively by the long term interest paid by the corporate sample for the industry.

Interest received, 1922–37, is interest received on tax-exempt obligations as reported in *Statistics of Income*. The industrial distribution of interest received on tax-exempt obligations by all corporations, as reported in *Statistics of Income* for 1919–21, is assumed to be the same as in 1922. The 1938 estimates are assumed to bear the same relation to total interest paid as in 1937.

Col. 3 Construction materials and furniture: in 1926 and later years net interest paid by metal building materials corporations, covered in *Statistics of Income* in the metals group, is included. Long term debt for these corporations is reported for 1930–33 in the special tabulation of *Statistics of Income* data. For the earlier years it is estimated by applying to the debt of the metals group the ratio of the debt of the metal building materials group to the total debt of the metals group. Basic figures for this ratio are from the special tabulation of *Statistics of Income* data for 1930. The ratio was extrapolated for the earlier years by the ratio of the gross sales of the metal building materials group to the sales of the total metals group. Total interest paid is estimated as outlined above; net interest is obtained by subtracting interest received on tax-exempt obligations (special tabulation of *Statistics of Income* data). For 1934 and later years net interest paid by metal building materials corporations is obtained by applying its ratio to net interest paid by the total metals group in 1933, extrapolated by the ratio of the gross income of the part to the whole, to net interest paid by the total metals group in the respective years.

Col. 6 Metal: excluded in 1926 and later years is net interest paid by metal building materials corporations (see the notes to col. 3). Included is net interest paid by shipbuilding corporations, covered in *Statistics of Income* under construction. Total long term debt is reported for 1930–35 in the special tabulation of the *Statistics of Income* data, and estimated for other years by a procedure similar to that used for dividends paid (see the notes to Table M 11, col. 6). Interest received is reported for 1926–37 in the special tabulation and is estimated for other years by a procedure similar to that used for dividends received.

TABLE M 14

Property Income by Major Industrial Divisions

Sum for each industrial division of net dividends paid (Table M 11) and net interest paid (Table M 13).

TABLE M 15

Entrepreneurial Withdrawals by Major Industrial Divisions

Product of the number of entrepreneurs (see the notes to Table M 28) and the estimated average withdrawal. The methods are similar for most industrial divisions.

Preliminary estimates of total withdrawals are obtained for 1919–37 by applying to the non-corporate value of product (see the notes to Table M 18) two estimated withdrawal ratios. The first, derived from *Statistics of Income,* is the ratio of dividends and officers' compensation to gross sales of corporations. The second is obtained by applying an adjustment factor to the corporate ratio of officers' compensation to gross sales, basic data for which are also from *Statistics of Income.* This adjustment factor is obtained as follows: from the 1931 *Statistics of Income* data for corporations having no net income, gross sales per corporation and the ratio of officers' compensation to gross sales, by asset classes, are derived. The regression line of the ratio of officers' compensation to sales on the logs of sales per corporation is computed and plotted. From this curve are read off ratios of officers' compensation to gross sales per corporation and per individual enterprise of the size indicated in each year by the actual sales per corporation and the value of product per entrepreneur. The relation of this expected ratio for the average individual concern to the expected ratio for the average corporation is the factor by which the ratio of officers' compensation to sales is adjusted to yield the second withdrawal ratio. The second withdrawal ratio for 1934, comparable with that for 1933, is extrapolated from 1933 to 1934 by the ratio of officers' compensation to gross sales of corporations filing unconsolidated returns as reported in *Statistics of Income.*

Both withdrawal ratios were applied to the estimated non-corporate value of product to yield two sets of preliminary estimates of total withdrawals, from which preliminary withdrawals per entrepreneur were computed. The first ratio yielded average levels of withdrawals per entrepreneur which, with a single exception, were in reasonable agreement with those that might be expected from average sales per entrepreneur; the second ratio yielded withdrawal estimates whose year to year changes were in reasonable agreement with the expected relative stability of what are essentially per family expenditure levels. The final estimate of average withdrawals was obtained by applying to the preliminary figure resulting from the second withdrawal ratio the ratio of the sum of the first withdrawal ratio for 1919–33 to the sum of the second for the same period. The average withdrawal for 1938 was extrapolated from 1937 by the average salary in the industry.

Col. 1 Food and tobacco: the above method gives unreasonably low results for the food and tobacco group. For it, the expected ratio of officers' compensation to gross sales for individual concerns of the size given is applied to the average value of product per entrepreneur to obtain a preliminary average withdrawal figure in each year. The average difference (per year) between the sum of the preliminary withdrawal figures and the sum of the average salary figures for 1919–35 is added to the average salary to yield the average withdrawal in each year.

Col. 9 Total: sum of col. 1–8.

TABLE M 16

Total Payments to Individuals by Major Industrial Divisions

Sum for each industrial division of wages and salaries (Table M 9), property income (Table M 14), and entrepreneurial withdrawals (Table M 15).

TABLE M 17

Entrepreneurial Net Savings by Major Industrial Divisions

Difference for each industrial division between entrepreneurial net income (Table M 18) and entrepreneurial withdrawals (Table M 15).

TABLE M 18

Entrepreneurial Net Income by Major Industrial Divisions

Entrepreneurial net income is obtained by multiplying the non-corporate value of product by an estimated net income ratio. The non-corporate value of product for each industrial division is obtained by multiplying the total value of product (see the notes to Table M 1) by the ratio of the non-corporate to the total, derived from the *Biennial Census of Manufactures* for 1919 and 1929, interpolated along a straight line for the intervening years, and kept constant at the 1929 level for all later years.

The net income ratio is, for all industries except food and tobacco, the corporate ratio to gross sales of the sum of statutory net income before taxes, officers' compensation, and estimated long term interest paid. The interest item is our estimate of total long term interest paid. The other items, except gross sales, 1919–21, and officers' compensation, 1925–27, are from *Statistics of Income*. Gross sales, 1919–21, are extrapolated from 1922 by *Statistics of Income* data on gross income. Officers' compensation in 1925, 1926, and 1927 is obtained by interpolating between 1924 and 1928 by corporate sales. The net income ratio is derived for all years, 1919–37. The 1934 ratio comparable with that for 1933 is estimated by applying to the 1933 figure the percentage change from 1933 to 1934 in the net income ratio, excluding the interest item, for unconsolidated returns as derived from the 1934 *Statistics of Income*.

Net income is extrapolated from 1937 to 1938 by corporate net income.

Col. 1 Food and tobacco: the ratio of net to gross income for the various subgroups and their relative weights in the non-corporate value of product made the net income ratio for food and tobacco as derived by the above method seem too low. It was therefore raised 75 per cent, the approximate adjustment based on the share of high net income industries in the total non-corporate value of product and the relation of their net income ratios to the net income ratio for all food and tobacco.

Col. 7 Chemical: since the use of the data for the group as a whole gave undue weight to petroleum refining, the non-corporate value of product is estimated separately for petroleum refining and chemicals proper.

The net income ratios for 1926 and later years for the minor divisions are based on statutory net income, since officers' compensation and long term interest are reported solely for the entire group. As corporate gross sales for the minor divisions are not available before 1926, preliminary estimates of entrepreneurial net profit are derived by applying to statutory net income of corporations the ratio of the non-corporate to the corporate value of product. These estimates are used to extrapolate the 1926 figure back to 1919. To the sum of the resulting partial net income figures for petroleum refining and chemicals proper is added the amount derived by applying, to the non-corporate value of product for the entire chemicals group, the ratio of officers' compensation and long term interest to gross sales.

Col. 9 Total: sum of col. 1–8.

TABLE M 19

Corporate Net Savings by Major Industrial Divisions

Difference between compiled net profits and total dividends paid. Compiled net profits are from *Statistics of Income* for 1922–37. The 1938 figures are extrapolated from 1937 by the corporate samples for each industrial division. Compiled net profits for 1919–21 are the sum of statutory net income after taxes (*Statistics of Income*) and dividends and interest received on government holdings. The latter two items are estimated on the assumption that the industrial distribution of the total as reported in the 1922 *Statistics of Income* applies to the totals reported for 1919, 1920, and 1921. For the derivation of total dividends see the notes to Table M 11.

Col. 3 Construction materials and furniture: included in 1926 and later years are the savings of metal building materials corporations, covered in *Statistics of Income* under the metals group. The basic data are reported in the special tabulation of *Statistics of Income* data for 1926–34. The estimate for 1934 comparable with that for 1933 is obtained by applying to the total savings of the metals group, comparable with that for 1933, the ratio of the savings of metal building materials corporations to the savings of all metals corporations recorded in the special tabulation on the basis of business reported in 1934. For 1935–37 the net profit of metal building materials corporations is obtained by applying to the net profit of metals corporations the ratio of statutory net income (after taxes) of the part to the whole, reported in *Statistics of Income*. From the resulting figure for net profit, total dividends paid are subtracted to yield net savings of metal building materials corporations.

Col. 6 Metal: excluded in 1926 and later years are the net savings of metal building materials corporations (see the notes to col. 3). Included are the net savings of shipbuilding corporations, covered in *Statistics of Income* under construction. Figures for 1926–37 are from the special tabulation of *Statistics of Income* data, except for 1934, classified by business reported in 1933, in which case the procedure outlined for metal building materials corporations in col. 3 is applied. For the years before 1926 shipbuilding corporate profit is the sum of statutory net income and dividends and interest received.

TABLE M 20

Corporate Net Savings by Minor Industrial Divisions

The method is outlined in the notes to Table M 19; the source is the special tabulation of *Statistics of Income* data.

TABLE M 21

Total Net Savings by Major Industrial Divisions

Sum for each industrial division of entrepreneurial savings (Table M 17) and corporate net savings (Table M 19).

TABLE M 22

Wage Earners by Major Industrial Divisions

Col. 1 Food and tobacco: see Table M 23, col. 1 and 2.
Col. 2 Textile and leather: see Table M 23, col. 10, 16, and 17.
Col. 3 Construction materials and furniture: see Table M 23, col. 22 and 23.
Col. 4 Paper: see the notes to Table M 5, col. 4.
Col. 5 Printing: see the notes to Table M 5, col. 5. For 1919–23 interpolation is by the FRB employment index for printing (*Federal Reserve Bulletin*, Nov. 1930).
Col. 6 Metal: see Table M 23, col. 24, 29, 30, and 31.
Col. 7 Chemical: see Table M 23, col. 32 and 33.
Col. 8 Misc. and rubber: see Table M 23, col. 34 and 35.
Col. 9 Total: sum of col. 1–8.

TABLE M 23

Wage Earners by Minor Industrial Divisions

The entries for odd years are the sums of the number of wage earners from the *Biennial Census of Manufactures* and grouped according to our classification. Unless otherwise noted, the interpolating and extrapolating series are identical with respect to coverage and source with those used in estimating total wages.

Col. 11 Woolen goods: for 1919–23 interpolation is by the FRB employment index for woolen and worsted manufactures (*Federal Reserve Bulletin,* Nov. 1930).

Col. 18 Lumber: for 1919–23 interpolation is by the FRB employment index for lumber (*Federal Reserve Bulletin,* Nov. 1930).

Col. 20 Heating apparatus: for 1919–23 interpolation is by the FRB employment index for heating apparatus (*Federal Reserve Bulletin,* Nov. 1930).

Col. 26 Shipbuilding: for 1919–23 interpolation is by the weighted average of employment in shipbuilding in Massachusetts, New York, Ohio, and Pennsylvania, with the 1923 Census employment figures as weights. The Massachusetts data are from the *Annual Report of the Department of Labor and Industries* of that state for the-year ending November 30, 1932. The New York data for 1919 and 1920 are from the *Labor Market Bulletin,* and for 1921–23 from the N. Y. Department of Labor Special Bulletin 171. The Ohio data are from BLS Bulletin 553. The Pennsylvania data are from the *Report on Productive Industries, Public Utilities and Miscellaneous Statistics* for that state.

Col. 27 Other transportation equipment excluding motor vehicles: for 1919–23 interpolation is by the FRB employment index for car building and repairing (*Federal Reserve Bulletin,* Nov. 1930).

Col. 33 Petroleum refining: for 1919–23 interpolation is by the sum of the number of wage earners, reported for Ohio in BLS Bulletin 553, and for Pennsylvania, in the *Report on Productive Industries, Public Utilities and Miscellaneous Statistics.*

Col. 34 Rubber tires: for 1919–23 interpolation is by the sum of the number of wage earners reported for Ohio and Pennsylvania

(see the notes to col. 33 for the sources) and for Massachusetts. The
Massachusetts data are for the rubber group excluding shoes (1931
Annual Report of the Department of Labor and Industries).

TABLE M 24

Salaried Employees by Major Industrial Divisions

The entries for odd years, except 1931, are the sums of the number of salaried employees from the *Biennial Census of Manufactures* and grouped according to our classification. The 1919, 1921,
and 1923 figures reported are adjusted to exclude salaried employees at central administrative offices on the basis of the ratio
for all manufacturing of the total excluding central administrative
offices to the total including central administrative offices as reported in the 1925 Census. Salaried employees reported in the
1933 Census exclude principal officers. These we estimate on the
basis of the ratio of the number of principal salaried officers to
other salaried employees as reported in the 1935 Census.

The method of estimating salaried employees is the same in
general for all industrial divisions. Salaried employees for intercensal years are estimated by multiplying the number of wage
earners (see the notes to Tables M 22 and M 23) by the ratio of
salaried employees to wage earners. The ratio of salaried employees
to wage earners is derived from Census data for odd years and
interpolated for other years by ratios calculated from state data.
The state data are from the sources cited in the notes to Tables
M 7 and M 8 and cover the same industries. However, Ohio employee data are available not only for 1929–37 but also for 1919–28
(BLS Bulletin 553). The Ohio industries covered in each year,
1919–29, are listed below for each industrial division. The data
as reported are monthly employment figures from which annual
averages are taken. The New York data are from the annual
survey which covers office employees in October. The number of
wage earners for New York used here are the difference between
total employees and office employees.

Col. 1 Food and tobacco: interpolation of the ratio of salaried employees to wage earners is by the ratio of salaried employees to
wage earners in Pennsylvania, New York, and Ohio. The Ohio

industries covered in 1919–29 are the food, liquor, and tobacco groups, and manufactured ice.

Col. 2 Textile and leather: see Table M 25, col. 3, 4, and 5.

Col. 3 Construction materials and furniture: see Table M 25, col. 10 and 11.

Col. 4 and 5 Paper and printing: the two are estimated as a whole and then divided. Interpolation of the ratio of salaried employees to wage earners for paper and printing is by the ratio for Pennsylvania, New York, and Ohio. The Ohio industries covered in 1919–29 are paper boxes, other paper including stationery, and printing and publishing.

The total of salaried employees in paper and printing is divided into subgroups on the basis of the percentage distribution in Census years, interpolated by the percentage distribution for Ohio and Pennsylvania, and extrapolated for 1938 by that for Pennsylvania alone.

Col. 6 Metal: interpolation of the ratio of salaried employees to wage earners is by the ratio for Pennsylvania, New York, and Ohio. The Ohio industries covered in 1919–29 are, by subgroups:

Iron and steel: blast furnaces, bolts and nuts, forgings, steel works, tinplate, wire and wirework

Machinery: calculating machines, foundry and machine shop products, gas engines, pumps, electric machines, agricultural implements, dairymen's supplies (after 1921), all vehicles except automobiles, cutlery and safes

Motor vehicles: automobiles and parts

Non-ferrous: metal and metal products other than iron and steel.

Col. 7 Chemical: see Table M 25, col. 16 and 17.

Col. 8 Misc. and rubber: see Table M 25, col. 18 and 19.

Col. 9 Total: sum of col. 1–8.

Col. 10 Central administrative offices: for 1919, 1921, and 1923 estimated by applying, to total salaried employees including those at central administrative offices, reported in the Census, the 1925 ratio of salaried employees at central administrative offices to the total including those at central administrative offices, derived from the 1925 *Biennial Census of Manufactures.* The 1925, 1929, and 1937 figures are reported in the Census. For 1920, 1922, 1924, 1926,

1927, 1928, 1930–36, and 1938 the figures are interpolated and extrapolated by the number of other salaried employees.

Col. 11 Total: sum of col. 9 and 10.

TABLE M 25

Salaried Employees by Minor Industrial Divisions

Estimated by the procedure described for Table M 24. The specific data used for each industrial division are indicated below.

Col. 1 and 2 Food and tobacco: the total of salaried employees in food and tobacco (see Table M 24) is distributed on the basis of ratios of those in food to those in food and tobacco, and of those in tobacco to those in food and tobacco, derived from Census data for odd years and interpolated for other years by the ratios for Pennsylvania and Ohio (for 1938 by the ratio for Pennsylvania alone). The estimates for each subgroup are adjusted by the ratio of the correct total for the group to the sum of the parts.

Col. 3 Wearing apparel: interpolation of the ratio of salaried employees to wage earners is by the ratio for Pennsylvania, New York, and Ohio. The Ohio industries covered in 1919–29 are men's clothing, women's clothing, boots and shoes, and hosiery; in 1923 and later years custom tailoring also is included.

Col. 4 Textile fabrics: interpolation of the ratio of salaried employees to wage earners is by the ratio in Pennsylvania, New York, and Ohio. The Ohio industries covered in 1919–29 are the textile group excluding the industries listed under col. 3.

Col. 5 Other leather: interpolation of the ratio of salaried employees to wage earners is by the ratio for Pennsylvania and Ohio. The Ohio industries covered in 1919–29 are the leather and leather products group excluding boots and shoes.

Col. 6 Lumber: salaried employees are estimated for the entire lumber group, including furniture, and then divided. Interpolation of the ratio of salaried employees to wage earners for the total lumber group is by the ratio for Pennsylvania, New York, and Ohio. The Ohio industries covered in 1919–29 are sawmill and planing mill products and furniture. The division of the total into lumber construction materials and furniture is by the method described for col. 1 and 2.

Col. 7 Stone, clay, and glass: interpolation of the ratio of salaried employees to wage earners is by the ratio for Pennsylvania, New York, and Ohio. The Ohio industries covered in 1919–29 are roofing materials and the stone, clay, and glass group excluding pottery.

Col. 8 Heating apparatus: interpolation of the ratio of salaried employees to wage earners is by the ratio for Pennsylvania and Ohio. The Ohio industries covered in 1919–29 are stoves and furnaces.

Col. 9 Other construction materials: interpolation of the ratio of salaried employees to wage earners is by the ratio for Pennsylvania and Ohio. The Ohio industries covered in 1919–29 are steel works and rolling mills; doors and shutters are added in 1921; boilers and tanks, in 1923.

Col. 10 Total construction materials: sum of col. 6–9.

Col. 11 Furniture: see the notes to col. 6.

Col. 12 Iron and steel: the total of salaried employees in the metals group (Table M 24, col. 6) is divided into iron and steel, machinery, motor vehicles, and non-ferrous metal by the procedure described for col. 1 and 2. The specific Ohio sample industries included under the minor group headings are indicated in the notes to Table M 24, col. 6.

Col. 13 Machinery: see the notes to col. 12.

Col. 14 Motor vehicles: see the notes to col. 12.

Col. 15 Non-ferrous metal: see the notes to col. 12.

Col. 16 Chemical excluding petroleum refining: interpolation of the ratio of salaried employees to wage earners is by the ratio for Pennsylvani ., New York, and Ohio. The Ohio industries covered in 1919–29 are the chemical group excluding petroleum refining.

Col. 17 Petroleum refining: interpolation of the ratio of salaried employees to wage earners is by the ratio for Pennsylvania and Ohio. The Ohio industry covered in 1919–29 is petroleum refining.

Col. 18 Rubber tires: interpolation of the ratio of salaried employees to wage earners is by the ratio for Pennsylvania and Ohio. The Ohio industry covered in 1919–29 is rubber tires and tubes.

Col. 19 Miscellaneous: interpolation of the ratio of salaried employees to wage earners is by the ratio for Pennsylvania and Ohio. The Ohio industries covered in 1919–29 are lumber excluding furniture and sawmill products, rubber excluding tires and tubes, pottery, and the miscellaneous group excluding agricultural implements, dairymen's supplies (for 1921 and later years), electric machines, ice, and roofing materials.

TABLE M 26

Employees by Major Industrial Divisions

Sum for each industrial division of wage earners (Table M 22) and salaried employees (Table M 24).

TABLE M 27

Employees by Minor Industrial Divisions

Sum for each industrial division of wage earners (Table M 23) and salaried employees (Table M 25).

TABLE M 28

Entrepreneurs by Major Industrial Divisions

The entries for odd years, except 1931, are the sums of the number of entrepreneurs from the *Biennial Census of Manufactures* and grouped according to our classification. We assumed that the number was the same in 1938 as in 1937. Interpolation, unless otherwise indicated, is by the number of failures reported in *Dun's Review* annually, the assumption being that a decline in the number of entrepreneurs from Census year to Census year is directly proportional and an increase inversely proportional to failures. The interpolating series for the various industrial divisions are as follows:

Col. 1 Food and tobacco: failures in milling and bakers and liquors and tobacco, 1919–35; in food and tobacco products, 1935–37.

Col. 2 Textiles and leather: failures in woolens and woolen goods, cottons and cotton goods, clothing and millinery, hats, gloves and furs, and leather, shoes and harness, 1919–35; in textiles, leather and furs, 1935–37.

Col. 3 Construction materials and furniture: failures in lumber and lumber products and glass, earthenware, and brick, 1919–37.

Col. 4 Paper: straight-line interpolation except for 1936 when the number of failures in paper and paper products is used.

Col. 5 Printing: failures in printing and engraving, 1919–35; in printing and publishing, 1935–37.

Col. 6 Metal: failures in iron and steel and machinery and tools, 1919–35; in iron and steel, machinery, automobiles, all other transportation equipment and non-ferrous metals, 1935–37.

Col. 7 Chemical: failures in chemicals and drugs and paints and oils, 1919–35; and, in addition, in petroleum, 1935–37.

Col. 8 Misc. and rubber: failures in all other manufacturing, 1919–35; and in rubber goods, general supplies, and all other miscellaneous manufacturing, 1935–37.

Col. 9 Total: sum of col. 1–8.

Construction

TABLES C1–C4

Whenever two entries are made for 1934 the first is comparable with those for preceding years in that the *Statistics of Income* data used are based on the old industrial classification; the second is comparable with those for succeeding years in that the *Statistics of Income* data used are based on the new industrial classification.

Net savings and net income, adjusted, exclude gains and losses from sales of capital assets, 1929–38, and from changes in inventory valuation, 1919–38. Net savings and net income without any specific designation are unadjusted, i.e., include these two types of gain and loss.

C 1 Gross Income (millions of dollars)

	PUBLIC UTILITY (1)	PUBLIC (2)	PRIVATE (3)	TOTAL (4)
1919	368	1,533	3,335	5,237
1920	422	1,042	4,297	5,762
1921	327	1,210	3,786	5,325
1922	419	1,294	4,827	6,540
1923	644	1,2.8	6,030	7,922
1924	723	1,454	6,597	8,775
1925	700	1,646	7,336	9,683
1926	761	1,650	7,893	10,305
1927	781	1,849	7,625	10,256
1928	741	1,923	7,276	9,940
1929	870	1,883	6,880	9,634
1930	983	1,949	4,919	7,852
1931	489	1,666	3,061	5,217
1932	123	895	1,645	2,664
1933	144	760	1,070	1,975
1934	158	1,017	1,277	2,452
1935	144	1,072	1,559	2,777
1936	267	1,328	2,511	4,107
1937	361	1,083	3,282	4,728
1938	374	1,576	2,766	4,717

C 2 Total Payments by Type (millions of dollars)

	WAGES (1)	SALARIES (2)	WAGES & SALARIES (3)	ENTREP. WITHDR. (4)	DIVIDENDS (5)	INTEREST (6)	PROP. INCOME (7)	PAY. TO INDIVIDUALS (8)
1919	1,364	244	1,608	240	15.3	4.0	19.3	1,868
1920	1,954	299	2,253	242	20.9	4.9	25.8	2,522
1921	1,357	293	1,651	223	32.4	7.8	40.2	1,915
1922	1,645	317	1,963	307	30.3	4.4	34.8	2,306
1923	2,560	368	2,929	306	37.5	6.0	43.4	3,279
1924	2,599	431	3,030	397	32.4	7.8	40.2	3,468
1925	2,653	416	3,070	567	58.4	10.4	68.7	3,706
1926	3,042	514	3,556	418	41.3	11.0	52.4	4,027
1927	2,901	496	3,398	419	47.4	11.3	58.7	3,875
1928	2,896	541	3,438	380	51.4	10.0	61.4	3,880
1929	2,923	517	3,441	436	60.0	13.2	73.2	3,950
1930	2,403	541	2,945	397	85.0	15.3	100	3,443
1931	1,577	399	1,976	266	40.1	13.5	53.6	2,296
1932	877	279	1,157	216	19.2	10.3	29.5	1,403
1933	564	200	764	175	18.7	8.6	27.3	967
1934	642	159	801	205	13.0	8.2	21.2	1,028
1934	642	159	801	197	15.2	1.7	16.9	1,016
1935	725	172	897	244	20.7	1.2	22.0	1,163
1936	1,036	225	1,261	347	36.6	1.9	38.4	1,647
1937	1,238	249	1,487	352	42.1	2.0	44.1	1,883
1938	1,057	232	1,290	371	29.4	2.0	31.4	1,693

C 3 Net Income Originating (millions of dollars)

	PAY. TO INDI- VIDUALS	ENTREPRENEURIAL Net savings	Net income	NET SAVINGS Corp.	Total	NET INCOME	NET SAVINGS, ADJUSTED Entrep.	Corp.	Total	NET INCOME, ADJ.
	(1)	(2)	(3)	(4)	(5)	(6)	(7)	(8)	(9)	(10)
1919	1,868	181	421	21.7	202	2,070	141	−6.3	134	2,002
1920	2,522	77.0	319	11.7	88.7	2,610	94.0	26.7	120	2,642
1921	1,915	−26.8	197	−28.5	−55.3	1,859	52.2	17.5	69.7	1,984
1922	2,306	44.4	352	7.8	52.3	2,358	22.4	−1.2	21.3	2,327
1923	3,279	79.7	386	22.7	102	3,382	47.7	9.7	57.4	3,337
1924	3,468	194	592	49.8	244	3,712	209	54.8	264	3,732
1925	3,706	204	771	42.3	246	3,952	208	43.3	251	3,957
1926	4,027	158	576	54.7	212	4,240	175	61.7	236	4,264
1927	3,875	109	528	51.3	160	4,036	159	76.3	235	4,111
1928	3,880	98.1	478	36.4	134	4,014	82.1	28.4	110	3,990
1929	3,950	98.6	534	36.5	135	4,085	89.2	31.6	120	4,071
1930	3,443	−36.9	360	−28.9	−65.7	3,377	24.2	19.5	43.6	3,486
1931	2,296	−101	165	−70.6	−172	2,124	−42.0	−25.6	−67.6	2,228
1932	1,403	−234	−18.1	−126	−361	1,042	−195	−105	−301	1,102
1933	967	−155	19.8	−84.1	−240	727	−167	−89.1	−256	711
1934	1,028	−91.0	114	−43.5	−134	894	−127	−55.9	−183	844
1934	1,016	−110	86.9	−49.2	−160	856	−146	−62.1	−208	808
1935	1,163	−70.2	174	−30.8	−101	1,062	−80.3	−34.7	−115	1,048
1936	1,647	−41.7	305	−21.8	−63.6	1,584	−60.5	−29.6	−90.1	1,557
1937	1,883	−23.0	329	−18.8	−41.8	1,842	−59.3	−32.5	−91.8	1,792
1938	1,693	−1.3	370	−0.7	−2.1	1,691	8.4	1.6	9.9	1,703

C 4   Persons Engaged (thousands)

| | EMPLOYEES | | | | ENTREPRENEURS |
| | Wage earners | Wage earners * | Salaried | Total | |
	(1)	(2)	(3)	(4)	(5)
1919	923	1,105	107	1,031	96.7
1920	1,057	1,264	114	1,171	90.3
1921	953	1,119	111	1,064	74.4
1922	1,217	1,403	127	1,345	108
1923	1,475	1,668	138	1,614	126
1924	1,507	1,671	156	1,663	159
1925	1,502	1,633	147	1,649	193
1926	1,723	1,836	176	1,900	174
1927	1,603	1,674	166	1,769	166
1928	1,596	1,631	181	1,778	163
1929	1,650	1,650	176	1,827	167
1930	1,429		181	1,610	167
1931	1,022		157	1,179	149
1932	650		133	784	121
1933	542		114	656	108
1934	613		109	723	120
1935	676		103	780	134
1936	867		118	985	151
1937	927		119	1,047	151
1938	821		119	941	151

* Second estimate.

TABLE C 1

Gross Income

Col. 1 Public utility: the estimate for 1929 is derived from the *Census of the Construction Industry* by approximating total public and public utility construction and subtracting estimated public construction (see the notes to col. 2).

In estimating total public and public utility construction in 1929 it is assumed that, in addition to work directly specified as such, all construction, other than building, is either public or public utility. Total public and public utility contract work is estimated for companies with annual volumes of $25,000 and over by applying to their reported total the ratio of public and public utility contracts, distributed by class, to the total so distributed. The procedure by which public and public utility contracts for firms with volumes under $25,000 were estimated was as follows:

A Total volume, under $25,000 (Census)
B Volume by class, under $25,000 (Census)
C Building volume by class, under $25,000 (Census)
D Ratio of C to B
E Estimated total building volume, under $25,000 (A × D)
F Estimated public and public utility building, under $25,000 (E × ratio for firms with volumes over $25,000)
G Other public and public utility construction, under $25,000 (A — E)
H Total public and public utility construction, under $25,000 (F + G)

Total public and public utility construction in 1929 is then a sum of the business of companies with volumes of over and under $25,000. As already indicated, from this total we subtract estimated public construction to derive public utility construction in 1929. The resulting estimate of public utility contract construction in 1929 is extrapolated to 1919 by the estimate of total new public utility construction as reported in *Construction Activity in the United States, 1915–37* (Bureau of Foreign and Domestic Commerce, 1938). The extrapolation from 1929 forward is by the F. W. Dodge Corporation series of public utility contracts for 37 states as collected by the National Bureau of Economic Research (Business Cycle Study).

Col. 2 Public: the 1929 estimate is computed from the *Census of the Construction Industry*, which shows a breakdown, by class of

ownership, of total construction including subcontracts let. It is
assumed that the ratio of public to the total as derived from this
breakdown applies to the total done by general contractors or
directly for owners and that all public contract construction is
covered in the Census. The extrapolation to 1919 is by the estimates of total new public construction as reported in *Construction
Activity in the United States, 1915–37*. The extrapolation forward
is by the F. W. Dodge Corporation series of public contracts for
37 states as collected by the National Bureau of Economic Research
(Business Cycle Study).

Col. 3 Private: includes, in addition to all construction other than
public and public utility, contract work for oil and gas wells which
is, primarily, the drilling of wells.

From *Construction Activity in the United States, 1915–37*, and
from articles in the *Survey of Current Business*, August 1939 and
February 1940, new non-farm residential construction, new non-
residential construction, public residential construction, and farm
construction are taken. Additions, alterations, and repairs done
under contract are estimated by applying, to the volume of new
construction, the ratio of additions, etc. to new construction reported in *Commodity Flow and Capital Formation,* Vol. One. It is
assumed that all new non-farm and one-half of farm construction
is done under contract.

From *Mineral Resources* and the *Minerals Yearbook* the number of wells drilled in each state and year is taken. The average cost
in each state in 1935 is given in *Petroleum and Natural Gas Production* (National Research Project on Reemployment Opportunities and Recent Changes in Industrial Techniques). The average
for gas wells is assumed to be two-thirds of that for oil wells (see
Federal Reserve Bulletin, Sept. 1939, p. 734). The 1935 prices are
used for each year in the period. Multiplying the number of wells
drilled by the average cost in 1935 yields an estimate of total cost.
The resulting series is used to interpolate between the 1919 figure
for total contract work as reported for oil and gas wells in the
Census of Mines and Quarries and the 1935 figure, computed as the
product of the average cost and the number of wells drilled on contract, the latter obtained by letter from the Bureau of Mines. Extrapolation from 1935 forward is also by this index.

Col. 4 Total: sum of col. 1–3.

TABLE C 2

Total Payments by Type

Col. 1 Wages: wages, 1919–29, are computed separately for public, public utility, and private construction by applying to the estimated value of construction (see the notes to Table C 1) the ratio of wages to the value of construction. The ratio for each group for 1929 is derived from the *Census of the Construction Industry*, Table 8, the classification of the establishments into the three groups being that used in *Commodity Flow and Capital Formation*, Vol. One.

Each of the three 1929 ratios is extrapolated from 1929 to 1919 by an index derived as follows. First, the ratio of total wages to total construction is calculated for 1929 from the Census, and estimated for 1921 by applying to the 1929 ratio the percentage change from 1921 to 1929 in the corresponding ratio for Ohio and Pennsylvania. Second, the ratios for 1919 and 1920 are extrapolated from 1921 by the ratio from Ohio and Pennsylvania data. Third, the ratio is interpolated for 1922–28 by the weighted average of the ratio of wages to the value of construction in Ohio and the ratio of compensation for maintenance of way and structures to total expense excluding depreciation on the maintenance of way and structures of Class I railroads, the Ohio ratio being given a weight of 2 and the railroad ratio, 1. The Ohio wage figures are from the *Monthly Labor Review*, February 1934. The Ohio construction figure for 1929 is based on wages reported in the *Monthly Labor Review* and the ratio of wages to the value of construction, derived from the *Census of the Construction Industry*. It is estimated for the years before 1929 by applying to the estimated total for the country the ratio of Ohio to the total, computed for 1929 and extrapolated to 1925 by the ratio of the Ohio value to the value for 37 states, and to 1919 by the ratio to the value for 27 states, as reported by the F. W. Dodge Corporation. The railroad data are from *Statistics of Railways*. The compensation for the first 6 months of 1921 for maintenance of way and structures is estimated on the basis of the ratio to total compensation in the second 6 months. It is adjusted to exclude switching and terminal companies by applying the 1922 ratio of the compensation for maintenance excluding switching and terminal companies to that including switching and terminal companies. Pennsylvania data on wages and construction are from the *Report on Productive Industries, Public Utilities and Miscellaneous Statistics.*

For the years after 1929 wages are the product of the estimated number of wage earners (see the notes to Table C 4) and the average wage. The average wage is computed from data in the *Census of the Construction Industry* for 1929 and 1935 and interpolated by a five-state average wage index compiled by the Bureau of Foreign and Domestic Commerce, National Income Division. The 1936–38 figures are extrapolated from 1935 by the BLS average wage index. The 1929 average wage is obtained by dividing wages by the number of wage earners as reported in the Census for companies with annual volumes of business of $25,000 or over. The 1935 average wage is based on various data in the *Census of the Construction Industry.* The steps are as follows:

a) From the partial data in the 1935 Census on the annual payroll and average number of wage earners at the construction site the average annual wage is computed.

b) For these same establishments the average annual wage based on the October figures is also computed because establishments giving occupational data report for one week in October. The ratios of the average annual wage and the number of wage earners, estimated on the basis of the annual figures, to those estimated on the basis of the October figures, are derived.

c) From Census occupational data the average wage of wage earners at the construction site is derived and adjusted by the ratio described above, as is the number of wage earners. The product of the two gives the estimated wages of wage earners at the construction site for establishments that report occupational data.

d) The latter item is subtracted from the total payroll of establishments that report occupational data to leave wages of other wage earners and salaries.

e) This total is divided into other wages and salaries on the basis of the relation between such wages and salaries as were reported for one week in October.

f) From estimated wages and salaries for establishments that report occupational data the ratio of each to the value of construction is computed. For these same establishments the ratio of total payrolls to value of construction also is computed, as is the corresponding ratio for all establishments.

g) The proportion of the latter to the former is applied to the ratios of wages to value and of salaries to value for establishments that report occupational data, thus yielding the final ratios of wages to value and salaries to value.

h) These ratios, applied to estimated construction in 1935, give total wages and total salaries paid.

i) The establishments that report occupational data indicate also their average number of employees during the year, from which is deducted the average number of wage earners at the construction site, estimated by the procedure outlined in step c.

j) The balance is divided into the number of other wage earners and of salaried employees on the basis of the number of each reported for one week.

k) Total wage earners in establishments that report occupational data are then derived and the ratio to total employees, for these same establishments, computed.

l) This ratio is applied to the total of employees reported by all establishments in the Census to give the number of wage earners covered by the Census.

m) Salaried employees are obtained by subtraction.

n) Average wage and salary figures are then computed.

Col. 2 Salaries: salaries, 1919–29, are estimated by applying to wages the ratio of salaries to wages, computed from the *Census of the Construction Industry* for 1929, and extrapolated to 1922 by Ohio and Wisconsin data. Ohio data on wages and salaries (from the *Monthly Labor Review,* Feb. 1934), and Wisconsin data on the percentage change from month to month (from the *Wisconsin Labor Market*) are converted into indexes and weighted indexes of wages and of salaries in Ohio and Wisconsin are derived with the 1929 salary figures reported in the *Census of the Construction Industry* as weights. The ratio of the index of salaries to the index of wages is used to extrapolate to 1922 the 1929 ratio of salaries to wages. To 1921 the extrapolation is by Ohio data; from 1921 to 1919, by the ratio of salaries to wages in Pennsylvania and Ohio. The sources are cited in the notes to col. 1.

For the years after 1929 salaries are the product of the estimated number of salaried employees (see the notes to Table C 4) and the average salary. The average salary is derived from the *Census of the Construction Industry* for 1929 and 1935 (see the notes to col. 1) and interpolated by the average salary in Ohio. This index is used also to extrapolate the 1935 figure through 1936–38.

Col. 3 Wages and salaries: sum of col. 1 and 2.

Col. 4 Entrepreneurial withdrawals: withdrawals in 1929 are based on data reported in the *Census of the Construction Industry* and are the sum of the withdrawals of proprietors of establishments with volumes of $25,000 or over and of smaller concerns.

The estimate of proprietors of establishments doing business of $25,000 or over covered by the Census is based on the number of proprietors reported, raised by the ratio of the total number of establishments to the number reporting proprietorship. The ratio of this number to the number of all proprietors covered by the Census is applied to our estimate of the number of all proprietors (see the notes to Table C 4) to yield the final estimate of proprietors of establishments with volumes of $25,000 or over. The number of proprietors of establishments with volumes of less than $25,000 covered by the Census is estimated by subtracting from the total number of such establishments the difference between the number of corporations covered in *Statistics of Income* and those reported in the Census as having volumes of $25,000 or over.

Proprietors' withdrawals are estimated by multiplying the average withdrawal by the estimated number. From data in the 1929 *Census of the Construction Industry* for establishments reporting proprietors' withdrawals, the per capita withdrawal of proprietors of establishments with annual volumes of $25,000 or over is computed. The average withdrawal for proprietors of smaller concerns is estimated as the average of the per capita wage and salary.

Estimates of total withdrawals for other years are extrapolated from 1929 by a preliminary estimate, obtained by applying to estimated non-corporate business the withdrawal ratio as derived from *Statistics of Income* corporate data.

Non-corporate business in 1929 is estimated by applying to estimated total contract construction the ratio of non-corporate to the total as derived from the Census. The non-corporate volume covered by the Census is the difference between the total reported and the estimated corporate. Corporate business is the sum of that for corporations with volumes of $25,000 or over (reported in the Census) and that for smaller corporations, estimated by multiplying their number by the average volume. The number of corporations with volumes under $25,000 is estimated by subtracting from the total (excluding shipbuilding) reported in *Statistics of Income* the number with volumes of $25,000 or over reported in the Census. Average value of construction for the smaller corporations is assumed to be the same as that derived from the Census for all establishments with volumes under $25,000. The ratio of the corporate to the total value reported in the Census is computed and the ratio for the non-corporate derived.

Non-corporate business for the years before 1929 is the difference between the total and the estimated corporate. The 1929 figure for the latter is extrapolated through 1922 by corporate gross sales, and through 1919 by corporate gross income as recorded in *Statistics of Income* (excluding shipbuilding). For the years after 1929 non-corporate is estimated on the basis of the ratio of non-corporate to total. For 1935 this ratio is computed from Census data for all establishments reporting on proprietors. Interpolated along a straight line between 1929 and 1935, it is kept constant thereafter.

The withdrawal ratio is the ratio of officers' compensation and total dividends paid to corporate gross sales. These items are reported in *Statistics of Income* 1919–37 except for (a) officers' compensation in 1925–27, which is estimated on the basis of the ratio to gross sales in 1924 and 1928, interpolated along a straight line and applied to gross sales in the respective years; (b) gross sales in 1919–21, extrapolated from 1922 by gross income as reported; (c) dividends paid in 1919–21, for the derivation of which, see the notes to col. 5. Shipbuilding is excluded throughout (see the notes to Table M 15). The estimate for 1938 is extrapolated from 1937 by corporate data for the industry.

Col. 5 Dividends: net dividends paid are the difference between total dividends paid and dividends received by corporations. Dividends paid, 1922–37, are from *Statistics of Income,* adjusted to exclude shipbuilding (see the notes to Table M 11, col. 6). The estimates of total dividends in 1919–21 are based on the ratio of dividends to corporate business in 1922, extrapolated to 1919 by the ratio of dividends to gross sales for lumber, stone, clay, and glass, and metal manufacturing corporations. The estimate for 1938 is extrapolated from 1937 by the corporate sample for the industry.

Dividends received, 1922–37, also are from *Statistics of Income* (excluding shipbuilding). Dividends received, 1919–21, are assumed to be the same percentage of total dividends received by all corporations (reported in *Statistics of Income*) as in 1922. Dividends received in 1938 are assumed to be the same percentage of dividends paid as in 1937.

Col. 6 Interest: net long term interest is the difference between total interest paid on long term debt and interest received on tax-exempt obligations. Total interest, 1922–35, is estimated by applying to the par value of long term debt the average interest rate for the industry, a rate based on sample corporate data for the industry.

Long term debt outstanding on December 31, 1921, 1923, 1924, and 1926–36 is from *Statistics of Income* (see the notes to Table M 13, col. 6). The 1921 figure, as reported in capital stock tax returns, is assumed to be complete. The 1923 and 1924 figures are raised by the ratio of the fair value of the stock of all corporations to the fair value of the stock of corporations reporting assets and liabilities. Long term debt reported for 1926–31 is raised by the 1931 ratio of compiled receipts of all corporations to compiled receipts of corporations reporting assets and liabilities. The compiled receipts ratios for 1932–35 are used to raise reported long term debt for the respective years. Estimates of long term debt outstanding on December 31, 1922 and 1925 are interpolated along a straight line. The December 31, 1934 figure, comparable with that reported for 1933, is estimated by applying to the 1933 figure the percentage change from 1933 to 1934 in the debt of sample corporations in the industry. The same percentage change is used to estimate the December 31, 1933 figure comparable with that reported for December 31, 1934.

The year-end figures are averaged to give the amount outstanding during the year; multiplying these averages by the estimated interest rate yields total long term interest, 1922–36. Estimates for

1919–21 are based on the ratio to total interest paid, computed for 1922, and extrapolated by the ratio for the lumber and stone, clay, and glass manufacturing groups. Total interest paid is reported in *Statistics of Income*. The 1936–38 estimates of total long term interest paid are extrapolated from 1935 by the corporate sample for the industry.

Interest received, 1922–37, is that received on tax-exempt obligations as reported in *Statistics of Income* (excluding shipbuilding). Receipts, 1919–21, are assumed to be the same percentage of interest received on tax-exempt obligations by all corporations (reported in *Statistics of Income*) as in 1922. Receipts in 1938 are assumed to bear the same relation to interest payments as in 1937.

Col. 7 Property income: sum of col. 5 and 6.

Col. 8 Total payments to individuals: sum of col. 3, 4, and 7.

TABLE C 3

Net Income Originating

Col. 1 Total payments to individuals: see Table C 2, col. 8.

Col. 2 Entrepreneurial net savings: estimates for 1919–37 are obtained by applying to non-corporate business (see the notes to Table C 2, col. 4) an estimated savings ratio—the corporate ratio to gross sales of statutory net income before taxes (from *Statistics of Income*) plus long term interest paid minus dividends paid. For total dividends and interest see the notes to Table C 2, col. 5 and 6. The 1934 ratio, comparable with the 1933, is based on the 1933 figure and the percentage change from 1933 to 1934 in the ratio for corporations filing unconsolidated returns (including shipbuilding). Interest is for all corporations, since the debt of those filing unconsolidated returns comprises over 90 per cent of the total. The 1938 estimate is extrapolated from 1937 by corporate savings (see the notes to col. 4).

Col. 3 Entrepreneurial net income: sum of col. 4, Table C 2, and col. 2, above.

Col. 4 Corporate net savings: difference between compiled net profits after taxes and total dividends paid. Compiled net profits (excluding shipbuilding) are from *Statistics of Income* for 1922–37 (see the notes to Table M 19, col. 6); for 1919–21 they are the sum of statutory net income after taxes (reported in *Statistics of Income*) and dividends and tax-exempt interest received. For the latter items and for total dividends paid see the notes to Table C 2, col. 5 and 6. The 1938 estimate is extrapolated from 1937 by the corporate sample for the industry.

Col. 5 Total net savings: sum of col. 2 and 4.

Col. 6 Net income originating: sum of col. 1 and 5.

TABLE C 4

Persons Engaged

Col. 1 Wage earners: for 1919–29 the number of wage earners is obtained by dividing the estimated total wage bill by the average wage paid (see the notes to Table C 2, col. 1, for the derivation of total wages for the period and the average wage in 1929).

Two estimates of the average wage are used, yielding two estimates of wage earners, which are averaged to obtain the final estimate. The first estimate of the average wage is extrapolated from 1929 by a weighted index of Ohio, Wisconsin, and Illinois data for 1923–29. This is extrapolated through 1922 by Ohio and Wisconsin data, through 1921 by Ohio data, and beyond 1921 by Ohio and Pennsylvania data. The sources of the Ohio and Pennsylvania data are cited in the notes to Table C 2, col. 1. Indexes of the average wage in Wisconsin and Illinois are derived from month to month changes in employment and payrolls as recorded in the *Wisconsin Labor Market* and the *Illinois Labor Bulletin*. The data are combined on the basis of the average number of wage earners in each state in 1929 as reported in the Census. The second estimate of the average wage also is extrapolated from 1929 but by the average wage of the construction materials manufacturing group.

The number of wage earners in 1929 and 1935 is described in the notes to Table C 2, col. 1. The 1930–34 and 1936–38 figures are averages of two estimates: one is interpolated and extrapolated by the six-state employment index compiled by the Bureau of Foreign and Domestic Commerce, National Income Division; the other by the ratio of the number of wage earners to value of construction in constant prices. The index of construction costs by which the value of construction is converted to constant prices is given in *Commodity Flow and Capital Formation*, Vol. One.

Col. 2 Wage earners, second estimate: the estimate of wage earners gainfully occupied in 1920 is based on the percentage change from 1920 to 1930 in the number in representative occupations reported for those years in the 1930 *Census of Population,* Vol. V. The percentage change is estimated for brick and stone masons and tile layers; carpenters; building painters, glaziers and varnishers; paper hangers; cement finishers; plasterers; plumbers and gas and steam fitters; roofers and slaters; building structural iron workers; carpenters' apprentices; plumbers' apprentices; building operatives; and building, general, and not specified laborers. The number attached in 1929 is by straight line interpolation between the Census dates. The percentage change from 1920 to 1929 is derived and applied to the number engaged in 1929 to yield the number engaged in 1920. The estimates for 1919 and 1921–28 are extrapolated and interpolated by the number of wage earners, derived as explained in the notes to col. 1.

Col. 3 Salaried employees: the method is similar to that used for wage earners, 1919–29. Only one estimate, however, that based on state data, is made. The 1929 average salary is extrapolated for 1922–28 by the weighted index of Ohio and Wisconsin data; for 1921, of Ohio data; and for 1920 and 1919, of Ohio and Pennsylvania data. Sources of these state materials are cited in the notes to col. 1.

For 1929 and 1935 estimates are derived as outlined in the notes to Table C 2, col. 1. For 1930–34 and 1936–38 the estimates are the product of the number of wage earners and the ratio of salaried employees to wage earners. This ratio, computed from Census data for 1929 and 1935, is interpolated by the ratio for Ohio. The Ohio figure is used also to extrapolate the ratio from 1935 through 1936–1938.

Col. 4 Total employees: sum of col. 1 and 3.

Col. 5 Entrepreneurs: the number of entrepreneurs in 1930 is from the 1930 *Census of Population,* Vol. V, Ch. 7, and comprises builders and building contractors, building owners, operators and proprietors, and contractors, builders, and proprietors in road, street, and bridge construction. The number of entrepreneurs is assumed to be the same in 1929 as in 1930. The 1920 figure is based on the percentage change from 1920 to 1930 as derived from data in the 1930 *Census of Population,* Vol. V, for builders and building contractors. Extrapolation for 1919 and interpolation between 1920 and 1929 are by non-corporate business (see the notes to Table C 2, col. 4); the average value per entrepreneur is computed for 1920 and 1929 and interpolated along a straight line. The average value per entrepreneur in 1919 is assumed to be the same as in 1920.

The 1935 estimate of entrepreneurs is based on non-corporate business (see the notes to Table C 2, col. 4) and the average value per entrepreneur derived from the *Census of the Construction Industry* for all establishments reporting information on proprietors and the value of construction of these establishments. Interpolation between 1930 and 1935 is by the number of construction establishments in Ohio. The number of entrepreneurs is assumed to be the same in 1936–38 as in 1935. The Ohio data for 1930–34 are from various issues of the *Monthly Labor Review* and for later years were received by letter from the Ohio Department of Industrial Relations, Division of Labor Statistics.

Transportation and Other Public Utilities

TABLES P 1 – P 2 1

Whenever two entries are made for 1934 the first is comparable with those for preceding years in that the *Statistics of Income* data used are based on the old industrial classification; the second is comparable with those for succeeding years in that the *Statistics of Income* data used are based on the new industrial classification.

Net savings and net income, adjusted, exclude gains and losses from sales of capital assets, 1929–38, and from changes in inventory valuation, 1919–38. Net savings and net income without any specific designation are unadjusted, i.e., include these two types of gain and loss.

P 1   Gross Income by Minor Industrial Divisions
(millions of dollars)

	ELEC. LIGHT & POWER	MFD. GAS	ELEC. LIGHT & POWER, & MFD. GAS	STEAM RR., PULLMAN, & RWY. EXPRESS	PIPE LINES	STREET RWY.	TELE-PHONE	TELE-GRAPH	COM-MUNICA-TION (7 + 8)
	(1)	(2)	(3)	(4)	(5)	(6)	(7)	(8)	(9)
1919	619	326	945	5,470		790			
1920	758	366	1,125	6,577	103	910	556	153	709
1921	835	405	1,240	5,884	116	916	609	136	746
1922	936	418	1,355	5,896	128	925	665	138	803
1923	1,130	443	1,573	6,653	131	954	721	144	866
1924	1,217	445	1,663	6,272	146	957	779	146	925
1925	1,365	448	1,813	6,481	164	972	865	162	1,028
1926	1,516	490	2,007	6,745	173	996	950	165	1,116
1927	1,680	509	2,189	6,479	195	992	1,023	170	1,194
1928	1,809	509	2,318	6,441	222	977	1,109	177	1,286
1929	1,969	505	2,475	6,600	251	989	1,210	188	1,398
1930	2,026	491	2,517	5,565	237	905	1,239	169	1,409
1931	2,015	461	2,476	4,426	222	791	1,200	142	1,343
1932	1,854	437	2,291	3,302	211	652	1,061	110	1,171
1933	1,788	403	2,192	3,256	217	600	967	109	1,076
1934	1,861	406	2,268	3,447	199	629	979	126	1,106
1935	1,938	402	2,340	3,639	197	634	1,033	130	1,164
1936	2,066	406	2,473	4,267	219	678	1,117	143	1,261
1937	2,198	409	2,608	4,398	248	685	1,180	146	1,326
1938	2,185	412	2,598	3,783	228	650	1,181	133	1,315

P 2   Net Income Originating by Major Industrial Divisions (millions of dollars)

	ELEC. LIGHT & POWER, & MFD. GAS	STEAM RR., PULLMAN, & RWY. EXPRESS	OTHER TRANSP. *	COMMUNICA-TION	TOTAL	TOTAL, ADJ.
	(1)	(2)	(3)	(4)	(5)	(6)
1919	424	3,938	1,182	417	5,963	5,958
1920	495	4,845	1,492	514	7,348	7,418
1921	524	3,815	1,215	532	6,087	6,337
1922	620	3,823	1,192	578	6,215	6,209
1923	778	4,438	1,239	637	7,094	7,057
1924	879	4,266	1,255	678	7,080	7,094
1925	1,070	4,487	1,259	747	7,564	7,600
1926	1,153	4,667	1,262	804	7,888	7,905
1927	1,253	4,465	1,229	841	7,790	7,829
1928	1,399	4,482	1,262	901	8,045	8,030
1929	1,563	4,653	1,305	988	8,511	8,505
1930	1,638	3,870	1,167	948	7,625	7,744
1931	1,533	2,973	987	871	6,366	6,452
1932	1,304	2,089	752	719	4,867	4,911
1933	1,187	2,121	757	654	4,720	4,709
1934	1,181	2,231	777	685	4,876	4,802
1934	1,114	2,231	803	685	4,833	4,764
1935	1,185	2,410	848	705	5,149	5,165
1936	1,271	2,810	977	784	5,843	5,834
1937	1,370	2,927	1,071	842	6,212	6,141
1938	1,316	2,415	957	823	5,513	5,529

* Pipe lines, street railways, and water transportation.

P 3   Net Income Originating by Minor Industrial Divisions
(millions of dollars)

	ELEC. LIGHT & POWER	MFD GAS	PIPE LINES	STREET RWY.	WATER TRANSP	TELE-PHONE	TELE-GRAPH
	(1)	(2)	(3)	(4)	(5)	(6)	(7)
1919	325	99.2	66.0	527	588	325	92.0
1920	381	113	92.3	629	771	397	117
1921	410	113	69.0	610	535	433	99.8
1922	502	117	97.4	625	469	472	106
1923	635	143	106	648	485	524	113
1924	730	149	112	627	515	565	112
1925	817	252	133	618	507	622	125
1926	944	209	128	602	531	668	136
1927	1,032	221	150	585	494	700	140
1928	1,204	194	175	567	519	757	144
1929	1,379	184	204	566	534	840	148
1930	1,452	186	176	523	468	822	126
1931	1,378	154	169	442	375	762	109
1932	1,145	159	134	338	280	645	74.0
1933	1,029	158	148	302	306	577	76.4
1934	1,012	169	129	315	332	601	83.6
1934	980	133	129	324	349	601	83.6
1935	1,041	143	126	324	398	619	86.0
1936	1,111	160	143	344	488	688	95.9
1937	1,188	181	162	344	563	744	98.3
1938	1,142	173	134	338	484	739	83.9

P 4　Total Payments by Type (millions of dollars)

	WAGES¹ (1)	SALARIES¹ (2)	WAGES & SALARIES² (3)	PENSIONS WAGES & COMP. FOR INJURY³ (4)	EMPL. COMP. (5)	ENTREP. WITHDR.⁴ (6)	DIVIDENDS (7)	INTEREST (8)	PROP. INCOME (9)	PAY. TO INDIVIDUALS (10)
1919	2,465	675	1,415	53.8	4,607	10.8	530	679	1,210	5,828
1920	3,216	864	1,866	78.9	6,026	8.9	486	714	1,201	7,257
1921	2,270	818	1,665	52.5	4,807	7.2	455	751	1,207	6,021
1922	2,117	836	1,619	55.9	4,630	7.7	566	784	1,350	5,988
1923	2,475	870	1,755	66.1	5,166	7.5	637	855	1,473	6,647
1924	2,290	871	1,871	67.1	5,100	5.8	707	893	1,601	6,707
1925	2,325	877	1,889	79.3	5,170	5.9	816	926	1,742	6,919
1926	2,405	893	2,000	85.5	5,382	5.7	866	945	1,811	7,199
1927	2,346	899	2,006	86.8	5,339	5.1	1,058	965	2,003	7,347
1928	2,264	891	2,070	81.5	5,308	5.2	1,047	985	2,031	7,344
1929	2,331	895	2,177	84.9	5,489	5.7	1,287	970	2,257	7,752
1930	1,997	852	2,139	85.7	5,073	5.7	1,426	990	2,416	7,495
1931	1,583	749	1,897	79.9	4,310	4.2	1,234	1,023	2,257	6,572
1932	1,122	564	1,545	70.7	3,302	3.0	974	1,065	2,039	5,345
1933	1,059	501	1,410	69.4	3,040	2.5	830	1,038	1,869	4,912
1934	1,164	524	1,508	74.2	3,272	2.6	833	984	1,818	5,093
1934	1,164	524	1,508	74.2	3,272	2.6	818	954	1,773	5,048
1935	1,269	562	1,593	82.7	3,508	2.9	932	923	1,855	5,366
1936	1,469	586	1,739	81.7	3,877	3.0	865	882	1,747	5,627
1937	1,588	628	1,940	123	4,280	3.2	948	854	1,803	6,087
1938	1,353	607	1,877	99.7	3,937	2.9	849	812	1,661	5,601

¹ Steam railroads, Pullman, and railway express.
² Other transportation, electric light and power and manufactured gas, and communication.
³ Steam railroads, Pullman, and railway express, and communication.
⁴ Electric light and power, and water transportation.

P 5　Net Income Originating (millions of dollars)

	PAY. TO INDIVIDUALS (1)	ENTREPRENEURIAL Net savings (2)	Net income (3)	NET SAVINGS Corp. (4)	Total (5)	NET INCOME (6)	NET SAVINGS, ADJUSTED Entrep. (7)	Corp. (8)	Total (9)	NET INCOME, ADJ. (10)
1919	5,828	8.2	19.0	126	134	5,963	8.2	121	129	5,958
1920	7,257	5.4	14.4	105	111	7,348	5.4	175	181	7,418
1921	6,021	−1.6	5.6	67.6	66.0	6,087	−1.6	317	316	6,337
1922	5,988	−0.5	7.2	227	226	6,215	−0.5	221	220	6,209
1923	6,647	0.1	7.4	447	447	7,094	0.1	410	410	7,057
1924	6,707	0.6	6.4	372	372	7,080	0.6	386	386	7,094
1925	6,919	1.1	6.9	644	645	7,564	1.1	680	681	7,600
1926	7,199	1.3	7.0	687	688	7,888	1.3	704	705	7,905
1927	7,347	0.2	5.2	442	442	7,790	0.2	481	481	7,829
1928	7,344	1.2	6.4	699	700	8,045	1.2	684	685	8,030
1929	7,752	2.0	7.8	756	758	8,511	1.9	751	753	8,505
1930	7,495	−1.8	3.9	151	129	7,625	−1.6	250	249	7,744
1931	6,572	−2.6	1.6	−205	−205	6,366	−1.8	−118	−120	6,452
1932	5,345	−2.3	0.7	−475	−477	4,867	−2.1	−431	−433	4,911
1933	4,912	−0.4	2.1	−190	−191	4,720	0.4	−203	−202	4,709
1934	5,093	0.4	3.0	−217	−217	4,876	0.3	−291	−291	4,802
1934	5,048	1.5	4.0	−215	−214	4,833	1.5	−285	−284	4,764
1935	5,366	0.8	3.7	−218	−217	5,149	2.7	−203	−200	5,165
1936	5,627	3.8	6.8	211	215	5,843	3.6	203	206	5,854
1937	6,087	4.5	7.7	120	125	6,212	4.5	50.6	54.9	6,141
1938	5,601	0.4	3.3	−89.1	−88.7	5,513	0.4	−72.8	−72.5	5,529

* Water transportation, and electric light and power.

P 6 Wages and Salaries by Major Industrial Divisions
(millions of dollars)

	ELEC. LIGHT & POWER, & MFD. GAS	STEAM RR., PULLMAN, & RWY. EXPRESS		OTHER TRANSP.*	COMMUNI- CATION	TOTAL
		Wages	Salaries			
	(1)	(2)	(3)	(4)	(5)	(6)
1919	217	2,463	675	891	307	4,553
1920	260	3,216	864	1,201	404	5,947
1921	263	2,270	818	999	402	4,754
1922	274	2,117	836	919	426	4,574
1923	345	2,473	870	939	471	5,099
1924	399	2,290	871	968	503	5,033
1925	415	2,325	877	947	527	5,091
1926	464	2,403	893	969	567	5,297
1927	479	2,346	899	940	585	5,252
1928	508	2,264	891	936	625	5,227
1929	533	2,331	895	942	701	5,404
1930	552	1,997	852	877	709	4,989
1931	506	1,583	749	756	635	4,230
1932	424	1,122	564	591	529	3,231
1933	392	1,059	501	559	457	2,970
1934	424	1,164	524	599	484	3,198
1935	442	1,269	562	656	494	3,425
1936	480	1,469	586	724	534	3,796
1937	536	1,588	628	801	602	4,157
1938	531	1,353	607	738	607	3,837

* Pipe lines, street railways, and water transportation.

P 7 Wages and Salaries by Minor Industrial Divisions (millions of dollars)

	ELEC. LIGHT & POWER (1)	MFD. GAS (2)	PIPE LINES (3)	STREET RWY. (4)	WATER TRANSP. (5)	TELEPHONE (6)	TELEGRAPH (7)
1919	140	77.2	26.9	368	495	236	70.6
1920	176	84.2	33.8	464	703	309	94.5
1921	185	78.1	31.7	438	529	322	80.0
1922	194	80.0	33.8	433	451	347	78.3
1923	252	93.7	37.8	439	462	385	86.0
1924	297	101	33.7	440	494	417	86.4
1925	310	105	37.5	433	475	434	92.4
1926	355	108	41.3	433	494	461	105
1927	367	112	49.0	420	471	483	102
1928	400	107	48.2	406	481	520	104
1929	432	100	50.1	411	480	585	116
1930	453	98.9	43.9	382	451	591	118
1931	422	83.8	39.5	335	380	531	103
1932	350	74.1	30.6	270	290	453	75.8
1933	317	75.5	30.2	227	301	390	67.1
1934	344	79.4	35.2	238	326	407	76.9
1935	361	81.3	37.6	236	382	418	76.4
1936	395	85.4	41.5	241	441	451	83.1
1937	446	90.4	48.8	242	510	511	90.4
1938	441	90.1	46.1	236	455	524	82.8

P 8 Pensions and Compensation for Injury, and Total Employee Compensation (millions of dollars)

	PENSIONS AND COMPENSATION FOR INJURY					EMPLOYEE COMPENSATION				
	Steam rr., Pull., & rwy. express (1)	Telephone (2)	Telegraph (3)	Commun. (4)	Total (5)	Elec. light & power, & mfd. gas (6)	Steam rr., Pull., & rwy. express (7)	Other transp.* (8)	Commun. (9)	Total (10)
1919	49.0	3.1	1.6	4.7	53.8	217	3,187	891	311	4,607
1920	72.7	4.2	2.0	6.2	78.9	260	4,154	1,201	410	6,026
1921	46.3	4.1	2.1	6.2	52.5	263	3,135	999	408	4,807
1922	48.9	4.8	2.2	7.0	55.9	274	3,003	919	433	4,630
1923	59.0	4.7	2.4	7.1	66.1	345	3,402	939	478	5,166
1924	60.0	4.6	2.5	7.1	67.1	399	3,221	968	510	5,100
1925	71.6	5.1	2.7	7.8	79.3	415	3,273	947	534	5,170
1926	77.1	5.7	2.7	8.4	85.5	464	3,374	969	575	5,382
1927	78.1	6.0	2.7	8.7	86.8	479	3,324	940	594	5,339
1928	72.1	6.8	2.7	9.5	81.5	508	3,228	936	634	5,308
1929	74.3	7.6	3.0	10.6	84.9	533	3,301	942	712	5,489
1930	72.6	7.8	3.2	11.0	85.7	552	2,922	877	720	5,073
1931	67.5	9.1	3.5	12.6	79.9	506	2,400	756	647	4,310
1932	59.0	8.6	3.1	11.7	70.7	424	1,745	591	541	3,302
1933	58.2	8.4	2.8	11.2	69.4	392	1,618	559	468	3,040
1934	61.5	9.8	2.8	12.6	74.2	424	1,750	599	497	3,272
1935	69.2	10.6	2.9	13.5	82.7	442	1,900	656	508	3,508
1936	67.2	11.4	3.1	14.5	81.7	480	2,123	724	549	3,877
1937	107	12.8	3.2	16.0	123	536	2,324	801	618	4,280
1938	85.0	13.4	3.3	16.7	99.7	531	2,043	738	624	3,937

* Pipe lines, street railways, and water transportation.

P 9   Dividends by Major Industrial Divisions (millions of dollars)

	ELEC. LIGHT & POWER, & MFD. GAS	STEAM RR., PULLMAN, & RWY. EXPRESS	OTHER TRANSP.*	COMMUNI- CATION	TOTAL
	(1)	(2)	(3)	(4)	(5)
1919	110	256	112	51.0	530
1920	108	236	91.5	51.0	486
1921	109	208	79.8	58.3	455
1922	145	225	125	70.7	566
1923	194	252	109	80.7	637
1924	233	277	104	91.7	707
1925	280	294	138	102	816
1926	294	337	122	111	866
1927	331	436	146	124	1,038
1928	395	366	156	129	1,047
1929	514	438	189	144	1,287
1930	604	441	211	169	1,426
1931	609	257	181	186	1,234
1932	520	76.8	186	190	974
1933	432	76.0	133	188	830
1934	397	126	122	188	833
1934	370	126	133	188	818
1935	395	127	223	186	932
1936	400	146	150	167	865
1937	454	165	160	167	948
1938	436	83.7	152	176	849

* Pipe lines, street railways, and water transportation.

P 10   Dividends by Minor Industrial Divisions
(millions of dollars)

	ELEC. LIGHT & POWER	MFD. GAS	PIPE LINES	STREET RWY.	WATER TRANSP.	TELE-PHONE	TELE-GRAPH
	(1)	(2)	(3)	(4)	(5)	(6)	(7)
1919	68.2	42.0	31.4	35.5	45.8	40.9	10.1
1920	71.3	36.9	30.8	32.3	28.4	40.9	10.1
1921	83.7	25.6	34.7	27.1	18.1	48.4	9.9
1922	123	22.3	60.2	47.0	18.2	60.2	9.8
1923	161	33.4	43.8	47.2	18.7	71.4	9.3
1924	185	48.2	44.5	46.9	13.5	82.3	9.4
1925	230	50.4	72.7	47.7	18.2	93.3	9.5
1926	246	48.0	55.1	46.9	20.4	99.9	11.8
1927	284	46.7	80.2	46.8	19.4	111	12.8
1928	356	38.7	87.5	46.4	22.2	116	13.2
1929	448	66.3	112	48.7	28.6	123	20.8
1930	536	67.9	142	39.1	30.2	147	22.0
1931	532	76.9	133	28.5	19.7	176	10.0
1932	432	87.5	156	17.9	12.4	187	3.1
1933	372	60.7	110	15.2	8.0	188	0.3
1934	328	68.8	91.0	19.2	11.9	187	0.5
1934	328	42.1	91.0	19.2	23.7	187	0.5
1935	331	64.0	144	21.6	56.5	181	4.3
1936	344	56.4	78.5	31.4	40.1	167	0.3
1937	395	59.5	81.9	38.0	41.0	165	2.2
1938	377	59.0	85.8	36.2	30.2	177	—0.8

P 11   Interest by Major Industrial Divisions (millions of dollars)

	ELEC. LIGHT & POWER, & MFD. GAS	STEAM RR., PULLMAN, & RWY. EXPRESS	OTHER TRANSP.*	COMMUNI- CATION	TOTAL
	(1)	(2)	(3)	(4)	(5)
1919	92.8	436	121	28.9	679
1920	100	461	120	32.3	714
1921	111	476	127	35.7	751
1922	129	488	137	29.0	784
1923	157	500	146	31.8	835
1924	193	525	141	33.4	893
1925	217	536	131	41.0	926
1926	253	527	123	41.3	945
1927	277	528	117	41.5	965
1928	307	527	112	36.5	983
1929	318	509	109	33.2	970
1930	339	518	102	29.5	990
1931	370	517	102	32.9	1,023
1932	404	510	105	46.3	1,065
1933	407	476	103	50.7	1,038
1934	386	447	99.7	51.3	984
1934	344	447	111	51.3	954
1935	347	416	111	47.7	923
1936	332	397	110	42.2	882
1937	311	393	107	42.6	854
1938	312	350	106	42.9	812

* Pipe lines, street railways, and water transportation.

P 12 Interest by Minor Industrial Divisions (millions of dollars)

	ELEC. LIGHT & POWER	MFD. GAS	PIPE LINES	STREET RWY.	WATER TRANSP.	TELE-PHONE	TELE-GRAPH
	(1)	(2)	(3)	(4)	(5)	(6)	(7)
1919	78.3	14.5	0.1	111	9.8	30.5	—1.6
1920	85.1	15.7	0.1	110	9.5	33.8	—1.5
1921	93.0	18.5	0.1	117	10.2	35.6	0.1
1922	114	15.1	0.3	127	9.8	29.0	..*
1923	142	15.0	0.4	135	10.1	31.6	0.2
1924	177	16.6	0.4	131	9.2	32.9	0.4
1925	195	21.7	0.4	123	7.7	40.3	0.7
1926	227	26.1	0.3	114	7.9	40.4	0.9
1927	249	28.3	0.4	109	7.9	39.9	1.6
1928	271	35.8	0.5	105	6.7	34.6	1.9
1929	280	37.5	0.5	103	6.1	31.1	2.1
1930	293	46.6	0.3	95.7	6.5	26.3	3.2
1931	321	49.0	2.1	92.3	8.4	29.3	3.6
1932	343	60.7	2.8	91.1	11.0	42.5	3.9
1933	343	64.5	3.8	87.7	12.4	46.5	4.2
1934	327	59.1	2.9	85.0	11.8	46.7	4.5
1934	295	49.0	2.9	93.7	14.8	46.7	4.5
1935	299	48.8	3.7	92.4	15.2	42.7	5.0
1936	285	46.6	3.3	92.3	15.1	37.2	4.9
1937	266	44.4	2.7	89.2	15.2	37.9	4.7
1938	268	43.7	1.9	88.9	15.9	38.5	4.4

* — $45,000.

P 13   Property Income by Major Industrial Divisions
(millions of dollars)

	ELEC. LIGHT & POWER, & MFD. GAS	STEAM RR., PULLMAN, & RWY. EXPRESS	OTHER TRANSP.*	COMMUNI-CATION	TOTAL
	(1)	(2)	(3)	(4)	(5)
1919	203	692	234	80.0	1,210
1920	208	697	211	83.3	1,201
1921	220	685	207	94.0	1,207
1922	274	714	262	99.0	1,350
1923	351	753	256	112	1,473
1924	427	802	246	125	1,601
1925	497	831	270	143	1,742
1926	547	864	245	153	1,811
1927	608	965	264	165	2,003
1928	702	894	268	166	2,031
1929	832	948	299	177	2,257
1930	944	960	314	198	2,416
1931	979	774	284	219	2,257
1932	924	586	291	237	2,039
1933	840	552	237	239	1,869
1934	783	573	221	239	1,818
1934	715	573	245	239	1,773
1935	743	544	334	233	1,855
1936	732	543	260	209	1,747
1937	765	559	267	210	1,803
1938	748	434	259	219	1,661

* Pipe lines, street railways, and water transportation.

P 14   Property Income by Minor Industrial Divisions
(millions of dollars)

	ELEC. LIGHT & POWER	MFD. GAS	PIPE LINES	STREET RWY.	WATER TRANSP.	TELE- PHONE	TELE- GRAPH
	(1)	(2)	(3)	(4)	(5)	(6)	(7)
1919	146	56.5	31.6	147	55.6	71.5	8.5
1920	156	52.5	30.9	143	37.9	74.7	8.6
1921	176	44.1	34.8	144	28.3	84.0	10.0
1922	237	37.4	60.4	174	28.0	89.2	9.8
1923	303	48.4	44.2	183	28.8	103	9.5
1924	363	64.8	44.9	178	22.7	115	9.8
1925	425	72.1	73.1	171	25.9	133	10.1
1926	473	74.2	55.4	161	28.3	140	12.7
1927	533	75.0	80.6	156	27.3	151	14.4
1928	627	74.4	88.0	151	28.9	150	15.1
1929	728	103	113	151	34.7	154	22.9
1930	829	114	142	134	36.7	173	25.2
1931	853	125	135	120	28.0	205	13.6
1932	776	148	159	109	23.5	230	7.0
1933	715	125	113	102	20.4	234	4.5
1934	655	127	93.9	104	23.7	234	5.1
1934	624	91.1	93.9	112	38.4	234	5.1
1935	630	112	148	114	71.7	224	9.3
1936	629	102	81.8	123	55.2	204	5.2
1937	661	103	84.6	127	56.2	203	6.9
1938	646	102	87.7	125	46.1	215	3.6

P 15   Total Payments to Individuals by Major Industrial
Divisions (millions of dollars)

	ELEC. LIGHT & POWER, & MFD. GAS	STEAM RR., PULLMAN, & RWY. EXPRESS	OTHER TRANSP.*	COMMUNI-CATION	TOTAL
	(1)	(2)	(3)	(4)	(5)
1919	423	3,880	1,133	391	5,828
1920	473	4,851	1,418	493	7,237
1921	487	3,820	1,210	502	6,021
1922	551	3,717	1,186	532	5,988
1923	700	4,156	1,199	590	6,647
1924	829	4,023	1,218	635	6,707
1925	914	4,105	1,220	678	6,919
1926	1,014	4,238	1,218	728	7,199
1927	1,090	4,289	1,208	760	7,347
1928	1,211	4,123	1,209	800	7,344
1929	1,366	4,250	1,246	889	7,752
1930	1,497	3,882	1,196	919	7,495
1931	1,487	3,174	1,043	867	6,572
1932	1,349	2,332	885	778	5,345
1933	1,234	2,171	798	708	4,912
1934	1,208	2,324	823	737	5,093
1934	1,139	2,324	847	737	5,048
1935	1,186	2,444	992	742	5,366
1936	1,214	2,667	987	759	5,627
1937	1,303	2,883	1,072	828	6,087
1938	1,281	2,477	999	843	5,601

* Pipe lines, street railways, and water transportation.

P 16 Entrepreneurial Withdrawals and Total Payments to Individuals by Minor Industrial Divisions (millions of dollars)

| | ENTREPRENEURIAL WITHDRAWALS | | TOTAL PAYMENTS TO INDIVIDUALS | | | | | | |
	Elec. light & power	Water transp.	Elec. light & power	Mfd. gas	Pipe lines	Street rwy.	Water transp.	TELE-PHONE	Tele-graph
	(1)	(2)	(3)	(4)	(5)	(6)	(7)	(8)	(9)
1919	3.2	7.6	289	133	58.5	515	558	311	80.7
1920	3.4	5.5	336	136	64.7	607	746	388	105
1921	3.4	3.8	365	122	66.5	582	561	410	92.0
1922	3.2	4.5	434	117	94.2	608	484	441	90.2
1923	2.8	4.5	558	142	82.0	622	495	492	97.9
1924	2.6	3.2	663	166	78.6	619	519	537	98.7
1925	2.3	3.6	737	177	110	604	505	573	105
1926	1.9	3.8	831	183	96.7	595	526	607	121
1927	1.5	3.6	902	187	129	576	502	641	119
1928	1.4	3.8	1,030	181	136	558	514	678	122
1929	1.2	4.6	1,162	204	163	563	519	747	142
1930	1.0	4.6	1,284	213	186	517	492	772	146
1931	0.9	3.3	1,277	209	174	456	412	746	120
1932	0.7	2.3	1,126	222	189	379	316	692	86.0
1933	0.6	1.8	1,033	200	144	330	324	633	74.4
1934	0.6	2.0	1,001	207	129	342	352	652	84.8
1934	0.6	1.9	969	170	129	351	366	652	84.8
1935	0.7	2.2	992	194	186	350	456	653	88.6
1936	0.7	2.3	1,026	188	123	364	499	667	91.4
1937	0.8	2.5	1,108	194	133	369	568	727	100
1938	0.8	2.1	1,088	192	133	361	504	754	89.6

P 17   Net Savings by Major Industrial Divisions
(millions of dollars)

	ELEC. LIGHT & POWER, & MFD. GAS	STEAM RR., PULLMAN, & RWY. EXPRESS	OTHER TRANSP.*	COMMUNI-CATION	TOTAL
	(1)	(2)	(3)	(4)	(5)
1919	1.3	58.1	49.3	25.7	134
1920	22.1	—6.5	74.1	21.4	111
1921	36.4	—5.2	4.5	30.3	66.0
1922	68.5	106	5.3	46.8	226
1923	78.1	282	40.2	46.7	447
1924	50.0	242	37.4	42.8	372
1925	155	382	38.7	68.8	645
1926	139	428	44.2	75.8	688
1927	163	176	21.5	81.2	442
1928	187	359	53.4	100	700
1929	196	403	59.5	98.9	758
1930	140	—11.6	—28.9	29.6	129
1931	46.4	—200	—55.7	4.5	—205
1932	—44.5	—242	—132	—58.5	—477
1933	—46.2	—49.7	—41.3	—53.9	—191
1934	—26.8	—93.1	—45.8	—51.6	—217
1934	—25.8	—93.1	—44.0	—51.6	—214
1935	—1.8	—34.1	—144	—37.2	—217
1936	57.1	143	—9.9	25.0	215
1937	67.6	44.3	—0.9	14.4	125
1938	35.4	—61.8	—42.0	—20.4	—88.7

* Pipe lines, street railways, and water transportation.

P 18   Net Savings by Minor Industrial Divisions
(millions of dollars)

	ELEC. LIGHT & POWER	MFD. GAS	PIPE LINES	STREET RWY.	WATER TRANSP.	TELE PHONE	TELE- GRAPH
	(1)	(2)	(3)	(4)	(5)	(6)	(7)
1919	35.7	—34.4	7.5	11.7	30.0	14.4	11.3
1920	45.2	—23.1	27.6	22.1	24.4	8.9	12.5
1921	44.9	—8.5	2.5	28.4	—26.4	22.6	7.7
1922	68.1	0.4	3.2	16.9	—14.8	30.6	16.2
1923	76.7	1.4	24.0	26.6	—10.4	31.6	15.1
1924	66.9	—17.0	33.7	8.0	—4.2	28.7	14.2
1925	80.3	75.1	23.1	13.9	1.7	48.9	19.9
1926	113	26.7	31.9	7.3	4.9	60.8	15.0
1927	129	34.7	20.7	9.2	—8.3	59.6	21.6
1928	174	12.6	39.4	9.1	4.9	78.9	21.7
1929	217	—20.3	41.4	2.9	15.2	93.0	6.0
1930	167	—27.1	—9.8	5.3	—24.4	50.3	—20.7
1931	101	—55.2	—4.9	—14.7	—36.1	15.6	—11.1
1932	18.5	—62.9	—55.7	—40.7	—36.5	—46.5	—12.0
1933	—4.1	—42.0	4.8	—28.3	—17.8	—55.8	1.9
1934	10.9	—37.7	0.2	—26.6	—19.5	—50.4	—1.2
1934	10.9	—36.7	0.2	—26.6	—17.6	—50.4	—1.2
1935	49.1	—50.8	—60.1	—26.1	—58.1	—34.6	—2.6
1936	85.5	—28.4	20.6	—20.1	—10.4	20.5	4.5
1937	79.9	—12.3	29.1	—25.1	—4.9	16.6	—2.2
1938	54.5	—19.1	1.0	—23.1	—19.9	—14.7	—5.7

P 19 Employees, by Major Industrial Divisions, and Total Entrepreneurs (thousands)

	ELEC. LIGHT & POWER, & MFD. GAS	STEAM RR., PULLMAN, & RWY. EXPRESS		OTHER TRANSP.[1]	COMMUNI-CATION	TOTAL	ENTRE-PRENEURS[2]
		Wage earners	Salaried em-ployees				
	(1)	(2)	(3)	(4)	(5)	(6)	(7)
1919	170	1,707	421	606	356	3,262	2.5
1920	175	1,804	457	683	381	3,502	2.4
1921	176	1,436	423	605	364	3,006	2.3
1922	193	1,373	441	634	381	3,024	2.2
1923	242	1,600	453	631	413	3,341	2.0
1924	259	1,500	446	615	423	3,245	1.7
1925	268	1,495	443	593	441	3,241	1.5
1926	296	1,528	447	599	453	3,325	1.3
1927	308	1,486	440	583	458	3,278	1.0
1928	320	1,412	425	570	477	3,206	1.0
1929	336	1,418	422	560	532	3,269	0.9
1930	342	1,254	399	526	519	3,043	0.8
1931	313	1,048	353	461	448	2,626	0.8
1932	273	859	292	400	402	2,228	0.7
1933	263	816	264	405	376	2,126	0.6
1934	278	853	267	419	374	2,192	0.7
1935	280	845	264	424	368	2,183	0.6
1936	296	920	270	438	377	2,303	0.6
1937	308	966	282	457	401	2,415	0.6
1938	298	795	263	415	386	2,158	0.6

[1] Pipe lines, street railways, and water transportation.
[2] Water transportation, and electric light and power.

P 20   Employees by Minor Industrial Divisions (thousands)

	ELEC. LIGHT & POWER	MFD. GAS	PIPE LINES	STREET RWY.	WATER TRANSP.	TELE- PHONE	TELE- GRAPH
	(1)	(2)	(3)	(4)	(5)	(6)	(7)
1919	108	62.6	18.6	294	293	279	76.3
1920	119	56.9	17.1	303	362	304	77.0
1921	123	52.8	19.9	279	305	291	73.0
1922	136	57.5	22.6	291	320	312	69.9
1923	177	65.0	24.3	291	315	339	74.0
1924	192	67.9	21.7	280	313	347	76.5
1925	198	70.0	23.7	270	299	360	81.7
1926	224	72.1	26.0	265	308	367	85.8
1927	234	74.2	30.2	254	298	375	83.5
1928	250	69.9	29.1	245	296	391	85.7
1929	271	64.6	26.4	241	291	436	96.1
1930	279	62.9	24.6	224	277	425	93.8
1931	259	53.7	22.7	200	238	367	81.1
1932	225	48.0	17.7	173	208	334	68.3
1933	213	49.4	20.5	157	228	311	65.4
1934	227	51.0	22.6	159	237	303	70.8
1935	229	50.7	23.3	152	248	299	68.8
1936	244	52.1	25.2	149	264	304	72.8
1937	256	51.9	26.4	145	286	325	75.4
1938	247	50.5	23.6	137	254	318	67.8

P 21 Comparison of Various Income Account Items for Steam Railroads Reported in *Statistics of Income* (SI) and *Statistics of Railways in the United States* (SR) (millions of dollars)

	GROSS INCOME		(1)	TOTAL EXPENSES		(4)	NET PROFIT		(7)	DIVIDENDS PAID		DIVIDENDS RECEIVED		NET DIVIDENDS PAID		(14)	NET PROFIT EXCL. DIVIDENDS RECEIVED		CORPORATE SAVINGS		(19)
	SI	SR	—	SI	SR	—	SI	SR	—	SI	SR	SI	SR	SI	SR	—	SI	SR	SI	SR	—
	(1)	(2)	(3)	(4)	(5)	(6)	(7)	(8)	(9)	(10)	(11)	(12)	(13)	(14)	(15)	(16)	(17)	(18)	(19)	(20)	(21)
1926	7,138	6,770	368	6,351	5,982	369	787	788	−1.0	347	362	144	35.5	203	327	−124	643	752	439	425	14.6
1927	7,162	6,500	661	6,530	5,865	665	631	634	−3.8	474	444	173	36.0	301	408	−107	458	599	156	190	−35.6
1928	7,261	6,480	781	6,502	5,725	776	759	755	4.5	452	401	157	44.6	294	356	−61.7	602	710	307	354	−46.3
1929	7,285	6,666	619	6,382	5,793	589	902	872	30.1	502	440	214	41.6	287	399	−111	687	830	399	431	−31.9
1930	6,073	5,640	433	5,644	5,158	485	429	482	−52.6	540	489	205	57.7	337	431	−94.4	226	424	−111	−7.3	−104
1931	4,851	4,483	368	4,905	4,377	528	−54.2	106	−160	324	310	113	53.4	211	257	−46.1	−167	52.9	−378	−204	−174
1932	3,679	3,359	320	3,942	3,479	463	−263	−120	−143	90.3	114	72.9	43.9	17.3	70.7	−53.4	−336	−164	−354	−235	−118
1933	3,587	3,322	265	3,805	3,254	551	−217	68.6	−285	83.5	118	66.9	42.4	16.6	75.9	−59.4	−284	26.2	−300	−49.7	−251
1934	3,731	3,497	234	3,945	3,421	524	−214	76.2	−290	144	170	76.4	44.4	68.2	126	−57.8	−290	31.7	−358	−94.2	−264
1935	3,859	3,676	182	3,994	3,544	450	−135	132	−268	132	165	73.0	38.2	59.5	127	−68.2	−208	94.6	−267	−33.1	−234
1936	4,497	4,301	196	4,512	3,985	526	−14.8	315	−330	178	188	78.9	29.2	99.6	159	−59.5	−93.7	286	−193	127	−320
1937	4,617	4,417	200	4,668	4,188	479	−50.7	228	−279	178	185	70.6	23.1	108	162	−54.0	−121	205	−229	43.0	−272
1938		3,776			3,740			35.2			99.5		15.9		83.7			19.4		−64.5	

Wages are separated from salaries for the most important division
in this group, steam railroads, on the basis of our grouping of the
various categories of workers in *Wage Statistics of Class I Steam
Railways* (Interstate Commerce Commission). This grouping is
shown in detail in General Note A.

For another industrial division, pipe lines, the basic data, reported by the Interstate Commerce Commission, must be adjusted
for incompleteness of coverage. Since this adjustment percentage
must be assumed to be the same for the various types of income
originating in the industry, it is described in General Note B.

GENERAL NOTE A

Grouping of
Wage Statistics of Class I Steam Railways in the United States (ICC)

SALARIED EMPLOYEES

1932 AND EARLIER YEARS	1933 AND LATER YEARS
Executives, Officials, and Staff Assistants *	
Executives, general officers, & assistants	Same *
Division officers, assistants, & staff assistants	Same *
Professional, Clerical, and General	
Architectural, chemical, & engineering assistants (A) *	
Architectural, chemical, & engineering assistants (B) *	
Subprofessional engineering & laboratory assistants	
Professional & subprofessional legal assistants	
	Professional & subprofessional assistants
Supervisory or chief clerks (major departments)	Same
Chief clerks (minor departments) & assistant chief clerks & supervisory cashiers	Same
Clerks & clerical specialists (A)	Same
Clerks (B)	
Clerks (C)	
	Clerks (B and C)
Mechanical device operators (office)	Same
Stenographers & secretaries (A)	Same
Stenographers & typists (B)	Same
Storekeepers, sales agents, & buyers	Same
Ticket agents & assistant ticket agents	Same
Traveling auditors or accountants	Same
Telephone switchboard operators & office assistants	Same
Messengers & office boys	Same
Elevator operators & other office attendants	Same
Lieutenants & sergeants of police	Same
Patrolmen	
Supervising traffic agents	

* Principal officers.

SALARIED EMPLOYEES (*cont.*)

1932 AND EARLIER YEARS	1933 AND LATER YEARS
Professional, Clerical, and General (concl.)	
Traffic agents, advertising & development agents	
Fire-prevention, smoke, & time-service inspectors, & office-building superintendents	
Claim agents & claim investigators	
Real estate & tax agents & investigators	
Examiners, instructors, & special investigators	
	Traffic & various other agents, inspectors, & investigators
	Claim agents or investigators
	Freight-claim agents or investigators
Maintenance of Way and Structures	Chief claim agents or investigators
Roadmasters & general foremen	
Assistant general foremen	
Supervising maintenance of way inspectors & scale inspectors	
Maintenance of way inspectors	
	Roadmasters, general foremen, & assistants
	Maintenance of way & scale inspectors
General foremen & supervising inspectors (signal, telegraph, & electrical transmission)	
Assistant general foremen (signal, telegraph, & electrical transmission) & signal & telegraph inspectors	
	General & assistant general foremen, & inspectors (signal, telegraph, & electrical transmission)
Maintenance of Equipment and Stores	
General foremen (M. E.)	
Assistant general foremen & department foremen (M. E.)	
	General, assistant general, & department foremen
General foremen (stores)	
Assistant general foremen (stores)	
	General & assistant general foremen (stores)
Equipment, shop, & electrical inspectors (M. E.)	
Material & supplies inspectors	
	Equipment, shop, electrical, material, & supplies inspectors
Transportation (other than Train, Engine, and Yard)	
Chief train dispatchers, train dispatchers, & train directors	
	Chief train dispatchers
	Train dispatchers
	Train directors

SALARIED EMPLOYEES *(concl.)*

1932 AND EARLIER YEARS	1933 AND LATER YEARS
Transportation (other than Train, Engine, and Yard) (concl.)	
Station agents (supervisory—major stations—non-telegraphers)	Same
Station agents (supervisory—smaller stations—non-telegraphers)	
Station agents (non-supervisory—smaller stations—non-telegraphers)	
	Station agents (smaller stations—non-telegraphers)
Station agents (telegraphers & telephoners)	Same
Chief telegraphers & telephoners or wire chiefs	Same
Clerk-telegraphers & clerk-telephoners	Same
Telegraphers, telephoners, & towermen	Same
Station masters & assistants	Same
Supervising baggage agents	Same
Baggage agents & assistants	Same
General foremen (freight stations, warehouses, grain elevators, & docks)	Same
Assistant general foremen (freight stations, warehouses, grain elevators, & docks)	Same
Stewards, restaurant & lodging-house managers, & dining-car supervisors	Same
Deck officers (ferryboats & towing vessels)	
Engine room officers (ferryboats & towing vessels)	
Transportation & dining service inspectors	Same
Parlor & sleeping car conductors	Same
Transportation (Yardmasters, Switch Tenders, and Hostlers)	
Yardmasters & assistants	
	Yardmasters
	Assistant yardmasters

WAGE EARNERS

Professional, Clerical, and General	
Watchmen (without police authority)	
	Patrolmen & watchmen
Misc. trades workers (other than plumbers)	Same
Motor-vehicle & motor-car operators	Same
Teamsters & stablemen	Same
Janitors & cleaners	Same
Maintenance of Way and Structures	
Bridge & building gang foremen (skilled labor)	Same
Bridge & building carpenters	Same
Bridge & building iron workers	Same
Bridge & building painters	Same
Masons, bricklayers, plasterers, & plumbers	Same
Skilled trades helpers	
Regular apprentices	
	Helpers & apprentices
Portable steam equipment operators	Same
Portable steam equipment operator helpers	Same
Pumping equipment operators	Same
Gang foremen (extra gang & work-train laborers)	Same

1932 AND EARLIER YEARS	1933 AND LATER YEARS
Maintenance of Way and Structures (concl.)	
Gang foremen (bridge & building, signal & telegraph laborers)	Same
Gang or section foremen	Same
Laborers (extra gang & work-train)	
	Extra gang men
Track & roadway section laborers	
	Section men
Maintenance of way laborers (other than track & roadway) & gardeners & farmers	Same
Gang foremen (signal & telegraph skilled-trades labor)	Same
Signalmen & signal maintainers	Same
Linemen & groundmen	Same
Assistant signalmen & assistant signal maintainers	Same
Signalmen & signal maintainer helpers	Same
Maintenance of Equipment and Stores	
Gang foremen & gang leaders (skilled labor)	Same
Blacksmiths	Same
Boilermakers	Same
Carmen (A)	
Carmen (B)	
	Carmen (A and B)
Carmen (C)	
Carmen (D)	
	Carmen (C and D)
Electrical workers (A)	Same
Electrical workers (B)	Same
Electrical workers (C)	Same
Machinists	Same
Molders	Same
Sheet-metal workers	Same
Skilled trades helpers	Same
Helper apprentices	Same
Regular apprentices	Same
Gang foremen laborers (shops, engine houses, power plants, & stores)	
	Gang foremen (shops, engine houses, & power plants)
	Gang foremen (stores and ice, reclamation, & timber-treating plants)
Coach cleaners	Same
Laborers (shops, engine houses, power plants & stores)	
Common laborers (shops, engine houses, power plants, & stores)	
	Classified laborers (shops, engine houses, & power plants)
	General laborers (shops, engine houses, & power plants)

WAGE EARNERS *(cont.)*

1932 AND EARLIER YEARS	1933 AND LATER YEARS
Maintenance of Equipment and Stores (concl.)	General laborers (stores & ice, reclamation, & timber-treating plants)
Stationary engineers (steam)	Same
Stationary firemen & oilers (steam & electrical plants)	
Coal passers & water tenders (steam station boiler rooms)	
	Stationary firemen, oilers, coal passers, & water tenders
Transportation (other than Train, Engine, and Yard)	
Baggage, parcel room, & station attendants	Same
Gang foremen (freight-station, warehouse, grain elevator, & dock labor)	Same
Callers, loaders, scalers, sealers, & perishable-freight inspectors	Same
Truckers (stations, warehouses, & platforms)	Same
Laborers (coal & ore docks & grain elevators)	Same
Common laborers (stations, warehouses, platforms, & grain elevators)	Same
Chefs & first cooks (dining cars & restaurants)	
Second & third cooks (dining cars & restaurants)	
	Chefs & cooks (restaurants or dining cars)
Waiters & lodging-house attendants	
Camp & crew cooks & kitchen helpers	
	Waiters, camp cooks, kitchen helpers, etc.
Barge, lighter & gasoline launch officers & workers	
Deck & engine-room workers (ferryboats & towing vessels)	
Deck & engine-room officers & workers (steamers)	
Floating equipment shore workers & attendants	
	Officers, workers, & attendants on barges, launches, ferryboats, towing vessels, & steamers, & shore workers
Train attendants	Same
Bridge operators & helpers	Same
Crossing & bridge flagmen & gatemen	Same
Foremen (laundry) & laundry workers	Same
Transportation (Yardmasters, Switch Tenders, and Hostlers)	
Switch tenders	Same
Outside hostlers	Same
Inside hostlers	Same
Outside hostler helpers	Same
Transportation (Train and Engine)	
Road passenger conductors	Same
Assistant road passenger conductors & ticket collectors	Same

WAGE EARNERS (*concl.*)

1932 AND EARLIER YEARS	1933 AND LATER YEARS
Transportation (Train and Engine) (*concl.*)	
Road freight conductors (through freight)	Same
Road freight conductors (local & way freight)	Same
Road passenger baggagemen	Same
Road passenger brakemen & flagmen	Same
Road freight brakemen & flagmen (through freight)	Same
Road freight brakemen & flagmen (local & way freight)	Same
Yard conductors & yard foremen	Same
Yard brakemen & yard helpers	Same
Road passenger engineers & motormen	Same
Road freight engineers & motormen (through freight)	Same
Road freight engineers & motormen (local & way freight)	Same
Yard engineers & motormen	Same
Road passenger firemen & helpers	Same
Road freight firemen & helpers (through freight)	Same
Road freight firemen & helpers (local & way freight)	Same
Yard firemen & helpers	Same

GENERAL NOTE B

Derivation of the
Raising Ratio for Statistics on the Pipe Line Industry (ICC)

From the *Report on Pipe Lines,* Part I, 72d Cong., 2d Sess., House Report 2192, it appears that:

a) The ICC *Selected Financial and Operating Data from Annual Reports of Pipe Line Companies* cover 80.92 per cent of the total oil line mileage of the country.

b) Of the companies reporting to the ICC, five are gasoline line companies with 2,738 miles of trunk lines. The Bureau of Foreign and Domestic Commerce, National Income Division, finds that these five companies have no gathering line mileage.

c) The House Report covers 105,738 miles of oil lines and 3,874 miles of gasoline lines. On the basis of the total oil mileage as of May 1, 1932 (111,660), the Bureau of Foreign and Domestic Commerce, National Income Division, estimates that the House Report covers 94.7 per cent of all oil line mileage. The gasoline line mileage coverage is regarded as complete.

From the above data the total gasoline and oil line mileage is found to be 115,534, of which 80.6 per cent is covered by the ICC Report and 94.9 per cent by the House Report.

After studying the companies that were not covered by the ICC, but were covered by the House, the Bureau of Foreign and Domestic Commerce, National Income Division, found that 65.2 per cent of the mileage of these companies belonged to companies that should more properly be included under petroleum refining. It is assumed that this is true also of the mileage not covered by the ICC. The computation yielding the percentage by which the ICC data are raised is then as follows:

$$(100.0\% \div 80.6\%) \times (100.0\% - 65.2\%) = 8.4\%.$$

TABLE P 1

Gross Income by Minor Industrial Divisions

Col. 1 Electric light and power: for 1917, 1922, 1927, 1932, and 1937, from the *Census of Central Electric Light and Power Stations*. Interpolation between 1917 and 1922, 1922 and 1927, is by the *Electric World* series of revenue from total sales (published in the *Survey of Current Business*). Interpolation between 1927 and 1932, 1932 and 1937, and extrapolation for 1938 are by the Edison Electric Institute series on total revenue from ultimate consumers, as given in their Statistical Bulletin 6.

Col. 2 Manufactured gas: for 1919, 1921, 1923, 1925, 1927, 1929, and 1931, from the *Biennial Census of Manufactures* (excluding the value of product of municipal plants). Interpolation for the intercensal years before 1929 is by the revenue from gas sales, reported in the American Gas Association Statistical Bulletin 9. Interpolation between 1929 and 1931 and extrapolation of the 1931 figure for 1932–38 are by the revenue from sales to consumers, reported in the American Gas Association Statistical Bulletin 36.

Col. 3 Electric light and power, and manufactured gas: sum of col. 1 and 2.

Col. 4 Steam railroads, Pullman, and railway express: operating revenue of steam railroads, from *Statistics of Railways;* of railway express and the Pullman Company, from the *Preliminary Abstract of Statistics of Common Carriers*.

Col. 5 Pipe lines: gross revenue for interstate pipe lines alone, from ICC *Selected Financial and Operating Data from Annual Reports of Pipe Line Companies*.

Col. 6 Street railways: estimates of operating revenues as prepared by the American Transit Association.

Col. 7 Telephone: gross operating revenue for 1917, 1922, 1927, 1932, and 1937, from the *Census of Telephones.* Interpolation and extrapolation are by the operating revenues of the American Telephone and Telegraph Company reported in *Bell Telephone Securities.*

Col. 8 Telegraph: reported for 1920–33 by the Interstate Commerce Commission and for 1934–38 by the Federal Communications Commission in *Selected Financial and Operating Data from Annual Reports of Telegraph, Cable and Radiotelegraph Carriers.* Radio communication is included for 1934–38 alone.

Col. 9 Communication: sum of col. 7 and 8.

TABLE P 2

Net Income Originating by Major Industrial Divisions

Sum for each industry of total payments and net savings in Tables P 15 and P 17, respectively.

Col. 5 Total: sum of col. 1–4.

TABLE P 3

Net Income Originating by Minor Industrial Divisions

Sum for each industry of total payments and net savings in Tables P 16 and P 18, respectively.

TABLE P 4

Total Payments by Type

Col. 1 Wages: see Table P 6, col. 2.
Col. 2 Salaries: see Table P 6, col. 3.
Col. 3 Wages and salaries: see Table P 6, col. 1, 4, and 5.
Col. 4 Pensions and compensation for injury: see Table P 8, col. 5.
Col. 5 Employee compensation: sum of col. 1–4.
Col. 6 Entrepreneurial withdrawals: see Table P 16, col. 1 and 2.
Col. 7 Dividends: see Table P 9, col. 5.
Col. 8 Interest: see Table P 11, col. 5.

Col. 9 Property income: sum of col. 7 and 8.

Col. 10 Payments to individuals: sum of col. 5, 6, and 9.

TABLE P 5

Net Income Originating

Col. 1 Total payments to individuals: see Table P 4, col. 10.

Col. 2 Entrepreneurial net savings:

 a) Electric light and power: total entrepreneurial net income is assumed to be withdrawn and savings are assumed to be zero.

 b) Water transportation: difference between entrepreneurial withdrawals (see the notes to Table P 16, col. 2) and net income (col. 3, below).

Col. 3 Entrepreneurial net income: sum of entrepreneurial net income in (a) the electric light and power industry and (b) water transportation.

 a) Electric light and power: see the notes to Table P 16, col. 1.

 b) Water transportation: product of corporate data and the ratio of unincorporated to incorporated tonnage. Statutory net income before taxes, total long term interest payments, and officers' compensation make up the corporate figure. To it is applied the ratio of tonnage operated by unincorporated firms to that operated by incorporated, derived for 1916 and 1926 from the *Census of Transportation by Water,* and interpolated for intercensal years along a straight line. The ratio is assumed to decline slightly, from 0.104 in 1926 to 0.100 in 1929, thus continuing the 1916–26 decline. After 1929 the ratio is held constant at the level for that year.

 Statutory net income is from *Statistics of Income.* Long term interest is described in the notes to Table P 12, col. 5. Officers' compensation, 1929–37, is from the special tabulation of *Statistics of Income* data. Officers' compensation, 1919–28, is estimated on the basis of the 1928 ratio of officers' compensation in water transportation to officers' compensation in all transportation and public utility corporations. Officers' compensation in transportation and other public utility corporations is reported in *Statistics of Income* for 1919–24 and 1928. For the years between 1924 and 1928 it is interpolated by compiled receipts, also reported in *Statistics of Income.*

Col. 4 Corporate net savings: see the notes to Table P 17.

Col. 5 Total net savings: sum of col. 2 and 4.

Col. 6 Net income originating: sum of col. 1 and 5.

TABLE P 6

Wages and Salaries by Major Industrial Divisions

Col. 1 Electric light and power, and manufactured gas: see Table P 7, col. 1 and 2.

Col. 2 and 3 Steam railroads, Pullman, and railway express: included with the wages paid by steam railroads and the Pullman Company are estimates of gratuities received by their employees. Railway express commissions are included with salaries.

a) Steam railroads: wages and salaries for all roads and switching and terminal companies, 1932–38, are from *Statistics of Railways.* Those for 1931 were received by letter from the Interstate Commerce Commission. Number and wages and salaries of employees of Class I roads, 1919–30, are from *Statistics of Railways,* as are the number of employees of Class II and III roads, 1922–30. The compensation of the latter, 1922–30, is estimated by multiplying their number of employees by the average annual pay of Class I road employees. Wages and salaries for all roads in 1919, 1920, and 1921 are the Class I figure raised by the ratio of operating expenses of all roads, excluding switching and terminal companies, to those of Class I roads. Total pay and number of employees of Class I switching and terminal companies, 1920–30, are from *Statistics of Railways;* pay of other switching and terminal companies, 1922–30, is estimated by multiplying their number of employees by the average pay in Class I switching and terminal companies. Total pay for all switching and terminal companies in 1920 and 1921 is estimated by raising the Class I figure by the ratio of total locomotives operated to those of Class I switching and terminal companies. The 1919 estimate is obtained by applying to railroad salaries and wages in 1919 the ratio of switching and terminal company salaries and wages to those of railroads in 1916.

The number and pay of Class I road employees is reported in detail by the Interstate Commerce Commission in *Wage Statistics of Class I Steam Railways.* Our grouping of the ICC data into wages and salaries forms the basis for the separation of the total pay of all railroads and switching and terminal companies into wages and salaries. Since the ICC listing of employees is revised somewhat after 1932, the wage and salary division for 1933–38 is not strictly comparable with that for the earlier years.

Gratuities are based on the gross revenue from dining and buffet car service and hotel and restaurant service on Class I railroads and switching and terminal companies as recorded in *Statistics of Railways* and the *Preliminary Abstract of Statistics of Common Carriers*. In 1920, 1921, 1924, 1927, and 1931–38 gratuities are estimated to be 10 per cent of gross revenue; in all other years in the period, 15 per cent.

b) Pullman Company: wages and salaries were obtained by letter from the Interstate Commerce Commission. Gratuities paid to porters are estimated by multiplying the average tip by the number of passengers tipping. The number of berth and chair passengers carried, 1919–21, was obtained by letter from the Interstate Commerce Commission. For later years it is reported in the *Preliminary Abstract of Statistics of Common Carriers*. From questionnaire returns from local porters' unions are computed the average tip and the percentage of berth and chair passengers tipping, 1929–32. For 1933–38 the 1932 figures are used. For the years before 1929 the average 1929 tips are used but the percentage of passengers tipping is assumed to decrease in years of depression and to increase in years of prosperity, the percentages ranging from 46 to 68. These percentages were suggested by the questionnaire returns for 1929–32.

c) Railway express: wages and salaries and commissions, 1925–38, are reported in the *Preliminary Abstract of Statistics of Common Carriers*. Data for 1921–24 were obtained by letter from the Interstate Commerce Commission. The combined item, wages and salaries, commissions and expenses, is reported for 1919 and 1920 in *Statistics of Express Companies*. The 1921 ratio of wages, salaries, and commissions to it is applied to obtain wages, salaries, and commissions for 1919 and 1920.

Col. 4 Other transportation: see Table P 7, col. 3–5.

Col. 5 Communication: see Table P 7, col. 6 and 7.

Col. 6 Total: sum of col. 1–5.

TABLE P 7

Wages and Salaries by Minor Industrial Divisions

Col. 1 Electric light and power: for 1917, 1922, 1927, 1932 (incomplete), and 1937, from the *Census of Central Electric Light and Power Stations.* The estimates for intercensal years and the total for 1932 are the product of the number of employees (see the notes to Table P 20) and the average pay. Interpolation between the 1917 and 1922 average pay figures is by those for New York (*Labor Market Bulletin* and the N. Y. Department of Labor Special Bulletin 171) and Pennsylvania (*Report on Productive Industries, Public Utilities and Miscellaneous Statistics*). Interpolation between the 1922 Census figure and the 1929 estimate is by an index of the average pay in New York, Pennsylvania, Wisconsin (*Wisconsin Labor Market*) and Illinois (*Illinois Labor Bulletin*). The averages for the four states are weighted by the amount of current generated in each Census year. The 1929 average pay is extrapolated from 1932 by an index derived by dividing the BLS payrolls index by its employment index. The same index is used in interpolating between 1929 and 1937 and extrapolating for 1938.

Col. 2 Manufactured gas: the *Biennial Census of Manufactures* reports wages and salaries and the number of employees in all and in commercial plants for the odd years 1919–29. The 1931 Census reports wages and the number of wage earners in all and in commercial plants. The 1933 Census reports wages and salaries and the number of employees in all plants. The number of wage earners in commercial plants and their pay in 1933 are based on their ratios to the totals in 1931; the number of salaried employees in commercial plants and their pay are based on their ratios to the totals in 1929. The 1933 pay figure reported excludes the pay of employees engaged in the distribution of gas although their number is reported. Their pay is estimated on the assumption that they receive the same average annual compensation as the other employees, and is added to the figure reported to yield total pay in 1933. The number of salaried employees and their pay in 1931 are derived from the ratios to wage earners and wages, respectively, in 1929 and 1933, interpolated along a straight line and applied to the number of wage earners and wages reported in 1931.

Estimates of total pay for intercensal years are the product of the number of employees (see the notes to Table P 20) and the average pay. From state data an index for interpolating between the Census figures on average pay for the years before 1929 was computed. For 1919–21 Pennsylvania and New York data are used; for 1921–23 Wisconsin data are added; and for 1923–29, Illinois data also. The sources of the state materials are those cited for col. 1. By weighting the index for each state by the number of its employees in 1929, as recorded in the Census, a single index is obtained. Interpolation of the average pay for the years between 1929 and 1931, 1931 and 1933, and extrapolation for the years since 1933 are by the BLS index of average pay in the electric light and power and manufactured gas industry.

Col. 3 Pipe lines: compensation of employees of companies reporting to the Interstate Commerce Commission, 1925–38, is from *Selected Financial and Operating Data from Annual Reports of Pipe Line Companies,* as are total operating expenses and miles of pipe line operated, 1920–32. Two-year moving totals of the net change in mileage operated are computed, the totals being centered at the earlier year. From the regression line of the ratio of compensation to operating expenses on the two-year moving total of net change in mileage operated the ratio of compensation to operating expenses is derived for 1921–24. The 1920 ratio is assumed to be the same as the 1921. The application of these ratios to total operating expenses yields total compensation, 1920–24. Total compensation in 1919 is obtained by applying to the 1920 estimate the percentage change from 1919 to 1920 in wages and salaries in petroleum refining. The figures for interstate companies are raised by the adjustment factor described in General Note B.

Col. 4 Street railways: for commercial railways, excluding bus operations, for 1917, 1922, 1927, 1932, and 1937, from the *Census of Electric Railways.* The 1937 figure is adjusted to include pay of employees of companies engaged in part year operations. Interpolation between and extrapolation of the Census data are by estimates of compensation prepared by the American Transit Association and obtained by letter.

Col. 5 Water transportation: for 1929–38 the sum of estimates for inland, lake, and foreign and coastwise transportation and for stevedores and longshoremen. Except for stevedores and longshoremen, the estimates are essentially those of the Bureau of Foreign and Domestic Commerce, National Income Division, as described in *National Income in the United States, 1929–35* (pp. 262-4). The estimates for stevedores and longshoremen also are based on Bureau of Foreign and Domestic Commerce sources and methods. Their compensation is the product of the number (see the notes to Table P 20) and the average pay. The latter is derived from partial data for 1929–32 on wages and overtime pay and the number of employees as obtained by the National Income Division from the United States Shipping Board. It is extrapolated through 1935 by the union scale of wages in 9 ports as indicated by data in the *Monthly Labor Review,* April 1936. On the advice of persons in the Bureau of Labor Statistics, the average wage for 1936–38 is assumed to be the same as for 1935.

For 1919–28 total compensation is the sum of estimates for vessel employees, shore employees, and longshoremen. All three are the product of the number employed (see the notes to Table P 20) and the average annual pay.

The average annual pay of vessel employees is an extrapolation of the 1929 figure. *Merchant Marine Statistics* records monthly wage rates of various classes of employees on vessels, 1923–29. These are extrapolated to 1919 by similar data, not quite as detailed, in the *Annual Report of the Bureau of Navigation.* A weighted average of these data is obtained with the number reported in the 1930 *Census of Population,* Vol. V, Ch. 7, as weights. The 1929 average pay figure is extrapolated to 1919 by the resulting index. Subsistence cost as estimated by the Bureau of Foreign and Domestic Commerce for 1929 is reduced to a per capita figure and extrapolated by the BLS index of wholesale prices of food products. Total subsistence cost is the product of per capita cost and the number of employees. The 1929 ratio of gratuities to wages and salaries is assumed to hold for the entire period; its application to wages and salaries yields total gratuities. The total wage and salary bill of vessel employees is the sum of cash payments, subsistence cost, and gratuities.

The average annual pay of shore employees, 1919–28, is obtained by applying to the average pay of vessel employees the ratio of the average pay of shore employees to that of vessel employees for 1929–34.

The 1929 average pay of longshoremen is extrapolated to 1919 by an index derived from union wage rates for freight handlers published by the Bureau of Labor Statistics for 1919–27 in the bulletins, *Union Scales of Wages and Hours of Labor,* and for 1928–35 in the *Monthly Labor Review,* April 1936.

Col. 6 Telephone: wages and salaries reported for 1917, 1922, 1927, 1932, and 1937 in the *Census of Telephones* are adjusted by the difference between the Bell System figures reported in the Census and those obtained by letter from the American Telephone and Telegraph Company. Intercensal year interpolation is by data for the Bell System. The 1938 estimate is extrapolated from 1937 by total compensation reported in *Selected Financial and Operating Data from Annual Reports of Telephone Carriers.*

Col. 7 Telegraph: wages and salaries and the number of telegraph and wireless employees in 1917, 1922, 1927, and 1932 (telegraph only) are reported in the *Census of Telegraphs.* The 1932 estimates for wireless companies are based on the ratio to telegraph company figures in 1927. Interpolation and extrapolation of the pay figures for intercensal years and for 1933 are by the Western Union Telegraph Company wages and salaries. The latter were obtained directly from the company by letter. For 1927–33 the final estimate of wages and salaries is an average of the one outlined above and another based on the number of employees (see the notes to Table P 20) and the average annual pay. Average pay, taken for 1927 and 1932 from the Census, is interpolated for the intervening years and extrapolated for 1933 by the average pay of Western Union Telegraph Company employees. Total wages and salaries, 1934–38, are reported by the Federal Communications Commission in *Selected Financial and Operating Data from Annual Reports of Telegraph, Cable and Radiotelegraph Carriers.*

TABLE P 8

Pensions and Compensation for Injury, and Total Employee
Compensation

PENSIONS, ETC.

Col. 1 Steam railroads, Pullman, and railway express:

a) *Steam railroads:* the items covered are relief, pensions, and compensation for injury. Relief payments are reported for Class I steam railroads in *Statistics of Railways*. For Class I switching and terminal companies for 1921 and later years they are reported in the *Preliminary Abstract of Statistics of Common Carriers*. The figures for 1919 and 1920 are assumed to be the same as for 1921. The relief payments of Class I railroads and switching and terminal companies are presumed to cover all relief payments of railroads. The references for relief apply also to pensions paid by Class I railroads and switching and terminal companies for all years except 1931–35 and 1937–38. For 1931–34 the estimates prepared by Murray W. Latimer for Industrial Relations Counselors, Inc. are used. For 1935 pensions reported are raised by the difference between the *Statistics of Railways* figure and Mr. Latimer's estimate for 1934. For 1937 and 1938 the pensions reported by the Railroad Retirement Board are included with those reported in *Statistics of Railways*. Class I pensions are raised to cover pensions for all steam railroads by the ratio of all wages and salaries to wages and salaries of Class I railroads. Compensation for injury on Class I railroads and switching and terminal companies is from the sources cited in the description of the relief figures. Figures for Class I companies are raised to the total by the ratio of total wages and salaries to those of Class I companies. Compensation for injury by switching and terminal companies in 1919 and 1920 is estimated by applying to the comparable item for railroads the ratio of wages and salaries of switching and terminal companies to railroad wages and salaries.

b) *Pullman Company:* for 1931–34 Mr. Latimer's estimates are used. The 1931 figure is extrapolated to 1919 by pensions of Class I steam railroads. Pensions in 1935 are assumed to be the same as in 1934, and were obtained for 1936–38 from the Interstate Commerce Commission.

c) *Railway express:* pensions and compensation for injury in 1919 and 1920 are reported in *Statistics of Express Companies,* and for all later years, in the *Preliminary Abstract of Statistics of Common Carriers*. For 1931–34, however, Mr. Latimer's estimates of pensions are substituted for those reported.

Col. 2 Telephone: pensions and benefits paid by the American Telephone and Telegraph Company were obtained by letter. For 1919–36 they are assumed to be the total for the industry. For 1937 and 1938 pensions paid by other companies reporting to the Federal Communications Commission are included.

Col. 3 Telegraph: totals for 1937 and 1938 are reported by the Federal Communications Commission in *Selected Financial and Operating Data from Annual Reports of Telegraph, Cable and Radiotelegraph Carriers.* They are estimated for 1919–36 on the basis of the ratio to wages and salaries, computed for 1937, and extrapolated for the earlier years by the corresponding ratio for the Western Union Telegraph Company. Their data were obtained by letter.

Col. 4 Communication: sum of col. 2 and 3.

Col. 5 Total: sum of col. 1 and 4.

EMPLOYEE COMPENSATION

Col. 6 Electric light and power, and manufactured gas: see Table P 6, col. 1.

Col. 7 Steam railroads, Pullman, and railway express: see col. 2 and 3, Table P 6, and col. 1, above.

Col. 8 Other transportation: see Table P 6, col. 4.

Col. 9 Communication: see col. 5, Table P 6, and col. 4, above.

Col. 10 Total: sum of col. 6–9.

TABLE P 9

Dividends by Major Industrial Divisions

Dividends are net originating in the industry and are the difference between total dividends paid and dividends received.

Col. 1 Electric light and power, and manufactured gas: see Table P 10, col. 1 and 2.

Col. 2 Steam railroads, Pullman, and railway express:

a) *Steam railroads:* dividend appropriations (including stock), dividend receipts, and stock dividends, from *Statistics of Railways.* Stock dividends are subtracted since only cash dividends are included in income originating.

b) *Pullman Company:* from the *Preliminary Abstract of Statistics of Common Carriers.*

c) *Railway express:* for 1919 and 1920, from *Statistics of Express Companies;* for other years, from the *Preliminary Abstract of Statistics of Common Carriers.*

Col. 3 Other transportation: see Table P 10, col. 3–5.

Col. 4 Communication: see Table P 10, col. 6 and 7.

Col. 5 Total: sum of col. 1–4.

Dividends by Minor Industrial Divisions

Dividends are net originating in the industry and are the difference between total dividends paid and dividends received.

Col. 1 Electric light and power: total dividends paid in 1917, 1922, 1927, 1932, and 1937, from the *Census of Central Electric Light and Power Stations.* Interpolation between Census years and extrapolation for 1938 are by dividend payments of the corporate sample for the industry.

Dividends received in 1917 and 1922 are assumed to be the same proportion of total investment income as for electric railways. In 1927 and 1932 they are assumed to be equal to total 'non-operating income' as reported in the Census. The ratio of dividends received to total dividends paid is computed for Census years and interpolated for intervening years along a straight line. The application of this ratio to dividends paid yields dividends received. The 1932 figure for dividends received is extrapolated through 1937 by that item, as indicated by *Statistics of Income* data in the tabulation by minor industrial divisions. The 1938 figure is assumed to be the same proportion of dividends paid as in 1937.

Col. 2 Manufactured gas: from the capital stock tax returns reported in *Statistics of Income* the par value of stocks with par value plus the fair value of no par value stock is obtained for December 31, 1921, 1923, and 1924. By applying to these capital stock figures the dividend rate derived for a corporate sample for the industry total dividends paid in 1921, 1923, and 1924 are computed. Dividends paid, 1926–37, are from the special tabulation of *Statistics of Income* data. Extrapolation for 1919, 1920, and 1938, and interpolation between 1921 and 1923, 1924 and 1926, are by dividend payments of the corporate sample for the industry.

Dividends received, 1926–37, are from the same source as dividends paid, and for 1938 are assumed to be the same proportion of dividends paid as in 1937. For this item, however, the 1934 figure comparable with those for the earlier years is estimated by applying to the 1933 figure the percentage change from 1933 to 1934 in dividend receipts of all transportation and public utility corporations filing unconsolidated returns in those years (see *Sta-*

tistics of Income for 1934, Part 2). For 1922–25 dividends received
are based on the ratio to total dividends paid. This ratio, computed
for 1926 from *Statistics of Income* data, is extrapolated by the corresponding ratio for the total transportation and public utilities
group as derived from *Statistics of Income*. The 1919–21 estimates
are extrapolated from 1922 by the dividend receipts of all corporations (*Statistics of Income*).

Col. 3 Pipe lines: total dividends paid by companies in interstate
commerce, 1920–38, are from *Selected Financial and Operating
Data from Annual Reports of Pipe Line Companies* (Interstate
Commerce Commission). The comparable 1919 estimate is based
on the percentage change from 1919 to 1920 in dividends of corporations in the industry reporting in *Moody's Industrials*. Dividends paid by interstate pipe lines are raised (see General Note B)
to obtain total dividends for the industry.

Dividends received by interstate pipe line companies, 1929–36,
were obtained by the Bureau of Foreign and Domestic Commerce,
National Income Division, from a special tabulation of ICC data;
for 1937–38 they are given in *Selected Financial and Operating
Data from Annual Reports of Pipe Line Companies*. They are
raised similarly to dividends paid to yield total dividends received.
For 1922–28 dividends received are based on the ratio to dividends
paid. This ratio, computed for 1929 from the ICC data, is extrapolated by the corresponding ratio for all transportation and
public utility corporations as derived from *Statistics of Income*.
Extrapolation of dividends received for 1919–21 is by dividend
receipts of all corporations as reported in *Statistics of Income*.

Col. 4 Street railways: basic figures for dividends paid in 1917, 1922,
1927, 1932, and 1937 are from the *Census of Electric Railways*. For
1917, 1922, and 1937 they are the sum of dividends paid by operating and by lessor companies as reported. For 1927 and 1932 dividends are reported for companies exclusively street railways and
for lessor companies. The data for the operating companies are
raised to include all operating companies on the basis of the ratio
of dividends paid by all operating companies to those of companies
exclusively street railways. This ratio, computed from Census data
for 1922, is extrapolated by the ratio of gross revenue of all operating companies to that of companies exclusively street railways
(computed for 1922, 1927, and 1932 from the Census). The resulting

dividend figures for 1927 and 1932, combined with dividends paid by lessor companies, yield total dividends paid in those years. Interpolation between Census years and extrapolation for 1938 are by the dividend payments of the corporate sample for the industry.

Dividends received also are reported for all Census years except 1937. For 1927 and 1932 they are for companies exclusively street railways and are raised by the ratio to dividends paid. This ratio, computed from Census data for 1922, is extrapolated for 1927 and 1932 by the ratio for companies exclusively street railways (computed for 1922, 1927, and 1932 from the Census).

The ratio of total dividends received to total dividends paid is interpolated along a straight line for the years before 1932. For the years after 1932 the 1932 ratio is used. Total dividends received are obtained by multiplying estimated dividends paid by this ratio. *Col. 5 Water transportation:* sources and methods are those cited for col. 2.

Col. 6 Telephone: total dividends paid in 1917 and 1922, from the *Census of Telephones.* Interpolation between these years is by the dividend payments of the Bell System as reported in *Bell Telephone Securities.* For 1923–34 the method is as follows: the ratio of dividends of companies other than Bell to dividends of Bell companies is derived for 1922 and extrapolated by the ratio of the operating revenue of the other companies to the operating revenue of the Bell System. The latter ratio for 1927 and 1932 is computed from the Census; for the other years it is interpolated and extrapolated along a straight line. By applying the ratio of dividends for other companies to Bell System dividends, as reported in *Bell Telephone Securities,* dividends for other companies are obtained which, added to Bell dividends, yield total dividends. For 1935–38 dividends paid are the sum of those for the Bell System, obtained by letter from the American Telephone and Telegraph Company, and those for other companies, reported in *Selected Financial and Operating Data from Annual Reports of Telephone Carriers.* The latter are not complete but since the gross revenue of companies reporting is almost 97 per cent of the 1937 total, we regarded the reported dividend figure as a total.

Dividends received in 1917 and 1922 are reported in the *Census of Telephones.* Interpolation for 1920 and 1921, and extrapolation from 1922 through 1933, are by the non-operating revenue of the

Bell companies as reported in *Bell Telephone Securities*. Extrapolation for 1934–37 is by dividends received by the American Telephone and Telegraph Company. Dividends received, reported for 1938 in *Selected Financial and Operating Data from Annual Reports of Telephone Carriers*, are considered complete. The 1919 estimate of dividends received is obtained by applying to 1919 dividends paid the ratio to dividends paid. This ratio, computed for 1917 from the Census and for 1920 from estimates outlined above, is interpolated along a straight line for the intervening years.

Col. 7 Telegraph: total dividends paid in 1917, 1922, 1927, and 1937, from the *Census of Telegraphs*. Interpolation between 1917 and 1922 is by dividend payments of the Western Union Telegraph Company, obtained by letter. Interpolation between 1922 and 1927 is by the dividends of companies reporting to the Interstate Commerce Commission. For 1922–38 these dividend figures are reported in *Selected Financial and Operating Data from Annual Reports of Telegraph, Cable and Radiotelegraph Carriers*. For 1927–38 they are combined with those of the Commercial Cable Company, obtained by letter, and form the basis for the interpolation between the 1927 and 1937 Census figures. For 1938 the Federal Communications Commission figures for telegraph and wireless companies are considered complete.

Dividends received in 1917, 1922, 1927, and 1937 are from the Census. Interpolation between 1917 and 1922 is by dividends received by the Western Union Telegraph Company, obtained by letter. Interpolation between 1922 and 1927 is by the interest and dividend receipts of the Western Union Telegraph Company as published. For 1928–36 dividends received are interpolated by the dividends received by companies reporting to the Interstate Commerce Commission, obtained by the Bureau of Foreign and Domestic Commerce, National Income Division. The 1938 figure published by the Federal Communications Commission is assumed to be complete.

TABLE P 11

Interest by Major Industrial Divisions

Interest is net originating in the industry and is the difference between interest paid and received. For some industrial divisions

interest received covers receipts on government obligations alone.
Col. 1 Electric light and power, and manufactured gas: see Table
P 12, col. 1 and 2.

Col. 2 Steam railroads, Pullman, and railway express:

a) *Steam railroads:* interest paid and received in 1921 and later
years, from *Statistics of Railways.* For 1919 and 1920 the reported
Class I railroad figures are raised by the ratio of interest for all
roads to that for Class I roads. This ratio, computed from the above
source for 1916 and 1921, is interpolated for the intervening years
along a straight line. The 1929–38 figures are corrected to allow for
defaulted interest as estimated from data for Class I railroads in
Statistics of Railways.

b) *Pullman Company:* interest paid and received in all years,
from the *Preliminary Abstract of Statistics of Common Carriers.*

c) *Railway express:* interest paid and received in 1919 and 1920,
from *Statistics of Express Companies;* for all other years, from the
Preliminary Abstract of Statistics of Common Carriers.

Col. 3 Other transportation: see Table P 12, col. 3–5.

Col. 4 Communication: see Table P 12, col. 6 and 7.

Col. 5 Total: sum of col. 1–4.

TABLE P 12

Interest by Minor Industrial Divisions

Interest is net originating in the industry and is the difference between interest paid and received. For some industrial divisions interest received covers receipts on government obligations alone.

Col. 1 Electric light and power: for 1917 the *Census of Central Electric Light and Power Stations* reports long and short term debt and
total interest payments. Interest payments on long term debt are
assumed to be in the same proportion to total interest as long term
debt is to total debt outstanding. The 1922 and 1927 Censuses
report long term debt outstanding; long term interest payments are
estimated by applying to the outstanding debt average interest
rates derived from a corporate sample for the industry. Total long
term interest, 1930–35, is derived from the special tabulation of
Statistics of Income data which shows long term debt outstanding
on December 31, 1930–35, for the companies that report balance
sheet items. The 1929 debt is assumed to be the same percentage of

the long term debt of all transportation and public utility companies as the 1930. The 1934 debt figure, comparable with that reported for 1933, is extrapolated from 1933 by the debt of companies in the electric light and power and gas industries included in the Standard Statistics Company sample and published in their August 14, 1936 *Composite of Financial Statements.* The same index is used in estimating the 1933 figure comparable with 1934 and later years. The debt figures thus obtained for 1929–35 are raised to total long term debt by the ratio of compiled receipts of all public utility companies to compiled receipts of companies reporting assets and liabilities. This ratio is computed from *Statistics of Income* for all transportation and public utility corporations for all years except 1929 and 1930, for which the 1931 ratio is used. The year-end debt figures are averaged to yield the average outstanding during the year. To it is applied the average interest rate of the corporate sample for the industry to obtain total long term interest payments. Interpolation between the estimates of long term interest for 1917 and 1922, 1922 and 1927, 1927 and 1930 is by the long term interest payments of the corporate sample for the industry. Estimates for 1936–38 are extrapolated from 1935 by the corporate sample for the industry.

Interest received in 1917 and 1922 is estimated by applying to the Census figure on income from investments the ratio of interest received to total income from investments in the electric railway industry. The ratio of interest received to interest paid is computed for 1917 and 1922 from Census data and extrapolated for 1927 and 1932 by the corresponding ratio in the electric railway industry. It is interpolated along a straight line for intercensal years and applied to estimated total interest paid to yield interest received. The 1932 figure is extrapolated through 1937 by the item as reported in the special tabulation of *Statistics of Income* data. The ratio of interest received to interest paid in 1938 is assumed to be the same as in 1937.

Col. 2 Manufactured gas: total interest paid in 1924 is estimated on the basis of the book value of long term debt on December 31, 1923 and 1924, reported in the capital stock tax returns in *Statistics of Income.* The figure reported is raised to the total by the ratio of the fair value of the stock of all companies to the fair value of the stock of companies submitting statements of assets and liabilities.

To the average for the year (average of the year-end figures) is applied the interest rate of the corporate sample for the industry to estimate long term interest paid in 1924. The 1930–33 estimates are made by a procedure similar to that used in estimating long term interest for the electric light and power industry. Interpolation between 1924 and 1930 and extrapolation from 1924 to 1919 are by the interest payments of the corporate sample for the industry. The 1934–35 estimates of interest paid are the product of the long term debt outstanding and the average interest rate. Long term debt as of December 31, reported in the special tabulation of *Statistics of Income* data, is raised to allow for corporations not reporting. The raising ratio is that of the compiled receipts of all transportation and other public utility corporations to those of corporations submitting balance sheet data. The 1934 debt figure comparable with 1933 is extrapolated by the debt of gas companies as recorded in the American Gas Association Statistical Bulletin 26. The same index is used in estimating the 1933 figure comparable with 1934 and later years. Average debt outstanding during the year is estimated by averaging year-end figures. The average interest rate is computed from the corporate sample for the industry. The 1936–38 estimates of interest paid are extrapolated from 1935 by the corporate sample for the industry.

Interest received on government obligations in 1926–37 is reported in the special tabulation of *Statistics of Income* data. The 1938 estimate is made on the assumption that the ratio of interest received to interest paid is the same as in 1937. Extrapolation from 1926 to 1922 is by interest received by the total transportation and public utility group, and from 1922 to 1919, by interest received by all corporations as reported in *Statistics of Income*.

Col. 3 Pipe lines: total interest paid by companies reporting to the Interstate Commerce Commission, 1934–38, from *Selected Financial and Operating Data from Annual Reports of Pipe Line Companies*. For 1929–33 it is obtained, by the Bureau of Foreign and Domestic Commerce, National Income Division, from the special tabulation of ICC data. For 1919–28 it is an extrapolation of the 1929 figure by an estimate based on long term debt outstanding and an estimated interest rate, For 1923 and later years long term debt outstanding is given in the ICC report. For earlier years it is estimated on the basis of reports for pipe line corporations in *Moody's Industrials,* as is the interest rate.

Interest received, 1929–38, is from the tabulation of ICC data obtained by the National Income Division. For earlier years it is estimated on the basis of the 1929 relation to interest paid. Both interest received and paid are raised to include companies not covered by the Interstate Commerce Commission (see General Note B).

Col. 4 Street railways: total interest paid on long term debt in 1917, 1922, and 1927, from the *Census of Electric Railways.* The 1917 and 1922 figures are the sum of interest payments by operating companies, excluding municipal, and lessor companies. In 1927 the figure reported for operating companies is for those exclusively street railways. This is raised to the total for all operating companies by the ratio of total interest payments to those of companies exclusively street railways. This ratio, computed from the Census for 1922, is extrapolated to 1927 by the ratio of total gross revenue to that of companies exclusively street railways (Census for 1922 and 1927).

The 1930–35 figures for long term interest are the product of the estimated long term debt and the estimated interest rate. Funded debt on December 31, 1930–35 is from the special tabulation of *Statistics of Income* data. For 1929 it is estimated by applying to funded debt for the entire transportation and public utility group, as reported in *Statistics of Income,* the 1930 ratio of electric railway debt to the total. The debt figures reported are raised to allow for corporations not reporting. The raising ratio is that of the compiled receipts of all transportation and other public utility corporations to those of corporations submitting balance sheet data. Funded debt in 1934, comparable with that reported in 1933, is estimated by the change from 1933 to 1934 in sample data for the industry collected by the Bureau of Foreign and Domestic Commerce, National Income Division. The 1933 figure comparable with that reported for 1934 is estimated by the same method. Year-end figures are averaged to yield the debt outstanding during the year. To it is applied the interest rate derived for Census years from data for operating companies and interpolated for the intervening years by the corporate sample for the industry. The estimates of interest paid in 1918–21, 1923–26, 1928–29, and 1936–38 are interpolated and extrapolated by the corporate sample for the industry.

For 1917, 1922, 1927, and 1932 the Census reports interest paid and received by operating companies. The ratio of interest received to interest paid is derived, interpolated along a straight line for intercensal years, and applied to the estimated interest paid in each year to yield the estimated interest received. For 1933–38 the 1932 ratio is used.

Col. 5 Water transportation: from the capital stock tax returns published in *Statistics of Income* we obtain long term debt as of December 31, 1921, 1923, and 1924. The figures for 1923 and 1924 are raised to the total by the ratio of the fair value of the stock of all companies to the fair value of the stock of companies submitting statements of assets and liabilities. The long term debt series for December 31, 1929–35, and long term interest, 1936–38, are derived from the same source material and by the same method as the series for street railways, described above. Extrapolation of long term debt for 1918, 1919, and 1920, and interpolation for 1922 and 1925–28 are by the corporate sample for the industry. To the average for the year (average of the year-end figures) is applied the interest rate of the corporate sample for the industry. From the resulting estimate of long term interest paid is subtracted interest received from government obligations (for the latter see the notes to col. 2).

Col. 6 Telephone: total interest paid on long term debt in 1917, 1922, and 1937, from the *Census of Telephones.* Interpolation between 1917 and 1922, 1922 and 1937, and extrapolation for 1938 are by interest payments of the Bell System. The American Telephone and Telegraph Company data, used as index, are reported in *Moody's Public Utilities* through 1922; since then they are derived from information given in *Bell Telephone Securities.*

Interest received in 1917, 1922, and 1937 is from the Census. Interpolation between 1917 and 1922, 1922 and 1937, and extrapolation for 1938 are by the Bell System non-operating revenue, 1917–33, and their interest revenues and miscellaneous earnings, 1933–38.

Col. 7 Telegraph: total interest paid, long term debt, and total debt in 1917, 1922, and 1927, from the *Census of Telegraphs.* Total long term interest for these years is derived by applying, to total interest paid, the ratio of long term to total debt. Interpolation between 1917 and 1922 is by long term interest paid by the Western Union Telegraph Company, obtained by letter. The 1923–37 estimates are the product of the estimated long term debt and the average interest rate. For 1923–37 the debt reported in *Selected Financial and Operating Data from Annual Reports of Telegraph, Cable and Radiotelegraph Carriers* plus that of the Commercial Cable Company for 1928–33, when that company did not report to the Commission, is considered the total. The interest rate is computed from the Census for 1922, 1927, and 1937 and is interpolated by the rate on Western Union Telegraph Company long term debt. Long term interest paid in 1938 is reported by the Federal Communications Commission.

Interest received in 1917, 1922, 1927, and 1937 is from the Census. Interpolation between 1917 and 1922 is by Western Union Telegraph Company interest receipts, obtained by letter. For 1923–37 interest received is computed from total interest paid and the ratio of the former to the latter. For 1922, 1927, and 1937 this ratio is derived from Census data. For the other years it is interpolated along a straight line. Interest receipts in 1938 are from the Federal Communications Commission report.

TABLE P 13

Property Income by Major Industrial Divisions

Sum for each industrial division of dividends (Table P 9) and interest (Table P 11).

TABLE P 14

Property Income by Minor Industrial Divisions

Sum for each industrial division of dividends (Table P 10) and interest (Table P 12).

TABLE P 15

Total Payments to Individuals by Major Industrial Divisions

Sum for each industrial division of wages and salaries (Table P 6), pensions and compensation for injury (Table P 8), property income (Table P 13), and entrepreneurial withdrawals (Table P 16).

Entrepreneurial Withdrawals and Total Payments to Individuals
by Minor Industrial Divisions

ENTREPRENEURIAL WITHDRAWALS

Col. 1 Electric light and power: the labor income of entrepreneurs
is the product of their number (see the notes to Table P 19) and
average employee compensation (see the notes to Tables P 7 and
P 20). To it is added the net income item derived, from the *Census
of Central Electric Light and Power Stations* for all Census years
except 1937, as the difference between total revenues and total
expenses. For 1937 the item added is 'authorized cash distributions'
as reported, since savings are assumed to be zero. The Census data
are for 1917, 1922, 1927, 1932, and 1937 and are interpolated along
a straight line for the intervening years except 1933–36; for those
years interpolation is by corporate net income.

Col. 2 Water transportation: withdrawals, 1919–33, are estimated
by applying, to the sum of compensation of corporate officers and
dividends paid, the ratio of tonnage operated by unincorporated
firms to corporate tonnage. The ratio and the series on officers'
compensation are described in the notes to Table P 5, col. 3; dividends, in the notes to Table P 10, col. 5. Withdrawals, 1934–37, are
extrapolated from 1933 by the compensation of corporate officers
as reported in *Statistics of Income.* The 1938 estimate is extrapolated from 1937 by total salary payments.

TOTAL PAYMENTS TO INDIVIDUALS

Col. 3–9 Total: sum for each industrial division of wages and
salaries (Table P 7), pensions and compensation for injury (Table
P 8), property income (Table P 14), and entrepreneurial withdrawals (col. 1 and 2, above).

TABLE P 17

Net Savings by Major Industrial Divisions

Col. 1 Electric light and power, and manufactured gas: see Table
P 18, col. 1 and 2.
Col. 2 Steam railroads, Pullman, and railway express: difference

between net income and total dividends paid (see the notes to Table P 9, col. 2). Net income is obtained as follows:

a) Steam railroads: net income of steam railroads, considered as a system, is reported for all years except 1919 and 1920 in *Statistics of Railways.* For these two years estimates are interpolated between 1917 and 1921 by the net income of Class I operating roads, of Class I non-operating roads, and of switching and terminal companies, also reported in *Statistics of Railways.* The 1919 figure covers corporate income alone, government income being excluded. For 1929 and later years net income is adjusted for interest defaults on the basis of data for Class I railroads reported in *Statistics of Railways.* For earlier years interest defaults are considered negligible.

b) Pullman Company: from the *Preliminary Abstract of Statistics of Common Carriers.*

c) Railway express: for 1919 and 1920, from *Statistics of Express Companies;* for later years, from the *Preliminary Abstract of Statistics of Common Carriers.*

Col. 3 Other transportation: see Table P 18, col. 3–5.

Col. 4 Communication: see Table P 18, col. 6 and 7.

Col. 5 Total: sum of col. 1–4.

TABLE P 18

Net Savings by Minor Industrial Divisions

Sum of savings of entrepreneurs and of corporations. Non-corporate enterprises are found in only two of the industries under consideration—electric light and power and water transportation. Entrepreneurial savings in these industries are described in the notes to Table P 5, col. 2. Corporate savings are the difference between net income and total dividends paid (see the notes to Table P 10). The method by which net income is estimated is indicated below for each industrial division.

Col. 1 Electric light and power: net income in 1917, 1922, 1927, 1932, and 1937 is from the *Census of Central Electric Light and Power Stations,* as are total revenues and total expenses of unincorporated firms. The difference between the last two items represents entrepreneurial net income which, when subtracted from the net income for the industry as a whole, leaves corporate net income.

Interpolation between Census years and extrapolation for 1938 are by the net income of the corporate sample for the industry.

Col. 2 Manufactured gas: net profits after taxes, 1926–37, are reported in the special tabulation of *Statistics of Income* data. For the years before 1926, they are estimated as the sum of statutory net income after taxes (*Statistics of Income*) and dividends and interest received on tax-exempt obligations (see the notes to Tables P 10 and P 12). Corporate savings for 1938 are extrapolated from 1937 by the corporate sample for the industry.

Col. 3 Pipe lines: net income in 1920 and later years for companies engaged in interstate commerce, from *Selected Financial and Operating Data from Annual Reports of Pipe Line Companies* (Interstate Commerce Commission). The 1919 estimate is an extrapolation of the 1920 figure by the corporate sample for the industry. The data for interstate companies are raised by the factor described in General Note B.

Col. 4 Street railways: net income (excluding that of state and municipal railways) in 1917, 1922, 1927, 1932, and 1937, from the *Census of Electric Railways*. Interpolation between 1917 and 1922, 1922 and 1927, is by the corporate sample for the industry. Interpolation for 1928–31 is by the net income reported for street railways in the special tabulation of *Statistics of Income* data. For 1932 and later years corporate savings are estimated directly. Interpolation for 1933–36 and extrapolation for 1938 are by the corporate savings of street railways reporting to the Interstate Commerce Commission.

Col. 5 Water transportation: sources and methods are those indicated for col. 2.

Col. 6 Telephone: net income in 1917 and 1922, from the *Census of Telephones*. Interpolation for intervening years is by the net income of the Bell System as reported in *Bell Telephone Securities*. For the years after 1922 net income is obtained by adding to the net income of the Bell System, as given in *Bell Telephone Securities,* the estimated net income of non-Bell companies. The latter is derived by applying to the net income of the Bell System the ratio of net income of non-Bell companies to that of the Bell System. This ratio, computed from Census data for 1922, is extrapolated for the other years by the ratio of the operating revenue of non-Bell companies to that of the Bell System. Operating revenues in 1922, 1927, 1932, and 1937 are from the Census. Interpolation of the ratio for intervening years is along a straight line. The 1938 net income reported by the Federal Communications Commission is assumed to be complete.

Col. 7 Telegraph: net income in 1917, 1922, and 1927, from the *Census of Telegraphs.* Interpolation between 1917 and 1922 is by the net income of the Western Union Telegraph Company, obtained by letter. Interpolation between 1922 and 1927 is by the net income of corporations reporting to the Interstate Commerce Commission. For 1934–38 the Federal Communications Commission reports the net income of telegraph and wireless companies and the figures are considered complete. Since for 1928–33 they cover telegraph companies alone, net income of wireless companies is interpolated by the net income of telegraph companies.

TABLE P 19

Employees by Major Industrial Divisions, and Total Entrepreneurs

EMPLOYEES

Col. 1 Electric light and power, and manufactured gas: see Table P 20, col. 1 and 2.

Col. 2 and 3 Steam railroads, Pullman, and railway express:

a) *Steam railroads:* the number of employees on all steam railroads, switching and terminal companies is reported annually since 1922 in *Statistics of Railways.* For 1920 and 1921 the number on Class I roads and switching and terminal companies is reported, and for 1919 the number on Class I roads alone. The number on all railroads for 1919–21 is obtained by applying to the figures for Class I roads the ratio of all employees to those on Class I roads. This ratio, derived from data reported for 1916 and 1922, is interpolated along a straight line for the intervening years. The estimates for all switching and terminal companies in 1920 and 1921 are obtained by applying to the Class I switching and terminal figure the ratio of locomotives used by all switching and terminal companies to those used by Class I switching and terminal companies. Total employees in 1919 are estimated by raising the figure for all railroads to include employees in switching and terminal companies. The ratio of employees on all railroads and switching and terminal companies to those on railroads alone is computed from data reported for 1916 and 1920 and interpolated for intervening years along a straight line. Employees are divided into wage earners and salaried employees by the method used to divide total pay into wages and salaries (see the notes to Table P 6, col. 2 and 3 and General Note A).

b) Pullman Company: the average number of employees, 1936–38, and the number of employees as of December 31 for all other years, from the *Preliminary Abstract of Statistics of Common Carriers.* For the years before 1936 the number of employees at year-ends are averaged.

c) Railway express: the average number of employees, 1934–38, and the number of employees as of December 31, 1925–33, from the *Preliminary Abstract of Statistics of Common Carriers.* For 1925–33 the number of employees at year-ends are averaged; for 1922–24, it is obtained by letter from the Interstate Commerce Commission; and for 1919–21, by dividing total wages and salaries paid by the average wage and salary. Average wage and salary figures are computed for 1922 from the ICC data and are extrapolated to 1919 by the steam railroad average wage and salary.

Col. 4 Other transportation: see Table P 20, col. 3–5.

Col. 5 Communication: see Table P 20, col. 6 and 7.

Col. 6 Total: sum of col. 1–5.

ENTREPRENEURS

Col. 7 Total: non-corporate enterprises are found in (a) electric light and power and (b) water transportation.

a) Electric light and power: the number of entrepreneurs is estimated by adding individual owners and unincorporated firm members. It is assumed that each unincorporated firm has two members. For 1917, 1922, 1927, 1932, and 1937 the number of individual owners and unincorporated firms is from the *Census of Central Electric Light and Power Stations.* Intercensal year estimates of entrepreneurs are interpolated along a straight line. The number of entrepreneurs is assumed to be the same in 1938 as in 1937.

b) Water transportation: for 1910 and 1930 the number of owners, from the occupation statistics of the *Census of Population.*

For 1919 and 1920 the number is assumed to be the same as in 1910 and interpolation between 1920 and 1930 is along a straight line. Extrapolation of the 1930 figure through 1934 is by the number of officers reported in the ICC special analysis, obtained by the Bureau of Foreign and Domestic Commerce, National Income Division. From 1935 through 1937 the extrapolation is by the number of salaried employees. The 1938 figure is assumed to be the same as the 1937.

TABLE P 20

Employees by Minor Industrial Divisions

Col. 1 Electric light and power: for 1917, 1922, 1927, 1932, and 1937, from the *Census of Central Electric Light and Power Stations*. Interpolation for 1919–21, 1923–26, is by a weighted average of employment indexes for electric light and power in New York (*Labor Market Bulletin* and N. Y. Department of Labor Special Bulletin 171), Ohio (BLS Bulletin 553), and Pennsylvania (*Report on Productive Industries, Public Utilities and Miscellaneous Statistics*) for the first period, and Wisconsin (derived from *Wisconsin Labor Market* data on month to month changes in employment), and Illinois (1929 *Annual Report of the Department of Labor*), in addition, for the second. The weights arc the kilowatt hours generated as reported in the Census, used for the 5 years centering at the Census year. The 1929–38 estimates are interpolated between and extrapolated from the 1932 and 1937 Census figures by the BLS employment index. The interpolation for 1928 is by the kilowatt hours generated in 1927–29 as reported in the National Electric Light Association Bulletin 7.

Col. 2 Manufactured gas: the number employed at commercial plants in 1919, 1921, 1923, 1925, 1927, and 1929, from the *Biennial Census of Manufactures;* for 1933 it is derived from the number employed in all plants as there reported. For the derivation of the 1931 estimates see the notes to Table P 7, col. 2. Interpolation for intercensal years and extrapolation for 1934–38 are by estimates prepared by the American Gas Association. The interpolating series for the years before 1929 is from the Association's Statistical Bulletin 9, and for 1930 and 1932, from Bulletin 17. The extrapolating series for 1934–37 is from Bulletin 32, and that for 1938, from Bulletin 36.

Col. 3 Pipe lines: for 1925–31 the number of employees as of December 31 in companies reporting to the Interstate Commerce Commission, from *Selected Financial and Operating Data from Annual Reports of Pipe Line Companies.* For 1932–38 this source reports the average for the year. Annual figures, 1926–31, are averages of year-end figures. The total for 1926 and later years is obtained by raising the figures for interstate companies by the factor described in General Note B. For 1919–25 the number is estimated by dividing the total compensation by the average pay. The average pay is computed for 1926 and extrapolated by the average pay in the petroleum refining industry.

Col. 4 Street railways: the number of employees in 1917, 1922, 1927, 1932, and 1937, from the *Census of Electric Railways* (excluding municipal and state railways). Interpolation for intercensal years and extrapolation for 1938 are by the American Transit Association estimates of the number of employees, obtained by letter.

Col. 5 Water transportation: the number of employees other than stevedores and longshoremen, 1929–38, is estimated by the procedure described in *National Income in the United States, 1929–35* (Bureau of Foreign and Domestic Commerce, pp. 262-4). The number of stevedores, 1929–38, is based on the number of man-years required for bulk and general cargo. The estimate of man-years, excluding inland traffic, 1929–32, was supplied by the United States Shipping Board, Division of Marine Development. The 1932 man-year figures for bulk and general cargo are extrapolated through 1938 by the tonnage of bulk and general cargo, excluding inland traffic. These estimates of man-years for 1929 and later years are raised to include inland transportation by the ratio of the tonnage of inland transportation to that of other water transportation. All the data on tonnage carried are from the *Annual Report of the Chief of Engineers* of the United States Army, Part II.

The number of employees for the years before 1929 is the sum of vessel employees, shore employees, and stevedores. Vessel employees are reported for 1916 and 1926 in the 1926 *Census of Transportation by Water,* and are for both freight and passenger vessels. Interpolation between 1916 and 1926, 1926 and 1929, is by tonnage cleared as recorded in the *Survey of Current Business*. The 1929 ratio of land to vessel employees is applied to vessel employees to yield land employees, 1919–28. The number of stevedores and long-shoremen, 1919–28, is extrapolated from 1929 by a preliminary series. The 1920 and 1930 figures in this series are the number of stevedores and longshoremen reported in the 1930 *Census of Population*, Vol. V, Ch. 1. Total tonnage of water-borne commerce, 1920–30 (*Annual Report of the Chief of Engineers*, Part II), is extrapolated for 1919 by the value of imports and exports by sea and of freight through the Sault Ste. Marie Canal, as reported in the *Statistical Abstract*. Average tonnage per stevedore is computed for 1920 and 1930, interpolated for 1921–29, and extrapolated for 1919 along a straight line. Total tonnage divided by the tonnage per man yields the preliminary estimate of stevedores, by which the final 1929 figure is extrapolated to 1919.

Col. 6 Telephone: the number of employees in 1917, 1922, 1927, 1932, and 1937, from the *Census of Telephones*. Interpolation between 1917 and 1922, 1922 and 1927, is by the number of employees of the Bell System (*Moody's Public Utilities* and the *Statistical Abstract*). Interpolation between 1927 and 1932, 1932 and 1937, and extrapolation for 1938 are by data reported by the Interstate Commerce Commission for 1927–33 and by the Federal Communications Commission for 1934–38 in *Selected Financial and Operating Data from Annual Reports of Telephone Carriers*.

Col. 7 Telegraph: the number of telegraph and wireless employees in 1917, 1922, and 1927 is from the *Census of Telegraphs*, as is that of telegraph in 1932. The 1932 estimate of wireless employees is based on the ratio to telegraph employees in 1927. Interpolation between 1917 and 1922, 1922 and 1927, is by Western Union Telegraph Company employment figures, obtained by letter. The Interstate Commerce Commission and the Federal Communications Commission report employment data in *Selected Financial and Operating Data from Annual Reports of Telegraph, Cable and Radiotelegraph Carriers*. These, together with Commercial Cable Company data, obtained by letter, provide an index by which interpolation between 1927 and 1932 and extrapolation for 1933 are made. The 1934–38 employment figures reported by the Federal Communications Commission are assumed to be complete.

TABLE P 21

Comparison of Various Income Account Items
for Steam Railroads Reported in
Statistics of Income and
Statistics of Railways in the United States

Col. 1, 4, 7, 10, and 12: from the special tabulation of *Statistics of Income* data. Gross income is the item reported as compiled receipts; total expense is total statutory deductions plus total tax; and net profit is compiled net profit less total tax.

Col. 2, 5, 8, 11, and 13: from Statement 34 of *Statistics of Railways.* Expenses and net profit were adjusted for defaulted interest for 1929 and later years (see the notes to Table P 11, col. 2). Gross income is the sum of railway operating revenues and other income; total expense is the sum of railway operating expenses, railway tax accruals, uncollectible railway revenues, equipment and joint facility rents, miscellaneous deductions from income, fixed charges and contingent charges; net profit is the reported net income item.

Col. 14: difference between col. 10 and 12.

Col. 15: difference between col. 11 and 13.

Col. 17: difference between col. 7 and 12.

Col. 18: difference between col. 8 and 13.

Col. 19: difference between col. 17 and 14.

Col. 20: difference between col. 18 and 15.

Trade

TABLES T1–T5

Whenever two entries are made for 1934 the first is comparable with those for preceding years in that the *Statistics of Income* data used are based on the old industrial classification; the second is comparable with those for succeeding years in that the *Statistics of Income* data used are based on the new industrial classification.

Net savings and net income, adjusted, exclude gains and losses from sales of capital assets, 1929–38, and from changes in inventory valuation, 1919–38. Net savings and net income without any specific designation are unadjusted, i.e., include these two types of gain and loss.

T 1 Gross Income (millions of dollars)

	WHOLESALE (1)	RETAIL (2)	TOTAL (3)
1919	64,094	36,549	100,643
1920	66,070	41,364	107,434
1921	47,566	32,954	80,521
1922	50,270	34,007	84,277
1923	58,938	38,897	97,835
1924	57,964	38,700	96,664
1925	63,061	42,283	105,344
1926	63,795	44,699	108,494
1927	63,484	43,699	107,183
1928	65,475	44,923	110,398
1929	68,950	46,989	115,939
1930	57,174	40,788	97,962
1931	44,405	33,480	77,885
1932	35,941	23,961	59,902
1933	32,151	23,607	55,758
1934	37,445	27,256	64,701
1935	44,877	30,770	75,647
1936	51,562	35,238	86,800
1937	56,458	37,052	93,510
1938	48,335	32,749	81,084

T 2 Total Payments by Type (millions of dollars)

	WAGES & SALARIES (1)	ENTREP. WITHDR. (2)	DIVIDENDS (3)	INTEREST (4)	PROP. INCOME (5)	PAY. TO INDIVIDUALS (6)
1919	5,430	2,197	400	33.1	433	8,061
1920	6,052	2,594	382	41.7	423	9,070
1921	5,171	2,176	320	40.0	360	7,708
1922	5,682	2,050	302	39.2	341	8,074
1923	6,389	2,072	369	22.0	391	8,853
1924	6,531	2,137	389	30.7	420	9,089
1925	6,986	2,091	440	30.7	470	9,548
1926	7,423	2,133	471	24.6	495	10,053
1927	7,290	2,109	495	30.8	526	9,926
1928	7,521	2,127	499	43.0	542	10,191
1929	8,012	2,231	565	55.6	621	10,865
1930	7,644	2,209	496	68.7	565	10,419
1931	6,644	2,144	386	66.1	452	9,241
1932	5,136	1,948	214	60.5	274	7,359
1933	4,513	1,796	178	49.1	227	6,537
1934	5,293	1,816	275	47.0	322	7,433
1934	5,293	1,816	339	36.3	375	7,486
1935	5,502	1,822	438	32.1	470	7,795
1936	5,848	1,921	669	30.1	699	8,469
1937	6,450	2,048	624	31.5	656	9,155
1938	6,258	2,085	482	31.3	513	8,857

T 3 Net Income Originating (millions of dollars)

	PAY. TO INDIVIDUALS (1)	NET SAVINGS Entrep. (2)	Corp. (3)	Total (4)	NET INCOME (5)	NET SAVINGS, ADJUSTED Entrep. (6)	Corp. (7)	Total (8)	NET INCOME, ADJ. (9)
1919	8,061	2,426	624	3,050	11,111	1,830	314	2,144	10,205
1920	9,070	419	8.5	427	9,498	1,491	910	2,401	11,472
1921	7,708	−458	−462	−920	6,788	1,195	622	1,818	9,527
1922	8,074	583	306	889	8,964	381	174	555	8,630
1923	8,853	840	460	1,301	10,154	833	456	1,290	10,143
1924	9,089	492	305	797	9,886	449	275	724	9,813
1925	9,548	539	393	933	10,481	364	253	618	10,166
1926	10,053	368	235	604	10,658	815	646	1,462	11,516
1927	9,926	290	173	464	10,390	380	261	642	11,568
1928	10,191	370	278	648	10,840	437	348	785	10,977
1929	10,865	171	68.8	240	11,105	308	200	508	11,374
1930	10,419	−553	−640	−1,194	9,225	297	261	559	10,978
1931	9,241	−846	−985	−1,831	7,410	−2.0	−207	−209	9,031
1932	7,359	−868	−1,037	−1,906	5,453	−438	−621	−1,060	6,298
1933	6,537	−141	−266	−408	6,128	−534	−778	−1,312	5,224
1934	7,433	−27.8	−65.8	−93.6	7,339	−136	−260	−396	7,036
1934	7,486	−17.9	−100	−118	7,368	−132	−294	−427	7,058
1935	7,795	−2.3	−71.2	−73.5	7,721	−121	−274	−396	7,399
1936	8,469	82.4	11.7	94.0	8,563	60.2	−32.0	28.2	8,498
1937	9,155	43.9	−42.5	1.4	9,156	−28.0	−165	−193	8,961
1938	8,857	34.9	−29.0	5.8	8,863	182	237	420	9,277

T 4 Wages and Salaries, and Entrepreneurial Net Income (millions of dollars)

	WAGES AND SALARIES Wholesale (1)	Retail (2)	Total (3)	ENTREPRENEURIAL WITHDRAWALS Wholesale (4)	Retail (5)	Total (6)	ENTREPRENEURIAL Net savings (7)	Net income (8)
1919	2,398	3,032	5,430	628	1,569	2,197	2,426	4,623
1920	2,522	3,529	6,052	730	1,864	2,594	419	3,013
1921	2,014	3,157	5,171	525	1,651	2,176	−458	1,718
1922	2,134	3,548	5,682	459	1,591	2,050	583	2,633
1923	2,453	3,936	6,389	459	1,613	2,072	840	2,913
1924	2,444	4,086	6,531	467	1,670	2,137	492	2,629
1925	2,644	4,341	6,986	440	1,650	2,091	539	2,631
1926	2,707	4,716	7,423	460	1,673	2,133	368	2,502
1927	2,742	4,548	7,290	470	1,638	2,109	290	2,399
1928	2,848	4,672	7,521	494	1,633	2,127	370	2,498
1929	3,003	5,008	8,012	531	1,699	2,231	171	2,403
1930	2,863	4,781	7,644	530	1,678	2,209	−553	1,655
1931	2,463	4,181	6,644	509	1,634	2,144	−846	1,298
1932	1,934	3,201	5,136	446	1,502	1,948	−868	1,080
1933	1,714	2,799	4,513	399	1,397	1,796	−141	1,654
1934	2,018	3,275	5,293	409	1,407	1,816	−27.8	1,789
1934	2,018	3,275	5,293	409	1,407	1,816	−17.9	1,798
1935	2,145	3,357	5,502	422	1,399	1,822	−2.3	1,819
1936	2,269	3,579	5,848	446	1,474	1,921	82.4	2,003
1937	2,505	3,944	6,450	475	1,573	2,048	43.9	2,092
1938	2,443	3,814	6,258	482	1,603	2,085	34.9	2,120

T 5   Persons Engaged (thousands)

	EMPLOYEES				ENTREPRENEURS		
	Wholesale	Retail	Total	Total *	Wholesale	Retail	Total
	(1)	(2)	(3)	(4)	(5)	(6)	(7)
1919			3,882	3,605	85.8	1,063	1,149
1920			4,269	3,636	86.3	1,093	1,179
1921			3,819	3,564	86.8	1,123	1,210
1922			4,029	3,891	87.3	1,152	1,240
1923			4,370	4,302	87.8	1,182	1,270
1924			4,514	4,390	88.3	1,212	1,300
1925			4,589	4,591	88.8	1,242	1,330
1926			4,729	4,796	89.3	1,271	1,361
1927			4,878	4,922	89.8	1,301	1,391
1928			4,929	4,924	90.3	1,331	1,421
1929	1,560	3,623	5,184	5,184	90.8	1,361	1,452
1930	1,484	3,495	4,980		91.7	1,356	1,448
1931	1,308	3,125	4,433		92.6	1,352	1,444
1932	1,149	2,685	3,833		93.6	1,347	1,440
1933	1,136	2,658	3,794		94.5	1,342	1,436
1934	1,257	2,950	4,207		95.9	1,298	1,394
1935	1,279	2,945	4,224		97.2	1,254	1,351
1936	1,320	3,062	4,383		100	1,289	1,389
1937	1,400	3,210	4,611		102	1,307	1,410
1938	1,352	3,051	4,403		103	1,312	1,416

* Second estimate.

TABLE T 1

Gross Income

Col. 1 Wholesale: from the Census of Wholesale Distribution for 1929 (revised in 1933), 1933, and 1935 we took total sales for each year. To the 1935 total as reported we added data for auxiliary units and chain store warehouses. We classified the 1929 total into perishable, semidurable, and durable commodities including building materials on the basis used in Commodity Flow and Capital Formation, Vol. One, and extrapolated each subtotal to 1919 by wholesalers' sales as estimated for that study. Interpolation for intercensal years and extrapolation for 1936–38 are by the sales estimates of the Market Data Section, Marketing Research Division of the Bureau of Foreign and Domestic Commerce (see Domestic Commerce).

Col. 2 Retail: from the Census of Retail Distribution for 1929, 1933, and 1935 we took total sales for each year, excluding restaurants and eating places which we include in the service industry. We classified the 1929 total into perishable, semidurable, consumers' durable, producers' durable commodities, and building materials on the basis used in *Commodity Flow and Capital Formation*, Vol. One, and extrapolated to 1919 by the series there reported for each subgroup. Interpolation for intercensal years and extrapolation for 1936–38 are by the sales estimates of the Market Data Section, Marketing Research Division of the Bureau of Foreign and Domestic Commerce (see *Domestic Commerce*).

Col. 3 Total: sum of col. 1 and 2.

TABLE T 2
Total Payments by Type

Col. 1 Wages and salaries: see Table T 4, col. 3.

Col. 2 Entrepreneurial withdrawals: see Table T 4, col. 6.

Col. 3 Dividends: net dividends are the difference between total dividends paid and dividends received, both reported for 1922–37 in *Statistics of Income*. The 1938 estimates are extrapolated from 1937 by the corporate sample for the industry. Total dividends paid, 1919–21, are extrapolated from 1922 by the dividend payments of the corporate sample for the industry. Dividends received, 1919–21, are estimated on the assumption that the industrial distribution of dividends received by all corporations, reported in *Statistics of Income,* is the same as in 1922.

Col. 4 Interest: net long term interest is the difference between total long term interest paid and interest received on tax-exempt obligations.

Total long term interest, 1922–35, is estimated by multiplying long term debt outstanding by the average interest rate. Long term debt outstanding on December 31, 1921, 1923, 1924, and 1926–35 is from *Statistics of Income*. The 1921 figures are assumed to be complete for the industry. Those for 1923 and 1924 are raised by the ratio of the fair value of the stock of all corporations to the fair value of the stock of corporations reporting assets and liabilities. The 1926–31 figures are raised by the 1931 ratio of compiled receipts of all corporations to the compiled receipts of corporations reporting assets and liabilities. Total figures for 1932–35 also are obtained by applying, to the figure reported, the compiled receipts ratios for the respective years.

Long term debt in 1934, comparable with 1933 and preceding years, is extrapolated from 1933 by the long term debt of corporations filing unconsolidated returns as reported in *Statistics of Income* and raised by the compiled receipts ratio. The latter applied to the long term debt figure for 1934, comparable with 1935 and later years, yields a comparable 1933 figure. Long term debt as of December 31, 1922 is interpolated by the debt of the corporate sample for the industry; as of December 31, 1925, along a straight line. Year-end figures are averaged to yield the debt outstanding during the year. To the resulting averages the average interest rate of the corporate sample for the industry is applied to yield total long term interest paid. Total interest paid in 1919–21 and in 1936–38 is extrapolated from 1922 and 1935, respectively, by the corporate sample for the industry.

Interest received, 1922–37, is from *Statistics of Income;* for 1919–21, it is estimated on the assumption that the industrial distribution of the total for the respective years, reported in *Statistics of Income,* is the same as in 1922. Interest received in 1938 is assumed to bear the same relation to interest paid as in 1937.

Col. 5 Property income: sum of col. 3 and 4.

Col. 6 Total payments to individuals: sum of col. 1, 2, and 5.

TABLE T 3

Net Income Originating

Col. 1 Total payments to individuals: see Table T 2, col. 6.

Col. 2 Entrepreneurial net savings: see Table T 4, col. 7.

Col. 3 Corporate net savings: difference between net profits after taxes and total dividends paid (see the notes to Table T 2, col. 3).

Net profits after taxes, 1922–37, are from *Statistics of Income;* for 1919–21, they are the sum of statutory net income (*Statistics of Income*) and dividends and interest received on tax-exempt obligations (see the notes to Table T 2, col. 3 and 4); for 1938 they are extrapolated from 1937 by the corporate sample for the industry.

Col. 4 Total net savings: sum of col. 2 and 3.

Col. 5 Net income originating: sum of col. 1 and 4.

TABLE T 4

Wages and Salaries, and Entrepreneurial Net Income

Col. 1 Wages and salaries, wholesale: for 1929, 1933, and 1935, from
the *Census of Wholesale Distribution;* the 1935 figure is adjusted
to include auxiliary units and chain store warehousing, Interpolation for intercensal years and extrapolation for 1936–38 are by the
BLS payrolls index.

For 1919–29 the entries are the sum of separate estimates for
perishable, semidurable, and durable commodities and building
materials, based on the relation of wages and salaries to sales.
Regression lines of the change in the ratio of wages and salaries to
sales on the percentage change in sales were derived from data on
operating cost studies for wholesale produce firms and for Ohio
wholesale grocers—the only samples available on this item for
wholesale trade. From these regression lines we read the change in
the ratio of wages and salaries to sales for the points corresponding
to the percentage change in our estimates of sales for the various
years. The readings from the two lines are averaged and are used
to extrapolate to 1919 the 1929 basic ratio of wages and salaries to
sales, computed from the *Census of Wholesale Distribution,* 1929
(revised in 1933). Wages and salaries in each year are the product of
this ratio and estimated sales. For the derivation of the sales figures
see the notes to Table T 1, col. 1.

Col. 2 Wages and salaries, retail: for 1929, 1933, and 1935, from the
Census of Retail Distribution, adjusted to exclude data reported
for restaurants and eating places, which we include in the service
industry, and to include salaries paid at central administrative
offices. Payrolls for central offices are reported for 1933 and 1935
and estimated for 1929 on the assumption that their ratio to sales
of chain stores (those reporting data for central offices) moves
similarly to the ratio of other payrolls to total sales. Interpolation
for intercensal years and extrapolation for 1936–38 are by the BLS
payrolls index.

Wages and salaries in retail trade, 1919–28, are the sum of estimates for (a) perishable, (b) semidurable, (c) consumers' durable,
(d) producers' durable, and (e) building materials. The estimates
are the product of the volume of sales (see the notes to Table T 1,

col. 2) and the ratio of wages and salaries to sales. For each sub-group the 1929 ratio of wages and salaries to sales is computed from the *Census of Retail Distribution,* and extrapolated for 1926 by the ratio for the sample cities covered in the 1926 *Census of Retail and Wholesale Trade.* A description of the series by which the ratio is extrapolated to 1919 and interpolated between 1926 and 1929 follows for each subgroup. The indexes indicated are derived from various operating cost studies. They are combined, when weighted indexes are used, by means of the 1929 sales figures.

a) Perishable commodities: interpolation between 1926 and 1929 is by the weighted average of the ratios of wages and salaries to sales for grocery and drug stores, as is the extrapolation from 1926 to 1924. For the years before 1924 extrapolation is by the ratio for grocery stores.

b) Semidurable commodities: interpolation and extrapolation for 1923–29 are by the ratio of wages and salaries to sales for department stores. The 1923 figure is extrapolated to 1920 by the weighted average of the ratios for department and shoe stores; the 1920, to 1919, by the ratio for shoe stores alone.

c) Consumers' durable commodities: interpolation and extrapolation for 1920–29 are by the weighted average of the ratios of wages and salaries to sales for department and jewelry stores; for 1919, by the ratio for jewelry stores alone.

d) Producers' durable commodities: interpolation and extrapolation for 1920–29 are by the ratio of wages and salaries to sales for hardware stores.

e) Building materials: interpolation and extrapolation for 1924–29 are by the weighted average of the ratios of wages and salaries to sales for building materials stores and hardware stores; for 1920–23, by the ratio for hardware stores alone.

Total wages and salaries in 1919 are estimated by applying to the 1920 total the percentage change from 1919 to 1920 in the sum of wages and salaries for the perishable, semidurable, and consumers' durable commodity groups.

Salaries at central administrative offices in the years before 1929 are based on the estimated sales of chain stores and the ratio of payrolls to sales. Chain store sales are based on the ratio to total sales reported for 1920, 1923, 1926, 1927, and 1929 in the *Chain Store Tells Its Story* (Institute of Distribution, Inc., 1940) and interpolated along a straight line for the intervening years. The ratio of payrolls to sales is assumed to move similarly to the ratio of other payrolls to total retail sales.

Col. 3 Total wages and salaries: sum of col. 1 and 2.

Col. 4 Entrepreneurial withdrawals, wholesale: total withdrawals are estimated by multiplying the number of entrepreneurs (see the notes to Table T 5, col. 5) by their estimated average annual withdrawal. The average withdrawal in 1929 and 1935 is assumed to equal the average salary paid executives as derived from the *Census of Wholesale Distribution.* Interpolation between 1929 and 1935 and extrapolation for 1936–38 are by an index derived by dividing the BLS payrolls index by that of employment. A preliminary estimate of withdrawals, 1919–29, is computed by applying to non-corporate business (see the notes to col. 7) the corporate withdrawal ratio. The withdrawal ratio is the ratio of the sum of dividends paid (see the notes to Table T 2, col. 3) and officers' compensation to gross sales *(Statistics of Income).* Officers' compensation is inter-polated for 1925–27 by corporate gross sales. Gross sales for 1922 is extrapolated to 1919 by the gross income series in *Statistics of Income.* The final 1929 total withdrawal figure is extrapolated through 1919 by the preliminary estimate described. Three-year moving averages of the average withdrawal are taken to yield the final average withdrawal for 1920–28. The 1920 average withdrawal is extrapolated to 1919 by the BLS cost of living index.

Col. 5 Entrepreneurial withdrawals, retail: obtained by multiply-ing the number of entrepreneurs (see the notes to Table T 5, col. 6) by their estimated average annual withdrawal. The average with-drawal in 1929 and 1933 is computed from the *Census of Retail Distribution;* for 1935 it is assumed to equal the average annual pay. Interpolation for intercensal years and extrapolation for 1936–38 are by an index derived by dividing the BLS payrolls index by that of employment. Estimates for the years before 1929 are made by the procedure described in the notes to col. 4.

Col. 6 Total entrepreneurial withdrawals: sum of col. 4 and 5.

Col. 7 Entrepreneurial net savings: product of non-corporate sales and the estimated savings ratio. Non-corporate sales are the differ-ence between total sales and retail and wholesale corporate sales. The total sales series is described in the notes to Table T 1. Retail corporate sales in 1929 are from the *Census of Retail Distribution.*

Corporate sales of restaurants and eating places are deducted from the Census total since we include this field in the service industry. The corporate figure for restaurants is estimated by applying to the total sales figure for restaurants the ratio of corporate to total sales for all trade.

The retail corporate sales figure for 1929 is extrapolated to 1927 and 1933 and from 1935 through 1937 by the gross income of retail corporations as reported in *Statistics of Income*. The 1934 and 1938 figures are assumed to be the same percentage of total retail sales as in 1933 añd 1937, respectively.

Wholesale corporate sales, 1927–38, are obtained by applying to total wholesale sales the estimated ratio of corporate to total sales. The ratio for 1929 and 1935 is computed from *Census of Wholesale Distribution* data. For intercensal years it is interpolated along a straight line and for 1936–38 it is kept constant at the 1935 level. For 1927 and 1928 the ratio is assumed to be the same as for 1929.

Total retail and wholesale corporate sales are extrapolated from 1927 to 1921 by *Statistics of Income* gross sales of corporations in trade; and from 1921 to 1919, by their gross income, from the same source.

The separation of total corporate sales in 1923 and 1924 into retail and wholesale is based on the ratio of retail corporate to wholesale corporate sales. The ratio for these years is an extrapolation of the 1930 ratio by the ratio of retail capital stock to wholesale capital stock. The capital stock figures are from capital stock tax returns in *Statistics of Income* for 1923 and 1924, and from the special tabulation of *Statistics of Income* asset and liability data for 1930. Total corporate sales in 1925 and 1926 are separated into retail and wholesale corporate by applying to total corporate sales the ratios of retail corporate and of wholesale corporate to total corporate (obtained by straight line interpolation), the resulting figures being adjusted proportionately to the correct total corporate sales. Retail and wholesale corporate sales for the years before 1923 are estimated by applying, to total corporate sales, the ratios of retail corporate to total retail sales and wholesale corporate to total wholesale sales. The ratios are extrapolated from 1923 on the assumption that the change in the ratio of retail corporate to total retail sales is one-half that for wholesale. The change in the wholesale ratio from 1923 to any of the earlier years is derived from the following formula (*a* being the change in the wholesale ratio): total retail sales × (ratio of retail corporate to total retail sales in 1923 − ½*a*) + total wholesale sales × (ratio of wholesale corporate to total wholesale sales in 1923 − *a*) = total corporate sales. Since all items except *a* are available, *a* can be found from this single equation. With *a* given, the ratios of retail corporate to total retail sales and wholesale corporate to total wholesale sales can be obtained. On the basis of the resulting ratios and total sales, preliminary totals for retail and wholesale corporate are derived and are adjusted on the basis of the ratio of the correct total corporate sales, as estimated above, to the sum of the preliminary estimates.

The net savings ratio is estimated as the ratio, to gross sales of corporations *(Statistics of Income)*, of statutory net income before taxes *(Statistics of Income)* plus total interest paid (see the notes to Table T 2, col. 4) minus total dividends paid (see the notes to Table T 2, col. 3). The 1934 ratio comparable with those for preceding years is extrapolated from 1933 by the savings ratio, excluding the interest item, for corporations filing unconsolidated returns, data for which are reported in the 1934 *Statistics of Income*. Net savings in 1938 are extrapolated from 1937 by corporate savings. *Col. 8 Entrepreneurial net income:* sum of col. 6 and 7.

TABLE T 5

Persons Engaged

EMPLOYEES

Col. 1 Wholesale: basic data for 1929, 1933, and 1935, from the *Census of Wholesale Distribution* (including auxiliary units and chain store warehouses). Our entries represent full-time employment equivalents. The 1933 estimate is the sum of the number of full-time employees reported and the part-time workers equated to full-time by dividing the part-time payroll, as reported, by the average full-time pay. The ratio of full- to full- and part-time employment is extrapolated from 1933 to 1929 by the corresponding ratio for retail trade (excluding restaurants and eating places). It is applied to the number of full- and part-time employees reported in 1929 to yield the full-time equivalent estimate. The 1935 figure is obtained by dividing the total payroll reported by the estimated average full-time pay which, in turn, is derived by dividing the total payroll by the total number of workers, full- and part-time, and correcting this average by the ratio of the full-time average pay to the full- and part-time average pay for those retailers that report full- and part-time data separately. Interpolation for intercensal years and extrapolation for 1936–38 of the number of employees are by the BLS employment index.

Col. 2 Retail: basic data for 1929, 1933, and 1935, from the *Census of Retail Distribution* (excluding restaurants and eating places). The methods used for the 1929 and 1933 estimates, and for the 1935, are the same as for wholesale trade in 1933 and 1935 (see the notes to col. 1). Interpolation for intercensal years and extrapolation for 1936–38 are by the BLS employment index.

Col. 3 Total: for 1929 and later years col. 3 is the sum of col. 1 and 2. For earlier years employment is estimated for trade as a whole. The 1926 figure is obtained by dividing the total wage and salary bill (see the notes to Table T 4, col. 3) by the estimated average pay. The average pay in 1926 is extrapolated from 1929 by a weighted index derived from data for Wisconsin (*Wisconsin Labor Market*), for Ohio (BLS Bulletin 613), and for 10 sample cities (1926 *Census of Retail and Wholesale Trade* and 1929 *Census of Retail Distribution*). The weights are the number of employees in 1929. Interpolation between 1926 and 1929 and extrapolation to 1919 is by an employment index based on Wisconsin, Ohio, Pennsylvania, and Iowa data. The weights are the respective employment figures in 1929. The sources for the Wisconsin and Ohio data, covering 1922–29 and 1919–29 respectively, are given above. The Pennsylvania data, 1923–27, are from J. F. Dewhurst's *Employment Fluctuations in Pennsylvania, 1921 to 1927;* the Iowa, 1927–29, from the *Iowa Employment Survey.*

Col. 4 Total, second estimate: from data reported in the 1930 *Census of Population,* Vol. V, Ch. 1, the change from 1920 to 1930 in the number in representative occupations is estimated. Salespeople; decorators, etc.; delivery men, stores; floorwalkers, etc.; laborers, porters, and helpers in stores; laborers, coal and lumber yards; fruit and vegetable graders and packers; meat cutters and clerks in stores are included. It is assumed that the proportion of unemployment is the same in 1920 and 1929. The 1929 figure (col. 3) is extrapolated to 1920 by the percentage change in the representative occupations. Interpolation for 1921–28 and extrapolation to 1919 are by sales of finished commodities, in 1929 prices (*Commodity Flow and Capital Formation*, Vol. One, Table V-7).

ENTREPRENEURS

Col. 5 Wholesale: from the *Census of Wholesale Distribution* for 1929, 1933, and 1935. The number in 1936–38 is based on the estimate of wholesale establishments prepared by the Bureau of Foreign and Domestic Commerce, Marketing Research Division. Estimates for intercensal years are by straight line interpolation. The 1929 figure is extrapolated to 1919 by the number of wholesale dealers and commercial brokers and commission men. The number as of January 1, 1920 and April 1, 1930 is reported in the 1930 *Census of Population*, Vol. V, Ch. 1. Figures for intercensal years and for 1919 are interpolated and extrapolated along a straight line.

Col. 6 Retail: from the *Census of Retail Distribution* for 1929, 1933, and 1935 (excluding restaurants and eating places). The method of interpolation and extrapolation is the same as for col. 5 except for 1936–38, when unpublished BLS estimates of entrepreneurs in retail trade are used as index. The *Census of Population* data, upon which the extrapolating series for 1919–29 is based, are for the number of retail dealers.

Col. 7 Total: sum of col. 5 and 6.

Finance

TABLES F1–F7

Net savings and net income, adjusted, exclude gains and losses from sales of capital assets, 1929–38, and from changes in inventory valuation, 1919–38. Net savings and net income without any specific designation are unadjusted, i.e., include these two types of gain and loss.

F 1   Net Income Originating by Major Industrial Divisions
(millions of dollars)

	BANKING (1)	INSURANCE (2)	REAL ESTATE (3)	TOTAL (4)	TOTAL, ADJ. (5)
1919	868	706	5,324	6,899	6,819
1920	957	727	5,787	7,471	7,418
1921	921	742	6,018	7,682	7,770
1922	923	783	6,551	8,258	8,255
1923	970	776	7,046	8,793	8,809
1924	1,035	865	7,699	9,600	9,608
1925	1,131	1,031	7,576	9,740	9,762
1926	1,180	1,127	7,507	9,815	9,837
1927	1,281	1,287	7,742	10,311	10,312
1928	1,401	1,435	8,033	10,870	10,874
1929	1,389	1,483	8,261	11,134	10,910
1930	1,139	1,326	7,295	9,761	9,740
1931	734	1,160	5,695	7,591	7,894
1932	415	937	4,141	5,493	5,905
1933	290	864	3,678	4,833	5,191
1934	490	1,041	3,503	5,035	5,071
1935	708	1,105	3,917	5,731	5,680
1936	881	1,144	4,086	6,112	5,976
1937	875	1,272	4,503	6,651	6,636
1938	814	1,274	4,462	6,551	6,538

F 2 Net Income Originating by Type (millions of dollars)

	WAGES & SALARIES (1)	ENTREP. WITHDR. (2)	DIVI-DENDS (3)	INTEREST (4)	NET RENT TO INDI-VIDUALS * (5)	PROP. INCOME (6)	PAY. TO INDI-VIDUALS (7)	NET SAVINGS (8)	NET INCOME (9)	NET SAVINGS, ADJ. (10)	NET INCOME, ADJ. (11)
1919	1,579	121	335	815	3,966	5,117	6,618	281	6,899	201	6,819
1920	1,651	147	405	882	4,287	5,576	7,375	96.1	7,471	43.1	7,418
1921	1,729	144	410	935	4,470	5,816	7,689	−7.6	7,682	80.4	7,770
1922	1,745	148	472	970	4,896	6,339	8,233	25.6	8,258	22.6	8,255
1923	1,816	172	531	1,121	5,165	6,818	8,808	−14.4	8,793	1.6	8,809
1924	1,973	189	506	1,223	5,631	7,361	9,525	75.5	9,600	83.5	9,608
1925	2,028	211	554	1,396	5,465	7,417	9,657	82.3	9,740	104	9,762
1926	2,241	226	549	1,516	5,141	7,208	9,675	139	9,815	161	9,837
1927	2,434	234	545	1,712	5,078	7,336	10,005	306	10,311	307	10,312
1928	2,657	245	660	1,981	4,941	7,583	10,466	404	10,870	408	10,874
1929	2,856	260	764	2,266	4,917	7,947	11,064	70.4	11,134	−153	10,910
1930	2,650	252	664	2,316	4,265	7,246	10,149	−388	9,761	−409	9,740
1931	2,385	229	593	2,298	3,026	5,918	8,534	−943	7,591	−639	7,894
1932	1,967	195	370	2,028	2,090	4,489	6,652	−1,158	5,493	−747	5,905
1933	1,743	176	204	1,552	2,114	3,870	5,791	−957	4,833	−600	5,191
1934	1,858	191	260	1,478	1,905	3,644	5,693	−658	5,035	−621	5,071
1935	1,953	201	277	1,493	2,143	3,913	6,067	−336	5,731	−386	5,680
1936	2,017	201	270	1,475	2,186	3,933	6,152	−39.6	6,112	−176	5,976
1937	2,120	225	285	1,465	2,579	4,329	6,675	−24.0	6,651	−39.1	6,656
1938	2,149	217	291	1,426	2,575	4,293	6,659	−108	6,551	−121	6,538

* Including imputed rent on owner-occupied residences.

F 3 Wages and Salaries by Minor Industrial Divisions (millions of dollars)

	BANKING					INSURANCE				REAL ESTATE	TOTAL
	Commercial incl. stock savings	Mutual savings	Fed. Res.	Insolvent	Total	Life	Other	Agencies	Total		
	(1)	(2)	(3)	(4)	(5)	(6)	(7)	(8)	(9)	(10)	(11)
1919	351	13.0	17.1	0.8	382	286	119	129	535	461	1,379
1920	437	15.2	19.5	0.7	472	328	150	162	641	537	1,651
1921	468	17.2	21.3	1.7	508	359	171	150	681	539	1,789
1922	475	17.5	19.5	2.5	515	382	171	151	704	525	1,745
1923	503	18.7	20.3	3.9	546	257	193	239	689	580	1,816
1924	535	20.0	18.7	5.7	579	284	225	263	773	621	1,973
1925	558	21.4	17.2	7.0	604	315	247	292	854	569	2,028
1926	593	22.7	16.8	7.9	640	340	275	311	926	673	2,241
1927	624	23.8	17.0	8.7	674	364	308	320	992	767	2,434
1928	652	25.1	17.3	8.4	703	394	334	331	1,060	873	2,637
1929	676	26.6	17.4	10.9	731	427	353	348	1,130	994	2,856
1930	653	27.9	17.4	14.1	712	431	365	338	1,135	802	2,650
1931	576	28.9	17.1	18.0	640	410	344	307	1,062	683	2,385
1932	484	29.7	17.6	23.3	555	343	298	273	915	496	1,967
1933	395	29.6	19.2	34.4	478	322	270	243	836	428	1,743
1934	413	30.8	20.3	30.4	495	338	274	263	876	486	1,858
1935	422	31.9	20.4	24.6	499	352	286	277	916	535	1,952
1936	446	33.1	19.9	18.2	517	364	308	276	948	550	2,017
1937	472	35.2	18.5	13.8	540	362	336	319	1,017	562	2,120
1938	483	36.5	18.9	12.6	551	367	353	305	1,026	571	2,149

F 4   Dividends and Interest by Major Industrial Divisions
(millions of dollars)

| | DIVIDENDS | | | | INTEREST | | | | |
	BANK-ING	INSUR-ANCE	REAL ESTATE	TOTAL	INSUR-ANCE	REAL ESTATE Corp.	Indiv.	Total	TOTAL
	(1)	(2)	(3)	(4)	(5)	(6)	(7)	(8)	(9)
1919	276	18.5	40.4	335	—13.5	297	531	829	815
1920	297	19.3	88.8	405	—16.9	287	612	899	882
1921	312	23.1	75.0	410	—18.8	278	676	954	935
1922	328	44.6	99.8	472	—19.4	245	744	989	970
1923	325	39.6	167	531	—19.8	278	862	1,141	1,121
1924	326	33.4	146	506	—21.8	271	973	1,245	1,223
1925	342	38.5	173	554	—22.5	294	1,124	1,419	1,396
1926	355	43.0	151	549	—22.6	298	1,241	1,539	1,516
1927	381	54.7	108	545	—23.8	299	1,436	1,736	1,712
1928	438	65.4	155	660	—23.8	420	1,584	2,005	1,981
1929	456	69.7	238	764	—32.0	432	1,865	2,298	2,266
1930	449	61.0	153	664	—24.1	434	1,906	2,341	2,316
1931	410	60.8	122	593	—21.5	450	1,869	2,320	2,298
1932	280	30.9	58.9	370	—20.9	375	1,674	2,049	2,028
1933	157	16.4	30.1	204	—21.2	252	1,320	1,573	1,552
1934	187	22.7	50.5	260	—25.0	235	1,267	1,503	1,478
1935	188	37.9	51.3	277	—26.6	220	1,299	1,519	1,493
1936	193	21.8	55.1	270	—27.5	199	1,304	1,503	1,475
1937	200	21.1	63.7	285	—30.7	199	1,296	1,496	1,465
1938	196	38.8	56.4	291	—30.9	197	1,260	1,457	1,426

F 5 Property Income by Major Industrial Divisions
(millions of dollars)

| | BANK-ING | INSUR-ANCE | REAL ESTATE | | | | TOTAL |
| | | | Dividends & interest | Net rent to individuals | Individuals' net imputed rent | Total | |
	(1)	(2)	(3)	(4)	(5)	(6)	(7)
1919	276	5.0	869	2,452	1,514	4,836	5,117
1920	297	2.4	988	2,375	1,912	5,276	5,576
1921	312	4.4	1,029	2,313	2,157	5,499	5,816
1922	328	25.2	1,089	2,643	2,253	5,986	6,339
1923	325	19.7	1,308	2,827	2,337	6,473	6,818
1924	326	11.6	1,392	2,973	2,658	7,023	7,361
1925	342	16.0	1,592	2,892	2,573	7,058	7,417
1926	355	20.4	1,690	2,735	2,406	6,832	7,208
1927	381	30.9	1,844	2,692	2,385	6,923	7,336
1928	438	41.6	2,161	2,698	2,243	7,102	7,583
1929	456	37.7	2,536	2,580	2,336	7,453	7,947
1930	449	36.9	2,494	1,982	2,282	6,760	7,246
1931	410	39.3	2,442	1,287	1,739	5,469	5,918
1932	280	10.0	2,108	806	1,284	4,199	4,489
1933	157	—4.8	1,603	898	1,216	3,717	3,870
1934	187	—2.3	1,553	857	1,048	3,459	3,644
1935	188	11.3	1,571	1,036	1,107	3,714	3,913
1936	193	—5.7	1,558	1,071	1,115	3,745	3,933
1937	200	—9.7	1,559	1,263	1,315	4,138	4,329
1938	196	7.9	1,514	1,154	1,420	4,089	4,293

F 6   Total Payments to Individuals and Net Savings by Major
Industrial Divisions (millions of dollars)

	TOTAL PAYMENTS				NET SAVINGS			
	Bank-ing	Insur-ance	Real estate	Total	Bank-ing	Insur-ance	Real estate	Total
	(1)	(2)	(3)	(4)	(5)	(6)	(7)	(8)
1919	658	661	5,298	6,618	210	44.3	26.9	281
1920	770	791	5,813	7,375	187	—64.7	—26.8	96.1
1921	820	830	6,038	7,689	100	—87.9	—20.4	—7.6
1922	843	877	6,511	8,233	80.1	—94.3	39.8	25.6
1923	871	881	7,054	8,808	99.3	—105	—8.6	—14.4
1924	905	974	7,645	9,525	129	—108	54.2	75.5
1925	947	1,082	7,628	9,657	184	—50.6	—51.6	82.3
1926	996	1,173	7,505	9,675	184	—46.2	1.7	139
1927	1,056	1,258	7,691	10,005	225	29.4	51.1	306
1928	1,142	1,347	7,976	10,466	259	87.8	57.2	404
1929	1,187	1,428	8,448	11,064	202	55.5	—187	70.4
1930	1,162	1,425	7,562	10,149	—22.7	—98.5	—266	—388
1931	1,050	1,331	6,152	8,534	—316	—170	—456	—943
1932	835	1,121	4,695	6,652	—420	—184	—554	—1,158
1933	636	1,008	4,146	5,791	—346	—143	—468	—957
1934	682	1,065	3,946	5,693	—192	—23.9	—442	—658
1935	687	1,129	4,250	6,067	20.8	—24.2	—332	—336
1936	711	1,144	4,296	6,152	170	0.3	—210	—39.6
1937	741	1,232	4,701	6,675	134	39.7	—198	—24.0
1938	747	1,251	4,660	6,659	66.6	23.2	—198	—108

F 7 Employees by Minor Industrial Divisions (thousands)

	BANKING					INSURANCE				REAL ESTATE	TOTAL
	Commercial incl. stock savings (1)	Mutual savings (2)	Fed. Res. (3)	Insolvent (4)	Total (5)	Life (6)	Other (7)	Agencies (8)	Total (9)	(10)	(11)
1919	288	8.0	13.8	0.5	310	131	55.9	113	301	329	940
1920	323	8.4	14.2	0.4	346	136	62.8	124	323	347	1,017
1921	316	8.7	14.2	1.0	340	144	68.2	129	342	324	1,007
1922	307	8.5	12.4	1.3	329	154	66.2	120	340	309	979
1923	322	9.0	12.8	2.1	346	103	74.1	171	349	341	1,037
1924	335	9.4	11.5	2.9	359	111	82.7	185	379	360	1,099
1925	345	9.9	10.4	3.5	369	119	85.2	196	401	329	1,100
1926	365	10.5	10.2	4.0	390	128	92.6	204	425	392	1,209
1927	379	10.8	10.1	4.4	405	140	104	210	454	447	1,306
1928	388	11.2	10.1	4.1	414	149	110	214	475	508	1,398
1929	396	11.7	10.0	5.3	423	156	114	229	500	576	1,500
1930	373	12.0	9.8	6.8	401	163	114	231	509	542	1,453
1931	320	12.1	9.4	8.6	350	168	105	226	499	495	1,346
1932	272	12.5	9.6	11.1	306	170	98.0	222	491	436	1,234
1933	229	12.9	11.1	17.2	270	173	91.4	212	476	431	1,178
1934	241	13.5	11.7	15.2	281	176	94.6	213	484	456	1,222
1935	232	13.9	11.6	12.3	270	179	101	212	493	476	1,240
1936	236	14.4	11.3	9.3	271	180			494	506	1,272
1937	246	14.6	10.5	7.2	278				506	534	1,319
1938	247	15.0	10.6	6.7	280				528	498	1,307

This group comprises banking, insurance, and real estate. The banking estimates cover commercial and savings banks, Federal Reserve banks, and insolvent banks, other than private. All other banking is included under miscellaneous industries. The insurance data cover all insurance companies and agencies. The real estate data cover corporations in the field and individuals' real estate holdings.

TABLE F 1

Net Income Originating by Major Industrial Divisions

Sum for each industry of wages and salaries (Table F 3), entrepreneurial withdrawals (for insurance only) (Table F 2, col. 2), property income (Table F 5), and net savings (Table F 6).

TABLE F 2

Net Income Originating by Type

Col. 1 Wages and salaries: see Table F 3, col. 11.

Col. 2 Entrepreneurial withdrawals: the estimates are for insurance alone. For 1935 this item is the product of the number of proprietors of agencies and the full-time salary of executives, both from the *Census of Business.* This 1935 figure is extrapolated for other years by total commissions and the salaries and expenses of agents of life insurance companies. For the derivation of the latter series see the notes to Table F 3.

Col. 3 Dividends: see Table F 4, col. 4.

Col. 4 Interest: see Table F 4, col. 9.

Col. 5 Net rent received by individuals: see Table F 5, col. 4 and 5.

Col. 6 Property income: sum of col. 3–5.

Col. 7 Total payments: sum of col. 1, 2, and 6.

Col. 8 Net savings: see Table F 6, col. 8.

Col. 9 Net income originating: sum of col. 7 and 8.

TABLE F 3

Wages and Salaries by Minor Industrial Divisions

Col. 1 Commercial and stock savings banks: wages and salaries of member banks of the Federal Reserve System are from the

Federal Reserve Bulletin, for calendar years 1923–38 and for years ending June 30 before 1923. The 1919–23 calendar year figures are averages of fiscal year data. Wages and salaries of non-member banks for 1935 are from the *Census of Business*. For 1934 and 1936–38 they are derived from data on wages and salaries for banks not members of the Federal Reserve System insured by the Federal Deposit Insurance Corporation (*Annual Report of the Federal Deposit Insurance Corporation*). The latter are raised to the total for non-member banks by the ratio of loans and investments of all banks not in the Federal Reserve System to the loans and investments of non-member banks reporting to the Federal Deposit Insurance Corporation. Adding the estimates for member and non-member banks, 1934–38, gives total wages and salaries for commercial banks. The ratio of wages and salaries to loans and investments is extrapolated for 1919–33 by the corresponding ratio for Federal Reserve member banks. Its application to total loans and investments yields estimates of total wages and salaries. Loans and investments of member banks are from the *Annual Report of the Federal Reserve Board* and those of all commercial and stock savings banks, from the *Annual Report of the Comptroller of the Currency.*

Col. 2 Mutual savings banks: total wages and salaries for 1935, from the *Census of Business;* for other years they are estimated by applying to total deposits (*Annual Report of the Comptroller of the Currency*) their ratio to deposits. The ratio is an extrapolation, on the basis of sample state data, of that derived for 1935. For the sample states the salary figures are from the respective state banking departments; the deposits, from the *Annual Report of the Comptroller of the Currency.* The states and years for which salaries are available are: 1919–29: Rhode Island, Ohio, and Massachusetts; 1929–35: Rhode Island, Ohio, Massachusetts, Delaware, New Jersey, New York, Vermont, Washington, Wisconsin, and California; 1935–38, the states listed for 1929–35 except California, and, in addition, Pennsylvania, Minnesota, New Hampshire, Maine, and Indiana.

Col. 3 Federal Reserve banks: total wages and salaries, from the *Annual Report of the Federal Reserve Board* and include the reimbursable salaries of fiscal agency departments.

Col. 4 Insolvent banks, other than private: from the Comptroller of the Currency, the Bureau of Foreign and Domestic Commerce, National Income Division, obtained estimates of salaries and wages paid by insolvent national banks, 1929–38, on which estimates for all insolvent banks, other than private, are based. The *Federal Reserve Bulletin,* September 1937, gives the number, deposits, and loans and investments of all suspended banks, by type of bank, 1921–36. For each item five-year totals are taken, the four years preceding and the current one being included. The ratios of salaries to each of these series are computed for insolvent national banks, 1929–36, and applied to the corresponding five-year totals for all insolvent banks. The final figures are averages of the three preliminary estimates thus derived. For the years before 1929 the same procedure is followed, using averages of the ratios for 1929–36. The number of insolvent banks before 1922 is from the *Annual Report of the Comptroller of the Currency.* Deposits are extrapolated from 1922 by liabilities, also from the comptroller's report. Since loans and investments were not reported before 1921, only two preliminary estimates are made for the early years and their average is used as an index to extrapolate for 1919–24 the final total salary for 1925. For 1937 the same procedure is followed since the basic data for only the two preliminary estimates are available. The 1938 estimate is made on the assumption that wages and salaries paid by insolvent banks other than national are the same as in 1937.

Col. 5 Total banking: sum of col. 1–4.

Col. 6 Life insurance companies: total payrolls for home and branch offices in 1935, from the *Census of Business.* Salaries for home offices are extrapolated for other years by the salaries of employees other than agents. The latter figure is reported for the years since 1929 in the *Life Insurance Year Book* (Spectator Company). This item, reported before 1929 as 'medical fees, salaries and other charges of employees', is corrected to eliminate the non-salary items on the basis of data for companies operating in Connecticut as given in the *Connecticut Insurance Report,* Part II. In this report medical fees and inspection of risks are shown separately from salaries and all other compensation of officers and employees. The ratio of the latter to the sum of the two is applied to the figure in the *Life Insurance Year Book* in the years before 1929 to give the estimated salaries of employees other than agents. The figure for branch offices is extrapolated by agents' salaries and expenses given for 1929 and later years in the *Life Insurance Year Book*. For the years before 1929 the item reported is 'commissions, salaries and expenses of agents'. Data from the *Connecticut Insurance Report*, Part II, for companies operating in Connecticut provide a basis for the segregation of commissions.

Col. 7 Insurance companies other than life: sum of salaries paid by fire and marine, casualty, surety, and miscellaneous companies at home and branch offices for 1935, from the *Census of Business*. The series used to extrapolate this total is the sum of preliminary estimates for fire and marine companies, and for casualty and all other companies.

For fire and marine companies this preliminary figure is obtained by applying to the total fire and marine insurance premiums as reported in the *Fire and Marine Insurance Year Book* (Spectator Company) the ratio of salaries, expenses, etc. of the officers and employees to premiums. This ratio is derived from data for companies operating in New York (*New York Insurance Report*, Part I). The resulting estimate of salaries and expenses of officers and employees is separated into salaries and other expenses on the basis of data in the *Connecticut Insurance Report*, Part I.

The same procedure is followed in deriving the preliminary estimate of salaries of casualty and miscellaneous insurance. Premiums are from the *Casualty, Surety, and Miscellaneous Insurance Year Book* and the ratio of salaries to salaries and expenses is that derived for the sample fire and marine companies mentioned above.

In addition to salaries and wages, loss adjustment expenses are also estimated for both fire and marine and casualty and miscellaneous insurance. The *Fire and Marine Insurance Year Book* shows loss adjustment expense for fire and marine companies, 1932–38. Estimates for 1919–31 are extrapolated from 1932 by a series obtained by applying to total fire premiums the ratio of loss adjustment expense to premiums for companies operating in Connecticut (*Connecticut Insurance Report*, Part I).

Adjustment expense for casualty and miscellaneous insurance companies, 1932–38, is from the *Casualty, Surety, and Miscellaneous Insurance Year Book*. The 1932 figure is extrapolated for all preceding years by a preliminary series estimated by applying, to total casualty and miscellaneous premiums, the ratio of adjust-

ment expense to premiums for companies operating in New York
(*New York Insurance Report*, Part III).

Col. 8 Insurance agencies: sum of salaries paid to selling and non-
selling employees.

   a) *Salaries of non-selling employees:* the total payroll of agencies
and brokerage offices in 1935 is reported in the *Census of Business*.
The salaries of selling employees are based on their percentage to
the total as indicated by data for one week reported in the *Census
of Business*. These are deducted and the balance is extrapolated
for other years by total commissions of all insurance companies.
The commissions paid by life insurance companies are recorded
separately for 1929 and later years in the *Life Insurance Year Book*.
For earlier years see the derivation, above, of the life insurance
salary item. For other insurance companies, commissions are the
sum of 'agents' compensation and allowances including brokerage'
of fire and marine insurance companies and 'total commissions' of
casualty and miscellaneous insurance companies. These items, reported in the *New York Insurance Report* (Parts I and III, respectively) for companies operating in New York, are raised by the ratio
of total premiums written to the premiums of companies operating
in New York.

   b) *Salaries of selling employees:* salaries paid by agencies are estimated for 1935 by applying to the total payroll reported in the
Census of Business the percentage indicated by Census data for one
week. The commissions of solicitors in branch offices are given for
1935 in the *Census of Business*. The commissions of solicitors in
agencies are estimated on the assumption that their number is the
same percentage of selling employees as in branch offices and that
their average annual commissions are the same as those of solicitors
in branch offices. The sum of the payroll of selling employees and
the commissions of solicitors in branch offices and agencies is the
basic figure for 1935. It is extrapolated for other years by total commissions paid. For the derivation of the series on commissions see
the notes on the salaries of non-selling employees, immediately
above.

Col. 9 Total insurance: sum of col. 6–8.

Col. 10 Real estate: total wages and salaries are obtained by applying to the estimated non-agricultural gross rent received by individuals and corporations in the real estate business the ratio of

salaries and wages to rent. The 1934 ratio, based on data for apartment houses reported in the *Real Estate Record,* April and August 1935, is assumed to apply to all real estate. Office buildings show a higher ratio and small private houses a lower. It is extrapolated back to 1929 and forward to 1935 by the ratio for New York State Housing Projects. The New York data are from the *Annual Report of the State Board of Housing.* For 1921–25 the ratio is based on that for office buildings, derived from data in the *Office Building Experience Exchange Report* (National Association of Building Owners and Managers). For 1926–28 the ratio is interpolated along a straight line; for 1919 and 1920 it is assumed to be the same as in 1921; for 1936–38 it is extrapolated from 1935 by the average of the New York State Board of Housing data and those for office buildings, weighted equally.

The gross rent bill, to which the ratio is applied, is estimated industry by industry, the basic data for most industries being the rent paid by corporations, as reported for 1933–37 in *Statistics of Income.* When the basic data are from other sources the fact is noted. The sources of other items referred to are mentioned in the notes for the specific industry.

Rent paid by steam railroads: the 1933 basic figure is extrapolated to 1921, and the 1937 to 1938, by rent paid by steam railroads, considered as a system. From 1921 to 1919 rent paid by Class I railroads, not consolidated, is used as index. The data for both indexes are from *Statistics of Railways.*

Rent paid by electric railways: the basic figures are extrapolated by a preliminary series of rent paid, obtained by applying to the operating revenue for the industry the ratio of rent to operating revenue, computed for 1917, 1922, 1927, and 1932 from data in the *Census of Electric Railways,* and interpolated along a straight line. The 1938 figure is assumed to be the same as the 1937.

Rent paid by telephone and telegraph companies: the basic figures are extrapolated by a preliminary series of rent paid. Rent paid by telephone companies is reported for 1917 and 1922 in the *Census of Telephones* and interpolated by 'rent and miscellaneous deductions' of the American Telephone and Telegraph Company as given in *Bell Telephone Securities.* The ratio in 1922 of the Census figure to that for the American Telephone and Telegraph Company is computed and extrapolated by the ratio of total operating revenue to that of the American Telephone and Telegraph Company. The application of this ratio to the American Telephone and Telegraph Company rent series yields the preliminary estimate of rent, 1922–32.

The preliminary telegraph rent series is based on the rent figure reported for 1917, 1922, and 1927 in the *Census of Telegraphs*. The Census data are interpolated for 1918–21 and 1923–26 by the preliminary estimates of the rent of telephone companies. Extrapolation from 1927 through 1932 is by the index of the preliminary telephone rent estimates.

The 1938 estimate for telephone and telegraph companies is extrapolated from 1937 by the 'rent and miscellaneous deductions' series reported for the Bell System in *Bell Telephone Securities*.

Rent paid by electric light and power companies: the basic figures are extrapolated by a preliminary series of rent paid, obtained by applying to the estimated operating revenue the ratio of rent to it. This ratio, computed for 1917 and 1922 from data in the *Census of Central Electric Light and Power Stations,* is interpolated and extrapolated by the corresponding ratio for telephone and telegraph companies. Rent paid is assumed to be the same in 1938 as in 1937.

Rent paid by manufactured gas companies: the basic figures are extrapolated by a preliminary series of rent paid, obtained by applying to the estimated operating revenue the ratio of rent to it. This ratio, computed from the basic material for 1933–37, is extrapolated by the corresponding ratio for the telephone and telegraph industry. Rent paid is assumed to be the same in 1938 as in 1937.

Rent paid by water transportation companies: from the basic figures the ratio of rent to gross income of corporations is computed for 1933–37. This ratio, extrapolated by the ratio of rent to operating revenue of electric railways, is applied to corporate gross income for all years to yield an estimate of rent paid by corporations. Corporate gross income in 1926 and later years is given in *Statistics of Income* and is extrapolated for earlier years by gross revenue as reported to the Interstate Commerce Commission. The estimated rent paid by corporations is raised to the total by the ratio of total tonnage to corporate tonnage. Total rent paid is assumed to be the same in 1938 as in 1937.

Rent paid by retail trade: for 1929, from the *Census of Retail Distribution.* For other years it is estimated on the basis of the ratio of rent to sales. The ratio to sales is computed for 1929 from Census data. It is estimated for 1935 by applying to the 1929 ratio the percentage change from 1929 to 1935 in the ratio of rent to sales in leased premises as reported in the 1935 *Census of Business.* For other years the ratio of rent to sales is obtained from the regression line of the absolute change in the percentage of rent to sales on the percentage change in sales. The regression line is fitted to data from various operating expense studies available for two-year periods, thus making it possible to derive figures on the change in the percentage of rent to sales and the percentage change in sales. The studies are those of the Harvard University Bureau of Business Research, Dun and Bradstreet, University of Nebraska College of Business Administration, Federal Trade Commission, University of Colorado Bureau of Business Research, National Stationers' Association, *The Progressive Grocer,* and the National Retail Hardware Association. The percentage change in sales from the preceding year having been computed for the entire period, the corresponding absolute change in the ratio of rent to sales is determined from the regression line and the resulting figures are used to extrapolate the 1929 ratio to 1919 and 1938. The 1919–28 figures thus obtained are applied directly to the sales figures for those years. Ratios obtained by this method for later years are used only in interpolating and extrapolating the 1929 and 1935 ratios originally estimated.

Rent paid by wholesale trade: rent paid by wholesalers in 1929 is from the *Census of Wholesale Distribution.* The ratio to sales is computed and extrapolated for all other years by the regression line of the absolute change in the percentage of rent to sales on the percentage change in sales. The sample data to which the regression line is fitted are from Dun and Bradstreet, Harvard University Bureau of Business Research, Cornell University Agricultural Experiment Station, and the Ohio State University Bureau of Business Research. Rent is estimated for all years other than 1929 by multiplying sales by the ratio of rent to sales.

Rent paid by manufacturing: from *Statistics of Income* the ratio of rent paid by corporations to corporate gross sales is derived for

1933–37. This ratio, extrapolated for other years by the corresponding ratio for trade, is applied to the estimated total value of product of manufacturing to yield total rent paid in all years.

Rent paid by mining: see the notes to manufacturing, above.

Rent paid by construction: see the notes to manufacturing, above. Corporate gross sales include, in this case, receipts from other operations.

Rent paid by life insurance companies: the rent paid by companies operating in Connecticut, reported in the *Connecticut Insurance Report,* Part II, is raised by the ratio of total premiums to premiums of companies operating in Connecticut to yield total rent paid in all years.

Rent paid by other industries: the sum of the estimates for the industries described above is used to extrapolate the basic figures for the other industries. From *Statistics of Income* for 1933–37 we take the rent paid by miscellaneous public utilities, service, finance excluding life insurance companies, and miscellaneous corporations.

The basic figure for personal service, other than corporate, is for 1933. Total receipts of laundries, cleaning and dyeing establishments, barber and beauty shops, hotels, window cleaning and linen supply firms are from the *Census of American Business;* of power laundries, from the *Census of Power Laundries;* of restaurants, from the *Census of Retail Distribution.* The corporate ratio of rent to gross income for the service group is applied to the sum of these gross receipts to yield total rent paid. From the total the corporate figure is subtracted.

The basic figure for rent paid by professional service is from the *Incomes of Physicians* (Committee on the Costs of Medical Care) and the *Practice of Dentistry and the Incomes of Dentists in Twenty States: 1929* (Committee on the Study of Dental Practice of the American Dental Association). The estimated rent bill is assumed to be the same for 1933 as for 1929. The basic figure for rent paid by other non-corporate service is estimated similarly to that for personal service, excluding from the industries grouped in this category, in addition to the personal service industries, cartage and trucking and storage establishments which are already covered in transportation and public utilities. For stockbrokers a basic figure for 1933 is estimated on the assumption that rent paid bears the same relation to partnership income reported on individual returns in *Statistics of Income* as it does to officers' compensation in the corporate field.

Residential rent paid: rent paid is estimated separately for each city with a population of 100,000 or over and for the group as a whole for cities of under 100,000. The *Census of Population, 1920* (Vol. III) and 1930 (Vol. VI) gives the total number of houses and the number rented on January 1, 1920 and April 1, 1930. The total number of houses and the ratio of the number rented to it are estimated for June 30, 1920–29 by straight line interpolation. The April 1930 figures are assumed to apply to June 30, 1930.

The estimates of houses for the years after 1930 are based on data for sample cities in the *Real Property Inventory, 1934* (Bureau of Foreign and Domestic Commerce). For the cities covered in the Inventory, the number of houses is estimated by straight line interpolation between the 1930 Census figure and the January 1, 1934 Inventory figure, and the extrapolation beyond 1934 is by the same annual increment. For the cities not covered in the Inventory the annual increment after 1930 is estimated by applying to the annual increment between 1920 and 1930 an estimated ratio of the former to the latter based on data on the age of structures reported in the Inventory. From this source we obtain data on the number of buildings erected during 1929–33 and 1919–28. These are added for all the Inventory cities of 100,000 or over and the ratio of twice the number erected during 1929–33 to the number erected in the earlier decade is applied to the 1920–30 annual increment for each city with a population of over 100,000 not covered in the Inventory. The same procedure is used for cities of under 100,000, the cities included in the Inventory being used to derive the ratio, which is then applied to the group as a whole.

The ratio of rented to all houses after 1930 is, for cities covered in the Inventory, based on a straight line interpolation between 1930 and January 1, 1934, and a straight line extrapolation from that date. For the cities not covered in the Inventory the ratio is extrapolated from 1930 by the average ratio for all Inventory cities of 100,000 or over. The same procedure is followed in estimating the ratio for cities of under 100,000, the sample data in this case consisting of only those Inventory cities that are under 100,000.

The total number of houses multiplied by the ratio of rented to it yields the estimate of rented houses in each year.

Average rent is based on the 1930 median rent paid as reported in the 1930 *Census of Population,* Vol. VI. This median rent figure for each city with a population of 100,000 or over is adjusted to the average rent paid by the ratio of the average to the median rent. The latter ratio is derived from a special survey of Census data for sample cities made by David L. Wickens in connection with the *Financial Survey of Urban Housing.* For the cities not covered in this special survey the ratio for that city in the survey with the closest median value is used. For the group of cities of under 100,000 the data in Wickens' special survey for all cities of under 100,000 are used to obtain the ratio of average to median rent. The resulting average rent for 1930 is extrapolated for other years by the BLS rent index for the specific city, whenever available. For the other cities, averages of the BLS indexes for cities falling into the same median rent groups are used. For the group of cities of under 100,000 the rent index used is an average of the National Industrial Conference Board rent indexes for cities of under 100,000 in their sample. Total rent paid is estimated by multiplying the number of rented houses by the average annual rent in each year.

Total rent bill of individuals and corporations in the real estate business: total rent paid, excluding that paid by agriculture, is the sum of the items listed above. From it the rent received by corporations not in real estate is subtracted. Rent received by all corporations, 1929–37, is reported in *Statistics of Income* and in 1938 is assumed to be the same percentage of total rent paid as in 1937. For 1922–24 *Statistics of Income* has the combined item 'rent and interest received' by corporations; rent receipts are assumed to have the same relation to rent and interest receipts as in 1929. For 1919 and 1920 rent receipts of all corporations are assumed to be the same percentage of total rent receipts as in 1922. Between 1924 and 1929 this percentage is interpolated along a straight line. On the basis of the total rent paid and the ratio of corporate receipts to it, the total rent receipts of corporations are estimated. Individuals' rent receipts are obtained by subtraction. Receipts of corporations in the real estate business in 1929 and later years are from the detailed tabulation of *Statistics of Income* data. For earlier years they are extrapolated by the rent receipts of all corporations.

The gross rent bill for the industry is the sum of rent receipts of individuals and of corporations in real estate.

Col. 11 Total: sum of col. 5, 9, and 10.

TABLE F 4

Dividends and Interest by Major Industrial Divisions

Col. 1 Banking: total dividends paid are assumed to be net. Available from 1926 through 1937 from the special tabulation of *Statistics of Income* data, they are extrapolated for earlier years and 1938 by a preliminary series, obtained by applying to the capital stock paid in of all banks other than private, as reported in the *Annual Report of the Comptroller of the Currency*, the average dividend rate of member banks. The dividend rate of member banks is based on total dividends paid and capital stock paid in, as reported in various issues of the *Federal Reserve Bulletin* and the *Annual Report of the Federal Reserve Board*, respectively.

Col. 2 Insurance: sum of total dividends paid to stockholders by life insurance companies and net dividends paid by insurance companies other than life. Life insurance companies' dividends are reported in the *Life Insurance Year Book* and are considered net. For 1926–37 the dividends of insurance companies other than life are the difference between total dividends paid and dividends received as reported in the special tabulation of *Statistics of Income* data. For earlier years and 1938 total dividends paid are extrapolated from 1926 and 1937, respectively, by the series on dividends paid to stockholders in the *Fire and Marine Insurance Year Book* and the *Casualty, Surety, and Miscellaneous Insurance Year Book*.

Dividends received in 1938 are extrapolated from 1937 by the series on dividends received in the *Fire and Marine Insurance Year Book* and the *Casualty, Surety, and Miscellaneous Insurance Year Book*. They are extrapolated for the years before 1926 by a preliminary series, the sum of estimates of dividends received by fire and marine and by casualty and miscellaneous companies. The procedure is the same for both groups. The *Connecticut Insurance Report*, Parts I and II, gives the total interest and dividend receipts of companies operating in Connecticut. On the basis of sample company data in the report short term interest is deducted. The balance is divided into interest and dividend receipts on the basis of the ratio of the weight derived for bond holdings to the sum of the weights derived for bond and stock holdings. The weight for bond holdings is the product of the percentage of total security holdings that are bonds (derived from sample company data in the Connecticut report) and the average interest rate on bond and mortgage debt for manufacturing, mining, trade, and steam railroads. The weight for stock holdings is the product of the average dividend rate for these same industries and the percentage that stocks are of the total security holdings of insurance companies as derived from sample company data. The resulting estimates of interest and dividend receipts of companies operating in Connecticut are raised by the ratio of total premiums to premiums of companies doing business in that state to yield the preliminary totals.

Col. 3 Real estate: difference between total dividends paid and dividends received. Dividends paid, 1926–37, are from the special tabulation of *Statistics of Income* data; they are extrapolated for earlier years and 1938 by the dividend payments of the corporate sample for the industry. Dividends received, 1926–37, also from the special tabulation, are estimated for 1922–25 by applying to dividends paid the ratio of dividends received to them. This ratio for 1926 is extrapolated by the corresponding ratio for the entire finance group, data for which appear in *Statistics of Income*. For 1919–21 dividends received are assumed to be the same percentage of dividends received by all corporations (reported in *Statistics of Income*) as in 1922. In 1938 dividends received are assumed to be the same percentage of dividends paid as in 1937.

Col. 4 Total: sum of col. 1–3.

Col. 5 Insurance: since there is no long term debt for insurance companies the net interest payments are negative. Interest receipts of companies other than life are alone considered. Reported for 1926–37 in the special tabulation of *Statistics of Income* data, they are extrapolated for 1919–25 by the preliminary series described in the notes on dividends received (col. 2). The 1938 figure is extrapolated from 1937 by interest received, reported in the *Fire and Marine Insurance Year Book* and the *Casualty, Surety, and Miscellaneous Insurance Year Book*.

Col. 6 Real estate, corporate: difference between total interest paid on long term debt and interest received on tax-exempt obligations. Total interest paid in 1930 and later years is estimated by applying to the par value of long term debt the average interest rate of the corporate sample for the industry. Long term debt outstanding on December 31, 1930–35 is from the special tabulation of *Statistics of Income* data. The figure for December 31, 1929 is assumed to be the same percentage of the long term debt of all finance corporations as in 1930. The figures for 1929–31 are raised by the 1931 ratio of compiled receipts of all corporations to compiled receipts of corporations reporting assets and liabilities. The compiled receipts ratios for 1932–35 are used to raise the reported figures for respective years. The year-end figures are averaged to yield long term debt outstanding during the year; multiplying these averages by the estimated interest rate yields total long term interest, 1930–35. The estimates of long term interest for earlier years and 1936–38 are extrapolated from 1930 and 1935, respectively, by the total long term interest of the corporate sample for the industry.

Interest received, 1926–37, is interest received on tax-exempt obligations as reported in the special tabulation of *Statistics of Income* data. It is assumed to be the same percentage of interest paid in 1938 as in 1937, and is extrapolated to 1922 by the comparable item for the entire finance group. It is assumed that the ratio to total interest receipts on tax-exempt obligations of all corporations is the same in 1919–21 as in 1922. The totals for 1919–21 appear in *Statistics of Income.*

Col. 7 Real estate, individual: based on the estimated total of individuals' urban mortgage debt, it is an estimate of total interest payments on mortgages other than those of real estate corporations. The figures for 1929–38 are the estimates of urban dwelling mortgages and other individuals' mortgages prepared by the Bureau of Foreign and Domestic Commerce, National Income Division. They are extrapolated for other years by the mortgage holdings of important lending agencies. Urban mortgage loans of over 90 per cent of life insurance companies are reported in the *Proceedings of the Annual Convention of the Association of Life Insurance Presidents.* These are raised to the total for all life insurance by the ratio of the assets of all companies to those of reporting companies. The urban mortgage loans of banks are based on data in the *Annual Report of the Comptroller of the Currency.* When the data are not classified in sufficient detail the method used is that outlined in *Internal Debts of the United States,* by Evans Clark

(Macmillan, 1933). Banks covered are national, state, loan and trust, stock savings, mutual savings, and private. Mortgage loans of building and loan associations, 1925–38, are from the *Annual Report of the Comptroller of the Currency.* For earlier years they are extrapolated from 1925 by total assets reported for the respective years. For the real estate bonds of title and mortgage guarantee companies we have estimates for 1921 and 1929 from *Internal Debts of the United States.* The sum of the above mentioned items for 1921 and 1929, interpolated for intervening years by the sum of all except title and mortgage guarantee companies, yields the preliminary series by which the 1929 figure for individuals' urban mortgage debt is extrapolated to 1919.

Total interest on individuals' urban mortgages is estimated by multiplying the estimated mortgage debt outstanding by the interest rate. For the years through 1928 the interest rate is assumed to be 6 per cent. For 1929–38 the interest rate is that derived by the Bureau of Foreign and Domestic Commerce, National Income Division.

To the interest on individuals' urban mortgages is added the interest on farm mortgages not paid by farm operators (see the notes to Table A 1, col. 6).

Col. 8 Real estate, total: sum of col. 6 and 7.

Col. 9 Total: sum of col. 5 and 8.

TABLE F 5

Property Income by Major Industrial Divisions

Col. 1 Banking: see Table F 4, col. 1.

Col. 2 Insurance: see Table F 4, col. 2 and 5.

Col. 3 Real estate: see Table F 4, col. 3 and 8.

Col. 4 Real estate, net rent received by individuals: difference between net rent before mortgage interest and the mortgage interest paid by individuals. Net urban rent before mortgage interest is obtained by applying to gross urban rent (see the notes to Table F 3) the ratio of net before interest to gross. The basic ratio of net to gross is for 1934 and is an average of the ratio for office buildings as derived from the *Office Building Experience Exchange Report* (National Association of Building Owners and Managers) and the ratio for apartment houses as derived from data in the *Real Estate*

Record, April and August 1935. It is extrapolated for other years by the ratio for office buildings.

From estimated net urban rent before mortgage interest, the estimated mortgage interest on individuals' rented property is subtracted to yield the net urban rent received by individuals. Net mortgage interest on individuals' rented property is estimated by applying to the total urban mortgage interest of individuals the ratio of gross rent received by individuals to the sum of gross rent and gross imputed rent of individuals (see the notes to col. 5). The net rent paid on agricultural property (Table A 1, col. 4) is added to the estimate for urban property to yield total net rent received by individuals.

Col. 5 Individuals' net imputed rent: gross imputed rent on owner-occupied dwellings is derived in a fashion similar to that for gross residential rent described in the notes to Table F 3. The number of owner-occupied dwellings is the difference between the total and the number rented. The 1930 *Census of Population,* Vol. VI median value of owner-occupied dwellings is adjusted to the average value by a method similar to that used to adjust the median rent of rented dwellings. Average imputed rent is obtained by applying to the average value the ratio of rent to value as derived from David L. Wickens' materials for the *Financial Survey of Urban Housing.* The basic average imputed rent is for 1929 and is extrapolated for other years by the indexes used to estimate average rent paid. Gross imputed rent is the product of the number of owner-occupied dwellings and the average imputed rent.

Net imputed rent is estimated by applying to gross imputed rent the ratio of net to gross before mortgage interest and subtracting from the result the estimated mortgage interest on owner-occupied dwellings. Mortgage interest (see the notes to Table F 4, col. 7) on owner-occupied dwellings is the difference between total interest on non-farm mortgages and that on rented non-farm property. The ratio of net to gross rent is derived from data reported for office buildings in the *Office Building Experience Exchange Report.* It is assumed that the relation of insurance, taxes, and depreciation and of heating, plumbing, alteration, repairs, and decoration to gross rent paid in office buildings is representative of that for private dwellings. The balance after deduction from gross rent of the expenses listed is the net figure from which the ratio of net to gross is estimated. As data for this ratio are available only since 1920 the 1919 ratio is assumed to be the same as the 1920.

Col. 6 Real estate, total: sum of col. 3–5.

Col. 7 Total: sum of col. 1, 2, and 6.

TABLE F 6

Total Payments to Individuals and Net Savings by Major Industrial Divisions

TOTAL PAYMENTS TO INDIVIDUALS

Col. 1–4: sum for each industrial division of wages and salaries (Table F 3), property income (Table F 5), and entrepreneurial withdrawals (insurance only) (Table F 2, col. 2).

NET SAVINGS

Col. 5 Banking: corporate savings are the difference between compiled net profits after taxes and total dividends paid (see the notes to Table F 4). Compiled net profits, 1926–37, are from the special tabulation of *Statistics of Income* data. Extrapolation of net savings for 1919 25 and for 1938 is by the difference between net additions to profits and dividends declared for members of the Federal Reserve System (*Federal Reserve Bulletin*). For the years before 1924 the data are reported for years ending June 30. Averages of fiscal years are used for calendar years.

Col. 6 Insurance: it is assumed that all the income of entrepreneurs is withdrawn and that there are, therefore, no entrepreneurial net savings. We estimated only corporate savings of insurance companies other than life; they are the difference between compiled net profits after taxes and total dividends paid. Compiled net profits, reported for 1926–37 in the special tabulation of *Statistics of Income* data, are extrapolated for 1938 from 1937 by the corporate sample for the industry. For the years before 1926 they are estimated as the sum of statutory net income after taxes (*Statistics of Income*), interest received on government obligations, and dividends received (see the notes to Table F 4).

Col. 7 Real estate: the derivation of corporate savings is the same as for insurance; for the sources and methods see the notes to col. 6.

Col. 8 Total: sum of col. 5–7.

Employees by Minor Industrial Divisions

Col. 1 Commercial and stock savings banks: the 1934 figure is based on the number of employees in the Federal Deposit Insurance Corporation *Call Report 1* for national, state member, and non-member banks. On the advice of P. T. Campbell of the Federal Deposit Insurance Corporation, part-time employees were equated to full-time by halving them. Employees of non-member banks are estimated on the basis of the number in insured non-member banks. The total in insured non-member banks is raised to the total in all non-member banks by the ratio of the deposits of the latter to the deposits of the former. Deposits of all non-member banks are recorded in the *Federal Reserve Bulletin.* The total is divided into full- and part-time on the basis of the breakdown for insured non-member banks, and the number of part-time is adjusted to the full-time equivalent by halving them.

The 1935 figure is based on *Census of Business* data. The item reported is total employment, full- and part-time, for national, state member, and non-member banks at the end of the year. The average for the year is estimated by interpolating along a straight line between the 1934 and the December 31, 1935 figures. Full-time and the full-time equivalent of part-time employees are assumed to have undergone the same percentage change from 1934 to 1935 as total employment, full- and part-time.

The number of employees in member banks, 1936–38, is from the *Federal Reserve Bulletin;* in insured non-member banks, by letter from the Federal Deposit Insurance Corporation; and in non-member banks not insured they were obtained by dividing wages and salaries paid by those banks by the estimated average salary. It is assumed that the average salary follows the movement of the average salary in insured banks.

The number of employees, 1919–33, is obtained by dividing total salaries paid (see the notes to Table F 3) by the estimated average salary. The average salary, computed for 1934, is extrapolated for other years by the average salary paid by Federal Reserve banks.

Col. 2 Mutual savings banks: obtained by dividing the total salary bill (see the notes to Table F 3) by the estimated average salary.

The average salary for December 1935 is derived from *Census of Business* data. It is extrapolated for 1936–38 by the average salary paid by insured mutual savings banks, and for 1919–34 by the average salary paid by Federal Reserve banks.

Col. 3 Federal Reserve banks: average number of employees, 1926–38, from the *Annual Report of the Federal Reserve Board.* For earlier years it is obtained by dividing total salaries paid by the estimated average salary. The latter is obtained by averaging pairs of December 31 figures computed from data on number and compensation in the *Annual Report of the Federal Reserve Board.*

Col. 4 Insolvent banks, other than private: obtained by dividing the total salary bill (see the notes to Table F 3) by the estimated average salary. The average salary for 1929–38 is estimated by the Bureau of Foreign and Domestic Commerce, National Income Division. For earlier years the 1929 figure is extrapolated by the average salary of active commercial banks.

Col. 5 Total banking: sum of col. 1–4.

Col. 6 Life insurance companies: the basic figure, for 1935, is derived from data for home and branch offices, full- and part-time, as reported in the 1935 *Census of Business.* The total of full- and part-time employees is adjusted to the full-time equivalent on the basis of the ratio of full-time employment to total full- and part-time employment for one week as reported for all home offices (life and other) and branch offices (life and other) separately. Full-time payroll divided by full-time number gives the average full-time salary, which, divided into the total part-time payroll, yields the estimated full-time equivalent of part-time employment. This procedure is followed for life and other insurance, home and branch offices, separately.

The 1935 figure is extrapolated to 1929 by figures on the employees of 61 companies, prepared by the Association of Life Insurance Presidents. For the years before 1929 the number of employees is obtained by dividing total salaries paid by the estimated average salary. The average salary for 1929 is computed and extrapolated to 1919 by the average salary paid by sample companies in the industry.

Col. 7 Other insurance companies: for the derivation of the basic figure for 1935 see the notes to col. 6. The average salary is computed for 1935 and extrapolated for other years by the average salary for sample companies in the industry. The number of employees is obtained by dividing total salaries by the estimated average salary. No estimate is available of the number engaged in loss adjustment.

Col. 8 Insurance agencies: sum of estimates of (a) non-selling employees and (b) selling employees.

a) Non-selling employees: for the derivation of the basic figure for 1935 see the notes to col. 6. For other years the procedure is that outlined in the notes to col. 7.

b) Selling employees: solicitors are included. The number of direct selling employees in agencies in 1935 is based on *Census of Business* data, and the adjustment for part-time employment is similar to that for life insurance companies. The number of solicitors in branch offices as reported is used; and the number of solicitors in agencies is assumed to be the same percentage of selling employees as in branch offices. The total of employees is extrapolated to 1929 by the number of agents reported for 61 life insurance companies by the Association of Life Insurance Presidents. The number before 1929 is obtained by dividing total salaries by the estimated average salary. The average salary, computed for 1929, is extrapolated for earlier years by the average salary of sample companies in the industry.

Col. 9 Total insurance: 1919–35, sum of col. 6–8; 1936–38, the total salary bill (see the notes to Table F 3) is divided by the estimated average salary. The average salary, computed for 1935, is extrapolated for 1936–38 by BLS data on employment and payrolls in insurance companies.

Col. 10 Real estate: for 1930, computed from data on the number gainfully occupied reported in the 1930 *Census of Population,* Vol. V, Ch. 7. We include all those covered under real estate and the following classified under domestic and personal service: all professional and clerical pursuits, all skilled trades, charwomen and cleaners, draymen, elevator tenders, firemen, guards, janitors and sextons, laborers, policemen, porters, and 'all other'. The number unemployed is estimated on the basis of Robert R. Nathan's unemployment figures for banking, brokerage, insurance and real estate, and domestic and personal service. The difference between the total gainfully occupied and the estimated unemployed is the number working in April 1930.

This estimate is extrapolated for 1929 and later years by Mr. Nathan's index of employment in banking, brokerage, insurance and real estate, and domestic and personal service. For the years before 1929 a preliminary estimate is made by dividing total salaries paid by a preliminary estimate of the average pay. The average pay is computed for 1929 and extrapolated to 1919 by the average pay of commercial banks and domestic service. The final figure for the number employed in 1920 is based on an estimate of the number gainfully occupied in 1920 and the assumption that the same percentage was unemployed as in 1929. The number gainfully occupied in 1920 is estimated by applying to the number gainfully occupied in 1930 the percentage change from 1920 to 1930 among managers, officials, and agents in real estate, and elevator tenders, janitors, porters, charwomen, and cleaners and laborers in domestic service (1930 *Census of Population,* Vol. V, Ch. 1). The 1929 estimate for gainfully occupied is interpolated between 1920 and 1930 along a straight line. The ratio of employed to gainfully occupied in 1929 is computed and applied to the estimated number gainfully occupied in 1920 to yield the number employed in that year. Final estimates of the number employed in 1919 are extrapolated from 1920 and in 1921-28 are interpolated between 1920 and 1929 by the preliminary series of the number employed.

Col. 11 Total: sum of col. 5, 9, and 10.

Service

Whenever two entries are made for 1934 the first is comparable with those for preceding years in that the *Statistics of Income* data used are based on the old industrial classification; the second is comparable with those for succeeding years in that the *Statistics of Income* data used are based on the new industrial classification.

Net savings and net income, adjusted, exclude gains and losses from sales of capital assets, 1929–38, and from changes in inventory valuation, 1919–38. Net savings and net income without any specific designation are unadjusted, i.e., include these two types of gain and loss.

Entrepreneurs and their net income for automobile repair shops and garages are included with employees and their compensation.

Salaried engineers and employees in hand trades and their compensation are included with entrepreneurs and their income.

S 1 Total Payments by Type (millions of dollars)

	WAGES & SALARIES (1)	ENTREP. WITHDR. (2)	DIVIDENDS (3)	INTEREST (4)	PROP. INCOME (5)	PAY. TO INDIVIDUALS (6)
1919	3,256	1,699	29.0	15.9	44.9	5,060
1920	4,072	1,853	80.4	14.9	95.2	6,020
1921	4,203	1,681	65.7	18.1	83.8	5,968
1922	4,498	2,404	48.8	22.8	71.6	6,973
1923	4,925	2,397	68.0	28.0	96.0	7,419
1924	5,238	2,691	71.2	33.2	104	8,033
1925	5,520	3,012	92.1	41.0	133	8,666
1926	5,905	3,000	105	47.7	153	9,059
1927	6,351	3,199	106	62.7	169	9,720
1928	6,433	3,430	99.1	73.0	172	10,036
1929	6,893	3,658	116	87.0	203	10,755
1930	6,390	3,505	112	99.0	211	10,108
1931	5,574	3,295	73.7	93.7	167	9,036
1932	4,415	3,230	54.5	110	164	7,810
1933	3,919	3,093	33.9	95.3	129	7,142
1934	4,395	2,780	41.8	86.9	128	7,304
1934	4,395	2,799	50.6	88.7	139	7,334
1935	4,792	2,818	54.3	104	159	7,770
1936	5,304	2,872	113	101	215	8,392
1937	5,914	3,218	120	95.6	215	9,348
1938	5,610	3,052	69.0	92.9	161	8,824

S 2 Net Income Originating (millions of dollars)

	PAY. TO INDIVIDUALS (1)	NET SAVINGS Entrep. (2)	Corp. (3)	Total (4)	NET INCOME (5)	NET SAVINGS, ADJ. Corp. (6)	Total (7)	NET INCOME, ADJ. (8)
1919	5,000	1,079	49.1	1,128	6,129	35.1	1,114	6,115
1920	6,020	826	5.6	831	6,852	0.6	826	6,847
1921	5,968	708	—25.0	683	6,652	—4.0	704	6,673
1922	6,973	383	25.9	408	7,382	24.9	407	7,381
1923	7,419	798	42.9	841	8,260	40.9	839	8,258
1924	8,033	566	44.2	610	8,644	47.2	613	8,647
1925	8,666	584	55.5	639	9,306	60.5	644	9,311
1926	9,059	1,031	23.1	1,054	10,114	29.1	1,060	10,120
1927	9,720	604	—6.4	597	10,318	—4.4	599	10,320
1928	10,036	637	7.0	644	10,680	13.0	650	10,686
1929	10,755	518	15.1	533	11,289	—7.9	510	11,266
1930	10,108	383	—79.7	303	10,411	—67.2	316	10,424
1931	9,036	—103	—206	—309	8,727	—135	—238	8,798
1932	7,810	—935	—476	—1,412	6,398	—372	—1,308	6,502
1933	7,142	—1,013	—357	—1,370	5,771	—317	—1,330	5,811
1934	7,304	—318	—240	—558	6,746	—239	—557	6,746
1934	7,334	—337	—239	—576	6,758	—238	—575	6,759
1935	7,770	—195	—211	—406	7,363	—206	—401	7,369
1936	8,392	105	—199	—94.0	8,298	—213	—108	8,284
1937	9,348	—49.4	—169	—218	9,130	—194	—243	9,105
1938	8,824	217	—169	48.0	8,872	—172	45.2	8,869

S 3 Wages and Salaries by Major Industrial Divisions
(millions of dollars)

	PROFESSIONAL (1)	PERSONAL (2)	DOMESTIC (3)	MISC. (4)	TOTAL (5)
1919	533	1,046	1,151	526	3,256
1920	624	1,322	1,305	819	4,072
1921	696	1,251	1,433	822	4,203
1922	748	1,384	1,553	811	4,498
1923	812	1,425	1,698	989	4,925
1924	879	1,476	1,801	1,080	5,238
1925	932	1,559	1,892	1,136	5,520
1926	993	1,642	1,971	1,298	5,905
1927	1,068	1,820	2,037	1,424	6,351
1928	1,148	1,746	2,039	1,499	6,433
1929	1,212	1,964	2,145	1,572	6,893
1930	1,245	1,858	1,843	1,443	6,390
1931	1,225	1,633	1,440	1,274	5,574
1932	1,148	1,302	1,055	909	4,415
1933	1,066	1,096	920	837	3,919
1934	1,074	1,322	1,050	947	4,395
1935	1,122	1,451	1,118	1,100	4,792
1936	1,196	1,574	1,260	1,274	5,304
1937	1,277	1,711	1,493	1,433	5,914
1938	1,316	1,666	1,303	1,325	5,610

S 4 Wages and Salaries by Minor Industrial Divisions
(millions of dollars)

	PROFESSIONAL				PERSONAL			
	Private education (1)	Religious (2)	Curative (3)	Other * (4)	Hotels (5)	Restaurants (6)	Power laund. & clean. & dye. (7)	Other (8)
1919	101	174	82.9	174	309	336	139	260
1920	124	201	100	198	345	467	177	332
1921	152	216	127	200	388	371	172	319
1922	176	228	142	201	412	436	182	353
1923	187	240	165	219	391	429	211	394
1924	198	258	184	238	376	487	228	385
1925	207	274	196	253	383	541	242	391
1926	224	283	212	273	415	540	259	426
1927	242	292	236	296	412	646	303	458
1928	255	301	264	325	408	585	320	431
1929	264	312	290	345	442	660	375	486
1930	272	311	300	360	416	669	374	398
1931	280	294	286	363	343	636	322	331
1932	276	266	261	345	253	555	257	235
1933	257	245	236	326	217	445	229	204
1934	252	246	243	331	266	582	247	226
1935	265	245	262	348	288	658	255	248
1936	276	250	295	373	310	705	279	279
1937	284	258	335	399	340	775	305	289
1938	286	265	358	405	333	761	297	274

* Including salaries of employees in legal and miscellaneous professions.

S 5 Wages and Salaries by Minor Industrial Subdivisions
(millions of dollars)

| | ASSISTANTS TO | | HOSPI-TALS | LEGAL | MISC. PROFES-SIONAL | ADV. | RECREA-TION & AMUSE-MENT | AUTO REPAIR SHOPS & GARAGES |
| | Physicians & surgeons | Dentists | | | | | | |
	(1)	(2)	(3)	(4)	(5)	(6)	(7)	(8)
1929	20.8	14.0	255	140	205	204	696	671
1930	20.4	13.5	267	147	213	176	622	644
1931	19.5	12.5	254	150	213	147	554	572
1932	17.5	10.7	233	147	197	101	362	445
1933	16.6	8.8	211	141	184	87.9	332	416
1934	17.0	9.1	217	143	188	115	360	472
1935	18.9	9.2	234	150	198	140	412	547
1936	21.2	10.4	263	160	213	161	493	620
1937	23.3	11.5	301	170	228	175	538	719
1938	23.7	11.6	323	174	231	150	495	679

S. 6 Entrepreneurial Net Income by Major Industrial Divisions
(millions of dollars)

| | CURATIVE | OTHER PROFES-SIONAL * | TOTAL PROFES-SIONAL | PERSONAL | MISC. | TOTAL |
	(1)	(2)	(3)	(4)	(5)	(6)
1919	714	845	1,559	843	375	2,778
1920	611	727	1,339	891	448	2,679
1921	526	636	1,163	829	396	2,390
1922	781	959	1,740	676	369	2,787
1923	850	1,075	1,926	855	413	3,195
1924	895	1,160	2,055	801	400	3,257
1925	1,033	1,356	2,389	807	400	3,597
1926	1,118	1,491	2,610	999	423	4,032
1927	1,042	1,410	2,453	953	397	3,803
1928	1,150	1,586	2,737	934	396	4,067
1929	1,184	1,666	2,851	938	386	4,177
1930	1,096	1,533	2,629	887	371	3,889
1931	961	1,182	2,144	726	321	3,192
1932	731	839	1,570	485	238	2,294
1933	676	764	1,440	425	214	2,080
1934	779	841	1,620	591	250	2,462
1935	840	901	1,742	621	259	2,623
1936	962	1,012	1,974	718	284	2,977
1937	1,038	1,109	2,147	714	306	3,168
1938	1,059	1,137	2,196	786	287	3,269

* Comprising private education, lawyers, engineers, and miscellaneous professions.

S 7 Entrepreneurial Net Income by Minor Industrial Divisions (millions of dollars)

	PHYSI-CIANS & SUR-GEONS	DENTISTS	TRAINED NURSES, PRIVATE DUTY	OTHER CURA-TIVE	LAWYERS	ENGI-NEERS	OTHER PROFES-SIONAL *	ADV.	RECREA-TION & AMUSE-MENT	HAND TRADES
	(1)	(2)	(3)	(4)	(5)	(6)	(7)	(8)	(9)	(10)
1929	665	245	143	130	614	492	559	39.7	121	225
1930	602	234	141	117	586	418	528	36.7	128	206
1931	530	202	125	102	519	237	425	27.2	113	180
1932	405	151	97.3	77.0	412	121	305	17.8	78.2	142
1933	379	135	92.3	69.4	380	105	277	10.4	65.6	138
1934	442	149	110	77.2	411	119	310	14.2	79.7	156
1935	475	156	127	81.4	444	125	331	11.3	79.8	168
1936	548	173	148	91.8	498	140	373	14.1	85.8	184
1937	590	186	163	97.7	558	148	402	14.9	90.7	201
1938	601	188	169	100	576	148	412	14.9	93.4	179

* Comprising private education and miscellaneous professions.

S 8 Employees by Major Industrial Divisions (thousands)

	PROFESSIONAL	PERSONAL	DOMESTIC	MISC.	TOTAL
	(1)	(2)	(3)	(4)	(5)
1919	594	915	1,692	426	3,629
1920	599	949	1,693	524	3,767
1921	610	926	1,733	541	3,810
1922	656	1,029	1,840	528	4,055
1923	722	1,056	1,967	605	4,351
1924	773	1,076	2,022	641	4,513
1925	784	1,161	2,084	661	4,692
1926	841	1,216	2,161	736	4,956
1927	870	1,265	2,214	796	5,147
1928	923	1,254	2,222	834	5,234
1929	971	1,401	2,303	860	5,536
1930	995	1,386	2,151	805	5,338
1931	991	1,308	1,926	752	4,979
1932	978	1,206	1,654	639	4,479
1933	975	1,116	1,571	616	4,279
1934	997	1,320	1,775	690	4,783
1935	1,033	1,423	1,860	776	5,094
1936	1,089	1,480	1,994	883	5,447
1937	1,138	1,550	2,118	917	5,724
1938	1,157	1,511	1,950	918	5,538

S 9   Employees by Minor Industrial Divisions (thousands)

	PROFESSIONAL					PERSONAL		
	Private educa- tion	Reli- gious	Cura- tive	Other *	Hotels	Restau- rants	Power laund. & clean. & dye.	Other
	(1)	(2)	(3)	(4)	(5)	(6)	(7)	(8)
1919	130	128	139	196	268	260	169	216
1920	140	127	135	197	255	300	176	216
1921	150	126	131	201	279	254	169	222
1922	160	128	158	209	302	305	183	238
1923	167	134	198	222	290	303	204	257
1924	174	139	221	237	271	325	213	265
1925	178	141	217	247	298	369	219	274
1926	186	143	251	260	305	384	241	285
1927	195	144	257	273	300	403	268	293
1928	200	146	288	287	295	391	272	294
1929	203	148	318	301	331	439	323	306
1930	203	148	326	316	317	452	320	295
1931	202	150	313	325	283	463	297	263
1932	200	150	300	327	243	464	273	225
1933	199	149	292	334	229	391	272	223
1934	202	149	304	341	266	522	289	242
1935	209	149	319	355	278	586	297	261
1936	215	149	352	371	289	603	315	271
1937	220	148	387	382	302	633	329	284
1938	221	148	396	391	295	629	316	270

* Including employees in legal and miscellaneous professions.

S 10   Employees by Minor Industrial Subdivisions (thousands)

	ASSISTANTS TO				MISC.		RECREATION	AUTO REPAIR
	Physicians & surgeons	Dentists	HOSPITALS	LEGAL	PROFES- SIONAL	ADV.	& AMUSE- MENT	SHOPS & GARAGES
	(1)	(2)	(3)	(4)	(5)	(6)	(7)	(8)
1929	25.1	14.3	279	96.1	205	67.7	390	402
1930	24.8	13.7	288	100	215	58.4	336	410
1931	24.3	13.0	276	106	219	51.2	298	402
1932	23.0	12.4	265	110	217	40.0	219	380
1933	23.1	11.7	257	114	220	36.2	216	362
1934	23.4	12.2	268	116	225	41.6	246	403
1935	24.9	12.7	282	121	233	44.2	274	458
1936	27.2	13.9	311	125	245	49.6	346	487
1937	28.5	14.6	344	129	252	52.4	346	518
1938	29.1	14.8	352	133	257	45.3	343	530

S 11 Entrepreneurs by Major Industrial Divisions (thousands)

	CURATIVE	OTHER PROFES- SIONAL *	TOTAL PROFES- SIONAL	PERSONAL	MISC.	TOTAL
	(1)	(2)	(3)	(4)	(5)	(6)
1919	248	201	450	402	370	1,222
1920	250	202	452	406	370	1,229
1921	256	205	461	396	361	1,220
1922	262	210	473	424	352	1,250
1923	269	219	488	452	344	1,284
1924	277	228	506	482	335	1,324
1925	287	235	522	512	326	1,361
1926	298	243	542	535	318	1,396
1927	310	252	562	561	309	1,433
1928	322	261	584	556	300	1,441
1929	335	270	605	588	292	1,486
1930	346	280	626	583	289	1,499
1931	354	288	643	582	284	1,509
1932	362	288	651	580	277	1,509
1933	370	293	664	616	276	1,557
1934	378	298	676	637	280	1,594
1935	387	304	691	654	277	1,623
1936	396	310	706	655	285	1,646
1937	406	316	722	656	285	1,664
1938	416	322	738	655	278	1,672

* Comprising private education, lawyers, engineers, and miscellaneous professions.

S 12 Entrepreneurs by Minor Industrial Divisions (thousands)

	PHYSI- CIANS & SUR- GEONS	DENTISTS	TRAINED NURSES, PRIVATE DUTY	OTHER CURA- TIVE	LAWYERS	ENGI- NEERS	OTHER PROFES- SIONAL *	ADV.	RECREA- TION & AMUSE- MENT	HAND TRADES
	(1)	(2)	(3)	(4)	(5)	(6)	(7)	(8)	(9)	(10)
1929	119	58.8	109	47.1	105	53.5	111	3.6	60.0	228
1930	121	59.9	118	46.7	109	53.6	117	3.7	61.5	224
1931	123	60.6	123	47.2	116	51.9	120	3.6	61.2	219
1932	125	61.4	128	47.7	117	50.1	121	3.3	61.1	213
1933	127	62.2	134	47.4	122	48.3	122	2.1	60.8	213
1934	128	62.8	139	46.8	126	48.3	123	2.6	58.8	219
1935	130	63.4	145	47.1	130	48.3	125	2.0	56.8	219
1936	132	64.0	151	47.5	134	48.3	127	2.2	58.4	224
1937	135	64.9	158	47.7	139	48.3	128	2.2	59.3	224
1938	137	65.7	164	48.1	143	48.3	130	2.2	59.5	216

* Comprising private education and miscellaneous professions.

TABLE S 1

Total Payments by Type

Col. 1 Wages and salaries: see Table S 3, col. 5.

Col. 2 Entrepreneurial withdrawals: estimated for entrepreneurs in (1) professional service, (2) personal service, (3) miscellaneous service.

1) Professional service: sum of estimates for:

a) Private education: commercial and correspondence schools are estimated separately. Total withdrawals are obtained by multiplying the number of entrepreneurs by their average withdrawal, which is assumed to be the same as the average pay of administrative and teaching employees (see the notes to Table S 4, col. 1). For the number of entrepreneurs see the notes to Table S 11, col. 2.

b) Trained nurses, private duty: estimated by multiplying the number (see Table S 11, col. 1) by the average income. Per capita cash income in 1926 is from *Nurses, Patients, and Pocketbooks* (Committee on the Grading of Nursing Schools, 1928); for 1929 it was obtained from the Committee on the Costs of Medical Care; and for 1934 and 1935 from *Facts about Nursing, 1938.* Interpolation and extrapolation of the figures for these four years are by the average of the per capita net income of physicians and surgeons and of dentists (see the notes to Table S 6, col. 1). The estimate of per capita payment in kind is the product of the estimated weeks of work per year and the weekly board allowance. Weeks of work are estimated by dividing the average annual pay by the daily rate of pay and by 7. The daily rate of pay in 1916 and 1926 is from *Nurses, Patients, and Pocketbooks,* and in 1936, from *Facts about Nursing.* For 1927–30 the 1926 figure is used; the 1935 figure is assumed to be the same as the 1936. Interpolation for 1919–25 and 1931–34 is along a straight line. The number of weeks of work is kept constant from 1936 to 1938. The weekly board allowance is that derived for domestic service (see the notes to Table S 3, col. 3).

c) Other professional service: lawyers, engineers including salaried engineers (since the latter cannot be segregated), and all entrepreneurs in the curative and other professional service fields not covered above. Withdrawals are obtained by applying to their estimated total net income the ratio of withdrawals to net income as derived from the data for entrepreneurs in manufacturing, mining, construction, and trade (for the net income series see the notes to Table S 6).

2) *Personal service:* total withdrawals are obtained by multiplying the number of entrepreneurs (see Table S 11, col. 4) by the average withdrawal, which is assumed to be the same as the average annual pay of employees in this field (see the notes to Table S 4, col. 5–8).

3) *Miscellaneous service:* sum of estimates for advertising, recreation and amusement, and hand trades.

 a) *Advertising:* estimated by the procedure outlined for 'other' professional service.

 b) *Recreation and amusement:* estimated by the procedure outlined for personal service.

 c) *Hand trades:* the total engaged cannot be separated into entrepreneurs and employees, and since entrepreneurs predominate, the compensation item is entered here rather than under wages and salaries. Total withdrawals are estimated by multiplying the number engaged (see the notes to Table S 11, col. 5) by the average income. The 1935 full-time pay for repair services and customs industries excluding automobiles, derived from the *Census of Business* (see notes to the advertising estimates in Table S 3, col. 4 for method), is extrapolated by the average wage in manufacturing to yield the series on average income.

Col. 3 Dividends: difference between total dividends paid and dividends received, both reported, 1922–37, in *Statistics of Income.* Dividends paid in 1922 are extrapolated through 1919 by the dividend payments of the corporate sample for the industry. Dividends received, 1919–21, are estimated by applying to total dividends received (reported in *Statistics of Income*) the industrial breakdown in 1922. The 1938 figure is extrapolated from 1937 by the corporate sample for the industry.

Col. 4 Interest: difference between total interest paid on long term debt and interest received on tax-exempt obligations.

 Total long term interest is estimated by multiplying long term debt outstanding by the average interest rate. Long term debt outstanding on December 31, 1921, 1923, 1924, and 1926–35 is from *Statistics of Income.* The 1921 figure is assumed to be the total for the industry. Those for 1923 and 1924 are raised by the ratio of the fair value of the stock of all corporations to the fair value of the stock of corporations reporting assets and liabilities. The 1926–31 figures are raised by the 1931 ratio of compiled receipts of all corporations to the compiled receipts of corporations reporting assets and liabilities. Totals for 1932–35 also are obtained by applying to the figure reported the compiled receipts ratios for the respective years.

Long term debt in 1934 comparable with prior years is extrapolated from 1933 by the long term debt of corporations filing unconsolidated returns as reported in *Statistics of Income* and raised by the compiled receipts ratios for the respective years. The same index applied to 1934 long term debt comparable with 1935 yields a comparable figure for 1933. Long term debt as of December 31, 1918–20, 1922, and 1925 is extrapolated and interpolated by the debt of the corporate sample for the industry. Year-end figures are averaged to yield debt outstanding during the year. To the latter the average interest rate of the corporate sample for the industry is applied to yield total long term interest paid. The estimates of interest paid, 1936–38, are extrapolated from 1935 by the corporate sample for the industry.

Interest received, 1922–37, is from *Statistics of Income*. Interest received, 1919–21, is estimated on the assumption that the industrial distribution of the total reported in *Statistics of Income* is the same as in 1922. Interest received in 1938 is assumed to be the same percentage of interest paid as in 1937.

Col. 5 Property income: sum of col. 3 and 4.
Col. 6 Total payments to individuals: sum of col. 1, 2, and 5.

TABLE S 2

Net Income Originating

Col. 1 Total payments to individuals: see Table S 1, col. 6.
Col. 2 Entrepreneurial net savings: sum of estimates for entrepreneurs in (1) professional service, (2) personal service, (3) miscellaneous service.
1) Professional service: sum of estimates for:
   a) Private education: entrepreneurial savings are estimated by applying to total withdrawals (see the notes to Table S 1, col. 2)

the ratio of savings to withdrawals as derived from data for entrepreneurs in trade.

b) Trained nurses, private duty: it is assumed that the entire net income is withdrawn.

c) Other professional service: lawyers, engineers including salaried engineers (since they cannot be segregated), and all entrepreneurs in the curative and other professional service fields not covered above. Their savings are the difference between their total net income (for the net income series see the notes to Table S 6) and their total withdrawals (see the notes to Table S 1, col. 2).

2) *Personal service:* estimated by the procedure outlined for private education.

3) *Miscellaneous service:* sum of estimates for:

a) Advertising: estimated by the procedure outlined for 'other' professional service.

b) Recreation and amusement: estimated by the procedure outlined for private education.

c) Hand trades: the same assumption is made as under (1) b. See the notes to Table S 1, col. 2, concerning the inclusion of data on employees.

Col. 3 Corporate net savings: difference between compiled net profits after taxes (reported for 1922–37 in *Statistics of Income*) and total dividends paid. For the years before 1922 net profits are estimated as the sum of statutory net income after taxes (*Statistics of Income*), dividends received, and interest received on tax-exempt obligations (see the notes to Table S 1, col. 3 and 4). Corporate savings are assumed to be the same in 1938 as in 1937.

Col. 4 Total net savings: sum of col. 2 and 3.

Col. 5 Net income originating: sum of col. 1 and 4.

TABLE S 3

Wages and Salaries by Major Industrial Divisions

Col. 1 Professional: see Table S 4, col. 1–4.

Col. 2 Personal: see Table S 4, col. 5–8.

Col. 3 Domestic: product of the number of employees (see Table S 8, col. 3) and the average pay. For 1929–36 average cash pay is estimated separately for nine groups of domestic servants: chauffeurs; cooks, male; cooks, female; housekeepers; laundresses;

nurses; waiters; waitresses; other servants. Average pay in 1937 and 1938 for domestic service is extrapolated from 1936 by an index prepared by the Bureau of Foreign and Domestic Commerce, National Income Division. For 1924–29 average pay estimates for each of the above groups are combined to yield an average pay figure for all domestic service; the weights used are the average of the number attached to 'domestic and personal service' in 1920 and 1930 as reported in the 1930 *Census of Population*, Vol. V, Ch. 1. The weighted average is extrapolated to 1919 by the annual pay of persons in the corresponding occupations in city and state employ. Data for laundry workers, housekeepers, chauffeurs, stewards, etc. are available for these early years from various state and city reports.

For each occupation wage rates for 1924–29 are based on the wage per week as of January 1 and July 1 of each year as reported by employment agencies throughout the country. The data are combined into an average for the year by weighting the figure for January 1, 1, that for July 1, 2, and that for January 1 of the following year, 1. The basic material for these years is from questionnaires sent out by the National Bureau. For 1929–36 the wage rate data are available only for January 1 of each year; for 1929–34 they are from questionnaires of the National Bureau and the Bureau of Foreign and Domestic Commerce, National Income Division, and for 1935 and 1936, from those of the Bureau of Foreign and Domestic Commerce. From the returns the most common type of wage is determined for each occupation, that is, whether without room and board, with room, with board, or with room and board, and data for the most prevalent type of payment are used throughout the period. The average wage for each occupation is computed for each geographic region and a weighted average derived for the United States; the weights used are the number in each geographic region attached to the specific occupational group as reported in the 1930 *Census of Population*, Vol. V, Ch. 1.

To the cash wage figures for each occupation we add an allowance for payments in kind, estimated for the week of January 1, 1929 (the date for which the largest number of questionnaires was returned) from the data reported, by determining the absolute difference between the rates with room and board, with room, with board, and without room and board. The estimate for the value of board as of January 1, 1929 is extrapolated by the BLS index of the cost of food, one of the components of its cost of living index; that for the value of room, by the weighted average of the BLS indexes of rent, fuel and light, and housefurnishings, the weights being those of the Bureau of Labor Statistics.

For the years before 1929 pairs of January 1 estimates of payments in kind are averaged and added to the respective annual average estimates of cash wages. For the years after 1929 the January 1 estimates of payments in kind are added directly to the January 1 estimates of cash wages and pairs of the resulting January 1 total wage figures are then averaged.

The weekly wage rates for all years since 1924 are multiplied by 52 to yield the estimated average annual wage. Since no sample wage data are available for 'other servants', the average annual wage for housekeepers is used.

Col. 4 Miscellaneous: sum of estimates for (1) advertising, (2) recreation and amusement, (3) automobile repair shops and garages.

1) Advertising: estimated by multiplying the number of employees (see the notes to Table S 8, col. 4) by the average pay. Average pay for 1933 and 1935 is computed from partial data on full- and part-time payroll and employment as reported in the *Census of American Business* and the *Census of Business*. On the basis of data for one week, also reported in the Census, average full-time pay is computed. Its ratio to the full- and part-time average is derived for the week reported and is used to adjust the full-and part-time average for the year to the full-time average. The average pay is extrapolated for all other years by the average salary in manufacturing, mining, steam railroads, Pullman, and railway express.

2) Recreation and amusement: sum of estimates for (a) motion picture production, (b) theatres, (c) all other recreation and amusement. For the description of the employee series referred to below see the notes to Table S 8, col. 4.

a) Motion picture production: for the odd years 1921–29 and for 1935 and 1937, reported in the *Biennial Census of Manufactures*. Partial data are reported for 1931 and 1933. The data reported for 1933 exclude principal officers' salaries, which are estimated by assuming the same ratio to other salaries as in 1929. For 1931 the figure reported is for 'productive employees' only. The

1931 total is estimated by applying to the total cost of production, given in the Census, the average of the 1929 and 1933 ratios of total payroll to total cost of production. The intercensal year estimates for 1922–28 are interpolated along a straight line. For years after 1929 interpolation and extrapolation are by an index derived from the percentage change in wages and salaries in identical establishments as reported by the California Division of Labor Statistics. Total salaries and wages for 1919 and 1920 are extrapolated from 1921 by salaries and wages in theatres (see (b) below).

b) Theatres: obtained by multiplying the number of employees (see the notes to Table S 8, col. 4) by the average pay. Average pay for 1933 and 1935 is from data for motion picture and vaudeville theatres and legitimate theatres reported in the *Census of American Business* and in the *Census of Business.* The adjustment of the average full- and part-time salary to full-time is similar to that described for advertising, (1) above. Average pay is extrapolated for all other years by the average wage paid in Ohio theatres. Ohio data for the early years are reported in BLS Bulletin 613; for the later years, obtained directly from the Ohio Division of Labor Statistics.

c) Other recreation and amusement: obtained by multiplying the number of employees (see the notes to Table S 8, col. 4) by the average pay. Average pay for 1933 is computed from data for recreation other than radio broadcasting in the *Census of American Business* and from estimates of employment and payrolls in the radio broadcasting field prepared by Herman S. Hettinger for the *Economics of American Broadcasting* (unpublished). Average pay for 1935 is derived from *Census of Business* data. The method used is similar to that described for advertising. Extrapolation and interpolation for other years are by the average pay in theatres and motion picture production.

3) Automobile repair shops and garages: the persons covered are those in small units not reporting to the *Census of Retail Distribution.* Since there are no data available that would make it possible to estimate wages and salaries separately from entrepreneurial income, the two are estimated as a single item. And inasmuch as wages and salaries form the major part of the item it is regarded as a labor rather than an entrepreneurial payment.

Total income is estimated by multiplying the number of persons engaged (see the notes to Table S 8, col. 4) by the average income. Average income in 1933 is estimated by subtracting operating expenses from gross receipts, adding the full-time payroll, and dividing the result by the sum of the number of proprietors and full-time employees (all items from the *Census of American Business*). The fields covered are auto brake shops, auto paint shops, auto radiator repair shops, auto top and body repair shops, auto laundries, garages, and parking lots.

Average income in 1935 is extrapolated from 1933 by the full-time average pay. The 1935 data are from the *Census of Business;* for the method by which full-time figures were estimated see (1) above. Extrapolation and interpolation for other years are by the average wage in manufacturing.

Col. 5 Total: sum of col. 1–4.

TABLE S 4

Wages and Salaries by Minor Industrial Divisions

Col. 1 Private education: sum of estimates for (1) elementary schools, (2) secondary schools, (3) commercial schools, (4) correspondence schools, (5) higher education, (6) special schools. Figures for school year periods are adjusted to a calendar year basis by weighting the current year figure, 2, and that for the following year, 1. The series on number of employees referred to below are described in the notes to Table S 9, col. 1.

1) Elementary schools: sum of estimates for school year periods for (a) Catholic, (b) non-Catholic.

a) Catholic schools: for 1929 and later years are from the Bureau of Foreign and Domestic Commerce, National Income Division. Total pay, 1919–28, estimated for teachers and principals separately from other employees, are the product of the number and the average pay. The per capita pay figures of principals and teachers and of other employees, as derived from 1929 data, are extrapolated for 1919–28 by the average pay of teachers, supervisors, and principals in public day schools.

b) Non-Catholic schools: the pay of teachers and principals and of other employees is the product of the number and the average pay. The average salary used for teachers and principals in 1930 is that in public elementary schools, derived by applying, to the salary figures for all public day schools, the ratio of pay in elementary schools to that in all public schools as computed from sample data from the Office of Education. Since the total and the sample for other years do not agree as closely as in 1930, the sample data for the other years are not used. Average pay in 1930 is extrapolated for other years by the average pay of teachers, supervisors, and principals in public day schools. The average salary of other employees is estimated by applying to the average salary of similar employees in public elementary and high schools the 1930 ratio of the average salary of teachers in non-Catholic elementary schools to the average salary of teachers in public elementary and high schools.

2) *Secondary schools:* estimated by the procedure outlined in (1).

3) *Commercial schools:* total salaries are estimated by multiplying the number of employees by the average pay. The average pay of teachers and administrative employees for 1929 and later years is derived from the Bureau of Foreign and Domestic Commerce questionnaire survey of commercial schools, as is the average pay of other employees. The former is extrapolated for the earlier years by the average pay of teachers and administrative employees in public elementary and secondary schools. To extrapolate the average pay of other employees, the average pay of similar employees in public elementary and secondary schools is used.

4) *Correspondence schools:* from the preliminary series on the number of employees and total salaries for 1929 and later years, obtained from questionnaires sent to correspondence schools by the Bureau of Foreign and Domestic Commerce, National Income Division, per capita pay is derived. The 1929 figure is extrapolated to 1919 by the average pay of employees in commercial schools. Total salaries are the product of the number of employees and the average salary.

5) *Higher education:* for the methods for school years see those outlined in the notes on wages and salaries in *public* higher education (Table G 2, col. 9). Basic materials, for even years, are from the *Biennial Survey of Education.* Interpolations are along a straight line. The ratios used to separate expenditures into salaries and other expenses are those for land-grant colleges. The index by which the average salary of the teaching staff is extrapolated from 1930 to other years is that for public universities. For 1934 the

salaries of 'other' employees and of those in libraries are obtained by multiplying the number by the average pay. The average pay of 'other' employees is assumed to be the same as in public elementary and secondary schools. For library employees the average pay is the 1932 figure extrapolated by the average pay of the faculty. Total salaries in higher education are extrapolated from 1936 through 1938 by the totals prepared by the Bureau of Foreign and Domestic Commerce, National Income Division.

6) Special schools: estimates for school years are made similarly to those for public special schools, the average pay figures being identical (see the notes to Table G 2, col. 9).

Col. 2 Religious service: total salaries of Catholic clergymen, including payments in kind, for 1929 and later years, from the Bureau of Foreign and Domestic Commerce, National Income Division. For other clergymen for the same period and for all clergymen before 1929, they are estimated by multiplying the number (see Table S 9, col. 2) by the estimated average salary. The average salary of non-Catholic clergymen in 1929 is derived from data on salaries and number of clergymen in the Protestant Episcopal Church, obtained from the Church Pension Fund; in the Methodist Episcopal Church, South, from their Publishing House; in the Congregational and Christian Churches, from the Bureau of Foreign and Domestic Commerce, National Income Division; and in the Methodist Episcopal Church, from the Editor of the *General Minutes.* The data for the Protestant Episcopal, the Methodist Episcopal, South, and the Methodist Episcopal Churches are available for the entire period; those for the Congregational Church, for 1929–38, and those for the Christian Churches, for 1929–31. An index of the average salary, computed on the basis of this material, is used to extrapolate the 1929 average salary of non-Catholic clergymen for later years and the average salary of all clergymen for the years before 1929.

Col. 3 Curative service: sum of estimates for (1) physicians' and surgeons' assistants, (2) dentists' assistants, (3) employees in private hospitals. For the employee series referred to below see the notes to Table S 9, col. 3.

1) Physicians' and surgeons' assistants: total salaries are estimated by multiplying the number of employees by the average pay. Average pay for 1929 and later years is derived from the questionnaire survey by the Bureau of Foreign and Domestic Commerce, National Income Division. The 1929 average is extrapolated for 1919–28 by the average salary in manufacturing, mining, steam railroads, Pullman, and railway express.

2) *Dentists' assistants:* estimates prepared by the method outlined in (1) above.

3) *Hospitals:* from the figures for 1935 on the annual expense and the percentage that the annual payroll is of total expense for various groups of hospitals, obtained from the files of the Bureau of Public Health Service by the Bureau of Foreign and Domestic Commerce, National Income Division, total cash salaries were derived. From data from the same source for one month on the number and average pay of full- and of part-time employees, the average maintenance cost per full- and per part-time paid employee, and the number and average maintenance cost per employee receiving only maintenance we estimated the total payroll including an allowance for maintenance for the given month. The ratio of the annual payroll to the payroll for the one month is derived and applied to the payroll, including the allowance for maintenance for the month, to yield the total payroll, including maintenance, for hospitals in 1935. This 1935 figure is extrapolated forward to 1938 and back to 1934 by total salaries as estimated by the Bureau of Foreign and Domestic Commerce, National Income Division.

For 1919–33, the 1934 figure is extrapolated by a preliminary series obtained by adding, to estimated wages and salaries, the estimated cost of maintenance. The wage and salary item is estimated by multiplying the number of beds by wages and salaries per bed. The number of beds in 1927 and later years is a total of the number in non-government hospitals and those in non-registered hospitals as reported in the annual Hospital Number of the *Journal of the American Medical Association*. From the Journal for the earlier years total beds in 1918, 1920, and 1923 are available, as is the number in non-government hospitals in 1923 and 1924. The bed capacity of non-registered hospitals is assumed to be negligible in these years. On the basis of the 1923 ratio of non-government to total hospital beds non-government beds in 1918 and 1920 are estimated. For 1919, 1921, 1922, 1925, and 1926 interpolation is along a straight line. Salaries and maintenance cost per bed,

1929–34, are from the questionnaire survey of the Bureau of Foreign and Domestic Commerce, National Income Division. The
1929 figure for salaries per bed is extrapolated to 1919 by the index
of the salaries per bed in New York hospitals. The New York data
are derived from figures on the number of beds and total wages
and salaries in the *Annual Report of the New York State Board of
Social Welfare.* Total maintenance cost, estimated for 1929 and
later years by multiplying the number of beds by the maintenance
cost per bed, is extrapolated to 1919 by the 1929 ratio to wages and
salaries.

Col. 4 Other professional service: sum of estimates for (1) lawyers'
employees and (2) employees in miscellaneous professional service.
Total salaries are estimated by multiplying the number of employees (see the notes to Table S 9, col. 4) by the average salary.

1) Lawyers' employees: professional salaries are estimated separately from non-professional. For 1929–38 average salaries are
those derived by the Bureau of Foreign and Domestic Commerce,
National Income Division, from questionnaire returns. Both series
are extrapolated to 1919 by the average salary in manufacturing,
mining, steam railroads, Pullman, and railway express.

2) Miscellaneous professional employees: the average salary for
1929 and later years is the average of the per capita salaries of
physicians' and surgeons' assistants, dentists' assistants, and lawyers' non-professional employees. The 1929 average is extrapolated
for the earlier years by the average salary in manufacturing, mining, steam railroads, Pullman, and railway express.

Col. 5 Hotels: sum of estimates of (1) cash wages and salaries,
(2) gratuities, (3) payments in kind. For the employee series referred
to below see the notes to Table S 9, col. 5.

1) Cash wages and salaries: salaries and wages for all year-round
hotels and for a sample of seasonal hotels, for 1933 from the *Census
of American Business* and for 1935 from the *Census of Business.*
The 1929 *Census of Hotels* covers year-round and seasonal hotels
of 25 rooms or more. The payroll of year-round hotels of 25 rooms
or more, interpolated between 1929 and 1933 by the BLS payrolls
index, is raised to the total for year-round hotels for those years by
the 1933 ratio of the payroll of all year-round to that of hotels
with 25 rooms or more. The 1929 ratio of the payroll for seasonal
hotels of 25 rooms or more to the payroll for year-round hotels of

25 rooms or more is applied to the payroll for the latter to obtain the estimated payroll for seasonal hotels of 25 rooms or more, 1929–33. On the basis of the sample data in the 1933 Census the ratio of the payroll of seasonal hotels of less than 25 rooms to that of seasonal hotels of 25 rooms or more is derived and applied to the estimate of the payroll for seasonal hotels of 25 rooms or more, 1929–33, to obtain the payroll of seasonal hotels of less than 25 rooms, 1929–33. The total for all hotels, 1929–33, is the sum of the parts. The payroll figure for all hotels is interpolated between 1933 and 1935 by the BLS payrolls index, which is used also to extrapolate the 1935 figure through 1938.

For the years before 1929 total payrolls are the product of the number of employees and the average pay. Average pay, as computed for 1929, is extrapolated to 1919 by the average pay of Ohio hotels (from BLS Bulletin 613). For 1922, when no Ohio data are available, the estimate is interpolated along a straight line between 1921 and 1923.

2) *Gratuities:* estimated for 1928 and later years at 10 per cent of the total receipts of hotels (based on the data reported in the 1933 *Census of American Business* and in the 1935 *Census of Business*). Receipts as reported are raised by the ratio of total payroll to the payroll of those reporting receipts. For 1929 receipts for both year-round and seasonal hotels of 25 rooms or more are reported in the *Census of Hotels.* Total receipts for all year-round hotels are estimated on the assumption that the percentage change from 1929 to 1933 in the ratio of receipts to payrolls in all year-round hotels is the same as for year-round hotels of 25 rooms or more. The same procedure is followed for all seasonal hotels with the further assumption that the 1933 data for those seasonal hotels reporting payrolls and receipts are representative of all seasonal hotels. Estimates for 1928, 1930–32, 1934, and 1936–38 are interpolated between and extrapolated from the resulting totals for 1929, 1933, and 1935 by the index of total sales given in *Hotel Operations in 1938* (Horwath and Horwath). For the years before 1928 gratuities are extrapolated by wages and salaries.

3) *Payments in kind:* sum of estimates for (a) board and (b) lodging.

a) *Board:* the 1935 *Census of Business* reports the number of meals served to employees in year-round hotels of 25 rooms or more and the number of employees receiving 1, 2, or 3 meals a day.

The total of meals served to employees is derived and divided by the estimated number of full-time employees to yield the number of meals per day per full-time employee. This figure divided by 3 (the number of meals in a full board allowance) is the proportion of employees receiving full board. This ratio applied to the estimate of full-time employees in 1929 and later years yields the total receiving full board. Multiplying the result by the estimated annual value of board per person (see the notes to Table S 3, col. 3) gives the total value of board received in 1929 and later years.

The 1929 figure is divided by total employees to yield the per capita board figure, which is extrapolated to 1919 by the BLS index of the cost of food. Total value of board received, 1919–28, is the product of the number of employees and the computed per capita board allowance.

b) Lodging: the 1935 *Census of Business* reports also the number of employees in year-round hotels of 25 rooms or more who receive lodging. The ratio of the number receiving lodging to the total in the group is applied to the estimated number of employees in all hotels to obtain the total receiving lodging. Multiplying the value of lodging per person (see the notes to Table S 3, col. 3) by the estimated number receiving lodging yields the estimated total value of lodging received by hotel employees in 1929 and later years.

The 1929 value per employee is derived and extrapolated to 1919 by a weighted average of BLS indexes of rent, fuel and light, and house furnishings. The weights are those used by the Bureau of Labor Statistics in obtaining their composite cost of living index. Total value of lodging, 1919–28, is the product of the number of employees and the derived per capita value.

Col. 6 Restaurants: sum of estimates of (1) cash wages and salaries, (2) gratuities, (3) payments in kind. For the employee series referred to below see the notes to Table S 9, col. 6.

1) Cash wages and salaries: for 1929, 1933, and 1935, from the *Census of Retail Distribution.* The 1929 figure is adjusted to include salaries paid to employees in central administrative offices by a method similar to that used for the trade estimates (see the notes to Table T 4, col. 2). Estimates for intercensal years and for 1936–38 are based on the sales figures prepared by the Bureau of Foreign and Domestic Commerce, Marketing Research Division;

and the ratio of payrolls to sales, computed for Census years and interpolated and extrapolated by the corresponding ratio for retail trade.

For the years before 1929 compensation is estimated by multiplying the number of employees by the average annual pay. Average pay is computed for 1929 and extrapolated by the average pay in Ohio restaurants (from BLS Bulletin 613). Since no Ohio data are available for 1922 the estimate for that year is by straight line interpolation between 1921 and 1923.

2) Gratuities: for 1929 and later years, estimated to be 10 per cent of receipts from the sale of meals in restaurants and eating places reported for 1929 in the *Census of Retail Distribution* and estimated for later years by applying, to the estimated total sales for the respective years, the 1929 ratio to total sales (*Domestic Commerce,* Feb. 20, 1940). For the years before 1929 gratuities are assumed to move similarly to cash wages and salaries.

3) Payments in kind: the 1929 per capita food allowance is estimated to be 2 meals a day costing 30 cents each. This per capita figure is extrapolated for the other years by the BLS index of the cost of food. The total food allowance is the product of the number of employees and the estimated per capita allowance.

Col. 7 Power laundries, and cleaning and dyeing establishments: sum of estimates of (1) wages and (2) salaries. For the employee series referred to below see the notes to Table S 9, col. 7.

1) Wages: for the odd years 1919–35, from the *Census of Power Laundries, Cleaning and Dyeing Establishments, and Rug Cleaning Establishments.* The 1933 Census figure is raised to allow for incomplete coverage on the basis of the estimated percentage of wage earners not reported in that year (see the *Census of Power Laundries,* 1933). Interpolation for 1932 and 1934 and extrapolation for 1936–38 are by the BLS payrolls index. For interpolation between 1919 and 1925, 1927 and 1931, weighted averages of the indexes of payrolls for Pennsylvania, Ohio, New York, and Massachusetts are used; for 1926, data for Pennsylvania, Ohio, and New York. The Pennsylvania data are actual wage figures given annually in the Pennsylvania *Report on Productive Industries, Public Utilities and Miscellaneous Statistics.* The Ohio data are actual wage figures from BLS Bulletin 613 except for 1922, which is estimated by multiplying the reported number of wage earners by the average wage (the latter a straight line interpolation between 1921 and 1923). The New York data are indexes published by the New York State Department of Labor in Special Bulletin 171. Wages in Massachusetts laundries are from a special tabulation supplied by R. F. Phelps, Director of Statistics. The weights used in combining the state data are the Census figures on wages in 1925.

2) *Salaries:* for 1919, 1925, 1927, 1929, 1933, and 1935, from the Census. The 1933 salaries, as reported in the Census, exclude those of principal salaried officers, which are estimated on the basis of the 1935 ratio of salaries of principal officers to other salaries. Other salaries in 1933 are first adjusted by the procedure followed in raising wages in that year. Estimates for intercensal years and 1936–38 are the product of the number of salaried workers and the estimated average salary. The average salary is computed for Census years and interpolated for other years by the average salary in Pennsylvania and Ohio. The state data are from the sources mentioned above.

Col. 8 Other personal service: all groups covered under the personal service category in the 1933 *Census of American Business* and the 1935 *Census of Business.* The entries are sums of estimates of (1) cash wages and salaries, (2) gratuities. For the employee series referred to below see the notes to Table S 9, col. 8.

1) *Cash wages and salaries:* the *Census of Business* reports total figures for 1935. The *Census of American Business* reports partial figures for 1933. The 1933 data for barber shops, beauty shops, cleaning and dyeing establishments, shoe repair and shoe shine shops are assumed comparable with those for 1935. The percentage change in their totals from 1933 to 1935 is applied to the 1935 figure for photographic studios to yield a 1933 figure, since the 1933 figure as reported for that field is definitely an understatement. The same procedure is followed in estimating payrolls of rug cleaning shops in 1933 since no information is given for that industry in that year. For all other personal service groups the total payroll as reported for 1933 is used.

For all other years total pay is estimated by multiplying the number of employees by the average pay. Average pay, computed for 1933 and 1935 from Census data, is extrapolated for the other years by the average wage of Ohio barbers and hairdressers. The

Ohio data for the years before 1932 are from BLS Bulletin 613; for later years they are obtained directly from the Ohio Division of Labor Statistics.

2) Gratuities: for 1933 and 1935 estimated to be 5 per cent of the total receipts of barber shops, beauty shops, and shoe shine parlors. Receipts are from the 1933 *Census of American Business* and the 1935 *Census of Business.* The 1935 Census, however, combines data for shoe shine and shoe repair shops. We assume that the distribution of total receipts in these two fields is the same in 1935 as in 1933. Gratuities for other years are estimated by applying to total payrolls the ratio of gratuities to payrolls. This ratio, computed from Census data in 1933 and 1935, is interpolated along a straight line for 1934. For the years before 1933 the 1933 ratio is used; for 1936–38, the 1935 ratio.

TABLE S 5

Wages and Salaries by Minor Industrial Subdivisions

Col. 1–3 Physicians' and surgeons' assistants, dentists' assistants, employees in private hospitals: see the notes to Table S 4, col. 3.
Col. 4 Lawyers' employees: see the notes to Table S 4, col. 4.
Col. 5 Miscellaneous professional service: see the notes to Table S 4, col. 4.
Col. 6–8 Advertising, recreation and amusement, and automobile repair shops and garages: see the notes to Table S 3, col. 4.

TABLE S 6

Entrepreneurial Net Income by Major Industrial Divisions

Col. 1 Curative: sum of estimates for (1) physicians and surgeons, (2) dentists, (3) trained nurses, private duty, (4) osteopaths, (5) veterinarians, (6) other curative service. The net income for each subgroup is estimated by multiplying the number of entrepreneurs (see the notes to Table S 11, col. 1) by the average net income.
1) Physicians and surgeons: average net income, 1929–36, is that prepared for the National Bureau of Economic Research study of professional incomes. The 1937 figure is extrapolated from 1936 by the index of dentists' income prepared by the Bureau of Foreign and Domestic Commerce, National Income Division. The

1938 average is assumed to be the same as the 1937. For 1919 it is that given in 'Financial Considerations of the Average Doctor' (*Canadian Medical Association Journal*, Feb. 1922). Interpolation between 1919 and 1929 is by the average of the indexes of per capita net income of entrepreneurs in the chemical manufacturing group and of per capita salary in universities.

2) *Dentists:* average net income, 1929–34, is that prepared for the National Bureau of Economic Research study of professional incomes. It is extrapolated to 1937 by the average income of non-salaried dentists as derived from the survey conducted by the Bureau of Foreign and Domestic Commerce, National Income Division, summarized in the *Survey of Current Business*, April 1939. The 1938 average is assumed to be the same as the 1937. The 1929 figure is extrapolated to 1919 by the per capita net income of physicians and surgeons. Net income from private practice of part-salaried dentists also is based on the National Income Division study.

3) *Trained nurses, private duty:* it is assumed that the entire net income is withdrawn. The withdrawal series is described in the notes to Table S 1, col. 2.

4) *Osteopaths:* average net income for 1929, 1933, 1935–38 is that for non-salaried osteopathic physicians as derived from the survey conducted by the Bureau of Foreign and Domestic Commerce, National Income Division, summarized in the *Survey of Current Business*, April 1939. Interpolation and extrapolation for other years are by the average of per capita net income of physicians and surgeons and of dentists.

5) *Veterinarians:* average net income for 1930, from the *Report of the Committee on Education* (American Veterinary Medical Association, 68th meeting). It is extrapolated for all other years by the average of per capita net income of physicians and surgeons and of dentists.

6) *Other curative service:* chiropractors and other healers. Their 1929 average income is the average for masseurs, religious healers, and chiropractors as given by the Committee on the Costs of Medical Care. Extrapolation for other years is by the average of per capita net income of physicians and surgeons and of dentists.

Col. 2 Other professional service: sum of estimates for (1) private education, (2) lawyers, (3) engineers, (4) entrepreneurs in miscellaneous professional fields. Except when indicated, the net income for each subgroup is estimated by multiplying the number of entrepreneurs (see the notes to Table S 11, col. 2) by the average net income.

1) Private education: net income is estimated by the procedure outlined below for personal service (col. 4).

2) Lawyers: average net income, 1929–36, is that prepared for the National Bureau of Economic Research study of professional incomes. The 1937 estimate is based on the assumption that the percentage change from 1936 to 1937 is the same as from 1935 to 1936. Average net income for 1938 is assumed to be the same as for 1937. It is extrapolated for 1919–28 by the average of per capita income of physicians and surgeons and of dentists.

3) Engineers: includes engineers who are employees in the professional service field, but since employers cannot be separated from employees and since independent practitioners predominate, the incomes of both are covered here. The average net income of independent engineers, 1929–32, is from the National Bureau of Economic Research study of professional incomes. The 1919 average is that given in the *Report of the Committee on Classification and Compensation of Engineers* (Engineering Council, Dec. 15, 1919). The median incomes of owners and of owners and employees are given in '1930 Earnings of Mechanical Engineers', *Mechanical Engineering,* September, November, and December 1931. The ratio of the latter to the former is applied to the net income of independent engineers, yielding the average net income of all engineers for 1919 and 1929–32. Estimates for all other years are interpolated and extrapolated by the average of per capita net income of physicians and surgeons and of dentists.

4) Miscellaneous professions: average net income for 1929 and later years is the average of per capita income of physicians and surgeons, dentists, osteopaths, veterinarians, other curative professionals (excluding trained nurses), lawyers, and engineers. The 1929 figure is extrapolated to 1919 by the average of per capita net income of physicians and surgeons and of dentists.

Col. 3 Total professional: sum of col. 1 and 2.

Col. 4 Personal: sum of withdrawals (see the notes to Table S 1, col. 2) and savings (see the notes to Table S 2, col. 2).

Col. 5 Miscellaneous: sum of estimates for (1) advertising, (2) recre-

ation and amusement, (3) hand trades. For the series on entrepreneurs referred to below see the notes to Table S 11, col. 5.

1) Advertising: net income is estimated by multiplying the number
of entrepreneurs by the average net income. Average net income
for 1930–32, obtained by letter from the American Association of
Advertising Agencies, is extrapolated for other years by the average
of per capita income of physicians and surgeons and of dentists.

2) Recreation and amusement: estimated by the procedure described above for personal service.

3) Hand trades: it is assumed that the entire net income is withdrawn. The withdrawal series is described in the notes to Table
S 1, col. 2.

Col. 6 Total: sum of col. 3–5.

TABLE S 7

Entrepreneurial Net Income by Minor Industrial Divisions

*Col. 1–4 Physicians and surgeons, dentists, trained nurses, and
other curative service:* see the notes to Table S 6, col. 1.

Col. 5–7 Lawyers, engineers, and other professionals: see the notes
to Table S 6, col. 2.

*Col. 8–10 Advertising, recreation and amusement, and hand
trades:* see the notes to Table S 6, col. 5.

TABLE S 8

Employees by Major Industrial Divisions

Col. 1 Professional: see the notes to Table S 9, col. 1–4.

Col. 2 Personal: see the notes to Table S 9, col. 5–8.

Col. 3 Domestic: for 1929 and later years, sum of estimates for
chauffeurs; cooks, male; cooks, female; housekeepers and stewards;
laundresses; nurses (not trained); waiters; waitresses; and other
servants. The number gainfully occupied in 1930 for each occupation is from the industrial classification of 'domestic and personal service' in the 1930 *Census of Population,* Vol. V, Ch. 7. To
the number gainfully occupied is applied the ratio of the number
employed to it. The ratio used is that prepared by Robert R.
Nathan, formerly of the Bureau of Foreign and Domestic Commerce, National Income Division. The resulting number employed

is extrapolated to 1929 and later years by the index of employment in domestic service, also prepared by Mr. Nathan.

The number gainfully occupied in 1930 is extrapolated to 1920 by representative occupations reported for 1920 and 1930 in the 1930 Census, Vol. V, Ch. 1. For example, the number of chauffeurs attached to domestic service in 1930 is from the Census, as is the total of chauffeurs, draymen and teamsters in 1920 and 1930. The percentage change in the latter from 1920 to 1930 is applied to the 1930 figure for chauffeurs gainfully occupied in domestic service to yield the estimated number gainfully occupied in 1920. The same procedure is followed for each occupation. The sum of the estimates for the various occupations yields the total gainfully occupied in domestic service in 1920, which the number actually employed in 1920 is assumed to equal.

The estimates of the total employed in 1919 and 1921–28 are extrapolated from 1920 and interpolated between 1920 and 1929 by a preliminary series, derived as follows: Extrapolating the 1929 payroll by consumer goods in 1929 prices (*Commodity Flow and Capital Formation*, Vol. One) yields an estimate of domestic pay in 1929 prices. This series is converted to pay in current prices by applying the index of the average pay in domestic service. Total pay, in current prices (see the notes to Table S 3, col. 3), divided by the estimated average pay yields the preliminary estimate of domestic employees.

Col. 4 Miscellaneous: sum of estimates for (1) advertising, (2) recreation and amusement, (3) automobile repair shops and garages.

1) Advertising: the total of employees attached to advertising in 1930 is reported in the 1930 *Census of Population*, Vol. V, Ch. 7. The number actually employed is computed by applying the ratio of employment to attachment in banking, brokerage, insurance and real estate, derived from Mr. Nathan's figures on employment and unemployment (*International Labour Review*, Jan. 1936). The number actually employed in 1930 is extrapolated to 1919 by the series on magazine and newspaper advertising lineage *(Survey of Current Business)*. It is extrapolated for the years after 1930 by the *Printers' Ink* index of advertising *(Survey of Current Business)*. *2) Recreation and amusement:* sum of estimates for (a) motion picture production, (b) theatres, (c) other recreation and amusement.

a) Motion picture production: sources and methods are those indicated for the wage and salary estimates described in the notes to Table S 3, col. 4. The 1931 figure is estimated by dividing the estimated payroll by the average compensation of 'productive employees' covered in the Census for that year.

b) Theatres: number of full-time employees in 1933 and 1935, derived from *Census of American Business* and *Census of Business* data. For 1933 data are recorded separately for full- and part-time employees. Part-time employment is equated to full-time by dividing the total part-time payroll by the average full-time pay. For 1935 the figures, as reported, are combined totals for full- and part-time. From Census data for one week, showing full-time and part-time separately, the ratio of the average full-time pay to the average full- and part-time pay is derived and applied to the average full- and part-time pay for the year to yield the estimated average full-time pay. The number of employees in theatres covered by the Census is derived by dividing the total payroll reported by the estimated full-time pay.

For all other years employees are estimated by multiplying the number of theatres by the number of employees per theatre. The number of moving picture and vaudeville theatres open in 1922, 1925, and 1928 is from the Bureau of Foreign and Domestic Commerce, Motion Picture Division; for 1929, from WPA files; and for later years, from the Film Boards of Trade. The number of motion picture and vaudeville theatres in 1919–21 is extrapolated from 1922 by the number of theatres in Ohio. The number in 1923, 1924, 1926, and 1927 is by straight line interpolation. The number of legitimate theatres reported in the Census is assumed to be the total. The 1933 figure is extrapolated to 1928 by the number of moving picture and vaudeville theatres. For 1919–27 the 1928 figure is used. The 1934 figure is by straight line interpolation between the Census dates; those for 1936–38 are assumed to remain at the 1935 level. The number of employees per theatre is computed for 1933 and 1935 on the basis of the number of theatres covered in the Census and is extrapolated for other years by the corresponding figure for Ohio theatres. The Ohio data for the years through 1932 are from BLS Bulletin 613; those for later years, from the Ohio Division of Labor Statistics.

c) Other recreation and amusement: difference between the total for all recreation and amusement and the estimated total for motion picture production and theatres combined. The total number attached to the industry in 1930 is the sum of those classified under recreation and amusement and under radio broadcasting in the 1930 *Census of Population,* Vol. V, Ch. 7. The number attached to the industry in 1920 is estimated by applying to the 1930 figure the percentage change from 1920 to 1930 in representative occupations reported in the Census. The number of entrepreneurs is deducted and the balance is adjusted for unemployment to yield the number of employees actually engaged in the field. The 1930 unemployment ratio is that derived by Mr. Nathan for recreation and amusement, data for which appear in the *International Labour Review,* January 1936. The number engaged in 1930 is extrapolated to 1929 and later years by the number of employees in moving picture production and in theatres. The number engaged in 1920 is derived from the number attached and the 1929 ratio of employment to attachment as computed from Mr. Nathan's figures on employment and unemployment in the field. Interpolation for 1921–28 and extrapolation to 1919 are by the number of employees in moving picture production and in theatres.

3) Automobile repair shops and garages: entrepreneurs in the field are included. The number gainfully occupied in auto repair shops in 1930 is that recorded in the 1930 *Census of Population,* Vol. V, Ch. 7. The number engaged is computed by applying, to the number gainfully occupied, the ratio of employment to attachment in the field, derived from Mr. Nathan's estimates of unemployment (*International Labour Review,* Jan. 1936). The number engaged in 1919 is from the *Biennial Census of Manufactures.* In addition to the number gainfully occupied in auto repair shops, the number gainfully occupied in garages, greasing stations, and auto laundries is reported for 1930. It is estimated for 1920 by applying to the 1930 figure the percentage change from 1920 to 1930 in representative occupations reported for both years in the 1930 *Census of Population,* Vol. V, Ch. 1. The number attached in 1920 is assumed to be actually engaged.

Both series, that for auto repair shops and that for garages, etc., are extrapolated and interpolated for all other years by the annual figures on total automobile registrations reported in *Automobile*

Facts and Figures. The sum of the two items gives the total engaged in the field. The larger firms, however, are covered in retail trade, data for which are reported for 1929, 1933, and 1935 in the *Census of Retail Distribution.* The ratio of those covered in retail trade to the total is computed for Census years and interpolated along a straight line for the intervening years. For 1919–28 the 1929 ratio is used; for 1936–38, the 1935 ratio. The application of the ratio to the total engaged yields the estimated number covered in trade. The balance is assumed to be the number in the service industry.

Col. 5 Total: sum of col. 1–4.

TABLE S 9

Employees by Minor Industrial Divisions

Col. 1 Private education: sum of estimates for (1) elementary schools, (2) secondary schools, (3) commercial schools, (4) correspondence schools, (5) higher education, (6) special schools. Figures for school years are adjusted to a calendar year basis by weighting the current year figure, 2, and that for the following year, 1.

1) Elementary schools: sum of estimates for school years for (a) Catholic, (b) non-Catholic.

a) Catholic schools: the number of principals and teachers for the even years since 1920 is from the National Catholic Welfare Conference of Directors of Catholic Colleges and Schools. The 1920 figure is extrapolated to 1918 by the number in all private elementary schools *(Biennial Survey of Education).* Estimates for all other years are by straight line interpolation. The number of other employees in 1929–35 is estimated on the basis of their ratio to the number of principals and teachers, derived from a special survey of Catholic dioceses by the Bureau of Foreign and Domestic Commerce, National Income Division. For 1919–28 the 1929 ratio is used; for 1936–38, the 1935 ratio.

b) Non-Catholic: the number of principals and teachers in 1932 and 1936 is from the United States Office of Education. The figures reported for other years are incomplete and therefore not used. Interpolation between and extrapolation of the 1932 and 1936 figures are by the corresponding estimates of principals and teachers in Catholic schools. The number of other employees is obtained

by applying to the number of principals and teachers the ratio for
Catholic schools of other employees to principals and teachers.

2) *Secondary schools*

a) Catholic: the National Catholic Welfare Conference of Directors of Catholic Colleges and Schools provided figures for 1915 and
for the even years since 1920. Estimates for the other years are by
straight line interpolation. The number of other employees is
estimated by the method indicated above for other employees in
Catholic elementary schools.

b) Non-Catholic: the figures for principals and teachers in 1926,
1928, 1932, and 1936 are from the United States Office of Education. The estimates of teachers and principals for other years and
those of other employees in all years are derived by the method
indicated above for employees in non-Catholic elementary schools.

3) *Commercial schools:* partial data on the number of instructors
are available for various years from Statistics of Private Commercial and Business Schools in the *Biennial Survey of Education.*
For 1918, 1920, and 1933 we have the total number of schools canvassed, the number replying to the questionnaire, and the number
not replying. For 1918 and 1920 the number of schools canvassed
is assumed to be the total in existence. For 1933 we have also the
number of those replying that have been discontinued since the
previous canvass (in 1929) and the number that have been organized. The ratio of the number discontinued to total replies, applied
to the total canvassed, yields the estimated total discontinued. The
number in existence is assumed to equal the difference between the
total canvassed and the estimated number discontinued. The ratio
of the number organized since 1929 to total replies, applied to the
number canvassed, yields the estimated total organized. The number of schools in existence in 1929 is the difference between the
total canvassed in 1933 and the estimated number organized since
1929. Estimates of total schools in existence in other years are by
straight line interpolation.

For 1918, 1920, 1925, 1929, and 1933 from the source cited above
we have the number of schools reporting instructors. For 1925,
1929, and 1933 we have also the number of schools with 100 or
more students and the number of their instructors. It is assumed
that the schools not reporting are smaller; therefore instructors
in schools not reporting are estimated by applying to the number

of schools the estimated number of instructors per school with fewer than 100 students. The latter figure, computed for 1925, 1929, and 1933 from the source cited above, is extrapolated to 1918 and 1920 by the number of instructors per school for all reporting schools. The total of instructors is the sum of the number reported and the estimate for schools not reporting. For 1922 we have the number of instructors reported but no comparable figure for the number of schools. The number of instructors reported is raised to the total by the ratio of the estimated total of instructors to the number reported in 1920 and 1925, interpolated along a straight line.

We now have estimates of the number of instructors for 1918, 1920, 1922, 1925, 1929, and 1933. Interpolation for 1919, 1921, 1923, 1924, 1926–28 is along a straight line. Interpolation between 1929 and 1933 and extrapolation through 1937 are by the number of administrative and teaching employees derived from a questionnaire survey by the Bureau of Foreign and Domestic Commerce, National Income Division. From the same survey the ratio of the number of other employees to the number of instructors is derived for 1929 and later years. This ratio applied to the estimated number of instructors yields an estimate of other employees. For 1919–28 the 1929 ratio is used. The total of employees is assumed to be the same in 1938 as in 1937.

4) Correspondence schools: the estimates for 1929 and later years are those prepared by the Bureau of Foreign and Domestic Commerce, National Income Division. The 1929 figure is extrapolated to 1919 by the number of employees in commercial schools.

5) Higher education: the number on the faculty for school years in even years through 1934 is from the *Biennial Survey of Education.* Estimates for other years before 1934 are interpolated along a straight line. The number engaged in library and research work is estimated for 1919–32 by dividing their estimated salaries by an average salary assumed to equal the average for the faculty. For 1934 the number is extrapolated from 1932 by the number of faculty employees; for 1933, along a straight line. The number of other employees is estimated for the years through 1932 by dividing their salary bill by the average salary paid similar employees in public elementary and secondary schools. The 1934 figure is obtained by the procedure used in estimating library workers; the

1933, by interpolating along a straight line. The total of employees for the years after 1934 is extrapolated by the number derived by the Bureau of Foreign and Domestic Commerce, National Income Division.

6) Special schools: the estimates of employees in private special schools are made similarly to those for public special schools, the index used to extrapolate the data for 1932 and later years being identical.

Col. 2 Religious service: the total of clergymen in 1920 and 1930 is from the 1930 *Census of Population,* Vol. V, Ch. 1.

Annual figures on Catholic clergymen are from the *Official Catholic Directory* and its editor. The number of non-Catholic clergymen is estimated for 1920 and 1930 by subtracting Catholic clergymen from the total. Extrapolation and interpolation for other years are by the number in the various denominations. For 1919–30 the number of clergymen in the Protestant Episcopal, Methodist Episcopal, South, Methodist Episcopal, Presbyterian, and American Baptist Churches is used as index. The figures for the Protestant Episcopal Church are from the Church Pension Fund. Those for the Methodist Episcopal Church, South, are from the editor of their *Yearbook.* Those for the Methodist Episcopal Church are from the editor of the *General Minutes* of the Methodist Episcopal Church. Those for the Presbyterian Church are from the office of the General Council of the Presbyterian Church in the United States. Those for the Baptist Church are from the *American Baptist Yearbook.* From 1930 to 1931 the index is composed of the number of clergymen in the churches mentioned excluding the Baptist Church; and, in addition, those in the Congregational and Christian Churches (obtained by the Bureau of Foreign and Domestic Commerce, National Income Division). For 1931–34 the index is derived from data for the same denominations as for 1930–31, except the Christian Churches. For 1934 and later years, data for only the Protestant Episcopal, the Methodist Episcopal, South, the Congregational, and the Methodist Episcopal Churches are available.

Col. 3 Curative service: sum of estimates for (1) physicians' and surgeons' assistants, (2) dentists' assistants, (3) employees in private hospitals.

1) Physicians' and surgeons' assistants: the number in 1928 is the estimate prepared by the Committee on the Costs of Medical Care. In all other years it is estimated by multiplying the number of physicians and surgeons (see the notes to Table S 11, col. 1) by the number of assistants per physician and surgeon. The ratio of assistants to private physicians and surgeons is computed for 1928. The ratio of physicians' and surgeons' attendants reported in the 1930 *Census of Population,* Vol. V, Ch. 1, to the estimated number of private practitioners is determined for 1920 and 1930. The intercensal year figures are interpolated along a straight line and the resulting series is used to extrapolate the 1928 ratio to 1920 and through 1929. The 1919 ratio is assumed to be the same as the 1920. The 1929 figure is extrapolated to 1936 by the number of assistants per physician and surgeon derived from the survey by the Bureau of Foreign and Domestic Commerce, National Income Division; to 1937 by the percentage change in the corresponding ratio for dentists. It is assumed to be the same in 1938 as in 1937.

2) *Dentists' assistants:* the number in 1920 and 1930, from the 1930 Census, Vol. V, Ch. 1. For 1919, 1921–29, and 1931–38 it is estimated by multiplying the number of dentists (see the notes to Table S 11, col. 1) by the number of assistants per dentist. The number of assistants per dentist is computed for 1920 and 1930. The 1930 figure is extrapolated through 1937 by the series derived from the survey by the Bureau of Foreign and Domestic Commerce, National Income Division. The number of assistants per dentist in 1938 is assumed to be the same as in 1937, and in 1929, as in 1930. Straight-line interpolation between 1920 and 1929 yields estimates for 1921–28. The 1919 figure is assumed to be the same as the 1920.

3) *Employees in hospitals:* from the files of the Bureau of Public Health Service the Bureau of Foreign and Domestic Commerce, National Income Division, obtained figures on employment for various groups of hospitals. Data for one month in 1935 are available for full-time employees, part-time employees, and the number receiving maintenance only. The number of part-time employees is equated to full-time on the assumption that full-time pay applies to both groups. Average full-time pay is obtained by dividing total full-time pay by the number of full-time employees. It is divided into total part-time pay to yield the estimated full-time equivalent of the number of part-time employees. Adding full-time, part-time, and maintenance employees yields the average number employed

during the month. The ratio of the annual payroll to the payroll for the month covered is divided by 12; the result applied to the average number of employees for the month yields the average number of employees for the year.

The resulting 1935 figure is extrapolated to 1929 by a preliminary estimate of the number of employees, which for 1929–34 is the product of the estimated number of beds (see the notes to Table S 4, col. 3) and the number of employees per bed (derived from the hospital survey by the Bureau of Foreign and Domestic Commerce, National Income Division, for 1929–34). The preliminary series is extrapolated to 1935 by an employment index derived by the Bureau of Foreign and Domestic Commerce, National Income Division, from data from the Ohio Hospital Association, the American Hospital Association, and the United Hospital Fund of New York. The final estimates for 1936–38 are derived by the method used by the Bureau of Foreign and Domestic Commerce, National Income Division.

Estimates for the years before 1929 are obtained by dividing total wages and salaries (see the notes to Table S 4, col. 3) by the annual pay. The latter is computed for 1929 and extrapolated to 1919 by the average pay in Ohio hospitals (BLS Bulletin 613). Annual pay in 1922, when no Ohio data are available, is an average of the 1921 and 1923 figures.

Col. 4 Other professional service: sum of estimates for (1) lawyers' employees and (2) employees in miscellaneous professional service. *1) Lawyers' employees:* sum of estimates for (a) professional and (b) non-professional.

a) Professional: the number of lawyers in professional service in 1930, recorded in the 1930 *Census of Population,* Vol. V, Ch. 7, is extrapolated for later years by the index of the number of lawyers prepared by the Bureau of Foreign and Domestic Commerce, National Income Division, from data reported in the *Martindale-Hubbell Law Directory* and in various city directories. The 1930 figure is extrapolated to 1919 by an estimate of total lawyers, for which the number of lawyers in 1920 and 1930 as reported in the 1930 Census, Vol. V, Ch. 1, is used. Extrapolation of the 1920 figure to 1919 and interpolation between 1920 and 1930 are by the totals as estimated from data in *Martindale's American Law Directory.*

For 1932 and later years lawyers in professional service are separated into those in independent practice and employees by the ratio of professional employees to entrepreneurs as derived from survey data collected by the Bureau of Foreign and Domestic Commerce, National Income Division. For the years before 1932 the average of the ratios for 1932–34 is applied. The resulting estimate of the number of lawyers who are employees is equated to the full-time number on the basis of the survey data. The ratio of full-time to full- and part-time employment is available, however, only for 1929–34. For 1935–38 the 1934 figure is used; for the years before 1929, an arbitrary ratio, slightly lower than that for 1929.

b) Non-professional: applying, to the number of independent lawyers (as described above), the ratio of non-professional employees to entrepreneurs yields the number of non-professional employees. The ratio for 1929 and later years is derived from the survey data. For the years before 1929 an arbitrary ratio, slightly lower than that for 1929, is used.

2) Employees in miscellaneous professional fields: difference between the total attached to professional service industries in 1930 (1930 *Census of Population,* Vol. V, Ch. 7) and the number covered in other service fields and in other industries. The comparable 1920 figure is extrapolated from 1930 by the number in occupations representative of the group as selected from the 1930 Census, Vol. V, Ch. 1. Of the total gainfully occupied in 1930 it is assumed that the following are self-employed or employers: architects, artists, authors, chemists, inventors, and teachers not in schools. The 1930 ratio of self-employed to all attached to miscellaneous professional service is computed and applied to the 1920 total of gainfully occupied to give the number of self-employed or employers. Extrapolation of and interpolation between the 1920 and 1930 figures for entrepreneurs are by an index of the number of physicians and surgeons, dentists, lawyers, engineers, and clergymen.

The number of employees attached to miscellaneous service in 1920 and 1930 is estimated by subtracting the estimated number of entrepreneurs from the total attached. The number of employees engaged in 1930 is estimated by applying to the number attached the ratio of employment to attachment as estimated for the professional group by Mr. Nathan. The number of employees engaged in 1929 and 1931 and later years is the product of the number of entrepreneurs and of employees per entrepreneur, computed for 1930 and extrapolated for other years by the ratio of employees to entrepreneurs for physicians and surgeons, dentists, and lawyers combined. Employees engaged in 1920 are estimated on the assumption that unemployment was the same as in 1929. The total gainfully occupied in 1929 was estimated by the procedure outlined for domestic service employees. The number of employees per entrepreneur is computed for 1920, interpolated between 1920 and 1929, and extrapolated to 1919 by the index used in extrapolating the 1930 figure. The total employed is estimated by multiplying the number of entrepreneurs by the ratio of employees to entrepreneurs.

Col. 5 Hotels: sum of employees in year-round and seasonal hotels. For year-round hotels the number in 1933 is from the *Census of American Business;* in 1935, from the *Census of Business.* For 1933 and 1929 the number of employees in year-round hotels of 25 rooms or more is also reported. The 1929 figure is from the *Census of Hotels.* For hotels of 25 rooms or more, interpolation between 1929 and 1933, and for all year-round hotels, between 1933 and 1935, and extrapolation for 1936–38 are by the BLS employment index. The ratio of total employees to the number in hotels of 25 rooms or more is computed for 1933 and applied to the estimates for year-round hotels of 25 rooms or more, 1929–32, to yield total employment in all year-round hotels.

Employees in seasonal hotels in 1929 and later years are estimated by dividing the total payroll by the average pay for year-round hotels. The sum of employees in year-round and seasonal hotels is adjusted for part-time employment on the basis of data in the 1933 *Census of American Business.* For that year the full-time average pay in year-round hotels is derived; when divided into the total payroll it yields the estimated full-time employment. The ratio of full-time to full- and part-time employment is computed and extrapolated to 1929 and to 1935 by the corresponding ratio for restaurants. The 1936–38 ratio is assumed to be the same as the 1935. Its application to the estimated number of employees yields an estimate of full-time employment in 1929 and later years.

Total employees for the years before 1929 are estimated by multiplying the number of hotels by the estimated number of full-time employees per hotel. The number of hotels in 1920–29 is reported in *Communication Agencies and Social Life* (Recent Social Trends Monograph, McGraw-Hill, 1933). The 1919 figure is assumed to be the same as the 1920. The number of employees per hotel is computed from Census data for 1929 and extrapolated to 1919 by the number of employees per hotel in Ohio (BLS Bulletin 613).

Col. 6 Restaurants: for 1929, 1933, and 1935, from the *Census of Retail Distribution.* For 1929 and 1933 full- and part-time employees are shown separately. The full-time equivalent of part-time employees is estimated by dividing the total part-time payroll by the average full-time pay. For 1935, when the combined figures for full- and part-time employment and payrolls alone are shown, average full-time pay is obtained by applying to average full- and part-time pay for the year the ratio of average full-time pay to average full- and part-time pay as derived from data for one week. Total full-time employment in 1935 is estimated by dividing the reported total payroll by this estimated full-time pay. The figure reported for 1929 is adjusted to include employees at central administrative offices by the method described in the notes to Table T 5. Estimates for intercensal years and for 1936–38 are obtained by dividing total employee compensation (see the notes to Table S 4, col. 6) by the estimated average pay. Average pay, computed for Census years, is extrapolated for other years by the average pay in hotels.

Employees in 1920 are estimated by applying, to the number of cooks and waiters gainfully occupied, the 1929 ratio of employees to the number of cooks and waiters gainfully occupied. The number of cooks and waiters in 1920 and 1930 is recorded in the 1930 *Census of Population,* Vol. V, Ch. 1. The 1929 figure is interpolated along a straight line. Interpolation of the number of employees between 1920 and 1929 is by total employees in Ohio restaurants as recorded in BLS Bulletin 613. The same index is used to estimate the 1919 figure.

Col. 7 Power laundries, and cleaning and dyeing establishments: sum of estimates of (1) wage earners and (2) salaried employees.

1) Wage earners: for 1919, 1925, 1927, 1929, 1931, 1933, and 1935, from the *Census of Power Laundries, Cleaning and Dyeing Establishments, and Rug Cleaning Establishments.* The 1933 Census figure is raised to allow for incomplete coverage by the estimated percentage of wage earners not reported in 1933 (see the 1933

Census). The BLS employment index is used to interpolate and extrapolate figures for 1932, 1934, and 1936–38. Interpolation between 1919 and 1925 is by weighted averages of the indexes of employment in Pennsylvania, Ohio, New York, and Massachusetts; between 1925 and 1927, by Pennsylvania, Ohio, New York, and Illinois data; between 1927 and 1931, by data for all five states. The Pennsylvania data are actual employment figures reported in the Pennsylvania *Report on Productive Industries, Public Utilities and Miscellaneous Statistics.* The Ohio data are actual employment figures reported in BLS Bulletin 613. The New York data are indexes recorded for 1919–21 in the *Labor Market Bulletin,* for 1921–30, in the New York Department of Labor Special Bulletin 171, and for 1931, in the *Industrial Bulletin.* The Massachusetts data are actual employment figures from a special tabulation by the Director of Statistics. The Illinois data are indexes recorded in the *Annual Report of the Department of Labor* of that state. The weights used in combining the state data are the Census figures on wage earners in 1925.

2) *Salaried employees:* total salaried employees also are reported for all Census years except 1931 and 1933. In 1933 the Census excludes principal salaried officers of corporations. The figure for other salaried employees is adjusted, in the manner in which wage earners are adjusted, to correct for incompleteness of coverage. Principal salaried officers are then obtained by applying to the estimate of other salaried employees the 1935 ratio of principal to other. For 1931 no data on salaried employees are available. Estimates for the intervening years are the product of the number of wage earners and the ratio of salaried employees to wage earners. The ratio is computed for Census years and interpolated and extrapolated for other years by the ratio for Pennsylvania and Ohio, derived from the sources cited above.

Col. 8 Other personal service: the basic figures are those reported in the 1933 *Census of American Business* and the 1935 *Census of Business.* The 1933 figures are raised by the procedure followed in raising wages and salaries (see the notes to Table S 4, col. 8). The 1933 total full- and part-time employment is adjusted to the full-time equivalent by adding to the number of full-time employees the estimate of the full-time equivalent of part-time employment, obtained by dividing the total part-time payroll by the average full-time pay. The adjustment to full-time employment in 1935 involves applying to the total full- and part-time employment reported for the year the ratio of the full-time equivalent of employment to full- and part-time employment as derived from data for one week. The ratio for the week is obtained by adding to the number of full-time employees reported the full-time equivalent of part-time employees (obtained by dividing the part-time payroll by the average full-time pay) and dividing the result by the sum of full- and part-time employees. The final estimates of full-time employee equivalents in 1933 and 1935 are extrapolated from 1933 to 1929 and from 1935 to 1938 by employment in retail trade, and interpolated for 1934 along a straight line. The number of employees in 1920 is obtained by applying to the number employed in 1929 the percentage change from 1920 to 1929 in the number gainfully occupied in representative occupations. For 1920 and 1930 this number is obtained by adding the data for barbers, hairdressers and manicurists, undertakers, photographers, shoemakers, cobblers and bootblacks recorded in the 1930 *Census of Population*, Vol. V, Ch. 1. The 1929 number gainfully occupied is interpolated along a straight line between 1920 and 1930. The number of employees in 1919 and 1921–28 is extrapolated from and interpolated between 1920 and 1929 by the number of employees in domestic service.

TABLE S 10

Employees by Minor Industrial Subdivisions

Col. 1–3 Physicians' and surgeons' assistants, dentists' assistants, and employees in private hospitals: see the notes to Table S 9, col. 3.

Col. 4 and 5 Lawyers' employees and miscellaneous professional service employees: see the notes to Table S 9, col. 4.

Col. 6–8 Advertising, recreation and amusement, and automobile repair shops and garages: see the notes to Table S 8, col. 4.

TABLE S 11

Entrepreneurs by Major Industrial Divisions

Col. 1 Curative service: sum of estimates for (1) physicians and surgeons, (2) dentists, (3) trained nurses, private duty, (4) osteopaths, (5) veterinarians, (6) other curative service.

1) *Physicians and surgeons:* number in 1918, 1921, 1923, 1925, 1927, and 1929, from the *Distribution of Physicians in the United States,* American Medical Association, Bureau of Medical Economics; in 1931, 1934, 1936, and 1938, from the American Medical Association. Estimates for the intervening years are interpolated along a straight line. Retired practitioners are estimated for 1918–29 on the assumption that their relation to the total is the same as in 1930, for which year we have the number of retired physicians and surgeons from the *Incomes of Physicians,* by Maurice Leven (Committee on the Costs of Medical Care, 1932). The number of active practitioners in these years is further reduced to allow for those not in private practice. For 1929 and later years the number in private practice is estimated by applying to total physicians and surgeons the ratio of the number in private practice to the total. The 1929 ratio is from the *Incomes of Physicians;* the 1938 from *Number of Physicians in the United States by County* (American Medical Association). The 1928 ratio of private to active physicians and surgeons is from 'Income from Medical Practice', *Journal of the American Medical Association,* May 16, 1931. Its application to the estimated number of active physicians and surgeons yields the number in private practice, 1919–28.

2) *Dentists:* number in private practice in 1930, by letter from the American Dental Association (also given in the 1930 *Census of Population,* Vol. V, Ch. 7); for 1936 we used the estimate of the National Bureau of Economic Research study of professional incomes. It is assumed that the ratio of dentists in private practice to the total is the same in 1936 as in 1930. Estimates of the number in private practice in 1929, 1931–35, and 1937–38 are extrapolated from and interpolated between 1930 and 1936 by the number in independent practice, also obtained by letter from the American Dental Association.

To the number in private practice is added the full-time equivalent of those dentists who work part-time on a salary basis. The materials essential to this computation are from the questionnaire survey by the Bureau of Foreign and Domestic Commerce, National Income Division. Figures for 1919–28 are extrapolated from 1929 by the number of dentists estimated from data for 1920 and 1930 reported in the 1930 Census, Vol. V, Ch. 1, and for the other years interpolated and extrapolated by the number of licenses issued

annually in nine states (Oklahoma, North Carolina, California,
Nebraska, New Hampshire, Iowa, Florida, Connecticut, and Pennsylvania).

3) Trained nurses, private duty: the number in 1920 and 1930 reported in the 1930 *Census of Population,* Vol. V, Ch. 7, includes
student nurses. The 1920 figure is adjusted to exclude them on the
basis of total graduates reported in *Nurses, Patients, and Pocketbooks.* For 1920 we assume three times as many students as there
were graduates. The number of students in 1930 is from *Facts
about Nursing, 1938.* Interpolation between the resulting figures
for 1920 and 1930 and extrapolation for other years are by the
series 'nurses in the profession' in *Nurses, Patients, and Pocketbooks.* The ratio of nurses on private duty to total trained nurses,
given by the Committee on the Costs of Medical Care, is used for all
years in the period. The number of nurses on private duty is the
product of the estimated number of trained nurses and this ratio.
It is assumed that nurses numbered the same in 1919 as in 1920.

4) Osteopaths: number in 1927, 1929, 1934–38, from the American
Osteopathic Association. Estimates for the intervening years are
interpolated along a straight line. The 1927 figure is extrapolated
to 1923 by Association membership figures. The 1923 figure is
extrapolated through 1920 by a second series on the number of
osteopaths. Basic data for this series are from the 1930 *Census of
Population,* Vol. V, Ch. 1, which reports the number in practice in
1920 and 1930. Intercensal year estimates are by straight line interpolation. It is assumed that osteopaths numbered the same in 1919
as 1920.

5) Veterinarians: number in 1920 and 1930, from the 1930 *Census
of Population,* Vol. V, Ch. 1. Intercensal year estimates are interpolated along a straight line and the 1919 figure is assumed to be
the same as the 1920. The number of practicing veterinarians in
1930 is from the *Report of the Committee on Education* (American
Veterinary Medical Association, 68th meeting). Its ratio to the
total is applied to the totals for 1919–30 to yield the number of
practicing veterinarians in those years. The 1930 number is kept
constant for all later years.

6) Other curative professionals: covers chiropractors and other
healers. For 1920 and 1930 the totals are from the 1930 *Census of
Population,* Vol. V, Ch. 1. Estimates for 1919 and 1921–29 are

extrapolated and interpolated by the number of Christian Science practitioners; for 1931–38, extrapolated by the number of Christian Science practitioners and chiropractors. The number of Christian Science practitioners in 1916, 1923, 1926, 1928, 1930, 1932, 1934, and 1936–38 is from the Christian Science Committee on Publication for the State of New York; for intervening years, interpolated along a straight line. The number of chiropractors for 1929, 1934, and 1938 is from the Chiropractic Health Bureau; for intervening years, interpolated along a straight line.

Col. 2 Other professional service: sum of estimates for (1) private education, (2) lawyers, (3) engineers, (4) entrepreneurs in miscellaneous professional fields.

1) Private education: sum of estimates for (a) commercial schools and (b) correspondence schools.

a) Commercial schools: entrepreneurs are estimated by applying to the number of teachers (see the notes to Table S 9, col. 1) the ratio of proprietors to teachers. For 1929 and later years this ratio is derived from survey data collected by the Bureau of Foreign and Domestic Commerce, National Income Division. For the years before 1929 the 1929 ratio is used.

b) Correspondence schools: entrepreneurs in 1929 and later years were estimated by the Bureau of Foreign and Domestic Commerce, National Income Division. The 1929 figure is extrapolated through 1919 by the number of entrepreneurs in commercial schools.

2) Lawyers: the sources and methods are indicated in the notes to Table S 9, col. 4.

3) Engineers: engineers that are employees of others in the professional service field are included. The 1930 total is from the 1930 *Census of Population,* Vol. V, Ch. 7. The 1920 total is interpolated between 1910 and 1930 by the totals in the occupational grouping (1930 Census, Vol. V, Ch. 1). Estimates for 1919 and 1921–28 are by straight line interpolation between the 1910, 1920, and 1930 figures. The 1933 estimate is from the American Association of Engineers. Those for 1931 and 1932 are by straight line interpolation. For the later years the 1933 figure is used.

4) Miscellaneous professionals: the derivation of the number of entrepreneurs in 1920 and 1930 is given in the notes to Table S 9, col. 4. Estimates for other years are interpolated between 1920 and

1930 and extrapolated for 1919 and 1931–38 by an index of physicians and surgeons, dentists, lawyers, engineers, and clergymen in practice.

Col. 3 Total professional: sum of col. 1 and 2.

Col. 4 Personal: sum of estimates for (1) hotels, (2) restaurants, (3) power laundries, and cleaning and dyeing establishments, (4) other personal service.

1) Hotels: number of entrepreneurs in 1929, 1933, and 1935, derived from the 1929 *Census of Hotels,* the 1933 *Census of American Business,* and the 1935 *Census of Business.* The data reported in the Censuses are indicated by asterisks in the accompanying tabulation.

		1929	*1933*	*1935*
A	No. of proprietors, year-round hotels with 25 rooms or more		*	*
B	No. of proprietors, year-round hotels, total		*	*
C	No. of proprietors, seasonal hotels with 25 rooms or more		*	
D	No. of proprietors, seasonal hotels, all reporting			*
E	No. of proprietors, seasonal hotels with 25 rooms or more, all reporting			*

Total proprietors of year-round hotels (B) in 1929 are estimated by applying to the 1929 A the 1933 ratio of B to A. Total proprietors of seasonal hotels in 1929 are estimated by applying to the 1929 C the 1933 ratio of D to E. Proprietors of seasonal hotels with 25 rooms or more (C) in 1933 are estimated by applying to the 1933 A the 1929 ratio of C to A; the result is then raised to the total by applying the ratio of D to E for that year. Total proprietors of seasonal hotels in 1935 are estimated by applying, to the 1935 B, the 1929 ratio of the estimated total of proprietors in seasonal hotels to the total of proprietors in year-round hotels (B). Total entrepreneurs in 1929, 1933, and 1935 are the sum of the number in year-round and seasonal hotels.

Interpolation between the resulting totals for 1929, 1933, and 1935 is by full-time employment. The 1929 estimate is extrapolated for the years before 1929 by the number of hotel keepers and managers. This item, reported for 1920 and 1930 in the 1930 *Census of Population,* Vol. V, Ch. 1, is interpolated for intercensal years by the number of hotels. The source for the latter is indicated in the notes to Table S 9, col. 5. The 1919 figure is assumed to be the same as the 1920.

2) *Restaurants:* number of entrepreneurs in 1929, 1933, and 1935, from the *Census of Retail Distribution*. Estimates for 1919–28 and 1930 are extrapolated from 1929 by a series on restaurant, café, and lunch room keepers. Their number in 1920 and 1930 is given by states in the 1930 *Census of Population*, Vol. V, Ch. 1. A series for Ohio is obtained by using the 1920 and 1930 Census figures and interpolating for intercensal years by the number of restaurants. The latter, used also in extrapolating the 1920 figure to 1919, is from BLS Bulletin 613. The resulting figures constitute the index by which the totals of restaurant, café, and lunch room keepers in 1919 and intercensal years are estimated. The 1931 and 1932 estimates of entrepreneurs are based on the 1929 and 1933 figures, and the increase in restaurants in 1933 over 1929 is distributed equally over the period. The 1934 figure is interpolated between 1933 and 1935 along a straight line. The figures for 1936–38 are assumed to be the same as that for 1935.

3) *Power laundries, and cleaning and dyeing establishments:* number of entrepreneurs in 1919, 1925, 1927, 1929, 1933, and 1935, from the *Census of Power Laundries, Cleaning and Dyeing Establishments, and Rug Cleaning Establishments.* The adjustment of the 1933 Census figure is similar to that for employees (see the notes to Table S 9, col. 7). The estimate for 1931 is interpolated by the number of establishments reported in the Census for 1929, 1931, and 1933 (the last adjusted to allow for incomplete coverage). Estimates for the other non-Census years are interpolated along a straight line except those for 1932 and 1936–38 when the number of establishments in Pennsylvania, Ohio, and Massachusetts is used as index. The sources of the state data are cited in the notes to Table S 9, col. 7.

4) *Other personal service:* number of entrepreneurs in 1933 and 1935, based on 1933 *Census of American Business* and 1935 *Census of Business*. The adjustments of the Census data are similar to those for employees (see the notes to Table S 9, col. 8). The 1929 estimate is based on the assumption that the percentage change in employees is an index of the percentage change in entrepreneurs. The ratio of the percentage change from 1933 to 1935 in entrepreneurs to that in employees is applied to the 1929–33 percentage

change in employees. The derived percentage change in entrepreneurs from 1929 to 1933 is applied to the 1933 estimate of entrepreneurs to yield the 1929 figure. Interpolation for 1930–32 and
1934 is along a straight line. The 1920 estimate is derived by the
method used to obtain the number of employees in that year. The
estimates for 1919 and 1921–28 are extrapolated from 1920 and
interpolated between 1920 and 1929 by the value of consumer
goods in 1929 prices (*Commodity Flow and Capital Formation,*
Vol. One). The number for 1936–38 is assumed to be the same as
that for 1935.

Col. 5 Miscellaneous: sum of estimates for (1) advertising, (2) recreation and amusement, (3) hand trades.

1) Advertising: number of entrepreneurs in 1930, from the 1930
Census of Population, Vol. V, Ch. 7. It is estimated for 1920 by
applying to the 1930 figure the percentage change from 1920 to
1930 in the occupational group 'agents, not classified' in the 1930
Census, Vol. V, Ch. 1. The number in 1919 is assumed to be the
same as the 1920. Estimates for 1921–29 are interpolated along a
straight line; for 1931–36 they are extrapolated from 1930 by the
number of proprietors reported by the American Association of
Advertising Agencies. The number is assumed to remain constant
from 1936 through 1938.

2) Recreation and amusement: number of entrepreneurs in 1920
and 1930, from the 1930 *Census of Population,* Vol. V, Ch. 1 (including keepers of billiard rooms, dance halls, skating rinks, etc.;
directors, managers and officials of motion picture production;
keepers of pleasure resorts, race tracks, etc.; and theatrical owners,
managers and officials). The number in 1919 is assumed to be the
same as in 1920. Estimates for 1921–29 are interpolated along a
straight line; for 1931 and later years they are extrapolated from
1930 by the number of entrepreneurs in retail trade.

3) Hand trades: employees in the field are included. From the number attached to independent hand trades in 1930, reported in the
1930 *Census of Population,* Vol. V, Ch. 7, shoemakers and milliners
were deducted, since they are covered by us in personal service and
trade. The number attached to hand trades in 1920 is estimated by
applying to the 1930 figure the percentage change from 1920 to
1930 in the number in representative occupations selected from
the 1930 Census, Vol. V, Ch. 1. The number attached in 1919 is

assumed to be the same as in 1920. Estimates for 1921–29 are interpolated along a straight line. The number engaged in 1930 is estimated by applying, to the number attached, the ratio of employment to attachment as derived from Mr. Nathan's data on employment and unemployment in hand trades (*International Labour Review*, Jan. 1936). The resulting figure is extrapolated for 1929 and later years by Mr. Nathan's series on employment in the field. The number engaged in 1920 is estimated on the assumption that unemployment in 1920 was the same as in 1929. Estimates for 1919 and 1921–28 are made similarly to those for the number attached to the industry.

Col. 6 Total: sum of col. 3–5.

TABLE S 12

Entrepreneurs by Minor Industrial Divisions

Col. 1–4 Physicians and surgeons, dentists, trained nurses in private duty, and other curative service: see the notes to Table S 11, col. 1.
Col. 5–7 Lawyers, engineers, and other professionals: see the notes to Table S 11, col. 2.
Col. 8–10 Advertising, recreation and amusement, and hand trades: see the notes to Table S 11, col. 5.

Government

TABLES G1–G7

G 1   Net Income Originating by Type (millions of dollars)

	WAGES & SALARIES	PENSIONS & RELIEF *	EMPL. COMP.	INTEREST	PAY. TO INDI- VIDUALS	NET SAVINGS	NET INCOME
	(1)	(2)	(3)	(4)	(5)	(6)	(7)
1919	3,646	380	4,026	1,044	5,071	—1,303	3,768˙
1920	3,385	491	3,877	1,246	5,123	1,894	7,017
1921	3,431	551	3,982	1,264	5,247	958	6,205
1922	3,410	545	3,956	1,326	5,282	854	6,136
1923	3,549	549	4,099	1,331	5,431	1,611	7,042
1924	3,732	549	4,281	1,279	5,560	1,717	7,277
1925	3,940	527	4,467	1,284	5,751	1,614	7,365
1926	4,147	532	4,680	1,281	5,962	2,151	8,113
1927	4,376	559	4,936	1,254	6,190	2,293	8,483
1928	4,575	576	5,152	1,240	6,392	1,897	8,289
1929	4,777	607	5,385	1,263	6,648	2,225	8,873
1930	4,904	644	5,549	1,266	6,816	2,104	8,920
1931	4,986	802	5,788	1,278	7,066	344	7,410
1932	4,808	908	5,716	1,364	7,081	—906	6,175
1933	4,364	1,790	6,154	1,461	7,616	—113	7,503
1934	4,504	2,690	7,194	1,568	8,763	—575	8,188
1935	4,901	2,849	7,751	1,489	9,240	—1,736	7,504
1936	5,334	3,539	8,874	1,537	10,412	—2,196	8,216
1937	5,598	2,947	8,546	1,681	10,227	497	10,724
1938	5,862	3,438	9,301	1,689	10,990	—175	10,815

* Relief payments included are, in millions of dollars:

1931	59	1933	1,128	1935	2,173	1937	2,190
1932	132	1934	2,087	1936	2,822	1938	2,621

G 2   Wages and Salaries (millions of dollars)

	FEDERAL					STATE	COUNTY	CITY	PUBLIC EDUC.	TOTAL
	Leg.	Judi-cial	Civil *	Military	Total					
	(1)	(2)	(3)	(4)	(5)	(6)	(7)	(8)	(9)	(10)
1919	10.1	3.3	728	1,324	2,066	155	149	582	692	3,646
1920	11.1	3.6	815	699	1,529	179	176	684	815	3,385
1921	10.7	3.6	792	511	1,318	193	209	726	982	3,431
1922	10.1	3.5	783	341	1,158	195	223	739	1,114	3,410
1923	10.2	3.6	834	296	1,144	205	231	791	1,175	3,549
1924	10.5	3.7	869	291	1,174	223	247	845	1,240	3,732
1925	11.1	3.8	918	303	1,236	246	247	887	1,322	3,940
1926	11.7	3.8	961	306	1,284	237	259	951	1,415	4,147
1927	11.9	4.9	986	300	1,303	263	281	1,027	1,501	4,376
1928	12.3	5.8	1,026	298	1,343	282	303	1,073	1,573	4,575
1929	13.0	5.5	1,073	304	1,396	296	325	1,128	1,630	4,777
1930	13.6	5.8	1,097	306	1,423	315	341	1,154	1,669	4,904
1931	13.7	5.9	1,119	303	1,442	336	358	1,177	1,670	4,986
1932	13.1	5.6	1,051	288	1,358	339	349	1,137	1,622	4,808
1933	12.1	5.3	941	261	1,220	330	318	1,013	1,481	4,364
1934	12.5	5.3	1,133	264	1,415	346	322	1,014	1,407	4,504
1935	13.9	5.7	1,363	295	1,678	381	336	1,040	1,465	4,901
1936	14.4	5.9	1,550	322	1,892	418	356	1,117	1,549	5,334
1937	14.5	6.0	1,545	342	1,908	470	381	1,182	1,656	5,598
1938	14.5	6.4	1,546	364	1,931	502	403	1,307	1,716	5,862

* Including the Post Office Department.

G 3   Pensions and Employee Compensation [1] (millions of dollars)

	PENSIONS					EMPLOYEE COMPENSATION				
	Fed.	State	County	City [2]	Total	Fed.	State	County	City [2]	Total
	(1)	(2)	(3)	(4)	(5)	(6)	(7)	(8)	(9)	(10)
1919	321	32.3	2.0	24.8	380	2,387	187	151	1,300	4,026
1920	406	53.8	2.9	29.0	491	1,935	233	179	1,528	3,877
1921	440	76.7	4.0	30.3	551	1,759	270	213	1,740	3,982
1922	445	68.6	3.5	27.6	545	1,583	264	226	1,881	3,956
1923	427	79.2	4.2	38.8	549	1,572	284	236	2,006	4,099
1924	403	95.8	5.1	44.8	549	1,578	319	252	2,131	4,281
1925	419	54.3	3.6	50.2	527	1,655	300	251	2,259	4,467
1926	451	28.1	2.6	50.3	532	1,736	265	261	2,417	4,680
1927	474	27.2	2.8	55.6	559	1,777	290	283	2,584	4,936
1928	483	27.9	3.2	62.7	576	1,826	310	306	2,709	5,152
1929	511	28.2	3.4	64.9	607	1,908	324	329	2,823	5,385
1930	539	29.0	3.7	72.8	644	1,962	344	345	2,896	5,549
1931	623	29.5	4.4	85.9	743	2,124	366	362	2,934	5,729
1932	645	30.6	4.7	95.6	776	2,135	370	354	2,856	5,584
1933	522	30.5	3.5	106	662	2,870	360	321	2,601	5,026
1934	451	33.1	3.9	114	603	3,953	379	325	2,535	5,107
1935	516	38.1	4.2	117	676	4,367	419	340	2,622	5,578
1936	550	41.1	4.2	122	717	5,265	459	360	2,789	6,052
1937	573	46.3	4.7	133	757	4,671	516	386	2,972	6,356
1938	601	50.3	5.4	160	817	5,154	553	408	3,184	6,680

[1] Excluding relief payments.   [2] Including public education.

G 4 Interest (millions of dollars)

| | FEDERAL | | | | | | |
	Public debt (1)	Postal savings (2)	Total (3)	STATE (4)	COUNTY (5)	CITY (6)	TOTAL (7)
1919	819	2.3	822	—5.8	37.8	190	1,044
1920	1,010	2.2	1,012	—8.4	40.7	201	1,246
1921	993	2.2	995	—6.8	47.6	228	1,264
1922	1,022	2.1	1,024	—0.3	53.6	248	1,326
1923	996	2.1	999	4.2	65.2	263	1,331
1924	910	2.2	912	8.5	77.7	280	1,279
1925	856	2.3	859	14.2	97.4	313	1,284
1926	809	2.3	812	15.5	104	349	1,281
1927	759	2.5	762	15.7	94.6	381	1,254
1928	705	2.6	708	18.7	101	412	1,240
1929	668	2.6	671	20.5	126	445	1,263
1930	620	2.7	622	26.5	121	496	1,266
1931	613	3.4	616	36.6	105	519	1,278
1932	637	7.3	645	47.0	110	562	1,364
1933	713	12.8	726	57.1	111	566	1,461
1934	817	17.3	834	61.7	108	564	1,568
1935	764	19.0	783	58.6	103	543	1,489
1936	794	19.2	813	55.0	96.5	572	1,537
1937	895	21.1	916	51.7	88.6	623	1,681
1938	919	21.9	941	48.1	81.9	618	1,689

G 5 Total Payments to Individuals (millions of dollars)

	FEDERAL (1)	STATE (2)	COUNTY (3)	CITY * (4)	TOTAL (5)
1919	3,209	181	189	1,490	5,071
1920	2,948	224	220	1,730	5,123
1921	2,754	263	260	1,968	5,247
1922	2,608	263	280	2,130	5,282
1923	2,571	288	301	2,269	5,431
1924	2,490	327	330	2,412	5,560
1925	2,514	315	348	2,573	5,751
1926	2,548	281	366	2,766	5,962
1927	2,539	305	378	2,966	6,190
1928	2,534	328	407	3,121	6,392
1929	2,579	345	455	3,269	6,648
1930	2,585	371	466	3,392	6,816
1931	2,741	403	468	3,453	7,066
1932	2,780	417	464	3,418	7,081
1933	3,596	417	433	3,168	7,616
1934	4,788	441	434	3,099	8,763
1935	5,151	478	444	3,166	9,240
1936	6,079	514	456	3,362	10,412
1937	5,588	568	474	3,596	10,227
1938	6,095	601	490	3,803	10,990

* Including public education.

G 6   Net Savings (millions of dollars)

	CHANGE IN SECURITY ASSETS					NET VALUE, CHANGE IN PUBLIC DEBT				
	FEDERAL			STATE		PUBLIC		State		NET
	Foreign	Other	Total	& LOCAL	TOTAL	CONSTR.	Federal	& local	Total	SAVINGS
	(1)	(2)	(3)	(4)	(5)	(6)	(7)	(8)	(9)	(10)
1919	2,052	66	2,118	149	2,268	1,520	4,539	552	5,091	—1,303
1920	312	49	361	104	465	826	—1,320	717	—603	1,894
1921	—24	110	86	268	354	1,149	—528	1,073	545	958
1922	4	—216	—212	347	135	1,277	—504	1,062	558	854
1923	256	—152	104	246	350	1,148	—983	870	—113	1,611
1924	232	—47	185	279	464	1,397	—972	1,116	144	1,717
1925	—12	0	—12	268	256	1,628	—745	1,015	270	1,614
1926	178	19	197	236	433	1,599	—1,072	953	—119	2,151
1927	186	—52	134	274	408	1,814	—1,088	1,017	—71	2,293
1928	—8	—1	—9	302	294	1,887	—729	1,013	284	1,897
1929	251	113	364	283	646	1,809	—912	1,142	230	2,225
1930	424	99	523	155	678	2,171	—405	1,150	745	2,104
1931	185	705	890	—209	681	1,980	1,644	673	2,317	344
1932	0.5	1,116	1,117	—112	1,006	1,246	2,929	229	3,158	—906
1933	119	1,169	1,288	302	1,590	634	2,591	—254	2,337	—113
1934	134	1,106	1,240	344	1,583	811	3,241	—272	2,969	—575
1935	0	283	283	301	584	742	2,868	194	3,062	—1,736
1936	0	396	396	139	535	1,372	4,013	90	4,103	—2,196
1937	1	1,093	1,094	22	1,116	1,092	1,732	—21	1,711	497
1938	1	945	946	72	1,019	1,185	2,142	237	2,379	—175

G 7   Employees (thousands)

	FEDERAL								PUBLIC	
	Leg.	Judi-cial	Civil*	Military	Total	STATE	COUNTY	CITY	EDUC.	TOTAL
	(1)	(2)	(3)	(4)	(5)	(6)	(7)	(8)	(9)	(10)
1919	4.6	1.8	693	1,087	1,786	160	150	567	832	3,497
1920	4.6	1.8	702	345	1,054	168	156	579	861	2,820
1921	4.6	1.8	604	389	1,000	166	166	548	907	2,787
1922	4.6	1.8	567	273	847	164	174	552	946	2,685
1923	4.6	1.8	554	250	810	167	179	586	971	2,715
1924	4.6	1.8	559	267	833	179	189	622	1,001	2,826
1925	4.6	1.8	568	261	835	197	184	631	1,042	2,891
1926	4.6	1.8	563	257	827	185	187	658	1,080	2,937
1927	4.6	1.8	561	260	828	203	195	675	1,104	3,007
1928	4.6	1.8	570	263	839	206	207	702	1,124	3,080
1929	4.6	1.8	588	267	862	212	217	715	1,155	3,162
1930	4.6	2.0	599	266	873	224	224	722	1,169	3,213
1931	4.7	2.0	611	262	880	238	233	727	1,174	3,254
1932	4.7	1.9	598	259	864	243	237	738	1,168	3,251
1933	4.7	1.8	593	255	855	243	233	723	1,142	3,199
1934	4.7	1.8	677	257	941	259	238	726	1,129	3,296
1935	4.9	1.9	774	268	1,050	283	244	729	1,150	3,457
1936	5.1	2.0	859	300	1,167	300	257	768	1,182	3,675
1937	5.2	2.1	862	320	1,190	325	270	792	1,222	3,801
1938	5.2	2.2	846	334	1,187	334	280	835	1,222	3,860

* Including the Post Office Department.

TABLE G 1

Net Income Originating by Type

Col. 1 Wages and salaries: see Table G 2.

Col. 2 Pensions and relief: see Table G 3 for pensions. For 1931–38 relief payments, a total of work and direct relief, are included. The work relief estimates are from the Bureau of Foreign and Domestic Commerce, National Income Division (see the *Survey of Current Business,* June 1940). The direct relief figures begin in 1933, and for 1933–35 are from the *Statistical Summary of Emergency Relief Activities, January 1933 through December 1935;* the 1936–38 figures are from the *Social Security Bulletin,* February 1940.

Col. 3 Employee compensation: sum of col. 1 and 2.

Col. 4 Interest: see Table G 4.

Col. 5 Total payments to individuals: sum of col. 3 and 4.

Col. 6 Net savings: see Table G 6.

Col. 7 Net income originating: sum of col. 5 and 6.

TABLE G 2

Wages and Salaries

FEDERAL

Col. 1 Legislative: for 1929–38, estimates prepared by the Bureau of Foreign and Domestic Commerce, National Income Division; for the description of their sources and methods see *National Income in the United States, 1929–35.* The 1929 estimate is extrapolated to 1919 by the figures on pay, reported as such by the Treasury Department in the *Combined Statement of the Receipts and Expenditures, Balances, etc. of the United States.*

Col. 2 Judicial: see the notes to col. 1.

Col. 3 Civil executive, including Post Office: see the notes to col. 1. The pay of Post Office employees is estimated separately from that of other civil executive departments.

Col. 4 Military: for cash pay see the notes to col. 1. Estimates are made separately for the Army, Navy, Marine Corps, and Coast Guard.

The estimates of allowance for subsistence in 1929 and later years are from the Bureau of Foreign and Domestic Commerce, National

Income Division. For 1919–28 allowance for subsistence is estimated by multiplying the per capita figures by the estimated military personnel (see the notes to Table G 7). Per capita subsistence
figures for 1929 are derived from the Bureau of Foreign and
Domestic Commerce estimates and extrapolated to 1919 by the
BLS index of the wholesale price of food.

Col. 5 Total: sum of col. 1–4.

STATE

Col. 6 Total: for 1919–31 and 1937, the product of operating expenditures and the ratio of salaries and wages to them. Salaries and
wages in sample states are used to interpolate between 1931 and
1937 and to extrapolate for 1938.

The ratio of salaries and wages to operating expenditures in 1926
is from the 'Extent, Costs and Significance of Public Employment
in the United States', by William E. Mosher and Sophie Polah,
National Municipal Review, Supplement, January 1932. This
ratio is extrapolated for other years by the ratios for sample states.

Operating expenditures are the sum of expenditures for general
operation and maintenance, excluding schools, and for public
service operation and maintenance (given for the fiscal years 1919,
1921–31, and 1937 in *Financial Statistics of States*). Since the 1921
figure reported is incomplete, it is raised by the 1922 ratio of total
expenditures to expenditures of those states reporting in 1921. The
1920 figure is interpolated between 1919 and 1921 by the operating
expenditures of sample states, as given in state auditors' reports
for 1919, 1920, 1921. The 1932 figure is based on partial data for
41 states as published by the Bureau of the Census. Since there is a
preponderance of fiscal year periods ending June 30, averages of
pairs of fiscal years are assumed to represent operations for calendar years.

The operating expenditures for the sample states are from *Financial Statistics of States*. Wages and salaries for these states, 1919–29,
are from state auditors' reports. For 1929 and later years they are
from questionnaire returns of the Bureau of Foreign and Domestic
Commerce, National Income Division.

The states and years for which wages and salaries are available
and for which the ratio of wages and salaries to operating expenditures is derived are:

1919-20 New York, Massachusetts, Illinois, Ohio, and Indiana

1920-21 New York, Massachusetts, Illinois, Ohio, Indiana, and Iowa

1921-23 New York, Massachusetts, Illinois, Ohio, Indiana, Iowa, West Virginia, and Washington

1923-24 New York, Massachusetts, Ohio, Indiana, Iowa, West Virginia, and Washington

1924-25 Massachusetts, Ohio, Indiana, Iowa, West Virginia, Washington, and Illinois

1925-26 Massachusetts, Ohio, Indiana, Iowa, West Virginia, Washington, and Illinois

1926-29 New York, Massachusetts, Illinois, Indiana, Iowa, West Virginia, and Washington

1929-31 Vermont, Massachusetts, Connecticut, New York, New Jersey, Ohio, Illinois, Wisconsin, Minnesota, Kansas, Delaware, Tennessee, Montana, Nevada, Pennsylvania, Indiana, Virginia, North Carolina, Washington, and Wyoming

1931 and 1937 The states listed for 1929-31 except Ohio and Indiana; and, in addition, South Dakota and Utah

The states whose wage and salary data are used to estimate the total wage and salary bill since 1931 are, by fiscal years:

1931-32 Those listed for 1929-31 except Massachusetts; and, in addition, Michigan

1932-34 Those listed for 1931-32 and, in addition, New Hampshire, Massachusetts, Rhode Island, Iowa, Georgia, Utah, and South Dakota

1934-35 Those listed for 1932-34 except Rhode Island and Kansas

1935-36 Those listed for 1934-35 except Ohio; and, in addition, Kansas and California

1936-37 Those listed for 1935-36 except Michigan and Georgia; and, in addition, Missouri, Maryland, Oklahoma, and Kentucky

1937-38 Those listed for 1936-37 except Maine, Vermont, New Jersey, Iowa, Missouri, Kentucky, Massachusetts, Oklahoma, Wyoming, and California; and, in addition, Michigan and Florida

In interpolating the total between 1919 and 1921 the operating expenditure figures of New York, Massachusetts, Illinois, Iowa, Ohio, and Indiana are used.

COUNTY

Col. 7 Total: in the Mosher and Polah report referred to above, total wages and salaries in 1926 are given by four geographic regions. They are estimated for the other years from 1919 through 1931 by applying to the estimated operating expenditures in each year the 1926 ratio of wages and salaries to operating expenditures.

The items included in operating expenditures are the same as for states and are reported for 1912 and 1931 in the *Census of Wealth, Debt and Taxation,* 1913, and *Financial Statistics of State and Local Governments,* 1932. Interpolation for intervening years is by the operating expenditures of the states in each geographic region. For 1932–35 the combined total of wages and salaries for states and cities is used as an index of county wages and salaries. For 1936–38 the estimates are extrapolated from 1935 by sample county data (from the Bureau of Foreign and Domestic Commerce, National Income Division).

CITY EXCLUDING PUBLIC EDUCATION

Col. 8 Total: estimated for (1) city-county consolidations, (2) cities over 500,000, (3) cities of 250,000–500,000, (4) cities of 100,000–250,000, (5) cities under 100,000. The fifth group, in which all the smaller municipalities are included, is divided for 1919–31 into cities of 50,000–100,000, 30,000–50,000, and under 30,000. The first group is estimated by adding the New York City data, available throughout the period, to the estimate for city-county consolidations excluding New York City.

a) The Larger Cities: The method for all groups of 50,000 or over for 1919–31 and of 100,000 or over for the years after 1931 is the same as that used in estimating state wages and salaries (see the notes to col. 6). Basic operating expenditures for the calendar years 1918, 1920, and 1922–36 are from *Financial Statistics of Cities.* The data for cities are incomplete in 1920 and are raised to the total by the average of the ratios in 1918 and 1922 of the total for all cities in the given size group to those reporting for 1920. Interpolation for 1919 and 1921 is by sample city data from auditors' reports. The 1926 ratio of wages and salaries to operating expenditures, from the Mosher and Polah report, is extrapolated for other years by sample data. For 1919–29 the sample city wage and salary data are from auditors' reports. For later years they are from questionnaire returns of the Bureau of Foreign and Domestic Commerce, National Income Division. The 1937–38 estimates of wages and salaries are extrapolated from 1936 by sample city data.

The cities whose operating expenditures are used to interpolate total operating expenditures between 1918, 1920, and 1922 are:

Group 1: For city-county consolidations, excluding New York City: Denver, Colo., and Washington, D. C.

Group 2: Chicago, Ill.

Group 3: Cincinnati, Ohio

Group 4: Oakland, Cal., Yonkers, N. Y., and Providence, R. I.

Group 5: For cities of 50,000-100,000: Saginaw, Mich., Rockford, Ill., Manchester, N. H., and Allentown, Pa.

The cities and years for which wages and salaries are available through 1938 and whose ratio of wages and salaries to operating expenditures is used to extrapolate the 1926 ratios back to 1919 and through 1936 are:

Group 1:

1919-29 Denver, Colo., and Washington, D. C.

1929-30 Denver, Colo., Washington, D. C., and Baltimore, Md.

1930-31 Denver, Colo., Washington, D. C., Baltimore, Md., and Philadelphia, Pa.

1931-32 Denver, Colo., Washington, D. C., and Philadelphia, Pa.

1932-33 Denver, Colo., Washington, D. C., Philadelphia, Pa., and St. Louis, Mo.

1933-35 Denver, Colo., Washington, D. C., Philadelphia, Pa., St. Louis, Mo., Baltimore, Md., and San Francisco, Cal.

1935-38 Denver, Colo., Washington, D. C., St. Louis, Mo., San Francisco, Cal., Philadelphia, Pa., and New Orleans, La.

Group 2:

1919-29 Chicago, Ill.

1929-30 Chicago, Ill., Los Angeles, Cal., Cleveland, Ohio, and Pittsburgh, Pa.

1930-31 Chicago, Ill., Detroit, Mich., Los Angeles, Cal., Cleveland, Ohio, Pittsburgh, Pa., and Buffalo, N. Y.

1931-32 Chicago, Ill., Detroit, Mich., Cleveland, Ohio, Pittsburgh, Pa., and Buffalo, N. Y.

1932-33 Chicago, Ill., Detroit, Mich., Cleveland, Ohio, Pittsburgh, Pa., Milwaukee, Wis., and Buffalo, N. Y.

1933-37 The entire group: Chicago, Ill., Detroit, Mich., Los Angeles, Cal., Cleveland, Ohio, Boston, Mass., Pittsburgh, Pa., Milwaukee, Wis., and Buffalo, N. Y. Since the total is available for 1926 and 1933 the final estimates for intervening years are interpolated by the estimates obtained by multiplying operating expenditures by the ratio of wages and salaries to them.

1937-38 The cities listed for 1933-37 except Milwaukee

Group 3:

1919-20 Cincinnati, Ohio

1920-22 Cincinnati, Ohio, and Rochester, N. Y.

1922-29 Cincinnati, Ohio, Rochester, N. Y., and Louisville, Ky.

1929-30 Cincinnati, Ohio, Newark, N. J., Kansas City, Mo., Seattle, Wash., Rochester, N. Y., Louisville, Ky., Portland, Ore., Columbus, Ohio, Houston, Texas, St. Paul, Minn., Akron, Ohio, Providence, R. I., Birmingham, Ala.

1930–32 The cities listed for 1929–30 and, in addition, Oakland, Cal., and Dallas, Texas

1932–33 The cities listed for 1930–32 and, in addition, Atlanta, Ga., Toledo, Ohio, and Minneapolis, Minn.

1933–34 The cities listed for 1932–33 except Louisville

1934–35 The cities listed for 1933–34 except Toledo

1935–36 The cities listed for 1934–35 except Newark and Houston; and, in addition, Louisville, Ky.

1936–37 The cities listed for 1935–36 except Akron; and, in addition, Toledo, Ohio

1937–38 The cities listed for 1936–37 except Kansas City, Rochester, Toledo, and Oakland

Group 4:

1919–29 Oakland, Cal., Yonkers, N. Y., and Providence, R. I.

1929–30 Salt Lake City, Utah, Cambridge, Mass., Duluth, Minn., Yonkers, N. Y., Bridgeport, Conn., Camden, N. J., Evansville, Ind., Fort Worth, Texas, Long Beach, Cal., New Bedford, Mass., Oklahoma City, Okla., Omaha, Nebr., Paterson, N. J., Reading, Pa., Richmond, Va., San Antonio, Texas, Scranton, Pa., South Bend, Ind., Tampa, Fla., Wichita, Kans., Albany, N. Y., Somerville, Mass., Spokane, Wash., Tacoma, Wash., El Paso, Texas, Norfolk, Va., Jacksonville, Fla., and Fort Wayne, Ind.

1930–32 The cities listed for 1929–30 and, in addition, San Diego, Cal.

1932–33 The cities listed for 1930–32 and, in addition, Springfield, Mass., Worcester, Mass., Elizabeth, N. J., Lynn, Mass., and Grand Rapids, Mich.

1933–34 The cities listed for 1932–33 and, in addition, Flint, Mich., and New Haven, Conn.

1934–35 The cities listed for 1933–34 and, in addition, Kansas City, Kans., and Utica, N. Y.

1935–36 The cities listed for 1934–35 except Yonkers and Scranton

1936–37 The cities listed for 1935–36 except San Diego and Worcester; and, in addition, Des Moines, Iowa

1937–38 The cities listed for 1936–37 except Cambridge, Flint, Paterson, and Des Moines

Group 5:

1919–29 Saginaw, Mich., Rockford, Ill., Manchester, N. H., and Allentown, Pa.

1929–30 Allentown, Pa., Savannah, Ga., Saginaw, Mich., Manchester, N. H., Lincoln, Nebr., Huntington, W. Va., Pueblo, Colo., Binghamton, N. Y., Rockford, Ill., Austin, Texas, Cedar Rapids, Iowa, Davenport, Iowa, East Orange, N. J., Hammond, Ind., Greensboro, N. C., Hoboken, N. J., Kalamazoo, Mich., McKeesport, Pa., St. Joseph, Mo., Topeka, Kans., Mt. Vernon, N. Y., Pasadena, Cal., and San Jose, Cal.

1930–31 The cities listed for 1929–30 and, in addition, Covington, Ky.

b) *The Smaller Cities:* The estimates of wages and salaries in cities with populations under 50,000 through 1931 are derived similarly to those for larger cities but the basic data are not available in as great detail.

Operating expenditures are estimated as follows:

For cities of 30,000–50,000 in 1918, 1920, and 1922–31 they are from *Financial Statistics of Cities.* Since the 1920 figure as reported is incomplete it is raised to the total by the average of the ratios in 1918 and 1922 of the totals to the cities reporting in 1920.

For cities of 2,500–30,000 and of 30,000 or over, operating expenditures, including school costs, in 1912 and 1931 are from the *Census of Wealth, Debt and Taxation,* 1913, and *Financial Statistics of State and Local Governments,* 1932, respectively. The ratio of the per capita cost for cities of 2,500–30,000 to that for cities of 30,000 or over is determined for 1912 and 1931, and interpolated along a straight line. This ratio is then used to extrapolate the 1912 ratio of per capita cost, excluding education, for cities of 2,500–30,000 (as determined from the *Census of Wealth, Debt and Taxation,* 1913) to that for cities of 30,000 or over. The resulting ratio applied to the per capita cost, excluding education, for cities of 30,000 or over yields an estimate of per capita cost, excluding education, for cities of 2,500–30,000. Total operating expenditures are estimated by multiplying the per capita by the population figures.

For municipalities with populations under 2,500 the 1931 per capita operating expenditures, including school costs, are from *Financial Statistics of State and Local Governments,* 1932. The estimated ratio of this figure to that for cities of 2,500–30,000 is extrapolated for other years by the relation between the cost in cities of 2,500–30,000 and that in cities of 30,000 or over. The resulting ratio is applied to the estimated per capita cost, excluding education, for cities of 2,500–30,000 to give operating expenditures per capita for municipalities under 2,500. Total operating expenditures are estimated by multiplying per capita cost by the population figures.

Total urban population is obtained by subtracting from the totals for the United States (*Statistical Abstract*) the estimated farm population (*Agricultural Situation*). Population figures for cities of 30,000 or over are from *Financial Statistics of Cities* except for 1919 and 1921 when straight-line interpolation is used. The estimates for cities under 30,000 are divided into those under 2,500 and those of 2,500–30,000 on the basis of the ratios derived for Census years and interpolated along a straight line for other years. Operating expenditures for 1919 and 1921 are estimated for the entire group of cities under 50,000 by multiplying the population figures by per capita cost, obtained by straight line interpolation of the 1918, 1920, and 1922 estimates.

Wages and salaries are estimated by the same method as for the other city groups, the 1926 ratio to operating expenditures as given in the Mosher and Polah report (see the notes to col. 6) being extrapolated by the ratio in sample cities. The estimates for cities of 30,000–50,000 are made on the assumption that the relation between salaries and wages and operating expenditures is the same for cities of 30,000–50,000 as for those under 50,000.

The cities and years for which wages and salaries are available for computing the ratio to operating expenditures are:

1919-21 Jamestown, N. Y., Jackson, Miss., Pittsfield, Mass., Portsmouth, Va., Bangor, Me., Fredericksburg, Va., and Red Wing, Minn.
1921-23 The cities listed for 1919-21 except Jamestown; and, in addition, New Castle, Pa.
1923-26 The cities listed for 1921-23 except Portsmouth
1926-27 The cities listed for 1921-23
1927-28 The cities listed for 1921-23 and, in addition, Jamestown
1928-29 The cities listed for 1927-28 except Portsmouth
1929-30 Pittsfield, Mass., New Castle, Pa., Waterloo, Iowa, Jamestown, N. Y., Wichita Falls, Texas, Dubuque, Iowa, Everett, Mass., Newport News. Va., Poughkeepsie, N. Y., Oshkosh, Wis., Moline, Ill., Jackson, Miss., Bangor, Maine, Fredericksburg, Va., and Red Wing, Minn.
1930-31 The cities listed for 1929-30 except Bangor; and, in addition, Port Arthur, Texas, Dearborn, Mich., Phoenix, Ariz., Everett, Wash., Plainfield, N. J., Tucson, Ariz., Baton Rouge, La., Bellingham, Wash., Amarillo, Texas, and Joplin, Mo.

The estimates of wages and salaries in cities under 100,000 for 1932–38 are based on their ratio to salaries in cities of 100,000 or over, the 1931 ratio being extrapolated by the ratios of the respective sample figures. The list of cities included in the sample of cities under 100,000 is available at the Bureau of Foreign and Domestic Commerce, National Income Division.

Col. 9 Public education: for all years except 1937 and 1938, estimated for (1) elementary and secondary schools, (2) special schools,

(3) higher schools. The basic data for the even school years 1918–36 are from the *Biennial Survey of Education*. The final calendar year figures are weighted averages of those for school years with the given year having a weight of 2 and the following year a weight of 1.

1) Elementary and secondary schools: the salaries paid supervisors, principals and teachers (also total expense figures) in day schools in cities of 100,000 or over are from Statistics of City School Systems in the *Biennial Survey of Education*. The ratio of salaries to expenses is applied in each Survey year to the total instruction expense at night, part-time, and summer schools for the same city group, also reported in the Survey, to yield the salaries paid supervisors, principals and teachers in these schools. This procedure is used for all years except 1934, for which the salaries of this group in part-time schools are given in the Survey. In 1934 also the figures for cities in county units are not reported with those for other cities. Data for the larger cities in county units are shown separately and have been added to make the series comparable. The 1936 figures for cities in county units are based on their ratio in 1934 to the figures for other cities. Total salaries for inter-Survey years are interpolated along a straight line.

The pay of other employees excluding janitors is the product of the estimated number (see the notes to Table G 7) and the average pay. Average pay for odd years since 1925 is derived from National Education Association sample data. Intervening year interpolation and extrapolation from 1925 to 1919 are by the average pay of the teaching staff.

School salaries in cities of 30,000–100,000, 10,000–30,000, and 2,500–10,000 are estimated by the same procedure as that outlined for schools in cities of 100,000 or over, with the following exceptions: (a) salaries of other employees in cities of 10,000–30,000 for the Survey years before 1926 are obtained by applying the 1926 ratio of salaries to total auxiliary expense as reported in the Survey to the comparable item for the earlier Survey years; estimates for inter-Survey years are interpolated along a straight line; (b) for cities of 2,500–10,000 the average salary of other employees is extrapolated from 1925 to 1919 by the average salary in cities of 10,000–30,000.

Salaries of teaching staffs in rural schools are estimated for Survey years by subtracting those for city day schools from the total

for all public day schools. Estimates for inter-Survey years are interpolated along a straight line. Since the 1918 Survey figure includes
only teachers' salaries the salaries of supervisors and principals are
estimated by multiplying their number (see the notes to Table G 7)
by the average salary. The average salary is assumed to have the
same relation to the average salary of teachers as it does in city day
schools. The pay of other employees excluding janitors is the
product of their number (see the notes to Table G 7) and the
average pay. Average pay is estimated by applying to the average
pay of teachers, etc. in rural schools the ratio of the average pay of
other employees to that of teachers in cities of 2,500–10,000.

Salaries of administrative officers are estimated for all schools as
a unit by multiplying the number (see the notes to Table G 7) by
the average pay. Average pay for odd years, 1925–37, is derived
from National Education Association sample data; for even years,
1926–36, interpolated along a straight line; for 1919–24, extrapolated by the average pay of the teaching staff.

Janitors' wages are estimated on the basis of total operating costs
of all schools reported in Statistics of State School Systems in the
Biennial Survey of Education and the ratio of wages to total cost
for those schools that report these items separately. Estimates for
inter-Survey years are interpolated along a straight line. For 1935
and 1936 janitors' wages are estimated by multiplying the number
(see the notes to Table G 7) by the average wage, the latter extrapolated by the average pay of other employees.

Bus drivers' wages are estimated to be 8.62 per cent of the total
cost of pupil transportation as reported in the Survey. For the
derivation of the percentage going to wages see the National Education Association *Research Bulletin,* May 1938.

For 1937 and 1938 wages and salaries in all elementary and high
schools combined are estimated by multiplying the number of employees (see the notes to Table G 7) by the average pay. Average
pay, computed for 1936, is extrapolated for 1937 and 1938 by
National Education Association data on employees and salaries in
city school systems. The NEA data are available for 1935, 1937,
and 1939; estimates for intervening years are interpolated along a
straight line.

2) *Special schools:* covers schools for blind, deaf, mentally deficient, and delinquent children. Total pay is estimated by multiply-

ing the number of employees (see the notes to Table G 7) by the average pay. The average pay of the teachers is assumed to be the same as that of teachers in public day schools; for attendants the average pay of other employees excluding janitors is used. The 1937 and 1938 estimates are assumed to be the same as the 1936.

3) *Higher schools:* negro land-grant colleges and universities are estimated separately from other higher schools which include junior colleges, normal schools, teachers' colleges, and universities.

Salaries of principals and instructors in normal schools and teachers' colleges, reported for 1918–30 in the *Biennial Survey of Education,* are interpolated for inter-Survey years along a straight line. Salaries of university teachers are estimated by multiplying the number (see the notes to Table G 7) by the average salary. Average salary is derived from Viva Boothe's *Salaries and the Cost of Living in Twenty-Seven State Universities and Colleges, 1913–1932* (Ohio State University Press, Nov. 1932). Total salaries for universities and colleges are based on the estimated salaries for instruction and the ratio of total salaries to the salaries for instruction as reported for land-grant colleges by the Office of Education in their bulletins, *Land-Grant Colleges and Universities,* for 1925–29. For the years back to 1919 the 1925 ratio is used; for 1930, the 1929 ratio. For salaries other than for instruction in teachers' colleges and normal schools the ratio of salaries other than for instruction and research to current expenditures excluding instruction, as derived for land-grant colleges from the above mentioned bulletins, is applied to the current expenditure figures for teachers' colleges and normal schools reported in the Survey and interpolated for intervening years along a straight line. For the years back to 1919 the 1925 ratio is used; for 1930, the 1929 ratio.

For 1931–38 the estimates of faculty salaries are based on the 1929 land-grant college ratios of salaries to total expenditures. Total expenditures are reported for individual colleges and universities in the *Biennial Survey of Education* for 1932 and 1934. For those that do not report expenditures but do report the number on the faculty, salaries are estimated on the basis of the average salary derived from the data for universities reporting both. Estimates for library workers' and other salaries in 1932 also are based on the 1929 ratio for land-grant colleges and universities. For 1933 and 1934 they are obtained by multiplying the estimated number (see the notes to Table G 7) by the average salary. The average salary of library workers in 1932 is extrapolated to 1933 and 1934 by the average salary of the faculty. The average pay of other employees is that of similar employees in elementary and high schools. The extrapolation of the total wage and salary bill after 1934 is by administrative and teaching salaries in elementary and secondary schools in cities of 30,000 or over.

Total wages and salaries in negro land-grant colleges and universities, 1926–29, are from the Office of Education bulletins, *Land-Grant Colleges and Universities*. For other years salaries are estimated by multiplying the number (see the notes to Table G 7) by the average salary. Average salary is computed for 1926–29 and extrapolated to 1919 and 1936 by the average salary in other higher public education.

The description of the estimates for higher education is not valid for 1929–38, since for these years we substituted estimates prepared by the Bureau of Foreign and Domestic Commerce, National Income Division. However, as the above description is referred to in the notes on the estimates of private education, we retained the notes on our original estimates of salaries in higher public education.

Col. 10 Total: sum of col. 5–9.

TABLE G 3

Pensions and Employee Compensation

PENSIONS

Col. 1 Federal: estimates for 1929–38, from the Bureau of Foreign and Domestic Commerce, National Income Division, and described in *National Income in the United States, 1929–35*. For 1919–28 they are the sum of (a) military and naval pensions, obtained from the Veterans' Administration, (b) military and naval retirement pay, extrapolated from 1929 by the pension figures, (c) civil retirement pay extrapolated from 1929 by civil salaries.

Col. 2 State: difference between total pensions paid and pension assessments; both are reported for the fiscal years 1919 and 1923–31 in *Financial Statistics of States,* but for 1921 and 1922 only total miscellaneous expense is reported and the 1921 figure does not cover all states. The miscellaneous expense item in 1921 is raised to include the states not reporting by the 1922 ratio of the total to that for the states reporting in 1921. Pensions for these two years are then estimated on the basis of the ratio of pensions to total miscellaneous expense for 1919 and 1923, interpolated along a straight line. Pensions paid in 1920 are interpolated between 1919 and 1921 by the total salary bill.

Pension assessments are combined with donations in the 1922 report. Donations are interpolated along a straight line between 1919 and 1923. Pension assessments are obtained by subtraction. The reported 1921 figure is raised to the total by the method used for pensions paid. The 1920 figure is interpolated between 1919 and 1921 along a straight line.

The estimate for 1932 is obtained by raising the data for the 41 states reporting to the Bureau of the Census by the 1931 ratio of the totals for all states to those for the 41 available in 1932 for both pensions paid and pension assessments. The extrapolation for later years is by pension payments of sample states from data collected by the Bureau of Foreign and Domestic Commerce, National Income Division.

Col. 3 County: for 1931 and 1932 from the Bureau of Foreign and Domestic Commerce, National Income Division, as derived from sample county pensions and the ratio of total county cost payments to sample county cost payments. The estimates for 1933–37 are extrapolated from 1932 by sample county pensions, collected by the National Income Division. The estimates for 1919–30 and 1938 are based on the county salary bill and the ratio of pensions to salaries. The ratio, computed for 1931 and 1937, is extrapolated for other years by the corresponding ratio for states and cities combined.

Col. 4 City, including public education: difference between pensions paid and pension assessments; both are reported for cities of 30,000 or over for 1918 and 1923–31 in *Financial Statistics of Cities,* but for 1920 and 1922 only total miscellaneous expenditures are reported. For 1919–22 the method of estimation is similar to that for states. Pensions, 1932–36, in cities of 100,000 or over are based on data from *Financial Statistics of Cities;* for 1937 and 1938 they are extrapolated by sample data collected by the Bureau of Foreign and Domestic Commerce, National Income Division. Pensions in cities of 30,000–100,000 in 1931 are extrapolated through 1938 by the sample for that city size group.

Pensions, 1919–31, in cities under 30,000 are based on the salary bill and the ratio of pensions to salaries. For 1931 the ratio for cities of 30,000–100,000 is used and is extrapolated by the corresponding ratio for cities of 30,000 or over. The 1931 estimate of pensions is extrapolated through 1938 by the sample data of the National Income Division, for that city size group.

Col. 5 Total: sum of col. 1–4.

EMPLOYEE COMPENSATION

Col. 6 Federal: sum of col. 5, Table G 2, and col. 1, above.

Col. 7 State: sum of col. 6, Table G 2, and col. 2, above.

Col. 8 County: sum of col. 7, Table G 2, and col. 3, above.

Col. 9 City, including public education: sum of col. 8 and 9, Table G 2, and col. 4, above.

Col. 10 Total: sum of col. 10, Table G 2, and col. 5, above.

TABLE G 4

Interest

Col. 1 Public debt: for fiscal years, from the *Annual Report of the Secretary of the Treasury.* Pairs of fiscal years are averaged to yield calendar year figures.

Col. 2 Postal savings: for 1920 and later years, from the *Annual Report of the Comptroller of the Currency.* The 1919 estimate is derived by applying the 1920 interest rate to 1919 deposits (from the same source). Pairs of fiscal years are averaged to yield calendar year figures.

Col. 3 Total federal: sum of col. 1 and 2.

Col. 4 State: pairs of fiscal years are averaged to yield calendar year figures after the estimates are made. Net interest is the difference between total interest paid and interest received.

Total interest paid in 1919 and 1921–31 is reported in *Financial Statistics of States.* The 1921 figure reported is not a total and is raised by the 1922 ratio of total interest to interest of the states that reported in 1921. The 1920 estimate is based on the gross new issues estimated by the *Commercial and Financial Chronicle* and the ratio of the net to the gross increase as derived from data in the *Bond Buyer,* 1928. The 1932 estimate is based on the percentage change from 1931 to 1932 in interest payments of the 41 states reporting to the Bureau of the Census in 1932. Extrapolation for later years is by the interest payments of sample states collected by the Bureau of Foreign and Domestic Commerce, National Income Division.

Interest received in 1919 and 1923–31 is reported in *Financial Statistics of States.* The 1922 estimate is the product of total receipts from rents and interest (*Financial Statistics of States*) and the ratio of interest to them. This ratio, computed for 1923, is extrapolated to 1921 by the ratio for states reporting in 1921, and interpolated between 1921 and 1923 along a straight line. Total interest received in 1921 is estimated on the basis of the percentage change from 1921 to 1922 in interest received by reporting states, as described above. The 1932 estimate of interest received is based on the percentage change from 1931 to 1932 in receipts from highway privileges, rents, and interest as indicated by partial data reported to the Bureau of the Census. Estimates for later years are extrapolated from 1932 by the sample data of the National Income Division.

Net interest in 1920 is estimated by applying to total interest paid in 1920 the ratio of net to total interest paid in 1919 and 1921, interpolated along a straight line.

Col. 5 County: total interest paid by county governments in 1912, from the *Census of Wealth, Debt and Taxation,* 1913; in 1931, from *Financial Statistics of State and Local Governments,* 1932. For 1922 and 1925–29 it is the difference between interest payments of state and local governments as derived by the National Industrial Conference Board and our estimates of state and city interest payments. Intervening year estimates are interpolated by the sum of state and city interest payments.

The ratio for states and cities of interest received to total receipts from highway privileges, rents, and interest is used to estimate interest received in 1931. Receipts from highway privileges, rents, and interest are reported in *Financial Statistics of State and Local Governments,* 1932. Interest received in 1919–30 is estimated by multiplying interest paid by the ratio of interest received to it, computed for counties in 1931 and extrapolated to 1919 by the corresponding ratio for states and cities.

Net interest is the difference between total interest paid and

interest received. For the years after 1931 both are extrapolated by
data for sample counties collected by the Bureau of Foreign and
Domestic Commerce, National Income Division.

Col. 6 City: payments by cities and all smaller municipalities including other civil divisions. Total interest paid in 1931 is from
Financial Statistics of State and Local Governments, 1932, and is
estimated for 1912 and 1922 by multiplying the total debt outstanding by the average interest rate. Total debt in 1912 is recorded
in the report mentioned above; that in 1922 in the *Census of
Wealth, Public Debt and Taxation*, 1922. The average interest
rate in 1912 is assumed to be the same as in cities of 2,500 or over.
The same figure is used for 1922 since the interest rate for larger
cities remained constant during the period. Interpolation between
1912, 1922, and 1931 is by the interest payments of cities of 30,000
or over as reported in *Financial Statistics of Cities.* For 1919 and
1921, when no reports were issued, the method is similar to that
for states for 1920. For 1920, when the Census coverage was incomplete, the total for the cities that reported is raised by the average
of the 1918 and 1922 ratios of all cities to those reporting in 1920.

Interest received is estimated on the basis of the ratio to interest
paid, derived for 1931 from *Financial Statistics of State and Local
Governments*, 1932, and *Financial Statistics of Cities.* In the
former, receipts from highway privileges, rents, and interest for
cities of 30,000 or over and for all other cities and civil divisions
are reported. From the latter we obtained the ratio of interest
received to receipts from highway privileges, rents, and interest
for cities of 30,000 or over and of 30,000–50,000. The ratio for the
latter is used also for cities with populations under 30,000. The
application of these ratios to the Census figures for receipts from
highway privileges, rents, and interest for cities of 30,000 or over
and for those of under 30,000 yields estimates of interest received
in 1931. The 1931 ratio of interest received to interest paid is
extrapolated to 1918 by the corresponding ratio for cities of 30,000
or over, estimated for 1918, 1920, 1922–31 from interest payments
and receipts recorded in *Financial Statistics of Cities.* Receipts
reported for 1920 are raised to include cities not covered. The
reported figure for 1922 includes receipts from highway privileges
and rents. To this is applied the estimated ratio of interest received
to receipts from highway privileges, rents, and interest computed

for 1922 from data for 1918, 1920, 1922, and 1923 in *Financial Statistics of Cities*.

Net interest paid is the difference between total interest paid and interest received. For 1919 and 1921 it is estimated on the basis of the ratio of net to total interest paid. The ratios in these years are by straight line interpolation between those for 1918, 1920, and 1922. For the years after 1931 only cities of 100,000 or over are covered in *Financial Statistics of Cities*. Net interest paid is computed for these cities and used as an index for net interest of all cities and minor civil divisions.

Col. 7 Total: sum of col. 3–6.

TABLE G 5

Total Payments to Individuals

Sum for each type of government of employee compensation (Table G 3) and interest (Table G 4). Relief payments (given in Table G 1, footnote 1) are added to the federal total in 1933 and later years.

TABLE G 6

Net Savings

Difference between net changes in assets and in liabilities. Complete figures are not available but information has increased throughout the period. The estimates are therefore crude; year to year changes are computed for comparable lists of items. Data on security assets and the public debt of state and local governments are reported for fiscal years only; calendar years are averages of pairs of fiscal years.

Col. 1 Federal, change in foreign security assets: see the notes to col. 3.

Col. 2 Federal, change in other security assets: see the notes to col. 3.

Col. 3 Federal, total change in security assets: federal security assets and the fiscal years for which annual changes can be determined are (1) foreign government securities and loans, 1918–39 (before 1920 termed 'credits advanced for war purposes'), (2) capital stock of the War Finance Corporation, 1918–20, (3) capital stock of war emergency corporations, 1920–29, (4) capital stock of other govern-

ment corporations, 1920–29, (5) other obligations and securities,
1920–39, (6) proprietary interest of the United States in government corporations, 1929–39, (7) federal securities held by United
States government trust funds and government agencies, 1918–29,
(8) federal securities held by United States government trust funds,
1929–39, (9) state and local securities held by United States government trust funds, 1930–39. All these items are given in the *Annual
Report of the Secretary of the Treasury on the State of the
Finances.*

Col. 4 State and local, change in security assets: the security assets
of state and local governments are their sinking fund holdings,
from the *Annual Report of the Secretary of the Treasury,* plus
estimated other security investments. The investments of states,
other than state securities in sinking funds, in 1918, 1919, and
1923–31 are from *Financial Statistics of States.* The 1920–22 estimates are obtained by applying to the estimated state debt in
1920–22 the ratios of such investments to state debt in 1919 and
1923, interpolated along a straight line; the 1932–37 estimates, by
extrapolating the 1931 ratio to debt by the ratio for city governments and applying it to the state debt for the respective years.
The 1938 estimate is extrapolated from 1937 by sinking fund
holdings.

Total state debt outstanding in 1918, 1919, and 1922–31 is from
Financial Statistics of States. The 1921 total is interpolated between 1919 and 1923 by the debt of the 30 states reporting in 1921.
The 1920 total is by straight line interpolation of the 1919 and
1921 figures. Estimates of state debt, 1932–36, are from *Long-Term
Debts in the United States* (Bureau of Foreign and Domestic Commerce). Total debt of local governments is the difference between
the total debt of state and local governments (given in the *Annual
Report of the Secretary of the Treasury*) and the estimated debt of
state governments.

Financial Statistics of Cities shows the debt and security holdings, other than sinking fund assets, of cities of 30,000 or over in
1918 and 1923–31, and of 100,000 or over in 1931–36. Data for the
latter are utilized to extrapolate through 1936 data for the former.
The ratio of these security holdings to debt is computed for 1918
and 1923 to date; the 1918 and 1923 ratios are interpolated along a
straight line to yield estimates for 1919–22. The application of

these ratios to the estimates of local government debt yields security holdings other than sinking fund assets.

Col. 5 Total change in security assets: sum of col. 3 and 4.

Col. 6 Net value, public construction: the net change in real property assets is assumed to 'equal the value of public construction less the estimated depreciation on government fixed assets. The construction figures are totals for federal, state, and local governments as given in *Construction Activity in the United States, 1915–37* (Domestic Commerce Series 99) and the *Survey of Current Business,* August 1939. The depreciation figures are the current price figures in *Capital Consumption and Adjustment* and unpublished estimates for recent years, estimated similarly to the published figures.

Col. 7 Federal, change in public debt: net debt for calendar years, from the *Annual Report of the Secretary of the Treasury.* The change in debt during the year is the difference between the amount outstanding at the end and at the beginning of the year.

Col. 8 State and local, change in public debt: net debt for fiscal years, from the *Annual Report of the Secretary of the Treasury.* Averages of pairs of fiscal year figures yield calendar year-end figures. The change in debt for the calendar year is the difference between year-end figures.

Col. 9 Total change in public debt: sum of col. 7 and 8.

Col. 10 Net savings: col. 5 plus col. 6 minus col. 9.

TABLE G 7

Employees

Col. 1 Legislative: estimates for 1929–38, from the Bureau of Foreign and Domestic Commerce, National Income Division, and described in *National Income in the United States, 1929–35.* For the earlier years the number is kept constant at the 1929 level.

Col. 2 Judicial: see the notes to col. 1.

Col. 3 Civil executive, including Post Office: see the notes to col. 1 for estimates for 1929–38. The 1929 estimates of employees in the Post Office Department and of other civil executive employees are extrapolated to 1919 by the number given in the *Annual Report of the United States Civil Service Commission.*

Col. 4 Military: see the notes to col. 1 for estimates for 1929–38.

The number in the Army, Navy, Marine Corps, and Coast Guard is extrapolated to 1919 by the number of active military personnel in the Army, the organized strength of the Navy, the active military personnel of the Marine Corps (all given in the *Statistical Abstract*), and the active military personnel of the Coast Guard (given in the *Annual Report of the Secretary of the Treasury*).

Col. 5 Total federal: sum of col. 1–4.

Col. 6 State: estimated by dividing the total salary bill by the average salary. The average salary for 1926 is derived from the Mosher and Polah report (see the notes to Table G 2, col. 6), adjustment being made for part-time employment. It is extrapolated for other years by the weighted average for sample states, the weights being the 1926 employment figures in the Mosher and Polah report. For the years before 1929 the sample is taken from data published in state auditors' reports. For 1929 and later years questionnaire material collected by the Bureau of Foreign and Domestic Commerce, National Income Division, is used.

The states and years for which average pay data are used are:

1919–21 New York (incl. county employees) and New Jersey
1921–26 New Jersey, California, Minnesota, Ohio, Texas, and Massachusetts
1926–27 New Jersey, California, Texas, and Massachusetts
1927–28 New Jersey and Massachusetts
1928–29 New Jersey, North Carolina, and Massachusetts
1929–30 Massachusetts, Connecticut, New York, New Jersey, Pennsylvania, Ohio, Minnesota, Kansas, Delaware, Virginia, North Carolina, Montana, Wyoming, Nevada, and Vermont
1930–32 The states listed for 1929–30 and, in addition, Michigan and Wisconsin
1932–33 The states listed for 1930–32 and, in addition, Maine, New Hampshire, Iowa, and South Dakota
1933–34 The states listed for 1932–33 except Kansas
1934–35 The states listed for 1933–34 except Ohio
1935–36 The states listed for 1934–35 except Massachusetts and Michigan; and, in addition, Indiana, Utah, and California
1936–37 The states listed for 1935–36 except Wisconsin; and, in addition, Ohio, Michigan, Maryland, and Kentucky
1937–38 Connecticut, New York, Pennsylvania, Minnesota, Delaware, North Carolina, Nevada, Indiana, Utah, Ohio, Illinois, Michigan, Maryland, and Georgia

Col. 7 County: the method is the same as that used for states. The basic average pay figure, for 1926 from the Mosher and Polah report (see the notes to Table G 2, col. 6), is extrapolated for 1919–25 and for 1927–35 by the average pay for state and city employees combined. Extrapolation from 1935 on is by the average pay in sample counties, derived from questionnaire material collected by the Bureau of Foreign and Domestic Commerce, National Income Division.

Col. 8 City: the method is essentially the same as that used for states. For 1929 and later years employees are estimated separately for city-county consolidations, cities of 500,000 or over, of 250,000–500,000, of 100,000–250,000, and under 100,000. In each case the average pay of the largest sample is considered to be the actual pay for the group for the year that the sample covers and is extrapolated by the samples for the other years. The sample data were collected by the Bureau of Foreign and Domestic Commerce, National Income Division.

For the years before 1929 employees are estimated for all groups of cities combined. The basic figures for average pay are for 1926 and 1929, the former derived from the Mosher and Polah report (see the notes to Table G 2, col. 6), the latter from the estimates by groups of cities. The cities used for interpolation between 1926 and 1929 and for extrapolation before 1926 are:

1919–21 New York, Washington, D. C., and San Francisco
1921–25 New York, Washington, D. C., San Francisco, and Cincinnati
1925–27 New York, Washington, D. C., San Francisco, Cincinnati, and Kalamazoo
1927–29 Washington, D. C., Cincinnati, and Kalamazoo

Col. 9 Public education: sum of employees in 1) elementary and high schools, 2) higher education, 3) special schools.
1) Elementary and high schools: the number of administrative employees as given in Statistics of State School Systems in the *Biennial Survey of Education* is interpolated along a straight line for the intervening years. Since the reported figure for 1936 is incomplete, it is raised to the total by the 1934 ratio of the total to those reporting in 1936.

The number of principals, supervisors and teachers in cities of 100,000 or over, 30,000–100,000, 10,000–30,000, and 2,500–10,000 is from Statistics of City School Systems in the *Biennial Survey of Education.* Inter-Survey year estimates are interpolated along a straight line. The number in rural schools is the difference between the *Biennial Survey of Education* figures for state day schools (from Statistics of State School Systems) and those for city day schools (from Statistics of City School Systems). Interpolation for intervening years is along a straight line.

The number of other employees excluding janitors and bus drivers is estimated separately for the various city groups and rural schools on the basis of their ratios to the number on the teaching staff. These ratios are derived for odd years, 1925–37, from the National Education Association sample data. The 1925 ratios are used for the earlier years. Examination of the ratio of other employees to those on the teaching staff for the various groups of cities reveals that the ratio declines with the size of the city. The ratio used for rural schools was selected after inspection of those for cities and is kept constant at 2 per cent for the entire period.

The number of janitors is obtained for odd years 1925–33 and for 1934 by dividing their total wages by the average wage. From the National Education Association sample data for odd years 1925–37 the average wage figure for janitors is derived. It is adjusted by the ratio of actual per capita pay to sample per capita pay of 'other' employees, the latter also derived from the National Education Association data. The average wage for 1934 is interpolated by the average pay of other employees. The estimate of janitors for 1925 is extrapolated back and that for 1934 forward by the number on teaching staffs. For all other years the estimates are by straight line interpolation.

The number of bus drivers is estimated by dividing their total wage bill by the average wage derived from bus transportation data.

For 1937 and 1938 employees in elementary and high schools as a whole are estimated. The totals for 1936 are extrapolated by National Education Association data on the number employed in schools covered in their surveys. The NEA data, available for 1935, 1937, and 1939, are raised to the total by their estimate of the percentage coverage of the sample and interpolated along a straight line to yield the extrapolating index of the number of employees.

2) *Higher education:* from the *Biennial Survey of Education* the number on the teaching staff is derived and interpolated along a straight line for intervening years. In estimating the number doing research and library work the assumption is made that per capita pay is the same as for teachers. These per capita figures divided into

the estimated salaries for research and library work yield the number employed in these activities. The number of 'other' employees is estimated by dividing their total pay by the average pay of 'other' employees in public elementary and high schools. For 1932–34, however, the number on the teaching staff is used as the index for the number of 'other' employees. For years after 1934 the total of employees is extrapolated by the number of teaching and administrative employees in elementary and secondary schools in cities of 30,000 or over.

The preceding estimates exclude figures for negro land-grant colleges. The number on the latter's faculties are reported in the Office of Education bulletins, *Land-Grant Colleges and Universities*. 'Other' employees in this group are assumed to have the same relation to the faculty as they do in other higher educational institutions.

The description of the estimates for higher education is not valid for 1929–38 since for these years we substituted estimates prepared by the Bureau of Foreign and Domestic Commerce, National Income Division. However, as the above description is referred to in the notes on the estimates of private education, we retained the notes on our original estimates of salaries in higher public education.

3) *Special schools:* the estimate of employees in these schools is not complete since it excludes Indian schools, which are combined with Alaskan schools, and employees other than teachers and attendants. The number excluded is probably negligible.

For 1918, 1922, 1927, and 1932 data are reported in the *Biennial Survey of Education* and include schools for the blind, deaf, feebleminded and subnormal, and delinquent. For inter-Survey years interpolation is along a straight line. The number of employees for 1932 is extrapolated through 1936 by the number of teachers in public elementary and secondary day schools. For 1937 and 1938 the 1936 figure is used.

For the minor adjustments in the basic Survey data and for the conversion of fiscal to calendar year figures see the notes to Table G 2.

Miscellaneous

TABLES Ms1 – Ms3

Whenever two entries are made for 1934 the first is comparable with those for preceding years in that the *Statistics of Income* data used are based on the old industrial classification; the second is comparable with those for succeeding years in that the *Statistics of Income* data used are based on the new industrial classification.

Net savings and net income, adjusted, exclude gains and losses from sales of capital assets, 1929–38, and from changes in inventory valuation, 1919–38. Net savings and net income without any specific designation are unadjusted, i.e., include these two types of gain and loss.

Ms 1   Total Payments by Type (millions of dollars)

| | WAGES & SALARIES | ENTREP. WITHDR. | PROPERTY INCOME | | | | PAY. TO INDIVIDUALS |
| | | | Dividends | Interest | Div. & int., international | Total | |
	(1)	(2)	(3)	(4)	(5)	(6)	(7)
1919	1,369	259	74.5	169	29.0	273	1,901
1920	1,531	307	82.8	178	43.0	304	2,143
1921	1,384	282	75.5	188	69.0	332	1,999
1922	1,517	333	77.2	183	86.0	347	2,198
1923	1,791	340	97.7	197	94.0	388	2,520
1924	1,842	375	96.1	213	129	438	2,656
1925	1,984	410	111	223	154	488	2,884
1926	2,150	413	120	225	110	455	3,019
1927	2,194	435	150	245	132	528	3,158
1928	2,256	463	189	272	149	611	3,331
1929	2,409	499	202	258	183	643	3,553
1930	2,259	476	110	256	224	591	3,327
1931	2,061	440	−30.7	246	301	516	3,017
1932	1,731	429	−87.0	236	264	413	2,574
1933	1,684	411	−100	211	220	331	2,427
1934	1,837	402	−121	199	108	185	2,425
1934	1,837	404	164	135	108	407	2,648
1935	2,057	438	218	107	41.0	367	2,863
1936	2,311	488	242	104	−23.0	324	3,124
1937	2,550	550	240	102	−76.0	267	3,367
1938	2,413	552	168	99.0	−44.0	223	3,189

Ms 2   Net Income Originating (millions of dollars)

| | PAY. TO INDIVIDUALS | ENTREPRENEURIAL | | NET SAVINGS | | NET INCOME | NET SAVINGS, ADJ. | | NET INCOME, ADJ. |
| | | Net savings | Net income | Corp. | Total | | Corp. | Total | |
	(1)	(2)	(3)	(4)	(5)	(6)	(7)	(8)	(9)
1919	1,901	157	416	186	343	2,245	182	339	2,241
1920	2,143	127	435	70.7	198	2,341	94.7	222	2,365
1921	1,999	101	383	−146	−45.0	1,954	−126	−25.0	1,974
1922	2,198	25.1	358	79.8	104	2,303	73.8	98.9	2,297
1923	2,520	88.3	428	113	202	2,722	114	203	2,723
1924	2,656	53.7	429	72.0	125	2,782	72.0	125	2,782
1925	2,884	52.3	463	135	188	3,072	131	184	3,068
1926	3,019	111	525	116	228	3,247	117	229	3,248
1927	3,158	50.6	486	49.0	99.6	3,258	49.0	99.6	3,258
1928	3,331	45.9	509	276	322	3,653	276	322	3,653
1929	3,553	29.5	529	283	313	3,866	−106	−77.4	3,476
1930	3,327	7.9	484	−739	−731	2,595	−478	−471	2,856
1931	3,017	−31.0	409	−1,131	−1,162	1,855	−407	−438	2,579
1932	2,574	−101	327	−1,018	−1,120	1,453	−345	−446	2,127
1933	2,427	−91.5	319	−900	−991	1,435	−326	−418	2,008
1934	2,425	−35.7	366	−527	−563	1,862	−251	−286	2,138
1934	2,648	−37.3	366	−244	−281	2,367	−218	−255	2,393
1935	2,863	−26.5	412	−207	−234	2,629	−269	−295	2,567
1936	3,124	−9.0	479	−102	−111	3,012	−193	−202	2,921
1937	3,367	−19.4	531	−169	−189	3,178	−177	−196	3,171
1938	3,189	−5.7	546	−169	−175	3,013	−178	−183	3,005

Ms 3   Persons Engaged (thousands)

	EMPLOYEES (1)	ENTREPRENEURS (2)	TOTAL (3)
1919	1,163	236	1,399
1920	1,164	249	1,413
1921	1,109	262	1,371
1922	1,198	275	1,473
1923	1,325	288	1,613
1924	1,355	301	1,656
1925	1,419	313	1,733
1926	1,506	326	1,833
1927	1,549	339	1,889
1928	1,580	352	1,932
1929	1,684	365	2,049
1930	1,617	357	1,975
1931	1,566	343	1,910
1932	1,491	322	1,814
1933	1,519	319	1,838
1934	1,571	339	1,910
1935	1,644	358	2,002
1936	1,734	378	2,112
1937	1,813	397	2,211
1938	1,767	412	2,179

TABLE Ms 1

Total Payments by Type

Col. 1 Wages and salaries: sum of estimates for subgroups. Estimates for 1929–38 are made separately for (1) common carrier buses, (2) sightseeing buses, (3) motor trucking and warehousing, (4) taxicabs, (5) air transportation, (6) harborcraft, (7) special banks, (8) brokerage, (9) fisheries, (10) unclassified. The figures for special banks are sums of estimates for joint stock land banks, the Regional Agricultural Credit Corporation, Federal Intermediate Credit Banks, Federal Land Banks, Banks for Cooperatives, Production Credit Corporation, Production Credit Association, Federal Home Loan Banks, and General Agents. For this period the estimates are derived by the method used by the Bureau of Foreign and Domestic Commerce, National Income Division, with materials supplied by it.

For 1919–28 the entries are the sum of estimates for (1) motor transportation, (2) miscellaneous banking and brokerage, (3) air transportation, (4) fisheries, (5) unclassified, including harborcraft. For each subgroup, wages and salaries are estimated by multiplying the number of employees (see the notes to Table Ms 3) by the average pay. The average pay in 1929 for each subgroup is extrapolated to 1919 by the estimated average pay of employees in construction, trade, and service.

Col. 2 Entrepreneurial withdrawals: for 1929–38 the entries are the sum of estimates for (1) motor trucking and warehousing, (2) taxicabs, (3) harborcraft, (4) brokerage, (5) fisheries. It is assumed that there are no entrepreneurs in the other fields. The estimates are derived by the method used by the Bureau of Foreign and Domestic Commerce, National Income Division, with materials supplied by it.

For 1919–28 the entries are the sum of estimates for (1) motor transportation, (2) harborcraft, (3) brokerage, (4) fisheries. Withdrawals are estimated by multiplying the number of entrepreneurs (see the notes to Table Ms 3) by the average withdrawal. The average withdrawal, computed for 1929, is extrapolated to 1919 for each subgroup by the estimated average withdrawal of entrepreneurs in construction, trade, and service.

Col. 3 Dividends: difference between total dividends paid and dividends received. The payments of all industries not covered separately are included: (1) forestry, fishing, and related industries, (2) air transportation, (3) autobus lines, etc., (4) cartage and storage, (5) radio broadcasting, (6) water companies, (7) 'other' public utilities, (8) joint stock land banks, (9) stock and bond brokers, etc., (10) loan companies, (11) corporations, nature of business not given. For all these industries both dividends paid and received in 1926–37 are from the special tabulation of *Statistics of Income* data. Net dividends for 1934 comparable with those for prior years are the difference between net dividends of all industries and net dividends of all industries other than miscellaneous. The 1933 figure for net dividends of all industries is the sum of dividends of miscellaneous and all other industries. The figure for 1934 comparable with that for 1933 is obtained by extrapolating the 1933 figure by the item for all industries other than miscellaneous.

Estimates of net dividends paid for the years before 1926 are extrapolated from 1926 by the total for all other industries. The

1938 figure is extrapolated from the 1937 figure by the corporate sample for the industry.

Col. 4 Interest: difference between total interest paid on long term debt and interest received on tax-exempt obligations. The industries covered are the same as for dividends.

Total interest payments, 1930–35, are estimated by applying to the par value of long term debt the average interest rate derived for all other industries. Long term debt outstanding on December 31, 1930–35, reported in the special tabulation of *Statistics of Income* data, is raised to the total by a ratio derived as follows:

From the capital stock tax returns for 1924, published in *Statistics of Income*, we derived the ratio of the fair value of the stock of all corporations to the fair value of the stock of corporations reporting assets and liabilities for industries related to agriculture; local transportation, etc.; water works; storage companies; 'all other' public utilities; lessors of public utilities; stocks and bonds, etc.; 'all other' financial combinations; combinations, predominant industry not ascertainable; nominal concerns; exempt corporations. The ratio for all corporations is also derived. The ratio for corporations in the miscellaneous industries is extrapolated for 1930–35 by the ratio for all corporations. The ratio for all corporations for 1931–35 is the ratio of compiled receipts of all corporations to those of corporations filing balance sheets. For 1930 the 1931 ratio is used.

The interest rate used is obtained by dividing total interest payments by the industrial divisions estimated separately by December 31 figures on their total long term debt outstanding.

Total interest payments for the years before 1930, for 1934 comparable with prior years, and for 1936–38 are extrapolated from 1930, 1933, and 1935, respectively, by total interest payments by all other industries.

Interest received on tax-exempt obligations is reported for 1926–37 (1934 comparable with 1935) in the special tabulation of *Statistics of Income* data. Estimates for 1919–25 are extrapolated from 1926, and for 1934 comparable with 1933, from 1933 by total interest received by all other industries. In 1938 interest received is assumed to have the same relation to interest paid as in 1937.

Col. 5 Dividends and interest, international: difference between receipts from long term foreign investments and payments to foreign investors. In estimating these two series for 1929 and later years the sources and methods of the Bureau of Foreign and Domestic Commerce, National Income Division, are used. The 1929 figures are extrapolated to 1919 by data supplied by Paul D. Dickens of the Bureau of Foreign and Domestic Commerce, Finance Division, and additional data from the *Balance of International Payments of the United States.*

Col. 6 Property income: sum of col. 3–5.

Col. 7 Total payments to individuals: sum of col. 1, 2, and 6.

TABLE Ms 2

Net Income Originating

Col. 1 Total payments to individuals: see Table Ms 1, col. 7.

Col. 2 Entrepreneurial net savings: sum of estimates for (1) motor trucking, (2) fisheries, (3) brokerage. It is assumed that for all other divisions the entire net income is withdrawn. The estimates for motor trucking and fisheries, 1929–38, are from the Bureau of Foreign and Domestic Commerce, National Income Division. For brokerage the estimates of individuals' savings, 1929–38, are derived on the assumption that the relation of withdrawals to savings is the same as that for entrepreneurs in manufacturing, mining, construction, and trade.

For the years before 1929 savings are estimated by applying to the estimated withdrawals the ratio of savings to withdrawals, computed for 1929 and extrapolated by the corresponding ratio for manufacturing, mining, construction, and trade.

Col. 3 Entrepreneurial net income: sum of col. 2, Table Ms 1, and col. 2, above.

Col. 4 Corporate net savings: difference between compiled net profits after taxes and total dividends paid. The industries covered are those listed in the notes to Table Ms 1, col. 3.

Compiled net profits after taxes are reported for 1926–37 in the special tabulation of *Statistics of Income* data. Dividend payments are described in the notes to Table Ms 1, col. 3. The resulting series on corporate savings, obtained by subtraction for 1926–37, is extrapolated for 1919–25, and for 1934 comparable with 1933, by total corporate savings of all other industries. Corporate savings in 1938 are assumed to be the same as in 1937.

Col. 5 Total net savings: sum of col. 2 and 4.
Col. 6 Net income originating: sum of col. 1 and 5.

TABLE Ms 3

Persons Engaged

Col. 1 Employees: for 1929 and later years, the sum of estimates of employees in (1) common carrier buses, (2) sightseeing buses, (3) motor trucking and warehousing, (4) taxicabs, (5) air transportation, (6) harborcraft, (7) special banks, (8) brokerage, (9) fisheries, (10) unclassified. For the institutions covered under (7) see the notes to Table Ms 1. For this period the sources and methods of the Bureau of Foreign and Domestic Commerce, National Income Division, are used.

For 1919–28 the estimates are the sum of employees in (1) motor transportation, (2) miscellaneous banking and brokerage, (3) air transportation, (4) fisheries, (5) unclassified, including harborcraft.

The method used to derive estimates for the years before 1929 is the same for all groups except the unclassified. In each case the number engaged in 1929 is the sum of employees and entrepreneurs. In the 1930 *Census of Population,* Vol. V, Ch. 1, figures on the gainfully occupied in representative occupations on January 1, 1920 and April 1, 1930 are reported. We assume that there was the same percentage of unemployment in 1920 as in 1929. Therefore, given the number engaged in 1929, we apply to it the percentage change from 1920 to 1929 in the number attached to representative occupations, the 1929 figure for which is obtained by interpolating along a straight line between Census dates. The estimates of the number engaged in 1921–28 are interpolated between 1920 and 1929 by the number engaged in all other industries; 1919 is extrapolated from 1920 by the same index. Employees are estimated by subtracting entrepreneurs (see the notes to col. 2) from the total engaged.

For (5), the unclassified division, the number engaged is extrapolated from 1929 by the number engaged in trade, service, and the other four miscellaneous divisions. Employees are estimated by subtracting entrepreneurs (see the notes to col. 2) from the total engaged.

The representative occupations used in estimating the 1920 figures for the number engaged are:

1) Motor transportation: chauffeurs, truck and tractor drivers; draymen, teamsters and carriage drivers; laborers, truck, transfer and cab companies; owners and managers, truck, transfer and cab companies

2) Miscellaneous banking and brokerage: commercial brokers and commission men, loan brokers, stock brokers and brokers, not elsewhere classified

3) Air transportation: aviators

4) Fisheries: fishermen and oystermen

Col. 2 Entrepreneurs: for the derivation of the estimates for 1929–38 see the notes to col. 1. For 1919–28 they are the sum of the estimates for the five divisions listed in the notes to col. 1, which were based on estimates of the total engaged in 1920 and 1929, as there described, and on the assumption that the percentage of entrepreneurs to the total engaged is the same in 1920 as in 1929. Figures for 1919 and for 1921–28 are extrapolated and interpolated along a straight line.

Col. 3 Total number engaged: sum of col. 1 and 2.

PART FIVE

Supplementary Data

PART FIVE assembles data supplementary to the basic estimates in Part Four. The series presented here were not included with the basic tables either because they are not available continuously or for all the relevant industrial divisions; or because they give information that does not relate directly either to income flow or to the number engaged. Yet it was thought that they would be of interest to readers who might wish to experiment with some breakdowns that could not be carried through continuously; to gauge the coverage of our samples; to observe the movements of some series on income flows, of which the basic estimates are derivatives at a remove (e.g., gross dividends and interest); to have at hand figures that would make possible variants of net savings of enterprises and of national income somewhat different from those in the basic tables.

No effort has been made to present all supplementary data. Only such series are given here as are readily accessible either in National Bureau files or in published sources; and even of these only those are presented that seem of most general interest as supplementary to the basic estimates in Part Four.

TABLE I

Compensation of Officers of Corporations

Tables I 1–3 provide series on the compensation of corporate officers. The comprehensive series, i.e., for all corporations in the country, are not continuous; for this and other reasons it did not seem advisable to include them in the basic tables in Part Four. For the years and industrial divisions covered they may be compared, however, with total salaries or compensation of employees in Part Four; and used to apportion these totals between payments to subordinate employees and to administrative personnel.

TABLE I 1

Compensation of Officers of Corporations,[1] 1919–1924, 1928–1937 (millions of dollars)

	AGR. & RELATED INDUS. (1)	MINING & QUARRY. (2)	MFG. (3)	CONSTRUC-TION (4)	TRANSP. & OTHER PUB. UTIL. (5)	TRADE (6)	SERVICE (7)	FINANCE (8)	NATURE OF BUSINESS NOT GIVEN (9)	TOTAL (10)
1919	18.0	50.1	822	59.1	66.6	604	75.2	263	33.9	1,993
1920	21.1	86.7	997	84.1	91.5	667	95.5	364	28.9	2,437
1921	18.3	63.9	878	84.1	82.3	642	95.4	375	17.9	2,258
1922	18.1	64.4	911	84.9	126	667	123	401	12.3	2,409
1923	18.4	62.5	960	93.4	135	729	134	422	18.9	2,575
1924	20.1	56.8	970	106	104	763	147	453	12.6	2,635
1928	23.2	55.4	1,107	155	107	926	209	612	2.9	3,199
1929	25.4	56.3	1,171	163	108	957	218	631	3.6	3,336
1930	24.0	50.9	1,095	158	104	888	215	598	2.7	3,138
1931	20.0	45.0	935	129	96.3	775	192	500	3.4	2,697
1932	16.2	38.4	734	88.1	85.1	616	155	397	1.2	2,132
1933	15.2	37.6	706	67.7	80.5	600	144	341	0.9	1,995
1934[2]	17.0	42.9	771	68.7	90.8	671	160	347	0.3	2,173
1934[3]	16.9	41.6	753	69.7	87.6	684	163	355	0.5	2,173
1935	18.6	42.6	812	76.6	95.2	744	179	375	0.7	2,345
1936	22.0	48.7	951	101	103	862	220	402	0.8	2,712
1937	22.0	50.1	1,004	110	104	875	230	411	1.0	2,809

1 *Statistics of Income.* Data not available for 1925–27.
2 Comparable with the earlier years in that data are based on the old industrial classification.
3 Comparable with the later years in that data are based on the new industrial classification.

TABLE I 2

Number and Salaries of Principal Salaried Officers
Manufacturing Corporations, 1929 and 1935

INDUSTRIAL DIVISION	1929		1935	
	NUMBER	SALARIES ($000)	NUMBER	SALARIES ($000)
	(1)	(2)	(3)	(4)
Food & tobacco	22,607	103,399	20,960	87,451
Food	22,038	99,485	20,476	84,197
Tobacco	569	3,914	484	3,254
Textile & leather	31,586	199,720	29,679	137,409
Wearing apparel	19,992	125,056	19,975	87,298
Textile fabrics	10,042	64,398	8,366	43,371
Other leather	1,552	10,266	1,338	6,740
Construction materials & furniture	22,598	126,689	16,363	61,330
Lumber	7,155	35,883	4,307	14,515
Stone, clay, & glass	5,862	30,337	4,129	16,331
Heating apparatus	1,617	11,921	1,490	7,552
Other construction materials	2,971	18,697	2,244	8,264
Furniture	4,993	29,851	4,193	14,668
Paper	4,174	30,878	3,978	25,706
Printing	19,916	124,391	18,587	90,747
Metal	33,188	244,932	27,350	145,734
Iron & steel	3,367	28,812	2,929	19,600
Machinery	20,641	152,520	17,013	88,944
Motor vehicles	1,825	16,801	1,164	8,082
Non-ferrous metal	7,355	46,799	6,244	29,108
Chemical	9,394	63,505	8,131	45,036
Chemical excl. petroleum refining	8,713	58,880	7,549	41,621
Petroleum refining	681	4,625	582	3,415
Miscellaneous & rubber	10,663	63,754	9,688	45,154
Rubber	286	3,357	121	1,432
Miscellaneous	10,377	60,397	9,567	43,722
Total	154,126	957,268	134,736	638,567

Biennial Census of Manufactures. We exclude central administrative offices.

TABLE I 3

Number and Salaries of Principal Salaried Officers
Steam Railroads, Pullman Company, and Railway Express

| | STEAM RAILROADS * | | PULLMAN COMPANY | | RAILWAY EXPRESS | |
	Number	Salaries ($000)	Number	Salaries ($000)	Number	Salaries ($000)
	(1)	(2)	(3)	(4)	(5)	(6)
1919	20,300	74,531	179	627	2,594	5,334
1920	23,598	100,674	186	634	2,560	6,116
1921	22,751	101,741	187	642	2,262	5,665
1922	24,067	100,600	192	736	2,150	5,032
1923	25,465	111,160	217	821	2,114	5,138
1924	25,944	110,910	250	929	2,135	5,381
1925	25,847	115,321	262	946	2,069	5,287
1926	28,253	118,803	256	967	2,218	5,738
1927	27,537	123,161	262	924	2,391	6,310
1928	27,993	125,640	274	946	2,328	6,196
1929	28,217	129,779	276	939	2,302	6,158
1930	27,659	129,480	258	937	2,377	6,143
1931	25,013	117,458	247	876	2,336	5,682
1932	14,200	73,892	246	742	2,010	4,549
1933	12,960	65,240	244	726	1,823	4,045
1934	12,693	64,813	242	776	2,042	5,054
1935	12,632	67,831	248	857	2,046	5,386
1936	12,752	70,474	268	902	2,077	5,511
1937	13,006	74,838	287	981	2,082	5,641
1938	12,675	73,350	283	995	1,930	5,415

Based on National Bureau grouping of Interstate Commerce Commission data.

* The data for 1933–38 are not comparable with those for the earlier years,
owing to a revision of the Interstate Commerce Commission occupational
classification.

TABLE II

Sample Corporate Data Collected by the
National Bureau

Table II describes the corporate samples compiled by the National Bureau for the years prior to 1930, for use mainly in estimating dividends for the early years in the period and long term debt and long term interest payments for all years prior to 1929. Since the National Bureau used the corporate sample collected by the Department of Commerce for years beginning with 1929, these tables cover the years through 1929 only.

For each industrial group in the sample the table shows in the second column the total (and the year) that is extrapolated or interpolated with the help of the sample. Comparison of this total with the entries in the following columns, which relate to the sample proper, indicate the extent of sample coverage relative to the comprehensive total.

TABLE II

Sample Corporate Data Collected by the National Bureau,[1] 1919–1930 (millions of dollars)

Debt and Capital Stock are at par value as of December 31
Debt and Interest are long term

	TOTALS[2]	1919	1920	1921	1922	1923	1924	1925	1926	1927	1928	1929	1930
				MINING									
1 Dividends paid	223.1 (1922)	83.0	94.1	87.4	79.2								
2 Debt	747.5 (1921) 1,011.7 (1923)			637.0	654.8	868.8							
3 Debt	1,200.4 (1924) 1,039.2 (1926)						804.4	778.4	793.8				
4 Int. paid	44.5 (1922)	21.8	28.1	33.5	34.1								
5 Debt					666.7	881.3	891.8	861.5	818.0	1,023.4	925.8		
6 Int. paid					39.1	50.6	51.1	49.2	46.8	56.6	50.7		
7 Int. rate (6 ÷ 5)					.0587	.0574	.0573	.0571	.0572	.0553	.0547		
			MANUFACTURING										
Food & Tobacco													
8 Dividends paid	181.8 (1922)	89.8	115.5	95.4	97.7								
9 Debt	627.2 (1921) 716.5 (1923)			432.4	438.4	492.9							
10 Debt	922.7 (1924) 730.5 (1926)						494.0	486.5	487.8				
11 Int. paid	37.9 (1922)	19.9	27.7	27.6	26.5								
12 Debt					448.6	499.9	501.3	501.5	498.3	515.2	515.1		
13 Int. paid					26.9	29.2	29.2	29.1	28.8	29.4	29.4		
14 Int. rate (13 ÷ 12)					.0600	.0584	.0583	.0581	.0578	.0573	.0570		
Textile & Leather													
15 Dividends paid	221.6 (1922)	35.6	39.5	28.7	30.7								
16 Int. paid	24.0 (1922)	2.8	2.8	3.0	5.7								
17 Debt					77.4	74.8	79.5	85.2	115.9	101.8	95.4		
18 Int. paid					4.8	4.7	5.0	5.6	7.3	6.4	5.9		
19 Int. rate (18 ÷ 17)					.0622	.0628	.0630	.0658	.0634	.0629	.0622		
Construction Materials & Furniture													
20 Dividends paid	129.7 (1922)	14.4	19.5	16.8	19.4								
21 Debt	198.4 (1921) 251.6 (1923)			27.7	40.5	55.5							

TABLE II (cont.)

Construction Materials & Furniture (concl.)

	TOTALS[2]	1919	1920	1921	1922	1923	1924	1925	1926	1927	1928	1929	1930
22 Debt	{285.5 (1924)} {264.5 (1926)}						62.9	52.5	51.4				
23 Int. paid	13.9 (1922)	1.5		1.7	2.5								
24 Debt					46.7	57.4	64.9	90.1	100.3	117.3	165.7	163.2	
25 Int. paid					3.1	3.6	4.1	5.4	6.0	7.0	9.5	9.4	
26 Int. rate (25 ÷ 24)					.0660	.0634	.0637	.0600	.0596	.0593	.0575	.0576	
Paper													
27 Dividends paid	36.9 (1922)	4.5	6.0	4.0	3.6								
28 Debt	{112.9 (1921)} {169.2 (1925)}			40.7	61.2	62.2							
29 Debt	{168.4 (1924)} {256.5 (1926)}						75.5	101.0	130.3				
30 Int. paid	6.3 (1922)	1.9		2.0	3.2								
31 Debt					68.0	75.4	75.5	101.0	166.9	204.4	187.6	225.0	
32 Int. paid					4.0	4.5	4.5	6.0	9.8	11.4	10.6	12.9	
33 Int. rate (32 ÷ 31)					.0591	.0594	.0594	.0596	.0589	.0559	.0564	.0571	
Printing & Publishing													
34 Dividends paid	{73.0 (1922)} {96.3 (1924)} {178.9 (1926)}	2.4	3.0	3.9	4.7								
35 Debt	4.4 (1922)						6.9	16.0	18.1				
36 Int. paid		0.30	0.27	0.38	0.33								
37 Debt					5.5	6.7	7.8	16.0	25.9	33.5	57.0		
38 Int. paid					0.35	0.42	0.50	0.98	1.6	1.9	3.3		
39 Int. rate (38 ÷ 37)					.0636	.0628	.0632	.0611	.0607	.0581	.0579		
Metal													
40 Dividends paid	307.1 (1922)	229.4	259.0	239.0	230.9								
41 Debt	{799.8 (1921)} {1,628.6 (1924)} {1,616.7 (1926)}			1,050.7	1,077.5	1,174.6							
42 Debt							1,186.2	1,153.9	1,008.5				
43 Int. paid	49.4 (1922)	48.9	55.4	58.9	60.0								
44 Debt					1,110.6	1,182.0	1,212.8	1,172.7	1,115.4	1,127.5	1,143.7		
45 Int. paid					61.7	65.2	66.5	64.1	60.0	59.4	57.4		
46 Int. rate (45 ÷ 44)					.0556	.0552	.0548	.0547	.0538	.0527	.0501		

Chemical

47 Dividends paid	296.5 (1922) 628.4 (1924) 806.6 (1926)										
48 Debt	23.5 (1922)	117.3	150.7	153.2	147.2		207.8	169.3	331.4		
49 Int. paid		4.7	7.9	22.1							
50 Debt					291.6	274.6	216.3	169.3	331.4	408.2	449.7
51 Int. paid					20.0	18.8	13.7	10.3	17.8	21.6	23.0
52 Int. rate (51 ÷ 50)					.0686	.0684	.0635	.0610	.0536	.0530	.0511

Rubber

53 Dividends paid	11.2 (1922) 191.7 (1924) 241.7 (1926)										
54 Debt	8.2 (1922)	17.4	31.2	15.4	12.0		138.0	164.8	190.7		
55 Int. paid		3.6	7.4	9.6							
56 Debt					8.8	141.5	138.0	164.8	190.7	180.5	189.4
57 Int. paid					142.5 8.8	8.8	8.5	10.2	11.6	11.0	11.4
58 Int. rate (57 ÷ 56)					.0620	.0619	.0617	.0612	.0606	.0608	.0599

Miscellaneous

59 Dividends paid	160.1 (1922)										
60 Debt		8.9	9.1	9.3	13.8	4.9	4.9	4.8	3.0	3.2	3.0
61 Int. paid					4.0	0.29	0.29	0.29	0.18	0.18	0.17
62 Int. rate (61 ÷ 60)					.0656	.0601	.0599	.0599	.0593	.0562	.0559

TRANSPORTATION AND OTHER PUBLIC UTILITIES

Electric Light & Power

63 Dividends paid [a]	64.6 (1917) 129.2 (1922) 129.2 (1927)										
64 Dividends paid		28.5	29.1	31.7	40.0	55.7	81.9	100.9	110.0	128.1	
65 Int. paid [4]	338.2 (1927) 61.6 (1917)										
66 Int. paid		34.3	36.1	38.4	43.5	71.1	80.2	84.5	92.2	97.6	
67 Int. paid	124.3 (1922) 124.3 (1922) 275.1 (1927) 275.1 (1927)				65.1	71.8					
68 Net income [5]	322.6 (1930) 94.5 (1917) 197.4 (1922) 197.4 (1922) 467.3 (1927)							135.0	136.8	153.8	160.7 170.3
69 Net income		35.0	38.1	41.2	57.3	61.5	76.3	82.2	101.4	117.8	136.9

TABLE II (cont.)

	TOTALS [2]	1919	1920	1921	1922	1923	1924	1925	1926	1927	1928	1929	1930
Manufactured Gas													
70 Dividends paid	{ 41.9 (1921) 72.1 (1923) 91.7 (1924) 93.9 (1926) }	24.1	24.0	18.7	23.2	41.4							
71 Dividends paid							41.3	43.8	44.7				
72 Capital stock				405.6		502.6	514.0						
73 Dividends paid				18.7		41.4	41.3						
74 Dividend rate (73 ÷ 72)				.0460		.0824	.0805						
75 Int. paid	{ 17.5 (1924) 47.0 (1930) }	15.7	17.0	20.0	16.8	16.8	18.3	20.8	22.2	21.5	24.6	23.5	27.0
76 Debt							353.8						
77 Int. paid							18.3						
78 Int. rate (77 ÷ 76)							.0520						
Electric Railways													
79 Dividends paid [6]	{ 73.3 (1917) 53.7 (1922) }	8.4	8.2	7.4	14.0								
80 Dividends paid	{ 53.7 (1922) 62.6 (1927) }				28.5	31.0	33.7	39.8	40.0	42.6			
81 Dividends paid [7]	{ 62.6 (1927) 30.6 (1932) }									42.9	43.9	47.8	
82 Int. paid [8]	{ 126.4 (1917) 138.8 (1922) }	31.6	31.8	34.0	37.5								
83 Int. paid	{ 138.8 (1922) 105.9 (1927) }				66.9	74.8	76.3	75.4	74.2	74.9			
84 Int. paid	{ 105.9 (1927) 104.9 (1930) }									73.9	69.6	67.7	60.4
85 Net income [9]	{ 81.9 (1917) 70.5 (1922) }	8.2	10.2	11.4	15.1								
86 Net income	{ 70.5 (1922) 67.6 (1927) }				26.3	31.9	26.1	31.1	29.9	33.2			
87 Net income [10]	{ 67.6 (1927) -8.5 (1932) }									41.4	39.3	45.8	
Pipe Lines													
88 Dividends paid	28.5 (1920)	20.4	20.0	9.7	34.2	34.7	34.0	39.5	20.0	47.8	46.6	43.5	
89 Debt		8.9	8.8										
90 Int. paid		0.55	0.55	0.60	1.8	1.8	1.8	1.9	1.0	2.4	2.3	2.2	
91 Int. rate (90 ÷ 89)		.0606	.0600	.0621	.0530	.0532	.0531	.0485	.0503	.0501	.0501	.0500	
92 Net income	53.9 (1930)	30.5	45.7										

Water Transportation

93 Dividends paid	20.4 (1921) / 22.6 (1923) / 15.9 (1924) / 24.1 (1926)	23.8	15.4	10.2	9.7	8.9	6.9					
94 Dividends paid								8.3	9.0			
95 Capital stock				181.7		270.7	275.8					
96 Dividends paid				5.9		8.9	8.9					
97 Dividend rate (96 ÷ 95)				.0325		.0330	.0252					
98 Debt [11]	224.6 (1921) / 243.2 (1923) / 197.1 (1924) / 145.7 (1929)	117.6	117.5	125.6	139.9	141.0						
99 Debt												
100 Debt		110.4	109.8	117.9	127.9	129.1	151.5	148.8	155.9	128.7	135.6	131.4
101 Int. paid		5.7	5.7	6.2	6.8	6.9	6.7	6.7	7.0	5.5	5.9	5.9
102 Int. rate (101 ÷ 100)		.0520	.0521	.0527	.0529	.0531	.0531	.0533	.0536	.0524	.0522	.0523

CONSTRUCTION

103 Debt	2.5	2.5	3.1	3.8	2.8	2.7	2.5	6.2	10.5
104 Int. paid	0.16	0.16	0.20	0.24	0.18	0.18	0.16	0.40	0.64
105 Int. rate (104 ÷ 103)	.0625	.0625	.0631	.0639	.0663	.0657	.0651	.0643	.0611

TRADE

106 Dividends paid	322.2 (1922) / 993.7 (1921) / 682.9 (1923) / 59.8 (1922)	29.8	28.7	24.2	23.4	15.0				
107 Debt		1.5	1.6	58.1	38.9					
108 Int. paid				1.5	1.8					
109 Debt										
110 Int. paid		3.8		3.8	2.4	3.6	6.3	9.0	10.4	9.1	11.4
111 Int. rate (110 ÷ 109)		.0647		.0610	.0598	.0571	.0572	.0575	.0568	.0566

(110 Int. paid values: 58.5, 39.5, 60.0, 110.3, 157.9, 180.2, 160.0, 202.2)

TABLE II (concl.)

	TOTALS²	1919	1920	1921	1922	1923	1924	1925	1926	1927	1928	1929	1930
Real Estate													
FINANCE													
112 Dividends paid	508.6 (1926)		2.5	2.2	3.3	5.3	4.8	6.3	8.3	5.7	8.7	8.8	
113 Dividends paid, preceding year	440.0 (1929)		1.5	2.5	2.5	3.3	5.3	5.2	8.2	5.4	6.4	8.7	
114 Int. paid			3.6	3.7	3.4	4.1	4.7	5.7	5.7				
115 Int. paid, preceding year			3.8	3.8	3.8	3.6	4.8	5.2	5.7				
SERVICE													
116 Dividends paid	56.3 (1922) ⎫ 358.1 (1921) ⎬	3.4	9.0	7.4	5.9								
117 Debt¹²	⎭	16.1	16.1	19.7	21.8	23.1							
118 Debt	505.4 (1923) ⎫ 618.3 (1924) ⎬ 888.8 (1926) ⎭						65.1	99.8	133.8				
119 Debt		16.1	18.8	32.0	43.9	56.0	70.2	117.2	165.1	294.4	321.4		
120 Int. paid		0.92	1.0	1.9	2.7	3.5	4.4	7.3	10.0	17.9	19.1		
121 Int. rate (120 ÷ 119)		.0572	.0551	.0591	.0624	.0632	.0627	.0623	.0607	.0608	.0595		

¹ The sources of other sample data collected by the National Bureau are given in the detailed notes in Part Four. Additional sample data have been supplied by the Bureau of Foreign and Domestic Commerce, National Income Division.

² Totals interpolated or extrapolated by the given sample.

³ The 1917 sample figure is $26.8 million.

⁴ The 1917 sample figure is $29.2 million.

⁵ The 1917 sample figure is $31.3 million.

⁶ The 1917 sample figure is $13.8 million.

⁷ The 1922 sample figure is $17.9 million.

⁸ The 1917 sample figure is $33.6 million.

⁹ The 1917 sample figure is $11.2 million.

¹⁰ The 1922 sample figure is −$8.8 million.

¹¹ The 1918 sample figure is $110.3 million.

¹² The 1918 sample figure is $16.5 million.

TABLE III

Gross Dividends and Long Term Interest Paid,
Dividends and Long Term Interest Received,
Total Interest Paid and Derived Short Term Interest Paid, All Corporations, by Industrial Divisions

Tables III 1–22 summarize the estimates of gross dividends and long term gross interest paid, as well as of dividends and long term interest received by corporations in various industrial divisions. These series of diminuends and subtrahends were the ones used to derive net dividends and net long term interest payments in the basic tables in Part Four.

For most industrial divisions we have in addition to gross long term interest paid a series on total interest paid (the latter usually reported in *Statistics of Income*). For these divisions we can derive estimates of short term interest paid by corporations. Such estimates are necessarily subject to wide margins of error but may be of value as rough approximations. They are not given for some public utilities for which gross long term interest paid and received is obtained from sources other than *Statistics of Income*.

Whenever two entries are given for 1934 the first is comparable with those for preceding years in that the *Statistics of Income* data used are based on the old industrial classification; the second is comparable with those for succeeding years in that the *Statistics of Income* data used are based on the new industrial classification.

TABLE III

1 Mining, Total (millions of dollars)

	GROSS DIV. PAID	DIV. REC.	GROSS LONG TERM INT. PAID	LONG TERM INT. REC.	TOTAL INT. PAID	DERIVED SHORT TERM INT. PAID
	(1)	(2)	(3)	(4)	(5)	(6)
1919	233	39.3	28.4	5.1	79.5	51.1
1920	265	55.5	36.6	6.3	94.9	58.3
1921	246	53.2	43.7	5.4	107	63.8
1922	223	83.9	44.5	11.2	80.8	36.3
1923	300	77.1	51.1	13.8	126	75.4
1924	255	42.6	63.4	12.1	139	76.4
1925	335	66.0	65.1	11.2	104	39.0
1926	402	76.0	60.3	13.8	96.6	36.4
1927	329	51.8	54.2	10.5	109	54.8
1928	311	57.6	52.7	10.7	99.3	46.6
1929	425	59.7	56.2	11.5	111	55.1
1930	302	53.6	54.6	10.1	85.4	30.8
1931	173	34.8	49.6	7.9	86.0	36.4
1932	102	20.5	46.9	7.4	79.1	32.1
1933	90.9	15.6	42.3	8.1	72.9	30.6
1934	189	74.8	38.0	8.1	78.1	40.0
1934	266	75.7	47.6	8.4	78.9	31.3
1935	257	71.7	45.6	8.6	73.9	28.3
1936	283	68.0	46.7	6.1	66.8	20.1
1937	381	85.6	41.7	5.9	68.7	27.0
1938	261	57.0	36.3	4.9		

TABLE III (cont.)

2 Mining by Minor Industrial Divisions, 1929–1938 (millions of dollars)

	1929	1930	1931	1932	1933	1934	1935	1936	1937	1938
Anthracite coal										
Gross div. paid	20.6	21.4	17.6	9.4	2.5	3.2	3.9	3.5	1.4	0.7
Div. received	5.0	8.2	8.2	3.3	1.7	1.8	1.2	0.4	0.3	0.1
Gross long term int. paid	9.2	9.1	9.7	10.4	10.2	9.9	11.0	10.8	9.4	9.1
Long term int. rec.	1.2	0.9	0.4	0.3	0.2	0.3	0.4	0.3	0.3	0.3
Total int. paid	10.2	10.3	12.6	11.2	11.2	10.9	9.5	9.2	9.3	
Derived short term int. paid	1.0	1.1	2.9	0.8	1.0	-0.6	-1.5	-1.6	-0.1	
Bituminous coal										
Gross div. paid	31.8	28.5	19.6	8.4	7.3	23.9	27.2	24.8	18.0	13.4
Div. received	5.0	4.5	4.0	1.7	3.1	5.3	16.2	8.4	6.2	4.6
Gross long term int. paid	18.1	17.7	15.0	13.0	10.8	8.7	9.2	8.7	7.6	6.7
Long term int. rec.	2.7	2.7	2.2	1.9	1.8	1.9	1.5	1.2	1.1	0.9
Total int. paid	27.8	25.3	21.2	18.5	15.4	16.3	16.3	15.1	13.9	
Derived short term int. paid	9.7	7.6	6.2	5.5	4.7	5.6	7.1	6.4	6.3	
Metal										
Gross div. paid	218	100	41.8	12.0	14.7	37.5	61.3	110	177	103
Div. received	23.7	8.1	4.0	0.9	1.5	20.8	19.1	30.8	48.2	28.2
Gross long term int. paid	6.3	6.2	6.6	7.5	7.4	7.0	7.5	9.6	8.3	7.0
Long term int. rec.	4.1	3.1	2.1	1.9	1.9	2.2	3.1	1.8	1.7	1.5
Total int. paid	29.7	13.4	13.3	14.3	14.3	11.3	11.0	11.5	12.2	
Derived short term int. paid	23.4	7.2	6.7	6.9	7.0	4.9	3.4	1.9	3.9	

Oil and gas

Gross div. paid	81.0	103	51.1	48.5	45.1	92.1	129	100	92.9	116	90.2
Div. received	11.6	24.1	13.9	12.1	7.0	31.5	31.9	27.6	23.3	25.1	19.4
Gross long term int. paid	11.1	10.7	11.3	11.8	10.7	9.6	14.8	12.6	12.1	10.9	8.2
Long term int. rec.	1.7	1.8	1.8	2.2	2.9	2.5	2.6	2.5	2.2	2.1	1.6
Total int. paid	22.9	17.8	23.5	23.2	20.5		28.1	26.3	20.4	23.8	
Derived short term int. paid	11.8	7.1	12.3	11.4	9.8		13.4	13.7	8.3	12.9	

Other

Gross div. paid	72.9	49.0	43.2	23.8	21.3	32.8	46.2	64.3	51.5	68.1	53.9
Div. received	14.5	8.8	4.7	2.6	2.4	15.4	15.6	7.8	5.1	5.8	4.6
Gross long term int. paid	11.5	10.9	7.0	4.3	3.2	2.8	4.3	5.3	5.6	5.5	5.3
Long term int. rec.	1.8	1.7	1.4	1.1	1.3	1.3	1.3	1.2	0.6	0.6	0.6
Total int. paid	20.5	18.7	15.3	11.9	11.4		12.3	10.9	10.7	9.5	5.6
Derived short term int. paid	9.0	7.8	8.3	7.6	8.2		7.9	5.6	5.1	4.0	0.6

TABLE III (cont.)

3 Manufacturing, Total (millions of dollars)

	GROSS DIV. PAID	DIV. REC.	GROSS LONG TERM INT. PAID	LONG TERM INT. REC.	TOTAL INT. PAID	DERIVED SHORT TERM INT. PAID
	(1)	(2)	(3)	(4)	(5)	(6)
1919	1,354	93.2	123	36.6		
1920	1,619	131	152	45.1		
1921	1,450	125	177	38.7		
1922	1,507	197	186	80.2		
1923	2,008	244	206	88.7		
1924	1,884	232	238	84.2		
1925	2,226	316	245	91.9		
1926	2,546	427	241	89.5		
1927	2,605	378	257	94.0		
1928	2,995	477	280	95.7		
1929	3,327	583	301	92.6		
1930	3,164	548	310	76.5		
1931	2,288	392	306	75.5		
1932	1,330	211	279	79.4		
1933	1,171	160	265	79.8	462	196
1934	2,116	819				
1934	1,612	388			369	
1935	2,196	613			344	
1936	2,956	545			338	
1937	2,959	524			375	
1938	1,741	328				

TABLE III (cont.)

4 Food and Tobacco (millions of dollars)

	GROSS DIV. PAID	DIV. REC.	GROSS LONG TERM INT. PAID	LONG TERM INT. REC.	TOTAL INT. PAID	DERIVED SHORT TERM INT. PAID
	(1)	(2)	(3)	(4)	(5)	(6)
1919	167	13.0	28.6	3.3	125	97.0
1920	215	18.4	39.6	4.1	157	117
1921	177	17.7	39.5	3.5	144	105
1922	181	27.9	37.9	7.3	108	70.8
1923	251	27.5	39.5	8.0	112	72.8
1924	273	24.5	47.8	7.4	119	71.2
1925	312	33.1	50.6	7.0	123	72.5
1926	327	53.2	44.8	8.4	132	87.5
1927	365	37.2	46.5	7.4	132	86.4
1928	384	30.5	49.6	7.5	133	83.4
1929	449	48.1	51.9	8.9	143	91.8
1930	483	48.8	55.2	6.9	125	69.8
1931	406	39.0	52.1	7.1	89.3	37.2
1932	330	38.6	47.6	11.3	77.6	30.0
1933	309	30.8	44.7	12.8	72.6	27.9
1934	450	154	42.3	11.1	73.0	30.7
1934	380	43.2	37.2	10.7	63.4	26.1
1935	419	83.7	34.0	6.6	62.7	28.7
1936	519	73.1	30.1	5.7	57.6	27.5
1937	470	61.1	31.1	4.7	62.1	31.0
1938	397	51.6	30.8	4.7		

TABLE III (cont.)

5   Textile and Leather (millions of dollars)

	GROSS DIV. PAID	DIV. REC.	GROSS LONG TERM INT. PAID	LONG TERM INT. REC.	TOTAL INT. PAID	DERIVED SHORT TERM INT. PAID
	(1)	(2)	(3)	(4)	(5)	(6)
1919	257	4.7	18.3	5.5	72.0	53.7
1920	283	6.7	18.2	6.7	108	90.5
1921	207	6.4	19.8	5.8	97.9	78.1
1922	221	10.1	24.0	12.1	87.6	63.7
1923	254	8.7	18.2	14.4	97.8	79.5
1924	213	10.4	15.7	12.5	96.9	81.2
1925	224	9.7	16.1	11.6	90.6	74.5
1926	218	10.1	14.3	12.0	89.1	74.8
1927	224	12.9	15.3	10.4	80.6	65.3
1928	245	14.4	16.8	9.4	85.3	68.5
1929	228	12.2	17.8	7.2	85.3	67.5
1930	180	12.1	15.9	6.5	73.5	57.7
1931	133	8.4	13.0	5.7	54.9	41.9
1932	79.5	5.2	9.1	8.5	41.9	32.7
1933	82.0	5.6	8.9	9.7	38.0	29.1
1934	124	9.5	6.5	7.1	37.6	31.1
1934	121	7.2	6.0	6.8	37.9	31.9
1935	125	10.4	7.2	5.2	37.1	29.9
1936	190	13.7	7.1	4.3	37.6	30.5
1937	186	15.9	7.8	4.0	40.9	33.1
1938	91.6	7.8	6.6	3.4		

TABLE III (cont.)

6 Construction Materials and Furniture (millions of dollars)

	GROSS DIV. PAID	DIV. REC.	GROSS LONG TERM INT. PAID	LONG TERM INT. REC.	TOTAL INT. PAID	DERIVED SHORT TERM INT. PAID
	(1)	(2)	(3)	(4)	(5)	(6)
1919	96.5	3.2	8.2	2.2	41.3	33.1
1920	130	4.5	9.4	2.8	50.7	41.3
1921	112	4.3	9.7	2.4	50.3	40.6
1922	129	6.8	13.9	5.0	57.9	44.0
1923	187	11.4	15.0	5.6	54.6	39.5
1924	171	12.8	16.8	5.6	58.6	41.8
1925	198	12.3	16.6	5.7	60.2	43.7
1926	262	17.0	19.6	7.6		
1927	236	17.0	20.3	6.5		
1928	232	15.1	24.3	7.1		
1929	233	15.3	28.6	6.2		
1930	193	15.1	30.5	4.8		
1931	120	12.5	30.4	4.2		
1932	54.9	6.0	22.7	4.7		
1933	44.9	3.9	21.3	5.3		
1934	92.6	13.3				
1934	85.3	7.7				
1935	110	16.6				
1936	195	25.9				
1937	205.0	22.7				
1938	91.5	10.1				

TABLE III (cont.)

7 Paper (millions of dollars)

	GROSS DIV. PAID	DIV. REC.	GROSS LONG TERM INT. PAID	LONG TERM INT. REC.	TOTAL INT. PAID	DERIVED SHORT TERM INT. PAID
	(1)	(2)	(3)	(4)	(5)	(6)
1919	45.8	0.9	4.9	0.9	12.3	7.4
1920	61.0	1.3	4.8	1.1	15.0	10.2
1921	50.2	1.3	5.2	0.9	15.8	10.6
1922	36.9	2.0	8.3	1.9	16.5	8.3
1923	60.3	3.2	10.0	1.8	19.1	9.1
1924	39.2	2.3	10.0	1.8	18.9	8.9
1925	64.3	3.4	11.3	1.6	21.9	10.6
1926	56.2	8.5	13.7	1.5	28.1	14.4
1927	65.9	9.3	15.0	1.7	29.6	14.6
1928	80.7	15.8	14.7	1.6	36.2	21.4
1929	79.5	22.4	17.1	1.8	33.4	16.3
1930	75.3	23.7	19.8	1.7	42.5	22.6
1931	46.0	9.5	18.6	1.6	39.7	21.1
1932	25.9	5.2	18.6	1.9	35.9	17.3
1933	30.1	2.9	18.7	2.0	33.1	14.5
1934	46.8	8.7	16.9	2.1	30.6	13.7
1934	44.6	5.0	14.3	2.1	25.5	11.2
1935	58.5	11.4	12.9	1.5	23.9	11.0
1936	76.3	15.1	12.3	1.2	21.1	8.8
1937	91.8	16.4	13.6	1.0	22.6	9.0
1938	32.4	5.8	11.6	0.9		

TABLE III (cont.)

8 Printing (millions of dollars)

	GROSS DIV. PAID	DIV. REC.	GROSS LONG TERM INT. PAID	LONG TERM INT. REC.	TOTAL INT. PAID	DERIVED SHORT TERM INT. PAID
	(1)	(2)	(3)	(4)	(5)	(6)
1919	38.0	2.9	3.9	1.4	9.3	5.4
1920	46.3	4.1	3.6	1.7	12.0	8.3
1921	61.2	4.0	5.0	1.4	14.1	9.1
1922	73.0	6.3	4.4	3.0	12.5	8.2
1923	74.6	6.7	4.4	3.2	14.4	10.0
1924	81.0	17.4	5.3	3.4	17.1	11.8
1925	99.6	11.2	7.9	4.0	19.4	11.5
1926	121	25.2	10.4	5.1	24.5	14.1
1927	137	27.8	12.2	3.4	27.0	14.7
1928	128	28.9	15.0	3.7	29.6	14.6
1929	152	19.9	16.9	3.8	32.9	16.0
1930	175	47.3	18.9	3.8	33.7	14.9
1931	111	16.5	19.1	3.6	32.3	13.2
1932	71.5	12.0	18.1	4.0	30.0	11.9
1933	47.8	12.2	17.3	3.9	27.8	10.5
1934	102	40.4	17.5	4.2	26.4	8.8
1934	82.0	15.4	12.8	4.2	20.2	7.5
1935	96.9	24.5	11.9	3.7	18.9	7.1
1936	132	27.1	11.7	3.0	19.0	7.3
1937	125	31.8	11.8	2.8	17.9	6.1
1938	99.2	25.1	12.5	2.9		

TABLE III (cont.)

9 Metal (millions of dollars)

	GROSS DIV. PAID	DIV. REC.	GROSS LONG TERM INT. PAID	LONG TERM INT. REC.
	(1)	(2)	(3)	(4)
1919	394	14.2	40.3	14.2
1920	445	19.7	45.6	17.5
1921	411	18.4	48.5	15.0
1922	397	28.8	49.4	30.7
1923	576	30.9	72.0	33.1
1924	660	36.5	90.5	35.8
1925	717	46.9	90.9	41.6
1926	855	58.0	84.2	38.7
1927	918	54.9	85.4	49.0
1928	1,022	65.1	94.9	47.2
1929	1,207	94.2	94.8	33.5
1930	1,050	99.7	87.8	31.6
1931	701	72.5	88.8	36.2
1932	338	38.0	79.8	29.9
1933	249	27.8	79.5	29.6
1934	567	188		
1934	473	88.5		
1935	724	193		
1936	1,031	144		
1937	1,125	145		
1938	484	62.5		

TABLE III (cont.)

10   Chemical (millions of dollars)

	GROSS DIV. PAID	DIV. REC.	GROSS LONG TERM INT. PAID	LONG TERM INT. REC.	TOTAL INT. PAID	DERIVED SHORT TERM INT. PAID
	(1)	(2)	(3)	(4)	(5)	(6)
1919	236	38.4	5.5	5.1	43.3	37.8
1920	303	54.3	9.2	6.3	56.8	47.6
1921	308	52.0	25.9	5.4	52.8	26.9
1922	296	82.1	23.5	11.2	98.8	75.3
1923	381	113	27.0	13.3	64.9	38.0
1924	342	98.1	33.3	12.9	62.9	29.6
1925	477	158	33.3	12.2	86.8	53.5
1926	544	198	34.0	12.6	92.4	58.4
1927	521	189	42.0	12.8	105	63.7
1928	771	276	43.8	16.5	120	77.0
1929	819	334	54.1	28.5	117	63.1
1930	864	264	59.8	18.7	140	80.3
1931	668	209	63.7	15.1	147	83.3
1932	378	99.2	65.0	14.6	141	76.9
1933	372	75.7	57.1	12.8	106	49.2
1934	648	362	51.5	11.5	96.7	45.2
1934	363	195	35.6	8.7	57.8	22.3
1935	570	257	37.7	6.8	53.9	16.2
1936	669	215	32.1	6.2	51.7	19.6
1937	623	207	28.7	5.5	51.5	22.8
1938	434	144	32.1	6.2		

TABLE III (cont.)

11 Miscellaneous and Rubber (millions of dollars)

	GROSS DIV. PAID	DIV. REC.	GROSS LONG TERM INT. PAID	LONG TERM INT. REC.	TOTAL INT. PAID	DERIVED SHORT TERM INT. PAID
	(1)	(2)	(3)	(4)	(5)	(6)
1919	119	15.8	13.6	4.1	43.8	30.1
1920	134	22.3	22.2	5.0	69.8	47.6
1921	122	21.4	23.4	4.3	75.8	52.4
1922	171	33.7	24.8	9.0	78.1	53.3
1923	222	42.4	20.6	9.2	81.4	60.9
1924	103	30.2	18.7	4.9	53.7	35.0
1925	132	41.2	19.2	8.4	43.2	24.0
1926	160	57.2	20.2	3.6	50.9	30.7
1927	135	28.9	21.1	2.8	52.2	31.1
1928	131	31.7	21.5	2.7	46.2	24.8
1929	156	37.5	20.6	2.7	45.1	24.5
1930	141	36.9	22.1	2.5	46.4	24.3
1931	100	25.2	21.2	2.0	41.9	20.7
1932	50.7	6.9	18.8	4.5	38.9	20.2
1933	35.5	1.9	18.0	3.7	31.0	13.0
1934	82.9	42.1	17.7	2.4	28.1	10.3
1934	62.3	26.1	14.7	2.5	19.7	4.9
1935	90.5	15.5	12.6	1.8	16.6	4.0
1936	141	30.7	10.6	1.7	14.9	4.3
1937	130	24.1	7.7	1.3	17.1	9.4
1938	110	20.9	7.6	1.0		

TABLE III (cont.)

12 Construction (millions of dollars)

	GROSS DIV. PAID	DIV. REC.	GROSS LONG TERM INT. PAID	LONG TERM INT. REC.	TOTAL INT. PAID	DERIVED SHORT TERM INT. PAID
	(1)	(2)	(3)	(4)	(5)	(6)
1919	16.6	1.3	4.6	0.6		
1920	23.1	2.2	5.6	0.7		
1921	34.9	2.6	8.4	0.6		
1922	34.6	4.3	6.3	1.8		
1923	43.0	5.6	8.2	2.2		
1924	36.2	3.8	10.5	2.7		
1925	66.9	8.5	12.6	2.2		
1926	53.0	11.7	13.7	2.6		
1927	72.0	24.7	14.2	2.9		
1928	60.4	9.1	13.7	3.7		
1929	73.4	13.4	16.4	3.2		
1930	110	25.1	19.1	3.7		
1931	60.1	19.9	17.3	3.8		
1932	36.7	17.5	14.9	4.6		
1933	28.4	9.7	12.8	4.2	20.4	7.6
1934	20.0	7.0	11.6	3.4		
1934	20.3	5.2	5.2	3.4	10.8	5.6
1935	26.8	6.0	3.9	2.6	10.0	6.2
1936	43.7	7.1	3.7	1.8	10.8	7.1
1937	47.8	5.8	3.4	1.4	10.6	7.2
1938	33.4	4.0	3.3	1.4		

TABLE III (cont.)

13   Electric Light and Power (millions of dollars)

	GROSS DIV. PAID	DIV. REC.	GROSS LONG TERM INT. PAID	LONG TERM INT. REC.
	(1)	(2)	(3)	(4)
1919	73.2	5.0	83.9	5.6
1920	76.0	4.7	91.7	6.6
1921	88.6	4.9	101	7.9
1922	129	6.3	124	10.3
1923	173	12.3	155	13.1
1924	204	19.0	194	16.8
1925	259	29.9	214	19.0
1926	286	39.3	249	22.7
1927	338	54.0	275	25.6
1928	420	64.1	299	27.7
1929	524	76.1	308	28.5
1930	622	85.9	322	29.6
1931	612	80.2	354	32.4
1932	493	61.1	377	34.4
1933	407	35.7	377	33.9
1934	361	33.5	364	37.4
1934	361	33.5	333	37.4
1935	359	27.7	327	28.6
1936	399	55.2	312	21.4
1937	434	38.9	299	22.8
1938	414	37.1	300	32.3

TABLE III (cont.)

14 Manufactured Gas (millions of dollars)

	GROSS DIV. PAID	DIV. REC.	GROSS LONG TERM INT. PAID	LONG TERM INT. REC.	TOTAL INT. PAID	DERIVED SHORT TERM INT. PAID
	(1)	(2)	(3)	(4)	(5)	(6)
1919	54.0	12.0	14.9	0.3		
1920	53.8	17.0	16.1	0.4		
1921	41.9	16.2	18.9	0.4		
1922	47.9	25.6	15.9	0.7		
1923	72.1	38.7	15.8	0.8		
1924	91.7	43.5	17.3	0.7		
1925	93.3	42.9	22.4	0.7		
1926	93.9	45.9	26.8	0.7		
1927	71.8	25.1	28.8	0.5		
1928	81.1	42.5	36.2	0.4		
1929	124	58.2	37.7	0.2	57.0	19.3
1930	139	71.4	47.0	0.4	73.0	26.0
1931	149	72.5	49.4	0.4	80.1	30.6
1932	198	111	61.2	0.5	88.3	27.2
1933	112	52.2	65.2	0.6	75.4	10.2
1934	96.4	27.6	60.1	1.0		
1934	90.8	48.7	49.9	0.9	71.6	21.7
1935	68.9	4.9	49.9	1.1	62.2	12.4
1936	59.8	3.4	47.5	0.9	58.6	11.1
1937	67.9	8.4	45.1	0.7	58.5	13.4
1938	67.3	8.3	44.4	0.7		

TABLE III (cont.)

15   Steam Railroads (millions of dollars)

	GROSS DIV. PAID	DIV. REC.	GROSS LONG TERM INT. PAID	LONG TERM INT. REC.	SHORT TERM INT. PAID
	(1)	(2)	(3)	(4)	(5)
1919	338	90.8	492	56.2	
1920	334	109	516	55.1	
1921	264	67.5	498	21.2	49.0
1922	273	60.9	514	24.7	31.7
1923	291	51.7	526	23.3	21.0
1924	306	42.1	564	36.9	15.0
1925	322	35.8	563	24.3	14.5
1926	362	35.5	564	34.9	15.3
1927	444	36.0	562	33.1	19.1
1928	401	44.6	558	28.6	16.0
1929	440	41.6	545	36.2	15.5
1930	489	57.7	551	34.8	15.1
1931	310	53.4	548	32.7	20.6
1932	114	43.9	536	27.6	27.8
1933	118	42.4	501	26.3	29.8
1934	170	44.4	471	25.0	32.6
1935	165	38.2	437	22.1	36.8
1936	172	29.2	415	20.1	41.4
1937	185	23.1	410	17.7	43.4
1938	99.5	15.9	363	13.7	48.2

TABLE III (cont.)

16   Street Railways (millions of dollars)

	GROSS DIV. PAID	DIV. REC.	GROSS LONG TERM INT. PAID	LONG TERM INT. REC.
	(1)	(2)	(3)	(4)
1919	39.7	4.1	118	6.5
1920	36.3	4.0	118	7.6
1921	30.7	3.6	126	9.2
1922	53.7	6.7	138	11.4
1923	54.8	7.7	148	12.3
1924	55.4	8.6	143	12.0
1925	57.5	9.7	134	11.4
1926	57.5	10.6	125	10.7
1927	58.4	11.6	119	10.3
1928	61.7	15.3	115	10.0
1929	69.2	20.6	112	9.9
1930	59.9	20.7	104	9.2
1931	47.1	18.6	101	9.0
1932	32.2	14.3	100	8.9
1933	27.3	12.1	96.3	8.6
1934	34.6	15.4	93.3	8.3
1934	34.6	15.4	102	9.2
1935	38.9	17.3	101	9.0
1936	56.5	25.1	101	9.0
1937	68.3	30.3	97.9	8.7
1938	65.1	28.9	97.6	8.7

TABLE III (cont.)

17 Water Transportation (millions of dollars)

	GROSS DIV. PAID	DIV. REC.	GROSS LONG TERM INT. PAID	LONG TERM INT. REC.	TOTAL INT. PAID	DERIVED SHORT TERM INT. PAID
	(1)	(2)	(3)	(4)	(5)	(6)
1919	47.6	1.7	10.9	1.2		
1920	30.8	2.5	10.9	1.4		
1921	20.4	2.4	11.5	1.2		
1922	21.9	3.7	12.3	2.5		
1923	22.6	3.9	12.9	2.8		
1924	15.9	2.4	11.7	2.5		
1925	21.3	3.1	10.3	2.6		
1926	24.1	3.7	10.2	2.3		
1927	22.5	3.1	9.0	1.1		
1928	25.6	3.4	8.0	1.3		
1929	33.4	4.8	7.9	1.7	12.2	4.3
1930	35.6	5.5	8.0	1.5	11.0	3.0
1931	22.6	3.0	10.1	1.8	13.6	3.5
1932	14.4	2.0	12.3	1.3	12.4	0.1
1933	9.5	1.4	13.6	1.2	11.2	—2.4
1934	43.0	31.1	12.9	1.1		
1934	40.5	16.8	16.0	1.2	15.3	—0.7
1935	74.2	17.7	16.4	1.2	13.8	—2.6
1936	45.6	5.5	16.4	1.3	11.2	—5.2
1937	45.9	4.9	16.4	1.2	11.3	—5.1
1938	33.8	3.6	17.1	1.2		

TABLE III (cont.)

18   Telephone (millions of dollars)

	GROSS DIV. PAID	DIV. REC.	GROSS LONG TERM INT. PAID	LONG TERM INT. REC.
	(1)	(2)	(3)	(4)
1919	45.3	4.3	36.6	6.1
1920	45.5	4.5	40.7	6.9
1921	53.4	5.0	44.1	8.5
1922	66.0	5.9	40.5	11.4
1923	78.9	7.5	46.3	14.7
1924	89.5	7.2	47.1	14.2
1925	100	7.2	54.5	14.2
1926	107	7.8	55.9	15.5
1927	119	8.2	56.2	16.3
1928	126	10.5	55.6	21.0
1929	140	17.1	65.2	34.1
1930	165	18.8	64.0	37.7
1931	191	14.7	58.8	29.6
1932	195	7.2	57.1	14.6
1933	193	5.0	56.7	10.1
1934	193	5.2	56.4	9.7
1935	188	6.2	50.9	8.2
1936	189	22.6	43.3	6.1
1937	190	24.6	42.4	4.5
1938	338 *	161 *	44.8	6.3

* Not comparable with the figures for preceding years, which are after sub-traction of inter-company payments.

TABLE III (cont.)

19 Telegraph (millions of dollars)

	GROSS DIV. PAID	DIV. REC.	GROSS LONG TERM INT. PAID	LONG TERM INT. REC.
	(1)	(2)	(3)	(4)
1919	10.5	0.4	2.5	4.1
1920	10.7	0.5	2.5	4.1
1921	10.5	0.7	2.8	2.7
1922	10.7	0.9	3.3	3.3
1923	10.3	1.0	3.1	3.0
1924	10.6	1.2	3.2	2.8
1925	10.5	1.1	3.3	2.6
1926	12.8	1.0	3.2	2.3
1927	14.2	1.4	4.7	3.1
1928	14.8	1.5	4.7	2.9
1929	22.5	1.6	4.7	2.6
1930	23.7	1.7	6.3	3.1
1931	11.7	1.6	6.4	2.8
1932	4.5	1.4	6.3	2.4
1933	2.8	2.5	6.3	2.1
1934	2.1	1.6	6.2	1.7
1935	6.2	1.9	6.4	1.4
1936	2.4	2.1	5.9	1.0
1937	4.5	2.4	5.3	0.6
1938	0.5	1.4	5.0	0.6

TABLE III (cont.)

20 Trade (millions of dollars)

	GROSS DIV. PAID	DIV. REC.	GROSS LONG TERM INT. PAID	LONG TERM INT. REC.	TOTAL INT. PAID	DERIVED SHORT TERM INT. PAID
	(1)	(2)	(3)	(4)	(5)	(6)
1919	410	9.4	42.5	9.3	252	209
1920	395	13.3	53.2	11.5	244	191
1921	333	12.8	49.9	9.9	221	171
1922	322	20.1	59.8	20.6	194	134
1923	393	24.6	46.9	24.9	219	172
1924	418	29.1	44.7	14.0	219	174
1925	506	66.2	43.4	12.7	246	202
1926	525	54.2	37.6	12.9	245	207
1927	553	58.3	42.6	11.7	348	306
1928	561	62.2	55.6	12.6	285	229
1929	624	59.3	67.3	11.8	276	209
1930	560	64.0	77.1	8.4	257	180
1931	433	47.3	78.3	12.1	217	139
1932	250	36.3	73.0	12.5	167	94.8
1933	213	34.4	63.7	14.6	150	86.5
1934	359	83.9	59.1	12.1	154	95.2
1934	398	59.5	48.4	12.1	150	101
1935	510	71.7	41.9	9.8	143	101
1936	750	81.2	39.4	9.2	143	104
1937	718	93.8	38.0	6.6	152	114
1938	554	72.4	37.8	6.5		

TABLE III (cont.)

21 Real Estate (millions of dollars)

	GROSS DIV. PAID	DIV. REC.	GROSS LONG TERM INT. PAID	LONG TERM INT. REC.	TOTAL INT. PAID	DERIVED SHORT TERM INT. PAID
	(1)	(2)	(3)	(4)	(5)	(6)
1919	73.5	33.0	300	2.6		
1920	135	46.7	290	3.2		
1921	119	44.7	280	2.8		
1922	170	70.5	250	5.7		
1923	275	107	285	6.7		
1924	251	104	280	8.7		
1925	303	130	303	8.6		
1926	308	157	306	8.2		
1927	419	310	321	21.4		
1928	492	336	433	13.0		
1929	333	94.9	440	7.2	511	71.3
1930	228	74.7	440	5.4	545	105
1931	169	47.6	457	6.7	530	72.5
1932	86.7	27.8	380	5.3		
1933	54.4	24.3	258	6.5	326	67.5
1934	75.9	25.4	240	5.2	338	97.2
1935	79.0	27.7	224	4.3	289	64.9
1936	86.4	31.3	202	3.2	200	—2.1
1937	93.8	30.2	202	2.8	187	—15.2
1938	83.1	26.7	199	2.8		

TABLE III (concl.)

22 Service (millions of dollars)

	GROSS DIV. PAID	DIV. REC.	GROSS LONG TERM INT. PAID	LONG TERM INT. REC.	TOTAL INT. PAID	DERIVED SHORT TERM INT. PAID
	(1)	(2)	(3)	(4)	(5)	(6)
1919	32.4	3.5	16.9	1.0	26.5	9.6
1920	85.3	4.9	16.1	1.3	26.2	10.1
1921	70.4	4.7	19.2	1.1	33.7	14.5
1922	56.3	7.5	25.1	2.2	40.8	15.7
1923	76.9	8.9	30.0	2.0	54.4	24.4
1924	85.1	13.9	35.2	2.0	53.9	18.7
1925	107	15.8	42.9	1.8	67.0	24.1
1926	125	19.8	49.9	2.2	80.4	30.5
1927	133	26.9	64.3	1.6	106	41.7
1928	134	35.2	77.1	4.1	117	40.4
1929	176	59.6	88.5	1.5	132	44.4
1930	166	53.2	100	1.9	138	38.0
1931	115	42.0	95.3	1.6	135	40.5
1932	72.0	17.5	112	2.4	204	92.0
1933	42.3	8.4	97.6	2.2	168	70.8
1934	58.4	16.6	89.2	2.3	165	76.4
1934	63.1	12.5	91.1	2.3	174	83.1
1935	71.1	16.8	106	1.9	200	94.3
1936	158	45.4	103	1.9	258	154
1937	153	33.5	97.5	1.9	246	148
1938	88.3	19.2	94.7	1.8		

TABLE IV

Gains and Losses from Sale of Capital Assets

Gains and losses from sale of capital assets are subtracted from the reported figures on net savings to yield an estimate of net savings (and of net product) consonant with the definitions developed in Volume I. The item is estimated by industrial divisions for years beginning with 1929, and may be of interest as suggesting the magnitude of this speculative element in the net income of enterprises.

For years prior to 1929 only a rough correction could be made. The corporate figures are averages of two estimates. The first is obtained by applying to estimated individuals' net gain on capital assets the geometric mean of the ratio of corporate to individual net gain in 1929 and 1935–37. Individuals' net capital gains are derived from *Statistics of Income* data for the successive years. The second is based on the net profit of real estate and holding corporations, reported in *Statistics of Income,* and the geometric mean of the ratio of corporate capital gains to it in 1929–34.

Entrepreneurial gains and losses from sale of capital assets are based on the corporate figures, the 1929 ratio of the former to the latter being extrapolated by the ratio of non-corporate to corporate depreciation. The depreciation figures are the accounting measures published in *Capital Consumption and Adjustment* (p. 262).

TABLE IV

1 Gains and Losses from Sale of Capital Assets, 1929–1938 (millions of dollars)

	1929	1930	1931	1932	1933	1934 [1]	1934 [2]	1935	1936	1937	1938
MINING											
Corp.	30.6	32.1	−12.0	−18.4	−14.4	15.5	17.1	15.1	18.2	21.4	13.6
Entrep.	4.1	2.6	−0.8	−2.2	−1.4	3.0	1.3	1.2	1.5	1.7	1.7
MANUFACTURING											
Corp.	68.9	−55.7	−203	−217	−235	4.8	0.4	35.7	38.5	19.0	9.2
Entrep.	3.3	−10.1	−19.4	−23.2	−20.3	−5.0	−0.6	2.3	3.0	1.8	1.1
CONSTRUCTION											
Corp.	4.6	−9.3	−19.0	−11.9	−8.1	1.5	2.0	3.7	4.7	2.7	2.7
Entrep.	8.7	−14.0	−27.5	−21.3	−15.3	5.9	4.4	9.3	11.8	6.3	3.3
TRANSPORTATION AND OTHER PUBLIC UTILITIES											
Manufactured gas											
Corp.	0.0	0.3	−2.9	−1.8	−7.0	6.6	3.2	0.4	0.6	1.0	0.8
Water transportation											
Corp.	1.2	−1.5	−8.0	−2.3	−7.7	0.3	−0.4	−18.9	2.0	2.3	0.8
Entrep.	0.1	−0.2	−0.8	−0.2	−0.8	0.0	0.0	−1.9	0.2	0.2	0.1
Total											
Corp.	1.2	−1.3	−10.9	−4.1	−14.7	6.9	2.8	−18.5	2.6	3.2	1.7
Entrep.	0.1	−0.2	−0.8	−0.2	−0.8	0.0	0.0	−1.9	0.2	0.2	0.1
TRADE											
Corp.	28.4	−29.1	−99.6	−54.7	−62.1	0.2	0.6	6.6	8.7	5.2	5.2
Entrep.	29.3	−28.0	−92.2	−48.8	−46.7	−6.0	0.0	2.3	5.1	5.9	4.6

TABLE IV (cont.)

	1929	1930	1931	1932	1933	1934[1]	1934[2]	1935	1936	1937	1938
FINANCE											
Banking Corp.	47.5	18.3	−82.5	−140	−142	−7.8	−7.8	61.9	122	−3.3	2.5
Insurance Corp.	35.2	−13.6	−70.1	−109	−114	−1.3	−1.3	2.3	9.1	2.1	−0.5
Real estate Corp.	141	19.3	−104	−143	−115	−31.8	−31.8	−6.9	9.7	12.3	12.3
Total	224	24.1	−257	−393	−371	−40.9	−40.9	57.4	141	11.2	14.3
SERVICE											
Corp.	23.0	2.4	−42.0	−91.5	−56.1	−11.3	−11.8	−4.0	13.2	8.8	8.8
MISCELLANEOUS											
Corp.	390	−258	−721	−672	−575	−277	−26.9	61.9	90.3	8.2	8.2
TOTAL											
Corp.	771	−295	−1,366	−1,463	−1,338	−300	−56.8	−157	317	79.7	63.7
Entrep.	45.5	−49.7	−140	−95.7	−84.4	−2.0	5.1	13.1	21.5	15.8	10.8

Since the income tax law for 1934 and later years limits the capital losses allowed to $2,000 plus capital gains, the series is not strictly comparable for the entire period.

[1] Comparable with 1929–33 in that *Statistics of Income* data used are those based on the old industrial classification.
[2] Comparable with 1935–38 in that *Statistics of Income* data used are those based on the new industrial classification.

TABLE IV (concl.)

2 Estimated Gains and Losses from Sale of Capital Assets, 1919–1928 (millions of dollars)

	1919	1920	1921	1922	1923	1924	1925	1926	1927	1928
Corporate	294	304	122	370	404	561	1,118	660	748	1,188
Entrepreneurial	31	28	9	29	29	40	80	45	46	74
Total	325	332	131	399	433	601	1,198	705	794	1,262

TABLES V AND VI

Both bad debts of corporations (or business enterprises at large) and taxes paid by them may in part be considered an element in their net savings transferred to individuals, and hence should be included in national income. For various reasons, discussed in Chapter 9, they have been excluded from our estimates of national income and net savings of enterprises. Such data relating to these two items as are readily accessible are summarized in Tables V and VI, for possible use as suggesting the magnitudes involved.

TABLE V

Bad Debts of Corporations,[1] 1927–1937 (millions of dollars)

	1927	1928	1929	1930	1931	1932	1933	1934 [2]	1934 [3]	1935	1936	1937
1 Agriculture	5.4	4.4	5.1	9.1	6.0	6.2	6.3	6.8	6.9	4.8	5.5	5.0
2 Mining	10.1	11.6	11.5	11.3	14.2	12.5	16.2	19.6	16.5	12.0	13.1	10.8
3 Manufacturing	242	246	266	290	315	335	318	280	250	197	204	185
4 Construction	15.3	16.6	21.0	20.6	20.2	17.4	14.5	13.6	13.6	11.3	11.7	10.7
5 Transp. & other public utilities	26.9	29.6	32.0	34.7	47.8	68.0	85.1	49.2	43.0	48.6	31.2	29.0
6 Trade	215	228	243	255	264	277	244	203	226	200	198	183
7 Service	16.3	18.6	20.9	27.2	26.3	33.8	34.2	38.5	43.6	34.9	40.9	29.8
8 Finance	281	247	339	329	487	561	529	567	579	452	394	301
9 Nature of business not given	1.1	1.8	1.1	0.9	1.5	1.7	0.7	2.7	1.7	2.5	1.4	0.5
10 Total	814	804	942	979	1,182	1,313	1,249	1,182	1,182	965	901	756

1 *Statistics of Income.*

2 Comparable with 1927–33 in that the data used are based on the old industrial classification.

3 Comparable with 1935–37 in that the data used are based on the new industrial classification.

TABLE VI

Taxes Paid by Non-Agricultural Corporations [1] and by Agriculture,[2] 1919–1937 (millions of dollars)

	AGR. (1)	MINING (2)	MFG. (3)	CONSTRUCTION (4)	TRANSP. & OTHER PUB. UTIL. (5)	TRADE (6)	SERVICE (7)	FINANCE (8)	NATURE OF BUSINESS NOT GIVEN (9)	TOTAL (10)
1919	352	144	1,770	74	242	458	49	288	46	3,423
1920	438	261	1,384	43	349	308	60	346	38	3,227
1921	496	119	793	29	524	236	54	371	21	2,643
1922	509	115	860	20	562	247	55	402	12	2,782
1923	513	130	986	22	625	281	65	417	16	3,055
1924	514	145	936	25	611	284	67	447	9	3,038
1925[3]	514	55	547	18	186	145	28	180	2	1,675
1926	521	161	1,139	33	776	317	87	559	1	3,594
1927	535	124	1,065	33	831	332	97	626	2	3,645
1928	550	117	1,118	31	881	328	97	780	1	3,903
1929	562	136	1,161	32	917	312	107	746	1	3,974
1930	567	104	952	32	851	288	105	647	1	3,547
1931	546	81	731	22	839	252	92	589	1	3,153
1932	493	70	647	17	807	213	132	464	1	2,844
1933	429	73	853	15	771	251	119	444	0.4	2,955
1934[4]	392	89	927	14	821	284	131	465	0.3	3,123
1934[5]	392	112	832	15	833	309	139	492	0.4	3,124
1935	389	115	1,315	19	846	354	167	518	0.4	3,723
1936	396	144	1,647	30	1,018	472	260	547	0.4	4,514
1937	403	200	2,059	47	1,158	564	301	580	0.4	5,312

1 *Statistics of Income.*
2 Bureau of Agricultural Economics.
3 Federal taxes only, except for agriculture.

4 Comparable with 1919–33 in that the data used are based on the old industrial classification.
5 Comparable with 1935–37 in that the data used are based on the new industrial classification.

TABLE VII

Data Underlying the Adjustment of Business Savings for Effects of Inventory Revaluation, by Industrial Divisions

The adjustment of net profit and savings of enterprises for the effects of revaluation of inventories (see discussion in Ch. 8) involves a comparison of changes in inventories at constant valuation with changes in current valuation. The relevant series are derived from the National Bureau's study of Commodity Flow and Capital Formation. For various industrial divisions, they indicate the magnitude of the adjustment made for every industry in every year of the period.

By means of these series any student can remove the adjustment and recalculate both net savings of enterprises and net income originating to a basis that includes the effects of changing inventory valuation.

TABLE VII

1   Mining (millions of dollars)

	CURRENT VALUATION		1929 VALUATION		CHANGE IN INVENTORY, RECONVERTED TO CURRENT VALUATION	BUSINESS SAVINGS DUE TO REVAL- UATION OF INVENTORY
	Inventory, Dec. 31	Change in inventory	Inventory, Dec. 31	Change in inventory		
	(1)	(2)	(3)	(4)	(5)	(6)
1918	550		450			
1919	1,017	+467	848	+398	+496	—29
1920	1,100	+84	811	—37	—81	+165
1921	761	—340	793	—18	—26	—314
1922	607	—154	538	—255	—278	+124
1923	731	+124	687	+149	+175	—51
1924	807	+76	765	+78	+85	—9
1925	749	—58	673	—92	—106	+48
1926	691	—58	610	—63	—73	+15
1927	740	+49	759	+149	+155	—106
1928	561	—179	559	—200	—202	+23
1929	754	+194	772	+213	+213	—19
1930	483	—271	587	—185	—174	—97
1931	515	+32	707	+120	+106	—74
1932	422	—93	581	—126	—96	+3
1933	415	+24	552	—29	—26	+50
1934	435	—10	482	—70	—70	+60
1935	373	—62	409	—73	—74	+12
1936	334	—39	355	—54	—56	+17
1937	402	+68	399	+44	+50	+18
1938	332	—70	346	—53	—58	—12

TABLE VII (cont.)

2 Manufacturing (millions of dollars)

	CURRENT VALUATION		1929 VALUATION		CHANGE IN INVENTORY, RECONVERTED TO CURRENT VALUATION	BUSINESS SAVINGS DUE TO REVALUATION OF INVENTORY
	Inventory, Dec. 31	Change in inventory	Inventory, Dec. 31	Change in inventory		
	(1)	(2)	(3)	(4)	(5)	(6)
1918	10,320		7,702			
1919	12,906	+2,586	8,892	+1,188	+1,684	+902
1920	13,484	+578	10,447	+1,555	+2,678	−2,100
1921	10,705	−2,779	10,412	−37	+34	−2,813
1922	12,118	+1,413	11,244	+835	+1,041	+372
1923	13,721	+1,603	12,625	+1,379	+1,474	+129
1924	13,270	−451	12,389	−236	−275	−176
1925	14,005	+735	13,067	+676	+684	+51
1926	13,727	−278	13,408	+342	+504	−782
1927	13,284	−443	13,346	−63	−60	−383
1928	13,362	+78	13,379	+34	+53	+25
1929	13,920	+558	14,301	+920	+920	−362
1930	12,264	−1,656	14,793	+492	+442	−2,098
1931	9,864	−2,400	13,733	−1,060	−883	−1,517
1932	7,950	−1,914	11,956	−1,777	−1,281	−633
1933	8,852	+902	11,675	−279	−209	+1,111
1934	9,152	+300	10,844	−831	−693	+993
1935	9,550	+398	10,840	−4	−3	+401
1936	10,986	+1,436	12,386	+1,546	+1,353	+83
1937	12,547	+1,561	13,728	+1,342	+1,255	+306
1938	11,162	−1,385	12,859	−869	−760	−625

TABLE VII (cont.)

3 Construction (millions of dollars)

	CURRENT VALUATION		1929 VALUATION		CHANGE IN INVENTORY, RECONVERTED TO CURRENT VALUATION	BUSINESS SAVINGS DUE TO REVALUATION OF INVENTORY
	Inventory, Dec. 31	Change in inventory	Inventory, Dec. 31	Change in inventory		
	(1)	(2)	(3)	(4)	(5)	(6)
1918	390		378			
1919	471	+81	389	+11	+13	+68
1920	588	+117	484	+95	+149	—32
1921	573	—15	592	+108	+110	—125
1922	587	+14	575	—17	—17	+31
1923	708	+121	642	+67	+76	+45
1924	778	+70	726	+84	+90	—20
1925	899	+121	844	+118	+126	—5
1926	998	+99	961	+117	+123	—24
1927	977	—21	1,015	+54	+54	—75
1928	800	—177	811	—204	—201	+24
1929	992	+192	1,002	+191	+191	+1
1930	581	—411	657	—345	—325	—86
1931	423	—158	537	—120	—100	—58
1932	424	+1	575	+38	+28	—27
1933	404	—20	501	—74	—60	+40
1934	483	+79	542	+41	+37	+42
1935	555	+72	621	+79	+71	+1
1936	642	+87	706	+85	+77	+10
1937	643	+1	666	—40	—40	+41
1938	641	—2	683	+17	+16	—18

TABLE VII (cont.)

4 Transportation and Other Public Utilities (millions of dollars)

	CURRENT VALUATION		1929 VALUATION		CHANGE IN INVENTORY, RECONVERTED TO CURRENT VALUATION	BUSINESS SAVINGS DUE TO REVAL-UATION OF INVENTORY
	Inventory, Dec. 31	Change in inventory	Inventory, Dec. 31	Change in inventory		
	(1)	(2)	(3)	(4)	(5)	(6)
1918	775		611			
1919	741	—34	580	—31	—39	+5
1920	1,147	+406	895	+315	+476	—70
1921	1,019	—128	1,003	+108	+122	—250
1922	869	—150	850	—153	—156	+6
1923	1,081	+212	1,009	+159	+175	+37
1924	939	—142	888	—120	—128	—14
1925	906	—33	892	+3	+3	—36
1926	950	+44	952	+61	+61	—17
1927	1,033	+83	1,079	+126	+122	—39
1928	1,008	—25	1,037	—41	—40	+15
1929	1,129	+121	1,154	+117	+117	+4
1930	982	—147	1,123	—31	—29	—118
1931	897	—85	1,110	—14	—11	—74
1932	749	—148	972	—137	—108	—40
1933	779	+30	976	+3	+3	+27
1934	636	—143	736	—240	—210	+67
1935	631	—5	726	—10	—9	+4
1936	699	+68	797	+71	+62	+6
1937	832	+133	865	+68	+66	+67
1938	699	—133	744	—121	—115	—18

TABLE VII (cont.)

5 Trade (millions of dollars)

	CURRENT VALUATION		1929 VALUATION		CHANGE IN INVENTORY, RECONVERTED TO CURRENT VALUATION	BUSINESS SAVINGS DUE TO REVAL- UATION OF INVENTORY
	Inventory, Dec. 31	Change in inventory	Inventory, Dec. 31	Change in inventory		
	(1)	(2)	(3)	(4)	(5)	(6)
1918	9,970		7,152			
1919	12,490	+2,520	8,332	+1,180	+1,614	+906
1920	12,742	+252	9,624	+1,292	+2,226	—1,974
1921	10,202	—2,540	9,838	+214	+199	—2,739
1922	10,678	+476	9,970	+132	+142	+334
1923	11,809	+1,131	11,036	+1,066	+1,120	+11
1924	11,706	—103	10,839	—197	—176	+73
1925	12,157	+451	10,982	+143	+136	+315
1926	12,075	—82	11,712	+730	+776	—858
1927	11,779	—296	11,594	—118	—118	—178
1928	12,022	+243	11,974	+380	+380	—137
1929	12,372	+350	12,650	+676	+676	—326
1930	10,169	—2,203	12,135	—515	—507	—1,696
1931	8,731	—1,438	12,126	—9	—8	—1,430
1932	7,080	—1,651	10,809	—1,317	—909	—742
1933	6,889	—191	9,041	—1,768	—1,204	+1,013
1934	7,160	+271	8,995	—46	—38	+309
1935	7,456	+296	8,972	—23	—18	+314
1936	8,042	+586	9,643	+671	+534	+52
1937	8,536	+494	10,007	+364	+310	+184
1938	7,942	—594	9,793	—214	—170	—424

TABLE VII (cont.)

6 Finance (millions of dollars)

	CURRENT VALUATION		1929 VALUATION		CHANGE IN INVENTORY, RECONVERTED TO CURRENT VALUATION	BUSINESS SAVINGS DUE TO REVAL- UATION OF INVENTORY
	Inventory, Dec. 31	Change in inventory	Inventory, Dec. 31	Change in inventory		
	(1)	(2)	(3)	(4)	(5)	(6)
1918	251		252			
1919	295	+44	222	−31	−36	+80
1920	337	+42	215	−7	−11	+53
1921	255	−82	220	+5	+6	−88
1922	278	+23	237	+17	+20	+3
1923	314	+36	281	+44	+52	−16
1924	444	+130	409	+128	+138	−8
1925	687	+243	662	+252	+265	−22
1926	1,004	+317	998	+337	+339	−22
1927	1,160	+156	1,155	+156	+157	−1
1928	733	−427	733	−422	−423	−4
1929	1,001	+268	1,001	+268	+268	0
1930	502	−499	504	−497	−496	−3
1931	271	−231	308	−196	−185	−46
1932	162	−109	204	−104	−91	−18
1933	153	−9	174	−29	−23	+14
1934	147	−6	162	−12	−10	+4
1935	119	−28	135	−27	−21	−7
1936	71	−48	80	−55	−43	−5
1937	51	−20	52	−28	−24	+4
1938	51	0	53	+1	+1	−1

TABLE VII (cont.)

7 Service (millions of dollars)

	CURRENT VALUATION		1929 VALUATION		CHANGE IN INVENTORY, RECONVERTED TO CURRENT VALUATION	BUSINESS SAVINGS DUE TO REVALUATION OF INVENTORY
	Inventory, Dec. 31	Change in inventory	Inventory, Dec. 31	Change in inventory		
	(1)	(2)	(3)	(4)	(5)	(6)
1918	63		60			
1919	85	+22	68	+8	+8	+14
1920	112	+27	83	+15	+22	+5
1921	103	−9	93	+10	+12	−21
1922	129	+26	116	+23	+25	+1
1923	134	+5	118	+3	+3	+2
1924	139	+5	125	+7	+8	−3
1925	154	+15	143	+18	+20	−5
1926	194	+40	186	+43	+46	−6
1927	187	−7	182	−5	−5	−2
1928	188	+1	188	+7	+7	−6
1929	202	+14	202	+14	+14	0
1930	255	+53	271	+69	+68	−15
1931	210	−45	253	−18	−16	−29
1932	152	−58	196	−57	−45	−13
1933	148	−4	172	−24	−20	+16
1934	173	+25	188	+16	+14	+11
1935	165	−8	180	−8	−7	−1
1936	178	+13	192	+12	+11	+1
1937	184	+6	182	−10	−10	+16
1938	184	0	188	+6	+6	−6

TABLE VII (concl.)

8   Miscellaneous (millions of dollars)

	CURRENT VALUATION		1929 VALUATION		CHANGE IN INVENTORY, RECONVERTED TO CURRENT VALUATION	BUSINESS SAVINGS DUE TO REVAL- UATION OF INVENTORY
	Inventory, Dec. 31	Change in inventory	Inventory, Dec. 31	Change in inventory		
	(1)	(2)	(3)	(4)	(5)	(6)
1918	71		50			
1919	83	+12	55	+5	+8	+4
1920	95	+12	77	+22	+36	−24
1921	72	−23	74	−3	−3	−20
1922	78	+6	74	0	0	+6
1923	89	+11	86	+11	+12	−1
1924	104	+15	100	+14	+15	0
1925	40	−64	37	−63	−68	+4
1926	15	−25	14	−23	−24	−1
1927	24	+9	23	+9	+9	0
1928	18	−6	17	−6	−6	0
1929	10	−8	10	−8	−8	0
1930	6	−4	7	−3	−2	−2
1931	7	+1	10	+3	+3	−2
1932	8	+1	13	+3	+2	−1
1933	2	−6	2	−11	−8	+2
1934	6	+4	5	+3	+2	+1
1935	4	−2	3	−2	−1	0
1936	6	+2	4	+1	+1	0
1937	2	−3	2	−3	−2	−1
1938	2	0	2	0	0	0

TABLE VIII

Data Underlying the Adjustment for the Difference
between Depreciation and Depletion Charges at
Cost and at Current Reproduction Prices

The adjustment of net savings of enterprises for the difference
between depreciation and depletion at cost and current reproduction prices (see Ch. 8) is derived from data in *Capital Consumption
and Adjustment* (Tables 29 and 31). The difference between the
accounting and economic measures, shown there, is corrected for
depreciation on farmers' property since our agricultural net savings are taken after deducting depreciation on a current price
basis. The distribution of the total corrected depreciation adjustment between incorporated and unincorporated firms is based on
Mr. Fabricant's estimates of corporate and non-corporate (excluding farmers') depreciation and depletion charges (see *Capital
Consumption and Adjustment,* p. 262).

TABLE VIII (millions of dollars)

	BUSINESS DEPRECIATION AND DEPLETION			ADJUSTMENT, DEPRECIATION ON FARMERS' PROPERTY	CORRECTED ADJUSTMENT, DEPRECIATION AND DEPLETION CHARGES		
	Accounting measures (1)	Economic measures (2)	Difference (1 − 2) (3)	(4)	Total (3 − 4) (5)	Corporate (6)	Entrepreneurial (7)
1919	3,906	5,867	−1,961	−584	−1,377	−1,073	−304
1920	4,208	6,804	−2,596	−774	−1,822	−1,461	−361
1921	4,040	5,078	−1,038	−277	−761	−633	−128
1922	4,388	4,931	−543	−136	−407	−335	−72
1923	4,586	5,670	−1,084	−230	−854	−715	−139
1924	4,688	5,564	−876	−191	−685	−574	−111
1925	4,908	5,672	−764	−164	−600	−503	−97
1926	5,475	6,166	−691	−144	−547	−462	−85
1927	5,416	6,097	−681	−128	−553	−474	−79
1928	5,728	6,286	−558	−102	−456	−391	−65
1929	6,093	6,759	−666	−113	−553	−476	−77
1930	6,042	6,385	−343	−57	−286	−249	−37
1931	5,770	5,765	+5	+14	−9	−8	−1
1932	5,381	4,956	+425	+72	+353	+306	+47
1933	5,143	4,702	+441	+77	+364	+313	+51
1934	5,075	5,017	+58	+14	+44	+38	+6
1935	5,091	5,105	−14	+1	−15	−13	−2
1936	5,160	5,362	−202	−17	−185	−160	−25
1937	5,380	6,046	−666	−94	−572	−497	−75
1938	5,460	6,079	−619	−95	−524	−454	−70

Index

THE COMPREHENSIVE INDEX covers in detail materials in Chapters 1–3, 8, 9, 11, and 12. References to materials in other chapters are general.

The tabular index covers materials in tables and directly related notes and comments. It is arranged by the narrowest industrial divisions and the types of income distinguished under each. Column 2, 'Derivation of Absolute Total', contains references to the text of Part Four. For those industry type of income cells for which there is no entry in Column 2 the absolute totals are sums of components referred to elsewhere in the index. Column 5, 'Analytical Material', contains references to tables showing averages, indexes, and measures of change over the period and during business cycles.

Comprehensive Index

Advertising
see Tabular index
Aggregate payments excluding entre-
preneurial savings, 48, 62, 136, 137
Adjustment for price changes in, 144
Average for selected periods, 137-9,
147, 149, 166, 167, 222, 223
Change during business cycles, 140-1,
148-50, 160, 205, 209
Change over the period, 137-9, 147-9,
178-83, 227-31, 248-50
Comparison with other estimates,
437, 442-9, 451-68
In current prices, 137-41
In 1929 prices, 147-50
Inclusion of
Compensation for injury, 136
Contributions, 63, 64, 136
Pensions, 63, 64, 136
Relief payments, 63, 64, 136
Industrial distribution, 78-80, 165-74,
178-83
Per population unit, 155-8
Percentage distribution by type, rea-
sons for, 220
Price index implicit in, 145, 146
Share of individuals' savings in, 280-3
see also Tabular index
Aggregate payments including entre-
preneurial savings, 62, 136, 137
Adjustment for price changes in, 144,
145
Average for selected periods, 137, 138,
166, 167
Change during business cycles, 140-1,
148-50, 160
Change over the period, 137, 138, 147,
178-81, 227-8
In current prices, 137, 138, 140, 141

Aggregate payments including entre-
preneurial savings (cont.)
Industrial distribution, 166
In 1929 prices, 147-50
Per population unit, 155-7
Price index implicit in, 145, 146
Share of individuals' and entrepre-
neurial savings in, 280-3
see also Tabular index
Agriculture
Coverage, 392
see also Tabular index
ALLEN, R. H., 105n
America's Capacity to Consume, 296,
423
Anthracite coal
see Tabular index
Auto repair shops and garages
see Tabular index
Average for the period, percentage dis-
tribution by industry
Aggregate payments, 166, 167
Dividends, 166, 167
Wages and salaries, 166, 167
Service income including entrepre-
neurial savings, 166, 167
Service income excluding entrepre-
neurial savings, 166, 167
Entrepreneurial net income, 166, 167
Entrepreneurial withdrawals, 166,
167
Interest, 166, 167
National income, 166, 167
Property income including rent, 166,
167

Bad debts, 413, 426, 427-8, 899
Banking
see Tabular index

917

Tabular Index

	ABSOLUTE TOTAL (1)	DERIVATION OF ABSOLUTE TOTAL (2)	PERCENTAGE SHARE IN Countrywide total (3)	Net income or total payments (4)	ANALYTICAL MATERIAL (5)	ERROR MARGIN & SUPPLEMENTARY DATA (6)
Agriculture						
Gross income	543	546				
Expenses	543	546				
Net income	163, 310, 358, 543, 544	546, 547	164, 166, 326		179, 184, 193, 205	510, 511, 512
Wages	544	546		374		
Wages & salaries			166, 332		184, 205, 233, 261	853
Employee compensation	314				233, 234	
Entrep. withdr.	316, 452, 544	546–7	166, 338	222, 358	184, 236, 257, 261	452
Entrep. savings	312	547	166, 338	222, 358, 374	184, 236, 257, 261	
Entrep. net income	544	547	166, 336	222	184, 205, 236, 257	
Service income excl. entrep. savings			166, 344		184, 236	
Service income incl. entrep. savings			166, 342		184, 236, 257	
Dividends	316, 544	547	166, 348	222, 358, 374	184, 198, 199, 200, 205, 239	
Interest	318, 544	547	166, 350	222, 358, 374	184, 198, 200, 239, 257, 261	
Dividends & interest			352		184, 239	
Property income incl. rent	318		166, 354	222	184, 198, 199, 205	
Total pay. excl. entrep. savings	314, 374, 456, 544	547	166, 330, 463	222, 358	179, 181, 205, 242	443, 456
Total pay. incl. entrep. savings			166, 328		179, 243	
Net savings of enterprises	450, 544	547		222, 358, 374	242, 257, 261	440, 450, 456, 899, 900
Wage earners	545	547				
Salaried employees	545	547–8				
Employees	314, 545	548	334			514, 516, 518
Entrepreneurs	316, 545	548	340			514, 516, 518
Number engaged			346			
Mining						
Gross income	551	559				
Net income	163, 310, 358, 552	560	164, 166, 326		179, 184, 193, 205	510, 511, 512

	ABSOLUTE TOTAL (1)	DERIVATION OF ABSOLUTE TOTAL (2)	PERCENTAGE SHARE IN Countrywide total (3)	PERCENTAGE SHARE IN Net income or total payments (4)	ANALYTICAL MATERIAL (5)	ERROR MARGIN & SUPPLEMENTARY DATA (6)
ANTHRACITE COAL (*cont.*)						
Service income excl. entrep. savings			166, 344		184	
Service income incl. entrep. savings			166, 342		184	
Dividends	554	565-6	166, 348		184, 198, 199, 200, 205	868
Interest	554	566-7	166, 350		184, 198, 199, 200	868
Dividends & interest			352		184	
Property income	555	567	166, 354		184, 198, 199, 200, 205	
Total pay. excl. entrep. savings	556	567	166, 330		179, 198, 199, 200, 205	
Total pay. incl. entrep. savings	556		166, 328		179	
Corp. savings	556	568				
Wage earners	557	569, 570	334			488
Salaried employees	557	569, 571	340			488
Employees			346			514, 516, 518
Entrepreneurs						
Number engaged						
BITUMINOUS COAL						
Gross income	551	558				
Net income			166, 326		179, 184, 193, 205	
Wages	553	560-1	166, 332			494
Salaries	553	565-4	166, 338		184, 205	488
Wages & salaries	555	567	166, 336			
Entrep. withdr.						
Entrep. net income					205	
Service income excl. entrep. savings			166, 344		184	
Service income incl. entrep. savings			166, 342		184	
Dividends	554	565-6	166, 348		184, 205	868

	ABSOLUTE TOTAL (1)	DERIVATION OF ABSOLUTE TOTAL (2)	PERCENTAGE SHARE IN Countrywide total (3)	Net income or total payments (4)	ANALYTICAL MATERIAL (5)	ERROR MARGIN & SUPPLEMENTARY DATA (6)
OIL & GAS						
Gross income	551	558	166, 326		179, 184, 193, 205	
Net income						
Wages	553	562				
Salaries	553	564				494
Wages & salaries	555	567	166, 332		184, 205	
Entrep. withdr.			166, 338		184	
Entrep. net income			166, 336		184, 199, 205	
Service income excl. entrep. savings						
Service income incl. entrep. savings			166, 344		184	
Dividends	554	565-6	166, 342		184, 205	869
Interest	554	566-7	166, 348		184, 199	869
Dividends & interest			166, 350		184	
Property income	555	567	352		184, 205	
Total pay. excl. entrep. savings	556	567	166, 354		179, 205	
Total pay. incl. entrep. savings			166, 330		179	
Corp. savings	556	568	166, 328			
Wage earners	557	569, 570				
Salaried employees	557	569, 571-2				494
Employees			334			514, 516, 518
Entrepreneurs			340			
Number engaged			346			
OTHER MINING						
Gross income	551	558-9	166, 326		179, 184, 193, 205	
Net income						
Wages	553	562-3				495
Salaries	553	564-5				495

Wages & salaries	555	567	166, 332		184, 205	
Entrep. withdr.			166, 338		205	
Entrep. net income			166, 336		184	
Service income excl. entrep. savings			166, 344			
Service income incl. entrep. savings					184	
Dividends	554	565-6	166, 342		184, 199, 205	869
Interest	554	566-7	166, 348		184, 199	869
Dividends & interest			166, 350		184	
Property income	555	567	352		184, 199, 205	
Total pay. excl. entrep. savings	556	567	166, 354		179, 205	
Total pay. incl. entrep. savings			166, 328		179	
Corp. savings	556	568				
Wage earners	557	569, 570-1				494
Salaried employees	557	569, 572				494
Employees			334			514, 516, 518
Entrepreneurs			340			
Number engaged			346			

Manufacturing

Gross income	576	610-1				
Net income	163, 310, 358, 577, 578	612	164, 166, 326		179, 184, 193, 205	510, 511, 513
Wages	578, 579	613		358, 374	233	
Salaries	578, 582	619		358, 374	233	853, 854
Wages & salaries	578, 584	612, 622	166, 332		184, 205, 233, 257	
Employee compensation	314			222	233	
Entrep. withdr.	316, 578, 590	627	166, 338	222, 358, 374	184, 236, 257, 261	
Entrep. savings	312, 578, 592	627		358, 374	184, 236, 257, 261	
Entrep. net income	593	629	166, 336	222	184, 198, 205, 236	893
Service income excl. entrep. savings			166, 344		184, 236	
Service income incl. entrep. savings			166, 342		184, 236	
Dividends	316, 578, 586	623	166, 348	222, 358, 374	184, 205, 239, 257, 261	870

	ABSOLUTE TOTAL (1)	DERIVATION OF ABSOLUTE TOTAL (2)	PERCENTAGE SHARE IN		ANALYTICAL MATERIAL (5)	ERROR MARGIN & SUPPLEMENTARY DATA (6)
			Countrywide total (3)	Net income or total payments (4)		
MANUFACTURING (cont.)						
Interest	318, 578, 588	624-5	166, 350	222, 358, 374	184, 198, 199, 200, 239, 257, 261	870
Dividends & interest			352		184, 239	
Property income	318, 578, 589	612, 625	166, 354	222	184, 205	
Total pay. excl. entrep. savings	314, 374, 452, 456, 578, 591	612, 627	166, 330, 463	222, 358	179, 181, 205, 242	452, 456
Total pay. incl. entrep. savings	310, 312, 578, 594	629-30	166, 328	222, 358, 374	179	893, 899, 900
Corp. savings	578, 596	612		222	242	904
Net savings of enterprises	597	630			242, 257, 261	
Wage earners	600	633, 634	334			854
Salaried employees	314, 602	636	340			
Employees	316, 604	637	346			514, 516, 518
Entrepreneurs						514, 516, 518
Number engaged						
FOOD & TOBACCO						
Gross income	576	610-1				
Net income	358, 577	612	166, 336		179, 184, 193, 199, 205	510, 511, 513
Wages	579	612		358, 374	233	
Salaries	582	616-7		358, 374	233	490, 854
Wages & salaries	584	622	166, 332		184, 205, 233, 257	
Employee compensation				222	233	
Entrep. withdr.	590	625-7	166, 338	222, 358, 374	184, 236, 257, 261	
Entrep. savings	592	627		358, 374	184, 198, 205, 236	
Entrep. net income	593	627-8	166, 336	222	184, 198, 205, 236	
Service income excl. entrep. savings			166, 344		184, 236	
Service income incl. entrep. savings			166, 342		184, 236	
Dividends	586	622-3	166, 348	222, 358, 374	184, 199, 205, 239	859, 871

Interest	588	624	166, 350	222, 358, 374	184, 198, 199, 200, 239, 257, 261	859, 871
Dividends & interest			352		184, 239	
Property income	589	625	166, 354	222	184, 199, 200, 205	
Total pay. excl. entrep. savings	374, 591	627	166, 330	222, 358	179, 205, 242	
Total pay. incl. entrep. savings			166, 328		179	
Corp. savings	594	629		222, 358, 374	199, 242	
Net savings of enterprises	596	630		222	242, 257, 261	
Wage earners	597	630				
Salaried employees	600	632–3				490, 854
Employees	602	636	334			514, 516, 518
Entrepreneurs	604	636	340			491, 514, 516, 518
Number engaged			346			
FOOD						
Wages	580	613				854
Salaries	583	619				
Wages & salaries	585	622				
Wage earners	598	631				
Salaried employees	601	634				854
Employees	603	636				
TOBACCO						
Wages	580	613				854
Salaries	583	619				
Wages & salaries	585	622				
Wage earners	598	631				
Salaried employees	601	634				854
Employees	603	636				
TEXTILE & LEATHER						
Gross income	576	610–1				510, 511, 513
Net income	360, 577	612	166, 326	360, 376	179, 184, 193, 198, 205	
Wages	579	612			233	
Salaries	582	616, 617		360, 376	233	854
Wages & salaries	584	622	166, 332		184, 205, 233	

	ABSOLUTE TOTAL (1)	DERIVATION OF ABSOLUTE TOTAL (2)	PERCENTAGE SHARE IN		ANALYTICAL MATERIAL (5)	ERROR MARGIN & SUPPLEMENTARY DATA (6)
			Countrywide total (3)	Net income or total payments (4)		
TEXTILE & LEATHER (*cont.*)						
Employee compensation	590			222	233	
Entrep. withdr.		625-7	166, 338	222, 360, 376	184, 236, 261	
Entrep. savings	592	627·		360, 376		
Entrep. net income	593	627-8	166, 336	222	184, 198, 200, 205, 236	
Service income excl. entrep. savings			166, 344		184, 236	
Service income incl. entrep. savings			166, 342		184, 236	
Dividends	586	622-3	166, 348	222, 360, 376	184, 205, 239, 257, 261	859, 872
Interest	588	624	166, 350	222, 360, 376	184, 198, 199, 200, 239	859, 872
Dividends & interest			352		184, 239	
Property income	589	625	166, 354	222	184, 205	
Total pay. excl. entrep. savings	376, 591	627	166, 330	222, 360	179, 205, 242	
Total pay. incl. entrep. savings			166, 328		179	
Corp. savings	594	629		222, 360, 376	198, 200, 242	
Net savings of enterprises	596	630		222	242	
Wage earners	597	630				
Salaried employees	600	633				854
Employees	602	636	334			514, 516, 518
Entrepreneurs	604	636	340			491, 514, 516, 518
Number engaged			346			
TOTAL WEARING APPAREL						
Wages	580	614				490, 854
Salaries	585	619				
Wages & salaries	585	622				
Dividends	587	623				
Corp. savings	595	630				
Wage earners	598	631				

Salaried employees	601	654	490, 854
Employees	603	656	
BOOTS & SHOES, OTHER THAN RUBBER			
Wages	580	613	
Wage earners	598	631	
BOOTS & SHOES, RUBBER			
Wages	580	613	
Wage earners	598	631	
HOSIERY & KNIT GOODS			
Wages	580	613	
Wage earners	598	631	
MEN'S CLOTHING			
Wages	580	613	488
Wage earners	598	631	488
WOMEN'S CLOTHING			
Wages	580	613	
Wage earners	598	631	
MILLINERY			
Wages	580	613	
Wage earners	598	631	
OTHER WEARING APPAREL			
Wages	580	613-4	487
Wage earners	598	631	487
TOTAL TEXTILE FABRICS			
Wages	580	614	490, 854
Salaries	583	619-20	
Wages & salaries	585	622	
Dividends	587	623	

	ABSOLUTE TOTAL (1)	DERIVATION OF ABSOLUTE TOTAL (2)	PERCENTAGE SHARE IN Countrywide total (3)	PERCENTAGE SHARE IN Net income or total payments (4)	ANALYTICAL MATERIAL (5)	ERROR MARGIN & SUPPLEMENTARY DATA (6)
TOTAL TEXTILE FABRICS (*cont.*)						
Corp. savings	595	630				
Wage earners	598	631				
Salaried employees	601	634				490, 854
Employees	603	636				
WOOLEN GOODS						
Wages	580	613, 614				488
Wage earners	598	631				488
COTTON GOODS						
Wages	580	613, 614				
Wage earners	598	631				
SILK & RAYON GOODS						
Wages	580	613				
Wage earners	598	631				
DYEING & FINISHING						
Wages	580	613				
Wage earners	598	631				
OTHER TEXTILE FABRICS						
Wages	580	613, 614				488
Wage earners	598	631				488
OTHER LEATHER						
Wages	580	613				
Salaries	583	619, 620				
Wages & salaries	585	622				490, 854
Dividends	587	623				

Corp. savings	595	630				
Wage earners	598	631				
Salaried employees	601	634				490, 854
Employees	603	636				
CONSTRUCTION MATERIALS & FURNITURE						
Gross income	576	610–1				
Net income	360, 577	612	166, 326		179, 184, 193, 205	510, 511, 513
Wages	579	612		360, 376	233	
Salaries	582	617		360, 376	233	854
Wages & salaries	584	622	166, 332		184, 205, 233, 257, 261	
Employee compensation				222	233	
Entrep. withdr.	590	625–7	166, 338	222, 360, 376	184, 236, 257	
Entrep. savings	592	627		360, 376		
Entrep. net income	593	627–8	166, 336	222	184, 205, 236	
Service income excl. entrep. savings			166, 344		184, 236	
Service income incl. entrep. savings			166, 342		184, 236	
Dividends	586	622–3	166, 348	222, 360, 376	184, 205, 239, 261	859, 873
Interest	588	624–5	166, 350	222, 360, 376	184, 199, 200, 239, 257, 261	860, 873
Dividends & interest			352		184, 239	
Property income	589	625	166, 354	222	184, 205	
Total pay. excl. entrep. savings	376, 591	627	166, 330	222, 360	179, 205, 242	
Total pay. incl. entrep. savings			166, 328		179	
Corp. savings	594	629		222, 360, 376	242	
Net savings of enterprises	596	630		222	242, 257, 261	
Wage earners	597	630				
Salaried employees	600	633				854
Employees	602	636	334			514, 516, 518
Entrepreneurs	604	636–7	340			492, 514, 516, 518
Number engaged			346			
TOTAL CONSTRUCTION MATERIALS						
Wages	581	614				
Salaries	583	621				

	ABSOLUTE TOTAL (1)	DERIVATION OF ABSOLUTE TOTAL (2)	PERCENTAGE SHARE IN		ANALYTICAL MATERIAL (5)	ERROR MARGIN & SUPPLEMENTARY DATA (6)
			Countywide total (3)	Net income or total payments (4)		
TOTAL CONSTRUCTION MATERIALS (*cont.*)						
Wages & salaries	585	622				
Wage earners	599	631				
Salaried employees	601	635				
Employees	603	636				
LUMBER						
Wages	581	613, 614				489
Salaries	585	619, 620				490, 854
Wages & salaries	585	622				
Dividends	587	623				
Corp. savings	595	630				
Wage earners	599	631				489
Salaried employees	601	634				490, 854
Employees	603	636				
STONE, CLAY, & GLASS						
Wages	581	613, 614				489
Salaries	583	619, 620				490, 854
Wages & salaries	585	622				
Dividends	587	623				
Corp. savings	595	630				
Wage earners	599	631				489
Salaried employees	601	634-5				490, 854
Employees	603	636				
METAL BUILDING MATERIALS						
Dividends	587	623				
Corp. savings	595	630				

PAPER (cont.)

	ABSOLUTE TOTAL (1)	DERIVATION OF ABSOLUTE TOTAL (2)	PERCENTAGE SHARE IN — Countrywide total (3)	PERCENTAGE SHARE IN — Net income or total payments (4)	ANALYTICAL MATERIAL (5)	ERROR MARGIN & SUPPLEMENTARY DATA (6)
Service income incl. entrep. savings			166, 342		184, 236	
Dividends	586	622–3	166, 348	222, 360, 376	184, 205, 239	860, 874
Interest	588	624	166, 350	222, 360, 376	184, 198, 199, 239, 257	860, 874
Dividends & interest			352		184, 239	
Property income	589	625	166, 354	222	184, 205	
Total pay. excl. entrep. savings	376, 591	627	166, 330	222, 360	179, 205, 242	
Total pay. incl. entrep. savings			166, 328		179	
Corp. savings	594	629		222, 360, 376	242	
Net savings of enterprises	596	630		222	242, 257, 261	
Wage earners	597	630				
Salaried employees	600	632–3	334			491, 854
Employees	602	636	340			514, 516, 518
Entrepreneurs	604	636–7	346			514, 516, 518
Number engaged						

PRINTING

	ABSOLUTE TOTAL (1)	DERIVATION OF ABSOLUTE TOTAL (2)	PERCENTAGE SHARE IN — Countrywide total (3)	PERCENTAGE SHARE IN — Net income or total payments (4)	ANALYTICAL MATERIAL (5)	ERROR MARGIN & SUPPLEMENTARY DATA (6)
Gross income	576	610–1			179, 184, 193, 199, 205	510, 511, 513
Net income	360, 577	612	166, 326			489
Wages	579	613		360, 376	233	
Salaries	582	616–7		360, 376	233	
Wages & salaries	584	622	166, 332		184, 199, 205, 233, 257	491, 854
Employee compensation				22x	233	
Entrep. withdr.	590	625–7	166, 338	222, 360, 376	184, 236, 257, 261	
Entrep. savings	592	627		360, 376		
Entrep. net income	593	627–8	166, 336	222	184, 205, 236	
Service income excl. entrep. savings			166, 344		184, 236	
Service income incl. entrep. savings			166, 342		184, 236	

Dividends	586	622-3	166, 348	222, 360, 376	184, 199, 205, 239, 257, 261	860, 875
Interest	588	624	166, 350	222, 360, 376	184, 198, 199, 200, 239, 257, 261	860, 875
Dividends & interest			352		184, 239	
Property income	589	625	166, 354	222	184, 199, 205	
Total pay. excl. entrep. savings	376, 591	627	166, 330	222, 360	179, 199, 205, 242	
Total pay. incl. entrep. savings			166, 328		179	
Corp. savings	594	629		222, 360, 376	242	
Net savings of enterprises	596	630		222	242, 257, 261	
Wage earners	597	630				489
Salaried employees	600	632-3				491, 854
Employees	602	636	334			514, 516, 518
Entrepreneurs	604	636-7	340			492, 514, 516, 518
Number engaged			346			

METAL

Gross income	576, 577	610-1	166, 326		179, 184, 193, 205	510, 511, 513
Net income	362, 377	612	166, 326	362, 378	255	
Wages	579	613		362, 378	255	
Salaries	582	616-8			233	491, 854
Wages & salaries	584	622	166, 332	222	184, 205, 233, 257	
Employee compensation				222, 362, 378	233	
Entrep. withdr.	590	625-7	166, 338	222, 362, 378	184, 226, 257, 261	
Entrep. savings	592	627		362, 378		
Entrep. net income	593	627-8	166, 336	222	184, 205, 236	
Service income excl. entrep. savings			166, 344		184, 226	
Service income incl. entrep. savings					184, 226	
Dividends	586	622-3	166, 342	222, 362, 378	184, 199, 205, 229, 257	860, 876
Interest	588	624-5	166, 348	222, 362, 378	184, 199, 200, 239, 257, 261	860, 876
Dividends & interest			166, 350		184, 239	
Property income	589	625	352	222	184, 199, 205	
Total pay. excl. entrep. savings	378, 591	627	166, 354	222, 362	179, 205, 242	
Total pay. incl. entrep. savings			166, 350		179	
Corp. savings	594	629-30	166, 328	222, 362, 378	242	

METAL (cont.)

	ABSOLUTE TOTAL (1)	DERIVATION OF ABSOLUTE TOTAL (2)	PERCENTAGE SHARE IN Countrywide total (3)	PERCENTAGE SHARE IN Net income or total payments (4)	ANALYTICAL MATERIAL (5)	ERROR MARGIN & SUPPLEMENTARY DATA (6)
METAL (cont.)						
Net savings of enterprises	596	630		222	242, 257, 261	
Wage earners	597	630				
Salaried employees	600	632–3				491, 854
Employees	602	636	334			514, 516, 518
Entrepreneurs	604	636–7	340			492, 514, 516, 518
Number engaged			346			
IRON & STEEL						
Wages	581	613, 614				489
Salaries	585	621				854
Wages & salaries	585	622				
Dividends	587	623				
Corp. savings	595	630				
Wage earners	599	631				489
Salaried employees	601	634–5				854
Employees	603	636				
TOTAL MACHINERY						
Wages	581	615				
Salaries	585	621				854
Wages & salaries	585	622				
Dividends	587	623				
Corp. savings	595	630				
Wage earners	599	631				
Salaried employees	601	635				854
Employees	603	636				
MACHINERY PROPER						
Wages	581	613				
Wage earners	599	631				

	ABSOLUTE TOTAL (1)	DERIVATION OF ABSOLUTE TOTAL (2)	PERCENTAGE SHARE IN		ANALYTICAL MATERIAL (5)	ERROR MARGIN & SUPPLEMENTARY DATA (6)
			Countrywide total (3)	Net income or total payments (4)		
CHEMICAL (cont.)						
Salaries	582	619		362, 378	233	854
Wages & salaries	584	622	166, 332	222	184, 205, 233, 257	
Employee compensation					233	
Entrep. withdr.	590	625-7	166, 338	222, 362, 261	184, 236, 257, 261	
Entrep. savings	592	627		362, 378	184, 205, 236	
Entrep. net income	593	627-9	166, 336	222	184, 236	
Service income excl. entrep. savings			166, 344		184, 236	
Service income incl. entrep. savings			166, 342		184, 236	
Dividends	586	622-3	166, 348	222, 362, 378	184, 205, 239, 257	861, 877
Interest	588	624	166, 350	222, 362, 378	184, 198, 199, 200, 239, 257, 261	861, 877
Dividends & interest			352		184, 239	
Property income	589	625	166, 354	222	184, 205	
Total pay. excl. entrep. savings	378, 591	627	166, 330	222, 362	179, 205, 242	
Total pay. incl. entrep. savings			166, 328		179	
Corp. savings	594	629			242	
Net savings of enterprises	596	630		222, 362, 378	242, 257, 261	
Wage earners	597	630				
Salaried employees	600	633	334			854
Employees	602	636				514, 516, 518
Entrepreneurs	604	636-7	340	222		492, 514, 516, 518
Number engaged			346			
CHEMICAL EXCLUDING PETROLEUM REFINING						
Wages	581	613, 615				
Salaries	583	619, 621				
Wages & salaries	585	622				
Dividends	587	623				491, 854

Corp. savings	595	630				
Wage earners	599	631				
Salaried employees	601	634-5				491, 854
Employees	603	636				
PETROLEUM REFINING						
Wages	581	613, 615-6				491, 854
Salaries	583	619, 621				
Wages & salaries	585	622				
Dividends	587	623				
Corp. savings	595	630				
Wage earners	599	631				
Salaried employees	601	634-5				491, 854
Employees	603	636				
MISCELLANEOUS & RUBBER						
Gross income	576	610-1				
Net income	362, 577	612	166, 326	362, 378	179, 184, 193, 205	510, 511, 513
Wages	579	613			233	
Salaries	582	619		562, 378	233	
Wages & salaries	584	622	166, 332		184, 205, 233, 257	854
Employee compensation				222	233	
Entrep. withdr.	590	625-7	166, 338	222, 362, 378	184, 236, 257, 261	
Entrep. savings	592	627		362, 378	184, 236, 257, 261	
Entrep. net income	593	627-8	166, 336	222	184, 198, 205, 236	
Service income excl. entrep. savings			166, 344		184, 236	
Service income incl. entrep. savings			166, 342		184, 236	
Dividends	586	622-3	166, 348	222, 362, 378	184, 205, 239	861, 878
Interest	588	624	166, 350	222, 362, 378	184, 198, 199, 200, 239, 257, 261	861, 878
Dividends & interest			352		184, 239	
Property income	589	625	166, 354	222	184, 205	
Total pay. excl. entrep. savings	378, 591	627	166, 330	222, 362	179, 205, 242	
Total pay. incl. entrep. savings			166, 328		179	

	ABSOLUTE TOTAL (1)	DERIVATION OF ABSOLUTE TOTAL (2)	PERCENTAGE SHARE IN Countrywide total (3)	Net income or total payments (4)	ANALYTICAL MATERIAL (5)	ERROR MARGIN & SUPPLEMENTARY DATA (6)
MISCELLANEOUS & RUBBER (cont.)						
Corp. savings	594	629		222, 362, 378	198, 242	
Net savings of enterprises	596	630		222	242, 257, 261	
Wage earners	597	630				
Salaried employees	600	633	334			854
Employees	602	636				514, 516, 518
Entrepreneurs	604	636–7	340			492, 514, 516, 518
Number engaged			346			
RUBBER TIRES						
Wages	581	615, 616				
Salaries	583	619, 621				854
Wages & salaries	585	622				
Dividends	587	623				861
Corp. savings	595	630				
Wage earners	599	631–2				
Salaried employees	601	634–5				491, 854
Employees	603	636				
MISCELLANEOUS						
Wages	581	615, 616				
Salaries	583	619, 621–2				491, 854
Wages & salaries	585	622				
Dividends	587	623				861
Corp. savings	595	630				
Wage earners	599	651				490
Salaried employees	601	634–6				491, 854
Employees	603	636				
Construction						
Gross income	641	645		164, 166, 326		
Net income	162, 510, 362, 642	653			179, 184, 193, 205	510, 511, 513

Transportation & Other Public Utilities

	ABSOLUTE TOTAL (1)	DERIVATION OF ABSOLUTE TOTAL (2)	PERCENTAGE SHARE IN Countrywide total (3)	PERCENTAGE SHARE IN Net income or total payments (4)	ANALYTICAL MATERIAL (5)	ERROR MARGIN & SUPPLEMENTARY DATA (6)
Net income	163, 310, 364, 660, 662	685, 687	164, 167, 326		179, 184, 195, 205	
Wages	662	685				
Salaries	662	685				853
Wages & salaries	662, 663	685, 688	167, 332	222, 364, 380	184, 205, 233, 257, 261	
Other employee compensation	662, 664	694				
Employee compensation	314, 662, 664	685, 694		222, 364, 380		
Entrep. withdr.	316, 662	685	167, 338	222, 364, 380	233	
Entrep. savings	312, 662	686		364, 380	261	
Entrep. net income	662	686	167, 336	222	205	893
Service income excl. entrep. savings			167, 344		184, 236	
Service income incl. entrep. savings			167, 342		184, 236	
Dividends	316, 662, 665	685, 694	167, 348	222, 364, 380	184, 198, 199, 200, 205, 239, 257	
Interest	318, 662, 667	685, 699	167, 350 352	222, 364, 380	184, 199, 200, 239, 257, 261	
Dividends & interest	318, 662, 669	686, 704	167, 354		184, 239	
Property income	314, 380, 662, 671	686, 704	167, 350	222, 364	184, 198, 199, 200, 205	
Total pay. excl. entrep. savings					179, 199, 205, 242	
Total pay. incl. entrep. savings			167, 328	222, 364	179	
Corp. savings	310, 312, 662	686		222, 364, 380	242	
Net savings of enterprises	450, 662, 675	687, 706		222	242, 257, 261	893, 899, 900
Employees	314, 675	709	534			450, 906
Entrepreneurs	316, 675	709–10	540			
Number engaged			546			

ELECTRIC LIGHT & POWER, & MANUFACTURED GAS

	ABSOLUTE TOTAL (1)	DERIVATION OF ABSOLUTE TOTAL (2)				
Gross income	659	684				
Net income	660	685				
Wages & salaries	663	687				

Employee compensation	664	694			
Dividends	665	694			
Interest	667	698, 699			
Property income	669	704			
Total pay. excl. entrep. savings	671	704			
Net savings of enterprises	673	705			
Employees	675	708			
ELECTRIC LIGHT & POWER					
Gross income	659	684			
Net income	364, 661	685	167, 326	179, 184, 193, 199, 205	510, 512, 513
Wages & salaries	664	689	167, 332	364, 380	184, 199, 205, 233, 261	492
Employee compensation				222	233	
Entrep. withdr.	672	705	167, 338	364, 380	236, 257	
Entrep. net income			167, 336	222, 364, 380	198, 205, 236	
Service income excl. entrep. savings			167, 344	222	184, 236	
Service income incl. entrep. savings					184, 236	
Dividends	666	695	167, 342	222, 364, 380	184, 199, 200, 205, 239	492, 861, 880
Interest	668	699-700	167, 348	222, 364, 380	184, 199, 200, 239, 257, 261	861, 880
Dividends & interest			352 / 167, 350	222	184, 239	
Property income	670	704	167, 354	222, 364	184, 199, 200, 205	
Total pay. excl. entrep. savings	380, 459, 672	705	167, 330, 465	222, 364, 380	179, 181, 199, 205, 242	
Total pay. incl. entrep. savings			167, 328	222	179	
Corp. savings				364, 380	242	
Net savings of enterprises	674	706-7		222	242, 257, 261	861
Employees	676	710	334			492, 515, 517, 519
Entrepreneurs			340			515, 517, 519
Number engaged			346			
MANUFACTURED GAS					
Gross income	659	684			
Net income	364, 661	685	167, 326	179, 184, 193, 199, 205	510, 512, 513
Wages & salaries	664	689-90	167, 332	364, 380	184, 199, 205, 233	492
Employee compensation					233	

	ABSOLUTE TOTAL (1)	DERIVATION OF ABSOLUTE TOTAL (2)	PERCENTAGE SHARE IN — Countrywide total (3)	PERCENTAGE SHARE IN — Net income or total payments (4)	ANALYTICAL MATERIAL (5)	ERROR MARGIN & SUPPLEMENTARY DATA (6)
MANUFACTURED GAS (cont.)						
Service income excl. entrep. savings			167, 344		184, 236	
Service income incl. entrep. savings			167, 542		184, 236	
Dividends	666	695–6	167, 548	222, 364, 380	184, 198, 199, 200, 205, 239	862, 881
Interest	668	699, 700–1	167, 550	222, 364, 380	184, 198, 199, 200, 239, 257, 261	862, 881
Dividends & interest			352		184, 239	
Property income	670	704	167, 354	222	184, 198, 199, 200, 205	461
Total pay. excl. entrep. savings	380, 461, 672	705	167, 330	222, 364	179, 199, 205, 243	
Total pay. incl. entrep. savings			167, 328		179	
Corp. savings				222, 364, 380	199, 200, 243	893
Net savings of enterprises	674	706, 707	334	222	243, 257	492, 515, 517, 519
Employees	676	710–1	346			
Number engaged						
STEAM RAILROADS, PULLMAN, & EXPRESS						
Gross income	659	684				677
Net income	364, 660	685	167, 326		179, 184, 193, 205	510, 512, 513
Wages	663	687–8		364, 380	233	
Salaries	663	687–8		364, 380	233	855
Wages & salaries			167, 332	225	184, 205, 233, 257, 261	
Other employee compensation	664	692–3				
Employee compensation	664	694		222, 364, 380	233	
Service income excl. entrep. savings			167, 344		184, 236	
Service income incl. entrep. savings			167, 342		184, 236	
Dividends	665	694	167, 348	222, 364, 380	184, 199, 200, 205, 239	677, 88‡

Interest	667	698, 699	167, 550	222, 364, 380	184, 198, 199, 200, 239, 257, 261	882
Dividends & interest					184, 239	
Property income	669	704	352	222	184, 198, 199, 200, 205	
Total pay. excl. entrep. savings	380, 458, 671	704	167, 354	222	184, 198, 199, 200, 205	458
Total pay. incl. entrep. savings		704	167, 350, 463	222, 364	179, 181, 205, 242	
			167, 328		179	
Corp. savings				222, 364, 380	242	
Net savings of enterprises	673	705–6		222	242, 257, 261	677
Wage earners	675	708–9				677
Salaried employees	675	708–9				855
Employees			334			515, 517, 519
Number engaged			346			

OTHER TRANSPORTATION

Net income	660	685
Wages & salaries	663	688
Employee compensation	664	694
Dividends	665	694
Interest	667	698, 699
Property income	669	704
Total pay. excl. entrep. savings	671	704
Net savings of enterprises	673	706
Employees	675	709

STREET RAILWAYS

Gross income	659	685				
Net income	364, 661	685	167, 326		179, 184, 195, 198, 205	510, 512, 513
Wages & salaries	664	690	167, 352	364, 380	184, 198, 205, 233	492
Employee compensation				222	233	
Service income excl. entrep. savings			167, 344		184, 236	
Service income incl. entrep. savihgs			167, 342		184, 236	
Dividends	666	695–7	167, 348	222, 364, 380	184, 205, 239	862, 883
Interest	668	699, 702–3	167, 350	222, 364, 380	184, 198, 200, 239, 257, 261	862, 883
Dividends & interest			352		184, 239	

	ABSOLUTE TOTAL (1)	DERIVATION OF ABSOLUTE TOTAL (2)	PERCENTAGE SHARE IN Countrywide total (3)	Net income or total payments (4)	ANALYTICAL MATERIAL (5)	ERROR MARGIN & SUPPLEMENTARY DATA (6)
STREET RAILWAYS (cont.)						
Property income	670	704	167, 354	222	184, 198, 200, 205	
Total pay. excl. entrep. savings	380, 458, 672	705	167, 330, 463	222, 364	179, 181, 198, 205, 242	458
Total pay. incl. entrep. savings			167, 328		179	
Corp. savings				222, 364, 380	198, 199, 242	862
Net savings of enterprises	674	706, 707		222	242, 257, 261	
Employees	676	711	334			492, 515, 517, 519
Number engaged			346			
WATER TRANSPORTATION						
Net income	366, 661	685	167, 326		179, 184, 193, 205	510, 512, 515
Wages & salaries	664	690-2	167, 332	366, 382	184, 205, 233, 257, 261	
Employee compensation				222	233	
Entrep. withdr.	672	705	167, 338	222, 366, 382	236	
Entrep. savings				366, 382		893
Entrep. net income			167, 326	222	205, 236	
Service income excl. entrep. savings					184, 236	
Service income incl. entrep. savings			167, 344		184, 236	
Dividends	666	697	167, 342	222, 366, 382	184, 205, 239, 257, 261	865, 884
Interest	668	699, 703	167, 348	222, 366, 382	184, 198, 199, 200, 239, 257, 261	865, 884
Dividends & interest			167, 350		184, 239	
Property income	670	704	352	222	184, 205	
Total pay. excl. entrep. savings	382, 458, 672	705	167, 330, 463	222, 366	179, 181, 205, 242	458
Total pay. incl. entrep. savings			167, 328		179	
Corp. savings				222, 366, 382	242	
Net savings of enterprises	674	707				893
Employees	676	711-2	334	222	242, 257, 261	515, 517, 519

Entrepreneurs		340				515, 517, 519
Number engaged		346				
PIPE LINES						
Gross income	659	684				
Net income	366, 661	685	167, 326	366, 382	179, 184, 193, 199, 205	510, 512, 515
Wages & salaries	664	690	167, 332	222	184, 205, 233, 261	233
Employee compensation					233	
Service income excl. entrep. savings			167, 344		236	236
Service income incl. entrep. savings					236	
Dividends	666	695-6	167, 342; 167, 348	222, 366, 382	184, 198, 199, 200, 205, 239, 257, 261	862
Interest	668	699, 701-2	167, 350; 352	222, 366, 382	198, 199, 200, 239	862
Dividends & interest					184, 239	
Property income	670	704	167, 354	222	184, 198, 199, 200, 205	461
Total pay. excl. entrep. savings	382, 461, 672	705	167, 330	222, 366	179, 199, 205, 242; 179	
Total pay. incl. entrep. savings			167, 328	222, 366, 382	242	
Corp. savings				222, 366, 382	242	
Net savings of enterprises	674	706, 707		222	242, 257, 261	862
Employees	676	711	334			515, 517, 519
Number engaged			346			
COMMUNICATION						
Gross income	659	685				
Net income	660	685				
Wages & salaries	663	688				
Other employee compensation	664	694				
Employee compensation	664	694				
Dividends	665	694				
Interest	667	698, 699				
Property income	669	704				
Total pay. excl. entrep. savings	458, 671	704	463		181	458
Net savings of enterpries	673	706				
Employees	675	709				

	ABSOLUTE TOTAL (1)	DERIVATION OF ABSOLUTE TOTAL (2)	PERCENTAGE SHARE IN Countywide total (3)	Net income or total payments (4)	ANALYTICAL MATERIAL (5)	ERROR MARGIN & SUPPLEMENTARY DATA (6)
TELEPHONE						
Gross income	659	685				
Net income	366, 661	685	167, 326		179, 184, 193, 199, 205	510, 512, 515
Wages & salaries	664	692	167, 332	223, 366, 382	184, 199, 200, 205, 233, 261	493
Other employee compensation	66,?	693				
Employee compensation				222, 366, 382	233	
Service income excl. entrep. savings			167, 344		184, 236	
Service income incl. entrep. savings			167, 342			
Dividends	666	695, 697–8	167, 348	222, 366, 382	184, 198, 199, 200, 205, 239, 257, 261	885
Interest	668	699, 703	167, 350	222, 366, 382	184, 198, 199, 200, 239, 257, 261	494, 885
Dividends & interest			352		184, 239	
Property income	670	704	167, 354	222	184, 199, 200, 205	
Total pay. excl. entrep. savings	382, 672	705	167, 350	222, 366	179, 199, 200, 205, 242	
Total pay. incl. entrep. savings			167, 328		179	
Corp. savings				222, 366, 382	242	
Net savings of enterprises	674	706, 707–8		222	242, 257, 261	
Employees	676	712	334			493, 515, 517, 519
Number engaged			346			
TELEGRAPH						
Gross income	659	685				
Net income	366, 661	685	167, 326		179, 184, 193, 205	510, 512, 515
Wages & salaries	664	692	167, 332	223, 366, 382	184, 205, 233	493
Other employee compensation	664	694				
Employee compensation				222, 366, 382	233	

Service income excl. entrep. savings					184, 236	493, 515, 517, 519
Service income incl. entrep. savings					184, 236	
Dividends	666	695, 698	167, 342	223, 366, 382	184, 198, 199, 205, 239	493, 886
Interest	668	699, 703-4	167, 348	223, 366, 382	199, 200, 239, 257, 261	886
Dividends & interest			167, 350		184, 239	
Property income	670	704	352	222	198, 199, 200, 205	
Total pay. excl. entrep. savings	382, 672	705	167, 354	222, 366	179, 205, 242	
Total pay. incl. entrep. savings			167, 330	222, 366	179	
Corp. savings		706, 708	167, 328	223, 366, 382	200, 242	
Net savings of enterprises	674			222	242, 257	
Employees	676	712	334	222		
Number engaged			346			

Trade

Gross income	717	720				
Net income	163, 310, 366, 718	721	164, 167, 326	366, 372, 382	179, 185, 193, 205	511, 512, 513
Wages & salaries	717, 718	724	167, 332	223	185, 205, 233	853
Employee compensation	314			223	233, 234	
Entrep. withdr.	316, 717, 718	724, 724-6	167, 338	223, 366, 382	185, 236, 257, 261	
Entrep. savings	312, 718			366, 382		893
Entrep. net income	718	726	167, 336	223, 372	185, 198, 205, 236, 237	
Service income excl. entrep. savings					185, 236	
Service income incl. entrep. savings			167, 344			
Dividends	316, 717	720	167, 342	223, 366, 382	185, 236, 237	863, 887
Interest	318, 717	720-1	167, 348	223, 366, 382	185, 199, 205, 239	863, 887
Dividends & interest			167, 350		185, 198, 199, 200, 239, 257, 261	
Property income	318, 717		352	223, 372	185, 239	
Total pay. excl. entrep. savings	314, 382, 459, 717, 718	721	167, 354	223, 366	185, 199, 205	443, 459
Total pay. incl. entrep. savings	372	721	167, 330, 463	223, 366	179, 181, 205, 242	
Corp. savings	310, 312, 718	721	167, 328	223, 366, 382	179, 198, 242	893, 899, 900
Net savings of enterprises	718	721		223	242, 257	907

	ABSOLUTE TOTAL (1)	DERIVATION OF ABSOLUTE TOTAL (2)	PERCENTAGE SHARE IN Countrywide total (3)	Net income or total payments (4)	ANALYTICAL MATERIAL (5)	ERROR MARGIN & SUPPLEMENTARY DATA (6)
TRADE (*cont.*)						
Employees	314, 719	727–8	334			515, 517, 519
Entrepreneurs	316, 719	728	340			515, 517, 519
Number engaged			346			
WHOLESALE						
Gross income	717	719				
Wages & salaries	718	722				
Entrep. withdr.	718	724				
Employees	719	726				493
Entrepreneurs	719	728				493
RETAIL						
Gross income	717	719–20				
Wages & salaries	718	722–4				
Entrep. withdr.	718	724				493
Employees	719	727				
Entrepreneurs	719	728				493
Finance						
Net income	163, 310, 368, 731, 732	738	164, 167, 326		179, 185, 193, 199, 200, 205	
Wages & salaries	732, 733	738, 749	167, 332	368, 384	185, 199, 200, 205, 233	853
Employee compensation	314			223	233	
Entrep. withdr.	316, 732	738	167, 338	223, 368, 384	185, 236, 257, 261	
Entrep. net income			167, 336	223	185, 199, 205, 236	
Service income excl. entrep. savings			167, 344		185, 236	
Service income incl. entrep. savings			167, 342		185, 236	
Dividends	316, 732, 734	738, 750	167, 348	223, 368, 384	185, 199, 205, 239, 257, 261	
Interest	318, 732, 734	738, 752	167, 350	223, 368, 384	185, 199, 200, 239, 261	

Dividends & interest	732					
Rent	318, 732, 735	738	352		185, 239	
Property income incl. rent	314, 384, 732, 736	738, 754	167, 354	368, 384	185, 198, 199, 200, 205	
Total pay. excl. entrep. savings		738, 754	167, 330	223	179, 199, 200, 205, 242	
Total pay. incl. entrep. savings		738	167, 328	223, 368	179	
Corp. savings	310, 312	738, 754		223, 368, 384	198, 199, 200, 242	894, 899, 900
Net savings of enterprises	732, 736			223	242	908
Employees	314, 737	758	334			
Number engaged			346			
BANKING						
Net income	368, 731	738	167, 326	368, 384	179, 185, 193, 199, 200, 205	511, 512, 515
Wages & salaries	733	740	167, 332	223	185, 199, 200, 205, 233	
Employee compensation					233	
Service income excl. entrep. savings			167, 344		185, 236	
Service income incl. entrep. savings					185, 236	
Dividends	734	749	167, 342	223, 368, 384	185, 199, 200, 205, 239, 257	
Dividends & interest			167, 348	223	185, 239	
Property income	735		352		185, 199, 200, 205, 239	
Total pay. excl. entrep. savings	384, 459, 736	752	167, 330, 464	223, 368, 384	179, 181, 200, 205, 242	459
Total pay. incl. entrep. savings		754	167, 328	223	179	
Corp. savings					198, 199, 200, 242	
Net savings of enterprises	736	754			242	894
Employees		756	334			
Number engaged	737		346			
COMMERCIAL INCLUDING STOCK SAVINGS						
Wages & salaries	733	738-9				515, 517, 519
Employees	737	755				
MUTUAL SAVINGS						
Wages & salaries	733	739				
Employees	737	755-6				

| | ABSOLUTE TOTAL (1) | DERIVATION OF ABSOLUTE TOTAL (2) | PERCENTAGE SHARE IN | | ANALYTICAL MATERIAL (5) | ERROR MARGIN & SUPPLEMENTARY DATA (6) |
			Countrywide total (3)	Net income or total payments (4)		
FEDERAL RESERVE						
Wages & salaries	753	759				
Employees	757	756				
INSOLVENT						
Wages & salaries	753	739-40				
Employees	757	756				
INSURANCE						
Net income	368, 731	738	167, 326		179, 185, 195, 199, 200, 205	511, 512, 515
Wages & salaries	733	742	167, 332	368, 384	185, 199, 205, 233, 261	
Employee compensation			233	233	233	
Entrep. withdr.			167, 338	233, 368, 384	185, 236, 257, 261	
Entrep. net income			167, 336	233	185, 199, 205, 236	
Service income excl. entrep. savings			167, 344		185, 236	
Service income incl. entrep. savings			167, 342		185, 236	
Dividends	734	749-50	167, 348	233, 368, 384	185, 199, 200, 205, 239	
Interest	734	750	167, 350	233, 368, 384	185, 198, 200, 239, 257	
Dividends & interest			352		185, 239	
Property income	735	752	167, 354	233	185, 198, 199, 200, 205	
Total pay. excl. entrep. savings	384, 461, 736	754	167, 330	233, 368	179, 205, 242	445, 461
Total pay. incl. entrep. savings			167, 328	233, 368, 384	179	
Corp. savings					198, 200, 242	894
Net savings of enterprises	756	754	334	233	242	
Employees	757	757				515, 517, 519
Number engaged			346			

LIFE						
Wages & salaries	733	740-1				
Employees	737	756				
OTHER						
Wages & salaries	733	741-2				
Employees	737	756-7				
AGENCIES						
Wages & salaries	733	742				
Employees	737	757				
REAL ESTATE						
Net income	368, 731	738	167, 326		179, 185, 193, 199, 200, 205	511, 512, 513
Wages & salaries	733	742-9	167, 332	368, 384	185, 199, 200, 205, 233	511, 512, 513
Employee compensation				223	233, 234	
Service income excl. entrep. savings						
Service income incl. entrep. savings			167, 344		185, 236	
Dividends	734	750	167, 342		185, 236, 237	
Corp. interest	734	750-1	167, 348	223, 368, 384	185, 205, 239, 257, 261	864, 888
Indiv. interest	734	751-2				
Interest, total	734	752	167, 350	223, 368, 384	185, 199, 200, 239	864, 888
Dividends & interest	735	752	352		185, 239	
Rent	452, 735	752-4		368, 384		459, 464
Property income incl. rent	735	754	167, 354	223	185, 198, 199, 200, 205	
Total pay. excl. entrep. savings	384, 461, 756	754	167, 350	223, 568	179, 199, 200, 205, 242	181, 443, 459
Total pay. incl. entrep. savings			167, 328		179, 243	
Corp. savings				223, 568, 384	198, 199, 200, 242	
Net savings of enterprises	736	754	334	223	242	894
Employees	737	757-8	346			
Number engaged						
Service						
Net income	165, 210, 368, 761	770	164, 167, 326	368, 372, 384	179, 185, 193, 199, 205	511, 512, 513
Wages & salaries	761, 762	767, 774	167, 332		185, 199, 205, 233, 234	853

SERVICE (cont.)

	ABSOLUTE TOTAL (1)	DERIVATION OF ABSOLUTE TOTAL (2)	PERCENTAGE SHARE IN — Countrywide total (3)	Net income or total payments (4)	ANALYTICAL MATERIAL (5)	ERROR MARGIN & SUPPLEMENTARY DATA (6)
Employee compensation	314, 761	767-8		223	233, 234	
Entrep. withdr.	316, 761	769-70	167, 338	223, 368, 384	185, 236, 257	
Entrep. savings	312, 761	786		368, 384		
Entrep. net income	763		167, 336	223, 372	185, 199, 205, 236, 237	
Service income excl. entrep. savings			167, 344		185, 236	
Service income incl. entrep. savings			167, 342		185, 236, 237	
Dividends	316, 761	768	167, 348	223, 368, 384	185, 199, 205, 239, 257, 261	864, 889
Interest	318, 761	768-9	167, 350	223, 368, 384	185, 198, 199, 200, 239, 257, 261	864, 889
Dividends & interest	318, 761	769	352		185, 239	
Property income	314, 384, 452, 461, 761	769	167, 354	223, 372	185, 199, 205	
Total pay. excl. entrep. savings	372	372	167, 330	223, 368	179, 199, 205, 242, 243	445, 452, 461
Total pay. incl. entrep. savings	310, 312, 761	770	167, 328		179	
Corp. savings	450, 761	770		223, 368, 384	198, 199, 242	894, 899, 900
Net savings of enterprises	314, 764	790		223	242, 257, 261	440, 450, 900
Employees	316, 766	807	334			515, 517, 519
Entrepreneurs			340			515, 517, 519
Number engaged			346			
PROFESSIONAL						
Wages & salaries	762	770	167, 332		185, 199, 200, 205	
Entrep. net income	763	785	167, 336		185, 199, 205	
Service income incl. entrep. savings			167		185	
Employees	764	786	334			515, 517, 519
Entrepreneurs	766	804	340			515, 517, 519
Number engaged			346			

	ABSOLUTE TOTAL (1)	DERIVATION OF ABSOLUTE TOTAL (2)	PERCENTAGE SHARE IN Countrywide total (3)	PERCENTAGE SHARE IN Net income or total payments (4)	ANALYTICAL MATERIAL (5)	ERROR MARGIN & SUPPLEMENTARY DATA (6)
OTHER PROFESSIONAL						
Wages & salaries	762	778				
Entrep. net income	763, 764	784-5, 786				
Employees	765	795-7				
Entrepreneurs	766	803-4, 807				
LEGAL						
Wages & salaries	763	785				
Entrep. net income	764	786				
Employees	765	800				
Entrepreneurs	766	807				
ENGINEERS						
Entrep. net income	764	786				
Entrepreneurs	766	807				
MISCELLANEOUS PROFESSIONAL						
Wages & salaries	763	785				
Employees	765	800				
PERSONAL						
Wages & salaries	762	770	167, 332		185, 199, 205	
Entrep. net income	765	785	167, 336		185, 205	
Service income incl. entrep. savings			167		185	
Employees	764	786	334			
Entrepreneurs	766	804-6	340			515, 517, 519
Number engaged			346			515, 517, 519

| | ABSOLUTE TOTAL (1) | DERIVATION OF ABSOLUTE TOTAL (2) | PERCENTAGE SHARE IN | | ANALYTICAL MATERIAL (5) | ERROR MARGIN & SUPPLEMENTARY DATA (6) |
			Countrywide total (3)	Net income or total payments (4)		
ADVERTISING (*cont.*)						
Employees	765	800				
Entrepreneurs	766	807				
RECREATION & AMUSEMENT						
Wages & salaries	763	783				
Entrep. net income	764	786				
Employees	765	800				
Entrepreneurs	766	807				
AUTO REPAIR SHOPS & GARAGES						
Wages & salaries	765	783				
Employees	765	800				
HAND TRADES						
Entrep. net income	764	786				
Entrepreneurs	766	807				
Government						
Net income	165, 310, 370, 811	815	164, 167, 326		179, 185, 193, 199, 205	511, 512, 515
Wages & salaries	811, 812	815, 826	167, 332	223, 370, 386	185, 199, 200, 205, 233, 257	
Other employee compensation	811, 812	815, 828				
Employee compensation	314, 811, 812	815, 828		223, 370, 386	233	
Service income excl. entrep. savings			167, 344		185, 236	
Service income incl. entrep. savings			167, 342		185, 236	
Interest	318, 811, 813	815, 851	167, 350	223, 370, 386	185, 199, 239, 261	
Dividends & interest			352		185, 239	
Property income	312		167, 354	223	185, 199, 205	
Total pay. excl. entrep. savings	314, 386, 459, 811, 813	815, 851	167, 350, 464	223, 370	179, 181, 199, 200, 205, 242	443, 459

Total pay. incl. entrep. savings					
Gov. savings	310, 312, 814	855	167, 328	223, 370, 386	179
Net savings	811, 814	815, 853		223	199, 242
Employees	314, 814	855-7	354		243, 257, 261
Number engaged			346		440, 814
FEDERAL					
Wages & salaries	812	816	167, 352	386	185, 198, 199, 200, 205, 233
Other employee compensation	812	826		386	233
Employee compensation	812	828		386	
Service income excl. entrep. savings			167, 344		185, 236
Service income incl. entrep. savings			167, 342		185
Interest	813	828	167, 350	386	185, 198, 200, 239
Dividends & interest			352		185, 239
Property income			167, 354		185, 198, 200, 205
Total pay. excl. entrep. savings	386, 813	831	167, 330		179, 198, 199, 200, 205
Total pay. incl. entrep. savings			167, 328		179
Employees	814	834	354		515, 517, 519
Number engaged			346		
LEGISLATIVE					
Wages & salaries	812	815			
Employees	814	833			
JUDICIAL					
Wages & salaries	812	815			
Employees	814	833			
CIVIL					
Wages & salaries	812	815			
Employees	814	833			
MILITARY					
Wages & salaries	812	815-6			
Employees	814	833-4			

	ABSOLUTE TOTAL (1)	DERIVATION OF ABSOLUTE TOTAL (2)	PERCENTAGE SHARE IN		ANALYTICAL MATERIAL (5)	ERROR MARGIN & SUPPLEMENTARY DATA (6)
			Countywide total (3)	Net income or total payments (4)		
STATE						
Wages & salaries	312	316–7	167, 332	386	185, 199, 200, 205, 233, 261	
Other employee compensation	312	326–7				
Employee compensation	312	328		386	233	
Service income excl. entrep. savings			167, 344		185, 236	
Service income incl. entrep. savings			167, 342		185	
Interest	313	328–9	167, 350	386	185, 199, 200, 239	
Dividends & interest			352		185, 239	
Property income			167, 354		185, 199, 200, 205	
Total pay. excl. entrep. savings	386, 313	351	167, 330		179, 199, 200, 205	515, 517, 519
Total pay. incl. entrep. savings			167, 328		179	
Employees	314	334	334			
Number engaged			346			
COUNTY						
Wages & salaries	312	317–8	167, 332	386	185, 199, 200, 205, 233	
Other employee compensation	312	327				
Employee compensation	312	328		386	233	
Service income excl. entrep. savings			167, 344		185, 236	
Service income incl. entrep. savings			167, 342		185	
Interest	313	329–30	167, 350	386	185, 199, 200, 239	
Dividends & interest			352		185, 239	
Property income			167, 354		185, 199, 200, 205	
Total pay. excl. entrep. savings	386, 313	351	167, 330		179, 199, 200, 205	
Total pay. incl. entrep. savings			167, 328		179	

Employees	814					
Number engaged		854-5	534, 346			515, 517, 519
CITY INCLUDING PUBLIC EDUCATION						
Wages & salaries	812	818-26	167, 532	386	185, 199, 200, 205, 233	
Other employee compensation	812	827-8			233	
Employee compensation	812	828		386	233	
Service income excl. entrep. savings			167, 344		185, 236	
Service income incl. entrep. savings					185	
Interest	815	890-1	167, 542	386	185, 199, 200, 239	
Dividends & interest			167, 550, 352		185, 239	
Property income			167, 554		185, 199, 200, 205	
Total pay. excl. entrep. savings	386, 813	831	167, 330		179, 199, 200, 205	
Total pay. incl. entrep. savings			167, 328		179	
Employees			534			
Number engaged			346			515, 517, 519
CITY						
Wages & salaries	812	818-22				
Employees	814	835				
PUBLIC EDUCATION						
Wages & salaries	812	822-6				
Employees	814	835-7				
Miscellaneous						
Net income	165, 310, 370, 841	846	164, 167, 326	370, 372, 386	179, 185, 195, 199, 205	511, 512, 513
Wages & salaries	841	842-3	167, 552		185, 199, 205, 233, 257, 261	853
Employee compensation	314			223	233, 234	
Entrep. withdr.	316, 841	843	167, 338	223, 370, 386	185, 236, 257, 261	
Entrep. savings	312, 841	845		370, 386		
Entrep. net income	841	845	167, 356	223, 372	185, 199, 205, 236, 257	
Service income excl. entrep. savings			167, 344		185, 236	

	ABSOLUTE TOTAL (1)	DERIVATION OF ABSOLUTE TOTAL (2)	PERCENTAGE SHARE IN Countrywide total (3)	Net income or total payments (4)	ANALYTICAL MATERIAL (5)	ERROR MARGIN & SUPPLEMENTARY DATA (6)
MISCELLANEOUS (cont.)						
Service income incl. entrep. savings						
Dividends	316, 841	843-4	167, 342	223, 370, 386	185, 236, 237	
Interest	318, 841	844	167, 348	223, 370, 386	185, 199, 200, 205, 239, 257	
Dividends & interest	841	844-5	352	223, 370, 386	185, 199, 200, 239, 257, 261	
Property income	318, 841	845	167, 354	223, 372	185, 239	
Total pay. excl. entrep. savings	314, 386, 452, 461, 841	845	167, 330	223, 370	185, 199, 200, 205	181, 443, 452, 461, 464
Total pay. incl. entrep. savings	372		167, 328		179, 199, 205, 242	
Corp. savings	310, 312, 841	845		223, 370, 386	179	
Net savings of enterprises	450, 841	846		223	242	894, 899, 900
Employes	314, 842	846-7	334		242, 257, 261	440, 450, 910
Entrepreneurs	316, 842	847	340			515, 517, 519
Number engaged	842	847	346			515, 517, 519
Commodity Producing						
Net income			168		180, 185, 203, 209	
Wages & salaries			168		185, 203, 209, 233, 255, 259	
Employee compensation				223	233	
Entrep. withdr.			168	223	185, 237, 255, 259	
Entrep. net income			168	223	185, 203, 209, 257	
Service income excl. entrep. savings						
Service income incl. entrep. savings			168		185, 237	
Dividends			168	223	185, 203, 209, 240, 255, 259	
Interest			168	223	185, 203, 240, 255, 259	
Dividends & interest					185, 240	
Property income			168	223	185, 203, 209	
Total pay. excl. entrep. savings			168, 464	223	180, 181, 203, 209, 242	
Total pay. incl. entrep. savings			168	223	180	

Corp. savings		225	203, 242
Net savings of enterprises		225	242, 255, 259
Commodity Transporting & Distributing			
Net income	168		180, 185, 203, 209
Wages & salaries	168	225	185, 203, 209, 233, 255, 259
Employee compensation	168	225	233
Entrep. withdr.	168	225	185, 237, 255, 259
Entrep. net income	168	225	185, 203, 209, 237
Service income excl. entrep. savings	168		185, 237
Service income incl. entrep. savings	168		185, 237
Dividends	168	225	185, 203, 209, 240, 255, 259
Interest	168	225	185, 203, 240, 255, 259
Dividends & interest	168		185, 240
Property income	168	225	185, 203, 209
Total pay. excl. entrep. savings	168, 464	225	180, 181, 203, 209, 242
Total pay. incl. entrep. savings	168		180
Corp. savings		225	203, 242
Net savings of enterprises		225	242, 255, 259
Services			
Net income	168		180, 185, 203, 209
Wages & salaries	168	225	185, 203, 209, 233, 255, 259
Employee compensation	168	225	233
Entrep. withdr.	168	225	185, 237, 255, 259
Entrep. net income	168	225	185, 203, 209, 237
Service income excl. entrep. savings	168		185, 237
Service income incl. entrep. savings	168		185, 237
Dividends	168	225	185, 203, 209, 240, 255, 259
Interest	168	225	185, 203, 240, 255, 259
Dividends & interest	168		185, 240
Property income incl. rent	168	225	185, 203, 209

		DERIVATION OF ABSOLUTE TOTAL	PERCENTAGE SHARE IN			
	ABSOLUTE TOTAL (1)	Countrywide total (2)	Countrywide total (3)	Net income or total payments (4)	ANALYTICAL MATERIAL (5)	ERROR MARGIN & SUPPLEMENTARY DATA (6)
SERVICES (cont.)						
Total pay. excl. entrep. savings			168, 464	223	180, 181, 203, 209, 242	
Total pay. incl. entrep. savings			168		180	
Corp. & gov. savings				223	203, 242	
Net savings of enterprises				223	243, 255, 259	
Non-durable						
Net income			168		203, 209	
Wages & salaries			168		203, 209	
Entrep. withdr.			168			
Entrep. net income			168		203, 209	
Service income excl. entrep. savings			168			
Service income incl. entrep. savings			168			
Dividends			168		203, 209	
Interest			168		203	
Property income incl. rent			168		203, 209	
Total pay. excl. entrep. savings			168		203, 209	
Total pay. incl. entrep. savings			168			
Corp. savings					203	
Durable						
Net income			168		203, 209	
Wages & salaries			168		203, 209	
Entrep. withdr.			168			
Entrep. net income			168		203, 209	
Service income excl. entrep. savings			168			
Service income incl. entrep. savings			168			

ABSOLUTE TOTAL (1)	DERIVATION OF ABSOLUTE TOTAL (2)	PERCENTAGE SHARE IN		ANALYTICAL MATERIAL (5)	ERROR MARGIN & SUPPLEMENTARY DATA (6)
		Countrywide total (3)	Net income or total payments (4)		
WITH LARGE PROPORTION OF INDIVIDUAL FIRMS (cont.)					
Total pay. excl. entrep. savings		168, 464	223	180, 181, 203, 209, 242	
Total pay. incl. entrep. savings		168		180	
Corp. savings			223	203, 242	
Net savings of enterprises			223	242, 255, 259	
Private Corporations					
Net income		168		180, 185, 203, 209	
Wages & salaries		168		185, 203, 209, 234, 255, 259	
Employee compensation		168	223	234	
Entrep. withdr.		168	223	185, 237, 255, 259	
Entrep. net income		168	223	185, 203, 209, 237	
Service income excl. entrep. savings		168		185, 237	
Service income incl. entrep. savings				185, 237	
Dividends		168	223	185, 203, 209, 240, 255, 259	
Interest		168	223	185, 203, 240, 255, 259	
Dividends & interest		168		185, 240	
Property income		168	223	185, 203, 209	
Total pay. excl. entrep. savings		168, 464	223	180, 181, 203, 209, 242	
Total pay. incl. entrep. savings		168		180	
Corp. savings			223	203, 242	
Net savings of enterprises			223	242, 255, 259	
Semi-public Corporations					
Net income		168		180, 185, 203, 209	
Wages & salaries		168		185, 203, 209, 234, 255, 259	
Employee compensation		168	223	234	
Entrep. withdr.		168	223	185, 237, 255, 259	
Entrep. net income		168	223	185, 203, 209, 237	

151

SOME NATIONAL BUREAU PUBLICATIONS

22749